W9-AFL-289

Bureau of Engraving

A COMPILATION

OF THE

MESSAGES AND PAPERS

OF THE

PRESIDENTS

1789 - 1902

BY

JAMES D. RICHARDSON

A REPRESENTATIVE FROM THE STATE OF TENNESSEE

VOLUME IX

PUBLISHED BY

BUREAU OF NATIONAL LITERATURE AND ART

1903

Copyright 1897,
BY
JAMES D. RICHARDSON

Prefatory Note

This volume comprises the papers of Benjamin Harrison and of Grover Cleveland (second term). The events of these two Administrations of eight years, though highly interesting, coming as they do down to March 4, 1897, are so recent and fresh in the public mind that I need not comment on them.

This volume is the last of the series, except the Appendix and Index volume. The work of compiling was begun by me in April, 1895, just after the expiration of the Fifty-third Congress. I then anticipated that I could complete the work easily within a year. Though I have given my entire time to the undertaking when not engaged in my official duties as a Representative, instead of completing it within the time mentioned it has occupied me for nearly four years. The labor has been far greater than the Joint Committee on Printing or I supposed it would be. I had no idea of the difficulties to overcome in obtaining the Presidential papers, especially the proclamations and Executive orders. In the Prefatory Note to Volume I, I said: ''I have sought to bring together in the several volumes of the series all Presidential proclamations, addresses, messages, and communications to Congress excepting those nominating persons to office and those which simply transmit treaties, and reports of heads of Departments which contain no recommendation from the Executive.'' But after the appearance of Volume I, and while preparing the contents of Volume II, I became convinced that I had made a mistake and that the work to be exhaustive should comprise every message of the Presidents transmitting reports of heads of Departments and other communications, no matter how brief or unintelligible the papers were in themselves, and that to make them intelligible I should insert editorial footnotes explaining them. Having acted upon the other idea in making up Volume I and a portion of Volume II, quite a number of such brief papers were intentionally omitted. Being convinced that all the papers of the Executives should be inserted, the plan was modified accordingly, and the endeavor was thereafter made to publish all of them.

In order, however, that the compilation may be "accurate and exhaustive," I have gone back and collected all the papers—those which should have appeared in Volumes I and II, as well as such as were unintentionally omitted from the succeeding volumes—excepting those simply making nominations, and shall publish them in an appendix in the last volume. While this may occasion some little annoyance to the reader who seeks such papers in chronological order, yet, inasmuch as they all appear at their proper places in the alphabetical Index, it is not believed that any serious inconvenience will result.

The editor and compiler has resorted to every possible avenue and has spared no effort to procure all public Presidential papers from the beginning of the Government to March 4, 1897. He has looked out for every reference to the work in the public prints, has endeavored to read all the criticisms made because of omissions, and has availed himself of all the papers to which his attention has been called by anyone; has diligently and earnestly sought for same himself, and has, as stated above, inserted all omitted papers in the Appendix, so that he feels warranted in saying that if he has given to the country all he could find and all any critic or reviewer has been able to find he has done his whole duty and reasonable complaint can not be made if any paper is still omitted. In view of the inaccessibility of many of the messages by reason of their not having been entered on the journals of either House of Congress, and of the fact that the Government itself does not possess many of the proclamations and Executive orders, it may be that there yet can be found a few papers omitted from this work; but with much confidence, amounting to a positive conviction, I feel that assurance may be safely given that only a few, if any at all, have been overlooked.

Congress in June, 1897, by law requested me to prepare an index to the entire compilation. I am now and have been for over two years engaged in this work. I hope to be able to give the last volume, which will include the Appendix and Index, as above stated, to Congress and the public in about two months. It would have been completed at this time but for the fact that in addition to making the Index simply an index to the various messages and other papers I have added to it the encyclopedic feature. There will therefore be found in the Index, in alphabetical order, a large number of encyclopedic definitions of words and phrases used by the Chief Executives, and of other politico-historical subjects. It is believed that this feature will not detract in any manner from the Index, but, on the other hand, will add largely to its value and to the value of the entire compilation.

JAMES D. RICHARDSON.

November 24, 1898.

Benjamin Harrison

March 4, 1889, to March 4, 1893

HOME, AT INDIANAPOLIS, INDIANA, OF

BENJAMIN HARRISON

With official portrait engraved from copy of original in steel

BENJAMIN HARRISON

Benjamin Harrison

BENJAMIN HARRISON, twenty-third President of the United States, was born at North Bend, Ohio, August 20, 1833. His father, John Scott Harrison, was the third son of General William Henry Harrison, ninth President of the United States, who was the third and youngest son of Benjamin Harrison, one of the signers of the Declaration of Independence. John Scott Harrison was twice married, his second wife being Elizabeth, daughter of Archibald Irwin, of Mercersburg, Pa. Benjamin was the second son of this marriage. His parents were resolutely determined upon the education of their children, and early in childhood Benjamin was placed under private instruction at home. In 1847 he and his elder brother were sent to a school on what was known as College Hill, a few miles from Cincinnati. After remaining there two years entered the junior class at Miami University, at Oxford, Ohio, where he was graduated in 1852. Was married October 20, 1853, to Caroline Scott, daughter of Dr. John W. Scott, who was then president of Oxford Female Seminary, from which Mrs. Harrison was graduated in 1852. After studying law under Storer & Gwynne in Cincinnati, Mr. Harrison was admitted to the bar in 1854, and began the practice of his profession at Indianapolis, Ind., which has since been his home. Was appointed crier of the Federal court, at a salary of $2.50 per day. This was the first money he had ever earned. Jonathan W. Gordon, one of the leaders of the Indianapolis bar, called young Harrison to his assistance in the prosecution of a criminal tried for burglary, and intrusted to him the plea for the State. He had taken ample notes of the evidence, but the case was closed at night, and the court-house being dimly lighted by tallow candles, he was unable to read them when he arose to address the court and jury. Laying them aside, he depended entirely upon his memory and found it perfect. He made an eloquent plea, produced a marked impression, and won the case. Since then he has always been an impromptu speaker. Formed a partnership later with William Wallace, but in 1860 the latter became clerk of Marion County, and the firm was changed to Harrison & Fishback, which was terminated by the entry of the senior partner into the Army in 1862. Was

3

chosen reporter of the supreme court of Indiana in 1860 on the Republican ticket. This was his first active appearance in the political field. When the Civil War began assisted in raising the Seventieth Indiana Regiment of Volunteers, taking a second lieutenant's commission and raising Company A of that regiment. Governor Morton tendered him the command of the regiment and he was commissioned its colonel. Mr. Harrison appointed a deputy reporter for the supreme court. In the ensuing autumn the Democratic State committee, considering his position as a civil officer vacated by this military appointment, nominated and elected a successor, although his term of office had not expired. Their view was sustained by the State supreme court; but in 1864, while Colonel Harrison was in the Army, the people of Indiana gave their judgment by reelecting him to the position of supreme-court reporter by an overwhelming majority. In 1862 the Seventieth Indiana went into the field with Harrison as its colonel, their objective point being Bowling Green, Ky. It was brigaded with the Seventy-ninth Ohio and the One hundred and second, One hundred and fifth, and One hundred and twenty-ninth Illinois regiments, under Brigadier-General Ward, of Kentucky, and this organization was kept unchanged until the close of the war. Colonel Harrison had the right of the brigade, and his command was occupied at first in guarding railroads and hunting guerrillas, his energies being largely spent in drilling his men. When General Rosecrans set out for Chattanooga General Ward was sent on duty to Nashville, and on January 2, 1864, his command was called to the front. Later this brigade became the First Brigade of the Third Division of the Twentieth Army Corps, under General Hooker, General Ward resuming its command. The campaign under General Sherman, upon which his regiment with its associate forces entered, was directed, as is now known, against the Confederate army of General Joseph E. Johnston, and not against any particular place. In the Federal advance one of the severest actions was fought at Resaca, Ga., May 14 and 15, 1864, and the Seventieth Indiana led the assault. His regiment participated in the fights at New Hope Church and at Golgotha Church, Kenesaw Mountain, and Peach Tree Creek. When Atlanta was taken by Sherman, September 2, 1864, Colonel Harrison received his first furlough to visit home, being assigned to special duty in a canvass of the State to recruit for the forces in the field. Returning to Chattanooga and then to Nashville, he was placed in command of a provisional brigade held in reserve at the battle at the latter place (December 15 and 16, 1864), and was but little engaged. When the fight was over he was sent in pursuit of the Confederate general Hood. Recalled from that pursuit, was next ordered to report to General Sherman at Savannah. While passing through New York he succumbed to an attack of scarlet fever, but in a few weeks was able to proceed on his way. Joining Sherman at Goldsboro, N. C., resumed command of his old brigade, and at the close of the war went with it to Washington to take part in the grand review of the armies. Was duly mustered out of the service June 8, 1865, not, however, until he had received a commission as brevet brigadier-general, dated January 23, 1865. Returning to Indianapolis after the war, resumed his office of reporter of the supreme court, but in 1867 declined a renomination, preferring to devote himself exclusively to the practice of law. Became a member of the firm of Porter, Harrison & Fishback, and, after subsequent changes, of that of Harrison, Miller & Elam. Took part in 1868 and 1872 in the Presidential campaigns in support of General Grant, traveling over Indiana and speaking to large audiences. In 1876 at first declined a nomination for governor on the Republican ticket, consenting to run only after the regular nominee had withdrawn. In this contest he received almost 2,000 more votes than his associates, but was defeated. Was a member of the Mississippi River Commission in 1879. In 1880, as chairman of the Indiana delegation in the Republican national convention, he cast nearly the entire vote of the State for James A. Garfield for President. President Garfield offered him a place in his Cabinet, but he declined it, preferring the United States Senatorship from Indiana, to which he had just been chosen, and which he held from 1881 to 1887. In the Senate he advocated the tariff views of his party, opposed President Cleveland's vetoes of pension bills, urged the reconstruction and upbuilding of the Navy, and labored and voted for civil-service reform. Was a delegate at large to the Republican national convention in 1884, and in 1888 at Chicago was nominated for the Presidency on the eighth ballot. The nomination was made unanimous, and in November he was elected, receiving 233 electoral votes to 168 for Grover Cleveland. Was inaugurated March 4, 1889. Was again nominated for the Presidency at the national Republican convention which met at Minneapolis in 1892, but was defeated at the November election, receiving 145 electoral votes, against 276 votes for Grover Cleveland. Upon his retiring from office located at Indianapolis, Ind., where he now resides.

INAUGURAL ADDRESS.

FELLOW-CITIZENS: There is no constitutional or legal requirement that the President shall take the oath of office in the presence of the people, but there is so manifest an appropriateness in the public induction to office of the chief executive officer of the nation that from the beginning of the Government the people, to whose service the official oath consecrates the officer, have been called to witness the solemn ceremonial. The oath taken in the presence of the people becomes a mutual covenant. The officer covenants to serve the whole body of the people by a faithful execution of the laws, so that they may be the unfailing defense and security of those who respect and observe them, and that neither wealth, station, nor the power of combinations shall be able to evade their just penalties or to wrest them from a beneficent public purpose to serve the ends of cruelty or selfishness.

My promise is spoken; yours unspoken, but not the less real and solemn. The people of every State have here their representatives. Surely I do not misinterpret the spirit of the occasion when I assume that the whole body of the people covenant with me and with each other to-day to support and defend the Constitution and the Union of the States, to yield willing obedience to all the laws and each to every other citizen his equal civil and political rights. Entering thus solemnly into covenant with each other, we may reverently invoke and confidently expect the favor and help of Almighty God—that He will give to me wisdom, strength, and fidelity, and to our people a spirit of fraternity and a love of righteousness and peace.

This occasion derives peculiar interest from the fact that the Presidential term which begins this day is the twenty-sixth under our Constitution. The first inauguration of President Washington took place in New York, where Congress was then sitting, on the 30th day of April, 1789, having been deferred by reason of delays attending the organization of the Congress and the canvass of the electoral vote. Our people have already worthily observed the centennials of the Declaration of Independence, of the battle of Yorktown, and of the adoption of the Constitution, and will shortly celebrate in New York the institution of the second great department of our constitutional scheme of government. When the centennial of the institution of the judicial department, by the organization of the Supreme Court, shall have been suitably observed, as I trust it will be, our nation will have fully entered its second century.

I will not attempt to note the marvelous and in great part happy contrasts between our country as it steps over the threshold into its second century of organized existence under the Constitution and that weak but wisely ordered young nation that looked undauntedly down the first century, when all its years stretched out before it.

Our people will not fail at this time to recall the incidents which accompanied the institution of government under the Constitution, or to find inspiration and guidance in the teachings and example of Washington and his great associates, and hope and courage in the contrast which thirty-eight populous and prosperous States offer to the thirteen States, weak in everything except courage and the love of liberty, that then fringed our Atlantic seaboard.

The Territory of Dakota has now a population greater than any of the original States (except Virginia) and greater than the aggregate of five of the smaller States in 1790. The center of population when our national capital was located was east of Baltimore, and it was argued by many well-informed persons that it would move eastward rather than westward; yet in 1880 it was found to be near Cincinnati, and the new census about to be taken will show another stride to the westward. That which was the body has come to be only the rich fringe of the nation's robe. But our growth has not been limited to territory, population, and aggregate wealth, marvelous as it has been in each of those directions. The masses of our people are better fed, clothed, and housed than their fathers were. The facilities for popular education have been vastly enlarged and more generally diffused.

The virtues of courage and patriotism have given recent proof of their continued presence and increasing power in the hearts and over the lives of our people. The influences of religion have been multiplied and strengthened. The sweet offices of charity have greatly increased. The virtue of temperance is held in higher estimation. We have not attained an ideal condition. Not all of our people are happy and prosperous; not all of them are virtuous and law-abiding. But on the whole the opportunities offered to the individual to secure the comforts of life are better than are found elsewhere and largely better than they were here one hundred years ago.

The surrender of a large measure of sovereignty to the General Government, effected by the adoption of the Constitution, was not accomplished until the suggestions of reason were strongly reenforced by the more imperative voice of experience. The divergent interests of peace speedily demanded a "more perfect union." The merchant, the shipmaster, and the manufacturer discovered and disclosed to our statesmen and to the people that commercial emancipation must be added to the political freedom which had been so bravely won. The commercial policy of the mother country had not relaxed any of its hard and oppressive features. To hold in check the development of our commercial marine, to prevent or retard the establishment and growth of manufactures in the States, and so to secure the American market for their shops and the carrying trade for their ships, was the policy of European statesmen, and was pursued with the most selfish vigor.

Petitions poured in upon Congress urging the imposition of discriminating duties that should encourage the production of needed things at home. The patriotism of the people, which no longer found a field of exercise in war, was energetically directed to the duty of equipping the young Republic for the defense of its independence by making its people self-dependent. Societies for the promotion of home manufactures and for encouraging the use of domestics in the dress of the people were organized in many of the States. The revival at the end of the century of the same patriotic interest in the preservation and development of domestic industries and the defense of our working people against injurious foreign competition is an incident worthy of attention. It is not a departure but a return that we have witnessed. The protective policy had then its opponents. The argument was made, as now, that its benefits inured to particular classes or sections.

If the question became in any sense or at any time sectional, it was only because slavery existed in some of the States. But for this there was no reason why the cotton-producing States should not have led or walked abreast with the New England States in the production of cotton fabrics. There was this reason only why the States that divide with Pennsylvania the mineral treasures of the great southeastern and central mountain ranges should have been so tardy in bringing to the smelting furnace and to the mill the coal and iron from their near opposing hillsides. Mill fires were lighted at the funeral pile of slavery. The emancipation proclamation was heard in the depths of the earth as well as in the sky; men were made free, and material things became our better servants.

The sectional element has happily been eliminated from the tariff discussion. We have no longer States that are necessarily only planting States. None are excluded from achieving that diversification of pursuits among the people which brings wealth and contentment. The cotton plantation will not be less valuable when the product is spun in the country town by operatives whose necessities call for diversified crops and create a home demand for garden and agricultural products. Every new mine, furnace, and factory is an extension of the productive capacity of the State more real and valuable than added territory.

Shall the prejudices and paralysis of slavery continue to hang upon the skirts of progress? How long will those who rejoice that slavery no longer exists cherish or tolerate the incapacities it put upon their communities? I look hopefully to the continuance of our protective system and to the consequent development of manufacturing and mining enterprises in the States hitherto wholly given to agriculture as a potent influence in the perfect unification of our people. The men who have invested their capital in these enterprises, the farmers who have felt the benefit of their neighborhood, and the men who work in shop or field will not fail to find and to defend a community of interest.

Is it not quite possible that the farmers and the promoters of the great mining and manufacturing enterprises which have recently been established in the South may yet find that the free ballot of the workingman, without distinction of race, is needed for their defense as well as for his own? I do not doubt that if those men in the South who now accept the tariff views of Clay and the constitutional expositions of Webster would courageously avow and defend their real convictions they would not find it difficult, by friendly instruction and cooperation, to make the black man their efficient and safe ally, not only in establishing correct principles in our national administration, but in preserving for their local communities the benefits of social order and economical and honest government. At least until the good offices of kindness and education have been fairly tried the contrary conclusion can not be plausibly urged.

I have altogether rejected the suggestion of a special Executive policy for any section of our country. It is the duty of the Executive to administer and enforce in the methods and by the instrumentalities pointed out and provided by the Constitution all the laws enacted by Congress. These laws are general and their administration should be uniform and equal. As a citizen may not elect what laws he will obey, neither may the Executive elect which he will enforce. The duty to obey and to execute embraces the Constitution in its entirety and the whole code of laws enacted under it. The evil example of permitting individuals, corporations, or communities to nullify the laws because they cross some selfish or local interest or prejudices is full of danger, not only to the nation at large, but much more to those who use this pernicious expedient to escape their just obligations or to obtain an unjust advantage over others. They will presently themselves be compelled to appeal to the law for protection, and those who would use the law as a defense must not deny that use of it to others.

If our great corporations would more scrupulously observe their legal limitations and duties, they would have less cause to complain of the unlawful limitations of their rights or of violent interference with their operations. The community that by concert, open or secret, among its citizens denies to a portion of its members their plain rights under the law has severed the only safe bond of social order and prosperity. The evil works from a bad center both ways. It demoralizes those who practice it and destroys the faith of those who suffer by it in the efficiency of the law as a safe protector. The man in whose breast that faith has been darkened is naturally the subject of dangerous and uncanny suggestions. Those who use unlawful methods, if moved by no higher motive than the selfishness that prompted them, may well stop and inquire what is to·be the end of this.

An unlawful expedient can not become a permanent condition of government. If the educated and influential classes in a community either practice or connive at the systematic violation of laws that seem to them to cross their convenience, what can they expect when the lesson that convenience or a supposed class interest is a sufficient cause for lawlessness has been well learned by the ignorant classes? A community where law is the rule of conduct and where courts, not mobs, execute its penalties is the only attractive field for business investments and honest labor.

Our naturalization laws should be so amended as to make the inquiry into the character and good disposition of persons applying for citizenship more careful and searching. Our existing laws have been in their administration an unimpressive and often an unintelligible form. We accept the man as a citizen without any knowledge of his fitness, and he assumes the duties of citizenship without any knowledge as to what they are.   The privileges of American citizenship are so great and its duties so grave that we may well insist upon a good knowledge of every person applying for citizenship and a good knowledge by him of our institutions. We should not cease to be hospitable to immigration, but we should cease to be careless as to the character of it.   There are men of all races, even the best, whose coming is necessarily a burden upon our public revenues or a threat to social order.   These should be identified and excluded.

We have happily maintained a policy of avoiding all interference with European affairs.   We have been only interested spectators of their contentions in diplomacy and in war, ready to use our friendly offices to promote peace, but never obtruding our advice and never attempting unfairly to coin the distresses of other powers into commercial advantage to ourselves.   We have a just right to expect that our European policy will be the American policy of European courts.

It is so manifestly incompatible with those precautions for our peace and safety which all the great powers habitually observe and enforce in matters affecting them that a shorter waterway between our eastern and western seaboards should be dominated by any European Government that we may confidently expect that such a purpose will not be entertained by any friendly power.

We shall in the future, as in the past, use every endeavor to maintain and enlarge our friendly relations with all the great powers, but they will not expect us to look kindly upon any project that would leave us subject to the dangers of a hostile observation or environment.   We have not sought to dominate or to absorb any of our weaker neighbors, but rather to aid and encourage them to establish free and stable governments resting upon the consent of their own people.   We have a clear right to expect, therefore, that no European Government will seek to establish colonial dependencies upon the territory of these independent American States.   That which a sense of justice restrains us from seeking they may be reasonably expected willingly to forego.

It must not be assumed, however, that our interests are so exclusively American that our entire inattention to any events that may transpire elsewhere can be taken for granted.   Our citizens domiciled for purposes of trade in all countries and in many of the islands of the sea demand and will have our adequate care in their personal and commercial rights. The necessities of our Navy require convenient coaling stations and dock and harbor privileges.   These and other trading privileges we will feel free to obtain only by means that do not in any degree partake of coercion, however feeble the government from which we ask such concessions.   But having fairly obtained them by methods and for purposes entirely consistent with the most friendly disposition toward all other powers, our consent will be necessary to any modification or impairment of the concession.

We shall neither fail to respect the flag of any friendly nation or the just rights of its citizens, nor to exact the like treatment for our own. Calmness, justice, and consideration should characterize our diplomacy. The offices of an intelligent diplomacy or of friendly arbitration in proper cases should be adequate to the peaceful adjustment of all international difficulties. By such methods we will make our contribution to the world's peace, which no nation values more highly, and avoid the opprobrium which must fall upon the nation that ruthlessly breaks it.

The duty devolved by law upon the President to nominate and, by and with the advice and consent of the Senate, to appoint all public officers whose appointment is not otherwise provided for in the Constitution or by act of Congress has become very burdensome and its wise and efficient discharge full of difficulty. The civil list is so large that a personal knowledge of any large number of the applicants is impossible. The President must rely upon the representations of others, and these are often made inconsiderately and without any just sense of responsibility. I have a right, I think, to insist that those who volunteer or are invited to give advice as to appointments shall exercise consideration and fidelity. A high sense of duty and an ambition to improve the service should characterize all public officers.

There are many ways in which the convenience and comfort of those who have business with our public offices may be promoted by a thoughtful and obliging officer, and I shall expect those whom I may appoint to justify their selection by a conspicuous efficiency in the discharge of their duties. Honorable party service will certainly not be esteemed by me a disqualification for public office, but it will in no case be allowed to serve as a shield of official negligence, incompetency, or delinquency. It is entirely creditable to seek public office by proper methods and with proper motives, and all applicants will be treated with consideration; but I shall need, and the heads of Departments will need, time for inquiry and deliberation. Persistent importunity will not, therefore, be the best support of an application for office. Heads of Departments, bureaus, and all other public officers having any duty connected therewith will be expected to enforce the civil-service law fully and without evasion. Beyond this obvious duty I hope to do something more to advance the reform of the civil service. The ideal, or even my own ideal, I shall probably not attain. Retrospect will be a safer basis of judgment than promises. We shall not, however, I am sure, be able to put our civil service upon a nonpartisan basis until we have secured an incumbency that fair-minded men of the opposition will approve for impartiality and integrity. As the number of such in the civil list is increased removals from office will diminish.

While a Treasury surplus is not the greatest evil, it is a serious evil. Our revenue should be ample to meet the ordinary annual demands upon our Treasury, with a sufficient margin for those extraordinary but scarcely less imperative demands which arise now and then. Expenditure should always be made with economy and only upon public necessity. Wastefulness, profligacy, or favoritism in public expenditures is criminal. But there is nothing in the condition of our country or of our people to suggest that anything presently necessary to the public prosperity, security, or honor should be unduly postponed.

It will be the duty of Congress wisely to forecast and estimate these extraordinary demands, and, having added them to our ordinary expenditures, to so adjust our revenue laws that no considerable annual surplus will remain. We will fortunately be able to apply to the redemption of the public debt any small and unforeseen excess of revenue. This is better than to reduce our income below our necessary expenditures, with the resulting choice between another change of our revenue laws and an increase of the public debt. It is quite possible, I am sure, to effect the necessary reduction in our revenues without breaking down our protective tariff or seriously injuring any domestic industry.

The construction of a sufficient number of modern war ships and of their necessary armament should progress as rapidly as is consistent with care and perfection in plans and workmanship. The spirit, courage, and skill of our naval officers and seamen have many times in our history given to weak ships and inefficient guns a rating greatly beyond that of the naval list. That they will again do so upon occasion I do not doubt; but they ought not, by premeditation or neglect, to be left to the risks and exigencies of an unequal combat. We should encourage the establishment of American steamship lines. The exchanges of commerce demand stated, reliable, and rapid means of communication, and until these are provided the development of our trade with the States lying south of us is impossible.

Our pension laws should give more adequate and discriminating relief to the Union soldiers and sailors and to their widows and orphans. Such occasions as this should remind us that we owe everything to their valor and sacrifice.

It is a subject of congratulation that there is a near prospect of the admission into the Union of the Dakotas and Montana and Washington Territories. This act of justice has been unreasonably delayed in the case of some of them. The people who have settled these Territories are intelligent, enterprising, and patriotic, and the accession of these new States will add strength to the nation. It is due to the settlers in the Territories who have availed themselves of the invitations of our land laws to make homes upon the public domain that their titles should be speedily adjusted and their honest entries confirmed by patent.

It is very gratifying to observe the general interest now being manifested in the reform of our election laws. Those who have been for years calling attention to the pressing necessity of throwing about the ballot box and about the elector further safeguards, in order that our elections might not only be free and pure, but might clearly appear to be so, will welcome the accession of any who did not so soon discover the need of reform. The National Congress has not as yet taken control of elections in that case over which the Constitution gives it jurisdiction, but has accepted and adopted the election laws of the several States, provided penalties for their violation and a method of supervision. Only the inefficiency of the State laws or an unfair partisan administration of them could suggest a departure from this policy.

It was clearly, however, in the contemplation of the framers of the Constitution that such an exigency might arise, and provision was wisely made for it. The freedom of the ballot is a condition of our national life, and no power vested in Congress or in the Executive to secure or perpetuate it should remain unused upon occasion. The people of all the Congressional districts have an equal interest that the election in each shall truly express the views and wishes of a majority of the qualified electors residing within it. The results of such elections are not local, and the insistence of electors residing in other districts that they shall be pure and free does not savor at all of impertinence.

If in any of the States the public security is thought to be threatened by ignorance among the electors, the obvious remedy is education. The sympathy and help of our people will not be withheld from any community struggling with special embarrassments or difficulties connected with the suffrage if the remedies proposed proceed upon lawful lines and are promoted by just and honorable methods. How shall those who practice election frauds recover that respect for the sanctity of the ballot which is the first condition and obligation of good citizenship? The man who has come to regard the ballot box as a juggler's hat has renounced his allegiance.

Let us exalt patriotism and moderate our party contentions. Let those who would die for the flag on the field of battle give a better proof of their patriotism and a higher glory to their country by promoting fraternity and justice. A party success that is achieved by unfair methods or by practices that partake of revolution is hurtful and evanescent even from a party standpoint. We should hold our differing opinions in mutual respect, and, having submitted them to the arbitrament of the ballot, should accept an adverse judgment with the same respect that we would have demanded of our opponents if the decision had been in our favor.

No other people have a government more worthy of their respect and love or a land so magnificent in extent, so pleasant to look upon, and so full of generous suggestion to enterprise and labor. God has placed upon our head a diadem and has laid at our feet power and wealth beyond definition or calculation. But we must not forget that we take these gifts upon the condition that justice and mercy shall hold the reins of power and that the upward avenues of hope shall be free to all the people.

I do not mistrust the future. Dangers have been in frequent ambush along our path, but we have uncovered and vanquished them all.   Passion has swept some of our communities, but only to give us a new demonstration that the great body of our people are stable, patriotic, and law-abiding.   No political party can long pursue advantage at the expense of public honor or by rude and indecent methods without protest and fatal disaffection in its own body.   The peaceful agencies of commerce are more fully revealing the necessary unity of all our communities, and the increasing intercourse of our people is promoting mutual respect.   We shall find unalloyed pleasure in the revelation which our next census will make of the swift development of the great resources of some of the States.   Each State will bring its generous contribution to the great aggregate of the nation's increase.   And when the harvests from the fields, the cattle from the hills, and the ores of the earth shall have been weighed, counted, and valued, we will turn from them all to crown with the highest honor the State that has most promoted education, virtue, justice, and patriotism among its people.

MARCH 4, 1889.

SPECIAL MESSAGE.

EXECUTIVE MANSION, *March 11, 1889.*

To the Senate of the United States:

I transmit herewith, in answer to the Senate resolution of the 11th ultimo, a report of the Secretary of State, with accompanying papers, in regard to the case of Louis Riel, otherwise known as Louis David Riel.*

BENJ. HARRISON.

PROCLAMATIONS.

BY THE PRESIDENT OF THE UNITED STATES OF AMERICA.

A PROCLAMATION.

The following provisions of the laws of the United States are hereby published for the information of all concerned:

Section 1956, Revised Statutes, chapter 3, Title XXIII, enacts that—

No person shall kill any otter, mink, marten, sable, or fur seal, or other fur-bearing animal within the limits of Alaska Territory or in the waters thereof; and every person guilty thereof shall for each offense be fined not less than $200 nor more than $1,000, or imprisoned not more than six months, or both; and all vessels, their tackle, apparel, furniture, and cargo, found engaged in violation of this section shall be forfeited; but the Secretary of the Treasury shall have power to authorize the killing of

---

*Tried and executed by the authorities of British North America for complicity in the rebellion in the Northwest Territory.

any such mink, marten, sable, or other fur-bearing animal, except fur seals, under such regulations as he may prescribe; and it shall be the duty of the Secretary to prevent the killing of any fur seal and to provide for the execution of the provisions of this section until it is otherwise provided by law, nor shall he grant any special privileges under this section.

*   *   *   *   *   *   *

Section 3 of the act entitled "An act to provide for the protection of the salmon fisheries of Alaska," approved March 2, 1889, provides that—

SEC. 3. That section 1956 of the Revised Statutes of the United States is hereby declared to include and apply to all the dominion of the United States in the waters of Bering Sea, and it shall be the duty of the President at a timely season in each year to issue his proclamation, and cause the same to be published for one month in at least one newspaper (if any such there be) published at each United States port of entry on the Pacific coast, warning all persons against entering such waters for the purpose of violating the provisions of said section, and he shall also cause one or more vessels of the United States to diligently cruise said waters and arrest all persons and seize all vessels found to be or to have been engaged in any violation of the laws of the United States therein.

Now, therefore, I, Benjamin Harrison, President of the United States, pursuant to the above-recited statutes, hereby warn all persons against entering the waters of Bering Sea within the dominion of the United States for the purpose of violating the provisions of said section 1956, Revised Statutes; and I hereby proclaim that all persons found to be or have been engaged in any violation of the laws of the United States in said waters will be arrested and punished as above provided, and that all vessels so employed, their tackle, apparel, furniture, and cargoes, will be seized and forfeited.

In testimony whereof I have hereunto set my hand and caused the seal of the United States to be affixed.

[SEAL.]   Done at the city of Washington, this 21st day of March, 1889, and of the Independence of the United States the one hundred and thirteenth.   BENJ. HARRISON.

By the President:

JAMES G. BLAINE, *Secretary of State.*

BY THE PRESIDENT OF THE UNITED STATES OF AMERICA.

A PROCLAMATION.

Whereas, pursuant to section 8 of the act of Congress approved March 3, 1885, entitled "An act making appropriations for the current and contingent expenses of the Indian Department and for fulfilling treaty stipulations with various Indian tribes for the year ending June 30, 1886, and for other purposes," certain articles of cession and agreement were made and concluded at the city of Washington on the 19th day of January, A. D. 1889, by and between the United States of America and the

Muscogee (or Creek) Nation of Indians, whereby the said Muscogee (or Creek) Nation of Indians, for the consideration therein mentioned, ceded and granted to the United States, without reservation or condition, full and complete title to the entire western half of the domain of the said Muscogee (or Creek) Nation in the Indian Territory, lying west of the division line surveyed and established under the treaty with said nation dated the 14th day of June, 1866, and also granted and released to the United States all and every claim, estate, right, or interest of any and every description in and to any and all land and territory whatever, except so much of the former domain of said Muscogee (or Creek) Nation as lies east of said line of division surveyed and established as aforesaid, and then used and occupied as the home of said nation, and which articles of cession and agreement were duly accepted, ratified, and confirmed by said Muscogee (or Creek) Nation of Indians by act of its council approved on the 31st day of January, 1889, and by the United States by act of Congress approved March 1, 1889; and

Whereas by section 12 of the act entitled "An act making appropriations for the current and contingent expenses of the Indian Department and for fulfilling treaty stipulations with various Indian tribes for the year ending June 30, 1890, and for other purposes," approved March 2, 1889, a sum of money was appropriated to pay in full the Seminole Nation of Indians for all the right, title, interest, and claim which said nation of Indians might have in and to certain lands ceded by article 3 of the treaty between the United States and said nation of Indians concluded June 14, 1866, and proclaimed August 16, 1866, said appropriation to become operative upon the execution by the duly appointed delegates of said nation specially empowered to do so of a release and conveyance to the United States of all right, title, interest, and claim of said nation of Indians in and to said lands in manner and form satisfactory to the President of the United States; and

Whereas said release and conveyance, bearing date the 16th day of March, 1889, has been duly and fully executed, approved, and delivered; and

Whereas section 13 of the act last aforesaid, relating to said lands, provides as follows:

SEC. 13. That the lands acquired by the United States under said agreement shall be a part of the public domain, to be disposed of only as herein provided; and sections 16 and 36 of each township, whether surveyed or unsurveyed, are hereby reserved for the use and benefit of the public schools to be established within the limits of said lands under such conditions and regulations as may be hereafter enacted by Congress.

That the lands acquired by conveyance from the Seminole Indians hereunder, except the sixteenth and thirty-sixth sections, shall be disposed of to actual settlers under the homestead laws only, except as herein otherwise provided (except that section 2301 of the Revised Statutes shall not apply): *And provided further,* That any person who, having attempted to but for any cause failed to secure a title in fee to a homestead under existing law, or who made entry under what is known as the commuted provision of the homestead law, shall be qualified to make a homestead entry upon said lands: *And provided further*, That the rights of honorably discharged Union soldiers and sailors in the late Civil War as defined and described in sections 2304 and 2305 of the Revised Statutes shall not be abridged: *And provided further*, That each entry shall be in square form as nearly as practicable, and no person be permitted to enter more than one quarter section thereof, but until said lands are opened for settlement by proclamation of the President no person shall be permitted to enter upon and occupy the same, and no person violating this provision shall ever be permitted to enter any of said lands or acquire any right thereto.

The Secretary of the Interior may, after said proclamation and not before, permit entry of said lands for town sites, under sections 2387 and 2388 of the Revised Statutes, but no such entry shall embrace more than one half section of land.

That all the foregoing provisions with reference to lands to be acquired from the Seminole Indians, including the provisions pertaining to forfeiture, shall apply to and regulate the disposal of the lands acquired from the Muscogee (or Creek) Indians by articles of cession and agreement made and concluded at the city of Washington on the 19th day of January, A. D. 1889.

Now, therefore, I, Benjamin Harrison, President of the United States, by virtue of the power in me vested by said act of Congress approved March 2, 1889, aforesaid, do hereby declare and make known that so much of the lands as aforesaid acquired from or conveyed by the Muscogee (or Creek) Nation of Indians and from or by the Seminole Nation of Indians, respectively, as is contained within the following-described boundaries, viz:

Beginning at a point where the degree of longitude 98 west from Greenwich, as surveyed in the years 1858 and 1871, intersects the Canadian River; thence north along and with the said degree to a point where the same intersects the Cimarron River; thence up said river, along the right bank thereof, to a point where the same is intersected by the south line of what is known as the Cherokee lands lying west of the Arkansas River, or as the "Cherokee Outlet," said line being the north line of the lands ceded by the Muscogee (or Creek) Nation of Indians to the United States by the treaty of June 14, 1866; thence east along said line to a point where the same intersects the west line of the lands set apart as a reservation for the Pawnee Indians by act of Congress approved April 10, 1876, being the range line between ranges 4 and 5 east of the Indian meridian; thence south on said line to a point where the same intersects the middle of the main channel of the Cimarron River; thence up said river, along the middle of the main channel thereof, to a point where the same intersects the range line between range 1 east and range 1 west (being the Indian meridian), which line forms the western boundary of the reservations set apart, respectively, for the Iowa and Kickapoo Indians by Executive orders dated, respectively, August 15, 1883; thence south along said range line or meridian to a point where the same intersects the right bank of the North Fork of the Canadian River; thence up said river, along the right bank thereof, to a point where the same is intersected by the west line of the reservation occupied by the Citizen band of Pottawatomies and the Absentee Shawnee Indians, set apart under the provisions of the treaty of February 27, 1867, between the United States and the Pottawatomie tribe of Indians, and referred to in the act of Congress approved May 23, 1872; thence south along the said west line of the aforesaid reservation to a point where the same intersects the middle of the main channel of the Canadian River; thence up the said river, along the middle of the main channel thereof, to a point opposite to the place of beginning, and thence north to the place of beginning (saving and excepting 1 acre of land in square form in the northwest corner of section 9, in township 16 north, range 2 west of the Indian meridian in Indian Territory, and also 1 acre of land in the southeast corner of the northwest quarter of section 15, township 16 north, range 7 west of the Indian meridian in the Indian Territory, which last-described 2 acres are hereby reserved for Government use and control), will, at and after the hour of 12 o'clock noon of the 22d day of April next, and not before, be open for settlement, under the terms of and subject to all the conditions, limitations, and restrictions contained in said act of Congress approved March 2, 1889, and the laws of the United States applicable thereto.

And it is hereby expressly declared and made known that no other parts or portions of the lands embraced within the Indian Territory than those herein specifically described and declared to be open to settlement at the time above named and fixed are to be considered as open to settlement under this proclamation or the act of March 2, 1889, aforesaid.

And warning is hereby again expressly given that no person entering upon and occupying said lands before said hour of 12 o'clock noon of the 22d day of April, A. D. 1889, hereinbefore fixed, will ever be permitted to enter any of said lands or acquire any rights thereto, and that the officers of the United States will be required to strictly enforce the provision of the act of Congress to the above effect.

In witness whereof I have hereunto set my hand and caused the seal of the United States to be affixed.

[SEAL.]   Done at the city of Washington, this 23d day of March, A. D. 1889, and of the Independence of the United States the one hundred and thirteenth.

BENJ. HARRISON.

By the President:

JAMES G. BLAINE,
Secretary of State.

BY THE PRESIDENT OF THE UNITED STATES OF AMERICA.

A PROCLAMATION.

A hundred years have passed since the Government which our forefathers founded was formally organized. At noon on the 30th day of April, 1789, in the city of New York, and in the presence of an assemblage of the heroic men whose patriotic devotion had led the colonies to victory and independence, George Washington took the oath of office as Chief Magistrate of the new-born Republic. This impressive act was preceded at 9 o'clock in the morning in all the churches of the city by prayer for God's blessing on the Government and its first President.

The centennial of this illustrious event in our history has been declared a general holiday by act of Congress, to the end that the people of the whole country may join in commemorative exercises appropriate to the day.

In order that the joy of the occasion may be associated with a deep thankfulness in the minds of the people for all our blessings in the past and a devout supplication to God for their gracious continuance in the future, the representatives of the religious creeds, both Christian and Hebrew, have memorialized the Government to designate an hour for prayer and thanksgiving on that day.

Now, therefore, I, Benjamin Harrison, President of the United States of America, in response to this pious and reasonable request, do recommend that on Tuesday, April 30, at the hour of 9 o'clock in the morning, the people of the entire country repair to their respective places of divine worship to implore the favor of God that the blessings of liberty, prosperity, and peace may abide with us as a people, and that His hand may lead us in the paths of righteousness and good deeds.

In witness whereof I have hereunto set my hand and caused the seal of the United States of America to be affixed.

[SEAL.]   Done in the city of Washington, this 4th day of April, A. D. 1889, and of the Independence of the United States the one hundred and thirteenth.

BENJ. HARRISON.

By the President:
JAMES G. BLAINE,
Secretary of State.

BY THE PRESIDENT OF THE UNITED STATES OF AMERICA.

A PROCLAMATION.

A highly favored people, mindful of their dependence on the bounty of Divine Providence, should seek fitting occasion to testify gratitude and ascribe praise to Him who is the author of their many blessings. It behooves us, then, to look back with thankful hearts over the past year and bless God for His infinite mercy in vouchsafing to our land enduring peace, to our people freedom from pestilence and famine, to our husbandmen abundant harvests, and to them that labor a recompense of their toil.

Now, therefore, I, Benjamin Harrison, President of the United States of America, do earnestly recommend that Thursday, the 28th day of this present month of November, be set apart as a day of national thanksgiving and prayer, and that the people of our country, ceasing from the cares and labors of their working day, shall assemble in their respective places of worship and give thanks to God, who has prospered us on our way and made our paths the paths of peace, beseeching Him to bless the day to our present and future good, making it truly one of thanksgiving for each reunited home circle as for the nation at large.

In witness whereof I have hereunto set my hand and caused the seal of the United States to be affixed.

[SEAL.]   Done at the city of Washington, this 1st day of November, A. D. 1889, and of the Independence of the United States the one hundred and fourteenth.

BENJ. HARRISON.

By the President:

JAMES G. BLAINE,
Secretary of State.

BY THE PRESIDENT OF THE UNITED STATES OF AMERICA.

A PROCLAMATION.

Whereas the Congress of the United States did by an act approved on the 22d day of February, 1889, provide that the inhabitants of the Territory of Dakota might upon the conditions prescribed in said act become the States of North Dakota and South Dakota; and

Whereas it was provided by said act that the area comprising the Territory of Dakota should for the purposes of the act be divided on the line of the seventh standard parallel produced due west to the western boundary of said Territory, and that the delegates elected as therein provided to the constitutional convention in districts north of said parallel should assemble in convention at the time prescribed in the act at the city of Bismarck; and

Whereas it was provided by the said act that the delegates elected as aforesaid should, after they had met and organized, declare on behalf of the people of North Dakota that they adopt the Constitution of the United States, whereupon the said convention should be authorized to form a constitution and State government for the proposed State of North Dakota; and

Whereas it was provided by said act that the constitution so adopted should be republican in form and make no distinction in civil or political rights on account of race or color, except as to Indians not taxed, and not be repugnant to the Constitution of the United States and the principles of the Declaration of Independence, and that the convention should, by an ordinance irrevocable without the consent of the United States and the people of said States, make certain provisions prescribed in said act; and

Whereas it was provided by said act that the constitutions of North Dakota and South Dakota should, respectively, incorporate an agreement, to be reached in accordance with the provision of the act, for an equitable division of all property belonging to the Territory of Dakota, the disposition of all public records, and also for the apportionment of the debts and liabilities of said Territory, and that each of said States should obligate itself to pay its proportion of such debts and liabilities the same as if they had been created by such States, respectively; and

Whereas it was provided by said act that the constitution thus formed for the people of North Dakota should, by an ordinance of the convention forming the same, be submitted to the people of North Dakota at an election to be held therein on the first Tuesday in October, 1889, for ratification or rejection by the qualified voters of said proposed State, and that the returns of said election should be made to the secretary of the Territory of Dakota, who, with the governor and chief justice thereof, or any two of them, should canvass the same, and if a majority of the legal votes cast should be for the constitution the governor should certify the result to the President of the United States, together with a statement of the votes cast thereon and upon separate articles or propositions, and a copy of said constitution, articles, propositions, and ordinances; and

Whereas it has been certified to me by the governor of the Territory of Dakota that within the time prescribed by said act of Congress a constitution for the proposed State of North Dakota has been adopted and the same ratified by a majority of the qualified voters of said proposed State in accordance with the conditions prescribed in said act; and

Whereas it is also certified to me by the said governor that at the same time that the body of said constitution was submitted to a vote of the people a separate article, numbered 20 and entitled "Prohibition," was also submitted and received a majority of all the votes cast for and against said article, as well as a majority of all the votes cast for and against the constitution, and was adopted; and

Whereas a duly authenticated copy of said constitution, article, ordinances, and propositions, as required by said act, has been received by me:

Now, therefore, I, Benjamin Harrison, President of the United States of America, do, in accordance with the provisions of the act of Congress aforesaid, declare and proclaim the fact that the conditions imposed by Congress on the State of North Dakota to entitle that State to admission to the Union have been ratified and accepted and that the admission of the said State into the Union is now complete.

In testimony whereof I have hereunto set my hand and caused the seal of the United States to be affixed.

[SEAL.]   Done at the city of Washington, this 2d day of November, A. D. 1889, and of the Independence of the United States of America the one hundred and fourteenth.

BENJ. HARRISON.

By the President:
    JAMES G. BLAINE,
        Secretary of State.

By the President of the United States of America.

A PROCLAMATION.

Whereas the Congress of the United States did by an act approved on the 22d day of February, 1889, provide that the inhabitants of the Territory of Dakota might upon the conditions prescribed in the said act become the States of North Dakota and South Dakota; and

Whereas it was provided by said act that the area comprising the Territory of Dakota should for the purposes of the act be divided on the line of the seventh standard parallel produced due west to the western boundary of said Territory, and that the delegates elected as therein provided to the constitutional convention in districts south of said parallel should at the time prescribed in the act assemble in convention at the city of Sioux Falls; and

Whereas it was provided by the said act that the delegates elected as aforesaid should, after they had met and organized, declare on behalf of the people of South Dakota that they adopt the Constitution of the United States, whereupon the said convention should be authorized to form a constitution and State government for the proposed State of South Dakota; and

Whereas it was provided by said act that the constitution so adopted should be republican in form and make no distinction in civil or political rights on account of race or color, except as to Indians not taxed, and not be repugnant to the Constitution of the United States and the principles of the Declaration of Independence, and that the convention should, by an ordinance irrevocable without the consent of the United States and the people of said States, make certain provisions prescribed in said act; and

Whereas it was provided by said act that the constitutions of North Dakota and South Dakota should, respectively, incorporate an agreement, to be reached in accordance with the provisions of the act, for an equitable division of all property belonging to the Territory of Dakota, the disposition of all public records, and also for the apportionment of the debts and liabilities of said Territory, and that each of said States should obligate itself to pay its proportion of such debts and liabilities the same as if they had been created by such States respectively; and

Whereas it was provided by said act that at the election for delegates to the constitutional convention in South Dakota, as therein provided, each elector might have written or printed on his ballot the words "For the Sioux Falls constitution" or the words "Against the Sioux Falls constitution;" that the votes on this question should be returned and canvassed in the same manner as the votes for the election of delegates, and if a majority of all votes cast on this question should be "For the Sioux Falls constitution" it should be the duty of the convention which might assemble at Sioux Falls, as provided in the act, to resubmit to the people of South Dakota, for ratification or rejection, at an election provided for in said act, the constitution framed at Sioux Falls and adopted November 3, 1885, and also the articles and propositions separately submitted at that election, including the question of locating the temporary seat of government, with such changes only as related to the name and boundary of the proposed State, to the reapportionment of the judicial and legislative districts, and such amendments as might be necessary in order to comply with the provisions of the act; and

Whereas it was provided by said act that the constitution formed for the people of South Dakota should, by an ordinance of the convention forming the same, be submitted to the people of South Dakota at an election to be held therein on the first Tuesday in October, 1889, for ratification or rejection by the qualified voters of said proposed State, and that the returns of said election should be made to the secretary of the Territory of Dakota, who, with the governor and chief justice thereof, or any two of them, should canvass the same, and if a majority of the legal votes cast should be for the constitution the governor should certify the result to the President of the United States, together with a statement of the votes cast thereon and upon separate articles or propositions, and a copy of said constitution, articles, propositions, and ordinances; and

Whereas it has been certified to me by the governor of the Territory of Dakota that at the aforesaid election for delegates the "Sioux Falls constitution" was submitted to the people of the proposed State of South Dakota, as provided in the said act; that a majority of all the votes cast on this question was "For the Sioux Falls constitution," and that the said constitution was at the time prescribed in the act resubmitted to the people of South Dakota, with proper changes and amendments, and has been adopted and ratified by a majority of the qualified voters of said proposed State in accordance with the conditions prescribed in said act; and

Whereas it is also certified to me by the said governor that at the same time that the body of said constitution was submitted to a vote of the people two additional articles were submitted separately, to wit, an article numbered 24, entitled "Prohibition," which received a majority of all the votes cast for and against said article, as well as a majority of all the votes cast for and against the constitution, and was adopted; and an article numbered 25, entitled "Minority representation," which did not receive a majority of the votes cast thereon or upon the constitution, and was rejected; and

Whereas a duly authenticated copy of said constitution, additional articles, ordinances, and propositions, as required by said act, has been received by me:

Now, therefore, I, Benjamin Harrison, President of the United States of America, do, in accordance with the act of Congress aforesaid, declare and proclaim the fact that the conditions imposed by Congress on the

State of South Dakota to entitle that State to admission to the Union have been ratified and accepted and that the admission of the said State into the Union is now complete.

In testimony whereof I have hereunto set my hand and caused the seal of the United States to be affixed.

[SEAL.]   Done at the city of Washington, this 2d day of November, A. D. 1889, and of the Independence of the United States of America the one hundred and fourteenth.

                                               BENJ. HARRISON.
By the President:
    JAMES G. BLAINE,
            Secretary of State.

BY THE PRESIDENT OF THE UNITED STATES OF AMERICA.

A PROCLAMATION.

Whereas the Congress of the United States did by an act approved on the 22d day of February, 1889, provide that the inhabitants of the Territory of Montana might upon the conditions prescribed in said act become the State of Montana; and

Whereas it was provided by said act that delegates elected as therein provided to a constitutional convention in the Territory of Montana should meet at the seat of government of said Territory, and that after they had met and organized they should declare on behalf of the people of Montana that they adopt the Constitution of the United States, whereupon the said convention should be authorized to form a State government for the proposed State of Montana; and

Whereas it was provided by said act that the constitution so adopted should be republican in form and make no distinction in civil or political rights on account of race or color, except as to Indians not taxed, and not be repugnant to the Constitution of the United States and the principles of the Declaration of Independence, and that the convention should, by an ordinance irrevocable without the consent of the United States and the people of said State, make certain provisions prescribed in said act; and

Whereas it was provided by said act that the constitution thus formed for the people of Montana should, by an ordinance of the convention forming the same, be submitted to the people of Montana at an election to be held therein on the 1st Tuesday in October, 1889, for ratification or rejection by the qualified voters of said proposed State, and that the returns of said election should be made to the secretary of said Territory, who, with the governor and chief justice thereof, or any two of them, should canvass the same, and if a majority of the legal votes cast should be for the constitution the governor should certify the result to the President of the United States, together with a statement of the votes cast

By the President of the United States of America

A Proclamation

Whereas the Congress of the United States did by an act approved on the twenty-second day of February one thousand eight hundred and eighty-nine, provide that the inhabitants of the Territory of Washington might, upon the conditions prescribed in said act, become the State of Washington;

And whereas it was provided by said act that delegates elected as therein provided, to a Constitutional convention in the Territory of Washington, should meet at the seat of government of said Territory; and that, after they had met and organized they should declare on behalf of the people of Washington that they adopt the Constitution of the United States; whereupon the said convention should be authorized to form a State Government for the proposed State of Washington;

And whereas it was provided by said act that the Constitution so adopted should be republican in form and make no distinction in civil or political rights on account of race or color, except as to Indians not taxed, and not be repugnant to the Constitution of the United States and

PRESIDENT BENJAMIN HARRISON'S PROCLAMATION ADMITTING THE TERRITORY OF WASHINGTON AS A STATE.

is now complete.

In Testimony Whereof, I have hereunto set my hand, and caused the seal of the United States to be affixed.

Done at the City of Washington this eleventh (11th) day of November, in the year of our Lord, one thousand, eight hundred, and eighty nine, and of the Independence of the United States of America the one hundred and fourteenth.

Benj Harrison

By the President:

James G. Blaine
Secretary of State

SIGNATURE OF PRESIDENT HARRISON TO PROCLAMATION
ADMITTING THE TERRITORY OF WASHINGTON INTO
THE UNION.

thereon and upon separate articles or propositions, and a copy of said constitution, articles, propositions, and ordinances; and

Whereas it has been certified to me by the governor of said Territory that within the time prescribed by said act of Congress a constitution for the proposed State of Montana has been adopted, and that the same, together with two ordinances connected therewith, has been ratified by a majority of the qualified voters of said proposed State in accordance with the conditions prescribed in said act; and

Whereas a duly authenticated copy of said constitution and ordinances, as required by said act, has been received by me:

Now, therefore, I, Benjamin Harrison, President of the United States of America, do, in accordance with the provisions of the act of Congress aforesaid, declare and proclaim the fact that the conditions imposed by Congress on the State of Montana to entitle that State to admission to the Union have been ratified and accepted and that the admission of the said State into the Union is now complete.

In testimony whereof I have hereunto set my hand and caused the seal of the United States to be affixed.

[SEAL.]   Done at the city of Washington, this 8th day of November, A. D. 1889, and of the Independence of the United States of America the one hundred and fourteenth.

BENJ. HARRISON.

By the President:

    JAMES G. BLAINE,
      Secretary of State.

BY THE PRESIDENT OF THE UNITED STATES OF AMERICA.

A PROCLAMATION.

Whereas the Congress of the United States did by an act approved on the 22d day of February, 1889, provide that the inhabitants of the Territory of Washington might upon the conditions prescribed in said act become the State of Washington; and

Whereas it was provided by said act that delegates elected as therein provided to a constitutional convention in the Territory of Washington should meet at the seat of government of said Territory, and that after they had met and organized they should declare on behalf of the people of Washington that they adopt the Constitution of the United States, whereupon the said convention should be authorized to form a State government for the proposed State of Washington; and

Whereas it was provided by said act that the constitution so adopted should be republican in form and make no distinction in civil or political rights on account of race or color, except as to Indians not taxed, and not be repugnant to the Constitution of the United States and the principles of the Declaration of Independence, and that the convention should, by an ordinance irrevocable without the consent of the United States and the people of said State, make certain provisions prescribed in said act; and

Whereas it was provided by said act that the constitution thus formed for the people of Washington should, by an ordinance of the convention forming the same, be submitted to the people of Washington at an election to be held therein on the first Tuesday in October, 1889, for ratification or rejection by the qualified voters of said proposed State, and that the returns of said election should be made to the secretary of said Territory, who, with the governor and chief justice thereof, or any two of them, should canvass the same, and if a majority of the legal votes cast should be for the constitution the governor should certify the result to the President of the United States, together with a statement of the votes cast thereon and upon separate articles or propositions, and a copy of said constitution, articles, propositions, and ordinances; and

Whereas it has been certified to me by the governor of said Territory that within the time prescribed by said act of Congress a constitution for the proposed State of Washington has been adopted, and that the same has been ratified by a majority of the qualified voters of said proposed State in accordance with the conditions prescribed in said act; and

Whereas it is also certified to me by the said governor that at the same time the body of said constitution was submitted to a vote of the people two separate articles, entitled "Woman suffrage" and "Prohibition," were likewise submitted, which said separate articles did not receive a majority of the votes cast thereon or upon the constitution, and were rejected; also that at the same election the question of the location of a permanent seat of government was so submitted, and that no place received a majority of all the votes cast upon said question; and

Whereas a duly authenticated copy of said constitution and articles, as required by said act, has been received by me:

Now, therefore, I, Benjamin Harrison, President of the United States of America, do, in accordance with the provisions of the act of Congress aforesaid, declare and proclaim the fact that the conditions imposed by Congress on the State of Washington to entitle that State to admission to the Union have been ratified and accepted and that the admission of the said State into the Union is now complete.

In testimony whereof I have hereunto set my hand and caused the seal of the United States to be affixed.

[SEAL.]   Done at the city of Washington, this 11th day of November, A. D. 1889, and of the Independence of the United States of America the one hundred and fourteenth.

BENJ. HARRISON.

By the President:
    JAMES G. BLAINE,
       Secretary of State.

EXECUTIVE ORDERS.

EXECUTIVE MANSION,
Washington March 11, 1889.

Whereas civil-service rules for the railway mail service were approved January 4, 1889, to go into effect March 15, 1889; and

Whereas it is represented to me by the Civil Service Commission in a communication of this date that it will be impossible to complete arrangements for putting said rules into full effect on said date, or sooner than May 1, 1889:

It is therefore ordered, That said railway mail rules shall take effect May 1, 1889, instead of March 15, 1889: *Provided,* That such rules shall become operative and take effect in any State or Territory as soon as an eligible register for such State or Territory shall be prepared, if it shall be prior to the date above fixed. BENJ. HARRISON.

AMENDMENT OF CIVIL-SERVICE RULES.

EXECUTIVE MANSION, *April 17, 1889.*

Special Departmental Rule No. 1 is hereby amended by including among the places excepted from examination thereunder in section 2 the following: ''and inspector of furniture.''

As amended so much of that section as relates to the office of Secretary of the Treasury will read as follows:

2. In the Department of the Treasury, in the office of the Secretary: Government actuary and inspector of furniture.

BENJ. HARRISON.

REGULATIONS FOR THE DISTRIBUTION OF ARMS, ORDNANCE STORES, QUARTERMASTER'S STORES, AND CAMP EQUIPAGE TO THE TERRITORIES AND THE DISTRICT OF COLUMBIA, PRESCRIBED BY THE PRESIDENT OF THE UNITED STATES IN CONFORMITY WITH THE SECOND SECTION OF THE ACT ENTITLED ''AN ACT TO AMEND SECTION 1661, REVISED STATUTES, MAKING AN ANNUAL APPROPRIATION TO PROVIDE ARMS AND EQUIPMENTS FOR THE MILITIA.''

EXECUTIVE MANSION, *April 23, 1889.*

1. Arms, ordnance stores, quartermaster's stores, and camp equipage shall be issued to the Territories on requisitions of the governors thereof, and to the District of Columbia on requisitions approved by the senior general of the District militia present for duty. Returns shall be made annually by the senior general of the District militia in the manner as required

by sections 3 and 4 of the act above referred to in the case of States and Territories.

2. It is forbidden to make issues to States and Territories in excess of the amount to their credit under the provisions of section 1661, Revised Statutes, as amended by the above act.

3. Any regulations established hitherto which in any way conflict with these are hereby revoked.

BENJ. HARRISON.

AMENDMENT OF CIVIL-SERVICE RULES.

MAY 4, 1889.

Special Departmental Rule No. 1 is hereby amended by including among the places excepted from examination thereunder in section 2 the following: "custodian of dies, rolls, and plates at the Bureau of Engraving and Printing, two subcustodians, keeper of the vault, and distributer of stock."

As amended so much of that section as relates to the office of the Secretary of the Treasury will read:

2. In the Department of the Treasury, in the office of the Secretary: Government actuary, inspector of furniture, custodian of dies, rolls, and plates at the Bureau of Engraving and Printing, two subcustodians, keeper of the vault, and distributer of stock.

BENJ. HARRISON.

AMENDMENTS OF CIVIL-SERVICE RULES.

EXECUTIVE MANSION, *May 27, 1889.*

Departmental Rule VIII is hereby amended as follows:

At the end of section 1 insert an additional clause, as follows:

(*d*) From the office of the President of the United States, after two years' continuous service therein immediately preceding the transfer, to any place in the classified service without examination, upon the requisition of the head of the Department to which the transfer is to be made and the certification of the Commission.

In section 2, line 1, after the word "authorized," insert the following: "except as provided in section 1, clause (*d*)."

BENJ. HARRISON.

BY THE PRESIDENT OF THE UNITED STATES.

EXECUTIVE ORDER.

EXECUTIVE MANSION, *May 29, 1889.*

It is hereby ordered, That the several Executive Departments and the Government Printing Office be closed on Thursday, the 30th instant, to enable the employees to participate in the decoration of the graves of the soldiers who fell during the rebellion.

BENJ. HARRISON.

EXECUTIVE MANSION, *June 7, 1889.*

In November, 1862, President Lincoln quoted the words of Washington to sustain his own views, and announced in a general order that—

The President, Commander in Chief of the Army and Navy, desires and enjoins the orderly observance of the Sabbath by the officers and men in the military and naval service. The importance for man and beast of the prescribed weekly rest, the sacred rights of Christian soldiers and sailors, a becoming deference to the best sentiment of a Christian people, and a due regard for the divine will demand that Sunday labor in the Army and Navy be reduced to the measure of strict necessity.

The truth so concisely stated can not be too faithfully regarded, and the pressure to ignore it is far less now than in the midst of war. To recall the kindly and considerate spirit of the orders issued by these great men in the most trying times of our history, and to promote contentment and efficiency, the President directs that Sunday-morning inspection will be merely of the dress and general appearance, without arms; and the more complete inspection under arms, with all men present, as required in paragraph 959, Army Regulations, 1889, will take place on Saturday.

BENJ. HARRISON.

By the President:

REDFIELD PROCTOR,
Secretary of War.

AMENDMENTS OF CIVIL-SERVICE RULES.

EXECUTIVE MANSION, *June 10, 1889.*

Special Departmental Rule No. 1 is hereby amended as follows:

In section 2, at the end of paragraph 1, insert the following: ''foremen of laborers, skilled laborers, elevator conductors, foreman of cabinet shop, and cabinetmakers.''

So that as amended so much of section 2 as relates to the office of the Secretary of the Treasury will read:

In the office of the Secretary: Government actuary, inspector of furniture, custodian of dies, rolls, and plates at the Bureau of Engraving and Printing, two subcustodians, keeper of the vault, and distributer of stock, foremen of laborers, skilled laborers, elevator conductors, foreman of cabinet shop, and cabinetmakers.

In section 3 strike out the last paragraph and insert in lieu thereof the following:

In the Geological Survey: General assistant, executive officer, chief photographer, editor, all scientific employees of the Geological Survey officially designated as follows: Chief geologist, geologist, assistant geologist, chief paleontologist, paleontologist, and assistant paleontologist, chief chemist, chemist, assistant chemist, chief physicist, physicist, assistant physicist, chief geographer, geographer, assistant geographer, chief topographer, topographer, assistant topographer, chief hydrographer, hydrographer, assistant hydrographer, supervising engineer, engineer, assistant engineer, paleontological draftsman, chief mechanician, mechanician, assistant mechanician.

BENJ. HARRISON.

AMENDMENT OF CIVIL-SERVICE RULES.

EXECUTIVE MANSION, *June 18, 1889.*

Departmental Rule X, Customs Rule VII, Postal Rule VII, and Railway Mail Rule VI are hereby amended by adding to each of said rules, at the end thereof, the following:

Provided, That certification may be made, subject to the other conditions of this rule, for the reinstatement of any person who served in the military or naval service of the United States in the late War of the Rebellion, and was honorably discharged therefrom, without regard to the length of time he has been separated from the service.

BENJ. HARRISON.

AMENDMENT OF CIVIL-SERVICE RULES.

JULY 26, 1889.

Clause (*h*) of section 2 of General Rule III is hereby amended by adding to that clause, at the end thereof, the following: "or for temporary appointment for not exceeding thirty days in any part of the classified service."

Approved:

BENJ. HARRISON.

AMENDMENT OF CIVIL-SERVICE RULES.

JULY 26, 1889.

Section 5 of Railway Mail Rule II is hereby amended by adding an additional clause, as follows:

(*c*) Printers, employed as such.

Approved:

BENJ. HARRISON.

AMENDMENT OF CIVIL-SERVICE RULES.

EXECUTIVE MANSION, *August 17, 1889.*

Clause 5 of Railway Mail Rule II is hereby amended by adding thereto the following clauses:

(*d*) Clerks employed exclusively as porters in handling mail matter in bulk, in sacks, or pouches, and not otherwise.

(*e*) Clerks employed exclusively on steamboats.

Approved:

BENJ. HARRISON.

AMENDMENT OF CIVIL-SERVICE RULES.

AUGUST 20, 1889.

Clause 2 of Special Departmental Rule No. 1 is hereby amended by including among the places excepted from examination in the office of the Supervising Architect the following: "engineers and draftsmen of classes 1, 2, 3, 4, and 5, not exceeding ten in all: *Provided*, That these ten places shall cease to be excepted places from and after June 30, 1890.''

As thus amended so much of clause 2 as relates to the office of the Supervising Architect will read as follows:

In the office of the Supervising Architect: Supervising Architect, assistant and chief clerk, confidential clerk to Supervising Architect, photographer, engineers and draftsmen of classes 1, 2, 3, 4, and 5, not exceeding ten in all: *Provided*, That these ten places shall cease to be excepted places from and after June 30, 1890.

Approved: BENJ. HARRISON.

AMENDMENT OF CIVIL-SERVICE RULES.

OCTOBER 29, 1889.

Section 2 of Special Departmental Rule No. 1 is hereby amended by adding to the places excepted from examination in the Bureau of Engraving and Printing the following: ''plate cleaners, transferrers, hardeners, provers, pressmen, machinists, plumbers, carpenters, and blacksmiths.''

Approved: BENJ. HARRISON.

AMENDMENTS OF CIVIL-SERVICE RULES.

Section 2 of Railway Mail Rule IV is hereby amended by substituting for clause (*b*) of said section the following:

(*b*) The Commission shall certify from the register of the State or Territory in which the vacancy exists the names of the three eligibles thereon having the highest averages, resident in the counties of said State or Territory through or on the borders of which the section of the road passes on which the person to be appointed is to serve, who have not been three times certified: *Provided*, That if there are not three eligibles resident in said counties, then certification shall be made in like manner from the counties of said State or Territory nearest to the line of said road in which there are three eligibles; or if there are not three eligibles upon the register of said State or Territory, then certification may be made from the register of any adjoining State or Territory: *Provided further*, That if upon the register of the State or Territory in which vacancy exists there are the names of eligibles having a claim of preference under section 1754, Revised Statutes, the names of such eligibles shall be certified before the names of other eligibles of higher grade.

At the end of the rule add an additional section, as follows:

7. In case of public and pressing exigency demanding the immediate employment of experienced railway mail clerks who can not be at once supplied in the manner provided for in section 2 of this rule, or by transfer under Rule V, or reappointment under Rule VI, there may be employed, without examination or certification, under such regulations as the Postmaster-General may prescribe, for a period not to exceed thirty days, which, with the consent of the Commission, may be extended to sixty days, any persons who have been in the railway mail service, who have the requisite knowledge and experience, who may be available. Every such employment and the reasons therefor shall be at once reported to the Commission.

Approved, November 1, 1889.   BENJ. HARRISON.

AMENDMENT OF CIVIL-SERVICE RULES.

Special Customs Rule No. 1 is hereby amended by adding to the places excepted from examination at the port of New York the following:

Office of the General Appraiser: Chief clerk and law clerk.

Approved, November 18, 1889.

BENJ. HARRISON.

FIRST ANNUAL MESSAGE.

EXECUTIVE MANSION,
Washington, December 3, 1889.

To the Senate and House of Representatives:

There are few transactions in the administration of the Government that are even temporarily held in the confidence of those charged with the conduct of the public business. Every step taken is under the observation of an intelligent and watchful people. The state of the Union is known from day to day, and suggestions as to needed legislation find an earlier voice than that which speaks in these annual communications of the President to Congress.

Good will and cordiality have characterized our relations and correspondence with other governments, and the year just closed leaves few international questions of importance remaining unadjusted. No obstacle is believed to exist that can long postpone the consideration and adjustment of the still pending questions upon satisfactory and honorable terms. The dealings of this Government with other states have been and should always be marked by frankness and sincerity, our purposes avowed, and our methods free from intrigue. This course has borne rich fruit in the past, and it is our duty as a nation to preserve the heritage of good repute which a century of right dealing with foreign governments has secured to us.

It is a matter of high significance and no less of congratulation that the first year of the second century of our constitutional existence finds as honored guests within our borders the representatives of all the independent States of North and South America met together in earnest conference touching the best methods of perpetuating and expanding the relations of mutual interest and friendliness existing among them. That the opportunity thus afforded for promoting closer international relations and the increased prosperity of the States represented will be used for the mutual good of all I can not permit myself to doubt. Our people will await with interest and confidence the results to flow from so auspicious a meeting of allied and in large part identical interests.

The recommendations of this international conference of enlightened statesmen will doubtless have the considerate attention of Congress and its cooperation in the removal of unnecessary barriers to beneficial intercourse between the nations of America. But while the commercial results which it is hoped will follow this conference are worthy of pursuit and of the great interests they have excited, it is believed that the crowning benefit will be found in the better securities which may be devised for the maintenance of peace among all American nations and the settlement of all contentions by methods that a Christian civilization can approve. While viewing with interest our national resources and products, the delegates will, I am sure, find a higher satisfaction in the evidences of unselfish friendship which everywhere attend their intercourse with our people.

Another international conference having great possibilities for good has lately assembled and is now in session in this capital. An invitation was extended by the Government, under the act of Congress of July 9, 1888, to all maritime nations to send delegates to confer touching the revision and amendment of the rules and regulations governing vessels at sea and to adopt a uniform system of marine signals. The response to this invitation has been very general and very cordial. Delegates from twenty-six nations are present in the conference, and they have entered upon their useful work with great zeal and with an evident appreciation of its importance. So far as the agreement to be reached may require legislation to give it effect, the cooperation of Congress is confidently relied upon.

It is an interesting, if not, indeed, an unprecedented, fact that the two international conferences have brought together here the accredited representatives of thirty-three nations.

Bolivia, Ecuador, and Honduras are now represented by resident envoys of the plenipotentiary grade. All the States of the American system now maintain diplomatic representation at this capital.

In this connection it may be noted that all the nations of the Western Hemisphere, with one exception, send to Washington envoys extraordinary and ministers plenipotentiary, being the highest grade accredited to this Government. The United States, on the contrary, sends envoys of lower grades to some of our sister Republics. Our representative in Paraguay and Uruguay is a minister resident, while to Bolivia we send a minister resident and consul-general. In view of the importance of our relations with the States of the American system, our diplomatic agents in those countries should be of the uniform rank of envoy extraordinary and minister plenipotentiary. Certain missions were so elevated by the last Congress with happy effect, and I recommend the completion of the reform thus begun, with the inclusion also of Hawaii and Hayti, in view of their relations to the American system of states.

I also recommend that timely provision be made for extending to

Hawaii an invitation to be represented in the international conference now sitting at this capital.

Our relations with China have the attentive consideration which their magnitude and interest demand. The failure of the treaty negotiated under the Administration of my predecessor for the further and more complete restriction of Chinese labor immigration, and with it the legislation of the last session of Congress dependent thereon, leaves some questions open which Congress should now approach in that wise and just spirit which should characterize the relations of two great and friendly powers. While our supreme interests demand the exclusion of a laboring element which experience has shown to be incompatible with our social life, all steps to compass this imperative need should be accompanied with a recognition of the claim of those strangers now lawfully among us to humane and just treatment.

The accession of the young Emperor of China marks, we may hope, an era of progress and prosperity for the great country over which he is called to rule.

The present state of affairs in respect to the Samoan Islands is encouraging. The conference which was held in this city in the summer of 1887 between the representatives of the United States, Germany, and Great Britain having been adjourned because of the persistent divergence of views which was developed in its deliberations, the subsequent course of events in the islands gave rise to questions of a serious character. On the 4th of February last the German minister at this capital, in behalf of his Government, proposed a resumption of the conference at Berlin. This proposition was accepted, as Congress in February last was informed.

Pursuant to the understanding thus reached, commissioners were appointed by me, by and with the advice and consent of the Senate, who proceeded to Berlin, where the conference was renewed. The deliberations extended through several weeks, and resulted in the conclusion of a treaty which will be submitted to the Senate for its approval. I trust that the efforts which have been made to effect an adjustment of this question will be productive of the permanent establishment of law and order in Samoa upon the basis of the maintenance of the rights and interests of the natives as well as of the treaty powers.

The questions which have arisen during the past few years between Great Britain and the United States are in abeyance or in course of amicable adjustment.

On the part of the government of the Dominion of Canada an effort has been apparent during the season just ended to administer the laws and regulations applicable to the fisheries with as little occasion for friction as was possible, and the temperate representations of this Government in respect of cases of undue hardship or of harsh interpretations have been in most cases met with measures of transitory relief. It is trusted that the attainment of our just rights under existing treaties and in virtue of the concurrent legislation of the two contiguous countries will not be long deferred and that all existing causes of difference may be equitably adjusted.

I recommend that provision be made by an international agreement for visibly marking the water boundary between the United States and Canada in the narrow channels that join the Great Lakes. The conventional line therein traced by the northwestern boundary survey years ago is not in all cases readily ascertainable for the settlement of jurisdictional questions.

A just and acceptable enlargement of the list of offenses for which extradition may be claimed and granted is most desirable between this country and Great Britain. The territory of neither should become a secure harbor for the evil doers of the other through any avoidable shortcoming in this regard. A new treaty on this subject between the two powers has been recently negotiated and will soon be laid before the Senate.

The importance of the commerce of Cuba and Puerto Rico with the United States, their nearest and principal market, justifies the expectation that the existing relations may be beneficially expanded. The impediments resulting from varying dues on navigation and from the vexatious treatment of our vessels on merely technical grounds of complaint in West India ports should be removed.

The progress toward an adjustment of pending claims between the United States and Spain is not as rapid as could be desired.

Questions affecting American interests in connection with railways constructed and operated by our citizens in Peru have claimed the attention of this Government. It is urged that other governments in pressing Peru to the payment of their claims have disregarded the property rights of American citizens. The matter will be carefully investigated with a view to securing a proper and equitable adjustment.

A similar issue is now pending with Portugal. The Delagoa Bay Railway, in Africa, was constructed under a concession by Portugal to an American citizen. When nearly completed the road was seized by the agents of the Portuguese Government. Formal protest has been made through our minister at Lisbon against this act, and no proper effort will be spared to secure proper relief.

In pursuance of the charter granted by Congress and under the terms of its contract with the Government of Nicaragua the Interoceanic Canal Company has begun the construction of the important waterway between the two oceans which its organization contemplates. Grave complications for a time seemed imminent, in view of a supposed conflict of jurisdiction between Nicaragua and Costa Rica in regard to the accessory privileges to be conceded by the latter Republic toward the construction of works on the San Juan River, of which the right bank is Costa Rican territory. I am happy to learn that a friendly arrangement has been effected between the two nations. This Government has held itself ready to promote in every proper way the adjustment of all questions that might present obstacles to the completion of a work of such transcendent importance to the commerce of this country, and, indeed, to the commercial interests of the world.

The traditional good feeling between this country and the French Republic has received additional testimony in the participation of our Government and people in the international exposition held at Paris during the past summer. The success of our exhibitors has been gratifying. The report of the commission will be laid before Congress in due season.

This Government has accepted, under proper reserve as to its policy in foreign territories, the invitation of the Government of Belgium to take part in an international congress, which opened at Brussels on the 16th of November, for the purpose of devising measures to promote the abolition of the slave trade in Africa and to prevent the shipment of slaves by sea. Our interest in the extinction of this crime against humanity in the regions where it yet survives has been increased by the results of emancipation within our own borders.

With Germany the most cordial relations continue. The questions arising from the return to the Empire of Germans naturalized in this country are considered and disposed of in a temperate spirit to the entire satisfaction of both Governments.

It is a source of great satisfaction that the internal disturbances of the Republic of Hayti are at last happily ended, and that an apparently stable government has been constituted. It has been duly recognized by the United States.

A mixed commission is now in session in this capital for the settlement of long-standing claims against the Republic of Venezuela, and it is hoped that a satisfactory conclusion will be speedily reached. This Government has not hesitated to express its earnest desire that the boundary dispute now pending between Great Britain and Venezuela may be adjusted amicably and in strict accordance with the historic title of the parties.

The advancement of the Empire of Japan has been evidenced by the recent promulgation of a new constitution, containing valuable guaranties of liberty and providing for a responsible ministry to conduct the Government.

It is earnestly recommended that our judicial rights and processes in Korea be established on a firm basis by providing the machinery necessary to carry out treaty stipulations in that regard.

The friendliness of the Persian Government continues to be shown by its generous treatment of Americans engaged in missionary labors and by the cordial disposition of the Shah to encourage the enterprise of our citizens in the development of Persian resources.

A discussion is in progress touching the jurisdictional treaty rights of the United States in Turkey. An earnest effort will be made to define those rights to the satisfaction of both Governments.

Questions continue to arise in our relations with several countries in respect to the rights of naturalized citizens. Especially is this the case with France, Italy, Russia, and Turkey, and to a less extent with Switzerland. From time to time earnest efforts have been made to regulate this subject by conventions with those countries. An improper use of naturalization should not be permitted, but it is most important that those who have been duly naturalized should everywhere be accorded recognition of the rights pertaining to the citizenship of the country of their adoption. The appropriateness of special conventions for that purpose is recognized in treaties which this Government has concluded with a number of European States, and it is advisable that the difficulties which now arise in our relations with other countries on the same subject should be similarly adjusted.

The recent revolution in Brazil in favor of the establishment of a republican form of government is an event of great interest to the United States. Our minister at Rio de Janeiro was at once instructed to maintain friendly diplomatic relations with the Provisional Government, and the Brazilian representatives at this capital were instructed by the Provisional Government to continue their functions. Our friendly intercourse with Brazil has therefore suffered no interruption.

Our minister has been further instructed to extend on the part of this Government a formal and cordial recognition of the new Republic so soon as the majority of the people of Brazil shall have signified their assent to its establishment and maintenance.

Within our own borders a general condition of prosperity prevails. The harvests of the last summer were exceptionally abundant, and the trade conditions now prevailing seem to promise a successful season to the merchant and the manufacturer and general employment to our working people.

The report of the Secretary of the Treasury for the fiscal year ending June 30, 1889, has been prepared and will be presented to Congress. It presents with clearness the fiscal operations of the Government, and I avail myself of it to obtain some facts for use here.

The aggregate receipts from all sources for the year were $387,050,-058.84, derived as follows:

From customs	$223,832,741.69
From internal revenue	130,881,513.92
From miscellaneous sources	32,335,803.23

The ordinary expenditures for the same period were $281,996,615.60, and the total expenditures, including the sinking fund, were $329,579,-929.25. The excess of receipts over expenditures was, after providing for the sinking fund, $57,470,129.59.

For the current fiscal year the total revenues, actual and estimated, are $385,000,000, and the ordinary expenditures, actual and estimated, are $293,000,000, making with the sinking fund a total expenditure of $341,321,116.99, leaving an estimated surplus of $43,678,883.01.

During the fiscal year there was applied to the purchase of bonds, in addition to those for the sinking fund, $90,456,172.35, and during the first quarter of the current year the sum of $37,838,937.77, all of which were credited to the sinking fund. The revenues for the fiscal year ending June 30, 1891, are estimated by the Treasury Department at $385,000,000, and the expenditures for the same period, including the sinking fund, at $341,430,477.70. This shows an estimated surplus for that year of $43,569,522.30, which is more likely to be increased than reduced when the actual transactions are written up.

The existence of so large an actual and anticipated surplus should have he immediate attention of Congress, with a view to reducing the receipts of the Treasury to the needs of the Government as closely as may be. The collection of moneys not needed for public uses imposes an unnecessary burden upon our people, and the presence of so large a surplus in the public vaults is a disturbing element in the conduct of private business. It has called into use expedients for putting it into circulation of very questionable propriety. We should not collect revenue for the purpose of anticipating our bonds beyond the requirements of the sinking fund, but any unappropriated surplus in the Treasury should be so used, as there is no other lawful way of returning the money to circulation, and the profit realized by the Government offers a substantial advantage.

The loaning of public funds to the banks without interest upon the security of Government bonds I regard as an unauthorized and dangerous expedient. It results in a temporary and unnatural increase of the banking capital of favored localities and compels a cautious and gradual recall of the deposits to avoid injury to the commercial interests. It is not to be expected that the banks having these deposits will sell their bonds to the Treasury so long as the present highly beneficial arrangement is continued. They now practically get interest both upon the bonds and their proceeds. No further use should be made of this method of getting the surplus into circulation, and the deposits now outstanding should be gradually withdrawn and applied to the purchase of bonds. It is fortunate that such a use can be made of the existing surplus, and for some time to come of any casual surplus that may exist after Congress has taken the necessary steps for a reduction of the revenue. Such legislation should be promptly but very considerately enacted.

I recommend a revision of our tariff law both in its administrative features and in the schedules. The need of the former is generally conceded, and an agreement upon the evils and inconveniences to be remedied and the best methods for their correction will probably not be difficult. Uniformity of valuation at all our ports is essential, and effective measures should be taken to secure it. It is equally desirable that questions affecting rates and classifications should be promptly decided.

The preparation of a new schedule of customs duties is a matter of great delicacy because of its direct effect upon the business of the country, and of great difficulty by reason of the wide divergence of opinion as to the objects that may properly be promoted by such legislation. Some disturbance of business may perhaps result from the consideration of this subject by Congress, but this temporary ill effect will be reduced to the minimum by prompt action and by the assurance which the country already enjoys that any necessary changes will be so made as not to impair the just and reasonable protection of our home industries. The inequalities of the law should be adjusted, but the protective principle should be maintained and fairly applied to the products of our farms as well as of our shops. These duties necessarily have relation to other things besides the public revenues. We can not limit their effects by fixing our eyes on the public Treasury alone. They have a direct relation to home production, to work, to wages, and to the commercial independence of our country, and the wise and patriotic legislator should enlarge the field of his vision to include all of these. The necessary reduction in our public revenues can, I am sure, be made without making the smaller burden more onerous than the larger by reason of the disabilities and limitations which the process of reduction puts upon both capital and labor. The free list can very safely be extended by placing thereon articles that do not offer injurious competition to such domestic products as our home labor can supply. The removal of the internal tax upon tobacco would relieve an important agricultural product from a burden which was imposed only because our revenue from customs duties was insufficient for the public needs. If safe provision against fraud can be devised, the removal of the tax upon spirits used in the arts and in manufactures would also offer an unobjectionable method of reducing the surplus.

A table presented by the Secretary of the Treasury showing the amount of money of all kinds in circulation each year from 1878 to the present time is of interest. It appears that the amount of national-bank notes in circulation has decreased during that period $114,109,729, of which $37,799,229 is chargeable to the last year. The withdrawal of bank circulation will necessarily continue under existing conditions. It is probable that the adoption of the suggestions made by the Comptroller of the Currency, namely, that the minimum deposit of bonds for the establishment of banks be reduced and that an issue of notes to the par value of the bonds be allowed, would help to maintain the bank circulation. But while this withdrawal of bank notes has been going on there has been a large increase in the amount of gold and silver coin in circulation and in the issues of gold and silver certificates.

The total amount of money of all kinds in circulation on March 1,

1878, was $805,793,807, while on October 1, 1889, the total was $1,405,-018,000. There was an increase of $293,417,552 in gold coin, of $57,554,100 in standard silver dollars, of $72,311,249 in gold certificates, of $276,619,715 in silver certificates, and of $14,073,787 in United States notes, making a total of $713,976,403. There was during the same period a decrease of $114,109,729 in bank circulation and of $642,481 in subsidiary silver. The net increase was $599,224,193. The circulation per capita has increased about $5 during the time covered by the table referred to.

The total coinage of silver dollars was on November 1, 1889, $343,-638,001, of which $283,539,521 were in the Treasury vaults and $60,-098,480 were in circulation. Of the amount in the vaults $277,319,944 were represented by outstanding silver certificates, leaving $6,219,577 not in circulation and not represented by certificates.

The law requiring the purchase by the Treasury of $2,000,000 worth of silver bullion each month, to be coined into silver dollars of 412½ grains, has been observed by the Department, but neither the present Secretary nor any of his predecessors has deemed it safe to exercise the discretion given by law to increase the monthly purchases to $4,000,000. When the law was enacted (February 28, 1878) the price of silver in the market was $1.204 per ounce, making the bullion value of the dollar 93 cents. Since that time the price has fallen as low as 91.2 cents per ounce, reducing the bullion value of the dollar to 70.6 cents. Within the last few months the market price has somewhat advanced, and on the 1st day of November last the bullion value of the silver dollar was 72 cents.

The evil anticipations which have accompanied the coinage and use of the silver dollar have not been realized. As a coin it has not had general use, and the public Treasury has been compelled to store it. But this is manifestly owing to the fact that its paper representative is more convenient. The general acceptance and the use of the silver certificate show that silver has not been otherwise discredited. Some favorable conditions have contributed to maintain this practical equality in their commercial use between the gold and silver dollars; but some of these are trade conditions that statutory enactments do not control and of the continuance of which we can not be certain.

I think it is clear that if we should make the coinage of silver at the present ratio free we must expect that the difference in the bullion values of the gold and silver dollars will be taken account of in commercial transactions; and I fear the same result would follow any considerable increase of the present rate of coinage. Such a result would be discreditable to our financial management and disastrous to all business interests. We should not tread the dangerous edge of such a peril. And, indeed, nothing more harmful could happen to the silver interests. Any safe legislation upon this subject must secure the equality of the two coins in their commercial uses.

I have always been an advocate of the use of silver in our currency.

We are large producers of that metal, and should not discredit it. To the plan which will be presented by the Secretary of the Treasury for the issuance of notes or certificates upon the deposit of silver bullion at its market value I have been able to give only a hasty examination, owing to the press of other matters and to the fact that it has been so recently formulated. The details of such a law require careful consideration, but the general plan suggested by him seems to satisfy the purpose—to continue the use of silver in connection with our currency and at the same time to obviate the danger of which I have spoken. At a later day I may communicate further with Congress upon this subject.

The enforcement of the Chinese exclusion act has been found to be very difficult on the northwestern frontier. Chinamen landing at Victoria find it easy to pass our border, owing to the impossibility with the force at the command of the customs officers of guarding so long an inland line. The Secretary of the Treasury has authorized the employment of additional officers, who will be assigned to this duty, and every effort will be made to enforce the law. The Dominion exacts a head tax of $50 for each Chinaman landed, and when these persons, in fraud of our law, cross into our territory and are apprehended our officers do not know what to do with them, as the Dominion authorities will not suffer them to be sent back without a second payment of the tax. An effort will be made to reach an understanding that will remove this difficulty.

The proclamation required by section 3 of the act of March 2, 1889, relating to the killing of seals and other fur-bearing animals, was issued by me on the 21st day of March,* and a revenue vessel was dispatched to enforce the laws and protect the interests of the United States. The establishment of a refuge station at Point Barrow, as directed by Congress, was successfully accomplished.

Judged by modern standards, we are practically without coast defenses. Many of the structures we have would enhance rather than diminish the perils of their garrisons if subjected to the fire of improved guns, and very few are so located as to give full effect to the greater range of such guns as we are now making for coast-defense uses. This general subject has had consideration in Congress for some years, and the appropriation for the construction of large rifled guns made one year ago was, I am sure, the expression of a purpose to provide suitable works in which these guns might be mounted. An appropriation now made for that purpose would not advance the completion of the works beyond our ability to supply them with fairly effective guns.

The security of our coast cities against foreign attacks should not rest altogether in the friendly disposition of other nations. There should be a second line wholly in our own keeping. I very urgently recommend an appropriation at this session for the construction of such works in our most exposed harbors.

I approve the suggestion of the Secretary of War that provision be made for encamping companies of the National Guard in our coast works

*See pp. 14-15.

for a specified time each year and for their training in the use of heavy guns. His suggestion that an increase of the artillery force of the Army is desirable is also, in this connection, commended to the consideration of Congress.

The improvement of our important rivers and harbors should be promoted by the necessary appropriations. Care should be taken that the Government is not committed to the prosecution of works not of public and general advantage and that the relative usefulness of works of that class is not overlooked. So far as this work can ever be said to be completed, I do not doubt that the end would be sooner and more economically reached if fewer separate works were undertaken at the same time, and those selected for their greater general interest were more rapidly pushed to completion. A work once considerably begun should not be subjected to the risks and deterioration which interrupted or insufficient appropriations necessarily occasion.

The assault made by David S. Terry upon the person of Justice Field, of the Supreme Court of the United States, at Lathrop, Cal., in August last, and the killing of the assailant by a deputy United States marshal who had been deputed to accompany Justice Field and to protect him from anticipated violence at the hands of Terry, in connection with the legal proceedings which have followed, suggest questions which, in my judgment, are worthy of the attention of Congress.

I recommend that more definite provision be made by law not only for the protection of Federal officers, but for a full trial of such cases in the United States courts. In recommending such legislation I do not at all impeach either the general adequacy of the provision made by the State laws for the protection of all citizens or the general good disposition of those charged with the execution of such laws to give protection to the officers of the United States. The duty of protecting its officers, as such, and of punishing those who assault them on account of their official acts should not be devolved expressly or by acquiescence upon the local authorities.

Events which have been brought to my attention happening in other parts of the country have also suggested the propriety of extending by legislation fuller protection to those who may be called as witnesses in the courts of the United States. The law compels those who are supposed to have knowledge of public offenses to attend upon our courts and grand juries and to give evidence. There is a manifest resulting duty that these witnesses shall be protected from injury on account of their testimony. The investigations of criminal offenses are often rendered futile and the punishment of crime impossible by the intimidation of witnesses.

The necessity of providing some more speedy method for disposing of the cases which now come for final adjudication to the Supreme Court becomes every year more apparent and urgent. The plan of providing some intermediate courts having final appellate jurisdiction of certain classes of questions and cases has, I think, received a more general approval from the bench and bar of the country than any other. Without attempting to discuss details, I recommend that provision be made for the establishment of such courts.

The salaries of the judges of the district courts in many of the districts are, in my judgment, inadequate. I recommend that all such salaries now below $5,000 per annum be increased to that amount. It is quite true that the amount of labor performed by these judges is very unequal, but as they can not properly engage in other pursuits to supplement their incomes the salary should be such in all cases as to provide an independent and comfortable support.

Earnest attention should be given by Congress to a consideration of the question how far the restraint of those combinations of capital commonly called "trusts" is matter of Federal jurisdiction. When organized, as they often are, to crush out all healthy competition and to monopolize the production or sale of an article of commerce and general necessity, they are dangerous conspiracies against the public good, and should be made the subject of prohibitory and even penal legislation.

The subject of an international copyright has been frequently commended to the attention of Congress by my predecessors. The enactment of such a law would be eminently wise and just.

Our naturalization laws should be so revised as to make the inquiry into the moral character and good disposition toward our Government of the persons applying for citizenship more thorough. This can only be done by taking fuller control of the examination, by fixing the times for hearing such applications, and by requiring the presence of some one who shall represent the Government in the inquiry. Those who are the avowed enemies of social order or who come to our shores to swell the injurious influence and to extend the evil practices of any association that defies our laws should not only be denied citizenship, but a domicile.

The enactment of a national bankrupt law of a character to be a permanent part of our general legislation is desirable. It should be simple in its methods and inexpensive in its administration.

The report of the Postmaster-General not only exhibits the operations of the Department for the last fiscal year, but contains many valuable suggestions for the improvement and extension of the service, which are commended to your attention. No other branch of the Government has so close a contact with the daily life of the people. Almost everyone uses the service it offers, and every hour gained in the transmission of the great commercial mails has an actual and possible value that only those engaged in trade can understand.

The saving of one day in the transmission of the mails between New York and San Francisco, which has recently been accomplished, is an incident worthy of mention.

The plan suggested of a supervision of the post-offices in separate districts that shall involve instruction and suggestion and a rating of the efficiency of the postmasters would, I have no doubt, greatly improve the service.

A pressing necessity exists for the erection of a building for the joint use of the Department and of the city post-office. The Department was partially relieved by renting outside quarters for a part of its force, but it is again overcrowded. The building used by the city office never was fit for the purpose, and is now inadequate and unwholesome.

The unsatisfactory condition of the law relating to the transmission through the mails of lottery advertisements and remittances is clearly stated by the Postmaster-General, and his suggestion as to amendments should have your favorable consideration.

The report of the Secretary of the Navy shows a reorganization of the bureaus of the Department that will, I do not doubt, promote the efficiency of each.

In general, satisfactory progress has been made in the construction of the new ships of war authorized by Congress. The first vessel of the new Navy, the *Dolphin*, was subjected to very severe trial tests and to very much adverse criticism; but it is gratifying to be able to state that a cruise around the world, from which she has recently returned, has demonstrated that she is a first-class vessel of her rate.

The report of the Secretary shows that while the effective force of the Navy is rapidly increasing by reason of the improved build and armament of the new ships, the number of our ships fit for sea duty grows very slowly. We had on the 4th of March last 37 serviceable ships, and though 4 have since been added to the list, the total has not been increased, because in the meantime 4 have been lost or condemned. Twenty-six additional vessels have been authorized and appropriated for; but it is probable that when they are completed our list will only be increased to 42—a gain of 5. The old wooden ships are disappearing almost as fast as the new vessels are added. These facts carry their own argument. One of the new ships may in fighting strength be equal to two of the old, but it can not do the cruising duty of two. It is important, therefore, that we should have a more rapid increase in the number of serviceable ships. I concur in the recommendation of the Secretary that the construction of 8 armored ships, 3 gunboats, and 5 torpedo boats be authorized.

An appalling calamity befell three of our naval vessels on duty at the Samoan Islands, in the harbor of Apia, in March last, involving the loss of 4 officers and 47 seamen, of two vessels, the *Trenton* and the *Vandalia*, and the disabling of a third, the *Nipsic*. Three vessels of the German navy, also in the harbor, shared with our ships the force of the hurricane and suffered even more heavily. While mourning the brave officers and men who died facing with high resolve perils greater than those of battle, it is most gratifying to state that the credit of the American Navy for seamanship, courage, and generosity was magnificently sustained in the storm-beaten harbor of Apia.

The report of the Secretary of the Interior exhibits the transactions of the Government with the Indian tribes. Substantial progress has been made in the education of the children of school age and in the allotment of lands to adult Indians. It is to be regretted that the policy of breaking up the tribal relation and of dealing with the Indian as an individual did not appear earlier in our legislation. Large reservations held in common and the maintenance of the authority of the chiefs and headmen have deprived the individual of every incentive to the exercise of thrift, and the annuity has contributed an affirmative impulse toward a state of confirmed pauperism.

Our treaty stipulations should be observed with fidelity and our legislation should be highly considerate of the best interests of an ignorant and helpless people. The reservations are now generally surrounded by white settlements. We can no longer push the Indian back into the wilderness, and it remains only by every suitable agency to push him upward into the estate of a self-supporting and responsible citizen. For the adult the first step is to locate him upon a farm, and for the child to place him in a school.

School attendance should be promoted by every moral agency, and those failing should be compelled. The national schools for Indians have been very successful and should be multiplied, and as far as possible should be so organized and conducted as to facilitate the transfer of the schools to the States or Territories in which they are located when the Indians in a neighborhood have accepted citizenship and have become otherwise fitted for such a transfer. This condition of things will be attained slowly, but it will be hastened by keeping it in mind; and in the meantime that cooperation between the Government and the mission schools which has wrought much good should be cordially and impartially maintained.

The last Congress enacted two distinct laws relating to negotiations with the Sioux Indians of Dakota for a relinquishment of a portion of their lands to the United States and for dividing the remainder into separate reservations. Both were approved on the same day—March 2. The one submitted to the Indians a specific proposition; the other (section 3 of the Indian appropriation act) authorized the President to appoint three commissioners to negotiate with these Indians for the accomplishment of the same general purpose, and required that any agreements made should be submitted to Congress for ratification.

On the 16th day of April last I appointed Hon. Charles Foster, of Ohio, Hon. William Warner, of Missouri, and Major-General George Crook, of the United States Army, commissioners under the last-named law. They were, however, authorized and directed first to submit to the Indians the definite proposition made to them by the act first mentioned, and only in the event of a failure to secure the assent of the requisite number to that proposition to open negotiations for modified terms under the other act. The work of the commission was prolonged and arduous, but the assent of the requisite number was, it is understood, finally obtained to the proposition made by Congress, though the report of the commission has not yet been submitted. In view of these facts, I shall not, as at present advised, deem it necessary to submit the agreement to Congress for ratification, but it will in due course be submitted for information. This agreement releases to the United States about 9,000,000 acres of land.

The commission provided for by section 14 of the Indian appropriation bill to negotiate with the Cherokee Indians and all other Indians owning or claiming lands lying west of the ninety-sixth degree of longitude for the cession to the United States of all such lands was constituted by the appointment of Hon. Lucius Fairchild, of Wisconsin, Hon. John F. Hartranft, of Pennsylvania, and Hon. Alfred M. Wilson, of Arkansas, and organized on June 29 last. Their first conference with the representatives of the Cherokees was held at Tahlequah July 29, with no definite results. General John F. Hartranft, of Pennsylvania, was prevented by ill health from taking part in the conference. His death, which occurred recently, is justly and generally lamented by a people he had served with conspicuous gallantry in war and with great fidelity in peace. The vacancy thus created was filled by the appointment of Hon. Warren G. Sayre, of Indiana.

A second conference between the commission and the Cherokees was begun November 6, but no results have yet been obtained, nor is it believed that a conclusion can be immediately expected. The cattle syndicate now occupying the lands for grazing purposes is clearly one of the agencies responsible for the obstruction of our negotiations with the Cherokees. The large body of agricultural lands constituting what is known as the ''Cherokee Outlet'' ought not to be, and, indeed, can not long be, held for grazing and for the advantage of a few against the public interests and the best advantage of the Indians themselves. The United States has now under the treaties certain rights in these lands. These will not be used oppressively, but it can not be allowed that those who by sufferance occupy these lands shall interpose to defeat the wise and beneficent purposes of the Government. I can not but believe that the advantageous character of the offer made by the United States to the Cherokee Nation for a full release of these lands as compared with other suggestions now made to them will yet obtain for it a favorable consideration.

Under the agreement made between the United States and the Muscogee (or Creek) Nation of Indians on the 19th day of January, 1889, an absolute title was secured by the United States to about 3,500,000 acres of land. Section 12 of the general Indian appropriation act approved March 2, 1889, made provision for the purchase by the United States from the Seminole tribe of a certain portion of their lands. The delegates of the Seminole Nation, having first duly evidenced to me their power to act in that behalf, delivered a proper release or conveyance to the United States of all the lands mentioned in the act, which was accepted by me and certified to be in compliance with the statute.

By the terms of both the acts referred to all the lands so purchased were declared to be a part of the public domain and open to settlement under the homestead law. But of the lands embraced in these purchases, being in the aggregate about 5,500,000 acres, 3,500,000 acres had already, under the terms of the treaty of 1866, been acquired by the United States for the purpose of settling other Indian tribes thereon and had been appropriated to that purpose. The land remaining and available for settlement consisted of 1,887,796 acres, surrounded on all sides by lands in the occupancy of Indian tribes. Congress had provided no civil government for the people who were to be invited by my proclamation to settle upon these lands, except as the new court which had been established at Muscogee or the United States courts in some of the adjoining States had power to enforce the general laws of the United States.

In this condition of things I was quite reluctant to open the lands to settlement; but in view of the fact that several thousand persons, many of them with their families, had gathered upon the borders of the Indian Territory with a view to securing homesteads on the ceded lands, and that delay would involve them in much loss and suffering, I did on the 23d day of March last issue a proclamation * declaring that the lands therein described would be open to settlement under the provisions of the law on the 22d day of April following at 12 o'clock noon. Two land districts had been established and the offices were opened for the transaction of business when the appointed time arrived.

It is much to the credit of the settlers that they very generally observed the limitation as to the time when they might enter the Territory. Care will be taken that those who entered in violation of the law do not secure the advantage they unfairly sought. There was a good deal of apprehension that the strife for locations would result in much violence and bloodshed, but happily these anticipations were not realized. It is estimated that there are now in the Territory about 60,000 people, and several considerable towns have sprung up, for which temporary municipal governments have been organized. Guthrie is said to have now a population of almost 8,000. Eleven schools and nine churches have been established, and three daily and five weekly newspapers are published in this city, whose charter and ordinances have only the sanction of the voluntary acquiescence of the people from day to day.

*See pp. 15-18.

Oklahoma City has a population of about 5,000, and is proportionately as well provided as Guthrie with churches, schools, and newspapers. Other towns and villages having populations of from 100 to 1,000 are scattered over the Territory.

In order to secure the peace of this new community in the absence o. civil government, I directed General Merritt, commanding the Department of the Missouri, to act in conjunction with the marshals of the United States to preserve the peace, and upon their requisition to use the troops to aid them in executing warrants and in quieting any riots or breaches of the peace that might occur. He was further directed to use his influence to promote good order and to avoid any conflicts between or with the settlers. Believing that the introduction and sale of liquors where no legal restraints or regulations existed would endanger the public peace, and in view of the fact that such liquors must first be introduced into the Indian reservations before reaching the white settlements, I further directed the general commanding to enforce the laws relating to the introduction of ardent spirits into the Indian country.

The presence of the troops has given a sense of security to the well-disposed citizens and has tended to restrain the lawless. In one instance the officer in immediate command of the troops went further than I deemed justifiable in supporting the *de facto* municipal government of Guthrie, and he was so informed, and directed to limit the interference of the military to the support of the marshals on the lines indicated in the original order. I very urgently recommend that Congress at once provide a Territorial government for these people. Serious questions, which may at any time lead to violent outbreaks, are awaiting the institution of courts for their peaceful adjustment. The American genius for self-government has been well illustrated in Oklahoma; but it is neither safe nor wise to leave these people longer to the expedients which have temporarily served them.

Provision should be made for the acquisition of title to town lots in the towns now established in Alaska, for locating town sites, and for the establishment of municipal governments. Only the mining laws have been extended to that Territory, and no other form of title to lands can now be obtained. The general land laws were framed with reference to the disposition of agricultural lands, and it is doubtful if their operation in Alaska would be beneficial.

We have fortunately not extended to Alaska the mistaken policy of establishing reservations for the Indian tribes, and can deal with them from the beginning as individuals with, I am sure, better results; but any disposition of the public lands and any regulations relating to timber and to the fisheries should have a kindly regard to their interests. Having no power to levy taxes, the people of Alaska are wholly dependent upon the General Government, to whose revenues the seal fisheries make a large annual contribution. An appropriation for education should neither be overlooked nor stinted.

The smallness of the population and the great distances between the settlements offer serious obstacles to the establishment of the usual Territorial form of government. Perhaps the organization of several sub-districts with a small municipal council of limited powers for each would be safe and useful.

Attention is called in this connection to the suggestions of the Secretary of the Treasury relating to the establishment of another port of entry in Alaska and of other needed customs facilities and regulations.

In the administration of the land laws the policy of facilitating in every proper way the adjustment of the honest claims of individual settlers upon the public lands has been pursued. The number of pending cases had during the preceding Administration been greatly increased under the operation of orders for a time suspending final action in a large part of the cases originating in the West and Northwest, and by the subsequent use of unusual methods of examination. Only those who are familiar with the conditions under which our agricultural lands have been settled can appreciate the serious and often fatal consequences to the settler of a policy that puts his title under suspicion or delays the issuance of his patent. While care is taken to prevent and to expose fraud, it should not be imputed without reason.

The manifest purpose of the homestead and preemption laws was to promote the settlement of the public domain by persons having a *bona fide* intent to make a home upon the selected lands. Where this intent is well established and the requirements of the law have been substantially complied with, the claimant is entitled to a prompt and friendly consideration of his case; but where there is reason to believe that the claimant is the mere agent of another who is seeking to evade a law intended to promote small holdings and to secure by fraudulent methods large tracts of timber and other lands, both principal and agent should not only be thwarted in their fraudulent purpose, but should be made to feel the full penalties of our criminal statutes. The laws should be so administered as not to confound these two classes and to visit penalties only upon the latter.

The unsettled state of the titles to large bodies of lands in the Territories of New Mexico and Arizona has greatly retarded the development of those Territories. Provision should be made by law for the prompt trial and final adjustment before a judicial tribunal or commission of all claims based upon Mexican grants. It is not just to an intelligent and enterprising people that their peace should be disturbed and their prosperity retarded by these old contentions. I express the hope that differences of opinion as to methods may yield to the urgency of the case.

The law now provides a pension for every soldier and sailor who was mustered into the service of the United States during the Civil War and is now suffering from wounds or disease having an origin in the service and in the line of duty. Two of the three necessary facts, viz, muster and disability, are usually susceptible of easy proof; but the third, origin in the service, is often difficult and in many deserving cases impossible to establish. That very many of those who endured the hardships of our most bloody and arduous campaigns are now disabled from diseases that had a real but not traceable origin in the service I do not doubt. Besides these there is another class composed of men many of whom served an enlistment of three full years and of reenlisted veterans who added a fourth year of service, who escaped the casualties of battle and the assaults of disease, who were always ready for any detail, who were in every battle line of their command, and were mustered out in sound health, and have since the close of the war, while fighting with the same indomitable and independent spirit the contests of civil life, been overcome by disease or casualty.

I am not unaware that the pension roll already involves a very large annual expenditure; neither am I deterred by that fact from recommending that Congress grant a pension to such honorably discharged soldiers and sailors of the Civil War as, having rendered substantial service during the war, are now dependent upon their own labor for a maintenance and by disease or casualty are incapacitated from earning it. Many of the men who would be included in this form of relief are now dependent upon public aid, and it does not, in my judgment, consist with the national honor that they shall continue to subsist upon the local relief given indiscriminately to paupers instead of upon the special and generous provision of the nation they served so gallantly and unselfishly. Our people will, I am sure, very generally approve such legislation. And I am equally sure that the survivors of the Union Army and Navy will feel a grateful sense of relief when this worthy and suffering class of their comrades is fairly cared for.

There are some manifest inequalities in the existing law that should be remedied. To some of these the Secretary of the Interior has called attention.

It is gratifying to be able to state that by the adoption of new and better methods in the War Department the calls of the Pension Office for information as to the military and hospital records of pension claimants are now promptly answered and the injurious and vexatious delays that have heretofore occurred are entirely avoided. This will greatly facilitate the adjustment of all pending claims.

The advent of four new States—South Dakota, North Dakota, Montana, and Washington—into the Union under the Constitution in the same month, and the admission of their duly chosen representatives to our National Congress at the same session, is an event as unexampled as it is interesting.

The certification of the votes cast and of the constitutions adopted in each of the States was filed with me, as required by the eighth section of the act of February 22, 1889, by the governors of said Territories, respectively. Having after a careful examination found that the several constitutions and governments were republican in form and not repugnant to the Constitution of the United States, that all the provisions of the act of Congress had been complied with, and that a majority of the votes cast in each of said proposed States was in favor of the adoption of the constitution submitted therein, I did so declare by a separate proclamation as to each—as to North Dakota and South Dakota on Saturday, November 2;* as to Montana on Friday, November 8,† and as to Washington on Monday, November 11.‡

Each of these States has within it resources the development of which will employ the energies of and yield a comfortable subsistence to a great population. The smallest of these new States, Washington, stands twelfth, and the largest, Montana, third, among the forty-two in area. The people of these States are already well-trained, intelligent, and patriotic American citizens, having common interests and sympathies with those of the older States and a common purpose to defend the integrity and uphold the honor of the nation.

The attention of the Interstate Commerce Commission has been called to the urgent need of Congressional legislation for the better protection of the lives and limbs of those engaged in operating the great interstate freight lines of the country, and especially of the yardmen and brakemen. A petition signed by nearly 10,000 railway brakemen was presented to the Commission asking that steps might be taken to bring about the use of automatic brakes and couplers on freight cars.

At a meeting of State railroad commissioners and their accredited representatives held at Washington in March last upon the invitation of the Interstate Commerce Commission a resolution was unanimously adopted urging the Commission "to consider what can be done to prevent the loss of life and limb in coupling and uncoupling freight cars and in handling the brakes of such cars." During the year ending June 30, 1888, over 2,000 railroad employees were killed in service and more than 20,000 injured. It is competent, I think, for Congress to require uniformity in the construction of cars used in interstate commerce and the use of improved safety appliances upon such trains. Time will be necessary to make the needed changes, but an earnest and intelligent beginning should be made at once. It is a reproach to our civilization that any class of American workmen should in the pursuit of a necessary and useful vocation be subjected to a peril of life and limb as great as that of a soldier in time of war.

The creation of an Executive Department to be known as the Department of Agriculture by the act of February 9 last was a wise and timely response to a request which had long been respectfully urged by the farmers of the country; but much remains to be done to perfect the organization of the Department so that it may fairly realize the

---

*See pp. 20-24.   † See pp. 24-25.   ‡ See pp. 25-26.

expectations which its creation excited. In this connection attention is called to the suggestions contained in the report of the Secretary, which is herewith submitted. The need of a law officer for the Department such as is provided for the other Executive Departments is manifest. The failure of the last Congress to make the usual provision for the publication of the annual report should be promptly remedied. The public interest in the report and its value to the farming community, I am sure, will not be diminished under the new organization of the Department.

I recommend that the weather service be separated from the War Department and established as a bureau in the Department of Agriculture. This will involve an entire reorganization both of the Weather Bureau and of the Signal Corps, making of the first a purely civil organization and of the other a purely military staff corps. The report of the Chief Signal Officer shows that the work of the corps on its military side has been deteriorating.

The interests of the people of the District of Columbia should not be lost sight of in the pressure for consideration of measures affecting the whole country. Having no legislature of its own, either municipal or general, its people must look to Congress for the regulation of all those concerns that in the States are the subject of local control. Our whole people have an interest that the national capital should be made attractive and beautiful, and, above all, that its repute for social order should be well maintained. The laws regulating the sale of intoxicating drinks in the District should be revised with a view to bringing the traffic under stringent limitations and control.

In execution of the power conferred upon me by the act making appropriations for the expenses of the District of Columbia for the year ending June 30, 1890, I did on the 17th day of August last appoint Rudolph Hering, of New York, Samuel M. Gray, of Rhode Island, and Frederick P. Stearns, of Massachusetts, three eminent sanitary engineers, to examine and report upon the system of sewerage existing in the District of Columbia. Their report, which is not yet completed, will be in due course submitted to Congress.

The report of the Commissioners of the District is herewith transmitted, and the attention of Congress is called to the suggestions contained therein.

The proposition to observe the four hundredth anniversary of the discovery of America by the opening of a world's fair or exposition in some one of our great cities will be presented for the consideration of Congress. The value and interest of such an exposition may well claim the promotion of the General Government.

On the 4th of March last the Civil Service Commission had but a single member. The vacancies were filled on the 7th day of May, and since then the Commissioners have been industriously, though with an inadequate force, engaged in executing the law. They were assured by me that a cordial support would be given them in the faithful and impartial enforcement of the statute and of the rules and regulations adopted in aid of it.

Heretofore the book of eligibles has been closed to everyone, except as certifications were made upon the requisition of the appointing officers. This secrecy was the source of much suspicion and of many charges of favoritism in the administration of the law. What is secret is always suspected; what is open can be judged. The Commission, with the full approval of all its members, has now opened the list of eligibles to the public. The eligible lists for the classified post-offices and custom-houses are now publicly posted in the respective offices, as are also the certifications for appointments. The purpose of the civil-service law was absolutely to exclude any other consideration in connection with appointments under it than that of merit as tested by the examinations. The business proceeds upon the theory that both the examining boards and the appointing officers are absolutely ignorant as to the political views and associations of all persons on the civil-service lists. It is not too much to say, however, that some recent Congressional investigations have somewhat shaken public confidence in the impartiality of the selections for appointment.

The reform of the civil service will make no safe or satisfactory advance until the present law and its equal administration are well established in the confidence of the people. It will be my pleasure, as it is my duty, to see that the law is executed with firmness and impartiality. If some of its provisions have been fraudulently evaded by appointing officers, our resentment should not suggest the repeal of the law, but reform in its administration. We should have one view of the matter, and hold it with a sincerity that is not affected by the consideration that the party to which we belong is for the time in power.

My predecessor, on the 4th day of January, 1889, by an Executive order to take effect March 15, brought the Railway Mail Service under the operation of the civil-service law.* Provision was made that the order should take effect sooner in any State where an eligible list was sooner obtained. On the 11th day of March Mr. Lyman, then the only member of the Commission, reported to me in writing that it would not be possible to have the list of eligibles ready before May 1, and requested that the taking effect of the order be postponed until that time, which was done,† subject to the same provision contained in the original order as to States in which an eligible list was sooner obtained.

As a result of the revision of the rules, of the new classification, and of the inclusion of the Railway Mail Service, the work of the Commission has been greatly increased, and the present clerical force is found to be inadequate. I recommend that the additional clerks asked by the Commission be appropriated for.

*See Vol. VIII, pp. 847–851. † See p. 27.

The duty of appointment is devolved by the Constitution or by the law, and the appointing officers are properly held to a high responsibility in its exercise. The growth of the country and the consequent increase of the civil list have magnified this function of the Executive disproportionally. It can not be denied, however, that the labor connected with this necessary work is increased, often to the point of actual distress, by the sudden and excessive demands that are made upon an incoming Administration for removals and appointments. But, on the other hand, it is not true that incumbency is a conclusive argument for continuance in office. Impartiality, moderation, fidelity to public duty, and a good attainment in the discharge of it must be added before the argument is complete. When those holding administrative offices so conduct themselves as to convince just political opponents that no party consideration or bias affects in any way the discharge of their public duties, we can more easily stay the demand for removals.

I am satisfied that both in and out of the classified service great benefit would accrue from the adoption of some system by which the officer would receive the distinction and benefit that in all private employments comes from exceptional faithfulness and efficiency in the performance of duty.

I have suggested to the heads of the Executive Departments that they consider whether a record might not be kept in each bureau of all those elements that are covered by the terms "faithfulness" and "efficiency," and a rating made showing the relative merits of the clerks of each class, this rating to be regarded as a test of merit in making promotions.

I have also suggested to the Postmaster-General that he adopt some plan by which he can, upon the basis of the reports to the Department and of frequent inspections, indicate the relative merit of postmasters of each class. They will be appropriately indicated in the Official Register and in the report of the Department. That a great stimulus would thus be given to the whole service I do not doubt, and such a record would be the best defense against inconsiderate removals from office.

The interest of the General Government in the education of the people found an early expression, not only in the thoughtful and sometimes warning utterances of our ablest statesmen, but in liberal appropriations from the common resources for the support of education in the new States. No one will deny that it is of the gravest national concern that those who hold the ultimate control of all public affairs should have the necessary intelligence wisely to direct and determine them. National aid to education has heretofore taken the form of land grants, and in that form the constitutional power of Congress to promote the education of the people is not seriously questioned. I do not think it can be successfully questioned when the form is changed to that of a direct grant of money from the public Treasury.

Such aid should be, as it always has been, suggested by some exceptional conditions. The sudden emancipation of the slaves of the South, the bestowal of the suffrage which soon followed, and the impairment of the ability of the States where these new citizens were chiefly found to adequately provide educational facilities presented not only exceptional but unexampled conditions. That the situation has been much ameliorated there is no doubt. The ability and interest of the States have happily increased.

But a great work remains to be done, and I think the General Government should lend its aid. As the suggestion of a national grant in aid of education grows chiefly out of the condition and needs of the emancipated slave and his descendants, the relief should as far as possible, while necessarily proceeding upon some general lines, be applied to the need that suggested it. It is essential, if much good is to be accomplished, that the sympathy and active interest of the people of the States should be enlisted, and that the methods adopted should be such as to stimulate and not to supplant local taxation for school purposes.

As one Congress can not bind a succeeding one in such a case and as the effort must in some degree be experimental, I recommend that any appropriation made for this purpose be so limited in annual amount and as to the time over which it is to extend as will on the one hand give the local school authorities opportunity to make the best use of the first year's allowance, and on the other deliver them from the temptation to unduly postpone the assumption of the whole burden themselves.

The colored people did not intrude themselves upon us. They were brought here in chains and held in the communities where they are now chiefly found by a cruel slave code. Happily for both races, they are now free. They have from a standpoint of ignorance and poverty— which was our shame, not theirs—made remarkable advances in education and in the acquisition of property. They have as a people shown themselves to be friendly and faithful toward the white race under temptations of tremendous strength. They have their representatives in the national cemeteries, where a grateful Government has gathered the ashes of those who died in its defense. They have furnished to our Regular Army regiments that have won high praise from their commanding officers for courage and soldierly qualities and for fidelity to the enlistment oath. In civil life they are now the toilers of their communities, making their full contribution to the widening streams of prosperity which these communities are receiving. Their sudden withdrawal would stop production and bring disorder into the household as well as the shop. Generally they do not desire to quit their homes, and their employers resent the interference of the emigration agents who seek to stimulate such a desire.

But notwithstanding all this, in many parts of our country where the colored population is large the people of that race are by various devices deprived of any effective exercise of their political rights and of many of their civil rights.   The wrong does not expend itself upon those whose votes are suppressed.   Every constituency in the Union is wronged.

It has been the hope of every patriot that a sense of justice and of respect for the law would work a gradual cure of these flagrant evils. Surely no one supposes that the present can be accepted as a permanent condition.   If it is said that these communities must work out this problem for themselves, we have a right to ask whether they are at work upon it.   Do they suggest any solution?   When and under what conditions is the black man to have a free ballot?   When is he in fact to have those full civil rights which have so long been his in law?   When is that equality of influence which our form of government was intended to secure to the electors to be restored?   This generation should courageously face these grave questions, and not leave them as a heritage of woe to the next.   The consultation should proceed with candor, calmness, and great patience, upon the lines of justice and humanity, not of prejudice and cruelty.   No question in our country can be at rest except upon the firm base of justice and of the law.

I earnestly invoke the attention of Congress to the consideration of such measures within its well-defined constitutional powers as will secure to all our people a free exercise of the right of suffrage and every other civil right under the Constitution and laws of the United States.   No evil, however deplorable, can justify the assumption either on the part of the Executive or of Congress of powers not granted, but both will be highly blamable if all the powers granted are not wisely but firmly used to correct these evils.   The power to take the whole direction and control of the election of members of the House of Representatives is clearly given to the General Government.   A partial and qualified supervision of these elections is now provided for by law, and in my opinion this law may be so strengthened and extended as to secure on the whole better results than can be attained by a law taking all the processes of such election into Federal control.   The colored man should be protected in all of his relations to the Federal Government, whether as litigant, juror, or witness in our courts, as an elector for members of Congress, or as a peaceful traveler upon our interstate railways.

There is nothing more justly humiliating to the national pride and nothing more hurtful to the national prosperity than the inferiority of our merchant marine compared with that of other nations whose general resources, wealth, and seacoast lines do not suggest any reason for their supremacy on the sea.   It was not always so, and our people are agreed, I think, that it shall not continue to be so.   It is not possible in this communication to discuss the causes of the decay of our shipping interests or the differing methods by which it is proposed to restore them.   The statement of a few well-authenticated facts and some general suggestions as to legislation is all that is practicable.   That the great steamship lines sailing under the flags of England, France, Germany, Spain, and Italy, and engaged in foreign commerce, were promoted and have since been and now are liberally aided by grants of public money in one form or another is generally known. That the American lines of steamships have been abandoned by us to an unequal contest with the aided lines of other nations until they have been withdrawn, or in the few cases where they are still maintained are subject to serious disadvantages, is matter of common knowledge.

The present situation is such that travelers and merchandise find Liverpool often a necessary intermediate port between New York and some of the South American capitals. The fact that some of the delegates from South American States to the conference of American nations now in session at Washington reached our shores by reversing that line of travel is very conclusive of the need of such a conference and very suggestive as to the first and most necessary step in the direction of fuller and more beneficial intercourse with nations that are now our neighbors upon the lines of latitude, but not upon the lines of established commercial intercourse.

I recommend that such appropriations be made for ocean mail service in American steamships between our ports and those of Central and South America, China, Japan, and the important islands in both of the great oceans as will be liberally remunerative for the service rendered and as will encourage the establishment and in some fair degree equalize the chances of American steamship lines in the competitions which they must meet. That the American States lying south of us will cordially cooperate in establishing and maintaining such lines of steamships to their principal ports I do not doubt.

We should also make provision for a naval reserve to consist of such merchant ships of American construction and of a specified tonnage and speed as the owners will consent to place at the use of the Government in case of need as armed cruisers. England has adopted this policy, and as a result can now upon necessity at once place upon her naval list some of the fastest steamships in the world. A proper supervision of the construction of such vessels would make their conversion into effective ships of war very easy.

I am an advocate of economy in our national expenditures, but it is a misuse of terms to make this word describe a policy that withholds an expenditure for the purpose of extending our foreign commerce. The enlargement and improvement of our merchant marine, the development of a sufficient body of trained American seamen, the promotion of rapid and regular mail communication between the ports of other countries and our own, and the adaptation of large and swift American merchant steamships to naval uses in time of war are public purposes of the highest concern. The enlarged participation of our people in the carrying trade, the new and increased markets that will be opened for the products of our farms and factories, and the fuller and better employment of our mechanics which will result from a liberal promotion of our foreign commerce insure the widest possible diffusion of benefit to all the States and to all our people. Everything is most propitious for the present inauguration of a liberal and progressive policy upon this subject, and we should enter upon it with promptness and decision.

The legislation which I have suggested, it is sincerely believed, will promote the peace and honor of our country and the prosperity and security of the people. I invoke the diligent and serious attention of Congress to the consideration of these and such other measures as may be presented having the same great end in view.

BENJ. HARRISON.

SPECIAL MESSAGES.

EXECUTIVE MANSION, *December 17, 1889.*
To the Senate and House of Representatives:

The act of Congress approved July 9, 1888, "for an international marine conference to secure greater safety for life and property at sea," and in virtue of which the present conference is now holding its sessions at Washington, provides by the third section that the labors of the conference shall terminate on the 1st day of January, 1890, or sooner, by direction of the President.

I transmit herewith a report from the Acting Secretary of State, accompanied with a letter from Rear-Admiral S. R. Franklin, United States Navy, president of the conference, stating that in all probability the labors of the conference can not be brought to a close by the time fixed by the present law.

In consideration of the many important questions now under discussion by the conference, which should if possible be satisfactorily determined before the final adjournment, I earnestly recommend that a further act be passed to enable the conference to continue its sessions for a period of two months from January 1, 1890.

BENJ. HARRISON.

EXECUTIVE MANSION, *December 18, 1889.*
To the Senate and House of Representatives:

I transmit herewith a communication of 16th instant from the Secretary of the Interior, submitting the report, with accompanying papers, of the commission appointed under the provisions of the act of March 2, 1889 (25 U. S. Statutes at Large, p. 1002), to conduct negotiations with the Cœur d'Alene tribe of Indians for the purchase and release by said tribe of such portions of its reservation not agricultural and valuable chiefly for minerals and timber as such tribe shall consent to sell, etc., together with the agreement entered into by said commission September 9, 1889, with said Indians. BENJ. HARRISON.

EXECUTIVE MANSION, *December 20, 1889.*

To the Senate and House of Representatives:

I transmit herewith a communication of the 16th instant from the Secretary of the Interior, submitting a draft of a bill "to provide for the reduction of the Round Valley Indian Reservation, in the State of California, and for other purposes." I invite your attention to the papers herein referred to, showing the necessity for the proposed legislation, and ask that the bill herewith receive careful and early consideration.

BENJ. HARRISON.

EXECUTIVE MANSION,
Washington, January 7, 1890.

To the Senate and House of Representatives:

I herewith inclose a report from the Secretary of State, with accompanying papers, in relation to the death of George Pauls, a German subject, at Wilmington, N. C., May 8, 1886, and the claim of his widow for compensation on that account. In view of the statements made by the Secretary of State, I earnestly recommend that an appropriation of $5,000 be made in behalf of Mrs. Pauls. BENJ. HARRISON.

EXECUTIVE MANSION,
Washington, January 13, 1890.

To the Senate and House of Representatives:

I transmit herewith a report of the Secretary of State of the 13th instant, recommending that the necessary means be provided to erect suitable buildings on the grounds so generously presented in the year 1884 to this Government for the use of its legation at Bangkok by His Majesty the King of Siam.

I commend the matter to the favorable consideration of Congress.

BENJ. HARRISON.

EXECUTIVE MANSION,
Washington, January 16, 1890.

To the Senate and House of Representatives:

I transmit herewith a report from the Secretary of State, in relation to the claim of the Government of Sweden and Norway, under the treaty between the United States and that Government of July 4, 1827, for the benefit of the lower rate of tonnage dues under the shipping acts of 1884 and 1886.

I recommend the immediate adoption by Congress of the necessary legislation to enable this Government to apply in the case of Sweden and Norway the same rule in respect to the levying of tonnage dues under the treaty of 1827 as was claimed and secured by this Government under the same instrument in 1828.

BENJ. HARRISON.

EXECUTIVE MANSION, *January 20, 1890.*

To the Senate and House of Representatives:

I transmit herewith a letter of Professor T. C. Mendenhall, chairman of a committee of the American Association for the Advancement of Science, and president of that association, and also the memorial prepared by said committee, relating to the preservation of the forests upon the public domain.

I very earnestly recommend that adequate legislation may be provided to the end that the rapid and needless destruction of our great forest areas may be prevented.

BENJ. HARRISON.

EXECUTIVE MANSION,
Washington, January 20, 1890.

To the Senate and House of Representatives:

I transmit herewith a letter from the Secretary of War, relating to the condition and needs of the band of Apache Indians now held at Mount Vernon Barracks and at Governors Island. The reports of General Crook and Lieutenant Howard, which accompany the letter of the Secretary, show that some of these Indians have rendered good service to the Government in the pursuit and capture of the murderous band that followed Natchez and Geronimo. It is a reproach that they should not in our treatment of them be distinguished from the cruel and bloody members of the tribe now confined with them.

I earnestly recommend that provision be made by law for locating these Indians upon lands in the Indian Territory.

BENJ. HARRISON.

EXECUTIVE MANSION,
Washington, January 27, 1890.

To the Senate of the United States:

I transmit, in reply to the resolution of the Senate of the 8th instant, a report from the Secretary of State, with accompanying documents, in relation to the execution of the acts of Congress approved May 6, 1882, and October 1, 1888, concerning Chinese.

BENJ. HARRISON.

EXECUTIVE MANSION, *February 10, 1890.*

To the Senate and House of Representatives:

In pursuance of the power vested in me by the terms of the last clause of section 3 of the act of Congress approved March 2, 1889, entitled "An act making appropriations for the current and contingent expenses of the Indian Department and for fulfilling treaty stipulations with various Indian tribes for the year ending June 30, 1890, and for other purposes," a commission, as therein authorized, was appointed, consisting of Charles Foster, of Ohio, William Warner, of Missouri, and General George Crook, of the United States Army. This commission was specially instructed to present to the Sioux Indians occupying the Great Sioux Reservation, for their acceptance thereof and consent thereto in manner and form as therein provided, the act of Congress approved March 2, 1889, entitled "An act to divide a portion of the reservation of the Sioux Nation of Indians in Dakota into separate reservations and to secure the relinquishment of the Indian title to the remainder, and for other purposes."

The report of the commission was submitted to me on the 24th day of December, 1889, and is, with the accompanying documents and a letter of the Secretary of the Interior, herewith transmitted for the information of Congress. It appears from the report of the commission that the consent of more than three-fourths of the adult Indians to the terms of the act last named was secured, as required by section 12 of the treaty of 1868, and upon a careful examination of the papers submitted I find such to be the fact, and that such consent is properly evidenced by the signatures of more than three-fourths of such Indians.

At the outset of the negotiations the commission was confronted by certain questions as to the interpretation and effect of the act of Congress which they were presenting for the acceptance of the Indians. Upon two or three points of some importance the commission gave in response to these inquiries an interpretation to the law, and it was the law thus explained to them that was accepted by the Indians. The commissioners had no power to bind Congress or the Executive by their construction of a statute, but they were the agents of the United States, first, to submit a definite proposition for the acceptance of the Indians, and, that failing, to agree upon modified terms to be submitted to Congress for ratification. They were dealing with an ignorant and suspicious people, and an explanation of the terms and effect of the offer submitted could not be avoided. Good faith demands that if the United States accepts the lands ceded the beneficial construction of the act given by our agents should be also admitted and observed.

The chief difficulty in the construction of the act grows out of its relation to prior treaties, which were by section 19 continued in force so far as they are not in conflict with the terms of the act. The seventh article of the treaty of 1868, relating to schools and schoolhouses, is by section 17 of the act continued in force for twenty years, "subject to such modifications as Congress shall deem most effective to secure to said Indians equivalent benefits of such education.''

Section 7 of the treaty of 1868 provides only for instruction in the ''elementary branches of an English education,'' while section 17 of the act, after continuing this section of the treaty in force, provides a fund which is to be applied ''for the promotion of industrial and other suitable education among said Indians.'' Again, section 7 of the treaty provides for the erection of a schoolhouse for every thirty children who can be induced to attend, while section 20 of the act requires the erection of not less than thirty schoolhouses, and more if found necessary.

The commissioners were asked by the Indians whether the cost of the English schools provided for in section 7 of the treaty and of the schoolhouses provided for in the same section and in section 20 of the act would be a charge against the proceeds of the lands they were now asked to cede to the United States. This question was answered in the negative, and I think the answer was correct. If the act, without reference to section 7 of the treaty, is to be construed to express the whole duty of the Government toward the Indians in the matter of schools, the extension for twenty years of the provisions of that section is without meaning.

The assurance given by the commissioners that the money appropriated by section 27 of the act to pay certain bands for the ponies taken by the military authorities in 1876 would not be a charge against the proceeds of the ceded lands was obviously a correct interpretation of the law.

The Indians were further assured by the commissioners that the amount appropriated for the expenses of the commission could not under the law be made a charge upon the proceeds of their lands. This, I think, is a correct exposition of the act.

It seems from the report of the commission that some of the Indians at the Standing Rock Agency asked whether if they accepted the act they could have the election to take their allotments under section 6 of the treaty of 1868 and have the benefits of sections 8 and 10 of that treaty, and were told that they could.

As the treaty is continued in force except where it contravenes the provisions of the act, I do not see any difficulty in admitting this interpretation.

It will be found that the commission has submitted many recommendations, some of them involving legislation and others appealing to powers already possessed by the executive department. The consent of the Indians to the act was not made dependent upon the adoption of any of these recommendations, but many of them are obviously just and promotive of the true interests of the Indians. So far as these require legislation they are earnestly commended to the attention of Congress.

The Secretary of the Interior has prepared and submits with his letter transmitting the report of the commission the draft of a bill embodying those recommendations of the commission requiring legislation.

The appropriations necessary to carry into effect the provisions of the act should be promptly made and be immediately available.

BENJ. HARRISON.

EXECUTIVE MANSION,
Washington, February 12, 1890

To the Senate and House of Representatives:

I transmit herewith a report from the Secretary of State, respecting the International Marine Conference which was held in the city of Washington in the year 1889, together with a copy of the proceedings of the conference, including the final act.

BENJ. HARRISON.

EXECUTIVE MANSION, *February 17 1890.*

To the Senate and House of Representatives:

I transmit herewith a communication of the 11th instant from the Secretary of the Interior, submitting a copy of a report from the Commissioner of Indian Affairs and accompanying draft of a bill to amend the first section of an act entitled "An act to provide for the allotment of lands in severalty to Indians on the various reservations, and to extend the protection of the laws of the United States and the Territories over the Indians, and for other purposes," approved February 8, 1887.

The matter is presented for the consideration and action of Congress.

BENJ. HARRISON.

EXECUTIVE MANSION, *February 18, 1890.*

To the Senate and House of Representatives:

I transmit herewith a communication of the 8th instant from the Secretary of the Interior, submitting a report of the Commissioner of Indian Affairs and accompanying agreement, made with the Sisseton and Wahpeton bands of Dakota or Sioux Indians, for the purchase and release of the surplus lands in the Lake Traverse Indian Reservation, in the States of North and South Dakota, the negotiations for said purchase and release having been conducted under the authority contained in the fifth section of the general allotment act of February 8, 1887 (24 U. S. Statutes at Large, p. 388), which provides, among other things, that the "purchase shall not be complete until ratified by Congress, and the form and manner of executing such release shall also be prescribed by Congress."

This agreement involves a departure from the terms of the general allotment act in at least one important particular. It gives to each member of the tribe 160 acres of land without regard to age or sex, while the general law gives this allotment only to heads of families. There are, I think, serious objections to the basis adopted in the general law, especially in its application to married women; but if the basis of the agreement herewith submitted is accepted, it would, I think, result in some cases, where there are large families of minor children, in excessive allotments to a single family. Whatever is done in this case will of course become in some sense a precedent in the cases yet to be dealt with.

Perhaps the question of the payment by the United States of the annuities which were forfeited by the act of February 16, 1863 (12 U. S. Statutes at Large, p. 652), should not have been considered in connection with this negotiation for the cession of these lands. But it appears that a refusal to consider this claim would have terminated the negotiation, and if the claim is just its allowance has already been too long delayed. The forfeiture declared by the act of 1863 unjustly included the annuities of certain Indians of these bands who were not only guilty of no fault, but who rendered meritorious services in the armies of the United States in the suppression of the Sioux outbreak and in the War of the Rebellion.

The agreement submitted, as I understand, provides for the payment of the annuities justly due to these friendly Indians to all the members of the two bands per capita. This is said to be the unanimous wish of the Indians, and a distribution to the friendly Indians and their descendants only would now be very difficult, if not impossible.

The agreement is respectfully submitted for the consideration of Congress.

BENJ. HARRISON.

Executive Mansion, *February 24, 1890.*

To the Senate and House of Representatives:

I transmit herewith a communication of 18th instant from the Secretary of the Interior, submitting copy of a report from the Commissioner of Indian Affairs, inclosing, with accompanying papers, a draft of a bill authorizing the removal of the Indians of the Papago or Gila Bend Reservation, in Maricopa County, Arizona Territory, to the Papago Indian Reservation, in Pima County, in said Territory, or to the Pima and Maricopa Indian reservations, commonly known as the Gila River and Salt River Indian reservations, respectively, in said Territory, and for other purposes.

The matter is presented for the early consideration and action of Congress.

BENJ. HARRISON.

Executive Mansion, *February 24, 1890.*

To the Senate and House of Representatives:

I transmit herewith a communication of the 18th instant from the Secretary of the Interior, submitting a copy of a report of the Commissioner of Indian Affairs and accompanying item for insertion in the bill making appropriations for the current and contingent expenses of the Indian Department, which makes provision for further compensation of Henry B. Carrington, special agent appointed under the act of March 2, 1889, "to provide for the sale of lands patented to certain members of the Flathead band of Indians in Montana Territory, and for other purposes," to secure the consent of the Indians thereto and appraise the lands and improvements thereof; for an appropriation to remove the Indians whose lands have been sold to the Jocko Reservation, and for additional legislation considered necessary to complete this matter, as suggested by the Commissioner of Indian Affairs.

I also transmit a copy of the report of Special Agent Carrington and its inclosures.

The matter is presented for the early consideration of Congress.

BENJ. HARRISON.

EXECUTIVE MANSION, *March 4, 1890.*

To the Senate and House of Representatives:

In pursuance of the authority and direction contained in the act of Congress approved January 14, 1889, entitled "An act for the relief and civilization of the Chippewa Indians in the State of Minnesota," three commissioners were appointed by the President on February 26, 1889, as therein authorized and directed, namely, Henry M. Rice, of Minnesota, Martin Marty, of Dakota, and Joseph B. Whiting, of Wisconsin, to negotiate with said Indians.

The commissioners have submitted their final report, with accompanying papers, showing the results of the negotiations conducted by them, and the same has been carefully reviewed by the Secretary of the Interior in his report to me thereon.

Being satisfied from an examination of the papers submitted that the cession and relinquishment by said Chippewa Indians of their title and interest in the lands specified and described in the agreement with the different bands or tribes of Chippewa Indians in the State of Minnesota was obtained in the manner prescribed in the first section of said act, and that more than the requisite number have signed said agreement, I have, as provided by said act, approved the said instruments in writing constituting the agreement entered into by the commissioners with said Indians.

The commissioners did not escape the embarrassment which unfortunately too often attends our negotiations with the Indians, namely, an indisposition to treat with the Government for further concessions while its obligations incurred under former agreements are unkept. I am sure it will be the disposition of Congress to consider promptly and in a just and friendly spirit the claims presented by these Indians through our commissioners, which have been formulated in the draft of a bill prepared by the Secretary of the Interior and submitted herewith.

The act of January 14, 1889 (25 U. S. Statutes at Large, p. 642), evidently contemplated the voluntary removal of the body of all these bands of Indians to the White Earth and Red Lake reservations; but a proviso in section 3 of the act authorized any Indian to take his allotment upon the reservation where he now resides. The commissioners report that quite a general desire was expressed by the Indians to avail themselves of this option. The result of this is that the ceded land can not be ascertained and brought to sale under the act until all of the allotments are made.

I recommend that the necessary appropriations to complete the surveys and allotments be made at once available, so that the work may be begun and completed at the earliest possible day.

A copy of the report made by the commissioners, with copies of all the papers submitted therewith, except the census rolls, is herewith presented for the information of the Congress. BENJ. HARRISON.

EXECUTIVE MANSION, *March 24, 1890.*

To the House of Representatives:

In answer to the resolution of the House of Representatives of the 8th instant, in relation to the employment by the Regular Army of the United States of Indian scouts for the purpose of pursuing hostile Indians in their raids in the territory of the United States and Mexico, and in regard to the proposed transfer of the Apache Chiricahua Indians from Mount Vernon Barracks, Ala., to Fort Sill, Ind. T., I transmit herewith a communication from the Secretary of State on the subject, together with the accompanying papers. BENJ. HARRISON.

EXECUTIVE MANSION, *March 29, 1890.*

To the Senate of the United States:

In compliance with the resolution of the Senate of the 28th instant, the House of Representatives concurring, I return herewith the bill (S. 1332) entitled "An act granting to the city of Colorado Springs, in the State of Colorado, certain lands therein described for water reservoirs." BENJ. HARRISON.

EXECUTIVE MANSION,
Washington, March 31, 1890.

To the Senate and House of Representatives:

I herewith transmit a report from the Secretary of State, in relation to the discriminating duty now imposed upon foreign works of art, and recommend that action thereon looking to the removal of the discrimination be taken by Congress during its present session, if practicable.

BENJ. HARRISON.

EXECUTIVE MANSION,
Washington, April 15, 1890.

To the House of Representatives:

I herewith transmit, in reply to the resolution of the House of Representatives of the 3d instant, a report from the Secretary of State, accompanied by certain correspondence in regard to the seizure of the schooner *Rebecca* by the Mexican customs authorities at Tampico in February, 1884.

BENJ. HARRISON.

EXECUTIVE MANSION,
Washington, April 18, 1890.

To the Senate and House of Representatives:

I transmit herewith the fifth annual report of the Commissioner of Labor.

BENJ. HARRISON.

EXECUTIVE MANSION, *April 18, 1890.*

To the House of Representatives:

In compliance with the resolution of the House of Representatives, the Senate concurring, I return herewith House bill No. 5179, entitled "An act fixing the rate of interest to be charged on arrearages of general and special taxes now due the District of Columbia if paid within a specified time."

BENJ. HARRISON.

EXECUTIVE MANSION, *April 21, 1890.*

To the Senate and House of Representatives:

In compliance with a resolution of the House of Representatives, the Senate concurring, I return herewith House bill No. 105, entitled "An act in relation to immediate transportation of dutiable goods, amendatory of the act of July 10, 1880."

BENJ. HARRISON.

EXECUTIVE MANSION,
Washington, April 21, 1890.

To the Senate of the United States:

In answer to the resolution of the Senate dated March 25 last, in relation to La Abra Silver Mining Company and the distribution or payment of moneys to that corporation on account of the award in its favor by the Mexican Government, I transmit herewith a report from the Secretary of State upon the subject, together with the accompanying papers.

BENJ. HARRISON.

EXECUTIVE MANSION, *April 30, 1890.*

To the Senate of the United States:

In compliance with a resolution of the Senate, the House of Representatives concurring, I return herewith Senate bill 895, entitled "An act to organize the Territory of Oklahoma, to establish courts in the Indian Territory, and for other purposes."

BENJ. HARRISON.

EXECUTIVE MANSION, *May 8, 1890.*

To the House of Representatives:

In answer to the resolution of the House of Representatives of March 31, 1890, respecting the importation into foreign countries of breadstuffs and provisions from the United States and the rates of duty imposed upon such articles, I transmit herewith a report from the Secretary of State on the subject, together with the accompanying papers.

BENJ. HARRISON.

EXECUTIVE MANSION, *May 13, 1890.*

To the Senate and House of Representatives:

I transmit herewith a communication of the 10th instant from the Secretary of the Interior, and the accompanying copies of correspondence, relative to the condition of the Northern Cheyenne Indians at the Pine Ridge Agency, S. Dak.

The desire of these Indians to be united upon some common reservation with their brethren now occupying the Tongue River Reserve, in Montana, is quite natural, and such an arrangement would, I think, promote the best interests of both of these bands.

BENJ. HARRISON.

EXECUTIVE MANSION, *May 17, 1890.*

To the Senate of the United States:

In compliance with a resolution of the Senate of this date, I return herewith the bill (S. 903) entitled "An act for the erection of a public building in Cedar Rapids, Iowa."

BENJ. HARRISON.

EXECUTIVE MANSION, *May 19, 1890.*

To the Senate and House of Representatives:

I inclose herewith a draft of a bill submitted by the Secretary of the Interior, providing for the survey and disposal of a tract of land situated in the city of Monterey, Cal., known as the "Cuartel" lot.

The lot referred to is one of the tracts excluded from the survey of the Pueblo lands of Monterey, Cal., by the decision of Acting Secretary of the Interior Muldrow of October 4, 1887 (6 Land Decisions, p. 179), on the ground that it was in a state of reservation for national purposes.

A communication from the Secretary of War to the Secretary of the Interior, copy herewith, states that this lot has been occupied at intervals by the War Department for military purposes, but as it is not within the limits of any declared military reservation the act of July 5, 1884 (23 U. S. Statutes at Large, p. 103), providing for a transfer to the Interior Department of abandoned military reservations, does not apply.

The lot is no longer required for military purposes, and a willingness is expressed by the War Department that the Department of the Interior should assume control of it. A copy of the tracing, with notes, is inclosed, showing an approximate survey and describing the situation of the lot.

I also inclose a copy of a report of the Commissioner of the General Land Office to the Secretary of the Interior, setting forth that under the decision of Mr. Muldrow the tract of land known as the "Cuartel" lot belongs to the United States by conquest and by treaty, and is in a state of reservation for national purposes, and respectfully submitting that Congress may continue its status as fixed by said decision or enact appropriate laws providing for its disposition as public land.

BENJ. HARRISON.

EXECUTIVE MANSION, *May 19, 1890.*

To the Senate and House of Representatives:

I transmit herewith a report of the International American Conference, recently in session at this capital, recommending the survey of a route for an intercontinental line of railroad to connect the systems of North America with those of the southern continent, and to be conducted under the direction of a board of commissioners representing the several American Republics.

Public attention has chiefly been attracted to the subject of improved water communication between the ports of the United States and those of Central and South America. The creation of new and improved steamship lines undoubtedly furnishes the readiest means of developing an increased trade with the Latin-American nations. But it should not be forgotten that it is possible to travel by land from Washington to the southernmost capital of South America, and that the opening of railroad communication with these friendly States will give to them and to us facilities for intercourse and the exchanges of trade that are of special value.

The work contemplated is vast, but entirely practicable. It will be interesting to all, and perhaps surprising to most of us, to notice how much has already been done in the way of railroad construction in Mexico and South America that can be utilized as part of an intercontinental line.

I do not hesitate to recommend that Congress make the very moderate appropriation for surveys suggested by the conference and authorize the appointment of commissioners and the detail of engineer officers to direct and conduct the necessary preliminary surveys.

BENJ. HARRISON.

EXECUTIVE MANSION, *May 21, 1890.*
To the Senate and House of Representatives:

I transmit herewith a communication of the 20th instant from the Secretary of the Interior and accompanying correspondence in the matter of the request of the Seminole Nation of Indians for negotiations with the Creek Nation of Indians for the purchase of an additional quantity of land, being about 25,000 acres, for the use of the Seminoles. The request is based upon the fact that former purchases do not embrace all of the lands upon which the Seminole Indians have made improvements, and which by the corrected survey were given to the Creeks. The money to be paid for these lands is to be reimbursed to the Government by the Seminoles.

BENJ. HARRISON.

EXECUTIVE MANSION, *May 26, 1890.*
To the House of Representatives:

In compliance with the resolutions of the House of Representatives of the 23d instant, the Senate concurring, I return herewith the bills H. R. Nos. 380 and 2007, entitled, respectively, "An act to amend an act entitled 'An act to authorize the Cairo and Tennessee River Railroad Company to construct bridges across the Tennessee and Cumberland rivers,' approved January 8, 1889," and "An act granting a pension to the widow of Adam Shrake."

BENJ. HARRISON.

EXECUTIVE MANSION, *May 27, 1890.*
To the Senate and House of Representatives:

I transmit herewith a letter from the Secretary of State, inclosing a report adopted by the International American Conference, recently in session at this capital, recommending the establishment of an international American bank, with its principal offices in the city of New York and branches in the commercial centers of the several other American Republics.

The advantages of such an institution to the merchants of the United States engaged in trade with Central and South America and the purposes intended to be accomplished are fully set forth in the letter of the Secretary of State and the accompanying report. It is not proposed to involve the United States in any financial responsibility, but only to give to the proposed bank a corporate franchise, and to promote public confidence by requiring that its condition and transactions shall be submitted to a scrutiny similar to that which is now exercised over our domestic banking system.

The subject is submitted for the consideration of Congress in the belief that it will be found possible to promote the end desired by legislation so guarded as to avoid all just criticism.

BENJ. HARRISON.

EXECUTIVE MANSION, *May 28, 1890.*

To the Senate and House of Representatives:

I transmit herewith a communication of the 26th instant from the Secretary of the Interior, and accompanying item of appropriation, to enable the President to continue the negotiations authorized by sections 14 and 15 of the Indian appropriation act approved March 2, 1889, with the Cherokee Indians and with all other Indians owning or claiming lands west of the ninety-sixth degree of longitude in the Indian Territory, for the cession to the United States of all their title, claim, or interest of every kind or character in and to said lands, etc.

The matter is presented for the favorable action of Congress.

BENJ. HARRISON.

EXECUTIVE MANSION, *June 2, 1890.*

To the House of Representatives:

In compliance with a resolution of the House of Representatives of the 29th ultimo, the Senate concurring, I return herewith the bill (H. R. 7345) entitled "An act authorizing and directing the Secretary of War to establish new harbor lines in Portage Lake, Houghton County, Mich."

BENJ. HARRISON.

EXECUTIVE MANSION, *June 2, 1890.*

To the Senate and House of Representatives:

The International American Conference, recently in session at this capital, recommended for adoption by the several American Republics—

1. A uniform system of customs regulations for the classification and valuation of imported merchandise;

2. A uniform nomenclature for the description of articles of merchandise imported and exported; and

3. The establishment at Washington of an international bureau of information.

The conference also at its final session decided to establish in the city of Washington, as a fitting memorial of its meeting, a Latin-American library, to be formed by contributions from the several nations, of historical, geographical, and literary works, maps, manuscripts, and official documents relating to the history and civilization of America, and expressed a desire that the Government of the United States should provide a suitable building for the shelter of such a library, to be solemnly dedicated upon the four hundredth anniversary of the discovery of America.

The importance of these suggestions is fully set forth in the letter of the Secretary of State and the accompanying documents, herewith transmitted, to which I invite your attention.

BENJ. HARRISON

EXECUTIVE MANSION, *June 6, 1890.*

To the Senate of the United States:

In response to the resolution of the Senate of the 26th of May, requesting me to "communicate to the Senate such information as may be in possession of the executive department relating to the alleged landing of an armed force from the United States revenue cutter *McLane* at Cedar Keys, Fla., and the alleged entry of houses of citizens by force, and their alleged pursuit of citizens of the United States in the surrounding country, and the authority under which the commanding officer of the cutter acted in any such matter," I submit for the information of the Senate the accompanying correspondence, which contains all the information possessed by the executive department relating to the matters inquired about.

It will be observed that the United States collector of customs at Cedar Keys had been driven from his office and from the town and the administration of the customs laws of the United States at that port suspended by the violent demonstrations and threats of one Cottrell, the mayor of the place, assisted by his town marshal, Mitchell. If it had been necessary, as I do not think it can be in any case, for a United States officer to appeal to the local authorities for immunity from violence in the exercise of his duties, the situation at Cedar Keys did not suggest or encourage such an appeal, for those to whom the appeal would have been addressed were themselves the lawless instruments of the threatened violence. It will always be agreeable to me if the local authorities, acting upon their own sense of duty, maintain the public order in such a way that the officers of the United States shall have no occasion to appeal for the intervention of the General Government; but when this is not done I shall deem it my duty to use the adequate powers vested in the Executive to make it safe and feasible to hold and exercise the offices established by the Federal Constitution and laws.

The means used in this case were, in my opinion, lawful and necessary, and the officers do not seem to have intruded upon any private right in executing the warrants placed in their hands. The letter dated August 4 last, which appears in the correspondence submitted, appealing to me to intervene for the protection of the citizens of Cedar Keys from the brutal violence of Cottrell, it will be noticed, was written before the appointment of the new collector. That the officers of the law should not have the full sympathy of every good citizen in their efforts to bring these men to merited punishment is matter of surprise and regret. It is a very grim commentary upon the condition of social order at Cedar Keys that only a woman, who had, as she says in her letter, no son or husband who could be made the victim of his malice, had the courage to file charges against this man, who was then holding a subordinate place in the customs service.

BENJ. HARRISON.

EXECUTIVE MANSION, *June 6, 1890.*

To the Senate of the United States:

In compliance with a resolution of the Senate of the 5th instant, the House of Representatives concurring, I return herewith the bill (S. 1293) entitled "An act for the relief of Charles F. Bowers."

BENJ. HARRISON.

EXECUTIVE MANSION, *June 16, 1890.*

To the Senate and House of Representatives:

I transmit herewith, for the information of Congress with a view to securing such legislation as may be appropriate, a communication from the Secretary of the Interior, relating to the destruction by fires, carelessly kindled or left, of the timber upon the public lands.

If proper penalties were imposed by law and a few convictions thereunder secured, I do not doubt that much waste of our forests would be prevented.

BENJ. HARRISON.

EXECUTIVE MANSION, *June 18, 1890.*

To the Senate of the United States:

In response to the resolution of the Senate of the 16th instant, relating to the negotiations by the Cherokee Commission for the purchase of certain lands in the Indian Territory, I respectfully state that on the 20th day of May and the 12th day of June, respectively, agreements were signed by the Iowa and the Sac and Fox tribes ceding to the United

States certain of their lands. The contracts and accompanying papers were received at the Interior Department on the 2d and 17th days of June, respectively, and are now under examination by the proper officers of that Department. When these examinations are concluded, the papers will, if found to be complete and conformable to law, be submitted to Congress.

BENJ. HARRISON.

EXECUTIVE MANSION, *June 19, 1890.*

To the Senate and House of Representatives:

I transmit herewith, for your information, a letter from the Secretary of State, inclosing a report of the International American Conference, which recommends that reciprocal commercial treaties be entered into between the United States and the several other Republics of this hemisphere.

It has been so often and so persistently stated that our tariff laws offered an insurmountable barrier to a large exchange of products with the Latin-American nations that I deem it proper to call especial attention to the fact that more than 87 per cent of the products of those nations sent to our ports are now admitted free. If sugar is placed upon the free list, practically every important article exported from those States will be given untaxed access to our markets, except wool. The real difficulty in the way of negotiating profitable reciprocity treaties is that we have given freely so much that would have had value in the mutual concessions which such treaties imply. I can not doubt, however, that the present advantages which the products of these near and friendly States enjoy in our markets, though they are not by law exclusive, will, with other considerations, favorably dispose them to adopt such measures, by treaty or otherwise, as will tend to equalize and greatly enlarge our mutual exchanges.

It will certainly be time enough for us to consider whether we must cheapen the cost of production by cheapening labor in order to gain access to the South American markets when we have fairly tried the effect of established and reliable steam communication and of convenient methods of money exchanges. There can be no doubt, I think, that with these facilities well established and with a rebate of duties upon imported raw materials used in the manufacture of goods for export our merchants will be able to compete in the ports of the Latin-American nations with those of any other country.

If after the Congress shall have acted upon pending tariff legislation it shall appear that under the general treaty-making power, or under any special powers given by law, our trade with the States represented in the conference can be enlarged upon a basis of mutual advantage, it will be promptly done.

BENJ. HARRISON.

EXECUTIVE MANSION, *June 24, 1890.*

To the House of Representatives:

In compliance with a resolution of the House of Representatives of the 23d instant, the Senate concurring, I return herewith the bill (H. R. 5702) "granting a pension to Ann Bryan."

BENJ. HARRISON.

EXECUTIVE MANSION, *June 25, 1890.*

To the Senate of the United States:

In compliance with a resolution of the Senate of the 23d instant, the House of Representatives concurring, I return herewith the bill (S. 145) "for the relief of the legal representatives of Henry S. French."

BENJ. HARRISON.

EXECUTIVE MANSION, *July 1, 1890.*

To the Senate and House of Representatives:

In my annual message I called attention to the urgent need of legislation for the adjustment of the claims under Mexican grants to lands in Arizona and New Mexico.

I now submit a correspondence which has passed between the Department of State and the Mexican Government concerning the rights of certain Mexican citizens to have their claims to lands ceded to the United States by the treaty adjusted and confirmed. I also submit a letter from the Secretary of the Interior, with accompanying papers, showing the number and extent of these claims and their present condition.

The United States owes a duty to Mexico to confirm to her citizens those valid grants that were saved by the treaty, and the long delay which has attended the discharge of this duty has given just cause of complaint.

The entire community where these large claims exist, and, indeed, all of our people, are interested in an early and final settlement of them. No greater incubus can rest upon the energies of a people in the development of a new country than that resulting from unsettled land titles.

The necessity for legislation is so evident and so urgent that I venture to express the hope that relief will be given at the present session of Congress.

BENJ. HARRISON.

EXECUTIVE MANSION, *July 2, 1890.*

To the Senate and House of Representatives:

In compliance with the provisions of section 14 of the act of March 2, 1889, I transmit herewith, for the consideration of Congress, an agreement concluded between the commissioners appointed under that section on behalf of the United States, commonly known as the Cherokee Commission, and the Sac and Fox Nation of Indians in the Indian Territory on the 12th day of June last.

The Sac and Fox Nation have a national council, and the negotiation was conducted with that body, which undoubtedly had competent authority to contract on behalf of the tribe for the sale of these lands. The letter of the Secretary of the Interior and the accompanying papers, which are submitted herewith, furnish all the information necessary to the consideration of the questions to be determined by Congress.

The only serious question presented is as to that article of the agreement which limits the distribution of the funds to be paid by the United States under it to the Sac and Fox Indians now in the Indian Territory. I very gravely doubt whether the remnant or band of this tribe now living in Iowa has any interest in these lands in the Indian Territory. The reservation there was apparently given in consideration of improvements upon the lands of the tribe in Kansas. The band now resident in Iowa upon lands purchased by their own means, as I am advised, left the Kansas reservation many years before the date of this treaty, and it would seem could have had no equitable interest in the improvements on the Kansas lands, which must have been the result of the labors of that portion of the tribe living upon them. The right of the Iowa band to a participation in the proceeds of the sale of the Kansas reservation was explicitly reserved in the treaty; but it seems to me upon a somewhat hasty examination of the treaty that the reservation in the Indian Territory was intended only for the benefit of those who should go there to reside. The Secretary of the Interior has expressed a somewhat different view of the effect of this treaty; but if the facts are, as I understand, that the Iowa band did not contribute to the improvements which were the consideration for the reservation and did not accept the invitation to settle upon the reservation lands in the Indian Territory, I do not well see how they have either an equitable or legal claim to participate in the proceeds of the sale of those lands.

The whole matter is submitted for the consideration of Congress.

BENJ. HARRISON.

EXECUTIVE MANSION,
Washington, July 2, 1890.

To the Senate and House of Representatives:

I transmit herewith a letter from the Secretary of State, inclosing the recommendations of the International American Conference for the establishment of improved facilities for postal and cable communication between the United States and the several countries of Central and South America.

I can not too strongly urge upon Congress the necessity of giving this subject immediate and favorable consideration and of making adequate appropriations to carry the recommendations into effect; and in this connection I beg leave to call attention to what was said on the subject in my annual message.* The delegates of the seventeen neighboring Republics, which have so recently been assembled in Washington at the invitation of this Government, have expressed their wish and purpose to cooperate with the United States in the adoption of measures to improve the means of communication between the several Republics of America. They recognize the necessity of frequent, regular, and rapid steamship service, both for the purpose of maintaining friendly intercourse and for the convenience of commerce, and realize that without such facilities it is useless to attempt to extend the trade between their ports and ours.

BENJ. HARRISON.

EXECUTIVE MANSION,
Washington, July 2, 1890.

To the Senate and House of Representatives:

I transmit herewith, for your information, a letter from the Secretary of State, inclosing a copy of a resolution passed by the International American Conference with reference to the celebration of the fourth centennial of the discovery of America.

BENJ. HARRISON.

EXECUTIVE MANSION, July 2, 1890.

To the Senate and House of Representatives:

I transmit herewith, as required by section 14 of the act of March 2, 1889, an agreement concluded on the 20th day of May last between the commissioners on behalf of the United States, commonly known as the Cherokee Commission, and the Iowa Indians residing in the Indian Territory.

A letter of the Secretary of the Interior, which is accompanied by communications from the Commissioner of Indian Affairs and the Assistant Attorney-General, is also submitted.

These papers present a full and clear statement of the matters of fact and questions of law which Congress will need to consider in passing upon the question of the ratification of the agreement, which is submitted for its consideration and such action as may be deemed proper.

BENJ. HARRISON.

EXECUTIVE MANSION,
Washington, July 11, 1890.

To the Senate and House of Representatives:

I transmit herewith a communication from the Secretary of State, including a report of the action of the International American Conference,

* See pp. 56–57.

lately in session in this city, concerning the protection of patents, trade-marks, and copyrights in commerce between the American Republics, to which I invite your attention.

BENJ. HARRISON.

EXECUTIVE MANSION,
Washington, July 11, 1890.

To the Senate and House of Representatives:

I invite your attention to the accompanying letter of the Secretary of State, submitting the recommendations of the International American Conference for the better protection of the public health against the spread of contagious diseases.

BENJ. HARRISON.

EXECUTIVE MANSION, *July 12, 1890.*

To the Senate and House of Representatives:

I transmit herewith a letter from the Secretary of State, inclosing a copy of a report upon weights and measures adopted by the International American Conference, recently in session at this capital.

BENJ. HARRISON.

EXECUTIVE MANSION, *July 12, 1890.*

To the Senate and House of Representatives:

I transmit herewith a letter from the Secretary of State, inclosing a copy of a report of the International American Conference, recently in session at this capital, recommending the establishment of an international American monetary union, and suggesting that the President be authorized to invite the several American nations to send delegates to its first meeting in Washington on the first Wednesday of January next; that authority also be granted for the appointment of three delegates on the part of the United States, and that an appropriation be made to meet the necessary expenses.

I commend these suggestions and hope they will receive the prompt consideration of Congress.

BENJ. HARRISON.

EXECUTIVE MANSION,
Washington, July 14, 1890.

To the Senate and House of Representatives:

I transmit herewith a letter from the Secretary of State, inclosing the recommendation of the International American Conference with reference to the adoption by the American Republics of a uniform code of international law, to which your attention is respectfully directed.

BENJ. HARRISON.

EXECUTIVE MANSION,
Washington, July 14, 1890.

To the Senate and House of Representatives:

I transmit herewith a letter from the Secretary of State, inclosing the recommendations of the International American Conference, recently in session at this capital, concerning a uniform system of port dues and consular fees to be adopted by the several American Republics, to which I invite your attention.

BENJ. HARRISON.

EXECUTIVE MANSION, *July 15, 1890.*

To the Senate and House of Representatives:

I transmit herewith a letter from the Secretary of State, inclosing a resolution adopted by the International American Conference for the erection of a memorial tablet in the diplomatic chamber of the Department of State to commemorate the meeting of that body.

BENJ. HARRISON.

EXECUTIVE MANSION, *July 15, 1890.*

To the Senate and House of Representatives:

I transmit herewith, for your information, certain reports on the subject of extradition adopted by the International American Conference at its recent sessions in this city.

BENJ. HARRISON.

EXECUTIVE MANSION, *July 15, 1890.*

To the Senate and House of Representatives:

I transmit two agreements concluded by the commission appointed under section 14 of the act of March 2, 1889, commonly known as the Cherokee Commission, with the Citizen band of Pottawatomie Indians and the band of Absentee Shawnees, respectively, for the cession of certain lands to the United States.

Letters from the Secretary of the Interior, the Commissioner of Indian Affairs, and the Assistant Attorney-General for the Department of the Interior relating to the same matter are also submitted.

BENJ. HARRISON.

EXECUTIVE MANSION, *July 17, 1890.*

To the Senate and House of Representatives:

The act making appropriations to provide for the expenses of the government of the District of Columbia for the fiscal year ending June 30, 1890, provides, among other things, that the President shall appoint three competent sanitary engineers to examine and report upon the system of sewerage existing in the District of Columbia, together with such suggestions and recommendations as may to them seem necessary and desirable for the modification and extension of the same, which report was to be transmitted to Congress by the President at its next session.

In pursuance of the authority thus conferred, on the 17th of August, 1889, I appointed Rudolph Hering, of New York, Samuel M. Gray, of Rhode Island, and Frederick P. Stearns, of Massachusetts, to make this examination and report.

The gentlemen named were believed to have such ability and experience as sanitary engineers as to guarantee an intelligent and exhaustive study of the problem submitted to them.

I transmit herewith their report, which has just been submitted to me, for the consideration of Congress. BENJ. HARRISON.

EXECUTIVE MANSION, *July 23, 1890.*
To the House of Representatives:

In response to the resolution of the House of Representatives requesting me, if in my judgment not incompatible with the public interest, to furnish to the House the correspondence since March 4, 1889, between the Government of the United States and the Government of Great Britain touching the subjects in dispute in the Bering Sea, I transmit a letter from the Secretary of State, which is accompanied by the correspondence referred to in the resolution. BENJ. HARRISON.

EXECUTIVE MANSION, *July 29, 1890.*
To the Senate and House of Representatives:

The recent attempt to secure a charter from the State of North Dakota for a lottery company, the pending effort to obtain from the State of Louisiana a renewal of the charter of the Louisiana State Lottery, and the establishment of one or more lottery companies at Mexican towns near our border have served the good purpose of calling public attention to an evil of vast proportions. If the baneful effects of the lotteries were confined to the States that give the companies corporate powers and a license to conduct the business, the citizens of other States, being powerless to apply legal remedies, might clear themselves of responsibility by the use of such moral agencies as were within their reach. But the case is not so. The people of all the States are debauched and defrauded. The vast sums of money offered to the States for charters are drawn from the people of the United States, and the General Government through its mail system is made the effective and profitable medium of intercourse between the lottery company and its victims. The use of the mails is quite as essential to the companies as the State license. It would be practically impossible for these companies to exist if the public mails were once effectively closed against their advertisements and remittances. The use of the mails by these companies is a prostitution of an agency only intended to serve the purposes of a legitimate trade and a decent social intercourse.

It is not necessary, I am sure, for me to attempt to portray the robbery of the poor and the widespread corruption of public and private morals which are the necessary incidents of these lottery schemes.

The national capital has become a subheadquarters of the Louisiana Lottery Company, and its numerous agents and attorneys are conducting here a business involving probably a larger use of the mails than that of any legitimate business enterprise in the District of Columbia. There seems to be good reason to believe that the corrupting touch of these agents has been felt by the clerks in the postal service and by some of the police officers of the District.

Severe and effective legislation should be promptly enacted to enable the Post-Office Department to purge the mails of all letters, newspapers, and circulars relating to the business.

The letter of the Postmaster-General which I transmit herewith points out the inadequacy of the existing statutes and suggests legislation that would be effective.

It may also be necessary to so regulate the carrying of letters by the express companies as to prevent the use of those agencies to maintain communication between the lottery companies and their agents or customers in other States.

It does not seem possible that there can be any division of sentiment as to the propriety of closing the mails against these companies, and I therefore venture to express the hope that such proper powers as are necessary to that end will be at once given to the Post-Office Department.

BENJ. HARRISON.

EXECUTIVE MANSION,
Washington, July 30, 1890.

To the Senate of the United States:

I transmit herewith a report from the Acting Secretary of State, in response to a resolution of the Senate of the 23d instant, calling for information touching the alleged arrest and imprisonment of A. J. Diaz by the Cuban authorities and the action which has been taken in respect thereto.

It will be seen that Mr. Diaz has been released.

BENJ. HARRISON.

EXECUTIVE MANSION, *August 8, 1890.*

To the Senate and House of Representatives:

I have received, under date of July 29 ultimo, a communication from Hon. George W. Steele, governor of the Territory of Oklahoma, in which, among other things, he says:

A delegation from township 16, range 1, in this county, has just left me, who came to represent that there are at this time twenty-eight families in that township who are in actual need of the necessaries of life, and they give it as their opinion that their township is not an exception, and that in the very near future a large propor-tion of the settlers of this Territory will have to have assistance.

This I have looked for, but have hoped to bridge over until after the legislature meets, when I thought some arrangement might be made for taking care of these needy people; but with little taxable property in the Territory, and very many necessary demands to be made and met, I doubt if the legislature will be able to make such provision until a crop is raised next year as will be adequate to the demands. * * *

Now I know whereof I speak, and I say there are a great many people in this Territory who have not the necessary means of providing meals for a day to come and are being helped by their very poor neighbors. No one regrets more than I do the necessity of making the foregoing statement, and I have hoped to bridge the matter over, as I have said before, until the legislature would meet and see if some provision could be made.

I now see the utter hopelessness of such a course, and I beg of you to call the attention of Congress to the condition of our people, with the earnest hope that pro-vision may be made whereby great suffering may be relieved; and I assure you that so far as I am able to prevent it not one ounce of provisions or a cent of money con-tributed to the above need shall be improperly used.

Information received by me from other sources leads me to believe that Governor Steele is altogether right in his impression that there will be, unless relief is afforded either by public appropriation or by organized individual effort, widespread suffering among the settlers in Oklahoma. Many of these people expended in travel and in providing shelter for their families all of their accumulated means. The crop prospects for this year are by reason of drought quite unfavorable, and the ability of the Territory itself to provide relief must be inadequate during this year.

I am advised that there is an unexpended balance of about $45,000 of the fund appropriated for the relief of the sufferers by flood upon the Mis-sissippi River and its tributaries, and I recommend that authority be given to use this fund to meet the most urgent necessities of the poorer people in Oklahoma. Steps have been taken to ascertain more particularly the condition of the people throughout the Territory, and if a larger relief should seem to be necessary the facts will be submitted to Congress. If the fund to which I have referred should be made available for relief in Oklahoma, care will be taken that so much of it as is necessary to be expended shall be judiciously applied to the most worthy and necessitous cases.

BENJ. HARRISON.

EXECUTIVE MANSION,
Washington, August 15, 1890.

To the Senate:

In compliance with the resolution of the Senate of the 26th of July, 1890, calling for all correspondence not already submitted to Congress and now on file in the Department of State touching the efforts made by this Government to secure the modification or repeal by the French Gov-ernment of its decree of 1881, prohibiting the importation into France of

American pork and kindred American products, I transmit herewith a report from the Acting Secretary on the subject, with the accompanying correspondence.

BENJ. HARRISON.

EXECUTIVE MANSION, *September 3, 1890.*

To the Senate and House of Representatives:

I transmit herewith a letter from the Secretary of State, which is accompanied by three reports adopted by the conference of American nations recently in session at Washington, relating to the subject of international arbitration. The ratification of the treaties contemplated by these reports will constitute one of the happiest and most hopeful incidents in the history of the Western Hemisphere.

BENJ. HARRISON.

EXECUTIVE MANSION, *October 1, 1890.*

To the House of Representatives:

I transmit herewith, in answer to the resolution of the House of Representatives of August 20, 1890, concerning the enforcement of proscriptive edicts against the Jews in Russia, a report from the Secretary of State upon the subject.

BENJ. HARRISON.

EXECUTIVE MANSION,
Washington, October 1, 1890.

To the Senate:

In response to the resolution of the Senate of September 17, 1890, I inclose a report from the Secretary of State, transmitting all the correspondence found among the files of his Department relating to the claim of Thomas T. Collins against the Government of Spain.

BENJ. HARRISON.

VETO MESSAGES.

EXECUTIVE MANSION, *April 26, 1890.*

To the House of Representatives:

I return herewith without my approval the bill (H. R. 7170) ''to authorize the city of Ogden, Utah, to assume an increased indebtedness.''

The purpose and effect of this bill is to relieve the city of Ogden from the limitation imposed by the act of July 30, 1886, upon all municipal corporations in the Territories as to the indebtedness which they may lawfully contract. The general law fixes the limit of 4 per cent upon the last assessment for taxation; this bill extends the limit as to the city of Ogden to 8 per cent. The purposes for which this legislation is asked are not peculiar or exceptional. They relate to schools, street improvements, and to sewerage, and are common to every prosperous and growing town and city. If the argument by which this measure is supported is adopted, the conclusion should be a repeal or modification of the general law; but in my opinion the limitation imposed by the act of 1886 is wise and wholesome and should not be relaxed.

The report of the governor of Utah for 1889 states the population of Ogden to be 15,000, the valuation for taxation $7,000,000, and the existing indebtedness $100,000. It will be noticed that under the existing limit the city has power to increase its indebtedness $180,000, which would seem to be enough to make a good beginning in the construction of sewers, while the cost of street improvements is usually met in large part by direct assessment upon the property benefited.

It is assumed in the report of the House committee that any city in the States similarly situated "would have the making of the needed improvements within its own power," while the fact is that almost all of our States have either by their constitutions or statutes limited the power of municipal corporations to incur indebtedness, and the limit is generally lower than that fixed by the act regulating this matter in the Territories. A large city debt retards growth and in the end defeats the purpose of those who think by mortgaging the future to attract population and property. I do not doubt that the citizens of Ogden will ultimately realize that the creation of a municipal debt of over half a million dollars by a city of 15,000 population—being $37 per capita—is unwise.

BENJ. HARRISON.

EXECUTIVE MANSION, *April 29, 1890.*

To the House of Representatives:

I return without my approval the bill (H. R. 848) "to authorize the construction of an addition to the public building in Dallas, Tex."

The bill authorizes the construction of a wing or addition to the present public building at a cost of $200,000. I find that the bill as originally introduced by the member representing the Congressional district in which Dallas is situated fixed $100,000 as the limit of the proposed expenditure, and it was so reported from the Committee on Public Buildings and Grounds after conferring with the Supervising Architect of the Treasury. A bill of the same tenor was introduced in the Senate by one of the Senators from that State, fixing the same limit of expenditure.

The public building at Dallas, for which a first appropriation of $75,000 was made in 1882, subsequently increased to $125,000, was only completed in 1889. It is probably inadequate now to the convenient transaction of

business, chiefly in that part assigned to the Post-Office Department.
The material and architectural style of any addition are fixed by the present building and its ground area by the available unoccupied space, as no
provision is made for buying additional ground.   The present building
is 85 by 56 feet, and Mr. John S. Witwer, the postmaster and the custodian of the building, writing to the Supervising Architect, advises that to
meet the present and prospective needs of the Government an addition at
least two-thirds as large as the present building should be provided.   It
will be seen from the following extract from a letter of the Supervising
Architect to the chairman of the Senate Committee on Public Buildings
and Grounds, dated February 17, 1890, that a building larger than that
suggested can be erected within the limit of $100,000.   He says:

From computations made in this office based upon data received it is found that an
extension or wing about 40 by 85 feet in dimensions, three stories high, with basement, giving 3,400 square feet, in addition to the 4,760 square feet of the first-floor
area of the building, of fireproof construction, can be erected on the present site within
the limit of cost proposed by said bill, namely, $100,000.

It may be possible that an expenditure of $325,000 for a public build-
ing at Dallas, if the questions of site, material, and architecture were all
undetermined, could be defended, but under existing conditions I do not
see how an appropriation of $200,000 can be justified when one-half that
sum is plainly adequate to such relief as the present site allows.

The legislation for the erection of public buildings has not proceeded,
so far as I can trace it, upon any general rules.   Neither population nor the
extent of the public business transacted has always indicated the points
where public buildings should first be built or the cost of the structures.
It can not be expected that, in the absence of some general law, the committees of Congress having charge of such matters will proceed in their
recommendations upon strict or equal lines.   The bills are individual, and
if comparisons are attempted the necessary element of probable future
growth is made to cover all apparent inequalities.   It will be admitted,
I am sure, that only a public need should suggest the expenditure of the
public money, and that if all such needs can not be at once supplied the
most general and urgent should have the preference.

I am not unfriendly to a liberal annual expenditure for the erection
of public buildings where the safe and convenient transaction of the public business demands it and the state of the revenues will permit.   It
would be wiser, in my opinion, to build more and less costly houses and
to fix by general law the amount of the annual expenditure for this purpose and some order of preference between the cities asking for public
buildings.

But in view of the pending legislation looking to a very large reduction
of our revenues and of the urgency and necessity of a large increase in
our expenditures in certain directions, I am of the opinion that appropriations for the erection of public buildings and all kindred expenditures

should be kept at the minimum until the effect of other probable legislation can be accurately measured.

The erection of a public building is largely a matter of local interest and convenience, while expenditures for enlarged relief and recognition to the soldiers and sailors of the war for the preservation of the Union, for necessary coast defenses, and for the extension of our commerce with other American States are of universal interest and involve considerations, not of convenience, but of justice, honor, safety, and general prosperity.

BENJ. HARRISON.

EXECUTIVE MANSION, *June 4, 1890.*

To the Senate of the United States:

I return without my approval the bill (S. 1306) ''for the erection of a public building at Hudson, N. Y.'' Hudson, from the best information attainable, is a city of only a little more than 10,000 population. If the postal receipts are a fair indication of the growth of the city, it has not been rapid, as they only increased about $4,000 in ten years. The gross postal receipts for the year 1888 were but $14,809, and the office force consists of three clerks and five carriers. There are no other Government officers at Hudson entitled under the law to offices or to an allowance for rent, unless it be a deputy collector of internal revenue.

It appears from the bill and the correspondence with the Supervising Architect that it is proposed to erect a two-story building, with fireproof vaults, heating and ventilating apparatus, and elevators, 40 by 80 feet in dimensions. The ground-floor area of 3,200 feet, to be devoted to the post-office, would give 400 square feet to each of the present employees. The second story and the basement, each having the same area, will be absolutely tenantless, unless authority is given by law to the custodian to rent the rooms to unofficial tenants. It seems to me to be very clear that the public needs do not suggest or justify such an expenditure as is contemplated by this bill.

BENJ. HARRISON.

EXECUTIVE MANSION, *June 12, 1890.*

To the House of Representatives:

I return without my approval the bill (H. R. 7175) to provide for the purchase of a site and the erection of a public building thereon at Tuscaloosa, in the State of Alabama.

Judged by its postal revenues and by the force employed in the office, the post-office at Tuscaloosa is not an important one. It has one clerk, at a salary of $450, and no carriers. The report of the Postmaster-General shows that the gross receipts for the year 1888 were $6,379 and the net revenue less than $4,000. The annual receipts have only increased about $3,000 in ten years. The rent now paid for a building affording 2,200 square feet of floor space is $275.

A general proposition to erect public buildings at this scale of expense in cities of the size of Tuscaloosa would not, I am sure, receive the sanction of Congress. It would involve the expenditure for buildings of ten times the present net revenues of such offices, and in the case under consideration would involve an increased cost for fuel, lights, and care greater than the rent now paid for the use of a room of ample size. I would not insist that it must always be shown that a proposed public building would yield an interest upon the investment, but in the present uncertain state of the public revenues and expenditures, resulting from pending and probable legislation, there is, in my opinion, an absolute necessity that expenditures for public buildings should be limited to cases where the public needs are very evident and very imperative. It is clear that this is not such a case.

BENJ. HARRISON.

EXECUTIVE MANSION, *June 17, 1890.*

To the Senate of the United States:

I return without my approval the bill (S. 1762) ''to change the boundaries of the Uncompahgre Reservation.''

This bill proposes to separate from the Ute Indian Reservation in Utah and restore to the public domain two ranges of townships along the east side of the reservation and bordering the Colorado State line. It is said that these lands are wholly worthless to the Indians for cultivation or for grazing purposes, and it must follow, I think, that they are equally worthless for such purposes to white men.

The object, then, of this legislation is to be sought not in any public demand for these lands for the use of settlers—for if they are susceptible of that use the Indians have a clear equity to take allotments upon them—but in that part of the bill which confirms the mineral entries, or entries for mineral uses, which have been unlawfully made ''or attempted to be made on said lands.'' It is evidently a private and not a public end that is to be promoted. It does not follow, of course, that this private end may not be wholly meritorious and the relief sought on behalf of these persons altogether just and proper. The facts, as I am advised, are that upon these lands there are veins or beds of asphaltum or gilsonite supposed to be of very great value.

Entries have been made in that vicinity, but upon public lands. which lands have been resold for very large amounts. It is not important, perhaps, that the United States should in parting with these lands realize their value, but it is essential, I think, that favoritism should have no part in connection with the sales. The bill confirms all attempted entries of these mineral lands at the price of $20 per acre (a price that is suggestive of something unusual) without requiring evidence of the expenditure of any money upon the claim, or even proof that the claimant was the discoverer of the deposits.

The bill requires "good faith," but it will be next to impossible for the officers of the Interior Department to show actual knowledge on the part of the claimant of the lines of the reservation. The case will practically be as to this matter in the hands of the claimant. But why should good faith at the moment of attempting the entry, without any requirement of expenditure, and followed, it may be, within twenty-four hours by actual notice that he was upon a reservation, give an advantage in the sale of these lands that may represent a very large sum of money?

In the second place, I do not think it wise, without notice even to the Indians, to segregate these lands from their reservation. It is true, I think, that they hold these lands by an Executive order, with a contract right to take allotments upon them, and that the lands in question are not likely to be sought as an allotment by any Indian. But the Indians have been placed on this reservation and its boundaries explained to them, and to take these lands in this manner is calculated to excite their distrust and fears, and possibly to create serious trouble.

BENJ. HARRISON.

EXECUTIVE MANSION, *June 20, 1890.*

To the House of Representatives:

I return without my approval the bill (H. R. 3934) "to authorize the board of supervisors of Maricopa County, Ariz., to issue certain bonds in aid of the construction of a certain railroad."

This bill proposes to confer authority upon the supervisors of the county of Maricopa to issue county bonds at the rate of $4,000 per mile in aid of a railroad to be constructed from Phœnix northwardly to the county line, a distance estimated at 50 miles, but probably somewhat longer. The bill seems to have passed the House of Representatives under an entire misapprehension of its true scope and effect. In the brief report submitted by the Committee on Territories it is said that "by the terms of the bill the county receives *bonds* in payment of the money proposed to be advanced," and in the course of the debate the Delegate from Arizona mistakenly stated in response to a request for information that the bill proposed a loan by the county, in exchange for which it was to receive the bonds of the railroad company. In fact, the bill does not provide for a loan to be secured by bonds, but for a subscription of stock. How far this mistake may have affected the passage of the bill can not of course be known.

The bill does not submit the question of granting this aid to a vote of the people of the county, but confers direct authority upon the supervisors to issue the bonds. It is said, however, that in April, 1889, an election was held to obtain the views of the people upon the question. It does not appear from any papers submitted to me who were the managers of this so-called election; what notice, if any, was given; what qualifications on the part of voters were insisted upon, if any, or in what form the question was presented. There was no law providing for such an election. Being wholly voluntary, the election was, of course, under the management of those who favored the subsidy, and was conducted without any legal restraints as to the voting or certification. I have asked for a statement of the vote by precincts, and have been given what purports to be the vote at twelve points. The total affirmative vote given was 1,975 and the negative 134. But of the affirmative vote 1,543 were given at Phœnix and 188 at Tempe, a town very near to Phœnix. If there were no other objections to this bill, I should deem this alone sufficient, that no provision is made for submitting to a vote of the people at an election, after due notice and under the sanction of law, the question whether this subscription shall be made.

But again, the bill proposes to suspend for this case two provisions of the act of Congress of July 30, 1886—first, that provision which forbids municipal corporations from subscribing to the stock of other corporations or loaning their credit to such corporations, and, second, that provision which forbids any municipal corporation from creating a debt in excess of 4 per cent of its taxable property as fixed by the last assessment. The condition of things then existing in Arizona had not a little to do with the enactment by Congress of this law, intended to give to the people of the Territories that protection against oppressive municipal debts which was secured to the people of most of the States by constitutional limitations. The wisdom of this legislation is not contested by the friends of this bill, but they claim that the circumstances here are so peculiar as to justify this exception. I do not think so. In the States the limitation upon municipal indebtedness is usually placed in the constitution, in order that it may be inflexible. If a showing of need, gain, or advantage is to overcome the barrier, then it is scarcely worth while to declare a limitation. Only a belief that the limit is inflexible will promote care and economy in administration. If this bill becomes a law, how can Congress refuse to any county in any of the Territories the right to subscribe to the stock of a railroad company, especially where the subscription would not exceed the debt limit, upon a showing of the advantages of better and cheaper communications?

Maricopa County is one of great extent. Its northern boundary is 95 miles long, its southern boundary 66, its eastern 45, and its western 102. This great area is to be taxed to construct a road which can, in the nature of things, be of advantage to but a fraction of it. There is no unity of interest or equality of advantage. It may very well be that a section of these lands along the line of the road, and especially town lots in Phœnix, would have an added value much greater than the increased burden imposed, but it is equally clear that much property in the county will receive no appreciable benefit.

The existing bonded indebtedness of Maricopa County is $272,000; the tax assessment of the county is about $5,000,000, and the population is estimated, by multiplying the vote cast in 1888 by 6, at about 12,000. It will be seen that the bonded debt, to say nothing of a floating debt, which is said to be small, is already largely in excess of the legal limit, and it is proposed to increase it by a subscription that will certainly involve $200,000, and possibly $250,000. If the bill becomes a law, the bonded indebtedness will very closely approximate 10 per cent of the assessed valuation of the property of the county.

The condition of things in the county of Yavapai, lying immediately north of Maricopa, and through which this road is also to run, though not directly affected by this legislation, is very instructive in this connection.

By an act of the legislature of Arizona passed the year before the act of Congress to which I have referred Yavapai County was authorized to subscribe $4,000 per mile to this line of road. The total length of the road in the county was 147 miles, and 74 miles, to Prescott, have been constructed. The secretary of the Territory, in response to an inquiry, states the debt of Yavapai County at $563,000 and the assessment for taxation at "between six and seven millions." There are 73 miles of road yet to be built from the present terminus, Prescott, to the south line of the county, for which Yavapai County must make a further issue of bonds of $292,000, making a total county debt of $855,000, or above 13 per cent upon the taxable assessment (taking that at $6,500,000), and a per capita county debt of nearly $85, taking the population at about 10,600, as stated in the report of the Senate committee. Surely no one will insist that the true and permanent prosperity of these communities will be promoted by loading their energies and their industries with these great debts. I feel the force of the suggestion that the freight charges now imposed upon the farm and orchard products of Maricopa County by the railroads now in operation are oppressive. But this bill does not afford much relief even in that direction. There would be but one competing point, viz, Phœnix. At all other points on the proposed road the people would be subject to the exaction of just such rates as are demanded by the other lines. If this bill contained some effective provision to secure reasonable freight rates to the people who are to be taxed to build the road, it would go far to secure my favorable consideration for it.

I have carefully examined the reports of the committees and every argument that has been submitted to me by the friends of the bill, but I can not bring myself to believe that the permanent welfare of the communities affected by it will be promoted by its passage.

BENJ. HARRISON.

EXECUTIVE MANSION, *July 9, 1890.*
To the House of Representatives:

I return herewith without my approval the bill (H. R. 5974) entitled "An act extending the time of payment to purchasers of land of the Omaha tribe of Indians in Nebraska, and for other purposes."

The United States holds the legal title of these lands, which have been sold for the benefit of the Omaha Indians to secure the unpaid purchase money, the time of payment of which it is proposed by this act to extend. There is no objection that I know of, either on the part of the United States or of the Indians, to the extension of the unpaid installments due from purchasers. This relief is probably due to the purchasers. The bill, however, contains the following provision:

That all the lands the payment for which is hereby extended shall be subject to taxation in all respects by and in the State of Nebraska as if fully paid for and patents issued.

Now, while it is entirely proper that the interest of the purchasers in these lands should share the burdens of the communities in which the lands are located, the title of the United States and the beneficial interest of the Indians in the lands should not be subjected to sale for the delinquency of the purchasers in paying tax assessments levied upon the lands. The effect of the provision which has been quoted would, in my opinion, give to the purchaser at a tax sale a title superior to the lien of the Government for purchase money. The bill should have contained a proviso that only the interest of the purchasers from the Government could be sold for taxes, and that the tax sale should be subject to the lien of the United States for unpaid purchase money.

BENJ. HARRISON.

EXECUTIVE MANSION, *September 30, 1890.*

To the House of Representatives:

I return herewith without my approval the joint resolution (H. Res. No. 39) declaring the retirement of Captain Charles B. Stivers, of the United States Army, legal and valid, and that he is entitled as such officer to his pay.

Captain Stivers was dismissed the service summarily by order of the President on July 15, 1863. A subsequent examination into the causes leading to this action seems to have satisfied the President that an injustice had been done to the officer, and on the 11th day of August, 1863, an order was issued revoking the order of dismissal and restoring Captain Stivers to duty as an officer of the Army. On December 30, 1864, by a proper order from the War Department, after examination, Captain Stivers was placed upon the retired list of the Army.

The Supreme Court has decided in the case of The United States *vs.* Corson (114 U. S. Reports, 619):

First. That at the time of the issuance of the order of dismissal the President had authority under the law to summarily dismiss an officer, and that the effect of such an order was absolutely to separate the officer from the service.

Second. That having been thus separated from the service he could not be restored except by nomination to the Senate and its advice and consent to the appointment.

Mr. Garland, as Attorney-General, gave an opinion to the Secretary of War in the case of Captain Stivers, based upon the decision of the Supreme Court to which I have referred, holding that Captain Stivers was not an officer on the retired list of the Army. The present Attorney-General, with whom I have conferred, takes the same view of the law. Indeed, the decision of the Supreme Court to which I have referred is so exactly in point that there can be no doubt as to the law of the case. It is undoubtedly competent for Congress by act or joint resolution to authorize the President, by and with the advice of the Senate, to appoint Captain Stivers to be a captain in the Army of the United States and to place him upon the retired list. It is also perfectly competent by suitable legislation for Congress to give to this officer the pay of his grade during the interval of time when he was improperly carried upon the army lists. But the joint resolution which I herewith return does not attempt to deal with the case in that way. It undertakes to declare that the retirement of Captain Stivers was legal and valid and that he always has been and is entitled to his pay as such officer. I do not think this is a competent method of giving the relief intended. The retirement under the law as it then existed was not legal and valid, as the highest judicial tribunal under the Constitution has declared, for the reason that Captain Stivers was not then an officer on the active list. That being so, it follows, of course, that he was not entitled to draw the pay of an office he did not hold.

The relief should have taken the form usual in such cases, which is to authorize the appointment of the officer to a place made for him on the retired list.

BENJ. HARRISON.

To the Senate: EXECUTIVE MANSION, *October 1, 1890.*

I return to the Senate without my approval the bill (S. 473) ''for the relief of the Portland Company, of Portland, Me.''

This bill confers upon the Court of Claims jurisdiction to inquire into and determine how much certain steam machinery built for the United States under contract, and to be used in the vessels *Agawam* and *Pontoosuc*, cost the contractors over and above the contract price and any allowances for extra work which have been made, and requires the court to enter judgment in favor of the claimant for the excess of cost above such contract price and allowances.

The bill differs from others which have been presented to me, and one of which I have approved, in that it does not make the further allowance to the contractors contingent upon the fact that the additional expense was the result of the acts of the Government through its officers' causing delays and increased cost in the construction of the work.

The bill in effect directs the court to ignore the contract entirely, except as payments under it are to be treated as credits, and to allow the contractors the cost of the work, and that without reference to their own negligence or want of skill in executing the work. There would seem to be no object in the Government's making a contract for work if the contract is only to be binding upon the parties in the event that the contractor realizes a profit.

I can not give my approval to the proposition applied here, which if allowed here should be given general application, that every contractor with the Government who during the early days of the war failed to realize, by reason of increase in the cost of labor and materials, a profit upon the contract shall now have access to the Court of Claims to recover upon the *quantum meruit* the cost of the work.

BENJ. HARRISON.

EXECUTIVE MANSION, *October 1, 1890.*

To the Senate:

I return without my approval Senate bill No. 1857, "for the relief of Charles P. Chouteau, survivor of Chouteau, Harrison & Valle."

This claim has been once presented to the Court of Claims and fully heard. This bill authorizes a rehearing. I find upon examination that every fact connected with the case necessary to the determination of the question whether the claim should be appropriated for has already been found and stated by the Court of Claims in a published opinion. Judgment was given against the claimant upon the ground that a settlement had been made and a receipt given in full. If in the opinion of Congress this receipt, given under the circumstances which accompanied it, should not be held a bar to such further appropriation as is equitable, all the facts have been found that can be necessary to determine the question what further payment should be made to the contractors. There can be no reason, as it seems to me, for a retrial of the case in the Court of Claims in the absence of any showing of newly discovered evidence. The result would only differ from the result already obtained in that under the bill which I return the court would enter a judgment instead of a finding, and the judgment could only be paid after Congressional action.

The finding which has already been made, as I have said, is a complete basis for any such action as Congress may think should be taken in the premises.

BENJ. HARRISON.

EXECUTIVE MANSION, *October 1, 1890.*

To the Senate:

I return without my approval the bill (S. 3830) "to prohibit bookmaking of any kind and pool selling in the District of Columbia for the purpose of gaming."

My objection to the bill is that it does not prohibit bookmaking and pool selling, but, on the contrary, expressly saves from the operation of its prohibitions and penalties the Washington Jockey Club "and any other regular organizations owning race tracks no less than 1 mile in length," etc.

If this form of gambling is to be prohibited, as I think it should be, the penalties should include all persons and all places.

BENJ. HARRISON.

PROCLAMATIONS.

By the President of the United States of America.

A PROCLAMATION.

Whereas it is provided in the act of Congress approved March 2, 1889, entitled "An act to divide a portion of the reservation of the Sioux Nation of Indians in Dakota into separate reservations and to secure the relinquishment of the Indian title to the remainder, and for other purposes"—

That this act shall take effect only upon the acceptance thereof and consent thereto by the different bands of the Sioux Nation of Indians, in manner and form prescribed by the twelfth article of the treaty between the United States and said Sioux Indians concluded April 29, 1868, which said acceptance and consent shall be made known by proclamation by the President of the United States, upon satisfactory proof presented to him that the same has been obtained in the manner and form required by said twelfth article of said treaty, which proof shall be presented to him within one year from the passage of this act; and upon failure of such proof and proclamation this act becomes of no effect and null and void.

And whereas satisfactory proof has been presented to me that the acceptance of and consent to the provisions of the said act by the different bands of the Sioux Nation of Indians have been obtained in manner and form as therein required:

Now, therefore, I, Benjamin Harrison, President of the United States, by virtue of the power in me vested, do hereby make known and proclaim the acceptance of said act by the different bands of the Sioux Nation of Indians and the consent thereto by them as required by the act, and said act is hereby declared to be in full force and effect, subject to all the provisions, conditions, limitations, and restrictions therein contained.

All persons will take notice of the provisions of said act and of the conditions, limitations, and restrictions therein contained, and be governed accordingly.

I furthermore notify all persons to particularly observe that by said act certain tracts or portions of the Great Reservation of the Sioux Nation in the Territory of Dakota, as described by metes and bounds, are set apart as separate and permanent reservations for the Indians receiving rations and annuities at the respective agencies therein named.

That any Indian receiving and entitled to rations and annuities at either of the agencies mentioned in this act at the time the same shall take effect, but residing upon any portion of said Great Reservation not included in either of the separate reservations herein established, may at his option, within one year from the time when this act shall take effect, and within one year after he has been notified of his said right of option, in such manner as the Secretary of the Interior shall direct, by recording his election with the proper agent at the agency to which he belongs, have the allotment to which he would be otherwise entitled on one of said separate reservations upon the land where such Indian may then reside.

That each member or the Ponca tribe of Indians now occupying a part of the old Ponca Reservation, within the limits of the said Great Sioux Reservation, shall be entitled to allotments upon said old Ponca Reservation in quantities as therein set forth, and that when allotments to the Ponca tribe of Indians and to such other Indians as allotments are provided for by this act shall have been made upon that portion of said reservation which is described in the act entitled "An act to extend the northern boundary of the State of Nebraska," approved March 28, 1882, the President shall, in pursuance of said act, declare that the Indian title is extinguished to all lands described in said act not so allotted hereunder, and thereupon all of said land not so allotted and included in said act of March 28, 1882, shall be open to settlement as provided in this act.

That protection is guaranteed to such Indians as may have taken allotments either within or without the said separate reservations under the provisions of the treaty with the Great Sioux Nation concluded April 29, 1868; and that provision is made in said act for the release of all title on the part of said Indians receiving rations and annuities on each separate reservation to the lands described in each of the other separate reservations, and to confirm in the Indians entitled to receive rations at each of said separate reservations, respectively, to their separate and exclusive use and benefit, all the title and interest of every name and nature secured to the different bands of the Sioux Nation by said treaty of April 29, 1868; and that said release shall not affect the title of any individual Indian to his separate allotment of land not included in any of said separate reservations, nor any agreement heretofore made with the Chicago, Milwaukee and St. Paul Railroad Company or the Dakota Central Railroad Company respecting certain lands for right of way, station grounds, etc., regarding which certain prior rights and privileges are reserved to and for the use of said railroad companies, respectively, upon the terms and conditions set forth in said act.

That it is therein provided that if any land in said Great Sioux Reservation is occupied and used by any religious society at the date of said act for the purpose of missionary or educational work among the Indians, whether situate outside of or within the limits of any of the separate reservations, the same, not exceeding 160 acres in any one tract, shall be granted to said society for the purposes and upon the terms and conditions therein named; and

Subject to all the conditions and limitations in said act contained, it is therein provided that all the lands in the Great Sioux Reservation outside of the separate reservations described in said act, except American Island, Farm Island, and Niobrara Island, regarding which islands special provisions are therein made, and sections 16 and 36 in each township thereof (which are reserved for school purposes), shall be disposed of by the United States, upon the terms, at the price, and in the manner therein set forth, to actual settlers only, under the provisions of the homestead law (except section 2301 thereof) and under the law relating to town sites.

That section 23 of said act provides—

That all persons who, between the 27th day of February, 1885, and the 17th day of April, 1885, in good faith entered upon or made settlements with intent to enter the same under the homestead or preemption laws of the United States upon any part of the Great Sioux Reservation lying east of the Missouri River, and known as the Crow Creek and Winnebago Reservation, which by the President's proclamation of date February 27, 1885, was declared to be open to settlement, and not included in the new reservation established by section 6 of this act, and who, being otherwise legally entitled to make such entries, located or attempted to locate thereon homestead, preemption, or town-site claims by actual settlement and improvement of any portion of such lands, shall for a period of ninety days after the proclamation of the President required to be made by this act have a right to reenter upon said claims and procure title thereto under the homestead or preemption laws of the United States and complete the same as required therein, and their said claims shall for such time have a preference over later entries; and when they shall have in other respects shown themselves entitled and shall have complied with the law regulating such entries, and, as to homesteads, with the special provisions of this act, they shall be entitled to have said lands, and patents therefor shall be issued as in like cases: *Provided*, That preemption claimants shall reside on their lands the same length of time before procuring title as homestead claimants under this act. The price to be paid for town-site entries shall be such as is required by law in other cases, and shall be paid into the general fund provided for by this act.

It is furthermore hereby made known that there has been and is hereby reserved from entry or settlement that tract of land now occupied by the agency and school buildings at the Lower Brulé Agency, to wit:

The west half of the southwest quarter of section 24, the east half of the southeast quarter of section 23, the west half of the northwest quarter of section 25, the east half of the northeast quarter of section 26, and the northwest fractional quarter of the southeast quarter of section 26, all in township 104 north of range 72 west of the fifth principal meridian.

That there is also reserved as aforesaid the following-described tract within which the Cheyenne River Agency, school, and certain other buildings are located, to wit: Commencing at a point in the center of the main channel of the Missouri River opposite Deep Creek, about 3 miles south of Cheyenne River; thence due west 5½ miles; thence due north to the Cheyenne River; thence down said river to the center of the main channel thereof to a point in the center of the Missouri River due east or opposite the mouth of said Cheyenne River; thence down the center of the main channel of the Missouri River to the place of beginning.

That in pursuance of the provisions contained in section 1 of said act the tract of land situate in the State of Nebraska and described in said act as follows, to wit: "Beginning at a point on the boundary line between the State of Nebraska and the Territory of Dakota where the range line between ranges 44 and 45 west of the sixth principal meridian, in the Territory of Dakota, intersects said boundary line; thence east along said boundary line 5 miles; thence due south 5 miles; thence due west 10 miles; thence due north to said boundary line; thence due east along said boundary line to the place of beginning," same is continued in a state of reservation so long as it may be needed for the use and protection of the Indians receiving rations and annuities at the Pine Ridge Agency.

Warning is hereby also expressly given to all persons not to enter or make settlement upon any of the tracts of land specially reserved by the terms of said act or by this proclamation, or any portion of any tracts of land to which any individual member of either of the bands of the Great Sioux Nation or the Ponca tribe of Indians shall have a preference right under the provisions of said act; and further, to in no wise interfere with the occupancy of any of said tracts by any of said Indians, or in any manner to disturb, molest, or prevent the peaceful possession of said tracts by them.

The surveys required to be made of the lands to be restored to the public domain under the provisions of the said act and as in this proclamation set forth will be commenced and executed as early as possible.

In witness whereof I have hereunto set my hand and caused the seal of the United States to be affixed.

[SEAL.]   Done at the city of Washington, this 10th day of February, A. D. 1890, and of the Independence of the United States the one hundred and fourteenth.

BENJ. HARRISON.

By the President:

JAMES G. BLAINE, *Secretary of State.*

BY THE PRESIDENT OF THE UNITED STATES OF AMERICA.

A PROCLAMATION.

Whereas that portion of the Indian Territory commonly known as the Cherokee Strip or Outlet has been for some years in the occupancy of an association or associations of white persons under certain contracts said to have been made with the Cherokee Nation, in the nature of a lease or leases for grazing purposes; and

Whereas an opinion has been given to me by the Attorney-General, concurring with the opinion given to my predecessor by the late Attorney-General, that whatever the right or title of said Cherokee Nation or of the United States to or in said lands may be, no right exists in said Cherokee Nation under the statutes of the United States to make such leases or grazing contracts, and that such contracts are wholly illegal and void; and

Whereas the continued use of said lands thereunder for grazing purposes is prejudicial to the public interests:

Now, therefore, I, Benjamin Harrison, President of the United States, do hereby proclaim and give notice—

First. That no cattle or live stock shall hereafter be brought upon said lands for herding or grazing thereon.

Second. That all cattle and other live stock now on said outlet must be removed therefrom not later than October 1, 1890, and so much sooner as said lands or any of them may be or become lawfully open to settlement by citizens of the United States; and that all persons connected with said cattle companies or associations must, not later than the time above indicated, depart from said lands.

In witness whereof I have hereunto set my hand and caused the seal of the United States to be affixed.

[SEAL.] Done at the city of Washington, this 17th day of February, A. D. 1890, and of the Independence of the United States of America the one hundred and fourteenth.

BENJ. HARRISON.

By the President:

JAMES G. BLAINE,
Secretary of State.

BY THE PRESIDENT OF THE UNITED STATES OF AMERICA.

A PROCLAMATION.

The following provisions of the laws of the United States are hereby published for the information of all concerned:

Section 1956, Revised Statutes, chapter 3, Title XXIII, enacts that—

No person shall kill any otter, mink, marten, sable, or fur seal, or other fur-bearing animal within the limits of Alaska Territory or in the waters thereof; and every person guilty thereof shall for each offense be fined not less than $200 nor more than $1,000, or imprisoned not more than six months, or both; and all vessels, their tackle, apparel, furniture, and cargo, found engaged in violation of this section shall be forfeited; but the Secretary of the Treasury shall have power to authorize the killing of any such mink, marten, sable, or other fur-bearing animal, except fur seals, under such regulations as he may prescribe; and it shall be the duty of the Secretary to prevent the killing of any fur seal and to provide for the execution of the provisions of this section until it is otherwise provided by law, nor shall he grant any special privileges under this section.

     *   *   *   *   *   *   *

Section 3 of the act entitled "An act to provide for the protection of the salmon fisheries of Alaska," approved March 2, 1889, provides that—

SEC. 3. That section 1956 of the Revised Statutes of the United States is hereby declared to include and apply to all the dominion of the United States in the waters of Bering Sea, and it shall be the duty of the President at a timely season in each year to issue his proclamation, and cause the same to be published for one month in at least one newspaper (if any such there be) published at each United States port of entry on the Pacific coast, warning all persons against entering such waters for the purpose of violating the provisions of said section, and he shall also cause one or more vessels of the United States to diligently cruise said waters and arrest all persons and seize all vessels found to be or to have been engaged in any violation of the laws of the United States therein.

Now, therefore, I, Benjamin Harrison, President of the United States, pursuant to the above-recited statutes, hereby warn all persons against entering the waters of Bering Sea within the dominion of the United States for the purpose of violating the provisions of said section 1956, Revised Statutes; and I hereby proclaim that all persons found to be or have been engaged in any violation of the laws of the United States in said waters will be arrested and punished as above provided, and that all vessels so employed, their tackle, apparel, furniture, and cargoes, will be seized and forfeited.

In testimony whereof I have hereunto set my hand and caused the seal of the United States to be affixed.

[SEAL.]   Done at the city of Washington, this 15th day of March, 1890, and of the Independence of the United States the one hundred and fourteenth.   BENJ. HARRISON.

By the President:
    JAMES G. BLAINE,
        Secretary of State.

PROCLAMATION.

SEPTEMBER 19, 1890.

To whom it may concern:

Whereas it has been represented to me that by reason of the drought which has prevailed in the Indian Territory and in the adjoining States the execution of my proclamation of February 17, 1890, requiring the removal of all live stock from the Cherokee Outlet on or before October 1 would work great hardship and loss, not only to the owners of stock herded upon the strip, but to the owners of cattle in the adjoining States; and

Whereas the owners of all cattle now herded upon the outlet have submitted to me a proposition in writing whereby they agree to remove one-half of their stock from the outlet on or before November 1 and the

62258

residue thereof and all their property and employees on or before December 1 next, and to abandon all claims in said outlet:

Now, therefore, I, Benjamin Harrison, President of the United States, do give notice and proclaim that the time heretofore fixed for the removal of the live stock herded upon said outlet is extended to November 1 as to one-half thereof and to December 1 next as to the residue thereof and as to all property and employees.   BENJ. HARRISON.

· BY THE PRESIDENT OF THE UNITED STATES OF AMERICA.

A PROCLAMATION.

Whereas it is provided in the act of Congress entitled "An act to extend the northern boundary of the State of Nebraska," approved March 28, 1882—

That the northern boundary of the State of Nebraska shall be, and hereby is, subject to the provisions hereinafter contained, extended so as to include all that portion of the Territory of Dakota lying south of the forty-third parallel of north latitude and east of the Keya Paha River and west of the main channel of the Missouri River; and when the Indian title to the lands thus described shall be extinguished the jurisdiction over said lands shall be, and hereby is, ceded to the State of Nebraska, and subject to all the conditions and limitations provided in the act of Congress admitting Nebraska into the Union, and the northern boundary of the State shall be extended to said forty-third parallel as fully and effectually as if said lands had been included in the boundaries of said State at the time of its admission to the Union; reserving to the United States the original right of soil in said lands and of disposing of the same: *Provided*, That this act, so far as jurisdiction is concerned, shall not take effect until the President shall by proclamation declare that the Indian title to said lands has been extinguished, nor shall it take effect until the State of Nebraska shall have assented to the provisions of this act; and if the State of Nebraska shall not by an act of its legislature consent to the provisions of this act within two years next after the passage hereof this act shall cease and be of no effect.

And whereas by section 13 of the act entitled "An act to divide a portion of the reservation of the Sioux Nation of Indians in Dakota into separate reservations and to secure the relinquishment of the Indian title to the remainder, and for other purposes," approved March 2, 1889, it is provided—

That when the allotments to the Ponca tribe of Indians and to such other Indians as allotments are provided for by this act shall have been made upon that portion of said reservation which is described in the act entitled "An act to extend the northern boundary of the State of Nebraska," approved March 28, 1882, the President shall, in pursuance of said act, declare that the Indian title is extinguished to all lands described in said act not so allotted hereunder, and thereupon all of said land not so allotted and included in said act of March 28, 1882, shall be open to settlement as provided in this act: *Provided*, That the allotments to Ponca and other Indians authorized by this act to be made upon the land described in the said act entitled "An act to extend the northern boundary of the State of Nebraska" shall be made within six months from the time this act shall take effect.

And whereas the State of Nebraska, by an act of its legislature approved May 23, 1882, entitled "An act declaring the assent of the State of Nebraska to an act of Congress of the United States entitled 'An act to extend the northern boundary of the State of Nebraska,' approved March 28, 1882," assented to and accepted the provisions of said act of Congress approved March 28, 1882; and

Whereas allotments have been made to the Ponca tribe of Indians under and in accordance with the provisions of said section 13 of the act of March 2, 1889, and no other Indians having selected or applied for allotments upon that portion of the reservation of the Sioux Nation of Indians described in the act of March 28, 1882, aforesaid, and the six months' limit of time within which said allotments were authorized to be made having expired on the 10th day of August, 1890:

Now, therefore, I, Benjamin Harrison, President of the United States, by virtue of the power in me vested by the act (section 13) of March 2, 1889, aforesaid, and in pursuance of the act of March 28, 1882, aforesaid, do hereby declare that the Indian title is extinguished to all lands described in said act of March 28, 1882, not allotted to the Ponca tribe of Indians as aforesaid and shown upon a schedule, in duplicate, of allotments made and certified jointly by George P. Litchfield, United States special agent, and James E. Helms, United States Indian agent, July 31, 1890, and approved by the Acting Commissioner of Indian Affairs October 14, 1890, and by the Acting Secretary of the Interior October 22, 1890, one copy of which schedule of allotments is now on file in the office of the Commissioner of Indian Affairs and the other in the office of the Commissioner of the General Land Office, Department of the Interior.

Be it known, however, that there is hereby reserved from entry or settlement that tract of land now occupied by the agency and school buildings of the old Ponca Agency, to wit: The south half of the southeast quarter of section 26 and the south half of the southwest quarter of section 25, all in township 32 north, range 7 west of the sixth principal meridian.

In witness whereof I have hereunto set my hand and caused the seal of the United States to be affixed.

[SEAL.]   Done at the city of Washington, this 23d day of October, A. D. 1890, and of the Independence of the United States the one hundred and fifteenth.   BENJ. HARRISON.

By the President:

ALVEY A. ADEE, *Acting Secretary of State.*

BY THE PRESIDENT OF THE UNITED STATES.

A PROCLAMATION.

By the grace and favor of Almighty God the people of this nation have been led to the closing days of the passing year, which has been full of the blessings of peace and the comforts of plenty. Bountiful compensation has come to us for the work of our minds and of our hands in every department of human industry.

Now, therefore, I, Benjamin Harrison, President of the United States of America, do hereby appoint Thursday, the 27th day of the present month of November, to be observed as a day of prayer and thanksgiving; and I do invite the people upon that day to cease from their labors, to meet in their accustomed houses of worship, and to join in rendering gratitude and praise to our beneficent Creator for the rich blessings He has granted to us as a nation and in invoking the continuance of His protection and grace for the future. I commend to my fellow-citizens the privilege of remembering the poor, the homeless, and the sorrowful. Let us endeavor to merit the promised recompense of charity and the gracious acceptance of our praise.

In testimony whereof I have hereunto set my hand and caused the seal of the United States to be affixed.

[SEAL.]   Done at the city of Washington, this 8th day of November, A. D. 1890, and of the Independence of the United States the one hundred and fifteenth.

BENJ. HARRISON.

By the President:

JAMES G. BLAINE, *Secretary of State.*

BY THE PRESIDENT OF THE UNITED STATES OF AMERICA.

A PROCLAMATION.

Whereas an act of Congress in regard to collision at sea was approved September 4, 1890, the said act being in the following words:

Be it enacted by the Senate and House of Representatives of the United States of America in Congress assembled, That in every case of collision between two vessels it shall be the duty of the master or person in charge of each vessel, if and so far as he can do so without serious danger to his own vessel, crew, and passengers (if any), to stay by the other vessel until he has ascertained that she has no need of further assistance, and to render to the other vessel, her master, crew, and passengers (if any), such assistance as may be practicable and as may be necessary in order to save them from any danger caused by the collision, and also to give to the master or person in charge of the other vessel the name of his own vessel and her port of registry, or the port or place to which she belongs, and also the name of the ports and places from which and to which she is bound. If he fails so to do, and no reasonable cause for such failure is shown, the collision shall, in the absence of proof to the contrary, be deemed to have been caused by his wrongful act, neglect, or default.

SEC. 2. That every master or person in charge of a United States vessel who fails, without reasonable cause, to render such assistance or give such information as aforesaid shall be deemed guilty of a misdemeanor, and shall be liable to a penalty of $1,000 or imprisonment for a term not exceeding two years; and for the above sum the vessel shall be liable and may be seized and proceeded against by process in any district court of the United States by any person; one-half such sum to be payable to the informer and the other half to the United States.

SEC. 3. That this act shall take effect at a time to be fixed by the President by proclamation issued for that purpose.

And whereas it is provided by section 3 of the said act that it shall take effect at a time to be fixed by the President by proclamation issued for that purpose:

Now, therefore, I, Benjamin Harrison, President of the United States of America, do hereby, in virtue of the authority vested in me by section 3 of the said act, proclaim the 15th day of December, 1890, as the day on which the said act shall take effect.

In testimony whereof I have hereunto set my hand and caused the seal of the United States of America to be affixed.

[SEAL.] Done at the city of Washington, this 18th day of November, A. D. 1890, and of the Independence of the United States the one hundred and fifteenth. BENJ. HARRISON.

By the President:
JAMES G. BLAINE, *Secretary of State.*

EXECUTIVE ORDERS.

AMENDMENT OF CIVIL-SERVICE RULES.

Special Departmental Rule No. 1 is hereby amended so as to include among the exceptions from examination in the Department of Agriculture the following:

Scientific or professional experts to be employed in investigations specially authorized by Congress, but not to include any persons regularly employed in that Department nor any persons whose duties are not scientific or professional, and who are not experts in the particular line of scientific or professional inquiry in which they are to be employed.

Approved, January 29, 1890. BENJ. HARRISON.

AMENDMENTS OF CIVIL-SERVICE RULES.

Section 1 of Postal Rule II is hereby amended by adding to the subjects of the clerk examination the following: "Reading addresses and physical tests;" and to the subjects of carrier examination the following: "Reading addresses."

Approved, January 29, 1890. BENJ. HARRISON.

AMENDMENT OF CIVIL-SERVICE RULES.

Special Customs Rule No. 1 is hereby amended by adding thereto the following:

In the customs district of New York: Detectives employed exclusively as such.

Approved, March 10, 1890. BENJ. HARRISON.

AMENDMENT OF CIVIL-SERVICE RULES.

That part of Special Departmental Rule No. 1 relating to the Coast and Geodetic Survey, as printed on page 66 of the Fifth Annual Report of the Commission, is hereby amended by striking out in line 3, after the word "to," the words "general office assistant," and inserting in lieu thereof the words "assistant in charge of office and topography;" so that as amended the clause will read: "confidential clerk to assistant in charge of office and topography."

Approved, March 10, 1890.

BENJ. HARRISON.

AMENDMENTS OF CIVIL-SERVICE RULES.

MARCH 28, 1890.

Departmental Rule VII is hereby amended by adding thereto the following section, to be numbered 7:

7. In case of temporary absence, from sickness or other unavoidable cause, of clerks, copyists, or employees of other grades for which examinations are held, there may be certified in the manner provided for in this rule, and employed under such regulations as the heads of the several Departments shall prescribe, substitutes for such clerks, copyists, or other employees so absent; and such substitutes so employed in any Department shall be appointed in the order of their employment as substitutes to the regular grades of that Department without further certification as vacancies to which they are eligible may occur therein while so employed as substitutes, every such appointment to be at once reported to the Commission: *Provided*, That no person while employed as a substitute in one Department shall be certified as a substitute to any other Department, and that no person employed as a substitute shall by reason of such employment be deprived of any right of certification for a regular place to which he may be entitled under the rules: *And provided further*, That service rendered as a substitute shall not be ground for reinstatement under Departmental Rule X. The time during which any substitute who shall be appointed to a regular place is actually employed as such shall be counted as a part of his period of probation. No substitute shall be employed in any Department otherwise than as herein provided.

Special Departmental Rule No. 2 is hereby revoked.

BENJ. HARRISON.

[From McPherson's Hand Book of Politics for 1890.]

EXECUTIVE MANSION, *April 24, 1890.*

To the Attorney-General:

I have had frequent occasion during the last six months to confer with you in reference to the obstructions offered in the counties of Leon, Gadsden, Madison, and Jefferson, in the State of Florida, to the execution of the process of the courts of the United States. It is not necessary to say more of the situation than that the officers of the United States are not suffered freely to exercise their lawful functions. This condition of things can not be longer tolerated. You will therefore instruct United States Marshal Weeks as soon as he has qualified to proceed at once to execute such writs of arrest as may be placed in his hands. If he apprehends resistance, he will employ such civil posse as may seem adequate to discourage resistance or to overcome it. He should proceed with calmness and moderation, which should always attend a public officer in the execution of his duty, and at the same time with a firmness and courage that will impress the lawless with a wholesome sense of the dangers and futility of resistance. You will assure the officers of the law and those who have foolishly and wickedly thought to set the law at defiance that every resource lodged with the Executive by the Constitution and the laws will as the necessity arises be employed to make it safe and feasible to hold a Federal commission and to execute the duties it imposes.

Very respectfully,

BENJ. HARRISON.

By the President of the United States.

EXECUTIVE ORDER.

Executive Mansion, *May 27, 1890.*

It is hereby ordered, That the several Executive Departments and the Government Printing Office be closed on Friday, the 30th instant, to enable the employees to participate in the decoration of the graves of the soldiers and sailors who fell in defense of the Union during the War of the Rebellion.

BENJ. HARRISON.

AMENDMENT OF CIVIL-SERVICE RULES.

United States Civil Service Commission,
Washington, D. C., *May 31, 1890.*

The PRESIDENT.

SIR: This Commission has the honor to recommend that Special Departmental Rule No. 1 be amended by adding to the exceptions from examination therein declared the following:

"In the Department of the Treasury, in the life-saving service: Topographer and hydrographer."

We have the honor to be, your obedient servants,

CHAS. LYMAN,
THEODORE ROOSEVELT,
HUGH S. THOMPSON,
United States Civil Service Commissioners.

Approved, June 3, 1890.

BENJ HARRISON.

EXECUTIVE MANSION,
Washington, July 14, 1890.*

The death of John C. Frémont, a major-general on the retired list of the Army of the United States, is an event calling for some appropriate expression of the national sorrow and of a grateful appreciation of his public services. His career was full of adventurous and useful discovery and of devoted and conspicuous service both in civil and military affairs. He opened the passes of the Rocky Mountains and gave value to his discoveries by aiding to create an American State on the Pacific Coast.

It is therefore ordered, That the national flag be displayed at half-mast upon all the buildings of the Executive Departments in this city until after the funeral shall have taken place.

By direction of the President:

E. W. HALFORD,
Private Secretary.

AMENDMENTS OF CIVIL-SERVICE RULES.

Departmental Rule VIII, section 1, clause (*b*), is hereby amended by inserting after the word "transacted" the following: "and from the office of the Solicitor of the Treasury;" and after the word "Department" where it last occurs the following: "or to said office;" so that as amended the clause will read:

(*b*) From a bureau of the Treasury Department in which business relating to the customs is transacted and from the office of the Solicitor of the Treasury to a classified customs district, and from such a district to such a bureau of the Treasury Department or to said office, upon requisition by the Secretary of the Treasury.

Approved, July 23, 1890.

BENJ. HARRISON.

AMENDMENT OF CIVIL-SERVICE RULES.

JULY 30, 1890.

Special Departmental Rule No. 1 is hereby amended by adding to the places excepted from examination in the Department of Agriculture the following:

Wood engravers.

BENJ. HARRISON.

AMENDMENT OF CIVIL-SERVICE RULES.

SEPTEMBER 2, 1890.*

Special Departmental Rule No. 1 is hereby amended by adding to the places excepted from examination therein the following:

In the Post-Office Department, office of the Postmaster-General: Stenographer as confidential clerk to the chief post-office inspector.

BENJ. HARRISON.

*Addressed to the heads of the Executive Departments, etc.

AMENDMENT OF CIVIL-SERVICE RULES.

OCTOBER 31, 1890.

Section 7 of Railway Mail Rule IV is hereby amended by inserting in line 7, after the word "days," the following: "or until the emergency ceases."

BENJ. HARRISON.

SECOND ANNUAL MESSAGE.

EXECUTIVE MANSION, *December 1, 1890.*

To the Senate and House of Representatives:

The reports of the several Executive Departments, which will be laid before Congress in the usual course, will exhibit in detail the operations of the Government for the last fiscal year. Only the more important incidents and results, and chiefly such as may be the foundation of the recommendations I shall submit, will be referred to in this annual message.

The vast and increasing business of the Government has been transacted by the several Departments during the year with faithfulness, energy, and success.

The revenues, amounting to above $450,000,000, have been collected and disbursed without revealing, so far as I can ascertain, a single case of defalcation or embezzlement. An earnest effort has been made to stimulate a sense of responsibility and public duty in all officers and employees of every grade, and the work done by them has almost wholly escaped unfavorable criticism. I speak of these matters with freedom because the credit of this good work is not mine, but is shared by the heads of the several Departments with the great body of faithful officers and employees who serve under them. The closest scrutiny of Congress is invited to all the methods of administration and to every item of expenditure.

The friendly relations of our country with the nations of Europe and of the East have been undisturbed, while the ties of good will and common interest that bind us to the States of the Western Hemisphere have been notably strengthened by the conference held in this capital to consider measures for the general welfare. Pursuant to the invitation authorized by Congress, the representatives of every independent State of the American continent and of Hayti met in conference in this capital in October, 1889, and continued in session until the 19th of last April. This important convocation marks a most interesting and influential epoch in the history of the Western Hemisphere. It is noteworthy that Brazil, invited while under an imperial form of government, shared as a republic in the deliberations and results of the conference. The recommendations of this conference were all transmitted to Congress at the last session.

The International Marine Conference, which sat at Washington last winter, reached a very gratifying result. The regulations suggested have been brought to the attention of all the Governments represented, and their general adoption is confidently expected. The legislation of Congress at the last session is in conformity with the propositions of the conference, and the proclamation therein provided for will be issued when the other powers have given notice of their adhesion.

The Conference of Brussels, to devise means for suppressing the slave trade in Africa, afforded an opportunity for a new expression of the interest the American people feel in that great work. It soon became evident that the measure proposed would tax the resources of the Kongo Basin beyond the revenues available under the general act of Berlin of 1884. The United States, not being a party to that act, could not share in its revision, but by a separate act the Independent State of the Kongo was freed from the restrictions upon a customs revenue. The demoralizing and destructive traffic in ardent spirits among the tribes also claimed the earnest attention of the conference, and the delegates of the United States were foremost in advocating measures for its repression. An accord was reached the influence of which will be very helpful and extend over a wide region. As soon as these measures shall receive the sanction of the Netherlands, for a time withheld, the general acts will be submitted for ratification by the Senate. Meanwhile negotiations have been opened for a new and completed treaty of friendship, commerce, and navigation between the United States and the Independent State of the Kongo.

Toward the end of the past year the only independent monarchical government on the Western Continent, that of Brazil, ceased to exist, and was succeeded by a republic. Diplomatic relations were at once established with the new Government, but it was not completely recognized until an opportunity had been afforded to ascertain that it had popular approval and support. When the course of events had yielded assurance of this fact, no time was lost in extending to the new Government a full and cordial welcome into the family of American Commonwealths. It is confidently believed that the good relations of the two countries will be preserved and that the future will witness an increased intimacy of intercourse and an expansion of their mutual commerce.

The peace of Central America has again been disturbed through a revolutionary change in Salvador, which was not recognized by other States, and hostilities broke out between Salvador and Guatemala, threatening to involve all Central America in conflict and to undo the progress which had been made toward a union of their interests. The efforts of this Government were promptly and zealously exerted to compose their differences, and through the active efforts of the representative of the United States a provisional treaty of peace was signed August 26, whereby the right of the Republic of Salvador to choose its own rulers was recognized. General Ezeta, the chief of the Provisional Government, has since been confirmed in the Presidency by the Assembly, and diplomatic recognition duly followed.

The killing of General Barrundia on board the Pacific mail steamer *Acapulco*, while anchored in transit in the port of San Jose de Guatemala, demanded careful inquiry. Having failed in a revolutionary attempt to invade Guatemala from Mexican territory, General Barrundia took passage at Acapulco for Panama. The consent of the representatives of the United States was sought to effect his seizure, first at Champerico, where the steamer touched, and afterwards at San Jose. The captain of the steamer refused to give up his passenger without a written order from the United States minister. The latter furnished the desired letter, stipulating as the condition of his action that General Barrundia's life should be spared and that he should be tried only for offenses growing out of his insurrectionary movements. This letter was produced to the captain of the *Acapulco* by the military commander at San Jose as his warrant to take the passenger from the steamer. General Barrundia resisted capture and was killed. It being evident that the minister, Mr. Mizner, had exceeded the bounds of his authority in intervening, in compliance with the demands of the Guatemalan authorities, to authorize and effect, in violation of precedent, the seizure on a vessel of the United States of a passenger in transit charged with political offenses, in order that he might be tried for such offenses under what was described as martial law, I was constrained to disavow Mr. Mizner's act and recall him from his post.

The Nicaragua Canal project, under the control of our citizens, is making most encouraging progress, all the preliminary conditions and initial operations having been accomplished within the prescribed time.

During the past year negotiations have been renewed for the settlement of the claims of American citizens against the Government of Chile, principally growing out of the late war with Peru. The reports from our minister at Santiago warrant the expectation of an early and satisfactory adjustment.

Our relations with China, which have for several years occupied so important a place in our diplomatic history, have called for careful consideration and have been the subject of much correspondence.

The communications of the Chinese minister have brought into view the whole subject of our conventional relations with his country, and at the same time this Government, through its legation at Peking, has sought to arrange various matters and complaints touching the interests and protection of our citizens in China.

In pursuance of the concurrent resolution of October 1, 1890, I have proposed to the Governments of Mexico and Great Britain to consider a conventional regulation of the passage of Chinese laborers across our southern and northern frontiers.

On the 22d day of August last Sir Edmund Monson, the arbitrator selected under the treaty of December 6, 1888, rendered an award to the effect that no compensation was due from the Danish Government to the United States on account of what is commonly known as the Carlos Butterfield claim.

Our relations with the French Republic continue to be cordial. Our representative at that court has very diligently urged the removal of the restrictions imposed upon our meat products, and it is believed that substantial progress has been made toward a just settlement.

The Samoan treaty, signed last year at Berlin by the representatives of the United States, Germany, and Great Britain, after due ratification and exchange, has begun to produce salutary effects. The formation of the government agreed upon will soon replace the disorder of the past by a stable administration alike just to the natives and equitable to the three powers most concerned in trade and intercourse with the Samoan Islands. The chief justice has been chosen by the King of Sweden and Norway on the invitation of the three powers, and will soon be installed. The land commission and the municipal council are in process of organization. A rational and evenly distributed scheme of taxation, both municipal and upon imports, is in operation. Malietoa is respected as King.

The new treaty of extradition with Great Britain, after due ratification, was proclaimed on the 25th of last March. Its beneficial working is already apparent.

The difference between the two Governments touching the fur-seal question in the Bering Sea is not yet adjusted, as will be seen by the correspondence which will soon be laid before the Congress. The offer to submit the question to arbitration, as proposed by Her Majesty's Government, has not been accepted, for the reason that the form of submission proposed is not thought to be calculated to assure a conclusion satisfactory to either party. It is sincerely hoped that before the opening of another sealing season some arrangement may be effected which will assure to the United States a property right derived from Russia, which was not disregarded by any nation for more than eighty years preceding the outbreak of the existing trouble.

In the tariff act a wrong was done to the Kingdom of Hawaii which I am bound to presume was wholly unintentional. Duties were levied on certain commodities which are included in the reciprocity treaty now existing between the United States and the Kingdom of Hawaii, without indicating the necessary exception in favor of that Kingdom. I hope Congress will repair what might otherwise seem to be a breach of faith on the part of this Government.

An award in favor of the United States in the matter of the claim of Mr. Van Bokkelen against Hayti was rendered on the 4th of December,

1888, but owing to disorders then and afterwards prevailing in Hayti the terms of payment were not observed. A new agreement as to the time of payment has been approved and is now in force. Other just claims of citizens of the United States for redress of wrongs suffered during the late political conflict in Hayti will, it is hoped, speedily yield to friendly treatment.

Propositions for the amendment of the treaty of extradition between the United States and Italy are now under consideration.

You will be asked to provide the means of accepting the invitation of the Italian Government to take part in an approaching conference to consider the adoption of a universal prime meridian from which to reckon longitude and time. As this proposal follows in the track of the reform sought to be initiated by the Meridian Conference of Washington, held on the invitation of this Government, the United States should manifest a friendly interest in the Italian proposal.

In this connection I may refer with approval to the suggestion of my predecessors that standing provision be made for accepting, whenever deemed advisable, the frequent invitations of foreign governments to share in conferences looking to the advancement of international reforms in regard to science, sanitation, commercial laws and procedure, and other matters affecting the intercourse and progress of modern communities.

In the summer of 1889 an incident occurred which for some time threatened to interrupt the cordiality of our relations with the Government of Portugal. That Government seized the Delagoa Bay Railway, which was constructed under a concession granted to an American citizen, and at the same time annulled the charter. The concessionary, who had embarked his fortune in the enterprise, having exhausted other means of redress, was compelled to invoke the protection of his Government. Our representations, made coincidently with those of the British Government, whose subjects were also largely interested, happily resulted in the recognition by Portugal of the propriety of submitting the claim for indemnity growing out of its action to arbitration. This plan of settlement having been agreed upon, the interested powers readily concurred in the proposal to submit the case to the judgment of three eminent jurists, to be designated by the President of the Swiss Republic, who, upon the joint invitation of the Governments of the United States, Great Britain, and Portugal, has selected persons well qualified for the task before them.

The revision of our treaty relations with the Empire of Japan has continued to be the subject of consideration and of correspondence. The questions involved are both grave and delicate; and while it will be my duty to see that the interests of the United States are not by any changes exposed to undue discrimination, I sincerely hope that such revision as will satisfy the legitimate expectations of the Japanese Government and maintain the present and long-existing friendly relations between Japan and the United States will be effected.

The friendship between our country and Mexico, born of close neighborhood and strengthened by many considerations of intimate intercourse and reciprocal interest, has never been more conspicuous than now nor more hopeful of increased benefit to both nations. The intercourse of the two countries by rail, already great, is making constant growth. The established lines and those recently projected add to the intimacy of traffic and open new channels of access to fresh areas of demand and supply. The importance of the Mexican railway system will be further enhanced to a degree almost impossible to forecast if it should become a link in the projected intercontinental railway. I recommend that our mission in the City of Mexico be raised to the first class.

The cordial character of our relations with Spain warrants the hope that by the continuance of methods of friendly negotiation much may be accomplished in the direction of an adjustment of pending questions and of the increase of our trade. The extent and development of our trade with the island of Cuba invest the commercial relations of the United States and Spain with a peculiar importance. It is not doubted that a special arrangement in regard to commerce, based upon the reciprocity provision of the recent tariff act, would operate most beneficially for both Governments. This subject is now receiving attention.

The restoration of the remains of John Ericsson to Sweden afforded a gratifying occasion to honor the memory of the great inventor, to whose genius our country owes so much, and to bear witness to the unbroken friendship which has existed between the land which bore him and our own, which claimed him as a citizen.

On the 2d of September last the commission appointed to revise the proceedings of the commission under the claims convention between the United States and Venezuela of 1866 brought its labors to a close within the period fixed for that purpose. The proceedings of the late commission were characterized by a spirit of impartiality and a high sense of justice, and an incident which was for many years the subject of discussion between the two Governments has been disposed of in a manner alike honorable and satisfactory to both parties. For the settlement of the claim of the Venezuela Steam Transportation Company, which was the subject of a joint resolution adopted at the last session of Congress, negotiations are still in progress, and their early conclusion is anticipated.

The legislation of the past few years has evinced on the part of Congress a growing realization of the importance of the consular service in fostering our commercial relations abroad and in protecting the domestic revenues. As the scope of operations expands increased provision must be made to keep up the essential standard of efficiency. The necessity of some adequate measure of supervision and inspection has been so often presented that I need only commend the subject to your attention.

The revenues of the Government from all sources for the fiscal year ending June 30, 1890, were $463,963,080.55 and the total expenditures for the same period were $358,618,584.52. The postal receipts have not heretofore been included in the statement of these aggregates, and for the purpose of comparison the sum of $60,882,097.92 should be deducted from both sides of the account. The surplus for the year, including the amount applied to the sinking fund, was $105,344,496.03. The receipts for 1890 were $16,030,923.79 and the expenditures $15,739,871 in excess of those of 1889. The customs receipts increased $5,835,842.88 and the receipts from internal revenue $11,725,191.89, while on the side of expenditures that for pensions was $19,312,075.96 in excess of the preceding year.

The Treasury statement for the current fiscal year, partly actual and partly estimated, is as follows: Receipts from all sources, $406,000,000; total expenditures, $354,000,000, leaving a surplus of $52,000,000, not taking the postal receipts into the account on either side. The loss of revenue from customs for the last quarter is estimated at $25,000,000, but from this is deducted a gain of about $16,000,000 realized during the first four months of the year.

For the year 1892 the total estimated receipts are $373,000,000 and the estimated expenditures $357,852,209.42, leaving an estimated surplus of $15,147,790.58, which, with a cash balance of $52,000,000 at the beginning of the year, will give $67,147,790.58 as the sum available for the redemption of outstanding bonds or other uses. The estimates of receipts and expenditures for the Post-Office Department, being equal, are not included in this statement on either side.

The act "directing the purchase of silver bullion and the issue of Treasury notes thereon," approved July 14, 1890, has been administered by the Secretary of the Treasury with an earnest purpose to get into circulation at the earliest possible dates the full monthly amounts of Treasury notes contemplated by its provisions and at the same time to give to the market for the silver bullion such support as the law contemplates. The recent depreciation in the price of silver has been observed with regret. The rapid rise in price which anticipated and followed the passage of the act was influenced in some degree by speculation, and the recent reaction is in part the result of the same cause and in part of the recent monetary disturbances. Some months of further trial will be necessary to determine the permanent effect of the recent legislation upon silver values, but it is gratifying to know that the increased circulation secured by the act has exerted, and will continue to exert, a most beneficial influence upon business and upon general values.

While it has not been thought best to renew formally the suggestion of an international conference looking to an agreement touching the full use of silver for coinage at a uniform ratio, care has been taken to observe closely any change in the situation abroad, and no favorable opportunity will be lost to promote a result which it is confidently believed would confer very large benefits upon the commerce of the world.

The recent monetary disturbances in England are not unlikely to suggest a reexamination of opinions upon this subject. Our very large supply of gold will, if not lost by impulsive legislation in the supposed interest of silver, give us a position of advantage in promoting a permanent and safe international agreement for the free use of silver as a coin metal.

The efforts of the Secretary to increase the volume of money in circulation by keeping down the Treasury surplus to the lowest practicable limit have been unremitting and in a very high degree successful. The tables presented by him showing the increase of money in circulation during the last two decades, and especially the table showing the increase during the nineteen months he has administered the affairs of the Department, are interesting and instructive. The increase of money in circulation during the nineteen months has been in the aggregate $93,866,813, or about $1.50 per capita, and of this increase only $7,100,000 was due to the recent silver legislation. That this substantial and needed aid given to commerce resulted in an enormous reduction of the public debt and of the annual interest charge is matter of increased satisfaction. There have been purchased and redeemed since March 4, 1889, 4 and 4½ per cent bonds to the amount of $211,832,450, at a cost of $246,620,741, resulting in the reduction of the annual interest charge of $8,967,609 and a total saving of interest of $51,576,706.

I notice with great pleasure the statement of the Secretary that the receipts from internal revenue have increased during the last fiscal year nearly $12,000,000, and that the cost of collecting this larger revenue was less by $90,617 than for the same purpose in the preceding year. The percentage of cost of collecting the customs revenue was less for the last fiscal year than ever before.

The Customs Administration Board, provided for by the act of June 10, 1890, was selected with great care, and is composed in part of men whose previous experience in the administration of the old customs regulations had made them familiar with the evils to be remedied, and in part of men whose legal and judicial acquirements and experience seemed to fit them for the work of interpreting and applying the new statute. The chief aim of the law is to secure honest valuations of all dutiable merchandise and to make these valuations uniform at all our ports of entry. It had been made manifest by a Congressional investigation that a system of undervaluation had been long in use by certain classes of importers, resulting not only in a great loss of revenue, but in a most intolerable discrimination against honesty. It is not seen how this legislation, when it is understood, can be regarded by the citizens of any country having commercial dealings with us as unfriendly. If any duty is supposed to be excessive, let the complaint be lodged there. It will surely not be claimed by any well-disposed people that a remedy may be sought and allowed in a system of quasi smuggling.

The report of the Secretary of War exhibits several gratifying results attained during the year by wise and unostentatious methods. The percentage of desertions from the Army (an evil for which both Congress and the Department have long been seeking a remedy) has been reduced during the past year 24 per cent, and for the months of August and September, during which time the favorable effects of the act of June 16 were felt, 33 per cent, as compared with the same months of 1889.

The results attained by a reorganization and consolidation of the divisions having charge of the hospital and service records of the volunteer soldiers are very remarkable. This change was effected in July, 1889, and at that time there were 40,654 cases awaiting attention, more than half of these being calls from the Pension Office for information necessary to the adjudication of pension claims. On the 30th day of June last, though over 300,000 new calls had come in, there was not a single case that had not been examined and answered.

I concur in the recommendations of the Secretary that adequate and regular appropriations be continued for coast-defense works and ordnance. Plans have been practically agreed upon, and there can be no good reason for delaying the execution of them, while the defenseless state of our great seaports furnishes an urgent reason for wise expedition.

The encouragement that has been extended to the militia of the States, generally and most appropriately designated the "National Guard," should be continued and enlarged. These military organizations constitute in a large sense the Army of the United States, while about five-sixths of the annual cost of their maintenance is defrayed by the States.

The report of the Attorney-General is under the law submitted directly to Congress, but as the Department of Justice is one of the Executive Departments some reference to the work done is appropriate here.

A vigorous and in the main an effective effort has been made to bring to trial and punishment all violators of the law, but at the same time care has been taken that frivolous and technical offenses should not be used to swell the fees of officers or to harass well-disposed citizens. Especial attention is called to the facts connected with the prosecution of violations of the election laws and of offenses against United States officers. The number of convictions secured, very many of them upon pleas of guilty, will, it is hoped, have a salutary restraining influence. There have been several cases where postmasters appointed by me have been subjected to violent interference in the discharge of their official duties and to persecutions and personal violence of the most extreme character. Some of these cases have been dealt with through the Department of Justice, and in some cases the post-offices have been abolished or suspended. I have directed the Postmaster-General to pursue this course in all cases where other efforts failed to secure for any postmaster not himself in fault an opportunity peacefully to exercise the duties of his office. But such action will not supplant the efforts of the Department of Justice to bring the particular offenders to punishment.

The vacation by judicial decrees of fraudulent certificates of naturalization, upon bills in equity filed by the Attorney-General in the circuit court of the United States, is a new application of a familiar equity jurisdiction. Nearly one hundred such decrees have been taken during the year, the evidence disclosing that a very large number of fraudulent certificates of naturalization have been issued. And in this connection I beg to renew my recommendation that the laws be so amended as to require a more full and searching inquiry into all the facts necessary to naturalization before any certificates are granted. It certainly is not too much to require that an application for American citizenship shall be heard with as much care and recorded with as much formality as are given to cases involving the pettiest property right.

At the last session I returned without my approval a bill entitled ''An act to prohibit bookmaking and pool selling in the District of Columbia,'' and stated my objection to be that it did not prohibit but in fact licensed what it purported to prohibit.* An effort will be made under existing laws to suppress this evil, though it is not certain that they will be found adequate.

The report of the Postmaster-General shows the most gratifying progress in the important work committed to his direction. The business methods have been greatly improved. A large economy in expenditures and an increase of four and three-quarters millions in receipts have been realized. The deficiency this year is $5,786,300, as against $6,350,183 last year, notwithstanding the great enlargement of the service. Mail routes have been extended and quickened and greater accuracy and dispatch in distribution and delivery have been attained. The report will be found to be full of interest and suggestion, not only to Congress, but to those thoughtful citizens who may be interested to know what business methods can do for that department of public administration which most nearly touches all our people.

The passage of the act to amend certain sections of the Revised Statutes relating to lotteries, approved September 19, 1890, has been received with great and deserved popular favor. The Post-Office Department and the Department of Justice at once entered upon the enforcement of the law with sympathetic vigor, and already the public mails have been largely freed from the fraudulent and demoralizing appeals and literature emanating from the lottery companies.

The construction and equipment of the new ships for the Navy have made very satisfactory progress. Since March 4, 1889, nine new vessels have been put in commission, and during this winter four more, including one monitor, will be added. The construction of the other vessels

*See pp. 93–94.

authorized is being pushed both in the Government and private yards with energy and watched with the most scrupulous care.

The experiments conducted during the year to test the relative resisting power of armor plates have been so valuable as to attract great attention in Europe. The only part of the work upon the new ships that is threatened by unusual delay is the armor plating, and every effort is being made to reduce that to the minimum. It is a source of congratulation that the anticipated influence of these modern vessels upon the *esprit de corps* of the officers and seamen has been fully realized. Confidence and pride in the ship among the crew are equivalent to a secondary battery. Your favorable consideration is invited to the recommendations of the Secretary.

The report of the Secretary of the Interior exhibits with great fullness and clearness the vast work of that Department and the satisfactory results attained. The suggestions made by him are earnestly commended to the consideration of Congress, though they can not all be given particular mention here.

The several acts of Congress looking to the reduction of the larger Indian reservations, to the more rapid settlement of the Indians upon individual allotments, and the restoration to the public domain of lands in excess of their needs have been largely carried into effect so far as the work was confided to the Executive. Agreements have been concluded since March 4, 1889, involving the cession to the United States of about 14,726,000 acres of land. These contracts have, as required by law, been submitted to Congress for ratification and for the appropriations necessary to carry them into effect. Those with the Sisseton and Wahpeton, Sac and Fox, Iowa, Pottawatomies and Absentee Shawnees, and Cœur d'Alene tribes have not yet received the sanction of Congress. Attention is also called to the fact that the appropriations made in the case of the Sioux Indians have not covered all the stipulated payments. This should be promptly corrected. If an agreement is confirmed, all of its terms should be complied with without delay and full appropriations should be made.

The policy outlined in my last annual message in relation to the patenting of lands to settlers upon the public domain* has been carried out in the administration of the Land Office. No general suspicion or imputation of fraud has been allowed to delay the hearing and adjudication of individual cases upon their merits. The purpose has been to perfect the title of honest settlers with such promptness that the value of the entry might not be swallowed up by the expense and extortions to which delay subjected the claimant. The average monthly issue of agricultural patents has been increased about 6,000.

The disability-pension act, which was approved on the 27th of June last, has been put into operation as rapidly as was practicable. The increased clerical force provided was selected and assigned to work, and

*See p. 49.

a considerable part of the force engaged in examinations in the field was recalled and added to the working force of the office. The examination and adjudication of claims have by reason of improved methods been more rapid than ever before. There is no economy to the Government in delay, while there is much hardship and injustice to the soldier. The anticipated expenditure, while very large, will not, it is believed, be in excess of the estimates made before the enactment of the law. This liberal enlargement of the general law should suggest a more careful scrutiny of bills for special relief, both as to the cases where relief is granted and as to the amount allowed.

The increasing numbers and influence of the non-Mormon population of Utah are observed with satisfaction. The recent letter of Wilford Woodruff, president of the Mormon Church, in which he advised his people "to refrain from contracting any marriage forbidden by the laws of the land," has attracted wide attention, and it is hoped that its influence will be highly beneficial in restraining infractions of the laws of the United States. But the fact should not be overlooked that the doctrine or belief of the church that polygamous marriages are rightful and supported by divine revelation remains unchanged. President Woodruff does not renounce the doctrine, but refrains from teaching it, and advises against the practice of it because the law is against it. Now, it is quite true that the law should not attempt to deal with the faith or belief of anyone; but it is quite another thing, and the only safe thing, so to deal with the Territory of Utah as that those who believe polygamy to be rightful shall not have the power to make it lawful.

The admission of the States of Wyoming and Idaho to the Union are events full of interest and congratulation, not only to the people of those States now happily endowed with a full participation in our privileges and responsibilities, but to all our people. Another belt of States stretches from the Atlantic to the Pacific.

The work of the Patent Office has won from all sources very high commendation. The amount accomplished has been very largely increased, and all the results have been such as to secure confidence and consideration for the suggestions of the Commissioner.

The enumeration of the people of the United States under the provisions of the act of March 1, 1889, has been completed, and the result will be at once officially communicated to Congress. The completion of this decennial enumeration devolves upon Congress the duty of making a new apportionment of Representatives "among the several States according to their respective numbers."

At the last session I had occasion to return with my objections several bills making provisions for the erection of public buildings for the reason that the expenditures contemplated were, in my opinion, greatly in excess of any public need. No class of legislation is more liable to abuse or to degenerate into an unseemly scramble about the public Treasury than this. There should be exercised in this matter a wise economy, based upon some responsible and impartial examination and report as to each case, under a general law.

The report of the Secretary of Agriculture deserves especial attention in view of the fact that the year has been marked in a very unusual degree by agitation and organization among the farmers looking to an increase in the profits of their business. It will be found that the efforts of the Department have been intelligently and zealously devoted to the promotion of the interests intrusted to its care.

A very substantial improvement in the market prices of the leading farm products during the year is noticed. The price of wheat advanced from 81 cents in October, 1889, to $1.00¾ in October, 1890; corn from 31 cents to 50¼ cents; oats from 19¼ cents to 43 cents, and barley from 63 cents to 78 cents. Meats showed a substantial but not so large an increase. The export trade in live animals and fowls shows a very large increase. The total value of such exports for the year ending June 30, 1890, was $33,000,000, and the increase over the preceding year was over $15,000,000. Nearly 200,000 more cattle and over 45,000 more hogs were exported than in the preceding year. The export trade in beef and pork products and in dairy products was very largely increased, the increase in the article of butter alone being from 15,504,978 pounds to 29,748,042 pounds, and the total increase in the value of meat and dairy products exported being $34,000,000. This trade, so directly helpful to the farmer, it is believed, will be yet further and very largely increased when the system of inspection and sanitary supervision now provided by law is brought fully into operation.

The efforts of the Secretary to establish the healthfulness of our meats against the disparaging imputations that have been put upon them abroad have resulted in substantial progress. Veterinary surgeons sent out by the Department are now allowed to participate in the inspection of the live cattle from this country landed at the English docks, and during the several months they have been on duty no case of contagious pleuro-pneumonia has been reported. This inspection abroad and the domestic inspection of live animals and pork products provided for by the act of August 30, 1890, will afford as perfect a guaranty for the wholesomeness of our meats offered for foreign consumption as is anywhere given to any food product, and its nonacceptance will quite clearly reveal the real motive of any continued restriction of their use, and that having been made clear the duty of the Executive will be very plain.

The information given by the Secretary of the progress and prospects of the beet-sugar industry is full of interest. It has already passed the experimental stage and is a commercial success. The area over which the sugar beet can be successfully cultivated is very large, and another field crop of great value is offered to the choice of the farmer.

The Secretary of the Treasury concurs in the recommendation of the

Secretary of Agriculture that the official supervision provided by the tariff law for sugar of domestic production shall be transferred to the Department of Agriculture.

The law relating to the civil service has, so far as I can learn, been executed by those having the power of appointment in the classified service with fidelity and impartiality, and the service has been increasingly satisfactory. The report of the Commission shows a large amount of good work done during the year with very limited appropriations.

I congratulate the Congress and the country upon the passage at the first session of the Fifty-first Congress of an unusual number of laws of very high importance. That the results of this legislation will be the quickening and enlargement of our manufacturing industries, larger and better markets for our breadstuffs and provisions both at home and abroad, more constant employment and better wages for our working people, and an increased supply of a safe currency for the transaction of business, I do not doubt. Some of these measures were enacted at so late a period that the beneficial effects upon commerce which were in the contemplation of Congress have as yet but partially manifested themselves.

The general trade and industrial conditions throughout the country during the year have shown a marked improvement. For many years prior to 1888 the merchandise balances of foreign trade had been largely in our favor, but during that year and the year following they turned against us. It is very gratifying to know that the last fiscal year again shows a balance in our favor of over $68,000,000. The bank clearings, which furnish a good test of the volume of business transacted, for the first ten months of the year 1890 show as compared with the same months of 1889 an increase for the whole country of about 8.4 per cent, while the increase outside of the city of New York was over 13 per cent. During the month of October the clearings of the whole country showed an increase of 3.1 per cent over October, 1889, while outside of New York the increase was 11.5 per cent. These figures show that the increase in the volume of business was very general throughout the country. That this larger business was being conducted upon a safe and profitable basis is shown by the fact that there were 300 less failures reported in October, 1890, than in the same month of the preceding year, with liabilities diminished by about $5,000,000.

The value of our exports of domestic merchandise during the last year was over $115,000,000 greater than the preceding year, and was only exceeded once in our history. About $100,000,000 of this excess was in agricultural products. The production of pig iron, always a good gauge of general prosperity, is shown by a recent census bulletin to have been 153 per cent greater in 1890 than in 1880, and the production of steel 290 per cent greater. Mining in coal has had no limitation except that resulting from deficient transportation. The general testimony is that labor is everywhere fully employed, and the reports for the last year show a smaller number of employees affected by strikes and lockouts than in any year since 1884. The depression in the prices of agricultural products had been greatly relieved and a buoyant and hopeful tone was beginning to be felt by all our people.

These promising influences have been in some degree checked by the surprising and very unfavorable monetary events which have recently taken place in England. It is gratifying to know that these did not grow in any degree out of the financial relations of London with our people or out of any discredit attached to our securities held in that market. The return of our bonds and stocks was caused by a money stringency in England, not by any loss of value or credit in the securities themselves. We could not, however, wholly escape the ill effects of a foreign monetary agitation accompanied by such extraordinary incidents as characterized this. It is not believed, however, that these evil incidents, which have for the time unfavorably affected values in this country, can long withstand the strong, safe, and wholesome influences which are operating to give to our people profitable returns in all branches of legitimate trade and industry. The apprehension that our tariff may again and at once be subjected to important general changes would undoubtedly add a depressing influence of the most serious character.

The general tariff act has only partially gone into operation, some of its important provisions being limited to take effect at dates yet in the future. The general provisions of the law have been in force less than sixty days. Its permanent effects upon trade and prices still largely stand in conjecture. It is curious to note that the advance in the prices of articles wholly unaffected by the tariff act was by many hastily ascribed to that act. Notice was not taken of the fact that the general tendency of the markets was upward, from influences wholly apart from the recent tariff legislation. The enlargement of our currency by the silver bill undoubtedly gave an upward tendency to trade and had a marked effect on prices; but this natural and desired effect of the silver legislation was by many erroneously attributed to the tariff act.

There is neither wisdom nor justice in the suggestion that the subject of tariff revision shall be again opened before this law has had a fair trial. It is quite true that every tariff schedule is subject to objections. No bill was ever framed, I suppose, that in all of its rates and classifications had the full approval even of a party caucus. Such legislation is always and necessarily the product of compromise as to details, and the present law is no exception. But in its general scope and effect I think it will justify the support of those who believe that American legislation should conserve and defend American trade and the wages of American workmen.

The misinformation as to the terms of the act which has been so widely disseminated at home and abroad will be corrected by experience, and the evil auguries as to its results confounded by the market reports, the savings banks, international trade balances, and the general prosperity of our people. Already we begin to hear from abroad and from our custom-houses that the prohibitory effect upon importations imputed to the act is not justified. The imports at the port of New York for the first three weeks of November were nearly 8 per cent greater than for the same period in 1889 and 29 per cent greater than in the same period of 1888. And so far from being an act to limit exports, I confidently believe that under it we shall secure a larger and more profitable participation in foreign trade than we have ever enjoyed, and that we shall recover a proportionate participation in the ocean carrying trade of the world.

The criticisms of the bill that have come to us from foreign sources may well be rejected for repugnancy. If these critics really believe that the adoption by us of a free-trade policy, or of tariff rates having reference solely to revenue, would diminish the participation of their own countries in the commerce of the world, their advocacy and promotion, by speech and other forms of organized effort, of this movement among our people is a rare exhibition of unselfishness in trade. And, on the other hand, if they sincerely believe that the adoption of a protective-tariff policy by this country inures to their profit and our hurt, it is noticeably strange that they should lead the outcry against the authors of a policy so helpful to their countrymen and crown with their favor those who would snatch from them a substantial share of a trade with other lands already inadequate to their necessities.

There is no disposition among any of our people to promote prohibitory or retaliatory legislation. Our policies are adopted not to the hurt of others, but to secure for ourselves those advantages that fairly grow out of our favored position as a nation. Our form of government, with its incident of universal suffrage, makes it imperative that we shall save our working people from the agitations and distresses which scant work and wages that have no margin for comfort always beget. But after all this is done it will be found that our markets are open to friendly commercial exchanges of enormous value to the other great powers.

From the time of my induction into office the duty of using every power and influence given by law to the executive department for the development of larger markets for our products, especially our farm products, has been kept constantly in mind, and no effort has been or will be spared to promote that end. We are under no disadvantage in any foreign market, except that we pay our workmen and workwomen better wages than are paid elsewhere—better abstractly, better relatively to the cost of the necessaries of life. I do not doubt that a very largely increased foreign trade is accessible to us without bartering for it either our home market for such products of the farm and shop as our own people can supply or the wages of our working people.

In many of the products of wood and iron and in meats and bread-stuffs we have advantages that only need better facilities of intercourse and transportation to secure for them large foreign markets. The reciprocity clause of the tariff act wisely and effectively opens the way to secure a large reciprocal trade in exchange for the free admission to our ports of certain products. The right of independent nations to make special reciprocal trade concessions is well established, and does not impair either the comity due to other powers or what is known as the "favored-nation clause," so generally found in commercial treaties. What is given to one for an adequate agreed consideration can not be claimed by another freely. The state of the revenues was such that we could dispense with any import duties upon coffee, tea, hides, and the lower grades of sugar and molasses. That the large advantage resulting to the countries producing and exporting these articles by placing them on the free list entitled us to expect a fair return in the way of customs concessions upon articles exported by us to them was so obvious that to have gratuitously abandoned this opportunity to enlarge our trade would have been an unpardonable error.

There were but two methods of maintaining control of this question open to Congress—to place all of these articles upon the dutiable list, subject to such treaty agreements as could be secured, or to place them all presently upon the free list, but subject to the reimposition of specified duties if the countries from which we received them should refuse to give to us suitable reciprocal benefits. This latter method, I think, possesses great advantages. It expresses in advance the consent of Congress to reciprocity arrangements affecting these products, which must otherwise have been delayed and unascertained until each treaty was ratified by the Senate and the necessary legislation enacted by Congress. Experience has shown that some treaties looking to reciprocal trade have failed to secure a two-thirds vote in the Senate for ratification, and others having passed that stage have for years awaited the concurrence of the House and Senate in such modifications of our revenue laws as were necessary to give effect to their provisions. We now have the concurrence of both Houses in advance in a distinct and definite offer of free entry to our ports of specific articles. The Executive is not required to deal in conjecture as to what Congress will accept. Indeed, this reciprocity provision is more than an offer. Our part of the bargain is complete; delivery has been made; and when the countries from which we receive sugar, coffee, tea, and hides have placed on their free lists such of our products as shall be agreed upon as an equivalent for our concession, a proclamation of that fact completes the transaction; and in the meantime our own people have free sugar, tea, coffee, and hides.

The indications thus far given are very hopeful of early and favorable action by the countries from which we receive our large imports of coffee and sugar, and it is confidently believed that if steam communication with these countries can be promptly improved and enlarged the next year will show a most gratifying increase in our exports of breadstuffs and provisions, as well as of some important lines of manufactured goods.

In addition to the important bills that became laws before the adjournment of the last session, some other bills of the highest importance were well advanced toward a final vote and now stand upon the calendars of the two Houses in favored positions. The present session has a fixed limit, and if these measures are not now brought to a final vote all the work that has been done upon them by this Congress is lost. The proper consideration of these, of an apportionment bill, and of the annual appropriation bills will require not only that no working day of the session shall be lost, but that measures of minor and local interest shall not be allowed to interrupt or retard the progress of those that are of universal interest. In view of these conditions, I refrain from bringing before you at this time some suggestions that would otherwise be made, and most earnestly invoke your attention to the duty of perfecting the important legislation now well advanced. To some of these measures, which seem to me most important, I now briefly call your attention.

I desire to repeat with added urgency the recommendations contained in my last annual message in relation to the development of American steamship lines.* The reciprocity clause of the tariff bill will be largely limited and its benefits retarded and diminished if provision is not contemporaneously made to encourage the establishment of first-class steam communication between our ports and the ports of such nations as may meet our overtures for enlarged commercial exchanges. The steamship, carrying the mails stately and frequently and offering to passengers a comfortable, safe, and speedy transit, is the first condition of foreign trade. It carries the order or the buyer, but not all that is ordered or bought. It gives to the sailing vessels such cargoes as are not urgent or perishable, and, indirectly at least, promotes that important adjunct of commerce. There is now both in this country and in the nations of Central and South America a state of expectation and confidence as to increased trade that will give a double value to your prompt action upon this question.

The present situation of our mail communication with Australia illustrates the importance of early action by Congress. The Oceanic Steamship Company maintains a line of steamers between San Francisco, Sydney, and Auckland consisting of three vessels, two of which are of United States registry and one of foreign registry. For the service done by this line in carrying the mails we pay annually the sum of $46,000, being, as estimated, the full sea and United States inland postage, which is the limit fixed by law. The colonies of New South Wales and New Zealand have been paying annually to these lines £37,000 for carrying the mails from Sydney and Auckland to San Francisco. The contract under which this payment has been made is now about to expire, and those colonies have refused to renew the contract unless the United States shall pay a more equitable proportion of the whole sum necessary to maintain the service.

*See pp. 56–58.

I am advised by the Postmaster-General that the United States receives for carrying the Australian mails, brought to San Francisco in these steamers, by rail to Vancouver, an estimated annual income of $75,000, while, as I have stated, we are paying out for the support of the steamship line that brings this mail to us only $46,000, leaving an annual surplus resulting from this service of $29,000. The trade of the United States with Australia, which is in a considerable part carried by these steamers, and the whole of which is practically dependent upon the mail communication which they maintain, is largely in our favor. Our total exports of merchandise to Australasian ports during the fiscal year ending June 30, 1890, were $11,266,484, while the total imports of merchandise from these ports were only $4,277,676. If we are not willing to see this important steamship line withdrawn, or continued with Vancouver substituted for San Francisco as the American terminal, Congress should put it in the power of the Postmaster-General to make a liberal increase in the amount now paid for the transportation of this important mail.

The South Atlantic and Gulf ports occupy a very favored position toward the new and important commerce which the reciprocity clause of the tariff act and the postal shipping bill are designed to promote. Steamship lines from these ports to some northern port of South America will almost certainly effect a connection between the railroad systems of the continents long before any continuous line of railroads can be put into operation. The very large appropriation made at the last session for the harbor of Galveston was justified, as it seemed to me, by these considerations. The great Northwest will feel the advantage of trunk lines to the South as well as to the East and of the new markets opened for their surplus food products and for many of their manufactured products.

I had occasion in May last to transmit to Congress a report adopted by the International American Conference upon the subject of the incorporation of an international American bank, with a view to facilitating money exchanges between the States represented in that conference.* Such an institution would greatly promote the trade we are seeking to develop. I renew the recommendation that a careful and well-guarded charter be granted. I do not think the powers granted should include those ordinarily exercised by trust, guaranty, and safe-deposit companies, or that more branches in the United States should be authorized than are strictly necessary to accomplish the object primarily in view, namely, convenient foreign exchanges. It is quite important that prompt action should be taken in this matter, in order that any appropriations for better communication with these countries and any agreements that may be made for reciprocal trade may not be hindered by the inconvenience of making exchanges through European money centers or burdened by the tribute which is an incident of that method of business.

The bill for the relief of the Supreme Court has after many years of

*See pp. 70-71.

discussion reached a position where final action is easily attainable, and it is hoped that any differences of opinion may be so harmonized as to save the essential features of this very important measure. In this connection I earnestly renew my recommendation that the salaries of the judges of the United States district courts be so readjusted that none of them shall receive less than $5,000 per annum.

The subject of the unadjusted Spanish and Mexican land grants and the urgent necessity for providing some commission or tribunal for the trial of questions of title growing out of them were twice brought by me to the attention of Congress at the last session. Bills have been reported from the proper committees in both Houses upon the subject, and I very earnestly hope that this Congress will put an end to the delay which has attended the settlement of the disputes as to the title between the settlers and the claimants under these grants. These disputes retard the prosperity and disturb the peace of large and important communities. The governor of New Mexico in his last report to the Secretary of the Interior suggests some modifications of the provisions of the pending bills relating to the small holdings of farm lands. I commend to your attention the suggestions of the Secretary of the Interior upon this subject.

The enactment of a national bankrupt law I still regard as very desirable. The Constitution having given to Congress jurisdiction of this subject, it should be exercised and uniform rules provided for the administration of the affairs of insolvent debtors. The inconveniences resulting from the occasional and temporary exercise of this power by Congress and from the conflicting State codes of insolvency which come into force intermediately should be removed by the enactment of a simple, inexpensive, and permanent national bankrupt law.

I also renew my recommendation in favor of legislation affording just copyright protection to foreign authors on a footing of reciprocal advantage for our authors abroad.

It may still be possible for this Congress to inaugurate by suitable legislation a movement looking to uniformity and increased safety in the use of couplers and brakes upon freight trains engaged in interstate commerce. The chief difficulty in the way is to secure agreement as to the best appliances, simplicity, effectiveness, and cost being considered. This difficulty will only yield to legislation, which should be based upon full inquiry and impartial tests. The purpose should be to secure the cooperation of all well-disposed managers and owners; but the fearful fact that every year's delay involves the sacrifice of 2,000 lives and the maiming of 20,000 young men should plead both with Congress and the managers against any needless delay.

The subject of the conservation and equal distribution of the water supply of the arid regions has had much attention from Congress, but has not as yet been put upon a permanent and satisfactory basis. The urgency of the subject does not grow out of any large present demand for the use of these lands for agriculture, but out of the danger that the water supply and the sites for the necessary catch basins may fall into the hands of individuals or private corporations and be used to render subservient the large areas dependent upon such supply. The owner of the water is the owner of the lands, however the titles may run. All unappropriated natural water sources and all necessary reservoir sites should be held by the Government for the equal use at fair rates of the homestead settlers who will eventually take up these lands. The United States should not, in my opinion, undertake the construction of dams or canals, but should limit its work to such surveys and observations as will determine the water supply, both surface and subterranean, the areas capable of irrigation, and the location and storage capacity of reservoirs. This done, the use of the water and of the reservoir sites might be granted to the respective States or Territories or to individuals or associations upon the condition that the necessary works should be constructed and the water furnished at fair rates without discrimination, the rates to be subject to supervision by the legislatures or by boards of water commissioners duly constituted. The essential thing to be secured is the common and equal use at fair rates of the accumulated water supply. It were almost better that these lands should remain arid than that those who occupy them should become the slaves of unrestrained monopolies controlling the one essential element of land values and crop results.

The use of the telegraph by the Post-Office Department as a means for the rapid transmission of written communications is, I believe, upon proper terms, quite desirable. The Government does not own or operate the railroads, and it should not, I think, own or operate the telegraph lines. It does, however, seem to be quite practicable for the Government to contract with the telegraph companies, as it does with railroad companies, to carry at specified rates such communications as the senders may designate for this method of transmission. I recommend that such legislation be enacted as will enable the Post-Office Department fairly to test by experiment the advantages of such a use of the telegraph.

If any intelligent and loyal company of American citizens were required to catalogue the essential human conditions of national life, I do not doubt that with absolute unanimity they would begin with "free and honest elections." And it is gratifying to know that generally there is a growing and nonpartisan demand for better election laws; but against this sign of hope and progress must be set the depressing and undeniable fact that election laws and methods are sometimes cunningly contrived to secure minority control, while violence completes the shortcomings of fraud.

In my last annual message I suggested that the development of the existing law providing a Federal supervision of Congressional elections offered an effective method of reforming these abuses.* The need of such a law has manifested itself in many parts of the country, and its wholesome restraints and penalties will be useful in all. The constitutionality of such legislation has been affirmed by the Supreme Court. Its probable effectiveness is evidenced by the character of the opposition that is made to it. It has been denounced as if it were a new exercise of Federal power and an invasion of the rights of States. Nothing could be further from the truth. Congress has already fixed the time for the election of members of Congress. It has declared that votes for members of Congress must be by written or printed ballot; it has provided for the appointment by the circuit courts in certain cases, and upon the petition of a certain number of citizens, of election supervisors, and made it their duty to supervise the registration of voters conducted by the State officers; to challenge persons offering to register; to personally inspect and scrutinize the registry lists, and to affix their names to the lists for the purpose of identification and the prevention of frauds; to attend at elections and remain with the boxes till they are all cast and counted; to attach to the registry lists and election returns any statement touching the accuracy and fairness of the registry and election, and to take and transmit to the Clerk of the House of Representatives any evidence of fraudulent practices which may be presented to them. The same law provides for the appointment of deputy United States marshals to attend at the polls, support the supervisors in the discharge of their duties, and to arrest persons violating the election laws. The provisions of this familiar title of the Revised Statutes have been put into exercise by both the great political parties, and in the North as well as in the South, by the filing with the court of the petitions required by the law.

It is not, therefore, a question whether we shall have a Federal election law, for we now have one and have had for nearly twenty years, but whether we shall have an effective law. The present law stops just short of effectiveness, for it surrenders to the local authorities all control over the certification which establishes the *prima facie* right to a seat in the House of Representatives. This defect should be cured. Equality of representation and the parity of the electors must be maintained or everything that is valuable in our system of government is lost. The qualifications of an elector must be sought in the law, not in the opinions, prejudices, or fears of any class, however powerful. The path of the elector to the ballot box must be free from the ambush of fear and the enticements of fraud; the count so true and open that none shall gainsay it. Such a law should be absolutely nonpartisan and impartial. It should give the advantage to honesty and the control to majorities. Surely there is nothing sectional about this creed, and if it shall happen that the penalties of laws intended to enforce these rights fall here and not there it is not because the law is sectional, but because, happily,

*See p. 56.

crime is local and not universal. Nor should it be forgotten that every law, whether relating to elections or to any other subject, whether enacted by the State or by the nation, has force behind it; the courts, the marshal or constable, the *posse comitatus*, the prison, are all and always behind the law.

One can not be justly charged with unfriendliness to any section or class who seeks only to restrain violations of law and of personal right. No community will find lawlessness profitable. No community can afford to have it known that the officers who are charged with the preservation of the public peace and the restraint of the criminal classes are themselves the product of fraud or violence. The magistrate is then without respect and the law without sanction. The floods of lawlessness can not be leveed and made to run in one channel. The killing of a United States marshal carrying a writ of arrest for an election offense is full of prompting and suggestion to men who are pursued by a city marshal for a crime against life or property.

But it is said that this legislation will revive race animosities, and some have even suggested that when the peaceful methods of fraud are made impossible they may be supplanted by intimidation and violence. If the proposed law gives to any qualified elector by a hair's weight more than his equal influence or detracts by so much from any other qualified elector, it is fatally impeached. But if the law is equal and the animosities it is to evoke grow out of the fact that some electors have been accustomed to exercise the franchise for others as well as for themselves, then these animosities ought not to be confessed without shame, and can not be given any weight in the discussion without dishonor No choice is left to me but to enforce with vigor all laws intended to secure to the citizen his constitutional rights and to recommend that the inadequacies of such laws be promptly remedied. If to promote with zeal and ready interest every project for the development of its material interests, its rivers, harbors, mines, and factories, and the intelligence, peace, and security under the law of its communities and its homes is not accepted as sufficient evidence of friendliness to any State or section, I can not add connivance at election practices that not only disturb local results, but rob the electors of other States and sections of their most priceless political rights.

The preparation of the general appropriation bills should be conducted with the greatest care and the closest scrutiny of expenditures. Appropriations should be adequate to the needs of the public service, but they should be absolutely free from prodigality.

I venture again to remind you that the brief time remaining for the consideration of the important legislation now awaiting your attention offers no margin for waste. If the present duty is discharged with diligence, fidelity, and courage, the work of the Fifty-first Congress may be confidently submitted to the considerate judgment of the people.

BENJ. HARRISON.

SPECIAL MESSAGES.

EXECUTIVE MANSION, *December 4, 1890.*

To the Senate and House of Representatives:

I transmit herewith a communication of the 3d instant from the Secretary of the Interior, accompanied by an agreement concluded by the Cherokee Commission with the Cheyenne and Arapahoe tribes of Indians for the cession of certain lands and for other purposes.

The agreement is submitted for the consideration of Congress, as required by law.   BENJ. HARRISON.

EXECUTIVE MANSION, *December 5, 1890.*

To the House of Representatives:

I transmit herewith, in response to the resolution of the House of Representatives of the 24th of September last, a report of the Secretary of State and accompanying correspondence, in relation to the killing of General J. Martine Barrundia by Guatemalan officers on board the Pacific mail steamer *Acapulco* in the port of San Jose, Guatemala, on the 28th of August last.   BENJ. HARRISON.

EXECUTIVE MANSION, *December 17, 1890.*

To the Senate and House of Representatives:

I herewith transmit a communication from the Secretary of State, in relation to a report upon the subject of cholera made by Dr. E. O. Shakespeare pursuant to the act of Congress approved March 3, 1885.

BENJ. HARRISON

EXECUTIVE MANSION, *December 17, 1890.*

To the Senate and House of Representatives:

I transmit herewith a letter from the Secretary of the Navy, accompanied by a letter from the secretary of the American Society of Mechanical Engineers, who transmits a memorial, addressed to the Government of the United States, in relation to the late Captain John Ericsson.

The matter is presented for such action as the Congress may deem proper.   BENJ. HARRISON.

EXECUTIVE MANSION, *December 17, 1890.*

To the Senate and House of Representatives:

I transmit herewith a letter from the Secretary of War, accompanied by a copy of a preliminary report of the board on gun factories and steel forgings for high-power guns, appointed by me under the provisions of an act entitled "An act making appropriations for fortifications," etc., approved August 18, 1890.

The report and accompanying papers are submitted for the information and early attention of Congress.

BENJ. HARRISON.

EXECUTIVE MANSION, *December 22, 1890.*

To the Senate and House of Representatives:

I transmit herewith a letter of the 18th instant from the Secretary of the Interior, in relation to the disposition of timber on certain Chippewa reservations in Wisconsin, together with copies of papers relating thereto. The matter is presented for the action of Congress.

BENJ. HARRISON.

EXECUTIVE MANSION, *December 23, 1890.*

To the Senate and House of Representatives:

The Territorial legislature of Oklahoma, now in session, will adjourn by limitation of law on to-morrow, the 24th instant. The act organizing the Territory provided (section 11) that certain chapters of the revised statutes of Nebraska should be in force until after the adjournment of the first session of the Territorial legislature.

The question of the location of the Territorial capital has so occupied the time of the legislature and so distracted and divided its members that no criminal code has been provided. It is urgently necessary that Congress should at once, by joint resolution or otherwise, continue the laws of Nebraska in force, and save pending criminal arrests and prosecutions at least. The reconvening of the legislature does not under the existing circumstances promise any relief.

BENJ. HARRISON.

EXECUTIVE MANSION, *December 23, 1890.*

To the Senate and House of Representatives:

I transmit herewith a letter of the Secretary of the Navy, accompanied by the report of the commission appointed by me by virtue of a provision in the naval appropriation bill approved June 30, 1890, for the purpose of selecting a suitable site "for a dry dock at some point on the shores of the Pacific Ocean, or the waters connected therewith, north of the parallel of latitude marking the northern boundary of California, including the waters of Puget Sound and also Lakes Union and Washington, in the State of Washington."

BENJ. HARRISON.

EXECUTIVE MANSION, *January 5, 1891.*

To the House of Representatives:

In further response to the resolution of the House of Representatives requesting me, if in my judgment not incompatible with the public interest, to furnish to the House the correspondence since March 4, 1889, between the Government of the United States and the Government of Great Britain touching the subjects in dispute in the Bering Sea, I transmit herewith a letter from the Secretary of State, which is accompanied by the correspondence which has taken place since my message of July 23, 1890.*

BENJ. HARRISON.

EXECUTIVE MANSION, *January 10, 1891.*

To the Senate and House of Representatives:

I transmit herewith a memorial of the legislative assembly of the Territory of Oklahoma, asking an appropriation for the relief of the destitute people of that Territory.

BENJ. HARRISON.

EXECUTIVE MANSION, *January 16, 1891.*

To the Senate and House of Representatives:

I transmit herewith the report of the World's Columbian Commission, with the accompanying papers.

BENJ. HARRISON.

EXECUTIVE MANSION, *January 19, 1891.*

To the Senate and House of Representatives:

I transmit herewith a communication of the 17th instant from the Secretary of the Interior, submitting the agreement entered into between the Crow Indians and the commission appointed to negotiate with them for the sale to the United States of the western portion of their reservation in Montana under the provisions of the act of September 25, 1890.

It is thought important by the Department that this matter receive the consideration of Congress during the present session.

BENJ. HARRISON.

EXECUTIVE MANSION, *January 26, 1891.*

To the Senate and House of Representatives:

I transmit herewith a letter of the Secretary of War, accompanied by the final report of the board on gun factories and steel forgings for high-power guns, and appendixes thereto.

BENJ. HARRISON.

* See p. 80.

EXECUTIVE MANSION, *January 26, 1891.*

To the Senate and House of Representatives:

I transmit herewith a letter of the Secretary of the Interior, accompanied by a letter from the Commissioner of Indian Affairs, who transmits a draft of a bill for compensating the Indians of the Crow Creek Reservation for the loss sustained by them by reason of their receiving less land per capita in their diminished reservations than is to be received by Indians occupying other diminished reservations.

The matter is presented for the early consideration of the Congress.

BENJ. HARRISON.

EXECUTIVE MANSION, *January 31, 1891.*

To the Senate and House of Representatives:

The sudden death of the Hon. William Windom, Secretary of the Treasury, in New York, on the evening of the 29th instant, has directed my attention to the present state of the law as to the filling of a vacancy occasioned by the death of the head of a Department.

I transmit herewith an opinion of the Attorney-General, from which it will be seen that under the statutes in force no officer in the Treasury Department or other person designated by me can exercise the duties of Secretary of the Treasury for a longer period than ten days. This limitation is, I am sure, unwise, and necessarily involves in such a case as that now presented undue haste and even indelicacy. The President should not be required to take up the question of the selection of a successor before the last offices of affection and respect have been paid to the dead. If the proprieties of an occasion as sad as that which now overshadows us are observed, possibly one-half of the brief time allowed is gone before, with due regard to the decencies of life, the President and those with whom he should advise can take up the consideration of the grave duty of selecting a head for one of the greatest Departments of the Government.

Hasty action by the Senate is also necessarily involved, and geographical limitations are practically imposed by the necessity of selecting some one who can reach the capital and take the necessary oath of office before the expiration of the ten days.

It may be a very proper restriction of the power of the President in this connection that he shall not designate for any great length of time a person to discharge these important duties who has not been confirmed by the Senate, but there would seem to be no reason why one of the assistant secretaries of the Department wherein the vacancy exists might not discharge the duties of Secretary until a successor is selected, confirmed, and qualified. The inconvenience of this limitation was made apparent at the time of the death of Secretary Folger. President Arthur in that case allowed one of the assistant secretaries, who had been designated to act in the absence of the Secretary, to continue in the discharge of such duties for ten days, then designated the same person to discharge the duties for a further term of ten days, and then made a temporary appointment as Secretary, in order to secure the consideration that he needed in filling this important place.

I recommend such a modification of the existing law as will permit the first or sole assistant, or, in the case of the Treasury Department, where the assistants are not graded, that one who may be designated by the President, to discharge the duties of the head of the Department until a successor is appointed and qualified.

BENJ. HARRISON.

To the Senate: Executive Mansion, *February 10, 1891.*

I transmit herewith the correspondence called for by the resolution of the Senate of the 6th instant, relating to the conduct of Commander Reiter in connection with the arrest and killing of General Barrundia.

BENJ. HARRISON.

Executive Mansion, *February 13, 1891.*

To the Senate and House of Representatives:

The Admiral of the Navy, David Dixon Porter, died at his residence in the city of Washington this morning at 8.15 o'clock, in the seventy-eighth year of his age. He entered the naval service as a midshipman February 2, 1829, and had been since continuously in service, having been made Admiral August 15, 1870. He was the son of Commodore David Porter, one of the greatest of our naval commanders. His service during the Civil War was conspicuously brilliant and successful, and his death ends a very high and honorable career. His countrymen will sincerely mourn his loss while they cherish with grateful pride the memory of his deeds. To officers of the Navy his life will continue to yield inspiration and encouragement.

BENJ. HARRISON.

Executive Mansion,
Washington, D. C., February 14, 1891.

To the Senate and House of Representatives:

I transmit herewith the sixth annual report of the Commissioner of Labor. This report relates to the cost of producing iron and steel and the materials of which iron is made in the United States and in Europe, and the earnings, the efficiency, and the cost of living of the men employed in such production.

BENJ. HARRISON.

EXECUTIVE MANSION, *February 14, 1891.*

To the Senate and House of Representatives:

The death of William Tecumseh Sherman, which took place to-day at his residence in the city of New York, at 1 o'clock and 50 minutes p. m., is an event that will bring sorrow to the heart of every patriotic citizen. No living American was so loved and venerated as he. To look upon his face, to hear his name, was to have one's love of country intensified. He served his country, not for fame, not out of a sense of professional duty, but for love of the flag and of the beneficent civil institutions of which it was the emblem. He was an ideal soldier, and shared to the fullest the *esprit de corps* of the Army; but he cherished the civil institutions organized under the Constitution, and was a soldier only that these might be perpetuated in undiminished usefulness and honor. He was in nothing an imitator.

A profound student of military science and precedent, he drew from them principles and suggestions, and so adapted them to novel conditions that his campaigns will continue to be the profitable study of the military profession throughout the world. His genial nature made him comrade to every soldier of the great Union Army. No presence was so welcome and inspiring at the camp fire or commandery as his. His career was complete; his honors were full. He had received from the Government the highest rank known to our military establishment and from the people unstinted gratitude and love. No word of mine can add to his fame. His death has followed in startling quickness that of the Admiral of the Navy; and it is a sad and notable incident that when the Department under which he served shall have put on the usual emblems of mourning four of the eight Executive Departments will be simultaneously draped in black, and one other has but to-day removed the crape from its walls.

BENJ. HARRISON.

EXECUTIVE MANSION, *February 26, 1891.*

To the Senate and House of Representatives:

I transmit herewith a report of the Secretary of State and accompanying documents, in relation to the execution of letters rogatory in foreign countries.

BENJ. HARRISON.

EXECUTIVE MANSION, *February 26, 1891.*

To the Senate of the United States:

I transmit herewith, in reply to the resolution of the Senate of the 9th instant, a report from the Secretary of State, accompanied by the papers relating to the commercial arrangement recently entered into with Brazil.

BENJ. HARRISON.

To the Senate: EXECUTIVE MANSION, *March 3, 1891.*

In accordance with the resolution of the Senate of this date, I return herewith Senate bill 1453, to provide for the purchase of a site and the erection of a public building thereon at Saginaw, in the State of Michigan.

BENJ. HARRISON.

VETO MESSAGES.

To the Senate: EXECUTIVE MANSION, *December 24, 1890.*

I return to the Senate, in which it originated, with my objections, the bill (No. 544) "to provide for the purchase of a site and the erection of a public building thereon at Bar Harbor, in the State of Maine." The statement of a few facts will show, I think, that the public needs do not justify the contemplated expenditure of $75,000 for the erection of a public building at Bar Harbor. Only one public office, the post-office, is to be accommodated. It appears from a report of the Postmaster-General that the rent paid by the United States for a room containing 875 square feet of floor space was in 1888 $300 and the expenditure for fuel and lights $60. One clerk was employed in the office and no carriers. The gross postal receipts for that year were $7,000. Bar Harbor is almost wholly a summer resort. The population of the town of Eden, of which Bar Harbor forms a part, as taken by the census enumerators, was less than 2,000. During one quarter of the year this population is largely increased by summer residents and visitors, but for the other three quarters is not much above the census enumeration. The postal receipts for 1890 by quarters show that for more than half the year the gross receipts of the post-office are about $8 per day. The salary of a janitor for the new building would be more than twice the present cost to the Government of rent, fuel, and lights. I can not believe that upon reconsideration the Congress will approve the contemplated expenditure.

BENJ. HARRISON.

EXECUTIVE MANSION, *January 26, 1891.*
To the House of Representatives:

I return herewith without my approval the bill (H. R. 12365) entitled "An act to authorize Oklahoma City, in Oklahoma Territory, to issue bonds to provide a right of way for the Choctaw Coal and Railway Company through said city." This bill authorizes the corporation of Oklahoma City to issue corporate bonds to the amount of $40,000 for the purpose of providing the right of way for a railroad company through the city, if the proposition shall receive the assent of a majority of the legal voters at an election to be called for that purpose.

It is attempted to distinguish this case from the ordinary case of a municipal grant to a railway company by the fact that this railway company had located its line through the lands afterwards settled upon under the town-site law before such settlement, and that the route thus located cuts the plat of the city diagonally and in a way to be very injurious to property interests.

Upon an examination of the facts it appears to me to be clear that no legal location was made by the railway company prior to the acquisition of the lands by the occupying settlers. Some preliminary surveys had been made, but no map of location had been filed with the Secretary of the Interior. If the rights of this company at this point of its road as to right of way are derived from the general statute of the United States upon that subject (U. S. Revised Statutes, Supplement, p. 87), then section 4 distinctly saves the right of any settler who had located prior to the filing of a profile of the road and the approval by the Secretary of the Interior thereof. And if, on the other hand, the rights of the company at the point indicated are derived from the act of Congress of February 18, 1888, "to authorize the Choctaw Coal and Railway Company to construct and operate a railway through the Indian Territory, and for other purposes," section 6 of that act also plainly protects the right of any occupying claimant. The latter statute, it seems to me, was intended to grant a right of way only through Indian lands, and if these lands were not such the general statute to which I have referred would apply; but in either event the conclusion is the same.

It appears from the report of the committee that its favorable action, and, I must assume, the favorable action of Congress, proceeded upon the theory that there was a real controversy, doubtful as to its issue, as to the right of the railroad company to hold the line of its survey through the city.

Stripped, then, of this claim the proposition is nakedly one to authorize Oklahoma City to donate $40,000 to the Choctaw Coal and Railway Company. The general statute of the United States prohibits such grants, and this must stand until repealed as a continuing expression of legislative opinion. If a departure from this rule is to be allowed at all, certainly it should only be where the circumstances are exceptional. Such circumstances, in my opinion, do not exist in this case. Already I have received from other cities in the Territory protests against special legislation of this sort, accompanied by the suggestion that if this policy is admitted other cities shall also be allowed to encourage the building of roads by donation.

Oklahoma City, according to the report of the Census Office, has a population of about 4,100, and this donation would be equivalent to nearly $10 per capita. Very little real estate, whether town-site or country property, in this Territory is yet subject to assessment for taxation. The people have not yet had time to accumulate, and Congress has received appeals for aid to relieve a prevailing distress which the Territorial authorities have found themselves unable to deal with. It does not seem to me, in view of all these facts, that the wholesome rule prescribed by the general statute should be departed from.

BENJ. HARRISON.

To the Senate:　　　　　　　　　　Executive Mansion, *February 26, 1891.*

I return to the Senate without my approval the bill (S. 4620) "to establish the Record and Pension Office of the War Department, and for other purposes."

This bill proposes to change the designation of one of the divisions of the War Department. It is now the "Record and Pension Division," and it is proposed that it shall hereafter be the "Record and Pension Office" of the War Department. The scope of the work assigned to this division or office is not changed, but the organization now existing under a classification made by the Secretary of War is by the bill made permanent and put beyond the control of the Secretary. The change of designation seems to have been intended to add dignity to the position, and the effect of the bill is probably to require that the chief of this office shall hereafter be appointed only by and with the advice and consent of the Senate, though it is not clear that any provision is made for a chief after the particular person designated in the bill has been separated from the place or in case he is not appointed.

The real object of the bill is disclosed in the following clause:

> The President is hereby authorized to nominate and, by and with the advice and consent of the Senate, to appoint the officer now in charge of said Record and Pension Division to be a colonel in the Army and chief of said office.

It is fairly to be implied from the bill that in the opinion of Congress the public interests would be promoted by making the contemplated change in the grade of this office and by giving the rank and pay of a colonel in the Army to the chief. A new and rather anomalous office is therefore created—that of "colonel in the Army and chief of the Record and Pension Office of the War Department"—but upon the condition that the President shall nominate a particular person to fill it. I do not think it is competent for Congress to designate the person who shall fill an office created by law, and practically nothing remains of the bill under consideration if this person is not to be appointed. The office is an important one, connected with the active civil administration of the War Department. I can not agree that the selection of the officer shall be taken out of the discretion of the Executive, where the responsibility for good administration necessarily rests. It is probably true that the officer intended to be benefited is peculiarly deserving and has had remarkable success in the discharge of the duties of the office; but these are considerations for the appointing power, and might safely have been left there.

If this particular appointment was backed by reasons so obvious as to secure the support of both Houses of Congress, it should have been assumed that these reasons could have been made obvious to the Executive by the ordinary methods. In connection with the Army and Navy retired lists, legislation akin to this has become quite frequent, too frequent in my opinion; but these laws have been regarded as grants of pensions rather than of offices.

If it is to be allowed that active places connected with the Executive Departments can be created upon condition that particular persons are or are not to be designated to fill them, the power of appointment might be wholly diverted from the Executive to the Congress.

BENJ. HARRISON.

To the Senate: EXECUTIVE MANSION, *March 2, 1891.*

I return herewith without my approval the bill (S. 3270) ''for the relief of the administratrix of the estate of George W. Lawrence.''

If I rightly construe this bill, it authorizes the Court of Claims to give judgment in favor of the contractor with the United States for the construction of the vessels named (*Agawam* and *Pontoosuc*) for the difference between the contract price and the actual cost to the contractor of building the vessels, subject only to the condition that nothing shall be allowed for any advance in the price of labor or material unless such advance occurred during the prolonged term for completing the work rendered necessary by delay resulting from the action of the Government. The bill is somewhat obscure, but I have, I think, correctly stated the legal effect of it.

Undoubtedly in contracts made for army and navy supplies and construction during the early days of the war there was not infrequently loss to the contractor by reason of the advance in the cost of labor resulting from the withdrawal of so large a body of men for service in the field and the indirect result of this upon the cost of material; but I can not believe that it is the purpose of Congress to reopen such contracts at this late day and to pay to the contractors the cost of the work or material which they stipulated to do or deliver at fixed prices. In the matter of another vessel constructed by this same claimant and in the case of one other similar claim I approved bills at the last session, but they carefully limited any finding by the Court of Claims to such losses as necessarily resulted from the interference by the Government with the progress of the work, thus creating delays and enhanced cost.

In those cases the Government only undertook to make good losses resulting directly and unavoidably from its own acts. If the principle which seems to me to be embodied in the bill under consideration is adopted, I do not see how the Congress can refuse in all cases of all sorts of contracts to make good the losses resulting from appreciation in the cost of labor and material. The expenditure that such a policy would entail is incalculable, and the policy itself is, in my judgment, indefensible.

The bill at the last session for the relief of this claimant in the case of another vessel constructed by him was, as I have said, carefully put upon the lines I have indicated, and if this claim could have been maintained upon those lines I assume that the bill would have been similar in its provisions.

BENJ. HARRISON.

PROCLAMATIONS.

By the President of the United States of America.

A PROCLAMATION.

Whereas satisfactory proof has been presented to me that provision has been made for adequate grounds and buildings for the uses of the World's Columbian Exposition, and that a sum not less than $10,000,000, to be used and expended for the purposes of said exposition, has been provided in accordance with the conditions and requirements of section 10 of an act entitled "An act to provide for celebrating the four hundredth anniversary of the discovery of America by Christopher Columbus by holding an international exhibition of arts, industries, manufactures, and the products of the soil, mine, and sea, in the city of Chicago, in the State of Illinois," approved April 25, 1890:

Now, therefore, I, Benjamin Harrison, President of the United States, by virtue of the authority vested in me by said act, do hereby declare and proclaim that such international exhibition will be opened on the 1st day of May, in the year 1893, in the city of Chicago, in the State of Illinois, and will not be closed before the last Thursday in October of the same year. And in the name of the Government and of the people of the United States I do hereby invite all the nations of the earth to take part in the commemoration of an event that is preeminent in human history and of lasting interest to mankind by appointing representatives thereto and sending such exhibits to the World's Columbian Exposition as will most fitly and fully illustrate their resources, their industries, and their progress in civilization.

In testimony whereof I have hereunto set my hand and caused the seal of the United States to be affixed.

[SEAL.]   Done at the city of Washington, this 24th day of December, 1890, and of the Independence of the United States the one hundred and fifteenth.

BENJ. HARRISON.

By the President:
    James G. Blaine, *Secretary of State.*

By the President of the United States of America.

A PROCLAMATION.

Whereas, pursuant to section 3 of the act of Congress approved October 1, 1890, entitled "An act to reduce the revenue and equalize duties on imports, and for other purposes," the Secretary of State of the United States of America communicated to the Government of the United States of Brazil the action of the Congress of the United States of America, with a view to secure reciprocal trade, in declaring the articles enumerated in said section 3, to wit, sugars, molasses, coffee, and hides, to be exempt from duty upon their importation into the United States of America; and

Whereas the envoy extraordinary and minister plenipotentiary of Brazil at Washington has communicated to the Secretary of State the fact that, in due reciprocity for and in consideration of the admission into the United States of America free of all duty of the articles enumerated in section 3 of said act, the Government of Brazil has by legal enactment authorized the admission, from and after April 1, 1891, into all the established ports of entry of Brazil, free of all duty, whether national, state, or municipal, of the articles or merchandise named in the following schedule, provided that the same be the product and manufacture of the United States of America:

I.—SCHEDULE OF ARTICLES TO BE ADMITTED FREE INTO BRAZIL.

Wheat.
Wheat flour.
Corn or maize and the manufactures thereof, including corn meal and starch.
Rye, rye flour, buckwheat, buckwheat flour, and barley.
Potatoes, beans, and pease.
Hay and oats.
Pork, salted, including pickled pork and bacon, except hams.
Fish, salted, dried, or pickled.
Cotton-seed oil.
Coal, anthracite and bituminous.
Rosin, tar, pitch, and turpentine.
Agricultural tools, implements, and machinery.
Mining and mechanical tools, implements, and machinery, including stationary and portable engines and all machinery for manufacturing and industrial purposes, except sewing machines.
Instruments and books for the arts and sciences.
Railway construction material and equipment.

And that the Government of Brazil has by legal enactment further authorized the admission into all the established ports of entry of Brazil, with a reduction of 25 per cent of the duty designated on the respective article in the tariff now in force or which may hereafter be adopted in the United States of Brazil, whether national, state, or municipal, of the articles or merchandise named in the following schedule, provided that the same be the product or manufacture of the United States of America:

2.—SCHEDULE OF ARTICLES TO BE ADMITTED INTO BRAZIL, WITH A REDUCTION OF DUTY OF 25 PER CENT.

Lard and substitutes therefor.
Bacon hams.
Butter and cheese.
Canned and preserved meats, fish, fruits, and vegetables.
Manufactures of cotton, including cotton clothing.
Manufactures of iron and steel, single or mixed, not included in the foregoing free schedule.
Leather and the manufactures thereof, except boots and shoes.
Lumber, timber, and the manufactures of wood, including cooperage, furniture of all kinds, wagons, carts, and carriages.
Manufactures of rubber.

And that the Government of Brazil has further provided that the laws and regulations adopted to protect its revenue and prevent fraud in the declarations and proof that the articles named in the foregoing schedules are the product or manufacture of the United States of America shall place no undue restrictions on the importer nor impose any additional charges or fees therefor on the articles imported;

And whereas the Secretary of State has, by my direction, given assurance to the envoy extraordinary and minister plenipotentiary of Brazil at Washington that this action of the Government of Brazil in granting exemption of duties to the products and manufactures of the United States of America is accepted as a due reciprocity for the action of Congress as set forth in section 3 of said act:

Now, therefore, be it known that I, Benjamin Harrison, President of the United States of America, have caused the above-stated modifications of the tariff law of Brazil to be made public for the information of the citizens of the United States of America.

In testimony whereof I have hereunto set my hand and caused the seal of the United States to be affixed.

[SEAL.]   Done at the city of Washington, this 5th day of February, 1891, and of the Independence of the United States of America the one hundred and fifteenth.

BENJ. HARRISON.

By the President:
JAMES G. BLAINE, *Secretary of State.*

BY THE PRESIDENT OF THE UNITED STATES OF AMERICA.

A PROCLAMATION.

Whereas it is provided by section 24 of an act approved March 3, 1891, entitled "An act to repeal timber-culture laws, and for other purposes "—

That the President of the United States may from time to time set apart and reserve in any State or Territory having public land bearing forests, in any part of the public lands wholly or in part covered with timber or undergrowth, whether of commercial value or not, as public reservations; and the President shall by public proclamation declare the establishment of such reservations and limits thereof.

Now, therefore, I, Benjamin Harrison, President of the United States, by virtue of the power in me vested, do hereby make known and proclaim that there has been and is hereby reserved from entry or settlement and set apart for a public forest reservation all that tract of land situate in the State of Wyoming contained within the following-described boundaries:

Beginning at a point on the parallel of 44° 50′ where said parallel is intersected by the meridian of 110° west longitude; thence due east along said parallel to the meridian of 109° 30′ west longitude; thence due south along said meridian to the forty-fourth parallel of north latitude; thence due west along said parallel to its point of intersection with the west boundary of the State of Wyoming; thence due north along said boundary line to its intersection with the south boundary of the Yellowstone National Park.

Warning is hereby expressly given to all persons not to enter or make settlement upon the tract of land reserved by this proclamation.

In witness whereof I have hereunto set my hand and caused the seal of the United States to be affixed.

[SEAL.]   Done at the city of Washington, this 30th day of March, A. D. 1891, and of the Independence of the United States the one hundred and fifteenth.   BENJ. HARRISON.

By the President:

JAMES G. BLAINE, *Secretary of State.*

BY THE PRESIDENT OF THE UNITED STATES OF AMERICA.

A PROCLAMATION.

The following provisions of the laws of the United States are hereby published for the information of all concerned:

Section 1956, Revised Statutes, chapter 3, Title XXIII, enacts that—

No person shall kill any otter, mink, marten, sable, or fur seal, or other fur-bearing animal within the limits of Alaska Territory or in the waters thereof; and every person guilty thereof shall for each offense be fined not less than $200 nor more than $1,000, or imprisoned not more than six months, or both; and all vessels, their tackle, apparel, furniture, and cargo, found engaged in violation of this section shall be forfeited; but the Secretary of the Treasury shall have power to authorize the killing of any such mink, marten, sable, or other fur-bearing animal, except fur seals, under such regulations as he may prescribe; and it shall be the duty of the Secretary to prevent the killing of any fur seal and to provide for the execution of the provisions of this section until it is otherwise provided by law, nor shall he grant any special privileges under this section.

*   *   *   *   *   *   *

Section 3 of the act entitled "An act to provide for the protection of the salmon fisheries of Alaska," approved March 2, 1889, provides that—

SEC. 3. That section 1956 of the Revised Statutes of the United States is hereby declared to include and apply to all the dominion of the United States in the waters of Bering Sea, and it shall be the duty of the President at a timely season in each year to issue his proclamation, and cause the same to be published for one month in at least one newspaper (if any such there be) published at each United States port of entry on the Pacific coast, warning all persons against entering such waters for the purpose of violating the provisions of said section, and he shall also cause one or more vessels of the United States to diligently cruise said waters and arrest all persons and seize all vessels found to be or to have been engaged in any violation of the laws of the United States therein.

Now, therefore, I, Benjamin Harrison, President of the United States, pursuant to the above-recited statutes, hereby warn all persons against entering the waters of Bering Sea within the dominion of the United States for the purpose of violating the provisions of said section 1956, Revised Statutes; and I hereby proclaim that all persons found to be or to have been engaged in any violation of the laws of the United States in said waters will be arrested and punished as above provided, and that all vessels so employed, their tackle, apparel, furniture, and cargoes, will be seized and forfeited.

In testimony whereof I have hereunto set my hand and caused the seal of the United States to be affixed.

[SEAL.]   Done at the city of Washington, this 4th day of April, 1891, and of the Independence of the United States the one hundred and fifteenth.

BENJ. HARRISON.

By the President:

JAMES G. BLAINE,
Secretary of State.

BY THE PRESIDENT OF THE UNITED STATES OF AMERICA.

A PROCLAMATION.

Whereas, pursuant to an act of Congress approved May 15, 1886, entitled "An act making appropriations for the current and contingent expenses of the Indian Department and for fulfilling treaty stipulations with various tribes for the year ending June 30, 1887, and for other purposes," an agreement was entered into on the 14th day of December, 1886, by John V. Wright, Jared W. Daniels, and Charles F. Larrabee, commissioners on the part of the United States, and the Arickaree, Gros Ventre, and Mandan tribes of Indians, residing on the Fort Berthold Reservation, in the then Territory of Dakota, now State of North Dakota, embracing a majority of all the male adult members of said tribes; and

Whereas by an act of Congress approved March 3, 1891, entitled "An act making appropriations for the current and contingent expenses of the Indian Department and for fulfilling treaty stipulations with various Indian tribes for the year ending June 30, 1892, and for other purposes," the aforesaid agreement of December 14, 1886, was accepted, ratified, and confirmed, except as to article 6 thereof, which was modified and changed on the part of the United States so as to read as follows:

That the residue of lands within said diminished reservation, after all allotments have been made as provided in article 3 of this agreement, shall be held by the said tribes of Indians as a reservation.

And whereas it is provided in said last above-mentioned act—

That this act shall take effect only upon the acceptance of the modification and changes made by the United States as to article 6 of the said agreement by the said tribes of Indians in manner and form as said agreement was assented to, which said acceptance and consent shall be made known by proclamation by the President of the United States, upon satisfactory proof presented to him that the said acceptance and consent have been obtained in such manner and form.

And whereas satisfactory proof has been presented to me that the acceptance of and consent to the provisions of the act last named by the different bands of Indians residing on said reservation have been obtained in manner and form as said agreement of December 14, 1886, was assented to:

Now, therefore, I, Benjamin Harrison, President of the United States, by virtue of the power in me vested, do hereby make known and proclaim the acceptance of and consent to the modification and changes made by the United States as to article 6 of said agreement by said tribe of Indians as required by the act, and said act is hereby declared to be in full force and effect, subject to all provisions, conditions, limitations, and restrictions therein contained.

All persons will take notice of the provisions of said act and of the conditions and restrictions therein contained, and be governed accordingly.

I furthermore notify all persons to particularly observe that a certain portion of the said Fort Berthold Reservation not ceded and relinquished by said agreement is reserved for allotment to, and also as a reservation for, the said tribes of Indians; and all persons are therefore hereby warned not to go upon any of the lands so reserved for any purpose or with any intent whatsoever, as no settlement or other rights can be secured upon said lands, and all persons found unlawfully thereon will be dealt with as trespassers and intruders; and I hereby declare all the lands sold, ceded, and relinquished to the United States under said agreement, namely, "all that portion of the Fort Berthold Reservation, as laid down upon the official map of the" (then) "Territory of Dakota published by the General Land Office in the year 1885, lying north of the forty-eighth parallel of north latitude, and also all that portion lying west of a north and south line 6 miles west of the most westerly point of the big bend of the Missouri River, south of the forty-eighth parallel of north latitude," open to settlement and subject to disposal as provided in section

25 of the act of March 3, 1891, aforesaid (26 U. S. Statutes at Large, p. 1035).

In witness whereof I have hereunto set my hand and caused the seal of the United States to be affixed.

[SEAL.]   Done at the city of Washington, this 20th day of May, A. D. 1891, and of the Independence of the United States the one hundred and fifteenth.

BENJ. HARRISON.

By the President:

WILLIAM F. WHARTON,
     Acting Secretary of State.

BY THE PRESIDENT OF THE UNITED STATES OF AMERICA.

A PROCLAMATION.

Whereas an agreement for a *modus vivendi* between the Government of the United States and the Government of Her Britannic Majesty in relation to the fur-seal fisheries in Bering Sea was concluded on the 15th day of June, A. D. 1891, word for word as follows:

AGREEMENT BETWEEN THE GOVERNMENT OF THE UNITED STATES AND THE GOVERNMENT OF HER BRITANNIC MAJESTY FOR A MODUS VIVENDI IN RELATION TO THE FUR-SEAL FISHERIES IN BERING SEA.

For the purpose of avoiding irritating differences and with a view to promote the friendly settlement of the questions pending between the two Governments touching their respective rights in Bering Sea, and for the preservation of the seal species, the following agreement is made without prejudice to the rights or claims of either party:

(1) Her Majesty's Government will prohibit until May next seal killing in that part of Bering Sea lying eastward of the line of demarcation described in article No. 1 of the treaty of 1867 between the United States and Russia, and will promptly use its best efforts to insure the observance of this prohibition by British subjects and vessels.

(2) The United States Government will prohibit seal killing for the same period in the same part of Bering Sea and on the shores and islands thereof the property of the United States (in excess of 7,500 to be taken on the islands for the subsistence and care of the natives), and will promptly use its best efforts to insure the observance of this prohibition by United States citizens and vessels.

(3) Every vessel or person offending against this prohibition in the said waters of Bering Sea outside of the ordinary territorial limits of the United States may be seized and detained by the naval or other duly commissioned officers of either of the high contracting parties, but they shall be handed over as soon as practicable to the authorities of the nation to which they respectively belong, who shall alone have jurisdiction to try the offense and impose the penalties for the same. The witnesses and proofs necessary to establish the offense shall also be sent with them.

(4) In order to facilitate such proper inquiries as Her Majesty's Government may desire to make with a view to the presentation of the case of that Government before arbitrators, and in expectation that an agreement for arbitration may be arrived at, it is agreed that suitable persons designated by Great Britain will be permitted at any time, upon application, to visit or to remain upon the seal islands during the present sealing season for that purpose.

Signed and sealed in duplicate at Washington, this 15th day of June, 1891, on behalf of their respective Governments, by William F. Wharton, Acting Secretary of State of the United States, and Sir Julian Pauncefote, G. C. M. G., K. C. B., H. B. M. envoy extraordinary and minister plenipotentiary.

WILLIAM F. WHARTON.　[SEAL.]

JULIAN PAUNCEFOTE.　[SEAL.]

Now, therefore, be it known that I, Benjamin Harrison, President of the United States of America, have caused the said agreement to be made public, to the end that the same and every part thereof may be observed and fulfilled with good faith by the United States of America and the citizens thereof.

In witness whereof I have hereunto set my hand and caused the seal of the United States to be affixed.

[SEAL.]　　Done at the city of Washington, this 15th day of June, A. D. 1891, and of the Independence of the United States the one hundred and fifteenth.

BENJ. HARRISON.

By the President:

WILLIAM F. WHARTON,
　　Acting Secretary of State.

BY THE PRESIDENT OF THE UNITED STATES OF AMERICA.

A PROCLAMATION.

Whereas it is provided by section 13 of the act of Congress of March 3, 1891, entitled "An act to amend Title LX, chapter 3, of the Revised Statutes of the United States, relating to copyrights," that said act "shall only apply to a citizen or a subject of a foreign state or nation when such foreign state or nation permits to citizens of the United States of America the benefit of copyright on substantially the same basis as its own citizens, or when such foreign state or nation is a party to an international agreement which provides for reciprocity in the granting of copyright, by the terms of which agreement the United States of America may at its pleasure become a party to such agreement;" and

Whereas it is also provided by said section that "the existence of either of the conditions aforesaid shall be determined by the President of the United States by proclamation made from time to time as the purposes of this act may require;" and

Whereas satisfactory official assurances have been given that in Belgium, France, Great Britain and the British possessions, and Switzerland the law permits to citizens of the United States the benefit of copyright on substantially the same basis as to the citizens of those countries:

Now, therefore, I, Benjamin Harrison, President of the United States of America, do declare and proclaim that the first of the conditions specified in section 13 of the act of March 3, 1891, is now fulfilled in respect to the citizens or subjects of Belgium, France, Great Britain, and Switzerland.

In testimony whereof I have hereunto set my hand and caused the seal of the United States to be affixed.

[SEAL.] Done at the city of Washington, this 1st day of July, 1891, and of the Independence of the United States the one hundred and fifteenth.

BENJ. HARRISON.

By the President:

WILLIAM F. WHARTON,
Acting Secretary of State.

BY THE PRESIDENT OF THE UNITED STATES OF AMERICA.

A PROCLAMATION.

Whereas, pursuant to section 3 of the act of Congress approved October 1, 1890, entitled "An act to reduce the revenue and equalize duties on imports, and for other purposes," the Secretary of State of the United States of America communicated to the Government of Spain the action of the Congress of the United States of America, with a view to secure reciprocal trade, in declaring the articles enumerated in said section 3, to wit, sugars, molasses, coffee, and hides, to be exempt from duty upon their importation into the United States of America; and

Whereas the envoy extraordinary and minister plenipotentiary of Spain at Washington has communicated to the Secretary of State the fact that, in reciprocity and compensation for the admission into the United States of America free of all duty of the articles enumerated in section 3 of said act, the Government of Spain will by due legal enactment and as a provisional measure admit, from and after September 1, 1891, into all the established ports of entry of the Spanish islands of Cuba and Puerto Rico the articles or merchandise named in the following transitory schedule, on the terms stated therein, provided that the same be the product or manufacture of the United States and proceed directly from the ports of said States:

TRANSITORY SCHEDULE.

Products or manufactures of the United States to be admitted into Cuba and Puerto Rico free of duties:

1. Meats, in brine, salted or smoked, bacon, hams, and meats preserved in cans, in lard or by extraction of air, jerked beef excepted.
2. Lard.
3. Tallow and other animal greases, melted or crude, unmanufactured.
4. Fish and shellfish, live, fresh, dried, in brine, smoked, pickled, oysters and salmon in cans.
5. Oats, barley, rye, and buckwheat, and flour of these cereals.
6. Starch, maizena, and other alimentary products of corn, except corn meal.
7. Cotton seed, oil and meal cake of said seed for cattle.
8. Hay, straw for forage, and bran.

9. Fruits, fresh, dried, and preserved, except raisins.

10. Vegetables and garden products, fresh and dried.

11. Resin of pine, tar, pitch, and turpentine.

12. Woods of all kinds, in trunks or logs, joists, rafters, planks, beams, boards, round or cylindric masts, although cut, planed, and tongued and grooved, including flooring.

13. Woods for cooperage, including staves, headings, and wooden hoops.

14. Wooden boxes, mounted or unmounted, except of cedar.

15. Woods, ordinary, manufactured into doors, frames, windows, and shutters, without paint or varnish, and wooden houses, unmounted, without paint or varnish.

16. Wagons and carts for ordinary roads and agriculture.

17. Sewing machines.

18. Petroleum, raw or unrefined, according to the classification fixed in the existing orders for the importation of this article in said islands.

19. Coal, mineral.

20. Ice.

Products or manufactures of the United States to be admitted into Cuba and Puerto Rico on payment of the duties stated:

21. Corn or maize, 25 cents per 100 kilograms.

22. Corn meal, 25 cents per 100 kilograms.

23. Wheat, from January 1, 1892, 30 cents per 100 kilograms.

24. Wheat flour, from January 1, 1892, $1 per 100 kilograms.

Products or manufactures of the United States to be admitted into Cuba and Puerto Rico at a reduction of duty of 25 per cent:

25. Butter and cheese.

26. Petroleum, refined.

27. Boots and shoes in whole or in part of leather or skins.

And whereas the envoy extraordinary and minister plenipotentiary of Spain in Washington has further communicated to the Secretary of State that the Government of Spain will in like manner and as a definitive arrangement admit, from and after July 1, 1892, into all the established ports of entry of the Spanish islands of Cuba and Puerto Rico the articles or merchandise named in the following schedules A, B, C, and D, on the terms stated therein, provided that the same be the product or manufacture of the United States and proceed directly from the ports of said States:

SCHEDULE A.

Products or manufactures of the United States to be admitted into Cuba and Puerto Rico free of duties:

1. Marble, jasper, and alabaster, natural or artificial, in rough or in pieces, dressed, squared, and prepared for taking shape.

2. Other stones and earthy matters, including cement, employed in building, the arts and industries.

3. Waters, mineral or medicinal.

4. Ice.

5. Coal, mineral.

6. Resin, tar, pitch, turpentine, asphalt, schist, and bitumen.

7. Petroleum, raw or crude, in accordance with the classification fixed in the tariff of said islands.

8. Clay, ordinary, in paving tiles, large and small, bricks, and roof tiles unglazed, for the construction of buildings, ovens, and other similar purposes.

9. Gold and silver coin.

10. Iron, cast, in pigs, and old iron and steel.

11. Iron, cast, in pipes, beams, rafters, and similar articles for the construction of buildings and in ordinary manufactures. (See repertory.)

12. Iron, wrought, and steel, in bars, rails and bars of all kinds, plates, beams, rafters, and other similar articles for construction of buildings.

13. Iron, wrought, and steel, in wire, nails, screws, nuts, and pipes.

14. Iron, wrought, and steel, in ordinary manufactures, and wire cloth unmanufac- tured. (See repertory.)

15. Cotton, raw, with or without seed.

16. Cotton seed, oil and meal cake of same for cattle.

17. Tallow and all other animal greases, melted or crude, unmanufactured.

18. Books and pamphlets, printed, bound and unbound.

19. Woods of all kinds, in trunks or logs, joists, rafters, planks, beams, boards, and round or cylindric masts, although cut, planed, tongued and grooved, including flooring.

20. Wooden cooperage, including staves, headings, and wooden hoops.

21. Wooden boxes, mounted or unmounted, except of cedar.

22. Woods, ordinary, manufactured into doors, frames, windows, and shutters, with- out paint or varnish, and wooden houses, unmounted, without paint or varnish.

23. Woods, ordinary, manufactured into all kinds of articles, turned or unturned, painted or varnished, except furniture. (See repertory.)

24. Manures, natural or artificial.

25. Implements, utensils, and tools for agriculture, the arts, and mechanical trades.

26. Machines and apparatus, agricultural, motive, industrial, and scientific, of all classes and materials, and loose pieces for the same, including wagons, carts, and handcarts for ordinary roads and agriculture.

27. Material and articles for public works, such as railroads, tramways, roads, canals for irrigation and navigation, use of waters, ports, light-houses, and civil con- struction of general utility, when introduced by authorization of the Government or if free admission is obtained in accordance with local laws.

28. Materials of all classes for the construction, repair in whole or in part of ves- sels, subject to specific regulations to avoid abuse in the importation.

29. Meats, in brine, salted and smoked, including bacon, hams, and meats preserved in cans, in lard or by extraction of air, jerked beef excepted.

30. Lard and butter.

31. Cheese.

32. Fish and shellfish, live, fresh, dried, in brine, salted, smoked, and pickled, oys- ters and salmon in cans.

33. Oats, barley, rye, and buckwheat, and flour of these cereals.

34. Starch, maizena, and other alimentary products of corn, except corn meal.

35. Fruits, fresh, dried, and preserved, except raisins.

36. Vegetables and garden products, fresh and dried.

37. Hay, straw for forage, and bran.

38. Trees, plants, shrubs, and garden seeds.

39. Tan bark.

SCHEDULE B.

Products or manufactures of the United States to be admitted into Cuba and Puerto Rico on payment of the duties stated:

40. Corn or maize, 25 cents per 100 kilograms.

41. Corn meal, 25 cents per 100 kilograms.

42. Wheat, 30 cents per 100 kilograms.

43. Wheat flour, $1 per 100 kilograms.

44. Carriages, cars and other vehicles for railroads or tramways, where authori- zation of the Government for free admission has not been obtained, 1 per cent *ad valorem.*

SCHEDULE C.

Products or manufactures of the United States to be admitted into Cuba and Puerto Rico at a reduction of duty of 50 per cent:

45. Marble, jasper, and alabaster of all kinds, cut into flags, slabs, or steps, and the same worked or carved in all kinds of articles, polished or not.

46. Glass and crystal ware, plate and window glass, and the same silvered, quicksilvered, and platinized.

47. Clay in tiles, large and small, and mosaic for pavement, colored tiles, roof tiles glazed, and pipes.

48. Stoneware and fine earthenware, and porcelain.

49. Iron, cast, in fine manufactures or those polished, with coating of porcelain or part of other metals. (See repertory.)

50. Iron, wrought, and steel, in axles, tires, springs, and wheels for carriages, rivets and their washers.

51. Iron, wrought, and steel, in fine manufactures or those polished, with coating of porcelain or part of other metals, not expressly comprised in other numbers of these schedules, and platform scales for weighing. (See repertory.)

52. Needles, pens, knives (table and carving), razors, penknives, scissors, pieces for watches, and other similar articles of iron and steel.

53. Tin plate in sheets or manufactured.

54. Copper, bronze, brass, and nickel, and alloys of same with common metals, in lump or bars, and all manufactures of the same.

55. All other common metals and alloys of the same, in lump or bars, and all manufactures of the same, plain, varnished, gilt, silvered, or nickeled.

56. Furniture of all kinds, of wood or metal, including school furniture, blackboards, and other materials for schools, and all kinds of articles of fine woods not expressly comprised in other numbers of these schedules. (See repertory.)

57. Rushes, esparto, vegetable hair, broom corn, willow, straw, palm, and other similar materials, manufactured into articles of all kinds.

58. Pastes for soups, rice flour, bread and crackers, and alimentary farinas not comprised in other numbers of these schedules.

59. Preserved alimentary substances and canned goods not comprised in other numbers of these schedules, including sausages, stuffed meats, mustards, sauces, pickles, jams, and jellies.

60. Rubber and gutta-percha and manufactures thereof, alone or mixed with other substances (except silk), and oilcloths and tarpaulin.

61. Rice, hulled or unhulled.

SCHEDULE D.

Products or manufactures of the United States to be admitted into Cuba and Puerto Rico at a reduction of duty of 25 per cent:

62. Petroleum, refined, and benzine.

63. Cotton, manufactured, spun or twisted, and in goods of all kinds, woven or knit, and the same mixed with other vegetable or animal fibers in which cotton is an equal or greater component part, and clothing exclusively of cotton.

64. Rope, cordage, and twine of all kinds.

65. Colors, crude and prepared, with or without oil, inks of all kinds, shoe blacking, and varnishes.

66. Soap, toilet, and perfumery.

67. Medicines, proprietary or patent and all others, and drugs.

68. Stearine and tallow manufactured in candles.

69. Paper for printing, for decorating rooms, of wood or straw, for wrapping and packing, and bags and boxes of same, sandpaper and pasteboard.

70. Leather and skins, tanned, dressed, varnished, or japanned, of all kinds, including sole leather or belting.

71. Boots and shoes in whole or in part of leather or skins.

72. Trunks, valises, traveling bags, portfolios, and other similar articles in whole or in part of leather.

73. Harness and saddlery of all kinds.

74. Watches and clocks of gold, silver, or other metals, with cases of stone, wood, or other material, plain or ornamented.

75. Carriages of two or four wheels and pieces of the same.

It is understood that flour which on its exportation from the United States has been favored with drawbacks shall not share in the foregoing reduction of duty.

The provisional arrangement as set forth in the transitory schedule shall come to an end on July 1, 1892, and on that date be substituted by the definitive arrangement as set forth in schedules A, B, C, and D.

And that the Government of Spain has further provided that the laws and regulations adopted to protect its revenue and prevent fraud in the declarations and proof that the articles named in the foregoing schedules are the product or manufacture of the United States of America shall place no undue restrictions on the importer nor impose any additional charges or fees therefor on the articles imported; and

Whereas the Secretary of State has, by my direction, given assurance to the envoy extraordinary and minister plenipotentiary of Spain at Washington that this action of the Government of Spain in granting exemption of duties to the products and manufactures of the United States of America on their importation into Cuba and Puerto Rico is accepted for those islands as a due reciprocity for the action of Congress as set forth in section 3 of said act:

Now, therefore, be it known that I, Benjamin Harrison, President of the United States of America, have caused the above-stated modifications of the tariff laws of Cuba and Puerto Rico to be made public for the information of the citizens of the United States of America.

In testimony whereof I have hereunto set my hand and caused the seal of the United States to be affixed.

[SEAL.]　　Done at the city of Washington, this 31st day of July, 1891, and of the Independence of the United States of America the one hundred and sixteenth.

BENJ. HARRISON.

By the President:

WILLIAM F. WHARTON, *Acting Secretary of State.*

BY THE PRESIDENT OF THE UNITED STATES OF AMERICA.

A PROCLAMATION.

Whereas, pursuant to section 3 of the act of Congress approved October 1, 1890, entitled "An act to reduce the revenue and equalize duties on imports, and for other purposes," the Secretary of State of the United States of America communicated to the Government of the Dominican

Republic the action of the Congress of the United States of America, with a view to secure reciprocal trade, in declaring the articles enumerated in said section 3, to wit, sugars, molasses, coffee, and hides, to be exempt from duty upon their importation into the United States of America; and

Whereas the envoy extraordinary and minister plenipotentiary of the Dominican Republic at Washington has communicated to the special plenipotentiary of the United States the fact that, in reciprocity and compensation for the admission into the United States of America free of all duty of the articles enumerated in section 3 of said act, the Government of the Dominican Republic will by due legal enactment admit, from and after September 1, 1891, into all the established ports of entry of the Dominican Republic the articles or merchandise named in the following schedules, on the terms stated therein, provided that the same be the product or manufacture of the United States and proceed directly from the ports of said States:

SCHEDULE A.

Articles to be admitted free of duty into the Dominican Republic:

1. Animals, live.
2. Meats of all kinds, salted or in brine, but not smoked.
3. Corn or maize, corn meal, and starch.
4. Oats, barley, rye, and buckwheat, and flour of these cereals.
5. Hay, bran, and straw for forage.
6. Trees, plants, vines, and seeds, and grains of all kinds for propagation.
7. Cotton-seed oil and meal cake of same.
8. Tallow, in cake or melted, and oil for machinery, subject to examination and proof respecting the use of said oil.
9. Resin, tar, pitch, and turpentine.
10. Manures, natural and artificial.
11. Coal, mineral.
12. Mineral waters, natural and artificial.
13. Ice.
14. Machines, including steam engines and those of all other kinds, and parts of the same, implements and tools for agricultural, mining, manufacturing, industrial, and scientific purposes, including carts, wagons, handcarts, and wheelbarrows, and parts of the same.
15. Material for the construction and equipment of railways.
16. Iron, cast and wrought, and steel, in pigs, bars, rods, plates, beams, rafters, and other similar articles for the construction of buildings, and in wire, nails, screws, and pipes.
17. Zinc, galvanized and corrugated iron, tin and lead in sheets, asbestus, tar paper, tiles, slate, and other material for roofing.
18. Copper in bars, plates, nails, and screws.
19. Copper and lead pipe.
20. Bricks, fire bricks, cement, lime, artificial stone, paving tiles, marble and other stones in rough, dressed or polished, and other earthy materials used in building.
21. Windmills.
22. Wire, plain or barbed, for fences, with hooks, staples, nails, and similar articles used in the construction of fences.
23. Telegraph wire and telegraphic, telephonic, and electrical apparatus of all kinds for communication and illumination.

24. Wood and lumber of all kinds for building, in logs or pieces, beams, rafters, planks, boards, shingles, flooring, joists, wooden houses, mounted or unmounted, and accessory parts of buildings.

25. Cooperage of all kinds, including staves, headings, and hoops, barrels and boxes, mounted or unmounted.

26. Materials for shipbuilding.

27. Boats and lighters.

28. School furniture, blackboards, and other articles exclusively for the use of schools.

29. Books, bound or unbound, pamphlets, newspapers and printed matter, and paper for printing newspapers.

30. Printers' inks of all colors, type, leads, and all accessories for printing.

31. Sacks, empty, for packing sugar.

32. Gold and silver coin and bullion.

SCHEDULE B.

Articles to be admitted into the Dominican Republic at a reduction of duty of 25 per cent:

33. Meats not included in Schedule A and meat products of all kinds except lard.

34. Butter, cheese, and condensed or canned milk.

35. Fish and shellfish, salted, dried, smoked, pickled, or preserved in cans.

36. Fruits and vegetables, fresh, canned, dried, pickled, or preserved.

37. Manufactures of iron and steel, single or mixed, not included in Schedule A.

38. Cotton, manufactured, spun or twisted, and in fabrics of all kinds, woven or knit, and the same fabrics mixed with other vegetable or animal fibers in which cotton is the equal or greater component part.

39. Boots and shoes in whole or in part of leather or skins.

40. Paper for writing, in envelopes, ruled or blank books, wall paper, paper for wrapping and packing, for cigarettes, in cardboard, boxes, and bags, sandpaper and pasteboard.

41. Tin plate and tinware for arts, industries, and domestic uses.

42. Cordage, rope, and twine of all kinds.

43. Manufactures of wood of all kinds not embraced in Schedule A, including wooden ware, implements for household use, and furniture in whole or in part of wood.

And that the Government of the Dominican Republic has further provided that the laws and regulations adopted to protect its revenue and prevent fraud in the declarations and proof that the articles named in the foregoing schedules are the product or manufacture of the United States of America shall place no undue restrictions on the importer nor impose any additional charges or fees therefor on the articles imported; and

Whereas the special plenipotentiary of the United States has, by my direction, given assurance to the envoy extraordinary and minister plenipotentiary of the Dominican Republic at Washington that this action of the Government of the Dominican Republic in granting exemption of duties to the products and manufactures of the United States of America on their importation into the Dominican Republic is accepted as a due reciprocity for the action of Congress as set forth in section 3 of said act:

Now, therefore, be it known that I, Benjamin Harrison, President of the United States of America, have caused the above-stated modifications of the tariff laws of the Dominican Republic to be made public for the information of the citizens of the United States of America.

In testimony whereof I have hereunto set my hand and caused the seal of the United States to be affixed.

[SEAL.]   Done at the city of Washington, this 1st day of August, 1891, and of the Independence of the United States of America the one hundred and sixteenth.

BENJ. HARRISON.

By the President:
WILLIAM F. WHARTON,
Acting Secretary of State.

BY THE PRESIDENT OF THE UNITED STATES OF AMERICA.

A PROCLAMATION.

Whereas it is provided by section 24 of an act approved March 3, 1891, entitled "An act to repeal timber-culture laws, and for other purposes"—

That the President of the United States may from time to time set apart and reserve in any State or Territory having public land bearing forests, in any part of the public lands wholly or in part covered with timber or undergrowth, whether of commercial value or not, as public reservations; and the President shall by public proclamation declare the establishment of such reservations and limits thereof.

And whereas the lands hereinafter described are public and forest bearing, and on the 30th of March last I issued a proclamation* intended to reserve the same as authorized in said act, but as some question has arisen as to the boundaries proclaimed being sufficiently definite to cover the forests intended to be reserved:

Now, therefore, I, Benjamin Harrison, President of the United States, for the purpose of removing any doubt and making the boundaries of said reservation more definite, by virtue of the power in me vested by said act, do hereby issue this my second proclamation and hereby set apart, reserve, and establish as a public reservation all that tract of land situate in the State of Wyoming embraced within the following boundary:

Beginning at a point on the parallel of 44° 50′ north latitude where said parallel is intersected by the east boundary of the Yellowstone National Park; thence due east along said parallel 24½ miles; thence due south to the parallel of 44° north latitude; thence due west along said parallel to its point of intersection with the west boundary of the State of Wyoming; thence due north along said boundary to its intersection with the south boundary of the Yellowstone National Park; thence due east along the south boundary of said park to the southeast corner thereof; thence due north along the east boundary of said park to the place of beginning.

And warning is hereby expressly given to all persons not to enter or make settlement upon the tract of land reserved by this proclamation.

*See pp. 142–143.

In witness whereof I have hereunto set my hand and caused the seal
of the United States to be affixed.

[SEAL.]   Done at the city of Washington, this 10th day of September,
A. D. 1891, and of the Independence of the United States the
one hundred and fifteenth.

BENJ. HARRISON.

By the President:

WILLIAM F. WHARTON, *Acting Secretary of State.*

BY THE PRESIDENT OF THE UNITED STATES OF AMERICA.

A PROCLAMATION.

Whereas by a written agreement made on the 12th day of June, 1890,
the Sac and Fox Nation of Indians, in the Territory of Oklahoma, ceded
and conveyed to the United States of America all title or interest of said
Indians in and to the lands particularly described in Article I of the agreement, except the quarter section of land on which the Sac and Fox
Agency is located, and provided that the section of land now designated
and set apart near the Sac and Fox Agency for a school and farm shall
not be subject either to allotment or to homestead entry; that every citizen of said nation shall have an allotment of land in quantity as therein
stated, to be selected within the tract of country so ceded, except in sections 16 and 36 in each Congressional township, and except the agency
quarter section and section set apart for school and farm, as above mentioned, or other lands selected in lieu thereof; that when the allotments
to the citizens of the Sac and Fox Nation are made the Secretary of the
Interior shall cause trust patents to issue therefor in the name of the allottees, and that as soon as such allotments are so made and approved by
the Department of the Interior, and the patents provided for are issued,
then the residue of said tract of country shall, as far as said Sac and Fox
Nation is concerned, become public lands of the United States, and, under
such restrictions as may be imposed by law, be subject to white settlement; and

Whereas by a certain other agreement with the Iowa tribe of Indians
residing on the Iowa Reservation, in said Territory, made on the 20th
day of May, 1890, said tribe surrendered and relinquished to the United
States all their title and interest in and to the lands of said Indians in
said Territory, and particularly described in Article I of said agreement,
and provided that each and every member of said tribe shall have an
allotment of 80 acres of land upon said reservation, and upon the approval
of such allotments by the Secretary of the Interior that trust patents
shall be issued therefor, and that there shall be excepted from the operation of said agreement a tract of land not exceeding 10 acres, in a square
form, including the church and schoolhouse and graveyard at or near the
Iowa village, which shall belong to said Iowa tribe of Indians in common,

subject to the conditions and limitations in said agreement expressed; that the chief of the Iowas may select an additional 10 acres, in a square form, for the use of said tribe in said reservation, conforming in boundaries to the legal subdivisions of land therein, which shall be held by said tribe in common, subject to the conditions and limitations as expressed in relation thereto; and

Whereas it is provided in the act of Congress approved February 13, 1891 (26 U. S. Statutes at Large, pp. 758, 759), section 7, accepting, ratifying, and confirming said agreements with the Sac and Fox Nation of Indians and the Iowa tribe of Indians—

That whenever any of the lands acquired by the agreements in this act ratified and confirmed shall by operation of law or proclamation of the President of the United States be open to settlement they shall be disposed of to actual settlers only, under the provisions of the homestead laws, except section 2301, which shall not apply: *Provided, however,* That each settler under and in accordance with the provisions of said homestead laws shall before receiving a patent for his homestead pay to the United States for the land so taken by him, in addition to the fees provided by law, the sum of $1.25 for each acre thereof; and such person, having complied with all the laws relating to such homestead settlement, may at his option receive a patent therefor at the expiration of twelve months from date of settlement upon said homestead; and any person otherwise qualified who has attempted to but for any cause failed to secure a title in fee to a homestead under existing law, or who made entry under what is known as the commuted provision of the homestead law, shall be qualified to make a homestead entry upon any of said lands.

And whereas by a certain other agreement with the Citizen band of Pottawatomie Indians, in said Territory, made on the 25th day of June, 1890, the said band of Indians ceded and absolutely surrendered to the United States all their title and interest in and to the lands in said Territory, and particularly described in Article I of said agreement, and provided that all allotments of land theretofore made, or then being made, or to be made, to members of said Citizen band of Pottawatomie Indians under the provisions of the general allotment act approved February 8, 1887, shall be confirmed; that in all allotments to be thereafter made no person shall have the right to select his or her allotment in sections 16 and 36 in any Congressional township, nor upon any land heretofore set apart in said tract of country for any use by the United States, or for schools, school-farm, or religious purposes; nor shall said sections 16 and 36 be subject to homestead entry, but shall be kept and used for school purposes; nor shall any lands set apart for any use of the United States, or for school, school-farm, or religious purposes, be subject to homestead entry, but shall be held by the United States for such purposes so long as the United States shall see fit to use them; and further, that the south half of section 7 and the north half of section 18, in township 6 north, range 5 east, theretofore set apart by a written agreement between said band of Indians and certain Catholic fathers for religious, school, and farm purposes, shall not be subject to allotment or homestead entry, but shall be held by the United States for the Sacred Heart Mission, the name under which said association of fathers are conducting the church, school, and farm on said lands; and

Whereas by a certain agreement with the Absentee Shawnee Indians, in said Territory, made on the 26th day of June, 1890, said last-named Indians ceded, relinquished, and surrendered to the United States all their title and interest in and to the lands in said Territory, and particularly described in Article I of said agreement, provided that all allotments of lands theretofore made, or then being made, or to be made, to said Absentee Shawnees under the provisions of the general allotment act approved February 8, 1887, shall be confirmed; that in all allotments to be thereafter made no person shall have the right to select his or her allotment in sections 16 and 36 in any Congressional township, nor in any land heretofore set apart in said tract of country for any use by the United States, or for school, school-farm, or religious purposes; nor shall said sections 16 and 36 be subject to homestead entry, but shall be held by the United States for such purposes so long as the United States shall see fit to use them; and

Whereas it is provided in the act of Congress accepting, ratifying, and confirming said agreements with the Citizen band of Pottawatomie Indians and the Absentee Shawnee Indians, approved March 3, 1891 (26 U. S. Statutes at Large, pp. 989–1044), section 16—

That whenever any of the lands acquired by either of the * * * foregoing agreements respecting lands in the Indian or Oklahoma Territory shall by operation of law or proclamation of the President of the United States be open to settlement they shall be disposed of to actual settlers only, under the provisions of the homestead and town-site laws, except section 2301 of the Revised Statutes of the United States, which shall not apply: *Provided, however,* That each settler on said lands shall before making a final proof and receiving a certificate of entry pay to the United States for the land so taken by him, in addition to the fees provided by law, and within five years from the date of the first original entry, the sum of $1.50 per acre, one-half of which shall be paid within two years; but the rights of honorably discharged Union soldiers and sailors as defined and described in sections 2304 and 2305 of the Revised Statutes of the United States shall not be abridged except as to the sum to be paid as aforesaid; and all the lands in Oklahoma are hereby declared to be agricultural lands, and proof of their nonmineral character shall not be required as a condition precedent to final entry.

And whereas allotments of land in severalty to said Sac and Fox Nation, said Iowa tribe, said Citizen band of Pottawatomies, and said Absentee Shawnee Indians have been made and approved, and provisional patents issued therefor, in accordance with law and the provisions of the beforementioned agreements with them respectively, and an additional 10 acres of land has been selected for the use of said Iowa tribe, to be held by said tribe in common, in accordance with the provisions of supplemental Article XII of the agreement with them; and

Whereas the lands acquired by the four several agreements hereinbefore mentioned have been divided into counties by the Secretary of the Interior, as required by said last-mentioned act of Congress before the same shall be open to settlement, and lands have been reserved for county-seat purposes, as therein required; and

Whereas it is provided by act of Congress for temporary government of Oklahoma, approved May 2, 1890, that there shall be reserved public highways 4 rods wide between each section of land in said Territory, the section lines being the centers of said highways, but no deduction shall be made from cash payments from each quarter section by reason thereof; and

Whereas all the terms, conditions, and considerations required by said several agreements made respectively with said tribes of Indians hereinbefore mentioned, and of the laws relating thereto, precedent to opening said several tracts of land to settlement, have been, as I hereby declare, provided for, paid, and complied with:

Now, therefore, I, Benjamin Harrison, President of the United States, by virtue of the power in me vested by the statutes hereinbefore mentioned, also an act of Congress entitled "An act making appropriations for the current and contingent expenses of the Indian Department and fulfilling treaty stipulations with various Indian tribes for the year ending June 30, 1890, and for other purposes," approved March 2, 1889, and by other the laws of the United States, and by said several agreements, do hereby declare and make known that all of the lands acquired from the Sac and Fox Nation of Indians, the Iowa tribe of Indians, the Citizen band of Pottawatomie Indians, and the Absentee Shawnee Indians by the four several agreements aforesaid, saving and excepting the lands allotted to the Indians as in said agreements provided, or otherwise reserved in pursuance of the provisions of said agreements and the said acts of Congress ratifying the same and other the laws relating thereto, will, at and after the hour of 12 o'clock noon (central standard time), Tuesday, the 22d day of this the present month of September, and not before, be opened to settlement, under the terms of and subject to all the conditions, limitations, reservations, and restrictions contained in said agreements, the statutes above specified, and the laws of the United States applicable thereto.

The lands to be so opened to settlement are for greater convenience particularly described in the accompanying schedule, entitled "Schedule of lands within the Sac and Fox, Iowa, Pottawatomie (and Absentee Shawnee) reservations, in Oklahoma Territory, opened to settlement by proclamation of the President dated September 18, 1891," and which schedule is made a part hereof.

Each entry shall be in square form as nearly as practicable; and no other lands in the Territory of Oklahoma are opened to settlement under this proclamation or the agreements ratifying the same.

Notice, moreover, is hereby given that it is by law enacted that until said lands are opened to settlement by proclamation no person shall be permitted to enter upon and occupy the same, and no person violating this provision shall be permitted to enter any of said lands or acquire any right thereto. The officers of the United States will be required to enforce this provision.

And further notice is hereby given that it has been duly ordered that the lands in the Territory of Oklahoma mentioned and included in this proclamation be, and the same are, attached to the Eastern and Oklahoma land districts in said Territory, severally, as follows:

1. All that portion of the Territory of Oklahoma commencing at the southwest corner of township 14 north, range 1 east; thence east on town line between townships 13 and 14 to the west boundary of the Creek country; thence north on said boundary line to the middle of main channel of the Cimarron River; thence up the Cimarron River, following the main channel thereof, to the Indian meridian; thence south on said meridian line to the place of beginning, is attached to the Eastern land district in Oklahoma Territory, the office of which is now located at Guthrie.

2. All that portion of said Territory commencing at the northwest corner of township 13 north, range 1 east; thence south on Indian meridian to the North Fork of the Canadian River; thence west up said river to the west boundary of the Pottawatomie Indian Reservation, according to Morrill's survey; thence south, following the line as run by O. T. Morrill under his contract of September 3, 1872, to the middle of the main channel of the Canadian River; thence east down the main channel of said river to the west boundary of the Seminole Indian Reservation; thence north with said west boundary to the North Fork of the Canadian River; thence east down said North Fork to the west boundary of the Creek Nation; thence north with said west boundary to its intersection with the line between townships 13 and 14 north of the Indian base; thence west on town line between townships 13 and 14 north to the place of beginning, is attached to the Oklahoma land district in said Territory, the office of which is now located at Oklahoma City.

In witness whereof I have hereunto set my hand and caused the seal of the United States to be affixed.

[SEAL.] Done at the city of Washington, this 18th day of September, A. D. 1891, and of the Independence of the United States the one hundred and sixteenth.

BENJ. HARRISON.

By the President:

WILLIAM F. WHARTON, *Acting Secretary of State.*

BY THE PRESIDENT OF THE UNITED STATES OF AMERICA.

A PROCLAMATION.

Whereas it is provided by section 24 of the act of Congress approved March 3, 1891, entitled "An act to repeal the timber-culture laws, and for other purposes"—

That the President of the United States may from time to time set apart and reserve in any State or Territory having public lands bearing forests, in any part of the public lands wholly or in part covered with timber or undergrowth, whether of commercial value or not, as public reservations; and the President shall by public proclamation declare the establishment of such reservation and the limits thereof.

And whereas the public lands in the State of Colorado within the limits hereinafter described are in part covered with timber, and it appears that the public good would be promoted by setting apart and reserving said lands as a public reservation:

Now, therefore, I, Benjamin Harrison, President of the United States, by virtue of the power in me vested by section 24 of the aforesaid act of Congress, do hereby make known and proclaim that there is hereby reserved from entry or settlement and set apart as a public reservation all those certain tracts, pieces, or parcels of land lying and being situate in the State of Colorado and particularly described as follows, to wit:

Beginning at a point between sections three (3) and four (4) on the north boundary of township five (5) south, range eighty-seven (87) west of the sixth principal meridian in Colorado; thence north 12 miles; thence east to the southeast corner of township two (2) south, range eighty-six (86) west; thence north between ranges numbered eighty-five (85) and eighty-six (86) west to the base line; thence west along the base line to the southwest corner of township one (1) north, range eighty-five (85) west; thence north between ranges numbered eighty-five (85) and eighty-six (86) west to a point between sections thirteen (13) and twenty-four (24) on the east boundary of township five (5) north, range eighty-six (86) west; thence west through the middle of township five (5) north to the center of township five (5) north, range ninety-one (91) west; thence south to a point between sections three (3) and four (4) on the north boundary of township two (2) north, range ninety-one (91) west; thence west six (6) miles to a point between sections three (3) and four (4) on the north boundary of township two (2) north, range ninety-two (92) west; thence south to a point on the base line between sections thirty-three (33) and thirty-four (34) of township one (1) north, range ninety-two (92) west; thence west along the base line to a point between sections three (3) and four (4) on the north boundary of township one (1) south, range ninety-two (92) west; thence south to a point between sections three (3) and four (4) on the north boundary of township two (2) south, range ninety-two (92) west; thence west to the northwest corner of township two (2) south, range ninety-three (93) west; thence south to the southwest corner of township three (3) south, range ninety-three (93) west; thence east to the northeast corner of township four (4) south, range ninety-two (92) west; thence south to the southeast corner of township four (4) south, range ninety-two (92) west; thence east to the place of beginning.

Excepting from the force and effect of this proclamation all land which may have been prior to the date hereof embraced in any valid entry or covered by a lawful filing duly made in the proper United States land office, and all mining claims duly located and held according to the laws of the United States and local rules and regulations not in conflict therewith.

Provided, That this exception shall not continue to apply to any particular tract of land unless the entryman or claimant continues to comply with the law under which the entry, filing, or location was made.

Warning is hereby expressly given to all persons not to enter or make settlement upon the tract of land reserved by this proclamation.

In witness whereof I have hereunto set my hand and caused the seal of the United States to be affixed.

[SEAL.]   Done at the city of Washington, this 16th day of October, A. D. 1891, and of the Independence of the United States the one hundred and sixteenth.   BENJ. HARRISON.

By the President:

WILLIAM F. WHARTON, *Acting Secretary of State.*

BY THE PRESIDENT OF THE UNITED STATES OF AMERICA.

A PROCLAMATION.

It is a very glad incident of the marvelous prosperity which has crowned the year now drawing to a close that its helpful and reassuring touch has been felt by all our people. It has been as wide as our country, and so special that every home has felt its comforting influence. It is too great to be the work of man's power and too particular to be the device of his mind. To God, the beneficent and the all-wise, who makes the labors of men to be fruitful, redeems their losses by His grace, and the measure of whose giving is as much beyond the thoughts of man as it is beyond his deserts, the praise and gratitude of the people of this favored nation are justly due.

Now, therefore, I, Benjamin Harrison, President of the United States of America, do hereby appoint Thursday, the 26th day of November present, to be a day of joyful thanksgiving to God for the bounties of His providence, for the peace in which we are permitted to enjoy them, and for the preservation of those institutions of civil and religious liberty which He gave our fathers the wisdom to devise and establish and us the courage to preserve. Among the appropriate observances of the day are rest from toil, worship in the public congregation, the renewal of family ties about our American firesides, and thoughtful helpfulness toward those who suffer lack of the body or of the spirit.

In testimony whereof I have hereunto set my hand and caused the seal of the United States to be affixed.

[SEAL.]   Done at the city of Washington, this 13th day of November, A. D. 1891, and of the Independence of the United States the one hundred and sixteenth.   BENJ. HARRISON.

By the President:

JAMES G. BLAINE, *Secretary of State.*

By the President of the United States of America.

A PROCLAMATION.

Whereas satisfactory proof has been given to me that no tonnage or light-house dues, or other equivalent tax or taxes, are imposed upon vessels of the United States in the ports of the island of Tobago, one of the British West India Islands:

Now, therefore, I, Benjamin Harrison, President of the United States of America, by virtue of the authority vested in me by section 11 of the act of Congress entitled "An act to abolish certain fees for official services to American vessels, and to amend the laws relating to shipping commissioners, seamen, and owners of vessels, and for other purposes," approved June 19, 1886, do hereby declare and proclaim that from and after the date of this my proclamation shall be suspended the collection of the whole of the tonnage duty which is imposed by said section of said act upon vessels entered in the ports of the United States from any of the ports of the island of Tobago.

Provided, That there shall be excluded from the benefits of the suspension hereby declared and proclaimed the vessels of any foreign country in whose ports the fees or dues of any kind or nature imposed on vessels of the United States, or the import or export duties on their cargoes, are in excess of the fees, dues, or duties imposed on the vessels of such country or on the cargoes of such vessels; but this proviso shall not be held to be inconsistent with the special regulation by foreign countries of duties and other charges on their own vessels, and the cargoes thereof, engaged in their coasting trade, or with the existence between such countries and other states of reciprocal stipulations founded on special conditions and equivalents, and thus not within the treatment of American vessels under the most-favored-nation clause in treaties between the United States and such countries.

And the suspension hereby declared and proclaimed shall continue so long as the reciprocal exemption of vessels belonging to citizens of the United States and their cargoes shall be continued in the said ports of the island of Tobago and no longer.

In witness whereof I have hereunto set my hand and caused the seal of the United States to be affixed.

[SEAL.] Done at the city of Washington, this 2d day of December, A. D. 1891, and of the Independence of the United States the one hundred and sixteenth.

BENJ. HARRISON.

By the President:
JAMES G. BLAINE,
Secretary of State.

EXECUTIVE ORDERS.

EXECUTIVE MANSION,
Washington, D. C., January 19, 1891.

The death of George Bancroft, which occurred in the city of Washington on Saturday, January 17, at 3.40 o'clock p. m., removes from among the living one of the most distinguished Americans. As an expression of the public loss and sorrow the flags of all the Executive Departments at Washington and the public buildings in the cities through which the funeral party is to pass will be placed at half-mast on to-morrow and until the body of this eminent statesman, scholar, and historian shall rest in the State that gave him to his country and to the world.

By direction of the President:

ELIJAH W. HALFORD, *Private Secretary.*

AMENDMENT OF CIVIL-SERVICE RULES.

JANUARY 26, 1891.

Special Departmental Rule No. 1 is hereby amended by adding to the exceptions from examination therein declared the following:

In the Department of Agriculture, in the office of the Secretary, division of illustration and engraving: One artist.

BENJ. HARRISON.

DEPARTMENT OF STATE,
Washington, January 30, 1891.

SIR:* The Hon. William Windom, Secretary of the Treasury of the United States, died suddenly last night, in the city of New York, at the hour of eleven minutes past 10 o'clock, in the sixty-fourth year of his age. Thus has passed away a man of pure life, an official of stainless integrity, distinguished by long and eminent service in both branches of Congress and by being twice called to administer the national finances. His death has caused deep regret throughout the country, while to the President and those associated with him in the administration of the Government it comes as a personal sorrow.

The President directs that all the Departments of the executive branch of the Government and the officers subordinate thereto shall manifest due respect to the memory of this eminent citizen in a manner consonant with the dignity of the office which he has honored by his devotion to public duty.

The President further directs that the Treasury Department in all its branches in this capital be draped in mourning for the period of thirty days, that on the day of the funeral the several Executive Departments

* Addressed to the heads of the Executive Departments, etc.

shall be closed, and that on all public buildings throughout the United States the national flag shall be displayed at half-mast.

Very respectfully,

JAMES G. BLAINE.

EXECUTIVE MANSION, *February 13, 1891.*

To the Heads of the Executive Departments:

In token of respect to the memory of Admiral David D. Porter, who died this morning, the President directs that the national flag be displayed at half-mast upon all public buildings throughout the United States until after his funeral shall have taken place, and that on the day of the funeral public business in the Departments at Washington be suspended.

E. W. HALFORD, *Private Secretary.*

GENERAL ORDERS No. 16.

HEADQUARTERS OF THE ARMY,
ADJUTANT-GENERAL'S OFFICE,
Washington, February 14, 1891.

I. The following order of the War Department is published to the Army:

WAR DEPARTMENT,
Washington, February 14, 1891.

The death of General Sherman is hereby announced in the fitting words of the President in his message to Congress:

[For message see p. 135.]

The following Executive order will be published to the Army:

EXECUTIVE MANSION,
Washington, D. C., February 14, 1891.

It is my painful duty to announce to the country that General William Tecumseh Sherman died this day at 1 o'clock and 50 minutes p. m., at his residence in the city of New York. The Secretary of War will cause the highest military honors to be paid to the memory of this distinguished officer. The national flag will be floated at half-mast over all public buildings until after the burial, and the public business will be suspended in the Executive Departments at the city of Washington and in the city where the interment takes place on the day of the funeral and in all places where public expression is given to the national sorrow during such hours as will enable every officer and employee to participate therein with their fellow-citizens.

BENJ. HARRISON.

The Major-General Commanding will issue the necessary orders to the Army.

It is ordered, That the War Department be draped in mourning for the period of thirty days, and that all business be suspended therein on the day of the funeral.

L. A. GRANT, *Acting Secretary of War.*

II. On the day of the funeral the troops at every military post will be paraded and this order read to them, after which all labors for the day will cease. The national flag will be displayed at half-staff from the time of the receipt of this order until the close of the funeral. On the day of the funeral a salute of seventeen guns will be fired at half-hour intervals, commencing at 8 o'clock a. m. The officers of the Army will wear the usual badges of mourning, and the colors of the several regiments and battalions will be draped in mourning for a period of six months.

The day and hour of the funeral will be communicated to department commanders by telegraph, and by them to their subordinate commanders. Other necessary orders will be issued hereafter relative to the appropriate funeral ceremonies.

By command of Major-General Schofield:

J. C. KELTON, *Adjutant-General.*

GENERAL ORDER.

NAVY DEPARTMENT, *February 16, 1891.*

The following Executive order, announcing the death of General William Tecumseh Sherman, is published for the information of the Navy and the Marine Corps:

[For Executive order see preceding page.]

In accordance with the order of the President, the Navy Department will be closed and all business suspended therein on the day of the funeral, and the flag at all yards and stations will be displayed at half-mast until after the burial of General Sherman, and in all places where public expression is given to the national sorrow business will be suspended at navy-yards or stations during such hours as will enable officers and employees of the Navy to participate therein with their fellow-citizens.

B. F. TRACY, *Secretary of the Navy.*

AMENDMENT OF CIVIL-SERVICE RULES.

FEBRUARY 18, 1891.

Special Departmental Rule No. 1 is hereby amended so as to include among the places excepted from examination therein the following:

In the Department of Agriculture, in the office of the Secretary: Private secretary to the chief of the division of statistics.

BENJ. HARRISON.

AMENDMENT OF CIVIL-SERVICE RULES.

FEBRUARY 21, 1891.

Special Departmental Rule No. 1 is hereby amended so as to include among the places excepted from examination therein the following:

In the Department of the Treasury, in the Coast and Geodetic Survey: Clerk to act as confidential clerk and cashier to the disbursing officer.

In the Post-Office Department, office of Assistant Attorney-General: Confidential clerk to the Assistant Attorney-General.

BENJ. HARRISON.

EXECUTIVE MANSION,
Washington, D. C., February 26, 1891.

In accordance with an act of Congress approved September 27, 1890, the following limits to the punishment of enlisted men, together with the accompanying regulations, are established for the government in time of peace of all courts-martial, and will take effect thirty days after the date of this order:

I. Subject to the modifications authorized in subdivision 3 of this section, the punishment for desertion shall not exceed the following:

1. In the case of a soldier who surrenders—

(*a*) When such surrender is made within thirty days after desertion, confinement at hard labor, with forfeiture of pay and allowances, for three months.

(*b*) When such surrender is made after an absence of more than thirty days and not more than ninety days, confinement at hard labor, with forfeiture of pay and allowances, for six months.

(*c*) When such surrender is made after an absence of more than ninety days, dishonorable discharge, with forfeiture of all pay and allowances, and confinement at hard labor for eighteen months: *Provided*, That in the case of a deserter who had not been more than three months in the service the confinement shall not exceed ten months.

2. In the case of a soldier who does not surrender—

(*a*) When at the time of desertion he shall have been less than three months in the service, dishonorable discharge, with forfeiture of all pay and allowances, and confinement at hard labor for one year.

(*b*) When at the time of desertion he shall have been three months or more, but less than six months, in the service, dishonorable discharge, with forfeiture of all pay and allowances, and confinement at hard labor for eighteen months.

(*c*) When at the time of desertion he shall have been six months or more in the service, dishonorable discharge, with forfeiture of all pay and allowances, and confinement at hard labor for two years and six months.

3. The foregoing limitations will be subject to modification under the following conditions:

(*a*) The punishment of a deserter may be increased by one year of confinement at hard labor in consideration of each previous conviction of desertion, and also by dishonorable discharge and forfeiture of all pay and allowances when not already authorized.

(*b*) The punishment for desertion when joined in by two or more soldiers in the execution of a conspiracy, or for desertion in the presence of an outbreak of Indians or of any unlawful assemblage which the troops may be opposing, shall not exceed dishonorable discharge, forfeiture of all pay and allowances, and confinement at hard labor for five years.

II. Except as herein otherwise indicated, punishments shall not exceed the limits prescribed in the following table:

Offenses.	Limit of punishment.
Under seventeenth article of war.	
Selling horse or arms, either or both	Three years' confinement at hard labor; for noncommissioned officer, reduction in addition thereto.*
Selling accouterments..............	Four months' confinement at hard labor; for noncommissioned officer, reduction in addition thereto.*
Selling clothing....................	Two months' confinement at hard labor; for noncommissioned officer, reduction in addition thereto.*
Losing or spoiling horse or arms through neglect.	Four months' confinement at hard labor; for noncommissioned officer, reduction in addition thereto.*
Losing or spoiling accouterments or clothing through neglect.	One month's confinement at hard labor; for noncommissioned officer, reduction in addition thereto.*
Under twentieth article of war.	
Behaving himself with disrespect toward his commanding officer.	Six months' confinement at hard labor and forfeiture of $10 per month for the same period; for noncommissioned officer, reduction in addition thereto.
Under twenty-fourth article of war.	
Refusal to obey or using violence to officer or roncommissioned officer while quelling quarrels or disorders.	Dishonorable discharge, with forfeiture of all pay and allowances, and imprisonment for 2 years.
Under thirty-first article of war.	
Lying out of quarters..............	Forfeiture of $2; corporal, $3; sergeant, $4.
Under thirty-second article of war.	
Absence without leave—	
Less than 1 hour (not including absence from a roll call).	Forfeiture of 50 cents; corporal, $1; sergeant, $2.
Less than 1 hour (including absence from a roll call).	Forfeiture of $1; corporal, $2; sergeant, $3; first sergeant or noncommissioned officer of higher grade, $4.
From 1 to 6 hours	Forfeiture of $2; corporal, $3; sergeant, $4; first sergeant or noncommissioned officer of higher grade, $5.
From 6 to 12 hours	Forfeiture of $3; corporal, $4; sergeant, $6; first sergeant or noncommissioned officer of higher grade, $7.
From 12 to 24 hours	Forfeiture of $5; corporal, $6; sergeant, $7; first sergeant or noncommissioned officer of higher grade, $10.

*In addition to the stoppages "sufficient for repairing the loss or damage," which the law requires the court-martial to adjudge. The court's action under this requirement in the case of sale or loss through neglect of clothing shall be limited to a confirmation of the charge made against the offender on his clothing account.

Offenses.	Limit of punishment.
Under thirty-second article of war—continued.	
Absence without leave—continued.	
From 24 to 48 hours	Forfeiture of $6 and 5 days' confinement at hard labor. For corporal, forfeiture of $8; sergeant, $10; first sergeant or noncommissioned officer of higher grade, $12; or for all noncommissioned officers, reduction.
From 2 to 9 days	Forfeiture of $10 and 10 days' confinement at hard labor; for noncommissioned officer, reduction in addition thereto.
From 10 to 29 days	Forfeiture of $20 and 1 month's confinement at hard labor; for noncommissioned officer, reduction in addition thereto.
From 30 to 90 days	Three months' confinement at hard labor and forfeiture of $10 per month for same period; for noncommissioned officer, reduction in addition thereto.
For more than 90 days.........	Dishonorable discharge and forfeiture of all pay and allowances and 3 months' confinement at hard labor.
Under thirty-third article of war.	
Failure to repair at the time fixed, etc., to the place of parade for—	
Reveille or retreat roll call	Forfeiture of 50 cents; corporal, $1; sergeant, $2; first sergeant, $3.
Guard detail	Forfeiture of $5; corporal, $8; sergeant, $10.
Fatigue detail...................	
Dress parade.....................	
The weekly inspection..........	
Target practice	Forfeiture of $2; corporal, $3; sergeant, $5.
Drill............................	
Guard mounting (by musician).	
Stable duty.....................	
Under thirty-eighth article of war.	
Drunkenness on—	
Guard	Six months' confinement at hard labor and forfeiture of $10 per month for the same period; for noncommissioned officer, reduction in addition thereto.
Duty as company cook..........	Forfeiture of $10.
Extra or special duty	
At drill.........................	
At target practice..............	
At parade	Forfeiture of $6; for noncommissioned officer, reduction and forfeiture of $10.
At inspection	
At inspection of company guard detail	
At stable duty	
Under fortieth article of war.	
Quitting guard	Six months' confinement at hard labor and forfeiture of $10 per month for the same period; for noncommissioned officer, reduction in addition thereto.
Under fifty-first article of war.	
Persuading soldiers to desert.......	Six months' confinement at hard labor and forfeiture of $10 per month for the same period; for noncommissioned officer, reduction in addition thereto.
Under sixtieth article of war	Dishonorable discharge, forfeiture of all pay and allowances, and 4 years' imprisonment.
Under sixty-second article of war.	
Manslaughter.....................	Dishonorable discharge, forfeiture of all pay and allowances, and 10 years' imprisonment.

Offenses.	Limit of punishment.
Under sixty-second article of war—continued.	
Assault with intent to kill..........	Dishonorable discharge, forfeiture of all pay and allowances, and 10 years' imprisonment.
Burglary	Dishonorable discharge, forfeiture of all pay and allowances, and 5 years' imprisonment.
Forgery ....,..........	Dishonorable discharge, forfeiture of all pay and allowances, and 4 years' imprisonment.
Perjury	Dishonorable discharge, forfeiture of all pay and allowances, and 4 years' imprisonment.
False swearing	Dishonorable discharge, forfeiture of all pay and allowances, and 2 years' imprisonment.
Robbery..............................	Dishonorable discharge, forfeiture of all pay and allowances, and 6 years' imprisonment.
Larceny or embezzlement of property of the value of—*	
More than $100.................	Dishonorable discharge, forfeiture of all pay and allowances, and 4 years' imprisonment.
$100 or less and more than $50..	Dishonorable discharge, forfeiture of all pay and allowances, and 3 years' imprisonment.
$50 or less and more than $20....	Dishonorable discharge, forfeiture of all pay and allowances, and 2 years' imprisonment.
$20 or less	Dishonorable discharge, forfeiture of all pay and allowances, and 1 year's imprisonment.
Disobedience of orders, involving willful defiance of the authority of a noncommissioned officer in charge of a guard or party.	Six months' confinement at hard labor and forfeiture of $10 per month for the same period; for noncommissioned officer, reduction in addition thereto.
Using threatening or insulting language or behaving in an insubordinate manner to a noncommissioned officer while in the execution of his office.	One month's confinement at hard labor and forfeiture of $10; for noncommissioned officer, reduction in addition thereto.
Absence from fatigue duty	Forfeiture of $4; corporal, $5; sergeant, $6.
Absence from extra or special duty.	Forfeiture of $4; corporal, $5; sergeant, $6.
Absence from duty as company or hospital cook.	Forfeiture of $10.
Introducing liquor into post or camp in violation of standing orders.	Forfeiture of $3; for noncommissioned officer, reduction and forfeiture of $5.
Drunkenness at post or in quarters.	Forfeiture of $3; for noncommissioned officer, reduction and forfeiture of $5.
Drunkenness and disorderly conduct, causing the offender's arrest and conviction by civil authorities at a place within 10 miles of his station.	Forfeiture of $10 and 7 days' confinement at hard labor; for noncommissioned officer, reduction and forfeiture of $12.
Noisy or disorderly conduct in quarters.	Forfeiture of $4; corporal, $7; sergeant, $10.
Abuse by noncommissioned officer of his authority over an inferior.	Reduction, 3 months' confinement at hard labor, and forfeiture of $10 per month for the same period.
Noncommissioned officer encouraging gambling.	Reduction and forfeiture of $5.
Noncommissioned officer making false report.	Reduction, forfeiture of $8, and 10 days' confinement at hard labor.
Sentinel allowing a prisoner under his charge to escape through neglect.	Six months' confinement at hard labor and forfeiture of $10 per month for the same period.

*In specifications to charges of larceny or embezzlement the value of the property shall be stated.

Offenses.	Limit of punishment.
Under sixty-second article of war—continued.	
Sentinel willfully suffering prisoner under his charge to escape.	Dishonorable discharge, forfeiture of all pay and allowances, and 1 year's imprisonment.
Sentinel allowing a prisoner under his charge to obtain liquor.	Two months' confinement at hard labor and forfeiture of $10 per month for the same period.
Sentinel or member of guard drinking liquor with prisoners.	Two months' confinement at hard labor and forfeiture of $10 per month for the same period.
Disrespect or affront to a sentinel..	Two months' confinement at hard labor and forfeiture of $10 per month for the same period; for noncommissioned officer, reduction in addition thereto.
Resisting or disobeying sentinel in lawful execution of his duty.	Six months' confinement at hard labor and forfeiture of $10 per month for the same period; for noncommissioned officer, reduction in addition thereto.
Lewd or indecent exposure of person.	Three months' confinement at hard labor and forfeiture of $10 per month for the same period; for noncommissioned officer, reduction in addition thereto.

III. (1) When a soldier shall be found guilty of an offense cognizable when committed for the first time by an inferior court-martial, his punishment therefor may exceed the prescribed limit by one-half if it shall appear that during his current enlistment and within two years preceding his trial he has been once convicted of one offense or more; it may be doubled if he has been twice so convicted, and it may be increased by one-half of the prescribed limit for every such previous conviction: *Provided*, That upon proof of five or more previous convictions the punishment may be that authorized for a fifth conviction, or dishonorable discharge with forfeiture of all pay and allowances. When found guilty of an offense cognizable only by a general court-martial, and on proof of five or more previous convictions within the two years, dishonorable discharge with forfeiture of all pay and allowances may be added to any confinement at hard labor. And when a noncommissioned officer shall be found guilty of an offense not punishable by reduction, reduction may be added to the punishment if it shall appear that he has been convicted of a military offense within one year and during his current enlistment.

(2) After arriving at the findings a court-martial may be opened to receive evidence of previous convictions. These convictions must be proved by the records of previous trials or by duly authenticated orders promulgating the same, showing the actual offenses of which the soldier was convicted, except in the cases of convictions by summary court, when a duly authenticated copy of the record of said court shall be deemed sufficient proof. Charges forwarded to the authority ordering a general court-martial or submitted to a summary garrison or regimental court must be accompanied by the proper evidence of such previous convictions as may have to be considered in determining upon a sentence. Paragraphs 1017 and 1018 of the Regulations are superseded by this order.

IV. This order prescribes the *maximum* limit of punishment for the offenses named, and this limit is intended for those cases where the severest punishment should be awarded. In other cases the punishment must be graded down according to the extenuating circumstances. Offenses not herein provided for remain punishable as authorized by the Articles of War and the custom of the service.

V. Summary courts are subject to the restrictions named in the eighty-third article of war. Soldiers against whom charges may be preferred for trial by summary court shall not be confined in the guardhouse, but shall be placed in arrest in quarters before and during trial and while awaiting sentence, unless in particular cases restraint may be deemed necessary.

VI. The following substitutions for punishments named in Section II of this order are authorized, at the discretion of the court:

Detention of pay to the extent of four times the amount of the forfeiture; two days' confinement at hard labor for $1 of forfeited pay; one day's solitary confinement on bread and water diet for two days' confinement at hard labor or for $1 of forfeited pay: *Provided*, That a noncommissioned officer not sentenced to reduction shall not be subject to confinement: *And provided*, That solitary confinement shall not exceed fourteen days at one time nor be repeated until fourteen days have elapsed, and shall not exceed eighty-four days in one year. Wherever the limit herein prescribed for an offense or offenses may be brought within the punishing power of inferior courts-martial, as defined by the eighty-third article of war, by substitution of punishment under the provisions of this section, the aforesaid courts shall be deemed to have jurisdiction of such offense or offenses.

VII. Sergeants shall not if they object thereto be brought to trial before regimental, garrison, or summary courts-martial without the authority of the officer competent to order their trial by general court-martial; nor shall sergeants of the post noncommissioned staff be reduced, but they may be dishonorably discharged whenever reduction is included in the limit of punishment. Paragraphs 105 and 254 of the Regulations, the latter as amended by General Orders, No. 67, series of 1890, Adjutant-General's Office, are modified accordingly.　　BENJ. HARRISON.

By the President:

REDFIELD PROCTOR, *Secretary of War.*

AMENDMENT OF CIVIL-SERVICE RULES.

MARCH 4, 1891.

Special Departmental Rule No. 1 is hereby amended so as to include among the places excepted from examination therein the following:

In the Department of Agriculture, in the office of the Secretary: Clerk to act as appointment clerk.　　BENJ. HARRISON.

AMENDMENT OF CIVIL-SERVICE RULES.

MARCH 16, 1891.

Special Departmental Rule No. 1 is hereby amended so as to include among the places excepted from examination therein the following:

In the Post-Office Department, office of the First Assistant Postmaster-General: Assistant superintenden: of free delivery. BENJ. HARRISON.

AMENDMENT OF CIVIL-SERVICE RULES.

APRIL 3, 1891.

Special Departmental Rule No. 1 is hereby amended so as to include among the places excepted from examination therein the following:

In the Treasury Department, office of the Secretary: One clerk in the office of the disbursing clerk. BENJ. HARRISON.

CIVIL SERVICE.—CLASSIFICATION OF INDIAN SERVICE.

DEPARTMENT OF THE INTERIOR,
Washington, April 13, 1891.

By direction of the President of the United States and in accordance with the third clause of section 6 of an act entitled "An act to regulate and improve the civil service of the United States," approved January 16, 1883—

It is ordered, That all physicians, school superintendents and assistant superintendents, school-teachers, and matrons in the Indian service be, and they are hereby, arranged in the following classes, without regard to salary or compensation:

Class 1. Physicians.
Class 2. School superintendents and assistant superintendents.
Class 3. School-teachers.
Class 4. Matrons.

Provided, That no person who may be required by law to be appointed to an office by and with the advice and consent of the Senate, and that no person who may be employed merely as a laborer or workman or in connection with any contract schools, shall be considered as within this classification, and no person so employed shall be assigned to the duties of a classified place.

It is further ordered, That no person shall be admitted to any place not excepted from examination by the civil-service rules in any of the classes above designated until he or she shall have passed an appropriate examination under the United States Civil Service Commission and his or her eligibility has been certified to by said Commission or the appropriate board of examiners.

JOHN W. NOBLE, *Secretary.*

EXECUTIVE MANSION, *April 13, 1891.*

The SECRETARY OF THE INTERIOR:

I approve of the within classification, and if you see no reason to suggest any further modification you will please put it in force.

BENJ. HARRISON.

AMENDMENTS OF CIVIL-SERVICE RULES.

APRIL 13, 1891.

Clause (*c*) of section 2 of General Rule III is hereby revoked, and clauses (*d*), (*e*), (*f*), (*g*), and (*h*) are lettered, respectively, (*c*), (*d*), (*e*), (*f*), and (*g*).

BENJ. HARRISON.

BY THE PRESIDENT OF THE UNITED STATES.

EXECUTIVE ORDER.

EXECUTIVE MANSION, *May 25, 1891.*

It is hereby ordered, That the several Executive Departments and the Government Printing Office be closed on Saturday, the 30th instant, to enable the employees to participate in the decoration of the graves of the soldiers and sailors who fell in defense of the Union during the War of the Rebellion.

BENJ. HARRISON.

EXECUTIVE MANSION,
Washington, D. C., July 6, 1891.

To the People of the United States:

The President, with a profound feeling of sorrow, announces the death of Hannibal Hamlin, at one time Vice-President of the United States, who died at Bangor, Me., on the evening of Saturday, July 4.

Few men in this country have filled more important and more distinguished public positions than Mr. Hamlin, and in recognition of his many eminent and varied services and as an expression of the great respect and reverence which are felt for his memory it is ordered that the national flag be displayed at half-mast upon the public buildings of the United States on the day of his funeral.

BENJ. HARRISON.

By the President:

WILLIAM F. WHARTON,
Acting Secretary of State.

AMENDMENTS OF CIVIL-SERVICE RULES.

EXECUTIVE MANSION, *August 6, 1891.*

The civil-service rules are hereby amended as follows:

GENERAL RULE II.

In line 1 strike out the word "four" and insert in lieu thereof the word "five." Add at the end of the rule the following:

5. The classified Indian service.

GENERAL RULE III.

Strike out paragraphs 1 and 2 of section 6 of General Rule III and insert in lieu thereof the following:

So far as practicable and useful, competitive examinations shall be established in the classified civil service to test fitness for promotion, under such regulations as the Commission may make. Until such regulations have been applied to any part of the classified service promotions therein shall be made in the manner prescribed by the rule applicable thereto.

DEPARTMENTAL RULE VI.

Strike out the first sentence of section 6 and transfer the remaining sentence to section 5. Change the numbers of sections 7, 8, 9, and 10 to 6, 7, 8, and 9, respectively.

CUSTOMS RULE III.

Strike out the first sentence of section 5 and transfer the remaining sentence to section 4. Change the numbers of sections 6, 7, 8, and 9 to 5, 6, 7, and 8, respectively.

POSTAL RULE III.

Strike out the first sentence of section 5 and transfer the remaining sentence to section 4. Change the numbers of sections 6, 7, 8, and 9 to 5, 6, 7, and 8, respectively.

RAILWAY MAIL RULE III.

Strike out the first sentence of section 7 and transfer the remaining sentence to section 4. Change the numbers of sections 8, 9, 10, 11, and 12 to 7, 8, 9, 10, and 11, respectively.

RAILWAY MAIL RULE II.

Insert an additional clause to section 5, as follows:

(*f*) Transfer clerks at junction points or stations where not more than two such clerks are employed.

RAILWAY MAIL RULE IV.

Insert an additional proviso at the end of clause (*b*) of section 2, as follows:

Provided further, That on a line on which the service does not require the full time of a clerk, and one can be employed jointly with the railroad company, the appointment may be made without examination and certification, with the consent of the Commission, upon a statement of the facts by the General Superintendent; but no clerk so appointed shall be eligible for transfer or appointment to any other place in the service.

In section 6, line 3, strike out the word "twenty" and insert in lieu thereof the word "ten."

In section 7, line 6, strike out the word "thirty" and insert in lieu thereof the word "sixty;" in the same line strike out the word "to" and insert in lieu thereof the words "in periods of;" in line 7 strike out the words "who have been in the railway mail service."

BENJ. HARRISON.

CIVIL SERVICE.—INDIAN RULES.

INDIAN RULE I.

The classified Indian service shall include all the physicians, school superintendents, assistant superintendents, school-teachers, and matrons in that service, classified under the provisions of section 6 of the act to regulate and improve the civil service of the United States, approved January 16, 1883.

INDIAN RULE II.

1. To test fitness for admission to the classified Indian service examinations of a practical character shall be provided on such subjects as the Commission may direct for physician, superintendent, assistant superintendent, teachers, and matrons.

2. The following age limitations shall apply to applicants for examination for the classified Indian service: For physician, not under 25 years of age nor over 45; for superintendent, not under 25 nor over 50; for assistant superintendent and for teacher, not under 20 nor over 50; for matron, not under 25 nor over 55: *Provided*, That these limitations shall not apply to the wives of superintendents of Indian schools who apply for the position of matron, nor shall the maximum limitations apply to persons allowed preference under section 1754, Revised Statutes, by the Commission.

3. Blank forms of application shall be furnished by the Commission, and the date of reception and also of approval by the Commission of each application shall be noted on the application paper.

INDIAN RULE III.

1. The papers of every examination shall be marked under regulations made by the Commission. Each competitor shall be graded on a scale of 100, according to the general average determined by the markings.

2. Immediately after the general average shall have been ascertained each competitor shall be notified that he has passed or has failed to pass.

3. A competitor who has failed to pass an examination may, with the consent of the Commission, be allowed reexamination at any time within six months from the date of failure without filing a new application; but if he be not allowed reexamination within six months he shall be required to file a new application before being again examined.

4. No eligible shall be allowed reexamination during the period of his eligibility unless he shall furnish satisfactory evidence to the Commission that at the time of his examination, because of illness or other good cause, he was incapable of doing himself justice; and his rating on such reexamination shall cancel and be a substitute for his rating on his former examination.

5. All competitors whose claim to preference under section 1754 of the Revised Statutes have been allowed by the Commission who attain a general average of 65 per cent or over, and all other competitors who attain a general average of 70 per cent or over, shall be eligible for appointment to the place for which they were examined. The names of all the competitors thus rendered eligible shall be entered in the order of grade on the proper register of eligibles.

6. When two or more eligibles are of the same grade, preference in certification shall be determined by the order in which the application papers are filed.

7. For the Indian service there shall be four districts and a separate register of eligibles for each grade of examination for each district, the names of males and females being listed separately on each register. The districts shall be comprised as follows: No. 1, of the States of Michigan, Wisconsin, Minnesota, Iowa, Nebraska, North Dakota, South Dakota, Montana, and Wyoming; No. 2, of the States of Idaho, Washington, Oregon, Nevada, and that part of California lying north of the thirty-seventh parallel of latitude, and the Territory of Utah; No. 3, of that part of California lying south of the thirty-seventh parallel of latitude, the Territories of Arizona, New Mexico, Oklahoma, the Indian Territory, and the States of Colorado, Kansas, Missouri, Arkansas, Louisiana, and Texas; No. 4, of all the States of the United States not embraced in any of the foregoing districts, together with the District of Columbia. Upon the written request of any eligible his name shall be entered upon the register of any one or more of the districts other than that in which he resides: *Provided*, That he shall state in writing his willingness to accept service wherever assigned in any such district.

8. The period of eligibility to appointment shall be one year from the date on which the name of the eligible is entered on the register unless otherwise determined by regulation of the Commission.

INDIAN RULE IV.

1. All vacancies, unless filled by promotion, transfer, or reappointment, shall be filled in the following manner:

(*a*) The Commissioner of Indian Affairs, through the Secretary of the Interior, shall, in form and manner to be prescribed by the Commission, request the certification to him of male or female eligibles from the district in which the vacancy exists.

(*b*) If fitness for the vacant place is tested by competitive examination, the Commission shall certify from the proper register of the district in which the vacancy exists the names of the three eligibles thereon of the sex called for having the highest averages: *Provided*, That the eligibles upon any register who have been allowed preference under section 1754 of the Revised Statutes shall be certified according to their grade before all other eligibles thereon: *And provided further*, That if the vacancy is in the grade of matron or teacher, and the wife of the superintendent of the school in which the vacancy exists is an eligible, she may be given preference in certification if the appointing officer so requests.

2. Of the three names certified to him the appointing officer shall select one, and if at the time of making this selection there are more vacancies than one he may select more than one: *Provided*, That if the appointing officer to whom certification has been made shall object in writing to any eligible named in the certificate, stating that because of physical incapacity or for other good cause particularly specified such eligible is not capable of properly performing the duties of the vacant place, the Commission may, upon investigation and ascertainment of the fact that the objection made is good and well founded, direct the certification of another eligible in place of the one objected to.

3. Each person thus designated for appointment shall be notified, and upon indicating acceptance shall be appointed for a probationary period—if a physician, for six months, and if a school employee, to expire at the end of the then current school year—at the end of which period, if his conduct and capacity be satisfactory to the appointing officer, he shall receive absolute appointment; but if his conduct and capacity be not satisfactory to said officer he shall be so notified, and this notification shall be his discharge from the service: *Provided*, That any probationer may be discharged during probation for misconduct or evident unfitness or incapacity.

4. The Commissioner of Indian Affairs shall require the officer under whom a probationer may be serving to carefully observe and report in writing upon the services rendered by and the character and qualifications of such probationer as to punctuality, industry, habits, ability, and adaptability. These reports shall be preserved on file, and the Commission may prescribe the form and manner in which they shall be made.

5. In case of the sudden occurrence of a vacancy in any school during a school term which the public interest requires to be immediately filled, the Commissioner of Indian Affairs is authorized, in his discretion, to provide for the temporary filling of the same until a regular appointment can be made under the provisions of sections 1, 2, and 3 of this rule, and when such regular appointment is made the temporary appointment shall terminate. All temporary appointments made under this authority and their termination shall at once be reported to the Commission.

INDIAN RULE V.

Until promotion regulations shall have been applied to the classified Indian service promotions therein may be made upon any test of fitness determined upon by the promoting officer if not disapproved by the Commission: *Provided*, That preference in promotion in any school shall be given to those longest in the service unless there are good reasons to the contrary; and when such reasons prevail they shall, through the proper channels, be reported to the Commission: *And provided further*, That no one shall be promoted to any grade he could not enter by original appointment under the minimum age limitation applied thereto by Indian Rule II, section 2, and that no one shall be promoted to the grade of physician from any other grade.

INDIAN RULE VI.

Subject to the conditions stated in Rule IV, transfers may be made after absolute appointment from one school to another and from one district to another under such regulations as the Commissioner of Indian Affairs, with the approval of the Secretary of the Interior, may prescribe.

INDIAN RULE VII.

Upon the requisition of the Commissioner of Indian Affairs, through the Secretary of the Interior, the Commission shall certify for reinstatement in a grade or class no higher than that in which he was formerly employed any person who within one year next preceding the date of the requisition has through no delinquency or misconduct been separated from the classified Indian service: *Provided*, That certification may be made, subject to the other conditions of this rule, for the reinstatement of any person who served in the military or naval service of the United States in the late War of the Rebellion and was honorably discharged therefrom, without regard to the length of time he has been separated from the service.

INDIAN RULE VIII.

The Commissioner of Indian Affairs shall report to the Commission—

(*a*) Every probational and every absolute appointment in the classified Indian service.

(*b*) Every refusal to make an absolute appointment and the reason therefor, and every refusal to accept an appointment.

(*c*) Every separation from the classified Indian service and the cause of such separation, whether death, resignation, or dismissal.

(*d*) Every restoration to the classified Indian service.

These rules shall take effect October 1, 1891.

BENJ. HARRISON.

AMENDMENT OF CIVIL-SERVICE RULES.

OCTOBER 9, 1891.

General Rule III, clause 6, is hereby amended by striking out the words "under such regulations as the Commission may make" and substituting therefor the following: "under regulations to be approved by the President;" so that as amended the clause will read as follows:

So far as practicable and useful competitive examinations shall be established in the classified civil service to test fitness for promotion under regulations to be approved by the President.

BENJ. HARRISON.

Whereas civil-service rules for the Indian service were approved to take effect October 1, 1891; and

Whereas it is represented to me by the Civil Service Commission in a communication of this date that no persons have as yet been examined for appointment to that service, and that it seems probable that complete arrangements for putting said rules into full effect will not be made sooner than March 1, 1892:

It is therefore ordered, That said Indian rules shall take effect March 1, 1892, instead of October 1, 1891: *Provided,* That said rules shall become operative and take effect in any district of the Indian service as soon as an eligible register for such district shall be provided, if it shall be prior to the date above fixed.

EXECUTIVE MANSION, *October 13, 1891.*

Upon the recommendation of the Commission the foregoing order is approved.

BENJ. HARRISON.

AMENDMENT OF CIVIL-SERVICE RULES.

NOVEMBER 24, 1891.

Special Departmental Rule No. 1 is hereby amended so as to include among the places excepted from examination the following:

In the Department of the Treasury, in the Bureau of Statistics: One confidential clerk to the Chief of the Bureau.

BENJ. HARRISON.

EXECUTIVE MANSION,
Washington, December 4, 1891.

SIR:* In my message to the first session of the Fifty-first Congress I said:

I have suggested to the heads of the Executive Departments that they consider whether a record might not be kept in each bureau of all those elements that are covered by the terms "faithfulness" and "efficiency," and a rating made showing the relative merits of the clerks of each class, this rating to be regarded as a test of merit in making promotions.

*Addressed to the heads of the Executive Departments.

In some of the Departments this suggestion has been acted upon in part at least, and I now direct that in your Department a plan be at once devised and put in operation for keeping an efficiency record of all persons within the classified service, with a view to placing promotions wholly upon the basis of merit.

It is intended to make provision for carrying into effect the stipulations of the civil-service law in relation to promotions in the classified service. To that end the rule requiring compulsory examination has been rescinded. In my opinion the examination for promotion of those who present themselves should be chiefly, if not wholly, upon their knowledge of the work of the bureau or Department to which they belong and the record of efficiency made by them during their previous service. I think the records of efficiency kept from day to day should be open to the inspection of the clerks.

Very respectfully, yours,

BENJ. HARRISON.

THIRD ANNUAL MESSAGE.

EXECUTIVE MANSION, *December 9, 1891.*

To the Senate and House of Representatives:

The reports of the heads of the several Executive Departments, required by law to be submitted to me, which are herewith transmitted, and the reports of the Secretary of the Treasury and the Attorney-General, made directly to Congress, furnish a comprehensive view of the administrative work of the last fiscal year relating to internal affairs. It would be of great advantage if these reports could have an attentive perusal by every member of Congress and by all who take an interest in public affairs. Such a perusal could not fail to excite a higher appreciation of the vast labor and conscientious effort which are given to the conduct of our civil administration.

The reports will, I believe, show that every question has been approached, considered, and decided from the standpoint of public duty and upon considerations affecting the public interests alone. Again I invite to every branch of the service the attention and scrutiny of Congress.

The work of the State Department during the last year has been characterized by an unusual number of important negotiations and by diplomatic results of a notable and highly beneficial character. Among these are the reciprocal trade arrangements which have been concluded, in the exercise of the powers conferred by section 3 of the tariff law, with the Republic of Brazil, with Spain for its West India possessions, and with Santo Domingo. Like negotiations with other countries have been much

advanced, and it is hoped that before the close of the year further definitive trade arrangements of great value will be concluded.

In view of the reports which had been received as to the diminution of
the seal herds in the Bering Sea, I deemed it wise to propose to Her
Majesty's Government in February last that an agreement for a closed
season should be made pending the negotiations for arbitration, which
then seemed to be approaching a favorable conclusion. After much correspondence and delays, for which this Government was not responsible,
an agreement was reached and signed on the 15th of June, by which Great
Britain undertook from that date and until May 1, 1892, to prohibit the
killing by her subjects of seals in the Bering Sea, and the Government of
the United States during the same period to enforce its existing prohibition against pelagic sealing and to limit the catch by the fur-seal company
upon the islands to 7,500 skins. If this agreement could have been
reached earlier in response to the strenuous endeavors of this Government, it would have been more effective; but coming even as late as it
did it unquestionably resulted in greatly diminishing the destruction of
the seals by the Canadian sealers.

In my last annual message I stated that the basis of arbitration proposed by Her Majesty's Government for the adjustment of the long-
pending controversy as to the seal fisheries was not acceptable. I am
glad now to be able to announce that terms satisfactory to this Government have been agreed upon and that an agreement as to the arbitrators
is all that is necessary to the completion of the convention. In view of
the advanced position which this Government has taken upon the subject of international arbitration, this renewed expression of our adherence
to this method for the settlement of disputes such as have arisen in the
Bering Sea will, I doubt not, meet with the concurrence of Congress.

Provision should be made for a joint demarcation of the frontier line
between Canada and the United States wherever required by the increasing border settlements, and especially for the exact location of the water
boundary in the straits and rivers.

I should have been glad to announce some favorable disposition of
the boundary dispute between Great Britain and Venezuela touching the
western frontier of British Guiana, but the friendly efforts of the United
States in that direction have thus far been unavailing. This Government
will continue to express its concern at any appearance of foreign encroachment on territories long under the administrative control of American
States. The determination of a disputed boundary is easily attainable by
amicable arbitration where the rights of the respective parties rest, as
here, on historic facts readily ascertainable.

The law of the last Congress providing a system of inspection for our
meats intended for export, and clothing the President with power to
exclude foreign products from our market in case the country sending
them should perpetuate unjust discriminations against any product of the

United States, placed this Government in a position to effectively urge the removal of such discriminations against our meats. It is gratifying to be able to state that Germany, Denmark, Italy, Austria, and France, in the order named, have opened their ports to inspected American pork products. The removal of these restrictions in every instance was asked for and given solely upon the ground that we have now provided a meat inspection that should be accepted as adequate to the complete removal of the dangers, real or fancied, which had been previously urged. The State Department, our ministers abroad, and the Secretary of Agriculture have cooperated with unflagging and intelligent zeal for the accomplishment of this great result. The outlines of an agreement have been reached with Germany looking to equitable trade concessions in consideration of the continued free importation of her sugars, but the time has not yet arrived when this correspondence can be submitted to Congress.

The recent political disturbances in the Republic of Brazil have excited regret and solicitude. The information we possessed was too meager to enable us to form a satisfactory judgment of the causes leading to the temporary assumption of supreme power by President Fonseca; but this Government did not fail to express to him its anxious solicitude for the peace of Brazil and for the maintenance of the free political institutions which had recently been established there, nor to offer our advice that great moderation should be observed in the clash of parties and the contest for leadership. These counsels were received in the most friendly spirit, and the latest information is that constitutional government has been reestablished without bloodshed.

The lynching at New Orleans in March last of eleven men of Italian nativity by a mob of citizens was a most deplorable and discreditable incident. It did not, however, have its origin in any general animosity to the Italian people, nor in any disrespect to the Government of Italy, with which our relations were of the most friendly character. The fury of the mob was directed against these men as the supposed participants or accessories in the murder of a city officer. I do not allude to this as mitigating in any degree this offense against law and humanity, but only as affecting the international questions which grew out of it. It was at once represented by the Italian minister that several of those whose lives had been taken by the mob were Italian subjects, and a demand was made for the punishment of the participants and for an indemnity to the families of those who were killed. It is to be regretted that the manner in which these claims were presented was not such as to promote a calm discussion of the questions involved; but this may well be attributed to the excitement and indignation which the crime naturally evoked. The views of this Government as to its obligations to foreigners domiciled here were fully stated in the correspondence, as well as its purpose to make an investigation of the affair with a view to determine whether there were present any circumstances that could under such rules of duty as we had indicated create an obligation upon the United States. The temporary absence of a minister plenipotentiary of Italy at this capital has retarded the further correspondence, but it is not doubted that a friendly conclusion is attainable.

Some suggestions growing out of this unhappy incident are worthy the attention of Congress. It would, I believe, be entirely competent for Congress to make offenses against the treaty rights of foreigners domiciled in the United States cognizable in the Federal courts. This has not, however, been done, and the Federal officers and courts have no power in such cases to intervene, either for the protection of a foreign citizen or for the punishment of his slayers. It seems to me to follow, in this state of the law, that the officers of the State charged with police and judicial powers in such cases must in the consideration of international questions growing out of such incidents be regarded in such sense as Federal agents as to make this Government answerable for their acts in cases where it would be answerable if the United States had used its constitutional power to define and punish crime against treaty rights.

The civil war in Chile, which began in January last, was continued, but fortunately with infrequent and not important armed collisions, until August 28, when the Congressional forces landed near Valparaiso and after a bloody engagement captured that city. President Balmaceda at once recognized that his cause was lost, and a Provisional Government was speedily established by the victorious party. Our minister was promptly directed to recognize and put himself in communication with this Government so soon as it should have established its *de facto* character, which was done. During the pendency of this civil contest frequent indirect appeals were made to this Government to extend belligerent rights to the insurgents and to give audience to their representatives. This was declined, and that policy was pursued throughout which this Government when wrenched by civil war so strenuously insisted upon on the part of European nations. The *Itata*, an armed vessel commanded by a naval officer of the insurgent fleet, manned by its sailors and with soldiers on board, was seized under process of the United States court at San Diego, Cal., for a violation of our neutrality laws. While in the custody of an officer of the court the vessel was forcibly wrested from his control and put to sea. It would have been inconsistent with the dignity and self-respect of this Government not to have insisted that the *Itata* should be returned to San Diego to abide the judgment of the court. This was so clear to the junta of the Congressional party, established at Iquique, that before the arrival of the *Itata* at that port the secretary of foreign relations of the Provisional Government addressed to Rear-Admiral Brown, commanding the United States naval forces, a communication, from which the following is an extract:

The Provisional Government has learned by the cablegrams of the Associated Press that the transport *Itata*, detained in San Diego by order of the United States for taking on board munitions of war, and in possession of the marshal, left the port, carrying on board this official, who was landed at a point near the coast, and then continued her voyage. * * * If this news be correct this Government would deplore the conduct of the *Itata*, and as an evidence that it is not disposed to support or agree to the infraction of the laws of the United States the undersigned takes advantage of the personal relations you have been good enough to maintain with him since your arrival in this port to declare to you that as soon as she is within reach of our orders his Government will put the *Itata*, with the arms and munitions she took on board in San Diego, at the disposition of the United States.

A trial in the district court of the United States for the southern district of California has recently resulted in a decision holding, among other things, that inasmuch as the Congressional party had not been recognized as a belligerent the acts done in its interest could not be a violation of our neutrality laws. From this judgment the United States has appealed, not that the condemnation of the vessel is a matter of importance, but that we may know what the present state of our law is; for if this construction of the statute is correct there is obvious necessity for revision and amendment.

During the progress of the war in Chile this Government tendered its good offices to bring about a peaceful adjustment, and it was at one time hoped that a good result might be reached; but in this we were disappointed.

The instructions to our naval officers and to our minister at Santiago from the first to the last of this struggle enjoined upon them the most impartial treatment and absolute noninterference. I am satisfied that these instructions were observed and that our representatives were always watchful to use their influence impartially in the interest of humanity, and on more than one occasion did so effectively. We could not forget, however, that this Government was in diplomatic relations with the then established Government of Chile, as it is now in such relations with the successor of that Government. I am quite sure that President Montt, who has, under circumstances of promise for the peace of Chile, been installed as President of that Republic, will not desire that in the unfortunate event of any revolt against his authority the policy of this Government should be other than that which we have recently observed. No official complaint of the conduct of our minister or of our naval officers during the struggle has been presented to this Government, and it is a matter of regret that so many of our own people should have given ear to unofficial charges and complaints that manifestly had their origin in rival interests and in a wish to pervert the relations of the United States with Chile.

The collapse of the Government of Balmaceda brought about a condition which is unfortunately too familiar in the history of the Central and South American States. With the overthrow of the Balmaceda Government he and many of his councilors and officers became at once fugitives for their lives, and appealed to the commanding officers of the foreign naval vessels in the harbor of Valparaiso and to the resident foreign ministers at Santiago for asylum. This asylum was freely given, according to my information, by the naval vessels of several foreign powers and by several of the legations at Santiago. The American minister as well as his colleagues, acting upon the impulse of humanity, extended asylum to political refugees whose lives were in peril. I have not been willing to direct the surrender of such of these persons as are still in the American legation without suitable conditions.

It is believed that the Government of Chile is not in a position, in view of the precedents with which it has been connected, to broadly deny the right of asylum, and the correspondence has not thus far presented any such denial. The treatment of our minister for a time was such as to call for a decided protest, and it was very gratifying to observe that unfriendly measures, which were undoubtedly the result of the prevailing excitement, were at once rescinded or suitably relaxed.

On the 16th of October an event occurred in Valparaiso so serious and tragic in its circumstances and results as to very justly excite the indignation of our people and to call for prompt and decided action on the part of this Government. A considerable number of the sailors of the United States steamship *Baltimore*, then in the harbor at Valparaiso, being upon shore leave and unarmed, were assaulted by armed men nearly simultaneously in different localities in the city. One petty officer was killed outright and seven or eight seamen were seriously wounded, one of whom has since died. So savage and brutal was the assault that several of our sailors received more than two and one as many as eighteen stab wounds. An investigation of the affair was promptly made by a board of officers of the *Baltimore*, and their report shows that these assaults were unprovoked, that our men were conducting themselves in a peaceable and orderly manner, and that some of the police of the city took part in the assault and used their weapons with fatal effect, while a few others, with some well-disposed citizens, endeavored to protect our men. Thirty-six of our sailors were arrested, and some of them while being taken to prison were cruelly beaten and maltreated. The fact that they were all discharged, no criminal charge being lodged against any one of them, shows very clearly that they were innocent of any breach of the peace.

So far as I have yet been able to learn no other explanation of this bloody work has been suggested than that it had its origin in hostility to those men as sailors of the United States, wearing the uniform of their Government, and not in any individual act or personal animosity. The attention of the Chilean Government was at once called to this affair, and a statement of the facts obtained by the investigation we had conducted was submitted, accompanied by a request to be advised of any other or qualifying facts in the possession of the Chilean Government that might tend to relieve this affair of the appearance of an insult to this Government. The Chilean Government was also advised that if such qualifying facts did not exist this Government would confidently expect full and prompt reparation.

It is to be regretted that the reply of the secretary for foreign affairs of the Provisional Government was couched in an offensive tone. To this no response has been made. This Government is now awaiting the result of an investigation which has been conducted by the criminal court at Valparaiso. It is reported unofficially that the investigation is about completed, and it is expected that the result will soon be communicated to this Government, together with some adequate and satisfactory response to the note by which the attention of Chile was called to this incident. If these just expectations should be disappointed or further needless delay intervene, I will by a special message bring this matter again to the attention of Congress for such action as may be necessary. The entire correspondence with the Government of Chile will at an early day be submitted to Congress.

I renew the recommendation of my special message dated January 16, 1890,* for the adoption of the necessary legislation to enable this Government to apply in the case of Sweden and Norway the same rule in respect to the levying of tonnage dues as was claimed and secured to the shipping of the United States in 1828 under Article VIII of the treaty of 1827.

The adjournment of the Senate without action on the pending acts for the suppression of the slave traffic in Africa and for the reform of the revenue tariff of the Independent State of the Kongo left this Government unable to exchange those acts on the date fixed, July 2, 1891. A *modus vivendi* has been concluded by which the power of the Kongo State to levy duties on imports is left unimpaired, and by agreement of all the signatories to the general slave-trade act the time for the exchange of ratifications on the part of the United States has been extended to February 2, 1892.

The late outbreak against foreigners in various parts of the Chinese Empire has been a cause of deep concern in view of the numerous establishments of our citizens in the interior of that country. This Government can do no less than insist upon a continuance of the protective and punitory measures which the Chinese Government has heretofore applied. No effort will be omitted to protect our citizens peaceably sojourning in China, but recent unofficial information indicates that what was at first regarded as an outbreak of mob violence against foreigners has assumed the larger form of an insurrection against public order.

The Chinese Government has declined to receive Mr. Blair as the minister of the United States on the ground that as a participant while a Senator in the enactment of the existing legislation against the introduction of Chinese laborers he has become unfriendly and objectionable to China. I have felt constrained to point out to the Chinese Government

* See pp. 59-60.

the untenableness of this position, which seems to rest as much on the unacceptability of our legislation as on that of the person chosen, and which if admitted would practically debar the selection of any representative so long as the existing laws remain in force.

You will be called upon to consider the expediency of making special provision by law for the temporary admission of some Chinese artisans and laborers in connection with the exhibit of Chinese industries at the approaching Columbian Exposition. I regard it as desirable that the Chinese exhibit be facilitated in every proper way.

A question has arisen with the Government of Spain touching the rights of American citizens in the Caroline Islands. Our citizens there long prior to the confirmation of Spain's claim to the islands had secured by settlement and purchase certain rights to the recognition and maintenance of which the faith of Spain was pledged. I have had reason within the past year very strongly to protest against the failure to carry out this pledge on the part of His Majesty's ministers, which has resulted in great injustice and injury to the American residents.

The Government and people of Spain propose to celebrate the four hundredth anniversary of the discovery of America by holding an exposition at Madrid, which will open on the 12th of September and continue until the 31st of December, 1892. A cordial invitation has been extended to the United States to take part in this commemoration, and as Spain was one of the first nations to express the intention to participate in the World's Columbian Exposition at Chicago, it would be very appropriate for this Government to give this invitation its friendly promotion.

Surveys for the connecting links of the projected intercontinental railway are in progress, not only in Mexico, but at various points along the course mapped out. Three surveying parties are now in the field under the direction of the commission. Nearly 1,000 miles of the proposed road have been surveyed, including the most difficult part, that through Ecuador and the southern part of Colombia. The reports of the engineers are very satisfactory, and show that no insurmountable obstacles have been met with.

On November 12, 1884, a treaty was concluded with Mexico reaffirming the boundary between the two countries as described in the treaties of February 2, 1848, and December 30, 1853. March 1, 1889, a further treaty was negotiated to facilitate the carrying out of the principles of the treaty of 1884 and to avoid the difficulties occasioned by reason of the changes and alterations that take place from natural causes in the Rio Grande and Colorado rivers in the portions thereof constituting the boundary line between the two Republics. The International Boundary Commission provided for by the treaty of 1889 to have exclusive jurisdiction of any question that may arise has been named by the Mexican Government. An appropriation is necessary to enable the United States to fulfill its treaty obligations in this respect.

The death of King Kalakaua in the United States afforded occasion to testify our friendship for Hawaii by conveying the King's body to his own land in a naval vessel with all due honors. The Government of his successor, Queen Liliuokalani, is seeking to promote closer commercial relations with the United States. Surveys for the much-needed submarine cable from our Pacific coast to Honolulu are in progress, and this enterprise should have the suitable promotion of the two Governments. I strongly recommend that provision be made for improving the harbor of Pearl River and equipping it as a naval station.

The arbitration treaty formulated by the International American Conference lapsed by reason of the failure to exchange ratifications fully within the limit of time provided; but several of the Governments concerned have expressed a desire to save this important result of the conference by an extension of the period. It is, in my judgment, incumbent upon the United States to conserve the influential initiative it has taken in this measure by ratifying the instrument and by advocating the proposed extension of the time for exchange. These views have been made known to the other signatories.

This Government has found occasion to express in a friendly spirit, but with much earnestness, to the Government of the Czar its serious concern because of the harsh measures now being enforced against the Hebrews in Russia. By the revival of antisemitic laws, long in abeyance, great numbers of those unfortunate people have been constrained to abandon their homes and leave the Empire by reason of the impossibility of finding subsistence within the pale to which it is sought to confine them. The immigration of these people to the United States—many other countries being closed to them—is largely increasing and is likely to assume proportions which may make it difficult to find homes and employment for them here and to seriously affect the labor market. It is estimated that over 1,000,000 will be forced from Russia within a few years. The Hebrew is never a beggar; he has always kept the law—life by toil—often under severe and oppressive civil restrictions. It is also true that no race, sect, or class has more fully cared for its own than the Hebrew race. But the sudden transfer of such a multitude under conditions that tend to strip them of their small accumulations and to depress their energies and courage is neither good for them nor for us.

The banishment, whether by direct decree or by not less certain indirect methods, of so large a number of men and women is not a local question. A decree to leave one country is in the nature of things an order to enter another—some other. This consideration, as well as the suggestion of humanity, furnishes ample ground for the remonstrances which we have presented to Russia, while our historic friendship for that Government can not fail to give the assurance that our representations are those of a sincere wellwisher.

The annual report of the Maritime Canal Company of Nicaragua shows that much costly and necessary preparatory work has been done during the year in the construction of shops, railroad tracks, and harbor piers and breakwaters, and that the work of canal construction has made some progress.

I deem it to be a matter of the highest concern to the United States that this canal, connecting the waters of the Atlantic and Pacific oceans and giving to us a short water communication between our ports upon those two great seas, should be speedily constructed and at the smallest practicable limit of cost. The gain in freights to the people and the direct saving to the Government of the United States in the use of its naval vessels would pay the entire cost of this work within a short series of years. The report of the Secretary of the Navy shows the saving in our naval expenditures which would result.

The Senator from Alabama (Mr. Morgan) in his argument upon this subject before the Senate at the last session did not overestimate the importance of this work when he said that "the canal is the most important subject now connected with the commercial growth and progress of the United States."

If this work is to be promoted by the usual financial methods and without the aid of this Government, the expenditures in its interest-bearing securities and stock will probably be twice the actual cost. This will necessitate higher tolls and constitute a heavy and altogether needless burden upon our commerce and that of the world. Every dollar of the bonds and stock of the company should represent a dollar expended in the legitimate and economical prosecution of the work. This is only possible by giving to the bonds the guaranty of the United States Government. Such a guaranty would secure the ready sale at par of a 3 per cent bond from time to time as the money was needed. I do not doubt that built upon these business methods the canal would when fully inaugurated earn its fixed charges and operating expenses. But if its bonds are to be marketed at heavy discounts and every bond sold is to be accompanied by a gift of stock, as has come to be expected by investors in such enterprises, the traffic will be seriously burdened to pay interest and dividends. I am quite willing to recommend Government promotion in the prosecution of a work which, if no other means offered for securing its completion, is of such transcendent interest that the Government should, in my opinion, secure it by direct appropriations from its Treasury.

A guaranty of the bonds of the canal company to an amount necessary to the completion of the canal could, I think, be so given as not to involve any serious risk of ultimate loss. The things to be carefully guarded are the completion of the work within the limits of the guaranty, the subrogation of the United States to the rights of the first-mortgage bondholders for any amounts it may have to pay, and in the meantime a control of the stock of the company as a security against mismanagement and loss. I most sincerely hope that neither party nor sectional lines will be drawn upon this great American project, so full of interest to the people of all our States and so influential in its effects upon the prestige and prosperity of our common country.

The island of Navassa, in the West Indian group, has, under the provisions of Title VII of the Revised Statutes, been recognized by the President as appertaining to the United States. It contains guano deposits, is owned by the Navassa Phosphate Company, and is occupied solely by its employees. In September, 1889, a revolt took place among these laborers, resulting in the killing of some of the agents of the company, caused, as the laborers claimed, by cruel treatment. These men were arrested and tried in the United States court at Baltimore, under section 5576 of the statute referred to, as if the offenses had been committed on board a merchant vessel of the United States on the high seas. There appeared on the trial and otherwise came to me such evidences of the bad treatment of the men that in consideration of this and of the fact that the men had no access to any public officer or tribunal for protection or the redress of their wrongs I commuted the death sentences that had been passed by the court upon three of them. In April last my attention was again called to this island and to the unregulated condition of things there by a letter from a colored laborer, who complained that he was wrongfully detained upon the island by the phosphate company after the expiration of his contract of service. A naval vessel was sent to examine into the case of this man and generally into the condition of things on the island. It was found that the laborer referred to had been detained beyond the contract limit and that a condition of revolt again existed among the laborers. A board of naval officers reported, among other things, as follows:

We would desire to state further that the discipline maintained on the island seems to be that of a convict establishment without its comforts and cleanliness, and that until more attention is paid to the shipping of laborers by placing it under Government supervision to prevent misunderstanding and misrepresentation, and until some amelioration is shown in the treatment of the laborers, these disorders will be of constant occurrence.

I recommend legislation that shall place labor contracts upon this and other islands having the relation that Navassa has to the United States under the supervision of a court commissioner, and that shall provide at the expense of the owners an officer to reside upon the island, with power to judge and adjust disputes and to enforce a just and humane treatment of the employees. It is inexcusable that American laborers should be left within our own jurisdiction without access to any Government officer or tribunal for their protection and the redress of their wrongs.

International copyright has been secured, in accordance with the conditions of the act of March 3, 1891, with Belgium, France, Great Britain and the British possessions, and Switzerland, the laws of those countries permitting to our citizens the benefit of copyright on substantially the same basis as to their own citizens or subjects.

With Germany a special convention has been negotiated upon this subject which will bring that country within the reciprocal benefits of our legislation.

The general interest in the operations of the Treasury Department has been much augmented during the last year by reason of the conflicting predictions, which accompanied and followed the tariff and other legislation of the last Congress affecting the revenues, as to the results of this legislation upon the Treasury and upon the country. On the one hand it was contended that imports would so fall off as to leave the Treasury bankrupt and that the prices of articles entering into the living of the people would be so enhanced as to disastrously affect their comfort and happiness, while on the other it was argued that the loss to the revenue, largely the result of placing sugar on the free list, would be a direct gain to the people; that the prices of the necessaries of life, including those most highly protected, would not be enhanced; that labor would have a larger market and the products of the farm advanced prices, while the Treasury surplus and receipts would be adequate to meet the appropriations, including the large exceptional expenditures for the refunding to the States of the direct tax and the redemption of the 4½ per cent bonds.

It is not my purpose to enter at any length into a discussion of the effects of the legislation to which I have referred; but a brief examination of the statistics of the Treasury and a general glance at the state of business throughout the country will, I think, satisfy any impartial inquirer that its results have disappointed the evil prophecies of its opponents and in a large measure realized the hopeful predictions of its friends. Rarely, if ever before, in the history of the country has there been a time when the proceeds of one day's labor or the product of one farmed acre would purchase so large an amount of those things that enter into the living of the masses of the people. I believe that a full test will develop the fact that the tariff act of the Fifty-first Congress is very favorable in its average effect upon the prices of articles entering into common use.

During the twelve months from October 1, 1890, to September 30, 1891, the total value of our foreign commerce (imports and exports combined) was $1,747,806,406, which was the largest of any year in the history of the United States. The largest in any previous year was in 1890, when our commerce amounted to $1,647,139,093, and the last year exceeds this enormous aggregate by over one hundred millions. It is interesting, and to some will be surprising, to know that during the year ending September 30, 1891, our imports of merchandise amounted to $824,715,270, which was an increase of more than $11,000,000 over the value of the imports of the corresponding months of the preceding year, when the imports of merchandise were unusually large in anticipation of the tariff legislation then pending. The average annual value of the imports of merchandise for the ten years from 1881 to 1890 was $692,186,522, and during the year ending September 30, 1891, this annual average was exceeded by $132,528,469.

The value of free imports during the twelve months ending September 30, 1891, was $118,092,387 more than the value of free imports during the corresponding twelve months of the preceding year, and there was during the same period a decrease of $106,846,508 in the value of imports of dutiable merchandise. The percentage of merchandise admitted free of duty during the year to which I have referred, the first under the new tariff, was 48.18, while during the preceding twelve months, under the old tariff, the percentage was 34.27, an increase of 13.91 per cent. If we take the six months ending September 30 last, which covers the time during which sugars have been admitted free of duty, the per cent of value of merchandise imported free of duty is found to be 55.37, which is a larger percentage of free imports than during any prior fiscal year in the history of the Government.

If we turn to exports of merchandise, the statistics are full of gratification. The value of such exports of merchandise for the twelve months ending September 30, 1891, was $923,091,136, while for the corresponding previous twelve months it was $860,177,115, an increase of $62,914,021, which is nearly three times the average annual increase of exports of merchandise for the preceding twenty years. This exceeds in amount and value the exports of merchandise during any year in the history of the Government. The increase in the value of exports of agricultural products during the year referred to over the corresponding twelve months of the prior year was $45,846,197, while the increase in the value of exports of manufactured products was $16,838,240.

There is certainly nothing in the condition of trade, foreign or domestic, there is certainly nothing in the condition of our people of any class, to suggest that the existing tariff and revenue legislation bears oppressively upon the people or retards the commercial development of the nation. It may be argued that our condition would be better if tariff legislation were upon a free-trade basis; but it can not be denied that all the conditions of prosperity and of general contentment are present in a larger degree than ever before in our history, and that, too, just when it was prophesied they would be in the worst state. Agitation for radical changes in tariff and financial legislation can not help but may seriously impede business, to the prosperity of which some degree of stability in legislation is essential.

I think there are conclusive evidences that the new tariff has created several great industries, which will within a few years give employment to several hundred thousand American working men and women. In view of the somewhat overcrowded condition of the labor market of the United States, every patriotic citizen should rejoice at such a result.

The report of the Secretary of the Treasury shows that the total receipts of the Government from all sources for the fiscal year ending June 30, 1891, were $458,544,233.03, while the expenditures for the same period were $421,304,470.46, leaving a surplus of $37,239,762.57.

The receipts of the fiscal year ending June 30, 1892, actual and estimated, are $433,000,000 and the expenditures $409,000,000. For the fiscal year ending June 30, 1893, the estimated receipts are $455,336,350 and the expenditures $441,300,093.

Under the law of July 14, 1890, the Secretary of the Treasury has purchased (since August 13) during the fiscal year 48,393,113 ounces of silver bullion at an average cost of $1.045 per ounce. The highest price paid during the year was $1.2025 and the lowest $0.9636. In exchange for this silver bullion there have been issued $50,577,498 of the Treasury notes authorized by the act. The lowest price of silver reached during the fiscal year was $0.9636 on April 22, 1891; but on November 1 the market price was only $0.96, which would give to the silver dollar a bullion value of 74¼ cents.

Before the influence of the prospective silver legislation was felt in the market silver was worth in New York about $0.955 per ounce. The ablest advocates of free coinage in the last Congress were most confident in their predictions that the purchases by the Government required by the law would at once bring the price of silver to $1.2929 per ounce, which would make the bullion value of a dollar 100 cents and hold it there. The prophecies of the antisilver men of disasters to result from the coinage of $2,000,000 per month were not wider of the mark. The friends of free silver are not agreed, I think, as to the causes that brought their hopeful predictions to naught. Some facts are known. The exports of silver from London to India during the first nine months of this calendar year fell off over 50 per cent, or $17,202,730, compared with the same months of the preceding year. The exports of domestic silver bullion from this country, which had averaged for the last ten years over $17,000,000, fell in the last fiscal year to $13,797,391, while for the first time in recent years the imports of silver into this country exceeded the exports by the sum of $2,745,365. In the previous year the net exports of silver from the United States amounted to $8,545,455. The production of the United States increased from 50,000,000 ounces in 1889 to 54,500,000 in 1890. The Government is now buying and putting aside annually 54,000,000 ounces, which, allowing for 7,140,000 ounces of new bullion used in the arts, is 6,640,000 more than our domestic products available for coinage.

I hope the depression in the price of silver is temporary and that a further trial of this legislation will more favorably affect it. That the increased volume of currency thus supplied for the use of the people was needed and that beneficial results upon trade and prices have followed this legislation I think must be very clear to everyone. Nor should it be forgotten that for every dollar of these notes issued a full dollar's worth of silver bullion is at the time deposited in the Treasury as a security for its redemption. Upon this subject, as upon the tariff, my recommendation is that the existing laws be given a full trial and that our business interests be spared the distressing influence which threats of radical changes always impart. Under existing legislation it is in the power of the Treasury Department to maintain that essential condition of national finance as well as of commercial prosperity—the parity in use of the coined dollars and their paper representatives. The assurance that these powers would be freely and unhesitatingly used has done much to produce and sustain the present favorable business conditions.

I am still of the opinion that the free coinage of silver under existing conditions would disastrously affect our business interests at home and abroad. We could not hope to maintain an equality in the purchasing power of the gold and silver dollar in our own markets, and in foreign trade the stamp gives no added value to the bullion contained in coins. The producers of the country, its farmers and laborers, have the highest interest that every dollar, paper or coin, issued by the Government shall be as good as any other. If there is one less valuable than another, its sure and constant errand will be to pay them for their toil and for their crops. The money lender will protect himself by stipulating for payment in gold, but the laborer has never been able to do that. To place business upon a silver basis would mean a sudden and severe contraction of the currency by the withdrawal of gold and gold notes and such an unsettling of all values as would produce a commercial panic. I can not believe that a people so strong and prosperous as ours will promote such a policy.

The producers of silver are entitled to just consideration, but they should not forget that the Government is now buying and putting out of the market what is the equivalent of the entire product of our silver mines. This is more than they themselves thought of asking two years ago. I believe it is the earnest desire of a great majority of the people, as it is mine, that a full coin use shall be made of silver just as soon as the cooperation of other nations can be secured and a ratio fixed that will give circulation equally to gold and silver. The business of the world requires the use of both metals; but I do not see any prospect of gain, but much of loss, by giving up the present system, in which a full use is made of gold and a large use of silver, for one in which silver alone will circulate. Such an event would be at once fatal to the further progress of the silver movement. Bimetallism is the desired end, and the true friends of silver will be careful not to overrun the goal and bring in silver monometallism with its necessary attendants—the loss of our gold to Europe and the relief of the pressure there for a larger currency. I have endeavored by the use of official and unofficial agencies to keep a close observation of the state of public sentiment in Europe upon this question and have not found it to be such as to justify me in proposing an international conference. There is, however, I am sure, a growing sentiment in Europe in favor of a larger use of silver, and I know of no more effectual way of promoting this sentiment than by accumulating gold here. A scarcity of gold in the European reserves will be the most persuasive argument for the use of silver.

The exports of gold to Europe, which began in February last and continued until the close of July, aggregated over $70,000,000. The net loss of gold during the fiscal year was nearly $68,000,000. That no serious monetary disturbance resulted was most gratifying and gave to Europe fresh evidence of the strength and stability of our financial institutions. With the movement of crops the outflow of gold was speedily stopped and a return set in. Up to December 1 we had recovered of our gold lost at the port of New York $27,854,000, and it is confidently believed that during the winter and spring this aggregate will be steadily and largely increased.

The presence of a large cash surplus in the Treasury has for many years been the subject of much unfavorable criticism, and has furnished an argument to those who have desired to place the tariff upon a purely revenue basis. It was agreed by all that the withdrawal from circulation of so large an amount of money was an embarrassment to the business of the country and made necessary the intervention of the Department at frequent intervals to relieve threatened monetary panics. The surplus on March 1, 1889, was $183,827,190.29. The policy of applying this surplus to the redemption of the interest-bearing securities of the United States was thought to be preferable to that of depositing it without interest in selected national banks. There have been redeemed since the date last mentioned of interest-bearing securities $259,079,350, resulting in a reduction of the annual interest charge of $11,684,675. The money which had been deposited in banks without interest has been gradually withdrawn and used in the redemption of bonds.

The result of this policy, of the silver legislation, and of the refunding of the 4½ per cent bonds has been a large increase of the money in circulation. At the date last named the circulation was $1,404,205,896, or $23.03 per capita, while on the 1st day of December, 1891, it had increased to $1,577,262,070, or $24.38 per capita. The offer of the Secretary of the Treasury to the holders of the 4½ per cent bonds to extend the time of redemption, at the option of the Government, at an interest of 2 per cent, was accepted by the holders of about one-half the amount, and the unextended bonds are being redeemed on presentation.

The report of the Secretary of War exhibits the results of an intelligent, progressive, and businesslike administration of a Department which has been too much regarded as one of mere routine. The separation of Secretary Proctor from the Department by reason of his appointment as a Senator from the State of Vermont is a source of **great regret** to me and to his colleagues in the Cabinet, as I am sure it will be to all those who have had business with the Department while under his charge.

In the administration of army affairs some especially good work has been accomplished. The efforts of the Secretary to reduce the percentage of desertions by removing the causes that promoted it have been so successful as to enable him to report for the last year a lower percentage of desertion than has been before reached in the history of the Army. The resulting money saving is considerable, but the improvement in the morale of the enlisted men is the most valuable incident of the reforms which have brought about this result.

The work of securing sites for shore batteries for harbor defense and the manufacture of mortars and guns of high power to equip them have made good progress during the year. The preliminary work of tests and plans which so long delayed a start is now out of the way. Some guns have been completed, and with an enlarged shop and a more complete equipment at Watervliet the Army will soon be abreast of the Navy in gun construction. Whatever unavoidable causes of delay may arise, there should be none from delayed or insufficient appropriations. We shall be greatly embarrassed in the proper distribution and use of naval vessels until adequate shore defenses are provided for our harbors.

I concur in the recommendation of the Secretary that the three-battalion organization be adopted for the infantry. The adoption of a smokeless powder and of a modern rifle equal in range, precision, and rapidity of fire to the best now in use will, I hope, not be longer delayed.

The project of enlisting Indians and organizing them into separate companies upon the same basis as other soldiers was made the subject of very careful study by the Secretary and received my approval. Seven companies have been completely organized and seven more are in process of organization. The results of six months' training have more than realized the highest anticipations. The men are readily brought under discipline, acquire the drill with facility, and show great pride in the right discharge of their duty and perfect loyalty to their officers, who declare that they would take them into action with confidence. The discipline, order, and cleanliness of the military posts will have a wholesome and elevating influence upon the men enlisted, and through them upon their tribes, while a friendly feeling for the whites and a greater respect for the Government will certainly be promoted.

The great work done in the Record and Pension Division of the War Department by Major Ainsworth, of the Medical Corps, and the clerks under him is entitled to honorable mention. Taking up the work with nearly 41,000 cases behind, he closed the last fiscal year without a single case left over, though the new cases had increased 52 per cent in number over the previous year by reason of the pension legislation of the last Congress.

I concur in the recommendation of the Attorney-General that the right in felony cases to a review by the Supreme Court be limited. It would seem that personal liberty would have a safe guaranty if the right of review in cases involving only fine and imprisonment were limited to the circuit court of appeals, unless a constitutional question should in some way be involved.

The judges of the Court of Private Land Claims, provided for by the act of March 3, 1891, have been appointed and the court organized. It is now possible to give early relief to communities long repressed in their development by unsettled land titles and to establish the possession and right of settlers whose lands have been rendered valueless by adverse and unfounded claims.

The act of July 9, 1888, provided for the incorporation and management of a reform school for girls in the District of Columbia; but it has remained inoperative for the reason that no appropriation has been made for construction or maintenance. The need of such an institution is very urgent. Many girls could be saved from depraved lives by the wholesome influences and restraints of such a school. I recommend that the necessary appropriation be made for a site and for construction.

The enforcement by the Treasury Department of the law prohibiting the coming of Chinese to the United States has been effective as to such as seek to land from vessels entering our ports. The result has been to divert the travel to vessels entering the ports of British Columbia, whence passage into the United States at obscure points along the Dominion boundary is easy. A very considerable number of Chinese laborers have during the past year entered the United States from Canada and Mexico.

The officers of the Treasury Department and of the Department of Justice have used every means at their command to intercept this immigration; but the impossibility of perfectly guarding our extended frontier is apparent. The Dominion government collects a head tax of $50 from every Chinaman entering Canada, and thus derives a considerable revenue from those who only use its ports to reach a position of advantage to evade our exclusion laws. There seems to be satisfactory evidence that the business of passing Chinamen through Canada to the United States is organized and quite active. The Department of Justice has construed the laws to require the return of any Chinaman found to be unlawfully in this country to China as the country from which he came, notwithstanding the fact that he came by way of Canada; but several of the district courts have in cases brought before them overruled this view of the law and decided that such persons must be returned to Canada. This construction robs the law of all effectiveness, even if the decrees could be executed, for the men returned can the next day recross our border. But the only appropriation made is for sending them back to China, and the Canadian officials refuse to allow them to reenter

Canada without the payment of the fifty-dollar head tax.   I recommend such legislation as will remedy these defects in the law.

In previous messages I have called the attention of Congress to the necessity of so extending the jurisdiction of the United States courts as to make triable therein any felony committed while in the act of violating a law of the United States.   These courts can not have that independence and effectiveness which the Constitution contemplates so long as the felonious killing of court officers, jurors, and witnesses in the discharge of their duties or by reason of their acts as such is only cognizable in the State courts.   The work done by the Attorney-General and the officers of his Department, even under the present inadequate legislation, has produced some notable results in the interest of law and order.

The Attorney-General and also the Commissioners of the District of Columbia call attention to the defectiveness and inadequacy of the laws relating to crimes against chastity in the District of Columbia.   A stringent code upon this subject has been provided by Congress for Utah, and it is a matter of surprise that the needs of this District should have been so long overlooked.

In the report of the Postmaster-General some very gratifying results are exhibited and many betterments of the service suggested.   A perusal of the report gives abundant evidence that the supervision and direction of the postal system have been characterized by an intelligent and conscientious desire to improve the service.   The revenues of the Department show an increase of over $5,000,000, with a deficiency for the year 1892 of less than $4,000,000, while the estimate for the year 1893 shows a surplus of receipts over expenditures.

Ocean mail post-offices have been established upon the steamers of the North German Lloyd and Hamburg lines, saving by the distribution on shipboard from two to fourteen hours' time in the delivery of mail at the port of entry and often much more than this in the delivery at interior places.   So thoroughly has this system, initiated by Germany and the United States, evidenced its usefulness that it can not be long before it is installed upon all the great ocean mail-carrying steamships.

Eight thousand miles of new postal service has been established upon railroads, the car distribution to substations in the great cities has been increased about 12 per cent, while the percentage of errors in distribution has during the past year been reduced over one-half.   An appropriation was given by the last Congress for the purpose of making some experiments in free delivery in the smaller cities and towns.   The results of these experiments have been so satisfactory that the Postmaster-General recommends, and I concur in the recommendation, that the free-delivery system be at once extended to towns of 5,000 population.   His discussion of the inadequate facilities extended under our present system to rural communities and his suggestions with a view to give these communities a fuller participation in the benefits of the postal service are worthy of your careful consideration. It is not just that the farmer, who receives his mail at a neighboring town, should not only be compelled to send to the post-office for it, but to pay a considerable rent for a box in which to place it or to wait his turn at a general-delivery window, while the city resident has his mail brought to his door. It is stated that over 54,000 neighborhoods are under the present system receiving mail at post-offices where money orders and postal notes are not issued. The extension of this system to these communities is especially desirable, as the patrons of such offices are not possessed of the other facilities offered in more populous communities for the transmission of small sums of money.

I have in a message to the preceding Congress expressed my views as to a modified use of the telegraph in connection with the postal service.* In pursuance of the ocean mail law of March 3, 1891, and after a most careful study of the whole subject and frequent conferences with ship-owners, boards of trade, and others, advertisements were issued by the Postmaster-General for 53 lines of ocean mail service—10 to Great Britain and the Continent, 27 to South America, 3 to China and Japan, 4 to Australia and the Pacific islands, 7 to the West Indies, and 2 to Mexico. It was not, of course, expected that bids for all these lines would be received or that service upon them all would be contracted for. It was intended, in furtherance of the act, to secure as many new lines as possible, while including in the list most or all of the foreign lines now occupied by American ships. It was hoped that a line to England and perhaps one to the Continent would be secured; but the outlay required to equip such lines wholly with new ships of the first class and the difficulty of establishing new lines in competition with those already established deterred bidders whose interest had been enlisted. It is hoped that a way may yet be found of overcoming these difficulties.

The Brazil Steamship Company, by reason of a miscalculation as to the speed of its vessels, was not able to bid under the terms of the advertisement. The policy of the Department was to secure from the established lines an improved service as a condition of giving to them the benefits of the law. This in all instances has been attained. The Postmaster-General estimates that an expenditure in American shipyards of about $10,000,000 will be necessary to enable the bidders to construct the ships called for by the service which they have accepted. I do not think there is any reason for discouragement or for any turning back from the policy of this legislation. Indeed, a good beginning has been made, and as the subject is further considered and understood by capitalists and shipping people new lines will be ready to meet future proposals, and we may date from the passage of this law the revival of American shipping interests and the recovery of a fair share of the carrying trade of the world. We were receiving for foreign postage nearly $2,000,000 under the old

*See p. 127.

system, and the outlay for ocean mail service did not exceed $600,000 per annum. It is estimated by the Postmaster-General that if all the contracts proposed are completed it will require $247,354 for this year in addition to the appropriation for sea and inland postage already in the estimates, and that for the next fiscal year, ending June 30, 1893, there would probably be needed about $560,000.

The report of the Secretary of the Navy shows a gratifying increase of new naval vessels in commission. The *Newark, Concord, Bennington,* and *Miantonomoh* have been added during the year, with an aggregate of something more than 11,000 tons. Twenty-four warships of all classes are now under construction in the navy-yards and private shops; but while the work upon them is going forward satisfactorily, the completion of the more important vessels will yet require about a year's time. Some of the vessels now under construction, it is believed, will be triumphs of naval engineering. When it is recollected that the work of building a modern navy was only initiated in the year 1883, that our naval constructors and shipbuilders were practically without experience in the construction of large iron or steel ships, that our engine shops were unfamiliar with great marine engines, and that the manufacture of steel forgings for guns and plates was almost wholly a foreign industry, the progress that has been made is not only highly satisfactory, but furnishes the assurance that the United States will before long attain in the construction of such vessels, with their engines and armaments, the same preeminence which it attained when the best instrument of ocean commerce was the clipper ship and the most impressive exhibit of naval power the old wooden three-decker man-of-war. The officers of the Navy and the proprietors and engineers of our great private shops have responded with wonderful intelligence and professional zeal to the confidence expressed by Congress in its liberal legislation. We have now at Washington a gun shop, organized and conducted by naval officers, that in its system, economy, and product is unexcelled. Experiments with armor plate have been conducted during the year with most important results. It is now believed that a plate of higher resisting power than any in use has been found and that the tests have demonstrated that cheaper methods of manufacture than those heretofore thought necessary can be used.

I commend to your favorable consideration the recommendations of the Secretary, who has, I am sure, given to them the most conscientious study. There should be no hesitation in promptly completing a navy of the best modern type large enough to enable this country to display its flag in all seas for the protection of its citizens and of its extending commerce. The world needs no assurance of the peaceful purposes of the United States, but we shall probably be in the future more largely a competitor in the commerce of the world, and it is essential to the dignity of this nation and to that peaceful influence which it should exercise on this hemisphere that its Navy should be adequate both upon the shores of the Atlantic and of the Pacific.

The report of the Secretary of the Interior shows that a very gratifying progress has been made in all of the bureaus which make up that complex and difficult Department.

The work in the Bureau of Indian Affairs was perhaps never so large as now, by reason of the numerous negotiations which have been proceeding with the tribes for a reduction of the reservations, with the incident labor of making allotments, and was never more carefully conducted. The provision of adequate school facilities for Indian children and the locating of adult Indians upon farms involve the solution of the "Indian question." Everything else—rations, annuities, and tribal negotiations, with the agents, inspectors, and commissioners who distribute and conduct them—must pass away when the Indian has become a citizen, secure in the individual ownership of a farm from which he derives his subsistence by his own labor, protected by and subordinate to the laws which govern the white man, and provided by the General Government or by the local communities in which he lives with the means of educating his children. When an Indian becomes a citizen in an organized State or Territory, his relation to the General Government ceases in great measure to be that of a ward; but the General Government ought not at once to put upon the State or Territory the burden of the education of his children.

It has been my thought that the Government schools and school buildings upon the reservations would be absorbed by the school systems of the States and Territories; but as it has been found necessary to protect the Indian against the compulsory alienation of his land by exempting him from taxation for a period of twenty-five years, it would seem to be right that the General Government, certainly where there are tribal funds in its possession, should pay to the school fund of the State what would be equivalent to the local school tax upon the property of the Indian. It will be noticed from the report of the Commissioner of Indian Affairs that already some contracts have been made with district schools for the education of Indian children. There is great advantage, I think, in bringing the Indian children into mixed schools. This process will be gradual, and in the meantime the present educational provisions and arrangements, the result of the best experience of those who have been charged with this work, should be continued. This will enable those religious bodies that have undertaken the work of Indian education with so much zeal and with results so restraining and beneficent to place their institutions in new and useful relations to the Indian and to his white neighbors.

The outbreak among the Sioux which occurred in December last is as to its causes and incidents fully reported upon by the War Department and the Department of the Interior. That these Indians had some just complaints, especially in the matter of the reduction of the appropriation for rations and in the delays attending the enactment of laws to enable the Department to perform the engagements entered into with them, is probably true; but the Sioux tribes are naturally warlike and turbulent, and their warriors were excited by their medicine men and chiefs, who preached the coming of an Indian messiah who was to give them power to destroy their enemies. In view of the alarm that prevailed among the white settlers near the reservation and of the fatal consequences that would have resulted from an Indian incursion, I placed at the disposal of General Miles, commanding the Division of the Missouri, all such forces as were thought by him to be required. He is entitled to the credit of having given thorough protection to the settlers and of bringing the hostiles into subjection with the least possible loss of life.

The appropriation of $2,991,450 for the Choctaws and Chickasaws contained in the general Indian appropriation bill of March 3, 1891, has not been expended, for the reason that I have not yet approved a release (to the Government) of the Indian claim to the lands mentioned. This matter will be made the subject of a special message, placing before Congress all the facts which have come to my knowledge.

The relation of the Five Civilized Tribes now occupying the Indian Territory to the United States is not, I believe, that best calculated to promote the highest advancement of these Indians. That there should be within our borders five independent states having no relations, except those growing out of treaties, with the Government of the United States, no representation in the National Legislature, its people not citizens, is a startling anomaly.

It seems to me to be inevitable that there shall be before long some organic changes in the relation of these people to the United States. What form these changes should take I do not think it desirable now to suggest, even if they were well defined in my own mind. They should certainly involve the acceptance of citizenship by the Indians and a representation in Congress. These Indians should have opportunity to present their claims and grievances upon the floor rather than, as now, in the lobby. If a commission could be appointed to visit these tribes to confer with them in a friendly spirit upon this whole subject, even if no agreement were presently reached the feeling of the tribes upon this question would be developed, and discussion would prepare the way for changes which must come sooner or later.

The good work of reducing the larger Indian reservations by allotments in severalty to the Indians and the cession of the remaining lands to the United States for disposition under the homestead law has been prosecuted during the year with energy and success. In September last I was enabled to open to settlement in the Territory of Oklahoma 900,000 acres of land, all of which was taken up by settlers in a single day. The rush for these lands was accompanied by a great deal of excitement, but was happily free from incidents of violence.

It was a source of great regret that I was not able to open at the same time the surplus lands of the Cheyenne and Arapahoe Reservation, amounting to about 3,000,000 acres, by reason of the insufficiency of the appropriation for making the allotments. Deserving and impatient settlers are waiting to occupy these lands, and I urgently recommend that a special deficiency appropriation be promptly made of the small amount needed, so that the allotments may be completed and the surplus lands opened in time to permit the settlers to get upon their homesteads in the early spring.

During the past summer the Cherokee Commission have completed arrangements with the Wichita, Kickapoo, and Tonkawa tribes whereby, if the agreements are ratified by Congress, over 800,000 additional acres will be opened to settlement in Oklahoma.

The negotiations for the release by the Cherokees of their claim to the Cherokee Strip have made no substantial progress so far as the Department is officially advised, but it is still hoped that the cession of this large and valuable tract may be secured. The price which the commission was authorized to offer—$1.25 per acre—is, in my judgment, when all the circumstances as to title and the character of the lands are considered, a fair and adequate one, and should have been accepted by the Indians.

Since March 4, 1889, about 23,000,000 acres have been separated from Indian reservations and added to the public domain for the use of those who desired to secure free homes under our beneficent laws. It is difficult to estimate the increase of wealth which will result from the conversion of these waste lands into farms, but it is more difficult to estimate the betterment which will result to the families that have found renewed hope and courage in the ownership of a home and the assurance of a comfortable subsistence under free and healthful conditions. It is also gratifying to be able to feel, as we may, that this work has proceeded upon lines of justice toward the Indian, and that he may now, if he will, secure to himself the good influences of a settled habitation, the fruits of industry, and the security of citizenship.

Early in this Administration a special effort was begun to bring up the work of the General Land Office. By faithful work the arrearages have been rapidly reduced. At the end of the last fiscal year only 84,172 final agricultural entries remained undisposed of, and the Commissioner reports that with the present force the work can be fully brought up by the end of the next fiscal year.

Your attention is called to the difficulty presented by the Secretary of the Interior as to the administration of the law of March 3, 1891, establishing a Court of Private Land Claims. The small holdings intended to be protected by the law are estimated to be more than 15,000 in number. The claimants are a most deserving class and their titles are supported by the strongest equities. The difficulty grows out of the fact that the lands have largely been surveyed according to our methods, while the holdings, many of which have been in the same family for generations, are laid out in narrow strips a few rods wide upon a stream and running back to the hills for pasturage and timber. Provision should be made for numbering these tracts as lots and for patenting them by such numbers and without reference to section lines.

The administration of the Pension Bureau has been characterized during the year by great diligence. The total number of pensioners upon the roll on the 30th day of June, 1891, was 676,160. There were allowed during the fiscal year ending at that time 250,565 cases. Of this number 102,387 were allowed under the law of June 27, 1890. The issuing of certificates has been proceeding at the rate of about 30,000 per month, about 75 per cent of these being cases under the new law. The Commissioner expresses the opinion that he will be able to carefully adjudicate and allow 350,000 claims during the present fiscal year. The appropriation for the payment of pensions for the fiscal year 1890-91 was $127,685,793.89 and the amount expended $118,530,649.25, leaving an unexpended surplus of $9,155,144.64.

The Commissioner is quite confident that there will be no call this year for a deficiency appropriation, notwithstanding the rapidity with which the work is being pushed. The mistake which has been made by many in their exaggerated estimates of the cost of pensions is in not taking account of the diminished value of first payments under the recent legislation. These payments under the general law have been for many years very large, as the pensions when allowed dated from the time of filing the claim, and most of these claims had been pending for years. The first payments under the law of June, 1890, are relatively small, and as the per cent of these cases increases and that of the old cases diminishes the annual aggregate of first payments is largely reduced. The Commissioner, under date of November 13, furnishes me with the statement that during the last four months 113,175 certificates were issued, 27,893 under the general law and 85,282 under the act of June 27, 1890. The average first payment during these four months was $131.85, while the average first payment upon cases allowed during the year ending June 30, 1891, was $239.33, being a reduction in the average first payments during these four months of $107.48.

The estimate for pension expenditures for the fiscal year ending June 30, 1893, is $144,956,000, which, after a careful examination of the subject, the Commissioner is of the opinion will be sufficient. While these disbursements to the disabled soldiers of the great Civil War are large, they do not realize the exaggerated estimates of those who oppose this beneficent legislation. The Secretary of the Interior shows with great fullness the care that is taken to exclude fraudulent claims, and also the gratifying fact that the persons to whom these pensions are going are men who rendered not slight but substantial war service.

The report of the Commissioner of Railroads shows that the total debt of the subsidized railroads to the United States was on December 31, 1890, $112,512,613.06. A large part of this debt is now fast approaching maturity, with no adequate provision for its payment. Some policy for dealing with this debt with a view to its ultimate collection should be at once adopted. It is very difficult, well-nigh impossible, for so large a body as the Congress to conduct the necessary negotiations and investigations. I therefore recommend that provision be made for the appointment of a commission to agree upon and report a plan for dealing with this debt.

The work of the Census Bureau is now far in advance and the great bulk of the enormous labor involved completed. It will be more strictly a statistical exhibit and less encumbered by essays than its immediate predecessors. The methods pursued have been fair, careful, and intelligent, and have secured the approval of the statisticians who have followed them with a scientific and nonpartisan interest. The appropriations necessary to the early completion and publication of the authorized volumes should be given in time to secure against delays, which increase the cost and at the same time diminish the value of the work.

The report of the Secretary exhibits with interesting fullness the condition of the Territories. They have shared with the States the great increase in farm products, and are bringing yearly large areas into cultivation by extending their irrigating canals. This work is being done by individuals or local corporations and without that system which a full preliminary survey of the water supply and of the irrigable lands would enable them to adopt. The future of the Territories of New Mexico, Arizona, and Utah in their material growth and in the increase, independence, and happiness of their people is very largely dependent upon wise and timely legislation, either by Congress or their own legislatures, regulating the distribution of the water supply furnished by their streams. If this matter is much longer neglected, private corporations will have unrestricted control of one of the elements of life and the patentees of the arid lands will be tenants at will of the water companies.

The United States should part with its ownership of the water sources and the sites for reservoirs, whether to the States and Territories or to individuals or corporations, only upon conditions that will insure to the settlers their proper water supply upon equal and reasonable terms. In the Territories this whole subject is under the full control of Congress, and in the States it is practically so as long as the Government holds the title to the reservoir sites and water sources and can grant them upon such conditions as it chooses to impose. The improvident granting of franchises of enormous value without recompense to the State or municipality from which they proceed and without proper protection of the public interests is the most noticeable and flagrant evil of modern legislation. This fault should not be committed in dealing with a subject that will before many years affect so vitally thousands of our people.

The legislation of Congress for the repression of polygamy has, after years of resistance on the part of the Mormons, at last brought them to the conclusion that resistance is unprofitable and unavailing. The power of Congress over this subject should not be surrendered until we have satisfactory evidence that the people of the State to be created would exercise the exclusive power of the State over this subject in the same way. The question is not whether these people now obey the laws of Congress against polygamy, but rather would they make, enforce, and maintain such laws themselves if absolutely free to regulate the subject? We can not afford to experiment with this subject, for when a State is once constituted the act is final and any mistake irretrievable. No compact in the enabling act could, in my opinion, be binding or effective.

I recommend that provision be made for the organization of a simple form of town government in Alaska, with power to regulate such matters as are usually in the States under municipal control. These local civil organizations will give better protection in some matters than the present skeleton Territorial organization. Proper restrictions as to the power to levy taxes and to create debt should be imposed.

If the establishment of the Department of Agriculture was regarded by anyone as a mere concession to the unenlightened demand of a worthy class of people, that impression has been most effectually removed by the great results already attained. Its home influence has been very great in disseminating agricultural and horticultural information, in stimulating and directing a further diversification of crops, in detecting and eradicating diseases of domestic animals, and, more than all, in the close and informal contact which it has established and maintains with the farmers and stock raisers of the whole country. Every request for information has had prompt attention and every suggestion merited consideration. The scientific corps of the Department is of a high order and is pushing its investigations with method and enthusiasm.

The inspection by this Department of cattle and pork products intended for shipment abroad has been the basis of the success which has attended our efforts to secure the removal of the restrictions maintained by the European Governments.

For ten years protests and petitions upon this subject from the packers and stock raisers of the United States have been directed against these restrictions, which so seriously limited our markets and curtailed the profits of the farm. It is a source of general congratulation that success has at last been attained, for the effects of an enlarged foreign market for these meats will be felt not only by the farmer, but in our public finances and in every branch of trade. It is particularly fortunate that the increased demand for food products resulting from the removal of the restrictions upon our meats and from the reciprocal trade arrangements to which I have referred should have come at a time when the agricultural surplus is so large. Without the help thus derived lower prices would have prevailed. The Secretary of Agriculture estimates that the restrictions upon the importation of our pork products into Europe lost us a market for $20,000,000 worth of these products annually.

The grain crop of this year was the largest in our history—50 per cent greater than that of last year—and yet the new markets that have been opened and the larger demand resulting from short crops in Europe have sustained prices to such an extent that the enormous surplus of meats and breadstuffs will be marketed at good prices, bringing relief and prosperity to an industry that was much depressed. The value of the grain crop of the United States is estimated by the Secretary to be this year $500,000,000 more than last; of meats $150,000,000 more, and of all products of the farm $700,000,000 more. It is not inappropriate, I think, here to suggest that our satisfaction in the contemplation of this marvelous addition to the national wealth is unclouded by any suspicion of the currency by which it is measured and in which the farmer is paid for the products of his fields.

The report of the Civil Service Commission should receive the careful attention of the opponents as well as the friends of this reform. The Commission invites a personal inspection by Senators and Representatives of its records and methods, and every fair critic will feel that such an examination should precede a judgment of condemnation either of the system or its administration. It is not claimed that either is perfect, but I believe that the law is being executed with impartiality and that the system is incomparably better and fairer than that of appointments upon favor. I have during the year extended the classified service to include superintendents, teachers, matrons, and physicians in the Indian service. This branch of the service is largely related to educational and philanthropic work and will obviously be the better for the change.

The heads of the several Executive Departments have been directed to establish at once an efficiency record as the basis of a comparative rating of the clerks within the classified service, with a view to placing promotions therein upon the basis of merit. I am confident that such a record, fairly kept and open to the inspection of those interested, will powerfully stimulate the work of the Departments and will be accepted by all as placing the troublesome matter of promotions upon a just basis.

I recommend that the appropriation for the Civil Service Commission be made adequate to the increased work of the next fiscal year.

I have twice before urgently called the attention of Congress to the necessity of legislation for the protection of the lives of railroad employees, but nothing has yet been done. During the year ending June 30, 1890, 369 brakemen were killed and 7,841 maimed while engaged in coupling cars.   The total number of railroad employees killed during the year was 2,451 and the number injured 22,390.   This is a cruel and largely needless sacrifice.   The Government is spending nearly $1,000,000 annually to save the lives of shipwrecked seamen; every steam vessel is rigidly inspected and required to adopt the most approved safety appliances.   All this is good.   But how shall we excuse the lack of interest and effort in behalf of this army of brave young men who in our land commerce are being sacrificed every year by the continued use of antiquated and dangerous appliances?   A law requiring of every railroad engaged in interstate commerce the equipment each year of a given per cent of its freight cars with automatic couplers and air brakes would compel an agreement between the roads as to the kind of brakes and couplers to be used, and would very soon and very greatly reduce the present fearful death rate among railroad employees.

The method of appointment by the States of electors of President and Vice-President has recently attracted renewed interest by reason of a departure by the State of Michigan from the method which had become uniform in all the States.   Prior to 1832 various methods had been used by the different States, and even by the same State.   In some the choice was made by the legislature; in others electors were chosen by districts, but more generally by the voters of the whole State upon a general ticket.   The movement toward the adoption of the last-named method had an early beginning and went steadily forward among the States until in 1832 there remained but a single State (South Carolina) that had not adopted it.   That State until the Civil War continued to choose its electors by a vote of the legislature, but after the war changed its method and conformed to the practice of the other States.   For nearly sixty years all the States save one have appointed their electors by a popular vote upon a general ticket, and for nearly thirty years this method was universal.

After a full test of other methods, without important division or dissent in any State and without any purpose of party advantage, as we must believe, but solely upon the considerations that uniformity was desirable and that a general election in territorial divisions not subject to change was most consistent with the popular character of our institutions, best preserved the equality of the voters, and perfectly removed the choice of President from the baneful influence of the "gerrymander," the practice of all the States was brought into harmony.   That this concurrence should now be broken is, I think, an unfortunate and even a threatening episode, and one that may well suggest whether the States that still give their approval to the old and prevailing method ought not to secure by a constitutional amendment a practice which has had the approval of all.   The recent Michigan legislation provides for choosing what are popularly known as the Congressional electors for President by Congressional districts and the two Senatorial electors by districts created for that purpose. This legislation was, of course, accompanied by a new Congressional apportionment, and the two statutes bring the electoral vote of the State under the influence of the "gerrymander."

These gerrymanders for Congressional purposes are in most cases buttressed by a gerrymander of the legislative districts, thus making it impossible for a majority of the legal voters of the State to correct the apportionment and equalize the Congressional districts. A minority rule is established that only a political convulsion can overthrow. I have recently been advised that in one county of a certain State three districts for the election of members of the legislature are constituted as follows: One has 65,000 population, one 15,000, and one 10,000, while in another county detached, noncontiguous sections have been united to make a legislative district. These methods have already found effective application to the choice of Senators and Representatives in Congress, and now an evil start has been made in the direction of applying them to the choice by the States of electors of President and Vice-President. If this is accomplished, we shall then have the three great departments of the Government in the grasp of the "gerrymander," the legislative and executive directly and the judiciary indirectly through the power of appointment.

An election implies a body of electors having prescribed qualifications, each one of whom has an equal value and influence in determining the result. So when the Constitution provides that "each State shall appoint" (elect), "in such manner as the legislature thereof may direct, a number of electors," etc., an unrestricted power was not given to the legislatures in the selection of the methods to be used. "A republican form of government" is guaranteed by the Constitution to each State, and the power given by the same instrument to the legislatures of the States to prescribe methods for the choice by the State of electors must be exercised under that limitation. The essential features of such a government are the right of the people to choose their own officers and the nearest practicable equality of value in the suffrages given in determining that choice.

It will not be claimed that the power given to the legislature would support a law providing that the persons receiving the smallest vote should be the electors or a law that all the electors should be chosen by the voters of a single Congressional district. The State is to choose, and under the pretense of regulating methods the legislature can neither vest the right of choice elsewhere nor adopt methods not conformable to republican institutions. It is not my purpose here to discuss the question whether a choice by the legislature or by the voters of equal single districts is a choice by the State, but only to recommend such regulation of this matter by constitutional amendment as will secure uniformity and prevent that disgraceful partisan jugglery to which such a liberty of choice, if it exists, offers a temptation.

Nothing just now is more important than to provide every guaranty for the absolutely fair and free choice by an equal suffrage within the respective States of all the officers of the National Government, whether that suffrage is applied directly, as in the choice of members of the House of Representatives, or indirectly, as in the choice of Senators and electors of President. Respect for public officers and obedience to law will not cease to be the characteristics of our people until our elections cease to declare the will of majorities fairly ascertained without fraud, suppression, or gerrymander. If I were called upon to declare wherein our chief national danger lies, I should say without hesitation in the overthrow of majority control by the suppression or perversion of the popular suffrage. That there is a real danger here all must agree; but the energies of those who see it have been chiefly expended in trying to fix responsibility upon the opposite party rather than in efforts to make such practices impossible by either party.

Is it not possible now to adjourn that interminable and inconclusive debate while we take by consent one step in the direction of reform by eliminating the gerrymander, which has been denounced by all parties as an influence in the selection of electors of President and members of Congress? All the States have, acting freely and separately, determined that the choice of electors by a general ticket is the wisest and safest method, and it would seem there could be no objection to a constitutional amendment making that method permanent. If a legislature chosen in one year upon purely local questions should, pending a Presidential contest, meet, rescind the law for a choice upon a general ticket, and provide for the choice of electors by the legislature, and this trick should determine the result, it is not too much to say that the public peace might be seriously and widely endangered.

I have alluded to the "gerrymander" as affecting the method of selecting electors of President by Congressional districts, but the primary intent and effect of this form of political robbery have relation to the selection of members of the House of Representatives. The power of Congress is ample to deal with this threatening and intolerable abuse. The unfailing test of sincerity in election reform will be found in a willingness to confer as to remedies and to put into force such measures as will most effectually preserve the right of the people to free and equal representation.

An attempt was made in the last Congress to bring to bear the constitutional powers of the General Government for the correction of fraud against the suffrage. It is important to know whether the opposition to such measures is really rested in particular features supposed to be objectionable or includes any proposition to give to the election laws of the United States adequacy to the correction of grave and acknowledged evils. I must yet entertain the hope that it is possible to secure a calm, patriotic consideration of such constitutional or statutory changes as may be necessary to secure the choice of the officers of the Government to the people by fair apportionments and free elections.

I believe it would be possible to constitute a commission, nonpartisan in its membership and composed of patriotic, wise, and impartial men, to whom a consideration of the question of the evils connected with our election system and methods might be committed with a good prospect of securing unanimity in some plan for removing or mitigating those evils. The Constitution would permit the selection of the commission to be vested in the Supreme Court if that method would give the best guaranty of impartiality. This commission should be charged with the duty of inquiring into the whole subject of the law of elections as related to the choice of officers of the National Government, with a view to securing to every elector a free and unmolested exercise of the suffrage and as near an approach to an equality of value in each ballot cast as is attainable.

While the policies of the General Government upon the tariff, upon the restoration of our merchant marine, upon river and harbor improvements, and other such matters of grave and general concern are liable to be turned this way or that by the results of Congressional elections and administrative policies, sometimes involving issues that tend to peace or war, to be turned this way or that by the results of a Presidential election, there is a rightful interest in all the States and in every Congressional district that will not be deceived or silenced by the audacious pretense that the question of the right of any body of legal voters in any State or in any Congressional district to give their suffrages freely upon these general questions is a matter only of local concern or control. The demand that the limitations of suffrage shall be found in the law, and only there, is a just demand, and no just man should resent or resist it. My appeal is and must continue to be for a consultation that shall "proceed with candor, calmness, and patience upon the lines of justice and humanity, not of prejudice and cruelty."

To the consideration of these very grave questions I invite not only the attention of Congress, but that of all patriotic citizens. We must not entertain the delusion that our people have ceased to regard a free ballot and equal representation as the price of their allegiance to laws and to civil magistrates.

I have been greatly rejoiced to notice many evidences of the increased unification of our people and of a revived national spirit. The vista that now opens to us is wider and more glorious than ever before. Gratification and amazement struggle for supremacy as we contemplate the population, wealth, and moral strength of our country. A trust momentous in its influence upon our people and upon the world is for a brief time committed to us, and we must not be faithless to its first condition—the defense of the free and equal influence of the people in the choice of public officers and in the control of public affairs.

BENJ. HARRISON.

SPECIAL MESSAGES.

EXECUTIVE MANSION, *December 16, 1891.*

To the Senate and House of Representatives:

I transmit herewith, for your information, a letter from the Secretary of State, inclosing the first annual report and copies of the bulletins of the Bureau of the American Republics.

BENJ. HARRISON.

EXECUTIVE MANSION, *December 23, 1891.*

To the Senate and House of Representatives:

I transmit herewith the report of the board appointed by me under a clause in the District of Columbia appropriation act approved August 6, 1890, "to consider the location, arrangement, and operation of electric wires in the District of Columbia," etc., to which the attention of Congress is respectfully invited.

BENJ. HARRISON.

EXECUTIVE MANSION, *December 23, 1891.*

To the Senate and House of Representatives:

My attention having been called to the necessity of bringing about a uniform usage and spelling of geographic names in the publications of the Government, the following Executive order was issued on the 4th day of September, 1890:

As it is desirable that uniform usage in regard to geographic nomenclature and orthography obtain throughout the Executive Departments of the Government, and particularly upon the maps and charts issued by the various Departments and bureaus, I hereby constitute a Board on Geographic Names and designate the following persons, who have heretofore cooperated for a similar purpose under the authority of the several Departments, bureaus, and institutions with which they are connected, as members of said board:

Professor Thomas C. Mendenhall, United States Coast and Geodetic Survey, chairman.

Andrew H. Allen, Department of State.

Captain Henry L. Howison, Light-House Board, Treasury Department.

Captain Thomas Turtle, Engineer Corps, War Department.

Lieutenant Richardson Clover, Hydrographic Office, Navy Department.

Pierson H. Bristow, Post-Office Department.

Otis T. Mason, Smithsonian Institution.

Herbert G. Ogden, United States Coast and Geodetic Survey.

Henry Gannett, United States Geological Survey.

Marcus Baker, United States Geological Survey.

To this board shall be referred all unsettled questions concerning geographic names which arise in the Departments, and the decisions of the board are to be accepted by these Departments as the standard authority in such matters.

Department officers are instructed to afford such assistance as may be proper to carry on the work of this board.

The members of this board shall serve without additional compensation and its organization shall entail no expense on the Government.

The report of the board thus constituted has been submitted to me, and is herewith transmitted for the information of Congress and with a view to its publication in suitable form if such action is deemed by Congress to be desirable.

BENJ. HARRISON.

EXECUTIVE MANSION, *January 5, 1892.*

To the Senate and House of Representatives:

The famine prevailing in some of the Provinces of Russia is so severe and widespread as to have attracted the sympathetic interest of a large number of our liberal and favored people. In some of the great grain-producing States of the West movements have already been organized to ·collect flour and meal for the relief of these perishing Russian families, and the response has been such as to justify the belief that a ship's cargo can very soon be delivered at the seaboard through the generous cooperation of the transportation lines. It is most appropriate that a people whose storehouses have been so lavishly filled with all the fruits of the earth by the gracious favor of God should manifest their gratitude by large gifts to His suffering children in other lands.

The Secretary of the Navy has no steam vessel at his disposal that could be used for the transportation of these supplies, and I therefore recommend that he be authorized to charter a suitable vessel to receive them if a sufficient amount should be offered, and to send them under the charge of a naval officer to such Russian port as may be most convenient for ready distribution to those most in need.

BENJ. HARRISON.

EXECUTIVE MANSION, *January 6, 1892.*

To the Senate and House of Representatives:

I transmit herewith, for the consideration of Congress, a communication of the 4th instant from the Secretary of the Interior, accompanied by an agreement concluded by and between the Cherokee Commission and the Wichita and affiliated bands of Indians in the Territory of Oklahoma, for the cession of certain lands and for other purposes.

BENJ. HARRISON.

EXECUTIVE MANSION, *January 6, 1892.*

To the Senate and House of Representatives:

I transmit herewith, for the consideration of Congress, a communication of the 4th instant from the Secretary of the Interior, submitting the agreement entered into between the Indians of the Colville Reservation, in the State of Washington, and the commissioners appointed under the provisions of the act of August 19, 1890, to negotiate with them for the cession of such portion of said reservation as said Indians may be willing to dispose of, that the same may be opened to white settlement.

BENJ. HARRISON.

EXECUTIVE MANSION, *January 6, 1892.*

To the Senate and House of Representatives:

I transmit herewith, for the consideration of Congress, a communication of the 4th instant from the Secretary of the Interior, accompanied by an agreement concluded by the Cherokee Commission with the Tonkawa Indians in Oklahoma Territory, for the cession of all their right, title, claim, and interest of every kind and character in and to the lands occupied by them in said Territory, and for other purposes.

BENJ. HARRISON.

EXECUTIVE MANSION, *January 11, 1892.*

To the Senate and House of Representatives:

I transmit herewith, for the consideration of Congress, a communication of the 8th instant from the Secretary of the Interior, submitting the agreements concluded by and between the Cherokee Commission and the Kickapoo tribe of Indians in the Territory of Oklahoma, for the cession of certain lands and for other purposes.

BENJ. HARRISON.

EXECUTIVE MANSION, *January 11, 1892.*

To the Senate and House of Representatives:

I transmit herewith, for the consideration of Congress, a communication of the 4th instant from the Secretary of the Interior, submitting the agreement entered into between the Indians of the Pyramid Lake Reservation and the commission appointed under the provisions of the Indian appropriation act of March 3, 1891, for the cession and relinquishment of the southern portion of their reservation in the State of Nevada.

BENJ. HARRISON.

EXECUTIVE MANSION, *January 11, 1892.*

To the Senate and House of Representatives:

I transmit herewith, for the consideration of Congress, a communication of the 4th instant from the Secretary of the Interior, submitting the agreement entered into between the Shoshone and Arapahoe Indians of the Shoshone or Wind River Reservation, in the State of Wyoming, and the commission appointed under the provisions of the Indian appropriation act of March 3, 1891, for the cession and relinquishment of a portion of their said reservation.

BENJ. HARRISON.

EXECUTIVE MANSION,
Washington. January 18, 1892.

To the Senate of the United States:

I transmit herewith to the Senate a report of the Secretary of State, in answer to the resolution of the Senate of the 12th instant, making inquiries regarding payments of the awards of the claims commission under the convention of July 4, 1868, between the United States and Mexico.

BENJ. HARRISON.

EXECUTIVE MANSION, *January 19, 1892.*

To the Senate and House of Representatives:

I transmit herewith a letter of the Secretary of the Navy, accompanied by the report of the commission appointed by me by virtue of a provision in the naval appropriation act approved June 30, 1890, "to select a suitable site, having due regard to commercial and naval interests, for a dry dock at some point on the shores of the Gulf of Mexico or the waters connected therewith."

The Secretary of the Navy approves the recommendations of the commission, and they are respectfully submitted for the consideration of the Congress.

BENJ. HARRISON.

EXECUTIVE MANSION, *January 25, 1892.*

To the Senate and House of Representatives:

In my annual message delivered to Congress at the beginning of the present session, after a brief statement of the facts then in the possession of this Government touching the assault in the streets of Valparaiso, Chile, upon the sailors of the United States steamship *Baltimore* on the evening of the 16th of October last, I said:

This Government is now awaiting the result of an investigation which has been conducted by the criminal court at Valparaiso. It is reported unofficially that the investigation is about completed, and it is expected that the result will soon be communicated to this Government, together with some adequate and satisfactory response to the note by which the attention of Chile was called to this incident. If these just expectations should be disappointed or further needless delay intervene, I will by a special message bring this matter again to the attention of Congress for such action as may be necessary.

In my opinion the time has now come when I should lay before the Congress and the country the correspondence between this Government and the Government of Chile from the time of the breaking out of the revolution against Balmaceda, together with all other facts in the possession of the executive department relating to this matter. The diplomatic correspondence is herewith transmitted, together with some correspondence between the naval officers for the time in command in Chilean waters and the Secretary of the Navy, and also the evidence taken at the Mare Island Navy-Yard since the arrival of the *Baltimore* at San Francisco. I do not deem it necessary in this communication to attempt any full analysis of the correspondence or of the evidence. A brief restatement of the international questions involved and of the reasons why the responses of the Chilean Government are unsatisfactory is all that I deem necessary.

It may be well at the outset to say that whatever may have been said in this country or in Chile in criticism of Mr. Egan, our minister at Santiago, the true history of this exciting period in Chilean affairs from the outbreak of the revolution until this time discloses no act on the part of Mr. Egan unworthy of his position or that could justly be the occasion of serious animadversion or criticism. He has, I think, on the whole borne himself in very trying circumstances with dignity, discretion, and courage, and has conducted the correspondence with ability, courtesy, and fairness.

It is worth while also at the beginning to say that the right of Mr. Egan to give shelter in the legation to certain adherents of the Balmaceda Government who applied to him for asylum has not been denied by the Chilean authorities, nor has any demand been made for the surrender of these refugees. That there was urgent need of asylum is shown by Mr. Egan's note of August 24, 1891, describing the disorders that prevailed in Santiago, and by the evidence of Captain Schley as to the pillage and violence that prevailed at Valparaiso. The correspondence discloses, however, that the request of Mr. Egan for a safe conduct from the country in behalf of these refugees was denied. The precedents cited by him in the correspondence, particularly the case of the revolution in Peru in 1865, did not leave the Chilean Government in a position to deny the right of asylum to political refugees, and seemed very clearly to support Mr. Egan's contention that a safe conduct to neutral territory was a necessary and acknowledged incident of the asylum. These refugees have very recently, without formal safe conduct, but by the acquiescence of the Chilean authorities, been placed on board the *Yorktown*, and are now being conveyed to Callao, Peru. This incident might be considered wholly closed but for the disrespect manifested toward this Government by the close and offensive police surveillance of the legation premises which was maintained during most of the period of the stay of the refugees therein. After the date of my annual message, and up to the time of the transfer of the refugees to the *Yorktown*, the legation premises seemed to have been surrounded by police in uniform and police agents or detectives in citizen's dress, who offensively scrutinized persons entering or leaving the legation, and on one or more occasions arrested members of the minister's family. Commander Evans, who by my direction recently visited Mr. Egan at Santiago, in his telegram to the Navy Department described the legation as "a veritable prison," and states that the police agents or detectives were after his arrival withdrawn during his stay. It appears further from the note of Mr. Egan of November 20, 1891, that on one occasion at least these police agents, whom he declares to be known to him, invaded the legation premises, pounding upon its windows and using insulting and threatening language toward persons therein. This breach of the right of a minister to freedom from police espionage and restraint seems to have been so flagrant that the Argentine minister, who was dean of the diplomatic corps, having observed it, felt called upon to protest against it to the Chilean minister of foreign affairs. The Chilean authorities have, as will be observed from the correspondence, charged the refugees and the inmates of the legation with insulting the police; but it seems to me incredible that men whose lives were in jeopardy and whose safety could only be secured by retirement and quietness should have sought to provoke a collision, which could only end in their destruction, or to aggravate their condition by intensifying a popular feeling that at one time so threatened the legation as to require Mr. Egan to appeal to the minister of foreign affairs.

But the most serious incident disclosed by the correspondence is that of the attack upon the sailors of the *Baltimore* in the streets of Valparaiso on the 16th of October last. In my annual message, speaking upon the information then in my possession, I said:

So far as I have yet been able to learn, no other explanation of this bloody work has been suggested than that it had its origin in hostility to those men as sailors of the United States, wearing the uniform of their Government, and not in any individual act or personal animosity.

We have now received from the Chilean Government an abstract of the conclusions of the fiscal general upon the testimony taken by the judge of crimes in an investigation which was made to extend over nearly three months. I very much regret to be compelled to say that this report does not enable me to modify the conclusion announced in my annual message. I am still of the opinion that our sailors were assaulted, beaten, stabbed, and killed not for anything they or any one of them had done, but for what the Government of the United States had done or was charged with having done by its civil officers and naval commanders. If that be the true aspect of the case, the injury was to the Government of the United States, not to these poor sailors who were assaulted in a manner so brutal and so cowardly.

Before attempting to give an outline of the facts upon which this conclusion rests I think it right to say a word or two upon the legal aspect of the case. The *Baltimore* was in the harbor of Valparaiso by virtue of that general invitation which nations are held to extend to the war vessels of other powers with which they have friendly relations. This invitation, I think, must be held ordinarily to embrace the privilege of such communication with the shore as is reasonable, necessary, and proper for the comfort and convenience of the officers and men of such vessels. Captain Schley testifies that when his vessel returned to Valparaiso on September 14 the city officers, as is customary, extended the hospitalities of the city to his officers and crew. It is not claimed that every personal collision or injury in which a sailor or officer of such naval vessel visiting the shore may be involved raises an international question, but I am clearly of the opinion that where such sailors or officers are assaulted by a resident populace, animated by hostility to the government whose uniform these sailors and officers wear and in resentment of acts done by their government, not by them, their nation must take notice of the event as one involving an infraction of its rights and dignity, not in a secondary way, as where a citizen is injured and presents his claim through his own government, but in a primary way, precisely as if its minister or consul or the flag itself had been the object of the same character of assault.

The officers and sailors of the *Baltimore* were in the harbor of Valparaiso under the orders of their Government, not by their own choice. They were upon the shore by the implied invitation of the Government of Chile and with the approval of their commanding officer; and it does not distinguish their case from that of a consul that his stay is more permanent or that he holds the express invitation of the local government to justify his longer residence. Nor does it affect the question that the injury was the act of a mob. If there had been no participation by the police or military in this cruel work and no neglect on their part to extend protection, the case would still be one, in my opinion, when its extent and character are considered, involving international rights.

The incidents of the affair are briefly as follows:

On the 16th of October last Captain Schley, commanding the United States steamship *Baltimore*, gave shore leave to 117 petty officers and sailors of his ship. These men left the ship about 1.30 p. m. No incident of violence occurred, none of our men were arrested, no complaint was lodged against them, nor did any collision or outbreak occur until about 6 o'clock p. m. Captain Schley states that he was himself on shore and about the streets of the city until 5.30 p. m.; that he met very many of his men who were upon leave; that they were sober and were conducting themselves with propriety, saluting Chilean and other officers as they met them. Other officers of the ship and Captain Jenkins, of the merchant ship *Keweenaw*, corroborate Captain Schley as to the general sobriety and good behavior of our men. The Sisters of Charity at the hospital to which our wounded men were taken when inquired of stated that they were sober when received. If the situation had been otherwise, we must believe that the Chilean police authorities would have made arrests. About 6 p. m. the assault began, and it is remarkable that the investigation by the judge of crimes, though so protracted, does not enable him to give any more satisfactory account of its origin than is found in the statement that it began between drunken sailors. Repeatedly in the correspondence it is asserted that it was impossible to learn the precise cause of the riot. The minister of foreign affairs, Matta, in his telegram to Mr. Montt under date December 31, states that the quarrel began between two sailors in a tavern and was continued in the street, persons who were passing joining in it.

The testimony of Talbot, an apprentice, who was with Riggin, is that the outbreak in which they were involved began by a Chilean sailor's spitting in the face of Talbot, which was resented by a knockdown. It appears that Riggin and Talbot were at the time unaccompanied by others of their shipmates. These two men were immediately beset by a crowd of Chilean citizens and sailors, through which they broke their way to a street car, and entered it for safety. They were pursued, driven from the car, and Riggin was so seriously beaten that he fell in the street apparently dead. There is nothing in the report of the Chilean investigation made to us that seriously impeaches this testimony. It appears from Chilean sources that almost instantly, with a suddenness that strongly implies meditation and preparation, a mob, stated by the police authorities at one time to number 2,000 and at another 1,000, was engaged in the assault upon our sailors, who are represented as resisting "with stones, clubs, and bright arms." The report of the *intendente* of October 30 states that the fight began at 6 p. m. in three streets, which are named; that information was received at the *intendencia* at 6.15, and that the police arrived on the scene at 6.30, a full half hour after the assault began. At that time he says that a mob of 2,000 men had collected, and that for several squares there was the appearance of a "real battlefield."

The scene at this point is very graphically set before us by the Chilean testimony. The American sailors, who after so long an examination have not been found guilty of any breach of the peace so far as the Chilean authorities are able to discover, unarmed and defenseless, are fleeing for their lives, pursued by overwhelming numbers, and fighting only to aid their own escape from death or to succor some mate whose life is in greater peril. Eighteen of them are brutally stabbed and beaten, while one Chilean seems from the report to have suffered some injury, but how serious or with what character of weapon, or whether by a missile thrown by our men or by some of his fellow-rioters, is unascertained.

The pretense that our men were fighting "with stones, clubs, and bright arms" is in view of these facts incredible. It is further refuted by the fact that our prisoners when searched were absolutely without arms, only seven penknives being found in the possession of the men arrested, while there were received by our men more than thirty stab wounds, every one of which was inflicted in the back, and almost every contused wound was in the back or back of the head. The evidence of the ship's officer of the day is that even the jackknives of the men were taken from them before leaving the ship.

As to the brutal nature of the treatment received by our men, the following extract from the account given of the affair by the La Patria newspaper, of Valparaiso, of October 17, can not be regarded as too friendly:

The Yankees, as soon as their pursuers gave chase, went by way of the Calle del Arsenal toward the city car station. In the presence of an ordinary number of citizens, among whom were some sailors, the North Americans took seats in the street car to escape from the stones which the Chileans threw at them. It was believed for an instant that the North Americans had saved themselves from popular fury, but such was not the case. Scarcely had the car begun to move when a crowd gathered around and stopped its progress. Under these circumstances and without any cessation of the howling and throwing of stones at the North Americans, the conductor entered the car, and, seeing the risk of the situation to the vehicle, ordered them to get out. At the instant the sailors left the car, in the midst of a hail of stones, the said conductor received a stone blow on the head. One of the Yankee sailors managed to escape in the direction of the Plaza Wheelright, but the other was felled to the ground by a stone. Managing to raise himself from the ground where he lay, he staggered in an opposite direction from the station. In front of the house of Señor Mazzini he was again wounded, falling then senseless and breathless.

No amount of evasion or subterfuge is able to cloud our clear vision of this brutal work. It should be noticed in this connection that the American sailors arrested, after an examination, were during the four days following the arrest every one discharged, no charge of any breach of the peace or other criminal conduct having been sustained against a single one of them. The judge of crimes, Foster, in a note to the *intendente* under date of October 22, before the dispatch from this Government of the following day, which aroused the authorities of Chile to a better sense of the gravity of the affair, says:

Having presided temporarily over this court in regard to the seamen of the United States cruiser *Baltimore*, who have been tried on account of the deplorable conduct which took place, etc.

The noticeable point here is that our sailors had been tried before the 22d of October, and that the trial resulted in their acquittal and return to their vessel. It is quite remarkable and quite characteristic of the management of this affair by the Chilean police authorities that we should now be advised that Seaman Davidson, of the *Baltimore*, has been included in the indictment, his offense being, so far as I have been able to ascertain, that he attempted to defend a shipmate against an assailant who was striking at him with a knife. The perfect vindication of our men is furnished by this report. One only is found to have been guilty of criminal fault, and that for an act clearly justifiable.

As to the part taken by the police in the affair, the case made by Chile is also far from satisfactory. The point where Riggin was killed is only three minutes' walk from the police station, and not more than twice that distance from the *intendencia;* and yet according to their official report a full half hour elapsed after the assault began before the police were upon the ground. It has been stated that all but two of our men have said that the police did their duty. The evidence taken at

Mare Island shows that if such a statement was procured from our men it was accomplished by requiring them to sign a writing in a language they did not understand and by the representation that it was a mere declaration that they had taken no part in the disturbance. Lieutenant McCrea, who acted as interpreter, says in his evidence that when our sailors were examined before the court the subject of the conduct of the police was so carefully avoided that he reported the fact to Captain Schley on his return to the vessel.

The evidences of the existence of animosity toward our sailors in the minds of the sailors of the Chilean navy and of the populace of Valparaiso are so abundant and various as to leave no doubt in the mind of anyone who will examine the papers submitted. It manifested itself in threatening and insulting gestures toward our men as they passed the Chilean men-of-war in their boats and in the derisive and abusive epithets with which they greeted every appearance of an American sailor on the evening of the riot. Captain Schley reports that boats from the Chilean war ships several times went out of their course to cross the bows of his boats, compelling them to back water. He complained of the discourtesy, and it was corrected. That this feeling was shared by men of higher rank is shown by an incident related by Surgeon Stitt, of the *Baltimore*. After the battle of Placilla he, with other medical officers of the war vessels in the harbor, was giving voluntary assistance to the wounded in the hospitals. The son of a Chilean army officer of high rank was under his care, and when the father discovered it he flew into a passion and said he would rather have his son die than have Americans touch him, and at once had him removed from the ward. This feeling is not well concealed in the dispatches of the foreign office, and had quite open expression in the disrespectful treatment of the American legation. The Chilean boatmen in the bay refused, even for large offers of money, to return our sailors, who crowded the Mole, to their ship when they were endeavoring to escape from the city on the night of the assault. The market boats of the *Baltimore* were threatened, and even quite recently the gig of Commander Evans, of the *Yorktown*, was stoned while waiting for him at the Mole.

The evidence of our sailors clearly shows that the attack was expected by the Chilean people, that threats had been made against our men, and that in one case, somewhat early in the afternoon, the keeper of one house into which some of our men had gone closed his establishment in anticipation of the attack, which he advised them would be made upon them as darkness came on.

In a report of Captain Schley to the Navy Department he says:

In the only interview that I had with Judge Foster, who is investigating the case relative to the disturbance, before he was aware of the entire gravity of the matter, he informed me that the assault upon my men was the outcome of hatred for our people among the lower classes because they thought we had sympathized with the Balmaceda Government on account of the *Itata* matter, whether with reason or without he could of course not admit; but such he thought was the explanation of the assault at that time.

Several of our men sought security from the mob by such complete or partial changes in their dress as would conceal the fact of their being seamen of the *Baltimore*, and found it then possible to walk the streets without molestation. These incidents conclusively establish that the attack was upon the uniform—the nationality—and not upon the men.

The origin of this feeling is probably found in the refusal of this Government to give recognition to the Congressional party before it had established itself, in the seizure of the *Itata* for an alleged violation of the neutrality law, in the cable incident, and in the charge that Admiral Brown conveyed information to Valparaiso of the landing at Quinteros. It is not my purpose to enter here any defense of the action of this Government in these matters. It is enough for the present purpose to say that if there was any breach of international comity or duty on our part it should have been made the subject of official complaint through diplomatic channels or for reprisals for which a full responsibility was assumed. We can not consent that these incidents and these perversions of the truth shall be used to excite a murderous attack upon our unoffending sailors and the Government of Chile go aquit of responsibility. In fact, the conduct of this Government during the war in Chile pursued those lines of international duty which we had so strongly insisted upon on the part of other nations when this country was in the throes of a civil conflict. We continued the established diplomatic relations with the government in power until it was overthrown, and promptly and cordially recognized the new government when it was established. The good offices of this Government were offered to bring about a peaceful adjustment, and the interposition of Mr. Egan to mitigate severities and to shelter adherents of the Congressional party was effective and frequent. The charge against Admiral Brown is too base to gain credence with anyone who knows his high personal and professional character.

Recurring to the evidence of our sailors, I think it is shown that there were several distinct assaults, and so nearly simultaneous as to show that they did not spread from one point. A press summary of the report of the fiscal shows that the evidence of the Chilean officials and others was in conflict as to the place of origin, several places being named by different witnesses as the locality where the first outbreak occurred. This if correctly reported shows that there were several distinct outbreaks, and so nearly at the same time as to cause this confusion. The La Patria, in the same issue from which I have already quoted, after describing the killing of Riggin and the fight which from that point extended to the Mole, says:

At the same time in other streets of the port the Yankee sailors fought fiercely with the people of the town, who believed to see in them incarnate enemies of the Chilean navy.

The testimony of Captain Jenkins, of the American merchant ship *Keweenaw*, which had gone to Valparaiso for repairs, and who was a witness of some part of the assault upon the crew of the *Baltimore*, is strongly corroborative of the testimony of our own sailors when he says that he saw Chilean sentries drive back a seaman seeking shelter upon a mob that was pursuing him. The officers and men of Captain Jenkins's ship furnish the most conclusive testimony as to the indignities which were practiced toward Americans in Valparaiso. When American sailors, even of merchant ships, can only secure their safety by denying their nationality, it must be time to readjust our relations with a government that permits such demonstrations.

As to the participation of the police, the evidence of our sailors shows that our men were struck and beaten by police officers before and after arrest, and that one at least was dragged with a lasso about his neck by a mounted policeman. That the death of Riggin was the result of a rifle shot fired by a policeman or soldier on duty is shown directly by the testimony of Johnson, in whose arms he was at the time, and by the evidence of Charles Langen, an American sailor, not then a member of the *Baltimore's* crew, who stood close by and saw the transaction. The Chilean authorities do not pretend to fix the responsibility of this shot upon any particular person, but avow their inability to ascertain who fired it further than that it was fired from a crowd. The character of the wound as described by one of the surgeons of the *Baltimore* clearly supports his opinion that it was made by a rifle ball, the orifice of exit being as much as an inch or an inch and a quarter in width. When shot the poor fellow was unconscious and in the arms of a comrade, who was endeavoring to carry him to a neighboring drug store for treatment. The story of the police that in coming up the street they passed these men and left them behind them is inconsistent with their own statement as to the direction of their approach and with their duty to protect them, and is clearly disproved. In fact Riggin was not behind but in front of the advancing force, and was not standing in the crowd, but was unconscious and supported in the arms of Johnson when he was shot.

The communications of the Chilean Government in relation to this cruel and disastrous attack upon our men, as will appear from the correspondence, have not in any degree taken the form of a manly and satisfactory expression of regret, much less of apology. The event was of so serious a character that if the injuries suffered by our men had been wholly the result of an accident in a Chilean port the incident was grave enough to have called for some public expression of sympathy and regret from the local authorities. It is not enough to say that the affair was lamentable, for humanity would require that expression even if the beating and killing of our men had been justifiable. It is not enough to say that the incident is regretted, coupled with the statement that the affair was not of an unusual character in ports where foreign sailors are accustomed to meet. It is not for a generous and sincere government to seek for words of small or equivocal meaning in which to convey to a friendly power an apology for an offense so atrocious as this. In the case of the assault by a mob in New Orleans upon the Spanish consulate in 1851, Mr. Webster wrote to the Spanish minister, Mr. Calderon, that the acts complained of were "a disgraceful and flagrant breach of duty and propriety," and that his Government "regrets them as deeply as Minister Calderon or his Government could possibly do;" that "these acts have caused the President great pain, and he thinks a proper acknowledgment is due to Her Majesty's Government." He invited the Spanish consul to return to his post, guaranteeing protection, and offered to salute the Spanish flag if the consul should come in a Spanish vessel. Such a treatment by the Government of Chile of this assault would have been more creditable to the Chilean authorities, and much less can hardly be satisfactory to a government that values its dignity and honor.

In our note of October 23 last, which appears in the correspondence, after receiving the report of the board of officers appointed by Captain Schley to investigate the affair, the Chilean Government was advised of the aspect which it then assumed and called upon for any facts in its possession that might tend to modify the unfavorable impressions which our report had created. It is very clear from the correspondence that before the receipt of this note the examination was regarded by the police authorities as practically closed. It was, however, reopened and protracted through a period of nearly three months. We might justly have complained of this unreasonable delay; but in view of the fact that the Government of Chile was still provisional, and with a disposition to be forbearing and hopeful of a friendly termination, I have awaited the report, which has but recently been made.

On the 21st instant I caused to be communicated to the Government of Chile by the American minister at Santiago the conclusions of this Government after a full consideration of all the evidence and of every suggestion affecting this matter, and to these conclusions I adhere. They were stated as follows:

First. That the assault is not relieved of the aspect which the early information of the event gave to it, viz, that of an attack upon the uniform of the United States Navy having its origin and motive in a feeling of hostility to this Government, and not in any act of the sailors or of any of them.

Second. That the public authorities of Valparaiso flagrantly failed in their duty to protect our men, and that some of the police and of the Chilean soldiers and sailors were themselves guilty of unprovoked assaults upon our sailors before and after arrest. He [the President] thinks the preponderance of the evidence and the inherent probabilities lead to the conclusion that Riggin was killed by the police or soldiers.

Third. That he [the President] is therefore compelled to bring the case back to the position taken by this Government in the note of Mr. Wharton of October 23 last * * * and to ask for a suitable apology and for some adequate reparation for the injury done to this Government.

In the same note the attention of the Chilean Government was called to the offensive character of a note addressed by Mr. Matta, its minister of foreign affairs, to Mr. Montt, its minister at this capital, on the 11th ultimo. This dispatch was not officially communicated to this Government, but as Mr. Montt was directed to translate it and to give it to the press of the country it seemed to me that it could not pass without official notice. It was not only undiplomatic, but grossly insulting to our naval officers and to the executive department, as it directly imputed untruth and insincerity to the reports of the naval officers and to the official communications made by the executive department to Congress. It will be observed that I have notified the Chilean Government that unless this note is at once withdrawn and an apology as public as the offense made I will terminate diplomatic relations.

The request for the recall of Mr. Egan upon the ground that he was not *persona grata* was unaccompanied by any suggestion that could properly be used in support of it, and I infer that the request is based upon official acts of Mr. Egan which have received the approval of this Government. But however that may be, I could not consent to consider such a question until it had first been settled whether our correspondence with Chile could be conducted upon a basis of mutual respect.

In submitting these papers to Congress for that grave and patriotic consideration which the questions involved demand I desire to say that I am of the opinion that the demands made of Chile by this Government should be adhered to and enforced. If the dignity as well as the prestige and influence of the United States are not to be wholly sacrificed, we must protect those who in foreign ports display the flag or wear the colors of this Government against insult, brutality, and death inflicted in resentment of the acts of their Government and not for any fault of their own. It has been my desire in every way to cultivate friendly and intimate relations with all the Governments of this hemisphere. We do not covet their territory. We desire their peace and prosperity. We look for no advantage in our relations with them except the increased exchanges of commerce upon a basis of mutual benefit. We regret every civil contest that disturbs their peace and paralyzes their development, and are always ready to give our good offices for the restoration of peace. It must, however, be understood that this Government, while exercising the utmost forbearance toward weaker powers, will extend its strong and adequate protection to its citizens, to its officers, and to its humblest sailor when made the victims of wantonness and cruelty in resentment not of their personal misconduct, but of the official acts of their Government.

Upon information received that Patrick Shields, an Irishman and probably a British subject, but at the time a fireman of the American steamer *Keweenaw*, in the harbor of Valparaiso for repairs, had been subjected to personal injuries in that city, largely by the police, I directed the Attorney-General to cause the evidence of the officers and crew of that vessel to be taken upon its arrival in San Francisco, and that testimony is also herewith transmitted. The brutality and even savagery of the treatment of this poor man by the Chilean police would be incredible if the evidence of Shields was not supported by other direct testimony and by the distressing condition of the man himself when he was finally able to reach his vessel. The captain of the vessel says:

He came back a wreck, black from his neck to his hips from beating, weak and stupid, and is still in a kind of paralyzed condition, and has never been able to do duty since.

A claim for reparation has been made in behalf of this man, for while he was not a citizen of the United States, the doctrine long held by us, as expressed in the consular regulations, is:

The principles which are maintained by this Government in regard to the protection, as distinguished from the relief, of seamen are well settled. It is held that the circumstance that the vessel is American is evidence that the seamen on board are such, and in every regularly documented merchant vessel the crew will find their protection in the flag that covers them.

I have as yet received no reply to our note of the 21st instant, but in my opinion I ought not to delay longer to bring these matters to the attention of Congress for such action as may be deemed appropriate.

BENJ. HARRISON.

EXECUTIVE MANSION, *January 25, 1892.*
To the Senate and House of Representatives:

I transmit herewith, for the consideration of Congress, a communication of the 23d instant from the Secretary of the Interior, submitting an extract from the report of the commission appointed under the act of January 12, 1891, entitled "An act for the relief of the Mission Indians in the State of California," and other papers relating to the exchange of lands with private individuals and the purchase of certain lands and improvements for the use and benefit of the Mission Indians, with draft of a bill to carry into effect the recommendations of said Mission Commission.

I have approved the report of the Mission Commission, except as much as relates to the purchase of lands from and exchange of lands with private individuals, which is also approved subject to the condition that Congress shall authorize the same.

The matter is presented with the recommendation for the early and favorable action of Congress.

BENJ. HARRISON.

EXECUTIVE MANSION,
Washington, January 25, 1892.
To the Senate of the United States:

Referring to a communication of June 11, 1890, concerning the adoption by the Committee on Foreign Relations of a resolution respecting the claim of William Webster against the Government of Great Britain, I herewith transmit a report of the Secretary of State, with accompanying documents, showing the action taken under that resolution.

BENJ. HARRISON.

EXECUTIVE MANSION,
Washington, January 25, 1892.

To the Senate and House of Representatives:

I transmit herewith a report of the Secretary of State, with accompaniments, in relation to the claim of the representatives of the late Hon. James Crooks, a British subject, against the Government of the United States for the seizure of the steamer *Lord Nelson* in 1812.

The favorable action of the Fiftieth and Fifty-first Congresses upon the bills heretofore introduced for the relief of the claimants makes it proper that I should recommend it anew for the consideration and final disposition of the present Congress.

BENJ. HARRISON.

EXECUTIVE MANSION, *January 28, 1892.*

To the Senate and House of Representatives:

I transmit herewith additional correspondence between this Government and the Government of Chile, consisting of a note of Mr. Montt, the Chilean minister at this capital, to Mr. Blaine, dated January 23; a reply of Mr. Blaine thereto of date January 27, and a dispatch from Mr. Egan, our minister at Santiago, transmitting the response of Mr. Pereira, the Chilean minister of foreign affairs, to the note of Mr. Blaine of January 21, which was received by me on the 26th instant. The note of Mr. Montt to Mr. Blaine, though dated January 23, was not delivered at the State Department until after 12 o'clock m. of the 25th, and was not translated and its receipt notified to me until late in the afternoon of that day.

The response of Mr. Pereira to our note of the 21st withdraws, with acceptable expressions of regret, the offensive note of Mr. Matta of the 11th ultimo, and also the request for the recall of Mr. Egan. The treatment of the incident of the assault upon the sailors of the *Baltimore* is so conciliatory and friendly that I am of the opinion that there is a good prospect that the differences growing out of that serious affair can now be adjusted upon terms satisfactory to this Government by the usual methods and without special powers from Congress. This turn in the affair is very gratifying to me, as I am sure it will be to the Congress and to our people. The general support of the efforts of the Executive to enforce the just rights of the nation in this matter has given an instructive and useful illustration of the unity and patriotism of our people.

Should it be necessary I will again communicate with Congress upon the subject.

BENJ. HARRISON.

EXECUTIVE MANSION, *February 2, 1892.*

To the Senate of the United States:

In reply to a resolution of the Senate of the 27th ultimo, requesting the President "to advise the Senate as to what action, if any, has been taken * * * to cause careful soundings to be made between San Francisco, Cal., and Honolulu * * * for the purpose of determining the practicability of laying a telegraphic cable between those two points, or between any point on the Pacific coast and the Kingdom of the Hawaiian Islands," I inclose herewith a communication from the Secretary of the Navy, dated January 30, 1892.

BENJ. HARRISON.

EXECUTIVE MANSION, *February 9, 1892.*

To the House of Representatives:

I transmit herewith, in answer to the resolution of the House of Representatives of the 13th of January last, a report from the Secretary of State and accompanying papers.*

BENJ. HARRISON.

EXECUTIVE MANSION, *February 10, 1892.*

To the Senate and House of Representatives:

I transmit herewith, as required by law, a communication of the 6th instant from the Secretary of the Interior, with the report of the Puyallup Indian Commission and accompanying papers.

BENJ. HARRISON.

EXECUTIVE MANSION, *February 16, 1892.*

To the Senate and House of Representatives:

There was passed by the last Congress "An act for the protection of the lives of the miners in the Territories," which was approved by me on the 3d day of March, 1891. That no appropriation was made to enable me to carry the act into effect resulted, I suppose, from the fact that it was passed so late in the session. This law recognizes the necessity of a responsible public inspection and supervision of the business of mining in the interest of the miners, and is in line with the legislation of most of the States.

The work of the miner has its unavoidable incidents of discomfort and danger, and these should not be increased by the neglect of the owners to provide every practicable safety appliance. Economies which involve a sacrifice of human life are intolerable.

---

*Correspondence with Spain, Brazil, Salvador, and the Dominican Republic relative to reciprocal trade relations; copies of commercial arrangements entered into with those countries; list of import and export duties imposed by Brazil, Salvador, and the Dominican Republic, and by Spain with respect to Cuba and Puerto Rico.

I transmit herewith memorials from several hundred miners working in the coal mines in the Indian Territory, asking for the appointment of an inspector under the act referred to. The recent frightful disaster at Krebs, in that Territory, in which sixty-seven miners met a horrible death, gives urgency to their appeal, and I recommend that a special appropriation be at once made for the salaries and the necessary expenses of the inspectors provided for in the law.

BENJ. HARRISON.

EXECUTIVE MANSION, *February 17, 1892.*

To the Senate and House of Representatives:

The Indian appropriation bill which was approved March 3, 1891, contains the following provision:

And the sum of $2,991,450 be, and the same is hereby, appropriated, out of any money in the Treasury not otherwise appropriated, to pay the Choctaw and Chickasaw nations of Indians for all the right, title, interest, and claim which said nations of Indians may have in and to certain lands now occupied by the Cheyenne and Arapahoe Indians under Executive order, said lands lying south of the Canadian River, and now occupied by the said Cheyenne and Arapahoe Indians; said lands have been ceded in trust by article 3 of the treaty between the United States and said Choctaw and Chickasaw nations of Indians which was concluded April 28, 1866, and proclaimed on the 10th day of August of the same year, and whereof there remains, after deducting allotments as provided by said agreement, a residue ascertained by survey to contain 2,393,160 acres; three-fourths of this appropriation to be paid to such person or persons as are or shall be duly authorized by the laws of said Choctaw Nation to receive the same, at such time and in such sums as directed and required by the legislative authority of said Choctaw Nation, and one-fourth of this appropriation to be paid to such person or persons as are or shall be duly authorized by the laws of said Chickasaw Nation to receive the same, at such times and in such sums as directed and required by the legislative authority of said Chickasaw Nation; this appropriation to be immediately available and to become operative upon the execution by the duly appointed delegates of said respective nations specially authorized thereto by law of releases and conveyances to the United States of all the right, title, interest, and claim of said respective nations of Indians in and to said land (not including Greer County, which is now in dispute), in manner and form satisfactory to the President of the United States; and said releases and conveyances, when fully executed and delivered, shall operate to extinguish all claim of every kind and character of said Choctaw and Chickasaw nations of Indians in and to the tract of country to which said releases and conveyances shall apply.

If this section had been submitted to me as a separate measure, especially during the closing hours of the session, I should have disapproved it; but as the Congress was then in its last hours a disapproval of the general Indian appropriation bill, of which it was a part, would have resulted in consequences so far-reaching and disastrous that I felt it my duty to approve the bill. But as a duty was devolved upon me by the section quoted, viz, the acceptance and approval of the conveyances provided for, I have felt bound to look into the whole matter, and in view of the facts which I shall presently mention to postpone any Executive action until these facts could be submitted to Congress. Very soon after the passage of the law it came to my knowledge that the Choctaw Legislature had entered into an agreement with three citizens of that tribe to pay to them as compensation for procuring this legislation 25 per cent of any appropriation that might be made by Congress. The amount to be secured by these three agents under this agreement out of the three-fourths interest in the appropriation of the Choctaw Nation is $560,896. I have information that a contract was made by the Chickasaws to pay about 10 per cent of their one-fourth interest to the agents and attorneys who represented them.

Within a month after the passage of the law R. J. Ward, one of the agents, who was to divide with his associates the enormous sum to be paid by the Choctaws, presented to me an affidavit dated April 4, 1891, which is herewith submitted. It appears from his statement that the action of the Choctaw Council in this matter was corruptly influenced by the execution of certain notes signed by Ward for himself and his associates in sums varying from $2,500 to $15,000. His associates deny any knowledge of this, but the giving and existence of these notes is not refuted. The statement of the two associates of Ward denying any knowledge or participation in this fraud is also submitted, together with other papers relating to the matter. Whatever may be the fact as to the use or nonuse of corrupt methods to secure this legislation from the Choctaw Council, I do not think the Congress of the United States should so legislate upon this matter as to give effect to such a contract, which I am sure must have been unnoticed when the measure was pending. If the relations of these Indians to the United States are those of a ward, Congress should protect them from such extortionate exactions. We can not assume that the expenses and services of a committee of three persons to represent this claim before Congress should justly assume such proportions. The making of such a contract seems to convey implications which I am sure are wholly unjust.

After the passage of the appropriation bill legislation was had by the Choctaw Nation looking to the completion of the contract made with their delegates as to the payment of this money; but subsequently, when it was supposed that this extraordinary arrangement might require me to bring the matter to the attention of Congress, an act was passed by the Choctaw General Council, approved October 19, 1891, declaring all contracts made by the Choctaw delegates with any attorneys in connection with this appropriation void and of no effect. A copy of this law will be found with the papers submitted. There has also been submitted to me an unofficial copy of the opinion of the attorney-general of the Choctaw Nation holding that this last legislation is unconstitutional and void. I am of the opinion that if this appropriation is to stand provision should be made for protecting these tribes against extortionate claims for compensation in procuring action by Congress. Copies of the several laws passed by the Choctaw Nation with reference to this matter will be found in the accompanying papers. It will be noticed that the distribution proposed is limited to Choctaws by blood, excluding the freedmen and the white men who have been given full citizenship from any participation. A protest against this method of distribution has been filed by a white citizen of the tribe, and also a representation by Hon. Thomas C. Fletcher, their attorney, on behalf of the freedmen. In view of the fact that the stipulations of the treaty of 1866 in behalf of the freedmen of these tribes have not, especially in the case of the Chickasaws, been complied with, it would seem that the United States should in a distribution of this money have made suitable provision in their behalf. The Chickasaws have steadfastly refused to admit the freedmen to citizenship, as they stipulated to do in the treaty referred to, and their condition in that tribe and in a lesser degree in the other strongly calls for the protective intervention of Congress.

After a somewhat careful examination of the question I do not believe that the lands for which this money is to be paid were, to quote the language of section 15 of the Indian appropriation bill, already set out, "ceded in trust by article 3 of the treaty between the United States and said Choctaw and Chickasaw nations of Indians which was concluded April 28, 1866," etc. It is agreed that that treaty contained no express limitation upon the uses to which the United States might put the territory known as the leased district. The lands were ceded by terms sufficiently comprehensive to have passed the full title of the Indians. The limitation upon the use to which the Government might put them is sought to be found in a provision of the treaty by which the United States undertook to exclude white settlers and in the expressions found in the treaties made at the same time with the Creeks and other tribes of the purpose of the United States to use the lands ceded by those tribes for the settlement of friendly Indians.

The stipulation as to the exclusion of white settlers might well have reference solely to the national lands retained by the Choctaw and Chickasaw tribes, and the reason for the nonincorporation in the treaty with them of a statement of the purpose of the Government in connection with the use of the lands is well accounted for by the fact that as to these lands the Government had already, under the treaty of 1855, secured the right to use them perpetually for the settlement of friendly Indians. This was not true as to the lands of the other tribes referred to. The United States paid to the Choctaws and Chickasaws $300,000, and the failure to insert the words that are called words of limitation in this treaty points, I think, clearly to the conclusion that the commissioners on the part of the Government and the Indians themselves must have understood that this Government was acquiring something more than a mere right to settle friendly Indians, which it already possessed, and something more than the mere release of the right which the Choctaws and Chickasaws had under the treaty of 1855 to select locations on these lands if they chose.

Undoubtedly it was the policy of this Government for the time to hold these and the adjacent lands as Indian country, and many of the expressions in the proclamations of my predecessors and in the reports of the Indian Bureau and of the Secretary of the Interior mean this and nothing more. This is quite different from a conditional title, which limits the grant to a particular use and works a reinvestment of full title in the Indian grantors when that use ceases. But those who hold most strictly that a use for Indian purposes, where it is expressed, is a limitation of title seem to agree that the United States might pass a fee absolute to other Indian tribes in the lands ceded for their occupancy. Certainly it was not intended that in settling friendly Indians upon these lands the Government was to be restrained in its policy of allotment and individual ownership. If for an adequate consideration, by treaty, the United States placed upon these lands other Indian tribes, it was competent to give them patents in fee for a certain and agreed reservation. This being so, when the policy of allotment is put into force the compensation for the unused lands should certainly go to the occupying tribe, which in the case supposed had paid a full consideration for the whole reservation.

It will hardly be contended that in such case this Government should pay twice for the lands. In the appropriation under discussion this principle is in part recognized, for no claim is made by the Choctaws and Chickasaws for the lands allotted to the Cheyennes and Arapahoes. The claim is for unallotted or surplus lands. The case of the Cheyennes and Arapahoes is this: In consideration of other lands the Government gave them a treaty reservation in the Cherokee Outlet, but never perfected it by paying the Cherokees the stipulated price and placing these Indians upon it. The Cheyennes and Arapahoes declined to go upon the strip and located themselves farther south, where they now are. The Government subsequently recognized their right to remain there, and set apart the lands now being allotted to members of that tribe and the lands for which payment is now claimed by the Choctaws and Chickasaws as the Cheyenne and Arapahoe Reservation. I think the United States must be held to have assented to the substitution of these lands for the treaty lands in the Cherokee Strip, and that being true, when the reservation is broken up, as now, by allotments, it would seem that the Cheyennes and Arapahoes were entitled to be compensated for these surplus lands. In fact, a commission which has been dealing with the tribes in the Indian Territory has concluded an arrangement with them by which the Government pays $1,500,000 for these surplus lands and for the release of any claim to the Cherokee Strip, so that in fact in this agreement with the Cheyennes and Arapahoes the Government has paid for the lands for which payment is now claimed by the Choctaws and Chickasaws.

It should not be forgotten also that the allotment to the Cheyennes and Arapahoes is still incomplete. The method of calculation which resulted in stating the claim of the Choctaws and Chickasaws at $2,991,450 is explained by a letter of Mr. J. S. Standley, one of the Choctaw delegates, dated April 6, 1891. The agent for the Cheyennes and Arapahoes wrote Mr. Standley that there were 600 Indians residing upon the lands south of the Canadian River, and who it was supposed would take allotments there, and upon this statement the legislation was based. Now it must be borne in mind that the Cheyennes and Arapahoes have the right to locate anywhere within their reservation, and that instead of 600 double that number might have taken their allotments south of the Canadian River upon these lands. This is not probable, but a later report indicates that the number will certainly be in excess of 600. If the sum to be paid to the Choctaws and Chickasaws depended upon a knowledge of the number of acres of unallotted land south of the Canadian River, it would seem to have been reasonable that the appropriation should have been delayed until the exact number of acres taken for allotment had been officially ascertained. This has not yet been done.

It is right also, I think, that Congress in dealing with this matter should have the whole question before it, for the declaration of Indian title contained in this item of appropriation extends to a very large body of land and will involve very large future appropriations. The Choctaw and Chickasaw leased district, embracing the lands in the Indian Territory between the ninety-eighth and one hundredth degrees of west longitude and extending north and south from the main Canadian River to the Red River, including Greer County, contains, according to the public surveys, 7,713,239 acres, or, excluding Greer County, 6,201,663 acres. This leased district is occupied as follows:

Greer County, by white citizens of Texas, 1,511,576 acres. The United States is now prosecuting a case in the courts to obtain a judicial declaration that this county is part of the Indian country. If a decision should be rendered in its favor, the claim of the Choctaws and Chickasaws to be paid for these lands at the rate named in this appropriation would at once be presented.

The Wichita Reservation is also upon the leased lands and is occupied by the Wichitas, Caddoes, Delawares, and remnants of other tribes by Department orders, made to depend upon the treaty with the Delawares in 1866 and some other unratified agreements with tribes or fragments of tribes in 1872. This reservation contains 743,610 acres.

The Kiowa, Comanche, and Apache Reservation is occupied by those Indians under a treaty proclaimed August 25, 1868, which provides that said district of country "shall be, and the same is hereby, set apart for the absolute and undisturbed use and occupation of the tribes herein named, and for such friendly tribes or individual Indians as from time to time they may be willing (with the consent of the United States) to admit among them." This reservation contains 2,968,893 acres.

The Cheyennes and Arapahoes, whose surplus lands are to be paid for by this appropriation, have occupied the country between the Washita and Canadian rivers, extending west to the one hundredth degree of longitude. This reservation contains 2,489,160 acres.

I have stated these facts in order that it may be seen what further appropriations are involved in a settlement for all these lands upon the basis which Congress has adopted. It does not seem to me to be a wise policy to deal with this question piecemeal. It would have been better, if a remnant of title remains in the Choctaws and Chickasaws to the lands in the leased district, to have settled the whole matter at once. Under the treaty of 1855 the Choctaws and Chickasaws quitclaimed any supposed interest of theirs in the lands west of the one hundredth degree. The boundary between the Louisiana purchase and the Spanish possessions by our treaty of 1819 with Spain was as to these lands fixed upon the one hundredth degree of west longitude.

Our treaty with the Choctaws and Chickasaws made in 1820 extended their grant to the limit of our possessions. It followed, of course, that these lands were included within the boundaries of the State of Texas when that State was admitted to the Union, and the release of the Choctaws and Chickasaws, whatever it was worth, operated for the benefit of the State of Texas and not of the United States. The lands became public lands of that State. For the release of this claim and for the lease of the lands west of the ninety-eighth degree the Government of the United States paid the sum of $800,000. In the calculations which have been made to arrive at the basis of the appropriation under discussion no part of this sum is treated as having been paid for the lease. I do not think that is just to the United States. It seems probable that a very considerable part of this consideration must have related to the leased lands, because these were the lands in which the Indian title was recognized, and the treaty gave to the United States a permanent right of occupation by friendly Indians. The sum of $300,000, paid under the treaty of 1866, is deducted, as I understand, in arriving at the sum appropriated. It seems to me that a considerable proportion of the sum of $800,000 previously paid should have been deducted in the same manner.

I have felt it to be my duty to bring these matters to the attention of Congress for such action as may be thought advisable.

BENJ. HARRISON.

EXECUTIVE MANSION *February 24, 1892.*
To the Senate and House of Representatives:

I transmit herewith, for the information of Congress, the annual report of the World's Columbian Commission; a supplementary report of the same commission, submitted February 16, 1892; the report of the board appointed by me under section 16 of the act of April 25, 1890, to have charge of the exhibit to be made by the Executive Departments, the Smithsonian Institution, the Fish Commission, and the National Museum; and the report of the board of lady managers, provided for by section 6 of the act referred to.

The information furnished by these reports as to the progress of the work is not only satisfactory, but highly gratifying. The plan and scope adopted and the site and buildings selected and now being erected are fully commensurate with the national and international character of the enterprise contemplated by the legislation of Congress. The Illinois corporation has fully complied with the condition of the law that $10,000,000 should be provided, and the Government commission reports that "the grounds and buildings will be the most extensive, adequate, and ornate ever devoted to such purposes." It seems, however, that from five to eight millions of dollars more will, in the opinion of the local board and the national commission, be necessary to prepare the exposition for a complete and successful inauguration. It will be noticed from the reports that it was first proposed by the local commission to ask of Congress a loan of $5,000,000, to be repaid from receipts, and that the national commission approved this suggestion. Subsequently the Illinois exposition corporation reconsidered its action and determined to ask a subscription of $5,000,000.

The supplementary report of the national commission seems to approve this amended proposition. I have not myself that detailed information as to the financial necessities of the enterprise which would enable me to form an independent judgment of the additional amount necessary, and am not, therefore, prepared to make any specific recommendation to Congress upon the subject. The committees of Congress having this matter in charge will undoubtedly obtain full and accurate information before final action. The exposition, notwithstanding the limitations which the act contains, is an enterprise to which the United States is so far committed that Congress ought not, I think, to withhold just and reasonable further support if the local corporation consents to proper conditions.

Liberality on the part of the United States is due to the foreign nations that have responded in a friendly way to the invitation of this Government to participate in the exposition, and will, I am sure, meet the approval of our people. The exposition will be one of the most illustrious incidents in our civic history.

I transmit also certain resolutions adopted by representatives of the National Guard of the various States appointed by the governors to attend a convention which was held in Chicago on the 27th of October, 1891, with a view to consider the subject of holding a military encampment at Chicago during the exposition.

BENJ. HARRISON.

EXECUTIVE MANSION, *February 25, 1892.*

To the Senate and House of Representatives:

I transmit herewith copy of a memorial of the Wichitas, Caddoes, and affiliated tribes of Indians in Oklahoma Territory in the matter of their claim to the lands they occupy, for consideration in connection with the agreement concluded by and between the Cherokee Commission and said Indians, and also with my communication of the 17th instant,* relative to the act to pay the Choctaw and Chickasaw Indians for certain lands now occupied by the Cheyenne and Arapahoe Indians.

BENJ. HARRISON.

EXECUTIVE MANSION,
Washington, March 8, 1892.

To the Senate:

I herewith transmit, with a view to its ratification, a convention signed at Washington the 29th of February, 1892, between the Governments of the United States and Her Britannic Majesty, submitting to arbitration the questions which have arisen between those Governments concerning the jurisdictional rights of the United States in the waters of the Bering Sea, and concerning also the preservation of the fur seal in and habitually resorting to the said sea and the rights of the citizens and subjects of either country as regards the taking of fur seal in or habitually resorting to the said waters.

The correspondence not heretofore submitted to Congress in relation to the Bering Sea matter is in course of preparation and will be transmitted without delay.

BENJ. HARRISON.

EXECUTIVE MANSION, *March 9, 1892.*

To the Senate and House of Representatives:

I transmit herewith, for the consideration of Congress, a communication of the 5th instant from the Secretary of the Interior, submitting the agreement concluded by and between the commissioners for the United States and the Cherokee Nation of Indians of the Indian Territory, for the cession of certain lands and for other purposes.

BENJ. HARRISON.

EXECUTIVE MANSION,
Washington, March 18, 1892.

To the Senate:

I herewith transmit, in answer to the resolution of the Senate of the 3d ultimo, a report from the Acting Secretary of State of the 17th instant,

*See pp. 229-234.

transmitting information relative to and his opinion as to the purchase of the unpublished correspondence and manuscripts of President James Monroe.

BENJ. HARRISON.

EXECUTIVE MANSION, *March 24, 1892.*

To the Senate and House of Representatives:

I transmit herewith a communication from the Board of Commissioners of the District of Columbia, accompanied by a letter from the chairman of the executive committee organized by the citizens of Washington for the reception and entertainment of the Twenty-sixth Annual Encampment of the Grand Army of the Republic, which is to be held in Washington during September next. An appeal is made for an appropriation by Congress of $100,000, one-half to be paid out of the District revenues, to aid in defraying the expenses attending this reception.

The event is one of very high and, as I believe, of national interest, and the attendance of the surviving Union soldiers will, I do not doubt, be larger than at any annual encampment that has ever been held. The public authorities of the cities or States, or both, in which the encampments have been held have, I believe, usually appropriated liberally to make the occasions worthy and the entertainment hospitable. The parade of the survivors of our great armies upon Pennsylvania avenue will bring vividly back to us those joyful and momentous days when the great victorious armies of the East and of the West marched through the streets of Washington in high parade and were received by our citizens with joyful acclaim. It seems to me that it will be highly appropriate for Congress suitably to aid in making this demonstration impressive and in extending to those soldiers whose lives a beneficent Providence has prolonged an opportunity to see in the security and peace, development and prosperity, which now so happily pervade the national capital the fruits of their sacrifice and valor.

BENJ. HARRISON.

EXECUTIVE MANSION, *April 1, 1892.*

To the Senate of the United States:

In compliance with a resolution of the 30th ultimo, the House of Representatives concurring, I return herewith the bill (S. 1057) entitled ''An act to punish the unlawful appropriation of the use of the property of another in the District of Columbia.''

BENJ. HARRISON.

EXECUTIVE MANSION,
Washington, April 1, 1892.

To the Senate:

I herewith transmit, in answer to the resolutions of the Senate of the 16th and 21st ultimo, a report from the Acting Secretary of State, with accompanying statistics, showing the duties imposed by the Governments of Venezuela and Colombia upon products of the United States imported into these countries.

BENJ. HARRISON.

EXECUTIVE MANSION,
Washington, April 4, 1892.

To the Senate:

I transmit, in reply to the resolution of the Senate passed in executive session on March 14, 1892, a report from the Secretary of State, with accompanying documents, in relation to the correspondence relating to the nonacceptance of Hon. Henry W. Blair as minister of the United States to the Government of China.

BENJ. HARRISON.

To the Senate: EXECUTIVE MANSION, *April 12, 1892.*

I transmit, in reply to the resolution of the Senate under date of December 15, 1891, a report from the Secretary of State, with accompanying documents, in relation to the correspondence had with regard to the impressment into its service and punishment by the Government of Italy of Nicolino Mileo, a naturalized citizen of the United States.

BENJ. HARRISON.

To the Senate: EXECUTIVE MANSION, *April 14, 1892.*

I herewith transmit, in response to the resolution passed in the Senate on the 10th of March, 1892, a report of the Secretary of State and the accompanying correspondence, had in relation to the claim of the Venezuela Steam Transportation Company for the said company's relief.

BENJ. HARRISON.

To the Senate: EXECUTIVE MANSION, *April 26, 1892.*

I have received the resolution of the Senate of April 23, requesting that, if not incompatible with the public interest, I inform the Senate what steps have been taken toward the securing of an international conference to consider the question of the free coinage of silver at the mints of the nations participating in such conference, or as to the enlarged use of silver in the currency system of said countries, and that I transmit to the Senate any correspondence between the United States and other governments upon the subject, and in response thereto beg respectfully to inform the Senate that in my opinion it would not be compatible with the public interest to lay before the Senate at this time the information requested, but that at the earliest moment after definite information can properly be given all the facts and any correspondence that may take place will be submitted to Congress.

It may not be inappropriate, however, to say here that, believing that the full use of silver as a coined metal upon an agreed ratio by the great commercial nations of the world would very highly promote the prosperity of all their people, I have not and will not let any favorable opportunity pass for the promotion of that most desirable result, or, if free international silver coinage is not presently attainable, then to secure the largest practicable use of that metal.
BENJ. HARRISON.

EXECUTIVE MANSION, *May 11, 1892.*
To the House of Representatives:

In compliance with the resolution of the House of Representatives, the Senate concurring, I return herewith the bill (H. R. 3927) entitled "An act to amend 'An act to provide for the performance of the duties of the office of President in case of the removal, death, resignation, or inability both of the President and Vice-President,' approved January 19, 1886."
BENJ. HARRISON.

EXECUTIVE MANSION, *May 11, 1892.*
To the Senate and House of Representatives:

I transmit herewith the seventh annual report of the Commissioner of Labor, which report relates to the cost of producing textiles and glass in the United States and in Europe. It also comprehends the wages and the cost of living of persons employed in the textile and glass industries.
BENJ. HARRISON.

EXECUTIVE MANSION, *May 25, 1892.*
To the Senate and House of Representatives:

I transmit herewith a communication of the Secretary of War, dated May 24, from which and from the accompanying papers it appears that the late General George W. Cullum, of the United States Army, has by will devised $250,000 to the Government of the United States for the erection of a memorial hall upon the grounds of the Military Academy at West Point, to be used as a "receptacle of statues, busts, mural tablets, and portraits of distinguished deceased officers and graduates of the Military Academy, of paintings of battle scenes, trophies of war, and such other objects as may tend to give elevation to the military profession."

This ample and patriotic gift is hampered by no conditions and involves no appropriation beyond the sum so generously donated.

The executors in order to facilitate action have prepared, and the same is herewith submitted, the outline of a bill to carry into effect the provisions of General Cullum's will.

There can be no occasion to urge upon Congress the immediate enactment of a suitable law to carry into effect the patriotic purpose expressed in the will.

I suggest that in the bill itself, or by a separate joint resolution, suitable expression be given of the public appreciation of this crowning service to the military profession and to his country rendered by General Cullum.

BENJ. HARRISON.

EXECUTIVE MANSION, May 25, 1892.

To the Senate and House of Representatives:

In accordance with the provisions of section 4119 of the Revised Statutes of the United States, I lay before you for revision a copy of the regulations for the consular courts of the United States in Korea, as decreed by the minister of this Government at Seoul March 31, 1892. I also transmit an accompanying report by the Acting Secretary of State.

BENJ. HARRISON.

EXECUTIVE MANSION, June 20, 1892.

To the Senate of the United States:

The following resolution was passed by the Senate on the 24th day of February last:

> *Resolved*, That the President be requested, if in his opinion not incompatible with the public interests, to inform the Senate of the proceedings recently had with the representatives of the Dominion of Canada and of the British Government as to arrangements for reciprocal trade between Canada and the United States.

In response thereto I now submit the following information:

On the 15th day of April last the Secretary of State submitted to me a report, which is herewith transmitted. Shortly after the report came into my possession I was advised by the Secretary that the British minister at this capital had informed him that the Canadian government desired a further conference on the subject of the discriminating canal tolls of which this country had complained. This information was accompanied by the suggestion that a response to the resolution of the Senate might properly be delayed until this further conference was held.

On the 3d instant the British minister, in connection with Hon. Mac-Kenzie Bowell and Hon. George E. Foster, members of the Canadian ministry, were received by the Secretary of State and a further conference took place. In both of the conferences referred to Hon. John W. Foster, at the request of the Secretary of State, appeared with him on behalf of this Government; and the report of the latter conference was submitted to me on the 6th instant by Mr. Foster, and is herewith transmitted. The result of the conference as to the practicability of arranging a reciprocity treaty with the Dominion of Canada is clearly stated in the letter of Mr. Blaine, and was anticipated, I think, by him and by every other thoughtful American who had considered the subject. A reciprocity treaty limited to the exchange of natural products would have been such only in form. The benefits of such a treaty would have inured almost wholly to Canada. Previous experiments on this line had been unsatisfactory to this Government. A treaty that should be reciprocal in fact and of mutual advantages must necessarily have embraced an important list of manufactured articles and have secured to the United States a free or favored introduction of these articles into Canada as against the world; but it was not believed that the Canadian ministry was ready to propose or assent to such an arrangement. The conclusion of the Canadian commissioners is stated in the report of Mr. Blaine as follows:

In the second place, it seemed to be impossible for the Canadian government, in view of its present political relations and obligations, to extend to American goods a preferential treatment over those of other countries. As Canada was a part of the British Empire, they did not consider it competent for the Dominion government to enter into any commercial arrangement with the United States from the benefits of which Great Britain and its colonies should be excluded.

It is not for this Government to argue against this announcement of Canadian official opinion. It must be accepted, however, I think, as the statement of a condition which places an insuperable barrier in the way of the attainment of that large and beneficial intercourse and reciprocal trade which might otherwise be developed between the United States and the Dominion.

It will be noticed that Mr. Blaine reports as one of the results of the conference "an informal engagement to repeal and abandon the drawback of 18 cents a ton given to wheat (grain) that is carried through to Montreal and shipped therefrom to Europe. By the American railways running from Ogdensburg and Oswego and other American ports the shippers paid the full 20 cents a ton, while in effect those by the way of Montreal pay only 2 cents. It was understood that the Canadian commissioners, who were all three members of the cabinet, would see to the withdrawal of this discrimination."

From the report of the recent conference by Mr. Foster it will be seen that the Canadian commissioners declare that this statement does not conform to their understanding, and that the only assurance they had intended to give was that the complaint of the Government of the United States should be taken into consideration by the Canadian ministry on their return to Ottawa. Mr. Foster, who was present at the first conference, confirms the statements of Mr. Blaine. While this misunderstanding is unfortunate, the more serious phase of the situation is that instead of rescinding the discriminating canal tolls of which this Government complains the Canadian ministry, after the return of the commissioners from their visit to Washington, on April 4, reissued, without any communication with this Government, the order continuing the discrimination, by which a rebate of 18 cents a ton is allowed upon grain going to Montreal, but not to American ports, and refusing this rebate even to grain going to Montreal if transshipped at an American port.

The report of Mr. Partridge, the Solicitor of the Department of State, which accompanies the letter of the Secretary of State, states these discriminations very clearly. That these orders as to canal tolls and rebates are in direct violation of Article XXVII of the treaty of 1871 seems to be clear. It is wholly evasive to say that there is no discrimination between Canadian and American vessels; that the rebate is allowed to both without favor upon grain carried through to Montreal or transshipped at a Canadian port to Montreal. The treaty runs:

To secure to the citizens of the United States the use of the Welland, St. Lawrence, and other canals in the Dominion on terms of equality with the inhabitants of the Dominion.

It was intended to give to consumers in the United States, to our people engaged in railroad transportation, and to those exporting from our ports equal terms in passing their merchandise through these canals. This absolute equality of treatment was the consideration for concessions on the part of this Government made in the same article of the treaty, and which have been faithfully kept.

It is a matter of regret that the Canadian government has not responded promptly to our request for the removal of these discriminating tolls.

The papers submitted show how serious the loss inflicted is upon our lake vessels and upon some of our lake ports. In view of the fact that the Canadian commissioners still contest with us the claim that these tolls are discriminating and insist that they constitute no violation of the letter or spirit of Article XXVII of the treaty, it would seem appropriate that Congress, if the view held by the Executive is approved, should with deliberation and yet with promptness take such steps as may be necessary to secure the just rights of our citizens.

In view of the delays which have already taken place in transmitting this correspondence to Congress, I have not felt justified in awaiting the further communication from the government of Canada which was suggested in the recent conference.

Should any proposition relating to this matter be received it will be immediately submitted for the consideration of the Senate, and if forwarded within the time suggested will undoubtedly anticipate any final action by Congress.

BENJ. HARRISON.

To the Senate: EXECUTIVE MANSION, *June 20, 1892.*

In response to the resolution of the Senate dated March 14, 1892, requesting that certain specified correspondence in regard to the claim of

Antonio Maximo Mora against the Government of Spain be communicated to it, if not incompatible with the public interests, I transmit herewith the report of the Acting Secretary of State on the matter.

BENJ. HARRISON.

To the Senate: EXECUTIVE MANSION, *June 27, 1892.*

In response to the resolution of the Senate dated April 6, 1892, directing the Secretary of State to send to the Senate, if not incompatible with the public interests, copies of all commercial agreements made with other countries, and also to report what steps have been taken to negotiate a reciprocal commercial treaty with Mexico, I submit herewith the reply of the Acting Secretary of State to that resolution.

BENJ. HARRISON.

To the Senate: EXECUTIVE MANSION, *July 1, 1892.*

For the information of the Senate and in further response to the resolution of the Senate of February 24 last, I transmit herewith a communication of the 24th ultimo from Mr. Herbert, the acting representative of the British Government at this capital, addressed to Mr. Wharton, Acting Secretary of State, upon the subject of Canadian canal tolls; also a memorandum prepared and submitted to me by Mr. Adee, Second Assistant Secretary of State, reviewing the communication of Mr. Herbert, and a letter of the 28th ultimo from Mr. John W. Foster, who, as I have previously stated, with Mr. Blaine represented this Government in the conferences with the Canadian commissioners.

The position taken by this Government, as expressed in my previous communication to the Senate, that the canal tolls and regulations of which complaint has been made are in violation of our treaty with Great Britain, is not shaken, but rather confirmed.

There can be no doubt that a serious discrimination against our citizens and our commerce exists, and quite as little doubt that this discrimination is not the incident but the purpose of the Canadian regulation.

It has not seemed to me that this was a case in which we could yield to the suggestion of further concessions on the part of the United States with a view to securing treaty rights for which a consideration has already been given.

BENJ. HARRISON.

EXECUTIVE MANSION, *July 21, 1892.*

To the Senate and House of Representatives:

I herewith transmit, for the information of Congress, a communication from the Secretary of State, forwarding certain bulletins of the American Republics.

BENJ. HARRISON.

EXECUTIVE MANSION,
Washington, July 23, 1892.

To the Senate of the United States:

I transmit, in reply to the resolution of the Senate passed in executive session on the 21st instant and addressed to the Secretary of State, a report of that officer, with accompanying documents, in further relation to the nonacceptance of the Hon. Henry W. Blair as minister of the United States to the Government of China, which question was the occasion of my recent message to the Senate of the 4th of April last.*

BENJ. HARRISON.

EXECUTIVE MANSION, *July 25, 1892.*

To the Senate:

I herewith transmit, in reply to the resolution of the Senate of June 6, 1892, a report from the Secretary of State, with its accompanying papers, in relation to guano deposits on Arcas Cays or Islands.

BENJ. HARRISON.

WASHINGTON, D. C., *July 27, 1892.*

To the Senate and House of Representatives:

I transmit herewith, with its accompaniments, a report from the Secretary of the Navy of the results of the survey made pursuant to the act of March 2, 1891, ''to enable the President to cause careful soundings to be made between San Francisco, Cal., and Honolulu, in the Kingdom of the Hawaiian Islands, for the purpose of determining the practicability of the laying of a telegraphic cable between those points.''

BENJ. HARRISON.

VETO MESSAGES.

EXECUTIVE MANSION, *July 19, 1892.*

To the Senate:

I return herewith without my approval the bill (S. 2729) entitled ''An act to amend an act entitled 'An act to establish circuit courts of appeals, and to define and regulate in certain cases the jurisdiction of the courts of the United States, and for other purposes.'''

The original act to which this amendment is proposed, constituting an intermediate court of appeals, had for its object the relief of the Supreme Court by limiting the cases which might be brought up for hearing in that court. The first section of the bill under consideration allows appeals in criminal cases where the sentence imposes no imprisonment and the fine is as much as $1,000. The effect of this provision will be to

* See p. 238.

bring to the Supreme Court many cases that in my opinion should be finally determined in the intermediate appellate court, and so in part to defeat the general purpose of Congress in constituting the intermediate court. But this objection would not alone have sufficient weight in my mind to induce me to return the bill. Section 3 of the bill is as follows:

That no appeal shall hereafter be allowed from judgments of the Court of Claims in cases under the act of March 3, 1891, entitled "An act to provide for the adjudication and payment of claims arising from Indian depredations," except where the adjudication involves the construction or application of the Constitution or the validity or construction of a treaty or the constitutionality of a law of the United States: *Provided, however*, That upon such appeal it shall be competent for the Supreme Court to require, by certiorari or otherwise, the whole case to be certified for its review and determination upon the facts as well as the law.

I am advised by the Attorney-General that under the Indian-depredations act 8,000 cases, involving an aggregate of damages claimed of about $30,000,000, have already been filed. A number of these cases involve as much as $100,000 each, while a few involve as much as $500,-000 each and one something over $1,000,000. The damages which may be awarded in these cases by the Court of Claims are to be paid out of the trust funds of the Indians held by the United States, or, if there are no such funds, out of the Treasury of the United States. The law referring these cases to the Court of Claims has had no judicial interpretation, and many novel and difficult questions are likely to arise. It is quite a startling proposition, and a very novel one, I think, that there shall be absolutely no opportunity for the review in an appellate court, in cases involving such large amounts, of questions involving the construction of the statute under which the court is proceeding, or those various questions of law, many of them new, which necessarily arise in such cases.

Neither the claimants, the Indians, nor the Government of the United States should be absolutely denied opportunity to bring their exceptions to review by some appellate tribunal. I would not suggest that an appeal should be allowed in all cases. Some limitation as to amount would be reasonable, and perhaps some discretion might be lodged in the Supreme Court as to granting appeals. The limitations, however, imposed by the section I have quoted are so severe and unreasonable, in my judgment, that I have felt compelled to return the bill to the Senate with a view to its reconsideration.

BENJ. HARRISON.

EXECUTIVE MANSION, *July 29, 1892.*

To the Senate:

I return herewith without my approval the bill (S. 1958) entitled "An act to submit to the Court of Private Land Claims, established by an act of Congress approved March 3, 1891, the title of William McGarrahan to the Rancho Panoche Grande, in the State of California, and for other purposes."

This bill came to me on the 20th instant, at a time when very many other bills were submitted for my consideration, and it has not been possible for me to make such an examination of the history of Mr. McGarrahan's claim as would be necessary to form an intelligent judgment as to its merits and just extent. It is quite possible that he has been wronged and that he has a claim for some reparation from the Government. I can not, however, think that this bill proceeds upon a just basis. It provides that Mr. McGarrahan shall file his claim as the assignee of Gomez in the Court of Private Land Claims for the lands described in the title, and that if the court establishes the grant to Gomez it shall be confirmed to McGarrahan. No evidence that he is the assignee of Gomez is, I think, required by the bill, which assumes that fact instead of submitting it to the court. If the claim is established, it is provided in substance that all lands part of said grant which have been conveyed by the Government or are in the occupancy of actual settlers, or "upon which there are any smelting or reduction works, or the lands claimed in connection with such reduction or smelting works," shall be excepted from the patent which the Secretary of the Interior is directed to issue to McGarrahan. By this provision the title of the New Idria Mining Company, which has long contested with McGarrahan the title to a large part of this property, is established and that company is relieved from any responsibility to account for the profits made in mining. On the other hand, the United States waives all benefit of judicial proceedings which have resulted in its favor and gives Mr. McGarrahan an opportunity *de novo* to try all such questions; and the decision, if in his favor, is not only to restore to him all the lands yet undisposed of, but the United States assumes to pay him the value of the lands appropriated by others and of their use for all these years and to account to him for all profits that have been made by the New Idria Mining Company or anyone else in quicksilver or other mining.

This seems to me to be wholly inadmissible. The amount involved must be enormously large, though at present incapable of any accurate estimate. If the title of the New Idria Company has been established by final decrees of court placing that title beyond question and that company beyond any call to respond for use and profits, why should the Government of the United States, waiving in its behalf these decrees, which would protect it also, assume a responsibility to account for the value of the lands and for their use and for the net value of minerals extracted by that company or others? It will be noticed in the quotation I have made from the act that this company is allowed to take all the land it may claim, but at the expense of the United States, not of Mr. McGarrahan.

The bill is so framed as to give full protection to the New Idria Mining Company to the full extent of its largest claim, while throwing upon the United States a responsibility which that company should bear if the title of Mr. McGarrahan is established.

The United States provided a proper tribunal for the trial of claims founded upon Mexican grants. This claim was there tried, and if fraud affected the judgment it is not, I think, chargeable to the Government; the contest was chiefly between rival claimants. In this state of the case it would seem that if the United States consents to open the litigation and to wipe out all judicial findings and decrees a less exacting measure of damages than that proposed in the bill should be agreed on.

It is not my purpose, as I have intimated, to express the opinion that Mr. McGarrahan is entitled to no relief. It seems to me, however, clear that he is not entitled to the relief given by this bill, and that it does not adequately protect the interests of the United States.

BENJ. HARRISON.

EXECUTIVE MANSION, *August 3, 1892.*

To the Senate:

I return herewith without my approval the bill (S. 1111) entitled "An act to amend the act of Congress approved March 3, 1887, entitled 'An act to provide for the bringing of suits against the Government of the United States.'"

If I may judge from the very limited discussion of this measure in Congress, the sweeping effects of it upon the administration of the public lands could hardly have been fully realized. From the beginning of the Government the administration of the public lands and the issuing of patents under the land laws have been an Executive function.

The jurisdiction of the courts as to contesting claims for patents has awaited the action of the General Land Office. Land offices have been established and maintained in all the districts where public lands were found, located with reference to the convenience of the settlers, and the proceedings have been informal and inexpensive. It is true that at times, by an administration of the Land Office unfriendly toward the settlers, unnecessary delays involving much hardship have intervened in the issuing of patents, but such is not the case now. The work of the Land Office within the last three years has been so efficient and so friendly to the *bona fide* settler that the large accumulation of cases there has been swept away, and the office, as I am informed by the Secretary of the Interior, is now engaged upon current business.

It seems to me that a transfer in whole or in part of this business to the courts, some of whose dockets are already loaded with cases, can not tend to expedition, while it is very manifest that, by reason of the greater formality in the taking and presentation of evidence which would be required in court and of the long distances which settlers would have to traverse in order to attend court, the costs in such cases would be enormously increased.

It is proposed by this bill to give what is called concurrent jurisdiction to the district courts of the United States and to the Court of Claims to hear and determine all claims for land patents under any law or grant of the United States. Whether concurrent with each other or with each other and the Land Office is not clear.

It is quite doubtful under the rulings of the Supreme Court whether the courts now provided by law for the Territories are "district courts of the United States" within the meaning of this bill. The effect of this legislation would, if they were held not to be such, be that as to all suits relating to lands in the Territories of New Mexico, Arizona, Utah, and Oklahoma no other forum is provided than the Court of Claims at Washington. In this state of the case a settler, or one who has taken a mineral claim in any of these Territories, would be subject to be brought to the city of Washington for the trial of his case.

In view of the fact that all recent legislation of Congress has been in the direction of subdividing judicial districts and of bringing the United States courts nearer to the litigants, I can only attribute to oversight the passage of this bill, which in my opinion would burden the homesteader and preemptor whose claim is contested, whether by another individual or by any corporation, by compelling him to appear at Washington and to conduct with the formality and expense incident to court proceedings the defense of his title. But even in the case of land contests arising in the States where district courts exist the plaintiff, it will be observed, by this act is given the option to sue in those courts or to bring his adversary to Washington to litigate the claim. Why should he have this advantage, one that is not given so far as I know in any other law fixing the forum of litigation between individuals? Not only is this true, but the Court of Claims was established for the trial of cases between individuals and corporations on the one side and the United States on the other, and so far as I now recall wholly for the trial of money claims.

There are no adequate provisions of law, if any at all, for conducting suits between individuals contesting private rights. The court has one bailiff and one messenger, no marshal, and is not provided, I think, either with the machinery or with the appropriation to send its processes to the most distant parts of the country. Yet it is apparent that under this bill the real issue would frequently be between rival claimants, and not between either and the United States. This court, too, is already burdened with business since the reference to it of the Indian depredation claims, the French spoliation claims, etc., and it certainly can not be thought that a more speedy settlement of land claims could be there obtained than is now given.

Again, the bill is so indefinite in its provisions that it can not be told, I think, what function, if any, remains to be discharged by the General Land Office. It was said in answer to an interrogatory when the bill was under consideration that it did not affect claims pending in the Land Office; and yet it seems to me that its effect is to allow any contestant in the Land Office at any stage of the proceedings there to transfer the whole controversy to the courts. He may take his chances of success in the Land Office, and if at any time he becomes apprehensive of an adverse decision he may begin *de novo* in the courts.

If it was intended to preserve the jurisdiction of the Land Office and to hold cases there until a judgment had been reached, the bill should have so provided, for it is capable of, and indeed seems to me compels, the construction that either party may forsake the Land Office at any stage of a contest. I am quite inclined to believe that if provision were made, as in section 1063 of the Revised Statutes, relating to claims in other departments, for the transfer to a proper court, under proper regulations, of certain contest cases involving questions affecting large classes of claims, it would be a relief to the Land Office and would tend to a more speedy adjustment of land titles in such cases, a result which would be in the interest of all our people.

Nothing is more disadvantageous to a community, its progress and peace, than unsettled land titles. This bill, however, as I have said, is so radical and seems to me to be so indefinite in its provisions that I can not give it my approval.

BENJ. HARRISON.

PROCLAMATIONS.

BY THE PRESIDENT OF THE UNITED STATES OF AMERICA.

A PROCLAMATION.

Whereas, pursuant to section 3 of the act of Congress approved October 1, 1890, entitled "An act to reduce the revenue and equalize duties on imports, and for other purposes," the Secretary of State of the United States of America communicated to the Government of Salvador the action of the Congress of the United States of America, with a view to secure reciprocal trade, in declaring the articles enumerated in said section 3 to be exempt from duty upon their importation into the United States of America; and

Whereas the envoy extraordinary and minister plenipotentiary of Salvador at Washington has communicated to the Secretary of State the fact that, in reciprocity for the admission into the United States of America free of all duty of the articles enumerated in section 3 of said act, the Government of Salvador will by due legal enactment, as a provisional measure and until a more complete arrangement may be negotiated and put in operation, admit free of all duty, from and after February 1, 1892, into all the established ports of entry of Salvador the articles or merchandise named in the following schedule, provided that the same be the product or manufacture of the United States:

SCHEDULE OF PRODUCTS AND MANUFACTURES WHICH THE REPUBLIC OF SALVA-
    DOR WILL ADMIT FREE OF ALL CUSTOMS, MUNICIPAL, AND ANY OTHER KIND
    OF DUTY.

1. Animals for breeding purposes.
2. Corn, rice, barley, and rye.
3. Beans.
4. Hay and straw for forage.
5. Fruits, fresh.
6. Preparations of flour in biscuits, crackers not sweetened, macaroni, vermicelli, and tallarin.
7. Coal, mineral.
8. Roman cement.
9. Hydraulic lime.
10. Bricks, fire bricks, and crucibles for melting.
11. Marble, dressed, for furniture, statues, fountains, gravestones, and building purposes.
12. Tar, vegetable and mineral.
13. Guano and other fertilizers, natural or artificial.
14. Plows and all other agricultural tools and implements.
15. Machinery of all kinds, including sewing machines, and separate or extra parts for the same.
16. Materials of all kinds for the construction and equipment of railroads.
17. Materials of all kinds for the construction and operation of telegraphic and telephonic lines.
18. Materials of all kinds for lighting by electricity and gas.
19. Materials of all kinds for the construction of wharves.
20. Apparatus for distilling liquors.
21. Wood of all kinds for building, in trunks or pieces, beams, rafters, planks, boards, shingles, or flooring.
22. Wooden staves, heads, and hoops, and barrels and boxes for packing, mounted or in pieces.
23. Houses of wood or iron, complete or in parts.
24. Wagons, carts, and carriages of all kinds.
25. Barrels, casks, and tanks of iron for water.
26. Tubes of iron and all other accessories necessary for water supply.
27. Wire, barbed, and staples for fences.
28. Plates of iron for building purposes.
29. Mineral ores.
30. Kettles of iron for making salt.
31. Kettles of iron for making sugar.
32. Molds for making sugar.
33. Guys for mining purposes.
34. Furnaces and instruments for assaying metals.
35. Scientific instruments.
36. Models of machinery and buildings.
37. Boats, lighters, tackle, anchors, chains, girtlines, sails, and all other articles for vessels, to be used in the ports, lakes, and rivers of the Republic.
38. Printing materials, including presses, type, ink, and all other accessories.
39. Printed books, pamphlets, and newspapers, bound or unbound, maps, photographs, printed music, and paper for music.
40. Paper for printing newspapers.
41. Quicksilver.
42. Loadstones.
43. Hops.

44. Sulphate of quinine.
45. Gold and silver in bars, dust, or coin.
46. Samples of merchandise the duties on which do not exceed $1.

It is understood that the packages or coverings in which the articles named in the foregoing schedule are imported shall be free of duty if they are usual and proper for the purpose.

And that the Government of Salvador has further stipulated that the laws and regulations adopted to protect its revenue and prevent fraud in the declarations and proof that the articles named in the foregoing schedule are the product or manufacture of the United States of America shall impose no additional charges on the importer nor undue restrictions on the articles imported; and

Whereas the Secretary of State has, by my direction, given assurance to the envoy extraordinary and minister plenipotentiary of Salvador at Washington that this action of the Government of Salvador in granting freedom of duties to the products and manufactures of the United States of America on their importation into Salvador and in stipulating for a more complete reciprocity arrangement is accepted as a due reciprocity for the action of Congress as set forth in section 3 of said act:

Now, therefore, be it known that I, Benjamin Harrison, President of the United States of America, have caused the above-stated modifications of the tariff laws of Salvador to be made public for the information of the citizens of the United States of America.

In testimony whereof I have hereunto set my hand and caused the seal of the United States to be affixed.

[SEAL.]   Done at the city of Washington, this 31st day of December, 1891, and of the Independence of the United States of America the one hundred and sixteenth.

                                          BENJ. HARRISON.
By the President:
    JAMES G. BLAINE, *Secretary of State.*

BY THE PRESIDENT OF THE UNITED STATES OF AMERICA.

A PROCLAMATION.

Whereas it is provided by section 24 of the act of Congress approved March 3, 1891, entitled "An act to repeal timber-culture laws, and for other purposes"—

That the President of the United States may from time to time set apart and reserve in any State or Territory having public land bearing forests, in any part of the public lands wholly or in part covered with timber or undergrowth, whether of commercial value or not, as public reservations; and the President shall by public proclamation declare the establishment of such reservation and the limits thereof.

And whereas the public lands in the Territory of New Mexico within the limits hereinafter described are in part covered with timber, and it appears that the public good would be promoted by setting apart and reserving said lands as a public reservation:

Now, therefore, I, Benjamin Harrison, President of the United States,

by virtue of the power in me vested by section 24 of the aforesaid act of Congress, do hereby make known and proclaim that there is hereby reserved from entry or settlement and set apart as a public reservation all those certain tracts, pieces, or parcels of land lying and being situate in the Territory of New Mexico and particularly described as follows, to wit:

Commencing at the standard corner to township seventeen (17) north, ranges thirteen (13) and fourteen (14) east (New Mexico principal base and meridian) on the fourth (4th) standard parallel north; thence northerly along the range line between ranges thirteen (13) and fourteen (14) east to the closing corner between ranges thirteen (13) and fourteen (14) east on the fifth (5th) standard parallel north; thence along said fifth (5th) standard parallel to the southeast corner of township twenty-one (21) north, range thirteen (13) east; thence north six (6) miles; thence west twelve (12) miles; thence due south to the fifth (5th) standard parallel; thence westerly on said fifth (5th) standard parallel to a point due north of the northwest corner of township seventeen (17) north, range eleven (11) east; thence south to the fourth (4th) standard parallel; thence westerly on said fourth (4th) standard parallel north seven and sixty-two one-hundredths (7.62) chains to the northwest corner of township sixteen (16) north, range eleven (11) east; thence southerly on the range line between townships sixteen (16) north, ranges ten (10) and eleven (11) east, three (3) miles and three and forty-three hundredths (3.43) chains to the corner to sections thirteen (13), eighteen (18), nineteen (19), and twenty-four (24) on said range line; thence easterly along the section lines to the range line between ranges eleven (11) and twelve (12) east; thence northerly three (3) miles and three (3) chains to the fourth (4th) standard parallel north; thence easterly on said fourth (4th) standard parallel eight (8) and fifty-hundredths (8.50) chains to the standard corner to township seventeen (17) north, ranges eleven (11) and twelve (12) east; thence northerly on the range line to the southwest corner of township eighteen (18) north, range twelve (12) east; thence easterly on the township line six (6) miles one and six-hundredths (1.06) chains to the southeast corner of township eighteen (18) north, range twelve (12) east; thence south six (6) miles to the fourth (4th) standard parallel north; thence east along said fourth (4th) standard parallel to the place of beginning.

Excepting from the force and effect of this proclamation all land which may have been prior to the date hereof embraced in any valid Spanish or Mexican grant or in any legal entry or covered by any lawful filing duly made in the proper United States land office, and all mining claims duly located and held according to the laws of the United States and rules and regulations not in conflict therewith.

Provided, That this exception shall not continue to apply to any particular tract of land unless the entryman or claimant continues to comply with the law under which the entry, filing, or location was made.

Warning is hereby expressly given to all persons not to enter or make settlement upon the tract of land reserved by this proclamation.

In witness whereof I have hereunto set my hand and caused the seal of the United States to be affixed.

[SEAL.]   Done at the city of Washington, this 11th day of January, A. D. 1892, and of the Independence of the United States the one hundred and sixteenth.

BENJ. HARRISON.

By the President:
JAMES G. BLAINE, *Secretary of State.*

BY THE PRESIDENT OF THE UNITED STATES OF AMERICA.

A PROCLAMATION.

Whereas, pursuant to section 3 of the act of Congress approved October 1, 1890, entitled "An act to reduce the revenue and equalize duties on imports, and for other purposes," the attention of the Government of Great Britain was called to the action of the Congress of the United States of America, with a view to secure reciprocal trade, in declaring the articles enumerated in said section 3 to be exempt from duty upon their importation into the United States of America; and

Whereas the envoy extraordinary and minister plenipotentiary of Great Britain at Washington has communicated to the Secretary of State the fact that, in view of the act of Congress above cited, the Government of Great Britain has by due legal enactment authorized the admission, from and after February 1, 1892, of the articles in merchandise named in the following schedules, on the terms stated therein, into the British colonies of Trinidad (which includes Tobago), Barbados, the Leeward Islands (consisting of the islands of Antigua, Montserrat, St. Christopher, Nevis, Dominica, with their respective dependencies, and the Virgin Islands), the Windward Islands (consisting of St. Lucia, St. Vincent, and their dependencies, but exclusive of Grenada and its dependencies), and into the colony of British Guiana on and after April 1, 1892:

TABLE No. 1.—APPLICABLE TO BRITISH GUIANA, TRINIDAD AND TOBAGO, BARBADOS, THE LEEWARD ISLANDS, AND THE WINDWARD ISLANDS EXCEPTING THE ISLAND OF GRENADA.

SCHEDULE A.

Articles to be admitted free of all customs duty and any other national, colonial, or municipal charges:

1. Animals, alive, to include only asses, sheep, goats, hogs, and poultry, and horses for breeding.
2. Beef, including tongues, smoked and dried.
3. Beef and pork preserved in cans.
4. Belting for machinery, of leather, canvas, or india rubber.
5. Boats and lighters.
6. Books,* bound or unbound, pamphlets, newspapers, and printed matter in all languages.
7. Bones and horns.
8. Bottles of glass or stone ware.
9. Bran, middlings, and shorts.

* The importation of books is subject to the provisions of copyright laws.

10. Bridges of iron or wood, or of both combined.

11. Brooms, brushes, and whisks of broom straw.

12. Candles, tallow.

13. Carts, wagons, cars, and barrows, with or without springs, for ordinary roads and agricultural use, not including vehicles of pleasure.

14. Clocks, mantel or wall.

15. Copper, bronze, zinc, and lead articles, plain and nickel plated, for industrial and domestic uses and for building.

16. Cotton seed and its products.

17. Crucibles and melting pots of all kinds.

18. Eggs.

19. Fertilizers of all kinds, natural and artificial.

20. Fish, fresh or on ice, and salmon and oysters in cans.

21. Fishing apparatus of all kinds.

22. Fruits and vegetables, fresh and dried, when not canned, tinned, or bottled.

23. Gas fixtures and pipes.

24. Gold and silver coin of the United States, and bullion.

25. Hay and straw for forage.

26. Houses of wood, complete.

27. Ice.

28. India-rubber and gutta-percha goods, including waterproof clothing made wholly or in part thereof.

29. Implements, utensils, and tools for agriculture, exclusive of cutlasses and forks.

30. Lamps and lanterns.

31. Lime of all kinds.

32. Locomotives, railway rolling stock, rails, railway ties, and all materials and appliances for railways and tramways.

33. Marble or alabaster, in the rough or squared, worked or carved, for building purposes or monuments.

34. Medicinal extracts and preparations of all kinds, including proprietary or patent medicines, but exclusive of quinine or preparations of quinine, opium, gange, and bhang.

35. Paper of all kinds for printing.

36. Paper of wood or straw for wrapping and packing, including surface coated or glazed.

37. Photographic apparatus and chemicals.

38. Printers' ink, all colors.

39. Printing presses, types, rules, spaces, and all accessories for printing.

40. Quicksilver.

41. Resin, tar, pitch, and turpentine.

42. Salt.

43. Sewing machines and all parts and accessories thereof.

44. Shipbuilding materials and accessories of all kinds, when used in the construction, equipment, or repair of vessels or boats of any kind, except rope and cordage of all kinds, including wire rope.

45. Starch of Indian corn or maize.

46. Steam and power engines, and machines, machinery, and apparatus, whether stationary or portable, worked by power or by hand, for agriculture, irrigation, mining, the arts and industries of all kinds, and all necessary parts and appliances for the erection or repair thereof or the communication of motive power thereto.

47. Steam boilers and steam pipes.

48. Sulphur.

49. Tan bark of all kinds, whole or ground.

50. Telegraph wire, telegraphic, telephonic, and electrical apparatus and appliances of all kinds for communication or illumination.

51. Trees, plants, vines, and seeds and grains of all kinds, for propagation or cultivation.

52. Varnish, not containing spirits.
53. Wall papers.
54. Watches when not cased in gold or silver, and watch movements uncased.
55. Water pipes of all classes, materials, and dimensions.
56. Wire for fences, the hooks, staples, nails, and the like appliances for fastening the same.
57. Yeast cake and baking powders.
58. Zinc, tin, and lead, in sheets, asbestus, and tar paper, for roofing.

It is understood that the packages or coverings in which the articles named in the foregoing schedule are imported shall be free of duty if they are usual and proper for the purpose.

SCHEDULE B.

Articles to be admitted at 50 per cent reduction of the duty designated in the respective customs tariff now in force in each of said colonies:
1. Bacon and bacon hams.
2. Boots and shoes made wholly or in part of leather.
3. Bread and biscuit.
4. Cheese.
5. Lard and its compounds.
6. Mules.
7. Oleomargarine.
8. Shooks and staves.

SCHEDULE C.

Articles to be admitted at 25 per cent reduction of the duty designated in the respective customs tariff now in force in each of said colonies:
1. Beef, salted or pickled.
2. Corn or maize.
3. Corn meal.
4. Flour of wheat.
5. Lumber of pitch pine, in rough or prepared for buildings.
6. Petroleum and its products, crude or refined.
7. Pork, salted or pickled.
8. Wheat.

It is understood that No. 4 of this schedule shall not apply to the colony of Trinidad, but it is stipulated that the duty on flour in said colony shall not exceed 75 cents per barrel.

And that the Government of Great Britain has by due legal enactment authorized the admission, from and after February 1, 1892, of the articles or merchandise named in the following schedules, on the terms stated therein, into the British colony of Jamaica and its dependencies:

TABLE No. 2.—APPLICABLE TO THE COLONY OF JAMAICA AND ITS DEPENDENCIES.

SCHEDULE A.

Articles to be admitted free of all customs duty and any other national, colonial, or municipal charges:
1. Animals, alive, and poultry.
2. Beef, including tongues, smoked and dried.
3. Beef and pork preserved in cans.
4. Belting for machinery, of leather, canvas, or india rubber.
5. Boats and lighters.
6. Books,* bound or unbound, pamphlets, newspapers, and printed matter in all languages.
7. Bones and horns.

*The importation of books is subject to the provisions of copyright laws.

8. Bottles of glass or stone ware.

9. Bran, middlings, and shorts.

10. Bridges of iron or wood, or of both combined.

11. Brooms, brushes, and whisks of broom straw.

12. Candles, tallow.

13. Carts, wagons, cars, and barrows, with or without springs, for ordinary roads and agricultural use, not including vehicles of pleasure.

14. Coal and coke.

15. Clocks, mantel or wall.

16. Cotton seed and its products, to include meal, meal cake, oil, and cottolene.

17. Crucibles and melting pots of all kinds.

18. Drawings, paintings, engravings, lithographs, and photographs

19. Eggs.

20. Fertilizers of all kinds, natural and artificial.

21. Fish, fresh or on ice, and oysters in cans.

22. Fishing apparatus of all kinds.

23. Fruits and vegetables, fresh and dried, when not canned, tinned, or bottled.

24. Gas fixtures and pipes.

25. Gold and silver coin of the United States, and bullion.

26. Hay and straw for forage.

27. Houses of wood, complete.

28. Ice.

29. India-rubber and gutta-percha goods, including waterproof clothing made wholly or in part thereof.

30. Implements, utensils, and tools for agriculture, exclusive of cutlasses and forks.

31. Iron, galvanized.

32. Iron for roofing.

33. Lamps and lanterns, not exceeding 10 shillings each in value.

34. Lime of all kinds.

35. Locomotives, railway rolling stock, rails, railway ties, and all materials and appliances for railways and tramways.

36. Marble or alabaster, in the rough or squared, worked or carved, for building purposes or monuments.

37. Paper of all kinds for printing.

38. Paper of wood or straw for wrapping and packing, including surface coated or glazed.

39. Photographic apparatus and chemicals.

40. Printers' ink, all colors.

41. Printing presses, types, rules, spaces, and all accessories for printing.

42. Proprietary or patent medicines, recommended by their proprietors as calculated to cure disease or alleviate pain in the human subject.

43. Quicksilver.

44. Resin, tar, pitch, and turpentine.

45. Sewing machines and all parts and accessories thereof.

46. Shipbuilding materials and accessories of all kinds, when used in the construction, equipment, or repair of vessels or boats of any kind, except rope and cordage of all kinds, including wire rope, and subject to specific regulations to avoid abuse in the importation.

47. Shooks and staves.

48. Starch of Indian corn or maize.

49. Steam and power engines, and machines, machinery, and apparatus, whether stationary or portable, worked by power or by hand, for agriculture, irrigation, mining, the arts and industries of all kinds, and all necessary parts and appliances for the erection or repair thereof or the communication of motive power thereto.

50. Steam boilers and steam pipes.
51. Sugar, refined.
52. Sulphur.
53. Tallow and animal greases.
54. Tan bark of all kinds, whole or ground.
55. Telegraph wire, telegraphic, telephonic, and electrical apparatus and appliances of all kinds for communication or illumination.
56. Trees, plants, vines, and seeds and grains of all kinds for propagation or cultivation.
57. Varnish, not containing spirits.
58. Wall papers.
59. Watches when not cased in gold or silver, and watch movements uncased.
60. Water pipes of all classes, materials, and dimensions.
61. Wire for fences, with the hooks, staples, nails, and the like appliances for fastening the same.
62. Yeast cake and baking powders.
63. Zinc, tin, and lead, in sheets, asbestos, and tar paper, for roofing.

It is understood that the packages or coverings in which the articles named in the foregoing schedule are imported shall be free of duty if they are usual and proper for the purpose.

SCHEDULE B.

Articles to be admitted at 50 per cent reduction of the duty designated in the customs tariff now in force:
1. Bacon and bacon hams.
2. Bread and biscuit.
3. Butter.
4. Cheese.
5. Lard and its compounds.

Lumber of pitch pine, in rough or prepared for buildings, to be reduced to 9 shillings per 1,000 feet.

SCHEDULE C.

Articles to be admitted at 25 per cent reduction of the duty designated in the customs tariff now in force:
1. Beef, salted or pickled.
2. Corn and maize.
3. Corn meal.
4. Oats.
5. Petroleum and its products, crude or refined.
6. Pork, salted or pickled.
7. Wheat.

And whereas the Secretary of State has, by my direction, given the assurance to the envoy extraordinary and minister plenipotentiary of Great Britain at Washington that this action of the Government of Great Britain in granting remissions and alterations of duties in the British colonies above mentioned is accepted as a due reciprocity for the action of Congress as set forth in section 3 of said act:

Now, therefore, be it known that I, Benjamin Harrison, President of the United States of America, have caused the above-stated modifications of the tariff laws of the aforesaid British colonies to be made public for the information of the citizens of the United States of America.

In testimony whereof I have hereunto set my hand and caused the seal of the United States to be affixed.

[SEAL.]   Done at the city of Washington, this 1st day of February, 1892, and of the Independence of the United States of America the one hundred and sixteenth.

BENJ. HARRISON.

By the President:

JAMES G. BLAINE, *Secretary of State.*

BY THE PRESIDENT OF THE UNITED STATES OF AMERICA.

A PROCLAMATION.

Whereas, pursuant to section 3 of the act of Congress approved October 1, 1890, entitled "An act to reduce the revenue and equalize duties on imports and for other purposes," the attention of the Government of the German Empire was called to the action of the Congress of the United States of America, with a view to secure reciprocal trade, in declaring the articles enumerated in said section 3 to be exempt from duty upon their importation into the United States of America; and

Whereas the chargé d'affaires of the German Empire at Washington has communicated to the special plenipotentiary of the United States the fact that, in view of the act of Congress above cited, the German Imperial Government has by due legal enactment authorized the admission, from and after February 1, 1892, into the German Empire of the articles or merchandise the product of the United States of America named in the following schedule, on the terms stated therein:

Schedules of articles to be admitted into Germany.

Articles.	Rate of duty per 100 kilo-grams.
	Marks.
1. Bran; malted germs...	Free.
2. Flax, raw, dried, broken, or hatcheled; also refuse portions............	Free.
3. Wheat...	3.50
4. Rye..	3.50
5. Oats...	2.80
6. Buckwheat..	2.00
7. Pulse..	1.50
8. Other kinds of grain not specially mentioned..........................	1.00
9. Barley...	2.00
10. Rape seed, turnip seed, poppy, sesame, peanuts, and other oleaginous products not specially mentioned...................................	2.00
11. Maize (Indian corn)...	1.60
12. Malt (malted barley)..	3.60
13. Anise, coriander, fennel, and caraway seed..........................	3.00
14. Agricultural productions not otherwise designated...................	Free.
15. Horsehair, raw, hatcheled, boiled, dyed, also laid in the form of tresses and spun; bristles; raw bed feathers..................................	Free.

Schedules of articles to be admitted into Germany—Continued.

Articles.	Rate of duty per 100 kilograms.
	Marks.
16. Bed feathers, cleaned and prepared...................................	Free.
17. Hides and skins, raw (green, salted, limed, dried), and stripped of the hair for the manufacture of leather...........................	Free.
18. Charcoal..	Free.
19. Bark of wood and tan bark..	Free.
20. Lumber and timber:	
(*a*) Raw or merely roughhewn with ax or saw, with or without bark; oaken barrel staves...................................	0.20
(*b*) Marked in the direction of the longitudinal axis, or prepared or cut otherwise than by roughhewing; barrel staves not included under (*a*); unpeeled osiers and hoops; hubs, fellies, and spokes...	0.30
(*c*) Sawed in the direction of the longitudinal axis; unplaned boards; sawed cantle woods and other articles sawn or hewn...	0.80
21. Wood in cut veneering; unglued, unstained parts of floors.............	5.00
22. Hops; also hop meal...	*14.00
23. Butter; also artificial butter..	17.00
24. Meat, slaughtered, fresh, with the exception of pork..................	15.00
25. Pork, slaughtered, fresh, and dressed meat, with the exception of bacon, fresh or prepared...	17.00
26. Game of all kinds (not alive).......................................	20.00
27. Cheese, except Strecchino, Gorgonzola, and Parmesan................	20.00
28. Fruit, seeds, berries, leaves, flowers, mushrooms, vegetables, dried, baked, pulverized, only boiled down or salted—all these products so far as they are not included under other numbers of the tariff; juices of fruits, berries, and turnips, preserved without sugar, to be eaten; dry nuts...	4.00
29. Mill products of grain and pulse, to wit, ground or shelled grains, peeled barley, groats, grits, flour, common cakes (bakers' products)..	7.30
30. Residue, solid, from the manufacture of fat oils, also ground..........	Free.
31. Goose grease and other greasy fats, such as oleomargarine, sperfett (a mixture of stearic fats with oil), beef marrow......................	10.00
32. Live animals and animal products not mentioned elsewhere; also beehives with live bees..	Free.
33. Horses (remarks)...each..	20.00
(*a*) Horses up to 2 years old..................................do...	10.00
(*b*) Colts following their dams....................................	Free.
34. Bulls and cows..	9.00
35. Oxen...	25.50
36. Calves less than 6 weeks old.......................................	3.00
37. Hogs...	5.00
38. Pigs weighing less than 10 kilograms................................	1.00
39. Sheep...	1.00
40. Lambs..	0.50
41. Wool, including animal hair not mentioned elsewhere, as well as stuffs made thereof:	
(*a*) Wool, raw, dyed, ground; also hair, raw, hatcheled, boiled, dyed; also curled...	Free.

*Gross.

And whereas the special plenipotentiary of the United States has, by my direction, given assurance to the chargé d'affaires of the German Empire at Washington that this action of the Government of the German Empire in granting exemption of duties to the products and manufactures of the United States of America on their importation into Germany is accepted as a due reciprocity for the action of Congress as set forth in section 3 of said act:

Now, therefore, be it known that I, Benjamin Harrison, President of the United States of America, have caused the above-stated modifications of the tariff laws of the German Empire to be made public for the information of the citizens of the United States of America.

In testimony whereof I have hereunto set my hand and caused the seal of the United States to be affixed.

[SEAL.] Done at the city of Washington, this 1st day of February, 1892, and of the Independence of the United States of America the one hundred and sixteenth.

BENJ. HARRISON.

By the President:
JAMES G. BLAINE,
Secretary of State.

BY THE PRESIDENT OF THE UNITED STATES OF AMERICA.

A PROCLAMATION.

Whereas it is provided by section 24 of the act of Congress approved March 3, 1891, entitled "An act to repeal timber-culture laws, and for other purposes"—

That the President of the United States may from time to time set apart and reserve in any State or Territory having public land bearing forests, in any part of the public lands wholly or in part covered with timber or undergrowth, whether of commercial value or not, as public reservations; and the President shall by public proclamation declare the establishment of such reservations and the limits thereof.

And whereas the public lands in the State of Colorado within the limits hereafter described are in part covered with timber, and it appears that the public good would be promoted by setting apart and reserving said lands as a public reservation:

Now, therefore, I, Benjamin Harrison, President of the United States, by virtue of the power in me vested by section 24 of the aforesaid act of Congress, do hereby make known and proclaim that there is hereby reserved from entry or settlement and set apart as a public reservation all those certain tracts, pieces, or parcels of land lying and being situate in the State of Colorado and particularly described as follows, to wit:

Commencing at the northeast corner of section four (4), township eleven (11) north, range sixty-seven (67) west of the sixth (6th) principal meridian; thence proceeding westerly along the township line between townships ten (10) and eleven (11) south to the northwest corner of section six (6), township eleven (11) south, range sixty-eight (68) west; thence southerly along the range line between ranges sixty-eight (68) and sixty-nine (69) west to the southwest corner of section eighteen (18), township thirteen (13) south, range sixty-eight (68) west; thence westerly along the section line to the northwest corner of section nineteen (19), township thirteen (13) south, range sixty-nine (69) west; thence southerly along the range line between ranges sixty-nine (69) and seventy (70) west to the southwest corner of section thirty-one (31), township thirteen (13) south, range sixty-nine (69) west; thence east along the township line between townships thirteen (13) and fourteen (14) south to the half-section corner on said township line of section two (2), township fourteen (14) south, range sixty-nine (69) west; thence southerly through the middle of sections two (2), eleven (11), and fourteen (14) to a point in the middle of the north line of section twenty-three (23) of said township and range; thence easterly along said northern section line to the northeast corner of said section; thence southerly between sections twenty-three (23) and twenty-four (24) to the middle of the east line of section twenty-three (23); thence easterly through the middle of section twenty-four (24) to the middle of the east line of said section twenty-four (24), township fourteen (14) south, range sixty-nine (69) west; thence southerly along the range line between ranges sixty-eight (68) and sixty-nine (69) west to the southwest corner of section thirty-one (31), township fifteen (15) south, range sixty-eight (68) west; thence east along the township line between townships fifteen (15) and sixteen (16) south to the southeast corner of section thirty-four (34), township fifteen (15) south, range sixty-seven (67) west; thence northerly along the section line to the northeast corner of the southeast quarter of section twenty-two (22), township fifteen (15) south, range sixty-seven (67) west; thence westerly to the northwest corner of the southeast quarter of section twenty-one (21) of said last-named township and range; thence southerly to the southwest corner of the southeast quarter of section twenty-eight (28) of said township and range; thence westerly along the section line to the corner common to sections twenty-five (25), thirty-one (31), and thirty-six (36) of said township and range; thence northerly on the section line to the corner common to sections one (1), six (6), and twelve (12) of said township and range; thence easterly along the section line to the corner common to sections five (5), six (6), and eight (8); thence southerly along the section line to the southwest corner of section eight (8) of said township and range; thence easterly along the section line to the corner common to sections ten (10), eleven (11), and fourteen (14) of said township and range; thence northerly along the section line to the northeast corner of section three (3); thence westerly to the northwest corner of section three (3) of said township and range; thence northerly along the section line to the corner common to sections sixteen (16), twenty-one (21), twenty-two (22), and fifteen (15), township fourteen (14) south, range sixty-seven (67) west; thence westerly along the section line to the northwest corner of section nineteen (19) of said township and range; thence northerly along the range line between ranges sixty-seven (67) and sixty-eight (68) to the northeast corner of section one (1), township fourteen (14) south, range sixty-eight (68) west; thence easterly along the township line between townships thirteen (13) and fourteen (14) south to the southeast corner of section thirty-three (33) of township thirteen (13) south, range sixty-seven (67) west; thence northerly along the section line to the place of beginning.

Excepting from the force and effect of this proclamation all surveyed land which may have been prior to the date hereof embraced in any legal entry or covered by any lawful filing duly made in the proper United States land office, all unsurveyed lands on which valid settlement has been made under any law of the United States, and all mining claims duly located and held according to the laws of the United States and rules and regulations not in conflict therewith.

Provided, That this exception shall not continue to apply to any particular tract of land unless the entryman, settler, or claimant continues to comply with the law under which the entry, filing, settlement, or location was made.

Warning is hereby expressly given to all persons not to enter or make settlement upon the tract of land reserved by this proclamation.

In witness whereof I have hereunto set my hand and caused the seal of the United States to be affixed.

[SEAL.]　　Done at the city of Washington, this 11th day of February, A. D. 1892, and of the Independence of the United States the one hundred and sixteenth.

BENJ. HARRISON.

By the President:

JAMES G. BLAINE,
　　Secretary of State.

BY THE PRESIDENT OF THE UNITED STATES OF AMERICA.

A PROCLAMATION.

The following provisions of the laws of the United States are hereby published for the information of all concerned:

Section 1956, Revised Statutes, chapter 3, Title XXIII, enacts that—

No person shall kill any otter, mink, marten, sable, or fur seal, or other fur-bearing animal within the limits of Alaska Territory or in the waters thereof; and every person guilty thereof shall for each offense be fined not less than $200 nor more than $1,000, or imprisoned not more than six months, or both; and all vessels, their tackle, apparel, furniture, and cargo, found engaged in violation of this section shall be forfeited; but the Secretary of the Treasury shall have power to authorize the killing of any such mink, marten, sable, or other fur-bearing animal, except fur seals, under such regulations as he may prescribe; and it shall be the duty of the Secretary to prevent the killing of any fur seal and to provide for the execution of the provisions of this section until it is otherwise provided by law, nor shall he grant any special privileges under this section.

Section 3 of the act entitled "An act to provide for the protection of the salmon fisheries of Alaska," approved March 2, 1889, provides that—

SEC. 3. That section 1956 of the Revised Statutes of the United States is hereby declared to include and apply to all the dominion of the United States in the waters of Bering Sea; and it shall be the duty of the President at a timely season in each year to issue his proclamation, and cause the same to be published for one month at least in one newspaper (if any such there be) published at each United States port of entry on the Pacific coast, warning all persons against entering said waters for the purpose of violating the provisions of said section; and he shall also cause one or more vessels of the United States to diligently cruise said waters and arrest all persons and seize all vessels found to be or to have been engaged in any violation of the laws of the United States therein.

Now, therefore, I, Benjamin Harrison, President of the United States, pursuant to the above-recited statutes, hereby warn all persons against entering the waters of Bering Sea within the dominion of the United States for the purpose of violating the provisions of said section 1956, Revised Statutes; and I hereby proclaim that all persons found to be or to have been engaged in any violation of the laws of the United States in said waters will be arrested and punished as above provided, and that all vessels so employed, their tackle, apparel, furniture, and cargoes, will be seized and forfeited.

In testimony whereof I have hereunto set my hand and caused the seal of the United States to be affixed.

[SEAL.]   Done at the city of Washington, this 15th day of February, 1892, and of the Independence of the United States the one hundred and sixteenth.   BENJ. HARRISON.

By the President:
JAMES G. BLAINE,
Secretary of State.

BY THE PRESIDENT OF THE UNITED STATES OF AMERICA.

A PROCLAMATION.

Whereas, pursuant to section 3 of the act of Congress approved October 1, 1890, entitled "An act to reduce the revenue and equalize duties on imports, and for other purposes," the Secretary of State of the United States of America communicated to the Government of Nicaragua the action of the Congress of the United States of America, with a view to secure reciprocal trade, in declaring the articles enumerated in said section 3 to be exempt from duty upon their importation into the United States of America; and

Whereas the envoy extraordinary and minister plenipotentiary of Nicaragua at Washington has communicated to the Secretary of State the fact that, in reciprocity for the admission into the United States of America free of all duty of the articles enumerated in section 3 of said act, the

Government of Nicaragua will by due legal enactment admit free of all duty, from and after April 15, 1892, into all the ports of entry of Nicaragua the articles or merchandise named in the following schedule, provided that the same be the product of the United States:

SCHEDULE OF ARTICLES WHICH THE REPUBLIC OF NICARAGUA WILL ADMIT FREE OF ALL KIND OF DUTY.

1. Animals, live.
2. Barley, Indian corn, wheat, oats, rye, and rice.
3. Seeds of all kinds for agriculture and horticulture.
4. Live plants of all kinds.
5. Corn meal.
6. Starch.
7. Beans, potatoes, and all other vegetables, fresh or dried.
8. Fruits, fresh or dried.
9. Hay, bran, and straw for forage.
10. Cotton-seed oil and all other products of said seed.
11. Tar, resin, and turpentine.
12. Asphalt, crude or manufactured in blocks.
13. Quicksilver for mining purposes.
14. Coal, mineral or animal.
15. Fertilizers for land.
16. Lime and cement.
17. Wood and lumber, in the rough or prepared for building purposes.
18. Houses of wood or iron.
19. Marble, in the rough or dressed, for fountains, gravestones, and building purposes.
20. Tools and implements for agricultural and horticultural purposes.
21. Wagons, carts, and handcarts.
22. Iron and steel, in rails for railroads and other similar uses, and structural iron and steel for bridges and building purposes.
23. Wire, for fences, with or without barbs, clamps, posts, clips, and other accessories of wire, not less than 3 lines in diameter.
24. Machinery of all kinds for agricultural purposes, arts, and trades, and parts of such machinery.
25. Motors of steam or animal power.
26. Forgers, water pumps of metal, pump hose, sledge hammers, drills for mining purposes, iron piping with its keys and faucets, crucibles for melting metals, iron water tanks, and lightning rods.
27. Roofs of galvanized iron, gutters, ridging, clamps, and screws for the same.
28. Printing materials.
29. Books, pamphlets, and other printed matter, and ruled paper for printed music, printing paper in sheets not less than 29 by 20 inches.
30. Geographical maps or charts and celestial and terrestrial spheres or globes.
31. Surgical and mathematical instruments.
32. Stones and fire bricks for smelting furnaces.
33. Vessels and boats of all kinds, fitted together or in parts.
34. Gold and silver in bullion, bars, or coin.

It is understood that the packages or coverings in which the articles named in the foregoing schedule are imported shall be free of duty if they are usual and proper for the purpose.

And that the Government of Nicaragua has further stipulated that the laws and regulations adopted to protect its revenue and prevent fraud in the declarations and proof that the articles named in the foregoing schedule are the product of the United States of America shall impose no undue restrictions on the importer nor additional charges on the articles imported; and

Whereas the Secretary of State has, by my direction, given assurance to the envoy extraordinary and minister plenipotentiary of Nicaragua at Washington that this action of the Government of Nicaragua in granting freedom of duties to the products of the United States of America on their importation into Nicaragua is accepted as a due reciprocity for the action of Congress as set forth in section 3 of said act:

Now, therefore, be it known that I, Benjamin Harrison, President of the United States of America, have caused the above-stated modifications of the tariff laws of Nicaragua to be made public for the information of the citizens of the United States of America.

In testimony whereof I have hereunto set my hand and caused the seal of the United States to be affixed.

[SEAL.]   Done at the city of Washington, this 12th day of March, 1892, and of the Independence of the United States of America the one hundred and sixteenth.

BENJ. HARRISON.

By the President:
WILLIAM F. WHARTON,
Acting Secretary of State.

BY THE PRESIDENT OF THE UNITED STATES OF AMERICA.

A PROCLAMATION.

Whereas in section 3 of an act passed by the Congress of the United States entitled "An act to reduce the revenue and equalize duties on imports, and for other purposes," approved October 1, 1890, it was provided as follows:

That with a view to secure reciprocal trade with countries producing the following articles, and for this purpose, on and after the 1st day of January, 1892, whenever and so often as the President shall be satisfied that the government of any country producing and exporting sugars, molasses, coffee, tea, and hides, raw and uncured, or any of such articles, imposes duties or other exactions upon the agricultural or other products of the United States which, in view of the free introduction of such sugar, molasses, coffee, tea, and hides into the United States, he may deem to be reciprocally unequal and unreasonable, he shall have the power and it shall be his duty to suspend, by proclamation to that effect, the provisions of this act relating to the free introduction of such sugar, molasses, coffee, tea, and hides the production of such country for such time as he shall deem just; and in such case and during such suspension duties shall be levied, collected, and paid upon sugar, molasses, coffee, tea, and hides the product of or exported from such designated country—

the duties hereinafter set forth; and

Whereas it has been established to my satisfaction and I find the fact to be that the Government of Colombia does impose duties or other exactions upon the agricultural and other products of the United States which, in view of the free introduction of such sugars, molasses, coffee, tea, and hides into the United States, in accordance with the provisions of said act, I deem to be reciprocally unequal and unreasonable:

Now, therefore, I, Benjamin Harrison, President of the United States of America, by virtue of the authority vested in me by section 3 of said act, by which it is made my duty to take action, do hereby declare and proclaim that the provisions of said act relating to the free introduction of sugars, molasses, coffee, tea, and hides the production of Colombia shall be suspended from and after this 15th day of March, 1892, and until such time as said unequal and unreasonable duties and exactions are removed by Colombia and public notice of that fact given by the President of the United States; and I do hereby proclaim that on and after this 15th day of March, 1892, there will be levied, collected, and paid upon sugars, molasses, coffee, tea, and hides the product of or exported from Colombia during such suspension duties as provided by said act, as follows:

All sugars not above No. 13 Dutch standard in color shall pay duty on their polariscopic tests as follows, namely:

All sugars not above No. 13 Dutch standard in color, all tank bottoms, sirups of cane juice or of beet juice, melada, concentrated melada, concrete and concentrated molasses, testing by the polariscope not above 75°, seven-tenths of 1 cent per pound, and for every additional degree or fraction of a degree shown by the polariscopic test two-hundredths of 1 cent per pound additional.

All sugars above No. 13 Dutch standard in color shall be classified by the Dutch standard of color and pay duty as follows, namely:

All sugars above No. 13 and not above No. 16 Dutch standard of color, 1⅜ cents per pound.

All sugars above No. 16 and not above No. 20 Dutch standard of color, 1⅝ cents per pound.

All sugars above No. 20 Dutch standard of color, 2 cents per pound.

Molasses testing above 56°, 4 cents per gallon.

Sugar drainings and sugar sweepings shall be subject to duty either as molasses or sugar, as the case may be, according to polariscopic test.

On coffee, 3 cents per pound.

On tea, 10 cents per pound.

Hides, raw or uncured, whether dry, salted, or pickled; Angora-goat skins, raw, without the wool, unmanufactured; asses' skins, raw or unmanufactured, and skins, except sheepskins, with the wool on, 1½ cents per pound.

In witness whereof I have hereunto set my hand and caused the seal of the United States to be affixed.

[SEAL.] Done at the city of Washington, this 15th day of March, 1892, and of the Independence of the United States of America the one hundred and sixteenth.

BENJ. HARRISON.

By the President:

WILLIAM F. WHARTON,
Acting Secretary of State.

BY THE PRESIDENT OF THE UNITED STATES OF AMERICA.

A PROCLAMATION.

Whereas in section 3 of an act passed by the Congress of the United States entitled "An act to reduce the revenue and equalize duties on imports, and for other purposes," approved October 1, 1890, it was provided as follows:

That with a view to secure reciprocal trade with countries producing the following articles, and for this purpose, on and after the 1st day of January, 1892, whenever and so often as the President shall be satisfied that the government of any country producing and exporting sugars, molasses, coffee, tea, and hides, raw and uncured, or any of such articles, imposes duties or other exactions upon the agricultural or other products of the United States which, in view of the free introduction of such sugar, molasses, coffee, tea, and hides into the United States, he may deem to be reciprocally unequal and unreasonable, he shall have the power and it shall be his duty to suspend, by proclamation to that effect, the provisions of this act relating to the free introduction of such sugar, molasses, coffee, tea, and hides the production of such country for such time as he shall deem just; and in such case and during such suspension duties shall be levied, collected, and paid upon sugar, molasses, coffee, tea, and hides the product of or exported from such designated country—

the duties hereinafter set forth; and

Whereas it has been established to my satisfaction and I find the fact to be that the Government of Hayti does impose duties or other exactions upon the agricultural and other products of the United States which, in view of the free introduction of such sugars, molasses, coffee, tea, and hides into the United States, in accordance with the provisions of said act, I deem to be reciprocally unequal and unreasonable:

Now, therefore, I, Benjamin Harrison, President of the United States of America, by virtue of the authority vested in me by section 3 of said act, by which it is made my duty to take action, do hereby declare and proclaim that the provisions of said act relating to the free introduction of sugars, molasses, coffee, tea, and hides the production of Hayti shall be suspended from and after this 15th day of March, 1892, and until such time as said unequal and unreasonable duties and exactions are removed by Hayti and public notice of that fact given by the President of the United States; and I do hereby proclaim that on and after this 15th day of March, 1892, there will be levied, collected, and paid upon sugars, molasses, coffee, tea, and hides the product of or exported from Hayti during such suspension duties as provided by said act, as follows:

All sugars not above No. 13 Dutch standard in color shall pay duty on their polariscopic tests as follows, namely:

All sugars not above No. 13 Dutch standard in color, all tank bottoms, sirups of cane juice or of beet juice, melada, concentrated melada, concrete and concentrated molasses, testing by the polariscope not above 75°, seven-tenths of 1 cent per pound and for every additional degree or fraction of a degree shown by the polariscopic test two-hundredths of 1 cent per pound additional.

All sugars above No. 13 Dutch standard in color shall be classified by the Dutch standard of color and pay duty as follows, namely:

All sugar above No. 13 and not above No. 16 Dutch standard of color, 1⅜ cents per pound.

All sugar above No. 16 and not above No. 20 Dutch standard of color, 1⅝ cents per pound.

All sugars above No. 20 Dutch standard of color, 2 cents per pound.

Molasses testing above 56°, 4 cents per gallon.

Sugar drainings and sugar sweepings shall be subject to duty either as molasses or sugar, as the case may be, according to polariscopic test.

On coffee, 3 cents per pound.

On tea, 10 cents per pound.

Hides, raw or uncured, whether dry, salted, or pickled; Angora-goat skins, raw, without the wool, unmanufactured; asses' skins, raw or unmanufactured, and skins, except sheepskins, with the wool on, 1½ cents per pound.

In witness whereof I have hereunto set my hand and caused the seal of the United States to be affixed.

[SEAL.]   Done at the city of Washington, this 15th day of March, 1892, and of the Independence of the United States of America the one hundred and sixteenth.

BENJ. HARRISON.

By the President:

WILLIAM F. WHARTON,
Acting Secretary of State.

By the President of the United States of America.

A PROCLAMATION.

Whereas in section 3 of an act passed by the Congress of the United States entitled "An act to reduce the revenue and equalize duties on imports, and for other purposes," approved October 1, 1890, it was provided as follows:

That with a view to secure reciprocal trade with countries producing the following articles, and for this purpose, on and after the 1st day of January, 1892, whenever and so often as the President shall be satisfied that the government of any country producing and exporting sugars, molasses, coffee, tea, and hides, raw and uncured, or any of such articles, imposes duties or other exactions upon the agricultural or other products of the United States which, in view of the free introduction of such sugar, molasses, coffee, tea, and hides into the United States, he may deem to be reciprocally unequal and unreasonable, he shall have the power and it shall be his duty to suspend, by proclamation to that effect, the provisions of this act relating to the free introduction of such sugar, molasses, coffee, tea, and hides the production of such country for such time as he shall deem just; and in such case and during such suspension duties shall be levied, collected, and paid upon sugar, molasses, coffee, tea, and hides the product of or exported from such designated country—

the duties hereinafter set forth; and

Whereas it has been established to my satisfaction and I find the fact to be that the Government of Venezuela does impose duties or other exactions upon the agricultural and other products of the United States which, in view of the free introduction of such sugars, molasses, coffee, tea, and hides into the United States, in accordance with the provisions of said act, I deem to be reciprocally unequal and unreasonable:

Now, therefore, I, Benjamin Harrison, President of the United States of America, by virtue of the authority vested in me by section 3 of said act, by which it is made my duty to take action, do hereby declare and proclaim that the provisions of said act relating to the free introduction of sugars, molasses, coffee, tea, and hides the production of Venezuela shall be suspended from and after this 15th day of March, 1892, and until such time as said unequal and unreasonable duties and exactions are removed by Venezuela and public notice of that fact given by the President of the United States; and I do hereby proclaim that on and after this 15th day of March, 1892, there will be levied, collected, and paid upon sugars, molasses, coffee, tea, and hides the product of or exported from Venezuela during such suspension duties as provided by said act, as follows:

All sugars not above No. 13 Dutch standard in color shall pay duty on their polariscopic tests as follows, namely:

All sugars not above No. 13 Dutch standard in color, all tank bottoms, sirups of cane juice or of beet juice, melada, concentrated melada, concrete and concentrated molasses, testing by the polariscope not above 75°, seven-tenths of 1 cent per pound, and for every additional degree or fraction of a degree shown by the polariscopic test two-hundredths of 1 cent per pound additional.

All sugars above No. 13 Dutch standard in color shall be classified by the Dutch standard of color and pay duty as follows, namely:

All sugar above No. 13 and not above No. 16 Dutch standard of color, 1⅜ cents per pound.

All sugar above No. 16 and not above No. 20 Dutch standard of color, 1⅝ cents per pound.

All sugars above No. 20 Dutch standard of color, 2 cents per pound.

Molasses testing above 56°, 4 cents per gallon.

Sugar drainings and sugar sweepings shall be subject to duty either as molasses or sugar, as the case may be, according to polariscopic test.

On coffee, 3 cents per pound.

On tea, 10 cents per pound.

Hides, raw or uncured, whether dry, salted, or pickled; Angora-goat skins, raw, without the wool, unmanufactured; asses' skins, raw or unmanufactured, and skins, except sheepskins, with the wool on, 1½ cents per pound.

In witness whereof I have hereunto set my hand and caused the seal of the United States to be affixed.

[SEAL.]   Done at the city of Washington, this 15th day of March, 1892, and of the Independence of the United States of America the one hundred and sixteenth.   BENJ. HARRISON.

By the President:

WILLIAM F. WHARTON,
   Acting Secretary of State.

By the President of the United States of America.

A PROCLAMATION.

Whereas it is provided by section 24 of an act approved March 3, 1891, entitled "An act to repeal timber-culture laws, and for other purposes"—

That the President of the United States may from time to time set apart and reserve in any State or Territory having public land bearing forests, in any part of the public lands wholly or in part covered with timber or undergrowth, whether of commercial value or not, as public reservations; and the President shall by public proclamation declare the establishment of such reservations and the limits thereof.

And whereas the lands hereinafter described are public and forest bearing, and on the 11th day of February last I issued a proclamation * intended to reserve the same as authorized in said act; but as some question has arisen as to the boundaries proclaimed being sufficiently definite to cover the lands intended to be reserved:

Now, therefore, I, Benjamin Harrison, President of the United States, for the purpose of removing any doubt and making the boundaries of said reservation more definite, by virtue of the power in me vested by said act, do hereby issue this my second proclamation and hereby set apart, reserve, and establish as a public reservation all that tract of land situate in the State of Colorado embraced within the following boundary:

Beginning at the northeast corner of section four (4), township eleven (11) south, range sixty-seven (67) west of the sixth (6th) principal meridian; thence westerly along the second (2d) correction line south between townships ten (10) and eleven (11) south to the northwest corner of section six (6), township eleven (11) south, range sixty-eight (68) west; thence southerly along the range line between ranges sixty-eight (68) and sixty-nine (69) west to the southwest corner of section eighteen (18), township thirteen (13) south, range sixty-eight (68) west; thence westerly along the section line between sections thirteen (13) and twenty-four (24), fourteen (14) and twenty-three (23), fifteen (15) and twenty-two (22), sixteen (16) and twenty-one (21), seventeen (17) and twenty (20), and eighteen (18) and nineteen (19) to the northwest corner of section nineteen (19), township thirteen (13) south, range sixty-nine (69) west; thence southerly along the range line between ranges sixty-nine (69) and seventy (70) west to the southwest corner of section thirty-one (31) of said township; thence easterly along the township line between townships thirteen (13) and fourteen (14) south to the quarter-section corner on said township line between section thirty-five (35), township thirteen (13) south, range sixty-nine (69) west, and section two (2), township fourteen (14) south, range sixty-nine (69) west; thence southerly through the middle of sections two (2), eleven (11), and fourteen (14), township fourteen (14) south, range sixty-nine (69) west, to the

*See pp. 260–262.

quarter-section corner on the section line between sections fourteen (14) and twenty-three (23) of said township and range; thence easterly along said section line to the northeast corner of section twenty-three (23) of said township and range; thence southerly along the section line to the quarter-section corner on said line between sections twenty-three (23) and twenty-four (24) of said township and range; thence easterly through the middle of section twenty-four (24) to the quarter-section corner on the range line between section nineteen (19), township fourteen (14) south, range sixty-eight (68) west, and section twenty-four (24), township fourteen (14) south, range sixty-nine (69) west; thence southerly along said range line to the southwest corner of section thirty-one (31), township fifteen (15) south, range sixty-eight (68) west; thence easterly along the third (3d) correction line south between townships fifteen (15) and sixteen (16) south to the southeast corner of section thirty-four (34), township fifteen (15) south, range sixty-seven (67) west; thence northerly along the section line between sections thirty-four (34) and thirty-five (35), twenty-six (26) and twenty-seven (27), to the point for the quarter-section corner on the section line between sections twenty-two (22) and twenty-three (23), township fifteen (15) south, range sixty-seven (67) west; thence westerly to a point for the legal center of section twenty-one (21) of said township and range; thence southerly to the southwest corner of the southeast quarter of section twenty-eight (28) of said township and range; thence westerly along the section line between sections twenty-eight (28) and thirty-three (33), twenty-nine (29) and thirty-two (32), thirty (30) and thirty-one (31), to the northwest corner of section thirty-one (31) of said township and range; thence northerly on the range line between ranges sixty-seven (67) and sixty-eight (68) west to the southwest corner of section six (6) of said township and range; thence easterly along the section line to the southeast corner of section six (6) of said township and range; thence southerly along the section line to the southwest corner of section eight (8) of said township and range; thence easterly along the section line to the southeast corner of section ten (10) of said township and range; thence northerly along the section line between sections ten (10) and eleven (11), two (2) and three (3), township fifteen (15) south, range sixty-seven (67) west, to the northeast corner of section three (3) of said township and range; thence westerly along the township line between townships fourteen (14) and fifteen (15) south to the northwest corner of section three (3), township fifteen (15) south, range sixty-seven (67) west; thence northerly along the section line between sections thirty-three (33) and thirty-four (34), twenty-seven (27) and twenty-eight (28), twenty-one (21) and twenty-two (22), to the northeast corner of section twenty-one (21), township fourteen (14) south, range sixty-seven (67) west; thence westerly along the section line between sections sixteen (16) and twenty-one (21), seventeen (17) and twenty (20), eighteen (18) and nineteen

(19), to the northwest corner of section nineteen (19) of said township and range; thence northerly along the range line between ranges sixty-seven (67) and sixty-eight (68) west to the northeast corner of section one (1), township fourteen (14) south, range sixty-eight (68) west; thence easterly along the township line between townships thirteen (13) and fourteen (14) south to the southeast corner of section thirty-three (33), township thirteen (13) south, range sixty-seven (67) west; thence northerly along the section line between sections thirty-three (33) and thirty-four (34), twenty-seven (27) and twenty-eight (28), twenty-one (21) and twenty-two (22), fifteen (15) and sixteen (16), nine (9) and ten (10), and three (3) and four (4) of townships thirteen (13), twelve (12), and eleven (11) south, range sixty-seven (67) west, to the place of beginning.

Excepting from the force and effect of this proclamation all lands which may have been prior to the date hereof embraced in any legal entry or covered by any lawful filing duly of record in the proper United States land office, or upon which any valid settlement has been made pursuant to law and the statutory period within which to make entry or filing of record has not expired, and all mining claims duly located and held according to the laws of the United States and rules and regulations not in conflict therewith.

Provided, That this exception shall not continue to apply to any particular tract of land unless the entryman, settler, or claimant continues to comply with the law under which the entry, filing, settlement, or location was made.

Warning is hereby expressly given to all persons not to enter or make settlement upon the tract of land reserved by this proclamation.

In witness whereof I have hereunto set my hand and caused the seal of the United States to be affixed.

[SEAL.] Done at the city of Washington, this 18th day of March, A. D. 1892, and of the Independence of the United States the one hundred and sixteenth.

BENJ. HARRISON.

By the President:

WILLIAM F. WHARTON,
Acting Secretary of State.

BY THE PRESIDENT OF THE UNITED STATES OF AMERICA.

A PROCLAMATION.

Whereas by the third article of the treaty between the United States of America and the Sisseton and Wahpeton bands of Dakota or Sioux Indians concluded February 19, 1867, proclaimed May 2, 1867 (15 U. S. Statutes at Large, p. 505), the United States set apart and reserved for certain of said Indians certain lands, particularly described, being situated partly in North Dakota and partly in South Dakota and known as the Lake Traverse Reservation; and

Whereas by agreement made with said Indians residing on said reservation dated December 12, 1889, they conveyed, as set forth in article 1 thereof, to the United States all their title and interest in and to all the unallotted lands within the limits of the reservation set apart as aforesaid remaining after the allotments shall have been made, which are provided for in article 4 of the agreement, as follows:

That there shall be allotted to each individual member of the bands of Indians parties hereto a sufficient quantity, which, with the lands heretofore allotted, shall make in each case 160 acres, and in case no allotment has been made to any individual member of said bands, then an allotment of 160 acres shall be made to such individual.

And whereas it is provided in article 2 of said agreement—

That the cession, sale, relinquishment, and conveyance of the lands described in article 1 of this agreement shall not take effect and be in force until the sum of $342,778.37, together with the sum of $18,400, shall have been paid to said bands of Indians, as set forth and stipulated in article 3 of this agreement.

And whereas it is provided in the act of Congress approved March 3, 1891 (26 U. S. Statutes at Large, pp. 1036–1038), section 30, accepting and ratifying the agreement with said Indians—

That the lands by said agreement ceded, sold, relinquished, and conveyed to the United States shall immediately, upon the payment to the parties entitled thereto of their share of the funds made immediately available by this act, and upon the completion of the allotments as provided for in said agreement, be subject only to entry and settlement under the homestead and town-site laws of the United States, excepting the sixteenth and thirty-sixth sections of said lands, which shall be reserved for common-school purposes and be subject to the laws of the State wherein located: *Provided*, That patents shall not issue until the settler or entryman shall have paid to the United States the sum of $2.50 per acre for the land taken up by such homesteader, and the title to the lands so entered shall remain in the United States until said money is duly paid by such entryman or his legal representatives, or his widow, who shall have the right to pay the money and complete the entry of her deceased husband in her own name and shall receive a patent for the same.

And whereas payment as required by said act has been made by the United States; and

Whereas allotments as provided for in said agreement, as now appears by the records of the Department of the Interior, will have been made, approved, and completed and all other terms and considerations required will have been complied with on the day and hour hereinafter fixed for opening said lands to settlement:

Now, therefore, I, Benjamin Harrison, President of the United States, do hereby declare and make known that all of the lands embraced in said reservation, saving and excepting the lands reserved for and allotted to said Indians and the lands reserved for other purposes in pursuance of the provisions of said agreement and the said act of Congress ratifying the same and other the laws relating thereto, will, at and after the hour of 12 o'clock noon (central standard time) on the 15th day of April, A. D. 1892, and not before, be opened to settlement under the terms of and subject to all the terms and conditions, limitations, reservations, and restrictions contained in said agreements, the statutes above specified, and the laws of the United States applicable thereto.

The lands to be opened for settlement are for greater convenience particularly described in the accompanying schedule, entitled "Schedule of lands within the Lake Traverse Reservation opened to settlement by proclamation of the President dated April 11, 1892," and which schedule is made a part hereof.

Warning, moreover, is hereby given that until said lands are opened to settlement as herein provided all persons save said Indians are forbidden to enter upon and occupy the same or any part thereof.

And further notice is hereby given that it has been duly ordered that the lands mentioned and included in this proclamation shall be, and the same are, attached to the Fargo and Watertown land districts, in said States, as follows:

1. All that portion of the Lake Traverse Reservation commencing at the northwest corner of said reservation; thence south 12° 2' west, following the west boundary of the reservation, to the new seventh standard parallel, or boundary line between the States of North and South Dakota; thence east, following the new seventh standard parallel to its intersection with the north boundary of said Indian reservation; thence northwesterly with said boundary to the place of beginning, is attached to the Fargo land district, the office of which is now located at Fargo, N. Dak.

2. All that portion of the Lake Traverse Reservation commencing at a point where the new seventh standard parallel intersects the west boundary of said reservation; thence southerly along the west boundary of said reservation to its extreme southern limit; thence northerly along the east boundary of said reservation to Lake Traverse; thence north with said lake to the northeast corner of the Lake Traverse Indian Reservation; thence westerly with the north boundary of said reservation to its intersection with the new seventh standard parallel, or boundary line between the States of North and South Dakota; thence with the new seventh standard parallel to the place of beginning, is attached to the Watertown land district, the office of which is now located at Watertown, S. Dak.

In witness whereof I have hereunto set my hand and caused the seal of the United States to be affixed.

[SEAL.]   Done at the city of Washington, this 11th day of April, A. D. 1892, and of the Independence of the United States the one hundred and sixteenth.

BENJ. HARRISON.

By the President:
　　JAMES G. BLAINE,
　　　　Secretary of State.

BY THE PRESIDENT OF THE UNITED STATES OF AMERICA.

A PROCLAMATION.

Whereas by a written agreement made on the —— day of October, 1890, the Cheyenne and Arapahoe tribes of Indians ceded, conveyed, transferred, relinquished, and surrendered all their claim, title, and interest in and to the lands described in article 2 of said agreement as follows, to wit:

Commencing at a point where the Washita River crosses the ninety-eighth degree of west longitude, as surveyed in the years 1858 and 1871; thence north on a line with said ninety-eighth degree to the point where it is crossed by the Red Fork of the Arkansas (sometimes called the Cimarron River.); thence up said river, in the middle of the main channel thereof, to the north boundary of the country ceded to the United States by the treaty of June 14, 1866, with the Creek Nation of Indians; thence west on said north boundary and the north boundary of the country ceded to the United States by the treaty of March 21, 1866, with the Seminole Indians to the one hundredth degree of west longitude; thence south on the line of said one hundredth degree to the point where it strikes the North Fork of the Red River; thence down said North Fork of the Red River to a point where it strikes the north line of the Kiowa and Comanche Reservation; thence east along said boundary to a point where it strikes the Washita River; thence down said Washita River, in the middle of the main channel thereof, to the place of beginning; and all other lands or tracts of country in the Indian Territory to which they have or may set up or allege any right, title, interest, or claim whatsoever.

Provided, That every member of said tribes shall have an allotment of 160 acres of land, as in said agreement provided, to be selected within the tract of country so ceded, except land in any part of said reservation now used or occupied for military, agency, school, school-farm, religious, or other public uses, or in sections 16 or 36 in each Congressional township, except, in cases where any Cheyenne or Arapahoe Indian has heretofore made improvements upon and now uses and occupies a part of said sections 16 and 36, such Indian may make his or her selection within the boundaries so prescribed so as to include his or her improvements; and except in that part of the lands by said agreement ceded, now occupied and claimed by the Wichita and affiliated bands of Indians described as follows, to wit:

Commencing at a point in the middle of the main channel of the Washita River where the ninety-eighth meridian of west longitude crosses the same; thence up the middle of the main channel of the said river to the line of 98° 40′ west longitude; thence up said line of 98° 40′ due north to the middle of the main channel of the main Canadian River; thence down the middle of the main Canadian River to where it crosses the ninety-eighth meridian; thence due south to the place of beginning.

And provided, That said sections 16 and 36 in each Congressional township in said reservation shall not become subject to homestead entry, but shall be held by the United States and finally sold for public-school purposes; and that when the allotments of lands shall have been selected and taken by the members of the Cheyenne and Arapahoe tribes as aforesaid and approved by the Secretary of the Interior the title thereto shall be held in trust for the allottees, respectively, for the period of twenty-five years in the manner and to the extent provided for in the act of Congress approved February 8, 1887 (24 U. S. Statutes at Large, p. 388); and

Whereas it is provided in the act of Congress accepting, ratifying, and confirming the said agreement with the Cheyenne and Arapahoe Indians, approved March 3, 1891 (26 U. S. Statutes at Large, pp. 989–1044), section 16—

That whenever any of the lands acquired by either of the * * * foregoing agreements respecting lands in the Indian or Oklahoma Territory shall by operation of law or proclamation of the President of the United States be opened to settlement they shall be disposed of to actual settlers only, under the provisions of the homestead and town-site laws, except section 2301 of the Revised Statutes of the United States, which shall not apply: *Provided, however*, That each settler on said lands shall before making a final proof and receiving a certificate of entry pay to the United States for the land so taken by him, in addition to the fees provided by law, and within five years from the date of the first original entry, the sum of $1.50 per acre, one-half of which shall be paid within two years; but the rights of honorably discharged Union soldiers and sailors as defined and described in sections 2304 and 2305 of the Revised Statutes of the United States shall not be abridged except as to the sum to be paid as aforesaid; and all the lands in Oklahoma are hereby declared to be agricultural lands, and proof of their nonmineral character shall not be required as a condition precedent to final entry.

And whereas allotments of land in severalty to said Cheyenne and Arapahoe Indians have been made and approved in accordance with law and the provisions of the before-mentioned agreement with them; and

Whereas the lands acquired by the said agreement hereinbefore mentioned have been divided into counties by the Secretary of the Interior, as required by said last-mentioned act of Congress, before the same shall be opened to settlement, and lands have been reserved for county-seat purposes as therein required, as follows, to wit:

For County C, the south one-half of section 19, township 16 north, range 11 west; for County D, the north one-half of section 13, township 18 north, range 17 west; for County E, the south one-half of section 15, township 17 north, range 22 west; for County F, the south one-half of section 8, township 13 north, range 23 west; for County G, the north one-half of section 25, township 13 north, range 17 west; for County H, the south one-half of section 13, township 9 north, range 16 west; and

Whereas it is provided by act of Congress for temporary government of Oklahoma, approved May 2, 1890, section 23 (26 U. S. Statutes at Large, p. 92), that there shall be reserved public highways 4 rods wide between each section of land in said Territory, the section lines being the center of said highways; but no deduction shall be made where cash payments are provided for in the amount to be paid for each quarter section of land by reason of such reservation; and

Whereas all the terms, conditions, and considerations required by said agreement made with said tribes of Indians and by the laws relating thereto precedent to opening said lands to settlement have been, as I hereby declare, complied with:

Now, therefore, I, Benjamin Harrison, President of the United States, by virtue of the power in me vested by the statutes hereinbefore mentioned, also an act of Congress entitled "An act making appropriations for the current and contingent expenses of the Indian Department and for fulfilling treaty stipulations with various Indian tribes for the year ending June 30, 1892, and for other purposes," approved March 3, 1891, and by other of the laws of the United States, and by said agreement, do hereby declare and make known that all of said lands hereinbefore described acquired from the Cheyenne and Arapahoe Indians by the agreement aforesaid, saving and excepting the lands allotted to the Indians as in said agreement provided, excepting also the lands hereinbefore described as occupied and claimed by the Wichita and affiliated bands of Indians, or otherwise reserved in pursuance of the provisions of said agreement and the said act of Congress ratifying the same, and other the laws relating thereto, will at the hour of 12 o'clock noon (central standard time), Tuesday, the 19th day of the present month of April, and not before, be opened to settlement under the terms of and subject to all the conditions, limitations, reservations, and restrictions contained in said agreement, the statutes above specified, and the laws of the United States applicable thereto.

The lands to be so opened to settlement are for greater convenience particularly described in the accompanying schedule, entitled "Schedule of lands within the Cheyenne and Arapahoe Indian Reservation, Oklahoma Territory, opened to settlement by proclamation of the President."

Each entry shall be in square form as nearly as applicable; and no other lands in the Territory of Oklahoma are opened to settlement under this proclamation, the agreement with the said Cheyenne and Arapahoe Indians, or the act ratifying the same.

Notice, moreover, is hereby given that it is by law enacted that until said lands are opened to settlement by proclamation no person shall be permitted to enter upon and occupy the same, and no person violating this provision shall be permitted to enter any of said lands or acquire any right thereto, and that the officers of the United States will be required to enforce this provision.

And further notice is hereby given that it has been duly ordered that the lands mentioned and included in this proclamation shall be, and the same are, attached to the Western land district, office at Kingfisher, and the Oklahoma land district, office at Oklahoma City, in said Territory of Oklahoma, as follows:

1. All of said lands lying north of the township line between townships 13 and 14 north are attached to the Western land district, the office of which is at Kingfisher, in said Territory.

2. All of said lands lying south of the township line between townships 13 and 14 north are attached to the Oklahoma land district, the office of which is at Oklahoma City, in the said Territory.

In witness whereof I have hereunto set my hand and caused the seal of the United States to be affixed.

[SEAL.]   Done at the city of Washington, this 12th day of April, A. D. 1892, and of the Independence of the United States the one hundred and sixteenth.

BENJ. HARRISON.

By the President:

JAMES G. BLAINE, *Secretary of State.*

BY THE PRESIDENT OF THE UNITED STATES OF AMERICA.

A PROCLAMATION.

Whereas it is provided by section 13 of the act of Congress of March 3, 1891, entitled "An act to amend Title LX, chapter 3, of the Revised Statutes of the United States, relating to copyrights," that said act "shall only apply to a citizen or subject of a foreign state or nation when such foreign state or nation permits to citizens of the United States of America the benefit of copyright on substantially the same basis as its own citizens, or when such foreign state or nation is a party to an international agreement which provides for reciprocity in the granting of copyright, by the terms of which agreement the United States of America may at its pleasure become a party to such agreement;" and

Whereas it is also provided by said section that "the existence of either of the conditions aforesaid shall be determined by the President of the United States by proclamation made from time to time as the purposes of this act may require;" and

Whereas in virtue of said section 13 of the aforesaid act of Congress a copyright agreement was signed at Washington on January 15, 1892, in the English and German languages, by the representatives of the United States of America and the German Empire, a true copy of the English version of which agreement is, word for word, as follows:

The President of the United States of America and His Majesty the German Emperor, King of Prussia, in the name of the German Empire, being actuated by the desire to extend to their subjects and citizens the full benefit of the legal provisions in force in both countries in regard to copyright, have to this end decided to conclude an agreement and have appointed as their plenipotentiaries:

The President of the United States of America, James G. Blaine, Secretary of State of the United States;

His Majesty the German Emperor, King of Prussia, Alfons Mumm von Schwarzenstein, his chargé d'affaires near the Government of the United States of America, who, being duly authorized, have concluded the following agreement, subject to due ratification:

ARTICLE I. Citizens of the United States of America shall enjoy in the German Empire the protection of copyright as regards works of literature and art, as well as photographs, against illegal reproduction, on the same basis on which such protection is granted to subjects of the Empire.

ART. II. The United States Government engages in return that the President of the United States shall, in pursuance of section 13 of the act of Congress of March 3, 1891, issue the proclamation therein provided for in regard to the extension of the provisions of that act to German subjects as soon as the Secretary of State shall have been officially notified that the present agreement has received the necessary legislative sanction in the German Empire.

ART. III. This agreement shall be ratified and the ratifications shall be exchanged at Washington as soon as possible.

The agreement shall go into operation at the expiration of three weeks from the date of the exchange of its ratifications, and shall be applicable only to works not published at the time when it shall have gone into operation. It shall remain in force until the expiration of three months from the day on which notice of a desire for the cessation of its effects shall have been given by one of the contracting parties.

Done in duplicate in the English and German languages, at the city of Washington, this 15th day of January, 1892.

> JAMES G. BLAINE. [SEAL.]
> A. v. MUMM. [SEAL.]

And whereas the official notification contemplated by Article II of the said agreement has been received by this Government:

Now, therefore, I, Benjamin Harrison, President of the United States of America, do declare and proclaim that the first of the conditions specified in section 13 of the act of March 3, 1891, is now fulfilled in respect to the subjects of the German Empire.

In testimony whereof I have hereunto set my hand and caused the seal of the United States to be affixed.

[SEAL.] Done at the city of Washington, the 15th day of April, 1892, and of the Independence of the United States the one hundred and sixteenth.

> BENJ. HARRISON.

By the President:
JAMES G. BLAINE, *Secretary of State.*

BY THE PRESIDENT OF THE UNITED STATES OF AMERICA.

A PROCLAMATION.

Whereas, pursuant to section 3 of the act of Congress approved October 1, 1890, entitled "An act to reduce the revenue and equalize duties on imports, and for other purposes," the Secretary of State of the United States of America communicated to the Government of Honduras the action of the Congress of the United States of America, with a view to secure reciprocal trade, in declaring the articles enumerated in said section 3 to be exempt from duty upon their importation into the United States of America; and

Whereas the consul-general of Honduras at New York has communicated to the Secretary of State the fact that, in reciprocity for the admission into the United States of America free of all duty of the articles enumerated in section 3 of said act, the Government of Honduras will by due legal enactment, as a provisional measure and until a more complete arrangement may be negotiated and put in operation, admit free of all duty, from and after May 25, 1892, into all the established ports of entry of Honduras the articles or merchandise named in the following schedule, provided that the same be the product or manufacture of the United States:

SCHEDULE OF PRODUCTS AND MANUFACTURES FROM THE UNITED STATES WHICH THE REPUBLIC OF HONDURAS WILL ADMIT FREE OF ALL CUSTOMS, MUNICIPAL, AND ANY OTHER KIND OF DUTY.

1. Animals for breeding purposes.
2. Corn, rice, barley, and rye.
3. Beans.
4. Hay and straw for forage.
5. Fruits, fresh.
6. Preparations of flour in biscuits, crackers not sweetened, macaroni, vermicelli, and tallarin.
7. Coal, mineral.
8. Roman cement.
9. Hydraulic lime.
10. Bricks, fire bricks, and crucibles for melting.
11. Marble, dressed, for furniture, statues, fountains, gravestones, and building purposes.
12. Tar, vegetable and mineral.
13. Guano and other fertilizers, natural or artificial.
14. Plows and all other agricultural tools and implements.
15. Machinery of all kinds, including sewing machines, and separate or extra parts of the same.
16. Materials of all kinds for the construction and equipment of railroads.
17. Materials of all kinds for the construction and operation of telegraphic and telephonic lines.
18. Materials of all kinds for lighting by electricity and gas.
19. Materials of all kinds for the construction of wharves.
20. Apparatus for distilling liquors.
21. Wood of all kinds for building, in trunks or pieces, beams, rafters, planks, boards, shingles, or flooring.
22. Wooden staves, heads, and hoops, and barrels and boxes for packing, mounted or in pieces.
23. Houses of wood or iron, complete or in parts.
24. Wagons, carts, and carriages of all kinds.
25. Barrels, casks, and tanks of iron for water.
26. Tubes of iron and all other accessories necessary for water supply.
27. Wire, barbed, and staples for fences.
28. Plates of iron for building purposes.
29. Mineral ores.
30. Kettles of iron for making salt.
31. Sugar boilers.
32. Molds for sugar.
33. Guys for mining purposes.
34. Furnaces and instruments for assaying metals.
35. Scientific instruments.
36. Models of machinery and buildings.
37. Boats, lighters, tackle, anchors, chains, girtlines, sails, and all other articles for vessels, to be used in the ports, lakes, and rivers of the Republic.

38. Printing materials, including presses, type, ink, and all other accessories.
39. Printed books, pamphlets, and newspapers, bound or unbound, maps, photographs, printed music, and paper for music.
40. Paper for printing newspapers.
41. Quicksilver.
42. Loadstones.
43. Hops.
44. Sulphate of quinine.
45. Gold and silver in bars, dust, or coin.
46. Samples of merchandise the duties on which do not exceed $1.

It is understood that the packages or coverings in which the articles named in the foregoing schedule are imported shall be free of duty if they are usual and proper for the purpose.

And that the Government of Honduras has further stipulated that the laws and regulations adopted to protect its revenue and prevent fraud in the declarations and proof that the articles named in the foregoing schedule are the product or manufacture of the United States of America shall impose no additional charges on the importer nor undue restrictions on the articles imported; and

Whereas the Secretary of State has, by my direction, given assurance to the consul-general of Honduras at New York that this action of the Government of Honduras in granting freedom of duties to the products and manufactures of the United States of America on their importation into Honduras and in stipulating for a more complete reciprocity arrangement is accepted as a due reciprocity for the action of Congress as set forth in section 3 of said act:

Now, therefore, be it known that I, Benjamin Harrison, President of the United States of America, have caused the above-stated modifications of the tariff laws of Honduras to be made public for the information of the citizens of the United States of America.

In testimony whereof I have hereunto set my hand and caused the seal of the United States to be affixed.

[SEAL.]　　Done at the city of Washington, this 30th day of April, 1892, and of the Independence of the United States of America the one hundred and sixteenth.　　BENJ. HARRISON.

By the President:
JAMES G. BLAINE, *Secretary of State.*

BY THE PRESIDENT OF THE UNITED STATES OF AMERICA.

A PROCLAMATION.

Whereas, pursuant to section 3 of the act of Congress approved October 1, 1890, entitled "An act to reduce the revenue and equalize duties on imports, and for other purposes," the Secretary of State of the United States of America communicated to the Government of Guatemala the action of the Congress of the United States of America, with a view to secure reciprocal trade, in declaring the articles enumerated in said section 3 to be exempt from duty upon their importation into the United States of America; and

Whereas the envoy extraordinary and minister plenipotentiary of Guatemala at Washington has communicated to the Secretary of State the fact that, in reciprocity for the admission into the United States of America free of all duty of the articles enumerated in section 3 of said act, the Government of Guatemala will by due legal enactment of the National Congress of that Republic admit free of all duty, from and after the 30th day after the passage of the said act by the Congress of Guatemala, into all the established ports of entry of that Republic the articles or merchandise named in the following schedule, provided that the same be the product or manufacture of the United States:

SCHEDULE OF ARTICLES THE PRODUCT OR MANUFACTURE OF THE UNITED STATES TO BE ADMITTED INTO GUATEMALA FREE OF ALL CUSTOMS DUTIES AND OF ANY NATIONAL OR MUNICIPAL DUES AND NATIONAL PORT CHARGES.

1. Live animals.
2. Barley, corn or maize, and rye.
3. Corn meal.
4. Potatoes, pease, and beans.
5. Fresh vegetables.
6. Rice.
7. Hay and straw for forage.
8. Tar, pitch, resin, turpentine, and asphalt.
9. Cotton-seed oil and other products of said seed.
10. Quicksilver.
11. Mineral coal.
12. Guano and other fertilizers.
13. Lumber and timber, in the rough or prepared for building purposes.
14. Houses of wood or iron, complete or in parts.
15. Fire bricks, lime, cement, shingles, and tiles of clay or glass for roofing and construction of buildings.
16. Marble in slabs, columns, cornices, door and window frames, and fountains, and dressed or undressed marble for buildings.
17. Piping of clay, glazed or unglazed, for aqueducts and sewers.
18. Wire, plain or barbed, for fences, with hooks and staples for same.
19. Printed books, bound or unbound; printed music; maps, charts, and globes.
20. Materials for the construction and equipment of railways.
21. Materials for electrical illumination.
22. Materials expressly for the construction of wharves.
23. Anchors and hoisting tackle.
24. Railings of cast or wrought iron.
25. Balconies of cast or wrought iron.
26. Window blinds of wood or metal.
27. Iron fireplaces or stoves.
28. Machinery, including steam machinery for agriculture and mining, and separate parts of the same.
29. Gold and silver, in bullion, dust, or coin.

It is understood that the packages or coverings in which the articles named in the foregoing schedule are imported shall enter free of duty if they are usual and proper for the purpose.

And whereas the Government of Guatemala has further stipulated that the laws and regulations adopted to protect its revenue and prevent fraud in the declarations and proof that the articles named in the foregoing schedule are the product or manufacture of the United States of America shall impose no undue restrictions on the importer and no additional charges on the articles imported; and

Whereas the Secretary of State has, by my direction, given assurance to the envoy extraordinary and minister plenipotentiary of Guatemala at Washington that this action of the Government of Guatemala in granting freedom of duties to the products and manufactures of the United States of America on their importation into Guatemala, is accepted as a due reciprocity for the action of Congress as set forth in section 3 of said act; and

Whereas the diplomatic representative of the United States of America at the city of Guatemala has been advised by the Government of Guatemala of the passage on April 30, 1892, of an act by the National Congress of that Republic approving the commercial arrangement concluded between the Governments of the two Republics and of the issue of a decree admitting, on and after the 30th day of May, 1892, the articles mentioned in the above schedule being the product or manufacture of the United States of America into the ports of Guatemala free of all duties whatsoever:

Now, therefore, be it known that I, Benjamin Harrison, President of the United States of America, have caused the above-stated modifications of the tariff laws of Guatemala to be made public for the information of the citizens of the United States of America.

In testimony whereof I have hereunto set my hand and caused the seal of the United States to be affixed.

[SEAL.] Done at the city of Washington, this 18th day of May, 1892, and of the Independence of the United States of America the one hundred and sixteenth.   BENJ. HARRISON.

By the President:
JAMES G. BLAINE,
Secretary of State.

BY THE PRESIDENT OF THE UNITED STATES OF AMERICA.

A PROCLAMATION.

Whereas, pursuant to section 3 of the act of Congress approved October 1, 1890, entitled "An act to reduce the revenue and equalize duties on imports, and for other purposes," the attention of the Government of Austria-Hungary was called to the action of the Congress of the United States of America, with a view to secure reciprocal trade, in declaring the articles enumerated in said section 3 to be exempt from duty upon their importation into the United States of America; and

Whereas the minister plenipotentiary of Austria-Hungary at Washington has communicated to the Secretary of State the fact that, in view of the act of Congress above cited, the Government of Austria-Hungary has by due legal enactment authorized the admission, from and after May 25, 1892, into Austria-Hungary of all the articles of merchandise the product of the United States of America named in the commercial treaties which Austria-Hungary has celebrated with Germany and other nations on the terms stated in said treaties; and

Whereas the Secretary of State has, by my direction, given assurance to the minister plenipotentiary of Austria-Hungary at Washington that this action of the Government of Austria-Hungary in granting exemption of duties to the products and manufactures of the United States of America on their importation into Austria-Hungary is accepted as a due reciprocity for the action of Congress as set forth in section 3 of said act:

Now, therefore, be it known that I, Benjamin Harrison, President of the United States of America, have caused the above-stated modifications of the tariff laws of Austria-Hungary to be made public for the information of the citizens of the United States of America.

In testimony whereof I have hereunto set my hand and caused the seal of the United States to be affixed.

[SEAL.] Done at the city of Washington, this 26th day of May, 1892, and of the Independence of the United States of America the one hundred and sixteenth.

BENJ. HARRISON.

By the President:

WILLIAM F. WHARTON, *Acting Secretary of State.*

BY THE PRESIDENT OF THE UNITED STATES OF AMERICA.

A PROCLAMATION.

Whereas it is provided by section 24 of the act of Congress approved March 3, 1891, entitled "An act to repeal timber-culture laws, and for other purposes"—

That the President of the United States may from time to time set apart and reserve in any State or Territory having public land bearing forests, in any part of the public lands wholly or in part covered with timber or undergrowth, whether of commercial value or not, as public reservations; and the President shall by public proclamation declare the establishment of such reservations and the limits thereof.

And whereas the public lands in the State of Oregon within the limits hereinafter described are in part covered with timber, and it appears that the public good would be promoted by setting apart and reserving said lands as a public reservation:

Now, therefore, I, Benjamin Harrison, President of the United States,

by virtue of the power in me vested by section 24 of the aforesaid act of Congress, do hereby make known and proclaim that there is hereby reserved from entry or settlement and set apart as a public reservation all those certain tracts, pieces, or parcels of land lying and being situate in the State of Oregon and particularly described as follows, to wit:

Beginning at the northwest corner of section six (6), township one (1) south, range six (6) east, Willamette meridian; thence easterly on the base line between townships one (1) north and one (1) south to the southwest corner of section thirty-two (32), township one (1) north, range six (6) east; thence northerly on the section line between sections thirty-one (31) and thirty-two (32) to the northwest corner of section thirty-two (32); thence easterly on the section line between sections twenty-nine (29) and thirty-two (32) to the northeast corner of section thirty-two (32); thence northerly on the section line between sections twenty-eight (28) and twenty-nine (29) to the northwest corner of section twenty-eight (28); thence easterly on the section line between sections twenty-one (21) and twenty-eight (28) to the northeast corner of section twenty-eight (28); thence northerly on the section line between sections twenty-one (21) and twenty-two (22) to the northwest corner of section twenty-two (22); thence easterly on the section line between sections fifteen (15) and twenty-two (22) and fourteen (14) and twenty-three (23) to the northeast corner of section twenty-three (23); thence northerly along the section line between sections thirteen (13) and fourteen (14) and eleven (11) and twelve (12) to the northwest corner of section twelve (12); thence easterly on the section line between sections one (1) and twelve (12) to the northeast corner of section twelve (12); thence northerly on the eastern boundary of section one (1) to the northeast corner of section one (1), all of said sections being in township one (1) north, range six (6) east; thence easterly to a point for the northeast corner of township one (1) north, range seven (7) east; thence southerly to a point for the southeast corner of section one (1), township one (1) north, range seven (7) east; thence easterly to a point for the northeast corner of section eight (8), township one (1) north, range eight (8) east; thence southerly to a point for the northeast corner of section thirty-two (32) of said township and range; thence easterly to a point for the northeast corner of section thirty-three (33) of said township and range; thence southerly to the southeast corner of section thirty-three (33) of said township and range; thence westerly along the base line to the northwest corner of section four (4), township one (1) south, range eight (8) east; thence southerly on the section line between sections four (4) and five (5) and eight (8) and nine (9) to the southeast corner of section eight (8); thence easterly along the section line between sections nine (9) and sixteen (16) to a point for the northeast corner of section sixteen (16); thence southerly along the section line between sections fifteen (15) and sixteen (16) to the southeast corner of section sixteen (16); thence easterly along the section line between sections fifteen (15) and twenty-two to the northeast corner of section twenty-two (22); thence southerly between sections twenty-two (22), twenty-three (23), twenty-six (26), twenty-seven (27), thirty-four (34), and thirty-five (35) to the southeast corner of section thirty-four (34); thence easterly along the southern boundary line of sections thirty-five (35) and thirty-six (36) to the southeast corner of section thirty-six (36), all of said sections being in township one (1) south, range eight (8) east; thence southerly to a point for the southeast corner of township two (2) south, range eight (8) east; thence westerly to the southeast corner of township two (2) south, range seven (7) east; thence northerly along the eastern boundary line of sections thirty-six (36), twenty-five (25), twenty-four (24), and thirteen (13), township two (2) south, range seven (7) east, to the southeast corner of section twelve (12) of said township and range; thence westerly along the section line between sections twelve (12) and thirteen (13), eleven (11) and fourteen (14), ten (10) and fifteen (15), nine (9) and sixteen (16), eight (8) and seventeen (17), and seven (7) and eighteen (18), township two (2) south, range seven (7) east, and sections twelve (12) and thirteen (13), eleven (11) and fourteen (14), ten (10) and fifteen (15), nine (9) and sixteen (16), eight (8) and seventeen (17), and seven (7) and eighteen (18), township two (2) south, range six (6) east, to the southwest corner of section seven (7) of said township and range; thence northerly along the western boundary of section seven (7) to the northwest corner of said section, township two (2) south, range six (6) east; thence westerly on the section line between sections one (1) and twelve (12), two (2) and eleven (11), three (3) and ten (10), and four (4) and nine (9) to the southwest corner of section four (4), township two (2) south, range five (5) east; thence northerly on the section line between sections four (4) and five (5) to the northwest corner of section four (4) in said township and range; thence easterly on the township line between townships one (1) and two (2) south, range five (5) east, to the southwest corner of section thirty-five (35), township one (1) south, range five (5) east; thence northerly on the section line between sections thirty-four (34), thirty-five (35), twenty-six (26), twenty-seven (27), twenty-two (22), and twenty-three (23) to the northwest corner of section twenty-three (23) of said township and range; thence easterly on the section line between sections fourteen (14) and twenty-three (23), thirteen (13) and twenty-four (24), to the northeast corner of section twenty-four (24) of said township and range; thence northerly along the range line between ranges five (5) and six (6) east to the place of beginning.

Excepting from the force and effect of this proclamation all lands which may have been prior to the date hereof embraced in any legal entry or covered by any lawful filing duly of record in the proper United States land office, or upon which any valid settlement has been made pursuant to law and the statutory period within which to make entry or filing of record has not expired, and all mining claims duly located and held according to the laws of the United States and rules and regulations not in conflict therewith.

Provided, That this exception shall not continue to apply to any particular tract of land unless the entryman, settler, or claimant continues to comply with the law under which the entry, filing, settlement, or location was made.

Warning is hereby expressly given to all persons not to enter or make settlement upon the tract of land reserved by this proclamation.

In witness whereof I have hereunto set my hand and caused the seal of the United States to be affixed.

[SEAL.]   Done at the city of Washington, this 17th day of June, A. D. 1892, and of the Independence of the United States the one hundred and sixteenth.

                                         BENJ. HARRISON.

By the President:
    WILLIAM F. WHARTON,
        Acting Secretary of State.

BY THE PRESIDENT OF THE UNITED STATES OF AMERICA.

A PROCLAMATION.

Whereas it is provided by section 24 of the act of Congress approved March 3, 1891, entitled "An act to repeal timber-culture laws, and for other purposes"—

That the President of the United States may from time to time set apart and reserve in any State or Territory having public land bearing forests, in any part of the public lands wholly or in part covered with timber or undergrowth, whether of commercial value or not, as public reservations; and the President shall by public proclamation declare the establishment of such reservations and the limits thereof.

And whereas the public lands in the State of Colorado within the limits hereinafter described are in part covered with timber, and it appears that the public good would be promoted by setting apart and reserving said lands as a public reservation:

Now, therefore, I, Benjamin Harrison, President of the United States, by virtue of the power in me vested by section 24 of the aforesaid act of Congress, do hereby make known and proclaim that there is hereby reserved from entry or settlement and set apart as a public reservation all those certain tracts, pieces, or parcels of land lying and being situate in the State of Colorado and particularly described as follows, to wit:

Township ten (10) south of ranges sixty-eight (68), sixty-nine (69), and seventy (70) west; township nine (9) south of ranges sixty-eight (68) and sixty-nine (69) west; township eight (8) south of range sixty-nine (69) west, and so much of township ten (10) south of range seventy-one (71) west, township nine (9) south of range seventy (70) west, township eight (8) south of range seventy (70) west, and township seven (7) south of range sixty-nine (69) west as lie to the eastward of the South Platte River.

Excepting from the force and effect of this proclamation all lands which may have been prior to the date hereof embraced in any legal entry or covered by any lawful filing duly of record in the proper United States land office, or upon which any valid settlement has been made pursuant to law and the statutory period within which to make entry or filing of record has not expired, and all mining claims duly located and held according to the laws of the United States and rules and regulations not in conflict therewith.

Provided, That this exception shall not continue to apply ₊o any particular tract of land unless the entryman, settler, or claimant continues to comply with the law under which the entry, filing, settlement, or location was made.

Warning is hereby expressly given to all persons not to enter or make settlement upon the tract of land reserved by this proclamation.

In witness whereof I have hereunto set my hand and caused the seal of the United States to be affixed.

[SEAL.]   Done at the city of Washington, this 23d day of June, A. D. 1892, and of the Independence of the United States the one hundred and sixteenth.

BENJ. HARRISON.

By the President:

WILLIAM F. WHARTON,
    Acting Secretary of State.

BY THE PRESIDENT OF THE UNITED STATES OF AMERICA.

A PROCLAMATION.

To whom it may concern:

Whereas the governor of the State of Idaho has represented to me that within said State there exist an insurrection and condition of domestic violence and resistance to the laws to meet and overcome which the resources at his command are unequal; and

Whereas he has further represented that the legislature of said State is not now in session and can not be promptly convened; and

Whereas by reason of said conditions the said governor, as chief executive of the State, has called upon me, as Chief Executive of the Government of the United States, for assistance in repressing said violence and restoring and maintaining the peace:

Now, therefore, I, Benjamin Harrison, President of the United States, by virtue of section 4, Article IV, of the Constitution of the United States and of the laws of Congress enacted in pursuance thereof, do hereby command all persons engaged in said insurrection and in resistance to the laws to immediately disperse and retire peaceably to their respective abodes.

In witness whereof I have hereunto set my hand and caused the seal of the United States to be affixed.

[SEAL.] Done at the city of Washington, this 15th day of July, A. D. 1892, and of the Independence of the United States the one hundred and seventeenth.

BENJ. HARRISON.

By the President:

JOHN W. FOSTER, *Secretary of State.*

BY THE PRESIDENT OF THE UNITED STATES OF AMERICA.

A PROCLAMATION.

Whereas by a joint resolution approved June 29, 1892, it was resolved by the Senate and House of Representatives of the United States of America in Congress assembled—

That the President of the United States be authorized and directed to issue a proclamation recommending to the people the observance in all their localities of the four hundredth anniversary of the discovery of America, on the 21st of October, 1892, by public demonstrations and by suitable exercises in their schools and other places of assembly.

Now, therefore, I, Benjamin Harrison, President of the United States of America, in pursuance of the aforesaid joint resolution, do hereby appoint Friday, October 21, 1892, the four hundredth anniversary of the discovery of America by Columbus, as a general holiday for the people of the United States. On that day let the people, so far as possible, cease from toil and devote themselves to such exercises as may best express honor to the discoverer and their appreciation of the great achievements of the four completed centuries of American life.

Columbus stood in his age as the pioneer of progress and enlightenment. The system of universal education is in our age the most prominent and salutary feature of the spirit of enlightenment, and it is peculiarly appropriate that the schools be made by the people the center of the day's demonstration. Let the national flag float over every schoolhouse in the country and the exercises be such as shall impress upon our youth the patriotic duties of American citizenship.

In the churches and in the other places of assembly of the people let there be expressions of gratitude to Divine Providence for the devout faith of the discoverer and for the divine care and guidance which has directed our history and so abundantly blessed our people.

In testimony whereof I have hereunto set my hand and caused the seal of the United States to be affixed.

[SEAL.] Done at the city of Washington, this 21st day of July, A. D. 1892, and of the Independence of the United States the one hundred and seventeenth.

BENJ. HARRISON.

By the President:

JOHN W. FOSTER, *Secretary of State.*

BY THE PRESIDENT OF THE UNITED STATES OF AMERICA.

A PROCLAMATION.

Whereas by reason of unlawful obstructions, combinations, and assemblages of persons it has become impracticable, in my judgment, to enforce by the ordinary course of judicial proceedings the laws of the United States within the State and district of Wyoming, the United States marshal, after repeated efforts, being unable by his ordinary deputies or by any civil posse which he is able to obtain to execute the process of the United States courts:

Now, therefore, be it known that I, Benjamin Harrison, President of the United States, do hereby command all persons engaged in such resistance to the laws and the process of the courts of the United States to cease such opposition and resistance and to disperse and retire peaceably to their respective abodes on or before Wednesday, the 3d day of August next.

In witness whereof I have hereunto set my hand and caused the seal of the United States to be affixed.

[SEAL.]   Done at the city of Washington, this 30th day of July, A. D. 1892, and of the Independence of the United States the one hundred and seventeenth.

BENJ. HARRISON.

By the President:

JOHN W. FOSTER,
  Secretary of State.

BY THE PRESIDENT OF THE UNITED STATES OF AMERICA.

A PROCLAMATION.

Whereas by an act of Congress approved July 26, 1892, entitled "An act to enforce reciprocal commercial relations between the United States and Canada, and for other purposes," it is provided—

That with a view of securing reciprocal advantages for the citizens, ports, and vessels of the United States, on and after the 1st day of August, 1892, whenever and so often as the President shall be satisfied that the passage through any canal or lock connected with the navigation of the St. Lawrence River, the Great Lakes, or the waterways connecting the same of any vessels of the United States, or of cargoes or passengers in transit to any port of the United States, is prohibited or is made difficult or burdensome by the imposition of tolls or otherwise which, in view of the free passage through the St. Marys Falls Canal now permitted to vessels of all nations, he shall deem to be reciprocally unjust and unreasonable, he shall have the power, and it shall be his duty, to suspend, by proclamation to that effect, for such time and to such extent (including absolute prohibition) as he shall deem just, the right of free passage through the St. Marys Falls Canal so far as it relates to vessels owned by the subjects of the government so discriminating against the citizens, ports, or vessels of the United States or to any cargoes, portions of cargoes, or passengers in transit to the ports of the government making such discrimination, whether carried in vessels of the United States or of other nations.

In such case and during such suspension tolls shall be levied, collected, and paid as follows, to wit: Upon freight of whatever kind or description not to exceed $2 per ton, upon passengers not to exceed $5 each, as shall be from time to time determined by the President: *Provided*, That no tolls shall be charged or collected upon freight or passengers carried to and landed at Ogdensburg, or any port west of Ogdensburg and south of a line drawn from the northern boundary of the State of New York through the St. Lawrence River, the Great Lakes, and their connecting channels to the northern boundary of the State of Minnesota.

SEC. 2. All tolls so charged shall be collected under such regulations as shall be prescribed by the Secretary of the Treasury, who may require the master of each vessel to furnish a sworn statement of the amount and kind of cargo and the number of passengers carried and the destination of the same, and such proof of the actual delivery of such cargo or passengers at some port or place within the limits above named as he shall deem satisfactory; and until such proof is furnished such freight and passengers may be considered to have been landed at some port or place outside of those limits, and the amount of tolls which would have accrued if they had been so delivered shall constitute a lien, which may be enforced against the vessel in default wherever and whenever found in the waters of the United States.

And whereas the government of the Dominion of Canada imposes a toll amounting to about 20 cents per ton on all freight passing through the Welland Canal in transit to a port of the United States, and also a further toll on all vessels of the United States and on all passengers in transit to a port of the United States, all of which tolls are without rebate; and

Whereas the government of the Dominion of Canada, in accordance with an order in council of April 4, 1892, refunds 18 cents per ton of the 20-cent toll at the Welland Canal on wheat, Indian corn, pease, barley, rye, oats, flaxseed, and buckwheat upon condition that they are originally shipped for and carried to Montreal or some port east of Montreal for export, and that if transshipped at an intermediate point such transshipment is made within the Dominion of Canada, but allows no such nor any other rebate on said products when shipped to a port of the United States or when carried to Montreal for export if transshipped within the United States; and

Whereas the government of the Dominion of Canada by said system of rebate and otherwise discriminates against the citizens of the United States in the use of said Welland Canal, in violation of the provisions of Article XXVII of the treaty of Washington concluded May 8, 1871; and

Whereas said Welland Canal is connected with the navigation of the Great Lakes, and I am satisfied that the passage through it of cargoes in transit to ports of the United States is made difficult and burdensome by said discriminating system of rebate and otherwise and is reciprocally unjust and unreasonable:

Now, therefore, I, Benjamin Harrison, President of the United States of America, by virtue of the power to that end conferred upon me by said act of Congress approved July 26, 1892, do hereby direct that from and after September 1, 1892, until further notice a toll of 20 cents per ton be levied, collected, and paid on all freight of whatever kind or description passing through the St. Marys Falls Canal in transit to any port of the Dominion of Canada, whether carried in vessels of the United States or of other nations; and to that extent I do hereby suspend from and after said date the right of free passage through said St. Marys Falls Canal of any and all cargoes or portions of cargoes in transit to Canadian ports.

In testimony whereof I have hereunto set my hand and caused the seal of the United States to be affixed.

[SEAL.]   Done at the city of Washington, this 18th day of August, A. D. 1892, and of the Independence of the United States of America the one hundred and seventeenth.

BENJ. HARRISON.

By the President:

JOHN W. FOSTER,
Secretary of State.

BY THE PRESIDENT OF THE UNITED STATES OF AMERICA.

A PROCLAMATION.

Whereas by a written agreement made on the 8th day of December, 1890, the Crow tribe of Indians, in the State of Montana, agreed to dispose of and sell to the United States, for certain considerations in said agreement specified, all that portion of the Crow Indian Reservation in the State of Montana lying west and south of the following lines, to wit:

Beginning in the mid-channel of the Yellowstone River at a point which is the northwest corner of section No. 36, township No. 2 north of range 27 east of the principal meridian of Montana; thence running in a southwesterly direction, following the top of the natural divide between the waters flowing into the Yellowstone and Clarks Fork rivers upon the west and those flowing into Pryor Creek and West Pryor Creek on the east, to the base of West Pryor Mountain; thence due south and up the north slope of said Pryor Mountain on a true meridian line to a point 15 miles due north from the established line between Montana and Wyoming; thence in a due easterly course on a parallel of latitude to a point where it intersects the mid-channel of the Big Horn River; thence following up the mid-channel of said river to a point where it crosses the Montana and Wyoming State line.

And whereas it is stipulated in the eleventh clause or section of said agreement that all lands upon that portion of the reservation by said agreement ceded which prior to the date thereof had been allotted in severalty to Indians of the Crow tribe shall be retained and enjoyed by them; and

Whereas it is provided in the twelfth clause or section of said agreement that, in accordance with the provisions of article 6 of the treaty of May 7, A. D. 1868, said cession of lands shall not be construed to deprive without his or her consent any individual Indian of the Crow tribe of his or her right to any tract of land selected by him or her in conformity with said treaty or as provided by the agreement approved by Congress April 11, A. D. 1882; and

Whereas it is further provided in said twelfth clause or section that in ratifying said agreement the Congress of the United States shall cause all such lands to be surveyed and certificates duly issued for the same to said Indians, as provided in the treaty of May 7, 1868, before said ceded portion of the reservation shall be opened for settlement; and

Whereas by the thirteenth clause or section of said agreement of December 8, 1890, it is made a condition of said agreement that it shall not be binding upon either party until ratified by the Congress of the United States, and when so ratified that said cession of lands so acquired by the United States shall not be opened for settlement until the boundary lines set forth and described in said agreement have been surveyed and definitely marked by suitable permanent monuments, erected every half mile wherever practicable, along the entire length of said boundary line; and

Whereas said agreement was duly ratified and confirmed by the thirty-first section of the act of Congress approved March 3, 1891; and

Whereas it is provided in section 34 of said act of March 3, 1891—

That whenever any of the lands acquired by the agreement with said Crow Indians hereby ratified and confirmed shall by operation of law or the proclamation of the President of the United States be open to settlement, they shall, except mineral lands, be disposed of to actual settlers only under the provisions of the homestead laws, except section 2301 of the Revised Statutes, which shall not apply: *Provided, however*, That each settler under and in accordance with the provisions of said homestead laws shall before receiving a patent for his homestead pay to the United States for the land so taken by him, in addition to the fees provided by law, and within five years from the date of the first original entry, the sum of $1.50 for each acre thereof, one-half of which shall be paid within two years; and any person otherwise qualified who has attempted to but for any cause failed to secure a title in fee to a homestead under existing law, or who made entry under what is known as the commuted provision of the homestead law, shall be qualified to make a homestead entry upon any of said lands in conformity with the provisions of this section; that any person who may be entitled to the privilege of selecting land in severalty under the provisions of article 6 of the treaty of May 7, 1868, with the Crow Indians, and which provisions were continued in force by the agreement with said Indians ratified and confirmed by the act of Congress approved April 11, 1882, or any other act or treaty, shall have the right for a period of sixty days to make such selections in any part of the territory by said agreement ceded, and such locations are hereby confirmed: *Provided further*, That all white persons who located upon said Crow Reservation by reason of an erroneous survey of the boundary and were afterwards allowed to file upon their location in the United States land office shall have thirty days in which to renew their filings, and their locations are hereby confirmed; and that in all cases where claims were located under the mining laws of the United States, and such location was made prior to December 1, 1890, by a locator qualified therefor who believed that he or she was so locating on lands outside the Crow Indian Reservation, such locator shall be allowed thirty days within which to relocate the said mining claims so theretofore located by them within the limits of the ceded portion of said Crow Indian Reservation, and upon such relocation such proceedings shall be had as are conformable to law and in accordance with the provisions of this act.

And whereas the boundary lines of said ceded lands have been duly surveyed and marked as stipulated in the thirteenth clause or section of said agreement; and

Whereas a written agreement was concluded with said Crow Indians on the 27th day of August, 1892, under and by virtue of the following clause in the Indian appropriation act of Congress approved July 13, 1892, to wit:

* * * To enable the Secretary of the Interior, in his discretion, to appoint a commission to negotiate with the Crow Indians of Montana for a modification of the agreement concluded with said Indians December 8, 1890, and ratified by Congress March 3, 1891, and to pay the necessary and actual expenses of said commissioners: *Provided*, That no such modification shall be valid unless assented to by a majority of the male adult members of the Crow tribe of Indians and be approved by the Secretary of the Interior.

Which said agreement was assented to by a majority of the male adult members of the Crow tribe of Indians, as attested by their signatures thereto, and has been duly approved by the Secretary of the Interior; and

Whereas it is stipulated and agreed in the first clause or section of said agreement of August 27, 1892, that the persons named in a schedule attached to and made a part of said agreement, marked "Schedule A," include all the members of said Crow tribe who are entitled to the benefits of the eleventh section of said agreement of December 8, 1890, and that each of said persons is entitled to the land therein described as his selection in full satisfaction of his claim under said section; and that the persons named in a schedule attached to and made a part of said agreement of August 27, 1892, marked "Schedule B," include all the members of said tribe who are entitled to the benefits of the twelfth section of said agreement of December 8, 1890, and of the proviso of the thirty-fourth section of the act of Congress approved March 3, 1891, extending the privilege of making selections on the ceded lands for a period of sixty days, and that each of the said persons therein named is entitled to retain the tract of land theretofore selected by him within the limits of the tract of land therein described as containing his selection of his claim under the said section (or the said proviso); and

Whereas it is stipulated and agreed by the second clause or section of said agreement of August 27, 1892, that all lands ceded by said agreement may be opened to settlement, upon the approval of the said agreement, by proclamation of the President:

Provided, That all lands within the ceded tract selected or set apart for the use of individual Indians and described in the aforesaid Schedules "A" and "B" shall be exempt from cession and shall remain a part of the Crow Indian Reservation, and shall continue under the exclusive control of the Interior Department until they shall have been surveyed and certificates or patents issued therefor as provided in the agreement of December 8, 1890, or until relinquished or surrendered by the Indian or Indians claiming the same: *Provided further*, That such lands shall be described as set forth in Schedules "A" and "B," and shall be exempted from settlement in the proclamation of the President opening the ceded lands, and that where lands so set apart are not described by legal subdivisions then the township or section or tract of land within whose limits such Indians' selections are located shall not be opened to settlement until the Indian allotments therein contained shall have been surveyed and proper evidence of title issued therefor.

Now, therefore, I, Benjamin Harrison, President of the United States, by virtue of the power in me vested by the agreements and statutes here- inbefore mentioned and by other the laws of the United States, do hereby declare and make known that all of the lands within that portion of the Crow Indian Reservation in Montana ceded to the United States by the said agreement of December 8, 1890, and hereinbefore described, except those hereinafter mentioned and described, are open to settlement under the terms of and subject to all the conditions, limitations, reservations, and restrictions contained in the thirty-fourth section of the act of Con- gress approved March 3, 1891, and hereinbefore quoted, and other laws applicable thereto.

The lands exempted from the operation of this proclamation, being those embraced in Schedules "A" and "B" attached to the agreement of August 27, 1892, are described as follows:

1.—SURVEYED LANDS.

IN TOWNSHIP 1 NORTH, RANGE 26 EAST.

Fractional section 24; the north half, the east half of southeast quarter, and west half of southwest quarter of fractional section 25; fractional section 26; lot 5 of frac- tional section 34; the north half of northeast quarter and the northeast quarter of northwest quarter of section 35; and the northeast quarter of northeast quarter of sec- tion 36.

IN TOWNSHIP 1 NORTH, RANGE 27 EAST.

Fractional section 7; lots 1, 2, 3, 4, 5, and 6, the southwest quarter of northeast quarter, the southeast quarter, and the south half of the southwest quarter of frac- tional section 8; the south half of northwest quarter of section 9; the north half of the northwest quarter and the southwest quarter of the northwest quarter of section 17; fractional section 18; the north half and the southwest quarter of section 19.

IN TOWNSHIP 3 SOUTH, RANGE 24 EAST.

The north half of the southwest quarter of section 3; the southeast quarter of the northeast quarter and lots 2, 3, and 4 of section 4; fractional section 5; the south- east quarter and the south half of the southwest quarter of section 6; section 7; west half of section 8; the east half of the northwest quarter and the southwest quarter of the northwest quarter of section 17; lots 1, 2, 3, 4, 5, and 6, the northeast quarter of the northeast quarter, the south half of the northeast quarter, and the southeast quarter of the northwest quarter and the south half of section 18; lots 1, 3, 4, and 5 and the east half of southwest quarter, section 19; and lots 1, 2, 3, and 4 in section 30.

IN TOWNSHIP 4 SOUTH, RANGE 23 EAST.

Lots 4, 5, 6, 7, 8, 9, and 13, the south half of northwest quarter, the southeast quar- ter of southeast quarter, and the northeast quarter of the southwest quarter, section 1; section 2; the north half, the southeast quarter, and the north half of southwest quarter, section 3; section 4; the east half and the southwest quarter of section 8; the north half and the southwest quarter of section 9; the east half and the southwest quarter of section 11; section 12; the north half, the south half of the southeast quarter, the east half of the southwest quarter, and lots 1, 2, and 3 of section 13; the north half, the southeast quarter, and the south half of the southwest quarter of section 14; the north half of section 17; the north half, the east half of the southeast quarter, and the north half of the southwest quarter of section 18; the northwest quarter of section 19; the east half and the northwest quarter of section 20; the south half of the northwest quarter of section 22; all of section 23 except the northwest quarter of northwest quarter; section 24; lots 2 and 3 in section 25; the north half of northeast quarter, the northwest quarter, the north half of the southwest quarter, and lots 1, 2, 5, 6, 7, and 8 of section 26; the south half of the southeast quarter of section 27; the northwest quarter of section 33; the fractional east half and the southwest quarter of section 34; lots 2, 3, 4, 5, 6, 7, 9, and 10 of section 35.

IN TOWNSHIP 5 SOUTH OF RANGE 23 EAST.

Lot 5 and southwest quarter of northwest quarter of section 2; lots 1, 2, 6, 7, 8, 9, 12, and 14 and southeast quarter of southeast quarter of section 3; the fractional east half, the south half of northwest quarter, and the southwest quarter of section 4; the south half of the northeast quarter and the north half of the southeast quarter of section 7; the south half of the north half and the south half of section 8; lots 1, 2, 3, 4, 6, 7, and 8 and the west half of section 9; lots 1, 2, 3, and 4, the west half of the northeast quarter, and the south half of section 10; the northwest quarter of section 15; section 16; the east half of the northeast quarter and the south half of section 17; the northwest quarter of the northeast quarter, the southeast quarter of the southeast quarter, the west half, and lots 1, 2, 4, and 5, section 20; the southwest quarter of section 21; the west half of southwest quarter, section 26; the south half of section 27; the west half of the northeast quarter, the northwest quarter, and the south half of section 28; lots 1, 2, 3, 4, 6, and 7, the northwest quarter, the south half of the southeast quarter, and the west half of the southwest quarter of section 29; the northeast quarter of northeast quarter, the northeast quarter of the southeast quarter, and the south half of the southeast quarter of section 30; the northeast quarter, the northeast quarter of the northwest quarter, and the southeast quarter of section 31; lots 3, 4, 5, 6, 9, and 10, the southwest quarter of the southeast quarter, and the southwest quarter of section 32; lot 1, the north half of the northeast quarter, and the northwest quarter of section 33; and the west half of the northeast quarter and the northwest quarter of section 34.

2.—UNSURVEYED LANDS WHICH WHEN SURVEYED WILL BE DESCRIBED AS FOLLOWS:

IN TOWNSHIP I NORTH OF RANGE 15 EAST.

The southwest quarter of the northwest quarter, the northwest quarter of the southwest quarter, and the south half of the southwest quarter of section 27; the southeast quarter of the northeast quarter and the east half of the southeast quarter of section 28; the east half of the northeast quarter of section 33; the north half, the north half of the southeast quarter, and the northeast quarter of the southwest quarter of section 34; the south half of the north half and the south half of section 35; and the southwest quarter of the northwest quarter, the southeast quarter, the north half of the southwest quarter, and the southwest quarter of the southwest quarter of section 36.

IN TOWNSHIP I NORTH, RANGE 16 EAST.

The southwest quarter of the southwest quarter of section 31.

IN TOWNSHIP I SOUTH OF RANGE 15 EAST.

The north half of the north half and the southeast quarter of the northeast quarter of section 1.

IN TOWNSHIP I SOUTH OF RANGE 16 EAST.

The north half of the northeast quarter and the southwest quarter of the northwest quarter of section 6, and the southeast quarter of the northeast quarter of section 24.

IN TOWNSHIP I SOUTH OF RANGE 18 EAST.

The southeast quarter of the southwest quarter of section 27; the northwest quarter of the southeast quarter and the south half of the southeast quarter of section 28; the north half of the northeast quarter of section 33; and the northeast quarter and the east half of the northwest quarter of section 34.

IN TOWNSHIP I SOUTH OF RANGE 17 EAST.

The east half of the northeast quarter, the east half of the northwest quarter, the southwest quarter of the northwest quarter, the northwest quarter of the southeast quarter, and the northeast quarter of the southwest quarter of section 19; the south half of the southeast quarter and the southeast quarter of the southwest quarter of section 28; and the north half of the northeast quarter and the northeast quarter of the northwest quarter of section 33.

IN TOWNSHIP I SOUTH OF RANGE 25 EAST.

The northeast quarter of the southeast quarter, the south half of the southeast quarter, and the southeast quarter of the southwest quarter of section 25, and the northeast quarter of the northwest quarter and the west half of section 36.

IN TOWNSHIP I SOUTH OF RANGE 26 EAST.

The south half of the southeast quarter of section 19; the southeast quarter, the northeast quarter of the southwest quarter, and the south half of the southwest quarter of section 20; the west half of the southwest quarter of section 21; the west half of the northwest quarter of section 28; the north half and the northwest quarter of the southwest quarter of section 29; the north half of the northeast quarter, the southeast quarter of the northeast quarter, the southwest quarter of the northwest quarter, the north half of the southeast quarter, and the southwest quarter of section 30.

IN TOWNSHIP 2 SOUTH OF RANGE 13 EAST.

The southwest quarter of the northwest quarter and the northwest quarter of the southwest quarter of section 27; the southeast quarter of the northeast quarter and the east half of the southeast quarter of section 28; and the east half, the east half of the northwest quarter, the northeast quarter of the southeast quarter, and the northeast quarter of the southwest quarter of section 33.

IN TOWNSHIP 2 SOUTH OF RANGE 18 EAST.

The southeast quarter and the east half of the southwest quarter of section 1

IN TOWNSHIP 2 SOUTH OF RANGE 20 EAST.

The east half, the east half of the northwest quarter, the southwest quarter of the northwest quarter, and the north half of the southwest quarter of section 28; the northeast quarter and the north half of the southeast quarter of section 29; the south half of the northeast quarter, the north half of the southeast quarter, and the southeast quarter of the southeast quarter of section 34; the south half of the north half and the south half of section 35; and the southwest quarter of the northwest quarter, the northwest quarter of the southeast quarter, the south half of the southeast quarter, and the southwest quarter of section 36.

IN TOWNSHIP 2 SOUTH OF RANGE 21 EAST.

The west half of the northeast quarter, the northwest quarter of the southeast quarter, the east half of the west half, and the southwest quarter of the southwest quarter of section 32.

IN TOWNSHIP 2 SOUTH OF RANGE 24 EAST.

The northeast quarter of the southeast quarter and the south half of the southeast quarter of section 21; the northeast quarter, the north half of the southeast quarter, and the southwest quarter of section 22; the west half of the northwest quarter of section 27; the northeast quarter of section 28; and the northeast quarter, the southeast quarter of the northwest quarter, the north half of the southeast quarter, and the southwest quarter of section 29.

IN TOWNSHIP 3 SOUTH OF RANGE 18 EAST.

The west half of section 14; the west half of the northeast quarter and the east half of the northwest quarter of section 23; the southwest quarter of the northeast quarter, the southeast quarter of the northwest quarter, the northwest quarter of the southeast quarter, and the northeast quarter of the southwest quarter of section 31; the northeast quarter, the south half of the northwest quarter, and the north half of the southwest quarter of section 32; the south half of the northeast quarter and the southeast quarter of section 33; the southwest quarter of the northeast quarter and the south half of the northwest quarter, the west half of the southeast quarter, and the southwest quarter of section 34; the south half of section 35; and the southeast quarter of the northeast quarter and the southeast quarter of section 36.

IN TOWNSHIP 3 SOUTH OF RANGE 19 EAST.

The northeast quarter, the north half of the southeast quarter, the southwest quarter of the southeast quarter, and the east half of the southwest quarter of section 12; the northwest quarter of section 29; the east half of the northeast quarter, the southwest quarter of the northeast quarter, the southeast quarter of the northwest quarter, and the south half of section 30; and the southwest quarter of the northwest quarter and the west half of the southwest quarter of section 31.

IN TOWNSHIP 3 SOUTH OF RANGE 20 EAST.

The northeast quarter, the north half of the northwest quarter, the southeast quarter of the northwest quarter, and the northeast quarter of the southeast quarter of section 1; the north half of the northeast quarter and the northeast quarter of the northwest quarter of section 2; the north half of the northwest quarter, the southwest quarter of the northwest quarter, and the west half of the southwest quarter of section 5; the southeast quarter of the northeast quarter, the southeast quarter, and the southeast quarter of the southwest quarter of section 6; and the west half of the northeast quarter and the northwest quarter of section 7.

IN TOWNSHIP 3 SOUTH OF RANGE 21 EAST.

The northwest quarter of the southwest quarter and the south half of the southwest quarter of section 5; the east half of the southeast quarter and the west half of section 6; the northeast quarter of the northeast quarter of section 7; and the north half of the northwest quarter of section 8.

IN TOWNSHIP 3 SOUTH OF RANGE 23 EAST.

The southeast quarter of the northeast quarter and the east half of the southeast quarter of section 12; the east half of section 13; the southeast quarter of the southeast quarter of section 23; the southeast quarter of the northeast quarter, the east half of the southeast quarter, and the southwest quarter of the southwest quarter of section 24; the east half of the east half, the west half of the northwest quarter, and the southwest quarter of section 25; the northeast quarter of the southeast quarter and the south half of the southeast quarter of section 26; the south half of the south half of section 34; the northeast quarter, the north half of the southeast quarter, the southwest quarter of the southeast quarter, and the south half of the southwest quarter of section 35; and the northwest quarter of section 36.

IN TOWNSHIP 4 SOUTH OF RANGE 18 EAST.

The northwest quarter of the northeast quarter and the north half of the northwest quarter of section 3; the north half of the northeast quarter of section 4; the southeast quarter of the southwest quarter of section 13; the west half of the northeast quarter, the east half of the northwest quarter, the southeast quarter, and the northeast quarter of the southwest quarter of section 24; the northeast quarter, the north half of the southeast quarter, the southwest quarter of the southeast quarter, and the southwest quarter of section 25; the south half of the southeast quarter of section 29; the northwest quarter of the northeast quarter and the northeast quarter of the . northwest quarter of section 32; the northeast quarter of the northeast quarter, the northwest quarter, the northeast quarter of the southeast quarter, and the south half of the southeast quarter of section 35; and the west half of the northeast quarter, the northwest quarter, and the northwest quarter of the southwest quarter of section 36

IN TOWNSHIP 6 SOUTH OF RANGE 18 EAST.

The east half of the southeast quarter and the southwest quarter of the southeast quarter of section 20, and the west half of the northeast quarter, the northeast quarter of the northwest quarter, and the south half of the northwest quarter of section 29.

IN TOWNSHIP 6 SOUTH OF RANGE 19 EAST.

The northeast quarter, the east half of the northwest quarter, the southwest quarter of the northwest quarter, the north half of the southeast quarter, and the northwest quarter of the southwest quarter of section 15; the southeast quarter of the northwest quarter and the northeast quarter of the southwest quarter of section 16; the south half of the northeast quarter and the north half of the southeast quarter of section 19; and the south half of the northwest quarter and the north half of the southwest quarter of section 20.

IN TOWNSHIP 6 SOUTH OF RANGE 23 EAST.

The north half of the northwest quarter and the north half of the southeast quarter of section 5; the south half of the southeast quarter of section 8; section 17; and the west half of the northwest quarter of section 16.

3.—TOWNSHIPS, SECTIONS, OR TRACTS OF LAND WITHIN WHICH INDIAN SELECTIONS ARE LOCATED.

TRACT I.

Beginning at a point in the mid-channel of the Yellowstone River 1½ miles below the mouth of the Clarks Fork River; thence running in a southwesterly direction along a line parallel to and 1½ miles distant from the mid-channel of the Clarks Fork River to the south line of township 2 south of range 24 east; thence west along said township line to the mid-channel of the Clarks Fork River; thence northeast along the mid-channel of the Clarks Fork River to the mid-channel of the Yellowstone River; thence northeast along the mid-channel of said river to the point of beginning.

TRACT 2.

All that part of township 2 south of range 24 east lying south of the Yellowstone River and west of the Clarks Fork River.

TRACT 3.

Sections 29, 31, and 32, township 5 south of range 21 east; sections 5, 6, 7, 8, 17, and 18, township 6 south of range 21 east; and sections 1, 2, 11, 12, 13, and 14, township 6 south of range 20 east.

TRACT 4.

Beginning at a point in the mid-channel of the Yellowstone River opposite the mouth of Duck Creek; thence running in a southwesterly direction along the mid-channel of the Yellowstone River to a point 1½ miles below the mouth of the Clarks Fork River; thence in a southwesterly direction along a line parallel to and 1½ miles distant from the mid-channel of the said Clarks Fork River to a point 1½ miles due south of the mid-channel of the said Yellowstone River; thence running in a northeasterly direction along a line parallel to and 1½ miles distant from the mid-channel of the Yellowstone River to the mid-channel of Duck Creek; thence in a northerly direction along the mid-channel of Duck Creek to the point of beginning.

TRACT 5.

All that part of townships 2 and 3 south of range 23 lying south of the mid-channel of the Yellowstone River and north of a line running parallel thereto and 1½ miles distant therefrom.

TRACT 6.

Beginning in the mid-channel of the main or West Fork of Red Lodge Creek at the point where it intersects the line known as the line of the Blake survey, and which was formerly supposed to be the south boundary of the Crow Indian Reserve; thence running due east along the lines of said Blake survey for a distance of 1 mile; thence running northeasterly along a line parallel to and 1 mile from the mid-channel of the said West Fork of said Red Lodge Creek for a distance of 10 miles; thence due west to the mid-channel of the said West Fork of said Red Lodge Creek; thence southwesterly along the mid-channel of the said West Fork of said creek to the place of beginning.

TRACT 7.

Townships 4 south of ranges 21 and 22 east.

TRACT 8.

All that part of the east half of township 1 south of range 26 east lying south of the Yellowstone River, and all that part of the west half of township 1 south of range 27 east lying south of the Yellowstone River.

TRACT 9.

Section 14, township 3 south of range 19 east.

TRACT 10.

Beginning in the mid-channel of the main or West Fork of Red Lodge Creek at the point where it intersects the line known as the line of the Blake survey, and which was formerly supposed to be the south boundary of the Crow Indian Reserve; thence running due east along the line of said Blake survey for a distance of 1 mile; thence running northeasterly along a line parallel to and 1 mile from the mid-channel of the said West Fork of said Red Lodge Creek for a distance of 10 miles; thence due west to the mid-channel of the said West Fork of said Red Lodge Creek; thence southwesterly along the mid-channel of the said West Fork of said Red Lodge Creek to the place of beginning.

In witness whereof I have hereunto set my hand and caused the seal of the United States to be affixed.

[SEAL.] Done at the city of Washington, this 15th day of October, A. D. 1892, and of the Independence of the United States the one hundred and seventeenth. BENJ. HARRISON.

By the President:

JOHN W. FOSTER, *Secretary of State.*

By the President of the United States of America.
A PROCLAMATION.

Whereas it is provided by section 13 of the act of Congress of March 3, 1891, entitled ''An act to amend Title LX, chapter 3, of the Revised Statutes of the United States, relating to copyrights,'' that said act ''shall only apply to a citizen or subject of a foreign state or nation when such foreign state or nation permits to citizens of the United States of America the benefit of copyright on substantially the same basis as its own citizens, or when such foreign state or nation is a party to an international agreement which provides for reciprocity in the granting of copyright, by the terms of which agreement the United States of America may at its pleasure become a party to such agreement;'' and

Whereas it is also provided by said section that '' the existence of either of the conditions aforesaid shall be determined by the President of the United States by proclamation made from time to time as the purposes of this act may require;'' and

Whereas satisfactory official assurances have been given that in Italy the law permits to citizens of the United States the benefit of copyright on substantially the same basis as to the subjects of Italy:

Now, therefore, I, Benjamin Harrison, President of the United States of America, do declare and proclaim that the first of the conditions specified in section 13 of the act of March 3, 1891, now exists and is fulfilled in respect to the subjects of Italy.

In testimony whereof I have hereunto set my hand and caused the seal of the United States to be affixed.

[SEAL.] Done at the city of Washington, this 31st day of October, 1892, and of the Independence of the United States the one hundred and seventeenth. BENJ. HARRISON.

By the President:

JOHN W. FOSTER, *Secretary of State.*

By the President of the United States of America.
A PROCLAMATION.

The gifts of God to our people during the past year have been so abundant and so special that the spirit of devout thanksgiving awaits not a call, but only the appointment of a day when it may have a common expression. He has stayed the pestilence at our door; He has given us more love for the free civil institutions in the creation of which His directing providence was so conspicuous; He has awakened a deeper reverence for law; He has widened our philanthropy by a call to succor the distress in other lands; He has blessed our schools and is bringing forward a patriotic and God-fearing generation to execute His great and benevolent designs for our country; He has given us great increase in material wealth and a wide diffusion of contentment and comfort in the homes of our people; He has given His grace to the sorrowing.

Wherefore, I, Benjamin Harrison, President of the United States, do call upon all our people to observe, as we have been wont, Thursday, the 24th day of this month of November, as a day of thanksgiving to God for His mercies and of supplication for His continued care and grace.

In testimony whereof I have hereunto set my hand and caused the seal of the United States to be affixed.

[SEAL.] Done at the city of Washington, this 4th day of November, 1892, and of the Independence of the United States the one hundred and seventeenth.

BENJ. HARRISON.

By the President:

JOHN W. FOSTER,
Secretary of State.

EXECUTIVE ORDERS.

AMENDMENT OF CIVIL-SERVICE RULES.

JANUARY 20, 1892.

Special Departmental Rule No. 1 is hereby amended by adding at the end of paragraph 10 the following: "and elevator conductors;" so that as amended the paragraph will read:

In all the Departments: Bookbinders and elevator conductors.

BENJ. HARRISON.

AMENDMENT OF CIVIL-SERVICE RULES.

UNITED STATES CIVIL SERVICE COMMISSION,
Washington, D. C., January 12, 1892.

The PRESIDENT.

SIR: We have the honor to recommend that Executive orders heretofore issued designating the places to be filled by noncompetitive examination under clause (*d*) of section 2 of General Rule III be amended so as to include among those places, in all the Departments where authorized by law and employed, "captains of the watch" and "lieutenants of the watch." The captains and lieutenants of the watch in the Treasury Department and the captain of the watch in the Post-Office Department are now included in this category, and the object of this recommendation is to place all the Departments on the same footing with respect to these places.

The occasion for the recommendation at this time is the receipt by this Commission of a request from the Secretary of the Interior for a noncompetitive examination of a person named by him for appointment as captain of the watch in the Interior Department.

The place is now subject to competitive examination, but the Commission sees no good reason why one rule should not apply to all the Departments; hence this recommendation.

If you approve the recommendation, your indorsement of approval on this letter and its return to the Commission is requested. As it is not a change of rule, it does not require to go to the Department of State for record.

We have the honor to be, your obedient servants,

CHAS. LYMAN,
HUGH S. THOMPSON,
Commissioners.

EXECUTIVE MANSION, *January 25, 1892.*

The within recommendation is approved.

BENJ HARRISON.

AMENDMENTS OF CIVIL-SERVICE RULES.

FEBRUARY 23, 1892.

Indian Rule VI is hereby amended by inserting after the word "appointment" the following: "from one agency to another;" so that as amended the rule will read:

Subject to the conditions stated in Rule IV, transfers may be made after absolute appointment from one agency to another, from one school to another, and from one district to another, under such regulations as the Commissioner of Indian Affairs, with the approval of the Secretary of the Interior, may prescribe.

Indian Rule IV, section 1, clause (*b*), is hereby amended by inserting after the word "averages" the following: "who have not been three times certified;" so that as amended the clause will read:

If fitness for the vacant place is tested by competitive examination, the Commission shall certify from the proper register of the district in which the vacancy exists the names of the three eligibles thereon, of the sex called for, having the highest averages, who have not been three times certified: *Provided,* That the eligibles upon any register who have been allowed preference under section 1754 of the Revised Statutes shall be certified, according to their grade, before all other eligibles thereon: *And provided further,* That if the vacancy is in the grade of matron or teacher, and the wife of the superintendent of the school in which the vacancy exists is an eligible, she may be given preference in certification if the appointing officer so requests.

Section 5 of the same rule is also hereby amended by inserting after the word "vacancy" the following: "in any agency or;" so that as amended the clause will read:

In case of the sudden occurrence of a vacancy in any agency or in any school during a school term which the public interest requires to be immediately filled the

Commissioner of Indian Affairs is authorized, in his discretion, to provide for the temporary filling of the same until a regular appointment can be made under the provisions of sections 1, 2, and 3 of this rule, and when such regular appointment is made the temporary appointment shall terminate. All temporary appointments made under this authority and their termination shall at once be reported to the Commission.

BENJ. HARRISON.

EXECUTIVE MANSION,
Washington, D. C., May 5, 1892.

In the exercise of the authority vested in the President by the seventeen hundred and fifty-third section of the Revised Statutes—

It is ordered, That the office of the United States Commission of Fish and Fisheries be, and the same is hereby, classified as a part of the classified departmental service and for the purpose of applying the civil-service rules thereto the officers, clerks, and other employees of said Commission are hereby arranged in the following classes, viz:

Class A.—All persons receiving an annual salary of less than $720, or a compensation at the rate of less than $720 per annum.

Class B.—All persons receiving an annual salary of $720 or more, or a compensation at the rate of $720 or more, but less than $840 per annum.

Class C.—All persons receiving an annual salary of $840 or more, or a compensation at the rate of $840 or more, but less than $900 per annum.

Class D.—All persons receiving an annual salary of $900 or more, or a compensation at the rate of $900 or more, but less than $1,000 per annum.

Class E.—All persons receiving an annual salary of $1,000 or more, or a compensation at the rate of $1,000 or more, but less than $1,200 per annum.

Class 1.—All persons receiving an annual salary of $1,200 or more, or a compensation at the rate of $1,200 or more, but less than $1,400 per annum.

Class 2.—All persons receiving an annual salary of $1,400 or more, or a compensation at the rate of $1,400 or more, but less than $1,600 per annum.

Class 3.—All persons receiving an annual salary of $1,600 or more, or a compensation at the rate of $1,600 or more, but less than $1,800 per annum.

Class 4.—All persons receiving an annual salary of $1,800 or more, or a compensation at the rate of $1,800 or more, but less than $2,000 per annum.

Class 5.—All persons receiving an annual salary of $2,000 or more, or a compensation at the rate of $2,000 per annum.

Provided, That no person who may be appointed to an office by and with the advice and consent of the Senate, and that no person who may be employed merely as a messenger, laborer, workman, or watchman, shall be considered as within this classification, and no person so employed shall be assigned to the duties of a classified place.

Provided further, That no person shall be admitted to any place not excepted from examination by the civil-service rules in any of the classes above designated until he or she shall have passed an appropriate examination under the United States Civil Service Commission and his or her eligibility has been certified to by said Commission.

BENJ. HARRISON

CIVIL SERVICE.—AMENDMENT OF EXECUTIVE ORDERS.

MAY 7, 1892.

Executive orders heretofore issued declaring the places subject to noncompetitive examination under clause (*d*) of section 2 of General Rule III are hereby amended so as to include among said places the following:

In the Commission of Fish and Fisheries: Fish culturists and machinists.

BENJ. HARRISON.

AMENDMENT OF CIVIL-SERVICE RULES.

MAY 7, 1892.

Special Departmental Rule No. 1 is hereby amended so as to include among the places excepted from examination therein the following:

In the Commission of Fish and Fisheries: Ichthyologist and editor, one scientific assistant, captains, officers, ships writers and crews on vessels of the Commission, and pilots.

BENJ. HARRISON

SEPTEMBER 16, 1892.

In order that the members of the Grand Army of the Republic employed in the public service in the city of Washington may have the opportunity of joining in the parade arranged for Tuesday, the 20th of September instant, and that all others may unite with the citizens of the District of Columbia in showing honor to the Union soldiers and sailors to be gathered in the national capital on that occasion—

It is hereby ordered, That the several Executive Departments and the Public Printing Office be closed on that day.

By the President:

BENJ. HARRISON.

AMENDMENT OF CIVIL-SERVICE RULES.

EXECUTIVE MANSION, *September 23, 1892.*

Departmental Rule X, Customs Rule VII, Postal Rule VII, and Indian Rule VII are hereby amended by inserting in the proviso of each of said rules, after the word "therefrom," the words "or the widow of any such person," and after the word "he" the words "or she;" so that as amended the proviso of each of said rules will read:

Provided, That certification may be made, subject to the other conditions of this rule, for the reinstatement of any person who served in the military or naval service in the late War of the Rebellion and was honorably discharged therefrom, or the widow of any such person, without regard to the length of time he or she has been separated from the service.

BENJ. HARRISON.

FOURTH ANNUAL MESSAGE.

EXECUTIVE MANSION, *December 6, 1892.*

To the Senate and House of Representatives:

In submitting my annual message to Congress I have great satisfaction in being able to say that the general conditions affecting the commercial and industrial interests of the United States are in the highest degree favorable. A comparison of the existing conditions with those of the most favored period in the history of the country will, I believe, show that so high a degree of prosperity and so general a diffusion of the comforts of life were never before enjoyed by our people.

The total wealth of the country in 1860 was $16,159,616,068. In 1890 it amounted to $62,610,000,000, an increase of 287 per cent.

The total mileage of railways in the United States in 1860 was 30,626. In 1890 it was 167,741, an increase of 448 per cent; and it is estimated that there will be about 4,000 miles of track added by the close of the year 1892.

The official returns of the Eleventh Census and those of the Tenth Census for seventy-five leading cities furnish the basis for the following comparisons:

In 1880 the capital invested in manufacturing was $1,232,839,670.

In 1890 the capital invested in manufacturing was $2,900,735,884.

In 1880 the number of employees was 1,301,388.

In 1890 the number of employees was 2,251,134.

In 1880 the wages earned were $501,965,778.

In 1890 the wages earned were $1,221,170,454.

In 1880 the value of the product was $2,711,579,899.

In 1890 the value of the product was $4,860,286,837.

I am informed by the Superintendent of the Census that the omission of certain industries in 1880 which were included in 1890 accounts in part for the remarkable increase thus shown, but after making full allowance for differences of method and deducting the returns for all industries not included in the census of 1880 there remain in the reports from these seventy-five cities an increase in the capital employed of $1,522,-745,604, in the value of the product of $2,024,236,166, in wages earned of $677,943,929, and in the number of wage earners employed of 856,029. The wage earnings not only show an increased aggregate, but an increase per capita from $386 in 1880 to $547 in 1890, or 41.71 per cent.

The new industrial plants established since October 6, 1890, and up to October 22, 1892, as partially reported in the American Economist, number 345, and the extension of existing plants 108; the new capital invested amounts to $40,449,050, and the number of additional employees to 37,285.

The Textile World for July, 1892, states that during the first six months of the present calendar year 135 new factories were built, of which 40 are cotton mills, 48 knitting mills, 26 woolen mills, 15 silk mills, 4 plush mills, and 2 linen mills. Of the 40 cotton mills 21 have been built in the Southern States. Mr. A. B. Shepperson, of the New York Cotton Exchange, estimates the number of working spindles in the United States on September 1, 1892, at 15,200,000, an increase of 660,000 over the year 1891. The consumption of cotton by American mills in 1891 was 2,396,-000 bales, and in 1892 2,584,000 bales, an increase of 188,000 bales. From the year 1869 to 1892, inclusive, there has been an increase in the consumption of cotton in Europe of 92 per cent, while during the same period the increased consumption in the United States has been about 150 per cent.

The report of Ira Ayer, special agent of the Treasury Department, shows that at the date of September 30, 1892, there were 32 companies manufacturing tin and terne plate in the United States and 14 companies building new works for such manufacture. The estimated investment in buildings and plants at the close of the fiscal year June 30, 1893, if existing conditions were to be continued, was $5,000,000 and the estimated rate of production 200,000,000 pounds per annum. The actual production for the quarter ending September 30, 1892, was 10,952,725 pounds.

The report of Labor Commissioner Peck, of New York, shows that during the year 1891, in about 6,000 manufacturing establishments in that State embraced within the special inquiry made by him, and representing 67 different industries, there was a net increase over the year 1890 of $31,315,130.68 in the value of the product and of $6,377,925.09 in the amount of wages paid. The report of the commissioner of labor for the State of Massachusetts shows that 3,745 industries in that State paid $129,416,248 in wages during the year 1891, against $126,030,303 in 1890, an increase of $3,335,945, and that there was an increase of $9,932,490 in the amount of capital and of 7,346 in the number of persons employed in the same period.

During the last six months of the year 1891 and the first six months of 1892 the total production of pig iron was 9,710,819 tons, as against

9,202,703 tons in the year 1890, which was the largest annual production ever attained. For the same twelve months of 1891–92 the production of Bessemer ingots was 3,878,581 tons, an increase of 189,710 gross tons over the previously unprecedented yearly production of 3,688,871 gross tons in 1890. The production of Bessemer steel rails for the first six months of 1892 was 772,436 gross tons, as against 702,080 gross tons during the last six months of the year 1891.

The total value of our foreign trade (exports and imports of merchandise) during the last fiscal year was $1,857,680,610, an increase of $128,-283,604 over the previous fiscal year. The average annual value of our imports and exports of merchandise for the ten fiscal years prior to 1891 was $1,457,322,019. It will be observed that our foreign trade for 1892 exceeded this annual average value by $400,358,591, an increase of 27.47 per cent. The significance and value of this increase are shown by the fact that the excess in the trade of 1892 over 1891 was wholly in the value of exports, for there was a decrease in the value of imports of $17,513,754.

The value of our exports during the fiscal year 1892 reached the highest figure in the history of the Government, amounting to $1,030,278,148, exceeding by $145,797,338 the exports of 1891 and exceeding the value of the imports by $202,875,686. A comparison of the value of our exports for 1892 with the annual average for the ten years prior to 1891 shows an excess of $265,142,651, or of 34.65 per cent. The value of our imports of merchandise for 1892, which was $829,402,462, also exceeded the annual average value of the ten years prior to 1891 by $135,-215,940. During the fiscal year 1892 the value of imports free of duty amounted to $457,999,658, the largest aggregate in the history of our commerce. The value of the imports of merchandise entered free of duty in 1892 was 55.35 per cent of the total value of imports, as compared with 43.35 per cent in 1891 and 33.66 per cent in 1890.

In our coastwise trade a most encouraging development is in progress, there having been in the last four years an increase of 16 per cent. In internal commerce the statistics show that no such period of prosperity has ever before existed. The freight carried in the coastwise trade of the Great Lakes in 1890 aggregated 28,295,959 tons. On the Mississippi, Missouri, and Ohio rivers and tributaries in the same year the traffic aggregated 29,405,046 tons, and the total vessel tonnage passing through the Detroit River during that year was 21,684,000 tons. The vessel tonnage entered and cleared in the foreign trade of London during 1890 amounted to 13,480,767 tons, and of Liverpool 10,941,800 tons, a total for these two great shipping ports of 24,422,568 tons, only slightly in excess of the vessel tonnage passing through the Detroit River. And it should be said that the season for the Detroit River was but 228 days, while of course in London and Liverpool the season was for the entire year. The vessel tonnage passing through the St. Marys Canal for the fiscal year

1892 amounted to 9,828,874 tons, and the freight tonnage of the Detroit River is estimated for that year at 25,000,000 tons, against 23,209,619 tons in 1891. The aggregate traffic on our railroads for the year 1891 amounted to 704,398,609 tons of freight, compared with 691,344,437 tons in 1890, an increase of 13,054,172 tons.

Another indication of the general prosperity of the country is found in the fact that the number of depositors in savings banks increased from 693,870 in 1860 to 4,258,893 in 1890, an increase of 513 per cent, and the amount of deposits from $149,277,504 in 1860 to $1,524,844,506 in 1890, an increase of 921 per cent. In 1891 the amount of deposits in savings banks was $1,623,079,749. It is estimated that 90 per cent of these deposits represent the savings of wage earners. The bank clearances for nine months ending September 30, 1891, amounted to $41,049,390,808. For the same months in 1892 they amounted to $45,189,601,947, an excess for the nine months of $4,140,211,139.

There never has been a time in our history when work was so abundant or when wages were as high, whether measured by the currency in which they are paid or by their power to supply the necessaries and comforts of life. It is true that the market prices of cotton and wheat have been low. It is one of the unfavorable incidents of agriculture that the farmer can not produce upon orders. He must sow and reap in ignorance of the aggregate production of the year, and is peculiarly subject to the depreciation which follows overproduction. But while the fact I have stated is true as to the crops mentioned, the general average of prices has been such as to give to agriculture a fair participation in the general prosperity. The value of our total farm products has increased from $1,363,-646,866 in 1860 to $4,500,000,000 in 1891, as estimated by statisticians, an increase of 230 per cent. The number of hogs January 1, 1891, was 50,625,106 and their value $210,193,925; on January 1, 1892, the number was 52,398,019 and the value $241,031,415. On January 1, 1891, the number of cattle was 36,875,648 and the value $544,127,908; on January 1, 1892, the number was 37,651,239 and the value $570,749,155.

If any are discontented with their state here, if any believe that wages or prices, the returns for honest toil, are inadequate, they should not fail to remember that there is no other country in the world where the conditions that seem to them hard would not be accepted as highly prosperous. The English agriculturist would be glad to exchange the returns of his labor for those of the American farmer and the Manchester workmen their wages for those of their fellows at Fall River.

I believe that the protective system, which has now for something more than thirty years continuously prevailed in our legislation, has been a mighty instrument for the development of our national wealth and a most powerful agency in protecting the homes of our workingmen from the invasion of want. I have felt a most solicitous interest to preserve to our working people rates of wages that would not only give daily bread, but supply a comfortable margin for those home attractions and family comforts and enjoyments without which life is neither hopeful nor sweet. They are American citizens—a part of the great people for whom our Constitution and Government were framed and instituted—and it can not be a perversion of that Constitution to so legislate as to preserve in their homes the comfort, independence, loyalty, and sense of interest in the Government which are essential to good citizenship in peace, and which will bring this stalwart throng, as in 1861, to the defense of the flag when it is assailed.

It is not my purpose to renew here the argument in favor of a protective tariff. The result of the recent election must be accepted as having introduced a new policy. We must assume that the present tariff, constructed upon the lines of protection, is to be repealed and that there is to be substituted for it a tariff law constructed solely with reference to revenue; that no duty is to be higher because the increase will keep open an American mill or keep up the wages of an American workman, but that in every case such a rate of duty is to be imposed as will bring to the Treasury of the United States the largest returns of revenue. The contention has not been between schedules, but between principles, and it would be offensive to suggest that the prevailing party will not carry into legislation the principles advocated by it and the pledges given to the people. The tariff bills passed by the House of Representatives at the last session were, as I suppose, even in the opinion of their promoters, inadequate, and justified only by the fact that the Senate and House of Representatives were not in accord and that a general revision could not therefore be undertaken.

I recommend that the whole subject of tariff revision be left to the incoming Congress. It is matter of regret that this work must be delayed for at least three months, for the threat of great tariff changes introduces so much uncertainty that an amount, not easily estimated, of business inaction and of diminished production will necessarily result. It is possible also that this uncertainty may result in decreased revenues from customs duties, for our merchants will make cautious orders for foreign goods in view of the prospect of tariff reductions and the uncertainty as to when they will take effect. Those who have advocated a protective tariff can well afford to have their disastrous forecasts of a change of policy disappointed. If a system of customs duties can be framed that will set the idle wheels and looms of Europe in motion and crowd our warehouses with foreign-made goods and at the same time keep our own mills busy; that will give us an increased participation in the "markets of the world" of greater value than the home market we surrender; that will give increased work to foreign workmen upon products to be consumed by our people without diminishing the amount of work to be done here; that will enable the American manufacturer to pay to his workmen from 50 to 100 per cent more in wages than is paid in the foreign mill, and yet to compete in our market and in foreign markets with the foreign producer; that will further reduce the cost of articles of wear and food without reducing the wages of those who produce them; that can be celebrated, after its effects have been realized, as its expectation has been in European as well as in American cities, the authors and promoters of it will be entitled to the highest praise. We have had in our history several experiences of the contrasted effects of a revenue and of a protective tariff, but this generation has not felt them, and the experience of one generation is not highly instructive to the next. The friends of the protective system with undiminished confidence in the principles they have advocated will await the results of the new experiment.

The strained and too often disturbed relations existing between the employees and the employers in our great manufacturing establishments have not been favorable to a calm consideration by the wage earner of the effect upon wages of the protective system. The facts that his wages were the highest paid in like callings in the world and that a maintenance of this rate of wages in the absence of protective duties upon the product of his labor was impossible were obscured by the passion evoked by these contests. He may now be able to review the question in the light of his personal experience under the operation of a tariff for revenue only. If that experience shall demonstrate that present rates of wages are thereby maintained or increased, either absolutely or in their purchasing power, and that the aggregate volume of work to be done in this country is increased or even maintained, so that there are more or as many days' work in a year, at as good or better wages, for the American workmen as has been the case under the protective system, everyone will rejoice. A general process of wage reduction can not be contemplated by any patriotic citizen without the gravest apprehension. It may be, indeed I believe is, possible for the American manufacturer to compete successfully with his foreign rival in many branches of production without the defense of protective duties if the pay rolls are equalized; but the conflict that stands between the producer and that result and the distress of our working people when it is attained are not pleasant to contemplate. The Society of the Unemployed, now holding its frequent and threatening parades in the streets of foreign cities, should not be allowed to acquire an American domicile.

The reports of the heads of the several Executive Departments, which are herewith submitted, have very naturally included a résumé of the whole work of the Administration with the transactions of the last fiscal year. The attention not only of Congress but of the country is again invited to the methods of administration which have been pursued and to the results which have been attained. Public revenues amounting to $1,414,079,292.28 have been collected and disbursed without loss from misappropriation, without a single defalcation of such importance as to attract the public attention, and at a diminished per cent of cost for collection. The public business has been transacted not only with fidelity, but progressively and with a view to giving to the people in the fullest possible degree the benefits of a service established and maintained for their protection and comfort.

Our relations with other nations are now undisturbed by any serious controversy. The complicated and threatening differences with Germany and England relating to Samoan affairs, with England in relation to the seal fisheries in the Bering Sea, and with Chile growing out of the *Baltimore* affair have been adjusted.

There have been negotiated and concluded, under section 3 of the tariff law, commercial agreements relating to reciprocal trade with the following countries: Brazil, Dominican Republic, Spain for Cuba and Puerto Rico, Guatemala, Salvador, the German Empire, Great Britain for certain West Indian colonies and British Guiana, Nicaragua, Honduras, and Austria-Hungary.*

Of these, those with Guatemala, Salvador, the German Empire, Great Britain, Nicaragua, Honduras, and Austria-Hungary have been concluded since my last annual message. Under these trade arrangements a free or favored admission has been secured in every case for an important list of American products. Especial care has been taken to secure markets for farm products, in order to relieve that great underlying industry of the depression which the lack of an adequate foreign market for our surplus often brings. An opening has also been made for manufactured products that will undoubtedly, if this policy is maintained, greatly augment our export trade. The full benefits of these arrangements can not be realized instantly. New lines of trade are to be opened. The commercial traveler must survey the field. The manufacturer must adapt his goods to the new markets and facilities for exchange must be established. This work has been well begun, our merchants and manufacturers having entered the new fields with courage and enterprise. In the case of food products, and especially with Cuba, the trade did not need to wait, and the immediate results have been most gratifying. If this policy and these trade arrangements can be continued in force and aided by the establishment of American steamship lines, I do not doubt that we shall within a short period secure fully one-third of the total trade of the countries of Central and South America, which now amounts to about $600,-000,000 annually. In 1885 we had only 8 per cent of this trade.

The following statistics show the increase in our trade with the countries with which we have reciprocal trade agreements from the date when such agreements went into effect up to September 30, 1892, the increase being in some almost wholly and in others in an important degree the result of these agreements:

The domestic exports to Germany and Austria-Hungary have in-

*See pp. 141–142, 152–155, 148–152, 281–283, 249–251, 258–260, 253–258, 263–265, 279–281, 283–284.

creased in value from $47,673,756 to $57,993,064, an increase of $10,-319,308, or 21.63 per cent. With American countries the value of our exports has increased from $44,160,285 to $54,613,598, an increase of $10,453,313, or 23.67 per cent. The total increase in the value of exports to all the countries with which we have reciprocity agreements has been $20,772,621. This increase is chiefly in wheat, flour, meat, and dairy products and in manufactures of iron and steel and lumber. There has been a large increase in the value of imports from all these countries since the commercial agreements went into effect, amounting to $74,294,525, but it has been entirely in imports from the American countries, consisting mostly of sugar, coffee, india rubber, and crude drugs. The alarmed attention of our European competitors for the South American market has been attracted to this new American policy and to our acquisition and their loss of South American trade.

A treaty providing for the arbitration of the dispute between Great Britain and the United States as to the killing of seals in the Bering Sea was concluded on the 29th of February last. This treaty was accompanied by an agreement prohibiting pelagic sealing pending the arbitration, and a vigorous effort was made during this season to drive out all poaching sealers from the Bering Sea. Six naval vessels, three revenue cutters, and one vessel from the Fish Commission, all under the command of Commander Evans, of the Navy, were sent into the sea, which was systematically patrolled. Some seizures were made, and it is believed that the catch in the Bering Sea by poachers amounted to less than 500 seals. It is true, however, that in the North Pacific, while the seal herds were on their way to the passes between the Aleutian Islands, a very large number, probably 35,000, were taken. The existing statutes of the United States do not restrain our citizens from taking seals in the Pacific Ocean, and perhaps should not unless the prohibition can be extended to the citizens of other nations. I recommend that power be given to the President by proclamation to prohibit the taking of seals in the North Pacific by American vessels in case, either as the result of the findings of the Tribunal of Arbitration or otherwise, the restraints can be applied to the vessels of all countries. The case of the United States for the Tribunal of Arbitration has been prepared with great care and industry by the Hon. John W. Foster, and the counsel who represent this Government express confidence that a result substantially establishing our claims and preserving this great industry for the benefit of all nations will be attained.

During the past year a suggestion was received through the British minister that the Canadian government would like to confer as to the possibility of enlarging upon terms of mutual advantage the commercial exchanges of Canada and of the United States, and a conference was held at Washington, with Mr. Blaine acting for this Government and the British minister at this capital and three members of the Dominion cabinet acting as commissioners on the part of Great Britain. The conference developed the fact that the Canadian government was only prepared to offer to the United States in exchange for the concessions asked the admission of natural products. The statement was frankly made that favored rates could not be given to the United States as against the mother country. This admission, which was foreseen, necessarily terminated the conference upon this question. The benefits of an exchange of natural products would be almost wholly with the people of Canada. Some other topics of interest were considered in the conference, and have resulted in the making of a convention for examining the Alaskan boundary and the waters of Passamaquoddy Bay adjacent to Eastport, Me., and in the initiation of an arrangement for the protection of fish life in the coterminous and neighboring waters of our northern border.

The controversy as to tolls upon the Welland Canal, which was presented to Congress at the last session by special message,* having failed of adjustment, I felt constrained to exercise the authority conferred by the act of July 26, 1892, and to proclaim a suspension of the free use of St. Marys Falls Canal to cargoes in transit to ports in Canada.† The Secretary of the Treasury established such tolls as were thought to be equivalent to the exactions unjustly levied upon our commerce in the Canadian canals.

If, as we must suppose, the political relations of Canada and the disposition of the Canadian government are to remain unchanged, a somewhat radical revision of our trade relations should, I think, be made. Our relations must continue to be intimate, and they should be friendly. I regret to say, however, that in many of the controversies, notably those as to the fisheries on the Atlantic, the sealing interests on the Pacific, and the canal tolls, our negotiations with Great Britain have continuously been thwarted or retarded by unreasonable and unfriendly objections and protests from Canada. In the matter of the canal tolls our treaty rights were flagrantly disregarded. It is hardly too much to say that the Canadian Pacific and other railway lines which parallel our northern boundary are sustained by commerce having either its origin or terminus, or both, in the United States. Canadian railroads compete with those of the United States for our traffic, and without the restraints of our interstate-commerce act. Their cars pass almost without detention into and out of our territory.

The Canadian Pacific Railway brought into the United States from China and Japan via British Columbia during the year ended June 30, 1892, 23,239,689 pounds of freight, and it carried from the United States, to be shipped to China and Japan via British Columbia, 24,068,346 pounds of freight. There were also shipped from the United States over this road from Eastern ports of the United States to our Pacific ports during the same year 13,912,073 pounds of freight, and there were received over this road at the United States Eastern ports from ports on the Pacific

Coast 13,293,315 pounds of freight. Mr. Joseph Nimmo, jr., former chief of the Bureau of Statistics, when before the Senate Select Committee on Relations with Canada, April 26, 1890, said that "the value of goods thus transported between different points in the United States across Canadian territory probably amounts to $100,000,000 a year."

There is no disposition on the part of the people or Government of the United States to interfere in the smallest degree with the political relations of Canada. That question is wholly with her own people. It is time for us, however, to consider whether, if the present state of things and trend of things is to continue, our interchanges upon lines of land transportation should not be put upon a different basis and our entire independence of Canadian canals and of the St. Lawrence as an outlet to the sea secured by the construction of an American canal around the Falls of Niagara and the opening of ship communication between the Great Lakes and one of our own seaports. We should not hesitate to avail ourselves of our great natural trade advantages. We should withdraw the support which is given to the railroads and steamship lines of Canada by a traffic that properly belongs to us and no longer furnish the earnings which lighten the otherwise crushing weight of the enormous public subsidies that have been given to them. The subject of the power of the Treasury to deal with this matter without further legislation has been under consideration, but circumstances have postponed a conclusion. It is probable that a consideration of the propriety of a modification or abrogation of the article of the treaty of Washington relating to the transit of goods in bond is involved in any complete solution of the question.

Congress at the last session was kept advised of the progress of the serious and for a time threatening difference between the United States and Chile. It gives me now great gratification to report that the Chilean Government in a most friendly and honorable spirit has tendered and paid as an indemnity to the families of the sailors of the *Baltimore* who were killed and to those who were injured in the outbreak in the city of Valparaiso the sum of $75,000. This has been accepted not only as an indemnity for a wrong done, but as a most gratifying evidence that the Government of Chile rightly appreciates the disposition of this Government to act in a spirit of the most absolute fairness and friendliness in our intercourse with that brave people. A further and conclusive evidence of the mutual respect and confidence now existing is furnished by the fact that a convention submitting to arbitration the mutual claims of the citizens of the respective Governments has been agreed upon. Some of these claims have been pending for many years and have been the occasion of much unsatisfactory diplomatic correspondence.

I have endeavored in every way to assure our sister Republics of Central and South America that the United States Government and its people have only the most friendly disposition toward them all. We do not covet their territory. We have no disposition to be oppressive or exacting in our dealings with any of them, even the weakest. Our interests and our hopes for them all lie in the direction of stable governments by their people and of the largest development of their great commercial resources. The mutual benefits of enlarged commercial exchanges and of a more familiar and friendly intercourse between our peoples we do desire, and in this have sought their friendly cooperation.

I have believed, however, while holding these sentiments in the greatest sincerity, that we must insist upon a just responsibility for any injuries inflicted upon our official representatives or upon our citizens. This insistence, kindly and justly but firmly made, will, I believe, promote peace and mutual respect.

Our relations with Hawaii have been such as to attract an increased interest, and must continue to do so. I deem it of great importance that the projected submarine cable, a survey for which has been made, should be promoted. Both for naval and commercial uses we should have quick communication with Honolulu. We should before this have availed ourselves of the concession made many years ago to this Government for a harbor and naval station at Pearl River. Many evidences of the friendliness of the Hawaiian Government have been given in the past, and it is gratifying to believe that the advantage and necessity of a continuance of very close relations is appreciated.

The friendly act of this Government in expressing to the Government of Italy its reprobation and abhorrence of the lynching of Italian subjects in New Orleans by the payment of 125,000 francs, or $24,330.90, was accepted by the King of Italy with every manifestation of gracious appreciation, and the incident has been highly promotive of mutual respect and good will.

In consequence of the action of the French Government in proclaiming a protectorate over certain tribal districts of the west coast of Africa eastward of the San Pedro River, which has long been regarded as the southeastern boundary of Liberia, I have felt constrained to make protest against this encroachment upon the territory of a Republic which was founded by citizens of the United States and toward which this country has for many years held the intimate relation of a friendly counselor.

The recent disturbances of the public peace by lawless foreign marauders on the Mexican frontier have afforded this Government an opportunity to testify its good will for Mexico and its earnest purpose to fulfill the obligations of international friendship by pursuing and dispersing the evil doers. The work of relocating the boundary of the treaty of Guadalupe Hidalgo westward from El Paso is progressing favorably.

Our intercourse with Spain continues on a friendly footing. I regret, however, not to be able to report as yet the adjustment of the claims of the American missionaries arising from the disorders at Ponape, in the Caroline Islands, but I anticipate a satisfactory adjustment in view of renewed and urgent representations to the Government at Madrid.

The treatment of the religious and educational establishments of American citizens in Turkey has of late called for a more than usual share of attention. A tendency to curtail the toleration which has so beneficially prevailed is discernible and has called forth the earnest remonstrance of this Government. Harassing regulations in regard to schools and churches have been attempted in certain localities, but not without due protest and the assertion of the inherent and conventional rights of our countrymen. Violations of domicile and search of the persons and effects of citizens of the United States by apparently irresponsible officials in the Asiatic *vilayets* have from time to time been reported. An aggravated instance of injury to the property of an American missionary at Bourdour, in the Province of Konia, called forth an urgent claim for reparation, which I am pleased to say was promptly heeded by the Government of the Porte. Interference with the trading ventures of our citizens in Asia Minor is also reported, and the lack of consular representation in that region is a serious drawback to instant and effective protection. I can not believe that these incidents represent a settled policy, and shall not cease to urge the adoption of proper remedies.

International copyright has been extended to Italy by proclamation* in conformity with the act of March 3, 1891, upon assurance being given that Italian law permits to citizens of the United States the benefit of copyright on substantially the same basis as to subjects of Italy. By a special convention proclaimed January 15, 1892, reciprocal provisions of copyright have been applied between the United States and Germany. Negotiations are in progress with other countries to the same end.

I repeat with great earnestness the recommendation which I have made in several previous messages that prompt and adequate support be given to the American company engaged in the construction of the Nicaragua ship canal. It is impossible to overstate the value from every standpoint of this great enterprise, and I hope that there may be time, even in this Congress, to give to it an impetus that will insure the early completion of the canal and secure to the United States its proper relation to it when completed.

The Congress has been already advised that the invitations of this Government for the assembling of an international monetary conference to consider the question of an enlarged use of silver were accepted by the nations to which they were addressed. The conference assembled at Brussels on the 22d of November, and has entered upon the consideration of this great question. I have not doubted, and have taken occasion to express that belief as well in the invitations issued for this conference as in my public messages, that the free coinage of silver upon an agreed international ratio would greatly promote the interests of our people and equally those of other nations. It is too early to predict what results may be accomplished by the conference. If any temporary check or delay

*See p. 301.

intervenes, I believe that very soon commercial conditions will compel the now reluctant governments to unite with us in this movement to secure the enlargement of the volume of coined money needed for the transaction of the business of the world.

The report of the Secretary of the Treasury will attract especial interest in view of the many misleading statements that have been made as to the state of the public revenues. Three preliminary facts should not only be stated but emphasized before looking into details: First, that the public debt has been reduced since March 4, 1889, $259,074,200, and the annual interest charge $11,684,469; second, that there have been paid out for pensions during this Administration up to November 1, 1892, $432,564,178.70, an excess of $114,466,386.09 over the sum expended during the period from March 1, 1885, to March 1, 1889; and, third, that under the existing tariff up to December 1 about $93,000,000 of revenue which would have been collected upon imported sugars if the duty had been maintained has gone into the pockets of the people, and not into the public Treasury, as before. If there are any who still think that the surplus should have been kept out of circulation by hoarding it in the Treasury, or deposited in favored banks without interest while the Government continued to pay to these very banks interest upon the bonds deposited as security for the deposits, or who think that the extended pension legislation was a public robbery, or that the duties upon sugar should have been maintained, I am content to leave the argument where it now rests while we wait to see whether these criticisms will take the form of legislation.

The revenues for the fiscal year ending June 30, 1892, from all sources were $425,868,260.22, and the expenditures for all purposes were $415,-953,806.56, leaving a balance of $9,914,453.66. There were paid during the year upon the public debt $40,570,467.98. The surplus in the Treasury and the bank redemption fund passed by the act of July 14, 1890, to the general fund furnished in large part the cash available and used for the payments made upon the public debt. Compared with the year 1891, our receipts from customs duties fell off $42,069,241.08, while our receipts from internal revenue increased $8,284,823.13, leaving the net loss of revenue from these principal sources $33,784,417.95. The net loss of revenue from all sources was $32,675,972.81.

The revenues, estimated and actual, for the fiscal year ending June 30, 1893, are placed by the Secretary at $463,336,350.44, and the expenditures at $461,336,350.44, showing a surplus of receipts over expenditures of $2,000,000. The cash balance in the Treasury at the end of the fiscal year it is estimated will be $20,992,377.03. So far as these figures are based upon estimates of receipts and expenditures for the remaining months of the current fiscal year, there are not only the usual elements of uncertainty, but some added elements. New revenue legislation, or even the expectation of it, may seriously reduce the public revenues during the period of uncertainty and during the process of business adjustment to the new conditions when they become known. But the Secretary has very wisely refrained from guessing as to the effect of possible changes in our revenue laws, since the scope of those changes and the time of their taking effect can not in any degree be forecast or foretold by him. His estimates must be based upon existing laws and upon a continuance of existing business conditions, except so far as these conditions may be affected by causes other than new legislation.

The estimated receipts for the fiscal year ending June 30, 1894, are $490,121,365.38, and the estimated appropriations $457,261,335.33, leaving an estimated surplus of receipts over expenditures of $32,860,-030.05. This does not include any payment to the sinking fund. In the recommendation of the Secretary that the sinking-fund law be repealed I concur. The redemption of bonds since the passage of the law to June 30, 1892, has already exceeded the requirements by the sum of $990,510,681.49. The retirement of bonds in the future before maturity should be a matter of convenience, not of compulsion. We should not collect revenue for that purpose, but only use any casual surplus. To the balance of $32,860,030.05 of receipts over expenditures for the year 1894 should be added the estimated surplus at the beginning of the year, $20,992,377.03, and from this aggregate there must be deducted, as stated by the Secretary, about $44,000,000 of estimated unexpended appropriations.

The public confidence in the purpose and ability of the Government to maintain the parity of all of our money issues, whether coin or paper, must remain unshaken. The demand for gold in Europe and the consequent calls upon us are in a considerable degree the result of the efforts of some of the European Governments to increase their gold reserves, and these efforts should be met by appropriate legislation on our part. The conditions that have created this drain of the Treasury gold are in an important degree political, and not commercial. In view of the fact that a general revision of our revenue laws in the near future seems to be probable, it would be better that any changes should be a part of that revision rather than of a temporary nature.

During the last fiscal year the Secretary purchased under the act of July 14, 1890, 54,355,748 ounces of silver and issued in payment therefor $51,106,608 in notes. The total purchases since the passage of the act have been 120,479,981 ounces and the aggregate of notes issued $116,-783,590. The average price paid for silver during the year was 94 cents per ounce, the highest price being $1.02¾ July 1, 1891, and the lowest 83 cents March 21, 1892. In view of the fact that the monetary conference is now sitting and that no conclusion has yet been reached, I withhold any recommendation as to legislation upon this subject.

The report of the Secretary of War brings again to the attention of Congress some important suggestions as to the reorganization of the infantry and artillery arms of the service, which his predecessors have before urgently presented. Our Army is small, but its organization should all the more be put upon the most approved modern basis. The conditions upon what we have called the "frontier" have heretofore required the maintenance of many small posts, but now the policy of concentration is obviously the right one. The new posts should have the proper strategic relations to the only "frontiers" we now have—those of the seacoast and of our northern and part of our southern boundary. I do not think that any question of advantage to localities or to States should determine the location of the new posts. The reorganization and enlargement of the Bureau of Military Information which the Secretary has effected is a work the usefulness of which will become every year more apparent. The work of building heavy guns and the construction of coast defenses has been well begun and should be carried on without check.

The report of the Attorney-General is by law submitted directly to Congress, but I can not refrain from saying that he has conducted the increasing work of the Department of Justice with great professional skill. He has in several directions secured from the courts decisions giving increased protection to the officers of the United States and bringing some classes of crime that escaped local cognizance and punishment into the tribunals of the United States, where they could be tried with impartiality.

The numerous applications for Executive clemency presented in behalf of persons convicted in United States courts and given penitentiary sentences have called my attention to a fact referred to by the Attorney-General in his report, namely, that a time allowance for good behavior for such prisoners is prescribed by the Federal statutes only where the State in which the penitentiary is located has made no such provision. Prisoners are given the benefit of the provisions of the State law regulating the penitentiary to which they may be sent. These are various, some perhaps too liberal and some perhaps too illiberal. The result is that a sentence for five years means one thing if the prisoner is sent to one State for confinement and quite a different thing if he is sent to another. I recommend that a uniform credit for good behavior be prescribed by Congress.

I have before expressed my concurrence in the recommendation of the Attorney-General that degrees of murder should be recognized in the Federal statutes, as they are, I believe, in all the States. These grades are founded on correct distinctions in crime. The recognition of them would enable the courts to exercise some discretion in apportioning punishment and would greatly relieve the Executive of what is coming to be a very heavy burden—the examination of these cases on application for commutation.

The aggregate of claims pending against the Government in the Court of Claims is enormous. Claims to the amount of nearly $400,000,000 for the taking of or injury to the property of persons claiming to be loyal during the war are now before that court for examination. When to these are added the Indian depredation claims and the French spoliation claims, an aggregate is reached that is indeed startling. In the defense of all these cases the Government is at great disadvantage. The claimants have preserved their evidence, whereas the agents of the Government are sent into the field to rummage for what they can find. This difficulty is peculiarly great where the fact to be established is the disloyalty of the claimant during the war. If this great threat against our revenues is to have no other check, certainly Congress should supply the Department of Justice with appropriations sufficiently liberal to secure the best legal talent in the defense of these claims and to pursue its vague search for evidence effectively.

The report of the Postmaster-General shows a most gratifying increase and a most efficient and progressive management of the great business of that Department. The remarkable increase in revenues, in the number of post-offices, and in the miles of mail carriage furnishes further evidence of the high state of prosperity which our people are enjoying. New offices mean new hamlets and towns, new routes mean the extension of our border settlements, and increased revenues mean an active commerce. The Postmaster-General reviews the whole period of his administration of the office and brings some of his statistics down to the month of November last. The postal revenues have increased during the last year nearly $5,000,000. The deficit for the year ending June 30, 1892, is $848,341 less than the deficiency of the preceding year. The deficiency of the present fiscal year it is estimated will be reduced to $1,552,423, which will not only be extinguished during the next fiscal year, but a surplus of nearly $1,000,000 should then be shown. In these calculations the payments to be made under the contracts for ocean mail service have not been included. There have been added 1,590 new mail routes during the year, with a mileage of 8,563 miles, and the total number of new miles of mail trips added during the year is nearly 17,000,000. The number of miles of mail journeys added during the last four years is about 76,000,000, this addition being 21,000,000 miles more than were in operation in the whole country in 1861.

The number of post-offices has been increased by 2,790 during the year, and during the past four years, and up to October 29 last, the total increase in the number of offices has been nearly 9,000. The number of free-delivery offices has been nearly doubled in the last four years, and the number of money-order offices more than doubled within that time.

For the three years ending June 30, 1892, the postal revenue amounted to $197,744,359, which was an increase of $52,263,150 over the revenue for the three years ending June 30, 1888, the increase during the last three years being more than three and a half times as great as the increase during the three years ending June 30, 1888. No such increase as that shown for these three years has ever previously appeared in the revenues of the Department. The Postmaster-General has extended to the post-offices in the larger cities the merit system of promotion introduced by my direction into the Departments here, and it has resulted there, as in the Departments, in a larger volume of work and that better done.

Ever since our merchant marine was driven from the sea by the rebel cruisers during the War of the Rebellion the United States has been pay-ing an enormous annual tribute to foreign countries in the shape of freight and passage moneys. Our grain and meats have been taken at our own docks and our large imports there laid down by foreign shipmasters. An increasing torrent of American travel to Europe has contributed a vast sum annually to the dividends of foreign shipowners. The balance of trade shown by the books of our custom-houses has been very largely reduced and in many years altogether extinguished by this constant drain. In the year 1892 only 12.3 per cent of our imports were brought in American vessels. These great foreign steamships maintained by our traffic are many of them under contracts with their respective Govern-ments by which in time of war they will become a part of their armed naval establishments. Profiting by our commerce in peace, they will become the most formidable destroyers of our commerce in time of war. I have felt, and have before expressed the feeling, that this condition of things was both intolerable and disgraceful. A wholesome change of pol-icy, and one having in it much promise, as it seems to me, was begun by the law of March 3, 1891. Under this law contracts have been made by the Postmaster-General for eleven mail routes. The expenditure involved by these contracts for the next fiscal year approximates $954,-123.33. As one of the results already reached sixteen American steam-ships, of an aggregate tonnage of 57,400 tons, costing $7,400,000, have been built or contracted to be built in American shipyards.

The estimated tonnage of all steamships required under existing con-tracts is 165,802, and when the full service required by these contracts is established there will be forty-one mail steamers under the American flag, with the probability of further necessary additions in the Brazilian and Argentine service. The contracts recently let for transatlantic serv-ice will result in the construction of five ships of 10,000 tons each, cost-ing $9,000,000 to $10,000,000, and will add, with the *City of New York* and *City of Paris*, to which the Treasury Department was authorized by legislation at the last session to give American registry, seven of the swiftest vessels upon the sea to our naval reserve. The contracts made with the lines sailing to Central and South American ports have increased the frequency and shortened the time of the trips, added new ports of call, and sustained some lines that otherwise would almost certainly have been withdrawn. The service to Buenos Ayres is the first to the Argen-tine Republic under the American flag. The service to Southampton,

Boulogne, and Antwerp is also new, and is to be begun with the steam-ships *City of New York* and *City of Paris* in February next.

I earnestly urge the continuance of the policy inaugurated by this leg-islation, and that the appropriations required to meet the obligations of the Government under the contracts may be made promptly, so that the lines that have entered into these engagements may not be embarrassed. We have had, by reason of connections with the transcontinental railway lines constructed through our own territory, some advantages in the ocean trade of the Pacific that we did not possess on the Atlantic. The construction of the Canadian Pacific Railway and the establishment under large subventions from Canada and England of fast steamship service from Vancouver with Japan and China seriously threaten our shipping interests in the Pacific. This line of English steamers receives, as is stated by the Commissioner of Navigation, a direct subsidy of $400,000 annually, or $30,767 per trip for thirteen voyages, in addition to some further aid from the Admiralty in connection with contracts under which the vessels may be used for naval purposes. The competing American Pacific mail line under the act of March 3, 1891, receives only $6,389 per round trip.

Efforts have been making within the last year, as I am informed, to establish under similar conditions a line between Vancouver and some Australian port, with a view of seizing there a trade in which we have had a large interest. The Commissioner of Navigation states that a very large per cent of our imports from Asia are now brought to us by English steamships and their connecting railways in Canada. With a view of promoting this trade, especially in tea, Canada has imposed a dis-criminating duty of 10 per cent upon tea and coffee brought into the Dominion from the United States. If this unequal contest between American lines without subsidy, or with diminished subsidies, and the English Canadian line to which I have referred is to continue, I think we should at least see that the facilities for customs entry and transportation across our territory are not such as to make the Canadian route a favored one, and that the discrimination as to duties to which I have referred is met by a like discrimination as to the importation of these articles from Canada.

No subject, I think, more nearly touches the pride, the power, and the prosperity of our country than this of the development of our merchant marine upon the sea. If we could enter into conference with other com-petitors and all would agree to withhold government aid, we could per-haps take our chances with the rest; but our great competitors have established and maintained their lines by government subsidies until they now have practically excluded us from participation. In my opinion no choice is left to us but to pursue, moderately at least, the same lines.

The report of the Secretary of the Navy exhibits great progress in the construction of our new Navy. When the present Secretary entered upon his duties, only 3 modern steel vessels were in commission. The vessels since put in commission and to be put in commission during the winter will make a total of 19 during his administration of the Department. During the current year 10 war vessels and 3 navy tugs have been launched, and during the four years 25 vessels will have been launched. Two other large ships and a torpedo boat are under contract and the work upon them well advanced, and the 4 monitors are awaiting only the arrival of their armor, which has been unexpectedly delayed, or they would have been before this in commission.

Contracts have been let during this Administration, under the appropriations for the increase of the Navy, including new vessels and their appurtenances, to the amount of $35,000,000, and there has been expended during the same period for labor at navy-yards upon similar work $8,000,000 without the smallest scandal or charge of fraud or partiality. The enthusiasm and interest of our naval officers, both of the staff and line, have been greatly kindled. They have responded magnificently to the confidence of Congress and have demonstrated to the world an unexcelled capacity in construction, in ordnance, and in everything involved in the building, equipping, and sailing of great war ships.

At the beginning of Secretary Tracy's administration several difficult problems remained to be grappled with and solved before the efficiency in action of our ships could be secured. It is believed that as the result of new processes in the construction of armor plate our later ships will be clothed with defensive plates of higher resisting power than are found on any war vessels afloat. We were without torpedoes. Tests have been made to ascertain the relative efficiency of different constructions, a torpedo has been adopted, and the work of construction is now being carried on successfully. We were without armor-piercing shells and without a shop instructed and equipped for the construction of them. We are now making what is believed to be a projectile superior to any before in use. A smokeless powder has been developed and a slow-burning powder for guns of large caliber. A high explosive capable of use in shells fired from service guns has been found, and the manufacture of gun cotton has been developed so that the question of supply is no longer in doubt.

The development of a naval militia, which has been organized in eight States and brought into cordial and cooperative relations with the Navy, is another important achievement. There are now enlisted in these organizations 1,800 men, and they are likely to be greatly extended. I recommend such legislation and appropriations as will encourage and develop this movement. The recommendations of the Secretary will, I do not doubt, receive the friendly consideration of Congress, for he has enjoyed, as he has deserved, the confidence of all those interested in the development of our Navy, without any division upon partisan lines. I earnestly express the hope that a work which has made such noble progress may not now be stayed. The wholesome influence for peace and the increased sense of security which our citizens domiciled in other lands feel when these magnificent ships under the American flag appear is already most gratefully apparent. The ships from our Navy which will appear in the great naval parade next April in the harbor of New York will be a convincing demonstration to the world that the United States is again a naval power.

The work of the Interior Department, always very burdensome, has been larger than ever before during the administration of Secretary Noble. The disability-pension law, the taking of the Eleventh Census, the opening of vast areas of Indian lands to settlement, the organization of Oklahoma, and the negotiations for the cession of Indian lands furnish some of the particulars of the increased work, and the results achieved testify to the ability, fidelity, and industry of the head of the Department and his efficient assistants.

Several important agreements for the cession of Indian lands negotiated by the commission appointed under the act of March 2, 1889, are awaiting the action of Congress. Perhaps the most important of these is that for the cession of the Cherokee Strip. This region has been the source of great vexation to the executive department and of great friction and unrest between the settlers who desire to occupy it and the Indians who assert title. The agreement which has been made by the commission is perhaps the most satisfactory that could have been reached. It will be noticed that it is conditioned upon its ratification by Congress before March 4, 1893. The Secretary of the Interior, who has given the subject very careful thought, recommends the ratification of the agreement, and I am inclined to follow his recommendation. Certain it is that some action by which this controversy shall be brought to an end and these lands opened to settlement is urgent.

The form of government provided by Congress on May 17, 1884, for Alaska was in its frame and purpose temporary. The increase of population and the development of some important mining and commercial interests make it imperative that the law should be revised and better provision made for the arrest and punishment of criminals.

The report of the Secretary shows a very gratifying state of facts as to the condition of the General Land Office. The work of issuing agricultural patents, which seemed to be hopelessly in arrear when the present Secretary undertook the duties of his office, has been so expedited that the bureau is now upon current business. The relief thus afforded to honest and worthy settlers upon the public lands by giving to them an assured title to their entries has been of incalculable benefit in developing the new States and the Territories.

The Court of Private Land Claims, established by Congress for the promotion of this policy of speedily settling contested land titles, is making satisfactory progress in its work, and when the work is completed a great impetus will be given to the development of those regions where unsettled claims under Mexican grants have so long exercised their repressive influence. When to these results are added the enormous cessions of Indian lands which have been opened to settlement, aggregating during this Administration nearly 26,000,000 acres, and the agreements negotiated and now pending in Congress for ratification by which about 10,000,000 additional acres will be opened to settlement, it will be seen how much has been accomplished.

The work in the Indian Bureau in the execution of the policy of recent legislation has been largely directed to two chief purposes: First, the allotment of lands in severalty to the Indians and the cession to the United States of the surplus lands, and, secondly, to the work of educating the Indian for his own protection in his closer contact with the white man and for the intelligent exercise of his new citizenship. Allotments have been made and patents issued to 5,900 Indians under the present Secretary and Commissioner, and 7,600 additional allotments have been made for which patents are now in process of preparation. The school attendance of Indian children has been increased during that time over 13 per cent, the enrollment for 1892 being nearly 20,000. A uniform system of school text-books and of study has been adopted and the work in these national schools brought as near as may be to the basis of the free common schools of the States. These schools can be transferred and merged into the common-school systems of the States when the Indian has fully assumed his new relation to the organized civil community in which he resides and the new States are able to assume the burden. I have several times been called upon to remove Indian agents appointed by me, and have done so promptly upon every sustained complaint of unfitness or misconduct. I believe, however, that the Indian service at the agencies has been improved and is now administered on the whole with a good degree of efficiency. If any legislation is possible by which the selection of Indian agents can be wholly removed from all partisan suggestions or considerations, I am sure it would be a great relief to the Executive and a great benefit to the service. The appropriation for the subsistence of the Cheyenne and Arapahoe Indians made at the last session of Congress was inadequate. This smaller appropriation was estimated for by the Commissioner upon the theory that the large fund belonging to the tribe in the public Treasury could be and ought to be used for their support. In view, however, of the pending depredation claims against this fund and other considerations, the Secretary of the Interior on the 12th of April last submitted a supplemental estimate for $50,000. This appropriation was not made, as it should have been, and the oversight ought to be remedied at the earliest possible date.

In a special message to this Congress at the last session* I stated the reasons why I had not approved the deed for the release to the United

*See pp. 229-234.

States by the Choctaws and Chickasaws of the lands formerly embraced in the Cheyenne and Arapahoe Reservation and remaining after allotments to that tribe. A resolution of the Senate expressing the opinion of that body that notwithstanding the facts stated in my special message the deed should be approved and the money, $2,991,450, paid over was presented to me May 10, 1892. My special message was intended to call the attention of Congress to the subject, and in view of the fact that it is conceded that the appropriation proceeded upon a false basis as to the amount of lands to be paid for and is by $50,000 in excess of the amount they are entitled to (even if their claim to the land is given full recognition at the rate agreed upon), I have not felt willing to approve the deed, and shall not do so, at least until both Houses of Congress have acted upon the subject. It has been informally proposed by the claimants to release this sum of $50,000, but I have no power to demand or accept such a release, and such an agreement would be without consideration and void.

I desire further to call the attention of Congress to the fact that the recent agreement concluded with the Kiowas and Comanches relates to lands which were a part of the ''leased district,'' and to which the claim of the Choctaws and Chickasaws is precisely that recognized by Congress in the legislation I have referred to. The surplus lands to which this claim would attach in the Kiowa and Comanche Reservation is 2,500,000 acres, and at the same rate the Government will be called upon to pay to the Choctaws and Chickasaws for these lands $3,125,000. This sum will be further augmented, especially if the title of the Indians to the tract now Greer County, Tex., is established. The duty devolved upon me in this connection was simply to pass upon the form of the deed; but as in my opinion the facts mentioned in my special message were not adequately brought to the attention of Congress in connection with the legislation, I have felt that I would not be justified in acting without some new expression of the legislative will.

The report of the Commissioner of Pensions, to which extended notice is given by the Secretary of the Interior in his report, will attract great attention. Judged by the aggregate amount of work done, the last year has been the greatest in the history of the office. I believe that the organization of the office is efficient and that the work has been done with fidelity. The passage of what is known as the disability bill has, as was foreseen, very largely increased the annual disbursements to the disabled veterans of the Civil War. The estimate for this fiscal year was $144,956,000, and that amount was appropriated. A deficiency amounting to $10,508,621 must be provided for at this session. The estimate for pensions for the fiscal year ending June 30, 1894, is $165,000,000. The Commissioner of Pensions believes that if the present legislation and methods are maintained and further additions to the pension laws are not made the maximum expenditure for pensions will be reached June 30, 1894, and will be at the highest point $188,000,000 per annum.

I adhere to the views expressed in previous messages that the care of the disabled soldiers of the War of the Rebellion is a matter of national concern and duty. Perhaps no emotion cools sooner than that of gratitude, but I can not believe that this process has yet reached a point with our people that would sustain the policy of remitting the care of these disabled veterans to the inadequate agencies provided by local laws. The parade on the 20th of September last upon the streets of this capital of 60,000 of the surviving Union veterans of the War of the Rebellion was a most touching and thrilling episode, and the rich and gracious welcome extended to them by the District of Columbia and the applause that greeted their progress from tens of thousands of people from all the States did much to revive the glorious recollections of the Grand Review when these men and many thousand others now in their graves were welcomed with grateful joy as victors in a struggle in which the national unity, honor, and wealth were all at issue.

In my last annual message I called attention to the fact that some legislative action was necessary in order to protect the interests of the Government in its relations with the Union Pacific Railway. The Commissioner of Railroads has submitted a very full report, giving exact information as to the debt, the liens upon the company's property, and its resources. We must deal with the question as we find it and take that course which will under existing conditions best secure the interests of the United States. I recommended in my last annual message that a commission be appointed to deal with this question, and I renew that recommendation and suggest that the commission be given full power.

The report of the Secretary of Agriculture contains not only a most interesting statement of the progressive and valuable work done under the administration of Secretary Rusk, but many suggestions for the enlarged usefulness of this important Department. In the successful efforts to break down the restrictions to the free introduction of our meat products in the countries of Europe the Secretary has been untiring from the first, stimulating and aiding all other Government officers at home and abroad whose official duties enabled them to participate in the work. The total trade in hog products with Europe in May, 1892, amounted to 82,000,000 pounds, against 46,900,000 in the same month of 1891; in June, 1892, the export aggregated 85,700,000 pounds, against 46,500,000 pounds in the same month of the previous year; in July there was an increase of 41 per cent and in August of 55 per cent over the corresponding months of 1891. Over 40,000,000 pounds of inspected pork have been exported since the law was put into operation, and a comparison of the four months of May, June, July, and August, 1892, with the same months of 1891 shows an increase in the number of pounds of our export of pork products of 62 per cent and an increase in value of 66½ per cent. The exports of dressed beef increased from 137,900,000 pounds in 1889 to 220,500,000 pounds in 1892, or about 60 per cent. During the past year there have been exported 394,607 head of live cattle, as against 205,786 exported in 1889. This increased exportation has been largely promoted by the inspection authorized by law and the faithful efforts of the Secretary and his efficient subordinates to make that inspection thorough and to carefully exclude from all cargoes diseased or suspected cattle. The requirement of the English regulations that live cattle arriving from the United States must be slaughtered at the docks had its origin in the claim that pleuro-pneumonia existed among American cattle and that the existence of the disease could only certainly be determined by a *post mortem* inspection.

The Department of Agriculture has labored with great energy and faithfulness to extirpate this disease, and on the 26th day of September last a public announcement was made by the Secretary that the disease no longer existed anywhere within the United States. He is entirely satisfied after the most searching inquiry that this statement was justified, and that by a continuance of the inspection and quarantine now required of cattle brought into this country the disease can be prevented from again getting any foothold. The value to the cattle industry of the United States of this achievement can hardly be estimated. We can not, perhaps, at once insist that this evidence shall be accepted as satisfactory by other countries; but if the present exemption from the disease is maintained and the inspection of our cattle arriving at foreign ports, in which our own veterinarians participate, confirms it, we may justly expect that the requirement that our cattle shall be slaughtered at the docks will be revoked, as the sanitary restrictions upon our pork products have been. If our cattle can be taken alive to the interior, the trade will be enormously increased.

Agricultural products constituted 78.1 per cent of our unprecedented exports for the fiscal year which closed June 30, 1892, the total exports being $1,030,278,030 and the value of the agricultural products $793,-717,676, which exceeds by more than $150,000,000 the shipment of agricultural products in any previous year.

An interesting and a promising work for the benefit of the American farmer has been begun through agents of the Agricultural Department in Europe, and consists in efforts to introduce the various products of Indian corn as articles of human food. The high price of rye offered a favorable opportunity for the experiment in Germany of combining corn meal with rye to produce a cheaper bread. A fair degree of success has been attained, and some mills for grinding corn for food have been introduced. The Secretary is of the opinion that this new use of the products of corn has already stimulated exportations, and that if diligently prosecuted large and important markets can presently be opened for this great American product.

The suggestions of the Secretary for an enlargement of the work of the Department are commended to your favorable consideration. It may, I think, be said without challenge that in no corresponding period has so much been done as during the last four years for the benefit of American agriculture.

The subject of quarantine regulations, inspection, and control was brought suddenly to my attention by the arrival at our ports in August last of vessels infected with cholera. Quarantine regulations should be uniform at all our ports. Under the Constitution they are plainly within the exclusive Federal jurisdiction when and so far as Congress shall legislate. In my opinion the whole subject should be taken into national control and adequate power given to the Executive to protect our people against plague invasions. On the 1st of September last I approved regulations establishing a twenty-day quarantine for all vessels bringing immigrants from foreign ports. This order will be continued in force. Some loss and suffering have resulted to passengers, but a due care for the homes of our people justifies in such cases the utmost precaution. There is danger that with the coming of spring cholera will again appear, and a liberal appropriation should be made at this session to enable our quarantine and port officers to exclude the deadly plague.

But the most careful and stringent quarantine regulations may not be sufficient absolutely to exclude the disease. The progress of medical and sanitary science has been such, however, that if approved precautions are taken at once to put all of our cities and towns in the best sanitary condition, and provision is made for isolating any sporadic cases and for a thorough disinfection, an epidemic can, I am sure, be avoided. This work appertains to the local authorities, and the responsibility and the penalty will be appalling if it is neglected or unduly delayed.

We are peculiarly subject in our great ports to the spread of infectious diseases by reason of the fact that unrestricted immigration brings to us out of European cities, in the overcrowded steerages of great steamships, a large number of persons whose surroundings make them the easy victims of the plague. This consideration, as well as those affecting the political, moral, and industrial interests of our country, leads me to renew the suggestion that admission to our country and to the high privileges of its citizenship should be more restricted and more careful. We have, I think, a right and owe a duty to our own people, and especially to our working people, not only to keep out the vicious, the ignorant, the civil disturber, the pauper, and the contract laborer, but to check the too great flow of immigration now coming by further limitations.

The report of the World's Columbian Exposition has not yet been submitted. That of the board of management of the Government exhibit has been received and is herewith transmitted. The work of construction and of preparation for the opening of the exposition in May next has progressed most satisfactorily and upon a scale of liberality and magnificence that will worthily sustain the honor of the United States.

The District of Columbia is left by a decision of the supreme court of the District without any law regulating the liquor traffic. An old statute of the legislature of the District relating to the licensing of various vocations has hitherto been treated by the Commissioners as giving them power to grant or refuse licenses to sell intoxicating liquors and as subjecting those who sold without licenses to penalties; but in May last the supreme court of the District held against this view of the powers of the Commissioners. It is of urgent importance, therefore, that Congress should supply, either by direct enactment or by conferring discretionary powers upon the Commissioners, proper limitations and restraints upon the liquor traffic in the District. The District has suffered in its reputation by many crimes of violence, a large per cent of them resulting from drunkenness and the liquor traffic. The capital of the nation should be freed from this reproach by the enactment of stringent restrictions and limitations upon the traffic.

In renewing the recommendation which I have made in three preceding annual messages that Congress should legislate for the protection of railroad employees against the dangers incident to the old and inadequate methods of braking and coupling which are still in use upon freight trains, I do so with the hope that this Congress may take action upon the subject. Statistics furnished by the Interstate Commerce Commission show that during the year ending June 30, 1891, there were forty-seven different styles of car couplers reported to be in use, and that during the same period there were 2,660 employees killed and 26,140 injured. Nearly 16 per cent of the deaths occurred in the coupling and uncoupling of cars and over 36 per cent of the injuries had the same origin.

The Civil Service Commission ask for an increased appropriation for needed clerical assistance, which I think should be given. I extended the classified service March 1, 1892, to include physicians, superintendents, assistant superintendents, school-teachers, and matrons in the Indian service, and have had under consideration the subject of some further extensions, but have not as yet fully determined the lines upon which extensions can most properly and usefully be made.

I have in each of the three annual messages which it has been my duty to submit to Congress called attention to the evils and dangers connected with our election methods and practices as they are related to the choice of officers of the National Government. In my last annual message I endeavored to invoke serious attention to the evils of unfair apportionments for Congress. I can not close this message without again calling attention to these grave and threatening evils. I had hoped that it was possible to secure a nonpartisan inquiry by means of a commission into evils the existence of which is known to all, and that out of this might grow legislation from which all thought of partisan advantage should be eliminated and only the higher thought appear of maintaining the freedom and purity of the ballot and the equality of the elector, without the guaranty of which the Government could never have been formed and without the continuance of which it can not continue to exist in peace and prosperity.

It is time that mutual charges of unfairness and fraud between the great parties should cease and that the sincerity of those who profess a desire for pure and honest elections should be brought to the test of their willingness to free our legislation and our election methods from everything that tends to impair the public confidence in the announced result. The necessity for an inquiry and for legislation by Congress upon this subject is emphasized by the fact that the tendency of the legislation in some States in recent years has in some important particulars been away from and not toward free and fair elections and equal apportionments. Is it not time that we should come together upon the high plane of patriotism while we devise methods that shall secure the right of every man qualified by law to cast a free ballot and give to every such ballot an equal value in choosing our public officers and in directing the policy of the Government?

Lawlessness is not less such, but more, where it usurps the functions of the peace officer and of the courts. The frequent lynching of colored people accused of crime is without the excuse, which has sometimes been urged by mobs for a failure to pursue the appointed methods for the punishment of crime, that the accused have an undue influence over courts and juries. Such acts are a reproach to the community where they occur, and so far as they can be made the subject of Federal jurisdiction the strongest repressive legislation is demanded. A public sentiment that will sustain the officers of the law in resisting mobs and in protecting accused persons in their custody should be promoted by every possible means. The officer who gives his life in the brave discharge of this duty is worthy of special honor. No lesson needs to be so urgently impressed upon our people as this, that no worthy end or cause can be promoted by lawlessness.

This exhibit of the work of the Executive Departments is submitted to Congress and to the public in the hope that there will be found in it a due sense of responsibility and an earnest purpose to maintain the national honor and to promote the happiness and prosperity of all our people, and this brief exhibit of the growth and prosperity of the country will give us a level from which to note the increase or decadence that new legislative policies may bring to us. There is no reason why the national influence, power, and prosperity should not observe the same rates of increase that have characterized the past thirty years. We carry the great impulse and increase of these years into the future. There is no reason why in many lines of production we should not surpass all other nations, as we have already done in some. There are no near frontiers to our possible development. Retrogression would be a crime.

BENJ. HARRISON.

SPECIAL MESSAGES.

EXECUTIVE MANSION, *December 7, 1892.*

To the Senate:

In response to the resolution of the Senate of April 11, 1892, requesting information in regard to the agreement between the United States and Great Britain of 1817 concerning the naval forces to be maintained by the two Governments on the Great Lakes, I transmit herewith a report of the Secretary of State and accompanying papers, giving all the information existing in that Department in regard to the agreement in question.

BENJ. HARRISON.

EXECUTIVE MANSION, *January 4, 1893.*

To the Senate and House of Representatives:

I transmit herewith, for the consideration of Congress, a communication of the 23d of December, 1892, from the Secretary of the Interior, accompanied by an agreement concluded by and between the Cherokee Commission and the Comanche, Kiowa, and Apache tribes of Indians in the Territory of Oklahoma, for the cession of certain lands and for other purposes.

BENJ. HARRISON.

EXECUTIVE MANSION, *January 4, 1893.*

To the Senate and House of Representatives:

I transmit herewith, for the consideration of Congress, a communication of the 23d of December, 1892, from the Secretary of the Interior, accompanied by an agreement concluded by and between the Cherokee Commission and the Pawnee tribe of Indians in the Territory of Oklahoma, for the cession of certain lands and for other purposes.

BENJ. HARRISON.

EXECUTIVE MANSION,
Washington, January 7, 1893.

To the Senate:

In response to the resolution of the Senate of January 6, 1893, calling on the Secretary of State for information whether the provisions of Senate bill No. 3513, absolutely suspending immigration for the period of one year, are in conflict with any treaties now existing between the United States and any foreign countries, I transmit herewith a report from the Secretary of State, giving the information called for.

BENJ. HARRISON.

EXECUTIVE MANSION,
Washington, January 11, 1893.

To the Senate:

In response to the resolutions of the Senate dated December 20, 1892, and January 5, 1893, respectively, I transmit herewith a report from the Secretary of State of the 10th instant, accompanying the reports of Mr. Walter T. Griffin, United States commercial agent at Limoges, France, and Mr. W. H. Edwards, United States consul-general at Berlin, Germany, which were called for by the aforesaid resolutions.

BENJ. HARRISON.

EXECUTIVE MANSION, *January 13, 1893.*

To the Senate and House of Representatives:

I transmit herewith, for your information, a letter from the Secretary of State, inclosing the annual report of the Bureau of American Republics for the year ending June 30, 1892.

BENJ. HARRISON.

EXECUTIVE MANSION,
Washington, January 25, 1893.

To the Senate of the United States:

In response to the resolution of the Senate of the 21st instant, relating to the alleged killing of Frank B. Riley, a sailor of the United States steamship *Newark*, in Genoa, Italy, I transmit herewith a report on the subject from the Secretary of State.

BENJ. HARRISON.

EXECUTIVE MANSION, *January 26, 1893.*

To the Senate and House of Representatives:

I transmit herewith, for the information of Congress, the third regular report of the World's Columbian Commission and the report of the president of the board of lady managers, with the accompanying papers.

BENJ. HARRISON.

EXECUTIVE MANSION, *January 31, 1893.*

To the Senate of the United States:

In compliance with a resolution of the Senate, the House of Representatives concurring, I return herewith the bill (S. 2625) entitled "An act to provide for the punishment of offenses on the high seas."

BENJ. HARRISON.

EXECUTIVE MANSION, *February 2, 1893.*

To the Senate and House of Representatives:

On the 23d of July last the following resolution of the House of Representatives was communicated to me:

Resolved, That the President be requested to inform the House, if not incompatible with the public interests, what regulations are now in force concerning the transportation of imported merchandise in bond or duty paid, and products or manufactures of the United States, from one port in the United States, over Canadian territory, to another port therein, under the provisions of section 3006 of the Revised Statutes; whether further legislation thereon is necessary or advisable, and especially whether a careful inspection of such merchandise should not be had at the frontiers of the United States upon the departure and arrival of such merchandise, and whether the interests of the United States do not require that each car containing such merchandise while in Canadian territory be in the custody and under the surveillance of an inspector of the customs department, the cost of such surveillance to be paid by the foreign carrier transporting such merchandise.

The resolution is limited in its scope to the subject of the transit of merchandise from one port in the United States, through Canadian territory, to another port in the United States, under the provisions of section 3006 of the Revised Statutes; but I have concluded that a review of our treaty obligations, if any, and of our legislation upon the whole subject of the transit of goods from, to, or through Canada is desirable, and therefore address this message to the Congress.

It should be known before new legislation is proposed whether the United States is under any treaty obligations which affect this subject growing out of the provisions of Article XXIX of the treaty of Washington. That article is as follows:

It is agreed that for the term of years mentioned in Article XXXIII of this treaty goods, wares, or merchandise arriving at the ports of New York, Boston, and Portland, and any other ports in the United States which have been or may from time to time be specially designated by the President of the United States, and destined for Her Britannic Majesty's possessions in North America, may be entered at the proper custom-house and conveyed in transit, without the payment of duties, through the territory of the United States, under such rules, regulations, and conditions for the protection of the revenue as the Government of the United States may from time to time prescribe; and under like rules, regulations, and conditions goods, wares, or merchandise may be conveyed in transit, without the payment of duties, from such possessions through the territory of the United States for export from the said ports of the United States.

It is further agreed that for the like period goods, wares, or merchandise arriving at any of the ports of Her Britannic Majesty's possessions in North America and destined for the United States may be entered at the proper custom-house and conveyed in transit, without the payment of duties, through the said possessions, under such rules and regulations and conditions for the protection of the revenue as the governments of the said possessions may from time to time prescribe; and under like rules, regulations, and conditions goods, wares, or merchandise may be conveyed in transit, without payment of duties, from the United States through the said possessions to other places in the United States, or for export from ports in the said possessions.

It will be noticed that provision is here made—

First. For the transit in bond, without the payment of duties, of goods arriving at specified ports of the United States, and at others to be designated by the President, destined for Canada.

Second. For the transit from Canada to ports of the United States, without the payment of duties, of merchandise for export.

Third. For the transit of merchandise arriving at Canadian ports, destined for the United States, through Canadian territory to the United States, without the payment of duties to the Dominion government.

Fourth. For the transit of merchandise from the United States to Canadian ports for export without the payment of duties.

Fifth. For the transit of merchandise, without the payment of duties, from the United States, through Canada, to other places in the United States.

The first and second of these provisions were concessions by the United States and were made subject to "such rules, regulations, and conditions for the protection of the revenue as the Government of the United States may from time to time prescribe." The third, fourth, and fifth provisions of the articles are concessions on the part of the Dominion of Canada and are made subject to "such rules and regulations and conditions for the protection of the revenue as the governments of the said possessions may from time to time prescribe." The first and second and the third and fourth of these provisions are reciprocal in their nature. The fifth, which provides for the transit of merchandise from one point in the United States, through Canada, to another point in the United States, is not met by a reciprocal provision for the passage of Canadian goods from one point in Canada to another point in Canada through the United States. If this article of the treaty is in force, the obligations assumed by the United States should be fully and honorably observed until such time as this Government shall free itself from them by methods provided in the treaty or recognized by international law. It is, however, no part of the obligation resting upon the United States under the treaty that it will use the concessions made to it by Canada. This Government would undoubtedly meet its full duty by yielding in an ample manner the concessions made by it to Canada. There could be no just cause of complaint by Great Britain or Canada if the compensating concession to the United States should not be exercised. We have not stipulated in the treaty that we will permit merchandise to be moved through Canadian territory from one point of the United States to another at the will of the shipper. The stipulation is on the part of Canada that it will permit such merchandise to enter its territory from the United States, to pass through it, and to return to the United States without the exaction of duties and without other burdens than such as may be necessary to protect its revenues.

The questions whether we shall continue to allow merchandise to pass from one point in the United States, through Canadian territory, to another point in the United States, and, if so, to what exactions and examinations it shall be subjected on reentering our territory, are wholly within the power of Congress without reference to the question whether Article XXIX is or is not in force.

The treaty of Washington embraced a number of absolutely independent subjects. Its purpose, as recited, was "to provide for an amicable settlement of all causes of difference between the two countries." It provided for four distinct arbitrations of unsettled questions, including the Alabama claims, for a temporary settlement of the questions growing out of the fisheries, and for various arrangements affecting commerce and intercourse between the United States and the British North American possessions. Some of its provisions were made terminable by methods pointed out in the treaty. Articles I to XVII, inclusive, provide for the settlement of the Alabama claims and of the claims of British subjects against the United States, and have been fully executed. Articles XVIII to XXV, inclusive, relate to the subject of the fisheries, and provide for a joint commission to determine what indemnity should be paid to Great Britain for the fishing privileges conceded. These articles have been terminated by the notice provided for in the treaty.

Article XXVI provides for the free navigation of the St. Lawrence, Yukon, Porcupine, and Stikine rivers. Article XXVII provides for the equal use of certain frontier canals and waterways, and contains no provision for termination upon notice. Article XXVIII opens Lake Michigan to the commerce of British subjects under proper regulations, and contains a provision for its abrogation, to which reference will presently be made. Article XXX provides for certain privileges of transshipment on the Lakes and northern waterways, and contains the same provision as Article XXIX as to the method by which it may be terminated. Article XXXI provides for the nonimposition of a Canadian export duty on lumber cut in certain districts in Maine and floated to the sea by the St. Johns River, and contains no limitation as to time and no provision for its abrogation. Article XXXII extended to Newfoundland in the event of proper legislation by that Province the fishery provisions of Articles XVIII to XXV, and was of course abrogated with those articles. Article XXXIII, which provides a method for the abrogation of certain articles of the treaty, I will presently quote at length. The remaining articles of the treaty, namely XXXV to XLII, provide for the arbitration of the dispute as to the Vancouver Island and De Haro Channel boundary, and have been fully executed. Articles XVIII, XIX, XXI, XXVIII, XXIX, and XXX each contains a provision limiting their life to "the term of years mentioned in Article XXXIII of this treaty." The articles between XVIII and XXX, inclusive, which do not contain this provision, are those that provide for an arbitration of the fishery question, which were of course terminable by the completion of the arbitration; Article XXVI, relating to the navigation of the St. Lawrence and other rivers, and Article XXVII, relating to the use of the canals. The question whether Article XXIX is still in force depends, so far as the construction of the treaty goes, upon the meaning of the words "the term of years mentioned in Article XXXIII." That article is as follows:

The foregoing Articles XVIII to XXV, inclusive, and Article XXX of this treaty shall take effect as soon as the laws required to carry them into operation shall have been passed by the Imperial Parliament of Great Britain, by the parliament of Canada, and by the legislature of Prince Edwards Island on the one hand and by the Congress of the United States on the other. Such assent having been given, the said articles shall remain in force for the period of ten years from the date at which they may come into operation, and, further, until the expiration of two years after either of the high contracting parties shall have given notice to the other of its wish to terminate the same; each of the high contracting parties being at liberty to give such notice to the other at the end of the said period of ten years or at any time afterwards.

The question of construction here presented is whether the reference to "the term of years mentioned in Article XXXIII" is to be construed as limiting the continuance of Article XXIX to the duration of Articles XVIII to XXV and XXX in such a way that the abrogation of those articles necessarily carried with it the other articles of the treaty which contained the reference to Article XXXIII already quoted, or whether the reference to this "term of years" in Articles XXVIII and XXIX was intended to provide a method of abrogation after ten years from the time of their taking effect, viz, a notice of two years of an intention to abrogate. The language of the treaty, considered alone, might support the conclusion that Article XXXIII was intended to provide a uniform method of abrogation for certain other articles. It will be noticed that the treaty does not expressly call for legislation to put Article XXIX into operation. Senator Edmunds, in the discussion in the Senate of the joint resolution terminating the fisheries article, took the view that no legislation was necessary. It seems to me, however, that such legislation was necessary, and Congress acted upon this view in the law of 1873, to which reference will presently be made. An examination of the discussion between the plenipotentiaries who framed the treaty furnishes this entry, which President Cleveland thought to be conclusive of the intention of the plenipotentiaries, viz:

The transit question was discussed, and it was agreed that any settlement that might be made should include a reciprocal arrangement in that respect for the period for which the fishery articles should be in force.

On March 1, 1873, Congress passed an act entitled "An act to carry into effect the provisions of the treaty between the United States and Great Britain signed in the city of Washington the 8th day of May, 1871, relating to the fisheries." The act consisted of five sections, the first and second of which provided for carrying into effect the provisions of the treaty "relating to the fisheries." The fourth section provided for carrying into effect section 30 of the treaty. These three sections furnished the legislation contemplated by Article XXXIII of the treaty to carry into effect Articles XVIII to XXV and XXX. The act, however, went further, as will be seen by an examination of section 3, which is as follows:

That from the date of the President's proclamation authorized by the first section of this act, and so long as the Articles XVIII to XXV, inclusive, and Article XXX of said treaty shall remain in force, according to the terms and conditions of Article XXXIII of said treaty, all goods, wares, or merchandise arriving at the ports of New York, Boston, and Portland, and any other ports in the United States which have been or may from time to time be specially designated by the President of the United States, and destined for Her Britannic Majesty's possessions in North America, may be entered at the proper custom-house and conveyed in transit, without the payment of duties, through the territory of the United States, under such rules, regulations, and conditions for the protection of the revenue as the Secretary of the Treasury may from time to time prescribe; and under like rules, regulations, and conditions goods, wares, or merchandise may be conveyed in transit, without the payment of duties, from such possessions through the territory of the United States, for export from the said ports of the United States.

It will be noticed that provision is here made for carrying into effect the two provisions of Article XXIX which I have already characterized as the concessions on the part of the United States, namely, the passage duty free from certain designated ports of the United States to Canada of imported goods, and the passage duty free to ports of the United States of Canadian goods for export. Section 3 of the law of 1873, which I have quoted, however, contains a legislative construction of Article XXIX of the treaty in the limitation that the provisions therein contained as to the transit of goods should continue in force only so long as Articles XVIII to XXV, inclusive, and XXX of the treaty should remain in force.

On March 3, 1883, Congress passed a joint resolution entitled as follows: "Joint resolution providing for the termination of articles numbered XVIII to XXV, inclusive, and article numbered XXX of the treaty between the United States of America and Her Britannic Majesty concluded at Washington May 8, 1871."

The resolution provided for the giving of notice of the abrogation of the articles of the treaty named in the title, and of no others. Section 3 contained the following provision:

And the act of Congress approved March 1, A. D. 1873, entitled * * * so far as it relates to the articles of said treaty so to be terminated, shall be and stand repealed and be of no force on and after the time of the expiration of said two years.

An examination of the debates at the time of the passage of this joint resolution very clearly shows that Congress made an attempt to save Article XXIX of the treaty and section 3 of the act of 1873. In the Senate on the 21st of February, 1883, the resolution being under consideration, several Senators, including Mr. Edmunds, the chairman of the Judiciary Committee, expressed the opinion that Article XXIX would not be affected by the abrogation of Articles XVIII to XXV and XXX, and an amendment was made to the resolution with a view to leave section 3 of the act of 1873 in force. The same view was taken in the debates in the House.

The subject again came before Congress in connection with the consideration of a bill (S. 3173) to "authorize the President of the United States to protect and defend the rights of American fishing vessels, American fishermen, American trading and other vessels in certain cases, and for other purposes."

In the course of the debate upon the bill in the Senate January 24, 1887, and in the House February 23 following, the prevailing opinion was, though not without some dissent, that Article XXIX was still in force.

On the 6th of July, 1887, in response to an inquiry by the Secretary of the Treasury, Mr. Bayard wrote a letter, a copy of which accompanies this message, in which he expresses the opinion that Article XXIX of the treaty was unaffected by the abrogation of the fisheries articles and was still in force. In August, 1888, however, Mr. Cleveland, in a message to Congress, expresses his opinion of the question in the following language:

In any event, and whether the law of 1873 construes the treaty or governs it, section 29 of such treaty, I have no doubt, terminated with the proceedings taken by our Government to terminate Articles XVIII to XXV, inclusive, and Article XXX of the treaty. * * *

If by any language used in the joint resolution it was intended to relieve section 3 of the act of 1873, embodying Article XXIX of the treaty, from its own limitations, or to save the article itself, I am entirely satisfied that the intention miscarried.

I have asked the opinion of the Attorney-General upon this question, and his answer accompanies this message. He is of the opinion that Article XXIX has been abrogated.

It should be added that the United States has continuously, through the Treasury Department, conducted our trade intercourse with Canada as if Article XXIX of the treaty and section 3 of the act of 1873 remained in force, and that Canada has continued to yield in practice the concessions made by her in that article. No change in our Treasury methods was made following Mr. Cleveland's message from which I have quoted. I am inclined to think that, using the aids which the protocol and the nearly contemporaneous legislation by Congress in the act of 1873 furnish in construing the treaty, the better opinion is that Article XXIX of the treaty is no longer operative. The enactment of section 3 of the act of 1873 was a clear declaration that legislation was necessary to put Article XXIX of the treaty into operation, and that under the treaty our obligation to provide such legislation terminated whenever Articles XVIII to XXV and XXX should be abrogated. This legislation was accepted by Great Britain as a compliance with our obligations under the treaty. No objection was made that our statute treated Article XXIX as having force only so long as the other articles named were in force.

But the question whether Article XXIX is in force has less practical

importance than has been supposed, for it does not, if in force, place
any restraints upon the United States as to the method of dealing with
imported merchandise destined for the United States arriving at a Canadian port for transportation to the United States, or of merchandise passing through Canadian territory from one place in the United States to
another. It would be no infraction either of the letter or of the spirit of
the treaty if we should stop, unload, and carefully inspect every vehicle
arriving at our border with such merchandise; nor, on the other hand,
would Canada violate her obligations under the treaty by a like treatment
of merchandise imported through the port of New York on its arrival in
Canada. Neither Government has placed itself under any restraint as to
merchandise intended for the use of its own people when such merchandise comes within its own territory. The question, therefore, as to how
we shall deal with merchandise imported by our own people through
a Canadian port and with merchandise passing from one place in the
United States to another through Canadian territory is wholly one of
domestic policy and law.

I turn now to consider the legislation of Congress upon this subject,
upon which, as it seems to me, the duties of the Treasury and the rights
of our people as to those phases of the transportation question to which
I have just alluded wholly depend. Sections 3005 and 3006 of the Revised Statutes, which are taken from the act of July 28, 1866, entitled
"An act to protect the revenue, and for other purposes" (14 U. S. Statutes at Large, p. 328), are as follows:

SEC. 3005. All merchandise arriving at the ports of New York, Boston, Portland in
Maine, or any other port specially designated by the Secretary of the Treasury, and
destined for places in the adjacent British Provinces, or arriving at the port of
[*Point Isabel*] [Brownsville] in Texas, or any other port specially designated by
the Secretary of the Treasury, and destined for places in the Republic of Mexico,
may be entered at the custom-house and conveyed in transit through the territory
of the United States without the payment of duties, under such regulations as the
Secretary of the Treasury may prescribe.

SEC. 3006. Imported merchandise in bond, or duty paid, and products or manufactures of the United States, may, with the consent of the proper authorities of the
British Provinces or Republic of Mexico, be transported from one port in the United
States to another port therein, over the territory of such Provinces or Republic, by
such routes and under such rules, regulations, and conditions as the Secretary of the
Treasury may prescribe; and the merchandise so transported shall, upon arrival in
the United States from such Provinces or Republic, be treated in regard to the liability to or exemption from duty or tax as if the transportation had taken place
entirely within the limits of the United States.

Section 3102 of the Revised Statutes is also related to this subject,
and is as follows:

To avoid the inspection at the first port of arrival, the owner, agent, master, or conductor of any such vessel, car, or other vehicle, or owner, agent, or other person having charge of any such merchandise, baggage, effects, or other articles, may apply to
any officer of the United States duly authorized to act in the premises to seal or close
the same, under and according to the regulations hereinafter authorized, previous

to their importation into the United States, which officer shall seal or close the same accordingly; whereupon the same may proceed to their port of destination without further inspection. Every such vessel, car, or other vehicle shall proceed without unnecessary delay to the port of its destination, as named in the manifest of its cargo, freight, or contents, and be there inspected. Nothing contained in this section shall be construed to exempt such vessel, car, or vehicle, or its contents, from such examination as may be necessary and proper to prevent frauds upon the revenue and violations of this title.

It will be noticed that section 3005 does not provide for the transit of merchandise through our territory from Canada to ports of the United States for export, nor have I been able to find any other law now in force that does provide for such transit. It would seem, therefore, that as to this concession made by the United States in Article XXIX of the treaty, legislation to put it into force was necessary, and that there is no such legislation unless section 3 of the act of 1873 was saved by the amendment to the joint resolution abrogating the fisheries articles and Article XXX, limiting the repeal to so much of said act as "relates to the articles of said treaty so to be terminated." The joint resolution certainly did not repeal section 3, and if that section has ceased to be operative it is by virtue of the limitation contained in the section itself. I think it did expire by its own express limitation.

The question has presented itself whether section 3 of the act of 1873 (U. S. Revised Statutes, sec. 2866) repealed by implication that section of the act of July, 1866, which is now section 3005 of the Revised Statutes; but I am of the opinion that the last-named section was not repealed. Section 3 of the act of 1873 was expressly intended to carry into effect a treaty obligation and was limited as to time. It contained no express repeal of the act of 1866, and while its provisions were broader than the last-named act, they were not inconsistent, save in the provision that while the act of 1873 was in force the additional ports in the United States at which Canadian goods might be received were to be designated by the President, whereas under the act of 1866 the designation was by the Secretary of the Treasury. The last-named act related also to intercourse with Mexico, and I think was unaffected by the act of 1873.

It will be seen that the law permits merchandise arriving at the ports of New York, Boston, Portland in Maine, and at other ports specially designated by the Secretary of the Treasury, for places in the adjacent British Provinces, to be entered at the custom-house of the port where it is landed and conveyed through the territory of the United States without the payment of duty, under regulations to be prescribed by the Secretary of the Treasury. As these goods come immediately and fully under the inspection of our customs officers at the principal ports, are entered there and remain until they cross our border into Canada fully under our supervision, there is little or no danger involved to our revenue. The regulations prescribed by the Treasury for conducting this traffic seem to me to be adequate.

As to merchandise imported into the United States from a contiguous foreign country, it is provided by section 3102 that the inspection at the first port of arrival in the United States may be avoided if the vehicle in which the same arrives has been sealed or closed by some officer of the United States duly authorized at some point in the contiguous country. When the act of closing or sealing conformably to the regulations of the Treasury has been effected, the car or other vehicle may proceed without unnecessary delay to the port of its destination, as named in the manifest of its cargo, freight, or contents, and be there inspected. This privilege, however, is subject to such examination at the point of entry to the United States as may be necessary to prevent fraud. It is important to be noticed that the merchandise to which this section refers is described in section 3100 as merchandise, etc., "imported into the United States from any contiguous foreign country."

A practice has grown up, and a traffic of considerable dimensions under it, of allowing merchandise from China and Japan, purchased and imported from those countries by our own citizens and landed at ports in the Dominion of Canada, to be there loaded into cars, which, being sealed by an officer of the United States or some one supposed to represent him, are forwarded through the territory of Canada, across the entire continent, and allowed to cross our frontier without other inspection than an examination of the seals. The real fact is that the American consul can not and does not either compare the manifest with the contents of the cars or attach the seals. The agents of the transportation companies are furnished by the consul with the seals and place them upon the cars. The practice of sealing such merchandise, notwithstanding it has been allowed by the Treasury for some years, I think is unauthorized. Such merchandise is not imported from a "contiguous country," but from China and Japan.

It has never become subject to the Canadian revenue laws as an importation from Japan to Canada, but by force of the treaty or by the courtesy of that government has been treated as subject to the revenue laws of the United States from the time of landing at the Canadian port. Our Treasury seal has been placed upon it; Canada only gives it passage. It is no more an importation from Canada than is a train load of wheat that starts from Detroit and is transported through Canada to another port of the United States. Section 3102 was enacted in 1864, two years before sections 3005 and 3006, and could not have had reference to the later methods of importing merchandise through one country to the other.

The practice to which I have referred not only equalizes the advantages of Canadian seaports with our own in the importation of goods for our domestic consumption, but makes the Canadian ports favored ports of entry. The detentions under this system at the Canadian ports are less than when the merchandise is landed at a port of the United States to be forwarded in bond to another port therein. Full effect should be given to section 3102 as to merchandise imported into the United States from Canada, so far as the appropriations enable the Treasury to provide the officers to do the work of closing and sealing. It will, however, be required that all this kind of work be done, and carefully done, by an officer of the United States, and that the duty shall in no case be delegated to the employees of the transportation companies. The considerations that it is quite doubtful whether a fraud committed in Canada by one of our agents upon our revenue would be punishable in our courts, and that such a fraud committed by anyone else certainly would not be, and that even if such acts are made penal by our statutes the criminal would be secure against extradition, seem to me to be conclusive against the policy of attempting to maintain such revenue agents in Canadian territory.

I come now to discuss another element of this international traffic, namely, the transportation of merchandise from one "port" in the United States to another "port" therein over the territory of Canada. This traffic is enormous in its dimensions, and very great interests have grown up in the United States in connection with it. Section 3006 authorizes this traffic, subject to "such rules, regulations, and conditions as the Secretary of the Treasury may prescribe;" but the important limitation is from "port" to "port." Section 3007 of the Revised Statutes, which exempts sealed cars from certain fees, preserves the terms of the preceding section—from "port" to "port." It seems to me that sections 3006 and 3007 contemplate the delivery of the sealed cars at a "port" of the United States, there to be examined by a revenue officer and their contents verified; but in practice the car, if the seal is found at the border to be intact, is passed to places not "ports" and is opened and unloaded by the consignee, no officer being present. The bill or manifest accompanying the merchandise and the unbroken seal on the car may furnish *prima facie* evidence that the amount and kind of merchandise named in the manifest and said to be contained in the car came from a port in the United States, but certainly it was not intended that the merchandise should go to the owner without an official ascertainment of the correspondence between the bill and the actual contents of the car.

I pass at this point any discussion of the question whether as a national policy this traffic should be promoted. It is enough to say that as the law stands it is authorized between "ports" of the United States, and that the rules, regulations, and conditions to be prescribed by the Secretary of the Treasury must not, in view of this declaration of the legislative will, be further restrictive of the traffic than may reasonably be necessary to protect the revenues of the United States. In determining whether further regulations are reasonably necessary to prevent frauds against our revenue it is not conclusive, at least, to say that frauds against the revenue under the existing system have not been discovered. The question is, Are the regulations such as to provide proper safeguards against fraud, or are they such as to make fraud easy to those who have the disposition to commit it? If all cars carrying this merchandise are carefully and honestly inspected at the point of lading and are securely closed during the transit, the revenue would be secure, for the proper lading of these cars is not subject to duty. Frauds can only be perpetrated by introducing products not subject to free entry. In practice the seals and locks provided by the Treasury Department do not give security that these cars, in the long transit in which they are free from observation by officers of the revenue, may not be opened and dutiable merchandise added.

The duplication of the seals used, composed of wire and lead, is easy, and the opening of locks scarcely less so. If, however, the cars, when they arrive in the United States, either at the point where our boundary is crossed or at some other port of the United States, were subject to the inspection of a revenue officer before the delivery to the consignee or owner, the manifest could be verified. The inspection, however, is now limited to an examination of the lock or seal. The car is not weighed or opened to verify its contents. I do not think this is an adequate protection against the surreptitious introduction into the cars, while on foreign territory, of dutiable articles. It will be seen by the letter of the Secretary of the Treasury that grain the product of the United States is now largely transported in American vessels to Canadian lake ports, and after being there placed in elevators is sent east in cars sealed by agents of the Treasury.

No observation is taken of this grain until its arrival in Canada, where only the amount and grade are noted by a Treasury agent, and a like amount in grade and quantity (though it may be not the identical grain) is by such agent billed and sealed in cars for carriage to the United States. I do not find any statute authorizing this practice. Section 3006, which authorizes this interstate trade through Canada, is limited to merchandise passing from ''port'' to ''port'' of the United States, and plainly means that such merchandise shall be taken up by our revenue officers at a ''port'' of the United States as a starting point.

The following are the conclusions at which I have arrived:

First. That Article XXIX of the treaty of Washington has been abrogated.

Second. That even if this article were in force there is no law in force to execute it.

Third. That when in force the treaty imposed no obligation upon the United States to use the concessions as to transit made by Canada, and no limitation upon the powers of the United States in dealing with merchandise imported for the use of our citizens through Canadian ports or passing from one place in the United States to another through Canada, upon the arrival of such merchandise at our border.

Fourth. That therefore, treaty or no treaty, the question of sealing cars containing such merchandise and the treatment of such sealed cars when they cross our border is and always has been one to be settled by our laws, according to our convenience and our interests as we may see them.

Fifth. That the law authorizing the sealing of cars in Canada containing foreign merchandise imported from a contiguous country does not apply to merchandise imported by our own people from countries not contiguous and carried through Canada for delivery to such owners.

Sixth. That the law did not contemplate the passing of sealed cars to any place not a ''port,'' nor the delivery of such cars to the owner or consignee, to be opened by him without the supervision of a revenue officer.

Seventh. That such a practice is inconsistent with the safety of the revenue.

The statutes relating to the transportation of merchandise between the United States and the British possessions should be the subject of revision. The Treasury regulations have given to these laws a construction and a scope that I do not think was contemplated by Congress. A policy adapted to the new conditions, growing in part out of the construction of the Canadian Pacific Railroad, should be declared, and the business placed upon a basis more just to our people and to our transportation companies.

If we continue the policy of supervising rates and requiring that they shall be equal and reasonable upon the railroads of the United States, we can not in fairness at the same time give these unusual facilities for competition to Canadian roads that are free to pursue the practices as to cut rates and favored rates that we condemn and punish if practiced by our own railroads.

I regret that circumstances prevented an earlier examination by me of these questions, but submit now these views in the hope that they may lead to a revision of the laws upon a safer and juster basis.

I transmit herewith the correspondence between the Secretary of the Treasury and the Attorney-General upon some phases of this question.

BENJ. HARRISON.

EXECUTIVE MANSION, *February 6, 1893.*

To the Senate and House of Representatives:

I transmit herewith, for the consideration of Congress, a communication from the Secretary of the Interior, dated 4th instant, accompanied by an agreement concluded by and between the Turtle Mountain Indians and the commission appointed under the provisions of the Indian appropriation act of July 13, 1892, to negotiate with the Turtle Mountain band of Chippewa Indians in North Dakota for the cession and relinquishment to the United States of whatever right or interest they have in and to any and all lands in said State to which they claim title, and for their removal to and settlement upon lands to be hereafter selected and determined upon by the Secretary of the Interior upon the recommendation of the proposed commissioners, subject to the approval of Congress.

BENJ. HARRISON.

Executive Mansion,
Washington, February 6, 1893.

To the Senate:

I transmit herewith, as desired by the resolution of the Senate of the 4th instant, a report from the Secretary of State of the 6th instant, with its accompanying correspondence, in relation to the draft of an uncompleted treaty with Hawaii made in 1854.

BENJ. HARRISON.

Executive Mansion,
Washington, D. C., February 8, 1893.

To the Senate and House of Representatives:

I transmit herewith the eighth annual report of the Commissioner of Labor. This report relates to industrial education in the United States and foreign countries.

BENJ. HARRISON.

Executive Mansion,
Washington, D. C., February 14, 1893.

To the Senate and House of Representatives:

I transmit herewith a special report of the Commissioner of Labor relating to compulsory insurance of workingmen in Germany and other countries.

BENJ. HARRISON.

Executive Mansion, *February 14, 1893.*

To the Senate and House of Representatives:

I transmit herewith a communication of the 13th instant from the Secretary of the Interior, transmitting copy of reports of Lieutenants Brown, Gurovits, and Suplee, United States Army, who were charged with the duty of inspecting the Navajo country, so that the Interior Department could be advised as to the practicability of restraining the Navajoes within their present reservations and of furnishing irrigation and water for their flocks, together with report of the Commissioner of Indian Affairs upon the matter with draft of an item of appropriation to carry the same into effect.

BENJ. HARRISON.

EXECUTIVE MANSION,
Washington, February 15, 1893.

To the Senate:

I transmit herewith, with a view to its ratification, a treaty of annexation concluded on the 14th day of February, 1893, between John W. Foster, Secretary of State, who was duly empowered to act in that behalf on the part of the United States, and Lorin A. Thurston, W. R. Castle, W. C. Wilder, C. L. Carter, and Joseph Marsden, the commissioners on the part of the Government of the Hawaiian Islands. The provisional treaty, it will be observed, does not attempt to deal in detail with the questions that grow out of the annexation of the Hawaiian Islands to the United States. The commissioners representing the Hawaiian Government have consented to leave to the future and to the just and benevolent purposes of the United States the adjustment of all such questions.

I do not deem it necessary to discuss at any length the conditions which have resulted in this decisive action. It has been the policy of the Administration not only to respect but to encourage the continuance of an independent government in the Hawaiian Islands so long as it afforded suitable guaranties for the protection of life and property and maintained a stability and strength that gave adequate security against the domination of any other power. The moral support of this Government has continually manifested itself in the most friendly diplomatic relations and in many acts of courtesy to the Hawaiian rulers.

The overthrow of the monarchy was not in any way promoted by this Government, but had its origin in what seems to have been a reactionary and revolutionary policy on the part of Queen Liliuokalani, which put in serious peril not only the large and preponderating interests of the United States in the islands, but all foreign interests, and, indeed, the decent administration of civil affairs and the peace of the islands. It is quite evident that the monarchy had become effete and the Queen's Government so weak and inadequate as to be the prey of designing and unscrupulous persons. The restoration of Queen Liliuokalani to her throne is undesirable, if not impossible, and unless actively supported by the United States would be accompanied by serious disaster and the disorganization of all business interests. The influence and interest of the United States in the islands must be increased and not diminished.

Only two courses are now open—one the establishment of a protectorate by the United States, and the other annexation full and complete. I think the latter course, which has been adopted in the treaty, will be highly promotive of the best interests of the Hawaiian people, and is the only one that will adequately secure the interests of the United States. These interests are not wholly selfish. It is essential that none of the other great powers shall secure these islands. Such a possession would not consist with our safety and with the peace of the world. This view of the situation is so apparent and conclusive that no protest has been heard from any government against proceedings looking to annexation. Every foreign representative at Honolulu promptly acknowledged the Provisional Government, and I think there is a general concurrence in the opinion that the deposed Queen ought not to be restored.

Prompt action upon this treaty is very desirable. If it meets the approval of the Senate, peace and good order will be secured in the islands under existing laws until such time as Congress can provide by legislation a permanent form of government for the islands. This legislation should be, and I do not doubt will be, not only just to the natives and all other residents and citizens of the islands, but should be characterized by great liberality and a high regard to the rights of all people and of all foreigners domiciled there. The correspondence which accompanies the treaty will put the Senate in possession of all the facts known to the Executive. BENJ. HARRISON.

EXECUTIVE MANSION,
Washington, February 16, 1893.

To the Senate:

I transmit herewith a letter from the Secretary of State of the 15th instant, covering a report, with accompanying correspondence, respecting relations between the United States and the Hawaiian Islands from September, 1820, to January, 1893. BENJ. HARRISON.

EXECUTIVE MANSION,
Washington, February 20, 1893.

To the Senate of the United States:

I transmit herewith a report submitted by the Acting Secretary of State in response to the resolution of the Senate of February 2 last, relating to the building of the Ozama River bridge at Santo Domingo City by American citizens. BENJ. HARRISON.

EXECUTIVE MANSION,
Washington, February 21, 1893.

To the Senate and House of Representatives:

I transmit herewith a communication of the Secretary of State, transmitting the official report of the American delegates to the International Monetary Conference convened at Brussels on November 22, 1892, with its accompaniments. BENJ. HARRISON.

EXECUTIVE MANSION, *February 25, 1893.*

To the Senate of the United States:

In compliance with a resolution of the Senate, the House of Representatives concurring, I return herewith the bill (S. 3811) entitled "An act to amend an act entitled 'An act to grant to the Mobile and Dauphin Island Railroad and Harbor Company the right to trestle across the shoal water between Cedar Point and Dauphin Island,' approved September 26, 1890.''

BENJ. HARRISON.

EXECUTIVE MANSION,
Washington, February 27, 1893.

To the Senate and House of Representatives:

I herewith transmit, for the information of Congress, a communication from the Acting Secretary of State, forwarding certain bulletins of the Bureau of the American Republics.

BENJ. HARRISON.

EXECUTIVE MANSION,
Washington, D. C., March 1, 1893.

To the Senate and House of Representatives:

I transmit herewith the fifth special report of the Commissioner of Labor. The report relates to the so-called ''Gothenburg system'' of regulating the liquor traffic, the system prevailing in Norway and Sweden.

BENJ. HARRISON.

VETO MESSAGE.

EXECUTIVE MANSION, *February 27, 1893.*

To the House of Representatives:

I return herewith without my approval an act (H. R. 9612) entitled ''An act to prescribe the number of district attorneys and marshals in the judicial districts of the State of Alabama.''

Under the present law there is a district attorney for the southern district of Alabama, a district attorney for the northern and middle districts, a marshal for the northern district, and a marshal for the southern and middle districts.

An examination of the records of the Attorney-General's office as to the amount of business in the courts in these districts leads me to believe that two districts would provide amply for the disposition of all public and private cases. The law creates two new officers, whose aggregate compensation may be $12,000 per annum, without, it seems to me, a justifying necessity. But the most serious objection to the legislation is that it creates at once upon the taking effect of the law the offices of district attorney and marshal for each of the three districts, and the effect, it seems to me, must be to abolish the offices as they now exist.

No provision is made for a continued discharge of the duties of marshal and district attorney by the present incumbents. A serious question would be raised as to whether these officers were not at once legislated out of office and vacancies created. As these vacancies could not be filled immediately, the business of the courts would seriously suffer. The law should at least have contained a provision for the continued discharge of their duties by the incumbents until the new officers were appointed and qualified.

BENJ. HARRISON.

PROCLAMATIONS.

By the President of the United States of America.

A PROCLAMATION.

Whereas it is provided by section 24 of the act of Congress approved March 3, 1891, entitled "An act to repeal timber-culture laws, and for other purposes"—

That the President of the United States may from time to time set apart and reserve in any State or Territory having public land bearing forests, in any part of the public lands wholly or in part covered with timber or undergrowth, whether of commercial value or not, as public reservations; and the President shall by public proclamation declare the establishment of such reservations and the limits thereof.

And whereas it is made to appear, by petition and otherwise, that the interests of the public and the welfare of the people of the State of Colorado will be materially benefited and subserved by the reservation of the public and forest lands hereinafter described:

Now, therefore, I, Benjamin Harrison, President of the United States, by virtue of the power in me vested by said act, do hereby set apart, reserve, and establish as a public reservation all that tract of land in the State of Colorado embraced in the following boundary and description, to wit:

Beginning at the confluence of the North Fork of the South Platte River with the South Platte River; thence up the middle of the channel of the North Fork of the South Platte River to the range line between township seven (7) south, ranges seventy-four (74) and seventy-five (75) west of the sixth (6th) principal meridian; thence northerly on said range line to the northeast corner of township seven (7) south, range seventy-five (75) west; thence westerly on the township line between townships six (6) and seven (7) south to the northwest corner of township seven (7) south, range seventy-six (76) west; thence southerly on the range line between ranges seventy-six (76) and seventy-seven (77) west to the northeast corner of section thirteen (13), township seven (7) south, range seventy-seven (77) west; thence westerly on the section line between sections twelve (12) and thirteen (13) to the northwest corner of section thirteen (13) of said township and range; thence southerly on the section line between sections thirteen (13) and fourteen (14), twenty-three (23) and twenty-four (24), and twenty-five (25) and twenty-six (26) to the northeast corner of section thirty-five (35) of said township and range; thence westerly on the section line between sections twenty-six (26) and thirty-five (35) and twenty-seven (27) and thirty-four (34) to the northwest corner of section thirty-four (34) of said township and range; thence southerly on the section line between sections thirty-three (33) and thirty-four (34) of said township and range and sections three (3) and four (4), nine (9) and ten (10), and fifteen (15) and sixteen (16), township eight (8) south, range seventy-seven (77) west, to the northeast corner of section twenty-one (21) of said last-named township and range; thence westerly on the section line between sections sixteen (16) and twenty-one (21), seventeen (17) and twenty (20), and eighteen (18) and nineteen (19) to the northwest corner of section nineteen (19) of said township and range; thence southerly on the range line between ranges seventy-seven (77) and seventy-eight (78) west to the northeast corner of section thirteen (13), township nine (9) south, range seventy-eight (78) west; thence westerly on the section line between sections twelve (12) and thirteen (13) and eleven (11) and fourteen (14) to the northwest corner of section fourteen (14) of said township and range; thence southerly on the section line between sections fourteen (14) and fifteen (15) to the southwest corner of said section fourteen (14); thence westerly on the section line between sections fifteen (15) and twenty-two (22) and sixteen (16) and twenty-one (21) to the northwest corner of section twenty-one (21) of said township and range; thence southerly on the section line between sections twenty (20) and twenty-one (21) and twenty-eight (28) and twenty-nine (29) to the southwest corner of section twenty-eight (28) of said township and range; thence easterly on the section line between sections twenty-eight (28) and thirty-three (33) to the southeast corner of said section twenty-eight (28); thence southerly on the section line between sections thirty-three (33) and thirty-four (34) of said township and range and sections three (3) and four (4), nine (9) and ten (10), and fifteen (15) and sixteen (16), township ten (10) south, range seventy-eight (78) west, to the northeast corner of section twenty-one (21) of said last-named township and range; thence westerly on the section line between sections sixteen (16) and twenty-one (21), seventeen (17) and twenty (20), and eighteen (18) and nineteen (19) to the northwest corner of section nineteen (19) of said township and range; thence southerly on the range line between ranges seventy-eight (78) and seventy-nine (79) west to the southwest corner of township ten (10) south, range seventy-eight (78) west; thence westerly on the second (2d) correction line south to the northwest corner of section one (1), township eleven (11) south, range seventy-nine (79) west;

thence southerly on the section line between sections one (1) and two (2), eleven (11) and twelve (12), thirteen (13) and fourteen (14), twenty-three (23) and twenty-four (24), twenty-five (25) and twenty-six (26), and thirty-five (35) and thirty-six (36) of said township and range and sections one (1) and two (2), eleven (11) and twelve (12), and thirteen (13) and fourteen (14), township twelve (12) south, range seventy-nine (79) west, to the southwest corner of section thirteen (13) of said last-named township and range; thence easterly on the section line between sections thirteen (13) and twenty-four (24) of said township and range and sections eighteen (18) and nineteen (19), seventeen (17) and twenty (20), sixteen (16) and twenty-one (21), and fifteen (15) and twenty-two (22), township twelve (12) south, range seventy-eight (78) west, to the quarter-section corner between said sections fifteen (15) and twenty-two (22); thence southerly through the middle of sections twenty-two (22), twenty-seven (27), and thirty-four (34) to the quarter-section corner on the south boundary of section thirty-four (34) of said township and range; thence easterly on the township line between townships twelve (12) and thirteen (13) south, range seventy-eight (78) west, to the northwest corner of township thirteen (13) south, range seventy-seven (77) west; thence southerly on the range line between ranges seventy-seven (77) and seventy-eight (78) west to the southwest corner of section six (6), township thirteen (13) south, range seventy-seven (77) west; thence easterly on the section line between sections six (6) and seven (7), five (5) and eight (8), and four (4) and nine (9) to the southeast corner of section four (4) of said township and range; thence northerly on the section line between sections three (3) and four (4) of said township and range and sections thirty-three (33) and thirty-four (34), township twelve (12) south, range seventy-seven (77) west, to the northeast corner of section thirty-three (33) of said last-named township and range; thence easterly on the section line between sections twenty-seven (27) and thirty-four (34) to the southeast corner of section twenty-seven (27) of said township and range; thence northerly on the section line between sections twenty-six (26) and twenty-seven (27), twenty-two (22) and twenty-three (23), fourteen (14) and fifteen (15), ten (10) and eleven (11), and two (2) and three (3) of said township and range and sections thirty-four (34) and thirty-five (35), township eleven (11) south, range seventy-seven (77) west, to the northeast corner of section thirty-four (34) of said township and range; thence westerly on the section line between sections twenty-seven (27) and thirty-four (34) to the northwest corner of said section thirty-four (34); thence northerly on the section line between sections twenty-seven (27) and twenty-eight (28) to the northeast corner of section twenty-eight (28) of said township and range; thence westerly on the section line between sections twenty-one (21) and twenty-eight (28), twenty (20) and twenty-nine (29), and nineteen (19) and thirty (30) to the northwest corner of section thirty (30) of said township and range;

thence northerly on the range line between ranges seventy-seven (77) and seventy-eight (78) west to the northeast corner of township eleven (11) south, range seventy-eight (78) west; thence easterly on the second (2d) correction line south to the southeast corner of township ten (10) south, range seventy-eight (78) west; thence northerly on the range line between ranges seventy-seven (77) and seventy-eight (78) west to the southwest corner of section eighteen (18), township nine (9) south, range seventy-seven (77) west; thence easterly on the section line between sections eighteen (18) and nineteen (19), seventeen (17) and twenty (20), sixteen (16) and twenty-one (21), and fifteen (15) and twenty-two (22) to the southeast corner of section fifteen (15) of said township and range; thence northerly on the section line between sections fourteen (14) and fifteen (15) and ten (10) and eleven (11) to the southwest corner of section two (2) of said township and range; thence easterly on the section line between sections two (2) and eleven (11) and one (1) and twelve (12) to the southeast corner of section one (1) of said township and range; thence northerly on the range line between ranges seventy-six (76) and seventy-seven (77) west to the southwest corner of township eight (8) south, range seventy-six (76) west; thence easterly on the township line between townships eight (8) and nine (9) south, range seventy-six (76) west, to the southeast corner of section thirty-one (31), township eight (8) south, range seventy-six (76) west; thence northerly on the section line between sections thirty-one (31) and thirty-two (32) to the southwest corner of section twenty-nine (29) of said township and range; thence easterly on the section line between sections twenty-nine (29) and thirty-two (32) to the southeast corner of said section twenty-nine (29); thence northerly on the section line between sections twenty-eight (28) and twenty-nine (29) and twenty (20) and twenty-one (21) to the southwest corner of section sixteen (16) of said township and range; thence easterly on the section line between sections sixteen (16) and twenty-one (21) to the southeast corner of said section sixteen (16); thence northerly on the section line between sections fifteen (15) and sixteen (16), nine (9) and ten (10), and three (3) and four (4) of said township and range, and sections thirty-three (33) and thirty-four (34), township seven (7) south, range seventy-six (76) west, to the southwest corner of section twenty-seven (27) of said township and range; thence easterly on the section line between sections twenty-seven (27) and thirty-four (34), twenty-six (26) and thirty-five (35), and twenty-five (25) and thirty-six (36) of said township and range, and sections thirty (30) and thirty-one (31), twenty-nine (29) and thirty-two (32), twenty-eight (28) and thirty-three (33), and twenty-seven (27) and thirty-four (34), township seven (7) south, range seventy-five (75) west, to the northwest corner of section thirty-five (35) of said township and range; thence southerly on the section line between sections thirty-four (34) and thirty-five (35) of said township and range and sections two (2) and three (3), ten (10) and eleven (11), fourteen (14) and fifteen (15), twenty-two (22) and twenty-three (23), twenty-six (26) and twenty-seven (27), and thirty-four (34) and thirty-five (35), township eight (8) south, range seventy-five (75) west, to the southwest corner of section thirty-five (35) of said township and range; thence easterly on the township line between townships eight (8) and nine (9) south, range seventy-five (75) west, to the northwest corner of township nine (9) south, range seventy-four (74) west; thence southerly on the range line between ranges seventy-four (74) and seventy-five (75) west to the southwest corner of township ten (10) south, range seventy-four (74) west; thence easterly on the second (2d) correction line south to the northwest corner of township eleven (11) south, range seventy-three (73) west; thence southerly on the range line between ranges seventy-three (73) and seventy-four (74) west to the northeast corner of section thirteen (13), township twelve (12) south, range seventy-four (74) west; thence westerly on the section line between sections twelve (12) and thirteen (13) and eleven (11) and fourteen (14) of said township and range to the quarter-section corner between said sections eleven (11) and fourteen (14); thence southerly through the middle of sections fourteen (14), twenty-three (23), and twenty-six (26) to the center of section twenty-six (26) of said township and range; thence easterly through the middle of sections twenty-six (26) and twenty-five (25) to the quarter-section corner on the range line between section twenty-five (25), township twelve (12) south, range seventy-four (74) west, and section thirty (30), township twelve (12) south, range seventy-three (73) west; thence southerly on said range line to the southwest corner of township twelve (12) south, range seventy-three (73) west; thence easterly on the township line between townships twelve (12) and thirteen (13) south to the southeast corner of township twelve (12) south, range seventy-three (73) west; thence southerly on the range line between ranges seventy-two (72) and seventy-three (73) west to the northeast corner of section twenty-four (24), township thirteen (13) south, range seventy-three (73) west; thence westerly on the section line between sections thirteen (13) and twenty-four (24), fourteen (14) and twenty-three (23), fifteen (15) and twenty-two (22), sixteen (16) and twenty-one (21), seventeen (17) and twenty (20), and eighteen (18) and nineteen (19) to the northwest corner of section nineteen (19) of said township and range; thence southerly on the range line between ranges seventy-three (73) and seventy-four (74) west to the quarter-section corner on the west boundary of section eighteen (18), township fourteen (14) south, range seventy-three (73) west; thence easterly through the middle of sections eighteen (18) and seventeen (17), sixteen (16), fifteen (15), fourteen (14), and thirteen (13), township fourteen (14) south, range seventy-three (73) west, and sections eighteen (18) and seventeen (17), township fourteen (14) south, range seventy-two (72) west, to the quarter-section corner between sections seventeen (17) and sixteen (16) of said last-named township and range; thence northerly on the section line between sections sixteen (16) and seventeen (17) and eight (8) and nine (9) to the northeast corner of section eight (8) of said township and range; thence easterly on the section line between sections four (4) and nine (9), three (3) and ten (10), two (2) and eleven (11), and one (1) and twelve (12) to the southeast corner of section one (1) of said township and range; thence northerly on the range line between ranges seventy-one (71) and seventy-two (72) west to the southwest corner of township thirteen (13) south, range seventy-one (71) west; thence easterly on the 'township line between townships thirteen (13) and fourteen (14) south to the southeast corner of section thirty-three (33), township thirteen (13) south, range seventy-one (71) west; thence northerly on the section line between sections thirty-three (33) and thirty-four (34), twenty-seven (27) and twenty-eight (28), twenty-one (21) and twenty-two (22), fifteen (15) and sixteen (16), nine (9) and ten (10), and three (3) and four (4) of said township and range, and between sections thirty-three (33) and thirty-four (34), twenty-seven (27) and twenty-eight (28), twenty-one (21) and twenty-two (22), fifteen (15) and sixteen (16), nine (9) and ten (10), and three (3) and four (4), township twelve (12) south, range seventy-one (71) west, and between sections thirty-three (33) and thirty-four (34), twenty-seven (27) and twenty-eight (28), twenty-one (21) and twenty-two (22), fifteen (15) and sixteen (16), nine (9) and ten (10), and three (3) and four (4), township eleven (11) south, range seventy-one (71) west, to the northeast corner of section four (4) of said last-named township and range; thence easterly on the second (2d) correction line south to the southeast corner of section thirty-three (33), township ten (10) south, range seventy-one (71) west; thence northerly on the section line between sections thirty-three (33) and thirty-four (34) of said township and range to the middle of the channel of the South Platte River; thence down the middle of the channel of the said river to its confluence with the North Fork of the South Platte River, the place of beginning, to be known as the South Platte Forest Reserve.

Excepting from the force and effect of this proclamation all lands which may have been prior to the date hereof embraced in any legal entry or covered by any lawful filing duly of record in the proper United States land office, or upon which any valid settlement has been made pursuant to law and the statutory period within which to make entry or filing of record has not expired, and all mining claims duly located and held according to the laws of the United States and rules and regulations not in conflict therewith.

Provided, That this exception shall not continue to apply to any particular tract of land unless the entryman, settler, or claimant continues to comply with the law under which the entry, filing, settlement, or location was made.

Warning is hereby expressly given to all persons not to enter or make settlement upon the tract of land reserved by this proclamation.

In witness whereof I have hereunto set my hand and caused the seal of the United States to be affixed.

[SEAL.] Done at the city of Washington, this 9th day of December, A. D. 1892, and of the Independence of the United States the one hundred and seventeenth.

BENJ. HARRISON.

By the President:

JOHN W. FOSTER,
Secretary of State.

BY THE PRESIDENT OF THE UNITED STATES OF AMERICA.

A PROCLAMATION.

Whereas it is provided by section 24 of the act of Congress approved March 3, 1891, entitled "An act to repeal timber-culture laws, and for other purposes"—

That the President of the United States may from time to time set apart and reserve in any State or Territory having public land bearing forests, in any part of the public lands wholly or in part covered with timber or undergrowth, whether of commercial value or not, as public reservations; and the President shall by public proclamation declare the establishment of such reservations and the limits thereof.

And whereas the public lands in the State of California within the limits hereinafter described are in part covered with timber, and it appears that the public good would be promoted by setting apart and reserving said lands as a public reservation:

Now, therefore, I, Benjamin Harrison, President of the United States, by virtue of the power in me vested by section 24 of the aforesaid act of Congress, do hereby make known and proclaim that there is hereby reserved from entry or settlement and set apart as a public reservation all those certain tracts, pieces, or parcels of land lying and being situate in the State of California and particularly described as follows, to wit:

Beginning at the northeast corner of township three (3) north, range six (6) west of the San Bernardino meridian; thence westerly on the surveyed and unsurveyed township line between townships three (3) and four (4) north, ranges six (6) and seven (7) west, to the northeast corner of township three (3) north, range eight (8) west; thence northerly on the unsurveyed and surveyed range line between ranges seven (7) and (8) west to the northeast corner of section twenty-four (24), township four (4) north, range eight (8) west; thence westerly on the surveyed and unsurveyed section line between sections thirteen (13) and twenty-four (24), fourteen (14) and twenty-three (23), fifteen (15) and twenty-two (22), sixteen (16) and twenty-one (21), seventeen (17) and twenty (20), and eighteen (18) and nineteen (19) of said township and range to the point for the northwest corner of section nineteen (19) of said township and range; thence northerly on the unsurveyed and surveyed range line between ranges eight (8) and nine (9) west to the northeast corner of township four (4) north, range nine (9) west; thence westerly on the township line between townships four (4) and five (5) north, range nine (9) west, to the southeast corner of township five (5) north, range ten (10) west; thence northerly on the range line between ranges nine (9) and ten (10) west to the northeast corner of section thirty-six (36) of said township and range; thence westerly on the section line between sections twenty-five (25) and thirty-six (36), twenty-six (26) and thirty-five (35), and twenty-seven (27) and thirty-four (34) to the southeast corner of section twenty-eight (28) of said township and range; thence northerly on the section line between sections twenty-seven (27) and twenty-eight (28) to the northeast corner of said section twenty-eight (28); thence westerly on the section line between sections twenty-one (21) and twenty-eight (28), twenty (20) and twenty-nine (29), and nineteen (19) and thirty (30) of said last-named township and range, and on the unsurveyed section line between sections twenty-four (24) and twenty-five (25), twenty-three (23) and twenty-six (26), twenty-two (22) and twenty-seven (27), twenty-one (21) and twenty-eight (28), twenty (20) and twenty-nine (29), and nineteen (19) and thirty (30), township five (5) north, range eleven (11) west, to the point for the northwest corner of section thirty (30) of said last-named township and range; thence southerly on the range line between ranges eleven (11) and twelve (12) west to the southeast corner of township five (5) north, range twelve (12) west; thence westerly on the township line between townships four (4) and five (5) north to the southwest corner of township five (5) north, range twelve (12) west; thence southerly on the range line between ranges twelve (12) and thirteen (13) west to the northeast corner of section twenty-four (24), township four (4) north, range thirteen (13) west; thence westerly on the section line between sections thirteen (13) and twenty-four (24), fourteen (14) and twenty-three (23), fifteen (15) and twenty-two (22), sixteen (16) and twenty-one (21), seventeen (17) and twenty (20), and eighteen (18) and nineteen (19) of said township and range, and sections thirteen (13) and twenty-four (24), fourteen (14) and twenty-three (23), fifteen (15) and twenty-two (22), sixteen (16) and twenty-one (21), seventeen (17) and twenty (20), and eighteen (18) and nineteen (19), township four (4) north, range fourteen (14) west, to the northwest corner of section nineteen (19) of said last-named township and range; thence southerly on the surveyed and unsurveyed range line between ranges fourteen (14) and fifteen (15) west to the point for the southwest corner of township three (3) north, range fourteen (14) west; thence easterly on the unsurveyed township line between townships two (2) and three (3) north, range fourteen (14) west, to a point for the northwest corner of section four (4), township two (2) north, range fourteen (14) west; thence southerly on the unsurveyed section line between sections four (4) and five (5) to the point for the southwest corner of said section four (4); thence easterly on the unsurveyed section line between sections four (4) and nine (9), three (3) and ten (10), two (2) and eleven (11), and one (1) and twelve (12) to a point for the southeast corner of section one (1) of said township and range; thence southerly on the range line between ranges thirteen (13) and fourteen (14) west to the southwest corner of section seven (7), township two (2) north, range thirteen (13) west; thence easterly on the surveyed and un-surveyed section line between sections seven (7) and eighteen (18), eight (8) and seventeen (17), nine (9) and sixteen (16), ten (10) and fifteen (15), eleven (11) and fourteen (14), and twelve (12) and (13) to a point for the northeast corner of section thirteen (13) of said township and range; thence southerly on the range line between ranges twelve (12) and thirteen (13) west to the southwest corner of township two (2) north, range twelve (12) west; thence easterly on the surveyed and unsurveyed town-ship line between townships one (1) and two (2) north, range twelve (12) west, to the point for the northwest corner of section one (1), township one (1) north, range twelve (12) west; thence southerly on the unsur-veyed section line between sections one (1) and two (2) to the point for the southwest corner of said section one (1); thence easterly on the un-surveyed section line between sections one (1) and twelve (12) to the point for the southeast corner of said section one (1); thence southerly on the range line between ranges eleven (11) and twelve (12) west to the southwest corner of section seven (7), township one (1) north, range eleven (11) west; thence easterly on the section line between sections seven (7) and eighteen (18), eight (8) and seventeen (17), nine (9) and sixteen (16), ten (10) and fifteen (15), eleven (11) and fourteen (14), and twelve (12) and thirteen (13) of said township and range, and sections seven (7) and eighteen (18), eight (8) and seventeen (17), nine (9) and sixteen (16), ten (10) and fifteen (15), eleven (11) and fourteen (14), and twelve (12) and thirteen (13), township one (1) north, range ten (10) west, to the southeast corner of section twelve (12) of said last-named township and range; thence southerly on the range line between ranges nine (9) and ten (10) west to the southwest corner of section eighteen (18), township one (1) north, range nine (9) west; thence easterly on the section line between sections eighteen (18) and nineteen (19), seventeen (17) and twenty (20), sixteen (16) and twenty-one (21), fifteen (15) and twenty-two (22), fourteen (14) and twenty-three (23), and thirteen (13) and twenty-four (24) of said township and range, and sections eighteen (18) and nineteen (19), seventeen (17) and twenty (20), sixteen (16) and twenty-one (21), fifteen (15) and twenty-two (22), fourteen (14) and twenty-three (23), and thirteen (13) and twenty-four (24), township one (1) north, range eight (8) west, to the southeast corner of section thir-teen (13) of said last-named township and range; thence northerly on the range line between ranges seven (7) and eight (8) west to the southwest corner of section seven (7), township one (1) north, range seven (7) west; thence easterly on the section line between sections seven (7) and eighteen

(18), eight (8) and seventeen (17), nine (9) and sixteen (16), ten (10) and fifteen (15), eleven (11) and fourteen (14), and twelve (12) and thirteen (13) of said township and range, and on the surveyed and unsurveyed section line between sections seven (7) and eighteen (18), eight (8) and seventeen (17), nine (9) and sixteen (16), ten (10) and fifteen (15), eleven (11) and fourteen (14), and twelve (12) and thirteen (13), township one (1) north, range six (6) west, to the point for the southeast corner of section twelve (12) of said last-named township and range; thence northerly on the unsurveyed and surveyed range line between ranges five (5) and six (6) west to the northeast corner of township three (?) north, range six (6) west, the place of beginning.

Excepting from the force and effect of this proclamation all lands which may have been prior to the date hereof embraced in any legal entry or covered by any lawful filing duly of record in the proper United States land office, or upon which any valid settlement has been made pursuant to law and the statutory period within which to make entry or filing of record has not expired, and all mining claims duly located and held according to the laws of the United States and rules and regulations not in conflict therewith.

Provided, That this exception shall not continue to apply to any particular tract of land unless the entryman, settler, or claimant continues to comply with the law under which the entry, filing, settlement, or location was made.

Warning is hereby expressly given to all persons not to enter or make settlement upon the tract of land reserved by this proclamation.

In witness whereof I have hereunto set my hand and caused the seal of the United States to be affixed.

[SEAL.]   Done at the city of Washington, this 20th day of December, A. D. 1892, and of the Independence of the United States the one hundred and seventeenth.

BENJ. HARRISON.

By the President:

JOHN W. FOSTER,
Secretary of State.

By the President of the United States of America.

A PROCLAMATION.

Whereas it is provided by section 24 of the act of Congress approved March 3, 1891, entitled "An act to repeal timber-culture laws, and for other purposes"—

That the President of the United States may from time to time set apart and reserve in any State or Territory having public land bearing forests, in any part of the public lands wholly or in part covered with timber or undergrowth, whether of commercial value or not, as public reservations; and the President shall by public proclamation declare the establishment of such reservations and the limits thereof.

And whereas it is provided by section 14 of said above-mentioned act that the public lands in the Territory of Alaska reserved for public purposes shall not be subject to occupation and sale; and

Whereas the public lands in the Territory of Alaska known as Afognak Island are in part covered with timber and are required for public purposes in order that salmon fisheries in the waters of the island, and salmon and other fish and sea animals, and other animals and birds, and the timber, undergrowth, grass, moss, and other growth in, on, and about said island may be protected and preserved unimpaired, and it appears that the public good would be promoted by setting apart and reserving said lands as a public reservation; and

Whereas the United States Commissioner of Fish and Fisheries has selected Afognak Bay, River, and Lake, with their tributary streams and the sources thereof, and the lands including the same on said Afognak Island and within 1 mile from the shores thereof, as a reserve for the purpose of establishing fish-culture stations and the use of the United States Commission of Fish and Fisheries, the boundary lines of which include the headsprings of the tributaries above mentioned and the lands the drainage of which is into the same:

Now, therefore, I, Benjamin Harrison, President of the United States, by virtue of the power in me vested by sections 24 and 14 of the aforesaid act of Congress and by other laws of the United States, do reserve and do hereby make known and proclaim that there is hereby reserved from occupation and sale and set apart as a public reservation, including use for fish-culture stations, said Afognak Island, Alaska, and its adjacent bays and rocks and territorial waters, including among others the Sea Lion Rocks and Sea Otter Island: *Provided*, That this proclamation shall not be so construed as to deprive any *bona fide* inhabitant of said island of any valid right he may possess under the treaty for the cession of the Russian possessions in North America to the United States, concluded at Washington on the 30th day of March, 1867.

Warning is hereby expressly given to all persons not to enter upon or to occupy the tract or tracts of land or waters reserved by this proclamation, or to fish in or use any of the waters herein described or mentioned, and that all persons or corporations now occupying said island or any of said premises except under said treaty shall depart therefrom.

In witness whereof I have hereunto set my hand and caused the seal of the United States to be affixed.

[SEAL.] Done at the city of Washington, this 24th day of December, A. D. 1892, and of the Independence of the United States the one hundred and seventeenth.

BENJ. HARRISON.

By the President:
JOHN W. FOSTER,
Secretary of State.

By the President of the United States of America.

A PROCLAMATION.

Whereas it is provided by section 24 of the act of Congress approved March 3, 1891, entitled "An act to repeal timber-culture laws, and for other purposes"—

That the President of the United States may from time to time set apart and reserve in any State or Territory having public land bearing forests, in any part of the public lands wholly or in part covered with timber or undergrowth, whether of commercial value or not, as public reservations; and the President shall by public proclamation declare the establishment of such reservations and the limits thereof.

And whereas the public lands in the State of Colorado within the limits hereinafter described are in part covered with timber, and it appears that the public good would be promoted by setting apart and reserving said lands as a public reservation:

Now, therefore, I, Benjamin Harrison, President of the United States, by virtue of the power in me vested by section 24 of the aforesaid act of Congress, do hereby make known and proclaim that there is hereby reserved from entry or settlement and set apart as a public reservation all those certain tracts, pieces, or parcels of land lying and being situate in the State of Colorado and particularly described as follows, to wit:

Beginning at the northeast corner of township seven (7) south, range ninety-three (93) west of the sixth (6th) principal meridian; thence westerly along the township line between townships six (6) and seven (7) south to the northwest corner of township seven (7) south, range ninety-three (93) west; thence southerly along the range line between ranges ninety-three (93) and ninety-four (94) west to the northwest corner of section nineteen (19), township seven (7) south, range ninety-three (93) west; thence westerly along the unsurveyed section line between sections thirteen (13) and twenty-four (24), fourteen (14) and twenty-three (23), fifteen (15) and twenty-two (22), sixteen (16) and twenty-one (21), seventeen (17) and twenty (20), and eighteen (18) and nineteen (19), township seven (7) south, range ninety-four (94) west, to the northwest corner of section nineteen (19) of said township and range; thence southerly along the range line between ranges ninety-four (94) and ninety-five (95) west to the northwest corner of township eight (8) south, range ninety-four (94) west; thence westerly along the township line between townships seven (7) and eight (8) south to the northwest corner of section three (3), township eight (8) south, range ninety-five (95) west; thence southerly along the section line between sections three (3) and four (4), nine (9) and ten (10), and fifteen (15) and sixteen (16) to the northwest corner of section twenty-two (22) of said township and range; thence westerly along the section line between sections sixteen (16) and twenty-one (21), seventeen (17) and twenty (20), and eighteen (18) and nineteen

(19) of said township and range, and sections thirteen (13) and twenty-four (24), fourteen (14) and twenty-three (23), and fifteen (15) and twenty-two (22), township eight (8) south, range ninety-six (96) west, to the northwest corner of section twenty-two (22) of said township and range; thence southerly along the section line between sections twenty-one (21) and twenty-two (22), twenty-seven (27) and twenty-eight (28), and thirty-three (33) and thirty-four (34) of said township and range to the northwest corner of section three (3), township nine (9) south, range ninety-six (96) west; thence westerly along the township line between townships eight (8) and nine (9) south to the northwest corner of section three (3), township nine (9) south, range ninety-seven (97) west; thence southerly along the section line between sections three (3) and four (4), nine (9) and ten (10), fifteen (15) and sixteen (16), twenty-one (21) and twenty-two (22), twenty-seven (27) and twenty-eight (28), and thirty-three (33) and thirty-four (34) to the southwest corner of section thirty-four (34) of said township and range; thence easterly along the township line between townships nine (9) and ten (10) south to the southeast corner of township nine (9) south, range ninety-six (96) west; thence northerly along the range line between ranges ninety-five (95) and ninety-six (96) west to the southeast corner of section thirteen (13), township nine (9) south, range ninety-six (96) west; thence easterly along the section line between sections eighteen (18) and nineteen (19), seventeen (17) and twenty (20), sixteen (16) and twenty-one (21), fifteen (15) and twenty-two (22), fourteen (14) and twenty-three (23), and thirteen (13) and twenty-four (24), township nine (9) south, range ninety-five (95) west, to the southeast corner of section thirteen (13) of said township and range; thence northerly along the range line between ranges ninety-four (94) and ninety-five (95) west to the southeast corner of township eight (8) south, range ninety-five (95) west; thence easterly along the township line between townships eight (8) and nine (9) south to the southwest corner of township eight (8) south, range ninety-two (92) west; thence southerly along the range line between ranges ninety-two (92) and ninety-three (93) west to the southwest corner of township ten (10) south, range ninety-two (92) west; thence westerly along the second (2d) correction line south between townships ten (10) and eleven (11) south to the northwest corner of township eleven (11) south, range ninety-six (96) west; thence southerly along the range line between ranges ninety-six (96) and ninety-seven (97) west to the northwest corner of township twelve (12) south, range ninety-six (96) west; thence westerly along the township line between townships eleven (11) and twelve (12) south to the northwest corner of fractional section two (2), fractional township twelve (12) south, fractional range ninety-eight (98) west; thence southerly along the range line between fractional range ninety-eight (98) west of the sixth (6th) principal meridian and range two (2) east of the Ute principal meridian to the southwest corner of fractional section thirty-five

(35), fractional township thirteen (13) south, fractional range ninety-eight (98) west of the sixth (6th) principal meridian; thence easterly along the township line between township thirteen (13) and fractional township fourteen (14) south to the southwest corner of township thirteen (13) south, range ninety-six (96) west; thence southerly along the range line between ranges ninety-six (96) and ninety-seven (97) west to the southwest corner of township fourteen (14) south, range ninety-six (96) west; thence easterly along the township line between townships fourteen (14) and fifteen (15) south to the southeast corner of section thirty-three (33), township fourteen (14) south, range ninety-five (95) west; thence northerly along the section line between sections thirty-three (33) and thirty-four (34), twenty-seven (27) and twenty-eight (28), twenty-one (21) and twenty-two (22), fifteen (15) and sixteen (16), nine (9) and ten (10), and three (3) and four (4), townships fourteen (14) and thirteen (13) south, range ninety-five (95) west, and sections thirty-three (33) and thirty-four (34), twenty-seven (27) and twenty-eight (28), and twenty-one (21) and twenty-two (22), township twelve (12) south, range ninety-five (95) west, to the southeast corner of section sixteen (16) of said township and range; thence easterly along the section line between sections fifteen (15) and twenty-two (22), fourteen (14) and twenty-three (23), and thirteen (13) and twenty-four (24), township twelve (12) south, range ninety-five (95) west, and sections eighteen (18) and nineteen (19), seventeen (17) and twenty (20), sixteen (16) and twenty-one (21), fifteen (15) and twenty-two (22), fourteen (14) and twenty-three (23), and thirteen (13) and twenty-four (24), township twelve (12) south, range (94) west, to the southwest corner of section eighteen (18), township twelve (12) south, range ninety-three (93) west; thence southerly along the range line between ranges ninety-three (93) and ninety-four (94) west to the southwest corner of township twelve (12) south, range ninety-three (93) west; thence easterly along the township line between townships twelve (12) and thirteen (13) south to the southeast corner of township twelve (12) south, range ninety-two (92) west; thence northerly along the range line between ranges ninety-one (91) and ninety-two (92) west to the southeast corner of township eleven (11) south, range ninety-two (92) west; thence easterly along the township line between townships eleven (11) and twelve (12) south to the southwest corner of township eleven (11) south, range ninety (90) west; thence southerly along the range line between ranges ninety (90) and ninety-one (91) west to the southwest corner of township twelve (12) south, range ninety (90) west; thence easterly along the township line between townships twelve (12) and thirteen (13) south to the southeast corner of township twelve (12) south, range eighty-nine (89) west; thence northerly along the surveyed and unsurveyed range line between ranges eighty-eight (88) and eighty-nine (89) west to the northeast corner of township eleven (11) south, range eighty-nine (89) west; thence easterly along the second (2d) correction line south to the southeast corner of township ten (10) south, range eighty-nine (89) west; thence northerly along the range line between ranges eighty-eight (88) and eighty-nine (89) west to the northeast corner of township nine (9) south, range eighty-nine (89) west; thence westerly along the township line between townships eight (8) and nine (9) south to the northeast corner of township nine (9) south, range ninety (90) west; thence northerly along the range line between ranges eighty-nine (89) and ninety (90) west to the northeast corner of township eight (8) south, range ninety (90) west; thence westerly along the surveyed and unsurveyed township line between townships seven (7) and eight (8) south to the northeast corner of township eight (8) south, range ninety-three (93) west; thence northerly along the range line between ranges ninety-two (92) and ninety-three (93) west to the northeast corner of township seven (7) south, range ninety-three (93) west, the place of beginning.

Excepting from the force and effect of this proclamation all lands which may have been prior to the date hereof embraced in any legal entry or covered by any lawful filing duly of record in the proper United States land office, or upon which any valid settlement has been made pursuant to law and the statutory period within which to make entry or filing of record has not expired, and all mining claims duly located and held according to the laws of the United States and rules and regulations not in conflict therewith.

Provided, That this exception shall not continue to apply to any particular tract of land unless the entryman, settler, or claimant continues to comply with the law under which the entry, filing, settlement, or location was made.

Warning is hereby expressly given to all persons not to enter or make settlement upon the tract of land reserved by this proclamation.

In witness whereof I have hereunto set my hand and caused the seal of the United States to be affixed.

[SEAL.]   Done at the city of Washington, this 24th day of December, A. D. 1892, and of the Independence of the United States the one hundred and seventeenth.

By the President: BENJ. HARRISON.

JOHN W. FOSTER, *Secretary of State.*

BY THE PRESIDENT OF THE UNITED STATES OF AMERICA.

A PROCLAMATION.

Whereas, pursuant to section 3 of the act of Congress approved October 1, 1890, entitled "An act to reduce the revenue and equalize duties on imports, and for other purposes," the Secretary of State of the United States of America communicated to the Government of Salvador the action of the Congress of the United States of America, with a view to secure reciprocal trade, in declaring the articles enumerated in said section 3 to be exempt from duty upon their importation into the United States of America; and

Whereas the minister for foreign affairs for the Republic of Salvador has communicated to the envoy extraordinary and minister plenipotentiary of the United States to Salvador that the Congress of Salvador has by due legal enactment authorized the executive power to conclude a definitive commercial arrangement with the United States to supersede the existing provisional arrangement; and

Whereas, in reciprocity for the admission into the United States of America free of all duty of the articles enumerated in section 3 of said act, the Government of Salvador will admit free of all duty from and after December 31, 1892, into all the established ports of entry of Salvador the articles or merchandise named in the following schedule, provided that the same is the manufacture or product of the United States:

PRODUCTS AND MANUFACTURES OF THE UNITED STATES TO BE ADMITTED INTO SALVADOR FREE OF CUSTOMS DUTIES AND OF ALL CHARGES, WHETHER NATIONAL OR PROVINCIAL.

1. Cotton-seed oil.
2. Live animals.
3. Tar, vegetable and mineral.
4. Wire, barbed, and staples for fences.
5. Apparatus for distilling liquors.
6. Plows, cultivators, hoes, axes, machetes, shovels, and rakes.
7. Quicksilver.
8. Barrels, casks, and tanks of iron for water.
9. Mineral ores.
10. Boats, lighters, tackle, anchors, chains, girtlines, sails, and all other articles for vessels, to be used in the ports, lakes, and rivers of the Republic.
11. Coal, mineral.
12. Roman cement and hydraulic lime.
13. Kettles for making salt.
14. Wooden staves, barrel heads and hoops.
15. Houses of wood and iron, complete and in parts.
16. Beans, potatoes, and onions.
17. Fruits, fresh.
18. Guano and other fertilizers, natural and artificial.
19. Guys for mining purposes.
20. Hay and straw for forage.
21. Furnaces and instruments for assaying metals.
22. Scientific instruments.
23. Loadstones.
24. Bricks, fire bricks, and crucibles for melting.
25. Hops.
26. Printed books, pamphlets and newspapers, bound or unbound, maps, photographs, printed music, and paper for music.
27. Corn, rice, barley, and rye.
28. **Marble, dressed, for furniture, statues, fountains, gravestones, and building purposes.**

29. Machinery of all kinds, including sewing machines, and separate or extra parts for the same.

30. Materials of all kinds for the construction and operation of railroads.

31. Materials of all kinds for the construction and operation of telegraphic and telephonic lines.

32. Materials of all kinds for lighting by electricity and gas.

33. Materials of all kinds for the construction of wharves in ports, lakes, or rivers.

34. Wood of all kinds for building, in trunks or pieces, beams, rafters, planks, boards, shingles, and flooring.

35. Molds for making sugar.

36. Models of machinery and buildings.

37. Printing materials, including presses, ink, and all other accessories.

38. Samples of merchandise the duties on which do not exceed $1.

39. Gold and silver in bars, dust, or coin.

40. Preparations of flour in biscuits, crackers, not sweetened, macaroni, vermicelli, and tallarin.

41. Plates of iron for building purposes.

42. Kettles for making sugar.

43. Sulphate of quinine.

44. Tubes of iron and all other accessories for water supply.

45. Wagons, carts, and carriages of all kinds, and separate parts for the same.

It is understood that the packages or coverings in which the articles named in the foregoing schedule are imported shall be free of duty if they are usual and proper for the purpose.

And whereas the Government of Salvador has further stipulated that the laws and regulations adopted to protect its revenue and prevent fraud in the declarations and proof that the articles named in the foregoing schedule are the product or manufacture of the United States of America shall impose no additional charges on the importer nor undue restrictions on the articles imported; and

Whereas the envoy extraordinary and minister plenipotentiary of the United States to Salvador has informed the Government of Salvador that its action in granting freedom of duties to the products and manufactures of the United States of America on their importation into Salvador is accepted as a due reciprocity for the action of Congress as set forth in section 3 of said act:

Now, therefore, be it known that I, Benjamin Harrison, President of the United States of America, have caused the above-stated modifications of the tariff laws of Salvador to be made public for the information of the citizens of the United States of America.

In testimony whereof I have hereunto set my hand and caused the seal of the United States to be affixed.

[SEAL.] Done at the city of Washington, this 27th day of December, A. D. 1892, and of the Independence of the United States the one hundred and seventeenth.

BENJ. HARRISON.

By the President:

JOHN W. FOSTER,
Secretary of State.

By the President of the United States of America.

A PROCLAMATION.

Whereas Congress by a statute approved March 22, 1882, and by statutes in furtherance and amendment thereof defined the crimes of bigamy, polygamy, and unlawful cohabitation in the Territories and other places within the exclusive jurisdiction of the United States and prescribed a penalty for such crimes; and

Whereas on or about the 6th day of October, 1890, the Church of the Latter-day Saints, commonly known as the Mormon Church, through its president issued a manifesto proclaiming the purpose of said church no longer to sanction the practice of polygamous marriages and calling upon all members and adherents of said church to obey the laws of the United States in reference to said subject-matter; and

Whereas it is represented that since the date of said declaration the members and adherents of said church have generally obeyed said laws and have abstained from plural marriages and polygamous cohabitation; and

Whereas by a petition dated December 19, 1891, the officials of said church, pledging the membership thereof to a faithful obedience to the laws against plural marriage and unlawful cohabitation, have applied to me to grant amnesty for past offenses against said laws, which request a very large number of influential non-Mormons residing in the Territories have also strongly urged; and

Whereas the Utah Commission in their report bearing date September 15, 1892, recommend that said petition be granted and said amnesty proclaimed, under proper conditions as to the future observance of the law, with a view to the encouragement of those now disposed to become law-abiding citizens; and

Whereas during the past two years such amnesty has been granted to individual applicants in a very large number of cases, conditioned upon the faithful observance of the laws of the United States against unlawful cohabitation, and there are now pending many more such applications:

Now, therefore, I, Benjamin Harrison, President of the United States, by virtue of the powers in me vested, do hereby declare and grant a full amnesty and pardon to all persons liable to the penalties of said act by reason of unlawful cohabitation under the color of polygamous or plural marriage who have since November 1, 1890, abstained from such unlawful cohabitation, but upon the express condition that they shall in the future faithfully obey the laws of the United States hereinbefore named, and not otherwise. Those who shall fail to avail themselves of the clemency hereby offered will be vigorously prosecuted.

In witness whereof I have hereunto set my hand and caused the seal of the United States to be affixed.

[SEAL.] Done at the city of Washington, this 4th day of January, A. D. 1893, and of the Independence of the United States the one hundred and seventeenth.

BENJ. HARRISON.

By the President:
JOHN W. FOSTER, *Secretary of State.*

BY THE PRESIDENT OF THE UNITED STATES OF AMERICA.

A PROCLAMATION.

Whereas it is provided by section 24 of the act of Congress approved March 3, 1891, entitled "An act to repeal timber-culture laws, and for other purposes"—

That the President of the United States may from time to time set apart and reserve in any State or Territory having public land bearing forests, in any part of the public lands wholly or in part covered with timber or undergrowth, whether of commercial value or not, as public reservations; and the President shall by public proclamation declare the establishment of such reservations and the limits thereof.

And whereas the public lands in the State of California within the limits hereinafter described are in part covered with timber, and it appears that the public good would be promoted by setting apart and reserving said lands as a public reservation:

Now, therefore, I, Benjamin Harrison, President of the United States, by virtue of the power in me vested by section 24 of the aforesaid act of Congress, do hereby make known and proclaim that there is hereby reserved from entry or settlement and set apart as a public reservation all those certain tracts, pieces, or parcels of land lying and being situate in the State of California and within the boundaries particularly described as follows, to wit:

Beginning at the northeast corner of township five (5) south, range thirty (30) east, on the first (1st) standard parallel south, Mount Diablo meridian, California; thence westerly along said first (1st) standard parallel to the northwest corner of township five (5) south, range twenty-one (21) east; thence southerly on the range line between ranges twenty (20) and twenty-one (21) east to the southwest corner of township six (6) south, range twenty-one (21) east; thence easterly on the township line between townships six (6) and seven (7) south to the southeast corner of township six (6) south, range twenty-one (21) east; thence southerly on the range line between ranges twenty-one (21) and twenty-two (22) east to the southwest corner of township seven (7) south, range twenty-two (22) east; thence easterly along the township line between townships seven (7) and eight (8) south to the southeast corner of township seven (7) south, range twenty-two (22) east; thence southerly along the range line between ranges twenty-two (22) and twenty-three (23) east to the southwest corner of township eight (8) south, range twenty-three (23) east; thence easterly along the second (2d) standard parallel south to the northeast corner of township nine (9) south, range twenty-three (23) east; thence southerly along the unsurveyed and surveyed range line between ranges twenty-three (23) and twenty-four (24) east to the southwest corner of township nine (9) south, range twenty-four (24) east; thence easterly along the township line between townships nine (9) and ten (10) south to the southeast corner of township nine (9) south, range twenty-four (24) east; thence southerly along the range line between ranges twenty-four (24) and twenty-five (25) east to the southwest corner of township ten (10) south, range twenty-five (25) east; thence easterly along the township line between townships ten (10) and eleven (11) south to the southeast corner of township ten (10) south, range twenty-five (25) east; thence southerly along the unsurveyed and surveyed range line between ranges twenty-five (25) and twenty-six (26) east to the southwest corner of township twelve (12) south, range twenty-six (26) east; thence easterly along the third (3d) standard parallel south to the northwest corner of township thirteen (13) south, range twenty-seven (27) east; thence southerly along the range line between ranges twenty-six (26) and twenty-seven (27) east to the southwest corner of township thirteen (13) south, range twenty-seven (27) east; thence easterly along the township line between townships thirteen (13) and fourteen (14) south to the southeast corner of township thirteen (13) south, range twenty-seven (27) east; thence northerly along the boundary line of "General Grant National Park" to the northwest corner, easterly to the northeast corner, southerly to the southeast corner, and westerly to the southwest corner of said park; thence southerly along the range line between ranges twenty-seven (27) and twenty-eight (28) east to the southwest corner of township fourteen (14) south, range twenty-eight (28) east; thence easterly along the township line between townships fourteen (14) and fifteen (15) south to the southwest corner of township fourteen (14) south, range thirty-one (31) east; thence southerly along the range line between ranges thirty (30) and thirty-one (31) east to the fourth (4th) standard parallel south; thence westerly along said fourth (4th) standard parallel to the northwest corner of township seventeen (17) south, range thirty-one (31) east; thence southerly along the range line between ranges thirty (30) and thirty-one (31) east to the southwest corner of township seventeen (17) south, range thirty-one (31) east; thence easterly along the township line between townships seventeen (17) and eighteen (18) south to the southeast corner of township seventeen (17) south, range thirty-one (31) east; thence southerly along the range line between ranges thirty-one (31) and thirty-two (32) east to the southwest corner of township eighteen (18) south, range thirty-two (32) east; thence westerly along the township line between townships eighteen (18) and nineteen (19) south to the northwest corner of township nineteen (19) south, range thirty (30) east; thence southerly along the range line between ranges twenty-nine (29) and thirty (30) east to the fifth (5th) standard parallel south; thence westerly along said fifth (5th) standard parallel to the northwest corner of township twenty-one (21) south, range thirty (30) east; thence southerly along the range line between ranges twenty-nine (29) and thirty (30) east to a point on said range line where it intersects the northern boundary line of the "Tule River Indian Reservation;" thence easterly and northeasterly along the northern boundary line of said reservation to the northeast corner thereof, located in the southwest quarter of section twenty-one (21), township twenty-one (21) south, range thirty-one (31) east; thence southerly along the eastern boundary of said reservation to the southeast corner thereof, located in the northwest quarter of section thirty-three (33), township twenty-two (22) south, range thirty-one (31) east; thence westerly and southwesterly along the southern boundary of said reservation to a point where it is intersected by the range line between ranges twenty-nine (29) and thirty (30) east; thence southerly along said range line to the southwest corner of township twenty-three (23) south, range thirty (30) east; thence easterly along the township line between townships twenty-three (23) and twenty-four (24) south to the southeast corner of township twenty-three (23) south, range thirty (30) east; thence southerly along the range line between ranges thirty (30) and thirty-one (31) east to the sixth (6th) standard parallel south; thence westerly along said sixth (6th) standard parallel to the northwest corner of township twenty-five (25) south, range thirty-one (31) east; thence southerly along the range line between ranges thirty (30) and thirty-one (31) east to the southwest corner of township twenty-six (26) south, range thirty-one (31) east; thence westerly along the township line between townships twenty-six (26) and twenty-seven (27) south to the northwest corner of township twenty-seven (27) south, range thirty (30) east; thence southerly along the range line between ranges twenty-nine (29) and thirty (30) east to the seventh (7th) standard parallel south; thence easterly along said seventh (7th) standard parallel to the southeast corner of township twenty-eight (28) south, range thirty-seven (37) east; thence northerly along the range line between ranges thirty-seven (37) and thirty-eight (38) east to the sixth (6th) standard parallel south; thence easterly along said sixth (6th) standard parallel to the southeast corner of township twenty-four (24) south, range thirty-seven (37) east; thence northerly along the range line between ranges thirty-seven (37) and thirty-eight (38) east to the northeast corner of township twenty-four (24) south, range thirty-seven (37) east; thence easterly along the township line between townships twenty-three (23) and twenty-four (24) south to the southeast corner of township twenty-three (23) south, range thirty-seven (37) east; thence northerly along the range line between ranges thirty-seven (37) and thirty-eight (38) east to the fifth (5th) standard parallel south; thence westerly along said fifth (5th) standard parallel south to the southeast corner of section thirty-one (31), township twenty (20) south, range thirty-seven (37) east; thence northerly along the western boundary line of sections thirty-two (32), twenty-nine (29), twenty (20), seventeen (17), eight (8), and five (5) to the northwest corner of section five (5) in said township and range; thence westerly along the township line between townships nineteen (19) and twenty (20) south to the southeast corner of township nineteen (19) south, range thirty-six (36) east; thence northerly along the range line between ranges thirty-six (36) and thirty-seven (37) east to the quarter-section corner on the east line of section thirty-six (36), township nineteen (19) south, range thirty-six (36) east, westerly on a line through the centers of sections thirty-six (36) and thirty-five (35) to the center of section thirty-five (35), northerly on a line through the centers of sections thirty-five (35), twenty-six (26), twenty-three (23), and fourteen (14) to the center of section fourteen (14), easterly on a line through the center of section fourteen (14) to the quarter-section corner between said section fourteen (14) and section thirteen (13), and northerly along the section lines on the west boundary of sections thirteen (13), twelve (12), and one (1) to the northwest corner of section one (1), all of said township and range; thence northerly along the section lines on the west boundary of sections thirty-six (36) and twenty-five (25), township eighteen (18) south, range thirty-six (36) east, to the northwest corner of said section twenty-five (25), easterly along the section line between sections twenty-four (24) and twenty-five (25) to the quarter-section corner between said sections, northerly through the centers of sections twenty-four (24) and thirteen (13) to the quarter-section corner between sections thirteen (13) and twelve (12), westerly along the section line to the southwest corner of section twelve (12), and northerly along the section lines on the west boundary of sections twelve (12) and one (1) to the northwest corner of section one (1) of said township and range; thence northerly along the section line on the west boundary of section thirty-six (36), township seventeen (17) south, range thirty-six (36) east, to the quarter-section corner between sections thirty-five (35) and thirty-six (36), westerly to the center of section thirty-five (35), northerly on a line through the centers of sections thirty-five (35), twenty-six (26), twenty-three (23), fourteen (14), and eleven (11) to the quarter-section corner between sections eleven (11) and two (2), westerly along the section line to the southwest corner of section two (2), and northerly along the section line to the northwest corner of section two (2), all of said township and range; thence westerly along the surveyed and unsurveyed line of the fourth (4th) standard parallel south to the southwest corner of township sixteen (16) south, range thirty-four (34) east; thence northerly along the range line between ranges thirty-three (33) and thirty-four

(34) east to the northwest corner of township fifteen (15) south, range thirty-four (34) east; thence easterly along the township line between townships fourteen (14) and fifteen (15) south to the southwest corner of township fourteen (14) south, range thirty-five (35) east; thence northerly on the range line between ranges thirty-four (34) and thirty-five (35) east to the northwest corner of township fourteen (14) south, range thirty-five (35) east; thence westerly along the township line between townships thirteen (13) and fourteen (14) south to the southwest corner of section thirty-five (35), township thirteen (13) south, range thirty-four (34) east, northerly along the section line to the quarter-section corner between sections thirty-four (34) and thirty-five (35), westerly to the center of section thirty-four (34), northerly on a line through the centers of sections thirty-four (34) and twenty-seven (27) to the center of section twenty-seven (27), easterly through section twenty-seven (27) to the quarter-section corner between sections twenty-seven (27) and twenty-six (26), northerly along the section lines on the west boundary of sections twenty-six (26), twenty-three (23), fourteen (14), eleven (11), and two (2) to the northwest corner of west lot one (1) in section two (2), easterly to the southwest corner of the east lot two (2) in section two (2), and northerly to the northwest corner of the west half of east lot six (6), section two (2), all of said township and range; thence westerly along the third (3d) standard parallel south to the southwest corner of section thirty-four (34), township twelve (12) south, range thirty-four (34) east, northerly along the section line to the quarter-section corner between sections thirty-four (34) and thirty-three (33), westerly to the center of section thirty-three (33), northerly to the quarter-section corner between sections thirty-three (33) and twenty-eight (28), westerly on the section line to the southwest corner of section twenty-eight (28), northerly along the section lines on the west boundary of sections twenty-eight (28), twenty-one (21), sixteen (16), nine (9), and four (4) to the quarter-section corner between sections four (4) and five (5), westerly to the center of section five (5), and northerly to the quarter-section corner on the north boundary of said section five (5), all of said township and range; thence westerly along the township line between townships eleven (11) and twelve (12) south to the southwest corner of section thirty-two (32), township eleven (11) south, range thirty-four (34) east, northerly along the section lines on the west boundary of sections thirty-two (32), twenty-nine (29), twenty (20), seventeen (17), and eight (8) to the quarter-section corner between sections seven (7) and eight (8), westerly on a line through the center of section seven (7), township eleven (11) south, range thirty-four (34) east, and sections twelve (12) and eleven (11), township eleven (11) south, range thirty-three (33) east, to the center of said section eleven (11), and northerly on a central line through sections eleven (11) and two (2) to the quarter-section corner on the north line of section two (2), township eleven (11) south, range thirty-three

(33) east; thence westerly on the township line between townships ten (10) and eleven (11) south to the southwest corner of section thirty-five (35), township ten (10) south, range thirty-three (33) east, northerly to the quarter-section corner between sections thirty-five (35) and thirty-four (34), westerly to the center of section thirty-four (34), northerly on a line through the centers of sections thirty-four (34), twenty-seven (27), and twenty-two (22) to the center of section twenty-two (22), easterly to the center of section twenty-three (23), northerly through the centers of sections twenty-three (23), fourteen (14), and eleven (11) to the center of section eleven (11), easterly to the quarter-section corner between sections eleven (11) and twelve (12), northerly along the section line to the northwest corner of section twelve (12), easterly along the section line to the quarter-section corner between sections twelve (12) and one (1), northerly to the center of section one (1), easterly to the quarter-section corner on the east line of section one (1), and northerly to the northeast corner of section one (1), all of said township and range; thence westerly along the unsurveyed township line between townships ten (10) and nine (9) south to the southeast corner of township nine (9) south, range thirty-two (32) east; thence northerly along the range line between ranges thirty-two (32) and thirty-three (33) east to the northeast corner of township nine (9) south, range thirty-two (32) east; thence westerly along the second (2d) standard parallel south to the southeast corner of township eight (8) south, range thirty-one (31) east; thence northerly along the surveyed and unsurveyed range line between ranges thirty-one (31) and thirty-two (32) east to the northeast corner of township eight (8) south, range thirty-one (31) east; thence westerly along the township line between townships seven (7) and eight (8) south to the southeast corner of township seven (7) south, range thirty (30) east; thence northerly along the range line between ranges thirty (30) and thirty-one (31) east to the northeast corner of township five (5) south, range thirty (30) east, the place of beginning.

Excepting from the force and effect of this proclamation all lands which may have been prior to the date hereof embraced in any legal entry or covered by any lawful filing duly of record in the proper United States land office, or upon which any valid settlement has been made pursuant to law and the statutory period within which to make entry or filing of record has not expired, and all mining claims duly located and held according to the laws of the United States and the rules and regulations not in conflict therewith.

Provided, That this exception shall not continue to apply to any particular tract of land unless the entryman, settler, or claimant continues to comply with the law under which the entry, filing, settlement, or location was made.

Warning is hereby expressly given to all persons not to enter or make settlement upon the tract of land reserved by this proclamation.

In witness whereof I have hereunto set my hand and caused the seal of the United States to be affixed.

[SEAL.] Done at the city of Washington, this 14th day of February, A. D. 1893, and of the Independence of the United States the one hundred and seventeenth.

BENJ. HARRISON.

By the President:

JOHN W. FOSTER, *Secretary of State.*

BY THE PRESIDENT OF THE UNITED STATES OF AMERICA.

A PROCLAMATION.

Whereas it is provided by section 24 of the act of Congress approved March 3, 1891, entitled "An act to repeal timber-culture laws, and for other purposes"—

That the President of the United States may from time to time set apart and reserve in any State or Territory having public land bearing forests, in any part of the public lands wholly or in part covered with timber or undergrowth, whether of commercial value or not, as public reservations; and the President shall by public proclamation declare the establishment of such reservations and the limits thereof.

And whereas the public lands in the State of Washington within the limits hereinafter described are in part covered with timber, and it appears that the public good would be promoted by setting apart and reserving said lands as a public reservation:

Now, therefore, I, Benjamin Harrison, President of the United States, by virtue of the power in me vested by section 24 of the aforesaid act of Congress, do hereby make known and proclaim that there is hereby reserved from entry or settlement and set apart as a public reservation all those certain tracts, pieces, or parcels of land lying and being situate in the State of Washington and within the boundaries particularly described as follows, to wit:

Beginning at the southwest corner of township thirteen (13) north, range fifteen (15) east of the Willamette base and meridian; thence northerly along the surveyed and unsurveyed range line between ranges fourteen (14) and fifteen (15) east, subject to the proper easterly or westerly offset on the fourth (4th) standard parallel north, to the point for the northeast corner of township eighteen (18) north, range fourteen (14) east; thence westerly along the unsurveyed township line between townships eighteen (18) and nineteen (19) north to the southeast corner of township nineteen (19) north, range seven (7) east; thence southerly along the unsurveyed range line between ranges seven (7) and eight (8) east, subject to the proper easterly or westerly offsets on the township line between townships seventeen (17) and eighteen (18) north, and the fourth (4th) standard parallel north to the point for the southwest corner of township thirteen (13) north, range eight (8) east; thence easterly along the unsurveyed township line between townships twelve (12) and thirteen (13) north to the southwest corner of township thirteen (13) north, range fifteen (15) east, the place of beginning.

Excepting from the force and effect of this proclamation all lands which may have been prior to the date hereof embraced in any legal entry or covered by any lawful filing duly of record in the proper United States land office, or upon which any valid settlement has been made pursuant to law and the statutory period within which to make entry or filing of record has not expired, and all mining claims duly located and held according to the laws of the United States and rules and regulations not in conflict therewith.

Provided, That this exception shall not continue to apply to any particular tract of land unless the entryman, settler, or claimant continues to comply with the law under which the entry, filing, settlement, or location was made.

Warning is hereby expressly given to all persons not to enter or make settlement upon the tract of land reserved by this proclamation.

In witness whereof I have hereunto set my hand and caused the seal of the United States to be affixed.

[SEAL.]   Done at the city of Washington, this 20th day of February, A. D. 1893, and of the Independence of the United States the one hundred and seventeenth.

By the President: BENJ. HARRISON.

JOHN W. FOSTER, *Secretary of State*.

BY THE PRESIDENT OF THE UNITED STATES OF AMERICA.

A PROCLAMATION.

Whereas it is provided by section 24 of the act of Congress approved March 3, 1891, entitled "An act to repeal timber-culture laws, and for other purposes"—

That the President of the United States may from time to time set apart and reserve in any State or Territory having public land bearing forests, in any part of the public lands wholly or in part covered with timber or undergrowth, whether of commercial value or not, as public reservations; and the President shall by public proclamation declare the establishment of such reservations and the limits thereof.

And whereas the public lands in the Territory of Arizona within the limits hereinafter described are in part covered with timber, and it appears that the public good would be promoted by setting apart and reserving said lands as a public reservation:

Now, therefore, I, Benjamin Harrison, President of the United States, by virtue of the power in me vested by section 24 of the aforesaid act of Congress, do hereby make known and proclaim that there is hereby reserved from entry or settlement and set apart as a public reservation all those certain tracts, pieces, or parcels of land lying and being situate in the Territory of Arizona and within the boundaries particularly described as follows, to wit :

Beginning at the point of intersection of the parallel of thirty-six (36) degrees thirty (30) minutes north latitude with the meridian of one hundred and eleven (111) degrees forty-five (45) minutes of longitude west from Greenwich ; thence westerly along said parallel of latitude to its intersection with the meridian of one hundred and twelve (112) degrees forty-five (45) minutes west longitude; thence southerly along said meridian of longitude to its intersection with the parallel of thirty-five (35) degrees forty-five (45) minutes north latitude; thence easterly along said parallel of latitude to its intersection with the meridian of one hundred and eleven (111) degrees forty-five (45) minutes west longitude ; thence northerly along said meridian of longitude to its intersection with the parallel of thirty-six (36) degrees thirty (30) minutes north latitude, the place of beginning.

Excepting from the force and effect of this proclamation all lands which may have been prior to the date hereof embraced in any legal entry or covered by any lawful filing duly of record in the proper United States land office, or upon which any valid settlement has been made pursuant to law and the statutory period within which to make entry or filing of record has not expired, and all mining claims duly located and held according to the laws of the United States and rules and regulations not in conflict therewith.

Provided, That this exception shall not continue to apply to any particular tract of land unless the entryman, settler, or claimant continues to comply with the law under which the entry, filing, settlement, or location was made.

Warning is hereby expressly given to all persons not to enter or make settlement upon the tract of land reserved by this proclamation.

In witness whereof I have hereunto set my hand and caused the seal of the United States to be affixed.

[SEAL.] Done at the city of Washington, this 20th day of February, A. D. 1893, and of the Independence of the United States the one hundred and seventeenth.

BENJ. HARRISON.

By the President :

JOHN W. FOSTER, *Secretary of State.*

BY THE PRESIDENT OF THE UNITED STATES OF AMERICA.

A PROCLAMATION.

Whereas by my proclamation of August 18, 1892,* and in pursuance of the authority conferred on me by an act of Congress approved July 26, 1892, entitled "An act to enforce the reciprocal commercial relations

* See pp. 290-292.

between the United States and Canada, and for other purposes," I directed "that from and after September 1, 1892, until further notice a toll of 20 cents per ton be levied, collected, and paid on all freight of whatever kind or description passing through the St. Marys Falls Canal in transit to any port of the Dominion of Canada, whether carried in vessels of the United States or of other nations," and to that extent thereby suspended "from and after said date the right of free passage through said St. Marys Falls Canal of any and all cargoes or portions of cargoes in transit to Canadian ports;" and

Whereas the above order was issued in consequence of the imposition by the government of the Dominion of Canada of a discriminating toll whereby unjust and unreasonable burdens were placed, in violation of Article XXVII of the treaty of Washington, upon the carrying of passengers and cargoes through the Welland Canal in transit to ports of the United States, as is fully set forth in the said proclamation; and

Whereas by an order in council dated February 13, 1893, the Governor-General of the Dominion of Canada has directed that—

For the season of 1893 the canal tolls for the passage of the following food products, wheat, Indian corn, pease, barley, rye, oats, flaxseed, and buckwheat, for passage eastward through the Welland Canal be 10 cents per ton, and for passage westward through the St. Lawrence canals only 10 cents per ton; payment of the said toll of 10 cents per ton for passage through the Welland Canal to entitle these products to free passage through the St. Lawrence canals.

And whereas I have received satisfactory assurances that this order revokes during the season of 1893 the discriminating provisions above referred to and secures to citizens of the United States equality with British subjects as regards the use of said canals:

Now, therefore, I, Benjamin Harrison, President of the United States of America, by virtue of the said act of Congress approved July 26, 1892, do hereby declare and proclaim that from and after the date hereof and until further notice the provisions of my said proclamation of August 18, 1892,* are suspended in so far as they direct that a toll of 20 cents per ton be levied, collected, and paid on all freight of whatever kind or description passing through the St. Marys Falls Canal in transit to any port of the Dominion of Canada, whether carried in vessels of the United States or of other nations.

In testimony whereof I have hereunto set my hand and caused the seal of the United States to be affixed.

[SEAL.] Done at the city of Washington, this 21st day of February, 1893, and of the Independence of the United States of America the one hundred and seventeenth.

BENJ. HARRISON.

By the President:

JOHN W. FOSTER,
Secretary of State.

* See pp. 290-292.

By the President of the United States of America.

A PROCLAMATION.

Whereas it is provided by section 24 of the act of Congress approved March 3, 1891, entitled "An act to repeal timber-culture laws, and for other purposes"—

That the President of the United States may from time to time set apart and reserve in any State or Territory having public land bearing forests, in any part of the public lands wholly or in part covered with timber or undergrowth, whether of commercial value or not, as public reservations; and the President shall by public proclamation declare the establishment of such reservations and the limits thereof.

And whereas the public lands in the State of California within the limits hereinafter described are in part covered with timber, and it appears that the public good would be promoted by setting apart and reserving said lands as a public reservation:

Now, therefore, I, Benjamin Harrison, President of the United States, by virtue of the power in me vested by section 24 of the aforesaid act of Congress, do hereby make known and proclaim that there is hereby reserved from entry or settlement and set apart as a public reservation all those certain tracts, pieces, or parcels of land lying and being situate in the State of California and within the boundaries particularly described as follows, to wit:

Beginning at the northeast corner of section thirteen (13), township five (5) south, range six (6) west, of the San Bernardino base and meridian; thence westerly along the surveyed and unsurveyed section line to the point for the southwest corner of section ten (10), said township and range; thence northerly along the surveyed and unsurveyed section line to the northwest corner of section three (3), said township and range; thence westerly along the surveyed and unsurveyed township line to the point for the northwest corner of section three (3), township five (5) south, range seven (7) west; thence southerly along the surveyed and unsurveyed section line to the southeast corner of section thirty-three (33), said township and range; thence easterly along the surveyed and unsurveyed township line to the northeast corner of township six (6) south, range seven (7) west; thence southerly to the southwest corner of township five (5) south, range six (6) west; thence easterly to the point for the quarter-section corner on the north line of section six (6), township six (6) south, range six (6) west; thence southerly on a central line to the center of section nineteen (19), said township and range; thence easterly to the quarter-section corner on the east boundary of said section nineteen (19); thence southerly on the section line to the point of intersection with the north boundary of the "Rancho Mission Viejo or La Paz;" thence in a southeasterly direction along said boundary line to the point of intersection with the township line between townships six (6) and seven (7) south; thence easterly along said township line to the southeast corner of township six (6) south, range six (6) west; thence northerly along the range line between ranges five (5) and six (6) west to the northeast corner of section thirteen (13), township five (5) south, range six (6) west, the place of beginning.

Excepting from the force and effect of this proclamation all lands which may have been prior to the date hereof embraced in any legal entry or covered by any lawful filing duly of record in the proper United States land office, or upon which any valid settlement has been made pursuant to law and the statutory period within which to make entry or filing of record has not expired, and all mining claims duly located and held according to the laws of the United States and rules and regulations not in conflict therewith.

Provided, That this exception shall not continue to apply to any particular tract of land unless the entryman, settler, or claimant continues to comply with the law under which the entry, filing, settlement, or location was made.

Warning is hereby expressly given to all persons not to enter or make settlement upon the tract of land reserved by this proclamation.

In witness whereof I have hereunto set my hand and caused the seal of the United States to be affixed.

[SEAL.] Done at the city of Washington, this 25th day of February, A. D. 1893, and of the Independence of the United States the one hundred and seventeenth.

BENJ. HARRISON.

By the President:

WILLIAM F. WHARTON,
Acting Secretary of State.

BY THE PRESIDENT OF THE UNITED STATES OF AMERICA.

A PROCLAMATION.

Whereas it is provided by section 24 of the act of Congress approved March 3, 1891, entitled "An act to repeal timber-culture laws, and for other purposes"—

That the President of the United States may from time to time set apart and reserve in any State or Territory having public land bearing forests, in any part of the public lands wholly or in part covered with timber or undergrowth, whether of commercial value or not, as public reservations; and the President shall by public proclamation declare the establishment of such reservations and the limits thereof.

And whereas the public lands in the State of California within the limits hereinafter described are in part covered with timber, and it appears that the public good would be promoted by setting apart and reserving said lands as a public reservation:

Now, therefore, I, Benjamin Harrison, President of the United States,

by virtue of the power in me vested by section 24 of the aforesaid act of Congress, do hereby make known and proclaim that there is hereby reserved from entry or settlement and set apart as a public reservation all those certain tracts, pieces, or parcels of land lying and being situate in the State of California and within the boundaries particularly described as follows, to wit:

Beginning at the northwest corner of township three (3) north, range five (5) west, San Bernardino meridian, California; thence southerly along the surveyed and unsurveyed range line between ranges five (5) and six (6) west to the northwest corner of section eighteen (18), township one (1) north, range five (5) west; thence easterly along the section line between sections seven (7) and eighteen (18) to the western boundary of the "Rancho Muscupiabe;" thence easterly, following the western and northern boundary of said rancho, to the point where said boundary intersects the section line between sections nineteen (19) and thirty (30), township one (1) north, range three (3) west; thence easterly along the section lines to the northeast corner of section twenty-five (25), said township and range; thence southerly along the range line between ranges two (2) and three (3) west to the San Bernardino base line; thence easterly along said base line to the northeast corner of section four (4), township one (1) south, range two (2) west, southerly along the unsurveyed and surveyed section lines to the northeast corner of section (16), easterly along the section lines to the northeast corner of section thirteen (13), and southerly to the southeast corner of section thirteen (13), all of said township and range; thence easterly to a point for the center of township one (1) south, range one (1) west; thence southerly to a point for the southwest corner of section thirty-four (34) in said township and range; thence easterly along the surveyed and unsurveyed township line between townships one (1) and two (2) south to the San Bernardino meridian; thence southerly along said meridian to the northeast corner of township three (3) south, range one (1) west; thence easterly through the Maronge Indian Reservation to the southeast corner of township two (2) south, range three (3) east; thence northerly along the surveyed and unsurveyed range line to the northeast corner of said township; thence easterly to a point for the southeast corner of township one (1) south, range four (4) east; thence northerly along the surveyed and unsurveyed range line between ranges four (4) and five (5) east to the northeast corner of section twenty-four (24), township three (3) north, range four (4) east; thence westerly along the surveyed and unsurveyed section lines to the southwest corner of section eighteen (18), township three (3) north, range (3) east; thence northerly along the range line between ranges two (2) and three (3) east to the northeast corner of township three (3) north, range two (2) east; thence westerly along the township line between townships three (3) and four (4) north to the northwest corner of township three (3) north, range (5) west, the place of beginning.

Excepting from the force and effect of this proclamation all lands which may have been prior to the date hereof embraced in any legal entry or covered by any lawful filing duly of record in the proper United States land office, or upon which any valid settlement has been made pursuant to law and the statutory period within which to make entry or filing of record has not expired, and all mining claims duly located and held according to the laws of the United States and rules and regulations not in conflict therewith.

Provided, That this exception shall not continue to apply to any particular tract of land unless the entryman, settler, or claimant continues to comply with the law under which the entry, filing, settlement, or location was made.

Warning is hereby expressly given to all persons not to enter or make settlement upon the tract of land reserved by this proclamation.

In witness whereof I have hereunto set my hand and caused the seal of the United States to be affixed.

[SEAL.]   Done at the city of Washington, this 25th day of February, A. D. 1893, and of the Independence of the United States the one hundred and seventeenth.

BENJ. HARRISON.

By the President:
  WILLIAM F. WHARTON,
    Acting Secretary of State.

BY THE PRESIDENT OF THE UNITED STATES OF AMERICA.

A PROCLAMATION.

Whereas public interests require that the Senate should be convened at 12 o'clock on the 4th day of March next to receive such communications as may be made by the Executive:

Now, therefore, I, Benjamin Harrison, President of the United States, do hereby proclaim and declare that an extraordinary occasion requires the Senate of the United States to convene at the Capitol, in the city of Washington, on the 4th day of March next, at 12 o'clock noon, of which all persons who shall at that time be entitled to act as members of that body are hereby required to take notice.

Given under my hand and the seal of the United States, at Washington, this 25th day of February, A. D. 1893, and of the Independence of the United States of America the one hundred and seventeenth.

[SEAL.]

BENJ. HARRISON.

By the President:
  WILLIAM F. WHARTON,
    Acting Secretary of State.

EXECUTIVE ORDERS.

AMENDMENT OF CIVIL-SERVICE RULES.

JANUARY 5, 1893.

Section 2 of Postal Rule I is hereby amended so as to read as follows:

The classification of the postal service made by the Postmaster-General under section 6 of the act of January 16, 1883, is hereby extended to all free-delivery post-offices; and hereafter whenever any post-office becomes a free-delivery office the said classification or any then existing classification made by the Postmaster-General under said section and act shall apply thereto; and the Civil Service Commission shall provide examinations to test the fitness of persons to fill vacancies in all free-delivery post-offices, and these rules shall be in force therein; but this shall not include any post-office made an experimental free-delivery office under the authority contained in the appropriation act of March 3, 1891. Every revision of the classification of any post-office under section 6 of the act of January 16, 1883, and every inclusion of a post-office within the classified postal service shall be reported to the President.

BENJ. HARRISON.

GENERAL ORDERS, NO. 4.

HEADQUARTERS OF THE ARMY,
ADJUTANT-GENERAL'S OFFICE,
Washington, January 19, 1893.

I. The following proclamation [order] has been received from the President:

EXECUTIVE MANSION,
Washington, D. C., January 18, 1893.

To the People of the United States:

The death of Rutherford B. Hayes, who was President of the United States from March 4, 1877, to March 4, 1881, at his home in Fremont, Ohio, at 11 p. m. yesterday, is an event the announcement of which will be received with very general and very sincere sorrow. His public service extended over many years and over a wide range of official duty. He was a patriotic citizen, a lover of the flag and of our free institutions, an industrious and conscientious civil officer, a soldier of dauntless courage, a loyal comrade and friend, a sympathetic and helpful neighbor, and the honored head of a happy Christian home. He has steadily grown in the public esteem, and the impartial historian will not fail to recognize the conscientiousness, the manliness, and the courage that so strongly characterized his whole public career.

As an expression of the public sorrow it is ordered that the Executive Mansion and the several Executive Departments at Washington be draped in mourning and the flags thereon placed at half-staff for a period of thirty days, and that on the day of the funeral all public business in the Departments be suspended, and that suitable military and naval honors, under the orders of the Secretaries of War and of the Navy, be rendered on that day.

Done at the city of Washington, this 18th day of January, A. D. 1893, [SEAL.] and of the Independence of the United States of America the one hundred and seventeenth.

BENJ. HARRISON.

By the President:

JOHN W. FOSTER, *Secretary of State.*

II. In compliance with the instructions of the President, on the day of the funeral, at each military post, the troops and cadets will be paraded and this order read to them, after which all labors of the day will cease.

The national flag will be displayed at half-staff.

At dawn of day thirteen guns will be fired, and afterwards at intervals of thirty minutes between the rising and setting of the sun a single gun, and at the close of the day a national salute of forty-four guns.

The officers of the Army will wear crape on the left arm and on their swords and the colors of the Battalion of Engineers, of the several regiments, and of the United States Corps of Cadets will be put in mourning for a period of six months.

The date of the funeral will be communicated to department commanders by telegraph, and by them to their subordinate commanders.

By command of Major-General Schofield:

R. WILLIAMS, *Adjutant-General.*

GENERAL ORDER NO. 406.

NAVY DEPARTMENT,
Washington, D. C., January 19, 1893.

The President of the United States announces the death of ex-President Rutherford B. Hayes in the following proclamation [order]:

[For order see preceding page.]

It is hereby directed, in pursuance of the instructions of the President, that on the day of the funeral, where this order may be received in time, otherwise on the day after its receipt, the ensign at each naval station and of each of the vessels of the United States Navy in commission be hoisted at half-mast from sunrise to sunset, and at each naval station and on board of flagships and vessels acting singly a gun be fired at intervals of every half hour from sunrise to sunset.

The officers of the Navy and Marine Corps will wear the usual badge of mourning attached to the sword hilt and on the left arm for a period of thirty days.

JAMES R. SOLEY,
Acting Secretary of the Navy.

EXECUTIVE MANSION,
Washington, January 27, 1893.

To the People of the United States:

It is my painful duty to announce to the people of the United States the death of James Gillespie Blaine, which occurred in this city to-day at 11 o'clock.

For a full generation this eminent citizen has occupied a conspicuous and influential position in the nation. His first public service was in the legislature of his State. Afterwards for fourteen years he was a member of the national House of Representatives, and was three times chosen its Speaker. In 1876 he was elected to the Senate. He resigned his seat in that body in 1881 to accept the position of Secretary of State in the Cabinet of President Garfield. After the tragic death of his chief he resigned from the Cabinet, and, devoting himself to literary work, gave to the public in his Twenty Years of Congress a most valuable and enduring contribution to our political literature. In March, 1889, he again became Secretary of State, and continued to exercise this office until June, 1892. His devotion to the public interests, his marked ability, and his exalted patriotism have won for him the gratitude and affection of his countrymen and the admiration of the world. In the varied pursuits of legislation, diplomacy, and literature his genius has added new luster to American citizenship.

As a suitable expression of the national appreciation of his great public services and of the general sorrow caused by his death, I direct that on the day of his funeral all the Departments of the executive branch of the Government at Washington be closed, and that on all public buildings throughout the United States the national flag shall be displayed at half-staff, and that for a period of thirty days the Department of State be draped in mourning.

Done at the city of Washington, this 27th day of January, A. D. 1893, and of the Independence of the United States of America the one hundred and seventeenth.

[SEAL.]

BENJ. HARRISON.

By the President:
JOHN W. FOSTER,
Secretary of State.

Grover Cleveland

March 4, 1893, to March 4, 1897

Grover Cleveland

[For portrait and biographical sketch see Vol. VIII, pp. 296–299.]

INAUGURAL ADDRESS.

MY FELLOW-CITIZENS: In obedience to the mandate of my country-men I am about to dedicate myself to their service under the sanction of a solemn oath. Deeply moved by the expression of confidence and per-sonal attachment which has called me to this service, I am sure my grati-tude can make no better return than the pledge I now give before God and these witnesses of unreserved and complete devotion to the inter-ests and welfare of those who have honored me.

I deem it fitting on this occasion, while indicating the opinions I hold concerning public questions of present importance, to also briefly refer to the existence of certain conditions and tendencies among our people which seem to menace the integrity and usefulness of their Government.

While every American citizen must contemplate with the utmost pride and enthusiasm the growth and expansion of our country, the sufficiency of our institutions to stand against the rudest shocks of violence, the wonderful thrift and enterprise of our people, and the demonstrated su-periority of our free government, it behooves us to constantly watch for every symptom of insidious infirmity that threatens our national vigor.

The strong man who in the confidence of sturdy health courts the sternest activities of life and rejoices in the hardihood of constant labor may still have lurking near his vitals the unheeded disease that dooms him to sudden collapse.

It can not be doubted that our stupendous achievements as a people and our country's robust strength have given rise to heedlessness of those laws governing our national health which we can no more evade than human life can escape the laws of God and nature.

Manifestly nothing is more vital to our supremacy as a nation and to the beneficent purposes of our Government than a sound and stable cur-rency. Its exposure to degradation should at once arouse to activity the most enlightened statesmanship, and the danger of depreciation in the purchasing power of the wages paid to toil should furnish the strongest incentive to prompt and conservative precaution.

In dealing with our present embarrassing situation as related to this subject we will be wise if we temper our confidence and faith in our national strength and resources with the frank concession that even these will not permit us to defy with impunity the inexorable laws of finance and trade. At the same time, in our efforts to adjust differences of opinion we should be free from intolerance or passion, and our judgments should be unmoved by alluring phrases and unvexed by selfish interests.

I am confident that such an approach to the subject will result in prudent and effective remedial legislation. In the meantime, so far as the executive branch of the Government can intervene, none of the powers with which it is invested will be withheld when their exercise is deemed necessary to maintain our national credit or avert financial disaster.

Closely related to the exaggerated confidence in our country's greatness which tends to a disregard of the rules of national safety, another danger confronts us not less serious. I refer to the prevalence of a popular disposition to expect from the operation of the Government especial and direct individual advantages.

The verdict of our voters which condemned the injustice of maintaining protection for protection's sake enjoins upon the people's servants the duty of exposing and destroying the brood of kindred evils which are the unwholesome progeny of paternalism. This is the bane of republican institutions and the constant peril of our government by the people. It degrades to the purposes of wily craft the plan of rule our fathers established and bequeathed to us as an object of our love and veneration. It perverts the patriotic sentiments of our countrymen and tempts them to pitiful calculation of the sordid gain to be derived from their Government's maintenance. It undermines the self-reliance of our people and substitutes in its place dependence upon governmental favoritism. It stifles the spirit of true Americanism and stupefies every ennobling trait of American citizenship.

The lessons of paternalism ought to be unlearned and the better lesson taught that while the people should patriotically and cheerfully support their Government its functions do not include the support of the people.

The acceptance of this principle leads to a refusal of bounties and subsidies, which burden the labor and thrift of a portion of our citizens to aid ill-advised or languishing enterprises in which they have no concern. It leads also to a challenge of wild and reckless pension expenditure, which overleaps the bounds of grateful recognition of patriotic service and prostitutes to vicious uses the people's prompt and generous impulse to aid those disabled in their country's defense.

Every thoughtful American must realize the importance of checking at its beginning any tendency in public or private station to regard frugality and economy as virtues which we may safely outgrow. The toleration of this idea results in the waste of the people's money by their chosen servants and encourages prodigality and extravagance in the home life of our countrymen.

Under our scheme of government the waste of public money is a crime against the citizen, and the contempt of our people for economy and frugality in their personal affairs deplorably saps the strength and sturdiness of our national character.

It is a plain dictate of honesty and good government that public expenditures should be limited by public necessity, and that this should be measured by the rules of strict economy; and it is equally clear that frugality among the people is the best guaranty of a contented and strong support of free institutions.

One mode of the misappropriation of public funds is avoided when appointments to office, instead of being the rewards of partisan activity, are awarded to those whose efficiency promises a fair return of work for the compensation paid to them. To secure the fitness and competency of appointees to office and remove from political action the demoralizing madness for spoils, civil-service reform has found a place in our public policy and laws. The benefits already gained through this instrumentality and the further usefulness it promises entitle it to the hearty support and encouragement of all who desire to see our public service well performed or who hope for the elevation of political sentiment and the purification of political methods.

The existence of immense aggregations of kindred enterprises and combinations of business interests formed for the purpose of limiting production and fixing prices is inconsistent with the fair field which ought to be open to every independent activity. Legitimate strife in business should not be superseded by an enforced concession to the demands of combinations that have the power to destroy, nor should the people to be served lose the benefit of cheapness which usually results from wholesome competition. These aggregations and combinations frequently constitute conspiracies against the interests of the people, and in all their phases they are unnatural and opposed to our American sense of fairness. To the extent that they can be reached and restrained by Federal power the General Government should relieve our citizens from their interference and exactions.

Loyalty to the principles upon which our Government rests positively demands that the equality before the law which it guarantees to every citizen should be justly and in good faith conceded in all parts of the land. The enjoyment of this right follows the badge of citizenship wherever found, and, unimpaired by race or color, it appeals for recognition to American manliness and fairness.

Our relations with the Indians located within our border impose upon us responsibilities we can not escape. Humanity and consistency require us to treat them with forbearance and in our dealings with them to honestly and considerately regard their rights and interests. Every effort should be made to lead them, through the paths of civilization and education, to self-supporting and independent citizenship. In the meantime, as the nation's wards, they should be promptly defended against the cupidity of designing men and shielded from every influence or temptation that retards their advancement.

The people of the United States have decreed that on this day the control of their Government in its legislative and executive branches shall be given to a political party pledged in the most positive terms to the accomplishment of tariff reform. They have thus determined in favor of a more just and equitable system of Federal taxation. The agents they have chosen to carry out their purposes are bound by their promises not less than by the command of their masters to devote themselves unremittingly to this service.

While there should be no surrender of principle, our task must be undertaken wisely and without heedless vindictiveness. Our mission is not punishment, but the rectification of wrong. If in lifting burdens from the daily life of our people we reduce inordinate and unequal advantages too long enjoyed, this is but a necessary incident of our return to right and justice. If we exact from unwilling minds acquiescence in the theory of an honest distribution of the fund of the governmental beneficence treasured up for all, we but insist upon a principle which underlies our free institutions. When we tear aside the delusions and misconceptions which have blinded our countrymen to their condition under vicious tariff laws, we but show them how far they have been led away from the paths of contentment and prosperity. When we proclaim that the necessity for revenue to support the Government furnishes the only justification for taxing the people, we announce a truth so plain that its denial would seem to indicate the extent to which judgment may be influenced by familiarity with perversions of the taxing power. And when we seek to reinstate the self-confidence and business enterprise of our citizens by discrediting an abject dependence upon governmental favor, we strive to stimulate those elements of American character which support the hope of American achievement.

Anxiety for the redemption of the pledges which my party has made and solicitude for the complete justification of the trust the people have reposed in us constrain me to remind those with whom I am to cooperate that we can succeed in doing the work which has been especially set before us only by the most sincere, harmonious, and disinterested effort. Even if insuperable obstacles and opposition prevent the consummation of our task, we shall hardly be excused; and if failure can be traced to our fault or neglect we may be sure the people will hold us to a swift and exacting accountability.

The oath I now take to preserve, protect, and defend the Constitution of the United States not only impressively defines the great responsibility

I assume, but suggests obedience to constitutional commands as the rule by which my official conduct must be guided. I shall to the best of my ability and within my sphere of duty preserve the Constitution by loyally protecting every grant of Federal power it contains, by defending all its restraints when attacked by impatience and restlessness, and by enforcing its limitations and reservations in favor of the States and the people.

Fully impressed with the gravity of the duties that confront me and mindful of my weakness, I should be appalled if it were my lot to bear unaided the responsibilities which await me. I am, however, saved from discouragement when I remember that I shall have the support and the counsel and cooperation of wise and patriotic men who will stand at my side in Cabinet places or will represent the people in their legislative halls.

I find also much comfort in remembering that my countrymen are just and generous and in the assurance that they will not condemn those who by sincere devotion to their service deserve their forbearance and approval.

Above all, I know there is a Supreme Being who rules the affairs of men and whose goodness and mercy have always followed the American people, and I know He will not turn from us now if we humbly and reverently seek His powerful aid.

MARCH 4, 1893.

SPECIAL MESSAGES.

EXECUTIVE MANSION,
Washington, March 9, 1893.

To the Senate of the United States:

I transmit herewith a report submitted by the Secretary of State in compliance with the resolution of the Senate of the 3d instant, calling for information relating to the capture and imprisonment of Captain Pharos B. Brubaker by Honduras officials.

GROVER CLEVELAND.

EXECUTIVE MANSION,
Washington, March 9, 1893.

To the Senate of the United States:

For the purpose of reexamination I withdraw the treaty of annexation between the United States and the Provisional Government of the Hawaiian Islands, now pending in the Senate, which was signed February 14, 1893, and transmitted to the Senate on the 15th of the same month, and I therefore request that said treaty be returned to me.

GROVER CLEVELAND.

PROCLAMATIONS.

BY THE PRESIDENT OF THE UNITED STATES OF AMERICA.

A PROCLAMATICN.

The following provisions of the laws of the United States are hereby published for the information of all concerned:

Section 1956, Revised Statutes, chapter 3, Title XXIII, enacts that—

No person shall kill any otter, mink, marten, sable, or fur seal, or other fur-bearing animal within the limits of Alaska Territory or in the waters thereof; and every person guilty thereof shall for each offense be fined not less than $200 nor more than $1,000, or imprisoned not more than six months, or both; and all vessels, their tackle, apparel, furniture, and cargo, found engaged in violation of this section shall be forfeited; but the Secretary of the Treasury shall have power to authorize the killing of any such mink, marten, sable, or other fur-bearing animal, except fur seals, under such regulations as he may prescribe; and it shall be the duty of the Secretary to prevent the killing of any fur seal and to provide for the execution of the provisions of this section until it is otherwise provided by law, nor shall he grant any special privileges under this section.

Section 3 of the act entitled "An act to provide for the protection of the salmon fisheries of Alaska," approved March 2, 1889, provides that—

SEC. 3. That section 1956 of the Revised Statutes of the United States is hereby declared to include and apply to all the dominion of the United States in the waters of Bering Sea; and it shall be the duty of the President at a timely season in each year to issue his proclamation, and cause the same to be published for one month in at least one newspaper (if any such there be) published at each United States port of entry on the Pacific coast, warning all persons against entering said waters for the purpose of violating the provisions of said section; and he shall also cause one or more vessels of the United States to diligently cruise said waters and arrest all persons and seize all vessels found to be or to have been engaged in any violation of the laws of the United States therein.

Articles I, II, and III of a convention between the United States of America and Great Britain for the renewal of the existing *modus vivendi* in Bering Sea, concluded April 18, 1892, are published for the same purpose:

ARTICLE I. Her Majesty's Government will prohibit during the pendency of the arbitration seal killing in that part of Bering Sea lying eastward of the line of demarcation described in Article No. I of the treaty of 1867 between the United States and Russia, and will promptly use its best efforts to insure the observance of this prohibition by British subjects and vessels.

ART. II. The United States Government will prohibit seal killing for the same period in the same part of Bering Sea and on the shores and islands thereof the property of the United States (in excess of 7,500 to be taken on the islands for the subsistence of the natives), and will promptly use its best efforts to insure the observance of this prohibition by United States citizens and vessels.

ART. III. Every vessel or person offending against this prohibition in the said waters of Bering Sea outside of the ordinary territorial limits of the United States may be seized and detained by the naval or other duly commissioned officers of either of the high contracting parties, but they shall be handed over as soon as practicable to the authorities of the nation to which they respectively belong, who alone shall have jurisdiction to try the offense and impose the penalties for the same. The witnesses and proof necessary to establish the offense shall also be sent with them.

Now, therefore, I, Grover Cleveland, President of the United States, hereby warn all persons against entering the waters of Bering Sea within the dominion of the United States for the purpose of violating the provisions of said section 1956 of the Revised Statutes and of the said articles of said convention, and I hereby proclaim that all persons found to be or to have been engaged in any violation of the laws of the United States or of the provisions of said convention in said waters will be arrested, proceeded against, and punished as above provided.

In testimony whereof I have hereunto set my hand and caused the seal of the United States to be affixed.

[SEAL.]   Done at the city of Washington, this 8th day of April, 1893, and of the Independence of the United States the one hundred and seventeenth.

                 GROVER CLEVELAND.

By the President:

W. Q. GRESHAM, *Secretary of State.*

BY THE PRESIDENT OF THE UNITED STATES OF AMERICA.

A PROCLAMATION.

Whereas it is provided by section 13 of the act of Congress of March 3, 1891, entitled "An act to amend Title LX, chapter 3, of the Revised Statutes of the United States, relating to copyrights," that said act "shall only apply to a citizen or subject of a foreign state or nation when such foreign state or nation permits to citizens of the United States of America the benefit of copyright on substantially the same basis as its own citizens, or when such foreign state or nation is a party to an international agreement which provides for reciprocity in the granting of copyright, by the terms of which agreement the United States of America may at its pleasure become a party to such agreement;" and

Whereas it is also provided by said section that "the existence of either of the conditions aforesaid shall be determined by the President of the United States by proclamation made from time to time as the purposes of this act may require;" and

Whereas satisfactory official assurances have been given that in Denmark the law permits to citizens of the United States the benefit of copyright on substantially the same basis as to the subjects of Denmark:

Now, therefore, I, Grover Cleveland, President of the United States of America, do declare and proclaim that the first of the conditions specified in section 13 of the act of March 3, 1891, now exists and is fulfilled in respect to the subjects of Denmark.

In testimony whereof I have hereunto set my hand and caused the seal
of the United States to be affixed.

[SEAL.]   Done at the city of Washington, this 8th day of May, 1893,
and of the Independence of the United States the one hundred
and seventeenth.

GROVER CLEVELAND.

By the President:

W. Q. GRESHAM, *Secretary of State.*

EXECUTIVE MANSION,
Washington, D. C., June 30, 1893.

Whereas the distrust and apprehension concerning the financial situation which pervade all business circles have already caused great loss and
damage to our people and threaten to cripple our merchants, stop the
wheels of manufacture, bring distress and privation to our farmers, and
withhold from our workingmen the wage of labor; and

Whereas the present perilous condition is largely the result of a financial policy which the executive branch of the Government finds embodied
in unwise laws, which must be executed until repealed by Congress:

Now, therefore, I, Grover Cleveland, President of the United States, in
performance of a constitutional duty, do by this proclamation declare that
an extraordinary occasion requires the convening of both Houses of the
Congress of the United States at the Capitol, in the city of Washington,
on the 7th day of August next, at 12 o'clock noon, to the end that the
people may be relieved through legislation from present and impending
danger and distress.

All those entitled to act as members of the Fifty-third Congress are
required to take notice of this proclamation and attend at the time and
place above stated.

Given under my hand and the seal of the United States, at the city of
Washington, on the 30th day of June, A. D. 1893, and of the
[SEAL.]   Independence of the United States the one hundred and seven-
teenth.

GROVER CLEVELAND.

By the President:

ALVEY A. ADEE, *Acting Secretary of State.*

BY THE PRESIDENT OF THE UNITED STATES OF AMERICA.

A PROCLAMATION.

Whereas an act of Congress amendatory of an act in relation to aiding
vessels wrecked or disabled in the waters conterminous to the United
States and the Dominion of Canada was approved May 24, 1890, the said
act being in the following words:

*Be it enacted by the Senate and House of Representatives of the United States of
America in Congress assembled,* That an act entitled "An act to aid vessels wrecked
or disabled in the waters conterminous to the United States and the Dominion of

Canada," approved June 19, 1878, be, and the same is hereby, amended so that the same will read as follows:

"That Canadian vessels and wrecking appurtenance may render aid and assistance to Canadian or other vessels and property wrecked, disabled, or in distress in the waters of the United States contiguous to the Dominion of Canada: *Provided*, That this act shall not take effect until proclamation by the President of the United States that the privilege of aiding American or other vessels and property wrecked, disabled, or in distress in Canadian waters contiguous to the United States has been extended by the government of the Dominion of Canada to American vessels and wrecking appliances of all descriptions. This act shall be construed to apply to the Welland Canal, the canal and improvement of the waters between Lake Erie and Lake Huron, and to the waters of the St. Marys River and Canal: *And provided further*, That this act shall cease to be in force from and after the date of the proclamation of the President of the United States to the effect that said reciprocal privilege has been withdrawn, revoked, or rendered inoperative by the said government of the Dominion of Canada."

And whereas an act of Congress making appropriation for the legislative, executive, and judicial expenses of the Government for the fiscal year ending June 30, 1894, and for other purposes, approved March 3, 1893, further amended the act of May 24, 1890, as follows:

That an act approved May 24, 1890, entitled "An act to amend an act entitled 'An act to aid vessels wrecked or disabled in the waters conterminous to the United States and the Dominion of Canada,' approved June 19, 1878," be, and is hereby, amended by striking out the words "the Welland Canal."

And whereas by an order in council dated May 17, 1893, the government of the Dominion of Canada has proclaimed an act entitled "An act respecting aid by United States wreckers in Canadian waters" to take effect June 1, 1893, said act reading as follows:

Her Majesty, by and with the advice and consent of the senate and house of commons of Canada, enacts as follows:

1. United States vessels and wrecking appliances may salve any property wrecked and may render aid and assistance to any vessels wrecked, disabled, or in distress in the waters of Canada contiguous to the United States.

2. Aid and assistance include all necessary towing incident thereto.

3. Nothing in the customs or coasting laws of Canada shall restrict the salving operations of such vessels or wrecking appliances.

4. This act shall come into force from and after a date to be named in a proclamation by the Governor-General, which proclamation may be issued when the Governor in council is advised that the privilege of salving any property wrecked or of aiding any vessels wrecked, disabled, or in distress in United States waters contiguous to Canada will be extended to Canadian vessels and wrecking appliances to the extent to which such privilege is granted by this act to United States vessels and wrecking appliances.

5. This act shall cease to be in force from and after a date to be named in a proclamation to be issued by the Governor-General to the effect that the said reciprocal privilege has been withdrawn, revoked, or rendered inoperative with respect to Canadian vessels or wrecking appliances in United States waters contiguous to Canada.

And whereas said proclamation of the Governor-General of Canada was communicated to this Government by Her Britannic Majesty's ambassador on the 2d day of June last:

Now, therefore, being thus satisfied that the privilege of aiding American or other vessels and property wrecked, disabled, or in distress in

Canadian waters contiguous to the United States has been extended by the government of the Dominion of Canada to American vessels and wrecking appliances of all descriptions, I, Grover Cleveland, President of the United States of America, in virtue of the authority conferred upon me by the aforesaid act of Congress approved May 24, 1890, do proclaim that the condition specified in the legislation of Congress aforesaid now exists and is fulfilled, and that the provisions of said act of May 24, 1890, whereby Canadian vessels and wrecking appliances may render aid and assistance to Canadian and other vessels and property wrecked, disabled, or in distress in the waters of the United States contiguous to the Dominion of Canada, including the canal and improvement of the waters between Lake Erie and Lake Huron and the waters of the St. Marys River and Canal, are now in full force and effect.

In testimony whereof I have hereunto set my hand and caused the seal of the United States of America to be hereunto affixed.

[SEAL.]   Done at the city of Washington, this 17th day of July, A. D. 1893, and of the Independence of the United States the one hundred and eighteenth.

GROVER CLEVELAND.

By the President:

W. Q. GRESHAM, *Secretary of State.*

BY THE PRESIDENT OF THE UNITED STATES OF AMERICA.

A PROCLAMATION.

Whereas it is provided by section 13 of the act of Congress of March 3, 1891, entitled "An act to amend Title LX, chapter 3, of the Revised Statutes of the United States, relating to copyrights," that said act "shall only apply to a citizen or subject of a foreign state or nation when such foreign state or nation permits to citizens of the United States of America the benefit of copyright on substantially the same basis as its own citizens, or when such foreign state or nation is a party to an international agreement which provides for reciprocity in the granting of copyright, by the terms of which agreement the United States of America may at its pleasure become a party to such agreement;" and

Whereas it is also provided by said section that "the existence of either of the conditions aforesaid shall be determined by the President of the United States by proclamation made from time to time as the purposes of this act may require;" and

Whereas satisfactory official assurances have been given that in Portugal the law permits to citizens of the United States the benefit of copyright on substantially the same basis as to the subjects of Portugal:

Now, therefore, I, Grover Cleveland, President of the United States of America, do declare and proclaim that the first of the conditions specified in section 13 of the act of March 3, 1891, now exists and is fulfilled in respect to the subjects of Portugal.

In testimony whereof I have hereunto set my hand and caused the seal of the United States to be affixed.

[SEAL.] Done at the city of Washington, this 20th day of July, A. D. 1893, and of the Independence of the United States the one hundred and eighteenth.

GROVER CLEVELAND.

By the President:

W. Q. GRESHAM, *Secretary of State.*

EXECUTIVE ORDERS.

AMENDMENT OF CIVIL-SERVICE RULES.

Departmental Rule VII is hereby amended by adding thereto the following section:

8. The First Comptroller of the Treasury having advised the Secretary of the Treasury that under the operation of section 5 of the legislative, executive, and judicial appropriation act making appropriations for the fiscal year ending June 30, 1894, the employment of substitutes in the departmental service must cease from and after July 1, 1893, it is hereby ordered, in view of the fact that the substitutes now employed were appointed by regular certification under section 7 of this rule, that such of said substitutes as shall not be appointed to regular places before the employment of substitutes shall cease shall be eligible for appointment to regular places by reinstatement under the provisions of Departmental Rule X, in the order of their employment as substitutes as provided in said section 7, notwithstanding the prohibition contained in the second proviso of said section; and said substitutes shall have preference for appointment in the manner herein provided over all other eligibles.

This section shall become inoperative and cease to be a part of the civil-service rules when all of the substitutes now employed in the several Departments shall have been appointed as herein provided or shall have ceased to be eligible for appointment by reason of the expiration of the time within which a reinstatement can be made under Rule X.

Approved, April 12, 1893. GROVER CLEVELAND.

EXECUTIVE MANSION, *May 8, 1893.*

It has become apparent after two months' experience that the rules heretofore promulgated regulating interviews with the President have wholly failed in their operation. The time which under these rules was set apart for the reception of Senators and Representatives has been almost entirely spent in listening to applications for office, which have been bewildering in volume, perplexing and exhausting in their iteration, and impossible of remembrance.

A due regard for public duty, which must be neglected if present conditions continue, and an observance of the limitations placed upon human endurance oblige me to decline from and after this date all personal interviews with those seeking appointments to office, except as I on my own motion may especially invite them. The same considerations make it impossible for me to receive those who merely desire to pay their respects except on the days and during the hours especially designated for that purpose.

I earnestly request Senators and Representatives to aid me in securing for them uninterrupted interviews by declining to introduce their constituents and friends when visiting the Executive Mansion during the hours designated for their reception. Applicants for office will only prejudice their prospects by repeated importunity and by remaining in Washington to await results.

GROVER CLEVELAND.

EXECUTIVE MANSION, *May 26, 1893.*

It is hereby ordered, That the several Executive Departments and the Government Printing Office be closed on Tuesday, the 30th instant, to enable the employees to participate in the decoration of the graves of the soldiers and sailors who fell in the defense of the Union during the War of the Rebellion.

GROVER CLEVELAND.

AMENDMENTS OF CIVIL-SERVICE RULES.

Special Departmental Rule No. 1 is hereby amended as follows: Include among the places excepted from examination therein the following:

6. In the Department of Agriculture:

In the office of the Secretary: The assistant chiefs of the following divisions: Of economic ornithology and mammalogy, of pomology, of microscopy, of vegetable pathology, of records and editing, and one property clerk.

In the Weather Bureau: The assistant chief of the Bureau, the three professors of meteorology of highest grade, executive officer, superintendent of telegraph lines, and one property clerk.

In the United States Commission of Fish and Fisheries the following: Scientific or professional experts to be temporarily employed in investigations authorized by Congress, but not to include any persons regularly employed in that Commission nor any person whose duties are not scientific or professional and who are not experts in the particular line of scientific inquiry in which they are to be employed.

EXECUTIVE MANSION, *June 6, 1893.*

The foregoing amendments are hereby approved.

GROVER CLEVELAND.

AMENDMENTS OF CIVIL-SERVICE RULES.

Postal Rule No. 2 is hereby amended as follows:

Strike out all of section 1 except the last paragraph, relating to noncompetitive examinations, and insert in lieu thereof the following:

1. To test the fitness for admission to the classified postal service one or more examinations shall be provided, as the Commission may determine, which shall not

include more than the following subjects: Orthography, copying, penmanship, arithmetic (fundamental rules, fractions, and percentage), elements of the geography of the United States, local delivery, reading addresses, physical tests: *Provided*, That when special examinations are needed to test fitness for any place requiring special or technical knowledge or skill the examination shall include, in addition to the special subjects required, such of the subjects of the regular examination as the Commission may determine.

Strike out section 2 and insert in lieu thereof the following:

No person shall be examined for the position of letter carrier if under 21 or over 40 years of age, and no person shall be examined for any other position in the classified postal service if under 18 years of age.

EXECUTIVE MANSION, *June 6, 1893.*
The foregoing amendments are hereby approved.

GROVER CLEVELAND.

EXECUTIVE MANSION,
Washington, June 16, 1893.

In accordance with section 16 of the act of Congress approved April 25, 1890, and entitled "An act to provide for celebrating the four hundredth anniversary of the discovery of America by Christopher Columbus by holding an international exhibition of arts, industries, manufactures, and the product of the soil, mine, and sea in the city of Chicago, in the State of Illinois," the designations of the following-named persons as members of the board of control and management of the Government exhibit at the World's Columbian Exhibition are hereby approved:

W. W. Rockhill, chief clerk of the Department of State, to represent that Department, *vice* William E. Curtis.

Lieutenant-Commander E. D. Taussig, United States Navy, to represent the Navy Department, *vice* Captain R. W. Meade, United States Navy.

Frank W. Clark, chemist, United States Geological Survey, to represent the Department of the Interior, *vice* Horace A. Taylor.

GROVER CLEVELAND.

SPECIAL SESSION MESSAGE.

EXECUTIVE MANSION, *August 8, 1893.*
To the Congress of the United States:

The existence of an alarming and extraordinary business situation, involving the welfare and prosperity of all our people, has constrained me to call together in extra session the people's representatives in Congress, to the end that through a wise and patriotic exercise of the legislative duty, with which they solely are charged, present evils may be mitigated and dangers threatening the future may be averted.

Our unfortunate financial plight is not the result of untoward events nor of conditions related to our natural resources, nor is it traceable to any of the afflictions which frequently check national growth and prosperity. With plenteous crops, with abundant promise of remunerative production and manufacture, with unusual invitation to safe investment, and with satisfactory assurance to business enterprise, suddenly financial distrust and fear have sprung up on every side. Numerous moneyed institutions have suspended because abundant assets were not immediately available to meet the demands of frightened depositors. Surviving corporations and individuals are content to keep in hand the money they are usually anxious to loan, and those engaged in legitimate business are surprised to find that the securities they offer for loans, though heretofore satisfactory, are no longer accepted. Values supposed to be fixed are fast becoming conjectural, and loss and failure have invaded every branch of business.

I believe these things are principally chargeable to Congressional legislation touching the purchase and coinage of silver by the General Government.

This legislation is embodied in a statute passed on the 14th day of July, 1890, which was the culmination of much agitation on the subject involved, and which may be considered a truce, after a long struggle, between the advocates of free silver coinage and those intending to be more conservative.

Undoubtedly the monthly purchases by the Government of 4,500,000 ounces of silver, enforced under that statute, were regarded by those interested in silver production as a certain guaranty of its increase in price. The result, however, has been entirely different, for immediately following a spasmodic and slight rise the price of silver began to fall after the passage of the act, and has since reached the lowest point ever known. This disappointing result has led to renewed and persistent effort in the direction of free silver coinage.

Meanwhile not only are the evil effects of the operation of the present law constantly accumulating, but the result to which its execution must inevitably lead is becoming palpable to all who give the least heed to financial subjects.

This law provides that in payment for the 4,500,000 ounces of silver bullion which the Secretary of the Treasury is commanded to purchase monthly there shall be issued Treasury notes redeemable on demand in gold or silver coin, at the discretion of the Secretary of the Treasury, and that said notes may be reissued. It is, however, declared in the act to be "the established policy of the United States to maintain the two metals on a parity with each other upon the present legal ratio or such ratio as may be provided by law." This declaration so controls the action of the Secretary of the Treasury as to prevent his exercising the discretion nominally vested in him if by such action the parity between gold and silver may be disturbed. Manifestly a refusal by the Secretary to pay these Treasury notes in gold if demanded would necessarily result in their discredit and depreciation as obligations payable only in silver, and would destroy the parity between the two metals by establishing a discrimination in favor of gold.

Up to the 15th day of July, 1893, these notes had been issued in payment of silver-bullion purchases to the amount of more than $147,000,000. While all but a very small quantity of this bullion remains uncoined and without usefulness in the Treasury, many of the notes given in its purchase have been paid in gold. This is illustrated by the statement that between the 1st day of May, 1892, and the 15th day of July, 1893, the notes of this kind issued in payment for silver bullion amounted to a little more than $54,000,000, and that during the same period about $49,-000,000 were paid by the Treasury in gold for the redemption of such notes.

The policy necessarily adopted of paying these notes in gold has not spared the gold reserve of $100,000,000 long ago set aside by the Government for the redemption of other notes, for this fund has already been subjected to the payment of new obligations amounting to about $150,000,000 on account of silver purchases, and has as a consequence for the first time since its creation been encroached upon.

We have thus made the depletion of our gold easy and have tempted other and more appreciative nations to add it to their stock. That the opportunity we have offered has not been neglected is shown by the large amounts of gold which have been recently drawn from our Treasury and exported to increase the financial strength of foreign nations. The excess of exports of gold over its imports for the year ending June 30, 1893, amounted to more than $87,500,000.

Between the 1st day of July, 1890, and the 15th day of July, 1893, the gold coin and bullion in our Treasury decreased more than $132,000,000, while during the same period the silver coin and bullion in the Treasury increased more than $147,000,000. Unless Government bonds are to be constantly issued and sold to replenish our exhausted gold, only to be again exhausted, it is apparent that the operation of the silver-purchase law now in force leads in the direction of the entire substitution of silver for the gold in the Government Treasury, and that this must be followed by the payment of all Government obligations in depreciated silver.

At this stage gold and silver must part company and the Government must fail in its established policy to maintain the two metals on a parity with each other. Given over to the exclusive use of a currency greatly depreciated according to the standard of the commercial world, we could no longer claim a place among nations of the first class, nor could our Government claim a performance of its obligation, so far as such an obligation has been imposed upon it, to provide for the use of the people the best and safest money.

If, as many of its friends claim, silver ought to occupy a larger place in our currency and the currency of the world through general international cooperation and agreement, it is obvious that the United States will not be in a position to gain a hearing in favor of such an arrangement so long as we are willing to continue our attempt to accomplish the result single-handed.

The knowledge in business circles among our own people that our Government can not make its fiat equivalent to intrinsic value nor keep inferior money on a parity with superior money by its own independent efforts has resulted in such a lack of confidence at home in the stability of currency values that capital refuses its aid to new enterprises, while millions are actually withdrawn from the channels of trade and commerce to become idle and unproductive in the hands of timid owners. Foreign investors, equally alert, not only decline to purchase American securities, but make haste to sacrifice those which they already have.

It does not meet the situation to say that apprehension in regard to the future of our finances is groundless and that there is no reason for lack of confidence in the purposes or power of the Government in the premises. The very existence of this apprehension and lack of confidence, however caused, is a menace which ought not for a moment to be disregarded. Possibly, if the undertaking we have in hand were the maintenance of a specific known quantity of silver at a parity with gold, our ability to do so might be estimated and gauged, and perhaps, in view of our unparalleled growth and resources, might be favorably passed upon. But when our avowed endeavor is to maintain such parity in regard to an amount of silver increasing at the rate of $50,000,000 yearly, with no fixed termination to such increase, it can hardly be said that a problem is presented whose solution is free from doubt.

The people of the United States are entitled to a sound and stable currency and to money recognized as such on every exchange and in every market of the world. Their Government has no right to injure them by financial experiments opposed to the policy and practice of other civilized states, nor is it justified in permitting an exaggerated and unreasonable reliance on our national strength and ability to jeopardize the soundness of the people's money.

This matter rises above the plane of party politics. It vitally concerns every business and calling and enters every household in the land. There is one important aspect of the subject which especially should never be overlooked. At times like the present, when the evils of unsound finance threaten us, the speculator may anticipate a harvest gathered from the misfortune of others, the capitalist may protect himself by hoarding or may even find profit in the fluctuations of values; but the wage earner—the first to be injured by a depreciated currency and the last to receive the benefit of its correction—is practically defenseless. He relies for work upon the ventures of confident and contented capital. This failing him, his condition is without alleviation, for he can neither prey on the misfortunes of others nor hoard his labor. One of the greatest statesmen our country has known, speaking more than fifty years ago, when a derangement of the currency had caused commercial distress, said:

The very man of all others who has the deepest interest in a sound currency and who suffers most by mischievous legislation in money matters is the man who earns his daily bread by his daily toil.

These words are as pertinent now as on the day they were uttered, and ought to impressively remind us that a failure in the discharge of our duty at this time must especially injure those of our countrymen who labor, and who because of their number and condition are entitled to the most watchful care of their Government.

It is of the utmost importance that such relief as Congress can afford in the existing situation be afforded at once. The maxim "He gives twice who gives quickly" is directly applicable. It may be true that the embarrassments from which the business of the country is suffering arise as much from evils apprehended as from those actually existing. We may hope, too, that calm counsels will prevail, and that neither the capitalists nor the wage earners will give way to unreasoning panic and sacrifice their property or their interests under the influence of exaggerated fears. Nevertheless, every day's delay in removing one of the plain and principal causes of the present state of things enlarges the mischief already done and increases the responsibility of the Government for its existence. Whatever else the people have a right to expect from Congress, they may certainly demand that legislation condemned by the ordeal of three years' disastrous experience shall be removed from the statute books as soon as their representatives can legitimately deal with it.

It was my purpose to summon Congress in special session early in the coming September, that we might enter promptly upon the work of tariff reform, which the true interests of the country clearly demand, which so large a majority of the people, as shown by their suffrages, desire and expect, and to the accomplishment of which every effort of the present Administration is pledged. But while tariff reform has lost nothing of its immediate and permanent importance and must in the near future engage the attention of Congress, it has seemed to me that the financial condition of the country should at once and before all other subjects be considered by your honorable body.

I earnestly recommend the prompt repeal of the provisions of the act passed July 14, 1890, authorizing the purchase of silver bullion, and that other legislative action may put beyond all doubt or mistake the intention and the ability of the Government to fulfill its pecuniary obligations in money universally recognized by all civilized countries.

GROVER CLEVELAND.

SPECIAL MESSAGE.

EXECUTIVE MANSION,
Washington, October 18, 1893.

To the Senate of the United States:

In response to the resolution of the Senate of the 10th instant, concerning the attitude of the Government of China with regard to an extension of the time for the registration of Chinese laborers in the United States under the act of May 5, 1892, I transmit a report of the Secretary of State on the subject.

GROVER CLEVELAND.

PROCLAMATIONS.

BY THE PRESIDENT OF THE UNITED STATES OF AMERICA.

A PROCLAMATION.

Whereas, pursuant to section 10 of the act of Congress approved March 3, 1893, entitled "An act making appropriations for current and contingent expenses and fulfilling treaty stipulations with Indian tribes for fiscal year ending June 30, 1894," the Cherokee Nation of Indians, by a written agreement made on the 17th day of May, 1893, has ratified the agreement for the cession of certain lands hereinafter described, as amended by said act of March 3, 1893, and thereby ceded, conveyed, transferred, relinquished, and surrendered all its title, claim, and interest of every kind and character in and to that part of the Indian Territory bounded on the west by the one hundredth degree (100°) of west longitude, on the north by the State of Kansas, on the east by the ninety-sixth degree (96°) of west longitude, and on the south by the Creek Nation, the Territory of Oklahoma, and the Cheyenne and Arapahoe Reservation created or defined by Executive order dated August 10, 1869: *Provided,* That any citizen of the Cherokee Nation who prior to the 1st day of November, 1891, was a *bona fide* resident upon and, further, had, as a farmer and for farming purposes, made permanent and valuable improvements upon any part of the land so ceded, and who has not disposed of the same, but desires to occupy the particular lands so improved as a homestead and for farming purposes, shall have the right to select one-eighth of a section of land, to conform, however, to the United States surveys; such selection to embrace, as far as the above limitation will admit, such improvements; the wife and children of any such citizen shall have the same right of selection that is above given to the citizen, and they shall have the preference in making selections to take any lands improved by the husband and father that he can not take until all of his improved land shall be taken; and that any citizen of the Cherokee Nation not a resident within the land so ceded who prior to the 1st day of November, 1891, had for farming purposes made valuable and permanent improvements upon any of the land so ceded shall have the right to select one-eighth of a section of land, to conform to the United States surveys; such selection to embrace, as far as the above limitation will admit, such improvements; but the allotments so provided for shall not exceed seventy (70) in number and the land allotted shall not exceed five thousand and six hundred (5,600) acres; and such allotments shall be made and confirmed under such rules and regulations as shall be prescribed by the Secretary of the Interior, and when so made and confirmed shall be conveyed to the allottees respectively by the United States in fee simple; and from the price to be paid to the Cherokee Nation for the cession so made there shall be deducted the sum of one dollar and forty cents ($1.40) for each acre so taken in allotment: *And provided,* That D. W. Bushyhead having made permanent or valuable improvements prior to the 1st day of November, 1891, on the lands so ceded, he may select a quarter section of the lands ceded, whether reserved or otherwise, prior to the opening of said lands to public settlement, but he shall be required to pay for such selection at the same rate per acre as other settlers, into the Treasury of the United States, in such manner as the Secretary of the Interior shall direct; and

Whereas it is provided in section 10 of the aforesaid act of Congress approved March 3, 1893, that—

Said lands, except the portion to be allotted as provided in said agreement, shall, upon the payment of the sum of $295,736, herein appropriated, to be immediately paid, become and be taken to be and treated as a part of the public domain; but in any opening of the same to settlement sections 16 and 36 in each township, whether surveyed or unsurveyed, shall be, and are hereby, reserved for the use and benefit of the public schools to be established within the limits of such lands, under such conditions and regulations as may be hereafter enacted by Congress. * * *

Sections 13, 14, 15, 16, 21, 22, 23, 24, 25, 26, 27, 28, and the east half of sections 17, 20, and 29, all in township No. 29 north of range No. 2 east of the Indian meridian, the same being lands reserved by Executive order dated July 12, 1884, for use of and in connection with the Chilocco Indian Industrial School, in the Indian Territory, shall not be subject to public settlement, but shall until the further action of Congress continue to be reserved for the purposes for which they were set apart in the said Executive order; and the President of the United States, in any order or proclamation which he shall make for the opening of the lands for settlement, may make such other reservations of lands for public purposes as he may deem wise and desirable.

The President of the United States is hereby authorized, at any time within six months after the approval of this act and the acceptance of the same by the Cherokee Nation as herein provided, by proclamation, to open to settlement any or all of the lands not allotted or reserved in the manner provided in section 13 of the act of Congress approved March 2, 1889, entitled "An act making appropriations for the current and contingent expenses of the Indian Department and for fulfilling treaty stipulations with various Indian tribes for the year ending June 30, 1890, and for other purposes" (25 U. S. Statutes at Large, p. 1005); and also subject to the provisions of the act of Congress approved May 2, 1890, entitled "An act to provide a temporary government for the Territory of Oklahoma, to enlarge the jurisdiction of the United States court in the Indian Territory, and for other purposes;" also subject to the second proviso of section 17, the whole of section 18, of the act of March 3, 1891, entitled "An act making appropriations for the current expenses of the Indian Department and for fulfilling treaty stipulations with various Indian tribes for the year ending June 30, 1892, and for other purposes;" except as to so much of said acts and sections as may conflict with the provisions of this act. Each settler on the lands so to be opened to settlement as aforesaid shall before receiving a patent for his homestead pay to the United States for the lands so taken by him, in addition to the fees provided by law, the sum of $2.50 per acre for any land east of $97\frac{1}{2}°$ west longitude, the sum of $1.50 per acre for any land between $97\frac{1}{2}°$ west longitude and $98\frac{1}{2}°$ west longitude, and the sum of $1 per acre for any land west of $98\frac{1}{2}°$ west longitude, and shall also pay interest upon the amount so to be paid for said land from the date of entry to the date of final payment therefor at the rate of 4 per cent per annum.

No person shall be permitted to occupy or enter upon any of the lands herein referred to except in the manner prescribed by the proclamation of the President opening the same to settlement, and any person otherwise occupying or entering upon any of said lands shall forfeit all right to acquire any of said lands. The Secretary of the Interior shall, under the direction of the President, prescribe rules and regulations, not inconsistent with this act, for the occupation and settlement of said lands, to be incorporated in the proclamation of the President, which shall be issued at least twenty days before the time fixed for the opening of said lands.

And whereas by a written agreement made on the 21st day of October, 1891, the Tonkawa tribe of Indians, in the Territory of Oklahoma, ceded, conveyed, and forever relinquished to the United States all their right, title, claim, and interest of every kind and character in and to the lands particularly described in Article I of the agreement: *Provided*, That the allotments of land to said Tonkawa tribe of Indians theretofore made or to be made under said agreement and the provisions of the general allotment act approved February 8, 1887, and an act amendatory thereof, approved February 28, 1891, shall be confirmed: *And provided*, That in all cases where the allottee has died since land has been set off and scheduled to such person the law of descent and partition in force in Oklahoma Territory shall apply thereto, any existing law to the contrary notwithstanding; and

Whereas by a certain other agreement with the Pawnee tribe of Indians, in said Territory, made on the 23d day of November, 1892, said tribe ceded, conveyed, released, relinquished, and surrendered to the United States all its title, claim, and interest of every kind and character in and to the lands particularly described in Article I of the agreement: *Provided*, That the allotments made or to be made to said Indians in the manner and subject to the conditions contained in said agreement shall be confirmed; and

Whereas it is provided in section 13 of the act of Congress accepting, ratifying, and confirming said agreements with the Tonkawa Indians and the Pawnee Indians, specified in sections 11 and 12 of the same act, approved March 3, 1893, entitled "An act making appropriations for current and contingent expenses and fulfilling treaty stipulations with Indian tribes for fiscal year ending June 30, 1894 ''—

That the lands acquired by the agreements specified in the two preceding sections are hereby declared to be a part of the public domain. Sections 16 and 36 in each township, whether surveyed or unsurveyed, are hereby reserved from settlement for the use and benefit of public schools, as provided in section 10 relating to lands acquired from the Cherokee Nation of Indians; and the lands so acquired by the agreements specified in the two preceding sections not so reserved shall be opened to settlement by proclamation of the President at the same time and in the manner and subject to the same conditions and regulations provided in section 10 relating to the opening of the lands acquired from the Cherokee Nation of Indians; and each settler on the lands so to be opened as aforesaid shall before receiving a patent for his homestead pay to the United States for the lands so taken by him, in addition to the fees provided by law, the sum of $2.50 per acre, and shall also pay interest upon the amount so to be paid for said land from the date of entry to the date of final payment at the rate of 4 per cent per annum.

And whereas the thirteenth section of the act approved March 2, 1889, the act approved May 2, 1890, and the second proviso of section 17 and the whole of section 18 of the act approved March 3, 1891, are referred to in the tenth section of the act approved March 3, 1893, and thereby made applicable in the disposal of the lands in the Cherokee Outlet hereinbefore mentioned, the provisions of which acts, so far as they affect the opening to settlement and the disposal of said lands, are more particularly set forth hereinafter in connection with the rules and regulations prescribed by the Secretary of the Interior for the occupation and settlement of the lands hereby opened according to said tenth section; and

Whereas the lands acquired by the three several agreements hereinbefore mentioned have been divided into counties by the Secretary of the Interior, as required by said last-mentioned act of Congress before the same shall be opened to settlement, and lands have been reserved for county-seat purposes, to be entered under sections 2387 and 2388 of the Revised Statutes of the United States, as therein required, as follows, to wit:

For County K, the southeast quarter of section 23 and the northeast quarter of section 26, township 28 north, range 2 east of the Indian meridian, excepting 4 acres reserved for the site of a court-house, to be designated by lot and block upon the official plat of survey of said reservation for county-seat purposes hereafter to be issued by the Commissioner of the General Land Office; said reservation to be additional to the reservations for parks, schools, and other public purposes required to be made by section 22 of the act of May 2, 1890.

For County L, the southwest quarter of section 1 and the southeast quarter of section 2, township 25 north, range 6 west of the Indian meridian, excepting 4 acres reserved for the site of a court-house, to be designated by lot and block upon the official plat of survey of said reservation for county-seat purposes hereafter to be issued by the Commissioner of the General Land Office; said reservation to be additional to the reservations for parks, schools, and other public purposes required to be made by section 22 of the act of May 2, 1890.

For County M, the south half of the northeast quarter and the north half of the southeast quarter of section 23 and the south half of the northwest quarter and the north half of the southwest quarter of section 24, township 27 north, range 14 west of the Indian meridian, excepting 1 acre reserved for Government use for the site of a land office and 4 acres to be reserved for the site of a court-house, which tracts are to be contiguous and to be designated by lot and block upon the official plat of survey of said reservation for county-seat purposes hereafter to be issued by the Commissioner of the General Land Office; said reservations to be additional to the reservations for parks, schools, and other public purposes required to be made by section 22 of the act of May 2, 1890.

For County N, the south half of section 25, township 23 north, range 21 west of the Indian meridian, excepting 1 acre reserved for Government use for the site of a land office and 4 acres to be reserved for the site of a court-house, which tracts are to be contiguous and to be designated by lot and block upon the official plat of survey of said reservation for county-seat purposes hereafter to be issued by the Commissioner of the General Land Office; said reservations to be additional to the reservations for parks, schools, and other public purposes required to be made by section 22 of the act of May 2, 1890.

For County O, the southeast quarter of section 7 and the southwest quarter of section 8, township 22 north, range 6 west of the Indian meridian, excepting 1 acre reserved for Government use for the site of a land office and 4 acres to be reserved for the site of a court-house, which tracts are to be contiguous and to be designated by lot and block upon the official plat of survey of said reservation for county-seat purposes hereafter to be issued by the Commissioner of the General Land Office; said reservations to be additional to the reservations for parks, schools, and other public purposes required to be made by section 22 of the act of May 2, 1890.

For County P, the northeast quarter of section 22 and the northwest quarter of section 23, township 21 north, range 1 west of the Indian meridian, excepting 1 acre reserved for Government use for the site of a land office and 4 acres reserved for the site of a court-house, which tracts are to be contiguous and to be designated by lot and block upon the official plat of survey of said reservation for county-seat purposes hereafter to be issued by the Commissioner of the General Land Office; said reservations to be additional to the reservations for parks, schools, and other public purposes required to be made by section 22 of the act of May 2, 1890; and

For County Q, the southeast quarter of section 31, the west half of the southwest quarter of section 32, township 22 north, range 5 east, lot 4 of section 5, and lot 1 of section 6, township 21 north, range 5 east of the

Indian meridian, excepting 4 acres reserved for the site of a court-house, to be designated by lot and block upon the official plat of survey of said reservation for county-seat purposes hereafter to be issued by the Commissioner of the General Land Office; said reservation to be additional to the reservations for parks, schools, and other public purposes required to be made by section 22 of the act of May 2, 1890.

Whereas it is provided by act of Congress for temporary government of Oklahoma, approved May 2, 1890, section 23 (26 U. S. Statutes at Large, p. 92), that there shall be reserved public highways 4 rods wide between each section of land in said Territory, the section lines being the center of said highways; but no deduction shall be made, where cash payments are provided for, in the amount to be paid for each quarter section of land by reason of such reservation; and

Whereas all the terms, conditions, and considerations required by said agreements made with said nation and tribes of Indians and by the laws relating thereto precedent to opening said lands to settlement have been, as I hereby declare, complied with:

Now, therefore, I, Grover Cleveland, President of the United States, by virtue of the power in me vested by the statutes hereinbefore mentioned and by other the laws of the United States and by said several agreements, do hereby declare and make known that all the lands acquired from the Cherokee Nation of Indians, the Tonkawa tribe of Indians, and the Pawnee tribe of Indians by the three several agreements aforesaid will at the hour of 12 o'clock noon (central standard time) on Saturday, the 16th day of the month of September, A. D. 1893, and not before, be opened to settlement under the terms of and subject to all the conditions, limitations, reservations, and restrictions contained in said agreements, the statutes above specified, the laws of the United States applicable thereto, and the conditions prescribed by this proclamation, saving and excepting lands described and identified as follows, to wit: The lands set apart for the Osage and Kansas Indians, being a tract of country bounded on the north by the State of Kansas, on the east by the ninety-sixth degree of west longitude, on the south and west by the Creek country and the main channel of the Arkansas River; the lands set apart for the Confederated Otoe and Missouria tribes of Indians, described as follows, to wit: Township 22 north, range 1 east; township 23 north, range 1 east; township 22 north, range 2 east; township 23 north, range 2 east; township 22 north, range 3 east; and that portion of township 23 north, range 3 east, lying west of the Arkansas River; and the lands set apart for the Ponca tribe of Indians, described as follows, to wit: Township 24 north, range 1 east; township 25 north, range 1 east; fractional township 24 north, range 2 east; fractional township 25 north, range 2 east; fractional township 24 north, range 3 east; fractional township 25 north, range 3 east; fractional township 24 north, range 4 east; fractional township 25 north, range 4 east, the said fractional townships lying on the right bank of the Arkansas

River; excepting also the lands allotted to the Indians as in said agreements provided; excepting also the lands reserved by Executive orders dated April 18, 1882, and January 17, 1883 (known as Camp Supply Military Reservation), described as follows, to wit: Township 24 north, range 22 west; the south half of township 25 north, range 22 west; and the southwest quarter of township 25 north, range 21 west; excepting also 1 acre of land in each of the reservations for county-seat purposes in Counties M, N, O, and P, which tracts are hereby reserved for Government use as sites for land offices, and 4 acres in each reservation for county-seat purposes hereinbefore named, which tracts are hereby reserved as sites for court-houses; and excepting also the reservations for the use of and in connection with the Chilocco Indian Industrial School and for county-seat purposes hereinbefore described; excepting also the saline lands covered by three leases made by the Cherokee Nation prior to March 3, 1893, known as the Eastern, Middle, and Western Saline reserves, under authority of the act of Congress of August 7, 1882 (22 U. S. Statutes at Large, p. 349), said lands being described and identified as follows: The Eastern Saline Reserve embracing all of section 6; lots 3 and 4 of section 4; the south half of the northeast quarter, the south half of the northwest quarter, the north half of the southwest quarter, and lots 1, 2, 3, and 4 of section 5; and the northeast quarter of the northwest quarter and lots 1 and 2 of section 7, township 25 north, range 9 west. All of sections 6, 7, 8, 17, 18, 19, 20, 21, 27, 28, 29, 30, 31, 32, and 33; the southwest quarter, the southwest quarter of the northwest quarter, and lots 2, 3, 4, 5, 6, and 7 of section 5; the southwest quarter, the southwest quarter of the northwest quarter, the southwest quarter of the southeast quarter, and lot 1 of section 9; the west half of the southwest quarter of section 15; the west half, the southeast quarter, the west half of the northeast quarter, and the southeast quarter of the northeast quarter of section 16; the west half, the west half of the southeast quarter, and the southeast quarter of the southeast quarter of section 22; the west half, the west half of the southeast quarter, the northeast quarter of the southeast quarter, and the southwest quarter of the northeast quarter of section 26; the northwest quarter, the north half of the southwest quarter, the west half of the northeast quarter, and the northeast quarter of the northeast quarter of section 34; and the northwest quarter of the northwest quarter of section 35, township 26 north, range 9 west. All of section 31; the southwest quarter of the southeast quarter, the southeast quarter of the southwest quarter, and lot 4 of section 30; and lots 3 and 4 of section 32, township 27 north, range 9 west. All of sections 1, 2, 3, 4, 9, 10, and 11; the southeast quarter, the south half of the northeast quarter, the east half of the southwest quarter, the southeast quarter of the northwest quarter, and lots 1, 2, and 3 of section 5; the east half, the southwest quarter, and the east half of the northwest quarter of section 8; the north half, the north half of the southwest quarter, the southwest quarter of the southwest quarter, and the northwest quarter of the southeast quarter of section 12; the northwest quarter, the northwest quarter of the northeast quarter, the north half of the southwest quarter, and the southwest quarter of the southwest quarter of section 14; the north half, the southeast quarter and the north half of the southwest quarter of section 15; and the northeast quarter and the north half of the northwest quarter of section 16, township 25 north, range 10 west. All of sections 1, 2, 3, 10, 11, 12, 13, 14, 15, 16, 21, 22, 23, 24, 25, 26, 27, 28, 33, 34, 35, and 36; the south half of the northeast quarter, the southeast quarter of the northwest quarter, the southeast quarter, the east half of the southwest quarter, and lots 1, 2, and 3 of section 4; the east half, the southwest quarter, the east half of the northwest quarter, and the southwest quarter of the northwest quarter of section 9; the southeast quarter of the southeast quarter of section 17; the east half of the northeast quarter and the east half of the southeast quarter of section 20; the southeast quarter and the east half of the northeast quarter of section 29; and the east half and the southeast quarter of the southwest quarter of section 32 of township 26 north, range 10 west. All of sections 22, 26, 27, 34, 35, and 36; the east half of the northeast quarter and the east half of the southeast quarter of section 21; the southwest quarter, the west half of the southeast quarter, the south half of the northwest quarter, and lots 1 and 6 of section 23; the southwest quarter, the west half of the southeast quarter, the southeast quarter of the southeast quarter, the south half of the northwest quarter, and lot 1 of section 25; the east half of section 28; and the east half and the southeast quarter of the southwest quarter of section 33, township 27 north, range 10 west. The Middle Saline Reserve embracing the southwest quarter of the northeast quarter, the southeast quarter of the northwest quarter, the west half of the southeast quarter, the east half of the southwest quarter, and lots 2, 3, 4, 5, 6, and 7 of section 6; and the northwest quarter of the northeast quarter, the northeast quarter of the northwest quarter, and lot 1 of section 7, township 26 north, range 18 west. The southwest quarter of the southeast quarter, the southeast quarter of the southwest quarter, and lot 7 of section 6; the west half of the northeast quarter, the east half of the northwest quarter, the west half of the southeast quarter, the east half of the southwest quarter, and lots 1, 2, 3, and 4 of section 7; the west half of the northeast quarter, the east half of the northwest quarter, the west half of the southeast quarter, the east half of the southwest quarter, and lots 1, 2, 3, and 4 of section 18; the west half of the northeast quarter, the east half of the northwest quarter, the west half of the southeast quarter, the east half of the southwest quarter, and lots 1, 2, 3, and 4 of section 19; the northwest quarter of the northeast quarter, the northeast quarter of the northwest quarter, and lots 1, 2, 3, 4, 6, 7, and 8 of section 30; and the west half of the northeast quarter, the east half of the northwest quarter, the west half of the southeast quarter, the east half of the southwest quarter, and lots 1, 2, 3, and 4 of section 31, township 27 north, range 18 west. All of sections 1 to 6, inclusive; the north half of the north half of sections 8, 9, 10, 11, and 12; and the north half of the northeast quarter, the northeast quarter of the northwest quarter, and lot 1 of section 7, township 26 north, range 19 west. All of sections 7 to 36, inclusive; the south half of the south half of sections 1, 2, 3, 4, and 5, and the south half of the southeast quarter, the southeast of the southwest quarter, and lot 7 of section 6, township 27 north, range 19 west. All of sections 1 and 2; the south half of the northeast quarter, the southeast quarter, and lots 1 and 2 of section 3; the north half of the northeast quarter of section 10; and the north half of the north half of sections 11 and 12, township 26 north, range 20 west. All of sections 11, 12, 13, 14, 23, 24, 25, 26, 35, and 36; the south half of the southeast quarter and lot 7 of section 1; the southwest quarter of the southwest quarter and lot 6 of section 2; the south half of the southeast quarter of section 3; and the east half of sections 10, 15, 22, 27, and 34, township 27 north, range 20 west. And the Western Saline Reserve embracing all of sections 18, 19, 30, and 31, township 29 north, range 20 west; and all of sections 13, 14, 23, 24, 25, 26, 35, and 36, township 29 north, range 21 west. Excepting also that section 13 in each township, which has not been otherwise reserved or disposed of, is hereby reserved for university, agricultural-college, and normal-school purposes, subject to the action of Congress; excepting also that section 33 in each township, which has not been otherwise reserved or disposed of, is hereby reserved for public buildings; excepting also sections 16 and 36 in each township, which are reserved by law for the use and benefit of the public schools; excepting also all selections and allotments made under the law and the agreements herein referred to, the lands covered by said selections and allotments to be particularly described and identified; said descriptions to be furnished by the Commissioner of the General Land Office and posted in the several booths hereinafter referred to as those where certain preliminary declarations are to be made prior to the day named in this proclamation as that when the strip will be open to settlement.

Said lands so to be opened as herein proclaimed shall be entered upon and occupied only in the manner and under the provisions following, to wit:

A strip of land 100 feet in width around and immediately within the outer boundaries of the entire tract of country to be opened to settlement under this proclamation is hereby temporarily set apart for the following purposes and uses, viz:

Said strip, the inner boundary of which shall be 100 feet from the exterior boundary of the country known as the Cherokee Outlet, shall be open to occupancy in advance of the day and hour named for the opening of said country by persons expecting and intending to make settlement pursuant to this proclamation. Such occupancy shall not be regarded as trespass or in violation of this proclamation or of the law under which it is made, nor shall any settlement rights be gained thereby.

The Commissioner of the General Land Office shall, under the direction of the Secretary of the Interior, establish on said 100-foot strip booths, to be located as follows: One in township 29 north, range 2 east; one in township 29 north, range 2 west; one in township 29 north, range 4 west; one in township 29 north, range 8 west; one in township 29 north, range 12 west; one in township 20 north, range 3 east; one in township 20 north, range 2 west; one in township 20 north, range 7 west; and one in township 20 north, range 26 west; and shall place in charge thereof three officers to each booth, who shall be detailed from the General Land Office. Said booths shall be open for the transaction of business on and after Monday, the 11th day of the month of September, A. D. 1893, from 7 a. m. to 12 m. and 1 p. m. to 6 p. m. each business day until the same shall be discontinued by the Secretary of the Interior, who is hereby authorized to discontinue the same at his discretion. Each party desiring to enter upon and occupy as a homestead any of the lands hereby opened to settlement will be required to first appear at one of the before-mentioned booths and make a declaration in writing, to be signed by the party in the presence of one of the officers in charge thereof, which shall be certified by such officer, according to the form hereto attached and made a part hereof marked A, showing his or her qualifications to make homestead entry for said lands, whereupon a certificate will be issued by the officers in charge of the booth to the party making the declaration, which shall be of the form hereto attached and made a part hereof marked D.

Where a party desires to file a soldier's declaratory statement in person, he will be required to make a declaration which shall be of the form hereto attached and made a part hereof marked B, the same to be made and subscribed before one of the officers in charge of the booth and certified by such officer, independently of the affidavit (Form 4–546) to be filed when he presents the certificate of Form D, there given him, to the district officers. Where a party desires to file a declaratory statement through an agent, it will be necessary for him previously to make the affidavit ordinarily required (Form 4–545) before some officer authorized to administer oaths and place the same in the hands of the agent, who, before being permitted to enter upon the lands to be opened in said outlet for the purpose of making the desired filing, will be required to appear before the officers in charge of some one of the booths, to present the said affidavit of the party authorizing him to act as such agent, and to make a declaration in writing, to be subscribed by him in the presence of one of such officers, which shall be certified by such officer, according to the form hereto attached and made a part hereof marked C, whereupon a certificate of Form D will be given him by said officer. The agent should be provided with affidavits of Form 4–545 made in duplicate—one for presentation to the officers in charge of the booth and the other for presentation to the district officers when formal filing is to be made.

Each party desiring to enter upon said lands for the purpose of settling upon a town lot will be required to first appear at one of the beforementioned booths and make a declaration in writing, to be signed by the party in the presence of one of the officers in charge thereof, which shall be certified by such officer, according to the form hereto attached and made a part hereof marked E, whereupon a certificate will be issued by the officers in charge of the booth to the party making the declaration, which shall be of the form hereto attached and made a part hereof marked F.

The said declarations made before the officers in charge shall be given consecutive numbers, beginning at No. 1 at each booth, and the certificate issued to the party making the declaration shall be given the same number as is given the declaration. The declaration shall be carefully preserved by the officers in charge of the booths, and when the booths are discontinued said declarations shall be transmitted, together with the duplicate affidavits (Form 4–545) hereinbefore required to be presented in case of agents proposing to act for soldiers in filing declaratory statements, to the General Land Office for filing as a part of the records pertaining to the disposal of said lands.

The certificate will be evidence only that the party named therein is permitted to go in upon the lands opened to settlement by this proclamation at the time specified herein, and the certificate of Form D must be surrendered when application to enter or file is presented to the district officers, and the party's right to make a filing, homestead entry, or settlement shall be passed upon by the district land officers at the proper time and in the usual manner. The holder of such certificate will be required when he makes his homestead affidavit, or, if a soldier or soldier's agent, when he files a declaratory statement at the district office, to allege under oath before the officers taking such homestead affidavit or to whom said declaratory statement is presented for filing that all the statements contained in the declaration made by him, upon which said certificate is based, are true in every particular, such oath to be added to affidavit of Form 4–102, as shown on form hereto attached and made a part hereof marked 102d.

After the hour and day hereinbefore named when said lands will be opened to settlement all parties holding such certificates (Form D or F) will be permitted to occupy or enter upon the lands so opened, and parties holding a certificate of Form D may initiate a homestead claim, either by settlement upon the land or by entry or filing at the proper district office; but no person not holding any such certificate shall be permitted to occupy or enter upon any of said lands until after the booths shall have been discontinued by direction of the Secretary of the Interior. Until then the officers of the United States are expressly charged to permit no party without a certificate to occupy or enter upon any of said lands.

The following rules and regulations have been prescribed by the Secretary of the Interior, under the direction of the President, as provided by section 10 of said act of March 3, 1893, for the occupation and settlement of the lands hereby opened, to wit:

The thirteenth section of the act approved March 2, 1889, the act approved May 2, 1890, the second proviso of section 17 and the whole of section 18 of the act approved March 3, 1891, are by section 10 of the act of March 3, 1893, made applicable in disposing of the lands under said section 10, and said lands are thereby rendered subject to disposal under the homestead and town-site laws only, with certain modifications, which laws as so modified contain provisions substantially as follows:

1. Any party will be entitled to initiate a homestead claim to a tract of said lands who is over 21 years of age or the head of a family; who is a citizen of the United States or has declared his intention to become such; who has not exhausted his homestead right either by perfecting a homestead entry for 160 acres of land under any law, excepting what is known as the commuted provision of the homestead law contained in section 2301 of the United States Revised Statutes, or by making or commuting a homestead entry since March 2, 1889; who has not entered since August 30, 1890, under the land laws of the United States or filed upon a quantity of land agricultural in character and not mineral which with the tracts sought to be entered in any case would make more than 320 acres; who is not the owner in fee simple of 160 acres of land in any State or Territory, and who has not entered upon or occupied the lands hereby opened in violation of this the President's proclamation opening the same to settlement and entry. (See section 2289, U. S. Revised Statutes; act of March 2, 1889, 25 U. S. Statutes at Large, p. 854; section 13 of the act of March 2, 1889, 25 U. S. Statutes at Large, p. 1005; act of August 30, 1890, 26 U. S. Statutes at Large, p. 391; section 20, act of May 2, 1890, 26 U. S. Statutes at Large, p. 91, and section 10, act of March 3, 1893, 27 U. S. Statutes at Large, p. 640.)

2. Each entry shall be in a compact body, according to the rectangular subdivisions of the public surveys, and in a square form, as nearly as reasonably practicable consistently with such surveys; and no person shall be permitted to enter more than one quarter section in quantity of said lands. (See section 13, act of March 2, 1889, 25 U. S. Statutes at Large, p. 1005.)

3. Parties who own and reside upon land (not acquired by them under the homestead law) not amounting in quantity to a quarter section may, if otherwise qualified, enter other land lying contiguous to their own to an amount which shall not with the land already owned by them exceed in the aggregate 160 acres. (See section 2289, U. S. Revised Statutes.)

4. Any party who has made a homestead entry prior to March 2, 1889, for less than one quarter section of land and who still owns and occupies the land so entered may, if otherwise qualified, enter an additional tract of land lying contiguous to the land embraced in the original entry, which

shall not with the land first entered exceed in the aggregate 160 acres; but such additional entry will not be permitted, or if permitted will be canceled, if the original entry should fail for any reason prior to patent or should appear to be illegal or fraudulent. The final proof of residence and cultivation made on the original entry, together with the payment of the prescribed price for the land, will be sufficient to entitle the party to a final certificate for the land so entered without further proof. (See section 5 of the act of March 2, 1889, 25 U. S. Statutes at Large, p. 854.)

5. Parties who have complied with the conditions of the law with regard to a homestead entry for less than 160 acres of land made prior to March 2, 1889, and have had the final papers issued therefor, may, if otherwise qualified, make an additional entry, by legal subdivisions, of so much land as added to the quantity previously so entered shall not exceed 160 acres. Parties making entry under the provisions set forth in this paragraph will be required to reside upon and cultivate the land embraced therein for the prescribed period and to submit proof of residence and cultivation of a like character with that required in ordinary homestead entries before the issuance of a final certificate. (See section 6, act of March 2, 1889, 25 U. S. Statutes at Large, p. 854.)

6. Any officer, soldier, seaman, or marine who served for not less than ninety days in the Army or Navy of the United States during the War of the Rebellion and who was honorably discharged and has remained loyal to the Government, or, in case of his death, his widow, or, in case of her death or remarriage, his minor orphan children, by a guardian duly appointed and officially accredited at the Department of the Interior, may, either in person or by agent, file a declaratory statement for a tract of land and have six months thereafter within which to make actual entry and commence residence and improvements upon the land. (See sections 2304, 2307, and 2309, U. S. Revised Statutes.)

7. Every person entitled under the preceding paragraph to enter a homestead who, or whose deceased husband or father, in case of the widow or minor children, may have prior to June 22, 1874, entered under the homestead laws a quantity of land less than 160 acres may, if otherwise qualified, enter so much land as when added to the quantity previously entered shall not exceed 160 acres; but the party must make affidavit that the entry is made for actual settlement and cultivation, and the proof of such settlement and cultivation prescribed by existing homestead laws and regulations thereunder will be required to be produced before the issue of final certificate. (See section 2306, U. S. Revised Statutes, and section 18 of the act of May 2, 1890, 26 U. S. Statutes at Large, p. 90.)

8. Parties may initiate claims under the homestead law either by settlement on the land or by entry at the district office. In the former case the party will have three months after settlement within which to file his application for the tract at the district office; in the latter case the party

will have six months after entry at that office within which to establish residence and begin improvements upon the land. (See sections 2290 and 2297, U. S. Revised Statutes, and section 3 of the act of May 14, 1880, 21 U. S. Statutes at Large, p. 140.)

9. The homestead affidavits required to be filed with the application must be executed before the register or receiver of the proper district land office (see section 2290, U. S. Revised Statutes) or before any other officer who may be found duly qualified at the time to administer such oaths, according to the provisions of the act of Congress of May 26, 1890 (26 U. S. Statutes at Large, p. 121).

10. Parties applying to make homestead entry will be required to tender with the application the legal fee and commissions, which are as follows: For an entry of over 80 acres a fee of $10, and for an entry of 80 acres or less a fee of $5, and in both cases, in addition, commissions of 2 per cent upon the Government price of the land, computed at the rate of $1.25 per acre, the ordinary minimum price of public lands under the general provisions of section 2357, United States Revised Statutes. (See sections 2238 and 2290, U. S. Revised Statutes.)

11. Homestead applicants appearing in great number at the local office to make entry at the time of opening will be required to form in line, in order that their applications may be presented and acted upon in regular order.

12. Soldiers' declaratory statements can only be made by the parties entitled or by their agents in person, and will not be received if sent by mail. A party acting as agent and appearing in line, as contemplated under the eleventh paragraph, will be allowed to make one entry or filing in his individual character, if he so desires, and to file one declaratory statement in his representative character as agent, if such he shall be, and thereupon he will be required to step out of line, giving place to the next person in order, and, if he desires to make any other filings, to take his place at the end of the line and await his proper turn before doing so, and thus to proceed in order until all the filings desired by him shall be made.

13. Section 2301 of the Revised Statutes of the United States, providing for commutation of homestead entries, is not applicable to said lands. (See section 18 of the act of May 2, 1890, 26 U. S. Statutes at Large, p. 90.)

14. Proof of five years' residence, cultivation, and improvement and the payment prescribed by the statute, as hereinbefore mentioned, must be made before a party will be entitled to a patent under the homestead law, and such proof is required to be made within seven years from the date of the entry. Commissions equal to 2 per cent upon the Government price for the land, computed at $1.25 per acre, under section 2357, United States Revised Statutes, must also be tendered with the final proof. Interest at 4 per cent per annum on the purchase price of the land must

be paid from the date of the entry to date of final payment of purchase money. (See sections 2238 and 2291, U. S. Revised Statutes, and sections 10 and 13 of the act of March 3, 1893, 27 U. S. Statutes at Large, p. 640.)

15. The parties named in paragraph 6 of these regulations are entitled to have the term of service in the Army or Navy under which the claim is made, not exceeding four years, deducted from the period of five years' residence or cultivation required as stated in the preceding paragraph, or, if the party was discharged from service on account of wounds or disabilities incurred in the line of duty, the whole term of enlistment, not exceeding four years, may be deducted. (See section 2305, U. S. Revised Statutes.)

16. Where a homestead settler dies before the consummation of his claim, the widow, or, in case of her death, the heirs or devisee, may continue settlement or cultivation and obtain title upon requisite proof at the proper time. If the widow proves up, title will pass to her; if she dies before proving up and the heirs or devisee make the proof, the title will vest in them, respectively. (See section 2291, U. S. Revised Statutes.)

17. Where both parents die, leaving infant children, the homestead may be sold for cash for the benefit of such children, and the purchaser will receive title from the United States. (See section 2292, U. S. Revised Statutes.)

18. In case of the death of a person after having entered a homestead the failure of the widow, children, or devisee of the deceased to fulfill the demands of the letter of the law as to residence on the lands will not necessarily subject the entry to forfeiture on the ground of abandonment. If the land is cultivated in good faith, the law will be considered as having been substantially complied with.

19. Town-site claims may be initiated upon said lands under the statutes by two methods, which are separate and distinct in character. The regulations under the first method are hereinafter set forth in paragraphs 20, 21, and 22, and under the second method in paragraphs 23 to 28, inclusive. Provision is further made for town-site entries in cases where lands entered under the homestead law are required for town-site purposes, as set forth in paragraph 30.

20. Parties having founded or who desire to found a city or town on the public lands must file with the recorder of the county in which land is situate a plat thereof, describing the exterior boundaries of the land according to the lines of public surveys. Such plat must state the name of the city or town, exhibit the streets, squares, blocks, lots, and alleys, and specify the size of the same, with measurements and area of each municipal subdivision the lots in which shall not exceed 4,200 square feet, with a statement of the extent and general character of the improvements. The plat and statement must be verified by the oath of the party, acting for and in behalf of the occupants and inhabitants of the town or

city. Within one month after filing the plat with the recorder of the county a verified copy of said plat and statement must be sent to the General Land Office, accompanied by the testimony of two witnesses that such town or city has been established in good faith, and a similar map and statement must be filed with the register and receiver of the proper district office. Thereafter the President may cause the lots embraced within the limits of such city or town to be offered at public sale to the highest bidder, subject to a minimum of $10 for each lot; and such lots as may not be disposed of at public sale shall thereafter be liable to private entry at such minimum or at such reasonable increase or diminution thereafter as the Secretary of the Interior may order from time to time, after at least three months' notice, in view of the increase or decrease in the value of the municipal property. Any actual settler upon any lot and upon any additional lot upon which he may have substantial improvements shall be entitled to prove up and purchase the same as a preemption, at such minimum, at any time before the day fixed for the public sale. (See section 2382, U. S. Revised Statutes.)

21. In case the parties interested shall fail or refuse within twelve months after founding a city or town to file in the General Land Office a transcript map, with the statement and testimony, as required in paragraph 20, the Secretary of the Interior may cause a survey and plat to be made of said city or town, and thereafter the lots will be sold at an increase of 50 per cent on the minimum price of $10 per lot. (See section 2384, U. S. Revised Statutes.)

22. When lots vary in size from the limitation of 4,200 square feet and the lots, buildings, and improvements cover an area greater than 640 acres, such variance as to size of lots or excess in area will prove no bar to entry, but the price of the lots may be increased to such reasonable amount as the Secretary of the Interior may by rule establish. (See section 2385, U. S. Revised Statutes.)

23. Under the second method lands actually settled upon and occupied as a town site, and therefore not subject to entry under the homestead laws, may be entered as a town site at the proper district land office. (See section 2387, U. S. Revised Statutes.)

24. If the town is incorporated, the entry may be made by the corporate authorities thereof through the mayor or other principal officer duly authorized so to do. If the town is not incorporated, the entry may be made by the judge of the county court for the county in which said town is situated. In either case the entry must be made in trust for the use and benefit of the occupants thereof according to their respective interests. The execution of such trust as to the disposal of lots and the proceeds of sales is to be conducted under regulations prescribed by the territorial laws. Acts of trustees not in accordance with such regulations are void. (See sections 2387 and 2391, U. S. Revised Statutes.)

25. The officer authorized to enter a town site may make entry at once,

or he may initiate an entry by filing a declaratory statement of the purpose of the inhabitants to make a town-site entry of the land described.
The entry or declaratory statement shall include only such land as is
actually occupied by the town and the title to which is in the United
States, and its exterior limits must conform to the legal subdivisions of
the public lands.   (See sections 2388 and 2389, U. S. Revised Statutes.)

26. The amount of land that may be entered under this method is proportionate to the number of inhabitants.   One hundred and less than 200
inhabitants may enter not to exceed 320 acres; 200 and less than 1,000
inhabitants may enter not to exceed 640 acres; and where the inhabitants number 1,000 and over an amount not to exceed 1,280 acres may
be entered, and for each additional 1,000 inhabitants, not to exceed 5,000
in all, a further amount of 320 acres may be allowed.   When the number
of inhabitants of a town is less than 100, the town site shall be restricted
to the land actually occupied for town purposes by legal subdivisions.
(See section 2389, U. S. Revised Statutes.)

27. Where an entry is made of less than the maximum quantity of land
allowed for town-site purposes, additional entries may be made of contiguous tracts occupied for town purposes which when added to the previous entry or entries will not exceed 2,560 acres; but no additional entry
can be allowed which will make the total area exceed the area to which
the town may be entitled by virtue of its population at date of additional
entry.   (See section 4 of the act of March 3, 1877, 19 U. S. Statutes at
Large, p. 392.)

28. The land must be paid for at the Government price per acre, and
proof must be furnished relating, first, to municipal occupation of the
land; second, number of inhabitants; third, extent and value of town
improvements; fourth, date when land was first used for town-site purposes; fifth, official character and authority of officer making entry; sixth,
if an incorporated town, proof of incorporation, which should be a certified
copy of the act of incorporation, and, seventh, that a majority of the occupants or owners of the lots within the town desire that such action be
taken.   Thirty days' publication of notice of intention to make proof
must be made and proof of publication furnished.   (See section 2387,
U. S. Revised Statutes.)

29. All surveys for town sites on said lands shall contain reservations
for parks (of substantially equal area if more than one park) and for
schools and other public purposes, embracing in the aggregate not less
than 10 nor more than 20 acres, and patents for such reservations, to be
maintained for such purposes, will be issued to the towns respectively
when organized as municipalities.   (See section 22, act of May 2, 1890,
26 U. S. Statutes at Large, p. 92.)

30. In case any of said lands which may be entered under the homestead laws by a person who is entitled to perfect his title thereto under
such laws are required for town-site purposes, the entryman may apply

to the Secretary of the Interior to purchase the lands embraced in said homestead, or any part thereof not less than a legal subdivision, for townsite purposes. The party must file in the district office with his application a plat of the proposed town site and evidence of his qualifications to perfect title under the homestead law and of his compliance with all the requirements of the law and the instructions thereunder, and must deposit with the Secretary of the Interior the sum of $10 per acre for all the lands embraced in such town site, except the lands to be donated and maintained for public purposes as mentioned in the preceding paragraph. (See section 22, act of May 2, 1890, 26 U. S. Statutes at Large, p. 92.)

Notice, moreover, is hereby given that it is by law enacted that no person shall be permitted to occupy or enter upon any of the lands herein referred to except in the manner prescribed by this proclamation, and any person otherwise occupying or entering upon any of said lands shall forfeit all right to acquire any of said lands, and that the officers of the United States will be required to enforce this provision.

And further notice is hereby given that four land districts have been established in Oklahoma Territory, with boundaries as follows:

The Perry district, bounded and described as follows: Beginning at the middle of the main channel of the Arkansas River where the same is intersected by the northern boundary of Oklahoma Territory; thence west to the northwest corner of township 29 north, range 2 west of the Indian meridian; thence south on the range line between ranges 2 and 3 west to the southwest corner of lot 3 of section 31, township 20 north, range 2 west; thence east to the southeast corner of lot 4 of section 36, township 20 north, range 4 east; thence south on the range line between ranges 4 and 5 east to the middle of the main channel of the Cimarron River; thence down said river, in the middle of the main channel thereof, to the western boundary of the Creek country; thence north to the northwest corner of the Creek country; thence east on the northern boundary of said Creek country to the middle of the main channel of the Arkansas River; thence up said river, in the middle of the main channel thereof, to the place of beginning; the local land office of which will be located at the town of Perry, in County P.

The Enid district, bounded and described as follows: Beginning at the northeast corner of township 29 north, range 3 west of the Indian meridian; thence west to the northwest corner of township 29 north, range 8 west; thence south on the range line between ranges 8 and 9 west to the southwest corner of lot 3 of section 31, township 20 north, range 8 west; thence east to the southeast corner of lot 4 of section 36, township 20 north, range 3 west; thence north on the range line between ranges 2 and 3 west to the place of beginning; the local land office of which will be located at the town of Enid, in County O.

The Alva district, bounded and described as follows: Beginning at the northeast corner of township 29 north, range 9 west of the Indian meridian; thence west to the northwest corner of township 29 north, range 16 west; thence south on the range line between ranges 16 and 17 west to the southwest corner of lot 3 of section 31, township 20 north, range 16 west; thence east to the southeast corner of lot 4 of section 36, township 20 north, range 9 west; thence north on the range line between ranges 8 and 9 west to the place of beginning; the local land office of which will be located at the town of Alva, in County M.

The Woodward land district, bounded and described as follows: Beginning at the northeast corner of township 29 north, range 17 west of the Indian meridian; thence west to the northwest corner of township 29 north, range 26 west; thence south to the southwest corner of lot 3 of section 32, township 20 north, range 26 west; thence east to the southeast corner of lot 4 of section 36, township 20 north, range 17 west; thence north on the range line between ranges 16 and 17 west to the place of beginning; the local land office of which will be located at the town of Woodward, in County N.

And further notice is hereby given that the line of 97½° west longitude, named herein for the purpose of disposing of the land hereby opened to settlement, is held to fall on the west line of sections 2, 11, 14, 23, 26, and 35 of the townships in range 3 west of the Indian meridian, and the line of 98½° of west longitude is held to fall on the line running due north and south through the centers of sections 4, 9, 16, 21, 28, and 33 of the townships in range 12 west of the Indian meridian, and said lines have been so laid down upon the township plats on file in the General Land Office.

In witness whereof I have hereunto set my hand and caused the seal of the United States to be affixed.

[SEAL.]   Done at the city of Washington, this 19th day of August, A. D. 1893, and of the Independence of the United States the one hundred and eighteenth.

GROVER CLEVELAND.

By the President:

W. Q. GRESHAM,
Secretary of State.

A.

DECLARATION REQUIRED BY PRESIDENT'S PROCLAMATION OF AUGUST 19, 1893, PREPARATORY TO OCCUPYING OR ENTERING UPON THE LANDS OF THE CHEROKEE OUTLET FOR THE PURPOSE OF MAKING A HOMESTEAD ENTRY.

No. ——.

BOOTH IN T. —— N., R. ——, ——, *1893.*

I, ——, of ——, being desirous of occupying or entering upon the lands opened to settlement by the President's proclamation of August 19, 1893, for the purpose of making a homestead entry, do solemnly declare that I am over 21 years of age or the head of a family; that I am a citizen of the United States (or have declared my intention to become such); that I have not perfected a homestead entry for 160 acres of land under any law except what is known as the commuted provision of the homestead law contained in section 2301, Revised Statutes, nor have I made or commuted a homestead entry since March 2, 1889;* —— that I have not entered since August 30, 1890, under the land laws of the United States or filed upon a quantity of land agricultural in character and not mineral which with the tracts now desired would make more than 320 acres; that I am not the owner in fee simple of 160 acres of land in any State or Territory; that I have not entered upon or occupied, nor will I enter upon or occupy, the lands to be opened to settlement by the President's proclamation of August 19, 1893, in violation of the requirements of said proclamation; that I desire to make entry for the purpose of actual settlement and cultivation, and not for the benefit of any other person, persons, or corporation; that I will faithfully and honestly endeavor to comply with all the requirements of law as to settlement, residence, and cultivation necessary to acquire title to the land I may select; that I am not acting as agent of any person, corporation, or syndicate in entering upon said lands, nor in collusion with any person, corporation, or syndicate to give them the benefit of the land I may enter, or any part thereof, or the timber thereon; that I do not apply to enter upon said lands for the purpose of speculation, but in good faith to obtain a home for myself; and that I have not, directly or indirectly, made and will not make any agreement or contract in any way or manner with any person or persons, corporation, or syndicate whatsoever by which the title which I may acquire from the Government of the United States should inure in whole or in part to the benefit of any person except myself. —— ——.

I certify that the foregoing declaration was made and subscribed before me this —— day of ——, 1893.

—— ——, *Officer in Charge.*

*NOTE.—If the party has made a homestead entry since March 2, 1889, but has failed or is unable to perfect title to the land covered thereby because of a valid adverse claim or other invalidity existing at the date of its inception, strike out the words "made or" and insert in the blank space *that I have made a homestead entry since March 2, 1889, but have failed or am unable to perfect title to the land covered thereby because of a valid adverse claim or other invalidity existing at the date of its inception.*

B.

DECLARATION REQUIRED BY PRESIDENT'S PROCLAMATION OF AUGUST 19, 1893, PREPARATORY TO OCCUPYING OR ENTERING UPON THE LANDS OF THE CHEROKEE OUTLET FOR THE PURPOSE OF FILING A SOLDIER'S DECLARATORY STATEMENT IN PERSON.

No. ——.

BOOTH IN T. —— N., R. ——, ——, *1893.*

I, ——, of —— County and State or Territory of ——, do solemnly declare that I served for a period of —— in the Army of the United States during the War of the Rebellion and was honorably discharged therefrom, as shown by a statement of such service herewith, and that I have remained loyal to the Government; that I have not perfected a homestead entry for 160 acres of land under any law except what is known as the commuted provision of the homestead law contained in section 2301, Revised Statutes, nor have I filed a declaratory statement under sections 2304 and 2309 of the Revised Statutes or made or commuted a homestead entry since March 2, 1889;* —— that I have not entered since August 30, 1890, under the land laws of the United States or filed upon a quantity of land agricultural in character and not mineral which with the tracts now desired would make more than 320 acres; that I am not the owner in fee simple of 160 acres of land in any State or Territory; that I have not entered upon or occupied, nor will I enter upon or occupy, the lands to be opened to settlement by the President's proclamation of August 19, 1893, in violation of said proclamation; that I intend to file a soldier's declaratory statement upon said lands, which location will be made for my exclusive use and benefit, for the purpose of my actual settlement and cultivation, and not, either directly or indirectly, for the use and benefit of any other person.

——— ———.

I certify that the foregoing declaration was made and subscribed before me this —— day of ———, 1893.

——— ———, *Officer in Charge.*

*NOTE.—If the party has made an entry or filing since March 2, 1889, to which he is unable to perfect title because of a valid adverse claim or other invalidity existing at the date of its inception, strike out the words "filed a declaratory statement under sections 2304 and 2309 of the Revised Statutes, or made or" and insert in the blank space *that I have made an entry or filing since March 2, 1889, but have failed or am unable to perfect title to the land covered thereby because of a valid adverse claim or other invalidity existing at the date of its inception.*

C.

DECLARATION REQUIRED BY PRESIDENT'S PROCLAMATION OF AUGUST 19, 1893, PREPARATORY TO ENTERING UPON THE LANDS OF THE CHEROKEE OUTLET FOR THE PURPOSE OF FILING A SOLDIER'S DECLARATORY STATEMENT AS AGENT.

No. ——.

BOOTH IN T. ——— N., R. ———, ———, *1893.*

I, ———, of ———, desiring to enter upon the Cherokee Outlet for the purpose of filing a soldier's declaratory statement under sections 2304 and 2309, United States Revised Statutes, as agent of ———, do hereby declare that I have no interest or authority in the matter, present or prospective, beyond the filing of such declaratory statement as the true and lawful attorney of the said ——— as provided by said sections 2304 and 2309.

——— ———.

I certify that the foregoing declaration was made and subscribed before me this —— day of ———, 1893.

——— ———, *Officer in Charge.*

D.

CERTIFICATE THAT MUST BE HELD BY PARTY DESIRING TO OCCUPY OR TO ENTER UPON THE LANDS OPENED TO SETTLEMENT BY THE PRESIDENT'S PROCLAMATION OF AUGUST 19, 1893, FOR THE PURPOSE OF MAKING A HOMESTEAD ENTRY OR FILING A SOLDIER'S DECLARATORY STATEMENT.

No. ——.

BOOTH IN T. ——— N., R. ———, ———, *1893.*

This certifies that ——— has this day made the declaration before me required by the President's proclamation of August 19, 1893, and he is therefore permitted to go in upon the lands opened to settlement by said proclamation at the time named therein for the purpose of making a homestead entry or filing a soldier's declaratory statement.

It is agreed and understood that this certificate will not prevent the district land officers from passing upon the holder's qualifications to enter or file for any of said lands at the proper time and in the usual manner, and that the holder will be required when he makes his homestead affidavit, or, if a soldier or a soldier's agent, when he files a declaratory statement at the district office, to allege under oath before the officer taking such homestead affidavit or to whom said declaratory statement is presented for filing that all of the statements contained in the declaration made by him, upon which this certificate is based, are true in every particular.

——— ———, *Officer in Charge.*

This certificate is not transferable. The holder will display the certificate, if demanded, after locating on claim.

E.

DECLARATION REQUIRED BY PRESIDENT'S PROCLAMATION OF AUGUST 19, 1893,
PREPARATORY TO OCCUPYING OR ENTERING UPON THE LANDS OF THE CHERO
KEE OUTLET FOR THE PURPOSE OF SETTLING UPON A TOWN LOT.

No. ——.

BOOTH IN T. —— N., R. ——, ——, *1893.*

I, ——, of ——, being desirous of occupying or entering upon lands opened
to settlement by the President's proclamation of August 19, 1893, do solemnly declare
that I have not entered upon or occupied, nor will I enter upon or occupy, any of the
lands to be opened to settlement by the President's proclamation of August 19, 1893,
in violation of the requirements of said proclamation, and that I desire to go in upon
said lands for the purpose of settling upon a town lot.   —— ——.

I certify that the foregoing declaration was made and subscribed before me this
—— day of ——, 1893.

—— ——, *Officer in Charge.*

F.

CERTIFICATE THAT MUST BE HELD BY PARTY DESIRING TO OCCUPY OR ENTER
UPON THE LANDS OPENED TO SETTLEMENT BY THE PRESIDENT'S PROCLAMATION
OF AUGUST 19, 1893, FOR THE PURPOSE OF SETTLING UPON A TOWN LOT.

No. ——.

BOOTH IN T. —— N., R. ——, ——, *1893.*

This certifies that —— has this day made the declaration before me required by
the President's proclamation of August 19, 1893, and he is therefore permitted to
go in upon the lands opened to settlement by said proclamation at the time named
therein for the purpose of settling upon a town lot.

—— ——, *Officer in Charge.*

This certificate is not transferable. The holder will display the certificate, if demanded, after
locating on claim.

4–102*d.*

AFFIDAVIT.

LAND OFFICE AT ——, ——, *1893.*

I, ——, of ——, applying to enter (or file for) a homestead, do solemnly swear
that I did not enter upon and occupy any portion of the lands described and declared open to entry in the President's proclamation dated August 19, 1893, prior to
12 o'clock noon of September 16, 1893; also that all of the statements contained in a
certain declaration made by me as foundation for obtaining permission to enter upon
the Cherokee Outlet in pursuance of requirements of the President's proclamation
opening said outlet to settlement are true in every particular.   —— ——.

Sworn to and subscribed before me this —— day of ——, 189—.

—— ——.

NOTE.—This affidavit must be made before the register or receiver of the proper district land
office or before some officer authorized to administer oaths and using a seal.

BY THE PRESIDENT OF THE UNITED STATES OF AMERICA.

A PROCLAMATION.

Whereas it is provided by section 24 of the act of Congress approved
March 3, 1891, entitled "An act to repeal timber-culture laws, and for
other purposes"—

That the President of the United States may from time to time set apart and reserve
in any State or Territory having public land bearing forests, in any part of the public

lands wholly or in part covered with timber or undergrowth, whether of commercial value or not, as public reservations; and the President shall by public proclamation declare the establishment of such reservations and the limits thereof.

And whereas the public lands in the State of Oregon within the limits hereinafter described are in part covered with timber, and it appears that the public good would be promoted by setting apart and reserving said lands as a public reservation:

Now, therefore, I, Grover Cleveland, President of the United States, by virtue of the power in me vested by section 24 of the aforesaid act of Congress, do hereby make known and proclaim that there is hereby reserved from entry or settlement and set apart as a public reservation all those certain tracts, pieces, or parcels of land lying and being situate in the State of Oregon and particularly described as follows, to wit:

Beginning at the meander corner at the intersection of the range line between ranges six (6) and seven (7) east, township two (2) north, Willamette meridian, Oregon, with the mean high-water mark on the south bank of the Columbia River in said State; thence northeasterly along said mean high-water mark to its intersection with the township line between townships two (2) and three (3) north; thence easterly along said township line to the northeast corner of township two (2) north, range eight (8) east; thence southerly along the range line between ranges eight (8) and nine (9) east to the southwest corner of township two (2) north, range nine (9) east; thence westerly along the township line between townships one (1) and two (2) north to the northwest corner of township one (1) north, range nine (9) east; thence southerly along the range line between ranges eight (8) and nine (9) east to the southwest corner of township one (1) north, range nine (9) east; thence easterly along the base line to the northeast corner of township one (1) south, range ten (10) east; thence southerly along the range line between ranges ten (10) and eleven (11) east to the southeast corner of township four (4) south, range ten (10) east; thence westerly along the township line between townships four (4) and five (5) south to the southwest corner of township four (4) south, range nine (9) east; thence southerly along the west boundary of township five (5) south, range nine (9) east, to its intersection with the west boundary of the Warm Springs Indian Reservation; thence southwesterly along said Indian-reservation boundary to the southwest corner of said reservation; thence southeasterly along the south boundary of said Indian reservation to a point on the north line of section three (3), township twelve (12) south, range nine (9) east, where said boundary crosses the township line between townships eleven (11) and twelve (12) south, range nine (9) east; thence easterly to the northeast corner of township twelve (12) south, range nine (9) east; thence southerly along the range line between ranges nine (9) and ten (10) east to the southeast corner of township thirteen (13) south, range nine (9) east; thence westerly along the third (3d) standard parallel south to the northeast corner of township fourteen (14) south, range nine (9) east; thence southerly along the range line between ranges nine (9) and ten (10) east to the southeast corner of township fifteen (15) south, range nine (9) east; thence easterly along the third (3d) standard parallel south to the northeast corner of township sixteen (16) south, range nine (9) east; thence southerly along the range line between ranges nine (9) and ten (10) east to the southeast corner of township twenty (20) south, range nine (9) east; thence easterly along the fourth (4th) standard parallel south to the northeast corner of township twenty-one (21) south, range nine (9) east; thence southerly along the range line between ranges nine (9) and ten (10) east to the southeast corner of township twenty-three (23) south, range nine (9) east; thence westerly along the township line between townships twenty-three (23) and twenty-four (24) south to the southeast corner of township twenty-three (23) south, range six (6) east; thence southerly along the range line between ranges six (6) and seven (7) east to the southwest corner of township twenty-five (25) south, range seven (7) east; thence westerly along the fifth (5th) standard parallel south to the point for the northwest corner of township twenty-six (26) south, range seven (7) east; thence southerly along the surveyed and unsurveyed west boundaries of townships twenty-six (26), twenty-seven (27), twenty-eight (28), twenty-nine (29), and thirty (30) south to the southwest corner of township thirty (30) south, range seven (7) east; thence westerly along the unsurveyed sixth (6th) standard parallel south to the point for the northwest corner of township thirty-one (31) south, range seven and one-half (7½) east; thence southerly along the surveyed and unsurveyed west boundaries of townships thirty-one (31), thirty-two (32), and thirty-three (33) south, range seven and one-half (7½) east, to the southwest corner of township thirty-three (33) south, range seven and one-half (7½) east; thence easterly along the township line between townships thirty-three (33) and thirty-four (34) south to the northeast corner of township thirty-four (34) south, range six (6) east; thence southerly along the east boundaries of townships thirty-four (34) and thirty-five (35) south, range six (6) east, to the point of intersection of the east boundary of township thirty-five (35) south, range six (6) east, with the west shore of Upper Klamath Lake; thence along said shore of said lake to its intersection with the range line between ranges six (6) and seven (7) east in township thirty-six (36) south; thence southerly along the range line between ranges six (6) and seven (7) east to the southeast corner of township thirty-seven (37) south, range six (6) east; thence westerly along the township line between townships thirty-seven (37) and thirty-eight (38) south to the southwest corner of township thirty-seven (37) south, range four (4) east; thence northerly along the range line between ranges three (3) and four (4) east to the northwest corner of township thirty-six (36) south, range four (4) east; thence easterly along the eighth (8th) standard parallel south to the southwest corner of township thirty-five (35) south, range four (4) east; thence northerly along the range line between ranges three (3) and four (4) east to the southwest corner of township thirty-one (31) south, range four (4) east; thence westerly along the township line between townships thirty-one (31) and thirty-two (32) south to the southwest corner of township thirty-one (31) south, range one (1) east; thence northerly along the surveyed and unsurveyed Willamette meridian to the northwest corner of township twenty (20) south, range one (1) east; thence easterly along the township line between townships nineteen (19) and twenty (20) south to the northeast corner of township twenty (20) south, range one (1) east; thence northerly along the range line between ranges one (1) and two (2) east to the northwest corner of township eighteen (18) south, range two (2) east; thence easterly along the township line between townships seventeen (17) and eighteen (18) south to the southeast corner of township seventeen (17) south, range two (2) east; thence northerly along the range line between ranges two (2) and three (3) east to the southwest corner of township seventeen (17) south, range three (3) east; thence easterly along the surveyed and unsurveyed township line between townships seventeen (17) and eighteen (18) south to the point for the southeast corner of township seventeen (17) south, range four (4) east; thence northerly along the surveyed and unsurveyed range line between ranges four (4) and five (5) east, subject to the proper easterly or westerly offsets on the third (3d), second (2d), and first (1st) standard parallels south, to the northwest corner of township five (5) south, range five (5) east; thence easterly along the township line between townships four (4) and five (5) south to the southeast corner of township four (4) south, range six (6) east; thence northerly along the range line between ranges six (6) and seven (7) east to the northwest corner of township four (4) south, range seven (7) east; thence easterly along the township line between townships three (3) and four (4) south to the southwest corner of section thirty-four (34), township three (3) south, range seven (7) east; thence northerly along the surveyed and unsurveyed section line between sections thirty-three (33) and thirty-four (34), twenty-seven (27) and twenty-eight (28), twenty-one (21) and twenty-two (22), fifteen (15) and sixteen (16), nine (9) and ten (10), and three (3) and four (4) to the northwest corner of section three (3) of said township and range; thence easterly along the surveyed and unsurveyed township line between townships two (2) and three (3) south to the point for the southeast corner of township two (2) south, range eight (8) east; thence northerly along the unsurveyed range line between ranges eight (8) and nine (9) east to the southeast corner of township one (1) south, range eight (8) east; thence westerly along the township line between townships one (1) and two (2) south to the southeast corner of section thirty-four (34), township one (1) south, range eight (8) east; thence northerly along the section line between sections thirty-four (34) and thirty-five (35), twenty-six (26) and twenty-seven (27), and twenty-two (22) and twenty-three (23) to the northeast corner of section twenty-two (22); thence westerly along the section line between sections fifteen (15) and twenty-two (22) to the southeast corner of section sixteen (16); thence northerly on the section line between sections fifteen (15) and sixteen (16) to the point for the northeast corner of section sixteen (16); thence westerly along the section line between sections nine (9) and sixteen (16) to the southeast corner of section eight (8); thence northerly along the section line between sections eight (8) and nine (9) and four (4) and five (5) to the northwest corner of section four (4), township one (1) south, range eight (8) east; thence easterly along the base line to the southeast corner of section thirty-three (33), township one (1) north, range eight (8) east; thence along the unsurveyed section lines northerly to the point for the northeast corner of section thirty-three (33), westerly to the point for the northeast corner of section thirty-two (32), northerly to the point for the northeast corner of section eight (8), westerly to the point for the southwest corner of section six (6); thence northerly along the unsurveyed range line between ranges seven (7) and eight (8) east to the point for the northwest corner of township one (1) north, range eight (8) east; thence westerly along the unsurveyed township line between townships one (1) and two (2) north to the northwest corner of township one (1) north, range seven (7) east; thence northerly along the surveyed and unsurveyed range line between ranges six (6) and seven (7) east to the meander corner at its intersection with the mean high-water mark on the south bank of the Columbia River, the place of beginning.

Excepting from the force and effect of this proclamation all lands which may have been prior to the date hereof embraced in any legal entry or covered by any lawful filing duly of record in the proper United States land office, or upon which any valid settlement has been made pursuant to law and the statutory period within which to make entry or filing of record has not expired, and all mining claims duly located and held according to the laws of the United States and rules and regulations not in conflict therewith.

Provided, That this exception shall not continue to apply to any particular tract of land unless the entryman, settler, or claimant continues to comply with the law under which the entry, filing, settlement, or location was made.

Warning is hereby expressly given to all persons not to enter or make settlement upon the tract of land reserved by this proclamation.

In witness whereof I have hereunto set my hand and caused the seal of the United States to be affixed.

[SEAL.] Done at the city of Washington, this 28th day of September, A. D. 1893, and of the Independence of the United States the one hundred and eighteenth.

GROVER CLEVELAND.

By the President:
ALVEY A. ADEE,
    Acting Secretary of State.

By the President of the United States of America.

A PROCLAMATION.

Whereas it is provided by section 24 of the act of Congress approved March 3, 1891, entitled "An act to repeal timber-culture laws, and for other purposes"—

That the President of the United States may from time to time set apart and reserve in any State or Territory having public land bearing forests, in any part of the public lands wholly or in part covered with timber or undergrowth, whether of commercial value or not, as public reservations; and the President shall by public proclamation declare the establishment of such reservations and the limits thereof.

And whereas the public lands in the State of Oregon within the limits hereinafter described are in part covered with timber, and it appears that the public good would be promoted by setting apart and reserving said lands as a public reservation:

Now, therefore, I, Grover Cleveland, President of the United States, by virtue of the power in me vested by section 24 of the aforesaid act of Congress, do hereby make known and proclaim that there is hereby reserved from entry or settlement and set apart as a public reservation all those certain tracts, pieces, or parcels of land lying and being situate in the State of Oregon and within the boundaries particularly described as follows, to wit:

Beginning at the northeast corner of section twenty-seven (27), township thirty-nine (39) south, range one (1) east, Willamette meridian; thence westerly along the surveyed and unsurveyed section line to the northwest corner of section twenty-five (25), township thirty-nine (39) south, range one (1) west; thence southerly along the section line to the southwest corner of section thirty-six (36), said township and range; thence westerly along the ninth (9th) standard parallel south to the northwest corner of section one (1), township forty (40) south, range one (1) west; thence southerly along the section line to the southwest corner of section thirteen (13), said township and range; thence easterly along the surveyed and unsurveyed section line to the point for the southeast corner of section fourteen (14), township forty (40) south, range one (1) east; thence northerly along the surveyed and unsurveyed section line to the northeast corner of section thirty-five (35), township thirty-nine (39) south, range one (1) east; thence westerly to the northwest corner of said section thirty-five (35); thence northerly to the northeast corner of section twenty-seven (27), said township and range, the place of beginning.

Excepting from the force and effect of this proclamation all lands which may have been prior to the date hereof embraced in any legal entry or covered by any lawful filing duly of record in the proper United States land office, or upon which any valid settlement has been made pursuant to law and the statutory period within which to make entry or filing of record has not expired, and all mining claims duly located and held according to the laws of the United States and rules and regulations not in conflict therewith.

Provided, That this exception shall not continue to apply to any particular tract of land unless the entryman, settler, or claimant continues to comply with the law under which the entry, filing, settlement, or location was made.

Warning is hereby expressly given to all persons not to enter or make settlement upon the tract of land reserved by this proclamation.

In witness whereof I have hereunto set my hand and caused the seal of the United States to be affixed.

[SEAL.] Done at the city of Washington, this 28th day of September, A. D. 1893, and of the Independence of the United States the one hundred and eighteenth.

GROVER CLEVELAND.

By the President:

ALVEY A. ADEE, *Acting Secretary of State.*

BY THE PRESIDENT OF THE UNITED STATES OF AMERICA.

A PROCLAMATION.

While the American people should every day remember with praise and thanksgiving the divine goodness and mercy which have followed them since their beginning as a nation, it is fitting that one day in each year should be especially devoted to the contemplation of the blessings we have received from the hand of God and to the grateful acknowledgment of His loving kindness.

Therefore, I, Grover Cleveland, President of the United States, do hereby designate and set apart Thursday, the 30th day of the present month of November, as a day of thanksgiving and praise to be kept and observed by all the people of our land. On that day let us forego our ordinary work and employments and assemble in our usual places of worship, where we may recall all that God has done for us and where from grateful hearts our united tribute of praise and song may reach the Throne of Grace. Let the reunion of kindred and the social meeting of friends lend cheer and enjoyment to the day, and let generous gifts of charity for the relief of the poor and needy prove the sincerity of our thanksgiving.

Witness my hand and the seal of the United States, which I have caused to be hereto affixed.

[SEAL.] Done at the city of Washington on the 3d day of November, A. D. 1893, and of the Independence of the United States the one hundred and eighteenth.

GROVER CLEVELAND.

By the President:

W. Q. GRESHAM, *Secretary of State.*

M P—VOL IX—28

EXECUTIVE ORDER.

AMENDMENTS OF CIVIL-SERVICE RULES.

UNITED STATES CIVIL SERVICE COMMISSION,
Washington, D. C.

Clause 2 of Departmental Rule VIII is hereby amended by inserting after the letter "*d*" in parentheses in line 2 the following: "until after absolute appointment and," and by striking out all after the word "transferred" in line 4 to and including the word "made" in line 7; so that as amended the clause will read:

2. No person may be transferred as herein authorized, except as provided in section 1, clause (*d*), until after absolute appointment and until the Commission shall have certified to the officer making the transfer requisition that the person whom it is proposed to transfer has passed an examination to test fitness for the place to which he is to be transferred: *Provided*, That no person who has been appointed from the copyist register shall be transferred to a place the salary of which is more than $900 per annum until one year after appointment.

EXECUTIVE MANSION,
Washington, August 19, 1893.

The above amendments to clause 2 of Departmental Rule VIII and said rule as so amended are hereby approved.

GROVER CLEVELAND.

FIRST ANNUAL MESSAGE.

EXECUTIVE MANSION,
Washington, December 4, 1893.

To the Congress of the United States:

The constitutional duty which requires the President from time to time to give to the Congress information of the state of the Union and recommend to their consideration such measures as he shall judge necessary and expedient is fittingly entered upon by commending to the Congress a careful examination of the detailed statements and well-supported recommendations contained in the reports of the heads of Departments, who are chiefly charged with the executive work of the Government. In an effort to abridge this communication as much as is consistent with its purpose I shall supplement a brief reference to the contents of these departmental reports by the mention of such executive business and incidents as are not embraced therein and by such recommendations as appear to be at this particular time appropriate.

While our foreign relations have not at all times during the past year been entirely free from perplexity, no embarrassing situation remains that will not yield to the spirit of fairness and love of justice which joined with consistent firmness, characterize a truly American foreign policy.

My predecessor having accepted the office of arbitrator of the long-standing Missions boundary dispute, tendered to the President by the Argentine Republic and Brazil, it has been my agreeable duty to receive the special envoys commissioned by those States to lay before me evidence and arguments in behalf of their respective Governments.

The outbreak of domestic hostilities in the Republic of Brazil found the United States alert to watch the interests of our citizens in that country, with which we carry on important commerce. Several vessels of our new Navy are now and for some time have been stationed at Rio de Janeiro. The struggle being between the established Government, which controls the machinery of administration, and with which we maintain friendly relations, and certain officers of the navy employing the vessels of their command in an attack upon the national capital and chief seaport, and lacking as it does the elements of divided administration, I have failed to see that the insurgents can reasonably claim recognition as belligerents.

Thus far the position of our Government has been that of an attentive but impartial observer of the unfortunate conflict. Emphasizing our fixed policy of impartial neutrality in such a condition of affairs as now exists, I deemed it necessary to disavow in a manner not to be misunderstood the unauthorized action of our late naval commander in those waters in saluting the revolted Brazilian admiral, being indisposed to countenance an act calculated to give gratuitous sanction to the local insurrection.

The convention between our Government and Chile having for its object the settlement and adjustment of the demands of the two countries against each other has been made effective by the organization of the claims commission provided for. The two Governments failing to agree upon the third member of the commission, the good offices of the President of the Swiss Republic were invoked, as provided in the treaty, and the selection of the Swiss representative in this country to complete the organization was gratifying alike to the United States and Chile.

The vexatious question of so-called legation asylum for offenders against the state and its laws was presented anew in Chile by the unauthorized action of the late United States minister in receiving into his official residence two persons who had just failed in an attempt at revolution and against whom criminal charges were pending growing out of a former abortive disturbance. The doctrine of asylum as applied to this case is not sanctioned by the best precedents, and when allowed tends to encourage sedition and strife. Under no circumstances can the representatives of this Government be permitted, under the ill-defined fiction of extraterritoriality, to interrupt the administration of criminal justice in the countries to which they are accredited. A temperate demand having been made by the Chilean Government for the correction of this conduct in the instance mentioned, the minister was instructed no longer to harbor the offenders.

The legislation of last year known as the Geary law, requiring the registration of all Chinese laborers entitled to residence in the United States and the deportation of all not complying with the provisions of the act within the time prescribed, met with much opposition from Chinamen in this country. Acting upon the advice of eminent counsel that the law was unconstitutional, the great mass of Chinese laborers, pending judicial inquiry as to its validity, in good faith declined to apply for the certificates required by its provisions. A test case upon proceeding by *habeas corpus* was brought before the Supreme Court, and on May 15, 1893, a decision was made by that tribunal sustaining the law.

It is believed that under the recent amendment of the act extending the time for registration the Chinese laborers thereto entitled who desire to reside in this country will now avail themselves of the renewed privilege thus afforded of establishing by lawful procedure their right to remain, and that thereby the necessity of enforced deportation may to a great degree be avoided.

It has devolved upon the United States minister at Peking, as dean of the diplomatic body, and in the absence of a representative of Sweden and Norway, to press upon the Chinese Government reparation for the recent murder of Swedish missionaries at Sung-pu. This question is of vital interest to all countries whose citizens engage in missionary work in the interior.

By Article XII of the general act of Brussels, signed July 2, 1890, for the suppression of the slave trade and the restriction of certain injurious commerce in the Independent State of the Kongo and in the adjacent zone of central Africa, the United States and the other signatory powers agreed to adopt appropriate means for the punishment of persons selling arms and ammunition to the natives and for the confiscation of the inhibited articles. It being the plain duty of this Government to aid in suppressing the nefarious traffic, impairing as it does the praiseworthy and civilizing efforts now in progress in that region, I recommend that an act be passed prohibiting the sale of arms and intoxicants to natives in the regulated zone by our citizens.

Costa Rica has lately testified its friendliness by surrendering to the United States, in the absence of a convention of extradition, but upon duly submitted evidence of criminality, a noted fugitive from justice. It is trusted that the negotiation of a treaty with that country to meet recurring cases of this kind will soon be accomplished. In my opinion treaties for reciprocal extradition should be concluded with all those countries with which the United States has not already conventional arrangements of that character.

I have deemed it fitting to express to the Governments of Costa Rica and Colombia the kindly desire of the United States to see their pending boundary dispute finally closed by arbitration in conformity with the spirit of the treaty concluded between them some years ago.

Our relations with the French Republic continue to be intimate and cordial.   I sincerely hope that the extradition treaty with that country, as amended by the Senate, will soon be operative.

While occasional questions affecting our naturalized citizens returning to the land of their birth have arisen in our intercourse with Germany, our relations with that country continue satisfactory.

The questions affecting our relations with Great Britain have been treated in a spirit of friendliness.

Negotiations are in progress between the two Governments with a view to such concurrent action as will make the award and regulations agreed upon by the Bering Sea Tribunal of Arbitration practically effective, and it is not doubted that Great Britain will cooperate freely with this country for the accomplishment of that purpose.

The dispute growing out of the discriminating tolls imposed in the Welland Canal upon cargoes of cereals bound to and from the lake ports of the United States was adjusted by the substitution of a more equitable schedule of charges, and my predecessor thereupon suspended his proclamation imposing discriminating tolls upon British transit through our canals.*

A request for additions to the list of extraditable offenses covered by the existing treaty between the two countries is under consideration.

During the past year an American citizen employed in a subordinate commercial position in Hayti, after suffering a protracted imprisonment on an unfounded charge of smuggling, was finally liberated on judicial examination.   Upon urgent representation to the Haytian Government a suitable indemnity was paid to the sufferer.

By a law of Hayti a sailing vessel, having discharged her cargo, is refused clearance until the duties on such cargo have been paid.   The hardship of this measure upon American shipowners, who conduct the bulk of the carrying trade of that country, has been insisted on with a view of securing the removal of this cause of complaint.

Upon receiving authentic information of the firing upon an American mail steamer touching at the port of Amapala because her captain refused to deliver up a passenger in transit from Nicaragua to Guatemala upon demand of the military authorities of Honduras, our minister to that country, under instructions, protested against the wanton act and demanded satisfaction.   The Government of Honduras, actuated by a sense of justice and in a spirit of the utmost friendship, promptly disavowed the illegal conduct of its officers and expressed sincere regret for the occurrence.

It is confidently anticipated that a satisfactory adjustment will soon be reached of the questions arising out of the seizure and use of American

*See pp. 377–378.

vessels by insurgents in Honduras and the subsequent denial by the successful Government of commercial privileges to those vessels on that account.

A notable part of the southeasterly coast of Liberia between the Cavally and San Pedro rivers, which for nearly half a century has been generally recognized as belonging to that Republic by cession and purchase, has been claimed to be under the protectorate of France in virtue of agreements entered into by the native tribes, over whom Liberia's control has not been well maintained.

More recently negotiations between the Liberian representative and the French Government resulted in the signature at Paris of a treaty whereby as an adjustment certain Liberian territory is ceded to France. This convention at last advices had not been ratified by the Liberian Legislature and Executive.

Feeling a sympathetic interest in the fortunes of the little Commonwealth, the establishment and development of which were largely aided by the benevolence of our countrymen, and which constitutes the only independently sovereign state on the west coast of Africa, this Government has suggested to the French Government its earnest concern lest territorial impairment in Liberia should take place without her unconstrained consent.

Our relations with Mexico continue to be of that close and friendly nature which should always characterize the intercourse of two neighboring republics.

The work of relocating the monuments marking the boundary between the two countries from Paso del Norte to the Pacific is now nearly completed.

The commission recently organized under the conventions of 1884 and 1889 it is expected will speedily settle disputes growing out of the shifting currents of the Rio Grande River east of El Paso.

Nicaragua has recently passed through two revolutions, the party at first successful having in turn been displaced by another. Our newly appointed minister by his timely good offices aided in a peaceful adjustment of the controversy involved in the first conflict. The large American interests established in that country in connection with the Nicaragua Canal were not molested.

The canal company has unfortunately become financially seriously embarrassed, but a generous treatment had been extended to it by the Government of Nicaragua. The United States are especially interested in the successful achievement of the vast undertaking this company has in charge. That it should be accomplished under distinctively American auspices, and its enjoyment assured not only to the vessels of this country as a channel of communication between our Atlantic and Pacific seaboards, but to the ships of the world in the interests of civilization, is a proposition which, in my judgment, does not admit of question.

Guatemala has also been visited by the political vicissitudes which have afflicted her Central American neighbors, but the dissolution of its Legislature and the proclamation of a dictatorship have been unattended with civil war.

An extradition treaty with Norway has recently been exchanged and proclaimed.

The extradition treaty with Russia signed in March, 1887, and amended and confirmed by the Senate in February last, was duly proclaimed last June.

Led by a desire to compose differences and contribute to the restoration of order in Samoa, which for some years previous had been the scene of conflicting foreign pretensions and native strife, the United States, departing from its policy consecrated by a century of observance, entered four years ago into the treaty of Berlin, thereby becoming jointly bound with England and Germany to establish and maintain Malietoa Laupepa as King of Samoa. The treaty provided for a foreign court of justice; a municipal council for the district of Apia, with a foreign president thereof, authorized to advise the King; a tribunal for the settlement of native and foreign land titles, and a revenue system for the Kingdom. It entailed upon the three powers that part of the cost of the new Government not met by the revenue of the islands.

Early in the life of this triple protectorate the native dissensions it was designed to quell revived. Rivals defied the authority of the new King, refusing to pay taxes and demanding the election of a ruler by native suffrage. Mataafa, an aspirant to the throne, and a large number of his native adherents were in open rebellion on one of the islands. Quite lately, at the request of the other powers and in fulfillment of its treaty obligation, this Government agreed to unite in a joint military movement of such dimensions as would probably secure the surrender of the insurgents without bloodshed.

The war ship *Philadelphia* was accordingly put under orders for Samoa, but before she arrived the threatened conflict was precipitated by King Malietoa's attack upon the insurgent camp. Mataafa was defeated and a number of his men killed. The British and German naval vessels present subsequently secured the surrender of Mataafa and his adherents. The defeated chief and ten of his principal supporters were deported to a German island of the Marshall group, where they are held as prisoners under the joint responsibility and cost of the three powers.

This incident and the events leading up to it signally illustrate the impolicy of entangling alliances with foreign powers.

More than fifteen years ago this Government preferred a claim against Spain in behalf of one of our citizens for property seized and confiscated in Cuba. In 1886 the claim was adjusted, Spain agreeing to pay unconditionally, as a fair indemnity, $1,500,000. A respectful but earnest note was recently addressed to the Spanish Government insisting upon prompt fulfillment of its long-neglected obligation.

Other claims preferred by the United States against Spain in behalf of American citizens for property confiscated in Cuba have been pending for many years.

At the time Spain's title to the Caroline Islands was confirmed by arbitration that Government agreed that the rights which had been acquired there by American missionaries should be recognized and respected. It is sincerely hoped that this pledge will be observed by allowing our missionaries, who were removed from Ponape to a place of safety by a United States war ship during the late troubles between the Spanish garrison and the natives, to return to their field of usefulness.

The reproduced caravel *Santa Maria*, built by Spain and sent to the Columbian Exposition, has been presented to the United States in token of amity and in commemoration of the event it was designed to celebrate. I recommend that in accepting this gift Congress make grateful recognition of the sincere friendship which prompted it.

Important matters have demanded attention in our relations with the Ottoman Porte.

The firing and partial destruction by an unrestrained mob of one of the school buildings of Anatolia College, established by citizens of the United States at Marsovan, and the apparent indifference of the Turkish Government to the outrage, notwithstanding the complicity of some of its officials, called for earnest remonstrance, which was followed by promise of reparation and punishment of the offenders.

Indemnity for the injury to the buildings has already been paid, permission to rebuild given, registration of the school property in the name of the American owners secured, and efficient protection guaranteed.

Information received of maltreatment suffered by an inoffensive American woman engaged in missionary work in Turkish Koordistan was followed by such representations to the Porte as resulted in the issuance of orders for the punishment of her assailants, the removal of a delinquent official, and the adoption of measures for the protection of our citizens engaged in mission and other lawful work in that quarter.

Turkey complains that her Armenian subjects obtain citizenship in this country not to identify themselves in good faith with our people, but with the intention of returning to the land of their birth and there engaging in sedition. This complaint is not wholly without foundation. A journal published in this country in the Armenian language openly counsels its readers to arm, organize, and participate in movements for the subversion of Turkish authority in the Asiatic provinces. The Ottoman Government has announced its intention to expel from its dominions Armenians who have obtained naturalization in the United States since 1868.

The right to exclude any or all classes of aliens is an attribute of sovereignty. It is a right asserted and, to a limited extent, enforced by the United States, with the sanction of our highest court. There being no naturalization treaty between the United States and Turkey, our minister at Constantinople has been instructed that, while recognizing the right of that Government to enforce its declared policy against naturalized Armenians, he is expected to protect them from unnecessary harshness of treatment.

In view of the impaired financial resources of Venezuela consequent upon the recent revolution there, a modified arrangement for the satisfaction of the awards of the late revisory claims commission, in progressive installments, has been assented to, and payments are being regularly made thereunder.

The boundary dispute between Venezuela and British Guiana is yet unadjusted. A restoration of diplomatic intercourse between that Republic and Great Britain and reference of the question to impartial arbitration would be a most gratifying consummation.

The ratification by Venezuela of the convention for the arbitration of the long-deferred claim of the Venezuelan Transportation Company is awaited.

It is hardly necessary for me to state that the questions arising from our relations with Hawaii have caused serious embarrassment. Just prior to the installation of the present Administration the existing Government of Hawaii had been suddenly overthrown and a treaty of annexation had been negotiated between the Provisional Government of the islands and the United States and submitted to the Senate for ratification. This treaty I withdrew for examination and dispatched Hon. James H. Blount, of Georgia, to Honolulu as a special commissioner to make an impartial investigation of the circumstances attending the change of government and of all the conditions bearing upon the subject of the treaty. After a thorough and exhaustive examination Mr. Blount submitted to me his report, showing beyond all question that the constitutional Government of Hawaii had been subverted with the active aid of our representative to that Government and through the intimidation caused by the presence of an armed naval force of the United States, which was landed for that purpose at the instance of our minister. Upon the facts developed it seemed to me the only honorable course for our Government to pursue was to undo the wrong that had been done by those representing us and to restore as far as practicable the status existing at the time of our forcible intervention. With a view of accomplishing this result within the constitutional limits of executive power, and recognizing all our obligations and responsibilities growing out of any changed conditions brought about by our unjustifiable interference, our present minister at Honolulu has received appropriate instructions to that end. Thus far no information of the accomplishment of any definite results has been received from him.

Additional advices are soon expected. When received they will be promptly sent to the Congress, together with all other information at hand, accompanied by a special Executive message fully detailing all the facts necessary to a complete understanding of the case and presenting a history of all the material events leading up to the present situation.

By a concurrent resolution passed by the Senate February 14, 1890, and by the House of Representatives on the 3d of April following the President was requested to "invite from time to time, as fit occasions may arise, negotiations with any government with which the United States has or may have diplomatic relations, to the end that any differences or disputes arising between the two governments which can not be adjusted by diplomatic agency may be referred to arbitration and be peaceably adjusted by such means." April 18, 1890, the International American Conference of Washington by resolution expressed the wish that all controversies between the republics of America and the nations of Europe might be settled by arbitration, and recommended that the government of each nation represented in that conference should communicate this wish to all friendly powers. A favorable response has been received from Great Britain in the shape of a resolution adopted by Parliament July 16 last, cordially sympathizing with the purpose in view and expressing the hope that Her Majesty's Government will lend ready cooperation to the Government of the United States upon the basis of the concurrent resolution above quoted.

It affords me signal pleasure to lay this parliamentary resolution before the Congress and to express my sincere gratification that the sentiment of two great and kindred nations is thus authoritatively manifested in favor of the rational and peaceable settlement of international quarrels by honorable resort to arbitration.

Since the passage of the act of March 3, 1893, authorizing the President to raise the grade of our envoys to correspond with the rank in which foreign countries accredit their agents here, Great Britain, France, Italy, and Germany have conferred upon their representatives at this capital the title of ambassador, and I have responded by accrediting the agents of the United States in those countries with the same title. A like elevation of mission is announced by Russia, and when made will be similarly met. This step fittingly comports with the position the United States hold in the family of nations.

During my former Administration I took occasion to recommend a recast of the laws relating to the consular service, in order that it might become a more efficient agency in the promotion of the interests it was intended to subserve. The duties and powers of consuls have been expanded with the growing requirements of our foreign trade. Discharging important duties affecting our commerce and American citizens abroad, and in certain countries exercising judicial functions, these officers should be men of character, intelligence, and ability.

Upon proof that the legislation of Denmark secures copyright to American citizens on equal footing with its own, the privileges of our copyright laws have been extended by proclamation to subjects of that country.*

The Secretary of the Treasury reports that the receipts of the Government from all sources during the fiscal year ended June 30, 1893, amounted to $461,716,561.94 and its expenditures to $459,374,674.29. There was collected from customs $205,355,016.73 and from internal revenue $161,027,623.93. Our dutiable imports amounted to $421,856,711, an increase of $52,453,907 over the preceding year, and importations free of duty amounted to $444,544,211, a decrease from the preceding year of $13,455,447. Internal-revenue receipts exceeded those of the preceding year by $7,147,445.32. The total tax collected on distilled spirits was $94,720,260.55, on manufactured tobacco $31,889,711.74, and on fermented liquors $32,548,983.07. We exported merchandise during the year amounting to $847,665,194, a decrease of $182,612,954 from the preceding year. The amount of gold exported was larger than any previous year in the history of the Government, amounting to $108,-680,844, and exceeding the amount exported during the preceding year by $58,485,517.

The sum paid from the Treasury for sugar bounty was $9,375,130.88, an increase over the preceding year of $2,033,053.09.

It is estimated upon the basis of present revenue laws that the receipts of the Government for the year ending June 30, 1894, will be $430,121,-365.38 and its expenditures $458,121,365.28, resulting in a deficiency of $28,000,000.

On the 1st day of November, 1893, the amount of money of all kinds in circulation, or not included in Treasury holdings, was $1,718,544,682, an increase for the year of $112,404,947. Estimating our population at 67,426,000 at the time mentioned, the per capita circulation was $25.49. On the same date there was in the Treasury gold bullion amounting to $96,657,273 and silver bullion which was purchased at a cost of $126,261,553.

The purchases of silver under the law of July 14, 1890, during the last fiscal year aggregated 54,008,162.59 fine ounces, which cost $45,531,-374.53. The total amount of silver purchased from the time that law became operative until the repeal of its purchasing clause, on the 1st day of November, 1893, was 168,674,590.46 fine ounces, which cost $155,-930,940.84. Between the 1st day of March, 1873, and the 1st day of November, 1893, the Government purchased under all laws 503,003,717 fine ounces of silver, at a cost of $516,622,948. The silver dollars that have been coined under the act of July 14, 1890, number 36,087,285. The seigniorage arising from such coinage was $6,977,098.39, leaving on hand in the mints 140,699,760 fine ounces of silver, which cost $126,-758,218.

Our total coinage of all metals during the last fiscal year consisted of

* See pp. 395-396.

97,280,875 pieces, valued at $43,685,178.80, of which there was $30,-038,140 in gold coin, $5,343,715 in silver dollars, $7,217,220.90 in subsidiary silver coin, and $1,086,102.90 in minor coins.

During the calendar year 1892 the production of precious metals in the United States was estimated to be 1,596,375 fine ounces of gold of the commercial and coinage value of $33,000,000 and 58,000,000 fine ounces of silver of the bullion or market value of $50,750,000 and of the coinage value of $74,989,900.

It is estimated that on the 1st day of July, 1893, the metallic stock of money in the United States, consisting of coin and bullion, amounted to $1,213,559,169, of which $597,697,685 was gold and $615,861,484 was silver.

One hundred and nineteen national banks were organized during the year ending October 31, 1893, with a capital of $11,230,000. Forty-six went into voluntary liquidation and 158 suspended. Sixty-five of the suspended banks were insolvent, 86 resumed business, and 7 remain in the hands of the bank examiners, with prospects of speedy resumption. Of the new banks organized, 44 were located in the Eastern States, 41 west of the Mississippi River, and 34 in the Central and Southern States. The total number of national banks in existence on October 31, 1893, was 3,796, having an aggregate capital of $695,558,120. The net increase in the circulation of these banks during the year was $36,886,972.

The recent repeal of the provision of law requiring the purchase of silver bullion by the Government as a feature of our monetary scheme has made an entire change in the complexion of our currency affairs. I do not doubt that the ultimate result of this action will be most salutary and far-reaching. In the nature of things, however, it is impossible to know at this time precisely what conditions will be brought about by the change, or what, if any, supplementary legislation may in the light of such conditions appear to be essential or expedient. Of course, after the recent financial perturbation, time is necessary for the reestablishment of business confidence. When, however, through this restored confidence, the money which has been frightened into hoarding places is returned to trade and enterprise, a survey of the situation will probably disclose a safe path leading to a permanently sound currency, abundantly sufficient to meet every requirement of our increasing population and business.

In the pursuit of this object we should resolutely turn away from alluring and temporary expedients, determined to be content with nothing less than a lasting and comprehensive financial plan. In these circumstances I am convinced that a reasonable delay in dealing with this subject, instead of being injurious, will increase the probability of wise action.

The monetary conference which assembled at Brussels upon our invitation was adjourned to the 30th day of November of the present year. The considerations just stated and the fact that a definite proposition

from us seemed to be expected upon the reassembling of the conference led me to express a willingness to have the meeting still further
postponed.

It seems to me that it would be wise to give general authority to the
President to invite other nations to such a conference at any time when
there should be a fair prospect of accomplishing an international agreement on the subject of coinage.

I desire also to earnestly suggest the wisdom of amending the existing
statutes in regard to the issuance of Government bonds. The authority
now vested in the Secretary of the Treasury to issue bonds is not as clear
as it should be, and the bonds authorized are disadvantageous to the
Government both as to the time of their maturity and rate of interest.

The Superintendent of Immigration, through the Secretary of the
Treasury, reports that during the last fiscal year there arrived at our ports
440,793 immigrants. Of these, 1,063 were not permitted to land under
the limitations of the law and 577 were returned to the countries from
whence they came by reason of their having become public charges.
The total arrivals were 141,034 less than for the previous year.

The Secretary in his report gives an account of the operation of the
Marine-Hospital Service and of the good work done under its supervision
in preventing the entrance and spread of contagious diseases.

The admonitions of the last two years touching our public health and
the demonstrated danger of the introduction of contagious diseases from
foreign ports have invested the subject of national quarantine with increased interest. A more general and harmonious system than now
exists, acting promptly and directly everywhere and constantly operating
by preventive means to shield our country from the invasion of disease,
and at the same time having due regard to the rights and duties of local
agencies, would, I believe, add greatly to the safety of our people.

The Secretary of War reports that the strength of the Army on the
30th day of September last was 25,778 enlisted men and 2,144 officers.

The total expenditures of the Department for the year ending June 30,
1893, amounted to $51,966,074.89. Of this sum $1,992,581.95 was for
salaries and contingent expenses, $23,377,828.35 for the support of the
military establishment, $6,077,033.18 for miscellaneous objects, and $20,-
518,631.41 for public works. This latter sum includes $15,296,876.46
for river and harbor improvements and $3,266,141.20 for fortifications
and other works of defense.

The total enrollment of the militia of the several States was on the 31st
of October of the current year 112,597 officers and enlisted men. The
officers of the Army detailed for the inspection and instruction of this
reserve of our military force report that increased interest and marked
progress are apparent in the discipline and efficiency of the organization.

Neither Indian outbreaks nor domestic violence have called the Army
into service during the year, and the only active military duty required

of it has been in the Department of Texas, where violations of the neutrality laws of the United States and Mexico were promptly and efficiently dealt with by the troops, eliciting the warm approval of the civil and military authorities of both countries.

The operation of wise laws and the influences of civilization constantly tending to relieve the country from the dangers of Indian hostilities, together with the increasing ability of the States, through the efficiency of the National Guard organizations, to protect their citizens from domestic violence, lead to the suggestion that the time is fast approaching when there should be a reorganization of our Army on the lines of the present necessities of the country. This change contemplates neither increase in number nor added expense, but a redistribution of the force and an encouragement of measures tending to greater efficiency among the men and improvement of the service.

The adoption of battalion formations for infantry regiments, the strengthening of the artillery force, the abandonment of smaller and unnecessary posts, and the massing of the troops at important and accessible stations all. promise to promote the usefulness of the Army. In the judgment of army officers, with but few exceptions, the operation of the law forbidding the reenlistment of men after ten years' service has not proved its wisdom, and while the arguments that led to its adoption were not without merit the experience of the year constrains me to join in the recommendation for its repeal.

It is gratifying to note that we have begun to attain completed results in the comprehensive scheme of seacoast defense and fortification entered upon eight years ago. A large sum has been already expended, but the cost of maintenance will be inconsiderable as compared with the expense of construction and ordnance. At the end of the current calendar year the War Department will have nine 12-inch guns, twenty 10-inch, and thirty-four 8-inch guns ready to be mounted on gun lifts and carriages, and seventy-five 12-inch mortars. In addition to the product of the Army Gun Factory, now completed at Watervliet, the Government has contracted with private parties for the purchase of one hundred guns of these calibers, the first of which should be delivered to the Department for test before July 1, 1894.

The manufacture of heavy ordnance keeps pace with current needs, but to render these guns available for the purposes they are designed to meet emplacements must be prepared for them. Progress has been made in this direction, and it is desirable that Congress by adequate appropriations should provide for the uninterrupted prosecution of this necessary work.

After much preliminary work and exhaustive examination in accordance with the requirements of the law, the board appointed to select a magazine rifle of modern type with which to replace the obsolete Springfield rifle of the infantry service completed its labors during the last year, and the work of manufacture is now in progress at the national armory at Springfield. It is confidently expected that by the end of the current year our infantry will be supplied with a weapon equal to that of the most progressive armies of the world.

The work on the projected Chickamauga and Chattanooga National Military Park has been prosecuted with zeal and judgment, and its opening will be celebrated during the coming year. Over 9 square miles of the Chickamauga battlefield have been acquired, 25 miles of roadway have been constructed, and permanent tablets have been placed at many historical points, while the invitation to the States to mark the positions of their troops participating in the battle has been very generally accepted.

The work of locating and preserving the lines of battle at the Gettysburg battlefield is making satisfactory progress on the plans directed by the last Congress.

The reports of the Military Academy at West Point and the several schools for special instruction of officers show marked advance in the education of the Army and a commendable ambition among its officers to excel in the military profession and to fit themselves for the highest service to the country.

Under the supervision of Adjutant-General Robert Williams, lately retired, the Bureau of Military Information has become well established and is performing a service that will put in possession of the Government in time of war most valuable information, and at all times serve a purpose of great utility in keeping the Army advised of the world's progress in all matters pertaining to the art of war.

The report of the Attorney-General contains the usual summary of the affairs and proceedings of the Department of Justice for the past year, together with certain recommendations as to needed legislation on various subjects. I can not too heartily indorse the proposition that the fee system as applicable to the compensation of United States attorneys, marshals, clerks of Federal courts, and United States commissioners should be abolished with as little delay as possible. It is clearly in the interest of the community that the business of the courts, both civil and criminal, shall be as small and as inexpensively transacted as the ends of justice will allow.

The system is therefore thoroughly vicious which makes the compensation of court officials depend upon the volume of such business, and thus creates a conflict between a proper execution of the law and private gain, which can not fail to be dangerous to the rights and freedom of the citizen and an irresistible temptation to the unjustifiable expenditure of public funds. If in addition to this reform another was inaugurated which would give to United States commissioners the final disposition of petty offenses within the grade of misdemeanors, especially those coming under the internal-revenue laws, a great advance would be made toward a more decent administration of the criminal law.

In my first message to Congress, dated December 8, 1885,* I strongly recommended these changes and referred somewhat at length to the evils of the present system. Since that time the criminal business of the Federal courts and the expense attending it have enormously increased. The number of criminal prosecutions pending in the circuit and district courts of the United States on the 1st day of July, 1885, was 3,808, of which 1,884 were for violations of the internal-revenue laws, while the number of such prosecutions pending on the 1st day of July, 1893, was 9,500, of which 4,200 were for violations of the internal-revenue laws. The expense of the United States courts, exclusive of judges' salaries, for the year ending July 1, 1885, was $2,874,733.11 and for the year ending July 1, 1893, $4,528,676.87.

It is therefore apparent that the reasons given in 1885 for a change in the manner of enforcing the Federal criminal law have gained cogency and strength by lapse of time.

I also heartily join the Attorney-General in recommending legislation fixing degrees of the crime of murder within Federal jurisdiction, as has been done in many of the States; authorizing writs of error on behalf of the Government in cases where final judgment is rendered against the sufficiency of an indictment or against the Government upon any other question arising before actual trial; limiting the right of review in cases of felony punishable only by fine and imprisonment to the circuit court of appeals, and making speedy provision for the construction of such prisons and reformatories as may be necessary for the confinement of United States convicts.

The report of the Postmaster-General contains a detailed statement of the operations of the Post-Office Department during the last fiscal year and much interesting information touching this important branch of the public service.

The business of the mails indicates with absolute certainty the condition of the business of the country, and depression in financial affairs inevitably and quickly reduces the postal revenues. Therefore a larger discrepancy than usual between the post-office receipts and expenditures is the expected and unavoidable result of the distressing stringency which has prevailed throughout the country during much of the time covered by the Postmaster-General's report. At a date when better times were anticipated it was estimated by his predecessor that the deficiency on the 30th day of June, 1893, would be but a little over a million and a half dollars. It amounted, however, to more than five millions. At the same time and under the influence of like anticipations estimates were made for the current fiscal year, ending June 30, 1894, which exhibited a surplus of revenue over expenditures of $872,245.71; but now, in view of the actual receipts and expenditures during that part of the current fiscal year already expired, the present Postmaster-General estimates

* See Vol. VIII, pp. 353-355.

that at its close instead of a surplus there will be a deficiency of nearly $8,000,000.

The post-office receipts for the last fiscal year amounted to $75,896,-933.16 and its expenditures to $81,074,104.90. This post-office deficiency would disappear or be immensely decreased if less matter were carried free through the mails, an item of which is upward of 300 tons of seeds and grain from the Agricultural Department.

The total number of post-offices in the United States on the 30th day of June, 1893, was 68,403, an increase of 1,284 over the preceding year. Of these, 3,360 were Presidential, an increase in that class of 204 over the preceding year.

Forty-two free-delivery offices were added during the year to those already existing, making a total of 610 cities and towns provided with free delivery on June 30, 1893. Ninety-three other cities and towns are now entitled to this service under the law, but it has not been accorded them on account of insufficient funds to meet the expenses of its establishment.

I am decidedly of the opinion that the provisions of the present law permit as general an introduction of this feature of mail service as is necessary or justifiable, and that it ought not to be extended to smaller communities than are now designated.

The expenses of free delivery for the fiscal year ending June 30, 1894, will be more than $11,000,000, and under legislation now existing there must be a constant increase in this item of expenditure.

There were 6,401 additions to the domestic money-order offices during the last fiscal year, being the largest increase in any year since the inauguration of the system. The total number of these offices at the close of the year was 18,434. There were 13,309,735 money orders issued from these offices, being an increase over the preceding year of 1,240,293, and the value of these orders amounted to $127,576,433.65, an increase of $7,509,632.58. There were also issued during the year postal notes amounting to $12,903,076.73.

During the year 195 international money-order offices were added to those already provided, making a total of 2,407 in operation on June 30, 1893. The number of international money orders issued during the year was 1,055,999, an increase over the preceding year of 72,525, and their value was $16,341,837.86, an increase of $1,221,506.31. The number of orders paid was 300,917, an increase over the preceding year of 13,503, and their value was $5,283,375.70, an increase of $94,094.83.

From the foregoing statements it appears that the total issue of money orders and postal notes for the year amounted to $156,821,348.24.

The number of letters and packages mailed during the year for special delivery was 3,375,693, an increase over the preceding year of nearly 22 per cent. The special-delivery stamps used upon these letters and packages amounted to $337,569.30, and the messengers' fees paid for their delivery amounted to $256,592.71, leaving a profit to the Government of $80,976.59.

The Railway Mail Service not only adds to the promptness of mail delivery at all offices, but it is the especial instrumentality which puts the smaller and way places in the service on an equality in that regard with the larger and terminal offices. This branch of the postal service has therefore received much attention from the Postmaster-General, and though it is gratifying to know that it is in a condition of high efficiency and great usefulness, I am led to agree with the Postmaster-General that there is room for its further improvement.

There are now connected to the Post-Office establishment 28,324 employees who are in the classified service. The head of this great Department gives conclusive evidence of the value of civil-service reform when, after an experience that renders his judgment on the subject absolutely reliable, he expresses the opinion that without the benefit of this system it would be impossible to conduct the vast business intrusted to him.

I desire to commend as especially worthy of prompt attention the suggestions of the Postmaster-General relating to a more sensible and businesslike organization and a better distribution of responsibility in his Department.

The report of the Secretary of the Navy contains a history of the operations of his Department during the past year and exhibits a most gratifying condition of the personnel of our Navy. He presents a satisfactory account of the progress which has been made in the construction of vessels and makes a number of recommendations to which attention is especially invited.

During the past six months the demands for cruising vessels have been many and urgent. There have been revolutions calling for vessels to protect American interests in Nicaragua, Guatemala, Costa Rica, Honduras, Argentina, and Brazil, while the condition of affairs in Honolulu has required the constant presence of one or more ships. With all these calls upon our Navy it became necessary, in order to make up a sufficient fleet to patrol the Bering Sea under the *modus vivendi* agreed upon with Great Britain, to detail to that service one vessel from the Fish Commission and three from the Revenue Marine.

Progress in the construction of new vessels has not been as rapid as was anticipated. There have been delays in the completion of unarmored vessels, but for the most part they have been such as are constantly occurring even in countries having the largest experience in naval shipbuilding. The most serious delays, however, have been in the work upon armored ships. The trouble has been the failure of contractors to deliver armor as agreed. The difficulties seem now, however, to have been all overcome, and armor is being delivered with satisfactory promptness. As a result of the experience acquired by shipbuilders and designers and material men, it is believed that the dates when vessels will be completed can now be estimated with reasonable accuracy. Great guns, rapid-fire guns, torpedoes, and powder are being promptly supplied.

The following vessels of the new Navy have been completed and are now ready for service: The double-turreted coast-defense monitor *Miantonomoh*, the double-turreted coast-defense monitor *Monterey*, the armored cruiser *New York*, the protected cruisers *Baltimore*, *Chicago*, *Philadelphia*, *Newark*, *San Francisco*, *Charleston*, *Atlanta*, and *Boston*, the cruiser *Detroit*, the gunboats *Yorktown*, *Concord*, *Bennington*, *Machias*, *Castine*, and *Petrel*, the dispatch vessel *Dolphin*, the practice vessel *Bancroft*, and the dynamite gunboat *Vesuvius*. Of these the *Bancroft*, *Machias*, *Detroit*, and *Castine* have been placed in commission during the current calendar year.

The following vessels are in process of construction: The second-class battle ships *Maine* and *Texas*, the cruisers *Montgomery* and *Marblehead*, and the coast-defense monitors *Terror*, *Puritan*, *Amphitrite*, and *Monadnock*, all of which will be completed within one year; the harbor-defense ram *Katahdin* and the protected cruisers *Columbia*, *Minneapolis*, *Olympia*, *Cincinnati*, and *Raleigh*, all of which will be completed prior to July 1, 1895; the first-class battle ships *Iowa*, *Indiana*, *Massachusetts*, and *Oregon*, which will be completed February 1, 1896, and the armored cruiser *Brooklyn*, which will be completed by August 1 of that year. It is also expected that the three gunboats authorized by the last Congress will be completed in less than two years.

Since 1886 Congress has at each session authorized the building of one or more vessels, and the Secretary of the Navy presents an earnest plea for the continuance of this plan. He recommends the authorization of at least one battle ship and six torpedo boats.

While I am distinctly in favor of consistently pursuing the policy we have inaugurated of building up a thorough and efficient Navy, I can not refrain from the suggestion that the Congress should carefully take into account the number of unfinished vessels on our hands and the depleted condition of our Treasury in considering the propriety of an appropriation at this time to begin new work.

The method of employing mechanical labor at navy-yards through boards of labor and making efficiency the sole test by which laborers are employed and continued is producing the best results, and the Secretary is earnestly devoting himself to its development. Attention is invited to the statements of his report in regard to the workings of the system.

The Secretary of the Interior has the supervision of so many important subjects that his report is of especial value and interest.

On the 30th day of June, 1893, there were on the pension rolls 966,012 names, an increase of 89,944 over the number on the rolls June 30, 1892. Of these there were 17 widows and daughters of Revolutionary soldiers, 86 survivors of the War of 1812, 5,425 widows of soldiers of that war, 21,518 survivors and widows of the Mexican War, 3,882 survivors and widows of Indian wars, 284 army nurses, and 475,645 survivors and widows and children of deceased soldiers and sailors of the War of the Rebellion. The latter number represents those pensioned on account of disabilities or death resulting from army and navy service. The number of persons remaining on the rolls June 30, 1893, who were pensioned under the act of June 27, 1890, which allows pensions on account of death and disability not chargeable to army service, was 459,155.

The number added to the rolls during the year was 123,634 and the number dropped was 33,690. The first payments on pensions allowed during the year amounted to $33,756,549.98. This includes arrears, or the accumulation between the time from which the allowance of pension dates and the time of actually granting the certificate.

Although the law of 1890 permits pensions for disabilities not related to military service, yet as a requisite to its benefits a disability must exist incapacitating applicants "from the performance of manual labor to such a degree as to render them unable to earn a support." The execution of this law in its early stages does not seem to have been in accord with its true intention, but toward the close of the last Administration an authoritative construction was given to the statute, and since that time this construction has been followed. This has had the effect of limiting the operation of the law to its intended purpose. The discovery having been made that many names had been put upon the pension roll by means of wholesale and gigantic frauds, the Commissioner suspended payments upon a number of pensions which seemed to be fraudulent or unauthorized pending a complete examination, giving notice to the pensioners, in order that they might have an opportunity to establish, if possible, the justice of their claims notwithstanding apparent invalidity.

This, I understand, is the practice which has for a long time prevailed in the Pension Bureau; but after entering upon these recent investigations the Commissioner modified this rule so as not to allow until after a complete examination interference with the payment of a pension apparently not altogether void, but which merely had been fixed at a rate higher than that authorized by law.

I am unable to understand why frauds in the pension rolls should not be exposed and corrected with thoroughness and vigor. Every name fraudulently put upon these rolls is a wicked imposition upon the kindly sentiment in which pensions have their origin; every fraudulent pensioner has become a bad citizen; every false oath in support of a pension has made perjury more common, and false and undeserving pensioners rob the people not only of their money, but of the patriotic sentiment which the survivors of a war fought for the preservation of the Union ought to inspire. Thousands of neighborhoods have their well-known fraudulent pensioners, and recent developments by the Bureau establish appalling conspiracies to accomplish pension frauds. By no means the least wrong done is to brave and deserving pensioners, who certainly ought not to be condemned to such association.

Those who attempt in the line of duty to rectify these wrongs should not be accused of enmity or indifference to the claims of honest veterans.

The sum expended on account of pensions for the year ending June 30, 1893, was $156,740,467.14.

The Commissioner estimates that $165,000,000 will be required to pay pensions during the year ending June 30, 1894.

The condition of the Indians and their ultimate fate are subjects which are related to a sacred duty of the Government and which strongly appeal to the sense of justice and the sympathy of our people.

Our Indians number about 248,000. Most of them are located on 161 reservations, containing 86,116,531 acres of land. About 110,000 of these Indians have to a large degree adopted civilized customs. Lands in severalty have been allotted to many of them. Such allotments have been made to 10,000 individuals during the last fiscal year, embracing about 1,000,000 acres. The number of Indian Government schools opened during the year was 195, an increase of 12 over the preceding year. Of this total 170 were on reservations, of which 73 were boarding schools and 97 were day schools. Twenty boarding schools and 5 day schools supported by the Government were not located on reservations. The total number of Indian children enrolled during the year as attendants of all schools was 21,138, an increase of 1,231 over the enrollment for the previous year.

I am sure that secular education and moral and religious teaching must be important factors in any effort to save the Indian and lead him to civilization. I believe, too, that the relinquishment of tribal relations and the holding of land in severalty may in favorable conditions aid this consummation. It seems to me, however, that allotments of land in severalty ought to be made with great care and circumspection. If hastily done, before the Indian knows its meaning, while yet he has little or no idea of tilling a farm and no conception of thrift, there is great danger that a reservation life in tribal relations may be exchanged for the pauperism of civilization instead of its independence and elevation.

The solution of the Indian problem depends very largely upon good administration. The personal fitness of agents and their adaptability to the peculiar duty of caring for their wards are of the utmost importance.

The law providing that, except in special cases, army officers shall be detailed as Indian agents it is hoped will prove a successful experiment.

There is danger of great abuses creeping into the prosecution of claims for Indian depredations, and I recommend that every possible safeguard be provided against the enforcement of unjust and fictitious claims of this description.

The appropriations on account of the Indian Bureau for the year ending June 30, 1894, amount to $7,954,962.99, a decrease as compared with the year preceding it of $387,131.95.

The vast area of land which but a short time ago constituted the public domain is rapidly falling into private hands.   It is certain that in the transfer the beneficent intention of the Government to supply from its domain homes to the industrious and worthy home seekers is often frustrated.   Though the speculator, who stands with extortionate purpose between the land office and those who, with their families, are invited by the Government to settle on the public lands, is a despicable character who ought not to be tolerated, yet it is difficult to thwart his schemes. The recent opening to settlement of the lands in the Cherokee Outlet, embracing an area of 6,500,000 acres, notwithstanding the utmost care in framing the regulations governing the selection of locations and notwithstanding the presence of United States troops, furnished an exhibition, though perhaps in a modified degree, of the mad scramble, the violence, and the fraudulent occupation which have accompanied previous openings of public land.

I concur with the Secretary in the belief that these outrageous incidents can not be entirely prevented without a change in the laws on the subject, and I hope his recommendations in that direction will be favorably considered.

I especially commend to the attention of the Congress the statements contained in the Secretary's report concerning forestry.   The time has come when efficient measures should be taken for the preservation of our forests from indiscriminate and remediless destruction.

The report of the Secretary of Agriculture will be found exceedingly interesting, especially to that large part of our citizens intimately concerned in agricultural occupations.

On the 7th day of March, 1893, there were upon its pay rolls 2,430 employees.   This number has been reduced to 1,850 persons.   In view of a depleted public Treasury and the imperative demand of the people for economy in the administration of their Government, the Secretary has entered upon the task of rationally reducing expenditures by the elimination from the pay rolls of all persons not needed for an efficient conduct of the affairs of the Department.

During the first quarter of the present year the expenses of the Department aggregated $345,876.76, as against $402,012.42 for the corresponding period of the fiscal year ending June 30, 1893.   The Secretary makes apparent his intention to continue this rate of reduction by submitting estimates for the next fiscal year less by $994,280 than those for the present year.

Among the heads of divisions in this Department the changes have been exceedingly few.   Three vacancies occurring from death and resignations have been filled by the promotion of assistants in the same divisions.

These promotions of experienced and faithful assistants have not only been in the interest of efficient work, but have suggested to those in the

Department who look for retention and promotion that merit and devotion to duty are their best reliance.

The amount appropriated for the Bureau of Animal Industry for the current fiscal year is $850,000. The estimate for the ensuing year is $700,000.

The regulations of 1892 concerning Texas fever have been enforced during the last year and the large stock yards of the country have been kept free from infection. Occasional local outbreaks have been largely such as could have been effectually guarded against by the owners of the affected cattle.

While contagious pleuro-pneumonia in cattle has been eradicated, animal tuberculosis, a disease widespread and more dangerous to human life than pleuro-pneumonia, is still prevalent. Investigations have been made during the past year as to the means of its communication and the method of its correct diagnosis. Much progress has been made in this direction by the studies of the division of animal pathology, but work ought to be extended, in cooperation with local authorities, until the danger to human life arising from this cause is reduced to a minimum.

The number of animals arriving from Canada during the year and inspected by Bureau officers was 462,092, and the number from transatlantic countries was 1,297. No contagious diseases were found among the imported animals.

The total number of inspections of cattle for export during the past fiscal year was 611,542. The exports show a falling off of about 25 per cent from the preceding year, the decrease occurring entirely in the last half of the year. This suggests that the falling off may have been largely due to an increase in the price of American export cattle.

During the year ending June 30, 1893, exports of inspected pork aggregated 20,677,410 pounds, as against 38,152,874 pounds for the preceding year. The falling off in this export was not confined, however, to inspected pork, the total quantity exported for 1892 being 665,490,616 pounds, while in 1893 it was only 527,308,695 pounds.

I join the Secretary in recommending that hereafter each applicant for the position of inspector or assistant inspector in the Bureau of Animal Industry be required, as a condition precedent to his appointment, to exhibit to the United States Civil Service Commission his diploma from an established, regular, and reputable veterinary college, and that this be supplemented by such an examination in veterinary science as the Commission may prescribe.

The exports of agricultural products from the United States for the fiscal year ending June 30, 1892, attained the enormous figure of $800,-000,000, in round numbers, being 78.7 per cent of our total exports. In the last fiscal year this aggregate was greatly reduced, but nevertheless reached 615,000,000, being 75.1 per cent of all American commodities exported.

A review of our agricultural exports with special reference to their destination will show that in almost every line the United Kingdom of Great Britain and Ireland absorbs by far the largest proportion. Of cattle the total exports aggregated in value for the fiscal year ending June 30, 1893, $26,000,000, of which Great Britain took considerably over $25,000,000. Of beef products of all kinds our total exports were $28,000,000, of which Great Britain took $24,000,000. Of pork products the total exports were $84,000,000, of which Great Britain took $53,000,000. In breadstuffs, cotton, and minor products like proportions sent to the same destination are shown.

The work of the statistical division of the Department of Agriculture deals with all that relates to the economics of farming.

The main purpose of its monthly reports is to keep the farmers informed as fully as possible of all matters having any influence upon the world's markets, in which their products find sale. Its publications relate especially to the commercial side of farming.

It is therefore of profound importance and vital concern to the farmers of the United States, who represent nearly one-half of our population, and also of direct interest to the whole country, that the work of this division be efficiently performed and that the information it has gathered be promptly diffused.

It is a matter for congratulation to know that the Secretary will not spare any effort to make this part of his work thoroughly useful.

In the year 1839 the Congress appropriated $1,000, to be taken from the Patent Office funds, for the purpose of collecting and distributing rare and improved varieties of seeds and for prosecuting agricultural investigations and procuring agricultural statistics. From this small beginning the seed division of the Department of Agriculture has grown to its present unwieldy and unjustifiably extravagant proportions.

During the last fiscal year the cost of seeds purchased was $66,548.61. The remainder of an appropriation of $135,000 was expended in putting them up and distributing them. It surely never could have entered the minds of those who first sanctioned appropriations of public money for the purchase of new and improved varieties of seeds for gratuitous distribution that from this would grow large appropriations for the purchase and distribution by members of Congress of ordinary seeds, bulbs, and cuttings which are common in all the States and Territories and everywhere easily obtainable at low prices.

In each State and Territory an agricultural experiment station has been established. These stations, by their very character and name, are the proper agencies to experiment with and test new varieties of seeds; and yet this indiscriminate and wasteful distribution by legislation and legislators continues, answering no purpose unless it be to remind constituents that their representatives are willing to remember them with gratuities at public cost.

Under the sanction of existing legislation there was sent out from the Agricultural Department during the last fiscal year enough of cabbage seed to plant 19,200 acres of land, a sufficient quantity of beans to plant 4,000 acres, beet seed enough to plant 2,500 acres, sweet corn enough to plant 7,800 acres, sufficient cucumber seed to cover 2,025 acres with vines, and enough muskmelon and watermelon seeds to plant 2,675 acres. The total quantity of flower and vegetable seeds thus distributed was contained in more than 9,000,000 packages, and they were sufficient if planted to cover 89,596 acres of land.

In view of these facts this enormous expenditure without legitimate returns of benefit ought to be abolished. Anticipating a consummation so manifestly in the interest of good administration, more than $100,000 has been stricken from the estimate made to cover this object for the year ending June 30, 1895; and the Secretary recommends that the remaining $35,000 of the estimate be confined strictly to the purchase of new and improved varieties of seeds, and that these be distributed through experiment stations.

Thus the seed will be tested, and after the test has been completed by the experiment station the propagation of the useful varieties and the rejection of the valueless may safely be left to the common sense of the people.

The continued intelligent execution of the civil-service law and the increasing approval by the people of its operation are most gratifying. The recent extension of its limitations and regulations to the employees at free-delivery post-offices, which has been honestly and promptly accomplished by the Commission, with the hearty cooperation of the Postmaster-General, is an immensely important advance in the usefulness of the system.

I am, if possible, more than ever convinced of the incalculable benefits conferred by the civil-service law, not only in its effect upon the public service, but also, what is even more important, in its effect in elevating the tone of political life generally.

The course of civil-service reform in this country instructively and interestingly illustrates how strong a hold a movement gains upon our people which has underlying it a sentiment of justice and right and which at the same time promises better administration of their Government.

The law embodying this reform found its way to our statute book more from fear of the popular sentiment existing in its favor than from any love for the reform itself on the part of legislators, and it has lived and grown and flourished in spite of the covert as well as open hostility of spoilsmen and notwithstanding the querulous impracticability of many self-constituted guardians. Beneath all the vagaries and sublimated theories which are attracted to it there underlies this reform a sturdy common-sense principle not only suited to this mundane sphere, but whose application our people are more and more recognizing to be absolutely essential to the most successful operation of their Government, if not to its perpetuity.

It seems to me to be entirely inconsistent with the character of this reform, as well as with its best enforcement, to oblige the Commission to rely for clerical assistance upon clerks detailed from other Departments. There ought not to be such a condition in any Department that clerks hired to do work there can be spared to habitually work at another place, and it does not accord with a sensible view of civil-service reform that persons should be employed on the theory that their labor is necessary in one Department when in point of fact their services are devoted to entirely different work in another Department.

I earnestly urge that the clerks necessary to carry on the work of the Commission be regularly put upon its roster and that the system of obliging the Commissioners to rely upon the services of clerks belonging to other Departments be discontinued. This ought not to increase the expense to the Government, while it would certainly be more consistent and add greatly to the efficiency of the Commission.

Economy in public expenditure is a duty that can not innocently be neglected by those intrusted with the control of money drawn from the people for public uses. It must be confessed that our apparently endless resources, the familiarity of our people with immense accumulations of wealth, the growing sentiment among them that the expenditure of public money should in some manner be to their immediate and personal advantage, the indirect and almost stealthy manner in which a large part of our taxes is exacted, and a degenerated sense of official accountability have led to growing extravagance in governmental appropriations.

At this time, when a depleted public Treasury confronts us, when many of our people are engaged in a hard struggle for the necessaries of life, and when enforced economy is pressing upon the great mass of our countrymen, I desire to urge with all the earnestness at my command that Congressional legislation be so limited by strict economy as to exhibit an appreciation of the condition of the Treasury and a sympathy with the straitened circumstances of our fellow-citizens.

The duty of public economy is also of immense importance in its intimate and necessary relation to the task now in hand of providing revenue to meet Government expenditures and yet reducing the people's burden of Federal taxation.

After a hard struggle tariff reform is directly before us. Nothing so important claims our attention and nothing so clearly presents itself as both an opportunity and a duty—an opportunity to deserve the gratitude of our fellow-citizens and a duty imposed upon us by our oft-repeated professions and by the emphatic mandate of the people. After full discussion our countrymen have spoken in favor of this reform, and they have confided the work of its accomplishment to the hands of those who are solemnly pledged to it.

If there is anything in the theory of a representation in public places of the people and their desires, if public officers are really the servants of the people, and if political promises and professions have any binding force, our failure to give the relief so long awaited will be sheer recreancy. Nothing should intervene to distract our attention or disturb our effort until this reform is accomplished by wise and careful legislation.

While we should stanchly adhere to the principle that only the necessity of revenue justifies the imposition of tariff duties and other Federal taxation and that they should be limited by strict economy, we can not close our eyes to the fact that conditions have grown up among us which in justice and fairness call for discriminating care in the distribution of such duties and taxation as the emergencies of our Government actually demand.

Manifestly if we are to aid the people directly through tariff reform, one of its most obvious features should be a reduction in present tariff charges upon the necessaries of life. The benefits of such a reduction would be palpable and substantial, seen and felt by thousands who would be better fed and better clothed and better sheltered. These gifts should be the willing benefactions of a Government whose highest function is the promotion of the welfare of the people.

Not less closely related to our people's prosperity and well-being is the removal of restrictions upon the importation of the raw materials necessary to our manufactures. The world should be open to our national ingenuity and enterprise. This can not be while Federal legislation through the imposition of high tariff forbids to American manufacturers as cheap materials as those used by their competitors. It is quite obvious that the enhancement of the price of our manufactured products resulting from this policy not only confines the market for these products within our own borders, to the direct disadvantage of our manufacturers, but also increases their cost to our citizens.

The interests of labor are certainly, though indirectly, involved in this feature of our tariff system. The sharp competition and active struggle among our manufacturers to supply the limited demand for their goods soon fill the narrow market to which they are confined. Then follows a suspension of work in mills and factories, a discharge of employees, and distress in the homes of our workingmen.

Even if the often-disproved assertion could be made good that a lower rate of wages would result from free raw materials and low tariff duties, the intelligence of our workmen leads them quickly to discover that their steady employment, permitted by free raw materials, is the most important factor in their relation to tariff legislation.

A measure has been prepared by the appropriate Congressional committee embodying tariff reform on the lines herein suggested, which will be promptly submitted for legislative action. It is the result of much patriotic and unselfish work, and I believe it deals with its subject consistently and as thoroughly as existing conditions permit.

I am satisfied that the reduced tariff duties provided for in the proposed legislation, added to existing internal-revenue taxation, will in the near future, though perhaps not immediately, produce sufficient revenue to meet the needs of the Government.

The committee, after full consideration and to provide against a temporary deficiency which may exist before the business of the country adjusts itself to the new tariff schedules, have wisely embraced in their plan a few additional internal-revenue taxes, including a small tax upon incomes derived from certain corporate investments.

These new adjustments are not only absolutely just and easily borne, but they have the further merit of being such as can be remitted without unfavorable business disturbance whenever the necessity of their imposition no longer exists.

In my great desire for the success of this measure I can not restrain the suggestion that its success can only be attained by means of unselfish counsel on the part of the friends of tariff reform and as a result of their willingness to subordinate personal desires and ambitions to the general good. The local interests affected by the proposed reform are so numerous and so varied that if all are insisted upon the legislation embodying the reform must inevitably fail.

In conclusion my intense feeling of responsibility impels me to invoke for the manifold interests of a generous and confiding people the most scrupulous care and to pledge my willing support to every legislative effort for the advancement of the greatness and prosperity of our beloved country.

GROVER CLEVELAND.

SPECIAL MESSAGES.

EXECUTIVE MANSION,
Washington, December 18, 1893.

To the Senate and House of Representatives:

In my recent annual message to the Congress I briefly referred to our relations with Hawaii and expressed the intention of transmitting further information on the subject when additional advices permitted.

Though I am not able now to report a definite change in the actual situation, I am convinced that the difficulties lately created both here and in Hawaii, and now standing in the way of a solution through Executive action of the problem presented, render it proper and expedient that the matter should be referred to the broader authority and discretion of Congress, with a full explanation of the endeavor thus far made to deal with the emergency and a statement of the considerations which have governed my action.

I suppose that right and justice should determine the path to be followed in treating this subject. If national honesty is to be disregarded and a desire for territorial extension or dissatisfaction with a form of government not our own ought to regulate our conduct, I have entirely misapprehended the mission and character of our Government and the behavior which the conscience of our people demands of their public servants.

When the present Administration entered upon its duties, the Senate had under consideration a treaty providing for the annexation of the Hawaiian Islands to the territory of the United States. Surely under our Constitution and laws the enlargement of our limits is a manifestation of the highest attribute of sovereignty, and if entered upon as an Executive act all things relating to the transaction should be clear and free from suspicion. Additional importance attached to this particular treaty of annexation because it contemplated a departure from unbroken American tradition in providing for the addition to our territory of islands of the sea more than 2,000 miles removed from our nearest coast.

These considerations might not of themselves call for interference with the completion of a treaty entered upon by a previous Administration, but it appeared from the documents accompanying the treaty when submitted to the Senate that the ownership of Hawaii was tendered to us by a Provisional Government set up to succeed the constitutional ruler of the islands, who had been dethroned, and it did not appear that such Provisional Government had the sanction of either popular revolution or suffrage. Two other remarkable features of the transaction naturally attracted attention. One was the extraordinary haste, not to say precipitancy, characterizing all the transactions connected with the treaty. It appeared that a so-called committee of safety, ostensibly the source of the revolt against the constitutional Government of Hawaii, was organized on Saturday, the 14th day of January; that on Monday, the 16th, the United States forces were landed at Honolulu from a naval vessel lying in its harbor; that on the 17th the scheme of a Provisional Government was perfected, and a proclamation naming its officers was on the same day prepared and read at the Government building; that immediately thereupon the United States minister recognized the Provisional Government thus created; that two days afterwards, on the 19th day of January, commissioners representing such Government sailed for this country in a steamer especially chartered for the occasion, arriving in San Francisco on the 28th day of January and in Washington on the 3d day of February; that on the next day they had their first interview with the Secretary of State, and another on the 11th, when the treaty of annexation was practically agreed upon, and that on the 14th it was formally concluded and on the 15th transmitted to the Senate. Thus between the initiation of the scheme for a Provisional Government in Hawaii, on the 14th day of January, and the submission to the Senate of the treaty of annexation concluded with such Government the entire interval was thirty-two days, fifteen of which were spent by the Hawaiian commissioners in their journey to Washington.

In the next place, upon the face of the papers submitted with the treaty it clearly appeared that there was open and undetermined an issue of fact of the most vital importance. The message of the President accompanying the treaty* declared that "the overthrow of the monarchy was not in any way promoted by this Government," and in a letter to the President from the Secretary of State, also submitted to the Senate with the treaty, the following passage occurs:

> At the time the Provisional Government took possession of the Government buildings no troops or officers of the United States were present or took any part whatever in the proceedings. No public recognition was accorded to the Provisional Government by the United States minister until after the Queen's abdication and when they were in effective possession of the Government buildings, the archives, the treasury, the barracks, the police station, and all the potential machinery of the Government.

But a protest also accompanied said treaty, signed by the Queen and her ministers at the time she made way for the Provisional Government, which explicitly stated that she yielded to the superior force of the United States, whose minister had caused United States troops to be landed at Honolulu and declared that he would support such Provisional Government.

The truth or falsity of this protest was surely of the first importance. If true, nothing but the concealment of its truth could induce our Government to negotiate with the semblance of a government thus created, nor could a treaty resulting from the acts stated in the protest have been knowingly deemed worthy of consideration by the Senate. Yet the truth or falsity of the protest had not been investigated.

I conceived it to be my duty, therefore, to withdraw the treaty from the Senate for examination, and meanwhile to cause an accurate, full, and impartial investigation to be made of the facts attending the subversion of the constitutional Government of Hawaii and the installment in its place of the Provisional Government. I selected for the work of investigation the Hon. James H. Blount, of Georgia, whose service of eighteen years as a member of the House of Representatives and whose experience as chairman of the Committee of Foreign Affairs in that body, and his consequent familiarity with international topics, joined with his high character and honorable reputation, seemed to render him peculiarly fitted for the duties intrusted to him. His report detailing his action under the instructions given to him and the conclusions derived from his investigation accompany this message.

These conclusions do not rest for their acceptance entirely upon Mr. Blount's honesty and ability as a man, nor upon his acumen and

*See pp. 348-349.

impartiality as an investigator. They are accompanied by the evidence upon which they are based, which evidence is also herewith transmitted, and from which it seems to me no other deductions could possibly be reached than those arrived at by the commissioner.

The report, with its accompanying proofs and such other evidence as is now before the Congress or is herewith submitted, justifies, in my opinion, the statement that when the President was led to submit the treaty to the Senate with the declaration that "the overthrow of the monarchy was not in any way promoted by this Government," and when the Senate was induced to receive and discuss it on that basis, both President and Senate were misled.

The attempt will not be made in this communication to touch upon all the facts which throw light upon the progress and consummation of this scheme of annexation. A very brief and imperfect reference to the facts and evidence at hand will exhibit its character and the incidents in which it had its birth.

It is unnecessary to set forth the reasons which in January, 1893, led a considerable proportion of American and other foreign merchants and traders residing at Honolulu to favor the annexation of Hawaii to the United States. It is sufficient to note the fact and to observe that the project was one which was zealously promoted by the minister representing the United States in that country. He evidently had an ardent desire that it should become a fact accomplished by his agency and during his ministry, and was not inconveniently scrupulous as to the means employed to that end. On the 19th day of November, 1892, nearly two months before the first overt act tending toward the subversion of the Hawaiian Government and the attempted transfer of Hawaiian territory to the United States, he addressed a long letter to the Secretary of State, in which the case for annexation was elaborately argued on moral, political, and economical grounds. He refers to the loss to the Hawaiian sugar interests from the operation of the McKinley bill and the tendency to still further depreciation of sugar property unless some positive measure of relief is granted. He strongly inveighs against the existing Hawaiian Government and emphatically declares for annexation. He says:

In truth, the monarchy here is an absurd anachronism. It has nothing on which it logically or legitimately stands. The feudal basis on which it once stood no longer existing, the monarchy now is only an impediment to good government—an obstruction to the prosperity and progress of the islands.

He further says:

As a Crown colony of Great Britain or a Territory of the United States the government modifications could be made readily and good administration of the law secured. Destiny and the vast future interests of the United States in the Pacific clearly indicate who at no distant day must be responsible for the government of these islands. Under a Territorial government they could be as easily governed as any of the existing Territories of the United States. * * * Hawaii has reached the parting of the ways. She must now take the road which leads to Asia, or the other, which outlets her in America, gives her an American civilization, and binds her to the care of American destiny.

He also declares:

One of two courses seems to me absolutely necessary to be followed—either bold and vigorous measures for annexation or a "customs union," an ocean cable from the Californian coast to Honolulu, Pearl Harbor perpetually ceded to the United States, with an implied but not expressly stipulated American protectorate over the islands. I believe the former to be the better, that which will prove much the more advantageous to the islands and the cheapest and least embarrassing in the end to the United States. If it was wise for the United States, through Secretary Marcy, thirty-eight years ago, to offer to expend $100,000 to secure a treaty of annexation, it certainly can not be chimerical or unwise to expend $100,000 to secure annexation in the near future. To-day the United States has five times the wealth she possessed in 1854, and the reasons now existing for annexation are much stronger than they were then. I can not refrain from expressing the opinion with emphasis that the golden hour is near at hand.

These declarations certainly show a disposition and condition of mind which may be usefully recalled when interpreting the significance of the minister's conceded acts or when considering the probabilities of such conduct on his part as may not be admitted.

In this view it seems proper to also quote from a letter written by the minister to the Secretary of State on the 8th day of March, 1892, nearly a year prior to the first step taken toward annexation. After stating the possibility that the existing Government of Hawaii might be overturned by an orderly and peaceful revolution, Minister Stevens writes as follows:

Ordinarily, in like circumstances, the rule seems to be to limit the landing and movement of United States forces in foreign waters and dominion exclusively to the protection of the United States legation and of the lives and property of American citizens; but as the relations of the United States to Hawaii are exceptional, and in former years the United States officials here took somewhat exceptional action in circumstances of disorder, I desire to know how far the present minister and naval commander may deviate from established international rules and precedents in the contingencies indicated in the first part of this dispatch.

To a minister of this temper, full of zeal for annexation, there seemed to arise in January, 1893, the precise opportunity for which he was watchfully waiting—an opportunity which by timely "deviation from established international rules and precedents" might be improved to successfully accomplish the great object in view; and we are quite prepared for the exultant enthusiasm with which, in a letter to the State Department dated February 1, 1893, he declares:

The Hawaiian pear is now fully ripe, and this is the golden hour for the United States to pluck it.

As a further illustration of the activity of this diplomatic representative, attention is called to the fact that on the day the above letter was written, apparently unable longer to restrain his ardor, he issued a proclamation whereby, "in the name of the United States," he assumed the protection of the Hawaiian Islands and declared that said action was "taken pending and subject to negotiations at Washington." Of course this assumption of a protectorate was promptly disavowed by our Government, but the American flag remained over the Government building at Honolulu and the forces remained on guard until April, and after Mr. Blount's arrival on the scene, when both were removed.

A brief statement of the occurrences that led to the subversion of the constitutional Government of Hawaii in the interests of annexation to the United States will exhibit the true complexion of that transaction.

On Saturday, January 14, 1893, the Queen of Hawaii, who had been contemplating the proclamation of a new constitution, had, in deference to the wishes and remonstrances of her cabinet, renounced the project for the present at least. Taking this relinquished purpose as a basis of action, citizens of Honolulu numbering from fifty to one hundred, mostly resident aliens, met in a private office and selected a so-called committee of safety, composed of thirteen persons, seven of whom were foreign subjects, and consisted of five Americans, one Englishman, and one German. This committee, though its designs were not revealed, had in view nothing less than annexation to the United States, and between Saturday, the 14th, and the following Monday, the 16th of January—though exactly what action was taken may not be clearly disclosed—they were certainly in communication with the United States minister. On Monday morning the Queen and her cabinet made public proclamation, with a notice which was specially served upon the representatives of all foreign governments, that any changes in the constitution would be sought only in the methods provided by that instrument. Nevertheless, at the call and under the auspices of the committee of safety, a mass meeting of citizens was held on that day to protest against the Queen's alleged illegal and unlawful proceedings and purposes. Even at this meeting the committee of safety continued to disguise their real purpose and contented themselves with procuring the passage of a resolution denouncing the Queen and empowering the committee to devise ways and means "to secure the permanent maintenance of law and order and the protection of life, liberty, and property in Hawaii." This meeting adjourned between 3 and 4 o'clock in the afternoon. On the same day, and immediately after such adjournment, the committee, unwilling to take further steps without the cooperation of the United States minister, addressed him a note representing that the public safety was menaced and that lives and property were in danger, and concluded as follows:

We are unable to protect ourselves without aid, and therefore pray for the protection of the United States forces.

Whatever may be thought of the other contents of this note, the absolute truth of this latter statement is incontestable. When the note was written and delivered the committee, so far as it appears, had neither a man nor a gun at their command, and after its delivery they became so panic-stricken at their position that they sent some of their number to interview the minister and request him not to land the United States forces till the next morning. But he replied that the troops had been ordered and whether the committee were ready or not the landing should take place. And so it happened that on the 16th day of January, 1893, between 4 and 5 o'clock in the afternoon, a detachment of marines from the United States steamer *Boston*, with two pieces of artillery, landed at Honolulu. The men, upward of 160 in all, were supplied with double cartridge belts filled with ammunition and with haversacks and canteens, and were accompanied by a hospital corps with stretchers and medical supplies.

This military demonstration upon the soil of Honolulu was of itself an act of war, unless made either with the consent of the Government of Hawaii or for the *bona fide* purpose of protecting the imperiled lives and property of citizens of the United States. But there is no pretense of any such consent on the part of the Government of the Queen, which at that time was undisputed and was both the *de facto* and the *de jure* Government. In point of fact the existing Government, instead of requesting the presence of an armed force, protested against it. There is as little basis for the pretense that such forces were landed for the security of American life and property. If so, they would have been stationed in the vicinity of such property and so as to protect it, instead of at a distance and so as to command the Hawaiian Government building and palace. Admiral Skerrett, the officer in command of our naval force on the Pacific station, has frankly stated that in his opinion the location of the troops was inadvisable if they were landed for the protection of American citizens, whose residences and places of business, as well as the legation and consulate, were in a distant part of the city; but the location selected was a wise one if the forces were landed for the purpose of supporting the Provisional Government. If any peril to life and property calling for any such martial array had existed, Great Britain and other foreign powers interested would not have been behind the United States in activity to protect their citizens. But they made no sign in that direction. When these armed men were landed the city of Honolulu was in its customary orderly and peaceful condition. There was no symptom of riot or disturbance in any quarter. Men, women, and children were about the streets as usual, and nothing varied the ordinary routine or disturbed the ordinary tranquillity except the landing of the *Boston's* marines and their march through the town to the quarters assigned them. Indeed, the fact that after having called for the landing of the United States forces on the plea of danger to life and property the committee of safety themselves requested the minister to postpone action exposed the untruthfulness of their representations of present peril to life and property. The peril they saw was an anticipation growing out of guilty intentions on their part and something which, though not then existing, they knew would certainly follow their attempt to overthrow the Government of the Queen without the aid of the United States forces.

Thus it appears that Hawaii was taken possession of by the United States forces without the consent or wish of the Government of the islands, or of anybody else so far as shown except the United States minister. Therefore the military occupation of Honolulu by the United States on the day mentioned was wholly without justification, either as an occupation by consent or as an occupation necessitated by dangers threatening American life and property. It must be accounted for in some other way and on some other ground, and its real motive and purpose are neither obscure nor far to seek.

The United States forces being now on the scene and favorably stationed, the committee proceeded to carry out their original scheme. They met the next morning, Tuesday, the 17th, perfected the plan of temporary government, and fixed upon its principal officers, ten of whom were drawn from the thirteen members of the committee of safety. Between 1 and 2 o'clock, by squads and by different routes to avoid notice, and having first taken the precaution of ascertaining whether there was anyone there to oppose them, they proceeded to the Government building to proclaim the new Government. No sign of opposition was manifest, and thereupon an American citizen began to read the proclamation from the steps of the Government building, almost entirely without auditors. It is said that before the reading was finished quite a concourse of persons, variously estimated at from 50 to 100, some armed and some unarmed, gathered about the committee to give them aid and confidence. This statement is not important, since the one controlling factor in the whole affair was unquestionably the United States marines, who, drawn up under arms and with artillery in readiness only 76 yards distant, dominated the situation.

The Provisional Government thus proclaimed was by the terms of the proclamation "to exist until terms of union with the United States had been negotiated and agreed upon." The United States minister, pursuant to prior agreement, recognized this Government within an hour after the reading of the proclamation, and before 5 o'clock, in answer to an inquiry on behalf of the Queen and her cabinet, announced that he had done so.

When our minister recognized the Provisional Government, the only basis upon which it rested was the fact that the committee of safety had in the manner above stated declared it to exist. It was neither a government *de facto* nor *de jure*. That it was not in such possession of the Government property and agencies as entitled it to recognition is conclusively proved by a note found in the files of the legation at Honolulu, addressed by the declared head of the Provisional Government to Minister Stevens, dated January 17, 1893, in which he acknowledges with expressions of appreciation the minister's recognition of the Provisional

Government, and states that it is not yet in the possession of the station house (the place where a large number of the Queen's troops were quartered), though the same had been demanded of the Queen's officers in charge. Nevertheless, this wrongful recognition by our minister placed the Government of the Queen in a position of most perilous perplexity. On the one hand she had possession of the palace, of the barracks, and of the police station, and had at her command at least 500 fully armed men and several pieces of artillery. Indeed, the whole military force of her Kingdom was on her side and at her disposal, while the committee of safety, by actual search, had discovered that there were but very few arms in Honolulu that were not in the service of the Government.

In this state of things, if the Queen could have dealt with the insurgents alone, her course would have been plain and the result unmistakable. But the United States had allied itself with her enemies, had recognized them as the true Government of Hawaii, and had put her and her adherents in the position of opposition against lawful authority. She knew that she could not withstand the power of the United States, but she believed that she might safely trust to its justice. Accordingly, some hours after the recognition of the Provisional Government by the United States minister, the palace, the barracks, and the police station, with all the military resources of the country, were delivered up by the Queen upon the representation made to her that her cause would thereafter be reviewed at Washington, and while protesting that she surrendered to the superior force of the United States, whose minister had caused United States troops to be landed at Honolulu and declared that he would support the Provisional Government, and that she yielded her authority to prevent collision of armed forces and loss of life, and only until such time as the United States, upon the facts being presented to it, should undo the action of its representative and reinstate her in the authority she claimed as the constitutional sovereign of the Hawaiian Islands.

This protest was delivered to the chief of the Provisional Government, who indorsed thereon his acknowledgment of its receipt. The terms of the protest were read without dissent by those assuming to constitute the Provisional Government, who were certainly charged with the knowledge that the Queen, instead of finally abandoning her power, had appealed to the justice of the United States for reinstatement in her authority; and yet the Provisional Government, with this unanswered protest in its hand, hastened to negotiate with the United States for the permanent banishment of the Queen from power and for a sale of her Kingdom.

Our country was in danger of occupying the position of having actually set up a temporary government on foreign soil for the purpose of acquiring through that agency territory which we had wrongfully put in its possession. The control of both sides of a bargain acquired in such a manner is called by a familiar and unpleasant name when found in private transactions. We are not without a precedent showing how scrupulously we avoided such accusations in former days. After the people of Texas had declared their independence of Mexico they resolved that on the acknowledgment of their independence by the United States they would seek admission into the Union. Several months after the battle of San Jacinto, by which Texan independence was practically assured and established, President Jackson declined to recognize it, alleging as one of his reasons that in the circumstances it became us "to beware of a too early movement, as it might subject us, however unjustly, to the imputation of seeking to establish the claim of our neighbors to a territory with a view to its subsequent acquisition by ourselves." This is in marked contrast with the hasty recognition of a government openly and concededly set up for the purpose of tendering to us territorial annexation.

I believe that a candid and thorough examination of the facts will force the conviction that the Provisional Government owes its existence to an armed invasion by the United States. Fair-minded people, with the evidence before them, will hardly claim that the Hawaiian Government was overthrown by the people of the islands or that the Provisional Government had ever existed with their consent. I do not understand that any member of this Government claims that the people would uphold it by their suffrages if they were allowed to vote on the question.

While naturally sympathizing with every effort to establish a republican form of government, it has been the settled policy of the United States to concede to people of foreign countries the same freedom and independence in the management of their domestic affairs that we have always claimed for ourselves, and it has been our practice to recognize revolutionary governments as soon as it became apparent that they were supported by the people. For illustration of this rule I need only to refer to the revolution in Brazil in 1889, when our minister was instructed to recognize the Republic "so soon as a majority of the people of Brazil should have signified their assent to its establishment and maintenance;" to the revolution in Chile in 1891, when our minister was directed to recognize the new Government "if it was accepted by the people," and to the revolution in Venezuela in 1892, when our recognition was accorded on condition that the new Government was "fully established, in possession of the power of the nation, and accepted by the people."

As I apprehend the situation, we are brought face to face with the following conditions:

The lawful Government of Hawaii was overthrown without the drawing of a sword or the firing of a shot by a process every step of which, it may safely be asserted, is directly traceable to and dependent for its success upon the agency of the United States acting through its diplomatic and naval representatives.

But for the notorious predilections of the United States minister for annexation the committee of safety, which should be called the committee of annexation, would never have existed.

But for the landing of the United States forces upon false pretexts respecting the danger to life and property the committee would never have exposed themselves to the pains and penalties of treason by undertaking the subversion of the Queen's Government.

But for the presence of the United States forces in the immediate vicinity and in position to afford all needed protection and support the committee would not have proclaimed the Provisional Government from the steps of the Government building.

And finally, but for the lawless occupation of Honolulu under false pretexts by the United States forces, and but for Minister Stevens's recognition of the Provisional Government when the United States forces were its sole support and constituted its only military strength, the Queen and her Government would never have yielded to the Provisional Government, even for a time and for the sole purpose of submitting her case to the enlightened justice of the United States.

Believing, therefore, that the United States could not, under the circumstances disclosed, annex the islands without justly incurring the imputation of acquiring them by unjustifiable methods, I shall not again submit the treaty of annexation to the Senate for its consideration, and in the instructions to Minister Willis, a copy of which accompanies this message, I have directed him to so inform the Provisional Government.

But in the present instance our duty does not, in my opinion, end with refusing to consummate this questionable transaction. It has been the boast of our Government that it seeks to do justice in all things without regard to the strength or weakness of those with whom it deals. I mistake the American people if they favor the odious doctrine that there is no such thing as international morality; that there is one law for a strong nation and another for a weak one, and that even by indirection a strong power may with impunity despoil a weak one of its territory.

By an act of war, committed with the participation of a diplomatic representative of the United States and without authority of Congress, the Government of a feeble but friendly and confiding people has been overthrown. A substantial wrong has thus been done which a due regard for our national character as well as the rights of the injured people requires we should endeavor to repair. The Provisional Government has not assumed a republican or other constitutional form, but has remained a mere executive council or oligarchy, set up without the assent of the people. It has not sought to find a permanent basis of popular support and has given no evidence of an intention to do so. Indeed, the representatives of that Government assert that the people of Hawaii are unfit for popular government and frankly avow that they can be best ruled by arbitrary or despotic power.

The law of nations is founded upon reason and justice, and the rules of conduct governing individual relations between citizens or subjects of a civilized state are equally applicable as between enlightened nations.

The considerations that international law is without a court for its en-forcement and that obedience to its commands practically depends upon good faith instead of upon the mandate of a superior tribunal only give additional sanction to the law itself and brand any deliberate infraction of it not merely as a wrong, but as a disgrace. A man of true honor protects the unwritten word which binds his conscience more scrupu-lously, if possible, than he does the bond a breach of which subjects him to legal liabilities, and the United States, in aiming to maintain itself as one of the most enlightened nations, would do its citizens gross injustice if it applied to its international relations any other than a high stand-ard of honor and morality. On that ground the United States can not properly be put in the position of countenancing a wrong after its com-mission any more than in that of consenting to it in advance. On that ground it can not allow itself to refuse to redress an injury inflicted through an abuse of power by officers clothed with its authority and wearing its uniform; and on the same ground, if a feeble but friendly state is in danger of being robbed of its independence and its sovereignty by a misuse of the name and power of the United States, the United States can not fail to vindicate its honor and its sense of justice by an earnest effort to make all possible reparation.

These principles apply to the present case with irresistible force when the special conditions of the Queen's surrender of her sovereignty are recalled. She surrendered, not to the Provisional Government, but to the United States. She surrendered, not absolutely and permanently, but temporarily and conditionally until such time as the facts could be considered by the United States. Furthermore, the Provisional Govern-ment acquiesced in her surrender in that manner and on those terms, not only by tacit consent, but through the positive acts of some members of that Government, who urged her peaceable submission, not merely to avoid bloodshed, but because she could place implicit reliance upon the justice of the United States and that the whole subject would be finally considered at Washington.

I have not, however, overlooked an incident of this unfortunate affair which remains to be mentioned. The members of the Provisional Gov-ernment and their supporters, though not entitled to extreme sympathy, have been led to their present predicament of revolt against the Govern-ment of the Queen by the indefensible encouragement and assistance of our diplomatic representative. This fact may entitle them to claim that in our effort to rectify the wrong committed some regard should be had for their safety. This sentiment is strongly seconded by my anxiety to do nothing which would invite either harsh retaliation on the part of the Queen or violence and bloodshed in any quarter. In the belief that the Queen, as well as her enemies, would be willing to adopt such a course as would meet these conditions, and in view of the fact that both the Queen and the Provisional Government had at one time apparently acquiesced in a reference of the entire case to the United States Government, and considering the further fact that in any event the Provisional Government by its own declared limitation was only "to exist until terms of union with the United States of America have been negotiated and agreed upon," I hoped that after the assurance to the members of that Government that such union could not be consummated I might compass a peaceful adjustment of the difficulty.

Actuated by these desires and purposes, and not unmindful of the inherent perplexities of the situation nor of the limitations upon my power, I instructed Minister Willis to advise the Queen and her supporters of my desire to aid in the restoration of the status existing before the lawless landing of the United States forces at Honolulu on the 16th of January last if such restoration could be effected upon terms providing for clemency as well as justice to all parties concerned. The conditions suggested, as the instructions show, contemplate a general amnesty to those concerned in setting up the Provisional Government and a recognition of all its *bona fide* acts and obligations. In short, they require that the past should be buried and that the restored Government should reassume its authority as if its continuity had not been interrupted These conditions have not proved acceptable to the Queen, and though she has been informed that they will be insisted upon and that unless acceded to the efforts of the President to aid in the restoration of her Government will cease, I have not thus far learned that she is willing to yield them her acquiescence. The check which my plans have thus encountered has prevented their presentation to the members of the Provisional Government, while unfortunate public misrepresentations of the situation and exaggerated statements of the sentiments of our people have obviously injured the prospects of successful Executive mediation.

I therefore submit this communication, with its accompanying exhibits, embracing Mr. Blount's report, the evidence and statements taken by him at Honolulu, the instructions given to both Mr. Blount and Minister Willis, and correspondence connected with the affair in hand.

In commending this subject to the extended powers and wide discretion of the Congress I desire to add the assurance that I shall be much gratified to cooperate in any legislative plan which may be devised for the solution of the problem before us which is consistent with American honor, integrity, and morality.   GROVER CLEVELAND.

EXECUTIVE MANSION,
Washington, December 18, 1893.

To the Senate of the United States:

In compliance with a resolution passed by the Senate on the 6th instant, I hereby transmit reports of the Secretaries of State and of the Navy, with copies of all instructions given to the respective diplomatic and naval representatives of the United States in the Hawaiian Islands since the 4th day of March, 1881, touching the matters specified in the resolution.

It has seemed convenient to include in the present communication to the Senate copies of the diplomatic correspondence concerning the political condition of Hawaii, prepared for transmission to the House of Representatives in response to a later resolution passed by that body on the 13th instant.

GROVER CLEVELAND.

EXECUTIVE MANSION,
Washington, December 18, 1893.

To the House of Representatives:

In compliance with a resolution passed by your honorable body on the 13th instant, I hereby transmit a report of the Secretary of State, with copies of the instructions given to Mr. Albert S. Willis, the representative of the United States now in the Hawaiian Islands, and also the correspondence since the 4th day of March, 1889, concerning the relations of this Government to those islands.

In making this communication I have withheld only a dispatch from the former minister to Hawaii, numbered 70, under date of October 8, 1892, and a dispatch from the present minister, numbered 3, under date of November 16, 1893, because in my opinion the publication of these two papers would be incompatible with the public interest.

GROVER CLEVELAND.

EXECUTIVE MANSION, *January 4, 1894.*

To the Senate of the United States:

I transmit herewith a report of the Secretary of State, submitted in compliance with the resolution of October 17 last, in the matter of the claim of certain persons against the Government of Spain for illegal arrest off the coast of Yucatan in the year 1850, and subsequent imprisonment.

GROVER CLEVELAND.

EXECUTIVE MANSION, *January 13, 1894.*

To the Congress:

I transmit herewith copies of all dispatches from our minister at Hawaii relating in any way to political affairs in that country, except such as have been heretofore laid before the Congress.

I also transmit a copy of the last instructions sent to our minister, dated January 12, 1894, being the only instructions to him not already sent to the Congress.

In transmitting certain correspondence with my message dated December 18, 1893, I withheld a dispatch from our present minister, numbered 3 and dated November 16, 1893, and also a dispatch from our former minister, numbered 70 and dated October 8, 1892. Inasmuch as the contents of the dispatch of November 16, 1893, are referred to in the dispatches of a more recent date, now sent to Congress, and inasmuch as there seems no longer to be sufficient reason for withholding said dispatch, a copy of the same is herewith submitted. The dispatch numbered 70 and dated October 8, 1892, above referred to, is still withheld for the reason that such a course still appears to be justifiable and proper.

GROVER CLEVELAND.

EXECUTIVE MANSION, *January 20, 1894.*

To the Congress:

I transmit herewith dispatches received yesterday from our minister at Hawaii, with certain correspondence which accompanied the same, including a most extraordinary letter, dated December 27, 1893, signed by Sanford B. Dole, minister of foreign affairs of the Provisional Government, addressed to our minister, Mr. Willis, and delivered to him a number of hours after the arrival at Honolulu of a copy of my message to Congress on the Hawaiian question, with copies of instructions given to our minister.

GROVER CLEVELAND.

EXECUTIVE MANSION, *January 22, 1894.*

To the Congress:

I transmit herewith copies of dispatches received from our minister to Hawaii after the arrival of those copies which accompanied my message of the 20th instant. I also inclose, for the information of Congress, copies of reports and a copy of an order just received by the Secretary of the Navy from Rear-Admiral Irwin, commanding our naval forces at Honolulu.

GROVER CLEVELAND.

EXECUTIVE MANSION, *February 2, 1894.*

To the Congress:

I transmit a communication from the Secretary of State, accompanying a dispatch received a few days ago from our minister at Hawaii.

GROVER CLEVELAND.

EXECUTIVE MANSION,
Washington, February 12, 1894.

To the Congress:

I transmit herewith two dispatches received a few days ago from our minister at Hawaii, and a reply to one of them from the Secretary of State, in which a correct version is given of an interview which occurred November 14, 1893, between the Secretary of State and Mr. Thurston, representing the Provisional Government at Washington.

GROVER CLEVELAND.

EXECUTIVE MANSION, *February 16, 1894.*

To the Senate and House of Representatives:

I transmit herewith, for the information of Congress, a communication from the Secretary of State, covering the report of the Director of the Bureau of the American Republics for the year 1893.

GROVER CLEVELAND.

EXECUTIVE MANSION, *February 19, 1894.*

To the House of Representatives:

I herewith transmit copies of certain dispatches recently received from our minister at Honolulu. GROVER CLEVELAND.

EXECUTIVE MANSION, *February 19, 1894.*

To the Senate:

On the evening of the 16th instant I received a copy of a resolution passed by the Senate, requesting the transmission to that body of all reports and dispatches from our minister at Hawaii, and especially a certain letter written to him by Mr. Dole, President of the Provisional Government.

On the same day I received from the State Department a copy of a dispatch from Minister Willis, accompanied by various exhibits. I was not able to send them to the Senate on that day. The Senate adjourned that afternoon until to-day, and thus prevented the submission until now of these papers.

The next day after the receipt of the Senate resolution, and on the 17th instant, other dispatches were received from Mr. Willis at the State Department. They were copied with all possible haste, and are now submitted at the first meeting of the Senate since their receipt. They include the letter mentioned in the Senate resolution and the answer of Minister Willis to the same.

Since the 18th day of December last, when I submitted to the "broader authority and discretion of the Congress" all matters connected with our relations with Hawaii, I have with the utmost promptness transmitted to the Congress all dispatches and reports relative to the subject, and I am not aware of any dispatches or documents in the remotest way connected with these relations which have come to the possession of the State Department or the Executive and been withheld from the Senate.

GROVER CLEVELAND.

EXECUTIVE MANSION,
Washington, March 7, 1894.

To the Senate of the United States:

I transmit herewith a report submitted by the Secretary of State in response to the resolution of the Senate dated January 23, 1894, requesting communication of correspondence exchanged between the Government of the United States and the Governments of Colombia, Venezuela, and Hayti.

GROVER CLEVELAND.

To the Congress: EXECUTIVE MANSION, *March 7, 1894.*

I transmit herewith copies of certain dispatches lately received from our minister at Hawaii, together with copies of the inclosures which accompanied such dispatches.

GROVER CLEVELAND.

EXECUTIVE MANSION, *March 8, 1894.*

To the Senate of the United States:

I transmit herewith a report furnished by the Secretary of State in response to a resolution of the Senate of the 1st instant, making inquiry respecting the present condition of the *Virginius* indemnity fund.

GROVER CLEVELAND.

EXECUTIVE MANSION,
To the Senate: *Washington, D. C., March 14, 1894.*

I herewith transmit a report* of the Secretary of State of the 14th instant, concerning the several inquiries in the resolution of the Senate addressed to him under date of the 9th instant.

GROVER CLEVELAND.

EXECUTIVE MANSION,
To the Senate: *Washington, March 19, 1894.*

I transmit herewith, with a view to its ratification, a convention concluded at this capital on the 17th instant between the United States and China concerning the subject of emigration between those two countries.

GROVER CLEVELAND.

EXECUTIVE MANSION,
To the Senate: *Washington, March 19, 1894.*

I transmit herewith a report from the Secretary of State, concerning the landing of British troops at Bluefields, Nicaragua, in answer to the resolution of the Senate of the 7th instant on that subject.

GROVER CLEVELAND.

---

*Relating to the coined silver money and the products of India, Russia, and the Argentine Republic.

EXECUTIVE MANSION, *March 19, 1894.*

To the Congress:

I transmit herewith a copy of a dispatch received from our minister at Hawaii, together with copies of the inclosures which accompanied said dispatch.

GROVER CLEVELAND.

EXECUTIVE MANSION,
Washington, April 3, 1894.

To the Senate:

I transmit herewith report from the Secretary of State, inclosing the final report of the agent of the United States before the Paris Tribunal, also the protocols thus far received and certain other papers relating to that arbitration.

GROVER CLEVELAND.

EXECUTIVE MANSION,
Washington, April 13, 1894.

To the Congress:

I transmit herewith copies of certain dispatches from the United States minister at Honolulu, received by the Secretary of State since my message of March 19, 1894.

GROVER CLEVELAND.

EXECUTIVE MANSION,
Washington, April 21, 1894.

To the Congress:

I transmit herewith a communication from the Secretary of State, covering a dispatch from the United States minister at Honolulu and reply thereto.

GROVER CLEVELAND.

EXECUTIVE MANSION,
Washington, D. C., May 1, 1894.

To the Senate and House of Representatives:

I transmit herewith the ninth annual report of the Commissioner of Labor. This report relates entirely to building and loan associations in the United States.

GROVER CLEVELAND.

EXECUTIVE MANSION,
Washington, May 9, 1894.

To the Senate of the United States:

I transmit herewith, in response to the resolution of the Senate of April 6, 1894, a report of the Secretary of State, containing the requested information as to the present condition of affairs in the Samoan Islands, with copies of the correspondence in relation thereto, including that with the Governments of Great Britain and Germany.

GROVER CLEVELAND.

EXECUTIVE MANSION,
Washington, *May 9, 1894.*

To the Congress:

I transmit herewith a communication from the Secretary of State, in regard to recent dispatches from the United States minister at Honolulu, received since my message of April 21, 1894, and also a dispatch from the minister dated April 14, 1894.

GROVER CLEVELAND.

EXECUTIVE MANSION,
Washington, *May 29, 1894.*

To the Congress:

I herewith transmit, having regard to my message of May 9, 1894, a communication from the Secretary of State, covering a dispatch from the United States minister at Honolulu.

GROVER CLEVELAND.

EXECUTIVE MANSION,
Washington, *June 20, 1894.*

To the Senate:

I transmit herewith, in response to the resolution of the Senate of December 20, 1893, a report from the Acting Secretary of State, covering the desired copies of correspondence in the matter of the claim of Antonio Maximo Mora against Spain.

GROVER CLEVELAND.

EXECUTIVE MANSION,
Washington, *June 23, 1894.*

To the Congress:

I herewith transmit a communication covering dispatches from the United States minister at Honolulu.

GROVER CLEVELAND.

EXECUTIVE MANSION, *June 25, 1894.*

To the Senate and House of Representatives:

The shocking intelligence has been received that the President of the French Republic met his death yesterday at the hands of an assassin. This terrible event which has overtaken a sister Republic can not fail to deeply arouse the sympathies of the American nation, while the violent termination of a career promising so much in aid of liberty and advancing civilization should be mourned as an affliction to mankind.

GROVER CLEVELAND.

EXECUTIVE MANSION, *June 29, 1894.*

To the Senate of the United States:

Answering a resolution of your honorable body dated the 13th instant, I transmit herewith a report* of the Secretary of State, with an

---

* Relating to the probable retaliatory action of foreign governments for the proposed imposition by the United States of a duty on sugar.

accompanying document, which contain all the information in my possession touching the matters embraced in said resolution.

GROVER CLEVELAND.

EXECUTIVE MANSION,
Washington, July 9, 1894.

To the Senate:

I transmit herewith, in further response to the Senate resolution of April 6, 1894, a report from the Secretary of State, accompanied by copies of certain correspondence relating to Samoan affairs.

GROVER CLEVELAND.

EXECUTIVE MANSION, *July 19, 1894.*

To the Senate of the United States:

In compliance with a resolution of the Senate of the 18th instant, the House of Representatives concurring, I return herewith the bill (S. 1105) entitled "An act for the relief of Albert Redstone."

GROVER CLEVELAND.

EXECUTIVE MANSION,
Washington, July 24, 1894.

To the Congress:

I herewith transmit a communication from the Secretary of State, covering a dispatch from the United States minister at Honolulu.

GROVER CLEVELAND.

EXECUTIVE MANSION,
Washington, D. C., July 27, 1894.

To the Senate and House of Representatives:

I transmit herewith the seventh special report of the Commissioner of Labor. This report relates to what is generally known as the slums of cities, and has been prepared in accordance with a joint resolution approved July 20, 1892.

GROVER CLEVELAND.

EXECUTIVE MANSION,
Washington, July 30, 1894.

To the Congress:

I herewith transmit a communication from the Secretary of State, covering two dispatches from the United States minister at Honolulu.

GROVER CLEVELAND.

VETO MESSAGES.

EXECUTIVE MANSION, *January 17, 1894.*

To the House of Representatives:

I return without my approval House bill No. 71, entitled "An act for the relief of purchasers of timber and stone lands under the act of June 3, 1878."

This bill permits the proofs and affidavits which under present statutes parties desiring to acquire certain public lands are required to make before the registers and receivers of the land offices within which such lands are located to be made before any commissioner of the United States circuit court or before the judge or clerk of any court of records of the county or parish in which the lands are situated.

A similar bill was passed by the Fifty-second Congress and was disapproved by the Commissioner of the General Land Office and the Secretary of the Interior. The successors of these officers oppose the present bill on the ground that in its operation it would open the door to fraud and to a perversion of the intentions of the Government in relation to the public lands.

It is difficult, with the most scrupulous care, to guard the alienation of our public lands from fraud and illegal practices. It is perfectly plain, however, that the prospect of accomplishing this result is better under present laws, which require the necessary proofs to be made before land officers who are appointed for that purpose and who are under the control of the General Land Office and amenable to its regulations, than it would be by substituting other officers over whom the Land Office has no control.

Certain rules and orders of the Land Office are now in force which regulate the taking of the necessary proofs and permit oral examinations by registers and receivers. These regulations are of the utmost importance if our land laws are to be justly and honestly administered.

I fully concur in the objections made to this bill by the officers having charge of the public lands in the last Administration and by their successors who are now charged with that responsibility. I am convinced that such a relaxation of our existing land laws as is contemplated by the bill under consideration would not be in the interest of good administration.

GROVER CLEVELAND.

EXECUTIVE MANSION, *January 20, 1894.*

To the House of Representatives:

I hereby return without my approval House bill No. 3289, entitled "An act to authorize the New York and New Jersey Bridge Companies to construct and maintain a bridge across the Hudson River between New York City and the State of New Jersey."

This bill authorizes the construction of a bridge over the North River between the States of New York and New Jersey, the terminus of which in the city of New York shall not be below Sixty-sixth street. It contemplates the construction of a bridge upon piers placed in the river. No mention is made of a single span crossing the entire river, nor is there anything in the bill indicating that it was within the intention of the Congress that there should be a bridge built without piers. I am by no means certain that the Secretary of War, who is invested by the terms of the bill with considerable discretion so far as the plans for the structure are concerned, would have the right to exact of the promoters of this enterprise the erection of a bridge spanning the entire river.

Much objection has been made to the location of any piers in the river for the reason that they would seriously interfere with the commerce which seeks the port of New York through that channel. It is certainly very questionable whether piers should be permitted at all in the North River at the point designated for the location of this bridge. It seems absolutely certain that within a few years a great volume of shipping will extend to that location, which would be seriously embarrassed by such obstruction.

I appreciate fully the importance of securing some means by which railroad traffic can cross this river, and no one can fail to realize the serious inconvenience to travel caused by lack of facilities of that character. At the same time, it is a plain dictate of wisdom and expediency that the commerce of the river be not unnecessarily interfered with by bridges or in any other manner.

Engineers whose judgment upon the matter can not be questioned, including the engineer of the company proposing to build this bridge, have expressed the opinion that the entire river can be spanned safely and effectively by a suspension bridge, or a construction not needing the use of piers.

The company to which the permission to bridge the river is granted in the bill under consideration was created by virtue of an act of the legislature of the State of New York which became a law, by reason of the failure of the governor to either approve or veto the same, on the 30th day of April, 1890. It may be safely assumed that the members of the legislature which passed this law knew what was necessary for the protection of the commerce of the city of New York and had informed themselves concerning the plan of a bridge that should be built in view of all the interests concerned.

By paragraph 24 of the law creating this company it is provided that "the said bridge shall be constructed with a single span over the entire river between towers or piers located between the span and the existing pier-head lines in either State," and that "no pier or tower or other obstruction of a permanent character shall be placed or built in the river between said towers or piers under this act.''

In view of such professional judgment, and considering the interests which would be interfered with by the location of piers in the river, and having due regard to the judgment of the legislature of the State of New York, it seems to me that a plan necessitating the use of piers in the bed of the river should be avoided. The question of increased expense of construction or the compromise of conflicting interests should not outweigh the other important considerations involved.

I notice the bill provides that the companies availing themselves of its privileges shall receive no greater pay for transporting the mails across the bridge than is allowed per mile to railroads using the same. If this is intended, as the language seems to import, to authorize this bridge company to charge the United States Government a toll for the carriage of its mails across the bridge equal to the amount which may be paid per mile by the Government for carrying the mails by railroads crossing the bridge, it seems to me it should not be allowed. The expense to the Government for carrying the mails over the structure should beyond any doubt be limited to the compensation paid the railroads for transportation.

An exceedingly important objection to the bill remains to be considered. In 1890 the North River Bridge Company was incorporated by an act of Congress for the purpose of constructing a bridge across the North River, the New York terminus of which was located at or near Twenty-third street in the city of New York. The proposition to construct the bridge at that point was a subject very carefully and thoroughly examined at that time and during the agitation of the project for a number of years prior to the passage of the act. As a result of such examination and much discussion, Congress granted permission to this company to construct a bridge having a single span and suspended from towers on each side of the river, and in the act especially prohibited the placing of any piers in the river, either of a temporary or of a permanent character, in connection with said bridge. This plan to bridge the river without piers was at that time considered feasible by the engineers of the company, and it accepted the terms of the act. Before this permission was finally granted a number of bills were introduced in the Congress covering the same subject, which were referred to Government engineers. Reports were made by these officers in every case insisting upon a construction with a single span and without piers in the bed of the river.

The eighth subdivision of the bill herewith returned provides that any company heretofore created for the purpose of bridging the river may avail itself of the provisions of the act, and makes such company subject to all its provisions. This, of course, has reference to the North River Bridge Company and releases that company from the prohibition of the act under which it was permitted to span the river and permits it to construct piers in the river. It seems to me that the language of the bill under consideration, so far as it relates to this particular feature, is equivalent to a new grant to that company, differing very materially from the grant which was thought expedient at the time it was before the Congress, and removes the guaranty that in the construction of its bridge there shall be no obstructions in the river such as were especially guarded against by the bill originally passed for its benefit. In effect a new charter is granted to a company not named in the bill, and with no apparent reason for the important enlargement of its privileges thus accomplished. It is entirely apparent that the reasons against obstructions in the North River which might interfere with commerce and navigation and the beneficial use of the harbor of New York are immensely strengthened when they are applied to a location in the river far below the location of the bridge which is permitted in the bill now before me.

Whatever question there may be about the injurious character of the obstruction at Sixty-sixth street in New York City, I believe there can be no doubt whatever that piers placed in the river more than 2 miles below, at Twenty-third street, would be very serious impediments. If this thoroughfare, so important to the commerce of the country and the State of New York, is to be crossed by bridges, each scheme for that purpose should be considered by itself and its merits and advisability determined by the circumstances which naturally belong to it. The objection to piers in the river for the purpose of supporting bridges is in any event so serious that the considerations which would determine the question of a bridge located at Sixty-sixth street ought not in such an indirect manner as is done by this bill be applied to a like structure at Twenty-third street.

GROVER CLEVELAND.

EXECUTIVE MANSION, *March 29, 1894.*

To the House of Representatives:

I return without my approval House bill No. 4956, entitled "An act directing the coinage of the silver bullion held in the Treasury, and for other purposes."

My strong desire to avoid disagreement with those in both Houses of Congress who have supported this bill would lead me to approve it if I could believe that the public good would not be thereby endangered and that such action on my part would be a proper discharge of official duty. Inasmuch, however, as I am unable to satisfy myself that the proposed legislation is either wise or opportune, my conception of the obligations and responsibilities attached to the great office I hold forbids the indulgence of my personal desire and inexorably confines me to that course which is dictated by my reason and judgment and pointed out by a sincere purpose to protect and promote the general interests of our people.

The financial disturbance which swept over the country during the last year was unparalleled in its severity and disastrous consequences. There seemed to be almost an entire displacement of faith in our financial ability and a loss of confidence in our fiscal policy. Among those who attempted to assign causes for our distress it was very generally conceded that the operation of a provision of law then in force which required the Government to purchase monthly a large amount of silver bullion and issue its notes in payment therefor was either entirely or to a large extent responsible for our condition. This led to the repeal on the 1st day of November, 1893, of this statutory provision.

We had, however, fallen so low in the depths of depression and timidity and apprehension had so completely gained control in financial circles that our rapid recuperation could not be reasonably expected. Our recovery has, nevertheless, steadily progressed, and though less than five months have elapsed since the repeal of the mischievous silver-purchase requirement a wholesome improvement is unmistakably apparent. Confidence in our absolute solvency is to such an extent reinstated and faith in our disposition to adhere to sound financial methods is so far restored as to produce the most encouraging results both at home and abroad. The wheels of domestic industry have been slowly set in motion and the tide of foreign investment has again started in our direction.

Our recovery being so well under way, nothing should be done to check our convalescence; nor should we forget that a relapse at this time would almost surely reduce us to a lower stage of financial distress than that from which we are just emerging.

I believe that if the bill under consideration should become a law it would be regarded as a retrogression from the financial intentions indicated by our recent repeal of the provision forcing silver-bullion purchases; that it would weaken, if it did not destroy, returning faith and confidence in our sound financial tendencies, and that as a consequence our progress to renewed business health would be unfortunately checked and a return to our recent distressing plight seriously threatened.

This proposed legislation is so related to the currency conditions growing out of the law compelling the purchase of silver by the Government that a glance at such conditions and a partial review of the law referred to may not be unprofitable.

Between the 14th day of August, 1890, when the law became operative, and the 1st day of November, 1893, when the clause it contained directing the purchase of silver was repealed, there were purchased by the Secretary of the Treasury more than 168,000,000 ounces of silver bullion. In payment for this bullion the Government issued its Treasury notes, of various denominations, amounting to nearly $156,000,000, which notes were immediately added to the currency in circulation among our people. Such notes were by the law made legal tender in payment of all debts, public and private, except when otherwise expressly stipulated, and were made receivable for customs, taxes, and all public dues, and when so received might be reissued. They were also permitted to be held by banking associations as a part of their lawful reserves.

On the demand of the holders these Treasury notes were to be redeemed in gold or silver coin, in the discretion of the Secretary of the Treasury; but it was declared as a part of this redemption provision that it was "the established policy of the United States to maintain the two metals on a parity with each other upon the present legal ratio or such ratio as may be provided by law." The money coined from such bullion was to be standard silver dollars, and after directing the immediate coinage of a little less than 28,000,000 ounces the law provided that as much of the remaining bullion should be thereafter coined as might be necessary to provide for the redemption of the Treasury notes issued on its purchase, and that "any gain or seigniorage arising from such coinage shall be accounted for and paid into the Treasury."

This gain or seigniorage evidently indicates so much of the bullion owned by the Government as should remain after using a sufficient amount to coin as many standard silver dollars as should equal in number the dollars represented by the Treasury notes issued in payment of the entire quantity of bullion. These Treasury notes now outstanding and in circulation amount to $152,951,280, and although there has been thus far but a comparatively small amount of this bullion coined, yet the so-called gain or seigniorage, as above defined, which would arise from the coinage of the entire mass has been easily ascertained to be a quantity of bullion sufficient to make when coined 55,156,681 standard silver dollars.

Considering the present intrinsic relation between gold and silver, the maintenance of the parity between the two metals, as mentioned in this law, can mean nothing less than the maintenance of such a parity in the estimation and confidence of the people who use our money in their daily transactions. Manifestly the maintenance of this parity can only be accomplished, so far as it is affected by these Treasury notes and in the estimation of the holders of the same, by giving to such holders on their redemption the coin, whether it is gold or silver, which they prefer. It follows that while in terms the law leaves the choice of coin to be paid on such redemption to the discretion of the Secretary of the Treasury, the exercise of this discretion, if opposed to the demands of the holder, is entirely inconsistent with the effective and beneficial maintenance of the parity between the two metals.

If both gold and silver are to serve us as money and if they together are to supply to our people a safe and stable currency, the necessity of preserving this parity is obvious. Such necessity has been repeatedly conceded in the platforms of both political parties and in our Federal statutes. It is nowhere more emphatically recognized than in the recent law which repealed the provision under which the bullion now on hand was purchased. This law insists upon the "maintenance of the parity in value of the coins of the two metals and the equal power of every dollar at all times in the markets and in the payment of debts.''

The Secretary of the Treasury has therefore, for the best of reasons, not only promptly complied with every demand for the redemption of these Treasury notes in gold, but the present situation as well as the letter and spirit of the law appear plainly to justify, if they do not enjoin upon him, a continuation of such redemption.

The conditions I have endeavored to present may be thus summarized:

First. The Government has purchased and now has on hand sufficient silver bullion to permit the coinage of all the silver dollars necessary to redeem in such dollars the Treasury notes issued for the purchase of said silver bullion, and enough besides to coin, as gain or seigniorage, 55,156,681 additional standard silver dollars.

Second. There are outstanding and now in circulation Treasury notes issued in payment of the bullion purchased amounting to $152,951,280. These notes are legal tender in payment of all debts, public and private, except when otherwise expressly stipulated; they are receivable for customs, taxes, and all public dues; when held by banking associations they may be counted as part of their lawful reserves, and they are redeemed by the Government in gold at the option of the holders. These advantageous attributes were deliberately attached to these notes at the time of their issue. They are fully understood by our people to whom such notes have been distributed as currency, and have inspired confidence in their safety and value, and have undoubtedly thus induced their continued and contented use as money, instead of anxiety for their redemption.

Having referred to some incidents which I deem relevant to the subject, it remains for me to submit a specific statement of my objections to the bill now under consideration.

This bill consists of two sections, excluding one which merely appropriates a sum sufficient to carry the act into effect. The first section provides for the immediate coinage of the silver bullion in the Treasury which represents the so-called gain or seigniorage, or which would arise from the coinage of all the bullion on hand, which gain or seigniorage this section declares to be $55,156,681. It directs that the money so coined or the certificates issued thereon shall be used in the payment of public expenditures, and provides that if the needs of the Treasury demand it the Secretary of the Treasury may, in his discretion, issue silver certificates in excess of such coinage, not exceeding the amount of seigniorage in said section authorized to be coined.

The second section directs that as soon as possible after the coinage of this seigniorage the remainder of the bullion held by the Government shall be coined into legal-tender standard silver dollars, and that they shall be held in the Treasury for the redemption of the Treasury notes issued in the purchase of said bullion. It provides that as fast as the bullion shall be coined for the redemption of said notes they shall not be reissued, but shall be canceled and destroyed in amounts equal to the coin held at any time in the Treasury derived from the coinage provided for, and that silver certificates shall be issued on such coin in the manner now provided by law. It is, however, especially declared in said section that the act shall not be construed to change existing laws relating to the legal-tender character or mode of redemption of the Treasury notes issued for the purchase of the silver bullion to be coined.

The entire bill is most unfortunately constructed. Nearly every sentence presents uncertainty and invites controversy as to its meaning and intent. The first section is especially faulty in this respect, and it is extremely doubtful whether its language will permit the consummation of its supposed purposes. I am led to believe that the promoters of the bill intended in this section to provide for the coinage of the bullion constituting the gain or seigniorage, as it is called, into standard silver dollars, and yet there is positively nothing in the section to prevent its coinage into any description of silver coins now authorized under any existing law.

I suppose this section was also intended, in case the needs of the Treasury called for money faster than the seigniorage bullion could actually be coined, to permit the issue of silver certificates in advance of such coinage; but its language would seem to permit the issuance of such certificates to double the amount of seigniorage as stated, one-half of which would not represent an ounce of silver in the Treasury. The debate upon this section in the Congress developed an earnest and positive difference of opinion as to its object and meaning. In any event, I am clear that the present perplexities and embarrassments of the Secretary of the Treasury ought not to be augmented by devolving upon him the execution of a law so uncertain and confused.

I am not willing, however, to rest my objection to this section solely on these grounds. In my judgment sound finance does not commend a further infusion of silver into our currency at this time unaccompanied by further adequate provision for the maintenance in our Treasury of a safe gold reserve.

Doubts also arise as to the meaning and construction of the second section of the bill. If the silver dollars therein directed to be coined are, as the section provides, to be held in the Treasury for the redemption of Treasury notes, it is suggested that, strictly speaking, certificates can not be issued on such coin "in the manner now provided by law," because these dollars are money held in the Treasury for the express purpose of redeeming Treasury notes on demand, which would ordinarily mean that they were set apart for the purpose of substituting them for these Treasury notes. They are not, therefore, held in such a way as to furnish a basis for certificates according to any provision of existing law.

If however, silver certificates can properly be issued upon these dollars, there is nothing in the section to indicate the characteristics and functions of these certificates. If they were to be of the same character as silver certificates in circulation under existing laws, they would at best be receivable only for customs, taxes, and all public dues; and under the language of this section it is, to say the least, extremely doubtful whether the certificates it contemplates would be lawfully received even for such purposes.

Whatever else may be said of the uncertainties of expression in this bill, they certainly ought not to be found in legislation affecting subjects so important and far-reaching as our finances and currency. In stating other and more important reasons for my disapproval of this section I shall, however, assume that under its provisions the Treasury notes issued in payment for silver bullion will continue to be redeemed as heretofore, in silver or gold, at the option of the holders, and that if when they are presented for redemption or reach the Treasury in any other manner there are in the Treasury coined silver dollars equal in nominal value to such Treasury notes, then and in that case the notes will be destroyed and silver certificates to an equal amount be substituted.

I am convinced that this scheme is ill advised and dangerous. As an ultimate result of its operation Treasury notes, which are legal tender for all debts, public and private, and which are redeemable in gold or silver at the option of the holder, will be replaced by silver certificates, which, whatever may be their character and description, will have none of these qualities. In anticipation of this result and as an immediate effect the Treasury notes will naturally appreciate in value and desirability. The fact that gold can be realized upon them and the further fact that their destruction has been decreed when they reach the Treasury must tend to their withdrawal from general circulation to be immediately presented for gold redemption or to be hoarded for presentation at a more convenient season. The sequel of both operations will be a large addition to the silver currency in our circulation and a corresponding reduction of gold in the Treasury. The argument has been made that these things will not occur at once, because a long time must elapse before the coinage of anything but the seigniorage can be entered upon. If the physical effects of the execution of the second section of this bill are not to be realized until far in the future, this may furnish a strong reason why it should not be passed so much in advance; but the postponement of its actual operation can not prevent the fear and loss of confidence and nervous precaution which would immediately follow its passage and bring about its worst consequences. I regard this section of the bill as embodying a plan by which the Government will be obliged to pay out its scanty store of gold for no other purpose than to force an unnatural addition of silver money into the hands of our people. This is an exact reversal of the policy which safe finance dictates if we are to preserve parity between gold and silver and maintain sensible bimetallism.

We have now outstanding more than $338,000,000 in silver certificates issued under existing laws. They are serving the purpose of money usefully and without question. Our gold reserve, amounting to only a little more than $100,000,000, is directly charged with the redemption of $346,000,000 of United States notes. When it is proposed to inflate our silver currency it is a time for strengthening our gold reserve instead of depleting it. I can not conceive of a longer step toward silver monometallism than we take when we spend our gold to buy silver certificates for circulation, especially in view of the practical difficulties surrounding the replenishment of our gold.

This leads me to earnestly present the desirability of granting to the Secretary of the Treasury a better power than now exists to issue bonds to protect our gold reserve when for any reason it should be necessary. Our currency is in such a confused condition and our financial affairs are apt to assume at any time so critical a position that it seems to me such a course is dictated by ordinary prudence.

I am not insensible to the arguments in favor of coining the bullion seigniorage now in the Treasury, and I believe it could be done safely and with advantage if the Secretary of the Treasury had the power to issue bonds at a low rate of interest under authority in substitution of that now existing and better suited to the protection of the Treasury.

I hope a way will present itself in the near future for the adjustment of our monetary affairs in such a comprehensive and conservative manner as will accord to silver its proper place in our currency; but in the meantime I am extremely solicitous that whatever action we take on this subject may be such as to prevent loss and discouragement to our people at home and the destruction of confidence in our financial management abroad.

GROVER CLEVELAND.

EXECUTIVE MANSION, *August 7, 1894.*
To the House of Representatives:

I herewith return without approval House bill No. 2637, entitled "An act for the relief of Eugene Wells, late captain, Twelfth Infantry, and second lieutenant, First Artillery, United States Army."

This bill authorizes the President to nominate and, by and with the advice and consent of the Senate, to appoint the beneficiary therein named a second lieutenant of artillery in the Army of the United States, and it directs that when so appointed he shall be placed upon the retired list on account of disability, thus dispensing with the usual examination and finding by a retiring board and all other ordinary prerequisites of retirement.

Appointments to the Army under the authority of special legislation which names the proposed appointee, and the purpose of which is the immediate retirement of the appointee, are open to serious objections,

though I confess I have been persuaded through sympathy and sentiment on a number of occasions to approve such legislation. When,
however, it is proposed to make the retirement compulsory and without
reference to age or previous examination, a most objectionable feature is
introduced.

The cases covered by the special enactments referred to are usually
such as should, if worthy of any consideration, be provided for under
general or private pension laws, leaving the retired list of the Army to
serve the legitimate purpose for which it was established.

A recent discussion in the House of Representatives upon a bill similar
to the one now before me drew from a member of the House Committee
on Military Affairs the declaration that hundreds of such bills were before
that committee and that there were fifty precedents for the passage of
the particular one then under discussion.

It seems to me that this condition suggests such an encroachment
upon the retired list of the Army as should lead to the virtual abandonment of the legislation referred to.

In addition to the objections to such legislation based upon sound
policy and good administration, there are facts connected with the case
covered by the bill now before me which, in my judgment, forbid its
favorable consideration.

The beneficiary named in this bill entered the military service as first
lieutenant in 1861. In September or October, 1870, then being a captain, a charge of conduct unbecoming an officer and a gentleman was
preferred against him with a view to his trial on said charge before a
court-martial.

The Articles of War provide that any officer convicted of this offense
shall be dismissed the service.

The first specification under this charge alleged that Captain Wells
did violently and without just cause or provocation assault First Lieutenant P. H. Breslin "by furiously striking and hitting him (Lieutenant
Breslin) upon the head with a hickory stick, the butt end of a billiard
cue, and did continue the assault (upon Lieutenant Breslin) until forced
to desist therefrom by First Lieutenant Carl Veitenhimer, Fourth United
States Infantry, thereby endangering the life of Lieutenant Breslin and
disgracing himself (Captain Wells) as an officer of the United States
Army."

The second specification alleged that Captain Wells "did become so
much under the influence of intoxicating liquor as to behave himself in
a scandalous manner by violently attacking the person of First Lieutenant P. H. Breslin, Fourth United States Infantry."

These offenses were charged to have been committed on the 3d day of
September, 1870, at Fort Fetterman, in Wyoming Territory.

On the 15th day of July, 1870, a law was passed, among other things,
to bring about a reduction of the Army, which law provided that the

President should before the 1st day of July, 1871, reduce the number of enlisted men in the Army to 30,000, and authorized him in his discretion to honorably discharge from the service of the United States officers of the Army who might apply therefor on or before January 1, 1871.

Before the trial by court-martial upon the charge then pending against him Captain Wells applied for his discharge under the provision of the law above recited, whereupon the charge against him was withdrawn and canceled, and on the 27th day of October, 1870, his application for a discharge was granted.

On the 6th day of July, 1875, he was again appointed to the Army as second lieutenant in the artillery, against which a remonstrance was made by certain officers in the Army.

In August, 1877, Second Lieutenant Wells was charged with being "drunk on duty, in violation of the thirty-eighth article of war."

He was also charged with "conduct to the prejudice of good order and military discipline."

The first specification under the latter charge alleged that the accused did "engage in an affray with First Lieutenant E. Van A. Andruss, First Artillery." The second specification under said charge alleged that the accused addressed his superior officer in a defiant and disrespectful manner and neglected and hesitated to promptly obey the order of said superior officer.

All these offenses were alleged to have been committed at Reading, Pa., on the 2d day of August, 1877.

Soon after these charges were preferred a court-martial was convened for the trial of the accused thereon. He pleaded not guilty to the charges and specifications, but was convicted of them all and sentenced "to be dismissed the service of the United States."

On the 6th day of October the proceedings, findings, and sentence of the court-martial were approved by the President, who ordered the sentence to be executed; and on the 13th day of October, 1877, in pursuance thereof, Lieutenant Eugene Wells was dismissed from the service.

Since that time repeated efforts have been made to vacate this judgment and restore the dismissed officer to the service. While a number of committees in Congress have made reports favorable to such action, at least two committees have recommended a denial of legislative relief. Both of these reports were made on behalf of House Committees on Military Affairs by distinguished soldiers, who, after patient examination and with an inclination to be not only just but generous to a fellow-soldier, were constrained to recommend a refusal of the application for restoration. One of these reports was made to the Forty-seventh and the other to the Forty-ninth Congress.

I am impressed with the belief that legislation of the kind proposed is of extremely doubtful expediency in any save very exceptional cases, and I am thoroughly convinced by the facts now before me that the discipline and efficiency of our Army, as well as justice to its meritorious members, do not permit my approval on any ground of the bill herewith returned.

GROVER CLEVELAND.

To the Senate: EXECUTIVE MANSION, *August 11, 1894.*

I hereby return without my approval Senate bill No. 1438, entitled "An act for the relief of Louis A. Yorke."

In the year 1886 the beneficiary named in this bill was a passed assistant paymaster in the Navy. In December of that year he appeared before a naval examining board convened pursuant to law for the purpose of passing upon his fitness to be promoted to the grade of paymaster.

The investigation of the board was conducted fairly and thoroughly. Much of the evidence relating to the candidate's moral fitness for promotion was documentary, and the examination touching his professional competency was of the usual character in such cases.

Considerable evidence was before the board showing quite a large amount of personal indebtedness owing by the candidate, and it appeared that in a few instances his accounts with the Navy Department had not been promptly settled. It was also shown that he had not at all times deposited the Government money intrusted to his care in the places required by law and the regulations of the Navy. In connection with his personal indebtedness incidents and circumstances were brought to light which certainly indicated that he entertained very lax ideas of honest dealing and fairness and which developed a disregard of the obligations and requirements of his position as an officer in the Navy. He was given abundant opportunity to meet and explain every damaging allegation and every adverse inference arising from the evidence, and his claim, not without foundation it appeared, that the charges against him were instigated by malice was doubtless given full weight.

The examining board on the evidence made the following decisions and findings:

The written examination of the candidate shows that he is deficient in his knowledge of the duties appertaining to the next higher grade; and the record evidence puts in question his moral fitness, and he has failed to establish both his professional and moral qualifications for promotion to the satisfaction of the board.

Therefore we hereby certify that Passed Assistant Paymaster Louis A. Yorke, United States Navy, has the mental fitness to perform efficiently all the duties, both at sea and on shore, of the next higher grade, but he has not the professional and moral qualifications required, and we do not recommend him for promotion.

After the board had thus disposed of the case and had adjourned it was, at the request of the candidate, reconvened by order of the Secretary of the Navy, who issued for its guidance the following directions, among others:

The board will inform Passed Assistant Paymaster Yorke of its findings and of the evidence upon which it finds him to be not morally qualified for promotion, and will afford him a further hearing and an opportunity to present such evidence as he may desire as to his moral fitness for promotion.

The board met pursuant to such order on the 4th day of January, 1887, when the findings of the board were read to the candidate for promotion, and also the evidence upon which said findings were based, and he was informed that the board would accord him a further hearing as to his moral fitness for promotion and would afford him a reasonable time in which to submit his case. Thereupon he requested the board to allow him until the 26th day of January to produce the necessary witnesses in his behalf. This request was granted, but on the day appointed, upon his representation that he was then unable to submit his defense, he was upon his request allowed another day for that purpose.

In availing himself of the opportunity thus afforded him to present evidence in defense or explanation of the matters charged against him he examined no witnesses and contented himself with presenting his own statement, containing little more than a reiteration of statements he had already made before the board at previous hearings, supplemented by slight documentary evidence which established no new facts in his favor.

The board thereupon reviewed all the evidence and proofs which had been submitted during the entire examination, and after full consideration decided that there was nothing in the additional evidence produced to warrant a modification of the original finding, and the board therefore again certified and decided that the candidate had not the moral qualifications to perform efficiently the duties of the grade to which he sought promotion.

The Secretary of the Navy transmitted the record, proceedings, and findings of said examining board to the President, with a recommendation that the same be approved and that the candidate be discharged from the Navy with one year's pay, pursuant to a statute passed on the 5th day of August, 1882, directing a discharge from the service in such cases.

Thereupon, and on the 19th day of February, 1887, the record, proceedings, and findings of said board were approved by the President, and Passed Assistant Paymaster Yorke was ordered discharged from the naval service with one year's pay.

The bill now under consideration provides that the action of the examining board above recited "be set aside and declared null and void." It also authorizes the President "to appoint the beneficiary to the office to which he would have been promoted but for said action and to retire him in that grade as of the date he was wholly retired."

The authority attempted by the bill to be given to the President to thus make an appointment to the office of paymaster in the Navy without the interposition of the Senate appears to be inadmissible under that clause of the Constitution which only permits the President to appoint certain officers "by and with the advice and consent of the Senate."

The bill provides for the immediate retirement of the beneficiary. He is now but 47 years old, thus lacking fifteen years of the time when he would be entitled to retirement on account of age. There is no suggestion that he is physically incapacitated. On the contrary, when he was examined for promotion a medical board certified that he was physically qualified to perform all his duties at sea, and the candidate himself not only certified to the same thing, but further declared that he was ''free from all bodily ailments.'' If this condition continues and if he should be restored to the Navy at all, he should be sent to duty on the active list instead of being retired. On the facts as presented he would seem to be out of place among those who, though still compensated by the Government, have been on account of age, long and honorable service, or disabilities incurred in the discharge of duty relieved from further activity.

A careful investigation of the facts submitted to the examining board and a consideration of all the statements made on behalf of the beneficiary named in the bill utterly fail, in my opinion, to justify the impeachment of the findings and determination of the board.

I have no doubt malicious feeling growing out of domestic difficulties entered into the affair and gave impetus to the search after inculpating evidence, but facts were nevertheless established beyond any reasonable doubt which abundantly uphold these findings.

I feel obliged to disapprove the bill herewith returned because I believe the power to appoint a paymaster in the Navy ought not, under the Constitution, be conferred upon the President alone; because if the beneficiary were restored to the Navy there would be no justice or propriety in placing him upon the retired list, and because upon the merits of the case I am of the opinion the judgment of the examining board ought not to be reversed.

GROVER CLEVELAND.

PROCLAMATIONS.

By the President of the United States of America.

A PROCLAMATION.

Whereas an act of Congress entitled ''An act to give effect to the award rendered by the Tribunal of Arbitration at Paris under the treaty between the United States and Great Britain concluded at Washington February 29, 1892, for the purpose of submitting to arbitration certain questions concerning the preservation of the fur seals,'' was approved April 6, 1894, and reads as follows:

Whereas the following articles of the award of the Tribunal of Arbitration constituted under the treaty concluded at Washington the 29th of February, 1892, between the United States of America and Her Majesty the Queen of the United Kingdom of

Great Britain and Ireland were delivered to the agents of the respective Governments on the 15th day of August, 1893:

"ARTICLE 1. The Governments of the United States and Great Britain shall forbid their citizens and subjects, respectively, to kill, capture, or pursue at any time and in any manner whatever the animals commonly called fur seals within a zone of 60 miles around the Pribilof Islands, inclusive of the territorial waters.

"The miles mentioned in the preceding paragraph are geographical miles, of 60 to a degree of latitude.

"ART. 2. The two Governments shall forbid their citizens and subjects, respectively, to kill, capture, or pursue in any manner whatever during the season extending each year from the 1st of May to the 31st of July, both inclusive, the fur seals on the high sea in the part of the Pacific Ocean, inclusive of the Bering Sea, which is situated to the north of the thirty-fifth degree of north latitude and eastward of the one hundred and eightieth degree of longitude from Greenwich till it strikes the water boundary described in Article I of the treaty of 1867 between the United States and Russia, and following that line up to Bering Strait.

"ART. 3. During the period of time and in the waters in which the fur-seal fishing is allowed only sailing vessels shall be permitted to carry on or take part in fur-seal fishing operations. They will, however, be at liberty to avail themselves of the use of such canoes or undecked boats, propelled by paddles, oars, or sails, as are in common use as fishing boats.

"ART. 4. Each sailing vessel authorized to fish for fur seals must be provided with a special license issued for that purpose by its Government, and shall be required to carry a distinguishing flag to be prescribed by its Government.

"ART. 5. The masters of the vessels engaged in fur-seal fishing shall enter accurately in their official log book the date and place of each fur-seal fishing operation, and also the number and sex of the seals captured upon each day. These entries shall be communicated by each of the two Governments to the other at the end of each fishing season.

"ART. 6. The use of nets, firearms, and explosives shall be forbidden in the fur-seal fishing. This restriction shall not apply to shotguns when such fishing takes place outside of Bering Sea during the season when it may be lawfully carried on.

"ART. 7. The two Governments shall take measures to control the fitness of the men authorized to engage in fur-seal fishing. These men shall have been proved fit to handle with sufficient skill the weapons by means of which this fishing may be carried on.

"ART. 8. The regulations contained in the preceding articles shall not apply to Indians dwelling on the coast of the territory of the United States or of Great Britain and carrying on fur-seal fishing in canoes or undecked boats not transported by or used in connection with other vessels, and propelled wholly by paddles, oars, or sails and manned by not more than five persons each in the way hitherto practiced by the Indians, provided such Indians are not in the employment of other persons, and provided that when so hunting in canoes or undecked boats they shall not hunt fur seals outside of territorial waters under contract for the delivery of the skins to any person.

"This exemption shall not be construed to affect the municipal law of either country, nor shall it extend to the waters of Bering Sea or the waters of the Aleutian passes.

"Nothing herein contained is intended to interfere with the employment of Indians as hunters or otherwise in connection with fur-sealing vessels as heretofore.

"ART. 9. The concurrent regulations hereby determined with a view to the protection and preservation of the fur seals shall remain in force until they have been in whole or in part abolished or modified by common agreement between the Governments of the United States and of Great Britain.

"The said concurrent regulations shall be submitted every five years to a new examination, so as to enable both interested Governments to consider whether, ir the light of past experience, there is occasion for any modification thereof.''

Now, therefore, be it enacted by the Senate and House of Representatives of tne United States of America in Congress assembled, That no citizen of the United States or person owing the duty of obedience to the laws or the treaties of the United States, nor any person belonging to or on board of a vessel of the United States, shall kill, capture, or pursue at any time or in any manner whatever outside of territorial waters any fur seal in the waters surrounding the Pribilof Islands within a zone of 60 geographical miles (60 to a degree of latitude) around said islands, exclusive of the territorial waters.

SEC. 2. That no citizen of the United States or person above described in section 1 of this act, nor any person belonging to or on board of a vessel of the United States, shall kill, capture, or pursue in any manner whatever during the season extending from the 1st day of May to the 31st day of July, both inclusive, in each year any fur seal on the high seas outside of the zone mentioned in section 1, and in that part of the Pacific Ocean, including Bering Sea, which is situated to the north of the thirty-fifth degree of north latitude and to the east of the one hundred and eightieth degree of longitude from Greenwich till it strikes the water boundary described in Article I of the treaty of 1867 between the United States and Russia, and following that line up to Bering Strait.

SEC. 3. No citizen of the United States or person above described in the first section of this act shall during the period and in the waters in which by section 2 of this act the killing of fur seals is not prohibited use or employ any vessel, nor shall any vessel of the United States be used or employed, in carrying on or taking part in fur-seal fishing operations, other than a sailing vessel propelled by sails exclusively and such canoes or undecked boats propelled by paddles, oars, or sails as may belong to and be used in connection with such sailing vessels; nor shall any sailing vessel carry on or take part in such operations without a special license obtained from the Government for that purpose and without carrying a distinctive flag prescribed by the Government for the same purpose.

SEC. 4. That every master of a vessel licensed under this act to engage in fur-seal fishing operations shall accurately enter in his official log book the date and place of every such operation, and also the number and sex of the seals captured each day; and on coming into port and before landing cargo the master shall verify on oath such official log book as containing a full and true statement of the number and character of his fur-seal fishing operations, including the number and sex of seals captured; and for any false statement willfully made by e person so licensed by the United States in this behalf he shall be subject to the penalties of perjury, and any seal skins found in excess of the statement in the official log book shall be forfeited to the United States.

SEC. 5. That no person or vessel engaging in fur-seal fishing operations under this act shall use or employ in such operations any net, firearm, air gun, or explosive: *Provided, however*, That this prohibition shall not apply to the use of shotguns in such operations outside of Bering Sea during the season when the killing of fur seals is not there prohibited by this act.

SEC. 6. That the foregoing sections of this act shall not apply to Indians dwelling on the coast of the United States and taking fur seals in canoes or undecked boats propelled wholly by paddles, oars, or sails, and not transported by or used in connection with other vessels or manned by more than five persons, in the manner heretofore practiced by the said Indians: *Provided, however*, That the exception made in this section shall not apply to Indians in the employment of other persons, or who shall kill, capture, or pursue fur seals outside of territorial waters under contract to deliver the skins to other persons, nor to the waters of Bering Sea or of the passes between the Aleutian Islands.

Sec. 7. That the President shall have power to make regulations respecting the special license and the distinctive flag mentioned in this act, and regulations otherwise suitable to secure the due execution of the provisions of this act, and from time to time to add to, modify, amend, or revoke such regulations as in his judgment may seem expedient.

Sec. 8. That, except in the case of a master making a false statement under oath in violation of the provisions of the fourth section of this act, every person guilty of a violation of the provisions of this act or of the regulations made thereunder shall for each offense be fined not less than $200 or imprisoned not more than six months, or both; and all vessels, their tackle, apparel, furniture, and cargo, at any time used or employed in violation of this act or of the regulations made thereunder shall be forfeited to the United States.

Sec. 9. That any violation of this act or the regulations made thereunder may be prosecuted either in the district court of Alaska or in any district court of the United States in California, Oregon, or Washington.

Sec. 10. That if any unlicensed vessel of the United States shall be found within the waters to which this act applies, and at a time when the killing of fur seals is by this act there prohibited, having on board seal skins or bodies of seals or apparatus or implements suitable for killing or taking seals, or if any licensed vessel shall be found in the waters to which this act applies having on board apparatus or implements suitable for taking seals, but forbidden then and there to be used, it shall be presumed that the vessel in the one case and the apparatus or implements in the other was or were used in violation of this act until it is otherwise sufficiently proved.

Sec. 11. That it shall be the duty of the President to cause a sufficient naval force to cruise in the waters to which this act is applicable to enforce its provisions; and it shall be the duty of the commanding officer of any vessel belonging to the naval or revenue service of the United States, when so instructed by the President, to seize and arrest all vessels of the United States found by him to be engaged, used, or employed in the waters last aforesaid in violation of any of the prohibitions of this act or of any regulations made thereunder, and to take the same, with all persons on board thereof, to the most convenient port in any district of the United States mentioned in this act, there to be dealt with according to law.

Sec. 12. That any vessel or citizen of the United States or person described in the first section of this act offending against the prohibitions of this act or the regulations thereunder may be seized and detained by the naval or other duly commissioned officers of Her Majesty the Queen of Great Britain, but when so seized and detained they shall be delivered as soon as practicable, with any witnesses and proofs on board, to any naval or revenue officer or other authorities of the United States, whose courts alone shall have jurisdiction to try the offense and impose the penalties for the same: *Provided, however*, That British officers shall arrest and detain vessels and persons as in this section specified only after, by appropriate legislation, Great Britain shall have authorized officers of the United States duly commissioned and instructed by the President to that end to arrest, detain, and deliver to the authorities of Great Britain vessels and subjects of that Government offending against any statutes or regulations of Great Britain enacted or made to enforce the award of the treaty mentioned in the title of this act.

Now, therefore, be it known that I, Grover Cleveland, President of the United States of America, have caused the said act specially to be proclaimed, to the end that its provisions may be known and observed; and I hereby proclaim that every person guilty of a violation of the provisions of said act will be arrested and punished as therein provided, and all vessels so employed, their tackle, apparel, furniture, and cargo, will be seized and forfeited.

In testimony whereof I have hereunto set my hand and caused the seal of the United States to be affixed.

[SEAL.]   Done at the city of Washington, this 9th day of April, A. D. 1894, and of the Independence of the United States the one hundred and eighteenth.

GROVER CLEVELAND.

By the President:

W. Q. GRESHAM,
Secretary of State.

BY THE PRESIDENT OF THE UNITED STATES OF AMERICA.

A PROCLAMATION.

Whereas satisfactory proof has been given to me that no light-house and light dues, tonnage dues, beacon and buoy dues, or other equivalent taxes of any kind are imposed upon vessels of the United States in the ports of the island of Grenada, one of the British West India Islands:

Now, therefore, I, Grover Cleveland, President of the United States of America, by virtue of the authority vested in me by section 11 of the act of Congress entitled "An act to abolish certain fees for official services to American vessels and to amend the laws relating to shipping commissioners, seamen, and owners of vessels, and for other purposes," approved June 19, 1886, and in virtue of the further act amendatory thereof, entitled "An act to amend the laws relating to navigation, and for other purposes," approved April 4, 1888, do hereby declare and proclaim that from and after the date of this my proclamation shall be suspended the collection of the whole of the tonnage duty which is imposed by said section 11 of the act approved June 19, 1886, upon vessels entered in the ports of the United States from any of the ports of the island of Grenada.

Provided, That there shall be excluded from the benefits of the suspension hereby declared and proclaimed the vessels of any foreign country in whose ports the fees or dues of any kind or nature imposed on vessels of the United States or the import or export duties on their cargoes are in excess of the fees, dues, or duties imposed on the vessels of such country or on the cargoes of such vessels; but this proviso shall not be held to be inconsistent with the special regulation by foreign countries of duties and other charges on their own vessels and the cargoes thereof engaged in their coasting trade, or with the existence between such countries and other states of reciprocal stipulations founded on special conditions and equivalents, and thus not within the treatment of American vessels under the most-favored-nation clause in treaties between the United States and such countries.

And the suspension hereby declared and proclaimed shall continue so long as the reciprocal exemption of vessels belonging to citizens of the United States and their cargoes shall be continued in the said ports of the island of Grenada, and no longer.

In witness whereof I have hereunto set my hand and caused the seal of the United States to be affixed.

[SEAL.]   Done at the city of Washington, this 2d day of May, A. D. 1894, and of the Independence of the United States the one hundred and eighteenth.

GROVER CLEVELAND.

By the President:
> W. Q. GRESHAM,
>   *Secretary of State.*

BY THE PRESIDENT OF THE UNITED STATES OF AMERICA.

A PROCLAMATION.

Whereas, by reason of unlawful obstructions, combinations, and assemblages of persons, it has become impracticable, in the judgment of the President, to enforce by the ordinary course of judicial proceedings the laws of the United States within the State of Illinois, and especially in the city of Chicago within said State; and

Whereas, for the purpose of enforcing the faithful execution of the laws of the United States and protecting its property and removing obstructions to the United States mails in the State and city aforesaid, the President has employed a part of the military forces of the United States:

Now, therefore, I, Grover Cleveland, President of the United States, do hereby admonish all good citizens and all persons who may be or may come within the city and State aforesaid against aiding, countenancing, encouraging, or taking any part in such unlawful obstructions, combinations, and assemblages; and I hereby warn all persons engaged in or in any way connected with such unlawful obstructions, combinations, and assemblages to disperse and retire peaceably to their respective abodes on or before 12 o'clock noon on the 9th day of July instant.

Those who disregard this warning and persist in taking part with a riotous mob in forcibly resisting and obstructing the execution of the laws of the United States or interfering with the functions of the Government or destroying or attempting to destroy the property belonging to the United States or under its protection can not be regarded otherwise than as public enemies.

Troops employed against such a riotous mob will act with all the moderation and forbearance consistent with the accomplishment of the desired end, but the stern necessities that confront them will not with certainty permit discrimination between guilty participants and those who are mingled with them from curiosity and without criminal intent. The only safe course, therefore, for those not actually unlawfully participating is to abide at their homes, or at least not to be found in the neighborhood of riotous assemblages.

While there will be no hesitation or vacillation in the decisive treatment of the guilty, this warning is especially intended to protect and save the innocent.

In testimony whereof I have hereunto set my hand and caused the seal of the United States to be hereto affixed.

[SEAL.]   Done at the city of Washington, this 8th day of July, A. D. 1894, and of the Independence of the United States the one hundred and nineteenth.

GROVER CLEVELAND.

By the President:

W. Q. GRESHAM,
    Secretary of State.

BY THE PRESIDENT OF THE UNITED STATES OF AMERICA.

A PROCLAMATION.

Whereas, by reason of unlawful obstructions, combinations, and assemblages of persons, it has become impracticable, in the judgment of the President, to enforce by the ordinary course of judicial proceedings the laws of the United States at certain points and places within the States of North Dakota, Montana, Idaho, Washington, Wyoming, Colorado, and California and the Territories of Utah and New Mexico, and especially along the lines of such railways traversing said States and Territories as are military roads and post routes and are engaged in interstate commerce and in carrying United States mails; and

Whereas, for the purpose of enforcing the faithful execution of the laws of the United States and protecting property belonging to the United States or under its protection, and of preventing obstructions of the United States mails and of commerce between the States and Territories, and of securing to the United States the right guaranteed by law to the use of such roads for postal, military, naval, and other Government service, the President has employed a part of the military forces of the United States:

Now, therefore, I, Grover Cleveland, President of the United States, do hereby command all persons engaged in or in any way connected with such unlawful obstructions, combinations, and assemblages to disperse and retire peaceably to their respective abodes on or before 3 o'clock in the afternoon on the 10th day of July instant.

In witness whereof I have hereunto set my hand and caused the seal of the United States to be hereto affixed.

[SEAL.]   Done at the city of Washington, this 9th day of July, A. D. 1894, and of the Independence of the United States the one hundred and nineteenth.

GROVER CLEVELAND.

By the President:

    W. Q. GRESHAM,
        Secretary of State.

BY THE PRESIDENT OF THE UNITED STATES OF AMERICA.

A PROCLAMATION.

Whereas an act of Congress entitled "An act to adopt regulations for preventing collisions at sea" was approved August 19, 1890, the said act being in the following words:

Be it enacted by the Senate and House of Representatives of the United States of America in Congress assembled, That the following regulations for preventing collisions at sea shall be followed by all public and private vessels of the United States upon the high seas and in all waters connected therewith navigable by seagoing vessels:

PRELIMINARY.

In the following rules every steam vessel which is under sail and not under steam is to be considered a sailing vessel, and every vessel under steam, whether under sail or not, is to be considered a steam vessel.

The words "steam vessel" shall include any vessel propelled by machinery.

A vessel is "under way" within the meaning of these rules when she is not at anchor or made fast to the shore or aground.

RULES CONCERNING LIGHTS, ETC.

The word "visible" in these rules when applied to lights shall mean visible on a dark night with a clear atmosphere.

ARTICLE 1. The rules concerning lights shall be complied with in all weathers from sunset to sunrise, and during such time no other lights which may be mistaken for the prescribed lights shall be exhibited.

ART. 2. A steam vessel when under way shall carry—

(*a*) On or in front of the foremast, or if a vessel without a foremast, then in the fore part of the vessel, at a height above the hull of not less than 20 feet, and if the breadth of the vessel exceeds 20 feet, then at a height above the hull not less than such breadth, so, however, that the light need not be carried at a greater height above the hull than 40 feet a bright white light so constructed as to show an unbroken light over an arc of the horizon of 20 points of the compass, so fixed as to throw the light 10 points on each side of the vessel—namely, from right ahead to 2 points abaft the beam on either side—and of such a character as to be visible at a distance of at least 5 miles.

(*b*) On the starboard side a green light so constructed as to show an unbroken light over an arc of the horizon of 10 points of the compass, so fixed as to throw the light from right ahead to 2 points abaft the beam on the starboard side, and of such a character as to be visible at a distance of at least 2 miles.

(*c*) On the port side a red light so constructed as to show an unbroken light over an arc of the horizon of 10 points of the compass, so fixed as to throw the light from right ahead to 2 points abaft the beam on the port side, and of such a character as to be visible at a distance of at least 2 miles.

(*d*) The said green and red side lights shall be fitted with inboard screens projecting at least 3 feet forward from the light, so as to prevent these lights from being seen across the bow.

(*e*) A steam vessel when under way may carry an additional white light similar in construction to the light mentioned in subdivision (*a*). These two lights shall be so placed in line with the keel that one shall be at least 15 feet higher than the other and in such a position with reference to each other that the lower light shall be forward of the upper one. The vertical distance between these lights shall be less than the horizontal distance.

ART. 3. A steam vessel when towing another vessel shall, in addition to her side lights, carry two bright white lights in a vertical line one over the other, not less than 6 feet apart, and when towing more than one vessel shall carry an additional bright white light 6 feet above or below such light if the length of the tow measuring from the stern of the towing vessel to the stern of the last vessel towed exceeds 600 feet. Each of these lights shall be of the same construction and character and shall be carried in the same position as the white light mentioned in article 2 (*a*), excepting the additional light, which may be carried at a height of not less than 14 feet above the hull.

Such steam vessel may carry a small white light abaft the funnel or aftermast for the vessel towed to steer by, but such light shall not be visible forward of the beam.

ART. 4. (*a*) A vessel which from any accident is not under command shall carry at the same height as a white light mentioned in article 2 (*a*), where they can best be seen, and if a steam vessel in lieu of that light, two red lights in a vertical line one over the other, not less than 6 feet apart, and of such a character as to be visible all around the horizon at a distance of at least 2 miles; and shall by day carry in a vertical line one over the other, not less than 6 feet apart, where they can best be seen, two black balls or shapes each 2 feet in diameter.

(*b*) A vessel employed in laying or in picking up a telegraph cable shall carry in the same position as the white light mentioned in article 2 (*a*), and if a steam vessel in lieu of that light, three lights in a vertical line one over the other, not less than 6 feet apart. The highest and lowest of these lights shall be red and the middle light shall be white, and they shall be of such a character as to be visible all around the horizon at a distance of at least 2 miles. By day she shall carry in a vertical line one over the other, not less than 6 feet apart, where they can best be seen, three shapes not less than 2 feet in diameter, of which the highest and lowest shall be globular in shape and red in color and the middle one diamond in shape and white.

(*c*) The vessels referred to in this article, when not making way through the water, shall not carry the side lights, but when making way shall carry them.

(*d*) The lights and shapes required to be shown by this article are to be taken by other vessels as signals that the vessel showing them is not under command and can not, therefore, get out of the way.

These signals are not signals of vessels in distress and requiring assistance. Such signals are contained in article 31.

ART. 5. A sailing vessel under way and any vessel being towed shall carry the same lights as are prescribed by article 2 for a steam vessel under way, with the exception of the white lights mentioned therein, which they shall never carry.

ART. 6. Whenever, as in the case of small vessels under way during bad weather, the green and red side lights can not be fixed, these lights shall be kept at hand, lighted and ready for use, and shall on the approach of or to other vessels be exhibited on their respective sides, in sufficient time to prevent collision, in such manner as to make them most visible and so that the green light shall not be seen on the port side nor the red light on the starboard side, nor, if practicable, more than 2 points abaft the beam on their respective sides.

To make the use of these portable lights more certain and easy the lanterns containing them shall each be painted outside with the color of the light they respectively contain and shall be provided with proper screens.

ART. 7. Steam vessels of less than 40 and vessels under oars or sails of less than 20 tons gross tonnage, respectively, when under way shall not be obliged to carry the lights mentioned in article 2 (*a*), (*b*), and (*c*), but if they do not carry them they shall be provided with the following lights:

First. Steam vessels of less than 40 tons shall carry—

(*a*) In the fore part of the vessel or on or in front of the funnel, where it can best be seen, and at a height above the gunwale of not less than 9 feet, a bright white light constructed and fixed as prescribed in article 2 (*a*) and of such a character as to be visible at a distance of at least 2 miles.

(*b*) Green and red side lights constructed and fixed as prescribed in article 2 (*b*) and (*c*) and of such a character as to be visible at a distance of at least 1 mile, or a combined lantern showing a green light and a red light from right ahead to 2 points abaft the beam on their respective sides. Such lanterns shall be carried not less than 3 feet below the white light.

Second. Small steamboats, such as are carried by seagoing vessels, may carry the white light at a less height than 9 feet above the gunwale, but it shall be carried above the combined lantern mentioned in subdivision 1 (*b*).

Third. Vessels under oars or sails of less than 20 tons shall have ready at hand a lantern with a green glass on one side and a red glass on the other, which on the approach of or to other vessels shall be exhibited, in sufficient time to prevent collision, so that the green light shall not be seen on the port side nor the red light on the starboard side.

The vessels referred to in this article shall not be obliged to carry the lights prescribed by article 4 (*a*) and article 11, last paragraph.

ART. 8. Pilot vessels when engaged on their station on pilotage duty shall not show the lights required for other vessels, but shall carry a white light at the masthead, visible all around the horizon, and shall also exhibit a flare-up light or flare-up lights at short intervals, which shall never exceed fifteen minutes.

On the near approach of or to other vessels they shall have their side lights lighted, ready for use, and shall flash or show them at short intervals to indicate the direction in which they are heading; but the green light shall not be shown on the port side nor the red light on the starboard side.

A pilot vessel of such a class as to be obliged to go alongside of a vessel to put a pilot on board may show the white light instead of carrying it at the masthead, and may, instead of the colored lights above mentioned, have at hand, ready for use, a lantern with a green glass on the one side and a red glass on the other, to be used as prescribed above.

Pilot vessels when not engaged on their station on pilotage duty shall carry lights similar to those of other vessels of their tonnage.

ART. 9. Fishing vessels and fishing boats when under way and when not required by this article to carry or show the lights therein named shall carry or show the lights prescribed for vessels of their tonnage under way.

(*a*) Vessels and boats when fishing with drift nets shall exhibit two white lights from any part of the vessel where they can best be seen. Such lights shall be placed so that the vertical distance between them shall be not less than 6 feet and not more than 10 feet, and so that the horizontal distance between them measured in a line with the keel shall be not less than 5 feet and not more than 10 feet. The lower of these two lights shall be the more forward, and both of them shall be of such a character as to show all around the horizon and to be visible at a distance of not less than 3 miles.

(*b*) Vessels when engaged in trawling, by which is meant the dragging of an apparatus along the bottom of the sea—

First. If steam vessels, shall carry in the same position as the white light mentioned in article 2 (*a*) a tricolored lantern so constructed and fixed as to show a white light from right ahead to 2 points on each bow and a green light and a red light over an arc of the horizon from 2 points on either bow to 2 points abaft the beam on the starboard and port sides, respectively, and not less than 6 nor more than 12 feet below the tricolored lantern, a white light in a lantern so constructed as to show a clear, uniform, and unbroken light all around the horizon.

Second. If sailing vessels of 7 tons gross tonnage and upward, shall carry a white light in a lantern so constructed as to show a clear, uniform, and unbroken light all around the horizon, and shall also be provided with a sufficient supply of red pyrotechnic lights, which shall each burn for at least 30 seconds, and shall be shown on the approach of or to other vessels in sufficient time to prevent collision.

In the Mediterranean Sea the vessels referred to in subdivision (*b*) 2 may use a flare-up light in lieu of a pyrotechnic light.

All lights mentioned in subdivision (*b*) 1 and 2 shall be visible at a distance of at least 2 miles.

Third. If sailing vessels of less than 7 tons gross tonnage, shall not be obliged to carry the white light mentioned in subdivision (*b*) 2 of this article, but if they do not carry such light they shall have at hand, ready for use, a lantern showing a bright white light, which shall on the approach of or to other vessels be exhibited where it can best be seen, in sufficient time to prevent collision; and they shall also show a red pyrotechnic light, as prescribed in subdivision (*b*) 2, or in lieu thereof a flare-up light.

(*c*) Vessels and boats when line fishing with their lines out and attached to their lines, and when not at anchor or stationary, shall carry the same lights as vessels fishing with drift nets.

(*d*) Fishing vessels and fishing boats may at any time use a flare-up light in addition to the lights which they are by this article required to carry and show. All flare-up lights exhibited by a vessel when trawling or fishing with any kind of dragnet shall be shown at the after part of the vessel, excepting that if the vessel is hanging by the stern to her fishing gear they shall be exhibited from the bow.

(*e*) Every fishing vessel and every boat when at anchor shall exhibit a white light visible all around the horizon at a distance of at least 1 mile.

(*f*) If a vessel or boat when fishing becomes stationary in consequence of her gear getting fast to a rock or other obstruction, she shall show the light and make the fog signal prescribed for a vessel at anchor, respectively. (See article 15 (*d*), (*e*), and last paragraph.)

(*g*) In fog, mist, falling snow, or heavy rain storms drift-net vessels attached to their nets, and vessels when trawling, dredging, or fishing with any kind of dragnet, and vessels line fishing with their lines out shall, if of 20 tons gross tonnage or upward, respectively, at intervals of not more than one minute make a blast—if steam vessels, with the whistle or siren, and if sailing vessels, with the fog horn—each blast to be followed by ringing the bell.

(*h*) Sailing vessels or boats fishing with nets or lines or trawls when under way shall in daytime indicate their occupation to an approaching vessel by displaying a basket or other efficient signal where it can best be seen.

The vessels referred to in this article shall not be obliged to carry the lights prescribed by article 4 (*a*) and article 11, last paragraph.

ART. 10. A vessel which is being overtaken by another shall show from her stern to such last-mentioned vessel a white light or a flare-up light.

The white light required to be shown by this article may be fixed and carried in a lantern, but in such case the lantern shall be so constructed, fitted, and screened that it shall throw an unbroken light over an arc of the horizon of 12 points of the compass—namely, for 6 points from right aft on each side of the vessel—so as to be visible at a distance of at least 1 mile. Such light shall be carried as nearly as practicable on the same level as the side lights.

ART. 11. A vessel under 150 feet in length when at anchor shall carry forward, where it can best be seen, but at a height not exceeding 20 feet above the hull, a white light in a lantern so constructed as to show a clear, uniform, and unbroken light visible all around the horizon at a distance of at least 1 mile.

A vessel of 150 feet or upward in length when at anchor shall carry in the forward part of the vessel, at a height of not less than 20 and not exceeding 40 feet above the hull, one such light, and at or near the stern of the vessel, and at such a height that it shall be not less than 15 feet lower than the forward light, another such light.

The length of a vessel shall be deemed to be the length appearing in her certificate of registry.

A vessel aground in or near a fairway shall carry the above light or lights and the two red lights prescribed by article 4 (*a*).

ART. 12. Every vessel may, if necessary in order to attract attention, in addition to the lights which she is by these rules required to carry, show a flare-up light or use any detonating signal that can not be mistaken for a distress signal.

ART. 13. Nothing in these rules shall interfere with the operation of any special rules made by the government of any nation with respect to additional station and signal lights for two or more ships of war or for vessels sailing under convoy, or with the exhibition of recognition signals adopted by shipowners which have been authorized by their respective governments and duly registered and published.

ART. 14. A steam vessel proceeding under sail only, but having her funnel up, shall carry in daytime forward, where it can best be seen, one black ball or shape 2 feet in diameter.

Sound Signals for Fog, etc.

ART. 15. All signals prescribed by this article for vessels under way shall be given—

1. By "steam vessels," on the whistle or siren.

2. By "sailing vessels" and "vessels towed," on the fog horn.

The words "prolonged blast" used in this article shall mean a blast of from four to six seconds' duration.

A steam vessel shall be provided with an efficient whistle or siren, sounded by steam or by some substitute for steam, so placed that the sound may not be intercepted by any obstruction, and with an efficient fog horn, to be sounded by mechanical means, and also with an efficient bell. (In all cases where the rules require a bell to be used a drum may be substituted on board Turkish vessels or a gong where such articles are used on board small seagoing vessels.) A sailing vessel of 20 tons gross tonnage or upward shall be provided with a similar fog horn and bell.

In fog, mist, falling snow, or heavy rain storms, whether by day or night, the signals described in this article shall be used as follows, viz:

(*a*) A steam vessel having way upon her shall sound at intervals of not more than two minutes a prolonged blast.

(*b*) A steam vessel under way, but stopped and having no way upon her, shall sound at intervals of not more than two minutes two prolonged blasts with an interval of about one second between them.

(*c*) A sailing vessel under way shall sound at intervals of not more than one minute, when on the starboard tack one blast, when on the port tack two blasts in succession, and when with the wind abaft the beam three blasts in succession.

(*d*) A vessel when at anchor shall at intervals of not more than one minute ring the bell rapidly for about five seconds.

(*e*) A vessel at anchor at sea, when not in ordinary anchorage ground and when in such a position as to be an obstruction to vessels under way, shall sound, if a steam vessel, at intervals of not more than two minutes, two prolonged blasts with her whistle or siren, followed by ringing her bell; or, if a sailing vessel, at intervals of not more than one minute two blasts with her fog horn, followed by ringing her bell.

(*f*) A vessel when towing shall, instead of the signals prescribed in subdivisions (*a*) and (*c*) of this article, at intervals of not more than two minutes sound three blasts in succession, namely, one prolonged blast followed by two short blasts. A vessel towed may give this signal, and she shall not give any other.

(*g*) A steam vessel wishing to indicate to another "The way is off my vessel; you may feel your way past me" may sound three blasts in succession, namely, short, long, short, with intervals of about one second between them.

(*h*) A vessel employed in laying or picking up a telegraph cable shall on hearing the fog signal of an approaching vessel sound in answer three prolonged blasts in succession.

(*i*) A vessel under way which is unable to get out of the way of an approaching vessel through being not under command or unable to maneuver as required by these rules shall on hearing the fog signal of an approaching vessel sound in answer four short blasts in succession.

Sailing vessels and boats of less than 20 tons gross tonnage shall not be obliged to give the above-mentioned signals, but if they do not they shall make some other efficient sound signal at intervals of not more than one minute.

SPEED OF SHIPS TO BE MODERATE IN FOG, ETC.

ART. 16. Every vessel shall in a fog, mist, falling snow, or heavy rain storm go at a moderate speed, having careful regard to the existing circumstances and conditions.

A steam vessel hearing, apparently forward of her beam, the fog signal of a vessel the position of which is not ascertained shall, so far as the circumstances of the case admit, stop her engines, and then navigate with caution until danger of collision is over.

STEERING AND SAILING RULES.

PRELIMINARY.—RISK OF COLLISION.

Risk of collision can, when circumstances permit, be ascertained by carefully watching the compass bearing of an approaching vessel. If the bearing does not appreciably change, such risk should be deemed to exist.

ART. 17. When two sailing vessels are approaching one another so as to involve risk of collision, one of them shall keep out of the way of the other as follows, namely:

(*a*) A vessel which is running free shall keep out of the way of a vessel which is closehauled.

(*b*) A vessel which is closehauled on the port tack shall keep out of the way of a vessel which is closehauled on the starboard tack.

(*c*) When both are running free with the wind on different sides, the vessel which has the wind on the port side shall keep out of the way of the other.

(*d*) When both are running free with the wind on the same side, the vessel which is to the windward shall keep out of the way of the vessel which is to leeward.

(*e*) A vessel which has the wind aft shall keep out of the way of the other vessel.

ART. 18. When two steam vessels are meeting end on or nearly end on, so as to involve risk of collision, each shall alter her course to starboard, so that each may pass on the port side of the other.

This article only applies to cases where vessels are meeting end on or nearly end on in such a manner as to involve risk of collision, and does not apply to two vessels which must if both keep on their respective courses pass clear of each other.

The only cases to which it does apply are when each of the two vessels is end on or nearly end on to the other; in other words, to cases in which by day each vessel sees the masts of the other in a line or nearly in a line with her own, and by night to cases in which each vessel is in such a position as to see both the side lights of the other.

It does not apply by day to cases in which a vessel sees another ahead crossing her own course, or by night to cases where the red light of one vessel is opposed to the red light of the other, or where the green light of one vessel is opposed to the green light of the other, or where a red light without a green light or a green light without a red light is seen ahead, or where both green and red lights are seen anywhere but ahead.

ART. 19. When two steam vessels are crossing, so as to involve risk of collision, the vessel which has the other on her own starboard side shall keep out of the way of the other.

ART. 20. When a steam vessel and a sailing vessel are proceeding in such directions as to involve risk of collision, the steam vessel shall keep out of the way of the sailing vessel.

ART. 21. Where by any of these rules one of two vessels is to keep out of the way, the other shall keep her course and speed.

ART. 22. Every vessel which is directed by these rules to keep out of the way of another vessel shall, if the circumstances of the case admit, avoid crossing ahead of the other.

ART. 23. Every steam vessel which is directed by these rules to keep out of the way of another vessel shall on approaching her, if necessary, slacken her speed or stop or reverse.

ART. 24. Notwithstanding anything contained in these rules every vessel overtaking any other shall keep out of the way of the overtaken vessel.

Every vessel coming up with another vessel from any direction more than 2 points abaft her beam—that is, in such a position with reference to the vessel which she is overtaking that at night she would be unable to see either of that vessel's side lights—shall be deemed to be an overtaking vessel, and no subsequent alteration of the bearing between the two vessels shall make the overtaking vessel a crossing vessel within the meaning of these rules or relieve her of the duty of keeping clear of the overtaken vessel until she is finally past and clear.

As by day the overtaking vessel can not always know with certainty whether she is forward of or abaft this direction from the other vessel, she should if in doubt assume that she is an overtaking vessel and keep out of the way.

ART. 25. In narrow channels every steam vessel shall, when it is safe and practicable, keep to that side of the fairway or mid-channel which lies on the starboard side of such vessel.

ART. 26. Sailing vessels under way shall keep out of the way of sailing vessels or boats fishing with nets or lines or trawls. This rule shall not give to any vessel or boat engaged in fishing the right of obstructing a fairway used by vessels other than fishing vessels or boats.

ART. 27. In obeying and construing these rules due regard shall be had to all dangers of navigation and collision and to any special circumstances which may render a departure from the above rules necessary in order to avoid immediate danger.

SOUND SIGNALS FOR VESSELS IN SIGHT OF ONE ANOTHER.

ART. 28. The words "short blast" used in this article shall mean a blast of about one second's duration.

When vessels are in sight of one another, a steam vessel under way, in taking any course authorized or required by these rules, shall indicate that course by the following signals on her whistle or siren, namely:

One short blast to mean, "I am directing my course to starboard."

Two short blasts to mean, "I am directing my course to port."

Three short blasts to mean, "My engines are going at full speed astern."

NO VESSEL UNDER ANY CIRCUMSTANCES TO NEGLECT PROPER PRECAUTIONS.

ART. 29. Nothing in these rules shall exonerate any vessel or the owner or master or crew thereof from the consequences of any neglect to carry lights or signals, or of any neglect to keep a proper lookout, or of the neglect of any precaution which may be required by the ordinary practice of seamen or by the special circumstances of the case.

RESERVATION OF RULES FOR HARBORS AND INLAND NAVIGATION.

ART. 30. Nothing in these rules shall interfere with the operation of a special rule duly made by local authority relative to the navigation of any harbor, river, or inland waters.

DISTRESS SIGNALS.

ART. 31. When a vessel is in distress and requires assistance from other vessels or from the shore, the following shall be the signals to be used or displayed by her, either together or separately, namely:

In the daytime—

First. A gun fired at intervals of about a minute.

Second. The international code signal of distress, indicated by N C.

Third. The distance signal, consisting of a square flag, having either above or below it a ball or anything resembling a ball.

Fourth. Rockets or shells as prescribed below for use at night.

Fifth. A continuous sounding with any fog-signal apparatus.

At night—

First. A gun fired at intervals of about a minute.

Second. Flames on the vessel (as from a burning tar barrel, oil barrel, etc.).

Third. Rockets or shells bursting in the air with a loud report and throwing stars of any color or description, fired one at a time at short intervals.

Fourth. A continuous sounding with any fog-signal apparatus.

SEC. 2. That all laws or parts of laws inconsistent with the foregoing regulations for preventing collisions at sea for the navigation of all public and private vessels of the United States upon the high seas and in all waters connected therewith navigable by seagoing vessels are hereby repealed.

SEC. 3. That this act shall take effect at a time to be fixed by the President by proclamation issued for that purpose.

And whereas an act of Congress entitled "An act to amend an act approved August 19, 1890, entitled 'An act to adopt regulations for preventing collisions at sea,'" was approved May 28, 1894, the said act being in the following words:

Be it enacted by the Senate and House of Representatives of the United States of America in Congress assembled, That article 7 of the act approved August 19, 1890, entitled "An act to adopt regulations for preventing collisions at sea," be amended to read as follows:

"ART. 7. Steam vessels of less than 40 and vessels under oars or sails of less than 20 tons gross tonnage, respectively, and rowing boats, when under way, shall not be required to carry the lights mentioned in article 2 (*a*), (*b*), and (*c*), but if they do not carry them they shall be provided with the following lights:

"First. Steam vessels of less than 40 tons shall carry—

"(*a*) In the fore part of the vessel or on or in front of the funnel where it can best be seen, and at a height above the gunwale of not less than 9 feet, a bright white light constructed and fixed as prescribed in article 2 (*a*) and of such a character as to be visible at a distance of at least 2 miles.

"(*b*) Green and red side lights constructed and fixed as prescribed in article 2 (*b*) and (*c*) and of such a character as to be visible at a distance of at least 1 mile, or a combined lantern showing a green light and a red light from right ahead to 2 points abaft the beam on their respective sides. Such lanterns shall be carried not less than 3 feet below the white light.

"Second. Small steamboats, such as are carried by seagoing vessels, may carry the white light at a less height than 9 feet above the gunwale, but it shall be carried above the combined lantern mentioned in subdivision 1 (*b*).

"Third. Vessels under oars or sails of less than 20 tons shall have ready at hand a lantern with a green glass on one side and a red glass on the other, which on the approach of or to other vessels shall be exhibited, in sufficient time to prevent collision, so that the green light shall not be seen on the port side nor the red light on the starboard side.

"Fourth. Rowing boats, whether under oars or sail, shall have ready at hand a lantern showing a white light, which shall be temporarily exhibited in sufficient time to prevent collision.

"The vessels referred to in this article shall not be obliged to carry the lights prescribed by article 4 (*a*) and article 11, last paragraph."

That article 9 be hereby repealed.

That article 21 be amended to read as follows:

"ART. 21. Where by any of these rules one of two vessels is to keep out of the way the other shall keep her course and speed.

"NOTE.—When, in consequence of thick weather or other causes, such vessel finds herself so close that collision can not be avoided by the action of the giving-way vessel alone, she also shall take such action as will best aid to avert collision." (See articles 27 and 29.)

That article 31 be amended to read as follows:

"DISTRESS SIGNALS.

"ART. 31. When a vessel is in distress and requires assistance from other vessels or from the shore the following shall be the signals to be used or displayed by her, either together or separately, namely:

"In the daytime—

"First. A gun or other explosive signal fired at intervals of about a minute.

"Second. The international code signal of distress indicated by N C.

"Third. The distance signal, consisting of a square flag, having either above or below it a ball or anything resembling a ball.

"Fourth. A continuous sounding with any fog-signal apparatus.

"At night—

"First. A gun or other explosive signal fired at intervals of about a minute.

"Second. Flames on the vessel (as from a burning tar barrel, oil barrel, etc.).

"Third. Rockets or shells throwing stars of any color or description, fired one at a time at short intervals.

"Fourth. A continuous sounding with any fog-signal apparatus."

And whereas it is provided by section 3 of the act approved August 19, 1890, that it shall take effect at a time to be fixed by the President by proclamation issued for that purpose:

Now, therefore, I, Grover Cleveland, President of the United States of America, do hereby, in virtue of the authority vested in me by section 3 of the act aforesaid, proclaim the 1st day of March, 1895, as the day on which the said act approved August 19, 1890, as amended by the act approved May 28, 1894, shall take effect.

In testimony whereof I have hereunto set my hand and caused the seal of the United States of America to be affixed.

[SEAL.] Done at the city of Washington, this 13th day of July, 1894, and of the Independence of the United States the one hundred and nineteenth.

GROVER CLEVELAND.

By the President:

W. Q. GRESHAM, *Secretary of State.*

BY THE PRESIDENT OF THE UNITED STATES OF AMERICA.

A PROCLAMATION.

Whereas Congress by a statute approved March 22, 1882, and by statutes in furtherance and amendment thereof defined the crimes of bigamy, polygamy, and unlawful cohabitation in the Territories and other places within the exclusive jurisdiction of the United States and prescribed a penalty for such crimes; and

Whereas on or about the 6th day of October, 1890, the Church of the Latter-day Saints, commonly known as the Mormon Church, through its president issued a manifesto proclaiming the purpose of said church no longer to sanction the practice of polygamous marriages and calling upon all members and adherents of said church to obey the laws of the United States in reference to said subject-matter; and

Whereas on the 4th day of January, A. D. 1893,* Benjamin Harrison, then President of the United States, did declare and grant a full pardon and amnesty to certain offenders under said acts upon condition of future obedience to their requirements, as is fully set forth in said proclamation of amnesty and pardon; and

Whereas upon the evidence now furnished me I am satisfied that the members and adherents of said church generally abstain from plural marriages and polygamous cohabitation and are now living in obedience to the laws, and that the time has now arrived when the interests of public justice and morality will be promoted by the granting of amnesty and pardon to all such offenders as have complied with the conditions of said proclamation, including such of said offenders as have been convicted under the provisions of said act:

Now, therefore, I, Grover Cleveland, President of the United States, by virtue of the powers in me vested, do hereby declare and grant a full amnesty and pardon to all persons who have in violation of said acts committed either of the offenses of polygamy, bigamy, adultery, or unlawful cohabitation under the color of polygamous or plural marriage, or who, having been convicted of violations of said acts, are now suffering deprivation of civil rights in consequence of the same, excepting all persons who have not complied with the conditions contained in said executive proclamation of January 4, 1893.

* See pp. 368–369.

In witness whereof I have hereunto set my hand and caused the seal of the United States to be affixed.

[SEAL.] Done at the city of Washington, this 25th day of September, A. D. 1894, and of the Independence of the United States the one hundred and nineteenth.

GROVER CLEVELAND.

By the President:

W. Q. GRESHAM, *Secretary of State.*

BY THE PRESIDENT OF THE UNITED STATES OF AMERICA.

A PROCLAMATION.

The American people should gratefully render thanksgiving and praise to the Supreme Ruler of the Universe, who has watched over them with kindness and fostering care during the year that has passed; they should also with humility and faith supplicate the Father of All Mercies for continued blessings according to their needs, and they should by deeds of charity seek the favor of the Giver of Every Good and Perfect Gift.

Therefore, I, Grover Cleveland, President of the United States, do hereby appoint and set apart Thursday, the 29th day of November instant, as a day of thanksgiving and prayer to be kept and observed by all the people of the land.

On that day let our ordinary work and business be suspended and let us meet in our accustomed places of worship and give thanks to Almighty God for our preservation as a nation, for our immunity from disease and pestilence, for the harvests that have rewarded our husbandry, for a renewal of national prosperity, and for every advance in virtue and intelligence that has marked our growth as a people.

And with our thanksgiving let us pray that these blessings may be multiplied unto us, that our national conscience may be quickened to a better recognition of the power and goodness of God, and that in our national life we may clearer see and closer follow the path of righteousness.

And in our places of worship and praise, as well as in the happy reunions of kindred and friends on that day, let us invoke divine approval by generously remembering the poor and needy. Surely He who has given us comfort and plenty will look upon our relief of the destitute and our ministrations of charity as the work of hearts truly grateful and as proofs of the sincerity of our thanksgiving.

Witness my hand and the seal of the United States, which I have caused to be hereto affixed.

[SEAL.] Done at the city of Washington on the 1st day of November, A. D. 1894, and of the Independence of the United States the one hundred and nineteenth.

GROVER CLEVELAND.

By the President:

W. Q. GRESHAM, *Secretary of State.*

A PROCLAMATION.

Whereas by the sixteenth section of the act of Congress approved March 2, 1889 (25 U. S. Statutes at Large, p. 888), the agreements entered into between the Chicago, Milwaukee and St. Paul Railway Company and the Sioux Indians for the right of way and occupation of certain lands for station purposes in that portion of the Sioux Reservation, in the State of South Dakota, relinquished by said Indians were ratified upon the condition that said railway company shall within three years after the said act takes effect construct, complete, and put into operation its line of road as therein provided for, due location of which was to be made within nine months after said act took effect; and in case of failure to so construct said road "the lands granted for right of way, station grounds, or other railway purposes as in this act provided shall without any further act or ceremony be declared by proclamation of the President forfeited, and shall without entry or further action on the part of the United States revert to the United States and be subject to entry under the other provisions of this act;" and

Whereas under previous proclamation* said act took effect on February 10, 1890, and more than three years have elapsed and no construction has been reported of the said road beyond the town of Chamberlain, in the State of South Dakota, as evidenced by the report of the Secretary of the Interior dated December 3, 1894:

Now, therefore, I, Grover Cleveland, President of the United States, do declare that the said lands granted for right of way and station purposes, to wit, that tract of land known as lots 2, 3, and 4 and the southeast quarter of the southwest quarter of section 10, and lots 1 and 9 in section 15, township 104 north, range 71 west, containing 188 acres, as shown by a plat approved January 24, 1891, being the tract selected by the Chicago, Milwaukee and St. Paul Railway Company under the sixteenth section of the act of March 2, 1889 (25 U. S. Statutes at Large, p. 888), also the 640 acres in said township 104 north, ranges 71 and 72 west, fifth principal meridian, in the State of South Dakota, plat of which was approved by the Secretary of the Interior January 24, 1889, and now on file in the General Land Office, are forfeited to the United States and will be subject to entry under the homestead laws as provided by said act of March 2, 1889, whenever the Secretary of the Interior shall give due notice to the local officers of this declaration of forfeiture.

Given under my hand, at the city of Washington, this 5th day of December, A. D. 1894.

GROVER CLEVELAND,
President of the United States.

By the President:

S. W. LAMOREUX,
  Commissioner of the General Land Office.

*See pp. 94-97.

EXECUTIVE ORDERS.

CIVIL SERVICE.—REVOCATION OF PROMOTION REGULATIONS.

DECEMBER 11, 1893.

The promotion regulations applied to the War Department May 7, 1887, under authority contained in amended Civil-Service Rule VI are hereby revoked, and hereafter promotions in that Department, until otherwise provided, will be made in accordance with the provisions of Departmental Rule IX and the order of the Secretary of War of March 2, 1892, or such other and further orders as the said Secretary may make not inconsistent with the civil-service rules and the order of the President of December 4, 1891, directing the keeping of an efficiency record with a view to the placing of promotions wholly upon the basis of merit.

GROVER CLEVELAND.

AMENDMENTS OF CIVIL-SERVICE RULES.

GENERAL RULE III.

Amend General Rule III by striking out clause (*e*) of section 2.

DEPARTMENTAL RULE II.

Amend Departmental Rule II by striking out the whole of section 1 and substituting therefor the following:

1. To test fitness for the classified departmental service there shall be a clerk-copyist examination and such supplementary and special examinations as the Commission may provide to meet the special requirements of the service. The clerk-copyist examination shall not include more than the following subjects: Orthography, copying, penmanship, arithmetic (fundamental rules, fractions, percentage, interest, and discount), elements of bookkeeping and accounts, elements of the English language, letter writing, elements of the geography, history, and government of the United States.

DEPARTMENTAL RULE VI.

Amend Departmental Rule VI as follows:

In section 1, line 1, strike out the words "copyist and of the clerk" and insert in lieu thereof the words "clerk-copyist," and in the same line strike out the final letter in the word "examinations." In section 4 strike out all after the word "the" where it occurs the second time in line 6 down to and including the word "separated" in line 8 and insert in lieu thereof the words "clerk-copyist," and strike out the final letter of the word "examinations" in line 9. In section 9, line 1, strike out the words "the copyist and the clerk" and insert in lieu thereof the word "all," and strike out all after the word "register" in line 3 to the end of the section.

DEPARTMENTAL RULE VII.

Amend Departmental Rule VII as follows:

In section 1, after the word "clerk" in line 3, insert a hyphen and the word "copyist." In section 3, after the word "the" where it occurs the second time in line 1, strike out the words "copyist or the clerk" and insert in lieu thereof the words "clerk-copyist." Strike out all of section 4 and change the numbering of the sections following as required.

DEPARTMENTAL RULE IX.

Amend Departmental Rule IX as follows:

In section 2, after the word "clerk" in line 1, insert a hyphen and the word "copyist." In section 3, after the word "clerk" in line 1, insert a hyphen and the word "copyist." Strike out the period at the end of section 5 and insert in lieu thereof a comma, and add to the section the following:

But the provisions of clause 1 of this rule shall cease to be operative when, by reason of the consolidation of the clerk and copyist examinations, there shall no longer be any persons in the departmental service to whom they apply.

POSTAL RULE IV.

Postal Rule IV is hereby amended by adding thereto the following section:

4. In case of the sudden occurrence of a vacancy in a position within the classified service of any post-office which the public interest requires shall be immediately filled, and which can not be so filled by certification from the eligible registers, such vacancy may be filled by temporary appointment until a regular appointment can be made under the provisions of sections 1 and 2 of this rule: *Provided*, Such temporary appointment shall in no case continue longer than ninety days: *And provided further*, That no person shall serve more than ninety days in any one year under such temporary appointment. Every such temporary appointment and also the discontinuance of the same shall at once be reported to the Commission.

Approved, January 5, 1894.

GROVER CLEVELAND.

AMENDMENT OF CIVIL-SERVICE RULES.

Departmental Rule VII is hereby amended by adding thereto the following section:

9. In case of the sudden occurrence of a vacancy in the position of observer in the Weather Bureau of the Department of Agriculture which the public interest requires shall be immediately filled, and which can not be so filled by certification from the eligible registers of the Commission, the Secretary of Agriculture may fill such vacancy by temporary appointment until a regular appointment can be made under the provisions of sections 1, 2, and 3 of this rule: *Provided*, Such temporary appointment shall in no case continue longer than ninety days. Every such temporary appointment and the discontinuance of the same shall at once be reported to the Commission.

Approved, January 5, 1894.

GROVER CLEVELAND.

CIVIL SERVICE.—EXECUTIVE ORDER WITHDRAWING FISH CULTURISTS FROM THE LIST OF PLACES TO BE FILLED BY NONCOMPETITIVE EXAMINATION.

EXECUTIVE MANSION, *January 20, 1894.*

So much of Executive orders heretofore issued under General Rule III, section 2, clause (*d*), as provides for the appointment of fish culturists upon noncompetitive examination is hereby revoked, and hereafter fish culturists will be appointed upon competitive examination.

GROVER CLEVELAND.

AMENDMENT OF CIVIL-SERVICE RULES.

SPECIAL INDIAN RULE NO. I.

EXECUTIVE MANSION, *March 6, 1894.*

Exceptions from examination are hereby made as follows: One superintendent and the necessary teachers, not exceeding four in number, for the organization and equipment of a normal school to be established at Albuquerque, N. Mex., this rule to expire by limitation six months after the date of its approval.

Approved:

GROVER CLEVELAND.

AMENDMENT OF CIVIL-SERVICE RULES.

EXECUTIVE MANSION, *March 20, 1894.*

So much of clause 6 of Special Departmental Rule No. 1, providing for exceptions from examination in the office of the Secretary in the Department of Agriculture, as excepts "clerk to act as appointment clerk" is hereby revoked, and that position will hereafter be treated as subject to competitive examination.

Approved:

GROVER CLEVELAND.

AMENDMENTS OF CIVIL-SERVICE RULES.

Section 6 of Special Departmental Rule No. 1 is hereby amended by striking from the list of excepted places in the Weather Bureau of the Department of Agriculture enumerated therein the following:

The three professors of meteorology of highest grade.

Said section is further amended by adding thereto the following:

Noncompetitive examinations shall be held, on such dates and at such places as the Commission may from time to time determine, to test the competency of inspectors and assistant inspectors in the Bureau of Animal Industry in the Department of Agriculture employed elsewhere than at Washington, who were so employed on the date inspectors and assistant inspectors were included in the classified service and have been continued in the service of the Department until opportunity has been provided for their noncompetitive examination. The results of such examination shall be reported by the Commission to the Secretary of Agriculture.

Approved, May 1, 1894.   GROVER CLEVELAND.

AMENDMENTS OF CIVIL-SERVICE RULES.

EXECUTIVE MANSION, *May 11, 1894.*

SPECIAL DEPARTMENTAL RULE NO. 1.

Special Departmental Rule No. 1 is hereby amended by adding to the exceptions from examination therein made in the Department of the Treasury the following:

In the office of the Second Auditor: One skilled laborer with duties exclusively of a carpenter and cabinetmaker.

In the Bureau of Engraving and Printing: Custodian of proving presses and modeler.

SPECIAL CUSTOMS RULE NO. 1.

Special Customs Rule No. 1, authorizing certain exceptions from examination in the classified customs service, is hereby amended by adding to the statement of places therein excepted the following:

In the customs district of Vermont: One deputy collector and inspector, to be stationed at Halifax during the winter and at Quebec during the time the St. Lawrence River is open to navigation.

RAILWAY MAIL RULE IV.

Railway Mail Rule IV, section 2, clause (*b*), of the civil-service rules is hereby amended by striking out all after the word "averages" in line 3 to and including the word "territory" in line 10, and the word "further" in line 10; so that as amended the clause will read:

The Commission shall certify from the register of the State or Territory in which the vacancy exists the names of the three eligibles thereon having the highest averages: *Provided*, That if upon the register of the State or Territory in which the vacancy exists there are the names of eligibles having a claim of preference under section 1754, Revised Statutes, the names of such eligibles shall be certified before the names of other eligibles of higher grade: *Provided further*, That on a line on which the service does not require the full time of a clerk, and one can be employed jointly with the railroad company, the appointment may be made without examination and certification, with the consent of the Commission, upon a statement of the facts by the general superintendent; but no clerk so appointed shall be eligible for transfer or appointment to any other place in the service.

Section 6 of said rule is hereby amended by adding after the word "substitutes" in line 6 the words "resident in the counties which are supplied wholly or in part by the road on which the vacancy exists;" so that as amended the section will read:

6. There may be certified and appointed in each State and Territory, in the manner provided for in this rule, such number of substitute clerks, not exceeding the ratio of one substitute to ten regular clerks, in such State or Territory as the Postmaster-General may authorize, and any vacancies occurring in class 1 in any State

or Territory in which substitutes have been appointed shall be filled by the appointment thereto of those substitutes resident in the counties which are supplied wholly or in part by the road on which the vacancy exists, in the order of their appointment as substitutes, without further certification. The time during which any substitute is actually employed in the service shall be counted as part of his probation.

GENERAL RULE III.

Section 2 of General Rule III is hereby amended by adding thereto the following clause:

(*h*) For the appointment of an Indian as assistant teacher in the Indian-school service.

INDIAN RULE IV.

Indian Rule IV is hereby amended by adding thereto the following section:

6. Upon the nomination by the Commissioner of Indian Affairs, through the Secretary of the Interior, of an Indian for appointment as assistant teacher, the Commission shall give such Indian noncompetitive examination under General Rule III, section 2, clause (*h*), upon passing which at the required grade he shall be certified and appointed for the probationary period provided for in section 3 of this rule, at the end of which period he shall be absolutely appointed or discharged from the service in accordance with the provisions of said section. Any Indian appointed assistant teacher as herein provided may be, any time after absolute appointment, appointed teacher upon the certification of the Commission that he has passed the teacher's examination.

Approved:

GROVER CLEVELAND.

CIVIL SERVICE.—AMENDMENT OF CLASSIFICATION OF THE INDIAN SERVICE AS MADE BY THE SECRETARY OF THE INTERIOR APRIL 13, 1891.

EXECUTIVE MANSION, *May 11, 1894.*

In the exercise of the power vested in the President by the third paragraph of section 6 of the act entitled "An act to regulate and improve the civil service of the United States," approved January 16, 1883, I hereby direct the Secretary of the Interior to revise the classification of the Indian service made by him, by direction of the President, on the 13th day of April, 1891, and to include in class 3 of said classification assistant teachers.

Approved:

GROVER CLEVELAND.

BY THE PRESIDENT OF THE UNITED STATES.

EXECUTIVE ORDER.

EXECUTIVE MANSION, *May 26, 1894.*

It is hereby ordered, That the several Executive Departments and the Government Printing Office be closed on Wednesday, the 30th instant, to enable the employees to participate in the decoration of the graves of the soldiers and sailors who fell in defense of the Union during the War of the Rebellion.

GROVER CLEVELAND.

AMENDMENT OF CIVIL-SERVICE RULES.

Special Indian Rule No. 1 is hereby amended by adding to the places excepted from examination therein the following:

Kindergarten teachers, to be employed as such, not exceeding twenty in number.

Approved, June 21, 1894.

GROVER CLEVELAND.

AMENDMENT OF CIVIL-SERVICE RULES.

Special Customs Rule No. 1 is hereby amended by adding to the places excepted from examination therein the following:

In the customs district of Boston, office of the collector: One superintendent of warehouses.

In the customs district of Philadelphia, office of the collector: Five chiefs of division.

Approved, June 21, 1894.

GROVER CLEVELAND.

AMENDMENTS OF CIVIL-SERVICE RULES.

EXECUTIVE MANSION, *July 9, 1894.*

DEPARTMENTAL RULE II.

Departmental Rule II, clause 3 (*f*), is hereby amended by adding at the end thereof the following words:

Except in the Department of Agriculture the chiefs of the following divisions: Entomology and economic ornithology and mammalogy.

SPECIAL DEPARTMENTAL RULE NO. 1.

Special Departmental Rule No. 1 is hereby amended by dropping from among the places therein excepted from examination the following:

In the Department of Agriculture, office of the Secretary, the assistant chiefs of the following divisions: Of entomology and of economic ornithology and mammalogy.

Approved:

GROVER CLEVELAND.

CIVIL SERVICE.—AMENDMENT OF CLASSIFICATION OF THE DEPARTMENT OF THE INTERIOR.

EXECUTIVE MANSION, *July 25, 1894.*

In the exercise of the power vested in the President by the third paragraph of section 6 of the act entitled "An act to regulate and improve the civil service of the United States," approved January 16, 1883, I hereby direct the Secretary of the Interior to revise the classification of the Department of the Interior so as to include therein the chief clerk and the assistant chief clerk at the Indian warehouse at New York.

Approved:

GROVER CLEVELAND.

AMENDMENT OF CIVIL-SERVICE RULES.

Special Departmental Rule No. 1 is hereby amended by adding to the places therein excepted from examination in the Department of the Treasury the following:

In the Bureau of Statistics: One expert in mechanical designs and in diagramming commercial and financial facts.

Approved, November 2, 1894.   GROVER CLEVELAND.

AMENDMENTS OF CIVIL-SERVICE RULES.

DEPARTMENTAL RULE II.

Departmental Rule II, clause 3 (*f*), is hereby amended by adding at the end thereof the following words: "and of pomology;" so that as amended the paragraph will read:

(*f*) Chiefs of divisions, except in the Department of Agriculture the chiefs of the following divisions: Entomology, economic ornithology and mammalogy, and of pomology.

SPECIAL DEPARTMENTAL RULE NO. I.

Special Departmental Rule No. 1 is hereby amended by dropping from among the places therein excepted from examination the following:

In the Department of Agriculture, office of the Secretary: The assistant chief of the division of pomology.

Approved, November 2, 1894.   GROVER CLEVELAND.

AMENDMENTS OF CIVIL-SERVICE RULES.

EXECUTIVE MANSION, *November 2, 1894.*

INDIAN RULE IV

Section 6 of Indian Rule IV is hereby amended by inserting the following proviso at the end of the first sentence:

Provided, That the certificates of graduation of the Indian graduates of the normal classes at Santa Fe, N. Mex.; Salem, Oreg.; Haskell Institute, Lawrence, Kans.; Carlisle, Pa., and Hampton, Va., may be accepted by the Commission as the basis of certification in lieu of the examination herein provided.

As amended the section will read:

6. Upon the nomination by the Commissioner of Indian Affairs, through the Secretary of the Interior, of an Indian for appointment as assistant teacher, the Commission shall give such Indian noncompetitive examination, under General Rule III, section 2, clause (*h*), upon passing which at the required grade he shall be certified and appointed for the probationary period provided for in section 3 of this rule, at the end of which period he shall be absolutely appointed or discharged from the

service in accordance with the provisions of said section: *Provided,* That the certificates of graduation of the Indian graduates of the normal classes at Santa Fe, N. Mex.; Salem, Oreg.; Haskell Institute, Lawrence, Kans.; Carlisle, Pa., and Hampton, Va., may be accepted by the Commission as the basis of certification in lieu of the examination herein provided for. Any Indian appointed assistant teacher as herein provided may at any time after absolute appointment be appointed teacher upon the certification of the Commission that he has passed the teacher examination.

SPECIAL INDIAN RULE NO. I.

Special Indian Rule No. 1 is hereby amended by inserting after the words "New Mexico" in line 3 the words "also one normal teacher each at the Salem (Oreg.) school and the Haskell Institute, Lawrence, Kans." As amended the rule will read:

Exceptions from examination are hereby made as follows: One superintendent and the necessary teachers, not exceeding four in number, for the organization and equipment of one normal school to be established at Santa Fe, N. Mex.; also one normal teacher each at the Salem (Oreg.) school and the Haskell Institute, Lawrence, Kans.; this rule to expire by limitation six months after the date of its approval.

Approved:

GROVER CLEVELAND.

AMENDMENTS OF CIVIL-SERVICE RULES.

Postal Rule II is hereby amended by striking out all of section 5 and inserting in lieu thereof the following:

5. Exceptions from examination in the classified postal service are hereby made as follows:

(*a*) Assistant postmaster or the chief assistant to the postmaster, by whatever designation known.

(*b*) One secretary to the postmaster, when authorized by law and allowed by the Post-Office Department.

(*c*) Cashier, when authorized by law and employed under that roster title.

(*d*) Assistant cashier, when authorized by law and employed under that roster title.

(*e*) Superintendents of station or branch post-offices at which letter carriers are employed.

(*f*) Printers and pressmen, when authorized by law and allowed by the Post-Office Department and employed as such.

6. No person appointed to a place under any exception made by any postal rule shall be transferred to any other place not also excepted from examination.

Postal Rule IV is hereby amended by inserting after the word "manner," in section 1, line 3, the following:

Provided, That superintendents of mail shall be selected from among the employees of the railway mail service or of the mailing division of the post-office at which they are respectively to serve.

Postal Rule VIII is hereby amended as follows:

In clause (*a*), line 2, after the word "by," insert the word "any," and in the same line strike out "II, clause 5."

Approved, November 2, 1894.

GROVER CLEVELAND.

AMENDMENT OF CIVIL-SERVICE RULES.

EXECUTIVE MANSION, *November 2, 1894.*

Departmental Rule VII, clause 1, is hereby amended by inserting at the end of line 6 the following:

Vacancies in places authorized to be filled by noncompetitive examination may be filled without examination for a period not exceeding thirty days, until a regular appointment can be made upon certification made by the Commission.

Every such appointment and the reasons therefor shall be at once reported to the Commission.

Approved:

GROVER CLEVELAND.

CIVIL SERVICE.—AMENDMENT OF CLASSIFICATION.

In pursuance of the authority contained in the third paragraph of section 6 of the act entitled "An act to regulate and improve the civil service of the United States," approved January 16, 1883, the heads of the several Executive Departments are hereby directed to amend their several classifications so as to include among the employees classified thereunder messengers, assistant messengers, and watchmen.

Approved, November 2, 1894.

GROVER CLEVELAND.

CIVIL SERVICE.—AMENDMENT OF CLASSIFICATION.

In pursuance of the authority contained in the third paragraph of section 6 of the act entitled "An act to regulate and improve the civil service of the United States," approved January 16, 1883, the Postmaster-General is hereby directed to amend the classification of the Post-Office Department so as to include among the classes covered thereby clerks to post-office inspectors.

Approved, November 2, 1894.

GROVER CLEVELAND.

AMENDMENTS OF CIVIL-SERVICE RULES.

GENERAL RULE III.

General Rule III is hereby amended by striking out clause (*b*) of section 2 and relettering the remaining clauses of the section accordingly.

DEPARTMENTAL RULES.

Departmental Rule II is hereby amended as follows:

In section 4, line 1, strike out the word "hereby," and insert after the word "made," at the end of the line, the words "by any departmental rule;" in line 2, after the word "shall," strike out the words "within one year after appointment;" substitute a period for the semicolon in line 3 and strike out the remainder of the section. As amended the section will read:

4. No person appointed to a place under the exceptions to examination made by any departmental rule shall be transferred from such place to a place not also excepted from examination.

Departmental Rule XI is hereby amended as follows:

In clause (*a*), line 2, insert the word "any" before the word "departmental," and strike out in line 3 all after the word "rule."

RAILWAY MAIL RULES.

Railway Mail Rule II is hereby amended as follows:

In section 6, line 2, after the word "shall," strike out the words "within one year after appointment;" substitute a period for the semicolon in line 3 and strike out the remainder of the section. As amended the section will read:

6. No person appointed to a place under any exception to examination hereby made shall be transferred to another place not also excepted from examination.

Approved, November 2, 1894.

GROVER CLEVELAND.

AMENDMENTS OF CIVIL-SERVICE RULES.

Customs Rule I is hereby amended as follows:

In section 2, line 2, strike out the word "fifty" and insert in lieu thereof the word "twenty."

Customs Rule II is hereby amended as follows:

In section 6, line 1, strike out the word "hereby," and after the word "made," at the end of the line, insert the words "by any customs rule;" in line 2, after the word "shall," strike out the words "within one year after appointment;" substitute a period for the semicolon in line 3 and strike out the remainder of the section. As amended the clause will read:

No person appointed to a place under any exception to examination made by any customs rule shall be transferred from such place to another place not also excepted from examination.

Customs Rule VIII is hereby amended as follows:

In clause (*a*), line 2, after the word "by," insert the word "any," and in the same line strike out "II, clause 5."

Approved, November 2, 1894.

GROVER CLEVELAND.

AMENDMENTS OF CIVIL-SERVICE RULES.

DEPARTMENTAL RULE VII.

Departmental Rule VII is hereby amended by adding to the first paragraph of section 1 the following proviso:

Provided further, That sea post clerks in the Post-Office Department shall be appointed by transfer from the classified railway mail service or the classified postal service, and shall be eligible at any time for retransfer to the service from which transferred, but shall not be transferred to any other department or branch of the service, nor to any other place in the Post-Office Department, without examination and certification by the Commission.

RAILWAY MAIL RULE II.

Railway Mail Rule II is hereby amended as follows:
In section 5 strike out clauses (*e*) and (*f*).

RAILWAY MAIL RULE IV.

Railway Mail Rule IV is hereby amended as follows:

In the last proviso of clause (*b*) of section 2, in line 2 of that proviso, after the word "line," insert the words "or at a transfer station or on a steamboat;" in the same line strike out the words "on which" and substitute therefor the word "where," and in line 3, after the word "railroad," insert the words "or steamboat;" so that as amended the proviso will read:

Provided further, That on a line or at a transfer station or on a steamboat where the service does not require the full time of a clerk, and one can be employed jointly with the railroad or steamboat company, the appointment may be made without examination and certification, with the consent of the Commission, upon a statement of the facts by the general superintendent; but no clerk so appointed shall be eligible for transfer or appointment to any other place in the service.

Approved, November 17, 1894.

GROVER CLEVELAND.

SECOND ANNUAL MESSAGE.

EXECUTIVE MANSION, *December 3, 1894.*
To the Congress of the United States:

The assemblage within the nation's legislative halls of those charged with the duty of making laws for the benefit of a generous and free people impressively suggests the exacting obligation and inexorable responsibility involved in their task. At the threshold of such labor now to be undertaken by the Congress of the United States, and in the discharge of an executive duty enjoined by the Constitution, I submit this communication, containing a brief statement of the condition of our national affairs and recommending such legislation as seems to me necessary and expedient.

The history of our recent dealings with other nations and our peaceful relations with them at this time additionally demonstrate the advantage of consistently adhering to a firm but just foreign policy, free from envious or ambitious national schemes and characterized by entire honesty and sincerity.

During the past year, pursuant to a law of Congress, commissioners were appointed to the Antwerp Industrial Exposition. Though the participation of American exhibitors fell far short of completely illustrating our national ingenuity and industrial achievements, yet it was quite creditable in view of the brief time allowed for preparation.

I have endeavored to impress upon the Belgian Government the needlessness and positive harmfulness of its restrictions upon the importation of certain of our food products, and have strongly urged that the rigid supervision and inspection under our laws are amply sufficient to prevent the exportation from this country of diseased cattle and unwholesome meat.

The termination of the civil war in Brazil has been followed by the general prevalence of peace and order. It appearing at an early stage of the insurrection that its course would call for unusual watchfulness on the part of this Government, our naval force in the harbor of Rio de Janeiro was strengthened. This precaution, I am satisfied, tended to restrict the issue to a simple trial of strength between the Brazilian Government and the insurgents and to avert complications which at times seemed imminent. Our firm attitude of neutrality was maintained to the end. The insurgents received no encouragement of eventual asylum from our commanders, and such opposition as they encountered was for the protection of our commerce and was clearly justified by public law.

A serious tension of relations having arisen at the close of the war between Brazil and Portugal by reason of the escape of the insurgent admiral Da Gama and his followers, the friendly offices of our representatives to those countries were exerted for the protection of the subjects of either within the territory of the other.

Although the Government of Brazil was duly notified that the commercial arrangement existing between the United States and that country based on the third section of the tariff act of 1890 was abrogated on August 28, 1894, by the taking effect of the tariff law now in force, that Government subsequently notified us of its intention to terminate such arrangement on the 1st day of January, 1895, in the exercise of the right reserved in the agreement between the two countries. I invite attention to the correspondence between the Secretary of State and the Brazilian minister on this subject.

The commission organized under the convention which we had entered into with Chile for the settlement of the outstanding claims of each Government against the other adjourned at the end of the period stipulated for its continuance leaving undetermined a number of American cases which had been duly presented. These claims are not barred, and negotiations are in progress for their submission to a new tribunal.

On the 17th of March last a new treaty with China in further regulation of emigration was signed at Washington, and on August 13 it received the sanction of the Senate. Ratification on the part of China and formal exchange are awaited to give effect to this mutually beneficial convention.

A gratifying recognition of the uniform impartiality of this country toward all foreign states was manifested by the coincident request of the Chinese and Japanese Governments that the agents of the United States should within proper limits afford protection to the subjects of the other during the suspension of diplomatic relations due to a state of war. This delicate office was accepted, and a misapprehension which gave rise to the belief that in affording this kindly unofficial protection our agents would exercise the same authority which the withdrawn agents of the belligerents had exercised was promptly corrected. Although the war between China and Japan endangers no policy of the United States, it deserves our gravest consideration by reason of its disturbance of our growing commercial interests in the two countries and the increased dangers which may result to our citizens domiciled or sojourning in the interior of China.

Acting under a stipulation in our treaty with Korea (the first concluded with a western power), I felt constrained at the beginning of the controversy to tender our good offices to induce an amicable arrangement of the initial difficulty growing out of the Japanese demands for administrative reforms in Korea, but the unhappy precipitation of actual hostilities defeated this kindly purpose.

Deploring the destructive war between the two most powerful of the eastern nations and anxious that our commercial interests in those countries may be preserved and that the safety of our citizens there shall not be jeopardized, I would not hesitate to heed any intimation that our friendly aid for the honorable termination of hostilities would be acceptable to both belligerents.

A convention has been finally concluded for the settlement by arbitration of the prolonged dispute with Ecuador growing out of the proceedings against Emilio Santos, a naturalized citizen of the United States.

Our relations with the Republic of France continue to be such as should exist between nations so long bound together by friendly sympathy and similarity in their form of government.

The recent cruel assassination of the President of this sister Republic called forth such universal expressions of sorrow and condolence from our people and Government as to leave no doubt of the depth and sincerity of our attachment. The resolutions passed by the Senate and House of Representatives on the occasion have been communicated to the widow of President Carnot.

Acting upon the reported discovery of Texas fever in cargoes of American cattle, the German prohibition against importations of live stock and fresh meats from this country has been revived. It is hoped that Germany will soon become convinced that the inhibition is as needless as it is harmful to mutual interests.

The German Government has protested against that provision of the customs tariff act which imposes a discriminating duty of one-tenth of 1 cent a pound on sugars coming from countries paying an export bounty thereon, claiming that the exaction of such duty is in contravention of Articles V and IX of the treaty of 1828 with Prussia.

In the interests of the commerce of both countries and to avoid even the accusation of treaty violation, I recommend the repeal of so much of the statute as imposes that duty, and I invite attention to the accompanying report of the Secretary of State, containing a discussion of the questions raised by the German protests.

Early in the present year an agreement was reached with Great Britain concerning instructions to be given to the naval commanders of the two Governments in Bering Sea and the contiguous North Pacific Ocean for their guidance in the execution of the award of the Paris Tribunal of Arbitration and the enforcement of the regulations therein prescribed for the protection of seal life in the waters mentioned. An understanding has also been reached for the payment by the United States of $425,000 in full satisfaction of all claims which may be made by Great Britain for damages growing out of the controversy as to fur seals in Bering Sea or the seizure of British vessels engaged in taking seal in those waters. The award and findings of the Paris Tribunal to a great extent determined the facts and principles upon which these claims should be adjusted, and they have been subjected by both Governments to a thorough examination upon the principles as well as the facts which they involve. I am convinced that a settlement upon the terms mentioned would be an equitable and advantageous one, and I recommend that provision be made for the prompt payment of the stated sum.

Thus far only France and Portugal have signified their willingness to adhere to the regulations established under the award of the Paris Tribunal of Arbitration.

Preliminary surveys of the Alaskan boundary and a preparatory examination of the question of protection of food fish in the contiguous waters of the United States and the Dominion of Canada are in progress.

The boundary of British Guiana still remains in dispute between Great Britain and Venezuela. Believing that its early settlement on some just basis alike honorable to both parties is in the line of our established policy to remove from this hemisphere all causes of difference with powers beyond the sea, I shall renew the efforts heretofore made to bring about a restoration of diplomatic relations between the disputants and to induce a reference to arbitration—a resort which Great Britain so conspicuously favors in principle and respects in practice and which is earnestly sought by her weaker adversary.

Since communicating the voluminous correspondence in regard to Hawaii and the action taken by the Senate and House of Representatives on certain questions submitted to the judgment and wider discretion of Congress the organization of a government in place of the provisional arrangement which followed the deposition of the Queen has been announced, with evidence of its effective operation. The recognition usual in such cases has been accorded the new Government.

Under our present treaties of extradition with Italy miscarriages of justice have occurred owing to the refusal of that Government to surrender its own subjects. Thus far our efforts to negotiate an amended convention obviating this difficulty have been unavailing.

Apart from the war in which the Island Empire is engaged, Japan attracts increasing attention in this country by her evident desire to cultivate more liberal intercourse with us and to seek our kindly aid in furtherance of her laudable desire for complete autonomy in her domestic affairs and full equality in the family of nations. The Japanese Empire of to-day is no longer the Japan of the past, and our relations with this progressive nation should not be less broad and liberal than those with other powers.

Good will, fostered by many interests in common, has marked our relations with our nearest southern neighbor. Peace being restored along her northern frontier, Mexico has asked the punishment of the late disturbers of her tranquillity. There ought to be a new treaty of commerce and navigation with that country to take the place of the one which terminated thirteen years ago. The friendliness of the intercourse between the two countries is attested by the fact that during this long period the commerce of each has steadily increased under the rule of mutual consideration, being neither stimulated by conventional arrangements nor retarded by jealous rivalries or selfish distrust.

An indemnity tendered by Mexico as a gracious act for the murder in 1887 of Leon Baldwin, an American citizen, by a band of marauders in Durango has been accepted and is being paid in installments.

The problem of the storage and use of the waters of the Rio Grande for irrigation should be solved by appropriate concurrent action of the two interested countries. Rising in the Colorado heights, the stream flows intermittently, yielding little water during the dry months to the irrigation channels already constructed along its course. This scarcity is often severely felt in the regions where the river forms a common boundary. Moreover, the frequent changes in its course through level sands often raise embarrassing questions of territorial jurisdiction.

Prominent among the questions of the year was the Bluefields incident, in what is known as the Mosquito Indian Strip, bordering on the Atlantic Ocean and within the jurisdiction of Nicaragua. By the treaty of 1860 between Great Britain and Nicaragua the former Government expressly recognized the sovereignty of the latter over the strip, and a limited form of self-government was guaranteed to the Mosquito Indians, to be exercised according to their customs, for themselves and other dwellers within its limits. The so-called native government, which grew to be largely made up of aliens, for many years disputed the sovereignty of Nicaragua over the strip and claimed the right to maintain therein a practically independent municipal government. Early in the past year efforts of Nicaragua to maintain sovereignty over the Mosquito territory led to serious disturbances, culminating in the suppression of the native government and the attempted substitution of an impracticable composite administration in which Nicaragua and alien residents were to participate. Failure was followed by an insurrection, which for a time subverted Nicaraguan rule, expelling her officers and restoring the old organization. This in turn gave place to the existing local government established and upheld by Nicaragua.

Although the alien interests arrayed against Nicaragua in these transactions have been largely American and the commerce of that region for some time has been and still is chiefly controlled by our citizens, we can not for that reason challenge the rightful sovereignty of Nicaragua over this important part of her domain.

For some months one, and during part of the time two, of our naval ships have been stationed at Bluefields for the protection of all legitimate interests of our citizens. In September last the Government at Managua expelled from its territory twelve or more foreigners, including two Americans, for alleged participation in the seditious or revolutionary movements against the Republic at Bluefields already mentioned; but through the earnest remonstrance of this Government the two Americans have been permitted to return to the peaceful management of their business. Our naval commanders at the scene of these disturbances by their constant exhibition of firmness and good judgment contributed largely to the prevention of more serious consequences and to the restoration of quiet and order. I regret that in the midst of these occurrences there happened a most grave and irritating failure of Nicaraguan justice. An American citizen named Wilson, residing at Rama, in the Mosquito territory, was murdered by one Argüello, the acting governor of the town. After some delay the murderer was arrested, but so insecurely confined or guarded that he escaped, and notwithstanding our repeated demands it is claimed that his recapture has been impossible by reason of his flight beyond Nicaraguan jurisdiction.

The Nicaraguan authorities, having given notice of forfeiture of their concession to the canal company on grounds purely technical and not embraced in the contract, have receded from that position.

Peru, I regret to say, shows symptoms of domestic disturbance, due probably to the slowness of her recuperation from the distresses of the war of 1881. Weakened in resources, her difficulties in facing international obligations invite our kindly sympathy and justify our forbearance in pressing long-pending claims. I have felt constrained to testify this sympathy in connection with certain demands urgently preferred by other powers.

The recent death of the Czar of Russia called forth appropriate expressions of sorrow and sympathy on the part of our Government with his bereaved family and the Russian people. As a further demonstration of respect and friendship our minister at St. Petersburg was directed to represent our Government at the funeral ceremonies.

The sealing interests of Russia in Bering Sea are second only to our own. A *modus vivendi* has therefore been concluded with the Imperial Government restrictive of poaching on the Russian rookeries and of sealing in waters which were not comprehended in the protected area defined in the Paris award.

Occasion has been found to urge upon the Russian Government equality of treatment for our great life-insurance companies whose operations have been extended throughout Europe. Admitting as we do foreign corporations to transact business in the United States, we naturally expect no less tolerance for our own in the ample fields of competition abroad.

But few cases of interference with naturalized citizens returning to Russia have been reported during the current year. One Krzeminski was arrested last summer in a Polish province on a reported charge of unpermitted renunciation of Russian allegiance, but it transpired that the proceedings originated in alleged malfeasance committed by Krzeminski while an imperial official a number of years ago. Efforts for his release, which promised to be successful, were in progress when his death was reported.

The Government of Salvador having been overthrown by an abrupt popular outbreak, certain of its military and civil officers, while hotly pursued by infuriated insurgents, sought refuge on board the United States war ship *Bennington*, then lying in a Salvadorean port. Although the practice of asylum is not favored by this Government, yet in view of the imminent peril which threatened the fugitives and solely from considerations of humanity they were afforded shelter by our naval commander, and when afterwards demanded under our treaty of extradition with Salvador for trial on charges of murder, arson, and robbery I directed that such of them as had not voluntarily left the ship be conveyed to one of our nearest ports where a hearing could be had before a judicial officer, in compliance with the terms of the treaty. On their arrival at San Francisco such a proceeding was promptly instituted before the United States district judge, who held that the acts constituting the alleged offenses were political and discharged all the accused except one Cienfuegos, who was held for an attempt to murder. Thereupon I was constrained to direct his release for the reason that an attempt to murder was not one of the crimes charged against him and upon which his surrender to the Salvadorean authorities had been demanded.

Unreasonable and unjust fines imposed by Spain on the vessels and commerce of the United States have demanded from time to time during the last twenty years earnest remonstrance on the part of our Government. In the immediate past exorbitant penalties have been imposed upon our vessels and goods by customs authorities of Cuba and Puerto Rico for clerical errors of the most trivial character in the manifests or bills of lading. In some cases fines amounting to thousands of dollars have been levied upon cargoes or the carrying vessels when the goods in question were entitled to free entry. Fines have been exacted even when the error had been detected and the Spanish authorities notified before the arrival of the goods in port.

This conduct is in strange contrast with the considerate and liberal treatment extended to Spanish vessels and cargoes in our ports in like cases. No satisfactory settlement of these vexatious questions has yet been reached.

The Mora case, referred to in my last annual message, remains unsettled. From the diplomatic correspondence on this subject which has been laid before the Senate it will be seen that this Government has offered to conclude a convention with Spain for disposal by arbitration of outstanding claims between the two countries, except the Mora claim, which, having been long ago adjusted, now only awaits payment as stipulated, and of course it could not be included in the proposed convention. It was hoped that this offer would remove parliamentary obstacles encountered by the Spanish Government in providing payment of the Mora indemnity. I regret to say that no definite reply to this offer has yet been made and all efforts to secure payment of this settled claim have been unavailing.

In my last annual message I adverted to the claim on the part of Turkey of the right to expel as persons undesirable and dangerous Armenians naturalized in the United States and returning to Turkish jurisdiction.* Numerous questions in this relation have arisen. While this Government acquiesces in the asserted right of expulsion, it will not consent that Armenians may be imprisoned or otherwise punished for no other reason than having acquired without imperial consent American citizenship.

Three of the assailants of Miss Melton, an American teacher in Mosul, have been convicted by the Ottoman courts, and I am advised that an appeal against the acquittal of the remaining five has been taken by the Turkish prosecuting officer.

A convention has been concluded with Venezuela for the arbitration of a long-disputed claim growing out of the seizure of certain vessels the property of citizens of the United States. Although signed, the treaty of extradition with Venezuela is not yet in force, owing to the insistence of that Government that when surrendered its citizens shall in no case be liable to capital punishment.

The rules for the prevention of collisions at sea which were framed by the maritime conference held in this city in 1889, having been concurrently incorporated in the statutes of the United States and Great Britain,

* See pp. 440-441.

have been announced to take effect March 1, 1895, and invitations have been extended to all maritime nations to adhere to them. Favorable responses have thus far been received from Austria, France, Portugal, Spain, and Sweden.

In my last annual message I referred briefly to the unsatisfactory state of affairs in Samoa under the operation of the Berlin treaty as signally illustrating the impolicy of entangling alliances with foreign powers,* and on May 9, 1894, in response to a resolution of the Senate, I sent a special message † and documents to that body on the same subject, which emphasized my previously expressed opinions. Later occurrences, the correspondence in regard to which will be laid before the Congress, further demonstrate that the Government which was devised by the three powers and forced upon the Samoans against their inveterate hostility can be maintained only by the continued presence of foreign military force and at no small sacrifice of life and treasure.

The suppression of the Mataafa insurrection by the powers and the subsequent banishment of the leader and eleven other chiefs, as recited in my last message, did not bring lasting peace to the islands. Formidable uprisings continued, and finally a rebellion broke out in the capital island, Upolu, headed in Aana, the western district, by the younger Tamasese, and in Atua, the eastern district, by other leaders. The insurgents ravaged the country and fought the Government's troops up to the very doors of Apia. The King again appealed to the powers for help, and the combined British and German naval forces reduced the Atuans to apparent subjection, not, however, without considerable loss to the natives. A few days later Tamasese and his adherents, fearing the ships and the marines, professed submission.

Reports received from our agents at Apia do not justify the belief that the peace thus brought about will be of long duration. It is their conviction that the natives are at heart hostile to the present Government, that such of them as profess loyalty to it do so from fear of the powers, and that it would speedily go to pieces if the war ships were withdrawn. In reporting to his Government on the unsatisfactory situation since the suppression of the late revolt by foreign armed forces, the German consul at Apia stated:

That peace will be lasting is hardly to be presumed. The lesson given by firing on Atua was not sufficiently sharp and incisive to leave a lasting impression on the forgetful Samoan temperament. In fact, conditions are existing which show that peace will not last and is not seriously intended. Malietoa, the King, and his chiefs are convinced that the departure of the war ships will be a signal for a renewal of war. The circumstance that the representatives of the villages of all the districts which were opposed to the Government have already withdrawn to Atua to hold meetings, and that both Atua and Aana have forbidden inhabitants of those districts which fought on the side of the Government to return to their villages, and have already partly burned down the latter, indicates that a real conciliation of the parties is still far off.

*See p. 439.   † See p. 477.

And in a note of the 10th ultimo, inclosing a copy of that report for the information of this Government, the German ambassador said:

The contents of the report awakened the Imperial Government's apprehension that under existing circumstances the peace concluded with the rebels will afford no assurance of the lasting restoration of tranquillity in the islands.

The present Government has utterly failed to correct, if indeed it has not aggravated, the very evils it was intended to prevent. It has not stimulated our commerce with the islands. Our participation in its establishment against the wishes of the natives was in plain defiance of the conservative teachings and warnings of the wise and patriotic men who laid the foundations of our free institutions, and I invite an expression of the judgment of Congress on the propriety of steps being taken by this Government looking to the withdrawal from its engagements with the other powers on some reasonable terms not prejudicial to any of our existing rights.

The Secretary of the Treasury reports that the receipts of the Government from all sources of revenue during the fiscal year ending June 30, 1894, amounted to $372,802,498.29 and its expenditures to $442,605,-758.87, leaving a deficit of $69,803,260.58. There was a decrease of $15,952,674.66 in the ordinary expense of the Government as compared with the fiscal year 1893.

There was collected from customs $131,818,530.62 and from internal revenue $147,168,449.70. The balance of the income for the year, amounting to $93,815,517.97, was derived from the sales of lands and other sources.

The value of our total dutiable imports amounted to $275,199,086, being $146,657,625 less than during the preceding year, and the importations free of duty amounted to $379,795,536, being $64,748,675 less than during the preceding year. The receipts from customs were $73,536,486.11 less and from internal revenue $13,836,539.97 less than in 1893.

The total tax collected from distilled spirits was $85,259,250.25, on manufactured tobacco $28,617,898.62, and on fermented liquors $31,414,-788.04.

Our exports of merchandise, domestic and foreign, amounted during the year to $892,140,572, being an increase over the preceding year of $44,495,378.

The total amount of gold exported during the fiscal year was $76,898,-061, as against $108,680,444 during the fiscal year 1893. The amount imported was $72,449,119, as against $21,174,381 during the previous year.

The imports of silver were $13,286,552 and the exports were $50,-451,265.

The total bounty paid upon the production of sugar in the United States for the fiscal year was $12,100,208.89, being an increase of $2,725,078.01

over the payments made during the preceding year. The amount of bounty paid from July 1, 1894, to August 28, 1894, the time when further payments ceased by operation of law, was $966,185.84. The total expenses incurred in the payment of the bounty upon sugar during the fiscal year was $130,140.85.

It is estimated that upon the basis of the present revenue laws the receipts of the Government during the current fiscal year, ending June 30, 1895, will be $424,427,748.44 and its expenditures $444,427,748.44, resulting in a deficit of $20,000,000.

On the 1st day of November, 1894, the total stock of money of all kinds in the country was $2,240,773,888, as against $2,204,651,000 on the 1st day of November, 1893, and the money of all kinds in circulation, or not included in the Treasury holdings, was $1,672,093,422, or $24.27 per capita upon an estimated population of 68,887,000. At the same date there was held in the Treasury gold bullion amounting to $44,615,-177.55 and silver bullion which was purchased at a cost of $127,772,988. The purchase of silver bullion under the act of July 14, 1890, ceased on the 1st day of November, 1893, and up to that time there had been purchased during the fiscal year 11,917,658.78 fine ounces, at a cost of $8,715,-521.32, an average cost of $0.7313 per fine ounce. The total amount of silver purchased from the time that law took effect until the repeal of its purchasing clause, on the date last mentioned, was 168,674,682.53 fine ounces, which cost $155,931,002.25, the average price per fine ounce being $0.9244.

The total amount of standard silver dollars coined at the mints of the United States since the passage of the act of February 28, 1878, is $421,-776,408, of which $378,166,793 were coined under the provisions of that act, $38,531,143 under the provisions of the act of July 14, 1890, and $5,078,472 under the act providing for the coinage of trade-dollar bullion.

The total coinage of all metals at our mints during the last fiscal year consisted of 63,485,220 pieces, valued at $106,216,730.06, of which there were $99,474,912.50 in gold coined, $758 in standard silver dollars, $6,024,140.30 in subsidiary silver coin, and $716,919.26 in minor coin.

During the calendar year 1893 the production of precious metals in the United States was estimated at 1,739,323 fine ounces of gold of the commercial and coinage value of $35,955,000 and 60,000,000 fine ounces of silver of the bullion or market value of $46,800,000 and of the coinage value of $77,576,000. It is estimated that on the 1st day of July, 1894, the stock of metallic money in the United States, consisting of coin and bullion, amounted to $1,251,640,958, of which $627,923,201 was gold and $624,347,757 was silver.

Fifty national banks were organized during the year ending October 31, 1894, with a capital of $5,285,000, and 79, with a capital of $10,475,-000, went into voluntary liquidation. Twenty-one banks, with a capital of $2,770,000, were placed in the hands of receivers. The total number of national banks in existence on the 31st day of October last was 3,756, being 40 less than on the 31st day of October, 1893. The capital stock paid in was $672,671,365, being $9,678,491 less than at the same time in the previous year, and the surplus fund and individual profits, less expenses and taxes paid, amounted to $334,121,082.10, which was $16,-089,780 less than on October 31, 1893. The circulation was decreased $1,741,563. The obligations of the banks to each other were increased $117,268,334 and the individual deposits were $277,294,489 less than at the corresponding date in the previous year. Loans and discounts were $161,206,923 more than at the same time the previous year, and checks and other cash items were $90,349,963 more. The total resources of the banks at the date mentioned amounted to $3,473,922,055, as against $3,109,563,284.36 in 1893.

From the report of the Secretary of War it appears that the strength of the Army on September 30, 1894, was 2,135 officers and 25,765 enlisted men. Although this is apparently a very slight decrease compared with the previous year, the actual effective force has been increased to the equivalent of nearly two regiments through the reorganization of the system of recruiting and the consequent release to regimental duty of the large force of men hitherto serving at the recruiting depots. The abolition of these depots, it is predicted, will furthermore effect an annual reduction approximating $250,000 in the direct expenditures, besides promoting generally the health, morale, and discipline of the troops.

The execution of the policy of concentrating the Army at important centers of population and transportation, foreshadowed in the last annual report of the Secretary, has resulted in the abandonment of fifteen of the smaller posts, which was effected under a plan which assembles organizations of the same regiments hitherto widely separated. This renders our small forces more readily effective for any service which they may be called upon to perform, increases the extent of the territory under protection without diminishing the security heretofore afforded to any locality, improves the discipline, training, and *esprit de corps* of the Army, besides considerably decreasing the cost of its maintenance.

Though the forces of the Department of the East have been somewhat increased, more than three-fourths of the Army is still stationed west of the Mississippi. This carefully matured policy, which secures the best and greatest service in the interests of the general welfare from the small force comprising our Regular Army, should not be thoughtlessly embarrassed by the creation of new and unnecessary posts through acts of Congress to gratify the ambitions or interests of localities.

While the maximum legal strength of the Army is 25,000 men, the effective strength, through various causes, is but little over 20,000 men. The purpose of Congress does not, therefore, seem to be fully attained by the existing condition. While no considerable increase in the Army is, in my judgment, demanded by recent events, the policy of seacoast fortification, in the prosecution of which we have been steadily engaged for some years, has so far developed as to suggest that the effective strength of the Army be now made at least equal to the legal strength. Measures taken by the Department during the year, as indicated, have already considerably augmented the effective force, and the Secretary of War presents a plan, which I recommend to the consideration of Congress, to attain the desired end. Economies effected in the Department in other lines of its work will offset to a great extent the expenditure involved in the proposition submitted. Among other things this contemplates the adoption of the three-battalion formation of regiments, which for several years has been indorsed by the Secretaries of War and the Generals Commanding the Army. Compact in itself, it provides a skeleton organization, ready to be filled out in the event of war, which is peculiarly adapted to our strength and requirements; and the fact that every other nation, with a single exception, has adopted this formation to meet the conditions of modern warfare should alone secure for the recommendation an early consideration.

It is hardly necessary to recall the fact that in obedience to the commands of the Constitution and the laws, and for the purpose of protecting the property of the United States, aiding the process of Federal courts, and removing lawless obstructions to the performance by the Government of its legitimate functions, it became necessary in various localities during the year to employ a considerable portion of the regular troops. The duty was discharged promptly, courageously, and with marked discretion by the officers and men, and the most gratifying proof was thus afforded that the Army deserves that complete confidence in its efficiency and discipline which the country has at all times manifested.

The year has been free from disturbances by Indians, and the chances of further depredations on their part are constantly becoming more remote and improbable.

The total expenditures for the War Department for the year ended June 30, 1894, amounted to $56,039,009.34. Of this sum $2,000,614.99 was for salaries and contingent expenses, $23,665,156.16 for the support of the military establishment, $5,001,682.23 for miscellaneous objects, and $25,371,555.96 for public works. This latter sum includes $19,-494,037.49 for river and harbor improvements and $3,947,863.56 for fortifications and other works of defense. The appropriations for the current year aggregate $52,429,112.78, and the estimates submitted by the Secretary of War for the next fiscal year call for appropriations amounting to $52,318,629.55.

The skill and industry of our ordnance officers and inventors have, it is believed, overcome the mechanical obstacles which have heretofore delayed the armament of our coasts, and this great national undertaking upon which we have entered may now proceed as rapidly as Congress shall determine. With a supply of finished guns of large caliber already on hand, to which additions should now rapidly follow, the wisdom of providing carriages and emplacements for their mount can not be too strongly urged.

The total enrollment of the militia of the several States is 117,533 officers and enlisted men, an increase of 5,343 over the number reported at the close of the previous year. The reports of militia inspections by Regular Army officers show a marked increase in interest and efficiency among the State organizations, and I strongly recommend a continuance of the policy of affording every practical encouragement possible to this important auxiliary of our military establishment.

The condition of the Apache Indians held as prisoners by the Government for eight years at a cost of half a million dollars has been changed during the year from captivity to one which gives them an opportunity to demonstrate their capacity for self-support and at least partial civilization. Legislation enacted at the late session of Congress gave the War Department authority to transfer the survivors, numbering 346, from Mount Vernon Barracks, in Alabama, to any suitable reservation. The Department selected as their future home the military lands near Fort Sill, Ind. T., where, under military surveillance, the former prisoners have been established in agriculture under conditions favorable to their advancement.

In recognition of the long and distinguished military services and faithful discharge of delicate and responsible civil duties by Major-General John M. Schofield, now the General Commanding the Army, it is suggested to Congress that the temporary revival of the grade of lieutenant-general in his behalf would be a just and gracious act and would permit his retirement, now near at hand, with rank befitting his merits.

The report of the Attorney-General notes the gratifying progress made by the Supreme Court in overcoming the arrears of its business and in reaching a condition in which it will be able to dispose of cases as they arise without any unreasonable delay. This result is of course very largely due to the successful working of the plan inaugurating circuit courts of appeals. In respect to these tribunals the suggestion is made in quarters entitled to the highest consideration that an additional circuit judge for each circuit would greatly strengthen these courts and the confidence reposed in their adjudications, and that such an addition would not create a greater force of judges than the increasing business of such courts requires. I commend the suggestion to the careful consideration of the Congress. Other important topics are adverted to in the report, accompanied by recommendations, many of which have been treated at large in previous messages, and at this time, therefore, need only be named. I refer to the abolition of the fee system as a measure of compensation to Federal officers; the enlargement of the powers of United States commissioners, at least in the Territories; the allowance of writs of error in criminal cases on behalf of the United States, and the establishment of degrees in the crime of murder. A topic dealt with by the Attorney-General of much importance is the condition of the administration of justice in the Indian Territory. The permanent solution of what is called the Indian problem is probably not to be expected at once, but meanwhile such ameliorations of present conditions as the existing system will admit of ought not to be neglected. I am satisfied there should be a Federal court established for the Territory, with sufficient judges, and that this court should sit within the Territory and have the same jurisdiction as to Territorial affairs as is now vested in the Federal courts sitting in Arkansas and Texas.

Another subject of pressing moment referred to by the Attorney-General is the reorganization of the Union Pacific Railway Company on a basis equitable as regards all private interests and as favorable to the Government as existing conditions will permit. The operation of a railroad by a court through a receiver is an anomalous state of things which should be terminated on all grounds, public and private, at the earliest possible moment. Besides, not to enact the needed enabling legislation at the present session postpones the whole matter until the assembling of a new Congress and inevitably increases all the complications of the situation, and could not but be regarded as a signal failure to solve a problem which has practically been before the present Congress ever since its organization.

Eight years ago in my annual message I urged upon the Congress as strongly as I could the location and construction of two prisons for the confinement of United States prisoners.* A similar recommendation has been made from time to time since, and a few years ago a law was passed providing for the selection of sites for three such institutions. No appropriation has, however, been made to carry the act into effect, and the old and discreditable condition still exists.

It is not my purpose at this time to repeat the considerations which make an impregnable case in favor of the ownership and management by the Government of the penal institutions in which Federal prisoners are confined. I simply desire to again urge former recommendations on the subject and to particularly call the attention of the Congress to that part of the report of the Secretary of War in which he states that the military prison at Fort Leavenworth, Kans., can be turned over to the Government as a prison for Federal convicts without the least difficulty and with an actual saving of money from every point of view.

Pending a more complete reform, I hope that by the adoption of the suggestion of the Secretary of War this easy step may be taken in the direction of the proper care of its convicts by the Government of the United States.

The report of the Postmaster-General presents a comprehensive statement of the operations of the Post-Office Department for the last fiscal year.

*See Vol. VIII, pp. 517-518.

The receipts of the Department during the year amounted to $75,-080,479.04 and the expenditures to $84,324,414.15.

The transactions of the postal service indicate with barometric certainty the fluctuations in the business of the country. Inasmuch, therefore, as business complications continued to exist throughout the last year to an unforeseen extent, it is not surprising that the deficiency of revenue to meet the expenditures of the Post-Office Department, which was estimated in advance at about $8,000,000, should be exceeded by nearly $1,225,000. The ascertained revenues of the last year, which were the basis of calculation for the current year, being less than estimated, the deficiency for the current year will be correspondingly greater, though the Postmaster-General states that the latest indications are so favorable that he confidently predicts an increase of at least 8 per cent in the revenues of the current year over those of the last year.

The expenditures increase steadily and necessarily with the growth and needs of the country, so that the deficiency is greater or less in any year, depending upon the volume of receipts.

The Postmaster-General states that this deficiency is unnecessary and might be obviated at once if the law regulating rates upon mail matter of the second class was modified. The rate received for the transmission of this second-class matter is 1 cent per pound, while the cost of such transmission to the Government is eight times that amount. In the general terms of the law this rate covers newspapers and periodicals. The extensions of the meaning of these terms from time to time have admitted to the privileges intended for legitimate newspapers and periodicals a surprising range of publications and created abuses the cost of which amounts in the aggregate to the total deficiency of the Post-Office Department. Pretended newspapers are started by business houses for the mere purpose of advertising goods, complying with the law in form only and discontinuing the publications as soon as the period of advertising is over. "Sample copies" of pretended newspapers are issued in great numbers for a like purpose only. The result is a great loss of revenue to the Government, besides its humiliating use as an agency to aid in carrying out the scheme of a business house to advertise its goods by means of a trick upon both its rival houses and the regular and legitimate newspapers. Paper-covered literature, consisting mainly of trashy novels, to the extent of many thousands of tons is sent through the mails at 1 cent per pound, while the publishers of standard works are required to pay eight times that amount in sending their publications. Another abuse consists in the free carriage through the mails of hundreds of tons of seed and grain uselessly distributed through the Department of Agriculture. The Postmaster-General predicts that if the law be so amended as to eradicate these abuses not only will the Post-Office Department show no deficiency, but he believes that in the near future all legitimate newspapers and periodical magazines might be properly transmitted through the mails to their subscribers free of cost. I invite your prompt consideration of this subject and fully indorse the views of the Postmaster-General.

The total number of post-offices in the United States on the 30th day of June, 1894, was 69,805, an increase of 1,403 over the preceding year. Of these, 3,428 were Presidential, an increase in that class of 68 over the preceding year.

Six hundred and ten cities and towns are provided with free delivery. Ninety-three other cities and towns entitled to this service under the law have not been accorded it on account of insufficient funds. The expense of free delivery for the current fiscal year will be more than $12,300,000, and under existing legislation this item of expenditure is subject to constant increase. The estimated cost of rural free delivery generally is so very large that it ought not to be considered in the present condition of affairs.

During the year 830 additional domestic money-order offices were established. The total number of these offices at the close of the year was 19,264. There were 14,304,041 money orders issued during the year, being an increase over the preceding year of 994,306. The value of these orders amounted to $138,793,579.49, an increase of $11,217,145.84. There were also issued during the year postal notes amounting to $12,-649,094.55.

During the year 218 international money-order offices were added to those already established, making a total of 2,625 such offices in operation June 30, 1894. The number of international money orders issued during the year was 917,823, a decrease in number of 138,176, and their value was $13,792,455.31, a decrease in amount of $2,549,382.55. The number of orders paid was 361,180, an increase over the preceding year of 60,263, and their value was $6,568,493.78, an increase of $1,285,118.08.

From the foregoing statements it appears that the total issue of money orders and postal notes for the year amounted to $165,235,129.35.

The number of letters and packages mailed during the year for special delivery was 3,436,970. The special-delivery stamps used upon these letters and packages amounted to $343,697. The messengers' fees paid for their delivery amounted to $261,209.70, leaving a balance in favor of the Government of $82,487.30.

The report shows most gratifying results in the way of economies worked out without affecting the efficiency of the postal service. These consist in the abrogation of steamship subsidy contracts, reletting of mail transportation contracts, and in the cost and amount of supplies used in the service, amounting in all to $16,619,047.42.

This report also contains a valuable contribution to the history of the Universal Postal Union, an arrangement which amounts practically to the establishment of one postal system for the entire civilized world. Special attention is directed to this subject at this time in view of the fact that the next congress of the union will meet in Washington in 1897, and it is hoped that timely action will be taken in the direction of perfecting preparations for that event.

The Postmaster-General renews the suggestion made in a previous report that the Department organization be increased to the extent of creating a direct district supervision of all postal affairs, and in this suggestion I fully concur.

There are now connected with the Post-Office establishment 32,661 employees who are in the classified service. This includes many who have been classified upon the suggestion of the Postmaster-General. He states that another year's experience at the head of the Department serves only to strengthen the conviction as to the excellent working of the civil-service law in this branch of the public service.

Attention is called to the report of the Secretary of the Navy, which shows very gratifying progress in the construction of ships for our new Navy. All the vessels now building, including the three torpedo boats authorized at the last session of Congress and excepting the first-class battle ship *Iowa*, will probably be completed during the coming fiscal year.

The estimates for the increase of the Navy for the year ending June 30, 1896, are large, but they include practically the entire sum necessary to complete and equip all the new ships not now in commission, so that unless new ships are authorized the appropriations for the naval service for the fiscal year ending June 30, 1897, should fall below the estimates for the coming year by at least $12,000,000.

The Secretary presents with much earnestness a plea for the authorization of three additional battle ships and ten or twelve torpedo boats. While the unarmored vessels heretofore authorized, including those now nearing completion, will constitute a fleet which it is believed is sufficient for ordinary cruising purposes in time of peace, we have now completed and in process of construction but four first-class battle ships and but few torpedo boats. If we are to have a navy for warlike operations, offensive and defensive, we certainly ought to increase both the number of battle ships and torpedo boats.

The manufacture of armor requires expensive plants and the aggregation of many skilled workmen. All the armor necessary to complete the vessels now building will be delivered before the 1st of June next. If no new contracts are given out, contractors must disband their workmen and their plants must lie idle. Battle ships authorized at this time would not be well under way until late in the coming fiscal year, and at least three years and a half from the date of the contract would be required for their completion. The Secretary states that not more than 15 per cent of the cost of such ships need be included in the appropriations for the coming year.

I recommend that provision be made for the construction of additional battle ships and torpedo boats.

The Secretary recommends the manufacture not only of a reserve supply of ordnance and ordnance material for ships of the Navy, but also a supply for the auxiliary fleet. Guns and their appurtenances should be provided and kept on hand for both these purposes. We have not to-day a single gun that could be put upon the ships *Paris* or *New York* of the International Navigation Company or any other ship of our reserve Navy.

The manufacture of guns at the Washington Navy-Yard is proceeding satisfactorily, and none of our new ships will be required to wait for their guns or ordnance equipment.

An important order has been issued by the Secretary of the Navy coordinating the duties of the several bureaus concerned in the construction of ships. This order, it is believed, will secure to a greater extent than has heretofore been possible the harmonious action of these several bureaus and make the attainment of the best results more certain.

During the past fiscal year there has been an unusual and pressing demand in many quarters of the world for the presence of vessels to guard American interests.

In January last, during the Brazilian insurrection, a large fleet was concentrated in the harbor of Rio de Janeiro. The vigorous action of Rear-Admiral Benham in protecting the personal and commercial rights of our citizens during the disturbed conditions afforded results which will, it is believed, have a far-reaching and wholesome influence whenever in like circumstances it may become necessary for our naval commanders to interfere on behalf of our people in foreign ports.

The war now in progress between China and Japan has rendered it necessary or expedient to dispatch eight vessels to those waters.

Both the Secretary of the Navy and the Secretary of the Treasury recommend the transfer of the work of the Coast Survey proper to the Navy Department. I heartily concur in this recommendation. Excluding Alaska and a very small area besides, all the work of mapping and charting our coasts has been completed. The hydrographic work, which must be done over and over again by reason of the shifting and varying depths of water consequent upon the action of streams and tides, has heretofore been done under the direction of naval officers in subordination to the Superintendent of the Coast Survey. There seems to be no good reason why the Navy should not have entire charge hereafter of such work, especially as the Hydrographic Office of the Navy Department is now and has been for many years engaged in making efficient maps entirely similar to those prepared by the Coast Survey.

I feel it my imperative duty to call attention to the recommendation of the Secretary in regard to the personnel of the line of the Navy. The stagnation of promotion in this the vital branch of the service is so great as to seriously impair its efficiency.

I consider it of the utmost importance that the young and middle-aged officers should before the eve of retirement be permitted to reach a grade entitling them to active and important duty.

The system adopted a few years ago regulating the employment of labor at the navy-yards is rigidly upheld and has fully demonstrated its usefulness and expediency. It is within the domain of civil-service reform inasmuch as workmen are employed through a board of labor selected at each navy-yard and are given work without reference to politics and in the order of their application, preference, however, being given to Army and Navy veterans and those having former navy-yard experience.

Amendments suggested by experience have been made to the rules regulating the system. Through its operation the work at our navy-yards has been vastly improved in efficiency and the opportunity to work has been honestly and fairly awarded to willing and competent applicants.

It is hoped that if this system continues to be strictly adhered to there will soon be as a natural consequence such an equalization of party benefit as will remove all temptation to relax or abandon it.

The report of the Secretary of the Interior exhibits the situation of the numerous and interesting branches of the public service connected with his Department. I commend this report and the valuable recommendations of the Secretary to the careful attention of the Congress.

The public land disposed of during the year amounted to 10,406,100.77 acres, including 28,876.05 of Indian lands.

It is estimated that the public domain still remaining amounts to a little more than 600,000,000 acres, including, however, about 360,000,000 acres in Alaska, as well as military reservations and railroad and other selections of lands yet unadjudicated.

The total cash receipts from sale of lands amounted to $2,674,285.79, including $91,981.03 received for Indian lands.

Thirty-five thousand patents were issued for agricultural lands, and 3,100 patents were issued to Indians on allotments of their holdings in severalty, the land so allotted being inalienable by the Indian allottees for a period of twenty-five years after patent.

There were certified and patented on account of railroad and wagon-road grants during the year 865,556.45 acres of land, and at the close of the year 29,000,000 acres were embraced in the lists of selections made by railroad and wagon-road companies and awaited settlement.

The selections of swamp lands and that taken as indemnity therefor since the passage of the act providing for the same in 1849 amount to nearly or quite 80,500,000 acres, of which 58,000,000 have been patented to States. About 138,000 acres were patented during the last year. Nearly 820,000 acres of school and education grants were approved during the year, and at its close 1,250,363.81 acres remained unadjusted.

It appears that the appropriation for the current year on account of special service for the protection of the public lands and the timber thereon is much less than those for previous years, and inadequate for an efficient performance of the work. A larger sum of money than has been appropriated during a number of years past on this account has been returned to the Government as a result of the labors of those employed in the particular service mentioned, and I hope it will not be crippled by insufficient appropriation.

I fully indorse the recommendation of the Secretary that adequate protection be provided for our forest reserves and that a comprehensive forestry system be inaugurated. Such keepers and superintendents as are necessary to protect the forests already reserved should be provided. I am of the opinion that there should be an abandonment of the policy sanctioned by present laws under which the Government, for a very small consideration, is rapidly losing title to immense tracts of land covered with timber, which should be properly reserved as permanent sources of timber supply.

The suggestion that a change be made in the manner of securing surveys of the public lands is especially worthy of consideration. I am satisfied that these surveys should be made by a corps of competent surveyors under the immediate control and direction of the Commissioner of the General Land Office.

An exceedingly important recommendation of the Secretary relates to the manner in which contests and litigated cases growing out of efforts to obtain Government land are determined. The entire testimony upon which these controversies depend in all their stages is taken before the local registers and receivers, and yet these officers have no power to subpœna witnesses or to enforce their attendance to testify. These cases, numbering three or four thousand annually, are sent by the local officers to the Commissioner of the General Land Office for his action. The exigencies of his other duties oblige him to act upon the decisions of the registers and receivers without an opportunity of thorough personal examination. Nearly 2,000 of these cases are appealed annually from the Commissioner to the Secretary of the Interior. Burdened with other important administrative duties, his determination of these appeals must be almost perfunctory and based upon the examination of others, though this determination of the Secretary operates as a final adjudication upon rights of very great importance.

I concur in the opinion that the Commissioner of the General Land Office should be relieved from the duty of deciding litigated land cases, that a nonpartisan court should be created to pass on such cases, and that the decisions of this court should be final, at least so far as the decisions of the Department are now final. The proposed court might be given authority to certify questions of law in matters of especial importance to the Supreme Court of the United States or the court of appeals for the District of Columbia for decision. The creation of such a tribunal would expedite the disposal of cases and insure decisions of a more satisfactory character. The registers and receivers who originally hear and decide these disputes should be invested with authority to compel witnesses to attend and testify before them.

Though the condition of the Indians shows a steady and healthy progress, their situation is not satisfactory at all points. Some of them to whom allotments of land have been made are found to be unable or disinclined to follow agricultural pursuits or to otherwise beneficially manage their land. This is especially true of the Cheyennes and Arapahoes, who, as it appears by reports of their agent, have in many instances never been located upon their allotments, and in some cases do not even know where their allotments are. Their condition has deteriorated. They are not self-supporting and they live in camps and spend their time in idleness.

I have always believed that allotments of reservation lands to Indians in severalty should be made sparingly, or at least slowly, and with the utmost caution. In these days, when white agriculturists and stock raisers of experience and intelligence find their lot a hard one, we ought not to expect Indians, unless far advanced in civilization and habits of industry, to support themselves on the small tracts of land usually allotted to them.

If the self-supporting scheme by allotment fails, the wretched pauperism of the allottees which results is worse than their original condition of regulated dependence. It is evident that the evil consequences of ill-advised allotment are intensified in cases where the false step can not be retraced on account of the purchase by the Government of reservation lands remaining after allotments are made and the disposition of such remaining lands to settlers or purchasers from the Government.

I am convinced that the proper solution of the Indian problem and the success of every step taken in that direction depend to a very large extent upon the intelligence and honesty of the reservation agents and the interest they have in their work. An agent fitted for his place can do much toward preparing the Indians under his charge for citizenship and allotment of their lands, and his advice as to any matter concerning their welfare will not mislead. An unfit agent will make no effort to advance the Indians on his reservation toward civilization or preparation for allotment of lands in severalty, and his opinion as to their condition in this and other regards is heedless and valueless.

The indications are that the detail of army officers as Indian agents will result in improved management on the reservations.

Whenever allotments are made and any Indian on the reservation has previously settled upon a lot and cultivated it or shown a disposition to improve it in any way, such lot should certainly be allotted to him, and this should be made plainly obligatory by statute.

In the light of experience and considering the uncertainty of the Indian situation and its exigencies in the future, I am not only disposed to be very cautious in making allotments, but I incline to agree with the Secretary of the Interior in the opinion that when allotments are made the balance of reservation land remaining after allotment, instead of being bought by the Government from the Indians and opened for settlement with such scandals and unfair practices as seem unavoidable, should remain for a time at least as common land or be sold by the Government on behalf of the Indians in an orderly way and at fixed prices, to be determined by its location and desirability, and that the proceeds, less expenses, should be held in trust for the benefit of the Indian proprietors.

The intelligent Indian-school management of the past year has been followed by gratifying results. Efforts have been made to advance the work in a sound and practical manner. Five institutes of Indian teachers have been held during the year, and have proved very beneficial through the views exchanged and methods discussed particularly applicable to Indian education.

Efforts are being made in the direction of a gradual reduction of the number of Indian contract schools, so that in a comparatively short time they may give way altogether to Government schools, and it is hoped that the change may be so gradual as to be perfected without too great expense to the Government or undue disregard of investments made by those who have established and are maintaining such contract schools.

The appropriation for the current year, ending June 30, 1895, applicable to the ordinary expenses of the Indian service amounts to $6,733,003.18, being less by $663,240.64 than the sum appropriated on the same account for the previous year.

At the close of the last fiscal year, on the 30th day of June, 1894, there were 969,544 persons on our pension rolls, being a net increase of 3,532 over the number reported at the end of the previous year.

These pensioners may be classified as follows: Soldiers and sailors survivors of all wars, 753,968; widows and relatives of deceased soldiers, 215,162; army nurses in the War of the Rebellion, 414. Of these pensioners 32,039 are surviving soldiers of Indian and other wars prior to the late Civil War and the widows or relatives of such soldiers.

The remainder, numbering 937,505, are receiving pensions on account of the rebellion, and of these 469,344 are on the rolls under the authority of the act of June 27, 1890, sometimes called the dependent-pension law.

The total amount expended for pensions during the year was $139,804,461.05, leaving an unexpended balance from the sum appropriated of $25,205,712.65.

The sum necessary to meet pension expenditures for the year ending June 30, 1896, is estimated at $140,000,000.

The Commissioner of Pensions is of the opinion that the year 1895, being the thirtieth after the close of the War of the Rebellion, must, according to all sensible human calculation, see the highest limit of the pension roll, and that after that year it must begin to decline.

The claims pending in the Bureau have decreased more than 90,000 during the year. A large proportion of the new claims filed are for increase of pension by those now on the rolls.

The number of certificates issued was 80,213.

The names dropped from the rolls for all causes during the year numbered 37,951.

Among our pensioners are 9 widows and 3 daughters of soldiers of the Revolution and 45 survivors of the War of 1812.

The barefaced and extensive pension frauds exposed under the direction of the courageous and generous veteran soldier now at the head of the Bureau leave no room for the claim that no purgation of our pension rolls was needed or that continued vigilance and prompt action are not necessary to the same end.

The accusation that an effort to detect pension frauds is evidence of unfriendliness toward our worthy veterans and a denial of their claims to the generosity of the Government suggests an unfortunate indifference to the commission of any offense which has for its motive the securing of a pension and indicates a willingness to be blind to the existence of mean and treacherous crimes which play upon demagogic fears and make sport of the patriotic impulse of a grateful people.

The completion of the Eleventh Census is now in charge of the Commissioner of Labor. The total disbursements on account of the work for the fiscal year ending June 30, 1894, amounted to $10,365,676.81. At the close of the year the number of persons employed in the Census Office was 679; at present there are about 400. The whole number of volumes necessary to comprehend the Eleventh Census will be 25, and they will contain 22,270 printed pages. The assurance is confidently made that before the close of the present calendar year the material still incomplete will be practically in hand, and the census can certainly be closed by the 4th of March, 1895. After that the revision and proof reading necessary to bring out the volumes will still be required.

The text of the census volumes has been limited as far as possible to the analysis of the statistics presented. This method, which is in accordance with law, has caused more or less friction and in some instances individual disappointment, for when the Commissioner of Labor took charge of the work he found much matter on hand which according to this rule he was compelled to discard. The census is being prepared according to the theory that it is designed to collect facts and certify them to the public, not to elaborate arguments or to present personal views.

The Secretary of Agriculture in his report reviews the operations of his Department for the last fiscal year and makes recommendations for the further extension of its usefulness. He reports a saving in expenditures during the year of $600,000, which is covered back into the Treasury. This sum is 23 per cent of the entire appropriation.

A special study has been made of the demand for American farm products in all foreign markets, especially Great Britain. That country received from the United States during the nine months ending September 30, 1894, 305,910 live beef cattle, valued at $26,500,000, as against 182,611 cattle, valued at $16,634,000, during the same period for 1893.

During the first six months of 1894 the United Kingdom took also 112,000,000 pounds of dressed beef from the United States, valued at nearly $10,000,000.

The report shows that during the nine months immediately preceding September 30, 1894, the United States exported to Great Britain 222,-676,000 pounds of pork; of apples, 1,900,000 bushels, valued at $2,500,-000, and of horses 2,811, at an average value of $139 per head. There was a falling off in American wheat exports of 13,500,000 bushels, and the Secretary is inclined to believe that wheat may not in the future be the staple export cereal product of our country, but that corn will continue to advance in importance as an export on account of the new uses to which it is constantly being appropriated.

The exports of agricultural products from the United States for the fiscal year ending June 30, 1894, amounted to $628,363,038, being 72.28 per cent of American exports of every description, and the United Kingdom of Great Britain took more than 54 per cent of all farm products finding foreign markets.

The Department of Agriculture has undertaken during the year two new and important lines of research. The first relates to grasses and forage plants, with the purpose of instructing and familiarizing the people as to the distinctive grasses of the United States and teaching them how to introduce valuable foreign forage plants which may be adapted to this country. The second relates to agricultural soils and crop production, involving the analyses of samples of soils from all sections of the American Union, to demonstrate their adaptability to particular plants and crops. Mechanical analyses of soils may be of such inestimable utility that it is foremost in the new lines of agricultural research, and the Secretary therefore recommends that a division having it in charge be permanently established in the Department.

The amount appropriated for the Weather Bureau was $951,100. Of that sum $138,500, or 14 per cent, has been saved and is returned to the Treasury.

As illustrating the usefulness of this service it may be here stated that the warnings which were very generally given of two tropical storms occurring in September and October of the present year resulted in detaining safely in port 2,305 vessels, valued at $36,283,913, laden with cargoes of probably still greater value. What is much more important and gratifying, many human lives on these ships were also undoubtedly saved.

The appropriation to the Bureau of Animal Industry was $850,000, and the expenditures for the year were only $495,429.24, thus leaving unexpended $354,570.76. The inspection of beef animals for export and interstate trade has been continued, and 12,944,056 head were inspected during the year, at a cost of 1¾ cents per head, against 4¾ cents for 1893. The amount of pork microscopically examined was 35,437,937 pounds, against 20,677,410 pounds in the preceding year. The cost of this inspection has been diminished from 8¾ cents per head in 1893 to 6½ cents in 1894.

The expense of inspecting the pork sold in 1894 to Germany and France by the United States was $88,922.10. The quantity inspected was greater by 15,000,000 pounds than during the preceding year, when the cost of such inspection was $172,367.08. The Secretary of Agriculture recommends that the law providing for the microscopic inspection of export and interstate meat be so amended as to compel owners of the meat inspected to pay the cost of such inspection, and I call attention to the arguments presented in his report in support of this recommendation.

The live beef cattle exported and tagged during the year numbered 353,535. This is an increase of 69,533 head over the previous year.

The sanitary inspection of cattle shipped to Europe has cost an average of 10¾ cents for each animal, and the cost of inspecting Southern cattle and the disinfection of cars and stock yards averages 2.7 cents per animal.

The scientific inquiries of the Bureau of Animal Industry have progressed steadily during the year. Much tuberculin and mallein have been furnished to State authorities for use in the agricultural colleges and experiment stations for the treatment of tuberculosis and glanders.

Quite recently this Department has published the results of its investigations of bovine tuberculosis, and its researches will be vigorously continued. Certain herds in the District of Columbia will be thoroughly inspected and will probably supply adequate scope for the Department to intelligently prosecute its scientific work and furnish sufficient material for purposes of illustration, description, and definition.

The sterilization of milk suspected of containing the bacilli of tuberculosis has been during the year very thoroughly explained in a leaflet by Dr. D. E. Salmon, the Chief of the Bureau, and given general circulation throughout the country.

The Office of Experiment Stations, which is a part of the United States Department of Agriculture, has during the past year engaged itself almost wholly in preparing for publication works based upon the reports of agricultural experiment stations and other institutions for agricultural inquiry in the United States and foreign countries.

The Secretary in his report for 1893 called attention to the fact that the appropriations made for the support of the experiment stations throughout the Union were the only moneys taken out of the National Treasury by act of Congress for which no accounting to Federal authorities was required. Responding to this suggestion, the Fifty-third Congress, in making the appropriation for the Department for the present fiscal year, provided that—

The Secretary of Agriculture shall prescribe the form of annual financial statement required by section 3 of said act of March 2, 1887; shall ascertain whether the expenditures under the appropriation hereby made are in accordance with the provisions of said act, and shall make report thereon to Congress.

In obedience to this law the Department of Agriculture immediately sent out blank forms of expense accounts to each station, and proposes in addition to make, through trusted experts, systematic examination of the several stations during each year for the purpose of acquiring by personal investigation the detailed information necessary to enable the Secretary of Agriculture to make, as the statute provides, a satisfactory report to Congress. The boards of management of the several stations with great alacrity and cordiality have approved the amendment to the law providing this supervision of their expenditures, anticipating that it will increase the efficiency of the stations and protect their directors and managers from loose charges concerning their use of public funds, besides bringing the Department of Agriculture into closer and more confidential relations with the experimental stations, and through their joint service largely increasing their usefulness to the agriculture of the country.

Acting upon a recommendation contained in the report of 1893, Congress appropriated $10,000 "to enable the Secretary of Agriculture to investigate and report upon the nutritive value of the various articles and commodities used for human food, with special suggestions of full, wholesome, and edible rations less wasteful and more economical than those in common use."

Under this appropriation the Department has prepared and now has nearly ready for distribution an elementary discussion of the nutritive value and pecuniary economy of food. When we consider that fully one-half of all the money earned by the wage earners of the civilized world is expended by them for food, the importance and utility of such an investigation is apparent.

The Department expended in the fiscal year 1893 $2,354,809.56, and out of that sum the total amount expended in scientific research was 45.6 per cent. But in the year ending June 30, 1894, out of a total expenditure of $1,948,988.38, the Department applied 51.8 per cent of that sum to scientific work and investigation. It is therefore very plainly observable that the economies which have been practiced in the administration of the Department have not been at the expense of scientific research.

The recommendation contained in the report of the Secretary for 1893 that the vicious system of promiscuous free distribution of its departmental documents be abandoned is again urged. These publications may well be furnished without cost to public libraries, educational institutions, and the officers and libraries of States and of the Federal Government; but from all individuals applying for them a price covering the cost of the document asked for should be required. Thus the publications and documents would be secured by those who really desire them for proper purposes. Half a million of copies of the report of the

Secretary of Agriculture are printed for distribution, at an annual cost of about $300,000. Large numbers of them are cumbering storerooms at the Capitol and the shelves of secondhand-book stores throughout the country. All this labor and waste might be avoided if the recommendations of the Secretary were adopted.

The Secretary also again recommends that the gratuitous distribution of seeds cease and that no money be appropriated for that purpose except to experiment stations. He reiterates the reasons given in his report for 1893 for discontinuing this unjustifiable gratuity, and I fully concur in the conclusions which he has reached.

The best service of the statistician of the Department of Agriculture is the ascertainment, by diligence and care, of the actual and real conditions, favorable or unfavorable, of the farmers and farms of the country, and to seek the causes which produce these conditions, to the end that the facts ascertained may guide their intelligent treatment.

A further important utility in agricultural statistics is found in their elucidation of the relation of the supply of farm products to the demand for them in the markets of the United States and of the world.

It is deemed possible that an agricultural census may be taken each year through the agents of the statistical division of the Department. Such a course is commended for trial by the chief of that division. Its scope would be:

(1) The area under each of the more important crops.

(2) The aggregate products of each of such crops.

(3) The quantity of wheat and corn in the hands of farmers at a date after the spring sowings and plantings and before the beginning of harvest, and also the quantity of cotton and tobacco remaining in the hands of planters, either at the same date or at some other designated time.

The cost of the work is estimated at $500,000.

Owing to the peculiar quality of the statistician's work and the natural and acquired fitness necessary to its successful prosecution, the Secretary of Agriculture expresses the opinion that every person employed in gathering statistics under the chief of that division should be admitted to that service only after a thorough, exhaustive, and successful examination at the hands of the United States Civil Service Commission. This has led him to call for such examination of candidates for the position of assistant statisticians, and also of candidates for chiefs of sections in that division.

The work done by the Department of Agriculture is very superficially dealt with in this communication, and I commend the report of the Secretary and the very important interests with which it deals to the careful attention of the Congress.

The advantages to the public service of an adherence to the principles of civil-service reform are constantly more apparent, and nothing is so encouraging to those in official life who honestly desire good government as the increasing appreciation by our people of these advantages. A vast majority of the voters of the land are ready to insist that the time and attention of those they select to perform for them important public duties should not be distracted by doling out minor offices, and they are growing to be unanimous in regarding party organization as something that should be used in establishing party principles instead of dictating the distribution of public places as rewards of partisan activity.

Numerous additional offices and places have lately been brought within civil-service rules and regulations, and some others will probably soon be included.

The report of the Commissioners will be submitted to the Congress, and I invite careful attention to the recommendations it contains.

I am entirely convinced that we ought not to be longer without a national board of health or national health officer charged with no other duties than such as pertain to the protection of our country from the invasion of pestilence and disease. This would involve the establishment by such board or officer of proper quarantine precautions, or the necessary aid and counsel to local authorities on the subject; prompt advice and assistance to local boards of health or health officers in the suppression of contagious disease, and in cases where there are no such local boards or officers the immediate direction by the national board or officer of measures of suppression; constant and authentic information concerning the health of foreign countries and all parts of our own country as related to contagious diseases, and consideration of regulations to be enforced in foreign ports to prevent the introduction of contagion into our cities and the measures which should be adopted to secure their enforcement.

There seems to be at this time a decided inclination to discuss measures of protection against contagious diseases in international conference, with a view of adopting means of mutual assistance. The creation of such a national health establishment would greatly aid our standing in such conferences and improve our opportunities to avail ourselves of their benefits.

I earnestly recommend the inauguration of a national board of health or similar national instrumentality, believing the same to be a needed precaution against contagious disease and in the interest of the safety and health of our people.

By virtue of a statute of the United States passed in 1888 I appointed in July last Hon. John D. Kernan, of the State of New York, and Hon. Nicholas E. Worthington, of the State of Illinois, to form, with Hon. Carroll D. Wright, Commissioner of Labor, who was designated by said statute, a commission for the purpose of making careful inquiry into the causes of the controversies between certain railroads and their employees which had resulted in an extensive and destructive strike, accompanied by much violence and dangerous disturbance, with considerable loss of life and great destruction of property.

The report of the commissioners has been submitted to me and will be transmitted to the Congress with the evidence taken upon their investigation.

Their work has been well done, and their standing and intelligence give assurance that the report and suggestions they make are worthy of careful consideration.

The tariff act passed at the last session of the Congress needs important amendments if it is to be executed effectively and with certainty. In addition to such necessary amendments as will not change rates of duty, I am still very decidedly in favor of putting coal and iron upon the free list.

So far as the sugar schedule is concerned, I would be glad, under existing aggravations, to see every particle of differential duty in favor of refined sugar stricken out of our tariff law. If with all the favor now accorded the sugar-refining interest in our tariff laws it still languishes to the extent of closed refineries and thousands of discharged workmen, it would seem to present a hopeless case for reasonable legislative aid. Whatever else is done or omitted, I earnestly repeat here the recommendation I have made in another portion of this communication, that the additional duty of one-tenth of a cent per pound laid upon sugar imported from countries paying a bounty on its export be abrogated. It seems to me that exceedingly important considerations point to the propriety of this amendment.

With the advent of a new tariff policy not only calculated to relieve the consumers of our land in the cost of their daily life, but to invite a better development of American thrift and create for us closer and more profitable commercial relations with the rest of the world, it follows as a logical and imperative necessity that we should at once remove the chief if not the only obstacle which has so long prevented our participation in the foreign carrying trade of the sea. A tariff built upon the theory that it is well to check imports and that a home market should bound the industry and effort of American producers was fitly supplemented by a refusal to allow American registry to vessels built abroad, though owned and navigated by our people, thus exhibiting a willingness to abandon all contest for the advantages of American transoceanic carriage. Our new tariff policy, built upon the theory that it is well to encourage such importations as our people need, and that our products and manufactures should find markets in every part of the habitable globe, is consistently supplemented by the greatest possible liberty to our citizens in the ownership and navigation of ships in which our products and manufactures may be transported. The millions now paid to foreigners for carrying American passengers and products across the sea should be turned into American hands. Shipbuilding, which has been protected to strangulation, should be revived by the prospect of profitable employment for ships when built, and the American sailor should be resurrected and again take his place—a sturdy and industrious citizen in time of peace and a patriotic and safe defender of American interests in the day of conflict.

The ancient provision of our law denying American registry to ships built abroad and owned by Americans appears in the light of present conditions not only to be a failure for good at every point, but to be nearer a relic of barbarism than anything that exists under the permission of a statute of the United States. I earnestly recommend its prompt repeal.

During the last month the gold reserved in the Treasury for the purpose of redeeming the notes of the Government circulating as money in the hands of the people became so reduced and its further depletion in the near future seemed so certain that in the exercise of proper care for the public welfare it became necessary to replenish this reserve and thus maintain popular faith in the ability and determination of the Government to meet as agreed its pecuniary obligations.

It would have been well if in this emergency authority had existed to issue the bonds of the Government bearing a low rate of interest and maturing within a short period; but the Congress having failed to confer such authority, resort was necessarily had to the resumption act of 1875, and pursuant to its provisions bonds were issued drawing interest at the rate of 5 per cent per annum and maturing ten years after their issue, that being the shortest time authorized by the act. I am glad to say, however, that on the sale of these bonds the premium received operated to reduce the rate of interest to be paid by the Government to less than 3 per cent.

Nothing could be worse or further removed from sensible finance than the relations existing between the currency the Government has issued, the gold held for its redemption, and the means which must be resorted to for the purpose of replenishing such redemption fund when impaired. Even if the claims upon this fund were confined to the obligations originally intended and if the redemption of these obligations meant their cancellation, the fund would be very small. But these obligations when received and redeemed in gold are not canceled, but are reissued and may do duty many times by way of drawing gold from the Treasury. Thus we have an endless chain in operation constantly depleting the Treasury's gold and never near a final rest. As if this was not bad enough, we have, by a statutory declaration that it is the policy of the Government to maintain the parity between gold and silver, aided the force and momentum of this exhausting process and added largely to the currency obligations claiming this peculiar gold redemption. Our small gold reserve is thus subject to drain from every side. The demands that increase our danger also increase the necessity of protecting this reserve against depletion, and it is most unsatisfactory to know that the protection afforded is only a temporary palliation.

It is perfectly and palpably plain that the only way under present conditions by which this reserve when dangerously depleted can be replenished is through the issue and sale of the bonds of the Government for gold, and yet Congress has not only thus far declined to authorize the issue of bonds best suited to such a purpose, but there seems a disposition in some quarters to deny both the necessity and power for the issue of bonds at all.

I can not for a moment believe that any of our citizens are deliberately willing that their Government should default in its pecuniary obligations or that its financial operations should be reduced to a silver basis. At any rate, I should not feel that my duty was done if I omitted any effort I could make to avert such a calamity. As long, therefore, as no provision is made for the final redemption or the putting aside of the currency obligation now used to repeatedly and constantly draw from the Government its gold, and as long as no better authority for bond issues is allowed than at present exists, such authority will be utilized whenever and as often as it becomes necessary to maintain a sufficient gold reserve, and in abundant time to save the credit of our country and make good the financial declarations of our Government.

Questions relating to our banks and currency are closely connected with the subject just referred to, and they also present some unsatisfactory features. Prominent among them are the lack of elasticity in our currency circulation and its frequent concentration in financial centers when it is most needed in other parts of the country.

The absolute divorcement of the Government from the business of banking is the ideal relationship of the Government to the circulation of the currency of the country.

This condition can not be immediately reached, but as a step in that direction and as a means of securing a more elastic currency and obviating other objections to the present arrangement of bank circulation the Secretary of the Treasury presents in his report a scheme modifying present banking laws and providing for the issue of circulating notes by State banks free from taxation under certain limitations.

The Secretary explains his plan so plainly and its advantages are developed by him with such remarkable clearness that any effort on my part to present argument in its support would be superfluous. I shall therefore content myself with an unqualified indorsement of the Secretary's proposed changes in the law and a brief and imperfect statement of their prominent features.

It is proposed to repeal all laws providing for the deposit of United States bonds as security for circulation; to permit national banks to issue circulating notes not exceeding in amount 75 per cent of their paid-up and unimpaired capital, provided they deposit with the Government as a guaranty fund, in United States legal-tender notes, including Treasury notes of 1890, a sum equal in amount to 30 per cent of the notes they desire to issue, this deposit to be maintained at all times, but whenever any bank retires any part of its circulation a proportional part of its guaranty fund shall be returned to it; to permit the Secretary of the Treasury to prepare and keep on hand ready for issue in case an increase in circulation is desired blank national-bank notes for each bank having circulation and to repeal the provisions of the present law imposing limitations and restrictions upon banks desiring to reduce or increase their circulation, thus permitting such increase or reduction within the limit of 75 per cent of capital to be quickly made as emergencies arise.

In addition to the guaranty fund required, it is proposed to provide a safety fund for the immediate redemption of the circulating notes of failed banks by imposing a small annual tax, say one-half of 1 per cent, upon the average circulation of each bank until the fund amounts to 5 per cent of the total circulation outstanding. When a bank fails its guaranty fund is to be paid into this safety fund and its notes are to be redeemed in the first instance from such safety fund thus augmented, any impairment of such fund caused thereby to be made good from the immediately available cash assets of said bank, and if these should be insufficient such impairment to be made good by *pro rata* assessment among the other banks, their contributions constituting a first lien upon the assets of the failed bank in favor of the contributing banks. As a further security it is contemplated that the existing provision fixing the individual liability of stockholders is to be retained and the bank's indebtedness on account of its circulating notes is to be made a first lien on all its assets.

For the purpose of meeting the expense of printing notes, official supervision, cancellation, and other like charges there shall be imposed a tax of say one-half of 1 per cent per annum upon the average amount of notes in circulation.

It is further provided that there shall be no national-bank notes issued of a less denomination than $10; that each national bank, except in case of a failed bank, shall redeem or retire its notes in the first instance at its own office or at agencies to be designated by it, and that no fixed reserve need be maintained on account of deposits.

Another very important feature of this plan is the exemption of State banks from taxation by the United States in cases where it is shown to the satisfaction of the Secretary of the Treasury and Comptroller of the Currency by banks claiming such exemption that they have not had outstanding their circulating notes exceeding 75 per cent of their paid-up and unimpaired capital; that their stockholders are individually liable for the redemption of their circulating notes to the full extent of their ownership of stock; that the liability of said banks upon their circulating notes constitutes under their State law a first lien upon their assets; that such banks have kept and maintained a guaranty fund in United States legal-tender notes, including Treasury notes of 1890, equal to 30 per cent of their outstanding circulating notes, and that such banks have promptly redeemed their circulating notes when presented at their principal or branch offices.

It is quite likely that this scheme may be usefully amended in some of its details, but I am satisfied it furnishes a basis for a very great improvement in our present banking and currency system.

I conclude this communication fully appreciating that the responsibility for all legislation affecting the people of the United States rests upon their representatives in the Congress, and assuring them that, whether in accordance with recommendations I have made or not, I shall be glad to cooperate in perfecting any legislation that tends to the prosperity and welfare of our country.

GROVER CLEVELAND.

SPECIAL MESSAGES.

EXECUTIVE MANSION, *December 6, 1894.*

To the Senate of the United States:

In compliance with the resolution of the Senate of the 24th of July, 1894, directing the Secretary of State to furnish copies of all papers, correspondence, diplomatic or otherwise, on file in the State Department in connection with the arrest and imprisonment at Arequipa, Peru, of Victor H. McCord, I transmit herewith the correspondence indicated.

GROVER CLEVELAND.

EXECUTIVE MANSION,
Washington, December 10, 1894.

To the Congress of the United States:

I transmit herewith a communication from the Secretary of State, inclosing the report, with accompanying papers, of the commission of the United States for the Columbian Historical Exposition in Madrid in 1892 and 1893, constituted in virtue of the act of Congress approved May 13, 1892.

GROVER CLEVELAND.

EXECUTIVE MANSION, *December 10, 1894.*

To the Senate and House of Representatives:

I transmit herewith the report on the Chicago strike of June and July, 1894, forwarded to me by the Strike Commission appointed July 26, 1894, under the provisions of section 6 of chapter 1063 of the laws of the United States, passed October 1, 1888.

The testimony taken by the commission and the suggestions and recommendations made to it accompany the report in the form of appendixes.

GROVER CLEVELAND.

EXECUTIVE MANSION,
Washington, December 11, 1894.

To the Senate of the United States:

In response to the resolution of the Senate dated December 6, 1894, requesting that copies of correspondence in regard to the claim of Antonio Maximo Mora against the Government of Spain exchanged since my last message to the Senate on the same subject, dated June 20, 1894,* be communicated to it, if not incompatible with the public interests, I transmit herewith the report of the Secretary of State on the matter, with accompanying copies of correspondence. GROVER CLEVELAND.

EXECUTIVE MANSION, *December 11, 1894.*

To the Senate of the United States:

I have received a copy of the following resolution of the Senate, passed on 3d instant:

Resolved, That the President be requested, if in his judgment it be not incompatible with the public interest, to communicate to the Senate any information he may have received in regard to alleged cruelties committed upon Armenians in Turkey, and especially whether any such cruelties have been committed upon citizens who have declared their intention to become naturalized in this country or upon persons because of their being Christians.

And further, to inform the Senate whether any expostulations have been addressed by this Government to the Government of Turkey in regard to such matters or any proposals made by or to this Government to act in concert with other Christian powers regarding the same.

In response to said resolution I beg leave to inform the Senate that I have no information concerning cruelties committed upon Armenians in Turkey or upon persons because of their being Christians, except such information as has been derived from newspapers and statements emanating from the Turkish Government denying such cruelties and two telegraphic reports from our minister at Constantinople.

One of these reports, dated November 28, 1894, is in answer to an inquiry by the State Department touching reports in the press alleging the killing of Armenians, and is as follows:

Reports in American papers of Turkish atrocities at Sassoun are sensational and exaggerated. The killing was in a conflict between armed Armenians and Turkish soldiers. The grand vizier says it was necessary to suppress insurrection, and that about fifty Turks were killed; between three and four hundred Armenian guns were picked up after the fight, and reports that about that number of Armenians were killed. I give credit to his statement.

The other dispatch referred to is dated December 2, 1894, and is as follows:

Information from British ambassador indicates far more loss of lives in Armenia, attended with atrocities, than stated in my telegram of 28th.

*See p. 478.

I have received absolutely no information concerning any cruelties committed "upon citizens who have declared their intention to become naturalized in this country," or upon any persons who had a right to claim or have claimed for any reason the protection of the United States Government.

In the absence of such authentic detailed knowledge on the subject as would justify our interference no "expostulations have been addressed by this Government to the Government of Turkey in regard to such matters."

The last inquiry contained in the resolution of the Senate touching these alleged cruelties seeks information concerning "any proposals made by or to this Government to act in concert with other Christian powers regarding the same."

The first proposal of the kind referred to was made by the Turkish Government through our minister on the 30th day of November, when the Sultan then expressed a desire that a consul of the United States be sent with a Turkish commission to investigate these alleged atrocities on Armenians. This was construed as an invitation on the part of the Turkish Government to actually take part with a Turkish commission in an investigation of these affairs and any report to be made thereon, and the proposition came before our minister's second dispatch was received and at a time when the best information in the possession of our Government was derived from his first report, indicating that the statements made in the press were sensational and exaggerated and that the atrocities alleged really did not exist. This condition very much weakened any motive for an interference based on considerations of humanity, and permitted us without embarrassment to pursue a course plainly marked out by other controlling incidents.

By a treaty entered into at Berlin in the year 1878 between Turkey and various other governments Turkey undertook to guarantee protection to the Armenians, and agreed that it would "periodically make known the steps taken to this effect to the powers, who will superintend their application."

Our Government was not a party to this treaty, and it is entirely obvious that in the face of the provisions of such treaty above recited our interference in the proposed investigation, especially without the invitation of any of the powers which had assumed by treaty obligations to secure the protection of these Armenians, might have been exceedingly embarrassing, if not entirely beyond the limits of justification or propriety.

The Turkish invitation to join the investigation set on foot by that Government was therefore, on the 2d day of December, declined. On the same day, and after this declination had been sent, our minister at Constantinople forwarded his second dispatch, tending to modify his former report as to the extent and character of Armenian slaughter. At the same time the request of the Sultan for our participation in the investigation was repeated, and Great Britain, one of the powers which joined in the treaty of Berlin, made a like request.

In view of changed conditions and upon reconsideration of the subject it was determined to send Mr. Jewett, our consul at Sivas, to the scene of the alleged outrages, not for the purpose of joining with any other government in an investigation and report, but to the end that he might be able to inform this Government as to the exact truth.

Instructions to this effect were sent to Mr. Jewett, and it is supposed he has already entered upon the duty assigned him.

I submit with this communication copies of all correspondence and dispatches in the State Department on this subject and the report to me of the Secretary of State thereon. GROVER CLEVELAND.

EXECUTIVE MANSION,
Washington, January 3, 1895.

To the Senate of the United States:

In response to the resolution of the Senate of the 4th ultimo, requesting "any reports or correspondence relating to affairs at Bluefields, in the Mosquito territory," and also information as to "whether any American citizens have been arrested or the rights of any American citizens at Bluefields have been interfered with during the past two years by the Government of Nicaragua," I transmit herewith a report from the Secretary of State, with accompanying papers. GROVER CLEVELAND.

EXECUTIVE MANSION, *January 9, 1895.*

To the Senate and House of Representatives:

I submit herewith certain dispatches from our minister at Hawaii and the documents which accompanied the same.

They disclose the fact that the Hawaiian Government desires to lease to Great Britain one of the uninhabited islands belonging to Hawaii as a station for a submarine telegraph cable to be laid from Canada to Australia, with a connection between the island leased and Honolulu.

Both the Hawaiian Government and the representatives of Great Britain in this negotiation concede that the proposed lease can not be effected without the consent of the United States, for the reason that in our reciprocity treaty with the King of Hawaii he agreed that as long as said treaty remained in force he would not "lease or otherwise dispose of or create any lien upon any port, harbor, or other territory in his dominion, or grant any special privilege or right of use therein, to any other power, state, or government."

At the request of the Hawaiian Government this subject is laid before the Congress for its determination upon the question of so modifying the treaty agreement above recited as to permit the proposed lease.

It will be seen that the correspondence which is submitted between the Hawaiian and British negotiators negatives the existence on the part of Hawaii of any suspicion of British unfriendliness or the fear of British aggression.

The attention of the Congress is directed to the following statement contained in a communication addressed to the Hawaiian Government by the representatives of Great Britain:

> We propose to inform the British Government of your inquiry whether they would accept the sovereignty of Nicker Island or some other uninhabited island on condition that no subsidy is required from you. As we explained, we have not felt at liberty to entertain that question ourselves, as we were definitely instructed not to ask for the sovereignty of any island, but only for a lease simply for the purpose of the cable.

Some of the dispatches from our minister, which are submitted, not only refer to the project for leasing an uninhabited island belonging to Hawaii, but contain interesting information concerning recent occurrences in that country and its political and social condition. This information is valuable because it is based upon the observation and knowledge necessarily within the scope of the diplomatic duties which are intrusted solely to the charge of this intelligent diplomatic officer representing the United States Government at Hawaii.

I hope the Congress will see fit to grant the request of the Hawaiian Government, and that our consent to the proposed lease will be promptly accorded. It seems to me we ought not by a refusal of this request to stand in the way of the advantages to be gained by isolated Hawaii through telegraphic communication with the rest of the world, especially in view of the fact that our own communication with that country would thereby be greatly improved without apparent detriment to any legitimate American interest.

GROVER CLEVELAND.

EXECUTIVE MANSION, *January 11, 1895.*

To the Senate of the United States:

In response to the resolution of the Senate of the 19th ultimo, requesting the record of the extradition proceedings in the case of General Ezeta, etc., I transmit herewith a letter from the Secretary of State, with accompanying papers.

GROVER CLEVELAND.

EXECUTIVE MANSION,
Washington, January 15, 1895.

To the Senate of the United States:

I transmit a report from the Secretary of State, with accompanying papers, in response to the resolution of the Senate of the 3d instant, requesting "all correspondence or other papers relating to the delivery by the United States consul at Shanghai of two Japanese citizens to the Chinese authorities," and information "whether the said Japanese were put to death after being tortured, and whether there was any understanding with the Chinese Government that officers of the United States should aid, assist, and give comfort to any Japanese citizen desiring to leave China, and whether the United States consul at Hankow was reprimanded by Chinese officials for aiding Japanese citizens to leave the country, and whether all information was refused to the United States consul at Ningpo when he made inquiries as to the charges against certain Japanese citizens arrested there."

GROVER CLEVELAND.

EXECUTIVE MANSION, *January 28, 1895.*

To the Senate and House of Representatives:

In my last annual message I commended to the serious consideration of the Congress the condition of our national finances, and in connection with the subject indorsed a plan of currency legislation which at that time seemed to furnish protection against impending danger.* This plan has not been approved by the Congress. In the meantime the situation has so changed and the emergency now appears so threatening that I deem it my duty to ask at the hands of the legislative branch of the Government such prompt and effective action as will restore confidence in our financial soundness and avert business disaster and universal distress among our people.

Whatever may be the merits of the plan outlined in my annual message as a remedy for ills then existing and as a safeguard against the depletion of the gold reserve then in the Treasury, I am now convinced that its reception by the Congress and our present advanced stage of financial perplexity necessitate additional or different legislation.

With natural resources unlimited in variety and productive strength and with a people whose activity and enterprise seek only a fair opportunity to achieve national success and greatness, our progress should not be checked by a false financial policy and a heedless disregard of sound monetary laws, nor should the timidity and fear which they engender stand in the way of our prosperity.

It is hardly disputed that this predicament confronts us to-day. Therefore no one in any degree responsible for the making and execution of our laws should fail to see a patriotic duty in honestly and sincerely attempting to relieve the situation. Manifestly this effort will not succeed unless it is made untrammeled by the prejudice of partisanship and with a steadfast determination to resist the temptation to accomplish party advantage. We may well remember that if we are threatened with

* See pp. 553-556.

financial difficulties all our people in every station of life are concerned; and surely those who suffer will not receive the promotion of party interests as an excuse for permitting our present troubles to advance to a disastrous conclusion. It is also of the utmost importance that we approach the study of the problems presented as free as possible from the tyranny of preconceived opinions, to the end that in a common danger we may be able to seek with unclouded vision a safe and reasonable protection.

The real trouble which confronts us consists in a lack of confidence, widespread and constantly increasing, in the continuing ability or disposition of the Government to pay its obligations in gold. This lack of confidence grows to some extent out of the palpable and apparent embarrassment attending the efforts of the Government under existing laws to procure gold and to a greater extent out of the impossibility of either keeping it in the Treasury or canceling obligations by its expenditure after it is obtained.

The only way left open to the Government for procuring gold is by the issue and sale of its bonds. The only bonds that can be so issued were authorized nearly twenty-five years ago and are not well calculated to meet our present needs. Among other disadvantages, they are made payable in coin instead of specifically in gold, which in existing conditions detracts largely and in an increasing ratio from their desirability as investments. It is by no means certain that bonds of this description can much longer be disposed of at a price creditable to the financial character of our Government.

The most dangerous and irritating feature of the situation, however, remains to be mentioned. It is found in the means by which the Treasury is despoiled of the gold thus obtained without canceling a single Government obligation and solely for the benefit of those who find profit in shipping it abroad or whose fears induce them to hoard it at home. We have outstanding about five hundred millions of currency notes of the Government for which gold may be demanded, and, curiously enough, the law requires that when presented and, in fact, redeemed and paid in gold they shall be reissued. Thus the same notes may do duty many times in drawing gold from the Treasury; nor can the process be arrested as long as private parties, for profit or otherwise, see an advantage in repeating the operation. More than $300,000,000 in these notes have already been redeemed in gold, and notwithstanding such redemption they are all still outstanding.

Since the 17th day of January, 1894, our bonded interest-bearing debt has been increased $100,000,000 for the purpose of obtaining gold to replenish our coin reserve. Two issues were made amounting to fifty millions each, one in January and the other in November. As a result of the first issue there was realized something more than $58,000,000 in gold. Between that issue and the succeeding one in November, comprising a period of about ten months, nearly $103,000,000 in gold were drawn from the Treasury. This made the second issue necessary, and upon that more than fifty-eight millions in gold was again realized. Between the date of this second issue and the present time, covering a period of only about two months, more than $69,000,000 in gold have been drawn from the Treasury. These large sums of gold were expended without any cancellation of Government obligations or in any permanent way benefiting our people or improving our pecuniary situation.

The financial events of the past year suggest facts and conditions which should certainly arrest attention.

More than $172,000,000 in gold have been drawn out of the Treasury during the year for the purpose of shipment abroad or hoarding at home.

While nearly $103,000,000 of this amount was drawn out during the first ten months of the year, a sum aggregating more than two-thirds of that amount, being about $69,000,000, was drawn out during the following two months, thus indicating a marked acceleration of the depleting process with the lapse of time.

The obligations upon which this gold has been drawn from the Treasury are still outstanding and are available for use in repeating the exhausting operation with shorter intervals as our perplexities accumulate.

Conditions are certainly supervening tending to make the bonds which may be issued to replenish our gold less useful for that purpose.

An adequate gold reserve is in all circumstances absolutely essential to the upholding of our public credit and to the maintenance of our high national character.

Our gold reserve has again reached such a stage of diminution as to require its speedy reenforcement.

The aggravations that must inevitably follow present conditions and methods will certainly lead to misfortune and loss, not only to our national credit and prosperity and to financial enterprise, but to those of our people who seek employment as a means of livelihood and to those whose only capital is their daily labor.

It will hardly do to say that a simple increase of revenue will cure our troubles. The apprehension now existing and constantly increasing as to our financial ability does not rest upon a calculation of our revenue. The time has passed when the eyes of investors abroad and our people at home were fixed upon the revenues of the Government. Changed conditions have attracted their attention to the gold of the Government. There need be no fear that we can not pay our current expenses with such money as we have. There is now in the Treasury a comfortable surplus of more than $63,000,000, but it is not in gold, and therefore does not meet our difficulty.

I can not see that differences of opinion concerning the extent to which silver ought to be coined or used in our currency should interfere with the counsels of those whose duty it is to rectify evils now apparent in our financial situation.   They have to consider the question of national credit and the consequences that will follow from its collapse.   Whatever ideas may be insisted upon as to silver or bimetallism, a proper solution of the question now pressing upon us only requires a recognition of gold as well as silver and a concession of its importance, rightfully or wrongfully acquired, as a basis of national credit, a necessity in the honorable discharge of our obligations payable in gold, and a badge of solvency.   I do not understand that the real friends of silver desire a condition that might follow inaction or neglect to appreciate the meaning of the present exigency if it should result in the entire banishment of gold from our financial and currency arrangements.

Besides the Treasury notes, which certainly should be paid in gold, amounting to nearly $500,000,000, there will fall due in 1904 one hundred millions of bonds issued during the last year, for which we have received gold, and in 1907 nearly six hundred millions of 4 per cent bonds issued in 1877.   Shall the payment of these obligations in gold be repudiated?   If they are to be paid in such a manner as the preservation of our national honor and national solvency demands, we should not destroy or even imperil our ability to supply ourselves with gold for that purpose.

While I am not unfriendly to silver and while I desire to see it recognized to such an extent as is consistent with financial safety and the preservation of national honor and credit, I am not willing to see gold entirely banished from our currency and finances.   To avert such a consequence I believe thorough and radical remedial legislation should be promptly passed.   I therefore beg the Congress to give the subject immediate attention.

In my opinion the Secretary of the Treasury should be authorized to issue bonds of the Government for the purpose of procuring and maintaining a sufficient gold reserve and the redemption and cancellation of the United States legal-tender notes and the Treasury notes issued for the purchase of silver under the law of July 14, 1890.   We should be relieved from the humiliating process of issuing bonds to procure gold to be immediately and repeatedly drawn out on these obligations for purposes not related to the benefit of our Government or our people.   The principal and interest of these bonds should be payable on their face in gold, because they should be sold only for gold or its representative, and because there would now probably be difficulty in favorably disposing of bonds not containing this stipulation.   I suggest that the bonds be issued in denominations of twenty and fifty dollars and their multiples and that they bear interest at a rate not exceeding 3 per cent per annum.   I do not see why they should not be payable fifty years from their date.   We of the present generation have large amounts to pay if we meet our obligations, and long bonds are most salable.   The Secretary of the Treasury might well be permitted at his discretion to receive on the sale of bonds the legal-tender and Treasury notes to be retired, and of course when they are thus retired or redeemed in gold they should be canceled.

These bonds under existing laws could be deposited by national banks as security for circulation, and such banks should be allowed to issue circulation up to the face value of these or any other bonds so deposited, except bonds outstanding bearing only 2 per cent interest and which sell in the market at less than par. National banks should not be allowed to take out circulating notes of a less denomination than $10, and when such as are now outstanding reach the Treasury, except for redemption and retirement, they should be canceled and notes of the denomination of $10 and upward issued in their stead. Silver certificates of the denomination of $10 and upward should be replaced by certificates of the denominations under $10.

As a constant means for the maintenance of a reasonable supply of gold in the Treasury, our duties on imports should be paid in gold, allowing all other dues to the Government to be paid in any other form of money.

I believe all the provisions I have suggested should be embodied in our laws if we are to enjoy a complete reinstatement of a sound financial condition. They need not interfere with any currency scheme providing for the increase of the circulating medium through the agency of national or State banks that may commend itself to the Congress, since they can easily be adjusted to such a scheme. Objection has been made to the issuance of interest-bearing obligations for the purpose of retiring the noninterest-bearing legal-tender notes. In point of fact, however, these notes have burdened us with a large load of interest, and it is still accumulating. The aggregate interest on the original issue of bonds, the proceeds of which in gold constituted the reserve for the payment of these notes, amounted to $70,326,250 on January 1, 1895, and the annual charge for interest on these bonds and those issued for the same purpose during the last year will be $9,145,000, dating from January 1, 1895.

While the cancellation of these notes would not relieve us from the obligations already incurred on their account, these figures are given by way of suggesting that their existence has not been free from interest charges and that the longer they are outstanding, judging from the experience of the last year, the more expensive they will become.

In conclusion I desire to frankly confess my reluctance to issuing more bonds in present circumstances and with no better results than have lately followed that course. I can not, however, refrain from adding to an assurance of my anxiety to cooperate with the present Congress in any reasonable measure of relief an expression of my determination to leave nothing undone which furnishes a hope for improving the situation or checking a suspicion of our disinclination or disability to meet with the strictest honor every national obligation.

GROVER CLEVELAND.

EXECUTIVE MANSION, *January 30, 1895.*

To the House of Representatives:

In compliance with a resolution of the House of Representatives of the 28th instant, the Senate concurring, I herewith return the bill (H. R. 6186) entitled "An act to pension Maria Davis."

GROVER CLEVELAND.

EXECUTIVE MANSION,
Washington, February 4, 1895.

To the Senate of the United States:

In response to the resolution of the Senate dated December 6, 1894, requesting that copies of correspondence in regard to the claim of Antonio Maximo Mora against the Government of Spain exchanged since my last message to the Senate on the same subject, dated June 20, 1894,* be communicated to it if not incompatible with the public interests, I transmit herewith a report of the Secretary of State, inclosing copies of further correspondence exchanged between the Governments of the United States and Spain since the date of my last message to the Senate, December 11, 1894.†

GROVER CLEVELAND.

EXECUTIVE MANSION,
Washington, February 4, 1895.

To the House of Representatives:

In response to the resolution of the House of Representatives of the 1st instant, calling for certain information touching the recent insurrection in the Hawaiian Islands, I transmit herewith a report of the Secretary of State, with accompanying papers.

GROVER CLEVELAND.

EXECUTIVE MANSION, *February 5, 1895.*

To the House of Representatives:

In compliance with a resolution of the House of Representatives of the 2d instant, the Senate concurring, I return herewith the bill (H.R.5377) entitled "An act granting a pension to Richard R. Knight."

GROVER CLEVELAND.

EXECUTIVE MANSION,
Washington, February 7, 1895.

To the Senate:

I transmit herewith, in response to a resolution of the Senate of the 16th ultimo, a report from the Secretary of State, accompanied by copies of certain correspondence touching the enforcement of the provisions of the tariff act of 1894.

GROVER CLEVELAND.

*See p. 478. †See p. 557.

EXECUTIVE MANSION, *February 8, 1895.*

To the Congress of the United States:

Since my recent communication to the Congress calling attention to our financial condition and suggesting legislation which I deemed essential to our national welfare and credit* the anxiety and apprehension then existing in business circles have continued.

As a precaution, therefore, against the failure of timely legislative aid through Congressional action, cautious preparations have been pending to employ to the best possible advantage, in default of better means, such Executive authority as may without additional legislation be exercised for the purpose of reenforcing and maintaining in our Treasury an adequate and safe gold reserve.

In the judgment of those especially charged with this responsibility the business situation is so critical and the legislative situation is so unpromising, with the omission thus far on the part of Congress to beneficially enlarge the powers of the Secretary of the Treasury in the premises, as to enjoin immediate Executive action with the facilities now at hand.

Therefore, in pursuance of section 3700 of the Revised Statutes, the details of an arrangement have this day been concluded with parties abundantly able to fulfill their undertaking whereby bonds of the United States authorized under the act of July 14, 1875, payable in coin thirty years after their date, with interest at the rate of 4 per cent per annum, to the amount of a little less than $62,400,000, are to be issued for the purchase of gold coin, amounting to a sum slightly in excess of $65,-000,000, to be delivered to the Treasury of the United States, which sum added to the gold now held in our reserve will so restore such reserve as to make it amount to something more than $100,000,000. Such a premium is to be allowed to the Government upon the bonds as to fix the rate of interest upon the amount of gold realized at 3¾ per cent per annum. At least one-half of the gold to be obtained is to be supplied from abroad, which is a very important and favorable feature of the transaction.

The privilege is especially reserved to the Government to substitute at par within ten days from this date, in lieu of the 4 per cent coin bonds, other bonds in terms payable in gold and bearing only 3 per cent interest if the issue of the same should in the meantime be authorized by the Congress.

The arrangement thus completed, which after careful inquiry appears in present circumstances and considering all the objects desired to be the best attainable, develops such a difference in the estimation of investors between bonds made payable in coin and those specifically made payable in gold in favor of the latter as is represented by three-fourths of a cent in annual interest. In the agreement just concluded the annual saving

*See pp. 561–565.

in interest to the Government if 3 per cent gold bonds should be substituted for 4 per cent coin bonds under the privilege reserved would be $539,159, amounting in thirty years, or at the maturity of the coin bonds, to $16,174,770.

Of course there never should be a doubt in any quarter as to the redemption in gold of the bonds of the Government which are made payable in coin. Therefore the discrimination, in the judgment of investors, between our bond obligations payable in coin and those specifically made payable in gold is very significant. It is hardly necessary to suggest that, whatever may be our views on the subject, the sentiments or preferences of those with whom we must negotiate in disposing of our bonds for gold are not subject to our dictation.

I have only to add that in my opinion the transaction herein detailed for the information of the Congress promises better results than the efforts previously made in the direction of effectively adding to our gold reserve through the sale of bonds, and I believe it will tend, as far as such action can in present circumstances, to meet the determination expressed in the law repealing the silver-purchasing clause of the act of July 14, 1890, and that, in the language of such repealing act, the arrangement made will aid our efforts to ''insure the maintenance of the parity in value of the coins of the two metals and the equal power of every dollar at all times in the markets and in the payment of debts.''

GROVER CLEVELAND.

EXECUTIVE MANSION, *February 8, 1895.*

To the Senate and House of Representatives:

I transmit herewith, for the information of the Congress, a copy of a telegraphic dispatch just received from Mr. Willis, our minister to Hawaii, with a copy of the reply thereto which was immediately sent by the Secretary of State.

GROVER CLEVELAND.

To the Senate: EXECUTIVE MANSION, *February 11, 1895.*

On the 8th day of January I received a copy of the following Senate resolution:

Resolved, That the President be requested, if not incompatible with the public interests, to communicate to the Senate all reports, documents, and other papers, including logs of vessels, relating to the enforcement of the regulations respecting fur seals adopted by the Governments of the United States and Great Britain in accordance with the decision of the Tribunal of Arbitration convened at Paris and the resolutions under which said reports are required to be made, as well as relating to the number of seals taken during the season of 1894 by pelagic hunters and by the lessees of the Pribilof and Commander islands; also relating to the steps which may have been taken to extend the said regulations to the Asiatic waters of the

North Pacific Ocean and Bering Sea and to secure the concurrence of other nations in said regulations, and, further, all papers not heretofore published, including communications of the agent of the United States before said tribunal at Paris, relating to the claims of the British Government on account of the seizure of the sealing vessels in Bering Sea.

In compliance with said request I herewith transmit sundry papers, documents, and reports which have been returned to me by the Secretary of State, the Secretary of the Treasury, and the Secretary of the Navy, to whom said resolution was referred. I am not in possession of any further information touching the various subjects embodied in such resolution.

It will be seen from a letter of the Secretary of the Navy accompanying the papers and documents sent from his Department that it is impossible to furnish at this time the complete log books of some of the naval vessels referred to in the resolution, but I venture to express the hope that the reports of the commanders of such vessels herewith submitted will be found to contain in substance so much of the matters recorded in said log books as are important in answering the inquiries addressed to me by the Senate. GROVER CLEVELAND.

EXECUTIVE MANSION,
Washington, February 12, 1895.

To the Senate and House of Representatives:

I transmit herewith, for the information of the Congress, a communication from the Secretary of State, covering the report of the Director of the Bureau of the American Republics for the year 1894.

GROVER CLEVELAND.

EXECUTIVE MANSION, *February 14, 1895.*

To the Senate and House of Representatives:

I transmit herewith the eighth special report of the Commissioner of Labor, which relates to " the housing of the working people " in different countries. GROVER CLEVELAND.

EXECUTIVE MANSION,
Washington, February 26, 1895.

To the Senate:

I transmit herewith, in response to a resolution of the Senate of the 29th ultimo, a report from the Secretary of State, accompanied by copies of correspondence touching Samoan affairs.

GROVER CLEVELAND.

VETO MESSAGES.

EXECUTIVE MANSION, *January 14, 1895.*

To the House of Representatives:

I herewith return without my approval House bill No. 7451, entitled "An act to authorize the entry of land for gravel pits and reservoir purposes and authorizing the grant of right of way for pipe lines."

The first section of this bill permits the sale to railroad companies, in the discretion of the Secretary of the Interior, under certain restrictions and at an appraised value, certain public lands to be used by said companies for gravel pits or the construction of reservoirs. It also permits grants of the right of way for pipe lines connecting such reservoirs with the railways of said companies.

The second, third, and fourth sections of the bill relate to the purchase by any citizen of the United States, or any association of citizens, or any ditch or water company, of public lands suitable for reservoir purposes at such a price as the Secretary of the Interior shall prescribe, not less than $2 per acre.

The right to purchase these lands is given by the sections last referred to "under rules and regulations prescribed by the Secretary of the Interior."

I think the expediency and propriety of disposing of these lands for the purposes specified should in each case be determined by the Secretary of the Interior, as well as the rules and regulations governing such disposition.

The objections to the bill, however, which appear to be the most serious are found in its fifth and last section, which provides:

That any State or any county or district organization duly organized under the laws of any State or Territory may apply for any of the storage-reservoir sites not reserved by the United States, situated on unentered public lands, for the storage of water for irrigating, mining, or other useful purposes, whereupon the Secretary of the Interior shall set aside and withdraw from public sale or other disposition such site or sites and permit the use thereof for either or all of such purposes.

These provisions do not seem to be in harmony with prior laws by which, under certain conditions, arid lands may be conveyed to States for the purpose of irrigation, and it is not clear what is intended by the words "any of the storage-reservoir sites not reserved by the United States."

The apparent purpose and effect of the section is to give to the organizations mentioned the right to select such land as may present eligible reservoir sites not reserved and upon unentered lands, and demand of the Secretary of the Interior a grant of the same, leaving no discretion on the subject to him or to any other officer of the Government; and these grants are to be made without any compensation to the Government and without any specific requirement of the amount or kind of work to be done or improvements to be made upon such sites.

The grants may be demanded not only for the storage of water for irrigating purposes, but for "mining and other useful purposes." Inasmuch as no officer of the Government is vested with any discretion in the premises, the pretext that the "purpose" to be accomplished is "useful" might result in the use of these sites in a manner prejudicial to the surrounding public domain and destructive of the utilization of such sites for irrigating purposes.

The wise and prudent safeguards which have been incorporated in other legislation relating to the disposition of arid public lands and their irrigation seem to have been to such an extent overlooked in the construction of the bill under consideration that, in my judgment, if it should become the law a beneficent policy which the Government has entered upon in the interest of agriculture would be seriously endangered.

GROVER CLEVELAND.

To the Senate: EXECUTIVE MANSION, *February 1, 1895.*

I herewith return without my approval Senate bill No. 2338, entitled "An act granting to the Gila Valley, Globe and Northern Railway Company a right of way through the San Carlos Indian Reservation, in the Territory of Arizona."

The reservation through which it is proposed to construct a railroad under the provisions of this bill is inhabited by tribes of Indians which in the past have been most troublesome and whose depredations on more than one occasion have caused loss of life, destruction of property, and serious alarm to the people of the surrounding country; and their condition as to civilization is not now so far improved as to give assurance that in the future they may not upon occasion make trouble.

The discontent among the Indians which has given rise to disturbances in the past has been largely caused by trespass upon their lands and interference with their rights by the neighboring whites. I am in very great doubt whether in any circumstances a road through their reservation should at this time be permitted, and especially since the route, which is rather indefinitely described in the bill, appears to pass through the richest and most desirable part of their lands. In any event, I am thoroughly convinced that the construction of the road should not be permitted without first obtaining the consent of these Indians. This is a provision which has been insisted upon, so far as I am aware, in all the like bills which have been approved for a long time, and I think it should especially be inserted in this bill if, even upon any conditions, it is thought expedient to permit a railroad to traverse this reservation.

The importance of this consent does not rest solely upon the extent to which the Indians have the right of ownership over this land. The fact that the procurement of this consent is the most effective means of allaying the discontent which might arise and perhaps develop into a train of lamentable and destructive outbreaks of violence particularly emphasizes its importance.

GROVER CLEVELAND.

EXECUTIVE MANSION, *February 5, 1895.*

To the House of Representatives:

I return herewith without approval House bill No. 5368, entitled "An act for the relief of H. W. McConnell."

The reports of both the Senate and House committees, which favorably reported this bill, disclose an intention to partially relieve the former postmaster at Jacksboro, in the State of Texas, from liability on account of two remittances of postal funds which he dispatched at different times during the year 1883 to be deposited at Dallas, in the same State, and which were lost by robberies of the stage conveying the same. In dealing with the first remittance the committees report that the postmaster should be relieved of liability to the amount of only $94, the loss of the remainder of the money being chargeable to his neglect and violation of postal regulations. As to the second remittance, the committees report that by reason of like neglect and violation of regulations the postmaster should be held responsible for the loss of all the money transmitted except the sum of $42.

For these two sums, amounting to $136, an appropriation is made for the benefit of H. W. McConnell.

The name of the postmaster intended to be relieved is H. H. McConnell, as appears by the records of the Post-Office Department. The person to whom the money appropriated should be paid is therefore not correctly named in the bill.

An examination of this postmaster's accounts discloses the further fact that the amount proposed to be appropriated for his relief is too large by $42, that being the sum allowed him by reason of the second stage robbery. This item has already been credited to him in the adjustment of his accounts at the Post-Office Department, and the claim for its reimbursement has been thereby extinguished.

GROVER CLEVELAND.

EXECUTIVE MANSION, *February 12, 1895.*

To the Senate:

I return herewith without approval Senate bill No. 143, entitled "An act for the relief of the heirs of D. Fulford."

This bill directs the Secretary of the Treasury "to redeem, in favor of the heirs at law of D. Fulford, four bonds of the United States, consols of 1867, of the denomination of $500, $100, $50, and $50, and known as five-twenties, said bonds having been destroyed by fire the 9th day of

July, 1872, and to pay to the heirs at law of said D. Fulford the amount of said bonds, together with accrued interest from July 1, 1872, to the date of the maturity of said bonds.''

The bill further provides that the heirs to whom the payment is to be made shall execute and file with the Secretary of the Treasury a bond ''conditioned to save harmless the United States from loss or liability on account of said bonds or the interest accrued thereon, and to contain such words as to cover any liability resulting from any mistake in the designation or description of the bonds, so that in no event shall the United States be called upon by a rightful claimant for a second payment thereof.''

The proposition is that the Government shall pay bonds alleged to have been destroyed by fire nearly twenty-three years ago.

The Secretary of the Treasury states that an application for the payment of these bonds, made by Mr. Fulford himself, was rejected by the Department because he was unable to describe the bonds in such a way as to permit their identification and because the evidence of their destruction by fire was inconclusive.

The Senate Committee on Claims, however, in their report on the bill under consideration, state that they are entirely satisfied that Mr. Fulford was the owner of four Government bonds, one for $500, one for $100, and two for $50, and that they were burned with his residence, which was destroyed by fire on the 9th day of July, 1872, and that while he could not furnish the numbers or descriptions of said bonds he understood all these bonds were of the class known as consols of 1867, and that he had collected the coupons thereon for the interest due July 1, 1872.

The particular class of bonds mentioned were dated July 1, 1867, and were payable or redeemable not less than five nor more than twenty years from their date. The short period expired, therefore, on the 1st day of July, 1872. That was the date when the last coupons on Mr. Fulford's bonds, which it is alleged were detached and collected, became due, and only nine days before the supposed destruction of the bonds by fire.

A letter from the Secretary of the Treasury dated July 20, 1892, attached to the report of the Senate committee made upon a bill similar to this which was pending at that time, discloses the fact that among the consols of 1867 then outstanding there were 107 of the denomination of $500, 167 of the denomination of $100, and 85 of the denomination of $50. This statement merely shows that there were numerous bonds precisely similar to those described as belonging to Mr. Fulford which had not in July, 1892, been redeemed, though the extreme limit of their maturity expired on the 1st day of July, 1887. The letter of the Secretary further discloses, however, that there were two of these outstanding bonds of the denomination of $500 and two of the denomination of $100 upon which coupons of interest had not been paid since July 1, 1872. Of course this lends plausibility to the suggestion that two of these four bonds, one of each denomination, were those destroyed when Mr. Fulford's house was burned in July, 1872; but this suggestion loses its force under the additional statement in the letter of the Secretary of the Treasury that in July, 1892, there were no consols of 1867 of the denomination of $50 whose last coupon was paid July 1, 1872. This shows conclusively that no fifty-dollar bonds of this class were destroyed by fire in Mr. Fulford's house and casts great uncertainty upon the description of the other bonds, inasmuch as the theory of the claimants seems to be that all the bonds destroyed belonged to the same class.

In 1893, upon an examination of the records of the Treasury Department, it was found that the two unpaid bonds for $500 reported in 1892 as outstanding, from which no coupons had been paid since July 1, 1872, still remained unredeemed, but that one of the two one-hundred-dollar bonds which were in that condition in 1892 had been since that time paid and canceled. I think it must be conceded that this late redemption of this bond greatly weakens any presumption that the other three will not be presented for payment.

It is perfectly clear that so far as this bill directs the payment to the persons therein named of two consols of 1867 of the denomination of $50 each on the ground that such bonds were destroyed by fire in July, 1872, it requires the payment of money to those not entitled to it, since it is shown that these consols could not have been destroyed at the time stated, because coupons due on all consols of that denomination unredeemed have been paid since that date.

While the objections to the payment of the amount of the other two bonds mentioned in the bill are less conclusive, there seem to be so much doubt and uncertainty concerning their description and character, and their identification as unredeemed consols of 1867 is so unsatisfactory, that, in my opinion, it is not safe to assume, as is done in this bill, that they are represented among those bonds of that class recorded as still outstanding whose coupons for some reason have not been presented for payment since July 1, 1872.

I do not believe that an indemnity bond could be drawn which, as against the strict rights of sureties, would protect the Government against double liability in case all the payments directed by this bill were made. Even if the payments were confined to the two larger consols described, there would be great difficulty in framing a bond which would surely indemnify the Government.

There should always be a willingness to save the holders of Government securities from damage through their loss or destruction, but, in my judgment, a bad precedent would be established by paying obligations whose destruction and identification are not more satisfactorily established than in this case.

GROVER CLEVELAND.

EXECUTIVE MANSION, *February 19, 1895.*
To the House of Representatives:

I return herewith without approval House bill No. 6244, entitled "An act to remove the charge of desertion from the military record of Jacob Eckert."

This bill directs the Secretary of War "to cause the records of the War Department to be so amended as to remove the charge of desertion from the service record of Jacob Eckert, of New Philadelphia, Ohio, late a private in Company B, Sixty-first Ohio Volunteer Infantry, and to grant an honorable discharge to said Jacob Eckert from the service of the United States Army as of date when said company was mustered out of service."

The regiment and company to which this soldier belonged, except such members as reenlisted as veterans, were mustered out of the service October 17, 1864.

Jacob Eckert did not reenlist and was not mustered out with his comrades for the reason that he was then under arrest on a charge of desertion. In November, 1864, he was tried by a general court-martial and convicted of having deserted on the 1st of September, 1864, and again on the 2d day of September, 1864, and upon such conviction he was sentenced to forfeit all pay due him from September 1, the date of his first desertion, until the expiration of his term of service, to be dishonorably discharged and confined at hard labor for twelve months.

This sentence was approved by the reviewing authority, and I assume the convicted soldier served his term of imprisonment, since the statement contained in the report of the House committee to whom this bill was referred that he was dishonorably discharged in 1865 can be accounted for in no other way.

It seems to me that the provisions of this bill amount to a legislative reversal of the judgment of a regularly constituted court and a legislative pardon of the offense of which this soldier was convicted. If this doubtful authority is to be exercised by Congress, it should be done in such a manner as not to restore a man properly convicted and sentenced as a deserter, without even the allegation of injustice, to the rights of pay, allowance, and pension belonging to those who faithfully and honorably served in the military service of their country according to the terms of their enlistment.

GROVER CLEVELAND.

EXECUTIVE MANSION, *February 20, 1895.*
To the Senate:

I return herewith without approval Senate bill No. 1526, entitled "An act for the relief of Henry Halteman."

This bill directs the Secretary of War "to grant an honorable discharge from the United States service to Henry Halteman, late of Company F, Second United States Artillery."

It is conceded that this soldier enlisted in the Regular Army on the 18th day of December, 1860, for the term of five years and that he deserted on the 18th day of August, 1865. The only excuse or palliation offered for his offense is found in the statement that his desertion was provoked by his company's being ordered to California so near the termination of his enlistment that his term would have expired before or soon after his company could have reached California, and "that his return would have been both tedious and somewhat perilous, if not expensive."

The fact must not be overlooked that this soldier enlisted in the Regular Army and that his term had no relation to the duration of the war or the immediate need of the Government for troops at the time of his desertion. The morale and discipline of the Regular Army are therefore directly involved in the proposed legislation.

The soldier's name remained on the records of the War Department as a deserter at large for twenty-three years, and until the year 1888. In August of that year application was made to the Department for the removal of the charge of desertion against him, which was refused on the ground that it was not shown that such charge was founded in error. Thereupon he applied for a discharge without character, as it is called, as of the date of his desertion. This was granted on the 21st day of September, 1888. Such discharges, which were not uncommon at that time, omitted the certificate of character which entitled the soldier to reenlistment.

In 1892 a bill similar to that now under consideration was referred to the Adjutant-General of the Army and was returned with an adverse report.

The record of the War Department on the subject of this soldier's separation from the Army is absolutely correct as it stands, and no sufficient reason is apparent why another record should be substituted. If this deserter is to be allowed an honorable discharge, I do not see why every deserter should not be absolved from the consequences of his unfaithfulness.

The effect of this bill if it should become a law would be to allow the beneficiary not only a pensionable status, but arrears of pay and clothing allowances up to the date of his desertion and travel allowance from the place of his desertion to the place of his enlistment.

It is not denied that all these things have been justly forfeited by deliberate and inexcusable desertion. In the case presented it seems to me that the laws and regulations adopted for the purpose of maintaining the discipline and efficiency of the Army ought not to be set aside.

GROVER CLEVELAND.

EXECUTIVE MANSION, *February 23, 1895.*

To the House of Representatives:

I return herewith without approval House bill No. 8165, entitled "An act authorizing the Kansas City, Oklahoma and Pacific Railway Company to construct and operate a railway through Indian reservations in the

Indian Territory and the Territories of Oklahoma and New Mexico, and for other purposes.''

This bill contains concessions more comprehensive and sweeping than any ever presented for my approval, and it seems to me the rights and interests of the Indians and the Government are the least protected.

The route apparently desired, though passing through or into one State and three Territories, is described as indefinitely as possible, and does not seem to be subject to the approval in its entirety of the Secretary of the Interior or any other governmental agency having relation to the interest involved.

There is no provision for obtaining the consent of the Indians through whose territory and reservations the railroad may be located.

Though it is proposed to build the railroad through territories having local courts convenient to their inhabitants, all controversies that may arise out of the location and building of the road are by the provisions of the bill to be passed upon by the United States circuit and district courts for the district of Kansas ''and such other courts as may be authorized by Congress.''

The bill provides that ''the civil jurisdiction of said courts is hereby extended within the limits of said Indian reservations, without distinction as to citizenship of the parties, so far as may be necessary to carry out the provisions of this act.'' This provision permits the subordination of the jurisdiction of Indian courts, which we are bound by treaty to protect, to the ''provisions of this act'' and to the interests and preferences of the railroad company for whose benefit the bill under consideration is intended.

A plan of appraisal is provided for in the bill in case an agreement can not be reached as to the amount of compensation to be paid for the taking of lands held by individual occupants according to the laws, customs, and usages of any of the Indian nations or tribes or by allotment or agreement with the Indians. It is, however, further provided that in case either party is dissatisfied with the award of the referees to be appointed an appeal may be taken to the district court held at Wichita, Kans., no matter where on the proposed route of the road the controversy may originate. If upon the hearing of said appeal the judgment of the court shall be for the same sum as the award of the referees, the costs shall be adjudged against the appellant, and if said judgment shall be for a smaller sum the costs shall be adjudged against the party claiming damages. It does not seem to me that the interests of an Indian occupant or allottee are properly regarded when he is obliged, if dissatisfied with an award for the taking of his land, to go to the district court of Kansas for redress, at the risk of incurring costs and expenses that may not only exceed the award originally made to him, but leave him in debt.

It is probable that there are other valid objections to this bill. I have only attempted to suggest enough to justify my action in disapproving it.

In constructing legislation of this description it should not be forgotten that the rights and interests of the Indians are important in every view and should be scrupulously protected.

GROVER CLEVELAND.

EXECUTIVE MANSION, *February 23, 1895.*
To the House of Representatives:

I return herewith without approval House bill No. 5740, entitled "An act incorporating the Society of American Florists."

No sufficient reason is apparent for the incorporation of this organization under Federal laws. There is not the least difficulty in the way of the accomplishment under State laws by the incorporators named in the bill of every purpose which can legitimately belong to their corporate existence. The creation of such a corporation by a special act of Congress establishes a vexatious and troublesome precedent.

There appears to be no limit in the bill to the value of the real and personal property which the proposed corporation may hold if acquired by donation or bequest. The limit of $50,000 applies only to property acquired by purchase.

A conclusive objection to the bill is found in the fact that it fails to carry out the purposes and objects of those interested in its passage. The promoters of the bill are florists, who undoubtedly seek to advance floriculture. The declared object of the proposed incorporation is, however, stated in the bill to be "the elevation and advancement of horticulture in all its branches, to increase and diffuse the knowledge thereof, and for kindred purposes in the interest of horticulture."

It is entirely clear that the interests of florists would be badly served by a corporation confined to the furtherance of garden culture.

GROVER CLEVELAND.

EXECUTIVE MANSION, *February 23, 1895.*
To the House of Representatives:

I return herewith without approval House bill No. 4658, entitled "An act granting a pension to Hiram R. Rhea and repealing an act approved March 3, 1871."

The person named in the title of this bill was pensioned under the provisions of a private act passed March 3, 1871. In 1892 a letter from the Commissioner of Pensions was presented to Congress exhibiting facts which established in a most satisfactory manner that the claim for pension allowed by said special act was a barefaced and impudent fraud, supported by deliberate perjury. This letter appears to be the moving cause of the passage of the bill now before me. Payment of pension under the fraudulent act has been suspended since January 28, 1893, and since that time no information has been received from the fraudulent pensioner.

The circumstances developed called for the repeal of the law of 1871 placing him upon the pension roll. This is accomplished in the second section of the bill under consideration, which section I would be glad to approve. This repeal, however, is accompanied by a provision in the first section of the bill directing the Secretary of the Interior to place upon the pension roll this identical fraudulent pensioner, under a certificate numbered precisely the same as that heretofore issued to him, "at a rate proportionate to the degree of disability from such gunshot wounds as may be shown to the satisfaction of said Secretary to have been received at the hands of Confederate soldiers or sympathizers while said Rhea was attempting to cooperate with the Union forces," etc.

Inasmuch as the letter of the Commissioner of Pensions to which reference has been made, and which forms part of the committee's report on this bill, is the basis of this repealing provision, and inasmuch as this letter furnishes evidence that the pensioner was when injured a very disreputable member of a band of armed rebels and was wounded by Union soldiers, I can not understand why the same bill which for this reason purges the pension rolls of his name should in the same breath undo this work and direct his name to be rewritten on the rolls.

If the facts before Congress justify the repeal of the law under which this man fraudulently received a pension for nearly twenty-two years, they certainly do not justify the provision directing his name to be put on the rolls again with a view to further examination of his case or for any other purpose.

GROVER CLEVELAND.

EXECUTIVE MANSION, *February 27, 1895.*

To the House of Representatives:

I return herewith without approval House bill No. 2051, entitled "An act to grant a pension to Eunice Putman."

This bill provides for a pension to the beneficiary therein named as the helpless daughter of John Putman, who served as a private in the War of the Rebellion from August 27, 1864, to June 2, 1865. In 1870, when the beneficiary was not 2 years old, her mother died, and her father married again in 1872. He applied for a pension in 1884, but died the same year. His claim was allowed, however, in 1891, and his pension which had accrued between the date of his application and his death was paid to his widow, Jeanette S. Putman. Immediately thereafter a pension was allowed the widow in her own right, dating from the soldier's death, in 1884, with $2 additional per month for each of the two minor children. The beneficiary was not included because she had reached the age of 16 years prior to her father's death.

The report of the committee to whom this bill was referred states that no claim for pension on account of the soldier's death has ever been filed in the Pension Bureau, and it seems that upon this theory it was proposed to pension the daughter. I do not suppose it was intended that a double pension should be allowed. In point of fact, the widow has already been pensioned, and no such pension allowance has been made for the minor children. There is no suggestion that the widow has died or remarried.

If this bill should become a law, two full pensions would be in force at the same time, one to the widow and another to the daughter, each predicated upon the services and death of the same soldier.

GROVER CLEVELAND.

EXECUTIVE MANSION, *February 27, 1895.*

To the House of Representatives:

I herewith return without approval House bill No. 6868, entitled "An act for the relief of Catherine Ott, widow of Joseph Ott."

An application by the beneficiary named in this bill, under the law of 1890, was rejected on the ground that her husband died in the service, and therefore had not been honorably discharged, as required by that law.

It appears that after he had served a number of years in a cavalry regiment, and having been once discharged for reenlistment, he was transferred to the Veteran Reserve Corps and was in that service at the time of his death.

In these circumstances the rejection of the beneficiary's claim on the ground stated is held, under present rulings of the Pension Bureau, to have been erroneous, and such claim can now be favorably adjudicated upon proof of continued widowhood of the applicant and the lack of other means of support than her daily labor.

If such proof is supplied, she would be entitled to a pension dating from July 14, 1890, which would be much more advantageous than the relief afforded by the bill herewith returned.

If the beneficiary can justly claim a pension dating from her application to the Pension Bureau in 1890, the benefits accruing to her therefrom should not be superseded by this special legislation, which allows relief only from the date of its enactment.

GROVER CLEVELAND.

EXECUTIVE MANSION, *February 28, 1895.*

To the House of Representatives:

I herewith return without approval House bill No. 8681, entitled "An act authorizing the Arkansas Northwestern Railway Company to construct and operate a railway through the Indian Territory, and for other purposes.''

The contemplated route of this railway, so far as it is disclosed in the bill, would run from a point in the southwestern corner of the State of Missouri, across the northeastern corner of the Indian Territory, to a point in the southeastern part of the State of Kansas. This route necessarily runs through the lands of the Cherokee Indians or through the small reservations of the Quapaws, the Peorias, the Ottawas, the Wyandottes, and the Senecas.

There is no provision in the bill requiring the consent of the Indians whose lands are to be thus traversed.

There is no provision requiring the entire line to be located and approved by the Secretary of the Interior before the work of building is commenced.

The bill provides for compensation to individual occupants or allottees by a process of appraisal by referees, with the right of appeal to the district court held at Fort Smith, in the State of Arkansas.

In the case of allotted land or land held in individual occupancy by the Indians great care should be exercised in interfering with their holdings. Their land is given them for cultivation and with a view of making them self-supporting and industrious citizens. If their land is invaded and cut up by railroads, the purpose of allotment is in danger of being defeated. Money compensation is of but little use to them, and no amount can compensate for the disturbance in the cultivation of their lands and their consequent discontent and discouragement.

These considerations, it seems to me, emphasize the necessity of the exact location of the entire line of the contemplated railroad and such control over it by the Secretary of the Interior as will enable him to avoid as much as possible interference with individual Indian occupants and other difficulties.

This supervision and regulation of the line can be done with much more safety and effectiveness in considering the entire line than it can be done in sections of 25 miles each, as is provided in the bill.

The United States circuit and district courts for the districts of Kansas and the district of Arkansas and such other courts as may be authorized by Congress are given concurrent jurisdiction of all controversies arising between the railway company and the nations and tribes of Indians through whose territory the railway shall be constructed, or between said company and the members of said nations or tribes, without reference to the amount in controversy, and the civil jurisdiction of said courts is extended within the limits of said Indian Territory, without distinction as to the citizenship of parties, so far as may be necessary to carry out the provisions of the act.

The requirement that an Indian shall be obliged to seek a distant court for the adjudication of his rights in his controversies, great and small, with this railway company would result in many cases to a denial of justice.

I am convinced of the growing necessity, in this period of change in our relations with the Indians, of caution and certainty in the grants given to railroads to pass through Indian lands and of the exercise of care in allowing interference with their occupation.

                                        GROVER CLEVELAND.

EXECUTIVE MANSION, *February 28, 1895.*

To the House of Representatives:

I herewith return without approval House bill No. 5624, entitled "An act to authorize the Oklahoma Central Railroad to construct and operate a railway through the Indian and Oklahoma Territories, and for other purposes."

The railroad proposed to be built under authority of this bill commences at a point in the Creek Nation called Sapulpa and runs through the Indian Territory to Oklahoma City, in Oklahoma, and thence through the Kiowa and Comanche Reservation to a point at or near the Red River, on the west line of said reservation.

There is no provision in this bill requiring the consent of the Indians through whose lands it is proposed to build the road.

The character and situation of these Indians are such as to make this consent important.

The first section gives the railroad company the right to build not only its line of road, but "such tracks, turn-outs, branches, sidings, and extensions as said company may deem it to their interest to construct."

If under an apparent grant to build a railroad the route of which is in a general way defined this company is to be allowed to build such branches and extensions as it may deem it to its interest to construct, the grant, I am sure, is more comprehensive than was intended by the Congress.

It seems to me that the entire line of the proposed railroad should be precisely located and subjected to the approval of the Secretary of the Interior before the work of construction is entered upon. This bill provides that it shall be approved in sections of 25 miles before construction on such sections shall be commenced.

Our relations to the Indians on reservations and their welfare and quiet are better preserved and protected when the entire line of road can be settled upon at one time and all uncertainty and doubt on the subject removed. The object sought by submitting the line to the supervision and determination of the Secretary of the Interior can be better and more intelligently accomplished if it is dealt with in its entirety instead of in sections.

                                        GROVER CLEVELAND.

PROCLAMATIONS.

BY THE PRESIDENT OF THE UNITED STATES OF AMERICA.

A PROCLAMATION.

The following provisions of the laws of the United States are hereby published for the information of all concerned:

Section 1956, Revised Statutes, chapter 3, Title XXIII, enacts that—

No person shall kill any otter, mink, marten, sable, or fur seal, or other fur-bearing animal within the limits of Alaska Territory or in the waters thereof; and every person guilty thereof shall for each offense be fined not less than $200 nor more than $1,000, or imprisoned not more than six months, or both; and all vessels, their tackle, apparel, furniture, and cargo, found engaged in violation of this section shall be forfeited; but the Secretary of the Treasury shall have power to authorize the killing of any such mink, marten, sable, or other fur-bearing animal, except fur seals, under such regulations as he may prescribe; and it shall be the duty of the Secretary to prevent the killing of any fur seal and to provide for the execution of the provisions of this section until it is otherwise provided by law, nor shall he grant any special privileges under this section.

Section 3 of the act entitled "An act to provide for the protection of the salmon fisheries of Alaska," approved March 2, 1889, provides—

SEC. 3. That section 1956 of the Revised Statutes of the United States is hereby declared to include and apply to all the dominion of the United States in the waters of Bering Sea; and it shall be the duty of the President at a timely season in each year to issue his proclamation, and cause the same to be published for one month in at least one newspaper (if any such there be) published at each United States port of entry on the Pacific coast, warning all persons against entering said waters for the purpose of violating the provisions of said section; and he shall also cause one or more vessels of the United States to diligently cruise said waters and arrest all persons and seize all vessels found to be or to have been engaged in any violation of the laws of the United States therein.

Now, therefore, I, Grover Cleveland, President of the United States, hereby warn all persons against entering the waters of Bering Sea within the dominion of the United States for the purpose of violating the provisions of said section 1956 of the Revised Statutes; and I hereby proclaim that all persons found to be or to have been engaged in any violation of the laws of the United States in said waters will be arrested, proceeded against, and punished as above provided.

In testimony whereof I have hereunto set my hand and caused the seal of the United States to be affixed.

[SEAL.] Done at the city of Washington, this 18th day of February, A. D. 1895, and of the Independence of the United States the one hundred and nineteenth.

GROVER CLEVELAND.

By the President:
    W. Q. GRESHAM,
        Secretary of State.

By the President of the United States of America.

A PROCLAMATION.

Whereas an act of Congress entitled "An act to postpone the enforcement of the act of August 19, 1890, entitled 'An act to adopt regulations for preventing collisions at sea,'" was approved February 23, 1895:

Now, therefore, I, Grover Cleveland, President of the United States of America, do hereby give notice that said act of August 19, 1890, as amended by the act of May 28, 1894, will not go into force on March 1, 1895, the date fixed in my proclamation of July 13, 1894,* but on such future date as may be designated in a proclamation of the President to be issued for that purpose.

In testimony whereof I have hereunto set my hand and caused the seal of the United States of America to be affixed.

[SEAL.]　　Done at the city of Washington, this 25th day of February, 1895, and of the Independence of the United States the one hundred and nineteenth.

GROVER CLEVELAND.

By the President:

W. Q. GRESHAM, *Secretary of State.*

By the President of the United States of America.

A PROCLAMATION.

Whereas, pursuant to section 1 of the act of Congress approved July 13, 1892, entitled "An act making appropriations for the current and contingent expenses of the Indian Department and for fulfilling treaty stipulations with various Indian tribes for the fiscal year ending June 30, 1893, and for other purposes," certain articles of agreement were made and concluded at the Yankton Indian Agency, S. Dak., on the 31st day of December, 1892, by and between the United States of America and the Yankton tribe of Sioux or Dakota Indians upon the Yankton Reservation, whereby the said Yankton tribe of Sioux or Dakota Indians, for the consideration therein mentioned, ceded, sold, relinquished, and conveyed to the United States all their claim, right, title, and interest in and to all the unallotted lands within the limits of the reservation set apart to said tribe by the first article of the treaty of April 19, 1858, between said tribe and the United States; and

Whereas it is further stipulated and agreed by article 8 that such part of the surplus lands by said agreement ceded and sold to the United States as may be occupied by the United States for agency, schools, and other purposes shall be reserved from sale to settlers until they are no longer required for such purposes, but all of the other lands so ceded and sold shall immediately after the ratification of the agreement by Congress be offered for

*See pp. 501–510.

sale through the proper land office, to be disposed of under the existing land laws of the United States to actual and *bona fide* settlers only; and

Whereas it is also stipulated and agreed by article 10 that any religious society or other organization shall have the right for two years from the date of the ratification of the said agreement within which to purchase the lands occupied by it under proper authority for religious or educational work among the Indians, at a valuation fixed by the Secretary of the Interior, which shall not be less than the average price paid to the Indians for the surplus lands; and

Whereas it is provided in the act of Congress accepting, ratifying, and confirming the said agreement, approved August 15, 1894, section 12 (Pamphlet Statutes, Fifty-third Congress, second session, pp. 314–319)—

That the lands by said agreement ceded to the United States shall upon proclamation by the President be opened to settlement, and shall be subject to disposal only under the homestead and town-site laws of the United States, excepting the sixteenth and thirty-sixth sections in each Congressional township, which shall be reserved for common-school purposes and be subject to the laws of the State of South Dakota: *Provided*, That each settler on said lands shall, in addition to the fees provided by law, pay to the United States for the land so taken by him the sum of $3.75 per acre, of which sum he shall pay 50 cents at the time of making his original entry and the balance before making final proof and receiving a certificate of final entry; but the rights of honorably discharged Union soldiers and sailors as defined and described in sections 2304 and 2305 of the Revised Statutes of the United States shall not be abridged except as to the sum to be paid as aforesaid.

That the Secretary of the Interior, upon proper plats and description being furnished, is hereby authorized to issue patents to Charles Picotte and Felix Brunot and W. T. Selwyn, United States interpreters, for not to exceed 1 acre of land each, so as to embrace their houses near the agency buildings upon said reservation, but not to embrace any buildings owned by the Government, upon the payment by each of said persons of the sum of $3.75.

That every person who shall sell or give away any intoxicating liquors or other intoxicants upon any of the lands by said agreement ceded, or upon any of the lands included in the Yankton Sioux Indian Reservation as created by the treaty of April 19, 1858, shall be punishable by imprisonment for not more than two years and by a fine of not more than $300.

And whereas all the terms, conditions, and considerations required by said agreement made with said tribes of Indians and by the laws relating thereto precedent to opening said lands to settlement have been, as I hereby declare, complied with:

Now, therefore, I, Grover Cleveland, President of the United States, by virtue of the power in me vested by the statutes hereinbefore mentioned, do hereby declare and make known that all of the lands acquired from the Yankton tribe of Sioux or Dakota Indians by the said agreement, saving and excepting the lands reserved in pursuance of the provisions of said agreement and the act of Congress ratifying the same, will, at and after the hour of 12 o'clock noon (central standard time) on the 21st day of May, 1895, and not before, be open to settlement under the terms of and subject to all the conditions, limitations, reservations, and restrictions contained in said agreement, the statutes hereinbefore specified, and the laws of the United States applicable thereto.

The lands to be so opened to settlement are for greater convenience particularly described in the accompanying schedule, entitled "Schedule of lands within the Yankton Reservation, S. Dak., to be opened to settlement by proclamation of the President," and which schedule is made a part hereof.

In witness whereof I have hereunto set my hand and caused the seal of the United States to be affixed.

[SEAL.]   Done at the city of Washington, this 16th day of May, A. D. 1895, and of the Independence of the United States the one hundred and nineteenth.

GROVER CLEVELAND.

By the President:

EDWIN F. UHL, *Acting Secretary of State.*

BY THE PRESIDENT OF THE UNITED STATES OF AMERICA.

A PROCLAMATION.

Whereas, pursuant to section 1 of the act of Congress approved July 13, 1892, entitled "An act making appropriations for the current and contingent expenses of the Indian Department and for fulfilling treaty stipulations with various Indian tribes for the fiscal year ending June 30, 1893, and for other purposes," certain articles of cession and agreement were made and concluded at the Siletz Agency, Oreg., on the 31st day of October, 1892, by and between the United States of America and the Alsea and other Indians on Siletz Reservation in Oregon, whereby said Alsea and other Indians, for the consideration therein mentioned, ceded and conveyed to the United States all their claim, right, title, and interest in and to all the unallotted lands within the limits of said reservation, except the five sections described in article 4 of the agreement, viz: Section 9, township 9 south, range 11 west of the Willamette meridian; and the west half of the west half of section 5, and the east half of section 6, and the east half of the west half of section 6, township 10 south, range 10 west; and the south half of section 8, and the north half of section 17, and section 16, township 9 south, range 9 west; and the east half of the northeast quarter and lot 3, section 20, and south half and south half of north half of section 21, township 8, range 10 west; and

Whereas it is further stipulated and agreed by article 6 that any religious society or other organization shall have the right for two years from the date of the ratification of this agreement within which to purchase the lands occupied by it with proper authority for religious or educational work among the Indians, at the rate of $2.50 per acre, the same to be conveyed to such society or organization by patent; and

Whereas it is provided in the act of Congress accepting, ratifying, and confirming said agreement, approved August 15, 1894 (Pamphlet Statutes, pp. 286–338), section 15, that—

The mineral lands shall be disposed of under the laws applicable thereto, and the balance of the land so ceded shall be disposed of until further provided by law under the town-site law and under the provisions of the homestead law: *Provided, however,* That each settler under and in accordance with the provisions of said homestead laws shall at the time of making his original entry pay the sum of 50 cents per acre in addition to the fees now required by law, and at the time of making final proof shall pay the further sum of $1 per acre, final proof to be made within five years from the date of entry; and three years' actual residence on the land shall be established by such evidence as is now required in homestead proofs as a prerequisite to title or patent.

And whereas it is provided—

That immediately after the passage of this act the Secretary of the Interior shall, under such regulations as he may prescribe, open said lands to settlement, after proclamation by the President and sixty days' notice.

And whereas all the terms, conditions, and considerations required by said agreement made with said tribe of Indians hereinbefore mentioned and the laws relating thereto precedent to opening said lands to settlement have been, as I hereby declare, provided for, paid, and complied with:

Now, therefore, I, Grover Cleveland, President of the United States, by virtue of the power in me vested by the statutes hereinbefore mentioned and by said agreement, do hereby declare and make known that all of the lands acquired from the Alsea and other Indians by said agreement will, at and after the hour of 12 o'clock noon (Pacific standard time) on the 25th day of July, 1895, and not before, be opened to settlement under the terms of and subject to all the conditions, limitations, reservations, and restrictions contained in said agreement, the statutes above specified, and the laws of the United States applicable thereto.

The lands to be so opened to settlement are for greater convenience particularly described in the accompanying schedule, entitled "Schedule of lands within the Siletz Indian Reservation, in Oregon, opened to settlement by proclamation of the President dated May 16, 1895," and which schedule is made a part hereof.

Warning is hereby given that no person entering upon and occupying said lands before said hour of 12 o'clock noon of the 25th day of July, 1895, hereinbefore fixed, will ever be permitted to enter any of said lands or acquire any rights thereto, and that the officers of the United States will be required to strictly enforce this provision, which is authorized by the act of August 15, 1894, hereinbefore mentioned.

In witness whereof I have hereunto set my hand and caused the seal of the United States to be affixed.

[SEAL.]   Done at the city of Washington, this 16th day of May, A. D. 1895, and of the Independence of the United States the one hundred and nineteenth.

GROVER CLEVELAND.

By the President:

EDWIN F. UHL, *Acting Secretary of State.*

BY THE PRESIDENT OF THE UNITED STATES OF AMERICA.

A PROCLAMATION.

Whereas by a written agreement made on the 9th day of September, 1891, the Kickapoo Nation of Indians, in the Territory of Oklahoma, ceded, conveyed, transferred, and relinquished, forever and absolutely, without any reservation whatever, all their claim, title, and interest of every kind and character in and to the lands particularly described in article 1 of the agreement: *Provided*, That in said tract of country there shall be allotted to each and every member, native and adopted, of said Kickapoo tribe of Indians 80 acres of land, in the manner and under the conditions stated in said agreement, and that when the allotments of land shall have been made and approved by the Secretary of the Interior the title thereto shall be held in trust for the allottees respectively for the period of twenty-five years in the manner and to the extent provided for in the act of Congress approved February 8, 1887 (24 U. S. Statutes at Large, p. 388); and

Whereas it is further stipulated and agreed by article 6 of the agreement that wherever in this reservation any religious society or other organization is now occupying any portion of said reservation for religious or educational work among the Indians the land so occupied may be allotted and confirmed to such society or organization, not, however, to exceed 160 acres of land to any one society or organization, so long as the same shall be so occupied and used: and such land shall not be subject to homestead entry; and

Whereas it is provided in the act of Congress accepting, ratifying, and confirming the said agreement with the Kickapoo Indians, approved March 3, 1893 (27 U. S. Statutes at Large, pp. 557–563), section 3—

That whenever any of the lands acquired by this agreement shall by operation of law or proclamation of the President of the United States be open to settlement or entry they shall be disposed of (except sections 16 and 36 in each township thereof) to actual settlers only under the provisions of the homestead and town-site laws, except section 2301 of the Revised Statutes of the United States, which shall not apply: *Provided, however,* That each settler on said lands shall before making a final proof and receiving a certificate of entry pay to the United States for the land so taken by him, in addition to the fees provided by law and within five years from the date of the first original entry, the sum of $1.50 an acre, one-half of which shall be paid within two years; but the rights of honorably discharged Union soldiers and sailors as defined and described in sections 2304 and 2305 of the Revised Statutes of the United States shall not be abridged except as to the sum to be paid as aforesaid. Until said lands are opened to settlement by proclamation of the President of the United States no person shall be permitted to enter upon or occupy any of said lands, and any person violating this provision shall never be permitted to make entry of any of said lands or acquire any title thereto: *Provided*, That any person having attempted to but for any cause failed to acquire a title in fee under existing law, or who made entry under what is known as the commuted provision of the homestead law, shall be qualified to make homestead entry upon said lands.

And whereas allotments of land in severalty to said Kickapoo Indians have been made and approved in accordance with law and the provisions of the before-mentioned agreement with them; and

Whereas it is provided by the act of Congress for the temporary government of Oklahoma, approved May 2, 1890, section 23 (26 U. S. Statutes at Large, p. 92), that there shall be reserved public highways 4 rods wide between each section of land in said Territory, the section lines being the center of said highways; but no deduction shall be made, where cash payments are provided for, in the amount to be paid for each quarter section of land by reason of such reservation; and

Whereas it is provided in the act of Congress approved February 10, 1894 (28 U. S. Statutes at Large, p. 37)—

That every homestead settler on the public lands on the left bank of the Deep Fork River in the former Iowa Reservation, in the Territory of Oklahoma, who entered less than 160 acres of land may enter under the homestead laws other lands adjoining the land embraced in his original entry when such additional lands become subject to entry, which additional entry shall not with the lands originally entered exceed in the aggregate 160 acres: *Provided*, That where such adjoining entry is made residence shall not be required upon the lands so entered, but the residence and cultivation by the settler upon and of the land embraced in his original entry shall be considered residence and cultivation for the same length of time upon the land embraced in his additional entry; but such lands so entered shall be paid for conformably to the terms of the act acquiring the same and opening it to homestead entry.

And whereas it is further provided in the act of Congress approved March 2, 1895 (28 U. S. Statutes at Large, p. 899)—

That any State or Territory entitled to indemnity school lands or entitled to select lands for educational purposes under existing law may select such lands within the boundaries of any Indian reservation in such State or Territory from the surplus lands thereof purchased by the United States, after allotments have been made to the Indians of such reservation and prior to the opening of such reservation to settlement.

And whereas all the terms, conditions, and considerations required by said agreement made with said tribes of Indians and by the laws relating thereto precedent to opening said lands to settlement have been, as I hereby declare, complied with:

Now, therefore, I, Grover Cleveland, President of the United States, by virtue of the power in me vested by the statutes hereinbefore mentioned and by other the laws of the United States and by the said agreement, do hereby declare and make known that all of said lands hereinbefore described, acquired from the Kickapoo Indians by the agreement aforesaid, will, at and after the hour of 12 o'clock noon (central standard time), Thursday, the 23d day of the month of May, A. D. 1895, and not before, be open to settlement under the terms of and subject to all the conditions, limitations, reservations, and restrictions contained in the said agreement, the statutes above specified, and the laws of the United States applicable thereto, saving and excepting such tracts as have been allotted, reserved, or selected under the laws herein referred to and such tracts as may be properly selected by the Territory of Oklahoma under and in accordance with the provisions of the act of March 2, 1895, hereinbefore quoted, prior to the time herein fixed for the opening of said lands to settlement.

The lands to be so opened to settlement are for greater convenience particularly described in the accompanying schedule, entitled "Schedule of lands within the Kickapoo Reservation, Oklahoma Territory, to be opened to settlement by proclamation of the President;" but notice is hereby given that should any of the lands described in the accompanying schedule be properly selected by the Territory of Oklahoma under and in accordance with the provisions of said act of Congress approved March 2, 1895, prior to the time herein fixed for the opening of said lands to settlement such tracts will not be subject to settlement or entry.

Notice, moreover, is hereby given that it is by law enacted that until said lands are opened to settlement by proclamation no person shall be permitted to enter upon or occupy the same, and any person violating this provision shall never be permitted to make entry of any of said lands or acquire any title thereto. The officers of the United States will be required to enforce this provision.

And further notice is hereby given that all of said lands lying north of the township line between townships 13 and 14 north are now attached to the Eastern land district, the office of which is at Guthrie, Oklahoma Territory, and all of said lands lying south of the township line between townships 13 and 14 north are now attached to the Oklahoma land district, the office of which is at Oklahoma, Oklahoma Territory.

In witness whereof I have hereunto set my hand and caused the seal of the United States to be affixed.

[SEAL.]   Done at the city of Washington, this 18th day of May, A. D. 1895, and of the Independence of the United States the one hundred and nineteenth.

GROVER CLEVELAND.

By the President:

EDWIN F. UHL,
Acting Secretary of State.

A PROCLAMATION

BY THE PRESIDENT OF THE UNITED STATES.

Walter Q. Gresham, Secretary of State of the United States, is dead.

The President in making this distressing announcement to his fellow-countrymen speaks from the depths of a personal affliction to remind them that they too have lost a pure and able public servant, a wise and patriotic guardian of all their rights and interests, a manly and loyal American, and a generous and lovable man.

As a suitable expression of national bereavement, I direct that the diplomatic representatives of the United States in all foreign countries display the flags over their embassies and legations at half-mast for ten days; that for a like period the flag of the United States be displayed at half-mast at all forts and military posts and at all naval stations and on all vessels of the United States.

I further order that on the day of the funeral the Executive Departments in the city of Washington be closed and that on all public buildings throughout the United States the national flag be displayed at half-mast.

Done at the city of Washington, this 28th day of May, A. D. 1895, and [SEAL.] of the Independence of the United States of America the one hundred and nineteenth.

GROVER CLEVELAND.

By the President:

EDWIN F. UHL,
Acting Secretary of State.

BY THE PRESIDENT OF THE UNITED STATES.

A PROCLAMATION.

Whereas the island of Cuba is now the seat of serious civil disturbances, accompanied by armed resistance to the authority of the established Government of Spain, a power with which the United States are and desire to remain on terms of peace and amity; and

Whereas the laws of the United States prohibit their citizens, as well as all others being within and subject to their jurisdiction, from taking part in such disturbances adversely to such established Government, by accepting or exercising commissions for warlike service against it, by enlistment or procuring others to enlist for such service, by fitting out or arming or procuring to be fitted out and armed ships of war for such service, by augmenting the force of any ship of war engaged in such service and arriving in a port of the United States, and by setting on foot or providing or preparing the means for military enterprises to be carried on from the United States against the territory of such Government:

Now, therefore, in recognition of the laws aforesaid and in discharge of the obligations of the United States toward a friendly power, and as a measure of precaution, and to the end that citizens of the United States and all others within their jurisdiction may be deterred from subjecting themselves to legal forfeitures and penalties, I, Grover Cleveland, President of the United States of America, do hereby admonish all such citizens and other persons to abstain from every violation of the laws hereinbefore referred to, and do hereby warn them that all violations of such laws will be rigorously prosecuted; and I do hereby enjoin upon all officers of the United States charged with the execution of said laws the utmost diligence in preventing violations thereof and in bringing to trial and punishment any offenders against the same.

In testimony whereof I have hereunto set my hand and caused the seal of the United States to be affixed.

[SEAL.]   Done at the city of Washington, this 12th day of June, A. D. 1895, and of the Independence of the United States of America the one hundred and nineteenth.

GROVER CLEVELAND.

By the President:

RICHARD OLNEY,
Secretary of State.

BY THE PRESIDENT OF THE UNITED STATES OF AMERICA.

A PROCLAMATION.

Whereas it is provided by section 13 of the act of Congress of March 3, 1891, entitled "An act to amend Title LX, chapter 3, of the Revised Statutes of the United States, relating to copyrights," that said act "shall only apply to a citizen or subject of a foreign state or nation when such foreign state or nation permits to citizens of the United States of America the benefit of copyright on substantially the same basis as its own citizens, or when such foreign state or nation is a party to an international agreement which provides for reciprocity in the granting of copyright, by the terms of which agreement the United States of America may at its pleasure become a party to such agreement;" and

Whereas it is also provided by said section that "the existence of either of the conditions aforesaid shall be determined by the President of the United States by proclamation made from time to time as the purposes of this act may require;" and

Whereas satisfactory official assurances have been given that in Spain and her provinces and colonial possessions the law permits to citizens of the United States the benefit of copyright on substantially the same basis as to the subjects of Spain:

Now, therefore, I, Grover Cleveland, President of the United States of America, do declare and proclaim that the first of the conditions specified in section 13 of the act of March 3, 1891, now exists and is fulfilled in respect to the subjects of Spain.

In testimony whereof I have hereunto set my hand and caused the seal of the United States to be affixed.

[SEAL.]   Done at the city of Washington, this 10th day of July, 1895, and of the Independence of the United States the one hundred and twentieth.

GROVER CLEVELAND.

By the President:

ALVEY A. ADEE,
Acting Secretary of State.

By the President of the United States.

A PROCLAMATION.

The constant goodness and forbearance of Almighty God which have been vouchsafed to the American people during the year which is just past call for their sincere acknowledgment and devout gratitude.

To the end, therefore, that we may with thankful hearts unite in extolling the loving care of our Heavenly Father, I, Grover Cleveland, President of the United States, do hereby appoint and set apart Thursday, the 28th day of the present month of November, as a day of thanksgiving and prayer to be kept and observed by all our people.

On that day let us forego our usual occupations and in our accustomed places of worship join in rendering thanks to the Giver of Every Good and Perfect Gift for the bounteous returns that have rewarded our labors in the fields and in the busy marts of trade, for the peace and order that have prevailed throughout the land, for our protection from pestilence and dire calamity, and for the other blessings that have been showered upon us from an open hand.

And with our thanksgiving let us humbly beseech the Lord to so incline the hearts of our people unto Him that He will not leave us nor forsake us as a nation, but will continue to us His mercy and protecting care, guiding us in the path of national prosperity and happiness, enduing us with rectitude and virtue, and keeping alive within us a patriotic love for the free institutions which have been given to us as our national heritage.

And let us also on the day of our thanksgiving especially remember the poor and needy, and by deeds of charity let us show the sincerity of our gratitude.

In witness whereof I have hereunto set my hand and caused the seal of the United States to be affixed.

[SEAL.]   Done at the city of Washington, this 4th day of November, A. D. 1895, and in the one hundred and twentieth year of the Independence of the United States.

GROVER CLEVELAND.

By the President:
RICHARD OLNEY,
Secretary of State.

By the President of the United States of America.

A PROCLAMATION.

Whereas section 17 of the act of August 28, 1894, entitled "An act to reduce taxation, to provide revenue for the Government, and for other purposes," prohibits "the importation of neat cattle and the hides of neat cattle from any foreign country into the United States;" and

Whereas it is provided by the act of Congress approved March 2, 1895, entitled "An act making appropriations for the Department of Agriculture for the fiscal year ending June 30, 1896"—

That whenever the Secretary of Agriculture shall certify to the President of the United States what countries or parts of countries are free from contagious or infectious diseases of domestic animals, and that neat cattle and hides can be imported from such countries without danger to the domestic animals of the United States, the President of the United States may suspend the prohibition of the importation of neat cattle and hides in the manner provided by law.

And whereas the Secretary of Agriculture has now certified to me that the countries of Norway, Sweden, Holland, Great Britain, Ireland, the Channel Islands, and the countries of North, Central, and South America, including Mexico, are so far free from contagious or infectious diseases of domestic animals that neat cattle may be imported from those countries into the United States, under the sanitary regulations prescribed by the Secretary of Agriculture, without danger to the domestic animals of the United States, and that so far as the countries above named, as well as all other countries from which hides are imported into the United States, are concerned, they are so far free from contagious or infectious diseases of domestic animals that hides of neat cattle can be imported from all parts of the world, under proper regulations prescribed by the Secretary of the Treasury, without danger to the domestic animals of the United States:

Now, therefore, I, Grover Cleveland, President of the United States, do hereby suspend the prohibition of the importation of neat cattle from the countries of Norway, Sweden, Holland, Great Britain, Ireland, the Channel Islands, and the countries of North, Central, and South America, including Mexico, and of the hides of neat cattle from all parts of the world; but all importations of neat cattle shall be made under the sanitary regulations prescribed by the Secretary of Agriculture and all importations of hides shall be made under proper regulations prescribed by the Secretary of the Treasury.

In testimony whereof I have hereunto set my hand and caused the seal of the United States to be affixed.

[SEAL.]　　Done at the city of Washington, this 8th day of November, 1895, and of the Independence of the United States of America the one hundred and twentieth.

By the President:　　　　　　　　　　GROVER CLEVELAND.

RICHARD OLNEY, *Secretary of State.*

BY THE PRESIDENT OF THE UNITED STATES OF AMERICA.

A PROCLAMATION.

Whereas, pursuant to section 5 of the act of Congress approved February 8, 1887 (24 U. S. Statutes at Large, p. 388), entitled "An act to provide for the allotment of lands in severalty to the Indians on the various reservations and to extend the protection of the laws of the United

States and the Territories over the Indians, and for other purposes,'' certain articles of cession and agreement were made and concluded at the Nez Percé Agency, Idaho, on the 1st day of May, 1893, by and between the United States of America and the Nez Percé Indians, whereby said Indians, for the consideration therein mentioned, ceded and conveyed to the United States all their claim, right, title, and interest to all the unallotted lands set apart as a home for their use and occupation by the second article of the treaty between said Indians and the United States concluded June 9, 1863 (14 U. S. Statutes at Large, p. 647), and included in the following boundaries, to wit:

Commencing at the northeast corner of Lake Wa-ha and running thence northerly to a point on the north bank of the Clearwater River 3 miles below the mouth of the Lapwai; thence down the north bank of the Clearwater to the mouth of the Hatwai Creek; thence due north to a point 7 miles distant; thence eastwardly to a point on the North Fork of the Clearwater 7 miles distant from its mouth; thence to a point on Oro Fino Creek 5 miles above its mouth; thence to a point on the North Fork of the South Fork of the Clearwater 1 mile above the bridge on the road leading to Elk City (so as to include all the Indian farms now within the forks); thence in a straight line westwardly to the place of beginning.

Saving and excepting the sixteenth and thirty-sixth sections of each Congressional township, which shall be reserved for common-school purposes and be subject to the laws of Idaho, and excepting the tracts described in articles 1 and 2 of the agreement, viz:

The said Nez Percé Indians hereby cede, sell, relinquish, and convey to the United States all their claim, right, title, and interest in and to all the unallotted lands within the limits of said reservation, saving and excepting the following-described tracts of lands, which are hereby retained by the said Indians, viz:

In township 34, range 4 west: Northeast quarter, north half and southeast of northwest quarter, northeast quarter of southwest quarter, north half and east half of southwest quarter, and the southeast quarter of southeast quarter, section 13; 440 acres.

In township 34, range 3 west: Sections 10, 15, 36; 1,920 acres.

In township 33, range 3 west: Section 1; northwest quarter of northeast quarter, north half of northwest quarter, section 12; 760 acres.

In township 35, range 2 west: South half of northeast quarter, northwest quarter, north half and southeast quarter of southwest quarter, southeast quarter, section 3; east half, east half of northwest quarter, southwest quarter, section 10; section 11; north half, north half of south half, section 21; east half of northeast quarter, section 20; sections 22, 27, 35; 4,200 acres.

In township 34, range 2 west: North half, southwest quarter, north half and southwest quarter and west half of southeast quarter of southeast quarter, section 13; section 14; north half, section 23; west half of east half and west half of northeast quarter, northwest quarter, north half of southwest quarter, west half of east half and northwest quarter and east half of southwest quarter of southeast quarter, section 24; section 29; 2,700 acres.

In township 33, range 2 west: West half and southeast quarter, section 6; sections 16, 22, 27; north half and north half of south half, section 34; 2,880 acres.

In township 34, range 1 west: West half, section 2; sections 3, 4; north half and southwest quarter, section 8; north half, section 9; north half and north half of southwest quarter, section 18; northwest quarter, section 17; 2,960 acres.

In township 37, range 1 east: Section 20; section 21, less south half of south half of southwest quarter of southeast quarter (10 acres); 1,270 acres.

In township 36, range 1 east: South half of sections 3, 4; sections 11, 12; 1,920 acres.

In township 36, range 2 east: Sections 16, 17, 18, 20; all of section 25 west of boundary line of reservation; sections 26, 27; 4,240 acres.

In township 35, range 2 east: North half of sections 16, 17; section 27; north half of section 34; 1,600 acres.

In township 34, range 2 east: East half and east half of west half of southeast quarter, section 24; 100 acres.

In township 34, range 3 east: South half of sections 19, 20; north half, north half of south half, southwest quarter and north half of southeast quarter of southwest quarter, north half of south half of southeast quarter, section 23; north half, north half and north half of southwest quarter and southeast quarter of southwest quarter, southeast quarter, section 24; north half and southeast quarter of northeast quarter, north half of northwest quarter, section 25; south half of northeast quarter of northeast quarter, section 26; section 29; northeast quarter of northeast quarter and south half, section 30; northwest quarter and north half of southwest quarter, section 31, northeast quarter, north half and southeast quarter of northwest quarter, section 32; northwest quarter, north half of southwest quarter, section 33; 3,700 acres.

In township 33, range 4 east: South half of southeast quarter, section 18; northeast quarter and fraction northeast of river in east half of northwest quarter, section 19; fraction west of boundary line of reservation in section 22; west half and southeast quarter of section 35; 1,440 acres.

In township 32, range 4 east: Fraction in west half of northeast quarter of southwest quarter, fraction in northwest quarter of southeast quarter, section 1; section 2; south half of section 6; west half and southeast quarter of northeast quarter of section 9; 1,410 acres.

In township 31, range 4 east: South half of northeast quarter, southeast quarter of northwest quarter, northeast quarter of southwest quarter, southeast quarter, section 17; northwest quarter, section 21; 480 acres.

Total, 32,020 acres.

ART. II. It is also stipulated and agreed that the place known as "the boom" on the Clearwater River, near the mouth of Lapwai Creek, shall be excepted from this cession and reserved for the common use of the tribe, with full right of access thereto, and that the tract of land adjoining said boom now occupied by James Moses shall be allotted to him in such manner as not to interfere with such right; also that there shall be reserved from said cession the land described as follows: "Commencing at a point at the margin of Clearwater River, on the south side thereof, which is 300 yards below where the middle thread of Lapwai Creek empties into said river; run thence up the margin of said Clearwater River at low-water mark 900 yards to a point; run thence south 250 yards to a point; thence southwesterly in a line to the southeast corner of a stone building partly finished as a church; thence west 300 yards to a point; thence from said point northerly in a straight line to the point of beginning; and also the adjoining tract of land lying southerly of said tract, on the south end thereof, commencing at the said corner of said church, and at the point 300 yards west thereof and run a line from each of said points, one of said lines running on the east side and the other on the west of said Lapwai Creek, along the foothills of each side of said creek, up the same sufficiently far so that a line being drawn east and west to intersect the aforesaid lines shall embrace within its boundaries, together with the first above-described tract of land, a sufficient quantity of land as to include and comprise 640 acres."

And excepting the land embraced in the William Craig donation claim, in township 35 north, range 3 west. (See case of Caldwell *vs.* Robinson, Federal Reporter, vol. 59, p. 653); and

Whereas it is further stipulated and agreed by article 6 of the agreement that any religious society or other organization now occupying under proper authority, for religious or educational work among the Indians, any of the lands ceded shall have the right for two years from the date of the ratification of this agreement within which to purchase the land so occupied, at the rate of $3 per acre, the same to be conveyed to such society or organization by patent in the usual form; and

Whereas it is further agreed by article 9 of the agreement that the lands by this agreement ceded, those retained, and those allotted to the said Nez Percé Indians shall be subject for a period of twenty-five years to all the laws of the United States prohibiting the introduction of intoxicants into the Indian country, and that the Nez Percé Indian allottees, whether under the care of an Indian agent or not, shall for a like period be subject to all the laws of the United States prohibiting the sale or other disposition of intoxicants to Indians; and

Whereas it is provided in the act of Congress accepting, ratifying, and confirming said agreement, approved August 15, 1894 (28 U. S. Statutes at Large, pp. 286–338), section 16—

That immediately after the issuance and receipt by the Indians of trust patents for the allotted lands, as provided for in said agreement, the lands so ceded, sold, relinquished, and conveyed to the United States shall be opened to settlement by proclamation of the President and shall be subject to disposal only under the homestead, town-site, stone and timber, and mining laws of the United States, excepting the sixteenth and thirty-sixth sections in each Congressional township, which shall be reserved for common-school purposes and be subject to the laws of Idaho: *Provided*, That each settler on said lands shall before making final proof and receiving a certificate of entry pay to the United States for the lands so taken by him, in addition to the fees provided by law, the sum of $3.75 per acre for agricultural lands, one-half of which shall be paid within three years from the date of original entry, and the sum of $5 per acre for stone, timber, and mineral lands, subject to the regulations prescribed by existing laws; but the rights of honorably discharged Union soldiers and sailors as defined and described in sections 2304 and 2305 of the Revised Statutes of the United States shall not be abridged except as to the sum to be paid as aforesaid.

And whereas all the terms, conditions, and considerations required by said agreement made with said tribe of Indians hereinbefore mentioned and the laws relating thereto precedent to opening said lands to settlement have been, as I hereby declare, provided for, paid, and complied with:

Now, therefore, I, Grover Cleveland, President of the United States, by virtue of the power in me vested by the statutes hereinbefore mentioned and by said agreement, do hereby declare and make known that all of the unallotted and unreserved lands acquired from the Nez Percé Indians by said agreement will, at and after the hour of 12 o'clock noon (Pacific standard time) on the 18th day of November, 1895, and not before, be opened to settlement under the terms of and subject to all the conditions, limitations, reservations, and restrictions contained in said agreement, the statutes above specified, and the laws of the United States applicable thereto.

The lands to be so opened to settlement are for greater convenience particularly described in the accompanying schedule, entitled "Schedule of lands within the Nez Percé Indian Reservation, Idaho, to be opened to settlement by proclamation of the President," and which schedule is made a part hereof.

In witness whereof I have hereunto set my hand and caused the seal of the United States to be affixed.

[SEAL.] Done at the city of Washington, this 8th day of November, A. D. 1895, and of the Independence of the United States the one hundred and twentieth.

GROVER CLEVELAND.

By the President:
RICHARD OLNEY,
Secretary of State.

EXECUTIVE ORDERS.

AMENDMENT OF CIVIL-SERVICE RULES.

Special Departmental Rule No. 1 is hereby amended by striking out the whole of the paragraph in section 3, Department of the Interior, relating to the Geological Survey and substituting in lieu thereof the following:

In the Geological Survey: Geologist, assistant geologist, paleontologist, assistant paleontologist, chief photographer, photographer, chief chemist, chemist, assistant chemist, chief engraver, engraver, assistant engraver, lithographic engraver, map printer, lithographic printer, assistant lithographic printer, map reviser, statistical experts temporarily employed.

Approved, December 4, 1894.

GROVER CLEVELAND.

AMENDMENT OF CIVIL-SERVICE RULES.

Departmental Rule VII is hereby amended by adding thereto the following section, to be numbered 9:

The Commission shall certify for transfer and reappointment to any classified non-excepted place in the departmental service, upon the requisition of the head of a Department, any person who at the time of making such requisition is holding an office outside the classified service in any Executive Department at Washington to which he was appointed from a classified place in the departmental service; and upon the requisition of any head of Department the Commission shall certify for reinstatement in the classified service of said Department any such officer who within one year next preceding the date of the requisition, by the abolition of his office or otherwise, has without delinquency or misconduct been separated from said office: *Provided*, That this section shall not authorize the reappointment to the classified service of any such officer or ex-officer who was appointed to his office from an excepted place, unless his appointment to such excepted place was by promotion from a nonexcepted place.

Approved, December 15, 1894. GROVER CLEVELAND.

AMENDMENTS OF CIVIL-SERVICE RULES.

EXECUTIVE MANSION, *January 3, 1895.*

Postal Rule II, clause 5, is amended by striking out paragraph (*e*) and relettering paragraph (*f*) as (*e*), so that as amended the clause will read:

5. Exceptions from examination in the classified postal service are hereby made as follows:

(*a*) Assistant postmaster, or the chief assistant to the postmaster, by whatever designation known.

(*b*) One secretary to the postmaster, when authorized by law and allowed by the Post-Office Department.

(*c*) Cashier, when authorized by law and employed under that roster title.

(*d*) Assistant cashier, when authorized by law and employed under that roster title.

(*e*) Printers and pressmen, when authorized by law and allowed by the Post-Office Department and employed as such.

Approved: GROVER CLEVELAND.

AMENDMENTS OF CIVIL-SERVICE RULES.

EXECUTIVE MANSION, *February 12, 1895.*

Departmental Rule VII, clause 8, is hereby amended to read as follows:

In case of the occurrence of a vacancy in any Department which the public interest requires shall be immediately filled, and which can not be so filled by certification from the eligible registers of the Commission, such vacancy may be filled by temporary appointment outside the civil service until a regular appointment can be made under the provisions of sections 1, 2, and 3 of this rule: *Provided,* That such temporary appointment shall in no case continue longer than ninety days, and shall expire by limitation at the end of that time: *And provided further,* That no person shall serve longer than the period herein prescribed in any one year under such temporary appointment.

The year limitation in regard to reappointment shall begin to run on the date of the original appointment.

Every such temporary appointment and the discontinuance of the same shall at once be reported to the Commission.

Postal Rule IV, clause 4, is hereby amended to read as follows:

4. In case of the occurrence of a vacancy in a position within the classified service of any post-office which the public interest requires shall be immediately filled, where there is no eligible remaining on the proper register, such vacancy may be filled by temporary appointment outside the civil service until a regular appointment can be made under the provisions of sections 1 and 2 of this rule: *Provided,* That such temporary appointment shall in no case continue longer than ninety days, and shall expire by limitation at the end of that time: *And provided further,* That no person shall serve more than ninety days in any one year under such temporary appointment.

The year limitation in regard to reappointment shall begin to run on the date of the original appointment.

Every such temporary appointment and also the discontinuance of the same shall at once be reported to the Commission.

Approved:

GROVER CLEVELAND.

AMENDMENTS OF CIVIL-SERVICE RULES.

GENERAL RULES.

General Rule II: Strike out the word "five" in line 1 and insert in lieu thereof the word "six," and add at the end of the rule a new clause, as follows:

6. The classified internal-revenue service.

General Rule III, section 5: Insert after the word "may" in line 1 the words "in its discretion," and after the word "appointment" in line 2 the following: "or an applicant who has been guilty of a crime or of infamous or notoriously disgraceful conduct." As amended the section will read:

5. The Commission may, in its discretion, refuse to examine an applicant who would be physically unable to perform the duties of the place to which he desires appointment or an applicant who has been guilty of a crime or of infamous or notoriously disgraceful conduct. The reason for any such action shall be entered on the minutes of the Commission.

Section 9: In line 1 strike out the word "departmental," and after the word "service" in the same line and in line 2 the words "and the classified railway mail service."

General Rule V: In line 2 change the order of words and insert other words so as to make the phrase amended read as follows: "and postmasters and customs and internal-revenue officers and custodians of public buildings."

General Rule IV, section 2: Insert after the word "may" in line 1 the words "in its discretion."

DEPARTMENTAL RULES.

Departmental Rule II: In section 1, line 2, after the word "such," insert the word "other" and strike out the words "supplementary and special." In section 2, line 2, strike out the words "supplementary and special" and insert in lieu thereof the word "other."

Departmental Rule IV: In section 1, after the semicolon following the word "age" in line 4, insert the following: "or for the position of messenger or assistant messenger who is not under 18 years of age, or for the position of page or messenger boy who is not under 14 nor over 18 years of age."

Departmental Rule V: In section 2, paragraph 6, line 1, after the word "postal," insert the words "internal-revenue."

Departmental Rule VI: In section 1, line 2, after the word "of," strike out the words "special and supplementary" and insert in lieu thereof the word "other." In section 4, line 7, after the words "clerk-copyist," insert the words "or the messenger and watchman." In section 5, line 3, after the word "printing," insert the words "or for page or messenger boy."

Departmental Rule VII: In section 3, at the beginning of line 2, before the word "register," insert the words "the messenger or the watchman." In the second paragraph of the same section, in line 2, after the word "assistant," insert the words "or page or messenger boy."

Departmental Rule VIII: In section 1 insert a clause, to be lettered (*c*), as follows:

(*c*) From a bureau of the Treasury Department in which business relating to the internal revenue is transacted to a classified internal-revenue district, and from such a district to such a bureau in the Treasury Department, upon requisition by the Secretary of the Treasury.

The remaining clauses of the section to be relettered (*d*) and (*e*), respectively. In section 2, line 2, strike out the letter "*d*" in parentheses and insert in lieu thereof the letter "*e*," and at the end of the section add the following proviso:

Provided, That a person may be transferred from a place in one Department to a place requiring no higher examination in another Department without examination.

Departmental Rule IX: Strike out the whole of section 1 and insert in lieu thereof the following:

1. Until promotion regulations have been applied to a Department under the provisions of section 6 of General Rule III promotions therein may be made as follows:

(*a*) Any person appointed from the appropriate register to the position of messenger, assistant messenger, watchman, or other subordinate position below the positions of clerk and copyist may at any time after absolute appointment, if not barred by age limitations, be transferred to any other of said subordinate positions, but shall not be promoted to the position of clerk or copyist or to any place the duties of which are clerical: *Provided*, That printers' assistants in the Bureau of Engraving and Printing, Treasury Department, shall only be eligible for transfer to the grade of operative in that Bureau.

Strike out sections 2, 3, and 5 and renumber section 4 as 2.

Approved, March 2, 1895.   GROVER CLEVELAND.

AMENDMENT OF CIVIL-SERVICE RULES.

EXECUTIVE MANSION, *March 18, 1895.*

Indian Rule IV is amended by adding at the end thereof a new section, to read as follows:

7. Graduates of Indian normal schools and of normal classes in Indian schools may be employed in the Indian-school service as assistant teachers or day-school

teachers without further examination: *Provided*, That certificates of satisfactory proficiency, of good moral character, and of physical soundness, signed by the proper officials, be transmitted at the time of appointment to the Civil Service Commission: *And provided further*, That until the 1st of July, 1896, graduates of the senior classes of Carlisle, Hampton, Lincoln Institute, Chilocco, Haskell Institute, and other Indian schools of equal grade may be included in the provisions of this rule. Such teachers shall become eligible for promotion to advanced positions on presentation to the Civil Service Commission of satisfactory certificates of efficiency and fidelity in their work and of a progressive spirit in their professional interests, signed by their immediate official superiors and by the superintendent of Indian schools, and forwarded with his approval by the Secretary of the Interior, the Commission reserving to itself the right to decide as to the satisfactoriness of such certificates.

Approved:

GROVER CLEVELAND.

EXECUTIVE MANSION, *March 20, 1895.*

The Executive order dated February 26, 1891,* establishing limits of punishment for enlisted men of the Army, under an act of Congress approved September 27, 1890, and which was published in General Orders, No. 21, 1891, Headquarters of the Army, is amended so as to prescribe as follows:

ARTICLE I.

In all cases of desertion the sentence may include dishonorable discharge and forfeiture of pay and allowances.

Subject to the modifications authorized in section 3 of this article, the limit of the term of confinement (at hard labor) for desertion shall be as follows:

SECTION 1. In case of surrender—

(*a*) When the deserter surrenders himself after an absence of not more than thirty days, one year.

(*b*) When the surrender is made after an absence of more than thirty days, eighteen months.

SEC. 2. In case of apprehension—

(*a*) When at the time of desertion the deserter shall not have been more than six months in the service, eighteen months.

(*b*) When he shall have been more than six months in the service, two and one-half years.

SEC. 3. The foregoing limitations are subject to modification under the following conditions:

(*a*) The punishment of a deserter may be increased by one year of confinement at hard labor in consideration of each previous conviction of desertion.

(*b*) The punishment for desertion when joined in by two or more soldiers in the execution of a conspiracy or for desertion in the presence of an outbreak of Indians or of any unlawful assemblage which the

*See pp. 167–172.

troops may be opposing shall not exceed dishonorable discharge, forfeiture of all pay and allowances, and confinement at hard labor for five years.

ARTICLE II.

Except as herein otherwise indicated punishments shall not exceed the limits prescribed in the following table:

Offenses.	Limits of punishment.
Under seventeenth article of war. Selling horse or arms, or both......	Dishonorable discharge, forfeiture of all pay and allowances, and confinement at hard labor for 3 years.
Selling accouterments..............	Four months' confinement at hard labor and forfeiture of $10 per month for the same period; for noncommissioned officer, reduction in addition thereto.
Selling clothing	Two months' confinement at hard labor and forfeiture of $10 per month for the same period; for noncommissioned officer, reduction in addition thereto.
Losing or spoiling horse or arms through neglect.	Four months' confinement at hard labor and forfeiture of $10 per month for the same period; for noncommissioned officer, reduction in addition thereto.
Losing or spoiling accouterments or clothing through neglect.	One month's confinement at hard labor and forfeiture of $10; for noncommissioned officer, reduction in addition thereto.
Under twentieth article of war. Behaving himself with disrespect to his commanding officer.	Six months' confinement at hard labor and forfeiture of $10 per month for the same period; for noncommissioned officer, reduction in addition thereto.
Under twenty-fourth article of war. Refusal to obey or using violence to officer or noncommissioned officer while quelling quarrels or disorders.	Dishonorable discharge, with forfeiture of all pay and allowances, and confinement at hard labor for 2 years.
Under thirty-first article of war. Lying out of quarters..............	Forfeiture of $2; corporal, $3; sergeant, $4.
Under thirty-second article of war. Absence without leave—*	
Less than 1 hour...............	Forfeiture of $1; corporal, $2; sergeant, $3; first sergeant or noncommissioned officer of higher grade, $4.
From 1 to 6 hours†.............	Forfeiture of $2; corporal, $3; sergeant, $4; first sergeant or noncommissioned officer of higher grade, $5.
From 6 to 12 hours.............	Forfeiture of $3; corporal, $4; sergeant, $6; first sergeant or noncommissioned officer of higher grade, $7.
From 12 to 24 hours............	Forfeiture of $5; corporal, $6; sergeant, $7; first sergeant or noncommissioned officer of higher grade, $10.
From 24 to 48 hours............	Forfeiture of $6 and 5 days' confinement at hard labor; for corporal, forfeiture of $8; sergeant, $10; first sergeant or noncommissioned officer of higher grade, $12, or, for all noncommissioned officers, reduction.
From 2 to 10 days..............	Forfeiture of $10 and 10 days' confinement at hard labor; for noncommissioned officer, reduction in addition thereto.
From 10 to 30 days.............	Forfeiture of $20 and 1 month's confinement at hard labor; for noncommissioned officer, reduction in addition thereto.

*Upon trial for desertion and conviction of absence without leave only, the court may, in addition to the limit prescribed for such absence, award a stoppage of the amount paid for apprehension.

†Including first and excluding last.

Offenses.	Limits of punishment.
Under thirty-second article of war—continued.	
Absence without leave—continued.	
From 30 to 90 days	Three months' confinement at hard labor and forfeiture of $10 per month for same period; for noncommissioned officer, reduction in addition thereto.
For 90 or more than 90 days	Dishonorable discharge and forfeiture of all pay and allowances and 6 months' confinement at hard labor.
Under thirty-third article of war.	
Failure to repair at the time fixed, etc., to the place of parade for—	
Reveille or retreat roll call and 11 p. m. inspection.	Forfeiture of $1; corporal, $2; sergeant, $3; first sergeant, $4.
Guard detail	Forfeiture of $5; corporal, $8; sergeant, $10.
Fatigue detail...................	
Dress parade....................	
The weekly inspection	
Target practice	Forfeiture of $2; corporal, $3; sergeant, $5.
Drill	
Guard mounting (by musician).	
Stable duty...................	
Under thirty-eighth article of war.	
Drunkenness on—	
Guard	Six months' confinement at hard labor and forfeiture of $10 per month for the same period; for noncommissioned officer, reduction in addition thereto.
Duty as company cook.........	Forfeiture of $20.
Extra or special duty	
At drill........................	
At target practice..............	
At parade	Forfeiture of $12; for noncommissioned officer, reduction and forfeiture of $20.
At inspection	
At inspection of company guard detail..............	
At stable duty.................	
Under fortieth article of war.	
Quitting guard....................	Six months' confinement at hard labor and forfeiture of $10 per month for the same period; for noncommissioned officer, reduction in addition thereto.
Under fifty-first article of war.	
Persuading soldiers to desert.......	Dishonorable discharge, forfeiture of all pay and allowances, and 1 year's confinement at hard labor.
Under sixtieth article of war	Dishonorable discharge, forfeiture of all pay and allowances, and 4 years' confinement at hard labor.
Under sixty-second article of war.	
Manslaughter......................	Dishonorable discharge, forfeiture of all pay and allowances, and 10 years' confinement at hard labor.
Assault with intent to kill.........	Dishonorable discharge, forfeiture of all pay and allowances, and 10 years' confinement at hard labor.
Burglary	Dishonorable discharge, forfeiture of all pay and allowances, and 5 years' confinement at hard labor.
Forgery	Dishonorable discharge, forfeiture of all pay and allowances, and 4 years' confinement at hard labor.
Perjury	Dishonorable discharge, forfeiture of all pay and allowances, and 4 years' confinement at hard labor.

Offenses.	Limits of punishment.
Under sixty-second article of war—continued.	
False swearing	Dishonorable discharge, forfeiture of all pay and allowances, and 2 years' confinement at hard labor.
Robbery...........................	Dishonorable discharge, forfeiture of all pay and allowances, and 6 years' confinement at hard labor.
Larceny or embezzlement of property of the value of—*	
More than $100.................	Dishonorable discharge, forfeiture of all pay and allowances, and 4 years' confinement at hard labor.
$100 or less and more than $50..	Dishonorable discharge, forfeiture of all pay and allowances, and 3 years' confinement at hard labor.
$50 or less and more than $20 ...	Dishonorable discharge, forfeiture of all pay and allowances, and 2 years' confinement at hard labor.
$20 or less	Dishonorable discharge, forfeiture of all pay and allowances, and 1 year's confinement at hard labor.
Fraudulent enlistment procured by false representation or concealment of a fact in regard to a prior enlistment or discharge or in regard to conviction of a civil or military crime.	Dishonorable discharge, forfeiture of all pay and allowances, and confinement at hard labor for 1 year.
Fraudulent enlistment, other cases of.	Dishonorable discharge, forfeiture of all pay and allowances, and confinement at hard labor for 6 months.
Disobedience of orders, involving willful defiance of the authority of a noncommissioned officer in the execution of his office.	Six months' confinement at hard labor and forfeiture of $10 per month for the same period; for noncommissioned officer, reduction in addition thereto.
Using threatening or insulting language or behaving in an insubordinate manner to a noncommissioned officer while in the execution of his office.	One month's confinement at hard labor and forfeiture of $10; for noncommissioned officer, reduction in addition thereto.
Absence from fatigue duty	Forfeiture of $4; corporal, $5; sergeant, $6.
Absence from extra or special duty.	Forfeiture of $4; corporal, $5; sergeant, $6.
Absence from duty as company or hospital cook.	Forfeiture of $10.
Introducing liquor into post or camp in violation of standing orders.	Forfeiture of $3; for noncommissioned officer, reduction and forfeiture of $5.
Drunkenness at post or in quarters.	Forfeiture of $3; for noncommissioned officer, reduction and forfeiture of $5.
Drunkenness and disorderly conduct, causing the offender's arrest and conviction by civil authorities at a place within 10 miles of his station.	Forfeiture of $10 and 7 days' confinement at hard labor; for noncommissioned officer, reduction and forfeiture of $12.
Noisy or disorderly conduct in quarters.	Forfeiture of $4; corporal, $7; sergeant, $10.
Abuse by noncommissioned officer of his authority over an inferior.	Reduction, 3 months' confinement at hard labor, and forfeiture of $10 per month for the same period.
Noncommissioned officer encouraging gambling.	Reduction and forfeiture of $5.
Noncommissioned officer making false report.	Reduction, forfeiture of $8, and 10 days' confinement at hard labor.
Sentinel allowing a prisoner under his charge to escape through neglect.	Six months' confinement at hard labor and forfeiture of $10 per month for the same period.
Sentinel willfully suffering prisoner under his charge to escape.	Dishonorable discharge, forfeiture of all pay and allowances, and 1 year's confinement at hard labor.

*In specifications to charges of larceny or embezzlement the value of the property shall be stated.

Offenses.	Limits of punishment.
Under sixty-second article of war—continued.	
Sentinel allowing a prisoner under his charge to obtain liquor.	Two months' confinement at hard labor and forfeiture of $10 per month for the same period.
Sentinel or member of guard drinking liquor with prisoners.	Two months' confinement at hard labor and forfeiture of $10 per month for the same period.
Disrespect or affront to a sentinel..	Two months' confinement at hard labor and forfeiture of $10 per month for the same period; for noncommissioned officer, reduction in addition thereto.
Resisting or disobeying sentinel in lawful execution of his duty.	Six months' confinement at hard labor and forfeiture of $10 per month for the same period; for noncommissioned officer, reduction in addition thereto.
Lewd or indecent exposure of person.	Three months' confinement at hard labor and forfeiture of $10 per month for the same period; for noncommissioned officer, reduction in addition thereto.

ARTICLE III.

SECTION 1. When a soldier shall be convicted of an offense the punishment for which, as authorized by Article II of this order or the custom of the service, does not exceed that which an inferior court-martial may award, the punishment so authorized may be increased by one-half for every previous conviction of one or more offenses within eighteen months preceding the trial and during the current enlistment: *Provided,* That the increase of punishment for five or more previous convictions shall not exceed that thus authorized when there are four previous convictions, and that when one or more of such five or more previous convictions shall have been by general court-martial or when such convictions shall have occurred within one year preceding the trial the limit of punishment shall be dishonorable discharge, forfeiture of all pay and allowances, and confinement at hard labor for three months.

When the conviction is of an offense punishable under Article II of this order or the custom of the service with a greater punishment than an inferior court-martial can award, but not punishable with dishonorable discharge, the sentence may on proof of five or more previous convictions within eighteen months and during the current enlistment impose dishonorable discharge and forfeiture of all pay and allowances in addition to the authorized confinement, and when this confinement is less than three months it may be increased to three months.

When a noncommissioned officer is convicted of an offense not punishable with reduction, he may, if he shall have been convicted of a military offense within a year and during the current enlistment, be sentenced to reduction in addition to the punishment already authorized.

SEC. 2. In every case when an offense on trial before a court-martial is of a character admitting of the introduction of evidence of previous convictions and the accused is convicted the court, after determining its findings, will be opened for the purpose of ascertaining whether there is such evidence, and, if so, of hearing it. These convictions must be proved by the records of previous trials or by duly authenticated orders promulgating the same, except in the cases of conviction by summary court, when a duly authenticated copy of the record of said court shall be deemed sufficient proof. Charges forwarded to the authority ordering a general court-martial or submitted to a summary, garrison, or regimental court must be accompanied by the proper evidence of such previous convictions as may have to be considered in determining upon a sentence.

ARTICLE IV.

When a soldier shall on one arraignment be convicted of two or more offenses none of which is punishable under Article II of this order or the custom of the service with dishonorable discharge, but the aggregate term of confinement for which may exceed six months, dishonorable discharge with forfeiture of pay and allowances may be awarded in addition to the authorized confinement.

ARTICLE V.

This order prescribes the *maximum* limit of punishment for the offenses named, and this limit is intended for those cases in which the severest punishment should be awarded. In other cases the punishment should be graded down according to the extenuating circumstances. Offenses not herein provided for remain punishable as authorized by the Articles of War and the custom of the service.

ARTICLE VI.

Summary courts are subject to the restrictions named in the eighty-third article of war. Soldiers against whom charges may be preferred for trial by summary court shall not be confined in the guardhouse, but shall be placed in arrest in quarters before and during trial and while awaiting sentence, except when in particular cases restraint may be necessary.

ARTICLE VII.

The following substitutions for punishments named in Article II of this order are authorized at the discretion of the court:

Two days' confinement at hard labor for $1 forfeiture; one day's solitary confinement on bread and water diet for two days' confinement at hard labor or for $1 forfeiture: *Provided*, That a noncommissioned officer not sentenced to reduction shall not be subject to confinement: *And provided*, That solitary confinement shall not exceed fourteen days at one time nor be repeated until fourteen days have elapsed, and shall not exceed eighty-four days in one year. Whenever the limit herein prescribed for an offense or offenses may be brought within the punishing power of inferior courts-martial, as defined by the eighty-third article of war, by substitution of punishment under the provisions of this article, the said courts have jurisdiction of such offense or offenses.

ARTICLE VIII.

Noncommissioned officers above the rank of corporal shall not, if they object thereto, be brought to trial before regimental, garrison, or summary courts-martial without the authority of the officer competent to order their trial by general court-martial, nor shall sergeants of the post noncommissioned staff or hospital stewards be reduced, but they may be dishonorably discharged whenever reduction is included in the limit of punishment.

GROVER CLEVELAND.

AMENDMENT OF CIVIL-SERVICE RULES.

EXECUTIVE MANSION, *April 15, 1895.*

Whereas on November 2, 1894, Departmental Rule II, section 4, Customs Rule II, section 6, Postal Rule II, section 6, Railway Mail Rule II, section 6, were amended to declare that no person appointed to a place under any exception to examination should be transferred from such place to another place not also excepted from examination; and

Whereas it was not my intention that these several amendments should be retroactive in their effect:

I therefore direct that the word "hereafter" be inserted after the word "person" in the first line of each of said sections as of the date of said amendments, viz, November 2, 1894.

Approved:

GROVER CLEVELAND.

CIVIL SERVICE.—INTERNAL-REVENUE RULES.

ADOPTING AND PROMULGATING ORDER.

MAY 7, 1895.

In the exercise of the power vested in him by the Constitution, by the seventeen hundred and fifty-third section of the Revised Statutes, and the act entitled "An act to regulate and improve the civil service of the United States," approved January 16, 1883, the President hereby makes and promulgates the following rules concerning the classified internal-revenue service, to be known as the Internal-Revenue Rules:

INTERNAL-REVENUE RULE I.

The classified internal-revenue service shall include all the clerks, storekeepers, storekeepers and gaugers, and gaugers classified under the provisions of section 6 of the act to regulate and improve the civil service of the United States, approved January 16, 1883.

INTERNAL-REVENUE RULE II.

1. To test fitness for admission to the classified internal-revenue service, examinations of a practical character shall be provided on such subjects as the Commission may direct.

2. The following age limitations shall apply to applicants for the classified internal-revenue service: For clerk, not under 18 years of age; for storekeepers, storekeepers and gaugers, and for gaugers, not under 21 years of age.

3. Blank forms of application shall be furnished by the secretaries of the several internal-revenue boards of examiners to any person desiring to be examined who applies therefor in person or by letter in his own handwriting.

4. The date of reception of each application and also of its approval by the board shall be noted on the application paper.

5. Exceptions from examination in the classified internal-revenue service are hereby made as follows:

6. No person appointed to a place excepted from examination by any internal-revenue rule shall be transferred from such place to another place not also excepted from examination.

INTERNAL-REVENUE RULE III.

1. The Commission shall appoint in each classified internal-revenue district a board of examiners, which shall—

(*a*) Conduct all examinations for admission to or promotion in the classified service of the internal-revenue district in which the board is located.

(*b*) Conduct such other examinations as the Commission may direct.

(*c*) Mark the papers of such examinations as the Commission may direct.

2. The papers of every examination shall be marked under the direction of the Commission, and each competitor shall be graded on a scale of 100, according to general average determined by the marks of the examiners.

3. Immediately after the general average shall have been ascertained each competitor shall be notified that he has passed or has failed to pass.

4. No competitor who has failed to pass an examination and no eligible during the period of his eligibility shall be allowed reexamination unless he shall furnish satisfactory evidence to the Commission that at the time of his examination he was, because of illness or other good cause, incapable of doing himself justice; and his rating on such reexamination, if an eligible, shall cancel and be a substitute for his rating on his previous examination.

5. All competitors whose claim to preference under section 1754, Revised Statutes, has been allowed by the Commission who attain a general average of 65 per cent or over, and all other competitors who attain a general average of 70 per cent or over, shall be eligible for appointment to the place for which they were examined, and the names of all the eligibles shall be entered in the order of grade on the proper register of eligibles.

6. When two or more eligibles are of the same grade, preference in certification shall be determined by the order in which their application papers were filed.

7. The period of eligibility shall be one year from the date on which the name of the eligible is entered on the register.

INTERNAL-REVENUE RULE IV.

1. All vacancies, unless filled by promotion, reduction, transfer, or reappointment, shall be filled in the following manner:

(*a*) When a vacancy occurs in any district, the collector thereof shall report the fact to the Commissioner of Internal Revenue, stating the class in which the vacancy occurs and whether in his judgment the place should be filled. If the Commissioner decides that the good of the public service requires that it be filled, he shall request the secretary of the board of examiners of that district to certify to him the names of persons eligible to the vacant place.

(*b*) If fitness for the vacant place is tested by competitive examination, the names of the three eligibles highest in grade on the proper register who have not been three times certified shall be certified; but if the request indicates the sex of the eligibles desired the three highest in grade of that sex shall be certified: *Provided*, That the eligibles upon any register who have been allowed preference under section 1754 of the Revised Statutes shall be certified, according to their grade, before all other eligibles thereon: *Provided further*, That no certification for an appointment shall be made under this clause while there are persons in the district in which any vacancy may exist, who have been removed from the service in that district on account of a reduction of the force or otherwise, who are eligible for reinstatement under Internal-Revenue Rule VII, and who are willing to reenter the service by reinstatement. Every collector of internal revenue shall keep a list of all such persons in his office, and said persons shall have preference for reinstatement to the service in the order of their separation therefrom.

(*c*) No eligible shall be certified more than three times.

2. Of the three names certified to him the Commissioner of Internal Revenue shall select one, and may select more than one if more than one vacancy exists at the time the certification is made. If the vacancy is in the class of clerk, the Commissioner shall certify the name of the person selected by him to the collector of the district in which the vacancy occurs and the collector shall make the appointment. If the vacancy is in the storekeepers', gaugers', or storekeepers and gaugers' class, the Commissioner of Internal Revenue shall certify the name to the Secretary of the Treasury with his recommendation that the person whose name is thus certified be appointed: *Provided*, That if any objection is made under section 3 of General Rule IV to any eligible certified, and is sustained by the Commission, another eligible shall be certified in the place of the one objected to.

3. Each person thus selected for appointment shall be notified, and upon indicating his acceptance shall be appointed for a probationary period of six months, at the end of which period, if his conduct and capacity be satisfactory to the appointing officer, he shall receive absolute appointment; but if his conduct and capacity be not satisfactory to said officer he shall be so notified, and this notification shall be his discharge from the service: *Provided*, That any probationer may be discharged during probation for misconduct or evident unfitness or incapacity.

4. The Commissioner of Internal Revenue shall require the collector under whom a probationer is serving to carefully observe and report in writing upon the services rendered by and the character and qualifications of such probationer as to punctuality, industry, habits, ability, and adaptability. These reports shall be preserved on file in the office of the collector, and copies thereof shall be filed with the Commissioner of Internal Revenue for such disposition as the Secretary of the Treasury may direct. The Civil Service Commission may prescribe the form and manner in which these reports shall be made.

5. In case of the occurrence of a vacancy in the classified service of any internal-revenue collection district which the public interest requires shall be immediately filled, and there is no eligible entitled to reinstatement under section 1, clause (*b*), of this rule or remaining on the proper register, such vacancy, if in the class of storekeeper, storekeeper and gauger, or clerk, may be filled without examination and certification by a temporary designation by the collector of the district of some suitable person to perform the duties of the position until a regular appointment can be made under the provisions of sections 1, 2, and 3 of this rule: *Provided*, That service under such temporary designation shall in no case continue longer than six months, and shall expire by limitation at the end of that time: *And provided further*, That no person shall serve more than six months in any one year under such temporary designation, the year limitation in regard to such designation to begin to run on the date thereof.

Every such temporary designation and also the discontinuance of the same shall at once be reported to the Commission.

INTERNAL-REVENUE RULE V.

Until promotion regulations shall have been applied to a classified internal-revenue collection district promotions therein may be made upon any test of fitness determined upon by the Commissioner of Internal Revenue, with the approval of the

Commission: *Provided*, That no employee shall be promoted to any grade he could not enter by appointment under the minimum age limitation applied thereto by section 2 of Internal-Revenue Rule II.

INTERNAL-REVENUE RULE VI.

Transfers may be made as follows:

From one classified internal-revenue collection district to another, from any classified internal-revenue collection district to a bureau in the Treasury Department in which business relating to the internal revenue is transacted, and from such a bureau in the Treasury Department to such a district, upon the requisition of the Secretary of the Treasury and the certification of the Commission, the appointment upon such transfer to be made by the Secretary of the Treasury, upon the recommendation of the Commissioner of Internal Revenue, if the place to be filled by such transfer is that of storekeeper, storekeeper and gauger, or gauger: *Provided*, That no person shall be transferred as herein authorized who is not within the age limitations prescribed by the civil-service rules for the place to which he is to be transferred and who has not been absolutely appointed, or, if appointed without civil-service examination, who has not served six months continuously in the district or bureau from which he is to be transferred.

INTERNAL-REVENUE RULE VII.

Upon the requisition of the Commissioner of Internal Revenue the secretary of the board of examiners for his district shall certify for reinstatement in a grade requiring no higher examination than the one in which he was formerly employed any person who within one year next preceding the date of the requisition has through no delinquency or misconduct been separated from the classified service of said district: *Provided*, That certification may be made, subject to the other conditions of this rule, for the reinstatement of any person who served in the military or naval service of the United States in the late War of the Rebellion and was honorably discharged therefrom, or the widow of any such person, without regard to the length of time he or she has been separated from the service.

INTERNAL-REVENUE RULE VIII.

Each collector in the classified internal-revenue service shall report to the board of examiners —

(*a*) Every probational and every absolute appointment and every appointment to an excepted or to an unclassified place in the internal-revenue service under him.

(*b*) Every refusal to make an absolute appointment and the reason therefor, and every refusal to accept an appointment.

(*c*) Every separation from the internal-revenue service under him and the cause of such separation, whether death, resignation, or dismissal.

(*d*) Every restoration to the internal-revenue service under him.

GROVER CLEVELAND.

AMENDMENT OF CUSTOMS RULE IV.

Customs Rule IV is hereby amended by adding thereto the following section, to be numbered 5:

5. In case of the occurrence of a vacancy in the classified service of any customs district which the public interest requires shall be immediately filled, and there is no eligible remaining on the proper register, such vacancy may be filled by temporary appointment without examination and certification until a regular appointment can be made under the provisions of sections 1 and 2 of this rule: *Provided*, That

such temporary appointment shall in no case continue longer than ninety days and shall expire by limitation at the end of that time: *And provided further,* That no person shall serve more than ninety days in any one year under such temporary appointment, the year limitation in regard to such appointment to begin to run on the date thereof.

Every such temporary appointment and also the discontinuance of the same shall at once be reported to the Commission.

Approved, May 18, 1895.

GROVER CLEVELAND.

AMENDMENT OF CIVIL-SERVICE RULES.

EXECUTIVE MANSION,
Washington, D. C., May 16, 1895.

Special Departmental Rule No. 1 is hereby amended as follows:

Include among the places excepted from examination therein the following:

6. In the Department of Agriculture: The chief of the dairy division.

Approved, May 24, 1895.

GROVER CLEVELAND, *President.*

CIVIL SERVICE.—EXECUTIVE ORDER REVOKED.

EXECUTIVE MANSION, *May 24, 1895.*

The Executive order heretofore issued under General Rule III, section 2, clause (*c*), that provides for the appointment of four clerks in the division of accounts and disbursements in the Department of Agriculture by noncompetitive examination is hereby revoked, and hereafter these positions will be filled through competitive examination.

Approved:

GROVER CLEVELAND.

CIVIL SERVICE.—AMENDMENT OF CLASSIFICATION.

EXECUTIVE MANSION, *May 24, 1895.*

In pursuance of the authority contained in the third paragraph of section 6 of the act entitled "An act to regulate and improve the civil service of the United States," approved January 16, 1883, the Secretary of Agriculture is hereby directed to amend the classification of the Department of Agriculture so as to include among the classes covered thereby clerks, microscopists, assistant microscopists, stock examiners, taggers, agents, and all other employees, except temporary laborers, in the Bureau of Animal Industry of the Department of Agriculture outside of Washington, D. C., all State statistical agents of the Department of Agriculture outside of Washington, D. C., and all messengers in the Weather Bureau of the Department of Agriculture outside of Washington, D. C. The classification when so amended shall take effect on July 1, 1895.

Approved:

GROVER CLEVELAND.

AMENDMENT OF CIVIL-SERVICE RULES.

EXECUTIVE MANSION, *May 24, 1895.*

Special Departmental Rule No. 1, section 6, is hereby amended by striking out the whole of said section and substituting therefor the following:

6. In the Department of Agriculture, in the office of the Secretary: Private secretary to the chief clerk, and wood engravers; scientific or professional experts employed for a period of not exceeding six months outside of Washington, D. C., in investigations specially authorized by Congress, but no such expert shall be reappointed as an expert unless the United States Civil Service Commission shall certify that such person has passed a suitable examination and is eligible for such appointment. This exception does not include any person to be employed in that Department in Washington, D. C., nor any person whose duties are not scientific or professional or who is not expert in the particular line of scientific or professional inquiry in which such person is to be employed.

Approved:

GROVER CLEVELAND.

AMENDMENT OF CIVIL-SERVICE RULES.

EXECUTIVE MANSION, *May 24, 1895.*

Special Departmental Rule No. 1, clause 3, is hereby amended by adding to the places excepted from examination in the Department of the Interior the following:

In the Bureau of Education: Specialist in foreign educational systems and specialist in education as a preventive of pauperism and crime.

Approved:

GROVER CLEVELAND.

AMENDMENTS OF CIVIL-SERVICE RULES.

DEPARTMENTAL RULE II.

EXECUTIVE MANSION, *May 24, 1895.*

Section 3 is hereby amended as follows: At the end of clause (*b*) add the following: "nor the cashier, nor the two clerks employed as assistant disbursing clerks in the division of accounts and disbursements in the Department of Agriculture."

At the end of clause (*c*) add the following: "but not including the disbursing clerk in the division of accounts and disbursements in the Department of Agriculture."

At the end of clause (*e*) add the following: "except those of the Weather Bureau and the Bureau of Animal Industry, in the Department of Agriculture."

At the end of clause (*f*) add the following: "except all chiefs of division in the Department of Agriculture."

The section as amended will read:

3. Exceptions from examination in the classified departmental service are hereby made as follows:

(*a*) One private secretary or one confidential clerk of the head of each classified Department and of each Assistant Secretary thereof, and also of each head of bureau appointed by the President by and with the advice and consent of the Senate.

(*b*) Direct custodians of money for whose fidelity another officer is under official bond; but this exception shall not include any officer below the grade of assistant cashier or assistant teller, nor the cashier, nor the two clerks employed as assistant disbursing clerks in the division of accounts and disbursements in the Department of Agriculture.

(*c*) Disbursing officers who give bonds, but not including the disbursing clerk in the division of accounts and disbursements in the Department of Agriculture.

(*d*) Persons employed exclusively in the secret service of the Government.

(*e*) Chief clerks, except those of the Weather Bureau and of the Bureau of Animal Industry, in the Department of Agriculture.

(*f*) Chiefs of division, except all chiefs of division in the Department of Agriculture.

GROVER CLEVELAND.

EXECUTIVE MANSION, *May 28, 1895.*

To the Heads of the Executive Departments:

As a mark of respect to the memory of the Hon. Walter Q. Gresham, late Secretary of State, the President directs that the several Executive Departments and the Government Printing Office, in the city of Washington, be closed on Wednesday, the 29th day of May, 1895, the day of the funeral.

HENRY T. THURBER,
Private Secretary.

EXECUTIVE MANSION, *May 28, 1895.*

It is hereby ordered, That the several Executive Departments and the Government Printing Office be closed on Thursday, the 30th instant, to enable the employees to participate in the decoration of the graves of the soldiers and sailors who fell in defense of the Union during the War of the Rebellion.

GROVER CLEVELAND.

CIVIL SERVICE.—GOVERNMENT PRINTING OFFICE RULES.

ADOPTING AND PROMULGATING ORDER.

EXECUTIVE MANSION, *June 13, 1895.*

In the exercise of the power vested in him by the Constitution, by the seventeen hundred and fifty-third section of the Revised Statutes, and the act entitled "An act to regulate and improve the civil service of the United States," approved January 16, 1883, the President hereby makes and promulgates the following rules concerning the classified service of the Government Printing Office, to be known as the Government Printing Office Rules:

RULE I.

1. The classified service of the Government Printing Office shall include all persons employed in that office except those appointed by and with the advice and consent of the Senate and unskilled laborers or workmen.

2. The officers, clerks, and other employees of the Government Printing Office are hereby arranged in the following classes:

Class 1.—All persons receiving an annual salary of less than $720, or a compensation at the rate of less than $720 per annum.

Class 2.—All persons receiving an annual salary of $720 or more, or a compensation at the rate of $720 or more, but less than $840 per annum.

Class 3.—All persons receiving an annual salary of $840 or more, or a compensation at the rate of $840 or more, but less than $900 per annum.

Class 4.—All persons receiving an annual salary of $900 or more, or a compensation at the rate of $900 or more, but less than $1,000 per annum.

Class 5.—All persons receiving an annual salary of $1,000 or more, or a compensation at the rate of $1,000 or more, but less than $1,200 per annum.

Class 6.—All persons receiving an annual salary of $1,200 or more, or a compensation at the rate of $1,200 or more, but less than $1,400 per annum.

Class 7.—All persons receiving an annual salary of $1,400 or more, or a compensation at the rate of $1,400 or more, but less than $1,600 per annum.

Class 8.—All persons receiving an annual salary of $1,600 or more, or a compensation at the rate of $1,600 or more, but less than $1,800 per annum.

Class 9.—All persons receiving an annual salary of $1,800 or more, or a compensation at the rate of $1,800 or more, but less than $2,000 per annum.

Class 10.—All persons receiving an annual salary of $2,000 or more, or a compensation at the rate of $2,000 or more per annum.

RULE II.

1. To test fitness for admission to the classified service of the Government Printing Office, examinations of a practical character shall be provided by the Commission. If the trade or occupation is such that a competitive test can not be made, the Commission shall provide regulations for the registration of applicants without competitive tests.

2. Any male citizen of the United States not under 21 or over 45 years of age and any female citizen not under 18 or over 35 years of age may be examined for positions in the Government Printing Office.

3. No application for a position in the Government Printing Office which belongs to one of the recognized mechanical trades shall be received from any applicant who has not served at least five years at the particular trade to which the position for which he applies belongs, one year of which service must have been rendered as a journeyman.

4. Blank forms of application shall be furnished by the Commission, and the date of reception and also of approval by the Commission of each application shall be entered on the application paper.

RULE III.

1. The grade or standing of every competitor shall be determined under regulations made by the Commission, and each competitor shall be duly notified whether or not he is eligible for appointment.

2. No competitor who has failed to obtain an eligible standing shall be admitted

to another test within six months from the date of failure unless he shall furnish satisfactory evidence to the Commission that at the time of his examination he was unable to do himself justice because of illness or other good cause.

3. No eligible shall be admitted to a test during the period of his eligibility unless he shall furnish satisfactory evidence to the Commission that at the time of his examination he was unable to do himself justice because of illness or other good cause.

4. All competitors whose claims of preference under section 1754 of the Revised Statutes have been allowed by the Commission who attain a general average of 65 per cent or over, and all other competitors who attain a general average of 70 per cent or over, shall be eligible for appointment to the place for which they were examined. The names of all competitors thus rendered eligible shall be entered in the order of grade on the proper register of eligibles.

5. The Commission shall establish regulations for the order of certification of applicants who are registered without competitive examinations under the provisions of Rule II, paragraph 1.

6. When two or more eligibles are of the same grade, preference in certification shall be determined by the order in which the application papers are filed.

7. The period of eligibility to appointment shall be one year from the date on which the name of the eligible is entered on the register, unless otherwise determined by regulations by the Commission.

RULE IV.

1. All vacancies, unless filled by promotion, transfer, or reappointment, shall be filled in the following manner:

(*a*) The Public Printer shall, in form and manner to be prescribed by the Commission, request the certification to him of either males or females, or both, eligible to the vacant place.

(*b*) If fitness for the vacant place is tested by competitive examination, the Commission shall certify from the proper register the names of the three eligibles thereon, of the sex or sexes called for, having the highest averages, who have not been three times certified: *Provided*, That the eligibles upon any register who have been allowed preference under section 1754 of the Revised Statutes shall be certified according to their grade before all other eligibles thereon: *And provided further*, That if the vacancy is in a position for which a competitive examination can not be provided certification shall be made of the names of the first three eligibles on the register, of the sex or sexes called for, who have not been three times certified.

2. Of the three names certified to him the Public Printer shall select one, and if at the time of making this selection there are more vacancies than one he may select more than one: *Provided*, That if the Public Printer shall object in writing to any eligible named in the certification, stating that because of physical incapacity or for other good cause particularly specified such eligible is not capable of properly performing the duties of the vacant place, the Commission may, upon investigation and ascertainment of the fact that the objection made is good and well founded, direct the certification of another eligible in place of the eligible to whom objection is made.

3. When a person designated for appointment shall have reported in person to the Public Printer, he shall be appointed for a probational period of six months, at the end of which period, if his conduct and capacity be satisfactory to the Public Printer, he shall receive absolute appointment; but if his conduct and capacity be not satisfactory he shall be notified that he will not receive absolute appointment, and this notification shall discharge him from the service. The Public Printer shall require the officer under whom the probationer may be serving to carefully observe and report in writing upon the services rendered by and the character and qualifications of

such probationer as to punctuality, industry, habits, ability, and adaptability. These reports shall be preserved on file, and the Commission may prescribe the form and manner in which they shall be made.

4. Any person appointed to a position which belongs to one of the recognized mechanical trades may upon reporting for appointment be subjected to a practical test under the supervision of a board designated by the Commission, and if he or she fails to attain a general average of 70 per cent on a maximum of 100 per cent he or she shall be rejected for appointment.

5. In case of public and pressing exigency, demanding the immediate employment of skilled and experienced workmen who can not be at once supplied in the manner provided for in section 2 of this rule, or by transfer under Rule VI, or reinstatement under Rule VII, there may be employed without examination or certification for a period not to exceed thirty days, which with the consent of the Commission may be extended in periods of thirty days each, any persons who have the requisite knowledge or experience who may be available: *Provided*, That no person shall serve more than ninety days in any one year under such temporary appointment. The year limitation in regard to appointment shall begin to run at the date of the original appointment. Every such temporary appointment and also the discontinuance of the same shall be at once reported to the Commission.

RULE V.

1. Until promotion regulations shall have been applied to the classified service of the Government Printing Office promotions therein may be made upon any test of fitness determined upon by the Public Printer if not disapproved by the Commission.

RULE VI.

1. Transfers may be made as follows:

(*a*) From a position in the classified service of the Government Printing Office requiring a knowledge of some mechanical trade to a position in any one of the Executive Departments requiring a knowledge of the same mechanical trade, upon requisition from the head of the Department to which the transfer is to be made and the consent of the Public Printer: *Provided*, That a person so transferred shall not be transferred to another position in one of the Executive Departments unless such other position requires a knowledge of the same mechanical trade upon which the original transfer was based, nor until he has served one year in the position to which he was originally transferred.

(*b*) From any Executive Department to the classified service of the Government Printing Office upon requisition from the Public Printer and the consent of the head of the Department from which the transfer is to be made.

2. No person shall be transferred as herein authorized until after absolute appointment and until the Commission shall have certified to the officer making the transfer requisition that the person whom it is proposed to transfer has passed an examination to test fitness for the place to which he or she is to be transferred. No person shall be transferred to any place from which he or she may be barred by age limitations for original entrance or by the rules regulating the apportionment of appointments among the several States and Territories and the District of Columbia.

RULE VII.

Upon requisition of the Public Printer the Commission shall certify for reinstatement in the Government Printing Office, in a grade requiring no higher examination than the one in which he was formerly employed, any person who within one year next preceding the date of the requisition has through no delinquency or misconduct been separated from the classified service of the Government Printing

Office: *Provided*, That certification may be made, subject to the other conditions of this rule, for the reinstatement of any person who served in the military or naval service of the United States in the late War of the Rebellion and was honorably discharged therefrom, or the widow of any such person, without regard to the length of time he or she has been separated from the service.

RULE VIII.

The Public Printer shall report to the Commission—

(*a*) Every probational and every absolute appointment to the service of the Government Printing Office.

(*b*) Every refusal to make an absolute appointment and the reason therefor, and every declination of an appointment.

(*c*) Every separation from the service of the Government Printing Office and the cause of such separation, whether death, resignation, or dismissal.

Approved:

GROVER CLEVELAND.

CIVIL SERVICE.—EXECUTIVE ORDER WITHDRAWING ENGINEERS AND ASSISTANT ENGINEERS FROM THE LIST OF PLACES TO BE FILLED BY NONCOMPETITIVE EXAMINATION.

So much of Executive orders heretofore issued under General Rule III, section 2, clause (*c*), as provides for the appointment of engineers and assistant engineers by noncompetitive examination is hereby revoked, and hereafter engineers and assistant engineers will be appointed by competitive examination.

Approved, June 25, 1895.

GROVER CLEVELAND.

In the exercise of the power vested in him by the Constitution, by the seventeen hundred and fifty-third section of the Revised Statutes, and the act entitled "An act to regulate and improve the civil service of the United States," approved January 16, 1883, the President hereby makes and promulgates the following rule to cancel and be in lieu of Customs Rule V of the Revised Civil-Service Rules:

CUSTOMS RULE V.

1. Until promotion regulations have been applied to a classified customs district the following promotions may be made therein at any time after absolute appointment:

(*a*) Any employee in any grade, upon any test of fitness determined upon by the nominating officer, to any vacant place in the class next above the one in which he may be serving, except to the positions of weigher and gauger.

(*b*) Any employee in any grade may be promoted or transferred to a vacancy in the lowest class of the grade of examiner after passing the examiner examination, to a vacancy in the lowest class of the grade of weigher after passing the weigher examination, to a vacancy in the lowest class of the grade of gauger after passing the gauger examination, or to a vacancy in the lowest class of any other grade than the one in which he may be serving upon passing the examination provided for that grade.

Approved, July 11, 1895.   GROVER CLEVELAND.

CIVIL SERVICE.—CLASSIFICATION OF THE PENSION AGENCIES OF THE INTERIOR DEPARTMENT.

EXECUTIVE MANSION, *July 15, 1895.*

In the exercise of the power vested in the President by the third paragraph of section 6 of the act entitled "An act to regulate and improve the civil service of the United States," approved January 16, 1883, I hereby direct the Secretary of the Interior to amend the classification of the Department of the Interior so as to include among the employees classified thereunder the officers, clerks, and other employees of the pension agencies of said Department.   GROVER CLEVELAND.

AMENDMENT OF CIVIL-SERVICE RULES.

DEPARTMENTAL RULE VIII.

Section 1, clause (*a*), is hereby amended as follows: Strike out the period after the word "made" in the second line, insert a semicolon, and add the following:

But transfers from a pension agency of the Interior Department may be made only as follows: From a pension agency of the Interior Department to the office of the Secretary of the Interior, or of the Assistant Attorney-General for the Interior Department, or to the Pension Office, or from any of the above-named offices to a pension agency, or from one pension agency to another pension agency, upon requisition of the Secretary of the Interior: *Provided,* That a transfer from a pension agency to a position in the Interior Department shall not be made when the person to be transferred would not be eligible to original appointment in the departmental service under the law requiring an apportionment of appointments among the States, Territories, and the District of Columbia according to population.

The section and clause as amended will read:

1. Transfers may be made as follows:

(*a*) From one Department to another, upon requisition by the head of the Department to which the transfer is to be made; but transfers from a pension agency of the Interior Department may be made only as follows: From a pension agency of the Interior Department to the office of the Secretary of the Interior, or of the Assistant Attorney-General for the Interior Department, or to the Pension Office, or from any of the above-named offices to a pension agency, or from one pension agency to another pension agency, upon requisition of the Secretary of the Interior: *Provided,* That a transfer from a pension agency to a position in the Interior Department shall not be made when the person to be transferred would not be eligible to original appointment in the departmental service under the law requiring an apportionment of appointments among the States, Territories, and the District of Columbia according to population.

Approved, July 15, 1895.   GROVER CLEVELAND.

Amendments of Civil-Service Rules.

DEPARTMENTAL RULE II.

Section 3, providing for exceptions from examination in the classified departmental service, is hereby amended as follows by the insertion of clause (*g*):

One designated clerk at each pension agency (designated to sign official checks for the pension agent).

Section 4 is hereby amended as follows: In the third line, after the word "examination," add the following proviso:

Provided, That any person employed in an excepted place in any office or bureau at the time when said office or bureau is brought into the classified service, or any person transferred directly from a nonexcepted to an excepted place in the office or bureau in which he is serving, may at any time be directly transferred from such excepted place to any nonexcepted place in the office or bureau in which he is serving.

The section as amended will read:

4. No person hereafter appointed to a place under the exceptions to examination made by any departmental rule shall be transferred from such place to a place not also excepted from examination: *Provided*, That any person employed in an excepted place in any office or bureau at the time when said office or bureau is brought into the classified service, or any person transferred directly from a nonexcepted to an excepted place in the office or bureau in which he is serving, may at any time be directly transferred from such excepted place to any nonexcepted place in the office or bureau in which he is serving.

Approved, July 15, 1895.

GROVER CLEVELAND.

AMENDMENT OF CIVIL-SERVICE RULES.

EXECUTIVE MANSION, *July 15, 1895.*

Special Departmental Rule I is hereby amended by striking out the whole of the paragraph in section 3, Department of the Interior, relating to the Geological Survey and substituting in lieu thereof the following:

In the Geological Survey: Professional experts and special agents employed for short periods at per diem salaries and paid only when actually employed.

Approved:

GROVER CLEVELAND.

Amendments of Civil-Service Rules.

DEPARTMENTAL RULE VII.

Section 2 is hereby amended as follows: At the end of the section, after the word "law," add the following proviso:

Provided, That appointments to positions at pension agencies shall not be charged to the apportionment.

The section as amended will read as follows:

2. Certifications hereunder shall be made in such a manner as to maintain as nearly as possible the apportionment of appointments among the several States and Territories and the District of Columbia as required by law: *Provided*, That appointments to positions at pension agencies shall not be charged to the apportionment.

Section 3, paragraph 2, is hereby amended as follows: In the second line, after the word "register," insert the following: "or when certification is made from any register to fill a vacancy at any pension agency."

The paragraph as amended will read:

When certification is made from a supplementary or special register or the printer's assistant or page and messenger-boy register, or when certification is made from any register to fill a vacancy at any pension agency, and there are more vacancies than one to be filled, the appointing officer may select from the three names certified more than one.

Section 6 is hereby amended as follows: Strike out the word "and" at the beginning of line 9, and in line 12, after the word "appointment," insert the following proviso:

And provided further, That at each pension agency at the time of the quarterly payment of pensions such temporary appointments may be made as the needs of the service may demand for a period not to exceed thirty days, which appointments shall not be extended or renewed until the date of the next quarterly payment of pensions.

The section as amended will read:

6. In case of the occurrence of a vacancy in any Department which the public interest requires shall be immediately filled, and which can not be so filled by certification from the eligible registers of the Commission, such vacancy may be filled by temporary appointment outside the civil service until a regular appointment can be made under the provisions of sections 1, 2, and 3 of this rule: *Provided*, That such temporary appointment shall in no case continue longer than ninety days, and shall expire by limitation at the end of that time: *Provided further*, That no person shall serve longer than the period herein prescribed in any one year under such temporary appointment. The year limitation in regard to reappointment shall begin to run on the date of the original appointment: *And provided further*, That at each pension agency at the time of the quarterly payment of pensions such temporary appointments may be made as the needs of the service may demand for a period not to exceed thirty days, which appointments shall not be extended or renewed until the date of the next quarterly payment of pensions. Every such temporary appointment and the discontinuance of the same shall at once be reported to the Commission.

Approved, July 15, 1895.

GROVER CLEVELAND.

CIVIL SERVICE.—AMENDMENT OF CLASSIFICATION.

EXECUTIVE MANSION, *July 15, 1895*.

In pursuance of the authority contained in the third paragraph of section 6 of the act entitled "An act to regulate and improve the civil service of the United States," approved January 16, 1883, the heads of the several

Executive Departments are hereby directed to amend their several classifications so as to include firemen among the employees classified thereunder.

GROVER CLEVELAND.

AMENDMENT OF CIVIL-SERVICE RULES.

EXECUTIVE MANSION, *July 15, 1895.*

Executive orders heretofore issued designating the places to be filled by noncompetitive examination under clause (*c*) of General Rule III are hereby amended so as to include among those places in the Department of the Interior, in the Geological Survey, the editor and the photographer.

Approved:

GROVER CLEVELAND.

AMENDMENT OF CIVIL-SERVICE RULES.

Special Departmental Rule I is hereby amended by adding to the list of places excepted from examination in the Treasury Department—

In the Bureau of Immigration: One statistician and stenographer, with power to act as immigrant inspector.

Approved, July 30, 1895.

GROVER CLEVELAND.

AMENDMENT OF CIVIL-SERVICE RULES.

Departmental Rule IX, clause 1, paragraph 2, is hereby amended by striking out in line 1 the words "appointed from the appropriate register to" and substituting therefor the word "occupying;" by adding before the word "messenger" in line 2 the following: "engineers, assistant engineers, firemen;" by striking out in line 3 the words "below the positions of clerk and copyist" and substituting therefor the words "the educational test for appointment to which is below the grade of the educational test required for the position of clerk or copyist;" and by adding in line 7, after the words "printers' assistants," the words "and skilled helpers." As amended the paragraph will read as follows:

Any person occupying the position of engineer, assistant engineer, fireman, messenger, assistant messenger, watchman, or other subordinate position the educational test for appointment to which is below the grade of the educational test required for the position of clerk or copyist may at any time after absolute appointment, if not barred by age limitations, be transferred to any other of said subordinate positions, but shall not be promoted to the position of clerk or copyist or to any place the duties of which are clerical: *Provided*, That printers' assistants and skilled helpers in the Bureau of Engraving and Printing, Treasury Department, shall only be eligible for transfer to the grade of operator in that Bureau.

Approved, August 5, 1895.

GROVER CLEVELAND.

CIVIL SERVICE.—EXECUTIVE ORDER WITHDRAWING COMPOSITORS AND PRESSMEN FROM THE LIST OF PLACES TO BE FILLED BY NONCOMPETITIVE EXAMINATION.

EXECUTIVE MANSION, *August 16, 1895.*

So much of Executive orders heretofore issued under General Rule III, section 2, clause (*c*), as provides for the appointment of compositors and pressmen by noncompetitive examination is hereby revoked, and hereafter compositors and pressmen will be appointed by competitive examination.

Approved:
GROVER CLEVELAND.

AMENDMENT OF CIVIL-SERVICE RULES.

EXECUTIVE MANSION, *August 22, 1895.*

Government Printing Office Rule II, section 2, is hereby amended by omitting in line 1, after the words "under 21," the words "or over 45," and in line 2, after the words "under 18," the words "or over 35." The section as amended will read as follows:

2. Any male citizen of the United States not under 21 years of age and any female citizen not under 18 years of age may be examined for positions in the Government Printing Office.

Approved:
GROVER CLEVELAND.

AMENDMENT OF CIVIL-SERVICE RULES.

EXECUTIVE MANSION, *September 5, 1895.*

Special Departmental Rule I is hereby amended by striking out from the list of places excepted from examination in all the Departments "bookbinders."

Approved:
GROVER CLEVELAND.

AMENDMENT OF CIVIL-SERVICE RULES.

Special Departmental Rule I is hereby amended to except from examination in the Department of the Treasury, in the Bureau of Printing and Engraving, forty-three compositors and eight pressmen now temporarily employed under authority of the sundry civil act of March 2, 1895, such employment to cease prior to March 14, 1896. Vacancies occurring in this force shall be filled only by competitive examination under the civil-service rules.

Approved, September 16, 1895.
GROVER CLEVELAND.

EXECUTIVE MANSION, *September 20, 1895.*

It being of great importance that the consuls and commercial agents of the United States shall possess the proper qualifications for their respective positions, to be ascertained either through a satisfactory record of previous actual service under the Department of State or through an appropriate examination:

It is hereby ordered, That any vacancy in a consulate or commercial agency now or hereafter existing the salary of which is not more than $2,500 nor less than $1,000, or the compensation of which, if derived from official fees, exclusive of notarial and other unofficial receipts, does not exceed $2,500 nor fall below $1,000, shall be filled (*a*) by a transfer or promotion from some other position under the Department of State of a character tending to qualify the incumbent for the position to be filled, or (*b*) by appointment of a person not under the Department of State, but having previously served thereunder to its satisfaction in a capacity tending to qualify him for the position to be filled, or (*c*) by the appointment of a person who, having furnished the customary evidence of character, responsibility, and capacity, and being thereupon selected by the President for examination, is found upon such examination to be qualified for the position.

For the purposes of this order notarial and unofficial fees shall not be regarded, but the compensation of a consulate or commercial agency shall be ascertained, if the office is salaried, by reference to the last preceding appropriation act, and if the office is not salaried by reference to the returns of official fees for the last preceding fiscal year.

The examination hereinbefore provided for shall be by a board of three persons designated by the Secretary of State, who shall also prescribe the subjects to which such examinations shall relate and the general mode of conducting the same by the board.

A vacancy in a consulate will be filled at discretion only when a suitable appointment can not be made in any of the modes indicated in the second paragraph of this order.

GROVER CLEVELAND.

EXECUTIVE MANSION,
Washington, September 30, 1895.

Lieutenant-General John M. Schofield having reached the age entitling him to relief from active military service, he is, in accordance with the provisions of law, hereby placed upon the retired list of the Army, to date September 29, 1895, with all the pay and allowances belonging to his rank upon such retirement.

It is with much regret that the President makes the announcement that the country is thus to lose from the command of its Army this distinguished general, who has done so much for its honor and efficiency. His gallantry in war challenges the admiration of all his countrymen, while they will not fail to gratefully remember and appreciate how faithfully he has served his country in times of peace by his splendid and successful performance of civil as well as military duty.

Lieutenant-General Schofield's career, exhibiting an unvarying love for his profession, a jealous care for its honor and good name, a just apprehension of the subordination it exacts, and a constant manifestation of the best traits of true Americanism, furnishes to the Army an example of inestimable value, and should teach all our people that the highest soldierly qualities are built upon the keenest sense of the obligations belonging to good citizenship.

GROVER CLEVELAND.

AMENDMENT OF CIVIL-SERVICE RULES.

EXECUTIVE MANSION, *November 6, 1895*.

Section 2 of Postal Rule I is hereby amended by inserting after the word "thereto" in line 6 the following:

And whenever, by order of the Postmaster-General, any post-office shall be consolidated with and made part of another post-office where free delivery is established, all the employees of the office thus consolidated whose names appear on the roster of said office approved by the Post-Office Department, and including the postmaster thereof, shall from the date of said order be employees of said free-delivery office, and the person holding on the date of said order the position of postmaster at the office thus consolidated with said free-delivery office may be assigned to any position therein and given any appropriate designation under the classification act which the Postmaster-General may direct.

The section as amended shall read as follows:

2. The classification of the postal service made by the Postmaster-General under section 6 of the act of January 16, 1883, is hereby extended to all free-delivery post-offices, and hereafter whenever any post-office becomes a free-delivery office the said classification or any then existing classification made by the Postmaster-General under said section and act shall apply thereto; and whenever, by order of the Postmaster-General, any post-office shall be consolidated with and made part of another post-office where free delivery is established, all the employees of the office thus consolidated whose names appear on the roster of said office approved by the Post-Office Department, and including the postmaster thereof, shall from the date of said order be employees of said free-delivery office, and the person holding on the date of said order the position of postmaster at the office thus consolidated with said free-delivery office may be assigned to any position therein and given any appropriate designation under the classification act which the Postmaster-General may direct; and the Civil Service Commission shall provide examinations to test the fitness of persons to fill vacancies in all free-delivery post-offices, and these rules shall be in force therein; but this shall not include any post-office made an experimental free-delivery office under the authority contained in the appropriation act of March 3, 1891. Every revision of the classification of any post-office under section 6 of the act of January 16, 1883, and every inclusion of a post-office within the classified postal service shall be reported to the President.

Approved:

GROVER CLEVELAND.

M P—VOL IX—40

THIRD ANNUAL MESSAGE.

EXECUTIVE MANSION, *December 2, 1895.*

To the Congress of the United States:

The present assemblage of the legislative branch of our Government occurs at a time when the interests of our people and the needs of the country give especial prominence to the condition of our foreign relations and the exigencies of our national finances. The reports of the heads of the several administrative Departments of the Government fully and plainly exhibit what has been accomplished within the scope of their respective duties and present such recommendations for the betterment of our country's condition as patriotic and intelligent labor and observation suggest.

I therefore deem my executive duty adequately performed at this time by presenting to the Congress the important phases of our situation as related to our intercourse with foreign nations and a statement of the financial problems which confront us, omitting, except as they are related to these topics, any reference to departmental operations.

I earnestly invite, however, not only the careful consideration but the severely critical scrutiny of the Congress and my fellow-countrymen to the reports concerning these departmental operations. If justly and fairly examined, they will furnish proof of assiduous and painstaking care for the public welfare. I press the recommendations they contain upon the respectful attention of those charged with the duty of legislation, because I believe their adoption would promote the people's good.

By amendatory tariff legislation in January last the Argentine Republic, recognizing the value of the large market opened to the free importation of its wools under our last tariff act, has admitted certain products of the United States to entry at reduced duties. It is pleasing to note that the efforts we have made to enlarge the exchanges of trade on a sound basis of mutual benefit are in this instance appreciated by the country from which our woolen factories draw their needful supply of raw material.

The Missions boundary dispute between the Argentine Republic and Brazil, referred to the President of the United States as arbitrator during the term of my predecessor, and which was submitted to me for determination, resulted in an award in favor of Brazil upon the historical and documentary evidence presented, thus ending a long-protracted controversy and again demonstrating the wisdom and desirability of settling international boundary disputes by recourse to friendly arbitration.

Negotiations are progressing for a revival of the United States and Chilean Claims Commission, whose work was abruptly terminated last year by the expiration of the stipulated time within which awards could be made.

The resumption of specie payments by Chile is a step of great interest and importance both in its direct consequences upon her own welfare and as evincing the ascendency of sound financial principles in one of the most influential of the South American Republics.

The close of the momentous struggle between China and Japan, while relieving the diplomatic agents of this Government from the delicate duty they undertook at the request of both countries of rendering such service to the subjects of either belligerent within the territorial limits of the other as our neutral position permitted, developed a domestic condition in the Chinese Empire which has caused much anxiety and called for prompt and careful attention. Either as a result of a weak control by the central Government over the provincial administrations, following a diminution of traditional governmental authority under the stress of an overwhelming national disaster, or as a manifestation upon good opportunity of the aversion of the Chinese population to all foreign ways and undertakings, there have occurred in widely separated provinces of China serious outbreaks of the old fanatical spirit against foreigners, which, unchecked by the local authorities, if not actually connived at by them, have culminated in mob attacks on foreign missionary stations, causing much destruction of property and attended with personal injuries as well as loss of life.

Although but one American citizen was reported to have been actually wounded, and although the destruction of property may have fallen more heavily upon the missionaries of other nationalities than our own, it plainly behooved this Government to take the most prompt and decided action to guard against similar or perhaps more dreadful calamities befalling the hundreds of American mission stations which have grown up throughout the interior of China under the temperate rule of toleration, custom, and imperial edict. The demands of the United States and other powers for the degradation and punishment of the responsible officials of the respective cities and provinces who by neglect or otherwise had permitted uprisings, and for the adoption of stern measures by the Emperor's Government for the protection of the life and property of foreigners, were followed by the disgrace and dismissal of certain provincial officials found derelict in duty and the punishment by death of a number of those adjudged guilty of actual participation in the outrages.

This Government also insisted that a special American commission should visit the province where the first disturbances occurred for the purpose of investigation. The latter commission, formed after much opposition, has gone overland from Tientsin, accompanied by a suitable Chinese escort, and by its demonstration of the readiness and ability of our Government to protect its citizens will act, it is believed, as a most influential deterrent of any similar outbreaks.

The energetic steps we have thus taken are all the more likely to result in future safety to our citizens in China because the Imperial Government is, I am persuaded, entirely convinced that we desire only the liberty and protection of our own citizens and redress for any wrongs they may have suffered, and that we have no ulterior designs or objects, political or otherwise. China will not forget either our kindly service to her citizens during her late war nor the further fact that, while furnishing all the facilities at our command to further the negotiation of a peace between her and Japan, we sought no advantages and interposed no counsel.

The Governments of both China and Japan have, in special dispatches transmitted through their respective diplomatic representatives, expressed in a most pleasing manner their grateful appreciation of our assistance to their citizens during the unhappy struggle and of the value of our aid in paving the way to their resumption of peaceful relations.

The customary cordial relations between this country and France have been undisturbed, with the exception that a full explanation of the treatment of John L. Waller by the expeditionary military authorities of France still remains to be given. Mr. Waller, formerly United States consul at Tamatav, remained in Madagascar after his term of office expired, and was apparently successful in procuring business concessions from the Hovas of greater or less value. After the occupation of Tamatav and the declaration of martial law by the French he was arrested upon various charges, among them that of communicating military information to the enemies of France, was tried and convicted by a military tribunal, and sentenced to twenty years' imprisonment.

Following the course justified by abundant precedents, this Government requested from that of France the record of the proceedings of the French tribunal which resulted in Mr. Waller's condemnation. This request has been complied with to the extent of supplying a copy of the official record, from which appear the constitution and organization of the court, the charges as formulated, and the general course and result of the trial, and by which it is shown that the accused was tried in open court and was defended by counsel; but the evidence adduced in support of the charges, which was not received by the French minister for foreign affairs till the first week in October, has thus far been withheld, the French Government taking the ground that its production in response to our demand would establish a bad precedent. The efforts of our ambassador to procure it, however, though impeded by recent changes in the French ministry, have not been relaxed, and it is confidently expected that some satisfactory solution of the matter will shortly be reached. Meanwhile it appears that Mr. Waller's confinement has every alleviation which the state of his health and all the other circumstances of the case demand or permit.

In agreeable contrast to the difference above noted respecting a matter of common concern, where nothing is sought except such a mutually satisfactory outcome as the true merits of the case require, is the recent resolution of the French Chambers favoring the conclusion of a permanent treaty of arbitration between the two countries.

An invitation has been extended by France to the Government and people of the United States to participate in a great international exposition at Paris in 1900 as a suitable commemoration of the close of this the world's marvelous century of progress. I heartily recommend its acceptance, together with such legislation as will adequately provide for a due representation of this Government and its people on the occasion.

Our relations with the States of the German Empire are in some aspects typical of a condition of things elsewhere found in countries whose productions and trade are similar to our own. The close rivalries of competing industries; the influence of the delusive doctrine that the internal development of a nation is promoted and its wealth increased by a policy which, in undertaking to reserve its home markets for the exclusive use of its own producers, necessarily obstructs their sales in foreign markets and prevents free access to the products of the world; the desire to retain trade in time-worn ruts, regardless of the inexorable laws of new needs and changed conditions of demand and supply, and our own halting tardiness in inviting a freer exchange of commodities, and by this means imperiling our footing in the external markets naturally open to us, have created a situation somewhat injurious to American export interests, not only in Germany, where they are perhaps most noticeable, but in adjacent countries. The exports affected are largely American cattle and other food products, the reason assigned for unfavorable discrimination being that their consumption is deleterious to the public health. This is all the more irritating in view of the fact that no European state is as jealous of the excellence and wholesomeness of its exported food supplies as the United States, nor so easily able, on account of inherent soundness, to guarantee those qualities.

Nor are these difficulties confined to our food products designed for exportation. Our great insurance companies, for example, having built up a vast business abroad and invested a large share of their gains in foreign countries in compliance with the local laws and regulations then existing, now find themselves within a narrowing circle of onerous and unforeseen conditions, and are confronted by the necessity of retirement from a field thus made unprofitable, if, indeed, they are not summarily expelled, as some of them have lately been from Prussia.

It is not to be forgotten that international trade can not be one-sided. Its currents are alternating, and its movements should be honestly reciprocal. Without this it almost necessarily degenerates into a device to gain advantage or a contrivance to secure benefits with only the semblance of a return. In our dealings with other nations we ought to be open-handed and scrupulously fair. This should be our policy as a producing nation, and it plainly becomes us as a people who love generosity and the moral aspects of national good faith and reciprocal forbearance.

These considerations should not, however, constrain us to submit to unfair discrimination nor to silently acquiesce in vexatious hindrances to the enjoyment of our share of the legitimate advantages of proper trade relations. If an examination of the situation suggests such measures on our part as would involve restrictions similar to those from which we suffer, the way to such a course is easy. It should, however, by no means be lightly entered upon, since the necessity for the inauguration of such a policy would be regretted by the best sentiment of our people and because it naturally and logically might lead to consequences of the gravest character.

I take pleasure in calling to your attention the encomiums bestowed on those vessels of our new Navy which took part in the notable ceremony of the opening of the Kiel Canal. It was fitting that this extraordinary achievement of the newer German nationality should be celebrated in the presence of America's exposition of the latest developments of the world's naval energy.

Our relations with Great Britain, always intimate and important, have demanded during the past year even a greater share of consideration than is usual.

Several vexatious questions were left undetermined by the decision of the Bering Sea Arbitration Tribunal. The application of the principles laid down by that august body has not been followed by the results they were intended to accomplish, either because the principles themselves lacked in breadth and definiteness or because their execution has been more or less imperfect. Much correspondence has been exchanged between the two Governments on the subject of preventing the exterminating slaughter of seals. The insufficiency of the British patrol of Bering Sea under the regulations agreed on by the two Governments has been pointed out, and yet only two British ships have been on police duty during this season in those waters.

The need of a more effective enforcement of existing regulations as well as the adoption of such additional regulations as experience has shown to be absolutely necessary to carry out the intent of the award have been earnestly urged upon the British Government, but thus far without effective results. In the meantime the depletion of the seal herds by means of pelagic hunting has so alarmingly progressed that unless their slaughter is at once effectively checked their extinction within a few years seems to be a matter of absolute certainty.

The understanding by which the United States was to pay and Great Britain to receive a lump sum of $425,000 in full settlement of all British claims for damages arising from our seizure of British sealing vessels unauthorized under the award of the Paris Tribunal of Arbitration was not confirmed by the last Congress, which declined to make the necessary appropriation. I am still of the opinion that this arrangement was a judicious and advantageous one for the Government, and I earnestly recommend that it be again considered and sanctioned. If, however, this does not meet with the favor of Congress, it certainly will hardly dissent from the proposition that the Government is bound by every consideration of honor and good faith to provide for the speedy adjustment of these claims by arbitration as the only other alternative. A treaty of arbitration has therefore been agreed upon, and will be immediately laid before the Senate, so that in one of the modes suggested a final settlement may be reached.

Notwithstanding that Great Britain originated the proposal to enforce international rules for the prevention of collisions at sea, based on the recommendations of the Maritime Conference of Washington, and concurred in, suggesting March 11, 1895, as the date to be set by proclamation for carrying these rules into general effect, Her Majesty's Government, having encountered opposition on the part of British shipping interests, announced its inability to accept that date, which was consequently canceled. The entire matter is still in abeyance, without prospect of a better condition in the near future.

The commissioners appointed to mark the international boundary in Passamaquoddy Bay according to the description of the treaty of Ghent have not yet fully agreed.

The completion of the preliminary survey of that Alaskan boundary which follows the contour of the coast from the southernmost point of Prince of Wales Island until it strikes the one hundred and forty-first meridian at or near the summit of Mount St. Elias awaits further necessary appropriation, which is urgently recommended. This survey was undertaken under the provisions of the convention entered into by this country and Great Britain July 22, 1892, and the supplementary convention of February 3, 1894.

As to the remaining section of the Alaskan boundary, which follows the one hundred and forty-first meridian northwardly from Mount St. Elias to the Frozen Ocean, the settlement of which involves the physical location of the meridian mentioned, no conventional agreement has yet been made. The ascertainment of a given meridian at a particular point is a work requiring much time and careful observations and surveys. Such observations and surveys were undertaken by the United States Coast and Geodetic Survey in 1890 and 1891, while similar work in the same quarters, under British auspices, is believed to give nearly coincident results; but these surveys have been independently conducted, and no international agreement to mark those or any other parts of the one hundred and forty-first meridian by permanent monuments has yet been made. In the meantime the valley of the Yukon is becoming a highway through the hitherto unexplored wilds of Alaska, and abundant mineral wealth has been discovered in that region, especially at or near the junction of the boundary meridian with the Yukon and its tributaries. In these circumstances it is expedient, and, indeed, imperative, that the jurisdictional limits of the respective Governments in this new region be speedily determined. Her Britannic Majesty's Government has proposed a joint delimitation of the one hundred and forty-first meridian by an international commission of experts, which, if Congress will authorize it and make due provision therefor, can be accomplished with no unreasonable delay. It is impossible to overlook the vital importance of continuing the work already entered upon and supplementing it by further effective measures looking to the exact location of this entire boundary line.

I call attention to the unsatisfactory delimitation of the respective jurisdictions of the United States and the Dominion of Canada in the Great Lakes at the approaches to the narrow waters that connect them. The waters in question are frequented by fishermen of both nationalities and their nets are there used. Owing to the uncertainty and ignorance as to the true boundary, vexatious disputes and injurious seizures of boats and nets by Canadian cruisers often occur, while any positive settlement thereof by an accepted standard is not easily to be reached. A joint commission to determine the line in those quarters on a practical basis, by measured courses following range marks on shore, is a necessity for which immediate provision should be made.

It being apparent that the boundary dispute between Great Britain and the Republic of Venezuela concerning the limits of British Guiana was approaching an acute stage, a definite statement of the interest and policy of the United States as regards the controversy seemed to be required both on its own account and in view of its relations with the friendly powers directly concerned. In July last, therefore, a dispatch was addressed to our ambassador at London for communication to the British Government in which the attitude of the United States was fully and distinctly set forth. The general conclusions therein reached and formulated are in substance that the traditional and established policy of this Government is firmly opposed to a forcible increase by any European power of its territorial possessions on this continent; that this policy is as well founded in principle as it is strongly supported by numerous precedents; that as a consequence the United States is bound to protest against the enlargement of the area of British Guiana in derogation of the rights and against the will of Venezuela; that considering the disparity in strength of Great Britain and Venezuela the territorial dispute between them can be reasonably settled only by friendly and impartial arbitration, and that the resort to such arbitration should include the whole controversy, and is not satisfied if one of the powers concerned is permitted to draw an arbitrary line through the territory in debate and to declare that it will submit to arbitration only the portion lying on one side of it. In view of these conclusions, the dispatch in question called upon the British Government for a definite answer to the question whether it would or would not submit the territorial controversy between itself and Venezuela in its entirety to impartial arbitration. The answer of the British Government has not yet been received, but is expected shortly, when further communication on the subject will probably be made to the Congress.

Early in January last an uprising against the Government of Hawaii was promptly suppressed. Martial law was forthwith proclaimed and numerous arrests were made of persons suspected of being in sympathy with the Royalist party. Among these were several citizens of the United States, who were either convicted by a military court and sentenced to death, imprisonment, or fine or were deported without trial. The United States, while denying protection to such as had taken the Hawaiian oath of allegiance, insisted that martial law, though altering the forms of justice, could not supersede justice itself, and demanded stay of execution until the proceedings had been submitted to this Government and knowledge obtained therefrom that our citizens had received fair trial. The death sentences were subsequently commuted or were remitted on condition of leaving the islands. The cases of certain Americans arrested and expelled by arbitrary order without formal charge or trial have had attention, and in some instances have been found to justify remonstrance and a claim for indemnity, which Hawaii has not thus far conceded.

Mr. Thurston, the Hawaiian minister, having furnished this Government abundant reason for asking that he be recalled, that course was pursued, and his successor has lately been received.

The deplorable lynching of several Italian laborers in Colorado was naturally followed by international representations, and I am happy to say that the best efforts of the State in which the outrages occurred have been put forth to discover and punish the authors of this atrocious crime. The dependent families of some of the unfortunate victims invite by their deplorable condition gracious provision for their needs.

These manifestations against helpless aliens may be traced through successive stages to the vicious *padroni* system, which, unchecked by our immigration and contract-labor statutes, controls these workers from the moment of landing on our shores and farms them out in distant and often rude regions, where their cheapening competition in the fields of bread-winning toil brings them into collision with other labor interests. While welcoming, as we should, those who seek our shores to merge themselves in our body politic and win personal competence by honest effort, we can not regard such assemblages of distinctively alien laborers, hired out in the mass to the profit of alien speculators and shipped hither and thither as the prospect of gain may dictate, as otherwise than repugnant to the spirit of our civilization, deterrent to individual advancement, and hindrances to the building up of stable communities resting upon the wholesome ambitions of the citizen and constituting the prime factor in the prosperity and progress of our nation. If legislation can reach this growing evil, it certainly should be attempted.

Japan has furnished abundant evidence of her vast gain in every trait and characteristic that constitutes a nation's greatness. We have reason for congratulation in the fact that the Government of the United States, by the exchange of liberal treaty stipulations with the new Japan, was the first to recognize her wonderful advance and to extend to her the consideration and confidence due to her national enlightenment and progressive character.

The boundary dispute which lately threatened to embroil Guatemala and Mexico has happily yielded to pacific counsels, and its determination has, by the joint agreement of the parties, been submitted to the sole arbitration of the United States minister to Mexico.

The commission appointed under the convention of February 18, 1889, to set new monuments along the boundary between the United States and Mexico has completed its task.

As a sequel to the failure of a scheme for the colonization in Mexico of negroes, mostly immigrants from Alabama under contract, a great number of these helpless and suffering people, starving and smitten with contagious disease, made their way or were assisted to the frontier, where, in wretched plight, they were quarantined by the Texas authorities. Learning of their destitute condition, I directed rations to be temporarily furnished them through the War Department. At the expiration of their quarantine they were conveyed by the railway companies at comparatively nominal rates to their homes in Alabama, upon my assurance, in the absence of any fund available for the cost of their transportation, that I would recommend to Congress an appropriation for its payment. I now strongly urge upon Congress the propriety of making such an appropriation. It should be remembered that the measures taken were dictated not only by sympathy and humanity, but by a conviction that it was not compatible with the dignity of this Government that so large a body of our dependent citizens should be thrown for relief upon the charity of a neighboring state.

In last year's message I narrated at some length the jurisdictional questions then freshly arisen in the Mosquito Indian Strip of Nicaragua. Since that time, by the voluntary act of the Mosquito Nation, the territory reserved to them has been incorporated with Nicaragua, the Indians formally subjecting themselves to be governed by the general laws and regulations of the Republic instead of by their own customs and regulations, and thus availing themselves of a privilege secured to them by the treaty between Nicaragua and Great Britain of January 28, 1860.

After this extension of uniform Nicaraguan administration to the Mosquito Strip, the case of the British vice-consul, Hatch, and of several of his countrymen who had been summarily expelled from Nicaragua and treated with considerable indignity provoked a claim by Great Britain upon Nicaragua for pecuniary indemnity, which, upon Nicaragua's refusal to admit liability, was enforced by Great Britain. While the sovereignty and jurisdiction of Nicaragua was in no way questioned by Great Britain, the former's arbitrary conduct in regard to British subjects furnished the ground for this proceeding.

A British naval force occupied without resistance the Pacific seaport of Corinto, but was soon after withdrawn upon the promise that the sum demanded would be paid. Throughout this incident the kindly offices of the United States were invoked and were employed in favor of as peaceful a settlement and as much consideration and indulgence toward Nicaragua as were consistent with the nature of the case. Our efforts have since been made the subject of appreciative and grateful recognition by Nicaragua.

The coronation of the Czar of Russia at Moscow in May next invites the ceremonial participation of the United States, and in accordance with usage and diplomatic propriety our minister to the imperial court has been directed to represent our Government on the occasion.

Correspondence is on foot touching the practice of Russian consuls within the jurisdiction of the United States to interrogate citizens as to their race and religious faith, and upon ascertainment thereof to deny to Jews authentication of passports or legal documents for use in Russia. Inasmuch as such a proceeding imposes a disability which in the case of succession to property in Russia may be found to infringe the treaty rights of our citizens, and which is an obnoxious invasion of our territorial jurisdiction, it has elicited fitting remonstrance, the result of which, it is hoped, will remove the cause of complaint. The pending claims of sealing vessels of the United States seized in Russian waters remain unadjusted. Our recent convention with Russia establishing a *modus vivendi* as to imperial jurisdiction in such cases has prevented further difficulty of this nature.

The Russian Government has welcomed in principle our suggestion for a *modus vivendi*, to embrace Great Britain and Japan, looking to the better preservation of seal life in the North Pacific and Bering Sea and the extension of the protected area defined by the Paris Tribunal to all Pacific waters north of the thirty-fifth parallel. It is especially noticeable that Russia favors prohibition of the use of firearms in seal hunting throughout the proposed area and a longer closed season for pelagic sealing.

In my last two annual messages I called the attention of the Congress to the position we occupied as one of the parties to a treaty or agreement by which we became jointly bound with England and Germany to so interfere with the government and control of Samoa as in effect to assume the management of its affairs.* On the 9th day of May, 1894, I transmitted to the Senate a special message,† with accompanying documents, giving information on the subject and emphasizing the opinion I have at all times entertained, that our situation in this matter was inconsistent with the mission and traditions of our Government, in violation of the principles we profess, and in all its phases mischievous and vexatious.

I again press this subject upon the attention of the Congress and ask for such legislative action or expression as will lead the way to our relief from obligations both irksome and unnatural.

* See pp. 439, 531–532.   † See p. 477.

Cuba is again gravely disturbed. An insurrection in some respects more active than the last preceding revolt, which continued from 1868 to 1878, now exists in a large part of the eastern interior of the island, menacing even some populations on the coast. Besides deranging the commercial exchanges of the island, of which our country takes the predominant share, this flagrant condition of hostilities, by arousing sentimental sympathy and inciting adventurous support among our people, has entailed earnest effort on the part of this Government to enforce obedience to our neutrality laws and to prevent the territory of the United States from being abused as a vantage ground from which to aid those in arms against Spanish sovereignty.

Whatever may be the traditional sympathy of our countrymen as individuals with a people who seem to be struggling for larger autonomy and greater freedom, deepened, as such sympathy naturally must be, in behalf of our neighbors, yet the plain duty of their Government is to observe in good faith the recognized obligations of international relationship. The performance of this duty should not be made more difficult by a disregard on the part of our citizens of the obligations growing out of their allegiance to their country, which should restrain them from violating as individuals the neutrality which the nation of which they are members is bound to observe in its relations to friendly sovereign states. Though neither the warmth of our people's sympathy with the Cuban insurgents, nor our loss and material damage consequent upon the futile endeavors thus far made to restore peace and order, nor any shock our humane sensibilities may have received from the cruelties which appear to especially characterize this sanguinary and fiercely conducted war, have in the least shaken the determination of the Government to honestly fulfill every international obligation, yet it is to be earnestly hoped on every ground that the devastation of armed conflict may speedily be stayed and order and quiet restored to the distracted island, bringing in their train the activity and thrift of peaceful pursuits.

One notable instance of interference by Spain with passing American ships has occurred. On March 8 last the *Allianca*, while bound from Colon to New York, and following the customary track for vessels near the Cuban shore, but outside the 3-mile limit, was fired upon by a Spanish gunboat. Protest was promptly made by the United States against this act as not being justified by a state of war, nor permissible in respect of vessels on the usual paths of commerce, nor tolerable in view of the wanton peril occasioned to innocent life and property. The act was disavowed, with full expression of regret and assurance of nonrecurrence of such just cause of complaint, while the offending officer was relieved of his command. Military arrests of citizens of the United States in Cuba have occasioned frequent reclamations. Where held on criminal charges their delivery to the ordinary civil jurisdiction for trial has been demanded and obtained in conformity with treaty provisions, and where merely detained by way of military precaution under a proclaimed state of siege, without formulated accusation, their release or trial has been insisted upon. The right of American consular officers in the island to prefer protests and demands in such cases having been questioned by the insular authority, their enjoyment of the privilege stipulated by treaty for the consuls of Germany was claimed under the most-favored-nation provision of our own convention and was promptly recognized.

The long-standing demand of Antonio Maximo Mora against Spain has at last been settled by the payment, on the 14th of September last, of the sum originally agreed upon in liquidation of the claim. Its distribution among the parties entitled to receive it has proceeded as rapidly as the rights of those claiming the fund could be safely determined.

The enforcement of differential duties against products of this country exported to Cuba and Puerto Rico prompted the immediate claim on our part to the benefit of the minimum tariff of Spain in return for the most favorable treatment permitted by our laws as regards the production of Spanish territories. A commercial arrangement was concluded in January last securing the treatment so claimed.

Vigorous protests against excessive fines imposed on our ships and merchandise by the customs officers of these islands for trivial errors have resulted in the remission of such fines in instances where the equity of the complaint was apparent, though the vexatious practice has not been wholly discontinued.

Occurrences in Turkey have continued to excite concern. The reported massacres of Christians in Armenia and the development there and in other districts of a spirit of fanatic hostility to Christian influences naturally excited apprehension for the safety of the devoted men and women who, as dependents of the foreign missionary societies in the United States, reside in Turkey under the guaranty of law and usage and in the legitimate performance of their educational and religious mission. No efforts have been spared in their behalf, and their protection in person and property has been earnestly and vigorously enforced by every means within our power.

I regret, however, that an attempt on our part to obtain better information concerning the true condition of affairs in the disturbed quarter of the Ottoman Empire by sending thither the United States consul at Sivas to make investigation and report was thwarted by the objections of the Turkish Government. This movement on our part was in no sense meant as a gratuitous entanglement of the United States in the so-called Eastern question nor as an officious interference with the right and duty which belong by treaty to certain great European powers calling for their intervention in political matters affecting the good government and religious freedom of the non-Mussulman subjects of the Sultan, but it arose solely from our desire to have an accurate knowledge of the conditions in our efforts to care for those entitled to our protection.

The presence of our naval vessels which are now in the vicinity of the disturbed localities affords opportunities to acquire a measure of familiarity with the condition of affairs and will enable us to take suitable steps for the protection of any interests of our countrymen within reach of our ships that might be found imperiled.

The Ottoman Government has lately issued an imperial *irade* exempting forever from taxation an American college for girls at Scutari. Repeated assurances have also been obtained by our envoy at Constantinople that similar institutions maintained and administered by our countrymen shall be secured in the enjoyment of all rights and that our citizens throughout the Empire shall be protected.

The Government, however, in view of existing facts, is far from relying upon such assurances as the limit of its duty. Our minister has been vigilant and alert in affording all possible protection in individual cases where danger threatened or safety was imperiled. We have sent ships as far toward the points of actual disturbance as it is possible for them to go, where they offer refuge to those obliged to flee, and we have the promise of other powers which have ships in the neighborhood that our citizens as well as theirs will be received and protected on board those ships. On the demand of our minister orders have been issued by the Sultan that Turkish soldiers shall guard and escort to the coast American refugees.

These orders have been carried out, and our latest intelligence gives assurance of the present personal safety of our citizens and missionaries. Though thus far no lives of American citizens have been sacrificed, there can be no doubt that serious loss and destruction of mission property have resulted from riotous conflicts and outrageous attacks.

By treaty several of the most powerful European powers have secured a right and have assumed a duty not only in behalf of their own citizens and in furtherance of their own interests, but as agents of the Christian world. Their right is to enforce such conduct of Turkish government as will restrain fanatical brutality, and if this fails their duty is to so interfere as to insure against such dreadful occurrences in Turkey as have lately shocked civilization. The powers declare this right and this duty to be theirs alone, and it is earnestly hoped that prompt and effective action on their part will not be delayed.

The new consulates at Erzerum and Harpoot, for which appropriation was made last session, have been provisionally filled by trusted employees of the Department of State. These appointees, though now in Turkey, have not yet received their exequaturs.

The arbitration of the claim of the Venezuela Steam Transportation Company under the treaty of January 19, 1892, between the United States and Venezuela, resulted in an award in favor of the claimant.

The Government has used its good offices toward composing the differences between Venezuela on the one hand and France and Belgium on the other growing out of the dismissal of the representatives of those powers on the ground of a publication deemed offensive to Venezuela. Although that dismissal was coupled with a cordial request that other more personally agreeable envoys be sent in their stead, a rupture of intercourse ensued and still continues.

In view of the growth of our interests in foreign countries and the encouraging prospects for a general expansion of our commerce, the question of an improvement in the consular service has increased in importance and urgency. Though there is no doubt that the great body of consular officers are rendering valuable services to the trade and industries of the country, the need of some plan of appointment and control which would tend to secure a higher average of efficiency can not be denied.

The importance of the subject has led the Executive to consider what steps might properly be taken without additional legislation to answer the need of a better system of consular appointments. The matter having been committed to the consideration of the Secretary of State, in pursuance of his recommendations an Executive order was issued on the 20th of September, 1895,* by the terms of which it is provided that after that date any vacancy in a consulate or commercial agency with an annual salary or compensation from official fees of not more than $2,500 or less than $1,000 should be filled either by transfer or promotion from some other position under the Department of State of a character tending to qualify the incumbent for the position to be filled, or by the appointment of a person not under the Department of State, but having previously served thereunder and shown his capacity and fitness for consular duty, or by the appointment of a person who, having been selected by the President and sent to a board for examination, is found upon such examination to be qualified for the position. Posts which pay less than $1,000 being usually, on account of their small compensation, filled by selection from residents of the locality, it was not deemed practicable to put them under the new system.

The compensation of $2,500 was adopted as the maximum limit in the classification for the reason that consular officers receiving more than that sum are often charged with functions and duties scarcely inferior in dignity and importance to those of diplomatic agents, and it was therefore thought best to continue their selection in the discretion of the Executive without subjecting them to examination before a board. Excluding 71 places with compensation at present less than $1,000 and 53 places above the maximum in compensation, the number of positions remaining within the scope of the order is 196. This number will undoubtedly be increased by the inclusion of consular officers whose remuneration in fees, now less than $1,000, will be augmented with the growth of our foreign commerce and a return to more favorable business conditions.

In execution of the Executive order referred to the Secretary of State has designated as a board to conduct the prescribed examinations the

*See p. 624.

Third Assistant Secretary of State, the Solicitor of the Department of State, and the Chief of the Consular Bureau, and has specified the subjects to which such examinations shall relate.

It is not assumed that this system will prove a full measure of consular reform. It is quite probable that actual experience will show particulars in which the order already issued may be amended and demonstrate that for the best results appropriate legislation by Congress is imperatively required.

In any event, these efforts to improve the consular service ought to be immediately supplemented by legislation providing for consular inspection. This has frequently been a subject of Executive recommendation, and I again urge such action by Congress as will permit the frequent and thorough inspection of consulates by officers appointed for that purpose or by persons already in the diplomatic or consular service. The expense attending such a plan would be insignificant compared with its usefulness, and I hope the legislation necessary to set it on foot will be speedily forthcoming.

I am thoroughly convinced that in addition to their salaries our ambassadors and ministers at foreign courts should be provided by the Government with official residences. The salaries of these officers are comparatively small and in most cases insufficient to pay, with other necessary expenses, the cost of maintaining household establishments in keeping with their important and delicate functions. The usefulness of a nation's diplomatic representative undeniably depends much upon the appropriateness of his surroundings, and a country like ours, while avoiding unnecessary glitter and show, should be certain that it does not suffer in its relations with foreign nations through parsimony and shabbiness in its diplomatic outfit. These considerations and the other advantages of having fixed and somewhat permanent locations for our embassies would abundantly justify the moderate expenditure necessary to carry out this suggestion.

As we turn from a review of our foreign relations to the contemplation of our national financial situation we are immediately aware that we approach a subject of domestic concern more important than any other that can engage our attention, and one at present in such a perplexing and delicate predicament as to require prompt and wise treatment.

We may well be encouraged to earnest effort in this direction when we recall the steps already taken toward improving our economic and financial situation and when we appreciate how well the way has been prepared for further progress by an aroused and intelligent popular interest in these subjects.

By command of the people a customs-revenue system designed for the protection and benefit of favored classes at the expense of the great mass of our countrymen, and which, while inefficient for the purpose of revenue, curtailed our trade relations and impeded our entrance to the markets of the world, has been superseded by a tariff policy which in principle is based upon a denial of the right of the Government to obstruct the avenues to our people's cheap living or lessen their comfort and contentment for the sake of according especial advantages to favorites, and which, while encouraging our intercourse and trade with other nations, recognizes the fact that American self-reliance, thrift, and ingenuity can build up our country's industries and develop its resources more surely than enervating paternalism.

The compulsory purchase and coinage of silver by the Government, unchecked and unregulated by business conditions and heedless of our currency needs, which for more than fifteen years diluted our circulating medium, undermined confidence abroad in our financial ability, and at last culminated in distress and panic at home, has been recently stopped by the repeal of the laws which forced this reckless scheme upon the country.

The things thus accomplished, notwithstanding their extreme importance and beneficent effects, fall far short of curing the monetary evils from which we suffer as a result of long indulgence in ill-advised financial expedients.

The currency denominated United States notes and commonly known as greenbacks was issued in large volume during the late Civil War and was intended originally to meet the exigencies of that period. It will be seen by a reference to the debates in Congress at the time the laws were passed authorizing the issue of these notes that their advocates declared they were intended for only temporary use and to meet the emergency of war. In almost if not all the laws relating to them some provision was made contemplating their voluntary or compulsory retirement. A large quantity of them, however, were kept on foot and mingled with the currency of the country, so that at the close of the year 1874 they amounted to $381,999,073.

Immediately after that date, and in January, 1875, a law was passed providing for the resumption of specie payments, by which the Secretary of the Treasury was required whenever additional circulation was issued to national banks to retire United States notes equal in amount to 80 per cent of such additional national-bank circulation until such notes were reduced to $300,000,000. This law further provided that on and after the 1st day of January, 1879, the United States notes then outstanding should be redeemed in coin, and in order to provide and prepare for such redemption the Secretary of the Treasury was authorized not only to use any surplus revenues of the Government, but to issue bonds of the United States and dispose of them for coin and to use the proceeds for the purposes contemplated by the statute.

In May, 1878, and before the date thus appointed for the redemption and retirement of these notes, another statute was passed forbidding their further cancellation and retirement. Some of them had, however, been previously redeemed and canceled upon the issue of additional national-bank circulation, as permitted by the law of 1875, so that the amount outstanding at the time of the passage of the act forbidding their further retirement was $346,681,016.

The law of 1878 did not stop at distinct prohibition, but contained in addition the following express provision:

And when any of said notes may be redeemed or be received into the Treasury under any law from any source whatever, and shall belong to the United States, they shall not be retired, canceled, or destroyed, but they shall be reissued and paid out again and kept in circulation.

This was the condition of affairs on the 1st day of January, 1879, which had been fixed upon four years before as the date for entering upon the redemption and retirement of all these notes, and for which such abundant means had been provided.

The Government was put in the anomalous situation of owing to the holders of its notes debts payable in gold on demand which could neither be retired by receiving such notes in discharge of obligations due the Government nor canceled by actual payment in gold. It was forced to redeem without redemption and to pay without acquittance.

There had been issued and sold $95,500,000 of the bonds authorized by the resumption act of 1875, the proceeds of which, together with other gold in the Treasury, created a gold fund deemed sufficient to meet the demands which might be made upon it for the redemption of the outstanding United States notes. This fund, together with such other gold as might be from time to time in the Treasury available for the same purpose, has been since called our gold reserve, and $100,000,000 has been regarded as an adequate amount to accomplish its object. This fund amounted on the 1st day of January, 1879, to $114,193,360, and though thereafter constantly fluctuating it did not fall below that sum until July, 1892. In April, 1893, for the first time since its establishment, this reserve amounted to less than $100,000,000, containing at that date only $97,011,330.

In the meantime, and in July, 1890, an act had been passed directing larger governmental monthly purchases of silver than had been required under previous laws, and providing that in payment for such silver Treasury notes of the United States should be issued payable on demand in gold or silver coin, at the discretion of the Secretary of the Treasury. It was, however, declared in the act to be "the established policy of the United States to maintain the two metals on a parity with each other upon the present legal ratio or such ratio as may be provided by law." In view of this declaration it was not deemed permissible for the Secretary of the Treasury to exercise the discretion in terms conferred on him by refusing to pay gold on these notes when demanded, because by such discrimination in favor of the gold dollar the so-called parity of the two metals would be destroyed and grave and dangerous consequences would be precipitated by affirming or accentuating the constantly widening disparity between their actual values under the existing ratio.

It thus resulted that the Treasury notes issued in payment of silver purchases under the law of 1890 were necessarily treated as gold obligations at the option of the holder. These notes on the 1st day of November, 1893, when the law compelling the monthly purchase of silver was repealed, amounted to more than $155,000,000. The notes of this description now outstanding added to the United States notes still undiminished by redemption or cancellation constitute a volume of gold obligations amounting to nearly $500,000,000.

These obligations are the instruments which ever since we had a gold reserve have been used to deplete it.

This reserve, as has been stated, had fallen in April, 1893, to $97,011,330. It has from that time to the present, with very few and unimportant upward movements, steadily decreased, except as it has been temporarily replenished by the sale of bonds.

Among the causes for this constant and uniform shrinkage in this fund may be mentioned the great falling off of exports under the operation of the tariff law until recently in force, which crippled our exchange of commodities with foreign nations and necessitated to some extent the payment of our balances in gold; the unnatural infusion of silver into our currency and the increasing agitation for its free and unlimited coinage, which have created apprehension as to our disposition or ability to continue gold payments; the consequent hoarding of gold at home and the stoppage of investments of foreign capital, as well as the return of our securities already sold abroad; and the high rate of foreign exchange, which induced the shipment of our gold to be drawn against as a matter of speculation.

In consequence of these conditions the gold reserve on the 1st day of February, 1894, was reduced to $65,438,377, having lost more than $31,000,000 during the preceding nine months, or since April, 1893. Its replenishment being necessary and no other manner of accomplishing it being possible, resort was had to the issue and sale of bonds provided for by the resumption act of 1875. Fifty millions of these bonds were sold, yielding $58,633,295.71, which was added to the reserve fund of gold then on hand. As a result of this operation this reserve, which had suffered constant and large withdrawals in the meantime, stood on the 6th day of March, 1894, at the sum of $107,446,802. Its depletion was, however, immediately thereafter so accelerated that on the 30th day of June, 1894, it had fallen to $64,873,025, thus losing by withdrawals more than $42,000,000 in five months and dropping slightly below its situation when the sale of $50,000,000 in bonds was effected for its replenishment.

This depressed condition grew worse, and on the 24th day of November, 1894, our gold reserve being reduced to $57,669,701, it became necessary to again strengthen it.

This was done by another sale of bonds amounting to $50,000,000, from which there was realized $58,538,500, with which the fund was increased to $111,142,021 on the 4th day of December, 1894.

Again disappointment awaited the anxious hope for relief. There was not even a lull in the exasperating withdrawals of gold. On the contrary, they grew larger and more persistent than ever. Between the 4th day of December, 1894, and early in February, 1895, a period of scarcely more than two months after the second reenforcement of our gold reserve by the sale of bonds, it had lost by such withdrawals more than $69,000,000 and had fallen to $41,340,181. Nearly $43,000,000 had been withdrawn within the month immediately preceding this situation.

In anticipation of impending trouble I had on the 28th day of January, 1895, addressed a communication* to the Congress fully setting forth our difficulties and dangerous position and earnestly recommending that authority be given the Secretary of the Treasury to issue bonds bearing a low rate of interest, payable by their terms in gold, for the purpose of maintaining a sufficient gold reserve and also for the redemption and cancellation of outstanding United States notes and the Treasury notes issued for the purchase of silver under the law of 1890. This recommendation did not, however, meet with legislative approval.

In February, 1895, therefore, the situation was exceedingly critical. With a reserve perilously low and a refusal of Congressional aid, everything indicated that the end of gold payments by the Government was imminent. The results of prior bond issues had been exceedingly unsatisfactory, and the large withdrawals of gold immediately succeeding their public sale in open market gave rise to a reasonable suspicion that a large part of the gold paid into the Treasury upon such sales was promptly drawn out again by the presentation of United States notes or Treasury notes, and found its way to the hands of those who had only temporarily parted with it in the purchase of bonds.

In this emergency, and in view of its surrounding perplexities, it became entirely apparent to those upon whom the struggle for safety was devolved not only that our gold reserve must, for the third time in less than thirteen months, be restored by another issue and sale of bonds bearing a high rate of interest and badly suited to the purpose, but that a plan must be adopted for their disposition promising better results than those realized on previous sales. An agreement was therefore made with a number of financiers and bankers whereby it was stipulated that bonds described in the resumption act of 1875, payable in coin thirty years after their date, bearing interest at the rate of 4 per cent per annum, and amounting to about $62,000,000, should be exchanged for gold, receivable by weight, amounting to a little more than $65,000,000.

This gold was to be delivered in such installments as would complete its delivery within about six months from the date of the contract, and

*See pp. 561-565.

at least one-half of the amount was to be furnished from abroad. It was also agreed by those supplying this gold that during the continuance of the contract they would by every means in their power protect the Government against gold withdrawals. The contract also provided that if Congress would authorize their issue bonds payable by their terms in gold and bearing interest at the rate of 3 per cent per annum might within ten days be substituted at par for the 4 per cent bonds described in the agreement.

On the day this contract was made its terms were communicated to Congress by a special Executive message,* in which it was stated that more than $16,000,000 would be saved to the Government if gold bonds bearing 3 per cent interest were authorized to be substituted for those mentioned in the contract.

The Congress having declined to grant the necessary authority to secure this saving, the contract, unmodified, was carried out, resulting in a gold reserve amounting to $107,571,230 on the 8th day of July, 1895. The performance of this contract not only restored the reserve, but checked for a time the withdrawals of gold and brought on a period of restored confidence and such peace and quiet in business circles as were of the greatest possible value to every interest that affects our people. I have never had the slightest misgiving concerning the wisdom or propriety of this arrangement, and am quite willing to answer for my full share of responsibility for its promotion. I believe it averted a disaster the imminence of which was, fortunately, not at the time generally understood by our people.

Though the contract mentioned stayed for a time the tide of gold withdrawal, its good results could not be permanent. Recent withdrawals have reduced the reserve from $107,571,230 on the 8th day of July, 1895, to $79,333,966. How long it will remain large enough to render its increase unnecessary is only matter of conjecture, though quite large withdrawals for shipment in the immediate future are predicted in well-informed quarters. About $16,000,000 has been withdrawn during the month of November.

The foregoing statement of events and conditions develops the fact that after increasing our interest-bearing bonded indebtedness more than $162,000,000 to save our gold reserve we are nearly where we started, having now in such reserve $79,333,966, as against $65,438,377 in February, 1894, when the first bonds were issued.

Though the amount of gold drawn from the Treasury appears to be very large as gathered from the facts and figures herein presented, it actually was much larger, considerable sums having been acquired by the Treasury within the several periods stated without the issue of bonds. On the 28th of January, 1895, it was reported by the Secretary of the Treasury that more than $172,000,000 of gold had been withdrawn for

*See pp. 567–568.

hoarding or shipment during the year preceding. He now reports that from January 1, 1879, to July 14, 1890, a period of more than eleven years, only a little over $28,000,000 was withdrawn, and that between July 14, 1890, the date of the passage of the law for an increased purchase of silver, and the 1st day of December, 1895, or within less than five and a half years, there was withdrawn nearly $375,000,000, making a total of more than $403,000,000 drawn from the Treasury in gold since January 1, 1879, the date fixed in 1875 for the retirement of the United States notes.

Nearly $327,000,000 of the gold thus withdrawn has been paid out on these United States notes, and yet every one of the $346,000,000 is still uncanceled and ready to do service in future gold depletions.

More than $76,000,000 in gold has since their creation in 1890 been paid out from the Treasury upon the notes given on the purchase of silver by the Government, and yet the whole, amounting to $155,000,000, except a little more than $16,000,000 which has been retired by exchanges for silver at the request of the holders, remains outstanding and prepared to join their older and more experienced allies in future raids upon the Treasury's gold reserve.

In other words, the Government has paid in gold more than nine-tenths of its United States notes and still owes them all. It has paid in gold about one-half of its notes given for silver purchases without extinguishing by such payment one dollar of these notes.

When, added to all this, we are reminded that to carry on this astounding financial scheme the Government has incurred a bonded indebtedness of $95,500,000 in establishing a gold reserve and of $162,315,400 in efforts to maintain it; that the annual interest charge on such bonded indebtedness is more than $11,000,000; that a continuance of our present course may result in further bond issues, and that we have suffered or are threatened with all this for the sake of supplying gold for foreign shipment or facilitating its hoarding at home, a situation is exhibited which certainly ought to arrest attention and provoke immediate legislative relief.

I am convinced the only thorough and practicable remedy for our troubles is found in the retirement and cancellation of our United States notes, commonly called greenbacks, and the outstanding Treasury notes issued by the Government in payment of silver purchases under the act of 1890.

I believe this could be quite readily accomplished by the exchange of these notes for United States bonds, of small as well as large denominations, bearing a low rate of interest. They should be long-term bonds, thus increasing their desirability as investments, and because their payment could be well postponed to a period far removed from present financial burdens and perplexities, when with increased prosperity and resources they would be more easily met.

To further insure the cancellation of these notes and also provide a way by which gold may be added to our currency in lieu of them, a feature in the plan should be an authority given to the Secretary of the Treasury to dispose of the bonds abroad for gold if necessary to complete the contemplated redemption and cancellation, permitting him to use the proceeds of such bonds to take up and cancel any of the notes that may be in the Treasury or that may be received by the Government on any account.

The increase of our bonded debt involved in this plan would be amply compensated by renewed activity and enterprise in all business circles, the restored confidence at home, the reinstated faith in our monetary strength abroad, and the stimulation of every interest and industry that would follow the cancellation of the gold-demand obligations now afflicting us. In any event, the bonds proposed would stand for the extinguishment of a troublesome indebtedness, while in the path we now follow there lurks the menace of unending bonds, with our indebtedness still undischarged and aggravated in every feature. The obligations necessary to fund this indebtedness would not equal in amount those from which we have been relieved since 1884 by anticipation and payment beyond the requirements of the sinking fund out of our surplus revenues.

The currency withdrawn by the retirement of the United States notes and Treasury notes, amounting to probably less than $486,000,000, might be supplied by such gold as would be used on their retirement or by an increase in the circulation of our national banks. Though the aggregate capital of those now in existence amounts to more than $664,000,000, their outstanding circulation based on bond security amounts to only about $190,000,000. They are authorized to issue notes amounting to 90 per cent of the bonds deposited to secure their circulation, but in no event beyond the amount of their capital stock, and they are obliged to pay 1 per cent tax on the circulation they issue.

I think they should be allowed to issue circulation equal to the par value of the bonds they deposit to secure it, and that the tax on their circulation should be reduced to one-fourth of 1 per cent, which would undoubtedly meet all the expense the Government incurs on their account. In addition they should be allowed to substitute or deposit in lieu of the bonds now required as security for their circulation those which would be issued for the purpose of retiring the United States notes and Treasury notes.

The banks already existing, if they desired to avail themselves of the provisions of law thus modified, could issue circulation, in addition to that already outstanding, amounting to $478,000,000, which would nearly or quite equal the currency proposed to be canceled. At any rate, I should confidently expect to see the existing national banks or others to be organized avail themselves of the proposed encouragements to issue circulation and promptly fill any vacuum and supply every currency need.

It has always seemed to me that the provisions of law regarding the capital of national banks, which operate as a limitation to their location, fail to make proper compensation for the suppression of State banks, which came near to the people in all sections of the country and readily furnished them with banking accommodations and facilities. Any inconvenience or embarrassment arising from these restrictions on the location of national banks might well be remedied by better adapting the present system to the creation of banks in smaller communities or by permitting banks of large capital to establish branches in such localities as would serve the people, so regulated and restrained as to secure their safe and conservative control and management.

But there might not be the necessity for such an addition to the currency by new issues of bank circulation as at first glance is indicated. If we should be relieved from maintaining a gold reserve under conditions that constitute it the barometer of our solvency, and if our Treasury should no longer be the foolish purveyor of gold for nations abroad or for speculation and hoarding by our citizens at home, I should expect to see gold resume its natural and normal functions in the business affairs of the country and cease to be an object attracting the timid watch of our people and exciting their sensitive imaginations.

I do not overlook the fact that the cancellation of the Treasury notes issued under the silver-purchasing act of 1890 would leave the Treasury in the actual ownership of sufficient silver, including seigniorage, to coin nearly $178,000,000 in standard dollars. It is worthy of consideration whether this might not from time to time be converted into dollars or fractional coin and slowly put into circulation, as in the judgment of the Secretary of the Treasury the necessities of the country should require.

Whatever is attempted should be entered upon fully appreciating the fact that by careless, easy descent we have reached a dangerous depth, and that our ascent will not be accomplished without laborious toil and struggle. We shall be wise if we realize that we are financially ill and that our restoration to health may require heroic treatment and unpleasant remedies.

In the present stage of our difficulty it is not easy to understand how the amount of our revenue receipts directly affects it. The important question is not the quantity of money received in revenue payments, but the kind of money we maintain and our ability to continue in sound financial condition. We are considering the Government's holdings of gold as related to the soundness of our money and as affecting our national credit and monetary strength.

If our gold reserve had never been impaired; if no bonds had ever been issued to replenish it; if there had been no fear and timidity concerning our ability to continue gold payments; if any part of our revenues were now paid in gold, and if we could look to our gold receipts as a means of maintaining a safe reserve, the amount of our revenues would be an influential factor in the problem. But, unfortunately, all the circumstances that might lend weight to this consideration are entirely lacking.

In our present predicament no gold is received by the Government in payment of revenue charges, nor would there be if the revenues were increased. The receipts of the Treasury, when not in silver certificates, consist of United States notes and Treasury notes issued for silver purchases. These forms of money are only useful to the Government in paying its current ordinary expenses, and its quantity in Government possession does not in the least contribute toward giving us that kind of safe financial standing or condition which is built on gold alone.

If it is said that these notes if held by the Government can be used to obtain gold for our reserve, the answer is easy. The people draw gold from the Treasury on demand upon United States notes and Treasury notes, but the proposition that the Treasury can on demand draw gold from the people upon them would be regarded in these days with wonder and amusement; and even if this could be done there is nothing to prevent those thus parting with their gold from regaining it the next day or the next hour by the presentation of the notes they received in exchange for it.

The Secretary of the Treasury might use such notes taken from a surplus revenue to buy gold in the market. Of course he could not do this without paying a premium. Private holders of gold, unlike the Government, having no parity to maintain, would not be restrained from making the best bargain possible when they furnished gold to the Treasury; but the moment the Secretary of the Treasury bought gold on any terms above par he would establish a general and universal premium upon it, thus breaking down the parity between gold and silver, which the Government is pledged to maintain, and opening the way to new and serious complications. In the meantime the premium would not remain stationary, and the absurd spectacle might be presented of a dealer selling gold to the Government and with United States notes or Treasury notes in his hand immediately clamoring for its return and a resale at a higher premium.

It may be claimed that a large revenue and redundant receipts might favorably affect the situation under discussion by affording an opportunity of retaining these notes in the Treasury when received, and thus preventing their presentation for gold. Such retention to be useful ought to be at least measurably permanent; and this is precisely what is prohibited, so far as United States notes are concerned, by the law of 1878, forbidding their further retirement. That statute in so many words provides that these notes when received into the Treasury and belonging to the United States shall be "paid out again and kept in circulation."

It will, moreover, be readily seen that the Government could not refuse to pay out United States notes and Treasury notes in current transactions when demanded, and insist on paying out silver alone, and still maintain the parity between that metal and the currency representing gold. Besides, the accumulation in the Treasury of currency of any kind exacted from the people through taxation is justly regarded as an evil, and it can not proceed far without vigorous protest against an unjustifiable retention of money from the business of the country and a denunciation of a scheme of taxation which proves itself to be unjust when it takes from the earnings and income of the citizen money so much in excess of the needs of Government support that large sums can be gathered and kept in the Treasury. Such a condition has heretofore in times of surplus revenue led the Government to restore currency to the people by the purchase of its unmatured bonds at a large premium and by a large increase of its deposits in national banks, and we easily remember that the abuse of Treasury accumulation has furnished a most persuasive argument in favor of legislation radically reducing our tariff taxation.

Perhaps it is supposed that sufficient revenue receipts would in a sentimental way improve the situation by inspiring confidence in our solvency and allaying the fear of pecuniary exhaustion. And yet through all our struggles to maintain our gold reserve there never has been any apprehension as to our ready ability to pay our way with such money as we had, and the question whether or not our current receipts met our current expenses has not entered into the estimate of our solvency. Of course the general state of our funds, exclusive of gold, was entirely immaterial to the foreign creditor and investor. His debt could only be paid in gold, and his only concern was our ability to keep on hand that kind of money.

On July 1, 1892, more than a year and a half before the first bonds were issued to replenish the gold reserve, there was a net balance in the Treasury, exclusive of such reserve, of less than $13,000,000, but the gold reserve amounted to more than $114,000,000, which was the quieting feature of the situation. It was when the stock of gold began rapidly to fall that fright supervened and our securities held abroad were returned for sale and debts owed abroad were pressed for payment. In the meantime extensive shipments of gold and other unfavorable indications caused restlessness and fright among our people at home. Thereupon the general state of our funds, exclusive of gold, became also immaterial to them, and they too drew gold from the Treasury for hoarding against all contingencies. This is plainly shown by the large increase in the proportion of gold withdrawn which was retained by our own people as time and threatening incidents progressed. During the fiscal year ending June 30, 1894, nearly $85,000,000 in gold was withdrawn from the Treasury and about $77,000,000 was sent abroad, while during the fiscal year ending June 30, 1895, over $117,000,000 was drawn out, of which only about $66,000,000 was shipped, leaving the large balance of such withdrawals to be accounted for by domestic hoarding.

Inasmuch as the withdrawal of our gold has resulted largely from fright, there is nothing apparent that will prevent its continuance or recurrence, with its natural consequences, except such a change in our financial methods as will reassure the frightened and make the desire for gold less intense. It is not clear how an increase in revenue, unless it be in gold, can satisfy those whose only anxiety is to gain gold from the Government's store.

It can not, therefore, be safe to rely upon increased revenues as a cure for our present troubles.

It is possible that the suggestion of increased revenue as a remedy for the difficulties we are considering may have originated in an intimation or distinct allegation that the bonds which have been issued ostensibly to replenish our gold reserve were really issued to supply insufficient revenue. Nothing can be further from the truth. Bonds were issued to obtain gold for the maintenance of our national credit. As has been shown, the gold thus obtained has been drawn again from the Treasury upon United States notes and Treasury notes. This operation would have been promptly prevented if possible; but these notes having thus been passed to the Treasury, they became the money of the Government, like any other ordinary Government funds, and there was nothing to do but to use them in paying Government expenses when needed.

At no time when bonds have been issued has there been any consideration of the question of paying the expenses of Government with their proceeds. There was no necessity to consider that question. At the time of each bond issue we had a safe surplus in the Treasury for ordinary operations, exclusive of the gold in our reserve. In February, 1894, when the first issue of bonds was made, such surplus amounted to over $18,000,000; in November, when the second issue was made, it amounted to more than $42,000,000, and in February, 1895, when bonds for the third time were issued, such surplus amounted to more than $100,000,000. It now amounts to $98,072,420.30.

Besides all this, the Secretary of the Treasury had no authority whatever to issue bonds to increase the ordinary revenues or pay current expenses.

I can not but think there has been some confusion of ideas regarding the effects of the issue of bonds and the results of the withdrawal of gold. It was the latter process, and not the former, that, by substituting in the Treasury United States notes and Treasury notes for gold, increased by their amount the money which was in the first instance subject to ordinary Government expenditure.

Although the law compelling an increased purchase of silver by the Government was passed on the 14th day of July, 1890, withdrawals of gold from the Treasury upon the notes given in payment on such purchases did not begin until October, 1891. Immediately following that date the withdrawals upon both these notes and United States notes increased very largely, and have continued to such an extent that since the passage of that law there has been more than thirteen times as much gold taken out of the Treasury upon United States notes and Treasury notes issued for silver purchases as was thus withdrawn during the eleven and a half years immediately prior thereto and after the 1st day of January, 1879, when specie payments were resumed.

It is neither unfair nor unjust to charge a large share of our present financial perplexities and dangers to the operation of the laws of 1878 and 1890 compelling the purchase of silver by the Government, which not only furnished a new Treasury obligation upon which its gold could be withdrawn, but so increased the fear of an overwhelming flood of silver and a forced descent to silver payments that even the repeal of these laws did not entirely cure the evils of their existence.

While I have endeavored to make a plain statement of the disordered condition of our currency and the present dangers menacing our prosperity and to suggest a way which leads to a safer financial system, I have constantly had in mind the fact that many of my countrymen, whose sincerity I do not doubt, insist that the cure for the ills now threatening us may be found in the single and simple remedy of the free coinage of silver. They contend that our mints shall be at once thrown open to the free, unlimited, and independent coinage of both gold and silver dollars of full legal-tender quality, regardless of the action of any other government and in full view of the fact that the ratio between the metals which they suggest calls for 100 cents' worth of gold in the gold dollar at the present standard and only 50 cents in intrinsic worth of silver in the silver dollar.

Were there infinitely stronger reasons than can be adduced for hoping that such action would secure for us a bimetallic currency moving on lines of parity, an experiment so novel and hazardous as that proposed might well stagger those who believe that stability is an imperative condition of sound money.

No government, no human contrivance or act of legislation, has ever been able to hold the two metals together in free coinage at a ratio appreciably different from that which is established in the markets of the world.

Those who believe that our independent free coinage of silver at an artificial ratio with gold of 16 to 1 would restore the parity between the metals, and consequently between the coins, oppose an unsupported and improbable theory to the general belief and practice of other nations and to the teaching of the wisest statesmen and economists of the world, both in the past and present, and, what is far more conclusive, they run counter to our own actual experiences.

Twice in our earlier history our lawmakers, in attempting to establish a bimetallic currency, undertook free coinage upon a ratio which accidentally varied from the actual relative values of the two metals not more than 3 per cent. In both cases, notwithstanding greater difficulties and cost of transportation than now exist, the coins whose intrinsic worth was undervalued in the ratio gradually and surely disappeared from our circulation and went to other countries where their real value was better recognized.

Acts of Congress were impotent to create equality where natural causes decreed even a slight inequality.

Twice in our recent history we have signally failed to raise by legislation the value of silver. Under an act of Congress passed in 1878 the Government was required for more than twelve years to expend annually at least $24,000,000 in the purchase of silver bullion for coinage. The act of July 14, 1890, in a still bolder effort, increased the amount of silver the Government was compelled to purchase and forced it to become the buyer annually of 54,000,000 ounces, or practically the entire product of our mines. Under both laws silver rapidly and steadily declined in value. The prophecy and the expressed hope and expectation of those in the Congress who led in the passage of the last-mentioned act that it would reestablish and maintain the former parity between the two metals are still fresh in our memory.

In the light of these experiences, which accord with the experiences of other nations, there is certainly no secure ground for the belief that an act of Congress could now bridge an inequality of 50 per cent between gold and silver at our present ratio, nor is there the least possibility that our country, which has less than one-seventh of the silver money in the world, could by its action alone raise not only our own but all silver to its lost ratio with gold. Our attempt to accomplish this by the free coinage of silver at a ratio differing widely from actual relative values would be the signal for the complete departure of gold from our circulation, the immediate and large contraction of our circulating medium, and a shrinkage in the real value and monetary efficiency of all other forms of currency as they settled to the level of silver monometallism. Everyone who receives a fixed salary and every worker for wages would find the dollar in his hand ruthlessly scaled down to the point of bitter disappointment, if not to pinching privation.

A change in our standard to silver monometallism would also bring on a collapse of the entire system of credit, which, when based on a standard which is recognized and adopted by the world of business, is many times more potent and useful than the entire volume of currency and is safely capable of almost indefinite expansion to meet the growth of trade and enterprise. In a self-invited struggle through darkness and uncertainty our humiliation would be increased by the consciousness that we had parted company with all the enlightened and progressive nations of the world and were desperately and hopelessly striving to meet the stress of modern commerce and competition with a debased and unsuitable currency and in association with the few weak and laggard nations which have silver alone as their standard of value.

All history warns us against rash experiments which threaten violent changes in our monetary standard and the degradation of our currency. The past is full of lessons teaching not only the economic dangers but the national immorality that follow in the train of such experiments. I will not believe that the American people can be persuaded after sober deliberation to jeopardize their nation's prestige and proud standing by encouraging financial nostrums, nor that they will yield to the false allurements of cheap money when they realize that it must result in the weakening of that financial integrity and rectitude which thus far in our history has been so devotedly cherished as one of the traits of true Americanism.

Our country's indebtedness, whether owing by the Government or existing between individuals, has been contracted with reference to our present standard. To decree by act of Congress that these debts shall be payable in less valuable dollars than those within the contemplation and intention of the parties when contracted would operate to transfer by the fiat of law and without compensation an amount of property and a volume of rights and interests almost incalculable.

Those who advocate a blind and headlong plunge to free coinage in the name of bimetallism, and professing the belief, contrary to all experience, that we could thus establish a double standard and a concurrent circulation of both metals in our coinage, are certainly reckoning from a cloudy standpoint. Our present standard of value is the standard of the civilized world and permits the only bimetallism now possible, or at least that is within the independent reach of any single nation, however powerful that nation may be. While the value of gold as a standard is steadied by almost universal commercial and business use, it does not despise silver nor seek its banishment. Wherever this standard is maintained there is at its side in free and unquestioned circulation a volume of silver currency sometimes equaling and sometimes even exceeding it in amount, both maintained at a parity notwithstanding a depreciation or fluctuation in the intrinsic value of silver.

There is a vast difference between a standard of value and a currency for monetary use. The standard must necessarily be fixed and certain. The currency may be in divers forms and of various kinds. No silver-standard country has a gold currency in circulation, but an enlightened and wise system of finance secures the benefits of both gold and silver as currency and circulating medium by keeping the standard stable and all other currency at par with it. Such a system and such a standard also give free scope for the use and expansion of safe and conservative credit, so indispensable to broad and growing commercial transactions and so well substituted for the actual use of money. If a fixed and stable standard is maintained, such as the magnitude and safety of our commercial transactions and business require, the use of money itself is conveniently minimized.

Every dollar of fixed and stable value has through the agency of confident credit an astonishing capacity of multiplying itself in financial work. Every unstable and fluctuating dollar fails as a basis of credit, and in its use begets gambling speculation and undermines the foundations of honest enterprise.

I have ventured to express myself on this subject with earnestness and plainness of speech because I can not rid myself of the belief that there lurk in the proposition for the free coinage of silver, so strongly approved and so enthusiastically advocated by a multitude of my countrymen, a serious menace to our prosperity and an insidious temptation of our people to wander from the allegiance they owe to public and private integrity. It is because I do not distrust the good faith and sincerity of those who press this scheme that I have imperfectly but with zeal submitted my thoughts upon this momentous subject. I can not refrain from begging them to reexamine their views and beliefs in the light of patriotic reason and familiar experience and to weigh again and again the consequences of such legislation as their efforts have invited. Even the continued agitation of the subject adds greatly to the difficulties of a dangerous financial situation already forced upon us.

In conclusion I especially entreat the people's representatives in the Congress, who are charged with the responsibility of inaugurating measures for the safety and prosperity of our common country, to promptly and effectively consider the ills of our critical financial plight. I have suggested a remedy which my judgment approves. I desire, however, to assure the Congress that I am prepared to cooperate with them in perfecting any other measure promising thorough and practical relief, and that I will gladly labor with them in every patriotic endeavor to further the interests and guard the welfare of our countrymen, whom in our respective places of duty we have undertaken to serve.

GROVER CLEVELAND.

SPECIAL MESSAGES.

To the Congress: EXECUTIVE MANSION, *December 17, 1895.*

In my annual message addressed to the Congress on the 3d instant I called attention to the pending boundary controversy between Great Britain and the Republic of Venezuela and recited the substance of a representation made by this Government to Her Britannic Majesty's Government suggesting reasons why such dispute should be submitted to arbitration for settlement and inquiring whether it would be so submitted.*

The answer of the British Government, which was then awaited, has since been received, and, together with the dispatch to which it is a reply, is hereto appended.

* See p. 632.

Such reply is embodied in two communications addressed by the British prime minister to Sir Julian Pauncefote, the British ambassador at this capital. It will be seen that one of these communications is devoted exclusively to observations upon the Monroe doctrine, and claims that in the present instance a new and strange extension and development of this doctrine is insisted on by the United States; that the reasons justifying an appeal to the doctrine enunciated by President Monroe are generally inapplicable "to the state of things in which we live at the present day," and especially inapplicable to a controversy involving the boundary line between Great Britain and Venezuela.

Without attempting extended argument in reply to these positions, it may not be amiss to suggest that the doctrine upon which we stand is strong and sound, because its enforcement is important to our peace and safety as a nation and is essential to the integrity of our free institutions and the tranquil maintenance of our distinctive form of government. It was intended to apply to every stage of our national life and can not become obsolete while our Republic endures. If the balance of power is justly a cause for jealous anxiety among the Governments of the Old World and a subject for our absolute noninterference, none the less is an observance of the Monroe doctrine of vital concern to our people and their Government.

Assuming, therefore, that we may properly insist upon this doctrine without regard to "the state of things in which we live" or any changed conditions here or elsewhere, it is not apparent why its application may not be invoked in the present controversy.

If a European power by an extension of its boundaries takes possession of the territory of one of our neighboring Republics against its will and in derogation of its rights, it is difficult to see why to that extent such European power does not thereby attempt to extend its system of government to that portion of this continent which is thus taken. This is the precise action which President Monroe declared to be "dangerous to our peace and safety," and it can make no difference whether the European system is extended by an advance of frontier or otherwise.

It is also suggested in the British reply that we should not seek to apply the Monroe doctrine to the pending dispute because it does not embody any principle of international law which "is founded on the general consent of nations," and that "no statesman, however eminent, and no nation, however powerful, are competent to insert into the code of international law a novel principle which was never recognized before and which has not since been accepted by the government of any other country."

Practically the principle for which we contend has peculiar, if not exclusive, relation to the United States. It may not have been admitted in so many words to the code of international law, but since in international councils every nation is entitled to the rights belonging to it, if the enforcement of the Monroe doctrine is something we may justly claim it has its place in the code of international law as certainly and as securely as if it were specifically mentioned; and when the United States is a suitor before the high tribunal that administers international law the question to be determined is whether or not we present claims which the justice of that code of law can find to be right and valid.

The Monroe doctrine finds its recognition in those principles of international law which are based upon the theory that every nation shall have its rights protected and its just claims enforced.

Of course this Government is entirely confident that under the sanction of this doctrine we have clear rights and undoubted claims. Nor is this ignored in the British reply. The prime minister, while not admitting that the Monroe doctrine is applicable to present conditions, states:

In declaring that the United States would resist any such enterprise if it was contemplated, President Monroe adopted a policy which received the entire sympathy of the English Government of that date.

He further declares:

Though the language of President Monroe is directed to the attainment of objects which most Englishmen would agree to be salutary, it is impossible to admit that they have been inscribed by any adequate authority in the code of international law.

Again he says:

They [Her Majesty's Government] fully concur with the view which President Monroe apparently entertained, that any disturbance of the existing territorial distribution in that hemisphere by any fresh acquisitions on the part of any European State would be a highly inexpedient change.

In the belief that the doctrine for which we contend was clear and definite, that it was founded upon substantial considerations and involved our safety and welfare, that it was fully applicable to our present conditions and to the state of the world's progress, and that it was directly related to the pending controversy, and without any conviction as to the final merits of the dispute, but anxious to learn in a satisfactory and conclusive manner whether Great Britain sought under a claim of boundary to extend her possessions on this continent without right, or whether she merely sought possession of territory fairly included within her lines of ownership, this Government proposed to the Government of Great Britain a resort to arbitration as the proper means of settling the question, to the end that a vexatious boundary dispute between the two contestants might be determined and our exact standing and relation in respect to the controversy might be made clear.

It will be seen from the correspondence herewith submitted that this proposition has been declined by the British Government upon grounds which in the circumstances seem to me to be far from satisfactory. It is deeply disappointing that such an appeal, actuated by the most friendly feelings toward both nations directly concerned, addressed to the sense of justice and to the magnanimity of one of the great powers of the world, and touching its relations to one comparatively weak and small, should have produced no better results.

The course to be pursued by this Government in view of the present condition does not appear to admit of serious doubt. Having labored faithfully for many years to induce Great Britain to submit this dispute to impartial arbitration, and having been now finally apprised of her refusal to do so, nothing remains but to accept the situation, to recognize its plain requirements, and deal with it accordingly. Great Britain's present proposition has never thus far been regarded as admissible by Venezuela, though any adjustment of the boundary which that country may deem for her advantage and may enter into of her own free will can not of course be objected to by the United States.

Assuming, however, that the attitude of Venezuela will remain unchanged, the dispute has reached such a stage as to make it now incumbent upon the United States to take measures to determine with sufficient certainty for its justification what is the true divisional line between the Republic of Venezuela and British Guiana. The inquiry to that end should of course be conducted carefully and judicially, and due weight should be given to all available evidence, records, and facts in support of the claims of both parties.

In order that such an examination should be prosecuted in a thorough and satisfactory manner, I suggest that the Congress make an adequate appropriation for the expenses of a commission, to be appointed by the Executive, who shall make the necessary investigation and report upon the matter with the least possible delay. When such report is made and accepted it will, in my opinion, be the duty of the United States to resist by every means in its power, as a willful aggression upon its rights and interests, the appropriation by Great Britain of any lands or the exercise of governmental jurisdiction over any territory which after investigation we have determined of right belongs to Venezuela.

In making these recommendations I am fully alive to the responsibility incurred and keenly realize all the consequences that may follow.

I am, nevertheless, firm in my conviction that while it is a grievous thing to contemplate the two great English-speaking peoples of the world as being otherwise than friendly competitors in the onward march of civilization and strenuous and worthy rivals in all the arts of peace, there is no calamity which a great nation can invite which equals that which follows a supine submission to wrong and injustice and the consequent loss of national self-respect and honor, beneath which are shielded and defended a people's safety and greatness.

GROVER CLEVELAND.

EXECUTIVE MANSION,
Washington, December 19, 1895.

To the Senate of the United States:

In response to the resolution of the Senate of the 4th instant, requesting the President, "if in his judgment not incompatible with the public interest, to communicate to the Senate all information which has been received by him or by the State Department in regard to injuries inflicted upon the persons or property of American citizens in Turkey and in regard to the condition of affairs there in reference to the oppression or cruelties practiced upon the Armenian subjects of the Turkish Government; also to inform the Senate whether all the American consuls in the Turkish Empire are at their posts of duty, and, if not, to state any circumstances which have interfered with the performance of the duties of such consuls,'' I transmit herewith a report from the Secretary of State.

GROVER CLEVELAND.

To the Congress: EXECUTIVE MANSION, *December 20, 1895.*

In my last annual message the evils of our present financial system were plainly pointed out and the causes and means of the depletion of Government gold were explained. It was therein stated that after all the efforts that had been made by the executive branch of the Government to protect our gold reserve by the issuance of bonds amounting to more than $162,000,000, such reserve then amounted to but little more than $79,000,000; that about $16,000,000 had been withdrawn from such reserve during the month next previous to the date of that message, and that quite large withdrawals for shipment in the immediate future were predicted.

The contingency then feared has reached us, and the withdrawals of gold since the communication referred to and others that appear inevitable threaten such a depletion in our Government gold reserve as brings us face to face to the necessity of further action for its protection. This condition is intensified by the prevalence in certain quarters of sudden and unusual apprehension and timidity in business circles.

We are in the midst of another season of perplexity caused by our dangerous and fatuous financial operations. These may be expected to recur with certainty as long as there is no amendment in our financial system. If in this particular instance our predicament is at all influenced by a recent insistence upon the position we should occupy in our relation to certain questions concerning our foreign policy, this furnishes a signal and impressive warning that even the patriotic sentiment of our people is not an adequate substitute for a sound financial policy.

Of course there can be no doubt in any thoughtful mind as to the complete solvency of our nation, nor can there be any just apprehension that the American people will be satisfied with less than an honest payment of our public obligations in the recognized money of the world. We should not overlook the fact, however, that aroused fear is unreasoning and must be taken into account in all efforts to avert possible loss and the sacrifice of our people's interests.

The real and sensible cure for our recurring troubles can only be effected by a complete change in our financial scheme. Pending that the executive branch of the Government will not relax its efforts nor abandon its determination to use every means within its reach to maintain before the world American credit, nor will there be any hesitation in exhibiting its confidence in the resources of our country and the constant patriotism of our people.

In view, however, of the peculiar situation now confronting us, I have ventured to herein express the earnest hope that the Congress, in default of the inauguration of a better system of finance, will not take a recess from its labors before it has by legislative enactment or declaration done something not only to remind those apprehensive among our own people that the resources of their Government and a scrupulous regard for honest dealing afford a sure guaranty of unquestioned safety and soundness, but to reassure the world that with these factors and the patriotism of our citizens the ability and determination of our nation to meet in any circumstances every obligation it incurs do not admit of question.

I ask at the hands of the Congress such prompt aid as it alone has the power to give to prevent in a time of fear and apprehension any sacrifice of the people's interests and the public funds or the impairment of our public credit in an effort by Executive action to relieve the dangers of the present emergency.

GROVER CLEVELAND.

EXECUTIVE MANSION,
Washington, December 30, 1895.

To the Senate of the United States:

In response to the resolution of the Senate of the 21st instant, relative to the refusal of the Turkish Government to grant exequaturs to the vice-consuls of the United States at Erzerum and Harpoot, I transmit herewith a report from the Secretary of State.

GROVER CLEVELAND.

EXECUTIVE MANSION,
Washington, January 10, 1896.

To the Senate of the United States:

I transmit herewith, in response to the Senate resolution of December 18, 1895, addressed to the Secretary of State, a report of that officer, with the accompanying correspondence, in relation to the arrest and imprisonment of Victor Hugo McCord at Arequipa, Peru, requested by said resolution.

GROVER CLEVELAND.

To the Congress: EXECUTIVE MANSION, *January 17, 1896.*

I desire to invite attention to the necessity for prompt legislation in order to remove the limitation of the time within which suits may be brought by the Government to annul unlawful or unauthorized grants of public lands.

By the act of March 3, 1887 (24 U. S. Statutes at Large, p. 556), the Secretary of the Interior is directed to adjust each of the railroad land grants which may be unadjusted, and it is provided, if it shall appear upon the completion of such adjustment or sooner that the lands have been from any cause erroneously certified or patented by the United States to or for the use of a company claiming under any of said grants, it shall be the duty of the Secretary of the Interior to demand a reconveyance of the title to all lands so erroneously certified or patented, and on failure of the company to make such reconveyance within ninety days the Attorney-General is required to institute and prosecute in the proper courts necessary proceedings to restore title to said lands to the United States. The demands made under this act have been numerous, and in some cases have resulted in the reinvestment of title to the lands in the United States upon demand, but in most cases the demand has been refused and suits have been necessary.

The work of adjustment has been unavoidably slow. The said act makes provision for the reinstatement of entries erroneously canceled on account of railroad withdrawals, and, upon certain conditions, provides for the confirmation of titles derived by purchase from the companies of lands shown to be excepted from the grants. It contemplates a disposition of every tract, described by the granting act, situated within the primary or granted limits; an inspection of each tract certified or patented to the company within such limit, to determine whether such certification or patenting was proper; the listing of those tracts shown to be erroneously certified, and the determination for what tracts lost to the grant indemnity is to be allowed.

It is necessary in making such an adjustment that all questions of conflicting claims, either between settlers and the road or between two roads the grants for which conflict or overlap, be finally disposed of, so that a proper disposition of the land can be shown in the adjustment. While adjustments have proceeded with the utmost rapidity consistent with a due regard for the rights of the settlers, of the United States, and the railroad companies, and while to this end the force of adjusters has been largely augmented in the General Land Office, many of the grants yet remain unadjusted.

In some of the grants, notably the corporation grants, the lack of surveys up to the present time made the completion of the work impossible.

Decisions rendered by the Interior Department in numerous conflicts have been carried into the courts. The construction of the Interior Department has generally been sustained when final determination has been reached, but many of the cases are still pending in the courts, not yet having been decided. Some of these cases, while involving immediately the title to only one particular tract, will when decided furnish a rule of construction to control the disposition of the title to thousands of acres of other lands in the same situation. Until the courts pass upon these questions final adjustments can not be made.

By section 8 of the act of March 3, 1891 (26 U. S. Statutes at Large, p. 1099), it is expressly enacted that suits by the United States to vacate and annul any patent theretofore issued "shall only be brought within five years from the passage of this act." This period of five years will expire on the 3d of March, 1896. Of course no suit by the United States to secure the cancellation of a patent in this class of cases after that date would be effective. Indeed, it is now too late to initiate proceedings looking to any such suit, inasmuch as demand has to be first made on the company, and thereafter ninety days must be allowed for compliance or refusal, in accordance with the provisions of the act of March 3, 1887. Before the expiration of this period the statute would bar the right of recovery by the Government, and the benefits of anticipated favorable decisions of the courts would be lost so far as they might determine the character and disposition of grants similar to those directly involved in pending cases.

It will be readily seen that if this act of limitations is to remain on the statute books the portion of the adjustment act referred to would be rendered nugatory. Indeed, there would be but little use in continuing the adjustment of many of the land grants, inasmuch as ascertained rights of the United States or of settlers could not be enforced by law.

Legislation establishing limitations against the right of the Government to sue is an innovation not entirely consistent with the general history of the rights of the Government, for it has uniformly been held that time did not bar the sovereign power from the assertion of a right.

The early adjudications of the Land Department construed the grants with a degree of liberality toward the grantees which later decisions of the courts and of the Department have not sustained. It seems clear that the further progress of adjustments will develop facts and transactions in connection with these land grants which ought to be the subjects of legal examination and scrutiny before they are allowed to become final and conclusive. The Government should not be prevented from going into the courts to right wrongs perpetrated by its agents or any other parties, and by which much of the public domain may be diverted from the people at large to corporate uses.

In these circumstances it seems to me that the act of 1891 should be so amended as not to apply to suits brought to recover title to lands certified or patented on account of railroad or other grants; and I respectfully urge upon Congress speedy action to the end suggested, so that the adjustment of these grants may proceed without the interposition of a bar, through lapse of time, against the right of recovery by the Government in proper cases.

GROVER CLEVELAND.

EXECUTIVE MANSION,
Washington, January 20, 1896.

To the House of Representatives:

In response to the resolution of the House of Representatives of December 28, 1895, I transmit herewith a report from the Secretary of State and accompanying papers, relating to certain speeches made by Thomas F. Bayard, ambassador of the United States to Great Britain.

In response to that part of said resolution which requests information as to the action taken by the President concerning the speeches therein referred to, I reply that no action has been taken thereon by the President except such as is indicated in the report and correspondence herewith submitted.

GROVER CLEVELAND.

EXECUTIVE MANSION,
Washington, January 22, 1896.

To the House of Representatives:

I transmit herewith, in compliance with the resolution of the House of Representatives of December 28, 1895, a report from the Secretary of State, with copies of all the correspondence of record in the Department of State in relation to the schooner *Henry Crosby,* fired upon while at anchor at Azua, Santo Domingo, December 10, 1893.

GROVER CLEVELAND.

EXECUTIVE MANSION, *January 22, 1896.*

To the Senate of the United States:

In response to the resolution adopted by the Senate on December 16, 1895, respecting what action had been taken in regard to the payment of the appropriation for the bounty on sugar contained in the sundry civil bill approved March 2, 1895, I herewith transmit a communication received from the Secretary of the Treasury, which contains all the information I have upon the subject.

GROVER CLEVELAND.

EXECUTIVE MANSION,
Washington, January 23, 1896.

To the Senate:

I transmit herewith a report from the Secretary of State, in answer to a resolution of the Senate of the 16th instant, requesting information in regard to the treatment of naturalized citizens of the United States of Armenian origin, and their families, by the Turkish Government.

GROVER CLEVELAND.

EXECUTIVE MANSION,
Washington, January 27, 1896.

To the House of Representatives:

I transmit herewith a report from the Secretary of State, with copies of all correspondence of record relating to the failure of the scheme for the colonization of negroes in Mexico, necessitating their return to their home in Alabama.

I referred to this matter in my message to Congress at the beginning of the present session, and for the reasons then given* I again urge the propriety of making an appropriation to cover the cost of transportation furnished by the railroad companies.

GROVER CLEVELAND.

EXECUTIVE MANSION,
Washington, January 30, 1896.

To the House of Representatives:

I transmit herewith a communication from the Secretary of State, accompanying the reports of the consuls of the United States on trade and commerce. In view of the evident value of this compilation to our business interests, I indorse the recommendation of the Secretary that Congress authorize the printing of a special edition of 10,000 copies of the General Summary of the Commerce of the World for distribution by the Department of State, and of 2,500 copies of Commercial Relations (including this summary) to enable the Department to meet the increasing demand for commercial information.

GROVER CLEVELAND.

EXECUTIVE MANSION,
Washington, February 3, 1896.

To the Congress:

In my last annual message allusion was made to the lawless killing of certain Italian laborers in the State of Colorado,† and it was added that "the dependent families of some of the unfortunate victims invite by their deplorable condition gracious provision for their needs."

It now appears that in addition to three of these laborers who were riotously killed two others, who escaped death by flight, incurred pitiable disabilities through exposure and privation.

Without discussing the question of the liability of the United States for these results, either by reason of treaty obligations or under the general rules of international law, I venture to urge upon the Congress the propriety of making from the public Treasury prompt and reasonable pecuniary provision for those injured and for the families of those who were killed.

*See p. 634.　　　　　　　　† See p. 633.

To aid in the consideration of the subject I append hereto a report of the Secretary of State, accompanied by certain correspondence which quite fully presents all the features of the several cases.

GROVER CLEVELAND.

To the House of Representatives:

Pursuant to the request made in a House resolution passed on the 30th day of January, 1896, I herewith transmit the report, with accompanying maps and exhibits, of the board of engineers under the provisions of chapter 189 of laws of 1895, for the purpose of ascertaining the feasibility, permanence, and cost of the construction and completion of the Nicaragua Canal by the route contemplated and provided for by the act which passed the Senate January 28, 1895, entitled "An act to amend an act entitled 'An act to incorporate the Maritime Canal Company of Nicaragua,' approved February 20, 1889."

GROVER CLEVELAND.

FEBRUARY 7, 1896.

EXECUTIVE MANSION,
Washington, February 10, 1896.

To the Senate of the United States:

I transmit herewith, in answer to the resolution of the Senate of December 18, 1895, a report by the Secretary of State, accompanied by copies of correspondence touching the establishment or attempted establishment of post routes by Great Britain or the Dominion of Canada over or upon United States territory in Alaska; also as to the occupation or attempted occupation by any means of any portion of that territory by the military or civil authorities of Great Britain or of Canada.

GROVER CLEVELAND.

EXECUTIVE MANSION,
Washington, February 10, 1896.

To the Senate:

I transmit herewith, for the consideration of the Senate with a view to its ratification, a convention signed at Washington the 8th instant between the Governments of the United States of America and of Her Britannic Majesty, providing for the settlement of the claims presented by Great Britain against the United States in virtue of the convention of February 29, 1892, and of the findings of the Paris Tribunal of Arbitration pursuant to article 8 of said convention, as well as of the additional claims specified in paragraph 5 of the preamble of the present convention.

GROVER CLEVELAND.

EXECUTIVE MANSION,
Washington, February 11, 1896.

To the Senate of the United States:

I transmit herewith, in answer to the resolution of the Senate of December 9, 1895, a report from the Secretary of State, accompanied by copies of correspondence and other papers in regard to the case of John L. Waller, a citizen of the United States, at present in the custody of the French Government.

It will be seen upon examination, as would of course be expected, that there is a slight conflict of evidence upon some of the features of Mr. Waller's case. Nevertheless, upon a fair and just consideration of all the facts and circumstances as presented, and especially in view of Mr. Waller's own letters, the conclusions set forth in the report of the Secretary of State do not appear to admit of any reasonable doubt nor to leave open to the Executive any other course of action than that adopted and acted upon as therein stated.

It is expected that Mr. Waller's release from imprisonment will be immediately forthcoming.

GROVER CLEVELAND.

[A similar message was sent to the House of Representatives in answer to a resolution of that body of December 28, 1895.]

EXECUTIVE MANSION,
Washington, February 11, 1896.

To the House of Representatives:

In response to the resolution of the House of Representatives of December 28 last, as follows—

Resolved, That the Secretary of State be directed to communicate to the House of Representatives, if not inconsistent with the public interests, copies of all correspondence relating to affairs in Cuba since February last—

I transmit herewith a communication from the Secretary of State and such portions of the correspondence requested as I deem it not inconsistent with the public interests to communicate.

GROVER CLEVELAND.

EXECUTIVE MANSION,
Washington, February 14, 1896.

To the Senate:

In response to the resolution of the Senate of January 7, 1896, I transmit herewith a report from the Secretary of State, with an accompanying report of the special agent of the United States sent to the Fiji Islands to investigate the claims of B. H. Henry and other American citizens for compensation for certain lands alleged to have been owned by them and claimed to have been appropriated by the British Government.

GROVER CLEVELAND.

EXECUTIVE MANSION,
Washington, February 14, 1896.

To the Senate of the United States:

I transmit, with the accompanying papers, a report from the Secretary of State, answering the resolution of the Senate of January 16, 1896, addressed to him, calling for information concerning the claims against Peru of Thomas W. Sparrow, N. B. Noland, and others, members of the commission known as the Hydrographic Commission of the Amazon, employed by the Government of Peru, for compensation for their services on said commission. GROVER CLEVELAND.

EXECUTIVE MANSION,
Washington, February 14, 1896.

To the Senate and House of Representatives:

I transmit herewith, for the information of Congress, a communication from the Secretary of State, covering the report of the Director of the Bureau of the American Republics for the year 1895.

GROVER CLEVELAND.

EXECUTIVE MANSION,
Washington, February 17, 1896.

To the House of Representatives:

I transmit herewith, in compliance with the resolution of the House of Representatives of February 1, 1896, a report from the Secretary of State, with copies of the correspondence of record in the Department of State in relation to the exclusion of life-insurance companies of the United States from transacting business in Germany.

GROVER CLEVELAND.

EXECUTIVE MANSION, *February 18, 1896.*

To the House of Representatives:

In compliance with a resolution of the House of Representatives, the Senate concurring, I return herewith Senate bill 879, entitled "An act to amend an act entitled 'An act to grant to the Gainesville, McAlester and St. Louis Railroad Company a right of way through the Indian Territory.'" GROVER CLEVELAND.

EXECUTIVE MANSION,
Washington, February 28, 1896.

To the Senate:

I transmit herewith, in response to the resolutions of the Senate of the 18th and 19th instant, a report of the Secretary of State, in regard to the claim of A. H. Lazare against the Government of Hayti.

GROVER CLEVELAND.

EXECUTIVE MANSION,
Washington, March 9, 1896.

To the Senate:

I transmit herewith, in answer to the resolution of the Senate of the 24th ultimo, a report from the Secretary of State, in relation to the claim of the legal representatives of Lieutenant George C. Foulke against the Government of the United States.

GROVER CLEVELAND.

To the Senate:

EXECUTIVE MANSION, *March 9, 1896.*

I transmit herewith, in response to the Senate's resolution of February 6, 1896, addressed to the Secretary of State, copies, in translation, of the decrees or orders of the Governments of Germany, France, Belgium, and Denmark placing restrictions upon the importation of certain American products.

GROVER CLEVELAND.

EXECUTIVE MANSION,
Washington, March 13, 1896.

To the Senate:

I transmit herewith, in response to a resolution of the Senate of March 2, a report from the Secretary of State, accompanied by copies of correspondence touching the arrest in Havana of Marcus E. Rodriguez, Luis Someillau y Azpeitia, and Luis Someillau y Vidal, citizens of the United States.

GROVER CLEVELAND.

EXECUTIVE MANSION,
Washington, March 13, 1896.

To the House of Representatives:

In response to the resolution of the House of Representatives of February 13, 1896, I transmit a report from the Secretary of State and accompanying papers, relating to the claim of Bernard Campbell against the Government of Hayti.

GROVER CLEVELAND.

EXECUTIVE MANSION, *April 14, 1896.*

To the Senate of the United States:

In compliance with a resolution of the Senate, the House of Representatives concurring, I return herewith the enrolled joint resolution (S. R. 116) authorizing the Public Printer to print the Annual Report of the United States Coast and Geodetic Survey in quarto form and to bind it in one volume.

GROVER CLEVELAND.

EXECUTIVE MANSION,
Washington, April 15, 1896.

To the Senate of the United States:

In response to the resolution of March 24, 1896, requesting that the Senate be furnished with the correspondence of the Department of State between November 5, 1875, and the date of the pacification of Cuba in 1878 relating to the subject of mediation or intervention by the United States in the affairs of that island, I transmit a report from the Secretary of State, forwarding such papers as seem to be called for by the resolution in question.

GROVER CLEVELAND.

EXECUTIVE MANSION,
Washington, April 30, 1896.

To the House of Representatives:

I transmit herewith, in response to the resolution of the House of Representatives of the 9th instant, addressed to the Secretary of State, a report of that officer, accompanied by copies of the correspondence in regard to the imprisonment of Mrs. Florence E. Maybrick.

GROVER CLEVELAND.

EXECUTIVE MANSION,
Washington, May 16, 1896.

To the Senate:

I transmit herewith, in response to the resolution of the Senate dated the 9th instant and addressed to the Secretary of State, a report of that officer, accompanied by copies of printed documents containing the information desired respecting the historical archives deposited in the Department of State.

GROVER CLEVELAND.

EXECUTIVE MANSION,
Washington, May 23, 1896.

To the Senate of the United States:

I transmit herewith, in response to a resolution of the Senate of the 16th instant, a report of the Secretary of State, to which are attached copies in English and Spanish of the original text of a protocol executed January 12, 1877, between the minister plenipotentiary of the United States of America to the Court of Spain and the minister of state of His Majesty the King of Spain.

It being, in my judgment, incompatible with the public service, I am constrained to refrain from communicating to the Senate at this time copies of the correspondence described in the third paragraph of said resolution.

GROVER CLEVELAND.

EXECUTIVE MANSION, *May 28, 1896.*

To the House of Representatives:

In compliance with a resolution of the House of Representatives of the 27th instant, the Senate concurring, I return herewith the bill (H. R. 5731) entitled "An act to regulate the practice of medicine and surgery, to license physicians and surgeons, and to punish persons violating the provisions thereof in the District of Columbia."

GROVER CLEVELAND.

EXECUTIVE MANSION, *June 3, 1896.*

To the House of Representatives:

In compliance with a resolution of the House of Representatives of the 2d instant, the Senate concurring, I return herewith the bill (H. R. 3279) entitled "An act to authorize the reassessment of water-main taxes or assessments in the District of Columbia, and for other purposes."

GROVER CLEVELAND.

EXECUTIVE MANSION, *June 8, 1896.*

To the Senate:

I transmit herewith a report of the Secretary of State, in answer to the resolution of the Senate of May 9, 1896, directing that "the Secretary of State, the Secretary of the Treasury, the Secretary of War, the Secretary of the Navy, the Secretary of the Interior, the Secretary of Agriculture, the Postmaster-General, and the Attorney-General cause a careful and thorough inquiry to be made regarding the number of aliens employed in their respective Departments, and to communicate the result of said inquiry to the Senate at the earliest practicable day."

GROVER CLEVELAND.

VETO MESSAGES.

EXECUTIVE MANSION, *February 28, 1896.*

To the House of Representatives:

I herewith return without my approval House bill No. 2769, entitled "An act to authorize the leasing of lands for educational purposes in Arizona."

This bill provides for the leasing of all the public lands reserved to the Territory of Arizona for the benefit of its universities and schools, "under such laws and regulations as may be hereafter prescribed by the legislature of said Territory."

If the proposed legislation granted no further authority than this, it would, in terms at least, recognize the safety and propriety of leaving the desirability of leasing these lands and the limitations and safeguards regulating such leasing to be determined by the local legislature chosen by the people to make their laws and protect their interests.

Instead of stopping here, however, the bill further provides that until such legislative action the governor, the secretary of the Territory, and the superintendent of public instruction shall constitute a board for the leasing of said lands under the rules and regulations heretofore prescribed by the Secretary of the Interior. It is specifically declared that it shall not be necessary to submit said leases to the Secretary of the Interior for approval, and that no leases shall be made for a longer term than five years nor for a term extending beyond the date of the admission of the Territory to statehood.

Under these provisions the lands reserved for university and school purposes, whose value largely depends upon their standing timber, and in which every citizen of the Territory has a deep interest, may be leased and denuded of their timber by officers none of whom have been chosen by the people, and without the sanction of any law or regulation made by their representatives in the local legislature. Even the measure of protection which would be afforded the citizens of the Territory by a submission to the Secretary of the Interior of the leases proposed, and thus giving him an opportunity to ascertain whether or not they comply with his regulations, is especially withheld.

It was hardly necessary to provide in this bill that these lands might be leased "under such laws and regulations as may be hereafter prescribed by the legislature of said Territory" if the action of the legislature was to be forestalled and rendered nugatory by the immediate and unrestrained action of the officers constituted "a board for the leasing of said lands" pending such legislative consideration. These are inconsistencies which are not satisfactorily accounted for by the suggestion that the time that would elapse before the legislature could consider the subject would be important.

The protests I have received from numerous and influential citizens of the Territory indicate considerable opposition to this bill among those interested in the preservation and proper management of these school lands.

GROVER CLEVELAND.

EXECUTIVE MANSION, *April 21, 1896.*

To the Senate:

I herewith return without my approval Senate bill No. 894, entitled "An act granting a pension to Nancy G. Allabach."

This bill provides for the payment of a pension of $30 a month to the beneficiary named as the widow of Peter H. Allabach.

This soldier served for nine months in the Army during the War of the Rebellion, having also served in the war with Mexico.

He was mustered out of his last service on the 23d day of May, 1863, and died on the 11th of February, 1892.

During his life he made no application for pension on account of disabilities. It is not now claimed that he was in the least disabled as an incident of his military service, nor is it alleged that his death, which occurred nearly twenty-nine years after his discharge from the Army, was in any degree related to such service.

His widow was pensioned after his death under the statute allowing pensions to widows of soldiers of the Mexican War without reference to the cause of the death of their husbands. Her case is also, indirectly, one of those provided for by the general act passed in 1890, commonly called the dependent-pension law.

It is proposed, however, by the special act under consideration to give this widow a pension of $30 a month without the least suggestion of the death or disability of her husband having been caused by his military service, and solely, as far as is discoverable, upon the ground that she is poor and needs the money.

This condition is precisely covered by existing general laws; and if a precedent is to be established by the special legislation proposed, I do not see how the same relief as is contained in this bill can be denied to the many thousand widows who in a similar situation are now on the pension rolls under general laws.

GROVER CLEVELAND.

To the Senate: EXECUTIVE MANSION, *April 21, 1896.*

I return herewith without my approval Senate bill No. 249, entitled "An act granting a pension to Charles E. Jones."

The beneficiary named in this bill was a photographer who accompanied one of the regiments of the Union Army in the War of the Rebellion. He was injured, apparently not very seriously, while taking photographs and when no battle was in actual progress. He was not enlisted, and was in no manner in the military service of the United States.

Aside from the question as to whether his present sad condition is attributable to the injury mentioned, it seems to me the extension of pension relief to such cases would open the door to legislation hard to justify and impossible to restrain from abuse.

GROVER CLEVELAND.

EXECUTIVE MANSION, *April 25, 1896.*
To the House of Representatives:

I herewith return without my approval House bill No. 1094, entitled "An act granting a pension to Francis E. Hoover."

It is proposed by this bill to grant a pension of $50 a month to the beneficiary named, who served as a private for about one year and nine months in the Union Army during the War of the Rebellion.

I do not understand it is claimed in any quarter that the present helpless condition of this soldier is at all attributable to his army service.

He himself never applied for a pension until after the passage of the law of 1890, providing for a pension for those who had served in the Army and are unable to maintain themselves by manual labor on account of disability not chargeable to army service. The committee of the House of Representatives in reporting this bill declare: "The testimony does not show the disease of the soldier to be of service origin."

The beneficiary is now receiving the largest pension permitted under the law of 1890.

His condition may well excite our sympathy, but to grant him a pension of $50 a month without the least suggestion that his pitiable disability is related to his army service, and in view of the fact that he is now receiving the highest pension allowed by a general law enacted to expressly meet such cases, it seems to me would result in an unfair discrimination as against many thousand worthy soldiers similarly situated, and would invite applications which, while difficult to refuse in the face of such a precedent, must certainly lead to the breaking down of all the limitations and restrictions provided by our laws regulating pensions.

The value of pension legislation depends as much upon fairness and justice in its administration as it does upon its liberality and generosity.

GROVER CLEVELAND.

EXECUTIVE MANSION, *May 19, 1896.*

To the House of Representatives:

I return herewith without approval House bill No. 1139, entitled "An act granting a pension to Caroline D. Mowatt."

The beneficiary mentioned in this bill was married in 1858 to Alfred B. Soule, who served as major of a Maine regiment of volunteers in the War of the Rebellion from September 10, 1862, to July 15, 1863, when he was mustered out of the service. He died in February, 1864, and in 1866 a pension was granted to the beneficiary as his widow at the rate of $25 a month, dating from the time of her husband's death, two years before.

The widow continued to receive the pension allowed her until June 17, 1869, when she was married to Henry T. Mowatt, which under the law terminated her pensionable right. It appears, however, that a small pension was allowed two minor children of the soldier at the time of their mother's remarriage, which continued until 1876, more than seven years after such remarriage, when the youngest of said children became 16 years of age.

In 1878, nine years after he became the second husband of the beneficiary, Henry T. Mowatt died.

Though twenty-seven years have passed since the beneficiary ceased to be the widow of the deceased soldier, and though she has been the widow of Henry T. Mowatt for eighteen years, it is proposed by the bill under consideration to again place her name upon the pension roll "as widow of Alfred B. Scule, late major of the Twenty-third Regiment Maine Volunteers."

Of course the propriety of the law which terminates the pension of a soldier's widow upon her remarriage will not be questioned. I suppose no one would suggest the renewal of such pension during the lifetime of her second husband. Her pensionable relation to the Government as the widow of her deceased soldier husband, under any reasonable pension theory, absolutely terminated with her remarriage.

If she is to be again pensioned because her second husband does not survive her, the transaction has more the complexion of an adjustment of a governmental insurance on the life of the second husband than the allowance of a pension on just and reasonable grounds.

Legislation of this description is sure to establish a precedent which it will be difficult to disclaim, and which if followed can not fail to lead to abuse.

GROVER CLEVELAND.

EXECUTIVE MANSION, *May 20, 1896.*

To the House of Representatives:

I return herewith without approval House bill No. 577, entitled "An act granting a pension to Lydia A. Taft."

In 1858 the beneficiary named in this bill became the wife of Lowell Taft, who afterwards enlisted in the Union Army as a private in a Connecticut regiment and served from August, 1862, until June, 1865. The records of the War Department show that he was captured by the enemy June 15, 1863, and paroled July 14, 1863.

No application for a pension was ever made by him, though he lived until 1891, when he died at a soldiers' home in Connecticut.

No suggestion is made that he incurred any disability in the service or that his death was in any manner related to such service.

In 1882, nearly twenty-four years after her marriage to the soldier and seventeen years after his discharge from the Army, the beneficiary obtained a divorce from him upon the grounds of habitual drunkenness and failure to afford her a support.

It is now proposed, five years after the soldier's death, to pension as his widow the wife who was divorced from him at her own instance fourteen years ago.

A government's generous care for widows deprived of a husband's support and companionship by the casualties or disabilities of war rests upon grounds which all must cheerfully approve; but it is difficult to place upon these grounds the case of this proposed beneficiary, who has renounced a wife's relation, with all its duties and all its rights, and who by her own act placed herself beyond the possibility of becoming the widow of her soldier husband.

If, as stated in the report of the House committee on this bill, the beneficiary for some reason contributed something toward the soldier's support after her divorce and paid the expense of his burial, the fact still remains that this soldier died in a soldiers' home wifeless and leaving no one surviving who, claiming to be his widow, should be allowed to profit by his death.

GROVER CLEVELAND.

EXECUTIVE MANSION, *May 21, 1896.*

To the House of Representatives:

I herewith return without approval House bill No. 1185, entitled "An act granting a pension to Rachel Patton."

John H. Patton, the husband of the beneficiary, was a captain in an Illinois regiment, and was killed in action June 25, 1863.

In December, 1863, the beneficiary was pensioned as his widow at the rate of $20 a month.

She received this pension for thirteen years and until 1876, when she married one William G. Culbertson. Thereupon, because of such marriage, her name was dropped from the pension rolls, pursuant to law.

In 1889, thirteen years after her remarriage and the termination of her pension, she procured a decree of divorce against her second husband on the ground of desertion.

She has a small income, but it does not appear that alimony was allowed her in the divorce proceedings.

It is proposed by this bill to pension her at the same rate which was allowed her while she remained the widow of the deceased soldier.

It can not be denied that the remarriage of this beneficiary terminated her pensionable relation to the Government as completely as if it never existed. The statute which so provides simply declares what is approved by a fair and sensible consideration of pension principles. As a legal proposition, the pensionable status of a soldier's widow, lost by her remarriage, can not be recovered by the dissolution of the second marriage. Waiving, however, the application of strictly legal principles to the subject, there does not appear to be any sentiment which should restore to the pension rolls as the widow of a deceased soldier a divorced wife who has relinquished the title of soldier's widow to again become a wife, and who to secure the expected advantages and comforts of a second marriage has been quite willing to forego the provision which was made for her by the Government solely on the grounds of her soldier widowhood.

GROVER CLEVELAND.

EXECUTIVE MANSION, *May 23, 1896.*

To the House of Representatives:

I herewith return without approval House bill No. 4804, entitled "An act to amend subdivision 10 of section 2238 of the Revised Statutes of the United States."

The subdivision of the section of the law proposed to be amended by this bill has reference to the fees allowed receivers and registers at public-land offices. This subdivision now reads as follows:

Tenth. Registers and receivers are allowed jointly at the rate of 15 cents per hundred words for testimony reduced by them to writing for claimants in establishing preemption and homestead rights.

The bill under consideration so amends this subdivision that in the first clause a compensation of 10 cents per hundred words is allowed to the registers and receivers for reducing to writing the testimony of claimants ''in all cases,'' instead of 15 cents per hundred words for reducing to writing testimony ''in establishing preemption and homestead rights,'' as provided in the old law.

Whether this reduction of fees preserves an adequate and just compensation to the officers affected I suppose has been duly considered by the Congress.

The bill, however, after providing for this change in compensation, contains the following words:

And in all cases where they [the registers and receivers] can secure a competent person to reduce the testimony to writing for a sum less per folio than the sum herein prescribed it shall be their duty to do so.

By the addition of these words the bill seems to give certain fees by way of official compensation to the officers named for certain services to be performed by them and at the same time to provide that if they can secure other persons willing to perform these services for a less sum than the amount allowed to them they shall forego their fees in favor of such persons.

It is very important that the fees and perquisites of public officers should be definitely and clearly fixed, so that the official may know precisely the items of his lawful compensation and the people be protected from extortion and imposition.

A public officer ought not to be expected to search very industriously for a person to underbid him for official work, and if such a person appeared the temptation to combination and conspiracy would in many cases lead to abuse.

It will be observed that the officers are not given by this amendment the option to do this work themselves at 10 cents per folio or secure a competent person to do it at a less rate, nor, if they desire, are they allowed to compete with those willing to accept a less compensation. They may charge a fixed rate for the service if performed by them, but in any event if they can procure another party to perform the services for a less sum they must do so.

I am convinced that this bill in its present form, perhaps through unfortunate phraseology, if it became a law would lead to confusion and uncertainty and would invite practices against which the public service ought to be carefully guarded.

GROVER CLEVELAND.

EXECUTIVE MANSION, *May 26, 1896.*

To the House of Representatives:

I return herewith without approval House bill No. 7161, entitled "An act for the relief of Benjamin F. Jones."

This bill directs the payment to the beneficiary, late postmaster at Beauregard, Miss., or to his order, of the sum of $50, in full compensation for services and expenses in carrying and distributing the mails between Wesson and Beauregard, in the State of Mississippi, in 1883.

It appears from the report of the House committee recommending the passage of this bill that on April 22, 1883, while Mr. Jones was postmaster at Beauregard, a cyclone destroyed every building in the place, including that in which the post-office was kept; that in consequence of this disaster the mails for Beauregard were for a period of thirty-five days, and until May 27, 1883, deposited at Wesson, 1 mile distant; that during that time it became necessary to transport such mails from Wesson to Beauregard, and that the postmaster caused this to be done, at an expense of $97.

A report from the Postmaster-General discloses the fact that this claim was presented to the Department in 1884 and was rejected on the ground that if the service was performed as alleged it was not authorized or directed by the Department.

In 1885 a suit was instituted against this postmaster and his sureties for a balance due the Government from him on his official accounts for the quarter ending June 30, 1883.

It will be observed that this quarter covered the period within which the alleged services were performed.

In the suit referred to a judgment was recovered by the Government against the postmaster for $190.45, being the balance found due from him. This judgment still remains unpaid.

In this condition of affairs it is quite plain that in fairness and justice no appropriation should be made in favor of the claimant.

It is the opinion of the Auditor of the Post-Office Department that even if this bill becomes a law payment of the money appropriated should be withheld under a section of the Revised Statutes which provides:

No money shall be paid to any person for his compensation who is in arrears to the United States until he has accounted for and paid into the Treasury all sums for which he may be liable.

GROVER CLEVELAND.

EXECUTIVE MANSION, *May 29, 1896.*

To the House of Representatives:

I return herewith without approval House bill No. 7977, entitled "An act making appropriations for the construction, repair, and preservation of certain public works on rivers and harbors, and for other purposes."

There are 417 items of appropriation contained in this bill, and every part of the country is represented in the distribution of its favors.

It directly appropriates or provides for the immediate expenditure of nearly $14,000,000 for river and harbor work. This sum is in addition to appropriations contained in another bill for similar purposes amounting to a little more than $3,000,000, which have already been favorably considered at the present session of Congress.

The result is that the contemplated immediate expenditures for the objects mentioned amount to about $17,000,000.

A more startling feature of this bill is its authorization of contracts for river and harbor work amounting to more than $62,000,000. Though the payments on these contracts are in most cases so distributed that they are to be met by future appropriations, more than $3,000,000 on their account are included in the direct appropriations above mentioned. Of the remainder, nearly $20,000,000 will fall due during the fiscal year ending June 30, 1898, and amounts somewhat less in the years immediately succeeding. A few contracts of a like character authorized under previous statutes are still outstanding, and to meet payments on these more than $4,000,000 must be appropriated in the immediate future.

If, therefore, this bill becomes a law, the obligations which will be imposed on the Government, together with the appropriations made for immediate expenditure on account of rivers and harbors, will amount to about $80,000,000. Nor is this all. The bill directs numerous surveys and examinations which contemplate new work and further contracts and which portend largely increased expenditures and obligations.

There is no ground to hope that in the face of persistent and growing demands the aggregate of appropriations for the smaller schemes, not covered by contracts, will be reduced or even remain stationary. For the fiscal year ending June 30, 1898, such appropriations, together with the installments on contracts which will fall due in that year, can hardly be less than $30,000,000; and it may reasonably be apprehended that the prevalent tendency toward increased expenditures of this sort and the concealment which postponed payments afford for extravagance will increase the burdens chargeable to this account in succeeding years.

In view of the obligation imposed upon me by the Constitution, it seems to me quite clear that I only discharge a duty to our people when I interpose my disapproval of the legislation proposed.

Many of the objects for which it appropriates public money are not related to the public welfare, and many of them are palpably for the benefit of limited localities or in aid of individual interests.

On the face of the bill it appears that not a few of these alleged improvements have been so improvidently planned and prosecuted that after an unwise expenditure of millions of dollars new experiments for their accomplishment have been entered upon.

While those intrusted with the management of public funds in the interest of all the people can hardly justify questionable expenditures for public work by pleading the opinions of engineers or others as to the practicability of such work, it appears that some of the projects for which appropriations are proposed in this bill have been entered upon without the approval or against the objections of the examining engineers.

I learn from official sources that there are appropriations contained in the bill to pay for work which private parties have actually agreed with the Government to do in consideration of their occupancy of public property.

Whatever items of doubtful propriety may have escaped observation or may have been tolerated in previous Executive approvals of similar bills, I am convinced that the bill now under consideration opens the way to insidious and increasing abuses and is in itself so extravagant as to be especially unsuited to these times of depressed business and resulting disappointment in Government revenue. This consideration is emphasized by the prospect that the public Treasury will be confronted with other appropriations made at the present session of Congress amounting to more than $500,000,000.

Individual economy and careful expenditure are sterling virtues which lead to thrift and comfort. Economy and the exaction of clear justification for the appropriation of public moneys by the servants of the people are not only virtues, but solemn obligations.

To the extent that the appropriations contained in this bill are instigated by private interests and promote local or individual projects their allowance can not fail to stimulate a vicious paternalism and encourage a sentiment among our people, already too prevalent, that their attachment to our Government may properly rest upon the hope and expectation of direct and especial favors and that the extent to which they are realized may furnish an estimate of the value of governmental care.

I believe no greater danger confronts us as a nation than the unhappy decadence among our people of genuine and trustworthy love and affection for our Government as the embodiment of the highest and best aspirations of humanity, and not as the giver of gifts, and because its mission is the enforcement of exact justice and equality, and not the allowance of unfair favoritism.

I hope I may be permitted to suggest, at a time when the issue of Government bonds to maintain the credit and financial standing of the country is a subject of criticism, that the contracts provided for in this bill would create obligations of the United States amounting to $62,000,000 no less binding than its bonds for that sum.

GROVER CLEVELAND.

To the Senate: EXECUTIVE MANSION, *May 29, 1896.*

I herewith return without approval Senate bill No. 147, entitled "An act granting a pension to Elvira Bachelder."

This bill provides for a pension to the beneficiary as dependent mother of "J. K. P. Bachelder, late a private in Company D, Seventh New Hampshire Volunteer Infantry."

On the merits of the case I am satisfied this mother deserves a pension. I withhold my approval of the bill intended to grant her this relief solely because I am advised that the law would be inoperative for the reason that the deceased soldier never served in the Seventh New Hampshire Infantry, and should have been described in the bill as a member of Company D, First New Hampshire Heavy Artillery.

GROVER CLEVELAND.

Executive Mansion, *May 29, 1896.*

To the House of Representatives:

I herewith return without approval House bill No. 900, entitled "An act to provide for the payment of the claim of William H. Mahoney."

This bill directs the Secretary of the Treasury to receive and pay to W. H. Mahoney, without the indorsement of N. A. Rogers, a certain bond issued by the United States in 1861 for the sum of $500, such payment to be made upon the giving by said Mahoney of a bond to hold harmless the United States against repayment of said bond.

The bond mentioned is one of a large issue which was authorized under an act passed March 2, 1861, and known as Oregon war-debt bonds. They were made payable in 1881.

In 1864 an act was passed directing the Secretary of the Treasury to issue or cause to be issued to E. F. and Samuel A. Ward duplicates of nineteen of these bonds, particularly described by their numbers and otherwise. Among others are mentioned "Nos. 1352 to 1359, inclusive." This of course includes the bond numbered 1358, which is directed to be paid in the bill under consideration. Nothing can now be discovered to indicate the occasion for the issuance of these duplicates, but from the fact that a bond of indemnity was required it is inferred that they were issued because of the loss or destruction of the original bonds.

Pursuant to this act a duplicate of the bond in question, among others, was issued and made payable to the order of Thomas Pritchard, attorney, who was the payee in the original bond.

In 1881 this duplicate was paid by the Treasury Department and is now in possession of the Government. The indorsement of the payee, "Thomas Pritchard, attorney," appears thereon and all other proper indorsements to show title in the party to whom the payment was made.

The Government has therefore once paid the amount of this bond to the party apparently entitled to it. If the beneficiary named in this bill has a better right to the money, the Government, not being in default, should be protected against double payment. I suppose to sustain a claim upon the indemnity bond given when the duplicate was issued in 1864 we should be prepared to show that the second payment on the original bond was made upon such a state of facts as compelled or at least justified it. The passage of an act simply directing such payment would alone not be sufficient. The bond directed to be given by this bill would afford the Government no protection, since it only provides against repayment of the bond in the future, whereas the payment we should suffer from has already been made.

I suggest that an act be passed directing the Secretary of the Treasury to investigate the entire subject with a view of determining to whom this money should be paid, in a manner to bind, if possible, by the results of the examination the party to whom it has already been paid, and who should refund if another has a better right.

GROVER CLEVELAND.

EXECUTIVE MANSION, *May 30, 1896.*

To the House of Representatives:

I return without approval House bill No. 6037, entitled "An act granting a pension to Mrs. Amanda Woodcock."

The bill provides for the granting of a pension to the beneficiary therein named, describing her as the "widow of Robert Woodcock, deceased, late a private in the Fourth United States Volunteer Infantry in the Mexican War."

My action in this case is based upon the following statement concerning the bill from the Pension Bureau:

The bill, if approved, would be inoperative, inasmuch as there was no such organization in the Mexican War as named in the bill (Fourth United States Volunteer Infantry), and the service alleged by the soldier having been in the Fourth Kentucky Volunteer Infantry.

GROVER CLEVELAND.

EXECUTIVE MANSION, *May 30, 1896.*

To the House of Representatives:

I herewith return without approval House bill No. 4526, entitled "An act granting a pension to Jonathan Scott."

This bill directs that the Secretary of the Interior place upon the pension roll, at the rate of $72 per month, subject to the provisions and limitations of the pension laws, the name of Jonathan Scott, late of Company M, Sixth Regiment Iowa Volunteer Cavalry.

The beneficiary was dropped from the pension roll in October, 1895, after a very thorough examination, for fraud, it appearing to the satisfaction of the Pension Bureau that the disability for which he was pensioned was not due to his army service. There certainly ought to be a strong presumption that the case was fairly and justly determined by the Bureau, and the evidence strongly tends to support the conclusion reached. If restored to the rolls, such restoration would still be "subject to the provisions and limitations of the pension laws," and he would not be exempt from further investigation if circumstances or newly developed facts justified such a course.

Whatever may be the merits of the case, however, I am advised by the Pension Bureau that the bill, if it becomes a law in its present form, would be inoperative for the reason that the beneficiary is therein described as having been a member of the Sixth Regiment of Iowa Volunteer Cavalry, whereas he actually served in the Fifth Regiment of the Volunteer Cavalry of that State.

GROVER CLEVELAND.

To the Senate: Executive Mansion, *June 1, 1896.*

I herewith return without approval Senate bill No. 149, entitled "An act granting a pension to Helen M. Jacob."

The purpose of this bill is to grant a pension of $12 per month to "Helen M. Jacob, of Rochester, Ind., widow of Benjamin Oden West."

It appears from the records of the War Department that Benjamin O. West served in the Mexican War from January to November in the year 1847. The beneficiary named in this bill was married to him in 1850, and he died in 1856. She was pensioned as his widow, and received such pension from the date of her husband's death until April 17, 1861. On that date she was married to William W. Jacob, whereupon her pension ceased, but two minor children were awarded pensions and continued in receipt of the same until January, 1873, when the youngest child became 16 years of age.

The entire absence of any fixed or reasonable principle or rule regulating private pension legislation at this time suggests the danger of its near approach in many cases to caprice and favoritism.

Though I have in a number of instances deferred to the judgment of Congress and refrained from interposing objections to bills of this character which seemed to me to be of doubtful merit, I am unwilling to follow such a wide departure from a palpably just pension theory and assent to the establishment of such an unfortunate precedent as this bill involves.

There is no duty or obligation due from the Government to a soldier's widow except it be worked out through the deceased soldier. She is pensioned only because he served his country and because through his death she as his wife has lost his support. In other words, she becomes a beneficiary of the Government because she is a soldier's widow. When she marries again, and thus displaces the memory of her soldier husband and surrenders all that belongs to soldier widowhood, she certainly ought not on the death of her second husband to be allowed to claim that she is again the soldier's widow.

GROVER CLEVELAND.

EXECUTIVE MANSION, *June 6, 1896.*

To the House of Representatives:

I hereby return without my approval House bill No. 8293, entitled "An act making appropriations to supply deficiencies in the appropriations for the fiscal year ending June 30, 1896, and for prior years, and for other purposes."

To the extent that the Constitution has devolved upon the President a participation in legislation I suppose his action on bills presented to him for approval involves a duty to be performed, like others pertaining to his office, with care and circumspection and in full view of his responsibility to the people and his obligation to subserve the public welfare. It is difficult to understand why under the Constitution it should be necessary to submit proposed legislation to Executive scrutiny and approval except to invoke the exercise of Executive judgment and invite independent Executive action.

The unpleasant incidents which accompany the use of the veto power would tempt its avoidance if such a course did not involve an abandonment of constitutional duty and an assent to legislation for which the Executive is not willing to share the responsibility.

I regret that I am constrained to disapprove an important appropriation bill so near the close of the present session of Congress. I have, however, by immediate action after the receipt of the bill, endeavored to delay as little as possible a reconsideration of this proposed legislation, though I am thus obliged to content myself with a less complete explanation of my objections than would otherwise be submitted.

This bill is in many of its features far removed from a legitimate deficiency bill, and it contains a number of appropriations which seem to me to be exceedingly questionable. Without noticing in detail many of these items, I shall refer to two of them which, in my judgment, justify my action in the premises.

The bill appropriates $1,027,314.09 for a partial payment upon claims which originated in depredations upon our commerce by French cruisers and vessels during the closing years of the last century. They have become quite familiar to those having Congressional experience, as they have been pressed for recognition and payment, with occasional intervals of repose, for nearly one hundred years.

These claims are based upon the allegations that France, being at war with England, seized and condemned many American vessels and cargoes in violation of the rules of international law and treaty provisions and contrary to the duty she owed to our country as a neutral power and to our citizens; that by reason of these acts claims arose in favor of such of our citizens as were damnified against the French nation, which claims our Government attempted to enforce, and that in concluding a treaty with France in the year 1800 these claims were abandoned or relinquished in consideration of the relinquishment of certain claims which France charged against us.

Upon these statements it is insisted by those interested that we as a nation having reaped a benefit in our escape from these French demands against us through the abandonment of the claims of our citizens against France, the Government became equitably bound as between itself and its citizens to pay the claims thus relinquished.

I do not understand it to be asserted that there exists any legal liability against the Government on account of its relation to these claims. At the term of the Supreme Court just finished the Chief Justice, in an opinion concerning them and the action of Congress in appropriating for their payment, said:

We think that payments thus prescribed to be made were purposely brought within the category of payments by way of gratuity—payments of grace and not of right.

From the time the plan was conceived to charge the Government with the payment of these claims they have abided in the atmosphere of controversy. Every proposition presented in their support has been stoutly disputed and every inference suggested in their favor has been promptly challenged.

Thus, inasmuch as it must, I think, be conceded that if a state of war existed between our country and France at the time these depredations were committed our Government was not justified in claiming indemnity for our citizens, it is asserted that we were at the time actually engaged in war with the French nation. This position seems to be sustained by an opinion of the Attorney-General of the United States written in 1798 and by a number of decisions of the Supreme Court delivered soon after that time.

We had certainly abrogated treaties with France, and our cruisers and armed ships were roaming the seas capturing her vessels and property.

So, also, when it is asserted that the validity of these claims was acknowledged in the treaty negotiations by the representatives of France, their declarations to a contrary purport are exhibited.

And when it is alleged that the abandonment of these claims against France was in consideration of great benefits to the Government, it is as confidently alleged that they were in point of fact abandoned because their enforcement was hopeless and that even if any benefit really accrued to us by insistence upon their settlement in the course of diplomatic negotiation such result gave no pretext for taxing the Government with liability to the claimants.

Without noticing other considerations and contentions arising from the alleged origin of these claims, a brief reference to their treatment in the past and the development of their presentation may be useful and pertinent.

It is, I believe, somewhat the fashion in interested quarters to speak of the failure by the Government to pay these claims as such neglect as amounts to repudiation and a denial of justice to citizens who have suffered. Of course the original claimants have for years been beyond the reach of relief; but as their descendants in each generation become more numerous the volume of advocacy, importunity, and accusation correspondingly increases. If injustice has been done in the refusal of these claims, it began early in the present century and may be charged against men then in public life more conversant than we can be with the facts involved and whose honesty and sense of right ought to be secure from suspicion.

As early as 1802 a committee of the House of Representatives reported the facts connected with these claims, but apparently without recommendation. No action was taken on the report. In 1803 a resolution declaring that indemnity ought to be paid was negatived by a vote of the same body. A favorable committee report was made in 1807, but it seems that no legislative action resulted. In 1818 an adverse report was made to the Senate, followed by the passage of a resolution declaring "that the relief asked by the memorialists and petitioners ought not to be granted." In 1822 and again in 1824 adverse committee reports on the subject were made to the House, concluding with similar resolutions.

The presumption against these claims arising from such unfavorable reports and resolutions and from the failure of Congress to provide for their payment at a time so near the events upon which they are based can not be destroyed by the interested cry of injustice and neglect of the rights of our citizens.

Until 1846 these claims were from time to time pressed upon the attention of Congress with varying fortunes, but never with favorable legislative action. In that year, however, a bill was passed for their ascertainment and satisfaction, and $5,000,000 were appropriated for their payment. This bill was vetoed by President Polk,* who declared that he could "perceive no legal or equitable ground upon which this large appropriation can rest." This veto was sustained by the House of Representatives.

Nine years afterwards, and in 1855, another bill was passed similar to the one last mentioned, and appropriating for the settlement of these claims a like sum of money. This bill was also vetoed,† President Pierce concluding a thorough discussion of its demerits with these words:

In view of what has been said there would seem to be no ground on which to raise a liability of the United States, unless it be the assumption that the United States are to be considered the insurer and the guarantor of all claims, of whatever nature, which any individual citizen may have against a foreign nation.

This veto was also sustained by the House of Representatives.

I think it will be found that in all bills proposed in former times for the payment of these claims the sum to be appropriated for that purpose did not exceed $5,000,000. It is now estimated that those already passed upon, with those still pending for examination in the Court of

---

*See Vol. IV, pp. 466-469.   †See Vol. V, pp. 307-322.

Claims, may amount to $25,000,000. This indicates either that the actual sufferers or those nearer to them in time and blood than the present claimants underestimated their losses or that there has been a great development in the manner of their presentation.

Nothwithstanding persistent efforts to secure payment from the Government and the importunity of those interested, no appropriation has ever been made for that purpose except a little more than $1,300,000, which was placed in the general deficiency bill in the very last hours of the session of Congress on March 3, 1891.

In the long list of beneficiaries who are provided for in the bill now before me on account of these claims 152 represent the owners of ships and their cargoes and 186 those who lost as insurers of such vessels or cargoes.

These insurers by the terms of their policies undertook and agreed "to bear and take upon themselves all risks and perils of the sea, men-of-war, fire, enemies, rovers, thieves, jettison, letters of mart and counter mart, surprisals, takings at sea, arrests, restraints, and detainments of all kings, princes, or people of what nation, condition, or quality whatsoever."

The premiums received on these policies were large, and the losses were precisely those within the contemplation of the insurers. It is well known that the business of insurance is entered upon with the expectation that the premiums received will pay all losses and yield a profit to the insurance in addition; and yet, without any showing that the business did not result in a profit to these insurance claimants, it is proposed that the Government shall indemnify them against the precise risks they undertook, notwithstanding the fact that the money appropriated is not to be paid except "by way of gratuity—payments as of grace and not of right."

The appropriations to indemnify against insurance losses rest upon weaker grounds, it seems to me, than those of owners; but in the light of all the facts and circumstances surrounding these spoliation claims, as they are called, none of them, in my opinion, should be paid by the Government.

Another item in this bill which seems to me especially objectionable is an appropriation in favor of Charles P. Chouteau, survivor, etc., of $174,445.75, in full satisfaction of all claims arising out of the construction of the ironclad steam battery *Etlah*.

The contract for the construction of this battery was made by the Government with Charles W. McCord during the war, and he was to be paid therefor the sum of $386,000. He was paid this sum and $210,991 for extras, and in May, 1866, gave his receipt in full. The assignee of McCord in bankruptcy assigned to Chouteau and his associates in 1868 all claims of McCord against the United States for the precise extras for which he had receipted in full two years before. Chouteau brought suit in the Court of Claims for such extras and was defeated. I can not gather from the facts I have been able to collect concerning this appropriation that it is justified on any ground.

In 1890 my immediate predecessor vetoed a bill allowing the matter to be examined again by the Court of Claims.*

If the additional payment proposed in this bill was made, the cost of the battery in question would be almost double that of the contract price.

I have determined to submit this incomplete presentation of my objections to this bill at once in order that the Congress may act thereon without embarrassment or the interruption of plans for an early adjournment.

GROVER CLEVELAND.

EXECUTIVE MANSION, *June 10, 1896.*
To the House of Representatives:

I herewith return without my approval House bill No. 225, entitled "An act to provide for the lease of Fort Omaha Military Reservation to the State of Nebraska."

This bill authorizes and directs the Secretary of War, when Fort Crook, near the city of Omaha, is ready for occupancy, to lease for a nominal rent to the State of Nebraska the possession of Fort Omaha Military Reservation, containing about 80 acres, with all the buildings, appurtenances, and improvements thereof. It is declared that the lease shall be conditional upon the use of said reservation by the State of Nebraska as a place of rendezvous and school of instruction for the National Guard of said State; that the State of Nebraska shall while it is in possession of said reservation keep the buildings and improvements thereon in as good condition and repair as at the date it shall enter into possession thereof, and that at any time when, in the judgment of the Secretary of War, the interests of the United States shall require such action he shall take possession of said military reservation for the use of the Government, together with all the buildings, appurtenances, and improvements thereon.

On the 23d day of July, 1888, an act was passed authorizing the Secretary of War to purchase suitable grounds, of not less than 640 acres in extent, to be situate within 10 miles of the city of Omaha, and to construct the necessary buildings thereon for a ten-company military post, to be known as Fort Omaha, and a necessary sum, not exceeding $200,000, was appropriated to enable the Secretary of War to carry out the provisions of said act.

The said act also authorized the Secretary of War, when the purchase of the new site should be effected, to sell the military reservation known as Fort Omaha and such of the buildings and improvements thereon as could not be economically removed to the new site, and to cause the said reservation, for the purposes of said sale, to be platted in blocks, streets,

*See p. 93.

and alleys, if in his judgment it would inure to the benefit of the Government in making a sale of such site.

The new site provided for by this act has been purchased, a large sum of money has been spent by the Government in preparing it for use, and I understand it will soon be ready for occupancy. The authority to sell the old site has not been exercised. This may be accounted for by the fact that the Government has not thus far been able to dispense with its use or because the depression in land values at Omaha has rendered it unadvisable.

The authority to sell and to remove any of the buildings from the old reservation to the new site still remains, however, unimpaired. In this condition of affairs it is now proposed to lease this land and these buildings to the State of Nebraska at a nominal rent, allowing the Government to repossess it only "when the interests of the United States shall require such action."

Of course it would be claimed that this language, in view of the statute of 1888, should not be construed as permitting the Government to retake the property for the purpose of selling it, because that is not stipulated in the bill. For that reason it would be plausibly urged that the lease was paramount to the power of sale contained in the law of 1888 and that the omission of any provision that possession might be resumed for the purpose of sale plainly indicated that "the interests of the United States" which allow such resumption contemplate some other and different emergency.

As a practical question, we all know that transactions of this character relating to Government property amount to a permanent alienation, or certainly pave the way for an absolute grant.

I do not think there should be anything done with this valuable property which will in the least embarrass the Government in its sale, and to that extent reimbursing itself for the cost of the new military post, which was plainly contemplated in the law of 1888.

GROVER CLEVELAND.

PROCLAMATIONS.

By the President of the United States of America.

A PROCLAMATION.

Whereas the Congress of the United States passed an act, which was approved on the 16th day of July, 1894, entitled "An act to enable the people of Utah to form a constitution and State government and to be admitted into the Union on an equal footing with the original States," which act provided for the election of delegates to a constitutional con-

By the President of the United States of America.

A Proclamation.

Whereas: The Congress of the United States passed an Act which was approved on the sixteenth day of July, eighteen hundred and ninety four, entitled "An Act to enable the people of Utah to form a Constitution and State Government and to be admitted into the Union on an equal footing with the original States," which Act provided for the election of delegates to a Constitutional Convention to meet, at the seat of government of the Territory of Utah, on the first Monday in March eighteen hundred and ninety-five, for the purpose of declaring the adoption of the Constitution of the United States by the people of the proposed State and forming a Constitution and State Government for such State;

And whereas, delegates were accordingly elected who met, organized and declared on behalf of the people of said proposed State their adoption of the Constitution of the United States, all as provided in said Act;

And whereas, said Convention, so organized, did, by ordinance irrevocable without the consent of the United States and the people of said State, as required

PRESIDENT CLEVELAND'S PROCLAMATION ON UTAH'S
ADMISSION TO THE UNION.

the United States to be affixed.

Done at the city of Washington this fourth day of January in the year of our Lord one thousand eight hundred and ninety six, and of the Independence of the United States of America the one hundred and twentieth.

Grover Cleveland

By the President

Richard Olney
Secretary of State.

PRESIDENT CLEVELAND'S SIGNATURE TO PROCLAMATION
ADMITTING UTAH INTO THE UNION.

vention to meet at the seat of government of the Territory of Utah on the first Monday in March, 1895, for the purpose of declaring the adoption of the Constitution of the United States by the people of the proposed State and forming a constitution and State government for such State; and

Whereas delegates were accordingly elected, who met, organized, and declared on behalf of the people of said proposed State their adoption of the Constitution of the United States, all as provided in said act; and

Whereas said convention, so organized, did, by ordinance irrevocable without the consent of the United States and the people of said State, as required by said act, provide that perfect toleration of religious sentiment shall be secured and that no inhabitant of said State shall ever be molested in person or property on account of his or her mode of religious worship, but that polygamous or plural marriages are forever prohibited, and did also by said ordinance make the other various stipulations recited in section 3 of said act; and

Whereas said convention thereupon formed a constitution and State government for said proposed State, which constitution, including said ordinance, was duly submitted to the people thereof at an election held on the Tuesday next after the first Monday of November, 1895, as directed by said act; and

Whereas the return of said election has been made and canvassed and the result thereof certified to me, together with a statement of the votes cast and a copy of said constitution and ordinance, all as provided in said act, showing that a majority of the votes lawfully cast at such election was for the ratification and adoption of said constitution and ordinance; and

Whereas the constitution and government of said proposed State are republican in form, said constitution is not repugnant to the Constitution of the United States and the Declaration of Independence, and all the provisions of said act have been complied with in the formation of said constitution and government:

Now, therefore, I, Grover Cleveland, President of the United States of America, in accordance with the act of Congress aforesaid and by authority thereof, announce the result of said election to be as so certified and do hereby declare and proclaim that the terms and conditions prescribed by the Congress of the United States to entitle the State of Utah to admission into the Union have been duly complied with and that the creation of said State and its admission into the Union on an equal footing with the original States is now accomplished.

In testimony whereof I have hereunto set my hand and caused the seal of the United States to be affixed.

[SEAL.] Done at the city of Washington, this 4th day of January, A. D. 1896, and of the Independence of the United States of America the one hundred and twentieth.

GROVER CLEVELAND.

By the President:

RICHARD OLNEY, *Secretary of State.*

BY THE PRESIDENT OF THE UNITED STATES OF AMERICA.

A PROCLAMATION.

Whereas it is provided by section 13 of the act of Congress of March 3, 1891, entitled "An act to amend Title LX, chapter 3, of the Revised Statutes of the United States, relating to copyrights," that said act "shall only apply to a citizen or subject of a foreign state or nation when such foreign state or nation permits to citizens of the United States of America the benefit of copyright on substantially the same basis as its own citizens, or when such foreign state or nation is a party to an international agreement which provides for reciprocity in the granting of copyright, by the terms of which agreement the United States of America may at its pleasure become a party to such agreement;" and

Whereas it is also provided by said section that "the existence of either of the conditions aforesaid shall be determined by the President of the United States by proclamation made from time to time as the purposes of this act may require;" and

Whereas satisfactory official assurances have been given that in the United States of Mexico the law permits to citizens of the United States of America the benefit of copyright on substantially the same basis as to the citizens of that Republic:

Now, therefore, I, Grover Cleveland, President of the United States of America, do declare and proclaim that the first of the conditions specified in section 13 of the act of March 3, 1891, now exists and is fulfilled in respect to the citizens of the United States of Mexico.

In testimony whereof I have hereunto set my hand and caused the seal of the United States to be affixed.

[SEAL.]   Done at the city of Washington, this 27th day of February, 1896, and of the Independence of the United States the one hundred and twentieth.

GROVER CLEVELAND.

By the President:

RICHARD OLNEY, *Secretary of State.*

BY THE PRESIDENT OF THE UNITED STATES OF AMERICA.

A PROCLAMATION.

Whereas in a suit between the United States and the State of Texas involving the title to and jurisdiction over all that territory lying between the North and South forks of the Red River and the one hundredth degree of longitude, known and styled as " Greer County, Tex.," the Supreme Court of the United States has decided that the title to and jurisdiction over said territory is vested in the United States; and

Whereas the Choctaw Nation claims that the title to these lands passed to said nation by virtue of treaties with the United States and that the title of said nation to said lands has not been extinguished, but that said Choctaw Nation has a right and interest therein; and

Whereas it is claimed that divers persons settled upon said lands prior to the 30th day of December, 1887, acting in good faith upon the belief that the same belonged to and were subject to the jurisdiction of the State of Texas and that Congress will be asked to extend to all such settlers suitable relief:

Now, therefore, I, Grover Cleveland, President of the United States, by virtue of the authority in me vested, not admitting in any wise the validity of such claim on behalf of the Choctaw Nation, but for the purpose of preserving the status of said lands intact until such time as said claim of the Choctaw Nation thereto may be duly determined, and that the settlers hereinbefore referred to shall not be disturbed until Congress shall have fully considered their claims for relief, do hereby withdraw said lands from disposition under the public-land laws of the United States and declare the same to be in a state of reservation until such time as this order of withdrawal may be revoked; and I do further warn and admonish all persons against entering upon said lands with a view to occupying the same or settling thereon under the public-land laws during the existence of this order.

In witness whereof I have hereunto set my hand and caused the seal of the United States to be affixed.

[SEAL.]   Done at the city of Washington, this 16th day of March, A. D. 1896, and of the Independence of the United States the one hundred and twentieth.

GROVER CLEVELAND.

By the President:

RICHARD OLNEY, *Secretary of State.*

BY THE PRESIDENT OF THE UNITED STATES OF AMERICA.

A PROCLAMATION.

The following provisions of the laws of the United States are published hereby for the information of all concerned:

Section 1956, Revised Statutes, chapter 3, Title XXIII, enacts that—

No person shall kill any otter, mink, marten, sable, or fur seal, or other fur-bearing animal within the limits of Alaska Territory or in the waters thereof; and every person guilty thereof shall for each offense be fined not less than $200 nor more than $1,000, or imprisoned not more than six months, or both; and all vessels, their tackle, apparel, furniture, and cargo, found engaged in violation of this section shall be forfeited; but the Secretary of the Treasury shall have power to authorize the killing of any such mink, marten, sable, or other fur-bearing animal, except fur seals, under such regulations as he may prescribe; and it shall be the duty of the Secretary to prevent the killing of any fur seal and to provide for the execution of the provisions of this section until it is otherwise provided by law, nor shall he grant any special privileges under this section.

Section 3 of the act entitled ''An act to provide for the protection of the salmon fisheries of Alaska,'' approved March 2, 1889, provides—

SEC. 3. That section 1956 of the Revised Statutes of the United States is hereby declared to include and apply to all the dominion of the United States in the waters of Bering Sea; and it shall be the duty of the President at a timely season in each year to issue his proclamation, and cause the same to be published for one month in at least one newspaper (if any such there be) published at each United States port of entry on the Pacific coast, warning all persons against entering said waters for the purpose of violating the provisions of said section; and he shall also cause one or more vessels of the United States to diligently cruise said waters and arrest all persons and seize all vessels found to be or to have been engaged in any violation of the laws of the United States therein.

The act entitled ''An act to extend to the North Pacific Ocean the provisions of the statutes for the protection of the fur seals and other fur-bearing animals,'' approved February 21, 1893, provides—

That whenever the Government of the United States shall conclude an effective international arrangement for the protection of fur seals in the North Pacific Ocean by agreement with any power or as a result of the decision of the Tribunal of Arbitration under the convention concluded between the United States and Great Britain February 29, 1892, and so long as such arrangement shall continue, the provisions of section 1956 of the Revised Statutes and all other provisions of the statutes of the United States, so far as the same may be applicable, relative to the protection of fur seals and other fur-bearing animals within the limits of Alaska or in the waters thereof shall be extended to and over all that portion of the Pacific Ocean included in such international arrangement. Whenever an effective international arrangement is concluded as aforesaid it shall be the duty of the President to declare that fact by proclamation and to designate the portion of the Pacific Ocean to which it is applicable and that this act has become operative, and likewise when such arrangement ceases to declare that fact and that this act has become inoperative; and his proclamation in respect thereto shall be conclusive. During the extension as aforesaid of said laws for the protection of fur seals or other fur-bearing animals all violations thereof in said designated portion of the Pacific Ocean shall be held to be the same as if committed within the limits of Alaska or in the waters thereof, but they may be prosecuted either in the district court of Alaska or in any district court of the United States in California, Oregon, or Washington.

An arrangement having been made for the protection of fur seals as a result of the decision of the Tribunal of Arbitration under the convention concluded as aforesaid February 29, 1892, which prohibits the killing of seals at any time within a radius of 60 miles around the Pribilof Islands or during May, June, and July of each year in that portion of the Pacific Ocean, inclusive of Bering Sea, situated to the north of the thirty-fifth degree of north latitude and eastward of the one hundred and eightieth degree of longitude from Greenwich until it strikes the water boundary described in Article I of the treaty of 1867 between the United States and Russia, and following that line up to Bering Strait:

Now, therefore, be it known that I, Grover Cleveland, President of the United States of America, hereby declare that the said act of Congress of February 21, 1893, has become operative; that in accordance therewith section 1956 of the Revised Statutes is applicable to the waters above mentioned, included in the award of the tribunal at Paris given under the said convention of February 29, 1892, and that I have caused the foregoing laws specially to be proclaimed to the end that their provisions may be known and observed.

I hereby proclaim that every person guilty of a violation of the provisions of said laws and of any other provisions of the statutes of the United States, so far as the same may be applicable, relative to the protection of fur-bearing animals within the limits of Alaska or in the waters thereof will be arrested and punished as therein provided, and all vessels so engaged, their tackle, apparel, furniture, and cargo, will be seized and forfeited.

In testimony whereof I have hereunto set my hand and caused the seal of the United States to be affixed.

[SEAL.]   Done at the city of Washington, this 14th day of April, A. D. 1896, and of the Independence of the United States the one hundred and twentieth.   GROVER CLEVELAND.

By the President:

RICHARD OLNEY,
Secretary of State.

BY THE PRESIDENT OF THE UNITED STATES OF AMERICA.

A PROCLAMATION.

Whereas it is provided by section 13 of the act of Congress of March 3, 1891, entitled "An act to amend Title LX, chapter 3, of the Revised Statutes of the United States, relating to copyrights," that said act "shall only apply to a citizen or subject of a foreign state or nation when such foreign state or nation permits to citizens of the United States of America the benefit of copyright on substantially the same basis as its own citizens, or when such foreign state or nation is a party to an international agreement which provides for reciprocity in the granting of copyright, by the terms of which agreement the United States of America may at its pleasure become a party to such agreement;" and

Whereas it is also provided by said section that "the existence of either of the conditions aforesaid shall be determined by the President of the United States by proclamation made from time to time as the purposes of this act may require;" and

Whereas satisfactory official assurances have been given that in the Republic of Chile the law permits to citizens of the United States of America the benefit of copyright on substantially the same basis as to the citizens of that Republic:

Now, therefore, I, Grover Cleveland, President of the United States of America, do declare and proclaim that the first of the conditions specified in section 13 of the act of March 3, 1891, now exists and is fulfilled in respect to the citizens of the Republic of Chile.

In testimony whereof I have hereunto set my hand and caused the seal of the United States to be affixed.

[SEAL.]   Done at the city of Washington, this 25th day of May, 1896, and of the Independence of the United States the one hundred and twentieth.   GROVER CLEVELAND.

By the President:

RICHARD OLNEY,
        Secretary of State.

BY THE PRESIDENT OF THE UNITED STATES OF AMERICA.

A PROCLAMATION.

Whereas by a proclamation dated the 12th day of June, A. D. 1895,* attention was called to the serious civil disturbances, accompanied by armed resistance to the established Government of Spain, then prevailing in the island of Cuba, and citizens of the United States and all other persons were admonished to abstain from taking part in such disturbances in contravention of the neutrality laws of the United States; and

Whereas said civil disturbances and armed resistance to the authority of Spain, a power with which the United States are on terms of peace and amity, continue to prevail in said island of Cuba; and

Whereas since the date of said proclamation said neutrality laws of the United States have been the subject of authoritative exposition by the judicial tribunal of last resort, and it has thus been declared that any combination of persons organized in the United States for the purpose of proceeding to and making war upon a foreign country with which the United States are at peace, and provided with arms to be used for such purpose, constitutes a ''military expedition or enterprise'' within the meaning of said neutrality laws, and that the providing or preparing of the means for such ''military expedition or enterprise,'' which is expressly prohibited by said laws, includes furnishing or aiding in transportation for such ''military expedition or enterprise;'' and

Whereas, by express enactment, if two or more persons conspire to commit an offense against the United States any act of one conspirator to effect the object of such conspiracy renders all the conspirators liable to fine and imprisonment; and

Whereas there is reason to believe that citizens of the United States and others within their jurisdiction fail to apprehend the meaning and operation of the neutrality laws of the United States as authoritatively interpreted as aforesaid, and may be misled into participation in transactions which are violations of said laws and will render them liable to the severe penalties provided for such violations:

Now, therefore, that the laws above referred to, as judicially con-

*See pp. 591-592.

strued, may be duly executed, that the international obligations of the United States may be fully satisfied, and that their citizens and all others within their jurisdiction, being seasonably apprised of their legal duty in the premises, may abstain from disobedience to the laws of the United States and thereby escape the forfeitures and penalties legally consequent thereon, I, Grover Cleveland, President of the United States, do hereby solemnly warn all citizens of the United States and all others within their jurisdiction against violations of the said laws, interpreted as hereinbefore explained, and give notice that all such violations will be vigorously prosecuted; and I do hereby invoke the cooperation of all good citizens in the enforcement of said laws and in the detection and apprehension of any offenders against the same, and do hereby enjoin upon all the executive officers of the United States the utmost diligence in preventing, prosecuting, and punishing any infractions thereof.

In testimony whereof I have hereunto set my hand and caused the seal of the United States to be affixed.

[SEAL.]   Done at the city of Washington, this 27th day of July, A. D. 1896, and of the Independence of the United States the one hundred and twenty-first.

GROVER CLEVELAND.

By the President:
    RICHARD OLNEY,
        Secretary of State.

BY THE PRESIDENT OF THE UNITED STATES.

THANKSGIVING PROCLAMATION.

The people of the United States should never be unmindful of the gratitude they owe the God of Nations for His watchful care, which has shielded them from dire disaster and pointed out to them the way of peace and happiness. Nor should they ever refuse to acknowledge with contrite hearts their proneness to turn away from God's teachings and to follow with sinful pride after their own devices.

To the end that these thoughts may be quickened it is fitting that on a day especially appointed we should join together in approaching the Throne of Grace with praise and supplication.

Therefore, I, Grover Cleveland, President of the United States, do hereby designate and set apart Thursday, the 26th day of the present month of November, to be kept and observed as a day of thanksgiving and prayer throughout our land.

On that day let all our people forego their usual work and occupation, and, assembled in their accustomed places of worship, let them with one accord render thanks to the Ruler of the Universe for our preservation as a nation and our deliverance from every threatened danger, for the peace that has dwelt within our boundaries, for our defense against disease and pestilence during the year that has passed, for the plenteous rewards that have followed the labors of our husbandmen, and for all the other blessings that have been vouchsafed to us.

And let us, through the mediation of Him who has taught us how to pray, implore the forgiveness of our sins and a continuation of heavenly favor.

Let us not forget on this day of thanksgiving the poor and needy, and by deeds of charity let our offerings of praise be made more acceptable in the sight of the Lord.

Witness my hand and the seal of the United States, which I have caused to be hereto affixed.

[SEAL.] Done at the city of Washington, this 4th day of November, A. D. 1896, and of the Independence of the United States of America the one hundred and twenty-first.

GROVER CLEVELAND

By the President:

RICHARD OLNEY,
Secretary of State.

BY THE PRESIDENT OF THE UNITED STATES.

A PROCLAMATION.

Whereas on June 21, 1890, the President of the United States by proclamation reserved certain lands in Juneau and Douglas City, Fort Wrangell and Sitka, in the Territory of Alaska, for public buildings, barracks, parade grounds, parks, wharves, coaling stations, etc., which are fully set forth and particularly described in said proclamation; and

Whereas a treaty of cession was exchanged and proclaimed on June 20, 1867, whereby the Russian Empire ceded to the United States the Territory of Alaska; and

Whereas said treaty, by Article II, provided, *inter alia*, that—

It is, however, understood and agreed that the churches which have been built in the ceded territory by the Russian Government shall remain the property of such members of the Greek Oriental Church resident in the territory as may choose to worship therein.

And whereas there were included among the lands hereinbefore referred to as reserved on June 21, 1890, certain lands in and about the town of Sitka, in said Territory of Alaska, which are claimed by the Holy Orthodox Catholic Apostolic Oriental Church, commonly styled the Greco-Russian Church, and described in the said treaty as the Greek Oriental Church:

Now, therefore, I, Grover Cleveland, President of the United States, by virtue of the authority in me vested, do hereby declare, proclaim, and make known that the Executive order of June 21, 1890, making said reservations of lands in the Territory of Alaska, therein particularly described, is hereby modified, and said reservations are diminished so that the following property, described in Inventory B attached to and referred to in the protocol of transfer signed by the representatives of Russia and the United States on October 26, 1867, and being in and about the town of Sitka aforesaid, be excluded therefrom, to wit:

The Cathedral Church of St. Michael, built of timber, situated in the center of the city.

The Church of Resurrection, of timber, commonly called the Kalochian Church, situated near the battery number at the palisade separating the city from the Indian village.

102. A double-storied timber building for bishop house, with outbuildings, appurtenances, and grounds.

35. A timber house for church warden.

98. A timber house for the deacon.

104
105 } Three timber houses, with their appurtenances and outbuildings,
114   for lodging of priests.

F
G
H } Four lots of ground belonging to the parsonages.
I

a The place commemorative of the old church.

b A tomb.

Three cemeteries, two outside palisades and one by the Church of the Resurrection.

In witness whereof I have hereunto set my hand and caused the seal of the United States to be affixed.

[SEAL.]   Done at the city of Washington, this 14th day of November, in the year 1896, and of the Independence of the United States the one hundred and twenty-first.

GROVER CLEVELAND.

By the President:

RICHARD OLNEY,
    Secretary of State.

BY THE PRESIDENT OF THE UNITED STATES.

A PROCLAMATION.

Whereas by a proclamation of the President of the United States dated January 26, 1888,* upon proof then appearing satisfactory that no tonnage or light-house dues or any equivalent tax or taxes whatever were

*See Vol. VIII, pp. 741-742.

imposed upon American vessels entering the ports of the Empire of Germany, either by the Imperial Government or by the governments of the German maritime States, and that vessels belonging to the United States of America and their cargoes were not required in German ports to pay any fee or due of any kind or nature or any import due higher or other than was payable by German vessels or their cargoes in the United States, the President did thereby declare and proclaim, from and after the date of his said proclamation of January 26, 1888, the suspension of the collection of the whole of the duty of 6 cents per ton, not to exceed 30 cents per ton per annum, imposed upon vessels entered in the ports of the United States from any of the ports of the Empire of Germany by section 11 of the act of Congress approved June 19, 1886, entitled "An act to abolish certain fees for official services to American vessels and to amend the laws relating to shipping commissioners, seamen, and owners of vessels, and for other purposes;" and

Whereas the President did further declare and proclaim in his proclamation of January 26, 1888, that the said suspension should continue so long as the reciprocal exemption of vessels belonging to citizens of the United States and their cargoes should be continued in the said ports of the Empire of Germany, and no longer; and

Whereas it now appears upon satisfactory proof that tonnage or light-house dues or a tax or taxes equivalent thereto are in fact imposed upon American vessels and their cargoes entered in German ports higher and other than those imposed upon German vessels or their cargoes entered in ports of the United States, so that said proclamation of January 26, 1888, in its operation and effect contravenes the meaning and intent of said section 11 of the act of Congress approved June 19, 1886:

Now, therefore, I, Grover Cleveland, President of the United States of America, by virtue of the aforesaid section 11 of the act aforesaid, as well as in pursuance of the terms of said proclamation itself, do hereby revoke my said proclamation of January 26, 1888, suspending the collection of the whole of the duty of 6 cents per ton, not to exceed 30 cents per ton per annum, which is imposed by the aforesaid section of said act upon vessels entered in the ports of the United States from any of the ports of the German Empire, this revocation of said proclamation to take effect on and after the 2d day of January, 1897.

In witness whereof I have hereunto set my hand and caused the seal of the United States to be affixed.

[SEAL.]   Done at the city of Washington, this 3d day of December, A. D. 1896, and of the Independence of the United States the one hundred and twenty-first.

GROVER CLEVELAND.

By the President:

RICHARD OLNEY,
            Secretary of State.

EXECUTIVE ORDERS.

AMENDMENT OF CIVIL-SERVICE RULES.

EXECUTIVE. MANSION, *December 2, 1895.*

Special Departmental Rule No. 1, clause 8, is hereby amended by striking from the list of places excepted from examination in the Department of Labor statistical experts and temporary experts.

Approved:

GROVER CLEVELAND.

AMENDMENT OF CIVIL-SERVICE RULES.

EXECUTIVE MANSION, *December 2, 1895.*

So much of Executive orders heretofore issued under General Rule III, section 2, clause (*c*), as provides for the appointment of special agents in the Department of Labor by noncompetitive examination is hereby revoked.

Approved:

GROVER CLEVELAND.

AMENDMENT OF CIVIL-SERVICE RULES.

EXECUTIVE MANSION, *January 18, 1896.*

Section 5 of Internal-Revenue Rule IV is hereby amended by adding at the end of the first paragraph thereof the following:

And provided further, That whenever an emergency shall arise requiring that a vacant position in any internal-revenue district shall be filled before a certificate can be issued by the Commission and an appointment made thereto in the manner provided in these rules, such position may be filled without regard to the provisions of these rules by temporary appointment for a period not to exceed fifteen days, and only for such period as may be required for the execution of the necessary details of an appointment thereto in accordance with said provisions; but no person shall receive such emergency appointment who within the sixty days next previous thereto has been separated from a position in said district to which he was temporarily appointed under the provisions of this section.

The section as amended shall read as follows:

5. In the case of the occurrence of a vacancy in the classified service of any internal-revenue collection district which the public interest requires shall be immediately filled and there is no eligible entitled to reinstatement under section 1, clause (*b*), of this rule or remaining on the proper register, such vacancy in the class of storekeeper, storekeeper and gauger, or clerk may be filled without examination and certification by a temporary designation by the collector of the district of some suitable person to perform the duties of the position until a regular appointment can be made under the provisions of sections 1, 2, and 3 of this rule: *Provided*, That service under such temporary designation shall in no case continue longer than six months, and shall expire by limitation at the end of that time: *And provided further*, That no person shall serve more than six months in any one year under such temporary

designation, the year limitation in regard to such designation to begin to run on the date thereof: *And provided further*, That whenever an emergency shall arise requiring that a vacant position in any internal-revenue district shall be filled before a certificate can be issued by the Commission and an appointment made thereto in the manner provided in these rules, such position may be filled without regard to the provisions of these rules by temporary appointment for a period not to exceed fifteen days, and only for such period as may be required for the execution of the necessary details of an appointment thereto in accordance with said provisions; but no person shall receive such emergency appointment who within the sixty days next previous thereto has been separated from a position in said district to which he was temporarily appointed under the provisions of this section.

Every such temporary designation, and also the discontinuance of the same, shall be at once reported to the Commission.

Approved:

GROVER CLEVELAND.

AMENDMENT OF CIVIL-SERVICE RULES.

EXECUTIVE MANSION, *January 18, 1896.*

Section 5 of Customs Rule II is hereby amended by adding thereto the following:

(*i*) Any person appointed to a position which requires only a portion of his time and attention for the performance of its duties, pays him a compensation not exceeding $300 per annum, and permits of his pursuing other regular business or occupation, such person being conveniently located for the performance of said duties.

The section as amended shall read as follows:

5. Exceptions from examination in the classified customs service are hereby made as follows:

(*a*) Deputy collectors who do not also act as inspectors, examiners, or clerks.
(*b*) Cashier of the collector.
(*c*) Assistant cashier of the collector.
(*d*) Auditor of the collector.
(*e*) Chief acting disbursing officer.
(*f*) Deputy naval officers.
(*g*) Deputy surveyors.
(*h*) One private secretary or one confidential clerk of each nominating officer.
(*i*) Any person appointed to a position which requires only a portion of his time and attention for the performance of its duties, pays him a compensation not exceeding $300 per annum, and permits of his pursuing other regular business or occupation, such person being conveniently located for the performance of said duties.

Approved:

GROVER CLEVELAND.

CIVIL SERVICE.—EXTENSION OF THE CLASSIFIED DEPARTMENTAL AND INDIAN SERVICES.

In the exercise of the power vested in the President by the third paragraph of section 6 of the act entitled "An act to regulate and improve the civil service of the United States," approved January 16, 1883, I hereby direct the Secretary of the Interior to amend the classification of the Interior Department so as to include among the positions classified thereunder and subject to competitive examination clerk, assistant clerk, issue clerk, property clerk, storekeeper, and all other clerical positions at Indian agencies and Indian schools; likewise to amend the classification of the Indian service so as to include among the positions classified thereunder supervisor of Indian schools, day-school inspector, disciplinarian, industrial teacher, teacher of industries, kindergarten teacher, farmer, nurse, assistant matron, and seamstress.

But Indians shall be eligible to appointment to any of said positions on such test of fitness as may be required by the Secretary of the Interior and without examination or certification by the Civil Service Commission; but they shall not be transferred from said positions to the departmental service.

Approved, March 20, 1896.

GROVER CLEVELAND.

AMENDMENT OF CIVIL-SERVICE RULES.

EXECUTIVE MANSION, *March 28, 1896.*

So much of the Executive orders heretofore issued under General Rule III, section 2, clause (*c*), as provides for the appointment of members of the board of pension appeals in the Department of the Interior by noncompetitive examination is hereby revoked, and these places will hereafter be treated as subject to competitive examination.

Approved:

GROVER CLEVELAND.

AMENDMENT OF CIVIL-SERVICE RULES.

EXECUTIVE MANSION, *March 28, 1896.*

Special Departmental Rule No. 1, clause 3, is hereby amended by striking from the list of places excepted from examination in the Department of the Interior assistant attorneys and law clerks, and these places will hereafter be treated as subject to competitive examination.

Approved:

GROVER CLEVELAND.

CIVIL-SERVICE RULES.

In the exercise of power vested in him by the Constitution and of authority given to him by the seventeen hundred and fifty-third section of the Revised Statutes and by an act to regulate and improve the civil service of the United States, approved January 16, 1883, the President hereby makes and promulgates the following rules and revokes all others:

RULE I.

1. The United States Civil Service Commission shall have authority to prescribe regulations in pursuance of and for the execution of the provisions of these rules and of the civil-service act.

2. The several terms hereinafter mentioned, wherever used in these rules or the regulations of the Commission, shall be construed as follows:

(*a*) The term "civil-service act" refers to "An act to regulate and improve the civil service of the United States," approved January 16, 1883.

(*b*) The term "classified service" refers to all that part of the executive civil service of the United States included within the provisions of the civil-service act.

(*c*) The term "grade" in connection with employees or positions refers to a group of employees or positions in the classified service arranged upon the basis of duties performed, without regard to salaries received.

(*d*) The term "class" in connection with employees or positions refers to a group of employees or positions in any grade arranged upon the basis of salaries received, in pursuance of the provisions of section 163 of the Revised Statutes and of section 6 of the civil-service act.

(*e*) The term "excepted position" refers to any position within the provisions of the civil-service act, but excepted from the requirement of competitive examination or registration for appointment thereto.

RULE II.

1. Any person in the executive civil service of the United States who shall willfully violate any of the provisions of the civil-service act or of these rules shall be dismissed from office.

2. No person in the executive civil service shall use his official authority or official influence for the purpose of interfering with an election or controlling the result thereof.

3. No person in the executive civil service shall dismiss, or cause to be dismissed, or make any attempt to procure the dismissal of, or in any manner change the official rank or compensation of, any other person therein because of his political or religious opinions or affiliations.

4. No question in any examination or form of application shall be so framed as to elicit information concerning, nor shall any inquiry be made concerning, nor any other attempt be made to ascertain, the political or religious opinions or affiliations of any applicant, competitor, or eligible; and all disclosures thereof shall be discountenanced, and no discrimination shall be exercised, threatened, or promised against or in favor of any applicant, competitor, or eligible because of his political or religious opinions or affiliations.

5. No recommendation of an applicant, competitor, or eligible involving any disclosure of his political or religious opinions or affiliations shall be received, filed, or considered by the Commission, by any board of examiners, or by any nominating or appointing officer.

6. In making removals or reductions or in imposing punishment for delinquency or misconduct penalties like in character shall be imposed for like offenses, and action thereupon shall be taken irrespective of the political or religious opinions or affiliations of the offenders.

7. A person holding a position on the date said position is classified under the civil-service act shall be entitled to all the rights and benefits possessed by persons of the same class or grade appointed upon examination under the provisions of said act.

RULE III.

1. All that part of the executive civil service of the United States which has been or may hereafter be classified under the civil-service act shall be arranged in branches as follows: The departmental service, the custom-house service, the post-office service, the Government printing service, and the internal-revenue service.

2. The departmental service shall include officers and employees as follows, except those in the service of the Government Printing Office and in the service of the several custom-houses, post-offices, and internal-revenue districts:

(*a*) All officers and employees, of whatever designation, except persons merely employed as laborers or workmen and persons who have been nominated for confirmation by the Senate, however or for whatever purpose employed, whether compensated by a fixed salary or otherwise, who are serving in or on detail from—

The several Executive Departments, the commissions, and offices in the District of Columbia.

The railway mail service.

The Indian service.

The several pension agencies.

The steamboat-inspection service.

The marine-hospital service.

The light-house service.

The life-saving service.

The several mints and assay offices.

The revenue-cutter service.

The force employed under custodians of public buildings.

The several subtreasuries.

The engineer department at large.

(*b*) All executive officers and employees outside of the District of Columbia not covered in (*a*), of whatever designation, whether compensated by a fixed salary or otherwise—

Who are serving in a clerical capacity or whose duties are in whole or in part of a clerical nature.

Who are serving in the capacity of watchman or messenger.

Who are serving in the capacity of physician, hospital steward, nurse, or whose duties are of a medical nature.

Who are serving in the capacity of draftsman, civil engineer, steam engineer, electrical engineer, computer, or fireman.

Who are in the service of the Supervising Architect's Office in the capacity of superintendent of construction, superintendent of repair, or foreman.

Who are in the service of the Treasury Department in any capacity except those in the life-saving service.

3. The custom-house service shall include the officers and employees serving in any customs district whose employees number as many as five who have been or may hereafter be classified under the civil-service act; and whenever in any customs district whose officers and employees number less than five the number of officers and employees shall be increased to as many as five the Secretary of the Treasury shall at once notify the Commission of such increase and the officers and employees in said district shall be included within the classified service from the date of said increase.

4. The post-office service shall include the officers and employees in any free-delivery post-office who have been or may hereafter be classified under the civil-service act; and whenever the free-delivery system shall be established in any post-office the Postmaster-General shall at once notify the Commission of such establishment and the officers or employees of said office shall be included within the classified service from the date of such establishment; and whenever by order of the Postmaster-General any post-office shall be consolidated with and made a part of a free-delivery post-office the Postmaster-General shall at once notify the Commission of such consolidation and from the date of said order the employees of the office thus made a part of the free-delivery office whose names appear on the roster of the Post-Office Department shall be employees of said free-delivery office, and the person holding on the date of said order the position of postmaster at the office thus made a part of said free-delivery office may be made an employee in said free-delivery office and may at the time of classification be assigned to any position therein and given any appropriate designation which the Postmaster-General may direct.

5. The Government printing service shall include the officers and employees in the Government Printing Office who have been or may hereafter be classified under the civil-service act.

6. The internal-revenue service shall include the officers and employees who have been or may hereafter be classified under the civil-service act in any internal-revenue district.

7. All officers and employees who have heretofore been classified under the civil-service act shall be considered as still classified and subject to the provisions of these rules.

8. The following-mentioned positions or employees shall not be subject to the provisions of these rules:

(*a*) Any position filled by a person whose place of private business is conveniently located for the performance of the duties of said position, or any position filled by a person remunerated in one sum both for services rendered therein and for necessary rent, fuel, and lights furnished for the performance of the duties thereof: *Provided*, That in either case the performance of the duties of said position requires only a portion of the time and attention of the occupant, paying him a compensation not exceeding, for his personal salary only, $300 per annum, and permitting of his pursuing other regular business or occupation.

(*b*) Any person in the military or naval service of the United States who is detailed for the performance of civil duties.

(*c*) Any person employed in a foreign country under the State Department or temporarily employed in a confidential capacity in a foreign country.

(*d*) Any position whose duties are of a quasi military or quasi naval character and for the performance of whose duties a person is enlisted for a term of years.

RULE IV.

1. In pursuance of the provisions of section 2 of the civil-service act, there shall be provided, to test fitness for admission to positions which have been or may hereafter be classified under the civil-service act, examinations of a practical and suitable character involving such subjects and tests as the Commission may direct.

2. No person shall be appointed to or be employed in any position which has been or may hereafter be classified under the civil-service act until he shall have passed the examination provided therefor or unless he is especially exempt from examination by the provisions of said act or the rules made in pursuance thereof.

3. In pursuance of the provisions of section 2 of the civil-service act, wherever competent persons can be found who are willing to compete, no noncompetitive examination shall be given except as follows:

(*a*) To test fitness for transfer or for promotion in a part of the service to which promotion regulations have not been applied.

(*b*) To test fitness for appointment of Indians as superintendents, teachers, teachers of industries, kindergartners, and physicians in the Indian service at large.

The noncompetitive examinations of Indians for the positions mentioned shall consist of such tests of fitness, not disapproved by the Commission, as may be determined upon by the Secretary of the Interior. A statement of the result of every noncompetitive test and all appointments, transfers, or promotions based thereon shall be immediately forwarded to the Commission.

4. In pursuance of the provisions of section 3 of the civil-service act, examinations shall be provided at such places and upon such dates as the Commission shall deem most practicable to subserve the convenience of applicants and the needs of the service.

5. In pursuance of the provisions of section 3 of the civil-service act, the Commission shall appoint from persons in the Government service such boards of examiners as it may deem necessary. The members of said boards shall perform such duties as the Commission may direct in connection with examinations, appointments, and promotions in any part of the service which has been or may hereafter be classified. The members of any board of examiners in the performance of their duties as such shall be under the direct and sole control and authority of the Commission. The duties performed by the members of any board of examiners in their capacity as such shall be considered part of the duties of the office in which they are serving, and time shall be allowed for the performance of said duties during the office hours of said office. The members of any board of examiners shall not all be adherents of one political party when persons of other political parties are available and competent to serve upon said board.

6. In pursuance of the provisions of section 3 of the civil-service act, all executive

officers of the United States shall facilitate civil-service examinations, and postmasters, customs officers, internal-revenue officers, and custodians of public buildings at places where such examinations are to be held shall for the purpose of such examinations permit and arrange for the use of suitable rooms under their charge and for heating, lighting, and furnishing the same.

RULE V.

1. Every applicant for examination must be a citizen of the United States, must be of proper age, and must make an application under oath upon a form prescribed by the Commission and accompanied by such certificates as may be prescribed.

2. No application for examination shall be accepted from any person serving in the Army, the Navy, or Marine Corps of the United States unless the written consent of the head of the department under which said person is enlisted is filed with his application.

3. The Commission may, in its discretion, refuse to examine an applicant or to certify an eligible who is physically so disabled as to be rendered unfit for the performance of the duties of the position to which he seeks appointment, or who has been guilty of a crime or of infamous or notoriously disgraceful conduct, or who has been dismissed from the service for delinquency or misconduct within one year next preceding the date of his application, or who has intentionally made a false statement in any material fact or practiced or attempted to practice any deception or fraud in securing his registration or appointment. Any of the foregoing disqualifications shall be good cause for the removal of an eligible from the service after his appointment.

4. No application for examination shall be accepted unless the applicant is within the age limitations fixed herein for entrance to the position to which he seeks to be appointed: *Provided*, That, subject to the other conditions of these rules, the application of any person whose claim of preference under the provisions of section 1754 of the Revised Statutes has been allowed by the Commission may be accepted without regard to his age. The age limitations for entrance to positions in the different branches of the service shall be as follows:

	Minimum.	Maximum.
Departmental service:		
Page or messenger boy	14	18
Apprentice (or student)	16	20
Printer's assistant and messenger	18	No limit.
Positions in railway mail service	18	35
Superintendent, physician, supervisor, day-school inspector, Indian service	25	55
All other positions in the Indian service	21	45
All other positions	20	No limit.
(These limitations shall not apply in the cases of wives of superintendents of Indian schools who apply for examination for the position of teacher or matron.)		
Custom-house service:		
Clerk and messenger	20	No limit.
Other positions	21	No limit.
Post-office service:		
Letter carrier	21	40
Other positions	18	No limit.
Government printing service:		
All positions (male)	21	No limit.
All positions (female)	18	No limit.
Internal-revenue service:		
Clerk	18	No limit.
Other positions	21	No limit.

5. No application shall be accepted for examination for a position which belongs to one of the recognized mechanical trades unless it shall be shown that the applicant has served as apprentice or as journeyman or as apprentice and journeyman at said trade for such periods as the Commission may prescribe.

RULE VI.

The following-named employees or positions which have been or may hereafter be classified under the civil-service act shall be excepted from the requirement of examination or registration:

Departmental service.—(*a*) Private secretaries or confidential clerks (not exceeding two) to the President or to the head of each of the eight Executive Departments; (*b*) Indians employed in the Indian service at large, except those employed as superintendents, teachers, teachers of industries, kindergartners, and physicians.

Custom-house service.—(*a*) One cashier in each customs district; (*b*) one chief or principal deputy or assistant collector in each customs district whose employees number as many as 150.

Post-office service.—(*a*) One assistant postmaster, or chief assistant to the postmaster, of whatever designation, at each post-office; (*b*) one cashier of each first-class post-office when employed under the roster title of cashier only.

Internal-revenue service.—One cashier in each internal-revenue district.

RULE VII.

1. Examination papers shall be rated on a scale of 100, and the subjects therein shall be given such relative weights as the Commission may prescribe. After a competitor's papers have been rated he shall be duly notified of the result thereof.

2. Every competitor who attains an average percentage of 70 or over shall be eligible for appointment to the position for which he was examined, and the names of eligibles shall be entered in the order of their average percentages on the proper register of eligibles: *Provided*, That the names of all competitors whose claims to preference under the provisions of section 1754 of the Revised Statutes have been allowed by the Commission, and who attain an average percentage of 65 or over, shall be placed in the order of their average percentages at the head of the proper register of eligibles.

3. For filling vacancies in positions for which competitive tests are not practicable the registration of applicants shall be in the order in which they fulfill the requirements prescribed therefor by regulation of the Commission: *Provided*, That persons who served in the military or naval service of the United States in the late War of the Rebellion and were honorably discharged therefrom, and persons who have been separated from such positions above mentioned through no delinquency or misconduct, shall be placed at the head of the proper register in the order of their fulfillment of said requirements.

4. The term of eligibility shall be one year from the date on which the name of the eligible is entered upon the register.

RULE VIII.

In pursuance of the provisions of section 2 of the civil-service act, whenever a vacancy occurs in any position which has been or may hereafter be classified under the civil-service act, and which is not an excepted position, the filling of said vacancy, unless filled through noncompetitive examination or by reinstatement, transfer, promotion, or reduction, shall be governed as follows:

1. The appointing or nominating officer shall request certification to him of the names of eligibles for the position vacant, and the Commission shall certify to said officer from the proper register the three names at the head thereof which have not been three times certified to the Department or office in which the vacancy

exists: *Provided*, That certification for temporary appointment shall not be counted as one of the three certifications to which an eligible is entitled: *And provided further*, That whenever the sex of those whose names are to be certified is fixed by any law, rule, or regulation or is specified in the request for certification the names of those of the sex so fixed or specified shall be certified, but in other cases certification shall be made without regard to sex.

2. Of the three names certified the nominating or appointing officer shall select one, and if at the time of selection there are more vacancies than one he may select more than one name, unless otherwise directed by the Commission.

3. If an eligible who is not entitled to certification is certified and appointed, his appointment shall be immediately revoked by the appointing officer upon notification from the Commission.

4. A person selected for appointment shall be notified of his selection by the appointing or nominating officer, and upon his acceptance shall receive from the appointing officer a certificate of appointment for a probationary period of six months, at the end of which period, if the conduct and capacity of the probationer are satisfactory to the appointing officer, his retention in the service shall be equivalent to his absolute appointment; but if his conduct or capacity be not satisfactory he shall be notified by the appointing officer that he will not receive absolute appointment because of such unsatisfactory conduct or want of capacity, and such notification shall discharge him from the service: *Provided*, That the probation of an employee in the Indian-school service shall terminate at the end of the school year in which he is appointed: *And provided further*, That the time which an employee has actually served as substitute in parts of the service where substitutes are authorized shall be counted as part of the probationary period of his regular appointment, but that time served under a temporary appointment shall not be so counted.

5. If the appointing or nominating officer shall object to an eligible named in the certificate, stating that because of some physical defect, mental unsoundness, or moral disqualification, particularly specified, said eligible would be incompetent or unfit for the performance of the duties of the vacant position, and if said officer shall sustain such objection with evidence satisfactory to the Commission, the Commission may certify the eligible on the register who is in average percentage next below those already certified in place of the one to whom objection is made and sustained.

6. Certifications for appointment of persons for service in or on direct detail from any Department or office in Washington, D. C., shall be so made as to maintain as nearly as possible the apportionment of such appointments among the several States and Territories and District of Columbia upon the basis of population, except to appointments in the Government Printing Office, to the position of printer's assistant, skilled helper, and operative in the Bureau of Engraving and Printing, to positions in the post quartermaster's office, in the pension agency, and other local offices in the District of Columbia, and to the positions of page and messenger boy and apprentice or student.

7. Within any part of the service to which promotion regulations have been or may hereafter be applied certification of those eligible to original appointment shall not be made for filling a vacancy in a position above the lowest class in any grade whenever there is any person eligible and willing to be promoted to said vacancy: *Provided*, That a vacancy in any position requiring the exercise of technical or professional knowledge may be filled by original appointment.

8. When two or more eligibles on a register have the same average percentage, preference in certification shall be determined by the order in which their applications were filed.

9. For filling vacancies in positions outside of the District of Columbia and in positions in the pension agency, the depot quartermaster's office, and other local offices in the District of Columbia the territory of the United States shall be arranged in

such sections or districts as the Commission may determine, and an eligible shall be certified in his order to vacancies in the section or district in which he resides, and, upon his written request, to vacancies in any one or more of the other sections or districts: *Provided*, That in the custom-house service, post-office service, or internal-revenue service an eligible shall be certified only to vacancies in the customs district, post-office, or internal-revenue district where he was examined.

10. In any part of the service in which the employment of substitutes is not prohibited by law there may be certified and appointed in the manner provided for in this rule only such number of substitutes as are actually needed for the performance of substitute duty.

11. In any part of the service in which substitutes are employed certifications of those eligible to original appointment shall be made for filling vacancies in substitute positions only, and vacancies in regular positions shall be filled by the appointment or promotion thereto of substitutes in the order of their original appointment as substitutes whenever there are substitutes of the required sex who are eligible and willing to be so appointed or promoted. Substitutes so appointed or promoted shall, however, be subject to the provisions of these rules relating to probation and permanent appointment.

12. Upon request of the appointing or nominating officer preference in certification may be given to the wife of the superintendent of an Indian school for filling a vacancy in the position of teacher or matron in said school.

13. Whenever there shall occur a vacancy which the public interest requires shall be immediately filled and which can not be so filled in time to meet the emergency by certification from the eligible registers, such vacancy may, subject to the approval of the Commission, be filled by temporary appointment without examination until a regular appointment can be made. Such temporary appointment shall in no case continue longer than ninety days, and shall expire by limitation at the end of that time. No person shall serve longer than ninety days in any one year under such temporary appointment or appointments, and in any event only until a regular appointment can be made through examination and certification. Said year limitation shall begin to run in the case of any person on the date of his first such appointment: *Provided*, That whenever an emergency shall arise requiring that a vacant position in any internal-revenue district shall be filled before a certificate can be issued by the Commission and an appointment made thereto in the manner provided in these rules such position may be filled without regard to the provisions of these rules by temporary appointment for a period not to exceed thirty days, and only for such period as may be required for the execution of the necessary details of an appointment thereto in accordance with said provisions; but no person shall receive such temporary appointment who within the ninety days next previous thereto has been separated from a position in said district to which he was temporarily appointed under the provisions of this section.

14. Whenever a temporary appointment shall be made through certification from the eligible registers of the Commission in the manner provided in these rules, such temporary appointment shall in no case continue longer than six months, and shall expire by limitation at the end of that period.

RULE IX.

A vacancy in any position which has been or may hereafter be classified under the civil-service act may, upon requisition of the proper officer and the certificate of the Commission, be filled by the reinstatement without examination of any person who within one year next preceding the date of said requisition has through no delinquency or misconduct been separated from a classified position at the date of said requisition and in that Department or office and that branch of the service in which said vacancy exists: *Provided*, That for original entrance to the position proposed to be filled by reinstatement there is not required by these rules, in the opinion of the Commission, an examination involving essential tests different from or higher than those involved in the examination for original entrance to the position formerly held by the person proposed to be reinstated: *And provided further*, That, subject to the other conditions of these rules, any person who served in the military or naval service of the United States in the late War of the Rebellion and was honorably discharged therefrom, or the widow of any such person, may be reinstated without regard to the length of time he or she has been separated from the service.

RULE X.

Within that part of the civil service of the United States which has been or may hereafter be classified under the civil-service act transfers shall be governed as follows:

1. A person in any Department or office may be transferred within the same Department or office and the same branch of the service upon any test of fitness, not disapproved by the Commission, which may be determined upon by the appointing officer, subject to the limitations of the provisos of section 2 of this rule.

2. A person who has received absolute appointment may be transferred without examination from any Department, office, or branch of the service upon requisition and consent of the proper officers and the certificate of the Commission: *Provided*, That no transfer shall be made of a person to a position within the same Department or office and the same branch of the service, or to a position in another Department, office, or branch of the service, if from original entrance to such position said person is barred by the age limitations prescribed therefor or by the provisions regulating apportionment, or if in said position there is not required, in the judgment of the Commission, the performance of the same class of work or the practice of the same mechanical trade performed or practiced in the position from which transfer is proposed: *And provided further*, That transfer shall not be made without examination, provided by the Commission, to a position for original entrance to which, in the judgment of the Commission, there is required by these rules an examination involving essential tests different from or higher than those involved in the examination required for original entrance to the position from which transfer is proposed; but a person employed in any grade shall not because of such employment be barred from the open competitive examination provided for original entrance to any other grade.

3. Upon requisition of the proper officer and the certificate of the Commission transfer may be made without examination from the office of the President of the United States, after continuous service therein for the two years next preceding the date of said requisition, to any position classified under the civil-service act, if in said position there is required, in the judgment of the Commission, the performance of the same class of work that is required to be performed in the position from which transfer is proposed.

4. Transfer shall not be made from an excepted position to a position not excepted: *Provided*, That a person holding an excepted position at the time said position is classified under the civil-service act, or a person holding an excepted position which he entered prior to the President's order of November 2, 1894, may, subject to the other conditions and provisions of this rule, be transferred to a position not excepted.

5. Transfer shall not be made from a position not classified under the civil-service act to a classified position: *Provided*, That a person who by promotion or transfer from a classified position has entered a position appointment to which is made by the President by and with the advice and consent of the Senate, and has served continuously therein from the date of said promotion or transfer, may be transferred from said Presidential appointment to the position from which he was so transferred or to any position to which transfer could be made therefrom.

6. Transfer shall not be made from a position outside the District of Columbia to a position within the District of Columbia except upon the certificate of the Commission, subject to the other conditions and provisions of this rule.

7. Any person who has been transferred from a classified position to another classified position may be retransferred to the position in which he was formerly employed or to any position to which transfer could be made therefrom without regard to the limitations of this rule.

8. All transfers herein authorized shall be made only after the issuance by the Commission of the certificates therefor, except those which may be specifically exempted from such condition by regulation of the Commission.

9. Whenever a person is proposed for transfer from one branch of the service to another branch of the service and from a part of the service not within the provisions regulating apportionment to a part of the service within said provisions, and the transfer is one which under the provisions of this rule may be allowed without examination, such person shall be required precedent to his transfer to file a statement under oath setting forth the same facts, accompanied by the same certificates or vouchers relating to residence, as may be required in an application for examination.

RULE XI.

1. In pursuance of the requirements of section 7 of the civil-service act, competitive tests or examinations shall, as far as practicable and useful, be established to test fitness for promotion in any part of the civil service of the United States which has been or may hereafter be classified under the civil-service act.

2. The details regulating promotions shall be formulated by the Commission after consultation with the heads of the several Departments, bureaus, or offices. It shall be the duty of the head of each Department, bureau, or office when such regulations have been formulated to promulgate the same, and any amendments or revocations thereof shall be approved by the Commission before going into effect.

3. The Commission shall, upon the nomination of the head of each Department, bureau, or office, designate and select a suitable number of persons, not less than three, in said Department, bureau, or office to be members of a board of promotion. In the Departments, bureaus, or offices in Washington and in all other offices the members of any board of examiners shall not all be adherents of one political party when persons of other political parties are available and competent to serve upon said board.

4. Until the regulations herein authorized have been approved for any Department, bureau, or office in which promotion regulations approved by the Commission are not in force promotions therein may be made from one class to another class which is in the same grade and from one grade to another grade upon any test of fitness, not disapproved by the Commission, which may be determined upon by the promoting officer: *Provided*, That no promotion of a person shall be made, except upon examination provided by the Commission, from one class to another class or from one grade to another grade if for original entrance to said class or grade to which promotion is proposed there is required by these rules an examination involving essential tests different from or higher than those involved in the examination required for original entrance to the class or grade from which promotion is proposed: *And provided further*, That no promotion of a person shall be made, except upon examination provided by the Commission, to a position in which, in the judgment of the Commission, there is not required the performance of the same class of work or the practice of the same mechanical trade which is required to be performed or practiced in the position from which promotion is proposed; but a person employed in any grade shall not because of such employment be barred from the open competitive examination provided for original entrance to any other grade: *And provided further*, That

no promotion of a person shall be made to a class or grade from original entrance to which such person is barred by the age limitations prescribed therefor or by the provisions regulating apportionment.

RULE XII.

1. In pursuance of the provisions of section 2 of the civil-service act every nominating or appointing officer in the executive civil service of the United States shall furnish to the Commission a list of all the positions and employments under his control and authority, together with the names, designations, compensations, and dates of appointment or employment of all persons serving in said positions or employments, said list to be arranged as follows: (*a*) Classified positions not excepted from examination; (*b*) classified positions excepted from examination; (*c*) unclassified positions.

2. Every nominating or appointing officer in the executive civil service shall report in detail to the Commission, in form and manner to be prescribed by the Commission, all changes as soon as made, and the dates thereof, in the service under his control and authority, setting forth among other things the following: The position to which an appointment or reinstatement is made; the position from which a separation is made, whether the same was caused by dismissal, resignation, or death, and the posiion from which and the position to which a transfer or promotion is made; the compensation of every position from which or to which a change is made; the name of every person appointed, reinstated, promoted, transferred, or separated from the service, and every failure to accept an appointment and the reasons therefor.

Approved, May 6, 1896. GROVER CLEVELAND.

EXECUTIVE MANSION,
Washington, D. C., May 7, 1896.

In the exercise of the authority vested in the President by the seventeen hundred and fifty-third (1753d) section of the Revised Statutes—

It is ordered, That the office of the Interstate Commerce Commission be, and the same is hereby, classified as a part of the classified departmental service, and for the purpose of applying the civil-service rules thereto the officers, clerks, and other employees of said Commission are hereby arranged in the following classes, viz:

Class A.—All persons receiving an annual salary of less than $720, or a compensation at the rate of less than $720 per annum.

Class B.—All persons receiving an annual salary of $720 or more, or a compensation at the rate of $720 or more, but less than $840 per annum.

Class C.—All persons receiving an annual salary of $840 or more, or a compensation at the rate of $840 or more, but less than $900 per annum.

Class D.—All persons receiving a salary of $900 or more, or a compensation at the rate of $900 or more, but less than $1,000 per annum.

Class E.—All persons receiving an annual salary of $1,000 or more, or a compensation at the rate of $1,000 or more, but less than $1,200 per annum.

Class 1.—All persons receiving an annual salary of $1,200 or more, or a compensation at the rate of $1,200 or more, but less than $1,400 per annum.

Class 2.—All persons receiving an annual salary of $1,400 or more per annum, or a compensation at the rate of $1,400 or more, but less than $1,600 per annum.

Class 3.—All persoLs receiving an annual salary of $1,600 or more per annum, or an annual compensation at the rate of $1,600 or more, but less than $1,800 per annum.

Class 4.—All persons receiving an annual salary of $1,800 or more per annum, or a compensation at the rate of $1,800 or more, but less than $2,000 per annum.

Class 5.—All persons receiving an annual salary of $2,000 or more or a compensation at the rate of $2,000 or more per annum.

Provided, That no person who may be appointed to an office by and with the advice and consent of the Senate and that no person who may be employed merely as a workman or laborer shall be considered as within this classification, and no person so employed shall be assigned to the duties of a classified place.

Provided further, That no person shall be admitted to any place not excepted from examination by the civil-service rules in any of the classes above designated until he or she shall have passed an appropriate examination under the United States Civil Service Commission and his or her eligibility has been certified to by said Commission.

GROVER CLEVELAND.

AMENDMENTS OF CIVIL-SERVICE RULES.

EXECUTIVE MANSION, *May 13, 1896.*

The civil-service rules are hereby amended as follows:

Rule III, clause 2 (*a*), is amended by adding after the words "the light-house service" the words "the life-saving service."

Paragraph (*b*) of the same rule and clause is amended by striking out after the words "who are in the service of the Treasury Department in any capacity" the words "except those in the life-saving service."

Approved:

GROVER CLEVELAND.

AMENDMENTS OF CIVIL-SERVICE RULES.

The civil-service rules as revised May 6, 1896, are hereby amended as follows:

Rule I, section 2, clause (*b*): In the third line, after the word "act," insert "and these rules;" so that as amended the clause will read:

(*b*) The term "classified service" refers to all that part of the executive civil service of the United States included within the provisions of the civil-service act and these rules,

Rule III, section 2, clause (*a*), is amended by adding thereto the following clause:

The Ordnance Department at large.

Rule III, section 2, clause (*a*), is amended by striking out after "persons" in the third line the words "who have been nominated for" and inserting in lieu thereof the words "whose appointments are subject to."

Rule III, section 2 clause (*b*), is amended by inserting in the second line, after the word "designation," the words "except persons merely employed as laborers or workmen and persons whose appointments are subject to confirmation by the Senate."

Rule III, section 2, clause (*b*), is amended by adding thereto the following words:

Who are employed in the Department of Justice under the annual appropriation for the investigation of official acts, records, and accounts of officers of the courts.

Rule III, section 3, is amended to read as follows:

3. The custom-house service shall include such officers and employees as have been or may hereafter be classified under the civil-service act who are serving in any customs district whose officers and employees number as many as five; and whenever in any customs district whose officers and employees number less than five the number of officers and employees shall be increased to as many as five the Secretary of the Treasury shall at once notify the Commission of such increase, and the officers and employees of said district shall be included within the classified service from the date of said increase.

Rule III, section 6, is amended by inserting in the second line, after the word "employees," the following: "in any internal-revenue district;" and in the third line, after the word "act," by striking out the following: "in any internal-revenue district;" so that as amended the section will read:

6. The internal-revenue service shall include the officers and employees in any internal-revenue district who have been or may hereafter be classified under the civil-service act.

Rule VI is amended by adding in the departmental service an additional clause, making exceptions from examination, to read as follows:

(*c*) Attorneys or assistant attorneys in any Department whose main duties are connected with the management of cases in court.

Amend Rule VI by striking out after "internal-revenue service" the words "one cashier in each internal-revenue district" and inserting in lieu thereof—

One employee in each internal-revenue district who shall act as cashier or chief deputy or assistant collector, as may be determined by the Treasury Department.

Amend Rule VIII by striking out section 3.

Rule IX is amended by striking out in the seventh line the word "classified" and inserting in lieu thereof after the word "position" in the same line the following: "included within the classified service;" so that as amended the line will read: "misconduct, been separated from a position included within the classified service at the."

Rule XI, section 2, is amended by striking out in line 1 the words "The details regulating" and inserting in their stead the words "Regulations to govern;" so that as amended the section will read:

2. Regulations to govern promotions shall be formulated by the Commission after consultation with the heads of the several Departments, bureaus, and offices. It shall be the duty of the head of each Department, bureau, or office when such regulations have been formulated to promulgate the same, and any amendments or revocations thereof shall be approved by the Commission before going into effect.

Rule XI, section 3: The word "examiners" in line 7 is changed to "promotion," making the section read:

3. The Commission shall, upon the nomination of the head of each Department, bureau, or office, designate and select a suitable number of persons, not less than three, in said Department, bureau, or office to be members of a board of promotion. In the Departments, bureaus, or offices in Washington and in all other offices the members of any board of promotion shall not all be adherents of one political party when persons of other political parties are available and competent to serve upon said board.

Approved, November 2, 1896.   GROVER CLEVELAND.

CIVIL SERVICE.—EXECUTIVE ORDER.

EXECUTIVE MANSION, *November 2, 1896.*

The regulations of the Navy Department governing the employment of labor at navy-yards having been adopted by the Civil Service Commission as a regulation of the Commission July 29, 1896, under the authority conferred by clause 1, Rule I, of the revised civil-service rules of May 6, 1896, it is hereby ordered that no modification of the existing regulations shall be made without the approval of the Civil Service Commission.   GROVER CLEVELAND.

FOURTH ANNUAL MESSAGE.

EXECUTIVE MANSION, *December 7, 1896.*

To the Congress of the United States:

As representatives of the people in the legislative branch of their Government, you have assembled at a time when the strength and excellence of our free institutions and the fitness of our citizens to enjoy popular rule have been again made manifest. A political contest involving momentous consequences, fraught with feverish apprehension, and creating aggressiveness so intense as to approach bitterness and passion has been waged throughout our land and determined by the decree of free and independent suffrage without disturbance of our tranquillity or the least sign of weakness in our national structure.

When we consider these incidents and contemplate the peaceful obedience and manly submission which have succeeded a heated clash of political opinions, we discover abundant evidence of a determination on the part of our countrymen to abide by every verdict of the popular will and to be controlled at all times by an abiding faith in the agencies established for the direction of the affairs of their Government.

Thus our people exhibit a patriotic disposition which entitles them to demand of those who undertake to make and execute their laws such faithful and unselfish service in their behalf as can only be prompted by a serious appreciation of the trust and confidence which the acceptance of public duty invites.

In obedience to a constitutional requirement I herein submit to the Congress certain information concerning national affairs, with the suggestion of such legislation as in my judgment is necessary and expedient. To secure brevity and avoid tiresome narration I shall omit many details concerning matters within Federal control which, though by no means unimportant, are more profitably discussed in departmental reports. I shall also further curtail this communication by omitting a minute recital of many minor incidents connected with our foreign relations which have heretofore found a place in Executive messages, but are now contained in a report of the Secretary of State, which is herewith submitted.

At the outset of a reference to the more important matters affecting our relations with foreign powers it would afford me satisfaction if I could assure the Congress that the disturbed condition in Asiatic Turkey had during the past year assumed a less hideous and bloody aspect and that, either as a consequence of the awakening of the Turkish Government to the demands of humane civilization or as the result of decisive action on the part of the great nations having the right by treaty to interfere for the protection of those exposed to the rage of mad bigotry and cruel fanaticism, the shocking features of the situation had been mitigated. Instead, however, of welcoming a softened disposition or protective intervention, we have been afflicted by continued and not unfrequent reports of the wanton destruction of homes and the bloody butchery of men, women, and children, made martyrs to their profession of Christian faith.

While none of our citizens in Turkey have thus far been killed or wounded, though often in the midst of dreadful scenes of danger, their safety in the future is by no means assured. Our Government at home and our minister at Constantinople have left nothing undone to protect our missionaries in Ottoman territory, who constitute nearly all the individuals residing there who have a right to claim our protection on the score of American citizenship. Our efforts in this direction will not be relaxed; but the deep feeling and sympathy that have been aroused among our people ought not to so far blind their reason and judgment as to lead them to demand impossible things. The outbreaks of blind fury which lead to murder and pillage in Turkey occur suddenly and without notice, and an attempt on our part to force such a hostile presence there as might be effective for prevention or protection would not only be resisted by the Ottoman Government, but would be regarded as an interruption of their plans by the great nations who assert their exclusive right to intervene in their own time and method for the security of life and property in Turkey.

Several naval vessels are stationed in the Mediterranean as a measure of caution and to furnish all possible relief and refuge in case of emergency.

We have made claims against the Turkish Government for the pillage and destruction of missionary property at Harpoot and Marash during uprisings at those places. Thus far the validity of these demands has not been admitted, though our minister, prior to such outrages and in anticipation of danger, demanded protection for the persons and property of our missionary citizens in the localities mentioned and notwithstanding that strong evidence exists of actual complicity of Turkish soldiers in the work of destruction and robbery.

The facts as they now appear do not permit us to doubt the justice of these claims, and nothing will be omitted to bring about their prompt settlement.

A number of Armenian refugees having arrived at our ports, an order has lately been obtained from the Turkish Government permitting the wives and children of such refugees to join them here. It is hoped that hereafter no obstacle will be interposed to prevent the escape of all those who seek to avoid the perils which threaten them in Turkish dominions.

Our recently appointed consul to Erzerum is at his post and discharging the duties of his office, though for some unaccountable reason his formal exequatur from the Sultan has not been issued.

I do not believe that the present somber prospect in Turkey will be long permitted to offend the sight of Christendom. It so mars the humane and enlightened civilization that belongs to the close of the nineteenth century that it seems hardly possible that the earnest demand of good people throughout the Christian world for its corrective treatment will remain unanswered.

The insurrection in Cuba still continues with all its perplexities. It is difficult to perceive that any progress has thus far been made toward the pacification of the island or that the situation of affairs as depicted in my last annual message has in the least improved. If Spain still holds Havana and the seaports and all the considerable towns, the insurgents still roam at will over at least two-thirds of the inland country. If the determination of Spain to put down the insurrection seems but to strengthen with the lapse of time and is evinced by her unhesitating devotion of largely increased military and naval forces to the task, there is much reason to believe that the insurgents have gained in point of numbers and character and resources and are none the less inflexible in their resolve not to succumb without practically securing the great objects for which they took up arms. If Spain has not yet reestablished her authority, neither have the insurgents yet made good their title to be regarded as an independent state. Indeed, as the contest has gone on the pretense that civil government exists on the island, except so far as Spain is able to maintain it, has been practically abandoned. Spain does keep on foot such a government, more or less imperfectly, in the large towns and their immediate suburbs; but that exception being made, the entire country is either given over to anarchy or is subject to the military occupation of one or the other party. It is reported, indeed, on reliable authority that at the demand of the commander in chief of the insurgent army the putative Cuban government has now given up all attempt to exercise its functions, leaving that government confessedly (what there is the best reason for supposing it always to have been in fact) a government merely on paper.

Were the Spanish armies able to meet their antagonists in the open or in pitched battle, prompt and decisive results might be looked for, and the immense superiority of the Spanish forces in numbers, discipline, and equipment could hardly fail to tell greatly to their advantage. But they are called upon to face a foe that shuns general engagements, that can choose and does choose its own ground, that from the nature of the country is visible or invisible at pleasure, and that fights only from ambuscade and when all the advantages of position and numbers are on its side. In a country where all that is indispensable to life in the way of food, clothing, and shelter is so easily obtainable, especially by those born and bred on the soil, it is obvious that there is hardly a limit to the time during which hostilities of this sort may be prolonged. Meanwhile, as in all cases of protracted civil strife, the passions of the combatants grow more and more inflamed and excesses on both sides become more frequent and more deplorable. They are also participated in by bands of marauders, who, now in the name of one party and now in the name of the other, as may best suit the occasion, harry the country at will and plunder its wretched inhabitants for their own advantage. Such a condition of things would inevitably entail immense destruction of property, even if it were the policy of both parties to prevent it as far as practicable; but while such seemed to be the original policy of the Spanish Government, it has now apparently abandoned it and is acting upon the same theory as the insurgents, namely, that the exigencies of the contest require the wholesale annihilation of property that it may not prove of use and advantage to the enemy.

It is to the same end that, in pursuance of general orders, Spanish garrisons are now being withdrawn from plantations and the rural population required to concentrate itself in the towns. The sure result would seem to be that the industrial value of the island is fast diminishing and that unless there is a speedy and radical change in existing conditions it will soon disappear altogether. That value consists very largely, of course, in its capacity to produce sugar—a capacity already much reduced by the interruptions to tillage which have taken place during the last two years. It is reliably asserted that should these interruptions continue during the current year, and practically extend, as is now threatened, to the entire sugar-producing territory of the island, so much time and so much money will be required to restore the land to its normal productiveness that it is extremely doubtful if capital can be induced to even make the attempt.

The spectacle of the utter ruin of an adjoining country, by nature one of the most fertile and charming on the globe, would engage the serious attention of the Government and people of the United States in any circumstances. In point of fact, they have a concern with it which is by no means of a wholly sentimental or philanthropic character. It lies so near to us as to be hardly separated from our territory. Our actual pecuniary interest in it is second only to that of the people and Government of Spain. It is reasonably estimated that at least from $30,000,000 to $50,000,000 of American capital are invested in plantations and in railroad, mining, and other business enterprises on the island. The volume of trade between the United States and Cuba, which in 1889 amounted to about $64,000,000, rose in 1893 to about $103,000,000, and in 1894, the year before the present insurrection broke out, amounted to nearly $96,000,000. Besides this large pecuniary stake in the fortunes of Cuba, the United States finds itself inextricably involved in the present contest in other ways, both vexatious and costly.

Many Cubans reside in this country, and indirectly promote the insurrection through the press, by public meetings, by the purchase and shipment of arms, by the raising of funds, and by other means which the spirit of our institutions and the tenor of our laws do not permit to be made the subject of criminal prosecutions. Some of them, though Cubans at heart and in all their feelings and interests, have taken out papers as naturalized citizens of the United States—a proceeding resorted to with a view to possible protection by this Government, and not unnaturally regarded with much indignation by the country of their origin. The insurgents are undoubtedly encouraged and supported by the widespread sympathy the people of this country always and instinctively feel for every struggle for better and freer government, and which, in the case of the more adventurous and restless elements of our population, leads in only too many instances to active and personal participation in the contest. The result is that this Government is constantly called upon to protect American citizens, to claim damages for injuries to persons and property, now estimated at many millions of dollars, and to ask explanations and apologies for the acts of Spanish officials whose zeal for the repression of rebellion sometimes blinds them to the immunities belonging to the unoffending citizens of a friendly power. It follows from the same causes that the United States is compelled to actively police a long line of seacoast against unlawful expeditions, the escape of which the utmost vigilance will not always suffice to prevent.

These inevitable entanglements of the United States with the rebellion in Cuba, the large American property interests affected, and considerations of philanthropy and humanity in general have led to a vehement demand in various quarters for some sort of positive intervention on the part of the United States. It was at first proposed that belligerent rights should be accorded to the insurgents—a proposition no longer urged because untimely and in practical operation clearly perilous and injurious to our own interests. It has since been and is now sometimes contended that the independence of the insurgents should be recognized; but imperfect and restricted as the Spanish government of the island may be, no other exists there, unless the will of the military officer in temporary command of a particular district can be dignified as a species of government. It is now also suggested that the United States should buy the island—a suggestion possibly worthy of consideration if there were any evidence of a desire or willingness on the part of Spain to entertain such a proposal. It is urged finally that, all other methods failing, the existing internecine strife in Cuba should be terminated by our intervention, even at the cost of a war between the United States and Spain—a war which its advocates confidently prophesy could neither be large in its proportions nor doubtful in its issue.

The correctness of this forecast need be neither affirmed nor denied. The United States has, nevertheless, a character to maintain as a nation, which plainly dictates that right and not might should be the rule of its conduct. Further, though the United States is not a nation to which peace is a necessity, it is in truth the most pacific of powers and desires nothing so much as to live in amity with all the world. Its own ample and diversified domains satisfy all possible longings for territory, preclude all dreams of conquest, and prevent any casting of covetous eyes upon neighboring regions, however attractive. That our conduct toward Spain and her dominions has constituted no exception to this national disposition is made manifest by the course of our Government, not only thus far during the present insurrection, but during the ten years that followed the rising at Yara in 1868. No other great power, it may safely be said, under circumstances of similar perplexity, would have manifested the same restraint and the same patient endurance. It may also be said that this persistent attitude of the United States toward Spain in connection with Cuba unquestionably evinces no slight respect and regard for Spain on the part of the American people. They in truth do not forget her connection with the discovery of the Western Hemisphere, nor do they underestimate the great qualities of the Spanish people nor fail to fully recognize their splendid patriotism and their chivalrous devotion to the national honor.

They view with wonder and admiration the cheerful resolution with which vast bodies of men are sent across thousands of miles of ocean and an enormous debt accumulated that the costly possession of the gem of the Antilles may still hold its place in the Spanish crown. And yet neither the Government nor the people of the United States have shut their eyes to the course of events in Cuba or have failed to realize the existence of conceded grievances which have led to the present revolt from the authority of Spain—grievances recognized by the Queen Regent and by the Cortes, voiced by the most patriotic and enlightened of Spanish statesmen, without regard to party, and demonstrated by reforms proposed by the executive and approved by the legislative branch of the Spanish Government. It is in the assumed temper and disposition of the Spanish Government to remedy these grievances, fortified by indications of influential public opinion in Spain, that this Government has hoped to discover the most promising and effective means of composing the present strife with honor and advantage to Spain and with the achievement of all the reasonable objects of the insurrection.

It would seem that if Spain should offer to Cuba genuine autonomy—a measure of home rule which, while preserving the sovereignty of Spain, would satisfy all rational requirements of her Spanish subjects—there should be no just reason why the pacification of the island might not be effected on that basis. Such a result would appear to be in the true interest of all concerned. It would at once stop the conflict which is now consuming the resources of the island and making it worthless for whichever party may ultimately prevail. It would keep intact the possessions of Spain without touching her honor, which will be consulted rather than impugned by the adequate redress of admitted grievances. It would put the prosperity of the island and the fortunes of its inhabitants within their own control without severing the natural and ancient ties which bind them to the mother country, and would yet enable them to test their capacity for self-government under the most favorable conditions. It has been objected on the one side that Spain should not promise autonomy until her insurgent subjects lay down their arms; on the other side, that promised autonomy, however liberal, is insufficient, because without assurance of the promise being fulfilled.

But the reasonableness of a requirement by Spain of unconditional surrender on the part of the insurgent Cubans before their autonomy is conceded is not altogether apparent. It ignores important features of the situation—the stability two years' duration has given to the insurrection; the feasibility of its indefinite prolongation in the nature of things, and, as shown by past experience, the utter and imminent ruin of the island unless the present strife is speedily composed; above all, the rank abuses which all parties in Spain, all branches of her Government, and all her leading public men concede to exist and profess a desire to remove. Facing such circumstances, to withhold the proffer of needed reforms until the parties demanding them put themselves at mercy by throwing down their arms has the appearance of neglecting the gravest of perils and inviting suspicion as to the sincerity of any professed willingness to grant reforms. The objection on behalf of the insurgents that promised reforms can not be relied upon must of course be considered, though we have no right to assume and no reason for assuming that anything Spain undertakes to do for the relief of Cuba will not be done according to both the spirit and the letter of the undertaking.

Nevertheless, realizing that suspicions and precautions on the part of the weaker of two combatants are always natural and not always unjustifiable, being sincerely desirous in the interest of both as well as on its own account that the Cuban problem should be solved with the least possible delay, it was intimated by this Government to the Government of Spain some months ago that if a satisfactory measure of home rule were tendered the Cuban insurgents and would be accepted by them upon a guaranty of its execution the United States would endeavor to find a way not objectionable to Spain of furnishing such guaranty. While no definite response to this intimation has yet been received from the Spanish Government, it is believed to be not altogether unwelcome, while, as already suggested, no reason is perceived why it should not be approved by the insurgents. Neither party can fail to see the importance of early action, and both must realize that to prolong the present state of things for even a short period will add enormously to the time and labor and expenditure necessary to bring about the industrial recuperation of the island. It is therefore fervently hoped on all grounds that earnest efforts for healing the breach between Spain and the insurgent Cubans upon the lines above indicated may be at once inaugurated and pushed to an immediate and successful issue. The friendly offices of the United States, either in the manner above outlined or in any other way consistent with our Constitution and laws, will always be at the disposal of either party.

Whatever circumstances may arise, our policy and our interests would constrain us to object to the acquisition of the island or an interference with its control by any other power.

It should be added that it can not be reasonably assumed that the hitherto expectant attitude of the United States will be indefinitely maintained. While we are anxious to accord all due respect to the sovereignty of Spain, we can not view the pending conflict in all its features and properly apprehend our inevitably close relations to it and its possible results without considering that by the course of events we may be drawn into such an unusual and unprecedented condition as will fix a limit to our patient waiting for Spain to end the contest, either alone and in her own way or with our friendly cooperation.

When the inability of Spain to deal successfully with the insurrection has become manifest and it is demonstrated that her sovereignty is extinct in Cuba for all purposes of its rightful existence, and when a hopeless struggle for its reestablishment has degenerated into a strife which means nothing more than the useless sacrifice of human life and the utter destruction of the very subject-matter of the conflict, a situation will be presented in which our obligations to the sovereignty of Spain will be superseded by higher obligations, which we can hardly hesitate to recognize and discharge. Deferring the choice of ways and methods until the time for action arrives, we should make them depend upon the precise conditions then existing; and they should not be determined upon without giving careful heed to every consideration involving our honor and interest or the international duty we owe to Spain. Until we face the contingencies suggested or the situation is by other incidents imperatively changed we should continue in the line of conduct heretofore pursued, thus in all circumstances exhibiting our obedience to the requirements of public law and our regard for the duty enjoined upon us by the position we occupy in the family of nations.

A contemplation of emergencies that may arise should plainly lead us to avoid their creation, either through a careless disregard of present duty or even an undue stimulation and ill-timed expression of feeling. But I have deemed it not amiss to remind the Congress that a time may arrive when a correct policy and care for our interests, as well as a regard for the interests of other nations and their citizens, joined by considerations of humanity and a desire to see a rich and fertile country intimately related to us saved from complete devastation, will constrain our Government to such action as will subserve the interests thus involved and at the same time promise to Cuba and its inhabitants an opportunity to enjoy the blessings of peace.

The Venezuelan boundary question has ceased to be a matter of difference between Great Britain and the United States, their respective Governments having agreed upon the substantial provisions of a treaty between Great Britain and Venezuela submitting the whole controversy to arbitration. The provisions of the treaty are so eminently just and fair that the assent of Venezuela thereto may confidently be anticipated.

Negotiations for a treaty of general arbitration for all differences between Great Britain and the United States are far advanced and promise to reach a successful consummation at an early date.

The scheme of examining applicants for certain consular positions to test their competency and fitness, adopted under an Executive order issued on the 20th of September, 1895,* has fully demonstrated the usefulness of this innovation. In connection with this plan of examination promotions and transfers of deserving incumbents have been quite extensively made, with excellent results.

*See p. 624.

During the past year 35 appointments have been made in the consular service, 27 of which were made to fill vacancies caused by death or resignation or to supply newly created posts, 2 to succeed incumbents removed for cause, 2 for the purpose of displacing alien consular officials by American citizens, and 4 merely changing the official title of incumbent from commercial agent to consul. Twelve of these appointments were transfers or promotions from other positions under the Department of State, 4 of those appointed had rendered previous service under the Department, 8 were made of persons who passed a satisfactory examination, 7 were appointed to places not included in the order of September 20, 1895, and 4 appointments, as above stated, involved no change of incumbency.

The inspection of consular offices provided for by an appropriation for that purpose at the last session of the Congress has been productive of such wholesome effects that I hope this important work will in the future be continued. I know of nothing that can be done with the same slight expense so improving to the service.

I desire to repeat the recommendation contained in my last annual message in favor of providing at public expense official residences for our ambassadors and ministers at foreign capitals. The reasons supporting this recommendation are strongly stated in the report of the Secretary of State, and the subject seems of such importance that I hope it may receive the early attention of the Congress.

We have during the last year labored faithfully and against unfavorable conditions to secure better preservation of seal life in the Bering Sea. Both the United States and Great Britain have lately dispatched commissioners to these waters to study the habits and condition of the seal herd and the causes of their rapid decrease. Upon the reports of these commissioners, soon to be submitted, and with the exercise of patience and good sense on the part of all interested parties, it is earnestly hoped that hearty cooperation may be secured for the protection against threatened extinction of seal life in the Northern Pacific and Bering Sea.

The Secretary of the Treasury reports that during the fiscal year ended June 30, 1896, the receipts of the Government from all sources amounted to $409,475,408.78. During the same period its expenditures were $434,678,654.48, the excess of expenditures over receipts thus amounting to $25,203,245.70. The ordinary expenditures during the year were $4,015,852.21 less than during the preceding fiscal year. Of the receipts mentioned there was derived from customs the sum of $160,021,751.67 and from internal revenue $146,830,615.66. The receipts from customs show an increase of $7,863,134.22 over those from the same source for the fiscal year ended June 30, 1895, and the receipts from internal revenue an increase of $3,584,537.91.

The value of our imported dutiable merchandise during the last fiscal year was $369,757,470 and the value of free goods imported $409,967,-470, being an increase of $6,523,675 in the value of dutiable goods and

$41,231,034 in the value of free goods over the preceding year. Our exports of merchandise, foreign and domestic, amounted in value to $882,606,938, being an increase over the preceding year of $75,068,773. The average *ad valorem* duty paid on dutiable goods imported during the year was 39.94 per cent and on free and dutiable goods taken together 20.55 per cent.

The cost of collecting our internal revenue was 2.78 per cent, as against 2.81 per cent for the fiscal year ending June 30, 1895. The total production of distilled spirits, exclusive of fruit brandies, was 86,588,703 taxable gallons, being an increase of 6,639,108 gallons over the preceding year. There was also an increase of 1,443,676 gallons of spirits produced from fruit as compared with the preceding year. The number of barrels of beer produced was 35,859,250, as against 33,589,784 produced in the preceding fiscal year, being an increase of 2,269,466 barrels.

The total amount of gold exported during the last fiscal year was $112,-409,947 and of silver $60,541,670, being an increase of $45,941,466 of gold and $13,246,384 of silver over the exportations of the preceding fiscal year. The imports of gold were $33,525,065 and of silver $28,-777,186, being $2,859,695 less of gold and $8,566,007 more of silver than during the preceding year.

The total stock of metallic money in the United States at the close of the last fiscal year, ended on the 30th day of June, 1896, was $1,228,-326,035, of which $599,597,964 was in gold and $628,728,071 in silver.

On the 1st day of November, 1896, the total stock of money of all kinds in the country was $2,285,410,590, and the amount in circulation, not including that in the Treasury holdings, was $1,627,055,641, being $22.63 per capita upon an estimated population of 71,902,000.

The production of the precious metals in the United States during the calendar year 1895 is estimated to have been 2,254,760 fine ounces of gold, of the value of $46,610,000, and 55,727,000 fine ounces of silver, of the commercial value of $36,445,000 and the coinage value of $72,051,-000. The estimated production of these metals throughout the world during the same period was 9,688,821 fine ounces of gold, amounting to $200,285,700 in value, and 169,189,249 fine ounces of silver, of the commercial value of $110,654,000 and of the coinage value of $218,738,100 according to our ratio.

The coinage of these metals in the various countries of the world during the same calendar year amounted to $232,701,438 in gold and $121,996,219 in silver.

The total coinage at the mints of the United States during the fiscal year ended June 30, 1896, amounted to $71,188,468.52, of which $58,-878,490 was in gold coins and $12,309,978.52 in standard silver dollars, subsidiary coins, and minor coins.

The number of national banks organized from the time the law authorizing their creation was passed up to October 31, 1896, was 5,051, and of this number 3,679 were at the date last mentioned in active operation, having authorized capital stock of $650,014,895, held by 288,902 share-holders, and circulating notes amounting to $211,412,620.

The total outstanding circulating notes of all national banks on the 31st day of October, 1896, amounted to $234,553,807, including unre-deemed but fully secured notes of banks insolvent and in process of liqui-dation. The increase in national-bank circulation during the year ending on that day was $21,099,429. On October 6, 1896, when the condition of national banks was last reported, the total resources of the 3,679 active institutions were $3,263,685,313.83, which included $1,893,268,839.31 in loans and discounts and $362,165,733.85 in money of all kinds on hand. Of their liabilities $1,597,891,058.03 was due to individual depositors and $209,944,019 consisted of outstanding circulating notes.

There were organized during the year preceding the date last men-tioned 28 national banks, located in 15 States, of which 12 were organ-ized in the Eastern States, with a capital of $1,180,000, 6 in the Western States, with a capital of $875,000, and 10 in the Southern States, with a capital of $1,190,000. During the year, however, 37 banks voluntarily abandoned their franchises under the national law, and in the case of 27 others it was found necessary to appoint receivers. Therefore, as com-pared with the year preceding, there was a decrease of 36 in the number of active banks.

The number of existing banks organized under State laws is 5,708.

The number of immigrants arriving in the United States during the fiscal year was 343,267, of whom 340,468 were permitted to land and 2,799 were debarred on various grounds prescribed by law and returned to the countries whence they came at the expense of the steamship com-panies by which they were brought in. The increase in immigration over the preceding year amounted to 84,731. It is reported that with some exceptions the immigrants of the past year were of a hardy labor-ing class, accustomed and able to earn a support for themselves, and it is estimated that the money brought with them amounted to at least $5,000,-000, though it was probably much in excess of that sum, since only those having less than $30 are required to disclose the exact amount, and it is known that many brought considerable sums of money to buy land and build homes. Including all the immigrants arriving who were over 14 years of age, 28.63 per cent were illiterate, as against 20.37 per cent of those of that age arriving during the preceding fiscal year. The num-ber of immigrants over 14 years old, the countries from which they came, and the percentage of illiterates among them were as follows: Italy, 57,515, with 54.59 per cent; Ireland, 37,496, with 7 per cent; Russia, 35,188, with 41.14 per cent; Austria-Hungary and provinces, 57,053, with 38.92 per cent; Germany, 25,334, with 2.96 per cent; Swe-den, 18,821, with 1.16 per cent; while from Portugal there came 2,067, of whom 77.69 per cent were illiterate. There arrived from Japan during the year only 1,110 immigrants, and it is the opinion of the immigration authorities that the apprehension heretofore existing to some extent of a large immigration from Japan to the United States is without any substantial foundation.

From the Life-Saving Service it is reported that the number of disasters to documented vessels within the limits of its operations during the year was 437. These vessels had on board 4,608 persons, of whom 4,595 were saved and 13 lost. The value of such vessels is estimated at $8,880,140 and of their cargoes $3,846,380, making the total value of property imperiled $12,726,520. Of this amount $11,292,707 was saved and $1,432,750 was lost. Sixty-seven of the vessels were totally wrecked. There were besides 243 casualties to small undocumented craft, on board of which there were 594 persons, of whom 587 were saved and 7 were lost. The value of the property involved in these latter casualties is estimated at $119,265, of which $114,915 was saved and $4,350 was lost. The life-saving crews during the year also rescued or assisted numerous other vessels and warned many from danger by signals, both by day and night. The number of disasters during the year exceeded that of any previous year in the history of the service, but the saving of both life and property was greater than ever before in proportion to the value of the property involved and to the number of persons imperiled.

The operations of the Marine-Hospital Service, the Revenue-Cutter Service, the Steamboat-Inspection Service, the Light-House Service, the Bureau of Navigation, and other branches of public work attached to the Treasury Department, together with various recommendations concerning their support and improvement, are fully stated in the report of the Secretary of the Treasury, to which the attention of the Congress is especially invited.

The report of the Secretary of War exhibits satisfactory conditions in the several branches of the public service intrusted to his charge.

The limit of our military force as fixed by law is constantly and readily maintained. The present discipline and morale of our Army are excellent, and marked progress and efficiency are apparent throughout its entire organization.

With the exception of delicate duties in the suppression of slight Indian disturbances along our southwestern boundary, in which the Mexican troops cooperated, and the compulsory but peaceful return, with the consent of Great Britain, of a band of Cree Indians from Montana to the British possessions, no active operations have been required of the Army during the year past.

Changes in methods of administration, the abandonment of unnecessary posts and consequent concentration of troops, and the exercise of care and vigilance by the various officers charged with the responsibility in the expenditure of the appropriations have resulted in reducing to a minimum the cost of maintenance of our military establishment.

During the past year the work of constructing permanent infantry and cavalry posts has been continued at the places heretofore designated. The Secretary of War repeats his recommendation that appropriations for barracks and quarters should more strictly conform to the needs of the service as judged by the Department rather than respond to the wishes and importunities of localities. It is imperative that much of the money provided for such construction should now be allotted to the erection of necessary quarters for the garrisons assigned to the coast defenses, where many men will be needed to properly care for and operate modern guns. It is essential, too, that early provision be made to supply the necessary force of artillery to meet the demands of this service.

The entire Army has now been equipped with the new magazine arms, and wise policy demands that all available public and private resources should be so employed as to provide within a reasonable time a sufficient number to supply the State militia with these modern weapons and provide an ample reserve for any emergency.

The organized militia numbers 112,879 men. The appropriations for its support by the several States approximate $2,800,000 annually, and $400,000 is contributed by the General Government. Investigation shows these troops to be usually well drilled and inspired with much military interest, but in many instances they are so deficient in proper arms and equipment that a sudden call to active duty would find them inadequately prepared for field service. I therefore recommend that prompt measures be taken to remedy this condition and that every encouragement be given to this deserving body of unpaid and voluntary citizen soldiers, upon whose assistance we must largely rely in time of trouble.

During the past year rapid progress has been made toward the completion of the scheme adopted for the erection and armament of fortifications along our seacoast, while equal progress has been made in providing the material for submarine defense in connection with these works.

It is peculiarly gratifying at this time to note the great advance that has been made in this important undertaking since the date of my annual message to the Fifty-third Congress at the opening of its second session, in December, 1893. At that time I informed the Congress of the approaching completion of nine 12-inch, twenty 10-inch, and thirty-four 8-inch high-power steel guns and seventy-five 12-inch rifled mortars.

This total then seemed insignificant when compared with the great work remaining to be done. Yet it was none the less a source of satisfaction to every citizen when he reflected that it represented the first installment of the new ordnance of American design and American manufacture and demonstrated our ability to supply from our own resources guns of unexcelled power and accuracy.

At that date, however, there were practically no carriages upon which to mount these guns and only thirty-one emplacements for guns and sixty-four for mortars. Nor were all these emplacements in condition to receive their armament. Only one high-power gun was at that time in position for the defense of the entire coast.

Since that time the number of guns actually completed has been increased to a total of twenty-one 12-inch, fifty-six 10-inch, sixty-one 8-inch high-power breech-loading steel guns, ten rapid-fire guns, and eighty 12-inch rifled mortars. In addition there are in process of construction one 16-inch-type gun, fifty 12-inch, fifty-six 10-inch, twenty-seven 8-inch high-power guns, and sixty-six 12-inch rifled mortars; in all, four hundred and twenty-eight guns and mortars.

During the same year, immediately preceding the message referred to, the first modern gun carriage had been completed and eleven more were in process of construction. All but one were of the nondisappearing type. These, however, were not such as to secure necessary cover for the artillery gunners against the intense fire of modern machine rapid-fire and high-power guns.

The inventive genius of ordnance and civilian experts has been taxed in designing carriages that would obviate this fault, resulting, it is believed, in the solution of this difficult problem. Since 1893 the number of gun carriages constructed or building has been raised to a total of 129, of which 90 are on the disappearing principle, and the number of mortar carriages to 152, while the 95 emplacements which were provided for prior to that time have been increased to 280 built and building.

This improved situation is largely due to the recent generous response of Congress to the recommendations of the War Department.

Thus we shall soon have complete about one-fifth of the comprehensive system the first step in which was noted in my message to the Congress of December 4, 1893.*

When it is understood that a masonry emplacement not only furnishes a platform for the heavy modern high-power gun, but also in every particular serves the purpose and takes the place of the fort of former days, the importance of the work accomplished is better comprehended.

In the hope that the work will be prosecuted with no less vigor in the future, the Secretary of War has submitted an estimate by which, if allowed, there will be provided and either built or building by the end of the next fiscal year such additional guns, mortars, gun carriages, and emplacements as will represent not far from one-third of the total work to be done under the plan adopted for our coast defenses, thus affording a prospect that the entire work will be substantially completed within six years. In less time than that, however, we shall have attained a marked degree of security.

The experience and results of the past year demonstrate that with a continuation of present careful methods the cost of the remaining work will be much less than the original estimate.

We should always keep in mind that of all forms of military preparation coast defense alone is essentially pacific in its nature. While it gives the sense of security due to a consciousness of strength, it is neither the

*See pp. 450–451.

purpose nor the effect of such permanent fortifications to involve us in foreign complications, but rather to guarantee us against them. They are not temptation to war, but security against it. Thus they are thoroughly in accord with all the traditions of our national diplomacy.

The Attorney-General presents a detailed and interesting statement of the important work done under his supervision during the last fiscal year.

The ownership and management by the Government of penitentiaries for the confinement of those convicted in United States courts of violations of Federal laws, which for many years has been a subject of Executive recommendation, have at last to a slight extent been realized by the utilization of the abandoned military prison at Fort Leavenworth as a United States penitentiary.

This is certainly a movement in the right direction, but it ought to be at once supplemented by the rebuilding or extensive enlargement of this improvised prison and the construction of at least one more, to be located in the Southern States. The capacity of the Leavenworth Penitentiary is so limited that the expense of its maintenance, calculated at a per capita rate upon the number of prisoners it can accommodate, does not make as economical an exhibit as it would if it were larger and better adapted to prison purposes; but I am thoroughly convinced that economy, humanity, and a proper sense of responsibility and duty toward those whom we punish for violations of Federal law dictate that the Federal Government should have the entire control and management of the penitentiaries where convicted violators are confined.

It appears that since the transfer of the Fort Leavenworth Military Prison to its new uses the work previously done by prisoners confined there, and for which expensive machinery has been provided, has been discontinued. This work consisted of the manufacture of articles for army use, now done elsewhere. On all grounds it is exceedingly desirable that the convicts confined in this penitentiary be allowed to resume work of this description.

It is most gratifying to note the satisfactory results that have followed the inauguration of the new system provided for by the act of May 28, 1896, under which certain Federal officials are compensated by salaries instead of fees. The new plan was put in operation on the 1st day of July, 1896, and already the great economy it enforces, its prevention of abuses, and its tendency to a better enforcement of the laws are strikingly apparent. Detailed evidence of the usefulness of this long-delayed but now happily accomplished reform will be found clearly set forth in the Attorney-General's report.

Our Post-Office Department is in good condition, and the exhibit made of its operations during the fiscal year ended June 30, 1896, if allowance is made for imperfections in the laws applicable to it, is very satisfactory. The total receipts during the year were $82,499,208.40. The total expenditures were $90,626,296.84, exclusive of the $1,559,898.27 which was earned by the Pacific Railroad for transportation and credited on their debt to the Government. There was an increase of receipts over the previous year of $5,516,080.21, or 7.1 per cent, and an increase of expenditures of $3,836,124.02, or 4.42 per cent. The deficit was $1,679,-956.19 less than that of the preceding year. The chief expenditures of the postal service are regulated by law and are not in the control of the Postmaster-General. All that he can accomplish by the most watchful administration and economy is to enforce prompt and thorough collection and accounting for public moneys and such minor savings in small expenditures and in letting those contracts, for post-office supplies and star service, which are not regulated by statute.

An effective coöperation between the Auditor's Office and the Post-Office Department and the making and enforcement of orders by the Department requiring immediate notification to their sureties of all delinquencies on the part of postmasters, and compelling such postmasters to make more frequent deposits of postal funds, have resulted in a prompter auditing of their accounts and much less default to the Government than heretofore.

The year's report shows large extensions of both star-route service and railway mail service, with increased postal facilities. Much higher accuracy in handling mails has also been reached, as appears by the decrease of errors in the railway mail service and the reduction of mail matter returned to the Dead-Letter Office.

The deficit for the last year, although much less than that of the last and preceding years, emphasizes the necessity for legislation to correct the growing abuse of second-class rates, to which the deficiency is mainly attributable. The transmission at the rate of 1 cent a pound of serial libraries, advertising sheets, ''house organs'' (periodicals advertising some particular ''house'' or institution), sample copies, and the like ought certainly to be discontinued. A glance at the revenues received for the work done last year will show more plainly than any other statement the gross abuse of the postal service and the growing waste of its earnings.

The free matter carried in the mails for the Departments, offices, etc., of the Government and for Congress, in pounds, amounted to 94,480,189.

If this is offset against buildings for post-offices and stations, the rental of which would more than compensate for such free postal service, we have this exhibit:

Weight of mail matter (other than above) transmitted through the mails for the year ending June 30, 1896.

Class.	Weight.	Revenue.
	Pounds.	
1. Domestic and foreign letters and postal cards, etc......	65,337,343	$60,624,464
2. Newspapers and periodicals, 1 cent per pound..........	348,988,648	2,996,403
3. Books, seeds, etc., 8 cents a pound......................	78,701,148	10,324,069
4. Parcels, etc., 16 cents a pound...........................	19,950,187	3,129,321
Total...	512,977,326	77,044,257

The remainder of our postal revenue, amounting to something more than $5,000,000, was derived from box rents, registry fees, money-order business, and other similar items.

The entire expenditures of the Department, including pay for transportation credited to the Pacific railroads, were $92,186,195.11, which may be considered as the cost of receiving, carrying, and delivering the above mail matter. It thus appears that though the second-class matter constituted more than two-thirds of the total that was carried, the revenue derived from it was less than one-thirtieth of the total expense.

The average revenue was—
From each pound of first-class matter ....cents.. 93.0
From each pound of second class* ....mills.. 8.5
From each pound of third class ....cents.. 13.1
From each pound of fourth class...do... 15.6

The growth in weight of second-class matter has been from 299,000,000 pounds in 1894 to 312,000,000 in 1895 and to almost 349,000,000 in 1896, and it is quite evident this increasing drawback is far outstripping any possible growth of postal revenues.

Our mail service should of course be such as to meet the wants and even the conveniences of our people at a direct charge upon them so light as perhaps to exclude the idea of our Post-Office Department being a money-making concern; but in the face of a constantly recurring deficiency in its revenues and in view of the fact that we supply the best mail service in the world it seems to me it is quite time to correct the abuses that swell enormously our annual deficit. If we concede the public policy of carrying weekly newspapers free in the county of publication, and even the policy of carrying at less than one-tenth of their cost other *bona fide* newspapers and periodicals, there can be no excuse for subjecting the service to the further immense and increasing loss involved in carrying at the nominal rate of 1 cent a pound the serial libraries, sometimes including trashy and even harmful literature, and other matter which under the loose interpretation of a loose statute have been gradually given second-class rates, thus absorbing all profitable returns derived from first-class matter, which pays three or four times more than its cost, and producing a large annual loss to be paid by general taxation. If such second-class matter paid merely the cost of its handling, our deficit would disappear and a surplus result which might be used to give the people still better mail facilities or cheaper rates of letter postage. I recommend that legislation be at once enacted to correct these abuses and introduce better business ideas in the regulation of our postal rates.

Experience and observation have demonstrated that certain improvements in the organization of the Post-Office Department must be secured before we can gain the full benefit of the immense sums expended in its administration. This involves the following reforms, which I earnestly recommend:

There should be a small addition to the existing inspector service, to be employed in the supervision of the carrier force, which now numbers

* Of the second class 52,348,297 was county-free matter.

13,000 men and performs its service practically without the surveillance exercised over all other branches of the postal or public service. Of course such a lack of supervision and freedom from wholesome disciplinary restraints must inevitably lead to imperfect service. There should also be appointed a few inspectors who could assist the central office in necessary investigation concerning matters of post-office leases, post-office sites, allowances for rent, fuel, and lights, and in organizing and securing the best results from the work of the 14,000 clerks now employed in first and second class offices.

I am convinced that the small expense attending the inauguration of these reforms would actually be a profitable investment.

I especially recommend such a recasting of the appropriations by Congress for the Post-Office Department as will permit the Postmaster-General to proceed with the work of consolidating post-offices. This work has already been entered upon sufficiently to fully demonstrate by experiment and experience that such consolidation is productive of better service, larger revenues, and less expenditures, to say nothing of the further advantage of gradually withdrawing post-offices from the spoils system.

The Universal Postal Union, which now embraces all the civilized world and whose delegates will represent 1,000,000,000 people, will hold its fifth congress in the city of Washington in May, 1897. The United States may be said to have taken the initiative which led to the first meeting of this congress, at Berne in 1874, and the formation of the Universal Postal Union, which brings the postal service of all countries to every man's neighborhood and has wrought marvels in cheapening postal rates and securing absolutely safe mail communication throughout the world. Previous congresses have met in Berne, Paris, Lisbon, and Vienna, and the respective countries in which they have assembled have made generous provision for their accommodation and for the reception and entertainment of the delegates.

In view of the importance of this assemblage and of its deliberations and of the honors and hospitalities accorded to our representatives by other countries on similar occasions, I earnestly hope that such an appropriation will be made for the expenses necessarily attendant upon the coming meeting in our capital city as will be worthy of our national hospitality and indicative of our appreciation of the event.

The work of the Navy Department and its present condition are fully exhibited in the report of the Secretary.

The construction of vessels for our new Navy has been energetically prosecuted by the present Administration upon the general lines previously adopted, the Department having seen no necessity for radical changes in prior methods, under which the work was found to be progressing in a manner highly satisfactory. It has been decided, however, to provide in every shipbuilding contract that the builder should pay all trial expenses, and it has also been determined to pay no speed premiums in future contracts. The premiums recently earned and some yet to be decided are features of the contracts made before this conclusion was reached.

On March 4, 1893, there were in commission but two armored vessels—the double-turreted monitors *Miantonomoh* and *Monterey*. Since that date, of vessels theretofore authorized, there have been placed in their first commission 3 first-class and 2 second-class battle ships, 2 armored cruisers, 1 harbor-defense ram, and 5 double-turreted monitors, including the *Maine* and the *Puritan*, just completed. Eight new unarmored cruisers and 2 new gunboats have also been commissioned. The *Iowa*, another battle ship, will be completed about March 1, and at least 4 more gunboats will be ready for sea in the early spring.

It is gratifying to state that our ships and their outfits are believed to be equal to the best that can be manufactured elsewhere, and that such notable reductions have been made in their cost as to justify the statement that quite a number of vessels are now being constructed at rates as low as those that prevail in European shipyards.

Our manufacturing facilities are at this time ample for all possible naval contingencies. Three of our Government navy-yards—those at Mare Island, Cal., Norfolk, Va., and Brooklyn, N. Y.—are equipped for shipbuilding, our ordnance plant in Washington is equal to any in the world, and at the torpedo station we are successfully making the highest grades of smokeless powder. The first-class private shipyards at Newport News, Philadelphia, and San Francisco are building battle ships; eleven contractors, situated in the States of Maine, Rhode Island, Pennsylvania, New Jersey, Maryland, Virginia, and the State of Washington, are constructing gunboats or torpedo boats; two plants are manufacturing large quantities of first-class armor, and American factories are producing automobile torpedoes, powder, projectiles, rapid-fire guns, and everything else necessary for the complete outfit of naval vessels.

There have been authorized by Congress since March, 1893, 5 battle ships, 6 light-draft gunboats, 16 torpedo boats, and 1 submarine torpedo boat. Contracts for the building of all of them have been let. The Secretary expresses the opinion that we have for the present a sufficient supply of cruisers and gunboats, and that hereafter the construction of battle ships and torpedo boats will supply our needs.

Much attention has been given to the methods of carrying on departmental business. Important modifications in the regulations have been made, tending to unify the control of shipbuilding as far as may be under the Bureau of Construction and Repair, and also to improve the mode of purchasing supplies for the Navy by the Bureau of Supplies and Accounts. The establishment under recent acts of Congress of a supply fund with which to purchase these supplies in large quantities and other modifications of methods have tended materially to their cheapening and better quality.

The War College has developed into an institution which it is believed will be of great value to the Navy in teaching the science of war, as well as in stimulating professional zeal in the Navy, and it will be especially useful in the devising of plans for the utilization in case of necessity of all the naval resources of the United States.

The Secretary has persistently adhered to the plan he found in operation for securing labor at navy-yards through boards of labor employment, and has done much to make it more complete and efficient. The naval officers who are familiar with this system and its operation express the decided opinion that its results have been to vastly improve the character of the work done at our yards and greatly reduce its cost.

Discipline among the officers and men of the Navy has been maintained to a high standard and the percentage of American citizens enlisted has been very much increased.

The Secretary is considering and will formulate during the coming winter a plan for laying up ships in reserve, thereby largely reducing the cost of maintaining our vessels afloat. This plan contemplates that battle ships, torpedo boats, and such of the cruisers as are not needed for active service at sea shall be kept in reserve with skeleton crews on board to keep them in condition, cruising only enough to insure the efficiency of the ships and their crews in time of activity.

The economy to result from this system is too obvious to need comment.

The Naval Militia, which was authorized a few years ago as an experiment, has now developed into a body of enterprising young men, active and energetic in the discharge of their duties and promising great usefulness. This establishment has nearly the same relation to our Navy as the National Guard in the different States bears to our Army, and it constitutes a source of supply for our naval forces the importance of which is immediately apparent.

The report of the Secretary of the Interior presents a comprehensive and interesting exhibit of the numerous and important affairs committed to his supervision. It is impossible in this communication to do more than briefly refer to a few of the subjects concerning which the Secretary gives full and instructive information.

The money appropriated on account of this Department and for its disbursement for the fiscal year ended June 30, 1896, amounted to more than $157,000,000, or a greater sum than was appropriated for the entire maintenance of the Government for the two fiscal years ended June 30, 1861.

Our public lands, originally amounting to 1,840,000,000 acres, have been so reduced that only about 600,000,000 acres still remain in Government control, excluding Alaska. The balance, being by far the most valuable portion, has been given away to settlers, to new States, and to railroads or sold at a comparatively nominal sum. The patenting of land in execution of railroad grants has progressed rapidly during the year, and since the 4th day of March, 1893, about 25,000,000 acres have thus been conveyed to these corporations.

I agree with the Secretary that the remainder of our public lands should be more carefully dealt with and their alienation guarded by better economy and greater prudence.

The commission appointed from the membership of the National Academy of Sciences, provided for by an act of Congress, to formulate plans for a national forestry system will, it is hoped, soon be prepared to present the result of thorough and intelligent examination of this important subject.

The total Indian population of the United States is 177,235, according to a census made in 1895, exclusive of those within the State of New York and those comprising the Five Civilized Tribes. Of this number there are approximately 38,000 children of school age. During the year 23,393 of these were enrolled in schools. The progress which has attended recent efforts to extend Indian-school facilities and the anticipation of continued liberal appropriations to that end can not fail to afford the utmost satisfaction to those who believe that the education of Indian children is a prime factor in the accomplishment of Indian civilization.

It may be said in general terms that in every particular the improvement of the Indians under Government care has been most marked and encouraging.

The Secretary, the Commissioner of Indian Affairs, and the agents having charge of Indians to whom allotments have been made strongly urge the passage of a law prohibiting the sale of liquor to allottees who have taken their lands in severalty. I earnestly join in this recommendation and venture to express the hope that the Indian may be speedily protected against this greatest of all obstacles to his well-being and advancement.

The condition of affairs among the Five Civilized Tribes, who occupy large tracts of land in the Indian Territory and who have governments of their own, has assumed such an aspect as to render it almost indispensable that there should be an entire change in the relations of these Indians to the General Government. This seems to be necessary in furtherance of their own interests, as well as for the protection of non-Indian residents in their territory. A commission organized and empowered under several recent laws is now negotiating with these Indians for the relinquishment of their courts and the division of their common lands in severalty and are aiding in the settlement of the troublesome question of tribal membership. The reception of their first proffers of negotiation was not encouraging, but through patience and such conduct on their part as demonstrated that their intentions were friendly and in the interest of the tribes the prospect of success has become more promising. The effort should be to save these Indians from the consequences of their own mistakes and improvidence and to secure to the real Indian his rights as against intruders and professed friends who profit by his retrogression. A change is also needed to protect life and property through the operation of courts conducted according to strict justice and strong enough to enforce their mandates.

As a sincere friend of the Indian, I am exceedingly anxious that these reforms should be accomplished with the consent and aid of the tribes and that no necessity may be presented for radical or drastic legislation. I hope, therefore, that the commission now conducting negotiations will soon be able to report that progress has been made toward a friendly adjustment of existing difficulties.

It appears that a very valuable deposit of gilsonite or asphaltum has been found on the reservation in Utah occupied by the Uncompahgre Ute Indians. Every consideration of care for the public interest and every sensible business reason dictate such management or disposal of this important source of public revenue as will except it from the general rules and incidents attending the ordinary disposition of public lands and secure to the Government a fair share at least of its advantages in place of its transfer for a nominal sum to interested individuals.

I indorse the recommendation made by the present Secretary of the Interior, as well as his predecessor, that a permanent commission, consisting of three members, one of whom shall be an army officer, be created to perform the duties now devolving upon the Commissioner and Assistant Commissioner of Indian Affairs. The management of the Bureau involves such numerous and diverse details and the advantages of an uninterrupted policy are so apparent that I hope the change suggested will meet the approval of the Congress.

The diminution of our enormous pension roll and the decrease of pension expenditure, which have been so often confidently foretold, still fail in material realization. The number of pensioners on the rolls at the close of the fiscal year ended June 30, 1896, was 970,678. This is the largest number ever reported. The amount paid exclusively for pensions during the year was $138,214,761.94, a slight decrease from that of the preceding year, while the total expenditures on account of pensions, including the cost of maintaining the Department and expenses attending pension distribution, amounted to $142,206,550.59, or within a very small fraction of one-third of the entire expense of supporting the Government during the same year. The number of new pension certificates issued was 90,640. Of these, 40,374 represent original allowances of claims and 15,878 increases of existing pensions.

The number of persons receiving pensions from the United States, but residing in foreign countries, at the close of the last fiscal year was 3,781, and the amount paid to them during the year was $582,735.38.

The sum appropriated for the payment of pensions for the current fiscal year, ending June 30, 1897, is $140,000,000, and for the succeeding year it is estimated that the same amount will be necessary.

The Commissioner of Pensions reports that during the last fiscal year 339 indictments were found against violators of the pension laws. Upon these indictments 167 convictions resulted.

In my opinion, based upon such statements as these and much other information and observation, the abuses which have been allowed to creep into our pension system have done incalculable harm in demoralizing our people and undermining good citizenship. I have endeavored within my sphere of official duty to protect our pension roll and make it what it should be, a roll of honor, containing the names of those disabled in their country's service and worthy of their country's affectionate remembrance. When I have seen those who pose as the soldiers' friends active and alert in urging greater laxity and more reckless pension expenditure, while nursing selfish schemes, I have deprecated the approach of a situation when necessary retrenchment and enforced economy may lead to an attack upon pension abuses so determined as to overlook the discrimination due to those who, worthy of a nation's care, ought to live and die under the protection of a nation's gratitude.

The Secretary calls attention to the public interests involved in an adjustment of the obligations of the Pacific railroads to the Government. I deem it to be an important duty to especially present this subject to the consideration of the Congress.

On January 1, 1897, with the amount already matured, more than $13,000,000 of the principal of the subsidy bonds issued by the United States in aid of the construction of the Union Pacific Railway, including its Kansas line, and more than $6,000,000 of like bonds issued in aid of the Central Pacific Railroad, including those issued to the Western Pacific Railroad Company, will have fallen due and been paid or must on that day be paid by the Government. Without any reference to the application of the sinking fund now in the Treasury, this will create such a default on the part of these companies to the Government as will give it the right to at once institute proceedings to foreclose its mortgage lien. In addition to this indebtedness, which will be due January 1, 1897, there will mature between that date and January 1, 1899, the remaining principal of such subsidy bonds, which must also be met by the Government. These amount to more than $20,000,000 on account of the Union Pacific lines and exceed $21,000,000 on account of the Central Pacific lines.

The situation of these roads and the condition of their indebtedness to the Government have been fully set forth in the reports of various committees to the present and prior Congresses, and as early as 1887 they were thoroughly examined by a special commission appointed pursuant to an act of Congress. The considerations requiring an adjustment of the Government's relations to the companies have been clearly presented and the conclusion reached with practical uniformity that if these relations are not terminated they should be revised upon a basis securing their safe continuance.

Under section 4 of the act of Congress passed March 3, 1887, the President is charged with the duty, in the event that any mortgage or other incumbrance paramount to the interest of the United States in the property of the Pacific railroads should exist and be lawfully liable to be enforced, to direct the action of the Departments of Treasury and of Justice in the protection of the interest of the United States by redemption or through judicial proceedings, including foreclosures of the Government liens.

In view of the fact that the Congress has for a number of years almost constantly had under consideration various plans for dealing with the conditions existing between these roads and the Government, I have thus far felt justified in withholding action under the statute above mentioned.

In the case of the Union Pacific Company, however, the situation has become especially and immediately urgent. Proceedings have been instituted to foreclose a first mortgage upon those aided parts of the main lines upon which the Government holds a second and subordinate mortgage lien. In consequence of those proceedings and increasing complications, added to the default occurring on the 1st day of January, 1897, a condition will be presented at that date, so far as this company is concerned, that must emphasize the mandate of the act of 1887 and give to Executive duty under its provisions a more imperative aspect. Therefore, unless Congress shall otherwise direct or shall have previously determined upon a different solution of the problem, there will hardly appear to exist any reason for delaying beyond the date of the default above mentioned such Executive action as will promise to subserve the public interests and save the Government from the loss threatened by further inaction.

The Department of Agriculture is so intimately related to the welfare of our people and the prosperity of our nation that it should constantly receive the care and encouragement of the Government. From small beginnings it has grown to be the center of agricultural intelligence and the source of aid and encouragement to agricultural efforts. Large sums of money are annually appropriated for the maintenance of this Department, and it must be confessed that the legislation relating to it has not always been directly in the interest of practical farming or properly guarded against waste and extravagance. So far, however, as public money has been appropriated fairly and sensibly to help those who actually till the soil, no expenditure has been more profitably made or more generally approved by the people.

Under the present management of the Department its usefulness has been enhanced in every direction, and at the same time strict economy has been enforced to the utmost extent permitted by Congressional action. From the report of the Secretary it appears that through careful and prudent financial management he has annually saved a large sum from his appropriations, aggregating during his incumbency and up to the close of the present fiscal year nearly one-fifth of the entire amount appropriated. These results have been accomplished by a conscientious study of the real needs of the farmer and such a regard for economy as the genuine farmer ought to appreciate, supplemented by a rigid adherence to civil-service methods in a Department which should be conducted in the interest of agriculture instead of partisan politics.

The Secretary reports that the value of our exports of farm products during the last fiscal year amounted to $570,000,000, an increase of $17,000,000 over those of the year immediately preceding. This statement is not the less welcome because of the fact that, notwithstanding such increase, the proportion of exported agricultural products to our total exports of all descriptions fell off during the year. The benefits of an increase in agricultural exports being assured, the decrease in its proportion to our total exports is the more gratifying when we consider that it is owing to the fact that such total exports for the year increased more than $75,000,000.

The large and increasing exportation of our agricultural products suggests the great usefulness of the organization lately established in the Department for the purpose of giving to those engaged in farming pursuits reliable information concerning the condition, needs, and advantages of different foreign markets. Inasmuch as the success of the farmer depends upon the advantageous sale of his products, and inasmuch as foreign markets must largely be the destination of such products, it is quite apparent that a knowledge of the conditions and wants that affect those markets ought to result in sowing more intelligently and reaping with a better promise of profit. Such information points out the way to a prudent foresight in the selection and cultivation of crops and to a release from the bondage of unreasoning monotony of production, a glutted and depressed market, and constantly recurring unprofitable toil.

In my opinion the gratuitous distribution of seeds by the Department as at present conducted ought to be discontinued. No one can read the statement of the Secretary on this subject and doubt the extravagance and questionable results of this practice. The professed friends of the farmer, and certainly the farmers themselves, are naturally expected to be willing to rid a Department devoted to the promotion of farming interests of a feature which tends so much to its discredit.

The Weather Bureau, now attached to the Department of Agriculture, has continued to extend its sphere of usefulness, and by an uninterrupted improvement in the accuracy of its forecasts has greatly increased its efficiency as an aid and protection to all whose occupations are related to weather conditions.

Omitting further reference to the operations of the Department, I commend the Secretary's report and the suggestions it contains to the careful consideration of the Congress.

The progress made in civil-service reform furnishes a cause for the utmost congratulation. It has survived the doubts of its friends as well as the rancor of its enemies and has gained a permanent place among the agencies destined to cleanse our politics and to improve, economize, and elevate the public service.

There are now in the competitive classified service upward of 84,000 places, more than half of these having been included from time to time since March 4, 1893. A most radical and sweeping extension was made by Executive order dated the 6th day of May, 1896,* and if fourth-class postmasterships are not included in the statement it may be said that practically all positions contemplated by the civil-service law are now classified. Abundant reasons exist for including these postmasterships, based upon economy, improved service, and the peace and quiet of neighborhoods. If, however, obstacles prevent such action at present, I earnestly hope that Congress will, without increasing post-office appropriations, so adjust them as to permit in proper cases a consolidation of these post-offices, to the end that through this process the result desired may to a limited extent be accomplished.

The civil-service rules as amended during the last year provide for a sensible and uniform method of promotion, basing eligibility to better positions upon demonstrated efficiency and faithfulness. The absence of fixed rules on this subject has been an infirmity in the system more and more apparent as its other benefits have been better appreciated.

The advantages of civil-service methods in their business aspects are too well understood to require argument. Their application has become a necessity to the executive work of the Government. But those who gain positions through the operation of these methods should be made to understand that the nonpartisan scheme through which they receive their appointments demands from them by way of reciprocity nonpartisan and faithful performance of duty under every Administration and cheerful fidelity to every chief. While they should be encouraged to decently exercise their rights of citizenship and to support through their suffrages the political beliefs they honestly profess, the noisy, pestilent, and partisan employee, who loves political turmoil and contention or who renders lax and grudging service to an Administration not representing his political views, should be promptly and fearlessly dealt with in such a way as to furnish a warning to others who may be likewise disposed.

The annual report of the Commissioners will be duly transmitted, and I commend the important matter they have in charge to the careful consideration of the Congress.

The Interstate Commerce Commission has during the last year supplied abundant evidence of its usefulness and the importance of the work committed to its charge.

Public transportation is a universal necessity, and the question of just and reasonable charges therefor has become of vital importance not only

*See pp. 701–711.

to shippers and carriers, but also to the vast multitude of producers and consumers. The justice and equity of the principles embodied in the existing law passed for the purpose of regulating these charges are everywhere conceded, and there appears to be no question that the policy thus entered upon has a permanent place in our legislation.

As the present statute when enacted was in the nature of the case more or less tentative and experimental, it was hardly expected to supply a complete and adequate system. While its wholesome effects are manifest and have amply justified its enactment, it is evident that all desired reforms in transportation methods have not been fully accomplished. In view of the judicial interpretation which some provisions of this statute have received and the defects disclosed by the efforts made for its enforcement, its revision and amendment appear to be essential, to the end that it may more effectually reach the evils designed to be corrected. I hope the recommendations of the Commission upon this subject will be promptly and favorably considered by the Congress.

I desire to recur to the statements elsewhere made concerning the Government's receipts and expenditures for the purpose of venturing upon some suggestions touching our present tariff law and its operation.

This statute took effect on the 28th day of August, 1894. Whatever may be its shortcomings as a complete measure of tariff reform, it must be conceded that it has opened the way to a freer and greater exchange of commodities between us and other countries, and thus furnished a wider market for our products and manufactures.

The only entire fiscal year during which this law has been in force ended on the 30th day of June, 1896. In that year our imports increased over those of the previous year more than $6,500,000, while the value of the domestic products we exported and which found markets abroad was nearly $70,000,000 more than during the preceding year.

Those who insist that the cost to our people of articles coming to them from abroad for their needful use should only be increased through tariff charges to an extent necessary to meet the expenses of the Government, as well as those who claim that tariff charges may be laid upon such articles beyond the necessities of Government revenue and with the additional purpose of so increasing their price in our markets as to give American manufacturers and producers better and more profitable opportunities, must agree that our tariff laws are only primarily justified as sources of revenue to enable the Government to meet the necessary expenses of its maintenance. Considered as to its efficiency in this aspect, the present law can by no means fall under just condemnation. During the only complete fiscal year of its operation it has yielded nearly $8,000,000 more revenue than was received from tariff duties in the preceding year. There was, nevertheless, a deficit between our receipts and expenditures of a little more than $25,000,000. This, however, was not unexpected.

The situation was such in December last, seven months before the close of the fiscal year, that the Secretary of the Treasury foretold a deficiency of $17,000,000. The great and increasing apprehension and timidity in business circles and the depression in all activities intervening since that time, resulting from causes perfectly well understood and entirely disconnected with our tariff law or its operation, seriously checked the imports we would have otherwise received and readily account for the difference between this estimate of the Secretary and the actual deficiency, as well as for a continued deficit. Indeed, it must be confessed that we could hardly have had a more unfavorable period than the last two years for the collection of tariff revenue. We can not reasonably hope that our recuperation from this business depression will be sudden, but it has already set in with a promise of acceleration and continuance.

I believe our present tariff law, if allowed a fair opportunity, will in the near future yield a revenue which, with reasonably economical expenditures, will overcome all deficiencies. In the meantime no deficit that has occurred or may occur need excite or disturb us. To meet any such deficit we have in the Treasury in addition to a gold reserve of one hundred millions a surplus of more than $128,000,000 applicable to the payment of the expenses of the Government, and which must, unless expended for that purpose, remain a useless hoard, or, if not extravagantly wasted, must in any event be perverted from the purpose of its exaction from our people. The payment, therefore, of any deficiency in the revenue from this fund is nothing more than its proper and legitimate use. The Government thus applying a surplus fortunately in its Treasury to the payment of expenses not met by its current revenues is not at all to be likened to a man living beyond his income and thus incurring debt or encroaching on his principal.

It is not one of the functions of our Government to accumulate and make additions to a fund not needed for immediate expenditure. With individuals it is the chief object of struggle and effort. The application of an accumulated fund by the Government to the payment of its running expenses is a duty. An individual living beyond his income and embarrassing himself with debt or drawing upon his accumulated fund of principal is either unfortunate or improvident. The distinction is between a government charged with the duty of expending for the benefit of the people and for proper purposes all the money it receives from any source, and the individual, who is expected to manifest a natural desire to avoid debt or to accumulate as much as possible and to live within the income derived from such accumulations, to the end that they may be increased or at least remain unimpaired for the future use and enjoyment of himself or the objects of his love and affection who may survive him.

It is immeasurably better to appropriate our surplus to the payment of justifiable expenses than to allow it to become an invitation to reckless appropriations and extravagant expenditures.

I suppose it will not be denied that under the present law our people obtain the necessaries of a comfortable existence at a cheaper rate than formerly. This is a matter of supreme importance, since it is the palpable duty of every just government to make the burdens of taxation as light as possible. The people should not be required to relinquish this privilege of cheaper living except under the stress of their Government's necessity made plainly manifest.

This reference to the condition and prospects of our revenues naturally suggests an allusion to the weakness and vices of our financial methods. They have been frequently pressed upon the attention of Congress in previous Executive communications and the inevitable danger of their continued toleration pointed out. Without now repeating these details, I can not refrain from again earnestly presenting the necessity of the prompt reform of a system opposed to every rule of sound finance and shown by experience to be fraught with the gravest peril and perplexity. The terrible Civil War, which shook the foundations of our Government more than thirty years ago, brought in its train the destruction of property, the wasting of our country's substance, and the estrangement of brethren. These are now past and forgotten. Even the distressing loss of life the conflict entailed is but a sacred memory which fosters patriotic sentiment and keeps alive a tender regard for those who nobly died. And yet there remains with us to-day in full strength and activity, as an incident of that tremendous struggle, a feature of its financial necessities not only unsuited to our present circumstances, but manifestly a disturbing menace to business security and an ever-present agent of monetary distress.

Because we may be enjoying a temporary relief from its depressing influence, this should not lull us into a false security nor lead us to forget the suddenness of past visitations.

I am more convinced than ever that we can have no assured financial peace and safety until the Government currency obligations upon which gold may be demanded from the Treasury are withdrawn from circulation and canceled. This might be done, as has been heretofore recommended, by their exchange for long-term bonds bearing a low rate of interest or by their redemption with the proceeds of such bonds. Even if only the United States notes known as greenbacks were thus retired it is probable that the Treasury notes issued in payment of silver purchases under the act of July 14, 1890, now paid in gold when demanded, would not create much disturbance, as they might from time to time, when received in the Treasury by redemption in gold or otherwise, be gradually and prudently replaced by silver coin.

This plan of issuing bonds for the purpose of redemption certainly appears to be the most effective and direct path to the needed reform. In default of this, however, it would be a step in the right direction if currency obligations redeemable in gold whenever so redeemed should be canceled instead of being reissued. This operation would be a slow remedy, but it would improve present conditions.

National banks should redeem their own notes. They should be allowed to issue circulation to the par value of bonds deposited as security for its redemption and the tax on their circulation should be reduced to one-fourth of 1 per cent.

In considering projects for the retirement of United States notes and Treasury notes issued under the law of 1890, I am of the opinion that we have placed too much stress upon the danger of contracting the currency and have calculated too little upon the gold that would be added to our circulation if invited to us by better and safer financial methods. It is not so much a contraction of our currency that should be avoided as its unequal distribution.

This might be obviated and any fear of harmful contraction at the same time removed by allowing the organization of smaller banks and in less populous communities than are now permitted, and also authorizing existing banks to establish branches in small communities under proper restrictions.

The entire case may be presented by the statement that the day of sensible and sound financial methods will not dawn upon us until our Government abandons the banking business and the accumulation of funds and confines its monetary operations to the receipt of the money contributed by the people for its support and to the expenditure of such money for the people's benefit.

Our business interests and all good citizens long for rest from feverish agitation and the inauguration by the Government of a reformed financial policy which will encourage enterprise and make certain the rewards of labor and industry.

Another topic in which our people rightfully take a deep interest may be here briefly considered. I refer to the existence of trusts and other huge aggregations of capital the object of which is to secure the monopoly of some particular branch of trade, industry, or commerce and to stifle wholesome competition. When these are defended, it is usually on the ground that though they increase profits they also reduce prices, and thus may benefit the public. It must be remembered, however, that a reduction of prices to the people is not one of the real objects of these organizations, nor is their tendency necessarily in that direction. If it occurs in a particular case it is only because it accords with the purposes or interests of those managing the scheme.

Such occasional results fall far short of compensating the palpable evils charged to the account of trusts and monopolies. Their tendency is to crush out individual independence and to hinder or prevent the free use of human faculties and the full development of human character. Through them the farmer, the artisan, and the small trader is in danger of dislodgment from the proud position of being his own master, watchful of all that touches his country's prosperity, in which he has an individual lot, and interested in all that affects the advantages of business of which he is a factor, to be relegated to the level of a mere appurtenance to a great machine, with little free will, with no duty but that of passive obedience, and with little hope or opportunity of rising in the scale of responsible and helpful citizenship.

To the instinctive belief that such is the inevitable trend of trusts and monopolies is due the widespread and deep-seated popular aversion in which they are held and the not unreasonable insistence that, whatever may be their incidental economic advantages, their general effect upon personal character, prospects, and usefulness can not be otherwise than injurious.

Though Congress has attempted to deal with this matter by legislation, the laws passed for that purpose thus far have proved ineffective, not because of any lack of disposition or attempt to enforce them, but simply because the laws themselves as interpreted by the courts do not reach the difficulty. If the insufficiencies of existing laws can be remedied by further legislation, it should be done. The fact must be recognized, however, that all Federal legislation on this subject may fall short of its purpose because of inherent obstacles and also because of the complex character of our governmental system, which, while making the Federal authority supreme within its sphere, has carefully limited that sphere by metes and bounds that can not be transgressed. The decision of our highest court on this precise question renders it quite doubtful whether the evils of trusts and monopolies can be adequately treated through Federal action unless they seek directly and purposely to include in their objects transportation or intercourse between States or between the United States and foreign countries.

It does not follow, however, that this is the limit of the remedy that may be applied. Even though it may be found that Federal authority is not broad enough to fully reach the case, there can be no doubt of the power of the several States to act effectively in the premises, and there should be no reason to doubt their willingness to judiciously exercise such power.

In concluding this communication its last words shall be an appeal to the Congress for the most rigid economy in the expenditure of the money it holds in trust for the people. The way to perplexing extravagance is easy, but a return to frugality is difficult. When, however, it is considered that those who bear the burdens of taxation have no guaranty of honest care save in the fidelity of their public servants, the duty of all possible retrenchment is plainly manifest.

When our differences are forgotten and our contests of political opinion are no longer remembered, nothing in the retrospect of our public service will be as fortunate and comforting as the recollection of official duty well performed and the memory of a constant devotion to the interests of our confiding fellow-countrymen.

GROVER CLEVELAND.

SPECIAL MESSAGES.

EXECUTIVE MANSION,
Washington, January 5, 1897.

To the Senate:

I transmit herewith, in response to a resolution of the Senate of the 22d ultimo, a report from the Secretary of State, accompanied by copies of correspondence concerning the death of Charles Govin, a citizen of the United States, in the island of Cuba.

GROVER CLEVELAND.

EXECUTIVE MANSION,
Washington, January 8, 1897.

To the House of Representatives:

I transmit herewith, in response to the resolution of the House of Representatives of May 8, 1896, requesting information as to what had been done by the Department of State to carry out the provision in the act of March 2, 1895, making appropriations for the Department of Agriculture for the year 1896, as to negotiations with Great Britain to secure the abrogation or modification of the regulations requiring the slaughter of cattle from the United States at the port of entry, a report from the Secretary of State, with accompanying papers.

GROVER CLEVELAND.

EXECUTIVE MANSION,
Washington, January 8, 1897.

To the House of Representatives:

I transmit herewith the report of the Secretary of State in response to the resolution of the House of Representatives of June 5, 1896, calling for information concerning the changes made in the force of his Department since the 4th day of March, 1893.

This report has been in my hands since the 9th day of December, 1896, and its transmission to the House of Representatives has been delayed by my inadvertence.

GROVER CLEVELAND.

EXECUTIVE MANSION, *January 11, 1897.*

To the Senate:

I transmit herewith a treaty for the arbitration of all matters in difference between the United States and Great Britain.

The provisions of the treaty are the result of long and patient deliberation and represent concessions made by each party for the sake of agreement upon the general scheme.

Though the result reached may not meet the views of the advocates of immediate, unlimited, and irrevocable arbitration of all international controversies, it is nevertheless confidently believed that the treaty can not fail to be everywhere recognized as making a long step in the right direction and as embodying a practical working plan by which disputes between the two countries will reach a peaceful adjustment as matter of course and in ordinary routine.

In the initiation of such an important movement it must be expected that some of its features will assume a tentative character looking to a further advance, and yet it is apparent that the treaty which has been formulated not only makes war between the parties to it a remote possibility, but precludes those fears and rumors of war which of themselves too often assume the proportions of national disaster.

It is eminently fitting as well as fortunate that the attempts to accomplish results so beneficent should be initiated by kindred peoples, speaking the same tongue and joined together by all the ties of common traditions, common institutions, and common aspirations. The experiment of substituting civilized methods for brute force as the means of settling international questions of right will thus be tried under the happiest auspices. Its success ought not to be doubtful, and the fact that its ultimate ensuing benefits are not likely to be limited to the two countries immediately concerned should cause it to be promoted all the more eagerly. The examples set and the lesson furnished by the successful operation of this treaty are sure to be felt and taken to heart sooner or later by other nations, and will thus mark the beginning of a new epoch in civilization.

Profoundly impressed as I am, therefore, by the promise of transcendent good which this treaty affords, I do not hesitate to accompany its transmission with an expression of my earnest hope that it may commend itself to the favorable consideration of the Senate.

GROVER CLEVELAND.

EXECUTIVE MANSION, *January 18, 1897.*

To the Senate and House of Representatives:

I transmit herewith the report of Messrs. James B. Angell, of Michigan, John E. Russell, of Massachusetts, and Lyman E. Cooley, of Illinois, who were appointed commissioners under the authority of a law passed March 2, 1895, to make inquiry and report, after conference with such similar commissioners as might be appointed on behalf of Great Britain or the Dominion of Canada, concerning the feasibility of the construction of such canals as will enable vessels engaged in ocean commerce to pass between the Great Lakes and the Atlantic Ocean, and the most convenient location and probable cost of such canals, together with other facts and information in said act specified relating to their construction and use.

The commissioners have prosecuted the work assigned them with great zeal and intelligence, resulting in the collection of a mass of information embodied in their report and its accompanying exhibits which is of great importance and interest as related to the project subjected to their examination.

The advantages of direct and unbroken water transportation of the products of our Western States and Territories from convenient points of shipment to our seaboard ports are plainly palpable. The report of the commissioners contains, in my opinion, demonstration of the feasibility of securing such transportation, and gives ground for the anticipation that better and more uninterrupted commerce, through the plan suggested, between the great West and foreign ports, with the increase of national prosperity which must follow in its train, will not long escape American enterprise and activity.

It will be observed that the report of the commissioners, though as comprehensive as the time and facilities at their disposal permitted, does not definitely deal with the cost of the work they were called upon to consider and omits some of the other details related to it. Thus far they have labored without compensation, and a part of the small sum appropriated for the payment of their expenses still remains unexpended.

I suggest to the Congress the propriety of making economical provision for such further prosecution of their work as will more fully develop the information necessary to an exact and complete understanding of this interesting and important subject. GROVER CLEVELAND.

EXECUTIVE MANSION,
Washington, January 22, 1897.

To the Senate of the United States:

In response to the resolution of the Senate of December 15, 1896, relating to Cuban affairs, I transmit a report from the Secretary of State, submitting a list of the claims filed in the Department of State by citizens of the United States against Spain arising out of the insurrection existing in the island of Cuba, and the accompanying correspondence relating to the vessel called the *Competitor* and the persons claiming American citizenship captured thereon, which I deem it not incompatible with the public interests to communicate. GROVER CLEVELAND.

EXECUTIVE MANSION,
Washington, January 25, 1897.

To the Senate of the United States:

I transmit herewith, in response to the Senate resolution of December 21, 1896, addressed to the Secretary of State, a report of that officer covering a list of persons claiming to be citizens of the United States who have been arrested on the island of Cuba since February 24, 1895, to the present time. GROVER CLEVELAND.

EXECUTIVE MANSION,
Washington, February 1, 1897.

To the Senate:

I transmit herewith, in response to a resolution of the Senate of the 6th ultimo, a report from the Secretary of State, accompanied by copies of correspondence concerning the arrest, imprisonment, trial, and condemnation to perpetual imprisonment in chains of Jules Sanguily, a citizen of the United States, by the authorities of Spain in Cuba.

GROVER CLEVELAND.

EXECUTIVE MANSION, *February 5, 1897.*

To the Senate and House of Representatives:

The World's Columbian Commission has delivered to me certain documents and exhibits which they desire should constitute the final report required by section 12 of the act of Congress passed April 25, 1890, providing for the celebration of the four hundredth anniversary of the discovery of America and the holding of an international exhibition in the city of Chicago.

The documents referred to embrace the reports of the president and secretary of the commission and a report of the executive committee on awards, with exhibits relating to the same. They are contained in five boxes of considerable size, which, instead of actually transmitting with this communication, I have deposited in the State Department subject to the action and direction of the Congress.

I am informed that the director-general of the exposition has made a report directly to the Congress, and that no report of the lady managers has yet been made.

The selection of such part of the material mentioned as may be considered necessary to constitute a final exhibit of the action of the commission and the results of the exposition is submitted to the discretion of Congress.

GROVER CLEVELAND.

EXECUTIVE MANSION,
Washington, February 8, 1897.

To the Senate and House of Representatives:

I transmit herewith a communication from the Secretary of State and accompanying reports from diplomatic and consular officers of the United States on the passport regulations of foreign countries. In view of the evident value of the information contained in these reports, especially to American citizens going abroad and sojourning or traveling in foreign lands, I approve the recommendation of the Secretary that Congress authorize the printing of a special edition of 3,000 copies of the work, to be distributed by the Department of State as indicated in the Secretary's report.

GROVER CLEVELAND.

EXECUTIVE MANSION, *February 8, 1897.*

To the Senate and House of Representatives:

I herewith submit the thirteenth annual report of the Civil Service Commission, containing a detailed statement of its important work and exhibiting the present condition of the classified service of the Government.

GROVER CLEVELAND.

EXECUTIVE MANSION, *February 10, 1897.*

To the Senate of the United States:

In compliance with a resolution of the Senate of the 9th instant, the House of Representatives concurring, I return herewith Senate bill No. 3328, entitled "An act to amend an act entitled 'An act to repeal the timber-culture laws, and for other purposes.'"

GROVER CLEVELAND.

EXECUTIVE MANSION,
Washington, February 11, 1897.

To the Senate of the United States:

In response to the resolution of the Senate of February 4, 1897, I transmit a report from the Secretary of State, submitting copies of correspondence relative to the arrest and detention of Gaspar A. Betancourt, a citizen of the United States, by the Spanish authorities in Cuba.

GROVER CLEVELAND.

EXECUTIVE MANSION,
Washington, February 11, 1897.

To the Senate of the United States:

In response to the resolution of the Senate of February 2, 1897, I transmit a report from the Secretary of State, relative to the killing of Segundo N. Lopez, son of M. F. Lopez, at Sagua la Grande, in Cuba.

GROVER CLEVELAND.

EXECUTIVE MANSION,
Washington, February 20, 1897.

To the Senate:

I transmit herewith, in answer to the resolution of the Senate of the 17th instant, a report from the Secretary of State, touching the reply of the British Government in regard to the failure of the negotiations of the Paris Tribunal to protect the fur-seal herd of Alaska.

GROVER CLEVELAND.

EXECUTIVE MANSION,
Washington, February 20, 1897.

To the Senate:

I transmit herewith, in answer to the resolution of the Senate of the 15th instant, a report from the Secretary of State, accompanied by copies of correspondence with the German Government in reference to American insurance companies.

GROVER CLEVELAND.

EXECUTIVE MANSION,
Washington, February 23, 1897.

To the Senate:

I transmit herewith, in response to the resolution of the Senate of February 6, 1897, a report from the Secretary of State, in regard to the persons claiming American citizenship captured on board of the *Competitor*.

GROVER CLEVELAND.

EXECUTIVE MANSION,
Washington, February 24, 1897

To the Congress:

I transmit herewith a communication from the Secretary of State, covering the report of the joint commission on behalf of the United States and Great Britain, dated December 31, 1896, relative to the preservation of the fisheries in waters contiguous to the United States and Canada, as provided by the joint agreement between the United States and Great Britain dated December 6, 1892.

GROVER CLEVELAND.

EXECUTIVE MANSION,
Washington, February 25, 1897.

To the Senate and House of Representatives:

I transmit herewith, for the information of the Congress, a communication from the Secretary of State, covering the report of the Director of the Bureau of the American Republics for the year 1896.

GROVER CLEVELAND.

EXECUTIVE MANSION,
Washington, February 26, 1897.

To the House of Representatives:

I transmit herewith a communication from the Secretary of State, accompanying the annual reports of the consuls of the United States upon foreign industries and commerce. In view of the value of these reports to the business interests throughout the country, I indorse the recommendation of the Secretary of State that Congress authorize the printing of a special edition of 10,000 copies of the general summary entitled Review of the World's Commerce, and of 5,000 copies of Commercial Relations (including this summary), to enable the Department of State to meet the demand for such information.   GROVER CLEVELAND.

To the Congress: EXECUTIVE MANSION, *March 1, 1897.*

I transmit herewith the report of the board of lady managers of the World's Columbian Commission.   GROVER CLEVELAND.

EXECUTIVE MANSION,
Washington, March 1, 1897.

To the Senate:

In response to the resolution of the Senate of the 24th ultimo, I transmit herewith a report from the Secretary of State, covering copies of the correspondence and reports of the consul-general of the United States at Havana relating to all American citizens now in prison in the island of Cuba not previously reported on.   GROVER CLEVELAND.

EXECUTIVE MANSION,
Washington, March 2, 1897.

To the Senate:

I transmit herewith, in response to the resolution of the Senate of February 24, 1897, a report from the Secretary of State, in relation to the claim of M. A. Cheek against the Siamese Government, with accompanying papers.   GROVER CLEVELAND.

EXECUTIVE MANSION,
Washington, March 2, 1897.

To the Senate:

I herewith transmit a report of the Secretary of State upon a resolution of the Senate relating to the arrest, imprisonment, and death of Dr. Ricardo Ruiz in the jail of Guanabacoa, on the island of Cuba. Agreeing with the suggestion of the Secretary, I have not thought it compatible with the public interest that the correspondence referred to in the resolution should be communicated pending the public and exhaustive investigation about to be instituted.

Though it seems to be clear that the consul-general should have professional aid in such investigation, that matter, together with the selection of the particular persons to act with him, properly devolves upon my successor in office.   GROVER CLEVELAND.

EXECUTIVE MANSION,
Washington, March 3, 1897.

To the Senate:

I transmit herewith, in reply to the resolution of the Senate of January 23, 1897, a report from the Secretary of State, accompanied by copies of the correspondence therein requested, relating to the Nicaraguan Canal or the Maritime Canal Company of Nicaragua, since 1887.

GROVER CLEVELAND.

VETO MESSAGES.

EXECUTIVE MANSION, *January 14, 1897.*

To the House of Representatives:

I return herewith without my approval House bill No. 9469, entitled "An act to constitute a new division of the eastern judicial district of Texas, and to provide for the holding of terms of court at Beaumont, Tex., and for the appointment of a clerk for said court."

It appears that terms of court are now held at four different places within the eastern judicial district of Texas and that parties having business in the courts are not seriously inconvenienced under present arrangements.

Both the Federal judge and district attorney in this district express themselves in opposition to the bill as unnecessary and an interruption to the transaction of the large volume of business now pending and constantly coming before the court.

I have before me certificates of the clerks of the present divisions of the courts showing that during the last five years the counties which it is proposed shall constitute the new division have contributed but forty-two cases to the calendars of the court.

Conclusive proof is also before me that the additional terms of court provided for in this bill would so interfere with the terms already appointed in the existing divisions that the proper administration of the civil as well as the criminal law would be impracticable.

The criminal docket of the terms held at Paris is so large that under present arrangements and with the utmost industry trials can not now be as promptly disposed of as the ends of justice require. This condition would be further aggravated if terms of the court should be held at Beaumont on the dates proposed in this bill, since they are fixed at such times as to necessarily curtail the period now devoted to the Paris terms.

On the grounds stated and because I am unable to discover how the public interests can possibly be promoted by the proposed legislation I am constrained to withhold my approval of the bill under consideration.

GROVER CLEVELAND.

EXECUTIVE MANSION, *February 22, 1897.*

To the House of Representatives:

I return herewith without my approval House bill No. 2189, entitled "An act granting a pension to Mrs. Mary A. Freeman."

A former husband of the beneficiary, named Andrew V. Pritchard, did service in the Mexican War, and on July 22, 1847, died of disease contracted in such service. Thereupon the beneficiary named in this bill was pensioned as his widow. She continued to receive this pension until 1852, when she married John Freeman, through which she of course lost her pensionable status. Two minor children of the soldier were, however, placed on the pension roll in her stead, and their pension was paid to them until the youngest became 16 years of age, in 1863.

John Freeman died in December, 1871, the beneficiary having been his wife for almost twenty years. It is now proposed to restore her to the pension roll as the widow of her former husband, the Mexican soldier, who died nearly fifty years ago, and notwithstanding the fact that less than five years after his death she relinquished her right to a pension and surrendered her widowhood to become the wife of another husband, with whom she lived for many years.

I am not willing, even by inaction, to be charged with acquiescence in what appears to be such an entire departure from the principle, as well as sentiment, connected with reasonable pension legislation.

GROVER CLEVELAND.

To the Senate: EXECUTIVE MANSION, *February 22, 1897.*

I return herewith without approval Senate bill No. 1323, entitled "An act granting a pension to Maria Somerlat, widow of Valentine Somerlat."

This beneficiary, under the name of Maria Somerlat, was pensioned in 1867 as the widow of Valentine Somerlat, a volunteer soldier, dating from his death, in 1864. She continued to draw the pension allowed her as such widow until 1881, when she married one Hiram Smith. Subsequently, but at what time does not appear, she was divorced from Smith in a suit that seems to have been begun by him, but in which she interposed a cross bill and obtained judgment in her favor. Notwithstanding her remarriage, through which she ceased to be the widow of the dead soldier, it is proposed to pension her again on account of his death.

The rule governing the operation of general pension laws which forfeits a widow's pension on her remarriage seems so reasonable and just and its relaxation must necessarily lead to such a departure from just principles and to such vexatious pension administration that I am convinced it ought to be strictly maintained.

I hope I may be permitted to call the attention of the Senate to the increasing latitude clearly discernible in special pension legislation. It has seemed to me so useless to attempt to stem the tide of this legislation by Executive interference that I have contented myself with nonacquiescence in numerous cases where I could not approve.

There have been already presented to me for Executive action during the present session of the Congress 206 special pension bills, of which I have actually examined 115. The entire number of such bills that have become laws during the four sessions of the Congress since March 4, 1893, is 391. Some of those presented at the present session are not based upon the least pretext that the death or disability involved is related to army service, while in numerous other cases it is extremely difficult to satisfactorily discover such relationship.

There is one feature of this legislation which I am sure deserves attention. I refer to the great number of special bills passed for the purpose of increasing the pensions of those already on the rolls. Of the 115 special pension bills which I have examined since the beginning of the present session of the Congress, 58 granted or restored pensions and 57 increased those already existing, and the appropriation of money necessary to meet these increases exceeds considerably the amount required to pay the original pensions granted or restored by the remaining 58 bills.

I can not discover that these increases are regulated by any rule or principle, and when we remember that there are nearly a million pensioners on our rolls and consider the importunity for such increase that must follow the precedents already made, the relation of the subject to a justifiable increase of our national revenues can not escape attention.

GROVER CLEVELAND.

EXECUTIVE MANSION, *February 22, 1897.*

To the House of Representatives:

I return herewith without my approval House bill No. 6902, entitled "An act granting a pension to Mrs. Mary A. Viel."

This beneficiary was married in 1862 to Major W. D. Sanger, then in the volunteer military service. He died in 1872, never having made any application for pension. His widow made no application for pension, but within three years after her husband's death, and in 1875, became the wife of Paul Viel. Eight years thereafter he died, leaving her his widow, and it is now proposed to pension her as the widow of the soldier, Major Sanger, though she long ago by her own deliberate act surrendered that title and all its incidents.

There is a further objection to granting this pension. I do not find that any claim is made that the death of the soldier, who was the beneficiary's first husband, was at all attributable to his army service. Neither he nor his widow, while she remained such, presented any such claim, nor is it found in reports of the committees in the Senate or House to whom the bill under consideration was referred. On the contrary, the

Senate Committee on Pensions in their report distinctly state that "there is no proof that soldier contracted disease while in the service or that he died of pensionable disabilities."

GROVER CLEVELAND.

EXECUTIVE MANSION, *March 1, 1897.*

To the Senate:

I return herewith without approval Senate bill No. 719, entitled "An act to restore a pension to Harriet M. Knowlton."

Major William Knowlton, a most worthy volunteer soldier, died of wounds received in battle on the 20th day of September, 1864.

In 1865 his widow, the beneficiary named in this bill, was pensioned at the rate of $25 a month, commencing on the day of her husband's death, with an additional allowance for four minor children dating from July, 1866.

She continued to receive this pension and allowance until November, 1867, when she married Albin P. Stinchfield.

Thereupon her name was dropped from the pension roll, she having by her remarriage lost her pensionable condition, and her children were pensioned at a small monthly rate from the date of their mother's remarriage until June 1, 1880, when the youngest became 16 years of age.

The beneficiary, after living with her second husband about twenty-two years, secured a divorce from him in the year 1889, and it is now proposed to pension the divorced wife as the widow of her deceased soldier husband at the rate she received while she was actually his widow, thirty years ago.

Her pensionable relation to the Government terminated with her remarriage, and her divorce from her second husband could not upon any ground of principle restore it. A departure from this rule, even in aid of cases of hardship, can not fail to establish precedents inviting the abandonment of reasonable and justifiable pension theories.

GROVER CLEVELAND.

EXECUTIVE MANSION, *March 1, 1897.*

To the House of Representatives:

I herewith return without approval House bill No. 1299, entitled "An act to pension Harriet Woodbury, of Windsor, Vt."

The beneficiary named in this bill was the wife of Aaron G. Firman at the time of his enlistment in 1863. He died October 2, 1864, and the beneficiary, as his widow, was pensioned in 1865, from the day of her soldier husband's death.

She continued to receive the pension allowed to her as such widow until July 14, 1866, when she married Samuel H. Woodbury. She was thereupon dropped from the pension roll pursuant to law, and in 1868 the minor son of the soldier was allowed a pension of $8 a month, commencing at the date of the remarriage of his mother. This pension was increased to $10 a month in 1873, from July 25, 1866, and was continued until 1880, when the minor child reached the age of 16 years.

On July 26, 1886, twenty years after the beneficiary ceased to be the widow of the soldier Aaron G. Firman and became the wife of the civilian Samuel H. Woodbury, he died and she became his widow.

It is now proposed by this bill to pension her again as the widow of the deceased soldier, notwithstanding her voluntary abandonment of that relation to become the wife of another more than thirty years ago.

No feature of our pension laws is so satisfactory and just as a fair allowance to the widows of our soldiers who have died' from causes attributable to their army service. When, however, such a beneficiary by remarriage surrenders her soldier widowhood and turns away from its tender and patriotic associations to assume again the relation and allegiance of wife to another husband, when she discards the soldier's name and in every way terminates her pensionable relationship to the Government, I am unable to discover any principle which justifies her restoration to that relationship upon the death of her second husband.

No one can be insensible to the sad plight of a widow in needy condition, but our pension laws should deal with soldiers' widows. I understand that only the existence of this relationship to a deceased soldier creates through him the Government's duty and justifies the application of public money to the relief of such widows.

GROVER CLEVELAND.

EXECUTIVE MANSION, *March 2, 1897.*

To the House of Representatives:

I herewith return without approval House bill No. 7864, entitled "An act to amend the immigration laws of the United States."

By the first section of this bill it is proposed to amend section 1 of the act of March 3, 1891, relating to immigration by adding to the classes of aliens thereby excluded from admission to the United States the following:

All persons physically capable and over 16 years of age who can not read and write the English language or some other language; but a person not so able to read and write who is over 50 years of age and is the parent or grandparent of a qualified immigrant over 21 years of age and capable of supporting such parent or grandparent may accompany such immigrant, or such a parent or grandparent may be sent for and come to join the family of a child or grandchild over 21 years of age similarly qualified and capable, and a wife or minor child not so able to read and write may accompany or be sent for and come and join the husband or parent similarly qualified and capable.

A radical departure from our national policy relating to immigration is here presented. Heretofore we have welcomed all who came to us from other lands except those whose moral or physical condition or history threatened danger to our national welfare and safety.   Relying upon the zealous watchfulness of our people to prevent injury to our political and social fabric, we have encouraged those coming from foreign countries to cast their lot with us and join in the development of our vast domain, securing in return a share in the blessings of American citizenship.

A century's stupendous growth, largely due to the assimilation and thrift of millions of sturdy and patriotic adopted citizens, attests the success of this generous and free-handed policy which, while guarding the people's interests, exacts from our immigrants only physical and moral soundness and a willingness and ability to work.

A contemplation of the grand results of this policy can not fail to arouse a sentiment in its defense, for however it might have been regarded as an original proposition and viewed as an experiment its accomplishments are such that if it is to be uprooted at this late day its disadvantages should be plainly apparent and the substitute adopted should be just and adequate, free from uncertainties, and guarded against difficult or oppressive administration.

It is not claimed, I believe, that the time has come for the further restriction of immigration on the ground that an excess of population overcrowds our land.

It is said, however, that the quality of recent immigration is undesirable.   The time is quite within recent memory when the same thing was said of immigrants who, with their descendants, are now numbered among our best citizens.

It is said that too many immigrants settle in our cities, thus dangerously increasing their idle and vicious population.   This is certainly a disadvantage.   It can not be shown, however, that it affects all our cities, nor that it is permanent; nor does it appear that this condition where it exists demands as its remedy the reversal of our present immigration policy.

The claim is also made that the influx of foreign laborers deprives of the opportunity to work those who are better entitled than they to the privilege of earning their livelihood by daily toil.   An unfortunate condition is certainly presented when any who are willing to labor are unemployed, but so far as this condition now exists among our people it must be conceded to be a result of phenomenal business depression and the stagnation of all enterprises in which labor is a factor.   With the advent of settled and wholesome financial and economic governmental policies and consequent encouragement to the activity of capital the misfortunes of unemployed labor should, to a great extent at least, be remedied. If it continues, its natural consequences must be to check the further immigration to our cities of foreign laborers and to deplete the ranks of those already there.   In the meantime those most willing and best entitled ought to be able to secure the advantages of such work as there is to do.

It is proposed by the bill under consideration to meet the alleged difficulties of the situation by establishing an educational test by which the right of a foreigner to make his home with us shall be determined. Its general scheme is to prohibit from admission to our country all immigrants ''physically capable and over 16 years of age who can not read and write the English language or some other language,'' and it is provided that this test shall be applied by requiring immigrants seeking admission to read and afterwards to write not less than twenty nor more than twenty-five words of the Constitution of the United States in some language, and that any immigrant failing in this shall not be admitted, but shall be returned to the country from whence he came at the expense of the steamship or railroad company which brought him.

The best reason that could be given for this radical restriction of immigration is the necessity of protecting our population against degeneration and saving our national peace and quiet from imported turbulence and disorder.

I can not believe that we would be protected against these evils by limiting immigration to those who can read and write in any language twenty-five words of our Constitution. In my opinion, it is infinitely more safe to admit a hundred thousand immigrants who, though unable to read and write, seek among us only a home and opportunity to work than to admit one of those unruly agitators and enemies of governmental control who can not only read and write, but delights in arousing by inflammatory speech the illiterate and peacefully inclined to discontent and tumult. Violence and disorder do not originate with illiterate laborers. They are, rather, the victims of the educated agitator. The ability to read and write, as required in this bill, in and of itself affords, in my opinion, a misleading test of contented industry and supplies unsatisfactory evidence of desirable citizenship or a proper apprehension of the benefits of our institutions. If any particular element of our illiterate immigration is to be feared for other causes than illiteracy, these causes should be dealt with directly, instead of making illiteracy the pretext for exclusion, to the detriment of other illiterate immigrants against whom the real cause of complaint can not be alleged.

The provisions intended to rid that part of the proposed legislation already referred to from obvious hardship appears to me to be indefinite and inadequate.

A parent, grandparent, wife, or minor child of a qualified immigrant, though unable to read and write, may accompany the immigrant or be sent for to join his family, provided the immigrant is capable of supporting such relative. These exceptions to the general rule of exclusion contained in the bill were made to prevent the separation of families, and yet neither brothers nor sisters are provided for. In order that relatives who are provided for may be reunited, those still in foreign lands must be sent for to join the immigrant here. What formality is necessary to constitute this prerequisite, and how are the facts of relationship and that the relative is sent for to be established? Are the illiterate relatives of immigrants who have come here under prior laws entitled to the advantage of these exceptions? A husband who can read and write and who determines to abandon his illiterate wife abroad will find here under this law an absolutely safe retreat. The illiterate relatives mentioned must not only be sent for, but such immigrant must be capable of supporting them when they arrive. This requirement proceeds upon the assumption that the foreign relatives coming here are in every case, by reason of poverty, liable to become a public charge unless the immigrant is capable of their support. The contrary is very often true. And yet if unable to read and write, though quite able and willing to support themselves and their relatives here besides, they could not be admitted under the provisions of this bill if the immigrant was impoverished, though the aid of his fortunate but illiterate relative might be the means of saving him from pauperism.

The fourth section of this bill provides—

That it shall be unlawful for any male alien who has not in good faith made his declaration before the proper court of his intention to become a citizen of the United States to be employed on any public works of the United States or to come regularly or habitually into the United States by land or water for the purpose of engaging in any mechanical trade or manual labor for wages or salary, returning from time to time to a foreign country.

The fifth section provides—

That it shall be unlawful for any person, partnership, company, or corporation knowingly to employ any alien coming into the United States in violation of the next preceding section of this act.

The prohibition against the employment of aliens upon any public works of the United States is in line with other legislation of a like character. It is quite a different thing, however, to declare it a crime for an alien to come regularly and habitually into the United States for the purpose of obtaining work from private parties, if such alien returns from time to time to a foreign country, and to constitute any employment of such alien a criminal offense.

When we consider these provisions of the bill in connection with our long northern frontier and the boundaries of our States and Territories, often but an imaginary line separating them from the British dominions, and recall the friendly intercourse between the people who are neighbors on either side, the provisions of this bill affecting them must be regarded as illiberal, narrow, and un-American.

The residents of these States and Territories have separate and especial interests which in many cases make an interchange of labor between their people and their alien neighbors most important, frequently with the advantage largely in favor of our citizens. This suggests the inexpediency of Federal interference with these conditions when not necessary to the correction of a substantial evil, affecting the general welfare. Such unfriendly legislation as is proposed could hardly fail to provoke retaliatory measures, to the injury of many of our citizens who now find employment on adjoining foreign soil.

The uncertainty of construction to which the language of these provisions is subject is a serious objection to a statute which describes a crime. An important element in the offense sought to be created by these sections is the coming "regularly or habitually into the United States." These words are impossible of definite and certain construction. The same may be said of the equally important words "returning from time to time to a foreign country."

A careful examination of this bill has convinced me that for the reasons given and others not specifically stated its provisions are unnecessarily harsh and oppressive, and that its defects in construction would cause vexation and its operation would result in harm to our citizens.

GROVER CLEVELAND.

POCKET VETOES.

["An act granting a pension to Mrs. Mary Gould Carr, widow of the late Brigadier and Brevet Major General Joseph B. Carr, United States Volunteers, deceased."]

DECEMBER 30, 1896.

This bill was presented to me on the 16th day of December, 1896. Congress, pursuant to a concurrent resolution adopted by both Houses of Congress, adjourned from the 22d day of December, 1896, to January 5, 1897. I have not approved the bill. GROVER CLEVELAND.

["An act to increase the pension of Caroline A. Hough, widow of Brigadier-General John Hough."]

DECEMBER 31, 1896.

This bill was presented to me on the 16th day of December, 1896. Congress, pursuant to a concurrent resolution adopted by both Houses of Congress, adjourned from the 22d day of December, 1896, to January 5, 1897. I have not approved the bill. GROVER CLEVELAND.

PROCLAMATIONS.

BY THE PRESIDENT OF THE UNITED STATES OF AMERICA.

A PROCLAMATION.

Whereas an act of Congress entitled "An act to adopt regulations for preventing collisions at sea" was approved August 19, 1890, the said act being in the following words:

Be it enacted by the Senate and House of Representatives of the United States of America in Congress assembled, That the following regulations for preventing collisions at sea shall be followed by all public and private vessels of the United States upon the high seas and in all waters connected therewith navigable by seagoing vessels:

PRELIMINARY.

In the following rules every steam vessel which is under sail and not under steam is to be considered a sailing vessel, and every vessel under steam, whether under sail or not, is to be considered a steam vessel.

The words "steam vessel" shall include any vessel propelled by machinery.

A vessel is "under way" within the meaning of these rules when she is not at anchor or made fast to the shore or aground.

RULES CONCERNING LIGHTS, ETC.

The word "visible" in these rules when applied to lights shall mean visible on a dark night with a clear atmosphere.

ARTICLE 1. The rules concerning lights shall be complied with in all weathers from sunset to sunrise, and during such time no other lights which may be mistaken for the prescribed lights shall be exhibited.

ART. 2. A steam vessel when under way shall carry—

(*a*) On or in front of the foremast, or if a vessel without a foremast, then in the fore part of the vessel, at a height above the hull of not less than 20 feet, and if the breadth of the vessel exceeds 20 feet, then at a height above the hull not less than such breadth, so, however, that the light need not be carried at a greater height above the hull than 40 feet a bright white light so constructed as to show an unbroken light over an arc of the horizon of 20 points of the compass, so fixed as to throw the light 10 points on each side of the vessel—namely, from right ahead to 2 points abaft the beam on either side—and of such a character as to be visible at a distance of at least 5 miles.

(*b*) On the starboard side a green light so constructed as to show an unbroken light over an arc of the horizon of 10 points of the compass, so fixed as to throw the light from right ahead to 2 points abaft the beam on the starboard side, and of such a character as to be visible at a distance of at least 2 miles.

(*c*) On the port side a red light so constructed as to show an unbroken light over an arc of the horizon of 10 points of the compass, so fixed as to throw the light from right ahead to 2 points abaft the beam on the port side, and of such a character as to be visible at a distance of at least 2 miles.

(*d*) The said green and red side lights shall be fitted with inboard screens projecting at least 3 feet forward from the light, so as to prevent these lights from being seen across the bow.

(*e*) A steam vessel when under way may carry an additional white light similar in construction to the light mentioned in subdivision (*a*). These two lights shall be so placed in line with the keel that one shall be at least 15 feet higher than the other, and in such a position with reference to each other that the lower light shall be forward of the upper one. The vertical distance between these lights shall be less than the horizontal distance.

ART. 3. A steam vessel when towing another vessel shall, in addition to her side lights, carry two bright white lights in a vertical line one over the other, not less than 6 feet apart, and when towing more than one vessel shall carry an additional bright white light 6 feet above or below such light, if the length of the tow measuring from the stern of the towing vessel to the stern of the last vessel towed exceeds 600 feet. Each of these lights shall be of the same construction and character and shall be carried in the same position as the white light mentioned in article 2 (*a*), excepting the additional light, which may be carried at a height of not less than 14 feet above the hull.

Such steam vessel may carry a small white light abaft the funnel or aftermast for the vessel towed to steer by, but such light shall not be visible forward of the beam.

ART. 4. (*a*) A vessel which from any accident is not under command shall carry at the same height as a white light mentioned in article 2 (*a*), where they can best be seen, and if a steam vessel in lieu of that light, two red lights in a vertical line one over the other, not less than 6 feet apart, and of such a character as to be visible all around the horizon at a distance of at least 2 miles, and shall by day carry in a vertical line one over the other, not less than 6 feet apart, where they can best be seen, two black balls or shapes each 2 feet in diameter.

(*b*) A vessel employed in laying or in picking up a telegraph cable shall carry in the same position as the white light mentioned in article 2 (*a*), and if a steam vessel in lieu of that light, three lights in a vertical line one over the other, not less than 6 feet apart. The highest and lowest of these lights shall be red and the middle light shall be white, and they shall be of such a character as to be visible all around the horizon at a distance of at least 2 miles. By day she shall carry in a vertical line one over the other, not less than 6 feet apart, where they can best be seen, three shapes not less than 2 feet in diameter, of which the highest and lowest shall be globular in shape and red in color and the middle one diamond in shape and white.

(*c*) The vessels referred to in this article when not making way through the water shall not carry the side lights, but when making way shall carry them.

(*d*) The lights and shapes required to be shown by this article are to be taken by other vessels as signals that the vessel showing them is not under command and can not, therefore, get out of the way.

These signals are not signals of vessels in distress and requiring assistance. Such signals are contained in article 31.

ART. 5. A sailing vessel under way and any vessel being towed shall carry the same lights as are prescribed by article 2 for a steam vessel under way, with the exception of the white lights mentioned therein, which they shall never carry.

ART. 6. Whenever, as in the case of small vessels under way during bad weather, the green and red side lights can not be fixed, these lights shall be kept at hand, lighted and ready for use, and shall on the approach of or to other vessels be exhibited on their respective sides, in sufficient time to prevent collision, in such manner as to make them most visible and so that the green light shall not be seen on the port side nor the red light on the starboard side, nor, if practicable, more than 2 points abaft the beam on their respective sides.

To make the use of these portable lights more certain and easy the lanterns containing them shall each be painted outside with the color of the light they respectively contain and shall be provided with proper screens.

ART. 7. Steam vessels of less than 40 and vessels under oars or sails of less than 20 tons gross tonnage, respectively, when under way shall not be obliged to carry the lights mentioned in article 2 (*a*), (*b*), and (*c*), but if they do not carry them they shall be provided with the following lights:

First. Steam vessels of less than 40 tons shall carry—

(*a*) In the fore part of the vessel or on or in front of the funnel, where it can best be seen, and at a height above the gunwale of not less than 9 feet, a bright white light constructed and fixed as prescribed in article 2 (*a*) and of such a character as to be visible at a distance of at least 2 miles.

(*b*) Green and red side lights constructed and fixed as prescribed in article 2 (*b*) and (*c*) and of such a character as to be visible at a distance of at least 1 mile, or a combined lantern showing a green light and a red light from right ahead to 2 points abaft the beam on their respective sides. Such lanterns shall be carried not less than 3 feet below the white light.

Second. Small steamboats, such as are carried by seagoing vessels, may carry the white light at a less height than 9 feet above the gunwale, but it shall be carried above the combined lantern mentioned in subdivision 1 (*b*).

Third. Vessels under oars or sails of less than 20 tons shall have ready at hand a lantern with a green glass on one side and a red glass on the other, which on the approach of or to other vessels shall be exhibited, in sufficient time to prevent collision, so that the green light shall not be seen on the port side nor the red light on the starboard side.

The vessels referred to in this article shall not be obliged to carry the lights prescribed by article 4 (*a*) and article 11, last paragraph.

ART. 8. Pilot vessels when engaged on their station on pilotage duty shall not show the lights required for other vessels, but shall carry a white light at the masthead, visible all around the horizon, and shall also exhibit a flare-up light or flare-up lights at short intervals, which shall never exceed fifteen minutes.

On the near approach of or to other vessels they shall have their side lights lighted ready for use and shall flash or show them at short intervals to indicate the direction in which they are heading; but the green light shall not be shown on the port side nor the red light on the starboard side.

A pilot vessel of such a class as to be obliged to go alongside of a vessel to put a pilot on board may show the white light instead of carrying it at the masthead, and may instead of the colored lights above mentioned have at hand ready for use a lantern with a green glass on the one side and a red glass on the other, to be used as prescribed above.

Pilot vessels when not engaged on their station on pilotage duty shall carry lights similar to those of other vessels of their tonnage.

ART. 9. Fishing vessels and fishing boats when under way and when not required by this article to carry or show the lights therein named shall carry or show the lights prescribed for vessels of their tonnage under way.

(*a*) Vessels and boats when fishing with drift nets shall exhibit two white lights from any part of the vessel where they can best be seen. Such lights shall be placed so that the vertical distance between them shall be not less than 6 feet and not more than 10 feet, and so that the horizontal distance between them measured in a line with the keel shall be not less than 5 feet and not more than 10 feet. The lower of these two lights shall be the more forward, and both of them shall be of such a character as to show all around the horizon and to be visible at a distance of not less than 3 miles.

(*b*) Vessels when engaged in trawling, by which is meant the dragging of an apparatus along the bottom of the sea—

First. If steam vessels, shall carry in the same position as the white light mentioned in article 2 (*a*) a tricolored lantern so constructed and fixed as to show a white light from right ahead to 2 points on each bow and a green light and a red light over an arc of the horizon from 2 points on either bow to 2 points abaft the beam on the starboard and port sides, respectively, and not less than 6 nor more than 12 feet below the tricolored lantern a white light in a lantern so constructed as to show a clear, uniform, and unbroken light all around the horizon.

Second. If sailing vessels of 7 tons gross tonnage and upward, shall carry a white light in a lantern so constructed as to show a clear, uniform, and unbroken light all around the horizon, and shall also be provided with a sufficient supply of red pyrotechnic lights, which shall each burn for at least thirty seconds and shall be shown on the approach of or to other vessels in sufficient time to prevent collision.

In the Mediterranean Sea the vessels referred to in subdivision (*b*) 2 may use a flare-up light in lieu of a pyrotechnic light.

All lights mentioned in subdivision (*b*) 1 and 2 shall be visible at a distance of at least 2 miles.

Third. If sailing vessels of less than 7 tons gross tonnage, shall not be obliged to carry the white light mentioned in subdivision (*b*) 2 of this article, but if they do not carry such light they shall have at hand, ready for use, a lantern showing a bright white light, which shall on the approach of or to other vessels be exhibited where it can best be seen in sufficient time to prevent collision; and they shall also show a red pyrotechnic light, as prescribed in subdivision (*b*) 2, or in lieu thereof a flare-up light.

(*c*) Vessels and boats when line fishing with their lines out and attached to their lines, and when not at anchor or stationary, shall carry the same lights as vessels fishing with drift nets.

(*d*) Fishing vessels and fishing boats may at any time use a flare-up light in addition to the lights which they are by this article required to carry and show. All flare-up lights exhibited by a vessel when trawling or fishing with any kind of drag-net shall be shown at the after part of the vessel, excepting that if the vessel is hanging by the stern to her fishing gear they shall be exhibited from the bow.

(*e*) Every fishing vessel and every boat when at anchor shall exhibit a white light visible all around the horizon at a distance of at least 1 mile.

(*f*) If a vessel or boat when fishing becomes stationary in consequence of her gear getting fast to a rock or other obstruction, she shall show the light and make the fog signal prescribed for a vessel at anchor, respectively. (See article 15 (*d*), (*e*), and last paragraph.)

(*g*) In fog, mist, falling snow, or heavy rain storms drift-net vessels attached to their nets, and vessels when trawling, dredging, or fishing with any kind of drag-net, and vessels line fishing with their lines out shall, if of 20 tons gross tonnage or upward, respectively, at intervals of not more than one minute make a blast—if steam vessels, with the whistle or siren, and if sailing vessels, with the fog horn—each blast to be followed by ringing the bell.

(*h*) Sailing vessels or boats fishing with nets or lines or trawls when under way shall in daytime indicate their occupation to an approaching vessel by displaying a basket or other efficient signal where it can best be seen.

The vessels referred to in this article shall not be obliged to carry the light prescribed by article 4 (*a*) and article 11, last paragraph.

ART. 10. A vessel which is being overtaken by another shall show from her stern to such last-mentioned vessel a white light or a flare-up light.

The white light required to be shown by this article may be fixed and carried in a lantern, but in such case the lantern shall be so constructed, fitted, and screened that it shall throw an unbroken light over an arc of the horizon of 12 points of the compass—namely, for 6 points from right aft on each side of the vessel—so as to be visible at a distance of at least 1 mile. Such light shall be carried as nearly as practicable on the same level as the side lights.

ART. 11. A vessel under 150 feet in length when at anchor shall carry forward, where it can best be seen, but at a height not exceeding 20 feet above the hull, a white light in a lantern so constructed as to show a clear, uniform, and unbroken light visible all around the horizon at a distance of at least 1 mile.

A vessel of 150 feet or upward in length when at anchor shall carry in the forward part of the vessel, at a height of not less than 20 and not exceeding 40 feet above the hull, one such light, and at or near the stern of the vessel, and at such a height that it shall be not less than 15 feet lower than the forward light, another such light.

The length of a vessel shall be deemed to be the length appearing in her certificate of registry.

A vessel aground in or near a fairway shall carry the above light or lights and the two red lights prescribed by article 4 (*a*).

ART. 12. Every vessel may, if necessary in order to attract attention, in addition to the lights which she is by these rules required to carry, show a flare-up light or use any detonating signal that can not be mistaken for a distress signal.

ART. 13. Nothing in these rules shall interfere with the operation of any special rules made by the government of any nation with respect to additional station and signal lights for two or more ships of war or for vessels sailing under convoy, or with the exhibition of recognition signals adopted by ship owners, which have been authorized by their respective governments and duly registered and published.

ART. 14. A steam vessel proceeding under sail only, but having her funnel up, shall carry in daytime forward, where it can best be seen, one black ball or shape 2 feet in diameter.

SOUND SIGNALS FOR FOG, ETC.

ART. 15. All signals prescribed by this article for vessels under way shall be given—

1. By "steam vessels," on the whistle or siren.

2. By "sailing vessels" and "vessels towed," on the fog horn.

The words "prolonged blast" used in this article shall mean a blast of from four to six seconds' duration.

A steam vessel shall be provided with an efficient whistle or siren, sounded by steam or by some substitute for steam, so placed that the sound may not be intercepted by any obstruction, and with an efficient fog horn, to be sounded by mechanical means, and also with an efficient bell. (In all cases where the rules require a bell to be used a drum may be substituted on board Turkish vessels or a gong where such articles are used on board small seagoing vessels.) A sailing vessel of 20 tons gross tonnage or upward shall be provided with a similar fog horn and bell.

In fog, mist, falling snow, or heavy rain storms, whether by day or night, the signals described in this article shall be used as follows, viz:

(*a*) A steam vessel having way upon her shall sound at intervals of not more than two minutes a prolonged blast.

(*b*) A steam vessel under way, but stopped and having no way upon her, shall sound at intervals of not more than two minutes two prolonged blasts, with an interval of about one second between them.

(*c*) A sailing vessel under way shall sound at intervals of not more than one minute, when on the starboard tack one blast, when on the port tack two blasts in succession, and when with the wind abaft the beam three blasts in succession.

(*d*) A vessel when at anchor shall at intervals of not more than one minute ring the bell rapidly for about five seconds.

(*e*) A vessel at anchor at sea, when not in ordinary anchorage ground and when in such a position as to be an obstruction to vessels under way, shall sound, if a steam vessel, at intervals of not more than two minutes, two prolonged blasts with her whistle or siren, followed by ringing her bell, or if a sailing vessel, at intervals of not more than one minute, two blasts with her fog horn, followed by ringing her bell.

(*f*) A vessel when towing shall, instead of the signals prescribed in subdivisions (*a*) and (*c*) of this article, at intervals of not more than two minutes sound three blasts in succession, namely, one prolonged blast followed by two short blasts. A vessel towed may give this signal, and she shall not give any other.

(*g*) A steam vessel wishing to indicate to another "The way is off my vessel; you may feel your way past me" may sound three blasts in succession—namely, short, long, short—with intervals of about one second between them.

(*h*) A vessel employed in laying or picking up a telegraph cable shall on hearing the fog signal of an approaching vessel sound in answer three prolonged blasts in succession.

(*i*) A vessel under way which is unable to get out of the way of an approaching vessel through being not under command or unable to maneuver as required by these rules shall on hearing the fog signal of an approaching vessel sound in answer four short blasts in succession.

Sailing vessels and boats of less than 20 tons gross tonnage shall not be obliged to give the above-mentioned signals, but if they do not they shall make some other efficient sound signal at intervals of not more than one minute.

SPEED OF SHIPS TO BE MODERATE IN FOG, ETC.

ART. 16. Every vessel shall in a fog, mist, falling snow, or heavy rain storms go at a moderate speed, having careful regard to the existing circumstances and conditions.

A steam vessel hearing, apparently forward of her beam, the fog signal of a vessel the position of which is not ascertained shall, so far as the circumstances of the case admit, stop her engines and then navigate with caution until danger of collision is over.

STEERING AND SAILING RULES.

PRELIMINARY.—RISK OF COLLISION.

Risk of collision can, when circumstances permit, be ascertained by carefully watching the compass bearing of an approaching vessel. If the bearing does not appreciably change, such risk should be deemed to exist.

ART. 17. When two sailing vessels are approaching one another so as to involve risk of collision, one of them shall keep out of the way of the other as follows, namely:

(*a*) A vessel which is running free shall keep out of the way of a vessel which is closehauled.

(*b*) A vessel which is closehauled on the port tack shall keep out of the way of a vessel which is closehauled on the starboard tack.

(*c*) When both are running free with the wind on different sides, the vessel which has the wind on the port side shall keep out of the way of the other.

(*d*) When both are running free with the wind on the same side, the vessel which is to the windward shall keep out of the way of the vessel which is to leeward.

(*e*) A vessel which has the wind aft shall keep out of the way of the other vessel.

ART. 18. When two steam vessels are meeting end on or nearly end on, so as to involve risk of collision, each shall alter her course to starboard, so that each may pass on the port side of the other.

This article only applies to cases where vessels are meeting end on or nearly end on in such a manner as to involve risk of collision, and does not apply to two vessels which must, if both keep on their respective courses, pass clear of each other.

The only cases to which it does apply are when each of the two vessels is end on or nearly end on to the other; in other words, to cases in which by day each vessel sees the masts of the other in a line or nearly in a line with her own, and by night to cases in which each vessel is in such a position as to see both the side lights of the other.

It does not apply by day to cases in which a vessel sees another ahead crossing her own course, or by night to cases where the red light of one vessel is opposed to the red light of the other, or where the green light of one vessel is opposed to the green light of the other, or where a red light without a green light or a green light without a red light is seen ahead, or where both green and red lights are seen anywhere but ahead.

ART. 19. When two steam vessels are crossing, so as to involve risk of collision, the vessel which has the other on her own starboard side shall keep out of the way of the other.

ART. 20. When a steam vessel and a sailing vessel are proceeding in such directions as to involve risk of collision, the steam vessel shall keep out of the way of the sailing vessel.

ART. 21. Where by any of these rules one of two vessels is to keep out of the way, the other shall keep her course and speed.

ART. 22. Every vessel which is directed by these rules to keep out of the way of another vessel shall, if the circumstances of the case admit, avoid crossing ahead of the other.

ART. 23. Every steam vessel which is directed by these rules to keep out of the way of another vessel shall on approaching her, if necessary, slacken her speed or stop or reverse.

ART. 24. Notwithstanding anything contained in these rules every vessel overtaking any other shall keep out of the way of the overtaken vessel.

Every vessel coming up with another vessel from any direction more than 2 points abaft her beam—that is, in such a position with reference to the vessel which she is overtaking that at night she would be unable to see either of that vessel's side lights—shall be deemed to be an overtaking vessel, and no subsequent alteration of the bearing between the two vessels shall make the overtaking vessel a crossing vessel within the meaning of these rules or relieve her of the duty of keeping clear of the overtaken vessel until she is finally past and clear.

As by day the overtaking vessel can not always know with certainty whether she is forward of or abaft this direction from the other vessel, she should if in doubt assume that she is an overtaking vessel and keep out of the way.

ART. 25. In narrow channels every steam vessel shall, when it is safe and practicable, keep to that side of the fairway or mid-channel which lies on the starboard side of such vessel.

ART. 26. Sailing vessels under way shall keep out of the way of sailing vessels or boats fishing with nets or lines or trawls. This rule shall not give to any vessel or boat engaged in fishing the right of obstructing a fairway used by vessels other than fishing vessels or boats.

ART. 27. In obeying and construing these rules due regard shall be had to all dangers of navigation and collision and to any special circumstances which may render a departure from the above rules necessary in order to avoid immediate danger.

SOUND SIGNALS FOR VESSELS IN SIGHT OF ONE ANOTHER.

ART. 28. The words "short blast" used in this article shall mean a blast of about one second's duration.

When vessels are in sight of one another, a steam vessel under way in taking any course authorized or required by these rules shall indicate that course by the following signals on her whistle or siren, namely:

One short blast to mean, "I am directing my course to starboard."

Two short blasts to mean, "I am directing my course to port."

Three short blasts to mean, "My engines are going at full speed astern."

NO VESSEL UNDER ANY CIRCUMSTANCES TO NEGLECT PROPER PRECAUTIONS.

ART. 29. Nothing in these rules shall exonerate any vessel or the owner or master or crew thereof from the consequences of any neglect to carry lights or signals, or of any neglect to keep a proper lookout, or of the neglect of any precaution which may be required by the ordinary practice of seamen or by the special circumstances of the case.

RESERVATION OF RULES FOR HARBORS AND INLAND NAVIGATION.

ART. 30. Nothing in these rules shall interfere with the operation of a special rule duly made by local authority relative to the navigation of any harbor, river, or inland waters.

DISTRESS SIGNALS.

ART. 31. When a vessel is in distress and requires assistance from other vessels or from the shore, the following shall be the signals to be used or displayed by her either together or separately, namely:

In the daytime—

First. A gun fired at intervals of about a minute.

Second. The international code signal of distress indicated by N C.

Third. The distance signal, consisting of a square flag, having either above or below it a ball or anything resembling a ball.

Fourth. Rockets or shells as prescribed below for use at night.

Fifth. A continuous sounding with any fog-signal apparatus.

At night—

First. A gun fired at intervals of about a minute.

Second. Flames on the vessel (as from a burning tar barrel, oil barrel, etc.).

Third. Rockets or shells bursting in the air with a loud report and throwing stars of any color or description, fired one at a time at short intervals.

Fourth. A continuous sounding with any fog-signal apparatus.

SEC. 2. That all laws or parts of laws inconsistent with the foregoing regulations for preventing collisions at sea, for the navigation of all public and private vessels of the United States upon the high seas and in all waters connected therewith navigable by seagoing vessels, are hereby repealed.

SEC. 3. That this act shall take effect at a time to be fixed by the President by proclamation issued for that purpose.

And whereas an act of Congress entitled "An act to amend an act approved August 19, 1890, entitled 'An act to adopt regulations for preventing collisions at sea,'" was approved May 28, 1894, the said act being in the following words:

Be it enacted by the Senate and House of Representatives of the United States of America in Congress assembled, That article 7 of the act approved August 19, 1890, entitled "An act to adopt regulations for preventing collisions at sea," be amended to read as follows:

"ART. 7. Steam vessels of less than 40 and vessels under oars or sails of less than 20 tons gross tonnage, respectively, and rowing boats, when under way, shall not be required to carry the lights mentioned in article 2 (*a*), (*b*), and (*c*), but if they do not carry them they shall be provided with the following lights:

"First. Steam vessels of less than 40 tons shall carry—

"(*a*) In the fore part of the vessel or on or in front of the funnel, where it can best be seen, and at a height above the gunwale of not less than 9 feet, a bright white light constructed and fixed as prescribed in article 2 (*a*) and of such a character as to be visible at a distance of at least 2 miles.

"(*b*) Green and red side lights constructed and fixed as prescribed in article 2 (*b*) and (*c*) and of such a character as to be visible at a distance of at least 1 mile, or a combined lantern showing a green light and a red light from right ahead to 2 points abaft the beam on their respective sides. Such lanterns shall be carried not less than 3 feet below the white light.

"Second. Small steamboats, such as are carried by seagoing vessels, may carry the white light at a less height than 9 feet above the gunwale, but it shall be carried above the combined lantern mentioned in subdivision 1 (*b*).

"Third. Vessels under oars or sails of less than 20 tons shall have ready at hand a lantern with a green glass on one side and a red glass on the other, which on the approach of or to other vessels shall be exhibited, in sufficient time to prevent collision, so that the green light shall not be seen on the port side nor the red light on the starboard side.

"Fourth. Rowing boats, whether under oars or sail, shall have ready at hand a lantern showing a white light, which shall be temporarily exhibited in sufficient time to prevent collision.

"The vessels referred to in this article shall not be obliged to carry the lights prescribed by article 4 (*a*) and article 11, last paragraph."

That article 9 be hereby repealed.

That article 21 be amended to read as follows:

"ART. 21. Where by any of these rules one of two vessels is to keep out of the way the other shall keep her course and speed.

"NOTE.—When in consequence of thick weather or other causes such vessel finds herself so close that collision can not be avoided by the action of the giving-way vessel alone, she also shall take such action as will best aid to avert collision." (See articles 27 and 29.)

That article 31 be amended to read as follows:

"DISTRESS SIGNALS.

"ART. 31. When a vessel is in distress and requires assistance from other vessels or from the shore, the following shall be the signals to be used or displayed by her, either together or separately, namely:

"In the daytime—

"First. A gun or other explosive signal fired at intervals of about a minute.

"Second. The international code signal of distress indicated by N C.

"Third. The distance signal, consisting of a square flag, having either above or below it a ball or anything resembling a ball.

"Fourth. A continuous sounding with any fog-signal apparatus.

"At night—

"First. A gun or other explosive signal fired at intervals of about a minute.

"Second. Flames on the vessel (as from a burning tar barrel, oil barrel, etc.).

"Third. Rockets or shells throwing stars of any color or description, fired one at a time at short intervals.

"Fourth. A continuous sounding with any fog-signal apparatus."

And whereas it was provided by section 3 of the said act of August 19, 1890, that it should take effect at a time to be fixed by the President by proclamation issued for that purpose; and

Whereas the President did, in virtue of the authority vested in him by the said section 3 of the act of August 19, 1890, issue a proclamation on the 13th day of July, 1894,* declaring the 1st day of March, 1895, as the day on which the said act approved August 19, 1890, as amended by the act approved May 28, 1894, should take effect; and

Whereas an act of Congress entitled "An act relating to lights on fishing vessels" was approved August 13, 1894, the said act being in the following words:

Be it enacted by the Senate and House of Representatives of the United States of America in Congress assembled, That article 10 of the act approved March 3, 1885, entitled "An act to adopt the 'Revised international regulations for preventing collisions at sea,'" so far as said article relates to lights for fishing vessels, is hereby reenacted and continued in force, anything in the act approved May 28, 1894, entitled "An act to amend an act approved August 19, 1890, entitled 'An act to adopt regulations for preventing collisions at sea,'" to the contrary notwithstanding.

And whereas the said article of the act approved March 3, 1885, entitled "An act to adopt the 'Revised international regulations for preventing collisions at sea,'" reenacted by the said act of August 13, 1894, is as follows:

ART. 10. Open boats and fishing vessels of less than 20 tons net registered tonnage when under way and when not having their nets, trawls, dredges, or lines in the water shall not be obliged to carry the colored side lights; but every such boat and vessel shall in lieu thereof have ready at hand a lantern with a green glass on the one side and a red glass on the other side, and on approaching to or being approached by another vessel such lantern shall be exhibited, in sufficient time to prevent collision, so that the green light shall not be seen on the port side nor the red light on the starboard side.

The following portion of this article applies only to fishing vessels and boats when in the sea off the coast of Europe lying north of Cape Finisterre:

(*a*) All fishing vessels and fishing boats of 20 tons net registered tonnage or upward when under way and when not having their nets, trawls, dredges, or lines in the water shall carry and show the same lights as other vessels under way.

(*b*) All vessels when engaged in fishing with drift nets shall exhibit two white lights from any part of the vessel where they can be best seen. Such lights shall be placed so that the vertical distance between them shall be not less than 6 feet and not more than 10 feet and so that the horizontal distance between them measured in a line with the keel of the vessel shall be not less than 5 feet and not more than 10 feet. The lower of these two lights shall be the more forward, and both of them shall be of such a character and contained in lanterns of such construction as to show all round the horizon on a dark night with a clear atmosphere for a distance of not less than 3 miles.

(*c*) All vessels when trawling, dredging, or fishing with any kind of dragnets shall exhibit from some part of the vessel where they can be best seen two lights. One of these lights shall be red and the other shall be white. The red light shall be above the white light and shall be at a vertical distance from it of not less than 6 feet and not more than 12 feet, and the horizontal distance between them, if any, shall not be more than 10 feet. These two lights shall be of such a character and contained in lanterns of such construction as to be visible all round the horizon on a dark night with a clear atmosphere, the white light to a distance of not less than 3 miles and the red light of not less than 2 miles.

(*d*) A vessel employed in line fishing with her lines out shall carry the same lights as a vessel when engaged in fishing with drift nets.

(*e*) If a vessel when fishing with a trawl, dredge, or any kind of dragnet becomes stationary in consequence of her gear getting fast to a rock or other obstruction, she shall show the light and make the fog signal for a vessel at anchor.

(*f*) Fishing vessels and open boats may at any time use a flare-up in addition to the lights which they are by this article required to carry and show. All flare-up lights exhibited by a vessel when trawling, dredging, or fishing with any kind of dragnet shall be shown at the after part of the vessel, excepting that if the vessel is hanging by the stern to her trawl, dredge, or dragnet they shall be exhibited from the bow.

(*g*) Every fishing vessel and every open boat when at anchor between sunset and sunrise shall exhibit a white light visible all round the horizon at a distance of at least 1 mile.

(*h*) In a fog a drift-net vessel attached to her nets, and a vessel when trawling, dredging, or fishing with any kind of dragnet, and a vessel employed in line fishing with her lines out shall at intervals of not more than two minutes make a blast with her fog horn and ring her bell alternately.

And whereas an act of Congress entitled "An act to postpone the enforcement of the act of August 19, 1890, entitled 'An act to adopt regulations for preventing collisions at sea,'" was approved February 23, 1895, the said act being in the following words:

Whereas the President, in accordance with the proposition of Great Britain to enforce on March 1, 1895, the "Revised international regulations for preventing collisions at sea," and on the representations of that Government that those regulations had received the general approval of the several foreign maritime powers, pursuant to section 3 of the act of August 19, 1890, entitled "An act to adopt regulations for preventing collisions at sea," issued on July 13, 1894, his proclamation* fixing March 1, 1895, as the time when the provisions of said act, as amended, embodying said revised international regulations, shall take effect; and

Whereas the Government of Great Britain has withdrawn from the position communicated to this Government on April 25, 1894, that no time should be lost in carrying those regulations into effect, and on January 16, 1895, announced to this Government that the Government of Great Britain now finds it impossible until Parliament has been consulted to fix a date for bringing the regulations into force, and earnestly requests this Government to consent to a temporary postponement of the enforcement of said regulations; and

Whereas it is desirable that the "Revised international regulations for preventing collisions at sea" shall be put into force simultaneously by the maritime powers: Therefore,

Be it enacted by the Senate and House of Representatives of the United States of America in Congress assembled, That said act of August 19, 1890, take effect not on March 1, 1895, but at a subsequent time, to be fixed by the President by proclamation issued for that purpose.

And whereas the President did, in virtue of the authority vested in him by the said act of February 23, 1895, issue a proclamation on the 25th day of February, 1895,† giving notice that the said act of August 19, 1890, as amended by the act of May 28, 1894, would not go into force on March 1, 1895, the date fixed in his said proclamation of July 13, 1894,* but on such future date as might be designated in a proclamation of the President to be issued for that purpose; and

Whereas an act of Congress entitled "An act to amend an act approved August 19, 1890, entitled 'An act to adopt regulations for preventing collisions at sea,'" was approved June 10, 1896, the said act being in the following words:

Be it enacted by the Senate and House of Representatives of the United States of America in Congress assembled, That article 15 of the act approved August 19, 1890, entitled "An act to adopt regulations for preventing collisions at sea," be amended to read as follows:

"ART. 15. All signals prescribed by this article for vessels under way shall be given—

"First. By 'steam vessels,' on the whistle or siren.

"Second. By 'sailing vessels' and 'vessels towed,' on the fog horn.

"The words 'prolonged blast' used in this article shall mean a blast of from four to six seconds' duration.

"A steam vessel shall be provided with an efficient whistle or siren, sounded by steam or some substitute for steam, so placed that the sound may not be intercepted by any obstruction, and with an efficient fog horn to be sounded by mechanical means, and also with an efficient bell. (In all cases where the rules require a bell to be used a drum may be substituted on board Turkish vessels or a gong where such articles are used on board small seagoing vessels.) A sailing vessel of 20 tons gross tonnage or upward shall be provided with a similar fog horn and bell.

"In fog, mist, falling snow, or heavy rain storms, whether by day or night, the signals described in this article shall be used as follows, namely:

"(*a*) A steam vessel having way upon her shall sound at intervals of not more than two minutes a prolonged blast.

*See pp. 501–510.   †See p. 584.

"(b) A steam vessel under way, but stopped and having no way upon her, shall sound at intervals of not more than two minutes two prolonged blasts with an interval of about one second between.

"(c) A sailing vessel under way shall sound at intervals of not more than one minute, when on the starboard tack one blast, when on the port tack two blasts in succession, and when with the wind abaft the beam three blasts in succession.

"(d) A vessel when at anchor shall at intervals of not more than one minute ring the bell rapidly for about five seconds.

"(e) A vessel when towing, a vessel employed in laying or in picking up a telegraph cable, and a vessel under way which is unable to get out of the way of an approaching vessel through being not under command or unable to maneuver as required by the rules shall, instead of the signals prescribed in subdivisions (a) and (c) of this article, at intervals of not more than two minutes sound three blasts in succession, namely, one prolonged blast followed by two short blasts. A vessel towed may give this signal, and she shall not give any other.

"Sailing vessels and boats of less than 20 tons gross tonnage shall not be obliged to give the above-mentioned signals, but if they do not they shall make some other efficient sound signal at intervals of not more than one minute."

SEC. 2. That said act of August 19, 1890, as amended, shall take effect at a subsequent time to be fixed by the President by proclamation issued for that purpose.

And whereas it was provided by section 2 of the act approved June 10, 1896, that the said act of August 19, 1890, as amended should take effect at a subsequent time to be fixed by the President by proclamation issued for that purpose:

Now, therefore, I, Grover Cleveland, President of the United States of America, do hereby, in virtue of the authority vested in me by section 3 of the act of August 19, 1890, and by section 2 of the act of June 10, 1896, proclaim the 1st day of July, 1897, as the day on which the said act approved August 19, 1890, as amended by the act approved May 28, 1894, by the act approved August 13, 1894, and by the act approved June 10, 1896, shall take effect.

In testimony whereof I have hereunto set my hand and caused the seal of the United States of America to be affixed.

[SEAL.]   Done at the city of Washington, this 31st day of December, 1896, and of the Independence of the United States the one hundred and twenty-first.   GROVER CLEVELAND.

By the President:

RICHARD OLNEY, *Secretary of State.*

BY THE PRESIDENT OF THE UNITED STATES OF AMERICA.

A PROCLAMATION.

Whereas it is provided by section 24 of the act of Congress approved March 3, 1891, entitled "An act to repeal timber-culture laws, and for other purposes" —

That the President of the United States may from time to time set apart and reserve in any State or Territory having public land bearing forests, in any part of the public lands wholly or in part covered with timber or undergrowth, whether of commercial value or not, as public reservations; and the President shall by public proclamation declare the establishment of such reservations and the limits thereof.

And whereas the public lands in the State of Utah within the limits hereinafter described are in part covered with timber, and it appears that the public good would be promoted by setting apart and reserving said lands as a public reservation:

Now, therefore, I, Grover Cleveland, President of the United States, by virtue of the power in me vested by section 24 of the aforesaid act of Congress, do hereby make known and proclaim that there is hereby reserved from entry or settlement and set apart as a public reservation all those certain tracts, pieces, or parcels of land lying and being situate in the State of Utah and within the boundaries particularly described as follows, to wit:

Beginning at the northwest corner of township one (1) south, range seven (7) east, Salt Lake meridian, Utah; thence easterly along the base line to the southeast corner of township one (1) north, range eight (8) east; thence northerly along the range line to the northeast corner of said township; thence easterly along the township line between townships one (1) and two (2) north to the southeast corner of township two (2) north, range thirteen (13) east; thence northerly along the range line to the northeast corner of said township; thence easterly along the surveyed and unsurveyed township line between townships two (2) and three (3) north to its point of intersection with the Green River; thence in a southeasterly direction along the middle of the channel of said river to the point for the unsurveyed range line between ranges twenty-two (22) and twenty-three (23) east; thence southerly along the unsurveyed and surveyed range line between said ranges to the point for the southeast corner of township two (2) south, range twenty-two (22) east; thence westerly along the unsurveyed and surveyed township line between townships two (2) and three (3) south to the northwest corner of township three (3) south, range nineteen (19) east; thence southerly along the west boundary of said township to its intersection with the east boundary of the Uintah Indian Reservation; thence northwesterly along said Indian-reservation boundary to the northeast corner of said reservation; thence southwesterly along the north boundary of said Indian reservation to the intersection therewith by the range line between ranges six (6) and seven (7) east; thence northerly along said range line, surveyed and unsurveyed, to the northwest corner of township one (1) south, range seven (7) east, the place of beginning.

Excepting from the force and effect of this proclamation all lands which may have been prior to the date hereof embraced in any legal entry or covered by any lawful filing duly of record in the proper United States land office, or upon which any valid settlement has been made pursuant to law and the statutory period within which to make entry or filing of record has not expired, and all mining claims duly located and held according to the laws of the United States and rules and regulations not in conflict therewith.

Provided, That this exception shall not continue to apply to any particular tract of land unless the entryman, settler, or claimant continues to comply with the law under which the entry, filing, settlement, or location was made.

Warning is hereby expressly given to all persons not to enter or make settlement upon the tract of land reserved by this proclamation.

In witness whereof I have hereunto set my hand and caused the seal of the United States to be affixed.

[SEAL.]   Done at the city of Washington, this 22d day of February, A. D. 1897, and of the Independence of the United States the one hundred and twenty-first.

GROVER CLEVELAND.

By the President:

RICHARD OLNEY, *Secretary of State.*

BY THE PRESIDENT OF THE UNITED STATES OF AMERICA.

A PROCLAMATION.

Whereas it is provided by section 24 of the act of Congress approved March 3, 1891, entitled "An act to repeal timber-culture laws, and for other purposes"—

That the President of the United States may from time to time set apart and reserve in any State or Territory having public land bearing forests, in any part of the public lands wholly or in part covered with timber or undergrowth, whether of commercial value or not, as public reservations; and the President shall by public proclamation declare the establishment of such reservations and the limits thereof.

And whereas the public lands in the State of California within the limits hereinafter described are in part covered with timber, and it appears that the public good would be promoted by setting apart and reserving said lands as a public reservation:

Now, therefore, I, Grover Cleveland, President of the United States, by virtue of the power in me vested by section 24 of the aforesaid act of Congress, do hereby make known and proclaim that there is hereby reserved from entry or settlement and set apart as a public reservation all those certain tracts, pieces, or parcels of land lying and being situate in the State of California and within the boundaries particularly described as follows, to wit:

Beginning at the southeast corner of township eight (8) south, range eight (8) east, San Bernardino base and meridian, California; thence northerly along the range line to the northeast corner of said township; thence westerly along the township line to the southwest corner of township seven (7) south, range eight (8) east; thence northerly along the range line to the northwest corner of said township; thence westerly along the township line to the southwest corner of township six (6) south, range seven (7) east; thence northerly along the range line to the northwest corner of said township; thence westerly along the unsurveyed and surveyed township line to the southwest corner of township five (5) south, range six (6) east; thence northerly along the range line to the northwest corner of said township; thence westerly along the first (1st) standard parallel south to the southwest corner of township four (4) south, range four (4) east; thence northerly along the range line to the northwest corner of said township; thence westerly along the unsurveyed and surveyed township line between townships three (3) and four (4) south to its intersection with the east boundary line of the "Rancho San Jacinto Neuvo y Potrero;" thence southeasterly along the boundary line of said rancho and the boundary line of "Rancho San Jacinto Viejo" to the most southeasterly point of said last-named rancho; thence westerly along the south boundary of said "Rancho San Jacinto Viejo" to the point of intersection by the section line between sections fifteen (15) and sixteen (16), township five (5) south, range one (1) east; thence southerly along the section line to the southwest corner of section thirty-four (34), township six (6) south, range one (1) east; thence easterly along the township line to the northwest corner of township seven (7) south, range two (2) east; thence southerly along the range line between ranges one (1) and two (2) east to the southwest corner of township eight (8) south, range two (2) east; thence along the second (2d) standard parallel south to the northwest corner of township nine (9) south, range two (2) east; thence southerly along the range line to the southwest corner of said township; thence easterly along the township line between townships nine (9) and ten (10) south to the southeast corner of township nine (9) south, range four (4) east; thence northerly along the range line to the northeast corner of said township; thence easterly along the second (2d) standard parallel south to the northwest corner of township nine (9) south, range seven (7) east; thence southerly along the range line to the southwest corner of section eighteen (18), said township; thence easterly along the section line to the southeast corner of section thirteen (13), said township; thence southerly along the range line between ranges seven (7) and eight (8) east to the southwest corner of township ten (10) south, range eight (8) east; thence easterly along the township line to the southeast corner of said township; thence northerly along the range line between ranges eight (8) and nine (9) east to the northeast corner of township nine (9) south, range eight (8) east; thence westerly along the second (2d) standard parallel south to the southeast corner of township eight (8) south, range eight (8) east, the place of beginning.

Excepting from the force and effect of this proclamation all irrigation rights and lands lawfully acquired therefor and all lands which may have been prior to the date hereof embraced in any legal entry or covered by any lawful filing duly of record in the proper United States land office, or upon which any valid settlement has been made pursuant to law and the statutory period within which to make entry or filing of record has not expired, and all mining claims duly located and held according to the laws of the United States and rules and regulations not in conflict therewith.

Provided, That this exception shall not continue to apply to any particular tract of land unless the entryman, settler, or claimant continues to comply with the law under which the entry, filing, settlement, or location was made.

Warning is hereby expressly given to all persons not to enter or make settlement upon the tract of land reserved by this proclamation.

In witness whereof I have hereunto set my hand and caused the seal of the United States to be affixed.

[SEAL.]   Done at the city of Washington, this 22d day of February, A. D. 1897, and of the Independence of the United States the one hundred and twenty-first.

GROVER CLEVELAND.

By the President:

RICHARD OLNEY,
Secretary of State.

BY THE PRESIDENT OF THE UNITED STATES OF AMERICA.

A PROCLAMATION.

Whereas it is provided by section 24 of the act of Congress approved March 3, 1891, entitled "An act to repeal timber-culture laws, and for other purposes"—

That the President of the United States may from time to time set apart and reserve in any State or Territory having public land bearing forests, in any part of the public lands wholly or in part covered with timber or undergrowth, whether of commercial value or not, as public reservations; and the President shall by public proclamation declare the establishment of such reservations and the limits thereof.

And whereas the public lands in the State of Washington within the limits hereinafter described are in part covered with timber, and it appears that the public good would be promoted by setting apart and reserving said lands as a public reservation:

Now, therefore, I, Grover Cleveland, President of the United States, by virtue of the power in me vested by section 24 of the aforesaid act of Congress, do hereby make known and proclaim that there is hereby reserved from entry or settlement and set apart as a public reservation all those certain tracts, pieces, or parcels of land lying and being situate in the State of Washington and within the boundaries particularly described as follows, to wit:

Beginning at the southeast corner of township four (4) north, range nine (9) east, Willamette base and meridian, Washington; thence northerly along the range line between ranges nine (9) and (10) east, subject to the proper offset on the first (1st) standard parallel north to the northwest corner of township six (6) north, range ten (10) east; thence easterly along the township line to the northeast corner of said township; thence northerly along the range line to the northwest corner of township seven (7) north, range eleven (11) east; thence easterly along the township line between townships seven (7) and eight (8) north to the northeast corner of township seven (7) north, range twelve (12) east; thence northerly along the surveyed and unsurveyed range line between ranges twelve (12) and thirteen (13) east, subject to the proper offset on the second (2d) standard parallel north, to the northwest corner of township (11) north, range thirteen (13) east; thence easterly along the surveyed and unsurveyed township line between townships eleven (11) and twelve (12) north to the southwest corner of township twelve (12) north, range (15) east; thence northerly along the surveyed and unsurveyed range line between ranges fourteen (14) and fifteen (15) east, subject to the proper offsets on the third (3d) and fourth (4th) standard parallels north to the point for the northeast corner of township eighteen (18) north, range fourteen (14) east; thence westerly along the unsurveyed and surveyed township line between townships eighteen (18) and nineteen (19) north to the southwest corner of township nineteen (19) north, range seven (7) east; thence southerly along the surveyed and unsurveyed range line between ranges six (6) and seven (7) east, subject to the proper offsets on the township line between townships seventeen (17) and eighteen (18) north and on the fourth (4th), third (3d), and second (2d) standard parallels north, to the point for the northeast corner of township five (5) north, range six (6) east; thence westerly along the unsurveyed township line between townships five (5) and (6) north to the southeast corner of township six (6) north, range four (4) east; thence southerly along the unsurveyed range line between ranges four (4) and five (5) east, subject to the proper offset on the first (1st) standard parallel north, to the point for the southwest corner of township four (4) north, range five (5) east; thence easterly along the unsurveyed and surveyed township line between townships three (3) and four (4) north to the southeast corner of township four (4) north, range nine (9) east, the place of beginning.

Excepting from the force and effect of this proclamation all lands which may have been prior to the date hereof embraced in any legal entry or covered by any lawful filing duly of record in the proper United States land office, or upon which any valid settlement has been made pursuant to law and the statutory period within which to make entry or filing of record has not expired, and all mining claims duly located and held according to the laws of the United States and rules and regulations not in conflict therewith.

Provided, That this exception shall not continue to apply to any particular tract of land unless the entryman, settler, or claimant continues to comply with the law under which the entry, filing, settlement, or location was made.

Warning is hereby expressly given to all persons not to enter or make settlement upon the tract of land reserved by this proclamation.

Whereas a portion of the land embraced within the limits above described was reserved by proclamation of February 20, 1893, and designated as "The Pacific Forest Reserve," and whereas it appearing proper that the entire area herein described should be distinguished by the name of the most notable landmark within its boundaries, the title "The Pacific Forest Reserve" is hereby abolished, and the reservation established by this proclamation shall be known as "The Mount Rainier Forest Reserve."

In witness whereof I have hereunto set my hand and caused the seal of the United States to be affixed.

[SEAL.]   Done at the city of Washington, this 22d day of February, A. D. 1897, and of the Independence of the United States the one hundred and twenty-first.

GROVER CLEVELAND.

By the President:

RICHARD OLNEY,
Secretary of State.

BY THE PRESIDENT OF THE UNITED STATES OF AMERICA.

A PROCLAMATION.

Whereas it is provided by section 24 of the act of Congress approved March 3, 1891, entitled "An act to repeal timber-culture laws, and for other purposes"—

That the President of the United States may from time to time set apart and reserve in any State or Territory having public land bearing forests, in any part of the public lands wholly or in part covered with timber or undergrowth, whether of commercial value or not, as public reservations; and the President shall by public proclamation declare the establishment of such reservations and the limits thereof.

And whereas the public lands in the State of California within the limits hereinafter described are in part covered with timber, and it appears that the public good would be promoted by setting apart and reserving said lands as a public reservation:

Now, therefore, I, Grover Cleveland, President of the United States, by virtue of the power in me vested by section 24 of the aforesaid act of Congress, do hereby make known and proclaim that there is hereby reserved from entry or settlement and set apart as a public reservation all those certain tracts, pieces, or parcels of land lying and being situate in the State of California and within the boundaries particularly described as follows, to wit:

Beginning at the southeast corner of township three (3) north, range twenty-four (24) east, Mount Diablo base and meridian, California; thence northerly along the range line to the northeast corner of said township; thence westerly along the township line to the northwest corner of said township; thence northerly along the range line to the township line between townships four (4) and five (5) north, range twenty-three (23) east; thence easterly along the township line to the southeast corner of township five (5) north, range twenty-three (23) east; thence northerly along the range line to the northeast corner of said township; thence westerly along the first (1st) standard parallel north to the southwest corner of township six (6) north, range twenty-two (22) east; thence northerly along the range line between ranges twenty-one (21) and twenty-two (22) east to the northeast corner of township seven (7) north, range twenty-one (21) east; thence westerly along the township line to the northwest corner of said township; thence northerly along the range line to the northeast corner of township eight (8) north, range twenty (20) east; thence westerly along the surveyed and unsurveyed township line between townships eight (8) and nine (9) north to the northwest corner of township eight (8) north, range seventeen (17) east; thence southerly along the range line to the southeast corner of township eight (8) north, range sixteen (16) east; thence easterly along the unsurveyed township line to the point for the southeast corner of township eight (8) north, range seventeen (17) east; thence southerly along the unsurveyed and surveyed range line between ranges seventeen (17) and eighteen (18) east, subject to the easterly offset on the first (1st) standard parallel north, to the southeast corner of township four (4) north, range seventeen (17) east; thence easterly along the township line to the northeast corner of township three (3) north, range eighteen (18) east; thence southerly along the range line to the southeast corner of said township; thence easterly along the township line between townships two (2) and three (3) north to the southeast corner of township three (3) north, range twenty-four (24) east, the place of beginning.

Excepting from the force and effect of this proclamation all lands which may have been prior to the date hereof embraced in any legal entry or covered by any lawful filing duly of record in the proper United States land office, or upon which any valid settlement has been made pursuant to law and the statutory period within which to make entry or filing of record has not expired, and all mining claims duly located and held according to the laws of the United States and rules and regulations not in conflict therewith.

Provided, That this exception shall not continue to apply to any particular tract of land unless the entryman, settler, or claimant continues to comply with the law under which the entry, filing, settlement, or location was made.

Warning is hereby expressly given to all persons not to enter or make settlement upon the tract of land reserved by this proclamation.

In witness whereof I have hereunto set my hand and caused the seal of the United States to be affixed.

[SEAL.] Done at the city of Washington, this 22d day of February, A. D. 1897, and of the Independence of the United States the one hundred and twenty-first.

GROVER CLEVELAND.

By the President:
RICHARD OLNEY,
Secretary of State.

BY THE PRESIDENT OF THE UNITED STATES OF AMERICA.

A PROCLAMATION.

Whereas it is provided by section 24 of the act of Congress approved March 3, 1891, entitled "An act to repeal timber-culture laws, and for other purposes"—

That the President of the United States may from time to time set apart and reserve in any State or Territory having public land bearing forests, in any part of the public lands wholly or in part covered with timber or undergrowth, whether of commercial value or not, as public reservations; and the President shall by public proclamation declare the establishment of such reservations and the limits thereof.

And whereas the public lands in the States of Idaho and Montana within the limits hereinafter described are in part covered with timber, and it appears that the public good would be promoted by setting apart and reserving said lands as a public reservation:

Now, therefore, I, Grover Cleveland, President of the United States, by virtue of the power in me vested by section 24 of the aforesaid act of Congress, do hereby make known and proclaim that there is hereby reserved from entry or settlement and set apart as a public reservation all those certain tracts, pieces, or parcels of land lying and being situate in the States of Idaho and Montana and within the boundaries particularly described as follows, to wit:

Beginning at the northeast corner of township thirty-six (36) north, range five (5) east, Boise meridian, Idaho; thence southerly along the surveyed and unsurveyed range line between ranges five (5) and six (6) east to the point of intersection with the Salmon River; thence in an easterly direction along the middle of the channel of said river to the point of intersection for the unsurveyed range line between ranges eighteen (18) and nineteen (19) east; thence northerly along said unsurveyed range line to the point of intersection with the boundary line between the States of Idaho and Montana; thence in an easterly direction along said State boundary line to the point for the unsurveyed range line between ranges nineteen (19) and twenty (20) west, principal meridian, Montana; thence northerly along said range line to the base line; thence westerly along said base line to the southeast corner of township one (1) north, range twenty (20) west; thence northerly along the range line to the northeast corner of said township; thence westerly along the surveyed and unsurveyed township line between townships one (1) and two (2) north to the point for the southeast corner of township two (2) north, range twenty-two (22) west; thence northerly along the unsurveyed range line between ranges twenty-one (21) and twenty-two (22) west, allowing for the proper offsets on the first (1st) and second (2d) standard parallels north, to the point for the northeast corner of township ten (10) north, range twenty-two (22) west; thence westerly along the unsurveyed township line between townships ten (10) and eleven (11) north to the point of intersection with the boundary line between the States of Montana and Idaho; thence along said State boundary line to the point for the unsurveyed township line between townships thirty-eight (38) and thirty-nine (39) north, Idaho; thence westerly along said township line to the point for the northwest corner of township thirty-eight (38) north, range ten (10) east; thence southerly along the unsurveyed range line between ranges nine (9) and ten (10) east to the point for the southwest corner of township thirty-seven (37) north, range ten (10) east; thence westerly along the unsurveyed seventh (7th) standard parallel north to the northeast corner of township thirty-six (36) north, range five (5) east, the place of beginning.

Excepting from the force and effect of this proclamation all lands which may have been prior to the date hereof embraced in any legal entry or covered by any lawful filing duly of record in the proper United States land office, or upon which any valid settlement has been made pursuant to law and the statutory period within which to make entry or filing of record has not expired, and all mining claims duly located and held according to the laws of the United States and rules and regulations not in conflict therewith.

Provided, That this exception shall not continue to apply to any particular tract of land unless the entryman, settler, or claimant continues to comply with the law under which the entry, filing, settlement, or location was made.

Warning is hereby expressly given to all persons not to enter or make settlement upon the tract of land reserved by this proclamation.

In witness whereof I have hereunto set my hand and caused the seal of the United States to be affixed.

[SEAL.]   Done at the city of Washington, this 22d day of February, A. D. 1897, and of the Independence of the United States the one hundred and twenty-first.

GROVER CLEVELAND.

By the President:

RICHARD OLNEY,
    Secretary of State.

BY THE PRESIDENT OF THE UNITED STATES OF AMERICA.

A PROCLAMATION.

Whereas it is provided by section 24 of the act of Congress approved March 3, 1891, entitled "An act to repeal timber-culture laws, and for other purposes"—

That the President of the United States may from time to time set apart and reserve in any State or Territory having public land bearing forests, in any part of the public lands wholly or in part covered with timber or undergrowth, whether of commercial value or not, as public reservations; and the President shall by public proclamation declare the establishment of such reservations and the limits thereof.

And whereas the public lands in the State of Washington within the limits hereinafter described are in part covered with timber, and it appears that the public good would be promoted by setting apart and reserving said lands as a public reservation:

Now, therefore, I, Grover Cleveland, President of the United States, by virtue of the power in me vested by section 24 of the aforesaid act of Congress, do hereby make known and proclaim that there is hereby reserved from entry or settlement and set apart as a public reservation all those certain tracts, pieces, or parcels of land lying and being situate in the State of Washington and within the boundaries particularly described as follows, to wit:

Beginning at the southeast corner of township twenty-one (21) north, range five (5) west, Willamette base and meridian, Washington; thence northerly along the surveyed and unsurveyed range line between ranges four (4) and five (5) west to the point for the northeast corner of township twenty-three (23) north, range five (5) west; thence easterly along the unsurveyed and surveyed township line to the point for the southeast corner of township twenty-four (24) north, range four (4) west; thence northerly along the unsurveyed range line to the point for the northeast corner of said township; thence easterly along the unsurveyed and surveyed sixth (6th) standard parallel north to the southeast corner of township twenty-five (25) north, range three (3) west; thence northerly along the surveyed and unsurveyed range line between ranges two (2) and three (3) west to the northeast corner of township twenty-nine (29) north, range three (3) west; thence westerly along the surveyed and unsurveyed seventh (7th) standard parallel north to the point for the southeast corner of township thirty (30) north, range nine (9) west; thence northerly along the unsurveyed and surveyed range line to the northeast corner of said township; thence westerly along the township line between townships thirty (30) and thirty-one (31) north to the northeast corner of township thirty (30) north, range fourteen (14) west; thence northerly along the range line to its intersection with the shore of the Strait of Juan de Fuca; thence northwesterly along said shore line to the east boundary of the Makah Indian Reservation; thence southerly along the east boundary to the southeast corner of said reservation and westerly along the south boundary thereof to the high-water mark on the Pacific coast; thence southerly along said coast line to the north boundary of the Quinaielt Indian Reservation; thence southeasterly along the north boundary to the eastern point of said reservation and southwesterly along the south boundary thereof to the point of intersection with the fifth (5th) standard parallel north; thence easterly along said parallel to the southeast corner of township twenty-one (21) north, range five (5) west, the place of beginning.

Excepting from the force and effect of this proclamation all lands which may have been prior to the date hereof embraced in any legal entry or covered by any lawful filing duly of record in the proper United States land office, or upon which any valid settlement has been made pursuant to law and the statutory period within which to make entry or filing of record has not expired, and all mining claims duly located and held according to the laws of the United States and rules and regulations not in conflict therewith.

Provided, That this exception shall not continue to apply to any particular tract of land unless the entryman, settler, or claimant continues to comply with the law under which the entry, filing, settlement, or location was made.

Warning is hereby expressly given to all persons not to enter or make settlement upon the tract of land reserved by this proclamation.

In witness whereof I have hereunto set my hand and caused the seal of the United States to be affixed.

[SEAL.]   Done at the city of Washington, this 22d day of February, A. D. 1897, and of the Independence of the United States the one hundred and twenty-first.

GROVER CLEVELAND.

By the President:
   RICHARD OLNEY,
     Secretary of State.

BY THE PRESIDENT OF THE UNITED STATES OF AMERICA.

A PROCLAMATION.

Whereas it is provided by section 24 of the act of Congress approved March 3, 1891, entitled "An act to repeal timber-culture laws, and for other purposes"—

That the President of the United States may from time to time set apart and reserve in any State or Territory having public land bearing forests, in any part of the public lands wholly or in part covered with timber or undergrowth, whether of commercial value or not, as public reservations; and the President shall by public proclamation declare the establishment of such reservations and the limits thereof.

And whereas the public lands in the State of South Dakota within the limits hereinafter described are in part covered with timber, and it appears that the public good would be promoted by setting apart and reserving said lands as a public reservation:

Now, therefore, I, Grover Cleveland, President of the United States, by virtue of the power in me vested by section 24 of the aforesaid act of Congress, do hereby make known and proclaim that there is hereby reserved from entry or settlement and set apart as a public reservation all those certain tracts, pieces, or parcels of land lying and being situate in the State of South Dakota and within the boundaries particularly described as follows, to wit:

Beginning at the northwest corner of township one (1) south, range seven (7) east, Black Hills meridian, South Dakota; thence westerly along the Black Hills base line to the southwest corner of township one (1) north, range six (6) east; thence northerly along the range line between ranges five (5) and six (6) east to the northwest corner of township two (2) north, range six (6) east; thence westerly along the unsurveyed township line between townships two (2) and three (3) north to the point of intersection with the boundary line between the States of South Dakota and Wyoming; thence southerly along said State boundary line to the point of intersection by the township line between townships six (6) and seven (7) south, Black Hills base line; thence easterly along said township line to the southwest corner of township six (6) south, range four (4) east; thence northerly along the range line to the northwest corner of said township; thence easterly along the township line between townships five (5) and six (6) south to the southwest corner of township five (5) south, range (6) east; thence northerly along the range line to the northwest corner of said township; thence easterly along the first (1st) standard parallel south to the southwest corner of township four (4) south, range seven (7) east; thence northerly along the range line between ranges six (6) and seven (7) east to the northwest corner of township one (1) south, range seven (7) east, the place of beginning.

Excepting from the force and effect of this proclamation all lands which may have been prior to the date hereof embraced in any legal entry or covered by any lawful filing duly of record in the proper United States land office, or upon which any valid settlement has been made pursuant to law and the statutory period within which to make entry or filing of record has not expired, and all mining claims duly located and held according to the laws of the United States and rules and regulations not in conflict therewith.

Provided, That this exception shall not continue to apply to any particular tract of land unless the entryman, settler, or claimant continues to comply with the law under which the entry, filing, settlement, or location was made.

Warning is hereby expressly given to all persons not to enter or make settlement upon the tract of land reserved by this proclamation.

In witness whereof I have hereunto set my hand and caused the seal of the United States to be affixed.

[SEAL.]   Done at the city of Washington, this 22d day of February, A. D. 1897, and of the Independence of the United States the one hundred and twenty-first.

GROVER CLEVELAND.

By the President:

RICHARD OLNEY,
Secretary of State.

BY THE PRESIDENT OF THE UNITED STATES OF AMERICA.

A PROCLAMATION.

Whereas it is provided by section 24 of the act of Congress approved March 3, 1891, entitled "An act to repeal timber-culture laws, and for other purposes"—

That the President of the United States may from time to time set apart and reserve in any State or Territory having public land bearing forests, in any part of the public lands wholly or in part covered with timber or undergrowth, whether of commercial value or not, as public reservations; and the President shall by public proclamation declare the establishment of such reservations and the limits thereof.

And whereas the public lands in the States of Idaho and Washington within the limits hereinafter described are in part covered with timber, and it appears that the public good would be promoted by setting apart and reserving said lands as a public reservation:

Now, therefore, I, Grover Cleveland, President of the United States, by virtue of the power in me vested by section 24 of the aforesaid act of Congress, do hereby make known and proclaim that there is hereby reserved from entry or settlement and set apart as a public reservation all that tract of land situate in the States of Idaho and Washington embraced within the following boundaries, to wit:

Bounded on the east by the summit of the ridges dividing the waters tributary to the Kootenai River and Priest Lake and River; on the west by the summit of the ridges dividing the waters tributary to the Pend Oreille River or Clark Fork of the Columbia River and Priest Lake and River; on the north by the international boundary line between the States of Idaho and Washington and the British possessions, connecting the east and west boundaries above described; on the south by the township line between townships fifty-six (56) and fifty-seven (57) north of the base line, Idaho, projected to connect the east and west boundaries above described.

Excepting from the force and effect of this proclamation all lands which may have been prior to the date hereof embraced in any legal entry or covered by any lawful filing duly of record in the proper United States land office, or upon which any valid settlement has been made pursuant to law and the statutory period within which to make entry or filing of record has not expired, and all mining claims duly located and held according to the laws of the United States and rules and regulations not in conflict therewith.

Provided, That this exception shall not continue to apply to any particular tract of land unless the entryman, settler, or claimant continues to comply with the law under which the entry, filing, settlement, or location was made.

Warning is hereby expressly given to all persons not to enter or make settlement upon the tract of land reserved by this proclamation.

In witness whereof I have hereunto set my hand and caused the seal of the United States to be affixed.

[SEAL.]   Done at the city of Washington, this 22d day of February, A. D. 1897, and of the Independence of the United States the one hundred and twenty-first.

By the President: GROVER CLEVELAND.

RICHARD OLNEY,
      Secretary of State.

BY THE PRESIDENT OF THE UNITED STATES OF AMERICA.

A PROCLAMATION.

Whereas it is provided by section 24 of the act of Congress approved March 3, 1891, entitled "An act to repeal timber-culture laws, and for other purposes"—

That the President of the United States may from time to time set apart and reserve in any State or Territory having public land bearing forests, in any part of the public lands wholly or in part covered with timber or undergrowth, whether of commercial value or not, as public reservations; and the President shall by public proclamation declare the establishment of such reservations and the limits thereof.

And whereas the public lands in the State of Washington within the limits hereinafter described are in part covered with timber, and it appears that the public good would be promoted by setting apart and reserving said lands as a public reservation:

Now, therefore, I, Grover Cleveland, President of the United States, by virtue of the power in me vested by section 24 of the aforesaid act of Congress, do hereby make known and proclaim that there is hereby reserved from entry or settlement and set apart as a public reservation all those certain tracts, pieces, or parcels of land lying and being situate in the State of Washington and within the boundaries particularly described as follows, to wit:

Beginning at the point for the southwest corner of township twenty-nine (29) north, range eight (8) east, Willamette meridian, Washington;

thence northerly along the unsurveyed range line between ranges seven (7) and eight (8) east to the point for the northwest corner of township thirty-two (32) north, range eight (8) east; thence easterly along the unsurveyed eighth (8th) standard parallel north to the point for the southwest corner of township thirty-three (33) north, range twelve (12) east; thence northerly along the unsurveyed range line between ranges eleven (11) and twelve (12) east to the point for the northwest corner of township thirty-six (36) north, range twelve (12) east; thence westerly along the unsurveyed ninth (9th) standard parallel north to the point for the southwest corner of township thirty-seven (37) north, range seven (7) east; thence northerly along the unsurveyed range line between ranges six (6) and seven (7) east to its point of intersection with the international boundary line between the State of Washington and the British possessions; thence easterly along said international boundary line to the point for the unsurveyed range line between ranges twenty-two (22) and twenty-three (23) east; thence southerly along said unsurveyed range line, subject to the proper easterly or westerly offsets on the ninth (9th) and eighth (8th) standard parallels north, to the point for the southeast corner of township twenty-nine (29) north, range twenty-two (22) east; thence westerly along the unsurveyed and surveyed seventh (7th) standard parallel north to the point for the southwest corner of township twenty-nine (29) north, range (8) east, the place of beginning.

Excepting from the force and effect of this proclamation all lands which may have been prior to the date hereof embraced in any legal entry or covered by any lawful filing duly of record in the proper United States land office, or upon which any valid settlement has been made pursuant to law and the statutory period within which to make entry or filing of record has not expired, and all mining claims duly located and held according to the laws of the United States and rules and regulations not in conflict therewith.

Provided, That this exception shall not continue to apply to any particular tract of land unless the entryman, settler, or claimant continues to comply with the law under which the entry, filing, settlement, or location was made.

Warning is hereby expressly given to all persons not to enter or make settlement upon the tract of land reserved by this proclamation.

In witness whereof I have hereunto set my hand and caused the seal of the United States to be affixed.

[SEAL.] Done at the city of Washington, this 22d day of February, A. D. 1897, and of the Independence of the United States the one hundred and twenty-first.

GROVER CLEVELAND.

By the President:

RICHARD OLNEY,
Secretary of State.

BY THE PRESIDENT OF THE UNITED STATES OF AMERICA.

A PROCLAMATION.

Whereas it is provided by section 24 of the act of Congress approved March 3, 1891, entitled "An act to repeal timber-culture laws, and for other purposes"—

That the President of the United States may from time to time set apart and reserve in any State or Territory having public land bearing forests, in any part of the public lands wholly or in part covered with timber or undergrowth, whether of commercial value or not, as public reservations; and the President shall by public proclamation declare the establishment of such reservations and the limits thereof.

And whereas the public lands in the State of Wyoming within the limits hereinafter described are in part covered with timber, and it appears that the public good would be promoted by setting apart and reserving said lands as a public reservation:

Now, therefore, I, Grover Cleveland, President of the United States, by virtue of the power in me vested by section 24 of the aforesaid act of Congress, do hereby make known and proclaim that there is hereby reserved from entry or settlement and set apart as a public reservation all those certain tracts, pieces, or parcels of land lying and being situate in the State of Wyoming and within the boundaries particularly described as follows, to wit:

Beginning at the southeast corner of township forty-three (43) north, range one hundred and ten (110) west, sixth (6th) principal meridian, Wyoming; thence northerly along the surveyed and unsurveyed range line between ranges one hundred and nine (109) and one hundred and ten (110) west to the point of intersection with the south boundary of the Yellowstone National Park Timber Land Reserve as established by proclamation of September 10, 1891;* thence westerly along said boundary to its intersection with the boundary line between the States of Wyoming and Idaho; thence southerly along said State boundary line to the point for the unsurveyed township line between townships forty-two (42) and forty-three (43) north; thence easterly along the unsurveyed and surveyed township line between townships forty-two (42) and forty-three (43) north to the southeast corner of township forty-three (43) north, range one hundred and ten (110) west, the place of beginning.

Excepting from the force and effect of this proclamation all lands which may have been prior to the date hereof embraced in any legal entry or covered by any lawful filing duly of record in the proper United States land office, or upon which any valid settlement has been made pursuant to law and the statutory period within which to make entry or filing of record has not expired, and all mining claims duly located and held according to the laws of the United States and rules and regulations not in conflict therewith.

* See pp. 155-156.

Provided, That this exception shall not continue to apply to any particular tract of land unless the entryman, settler, or claimant continues to comply with the law under which the entry, filing, settlement, or location was made.

Warning is hereby expressly given to all persons not to enter or make settlement upon the tract of land reserved by this proclamation.

In witness whereof I have hereunto set my hand and caused the seal of the United States to be affixed.

[SEAL.]   Done at the city of Washington, this 22d day of February, A. D. 1897, and of the Independence of the United States the one hundred and twenty-first.

GROVER CLEVELAND.

By the President:

RICHARD OLNEY,
Secretary of State.

BY THE PRESIDENT OF THE UNITED STATES OF AMERICA.

A PROCLAMATION.

Whereas it is provided by section 24 of the act of Congress approved March 3, 1891, entitled "An act to repeal timber-culture laws, and for other purposes"—

That the President of the United States may from time to time set apart and reserve in any State or Territory having public land bearing forests, in any part of the public lands wholly or in part covered with timber or undergrowth, whether of commercial value or not, as public reservations; and the President shall by public proclamation declare the establishment of such reservations and the limits thereof.

And whereas the public lands in the State of Montana within the limits hereinafter described are in part covered with timber, and it appears that the public good would be promoted by setting apart and reserving said lands as a public reservation:

Now, therefore, I, Grover Cleveland, President of the United States, by virtue of the power in me vested by section 24 of the aforesaid act of Congress, do hereby make known and proclaim that there is hereby reserved from entry or settlement and set apart as a public reservation all those certain tracts, pieces, or parcels of land lying and being situate in the State of Montana and within the boundaries particularly described as follows, to wit:

Beginning at the point on the south boundary of the Blackfeet Indian Reservation where said boundary line is intersected by the range line between ranges eight (8) and nine (9) west, principal meridian, Montana; thence southwesterly along the south boundary to the southwest corner of said reservation and northwesterly along the west boundary thereof as defined and described in the act of Congress approved June 10, 1896,

entitled "An act making appropriations for current and contingent expenses of the Indian Department and fulfilling treaty stipulations with
various Indian tribes for the fiscal year ending June 30, 1897, and for other
purposes," to the point where the unsurveyed range line between ranges
twelve (12) and thirteen (13) west will intersect said boundary line;
thence southerly along said unsurveyed range line to the point for the
northeast corner of township twenty-nine (29) north, range thirteen (13)
west; thence westerly along the unsurveyed township line to the point
for the northwest corner of said township; thence southerly along the
unsurveyed range line to the point for the southwest corner of section
eighteen (18), said township; thence westerly along the unsurveyed section line to the point for the northwest corner of section nineteen (19),
township twenty-nine (29) north, range fourteen (14) west; thence southerly along the unsurveyed range line to the point for the southwest corner
of said township twenty-nine (29) north, range fourteen (14) west; thence
westerly along the unsurveyed seventh (7th) standard parallel north to
the point for the southeast corner of township twenty-nine (29) north,
range seventeen (17) west; thence northerly along the unsurveyed range
line to the point for the northeast corner of said township; thence westerly along the unsurveyed township line to the point for the northwest
corner of section three (3), said township; thence northerly along the
unsurveyed section line to the point for the northeast corner of section
four (4), township thirty (30) north, range seventeen (17) west; thence
westerly along the unsurveyed township line to the point for the northwest corner of section three (3), township thirty (30) north, range nineteen (19) west; thence southerly along the unsurveyed and surveyed
section line, subject to the proper offset on the seventh (7th) standard
parallel north, to the southeast corner of section twenty-one (21), township
twenty-eight (28) north, range nineteen (19) west; thence easterly along
the unsurveyed section line to the point for the southeast corner of section
twenty-four (24), said township; thence southerly along the unsurveyed
and surveyed range line to the southeast corner of township twenty-seven
(27) north, range nineteen (19) west; thence easterly along the surveyed
and unsurveyed township line to the point for the northwest corner of section three (3), township twenty-six (26) north, range eighteen (18) west;
thence southerly along the unsurveyed section line to the point for the
southwest corner of section thirty-four (34), said township; thence westerly along the unsurveyed and surveyed township line to its intersection
with the east shore of Flathead Lake; thence southerly along the shore
of said lake to the north boundary of the Flathead Indian Reservation;
thence easterly along the north boundary to the northeast corner of said
reservation and southerly along the east boundary thereof to the point
where said boundary line will be intersected by the unsurveyed fourth
(4th) standard parallel north; thence easterly along said unsurveyed parallel to the point for the southeast corner of township seventeen (17)

north, range seven (7) west; thence northerly along the unsurveyed range line to the point for the northeast corner of said township; thence westerly along the unsurveyed township line to the point for the northwest corner of said township; thence northerly along the unsurveyed range line to the point for the northeast corner of township eighteen (18) north, range eight (8) west; thence westerly along the unsurveyed township line to the point for the southeast corner of township nineteen (19) north, range nine (9) west; thence northerly along the unsurveyed and surveyed range line between ranges eight (8) and nine (9) west, subject to the proper offsets on the fifth (5th), sixth (6th), and seventh (7th) standard parallels north, to the point of intersection with the south boundary of the Blackfeet Indian Reservation, the place of beginning.

Excepting from the force and effect of this proclamation all lands which may have been prior to the date hereof embraced in any legal entry or covered by any lawful filing duly of record in the proper United States land office, or upon which any valid settlement has been made pursuant to law and the statutory period within which to make entry or filing of record has not expired, and all mining claims duly located and held according to the laws of the United States and rules and regulations not in conflict therewith.

Provided, That this exception shall not continue to apply to any particular tract of land unless the entryman, settler, or claimant continues to comply with the law under which the entry, filing, settlement, or location was made.

Warning is hereby expressly given to all persons not to enter or make settlement upon the tract of land reserved by this proclamation.

The rights and privileges reserved to the Indians of the Blackfeet Indian Reservation by Article I of the agreement set forth in and accepted, ratified, and confirmed by the act of Congress approved June 10, 1896, hereinbefore referred to, respecting that portion of their reservation relinquished to the United States by said Article I shall be in no way infringed or modified by reason of the fact that a part of the area so relinquished is embraced within the limits of the boundaries herein described and set apart as a forest reservation, nor shall the right of occupation, location, and purchase of said relinquished lands under the provisions of the mineral-land laws accorded by said act of Congress be abridged.

In witness whereof I have hereunto set my hand and caused the seal of the United States to be affixed.

[SEAL.]   Done at the city of Washington, this 22d day of February, A. D. 1897, and of the Independence of the United States the one hundred and twenty-first.

GROVER CLEVELAND.

By the President:
RICHARD OLNEY,
   Secretary of State.

By the President of the United States of America.

A PROCLAMATION.

Whereas it is provided by section 24 of the act of Congress approved March 3, 1891, entitled "An act to repeal timber-culture laws, and for other purposes"—

That the President of the United States may from time to time set apart and reserve in any State or Territory having public land bearing forests, in any part of the public lands wholly or in part covered with timber or undergrowth, whether of commercial value or not, as public reservations; and the President shall by public proclamation declare the establishment of such reservations and the limits thereof.

And whereas the public lands in the State of Wyoming within the limits hereinafter described are in part covered with timber, and it appears that the public good would be promoted by setting apart and reserving said lands as a public reservation:

Now, therefore, I, Grover Cleveland, President of the United States, by virtue of the power in me vested by section 24 of the aforesaid act of Congress, do hereby make known and proclaim that there is hereby reserved from entry or settlement and set apart as a public reservation all those certain tracts, pieces, or parcels of land lying and being situate in the State of Wyoming and within the boundaries particularly described as follows, to wit:

Beginning at the southeast corner of township forty-eight (48) north, range eighty-four (84) west, sixth (6th) principal meridian, Wyoming; thence northerly along the range line to the northeast corner of said township; thence westerly along the twelfth (12th) standard parallel north to the southeast corner of township forty-nine (49) north, range eighty-four (84) west; thence northerly along the range line to the northeast corner of section thirteen (13), township fifty (50) north, range eighty-four (84) west; thence westerly along the section line to the northeast corner of section seventeen (17), said township; thence northerly along the section line to the southeast corner of section twenty-nine (29), township fifty-one (51) north, range eighty-four (84) west; thence easterly along the section line to the southeast corner of section twenty-six (26), said township; thence northerly along the section line to the northeast corner of section two (2), township fifty-two (52) north, range eighty-four (84) west; thence westerly along the thirteenth (13th) standard parallel north to the southeast corner of section thirty-five (35), township fifty-three (53) north, range eighty-four (84) west; thence northerly along the section line to the northeast corner of section fourteen (14), said township; thence westerly along the section line to the northeast corner of section fourteen (14), township fifty-three (53) north, range eighty-five (85) west; thence northerly along the section line to the northeast corner of section two (2), said township; thence westerly along the township line to the northeast corner of section two (2), township fifty-three (53) north, range eighty-six (86) west; thence northerly along the section line to the northeast corner of section two (2), township fifty-four (54) north, range eighty-six (86) west; thence westerly along the township line to the southeast corner of township fifty-five (55) north, range eighty-seven (87) west; thence northerly along the range line to the northeast corner of said township; thence westerly along the township line to the northwest corner of said township; thence southerly along the range line to the southwest corner of said township; thence westerly along the township line to the northwest corner of township fifty-four (54) north, range eighty-eight (88) west; thence northerly along the range line between ranges eighty-eight (88) and eighty-nine (89) west to the northwest corner of township fifty-six (56) north, range eighty-eight (88) west; thence westerly along the fourteenth (14th) standard parallel north to the southwest corner of township fifty-seven (57) north, range eighty-eight (88) west; thence northerly along the range line between ranges eighty-eight (88) and eighty-nine (89) west to the point of intersection with the boundary line between the States of Wyoming and Montana; thence westerly along said State boundary line to the point for the unsurveyed range line between ranges ninety-two (92) and ninety-three (93) west; thence southerly along said unsurveyed range line to the fourteenth (14th) standard parallel north; thence easterly along said standard parallel to the northeast corner of township fifty-six (56) north, range ninety-three (93) west; thence southerly along the range line between ranges ninety-two (92) and ninety-three (93) west to the northwest corner of township fifty-four (54) north, range ninety-two (92) west; thence easterly along the township line to the northeast corner of said township; thence southerly along the range line to the southeast corner of said township; thence easterly along the township line to the northeast corner of township fifty-three (53) north, range ninety-one (91) west; thence southerly along the range line to the southeast corner of said township; thence easterly along the thirteenth (13th) standard parallel north to the northwest corner of township fifty-two (52) north, range eighty-eight (88) west; thence southerly along the range line between ranges eighty-eight (88) and eighty-nine (89) west to the southwest corner of township fifty-one (51) north, range eighty-eight (88) west; thence easterly along the township line to the southeast corner of said township; thence southerly along the range line between ranges eighty-seven (87) and eighty-eight (88) west to the southwest corner of township forty-nine (49) north, range eighty-seven (87) west; thence easterly along the twelfth (12th) standard parallel north to the northwest corner of township forty-eight (48) north, range eighty-seven (87) west; thence southerly along the range line to the southwest corner of said township; thence easterly along the township line between townships forty-seven (47) and forty-eight (48) north to the southeast corner of township forty-eight (48) north, range eighty-four (84) west, the place of beginning.

Excepting from the force and effect of this proclamation all lands which may have been prior to the date hereof embraced in any legal entry or covered by any lawful filing duly of record in the proper United States land office, or upon which any valid settlement has been made pursuant to law and the statutory period within which to make entry or filing of record has not expired, and all mining claims duly located and held according to the laws of the United States and rules and regulations not in conflict therewith.

Provided, That this exception shall not continue to apply to any particular tract of land unless the entryman, settler, or claimant continues to comply with the law under which the entry, filing, settlement, or location was made.

Warning is hereby expressly given to all persons not to enter or make settlement upon the tract of land reserved by this proclamation.

In witness whereof I have hereunto set my hand and caused the seal of the United States to be affixed.

[SEAL.]   Done at the city of Washington, this 22d day of February, A. D. 1897, and of the Independence of the United States the one hundred and twenty-first.

GROVER CLEVELAND.

By the President:

RICHARD OLNEY,
Secretary of State.

BY THE PRESIDENT OF THE UNITED STATES OF AMERICA.

A PROCLAMATION.

Whereas it is provided by section 24 of the act of Congress approved March 3, 1891, entitled "An act to repeal timber-culture laws, and for other purposes"—

That the President of the United States may from time to time set apart and reserve in any State or Territory having public land bearing forests, in any part of the public lands wholly or in part covered with timber or undergrowth, whether of commercial value or not, as public reservations; and the President shall by public proclamation declare the establishment of such reservations and the limits thereof.

And whereas the public lands in the State of Montana within the limits hereinafter described are in part covered with timber, and it appears that the public good would be promoted by setting apart and reserving said lands as a public reservation:

Now, therefore, I, Grover Cleveland, President of the United States, by virtue of the power in me vested by section 24 of the aforesaid act of Congress, do hereby make known and proclaim that there is hereby reserved from entry or settlement and set apart as a public reservation all those certain tracts, pieces, or parcels of land lying and being situate in the State of Montana and within the boundaries particularly described as follows, to wit:

Beginning at the southwest corner of township thirty-three (33) north, range twenty-five (25) west, principal meridian, Montana; thence east-erly along the surveyed and unsurveyed eighth (8th) standard parallel north to the northeast corner of township thirty-two (32) north, range twenty-two (22) west; thence southerly along the range line between ranges twenty-one (21) and twenty-two (22) west to the southeast cor-ner of section thirteen (13) of said township thirty-two (32) north, range twenty-two (22) west; thence easterly along the unsurveyed section line to the point for the southeast corner of section thirteen (13), township thirty-two (32) north, range eighteen (18) west; thence southerly along the unsurveyed range line between ranges seventeen (17) and eighteen (18) west to the northwest corner of township thirty-one (31) north, range seventeen (17) west; thence easterly along the township line be-tween townships thirty-one (31) and thirty-two (32) north to the north-west corner of section two (2), township thirty-one (31) north, range seventeen (17) west; thence along the section lines southerly to the southwest corner of section twenty-three (23) and easterly to the north-east corner of section twenty-five (25), said township; thence southerly along the range line between ranges sixteen (16) and seventeen (17) west to the southeast corner of said township thirty-one (31) north, range seventeen (17) west; thence easterly along the unsurveyed township line between townships thirty (30) and thirty-one (31) north to the point for the southeast corner of township thirty-one (31) north, range sixteen (16) west; thence southerly along the unsurveyed range line between ranges fifteen (15) and sixteen (16) west to the point for the southwest corner of township thirty (30) north, range fifteen (15) west; thence east-erly along the unsurveyed township line between townships twenty-nine (29) and thirty (30) north to the point for the southeast corner of said township thirty (30) north; thence northerly along the unsurveyed range line between ranges fourteen (14) and fifteen (15) west to the point for the southeast corner of section thirteen (13), said township thirty (30) north, range fifteen (15) west; thence along the unsurveyed section lines easterly to the point for the southeast corner of section sixteen (16) and northerly to the point for the northeast corner of section four (4), town-ship thirty (30) north, range fourteen (14) west; thence easterly along the unsurveyed township line between townships thirty (30) and thirty-one (31) north to the point for the southeast corner of township thirty-one (31) north, range fourteen (14) west; thence northerly along the unsur-veyed range line between ranges thirteen (13) and fourteen (14) west to the point where it will intersect the west boundary of the Blackfeet Indian Reservation as said boundary is defined and described in the act of Con-gress approved June 10, 1896, entitled "An act making appropriations for current and contingent expenses of the Indian Department and fulfilling treaty stipulations with various Indian tribes for the fiscal year ending June 30, 1897, and for other purposes;" thence northwesterly along the boundary of said Indian reservation to its point of intersection with the international boundary line between the State of Montana and the British possessions; thence westerly along said international boundary line to the point for the unsurveyed range line between ranges twenty-five (25) and twenty-six (26) west; thence southerly along the unsurveyed range line between ranges twenty-five (25) and twenty-six (26) west to the ninth (9th) standard parallel north; thence easterly along said parallel to the northeast corner of township thirty-six (36) north, range twenty-six (26) west; thence southerly along the range line between ranges twenty-five (25) and twenty-six (26) west to the southwest corner of township thirty-three (33) north, range twenty-five (25) west, the place of beginning.

Excepting from the force and effect of this proclamation all lands which may have been prior to the date hereof embraced in any legal entry or covered by any lawful filing duly of record in the proper United States land office, or upon which any valid settlement has been made pursuant to law and the statutory period within which to make entry or filing of record has not expired, and all mining claims duly located and held according to the laws of the United States and rules and regulations not in conflict therewith.

Provided, That this exception shall not continue to apply to any particular tract of land unless the entryman, settler, or claimant continues to comply with the law under which the entry, filing, settlement, or location was made.

Warning is hereby expressly given to all persons not to enter or make settlement upon the tract of land reserved by this proclamation.

The rights and privileges reserved to the Indians of the Blackfeet Indian Reservation by Article I of the agreement set forth in and accepted, ratified, and confirmed by the act of Congress approved June 10, 1896, hereinbefore referred to, respecting that portion of their reservation relinquished to the United States by said Article I shall be in no way infringed or modified by reason of the fact that a part of the area so relinquished is embraced within the limits of the boundaries herein described and set apart as a forest reservation, nor shall the right of occupation, location, and purchase of said relinquished lands under the provisions of the mineral-land laws accorded by said act of Congress be abridged.

In witness whereof I have hereunto set my hand and caused the seal of the United States to be affixed.

[SEAL.]   Done at the city of Washington, this 22d day of February, A. D. 1897, and of the Independence of the United States the one hundred and twenty-first.

GROVER CLEVELAND.

By the President:

RICHARD OLNEY, *Secretary of State.*

By the President of the United States of America.

A PROCLAMATION.

Whereas public interests require that the Senate should be convened at 12 o'clock on the 4th day of March next to receive such communications as may be made by the Executive:

Now, therefore, I, Grover Cleveland, President of the United States of America, do hereby proclaim and declare that an extraordinary occasion requires the Senate of the United States to convene at the Capitol, in the city of Washington, on the 4th day of March next, at 12 o'clock noon, of which all persons who shall at that time be entitled to act as members of that body are hereby required to take notice.

Given under my hand and the seal of the United States, at Washington,

[SEAL.] the 24th day of February, A. D. 1897, and of the Independence of the United States the one hundred and twenty-first.

GROVER CLEVELAND.

By the President:

RICHARD OLNEY,
Secretary of State.

EXECUTIVE ORDERS.

AMENDMENT OF CIVIL-SERVICE RULES.

EXECUTIVE MANSION, *December 23, 1896.*

Amend clause 2 (*b*) of Rule III by adding at the end thereof the following:

And all officers and employees in the penitentiary service who are by law subject to classification.

Approved:

GROVER CLEVELAND.

AMENDMENT OF CIVIL-SERVICE RULES.

EXECUTIVE MANSION, *January 2, 1897.*

Amend Rule VIII by striking out section 12 and substituting therefor the following:

Whenever there are no names of eligibles upon a register for any grade in which a vacancy exists, and the public interest requires that it must be filled before eligibles can be provided by the Commission, such vacancy may, subject to the approval of the Commission, be filled by appointment without examination and certification for such part of three months as will enable the Commission to provide eligibles. Such temporary appointment shall expire by limitation as soon as an eligible shall be provided, and no person shall serve longer than three months in any one year under such temporary appointment or appointments unless by special authority of the Commission previously obtained. Said year limitation shall commence from the date of such first appointment: *Provided*, That whenever an emergency shall arise requiring that a vacancy shall be filled before a certification can be issued and an appointment made thereto in the manner provided in these rules, such vacancy may be filled without regard to the provisions of these rules for such part of thirty days as may be required for the issuance of a certificate and the execution of the necessary details of an appointment thereto in accordance with said provisions. Such appointment shall in no case continue longer than thirty days.

Approved:

GROVER CLEVELAND.

AMENDMENT OF CIVIL-SERVICE RULES.

EXECUTIVE MANSION, *January 2, 1897.*

Amend Rule V, section 4, prescribing age limitations for the classified service, by striking out the table after the tenth line and substituting therefor the following:

	Minimum.	Maximum.
Departmental service:		
Page, messenger boy, apprentice, or student	14	20
Printer's assistant and messenger	18	No limit.
Positions in the railway mail service	18	35
Internes and hospital stewards in the marine-hospital service and acting second assistant engineer in the revenue-cutter service	21	30
Cadet in the revenue-cutter service and aid in the Coast and Geodetic Survey	18	25
Surfmen in the life-saving service	18	45
Superintendent, physician, supervisor, day-school inspector, and disciplinarian in the Indian service; inspector and assistant inspector of hulls, an inspector and an assistant inspector of boilers, in the steamboat-inspection service	25	55
All other positions	20	No limit.
(The age limitation shall not apply in the case of the wife of the superintendent of an Indian school who applies for examination for the position of teacher or matron.)		
Custom-house service:		
All positions	20	No limit.
Post-office service:		
Letter carrier	21	40
All other positions	18	No limit.
Government printing service:		
All positions (male)	21	No limit.
All positions (female)	18	No limit.
Internal-revenue service:		
All positions	21	No limit.

Approved:

GROVER CLEVELAND.

CIVIL SERVICE.—CLASSIFICATION OF THE OFFICE OF THE PRESIDENT.

EXECUTIVE OFFICE,
Washington, D. C., January 12, 1897.

In accordance with the third clause of section 6 of the act entitled "An act to regulate and improve the civil service of the United States," approved January 16, 1883—

It is ordered, That the officers and employees in or under this office included within the provisions of the civil-service law and rules be, and they are hereby, arranged in the following classes:

Class A.—All persons receiving an annual salary of less than $720, or a compensation at the rate of less than $720 per annum.

Class B.—All persons receiving an annual salary of $720 or more, or a compensation at the rate of $720 or more, but less than $840 per annum.

Class C.—All persons receiving an annual salary of $840 or more, or a compensation at the rate of $840 or more, but less than $900 per annum.

Class D.—All persons receiving an annual salary of $900 or more, or a compensation at the rate of $900 or more, but less than $1,000 per annum.

Class E.—All persons receiving an annual salary of $1,000 or more, or a compensation at the rate of $1,000 or more, but less than $1,200 per annum.

Class 1.—All persons receiving an annual salary of $1,200 or more, or a compensation at the rate of $1,200 or more, but less than $1,400 per annum.

Class 2.—All persons receiving an annual salary of $1,400 or more, or a compensation at the rate of $1,400 or more, but less than $1,600 per annum.

Class 3.—All persons receiving an annual salary of $1,600 or more, or a compensation at the rate of $1,600 or more, but less than $1,800 per annum.

Class 4.—All persons receiving an annual salary of $1,800 or more, or a compensation at the rate of $1,800 or more, but less than $2,000 per annum.

Class 5.—All persons receiving an annual salary of $2,000 or more, or a compensation at the rate of $2,000 or more, but less than $2,500 per annum.

Class 6.—All persons receiving an annual salary of $2,500 or more, or a compensation at the rate of $2,500 or more per annum.

It is provided, That this classification shall not include persons appointed to an office by and with the advice and consent of the Senate nor persons employed as mere laborers or workmen; but all positions whose occupants are designated as laborers or workmen, and who were prior to May 6, 1896, and are now regularly assigned to work of the same grade as that performed by classified employees, shall be included within this classification. Hereafter no person who is appointed as a laborer or workman, without examination under the civil-service rules, shall be assigned to work of the same grade as that performed by classified employees.

It is also ordered, That no person shall be admitted into any place not excepted from examination by the civil-service rules in any of the classes above designated until he shall have passed an appropriate examination prepared by the United States Civil Service Commission and his eligibility has been certified to this office by said Commission.

By direction of the President:

HENRY T. THURBER, *Private Secretary.*

EXECUTIVE MANSION,
Washington, January 12, 1897.

Hon. JUDSON HARMON,
   Attorney-General of the United States.

DEAR SIR: The bill which has been for some time pending before the Congress providing for the adjustment and extension of the indebtedness of the Pacific railroads to the Government of the United States has been defeated in the House of Representatives.

In the case of the Union Pacific Railroad and the Kansas Pacific Railroad, a default in the payment of their indebtedness having occurred and suits having been commenced for the foreclosure of the lien upon said roads which is paramount to the lien and security of the United States, you are hereby directed, pursuant to the provisions of an act of Congress passed March 3, 1887, after taking such precautions and perfecting such arrangements as are possible to assure as far as practicable the payment of their indebtedness to the Government as a result of the suits now pending or others to be instituted, to take such proceedings in the courts as shall be needful to protect and defend the rights and interests of the United States in respect of such indebtedness, and to take steps to foreclose the mortgages or liens of the United States upon the property of these railroad companies.

In the case of the other aided Pacific railroads, as to which no foreclosure suits are pending, a different situation is presented, which requires further consideration before deciding the course to be taken by the Government.

Yours, truly,   GROVER CLEVELAND.

AMENDMENT OF CIVIL-SERVICE RULES.

Rule VI of the civil-service rules is hereby amended by adding to the exceptions from examination in the departmental service a new clause, to read as follows:

(*d*) Assistant Secretary Smithsonian Institution, in charge of United States National Museum.

Approved, January 27, 1897.   GROVER CLEVELAND.